European Community Law
Text and Materials

European Community Law

Text and Materials

David Pollard LLB
Chevalier des Palmes Académiques;
Senior Lecturer, Faculty of Law,
University of Leicester

Malcolm Ross LLB, MPhil
Jean Monnet Senior Lecturer
in European Community Law,
University of Leicester

Butterworths
London, Dublin, Edinburgh
1994

United Kingdom	Butterworth & Co (Publishers) Ltd, Halsbury House, 35 Chancery Lane, LONDON WC2A 1EL and 4 Hill Street, EDINBURGH EH2 3JZ
Australia	Butterworths, SYDNEY, MELBOURNE, BRISBANE, ADELAIDE, PERTH, CANBERRA and HOBART
Canada	Butterworths Canada Ltd, TORONTO and VANCOUVER
Ireland	Butterworth (Ireland) Ltd, DUBLIN
Malaysia	Malayan Law Journal Sdn Bhd, KUALA LUMPUR
New Zealand	Butterworths of New Zealand Ltd, WELLINGTON and AUCKLAND
Puerto Rico	Butterworth of Puerto Rico, Inc, SAN JUAN
Singapore	Butterworths Asia, SINGAPORE
South Africa	Butterworths Publishers (Pty) Ltd, DURBAN
USA	Butterworth Legal Publishers, CARLSBAD, California and SALEM, New Hampshire

A CIP Catalogue record for this book is available from the British Library.

ISBN 0 406 01621 6

Typeset by Columns Design and Production Services Ltd, Reading
Printed and bound in Great Britain by Butler and Tanner Ltd, Frome and London

Non Vitae sed Europae discimus.

(Seneca)

Freude, schöner Götterfunken,
Tochter aus Elysium,
Wir betreten feuertrunken,
Himmlische, dein Heiligtum.

Deine Zauber binden wieder,
Was die Mode streng geteilt,
Alle Menschen werden Brüder,
Wo dein sanfter Flügel weilt.

(Schiller)

Preface

We have two reasons for creating this work – to provide a portable library on Community law for students and to organise that library in a way which illustrates Community law as it has developed, as it currently exists and as it will be.

We have taught Community law for more years than we care to remember to students of law and social science and to legal practitioners, both from the United Kingdom and from many other jurisdictions. For students of law (who often will have no recent history, political science or knowledge of economics) and for social science students (where knowledge of the working of Community institutions and the operation of Community law is an essential element of their studies) any understanding of Community law depends on accessibility to its source materials. Community law presents a wonderful challenge to those seeking an insight into the development of a 'new legal order' (still not yet 40 years old), not least because of the variety of those source materials, whose creators and draftsmen come from widely differing constitutional and legal backgrounds. However, the current state of university and other public library holdings means, sadly, that individual access to some materials is practically impossible and that there is no access at all to other materials. It is appreciated that many students (and teachers) do not have ready access to a European Documentation Centre. The primary materials selected consist of the Treaties (from the Treaty of Rome to the Treaty of Maastricht), Community secondary legislation (regulations, directives and decisions), and judgments of the European Court of Justice, together with opinions of Advocates General. Primary materials, however, do not present a complete picture of Community law, as we analyse it, and we include as essential study tools many less readily available source materials (including reports made by Community institutions, questions and debates in the European Parliament, reports and materials from national institutions and jurisdictions, and selected periodical literature).

To this, we add selected lists of further reading, which experience has shown to be of particular use to students, and a connecting explanatory text, designed to explain (and perhaps to justify) that, although we cover the principal aspects of Community law which a student needs to know, we do this in a way which departs to some degree from the formats which tend to dominate other texts. This departure is necessary to show some of the linking themes which have emerged with the increasing maturity of Community law and to demonstrate the shifting nature of the dividing line between Community and national competence.

European Community law is dynamic, different and diverse. It is an independent system of law in its own right, is superimposed on and forms an integral part of the domestic legal, political and economic systems of 12 nations. It is more than a system of inter-nation co-operation. Its subjects include the constitutional and legal institutions of the Member States, together with their corporate commercial organisations, individual manufacturers, farmers and traders, members of many professions, employees and their families. It has repercussions on the macro and micro economies of the Member States and on global economic activity. In a short time it has progressed in leaps and bounds from a customs union to an economic and monetary union and seems set to emerge as some form of federal organisation. We identify Community law, as it currently exists and as it is (or ought to be) taught, as presenting five principal elements: the embryo European Union, the European constitution, the relationship between Community law and the Member States, the European citizen and the European trader. These five are, in turn, themselves divided into clearly defined and labelled sections (each with its introductory text and assembled materials), thus facilitating the selection of specific study modules appropriate to the width and depth of study for individual courses of Community law.

Our approach is not limited to Community law as it has developed and as it currently exists, and we consistently and constantly herald the 'even newer' legal (and possibly federal) order which is to come. With regard to the Community's current characteristics, we emphasise the fluidity of Community law and consider the catalysts for future changes, together with the instruments for channelling and implementing them. This is epitomised in the saga of the Maastricht Treaty of Union, which has been contemporeous with the gestation period of this work, and we point to the future and Community action already contemplated under that Treaty. It may well be that, in the not too distant future, there will be a federal Europe, with a 'true' constitution, European citizenship and European traders trading in a single currency and in accordance with common commercial policies – that will have to await a future edition of this work.

David Pollard   Leicester
Malcolm Ross   1 July 1994

Acknowledgments

This work could not have been created without the generosity of copyright owners of the materials extracted in giving their kind permission to reproduce those extracts. Consequently, the sincere thanks of the authors and publishers are extended to:

the American Society of Comparative Law Inc;

British Institute of International and Comparative Law;

the Commission of the European Community;

the Council of Ministers of the European Community;

the Court of Justice of the European Community;

the European Parliament, Directorate-General for Information and Public Relations, European Parliament Document Service, and 'European Parliament News';

Hella Pick and Guardian Newspapers Ltd;

Her Majesty's Stationery Office;

the Incorporated Council of Law Reporting for England and Wales;

Kluwer Academic Publishers;

Longman Group UK Ltd;

Macmillan Ltd;

the Modern Law Review Ltd and Basil Blackwell Ltd;

Oxford University Press;

Pinter Publishers Ltd;

Sage Publications Ltd;

Sweet and Maxwell Ltd;

Times Newspapers Ltd.

Malcolm also wishes to thank Mandy Archer for her wizardry and good humour.

Contents

Section Two
Establishing the Community Dimension   26

Section Three
The Pressures and Agents for Change   66

CHAPTER TWO
THE EUROPEAN CONSTITUTION 127

The creation of a European constitution 127

Section One
The Government of the Community 131

1 The European Parliament 131
2 The Council 133
3 The Commission 135
4 The Economic and Social Committee and the Committee of the Regions
   135

Section Two
Community Legislation   168

Section Three
The European Court of Justice   197

CHAPTER THREE
COMMUNITY LAW AND THE MEMBER STATES   287

The supremacy of Community law   287

Section One
Enforcing Community Obligations   290

Section Two
The Reference Procedure   314

Section Four
Social Policy   550

Introduction   550

Section Two
Competition Policy   729

Table of Statutes

References in this Table to *Statutes* are to Halsbury's Statutes of England (Fourth Edition) showing the volume and page at which the annotated text of the Act may be found.

Page numbers printed in **bold** type indicate where the section of the Act is set out in part or in full.

Table of EC Legislation

Page numbers printed in **bold** type indicate where an article or rule is set out in part or in full.

List of Cases

Page numbers printed in **bold** type indicate where the case is set out.

PAGE

xxxiii

M

N

O

P

Q

R

Chapter One

The European Community: an Evolving Union

This chapter explores the principal characteristics of the European Community. The materials not only illustrate the menu of activities set out in the founding Treaties but also provide a sample of the range of ingredients used to create new developments and a flavour of Community law in action. Three aspects of the Community recur throughout the chapter: the broad range of its activity, the fluidity of its evolution and the diversity of inputs into that process. Examination of these considerations can help answer the basic questions which arise in relation to the Community: what is it for, which factors help or hinder progress in achieving its goals and how are conflicts of interest resolved? Since this book has been designed primarily with the law student in mind, the perspective adopted focuses closely on the role of the Treaties and their interpretation by the European Court of Justice. But this is deliberately balanced by materials which stress the historical, political, economic and social influences upon the development of the Community.

1 The breadth of Community activities

An initial glance at the objectives of the Treaties might focus upon their various references to the creation of a customs union, a common market [A1] and a single internal market [A30]. It may not therefore be immediately obvious why the European Court of Justice should have had to give judgments upon matters as diverse as the protection of wild birds [A37], the dissemination of information about abortion clinics [A19] or the extent to which individuals have a right to a particular spelling of their name [A21]. Similar surprise might be expressed at legislative activity in fields including the monitoring of drug abuse [A48], the return of items of cultural heritage to their original Member State [A43], the content of driving tests [A17] and the regulation of property timeshares [A42]. However, these issues have already arisen under the original EEC Treaty as amended by the Single European Act.

The Maastricht Treaty on European Union [A2], [A3], [A4], undoubtedly encompasses a wider picture of Community activities. In some fields, for example social and environmental policies, this means an extension of influence clearly built upon the foundations already made by the amendments brought about by the Single European Act [A6], [A7]. Other aims, such as the targets in relation to economic and monetary policy [A4], [A14], are

1

made much more explicit than ever before. Areas of policy which would previously have been seen as national preserves are now subject to some form of
Community-level direction, influence or review. Thus, aspects of criminal law
[A16], [A47], [A48], [A49], defence and foreign policy [A15] can no longer
be assumed to be governed by unilateral national decisions.

This vast scope for Community action is brought about in three ways. First,
the objectives of the Treaties are couched in open-ended and ambitious
terms. An 'ever closer union of the peoples' [A3] is not a concept that is easily pinned down. Secondly, such limitations on powers as might be deduced
from a textual approach to the Treaties have not met with favour before the
European Court of Justice, an institution given to purposive and expansive
techniques of interpretation. Its invention and exposition of fundamental
principles of Community law, purportedly derived from the Treaties and the
common legal traditions of the Member States, has contributed a constitutional character to the Community in the face of efforts in some quarters to
maintain it as an inter-governmental club (see also Chapter Two, Sections
Three and Four). Thirdly, there are structures and mechanisms built into
the Treaties which permit revision and extension. Devices such as Article 235
[A35] allow for goals which are compatible with the EC Treaty to be pursued
in the absence of specific powers. In combination, these factors provide a sufficient legal armoury to implement the political will needed to progress from
customs union to European Union via the single internal market.

The most important consequence of the size of the sphere of Community
activity is that it dictates the division of competence between national and
Community levels of law making. Of itself, a Community competence does
not oust national activity. Crucial importance is therefore attached to the
part played by the European Court of Justice in determining whether, and in
what circumstances, an exclusive competence for the Community can be
established [A53]. However, in any event, the principle of supremacy
demands that in the case of conflict between Community and national rules,
the former prevails (see also Chapter Three).

It should quickly emerge from the materials in this chapter that the cate-
gorisation of any dispute or issue as having nothing to do with European
Community law is not easily made. The emphasis therefore shifts to whether
particular national laws are justified – the effect of the breadth of
Community competence is not to demand that lawful action can only take
place at a harmonised Community level but to subject national measures to a
requirement of compatibility with Community goals. Diversity between
national laws is not intrinsically objectionable, as shown by the Sunday trading cases [A18]. But the non-application of Article 30 to the Shops Act 1950
was reasoned on the basis that the purpose of the domestic rules was compatible with Community law and that any effect on trade was not excessive.

Fears that the Community is an encroaching monolith have led to a reappraisal of the proper balance between local, national, Community and
international action. This tension surfaces in the Maastricht Treaty, where
the explicit ambitions of economic and monetary union are placed alongside
the notion of subsidiarity [A22]–[A29]. One of the many issues to be resolved
in the Community's continuing development is whether the latter acts to
curb the scope of Community competence or whether it only redistributes
the institutional application of established Community goals. Seen in this
second sense, subsidiarity performs a function equivalent to the established

Community law principle of proportionality, ensuring that competences are exercised in necessary and effective fashion. It does not redefine the allocation of those competences.

2   The fluidity of developments

This second theme explores the dynamics which have influenced the creation of the Community to date and which may engender the creation of the European Union and the expansion of the European Economic Area [A56], [A57] in the post-Maastricht phase of Community growth. Lawyers may wish to focus most closely on the comparative contributions of legislative and judicial institutions as catalysts for change. Chapter Three explains further how the European Court of Justice has striven from its earliest judgments to entrench Community law by providing individuals with the tools to rely on it in their national courts. In subsequent decisions the court has revealed the obligation to interpret national law in accordance with Community law and has declared Community law remedies to exist in particular circumstances. The court's willingness to establish fundamental general principles of Community law and to look for inspiration at other sources, such as the European Convention on Human Rights, further underscores its dynamic contribution [A52]. As arbiter of inter-institutional disputes the court has had further opportunities to set the agenda for legal change. The various tensions can clearly be seen in its approach to the *Titanium Dioxide* case [A38], especially its reference to the role of the European Parliament as crucial in determining the appropriate legal basis for the measure under challenge.

The legislative contribution to change is most obviously evident in the harmonisation programme adopted to create the single internal market [A30]–[A34]. Achieving specific Community regulation of an area raises important questions as to the effect on the applicability of other Treaty rules [A37]. However, a Community legal instrument, whether a directive, regulation or decision, may not itself be a cause of change, only its manifestation. It may therefore be more instructive to examine the forces which produce the legislation. For example, the Regulation on Drug Abuse Monitoring [A48] can be seen as a 'top-down' enactment driven by the political agreement of the Heads of Government acting as the European Council. This may be compared with the location of the initiative behind the legislation in point in the *Titanium Dioxide* saga. But there are democratic risks if the evolution of regulatory processes is diverted into narrow arguments about legal base as a smokescreen for institutional muscle flexing [A41], [A46].

The European Community's development is not just shaped by its internal goals and conflicts; it is also driven by global events and relations. Expansion in the political sense involves discussion of the enlargement of the Community and the character of emerging relationships with other countries [A54], [A55]. The establishment of the European Economic Area alongside the amendment of the Community under the Maastricht Treaty has highlighted the central question of whether a plethora of 'European' goals and systems are mutually compatible and workable. Examination of the court's opinions in relation to the EEA agreement [A56], [A57] are particularly instructive both as to its views about the Community and its own institutional role. The precise relationship between the content and

structures of Community law and the European Convention on Human
Rights is a further area awaiting definitive treatment [A52].

In nearly 40 years of existence, the Community has moved far beyond its
formative tasks of achieving a customs union. The protection afforded by
Community law, particularly as a result of the court's activity, now exceeds
the sum of individual components such as the fundamental freedoms associated with free movement. Legislative proposals no longer strive to seek their
justifications wholly from those relatively narrow freedoms, but reveal other
aspirations [A45]. Later chapters of this book will demonstrate how the economic focus of the Community has been overtaken by other concerns to
secure social and political protection. Put crudely, Community law is now
geared towards recognition of 'persons' rather than just 'workers'. More
attention is also now directed towards creating a bundle of enforceable individual rights rather than the enjoyment of limited freedoms. It is the extent
of the synthesis of these two strands of development which will principally
determine the actual value to be attached to notions of Community citizenship, expressly articulated in the Maastricht Treaty [A50], [A51].

As Holland observes [A58], there is nothing inevitable about European
integration. Nor, it might be added, is the pace of progression or the form of
any such integration as might evolve limited to a single blueprint. A two-
speed approach has at least been threatened by developments in relation to
social policy [A8], [A9]. As far as methods are concerned, it is especially striking that the presence of a Community dimension to policy and regulation
can already take so many different forms. At one extreme there are directly
effective Community law rights which must be protected by national courts.
Some issues are subject to a mix of Community and international regulation
[A44]. Other matters, such as the justice and home affairs 'pillar' [A16] of
the Maastricht Treaty are for the moment left to inter-governmental co-operation. But today's co-operation may become tomorrow's binding union. The
fact that the 'F' word was too strong for the time at which it was aired meant
that the Maastricht Treaty does not expressly refer to federalism. But if the
breadth of Community objectives is coupled with the dynamics of the
Community in action, then it can be seen that the means are already in place
to bring it about.

3 The diversity of influences

The third principal theme of this chapter, closely intertwined with the other
two strands of analysis, is that the Community cannot and should not be
viewed in isolation or from a narrow legalistic perspective, for it is a multi-
disciplinary and multi-layered edifice. Economic, political and social dimensions form not only spheres of Community activity but also agents for change
which, in turn, may emanate from local, national, Community or international sources. The discussion of the importance of the Irish language in *Groener*
[A20] and the spelling of a name in *Konstantinidis* [A21] show how fundamental the considerations addressed by Community law can be. Some
measure of the extreme sensitivity of the questions at issue in those cases can
be gleaned from the difference between the panoramic approach taken by
the Advocates General and the relatively cautious answers provided by the
court. Whilst generally renowned for its dynamism and initiative in spear-
heading integration by means of law, the court faces stern choices when

confronted by cases involving such national sensibilities. These were clearly visible in its handling of the Irish abortion controversy **[A19]**.

Nevertheless, it is increasingly evident that the court is distilling essential and protectable interests bridging the different aspects of the Treaty to provide a core of legitimising criteria which can be deployed in any situation. In the Sunday trading cases, for example, the national rules were held compatible with Article 30 because they pursue acceptable socio-cultural objectives. The result, when applied generally, is the creation of an *acquis communautaire* which has a coherence and permanence which goes deeper than the diverse articles of the Treaties. Examples of these common threads of judicial reasoning will be apparent from the substantive materials contained in Chapters Three, Four and Five of this book.

The Treaties themselves are littered with references which derive from, and demand understanding of, a range of pressures and disciplines. The lawyer's interest in such inputs, therefore, must at the very least involve the examination of the justiciability of the concepts which they introduce. Will the strengthening of economic and social cohesion, as demanded by Article B of the Common Provisions of the Maastricht Treaty **[A3]**, be recognisable and measurable if and when it happens? Even something as apparently straightforward as the obligation of Member States to facilitate the achievement of the Community's tasks under Article 5 EEC **[A5]** becomes a moving target for the lawyer seeking to demonstrate its breach.

Since it occupies a prominent place on the political agenda, perhaps the most telling example of the current challenge to lawyers is the unravelling of the notion of subsidiarity. This concept appears in a variety of guises: contrast may be made between the political view expounded by the European Council at Edinburgh **[A25]** and the more legalistic approach adopted by Toth **[A23]**. Some of the tensions generated by the issue can be seen from the different perspectives expressed within the European Parliament **[A24]**. The European Court of Justice will at some point need to determine whether Article 3b of the EC Treaty **[A22]** is a political exhortation without legal effect, a fundamental source of inspiration against which to judge the validity of the application of other Community law measures or a meaningful self-standing Community legal principle capable of enforcement by individuals against private and public defendants. Nor should the contribution of national courts be understated, although there are the obvious risks that their own views of subsidiarity may be some distance from those of the European Court of Justice **[A39]**, **[A40]**.

This chapter demonstrates that the challenges and opportunities presented by Community law are spectacular in their diversity and enormity. But the scope for mythology and propaganda is equally considerable **[A27]**. The Maastricht Treaty 'marks a new stage in the process of creating an ever closer union among the peoples of Europe, in which decisions are taken as closely as possible to the citizen' **[A3]**. Yet, as Holland notes **[A58]**, there remains a marked 'democratic deficit' in the Community institutional framework. The materials which follow indicate the sources and tools of Community evolution. What cannot be put on the page is the political energy which determines the speed and direction of that development.

SECTION ONE

THE GOALS AND MODELS TO BE PURSUED

MATERIALS

[A1]   Treaty establishing the European Economic Community

PRINCIPLES

Article 1

By this Treaty, the High Contracting Parties establish among themselves a EUROPEAN ECONOMIC COMMUNITY.

Article 2

The Community shall have as its task, by establishing a common market and progressively approximating the economic policies of Member States, to promote throughout the Community a harmonious development of economic activities, a continuous and balanced expansion, an increase in stability, an accelerated raising of the standard of living and closer relations between the States belonging to it.

Article 3

For the purposes set out in Article 2, the activities of the Community shall include, as provided in this Treaty and in accordance with the timetable set out therein:

(a)   the elimination, as between Member States, of customs duties and of quantitative restrictions on the import and export of goods, and of all other measures having equivalent effect;
(b)   the establishment of a common customs tariff and of a common commercial policy towards third countries;
(c)   the abolition, as between Member States, of obstacles to freedom of movement for persons, services and capital;
(d)   the adoption of a common policy in the sphere of agriculture;
(e)   the adoption of a common policy in the sphere of transport;
(f)   the institution of a system ensuring that competition in the common market is not distorted;
(g)   the application of procedures by which the economic policies of

Member States can be co-ordinated and disequilibria in their balances of payments remedied;

(h)   the approximation of the laws of Member States to the extent required for the proper functioning of the common market;

(i)   the creation of a European Social Fund in order to improve employment opportunities for workers and to contribute to the raising of their standard of living;

(j)   the establishment of a European Investment Bank to facilitate the economic expansion of the Community by opening up fresh resources;

(k)   the association of the overseas countries and territories in order to increase trade and to promote jointly economic and social development.

[A2]   Preamble to the Maastricht Treaty on European Union

His Majesty the King of the Belgians, Her Majesty the Queen of Denmark, the President of the Federal Republic of Germany, the President of the Hellenic Republic, His Majesty the King of Spain, the President of the French Republic, the President of Ireland, the President of the Italian Republic, His Royal Higness the Grand Duke of Luxembourg, Her Majesty the Queen of the Netherlands, the President of the Portuguese Republic, Her Majesty the Queen of the United Kingdom of Great Britain and Northern Ireland,

RESOLVED to mark a new stage in the process of European integration undertaken with the establishment of the European Communities,

RECALLING the historic importance of the ending of the division of the European continent and the need to create firm bases for the construction of the future Europe,

CONFIRMING their attachment to the principles of liberty, democracy and respect for human rights and fundamental freedoms and of the rule of law,

DESIRING to deepen the solidarity between their peoples while respecting their history, their culture and their traditions,

DESIRING to enhance further the democratic and efficient functioning of the institutions so as to enable them better to carry out, within a single institutional framework, the tasks entrusted to them,

RESOLVED to achieve the strengthening and the convergence of their economies and to establish an economic and monetary union including, in accordance with the provisions of this Treaty, a single and stable currency,

DETERMINED to promote economic and social progress for their peoples, within the context of the accomplishment of the internal market and of reinforced cohesion and environmental protection, and to implement policies ensuring that advances in economic integration are accompanied by parallel progress in other fields,

RESOLVED to establish a citizenship common to nationals of their countries,

RESOLVED to implement a common foreign and security policy including the eventual framing of a common defence policy, which might in time lead to a common defence, thereby reinforcing the European identity and its independence in order to promote peace, security and progress in Europe and in the world,

REAFFIRMING their objective to facilitate the free movement of persons, while ensuring the safety and security of their peoples, by including provisions on justice and home affairs in this Treaty,

RESOLVED to continue the process of creating an ever closer union among the peoples of Europe, in which decisions are taken as closely as possible to the citizen in accordance with the principle of subsidiarity,

IN VIEW of further steps to be taken in order to advance European integration,

HAVE DECIDED to establish a European Union . . .

[A3]   Maastricht Treaty: common provisions of the European Union

TITLE I

COMMON PROVISIONS

Article A

By this Treaty, the High Contracting Parties establish among themselves a European Union, hereinafter called 'the Union'.

This Treaty marks a new stage in the process of creating an ever closer union among the peoples of Europe, in which decisions are taken as closely as possible to the citizen.

The Union shall be founded on the European Communities, supplemented by the policies and forms of co-operation established by this Treaty. Its task shall be to organise, in a manner demonstrating consistency and solidarity, relations between the Member States and between their peoples.

Article B

The Union shall set itself the following objectives:

- to promote economic and social progress which is balanced and sustainable, in particular through the creation of an area without internal frontiers, through the strengthening of economic and social cohesion and through the establishment of economic and monetary union, ultimately including a single currency in accordance with the provisions of this Treaty;
- to assert its identity on the international scene, in particular through the implementation of a common foreign and security policy including the eventual framing of a common defence policy, which might in time lead to a common defence;
- to strengthen the protection of the rights and interests of the nationals of its Member States through the introduction of a citizenship of the Union;
- to develop close co-operation on justice and home affairs;
- to maintain in full the *acquis communautaire* and build on it with a view to considering, through the procedure referred to in Article N(2) [the 1996 Inter-Governmental Conference], to what extent the policies and forms of co-operation introduced by this Treaty may need to be revised with the aim of ensuring the effectiveness of the mechanisms and the institutions of the Community.

The objectives of the Union shall be achieved as provided in this Treaty and in accordance with the conditions and the timetable set out therein while respecting the principle of subsidiarity as defined in Article 3b of the Treaty establishing the European Community **[A22]**.

Article C

The Union shall be served by a single institutional framework which shall ensure the consistency and the continuity of the activities carried out in order to attain its objectives while respecting and building upon the *acquis communautaire*.

The Union shall in particular ensure the consistency of its external activities as a whole in the context of its external relations, security, economic and development policies. The Council and the Commission shall be responsible for ensuring such consistency. They shall ensure the implementation of these policies, each in accordance with its respective powers.

Article D

The European Council shall provide the Union with the necessary impetus for its development and shall define the general political guidelines thereof.

The European Council shall bring together the Heads of State or of Government of the Member States and the President of the Commission. They shall be assisted by the Ministers for Foreign Affairs of the Member States and by a Member of the Commission. The European Council shall meet at least twice a year, under the chairmanship of the Head of State or of Government of the Member State which holds the Presidency of the Council.

The European Council shall submit to the European Parliament a report after each of its meetings and a yearly written report on the progress achieved by the Union.

Article E

The European Parliament, the Council, the Commission and the Court of Justice shall exercise their powers under the conditions and for the purposes provided for, on the one hand, by the provisions of the Treaties establishing the European Communities and of the subsequent Treaties and Acts modifying and supplementing them and, on the other hand, by the other provisions of this Treaty.

Article F

1. The Union shall respect the national identities of its Member States, whose systems of government are founded on the principles of democracy.

2. The Union shall respect fundamental rights, as guaranteed by the European Convention for the Protection of Human Rights and Fundamental Freedoms signed in Rome on 4 November 1950 and as they result from the constitutional traditions common to the Member States, as general principles of Community law.

3. The Union shall provide itself with the means necessary to attain its objectives and carry through its policies.

[A4]   Maastricht Treaty provisions amending the EEC Treaty with a view to establishing the European Community

Article G

The Treaty establishing the European Economic Community shall be amended in accordance with the provisions of this Article, in order to establish a European Community.

A.   Throughout the Treaty :

(1) The term 'European Economic Community' shall be replaced by the term 'European Community'.

B.   In Part One 'Principles':

(2) *Article 2 shall be replaced by the following* :

Article 2

The Community shall have as its task, by establishing a common market and an economic and monetary union and by implementing the common policies or activities referred to in Articles 3 and 3a, to promote throughout the Community a harmonious and balanced development of economic activities, sustainable and non-inflationary growth respecting the environment, a high degree of convergence of economic performance, a high level of employment and of social protection, the raising of the standard of living and quality of life, and economic and social cohesion and solidarity among Member States.

(3) *Article 3 shall be replaced by the following*:

Article 3

For the purposes set out in Article 2, the activities of the Community shall include, as provided in this Treaty and in accordance with the timetable set out therein :

(a)   the elimination, as between Member States, of customs duties and quantitative restrictions on the import and export of goods, and of all other measures having equivalent effect;
(b)   a common commercial policy;
(c)   an internal market characterised by the abolition, as between Member States, of obstacles to the free movement of goods, persons, services and capital;
(d)   measures concerning the entry and movement of persons in the internal market as provided for in Article 100c;
(e)   a common policy in the sphere of agriculture and fisheries;
(f)   a common policy in the sphere of transport;
(g)   a system ensuring that competition in the internal market is not distorted;
(h)   the approximation of the laws of Member States to the extent required for the functioning of the common market;
(i)   a policy in the social sphere comprising a European Social Fund;

(j)   the strengthening of economic and social cohesion;
(k)   a policy in the sphere of the environment;
(l)   the strengthening of the competitiveness of Community industry;
(m)   the promotion of research and technological development;
(n)   encouragement for the establishment and development of trans-European networks;
(o)   a contribution to the attainment of a high level of health protection;
(p)   a contribution to education and training of quality and to the flowering of the cultures of the Member States;
(q)   a policy in the sphere of development co-operation;
(r)   the association of the overseas countries and territories in order to increase trade and promote jointly economic and social development;
(s)   a contribution to the strengthening of consumer protection;
(t)   measures in the spheres of energy, civil protection and tourism.

(4) *The following Article shall be inserted*:

Article 3a

1. For the purposes set out in Article 2, the activities of the Member States and the Community shall include, as provided in this Treaty and in accordance with the timetable set out therein, the adoption of an economic policy which is based on the close co-ordination of Member States' economic policies, on the internal market and on the definition of common objectives, and conducted in accordance with the principle of an open market economy with free competition.

2. Concurrently with the foregoing, and as provided in this Treaty and in accordance with the timetable and the procedures set out therein, these activities shall include the irrevocable fixing of exchange rates leading to the introduction of a single currency, the ECU, and the definition and conduct of a single monetary policy and exchange rate policy the primary objective of both of which shall be to maintain price stability and, without prejudice to this objective, to support the general economic policies in the Community, in accordance with the principle of an open market economy with free competition.

3. These activities of the Member States and the Community shall entail compliance with the following guiding principles: stable prices, sound public finances and monetary conditions and a sustainable balance of payments.

[A5]   The Member States' duty of solidarity: Article 5 EEC

Article 5

Member States shall take all appropriate measures, whether general or particular, to ensure fulfilment of the obligations arising out of this Treaty or resulting from action taken by the institutions of the Community. They shall facilitate the achievement of the Community's tasks.

They shall abstain from any measure which could jeopardise the attainment of the objectives of this Treaty.

Note. This provision, which remains unaltered by the Maastricht Treaty, attracted little attention in the early days of the Community's development.

However, it has increasingly formed the cornerstone of the court's reasoning when seeking to justify its invention or revelation of new dimensions in the scope or application of Community law **[C31]**, **[C33]**, **[C48]**.

[A6]   Title XI of EC Treaty: consumer protection

Article 129a

1. The Community shall contribute to the attachment of a high level of consumer protection through:

(a)   measures adopted pursuant to Article 100a **[A33]**, **[A34]** in the context of the completion of the internal market;
(b)   specific action which supports and supplements the policy pursued by the Member States to protect the health, safety and economic interests of consumers and to provide adequate information to consumers.

2. The Council, acting in accordance with the procedure referred to in Article 189b **[B19]** and after consulting the Economic and Social Committee, shall adopt the specific action referred to in paragraph 1(b).
3. Action adopted pursuant to paragraph 2 shall not prevent any Member State from maintaining or introducing more stringent protective measures. Such measures must be compatible with this Treaty. The Commission shall be notified of them.

[A7]   Title XVI of EC Treaty: environment

Article 130r

1. Community policy on the environment shall contribute to pursuit of the following objectives:

– preserving, protecting and improving the quality of the environment;
– protecting human health;
– prudent and rational utilisation of natural resources;
– promoting measures at international level to deal with regional or world-wide environmental problems.

2. Community policy on the environment shall aim at a high level of protection taking into account the diversity of situations in the various regions of the Community. It shall be based on the precautionary principle and on the principles that preventive action should be taken, that environmental damage should as a priority be rectified at source and that the polluter should pay. Environmental protection requirements must be integrated into the definition and implementation of other Community policies.

In this context, harmonisation measures answering these requirements shall include, where appropriate, a safeguard clause allowing Member States to take provisional measures, for non-economic environmental reasons, subject to a Community inspection procedure.
3. In preparing its policy on the environment, the Community shall take account of:

- available scientific and technical data;
- environmental conditions in the various regions of the Community;
- the potential benefits and costs of action or lack of action;
- the economic and social development of the Community as a whole and the balanced development of its regions.

4. Within their respective spheres of competence, the Community and the Member States shall co-operate with third countries and with the competent international organisations. The arrangements for Community co-operation may be the subject of agreements between the Community and the third parties concerned, which shall be negotiated and concluded in accordance with Article 228.

The previous subparagraph shall be without prejudice to Member States' competence to negotiate in international bodies and to conclude international agreements.

Article 130s

1. The Council, acting in accordance with the procedure referred to in Article 189c and after consulting the Economic and Social Committee, shall decide what action is to be taken by the Community in order to achieve the objectives referred to in Article 130r.

2. By way of derogation from the decision-making procedure provided for in paragraph 1 and without prejudice to Article 100a, the Council, acting unanimously on a proposal from the Commission and after consulting the European Parliament and the Economic and Social Committee, shall adopt:

- provisions primarily of a fiscal nature;
- measures concerning town and country planning, land use with the exception of waste management and measures of a general nature, and management of water resources;
- measures significantly affecting a Member State's choice between different energy sources and the general structure of its energy supply.

The Council may, under the conditions laid down in the preceding subparagraph, define those matters referred to in this paragraph on which decisions are to be taken by a qualified majority.

3. In other areas, general action programmes setting out priority objectives to be attained shall be adopted by the Council, acting in accordance with the procedure referred to in Article 189b and after consulting the Economic and Social Committee.

The Council, acting under the terms of paragraph 1 or paragraph 2 according to the case, shall adopt the measures necessary for the implementation of these programmes.

[A8]   Maastricht Protocol on social policy

THE HIGH CONTRACTING PARTIES,

NOTING that eleven Member States, that is to say the Kingdom of Belgium, the Kingdom of Denmark, the Federal Republic of Germany, the Hellenic Republic, the Kingdom of Spain, the French Republic, Ireland, the

Italian Republic, the Grand Duchy of Luxembourg, the Kingdom of the Netherlands, and the Portuguese Republic, wish to continue along the path laid down in the 1989 Social Charter; that they have adopted among themselves an Agreement to this end; that this Agreement is annexed to this Protocol; that this Protocol and the said Agreement are without prejudice to the provisions of this Treaty, particularly those relating to social policy which constitute an integral part of the *acquis communautaire*:

1.   Agree to authorise those eleven Member States to have recourse to the institutions, procedures and mechanisms of the Treaty for the purposes of taking among themselves and applying as far as they are concerned the acts and decisions required for giving effect to the above mentioned Agreement.
2.   The United Kingdom of Great Britain and Northern Ireland shall not take part in the deliberations and the adoption by the Council of Commission proposals made on the basis of this Protocol and the above mentioned Agreement.
     By way of derogation from Article 148(2) of the Treaty, acts of the Council which are made pursuant to this Protocol and which must be adopted by a qualified majority shall be deemed to be so adopted if they have received at least forty-four votes in favour. The unanimity of the members of the Council, with the exception of the United Kingdom of Great Britain and Northern Ireland, shall be necessary for acts of the Council which must be adopted unanimously and for those amending the Commission proposal.
     Acts adopted by the Council and any financial consequences other than administrative costs entailed for the institutions shall not be applicable to the United Kingdom of Great Britain and Northern Ireland.
3.   This Protocol shall be annexed to the Treaty establishing the European Community.

[A9]   Maastricht Agreement on Social Policy

AGREEMENT ON SOCIAL POLICY CONCLUDED BETWEEN THE MEMBER STATES OF THE EUROPEAN COMMUNITY WITH THE EXCEPTION OF THE UNITED KINGDOM OF GREAT BRITAIN AND NORTHERN IRELAND

The undersigned eleven HIGH CONTRACTING PARTIES, that is to say the Kingdom of Belgium, the Kingdom of Denmark, the Federal Republic of Germany, the Hellenic Republic, the Kingdom of Spain, the French Republic, Ireland, the Italian Republic, the Grand Duchy of Luxembourg, the Kingdom of the Netherlands and the Portuguese Republic (hereinafter referred to as 'the Member States'),
WISHING to implement the 1989 Social Charter on the basis of the *acquis communautaire*,
CONSIDERING the Protocol on social policy,
HAVE AGREED as follows:

Article 1
The Community and the Member States shall have as their objectives the promotion of employment, improved living and working conditions, proper social protection, dialogue between management and labour, the development of human resources with a view to lasting high employment and the combating of exclusion. To this end the Community and the Member States shall implement measures which take account of the diverse forms of national practices, in particular in the field of contractual relations, and the need to maintain the competitiveness of the Community economy.

Article 2
1. With a view to achieving the objectives of Article 1, the Community shall support and complement the activities of the Member States in the following fields:

- improvement in particular of the working environment to protect workers' health and safety;
- working conditions;
- the information and consultation of workers;
- equality between men and women with regard to labour market opportunities and treatment at work;
- the integration of persons excluded from the labour market, without prejudice to Article 127 of the Treaty establishing the European Community (hereinafter referred to as 'the Treaty').

2. To this end, the Council may adopt, by means of directives, minimum requirements for gradual implementation, having regard to the conditions and technical rules obtaining in each of the Member States. Such directives shall avoid imposing administrative, financial and legal constraints in a way which would hold back the creation and development of small and medium-sized undertakings.

The Council shall act in accordance with the procedure referred to in Article 189c of the Treaty after consulting the Economic and Social Committee.

3. However, the Council shall act unanimously on a proposal from the Commission, after consulting the European Parliament and the Economic and Social Committee, in the following areas:

- social security and social protection of workers;
- protection of workers where their employment contract is terminated;
- representation and collective defence of the interests of workers and employers, including co-determination, subject to paragraph 6;
- conditions of employment for third country nationals legally residing in Community territory;
- financial contributions for promotion of employment and job creation, without prejudice to the provisions relating to the Social Fund.

4. A Member State may entrust management and labour, at their joint request, with the implementation of directives adopted pursuant to paragraphs 2 and 3.

In this case, it shall ensure that, no later than the date on which a directive must be transposed in accordance with Article 189, management and labour have introduced the necessary measures by agreement, the

Member State concerned being required to take any necessary measure enabling it at any time to be in a position to guarantee the results imposed by that directive.

5. The provisions adopted pursuant to this Article shall not prevent any Member State from maintaining or introducing more stringent protective measures compatible with the Treaty.

6. The provisions of this Article shall not apply to pay, the right of association, the right to strike or the right to impose lock outs.

Article 3

1. The Commission shall have the task of promoting the consultation of management and labour at Community level and shall take any relevant measure to facilitate their dialogue by ensuring balanced support for the parties.

2. To this end, before submitting proposals in the social policy field, the Commission shall consult management and labour on the possible direction of Community action.

3. If, after such consultation, the Commission considers Community action advisable, it shall consult management and labour on the content of the envisaged proposal. Management and labour shall forward to the Commission an opinion or, where appropriate, a recommendation.

4. On the occasion of such consultation, management and labour may inform the Commission of their wish to initiate the process provided for in Article 4. The duration of the procedure shall not exceed nine months, unless the management and labour concerned and the Commission decide jointly to extend it.

Article 4

1. Should management and labour so desire, the dialogue between them at Community level may lead to contractual relations, including agreements.

2. Agreements concluded at Community level shall be implemented either in accordance with the procedures and practices specific to management and labour and the Member States or, in matters covered by Article 2, at the joint request of the signatory parties, by a Council decision on a proposal from the Commission.

The Council shall act by qualified majority, except where the agreement in question contains one or more provisions relating to one of the areas referred to in Article 2(3), in which case it shall act unanimously.

Article 5

With a view to achieving the objectives of Article I and without prejudice to the other provisions of the Treaty, the Commission shall encourage co-operation between the Member States and facilitate the co-ordination of their action in all social policy fields under this Agreement.

Article 6

1. Each Member State shall ensure that the principle of equal pay for male and female workers for equal work is applied.

2. For the purpose of this Article, 'pay' means the ordinary basic or

minimum wage or salary and any other consideration, whether in cash or in kind, which the worker receives directly or indirectly, in respect of his employment, from his employer.

Equal pay without discrimination based on sex means:

(a) that pay for the same work at piece rates shall be calculated on the basis of the same unit of measurement;
(b) that pay for work at time rates shall be the same for the same job.

3. This Article shall not prevent any Member State from maintaining or adopting measures providing for specific advantages in order to make it easier for women to pursue a vocational activity or to prevent or compensate for disadvantages in their professional careers.

[A10] Title IX of EC Treaty: culture

Article 128

1. The Community shall contribute to the flowering of the cultures of the Member States, while respecting their national and regional diversity and at the same time bringing the common cultural heritage to the fore.

2. Action by the Community shall be aimed at encouraging co-operation between Member States and, if necessary, supporting and supplementing their action in the following areas:

– improvement of the knowledge and dissemination of the culture and history of the European peoples;
– conservation and safeguarding of cultural heritage of European significance;
– non-commercial cultural exchanges;
– artistic and literary creation, including the audiovisual sector.

3. The Community and the Member States shall foster co-operation with third countries and the competent international organisations in the sphere of culture, in particular the Council of Europe.

4. The Community shall take cultural aspects into account in its action under other provisions of this Treaty.

5. In order to contribute to the achievement of the objectives referred to in this Article, the Council:

– acting in accordance with the procedure referred to in Article 189b [B19] and after consulting the Committee of the Regions, shall adopt incentive measures, excluding any harmonisation of the laws and regulations of the Member States. The Council shall act unanimously throughout the procedures referred to in Article 189b;
– acting unanimously on a proposal from the Commission, shall adopt recommendations.

[A11]   Written Question No 1285/91 by Mr Leen van der Waal (NI) to the Commission of the European Communities (10 June 1991) (OJ 1992 C309/4)

Subject: Cultural activities of the Commission.

1. Does the Commission consider that there is such a thing as European culture? If so, what is it?
2. What is the Commission's legal basis for its intention to undertake cultural activities at European level?
3. Can the Commission define precisely what it means by the specifically 'European dimension' and by the 'common roots' through which European creativity is nourished?
4. There is currently a great deal of uncertainty in the Member States about the applicability of the EEC Treaty to the cultural sector. In particular there is concern about the powers remaining to the Member States with regard to their own national cultural policies.

(a)   Does the Commission agree that the pursuit of an independent cultural policy should remain a matter for the Member States?
(b)   Can the Commission make clear that the activities it has announced to promote the 'European dimension' do not impinge upon the area of responsibility of the Member States?

[A12]   Answer given by Mr Dondelinger on behalf of the Commission (19 August 1992)

The Honourable Member will be aware that the Maastricht Treaty contains new provisions for Community cultural action (Article 128). . .

To help the Council and Parliament establish a reference framework and determine priorities before the end of this year, the Commission adopted a communication on new prospects for Community cultural action on 29 April 1992. It highlights the principle of subsidiarity, the idea being that the Community should opt for activities that supplement those of the Member States with the primary objective of removing barriers, improving information flows and thereby generating added value at Community level.

The Commission further proposes greater co-operation with the professionals and the treaties in the Member States in close collaboration with the European Parliament and the new Committee of the Regions.

In all events, new action cannot be launched until the Maastricht Treaty has come into force; it will have to comply with the procedures of Articles 128 and 189b, which require unanimity in the Council.

[A13]   Title XIV of EC Treaty: economic and social cohesion

Article 130a

In order to promote its overall harmonious development, the Community shall develop and pursue its actions leading to the strengthening of its economic and social cohesion.

In particular, the Community shall aim at reducing disparities between the levels of development of the various regions and the backwardness of the least-favoured regions, including rural areas.

Article 130b

Member States shall conduct their economic policies and shall co-ordinate them in such a way as, in addition, to attain the objectives set out in Article 130a. The formulation and implementation of the Community's policies and actions and the implementation of the internal market shall take into account the objectives set out in Article 130a and shall contribute to their achievement. The Community shall also support the achievement of these objectives by the action it takes through the Structural Funds (European Agricultural Guidance and Guarantee Fund, Guidance Section; European Social Fund; European Regional Development Fund), the European Investment Bank and the other existing financial instruments.

The Commission shall submit a report to the European Parliament, the Council, the Economic and Social Committee and the Committee of the Regions every three years on the progress made towards achieving economic and social cohesion and on the manner in which the various means provided for in this Article have contributed to it. This report shall, if necessary, be accompanied by appropriate proposals.

If specific actions prove necessary outside the Funds and without prejudice to the measures decided upon within the framework of the other Community policies, such actions may be adopted by the Council acting unanimously on a proposal from the Commission and after consulting the European Parliament, the Economic and Social Committee and the Committee of the Regions.

[A14]   Title VI of EC Treaty: economic and monetary policy

CHAPTER 1

ECONOMIC POLICY

Article 102a

Member States shall conduct their economic policies with a view to contributing to the achievement of the objectives of the Community, as defined in Article 2, and in the context of the broad guidelines referred to in Article 103(2). The Member States and the Community shall act in accordance with the principle of an open market economy with free competition, favouring an efficient allocation of resources, and in compliance with the principles set out in Article 3a.

Article 103

1. Member States shall regard their economic policies as a matter of common concern and shall co-ordinate them within the Council, in accordance with the provisions of Article 102a.

2. The Council shall, acting by a qualified majority on a recommendation from the Commission, formulate a draft for the broad guidelines of the economic policies of the Member States and of the Community, and shall report its findings to the European Council.

The European Council shall, acting on the basis of the report from the Council, discuss a conclusion on the broad guidelines of the economic policies of the Member States and of the Community.

On the basis of this conclusion, the Council shall, acting by a qualified majority, adopt a recommendation setting out these broad guidelines. The Council shall inform the European Parliament of its recommendation.

3. In order to ensure closer co-ordination of economic policies and sustained convergence of the economic performances of the Member States, the Council shall, on the basis of reports submitted by the Commission, monitor economic developments in each of the Member States and in the Community as well as the consistency of economic policies with the broad guidelines referred to in paragraph 2, and regularly carry out an overall assessment.

For the purpose of this multilateral surveillance, Member States shall forward information to the Commission about important measures taken by them in the field of their economic policy and such other information as they deem necessary.

4. Where it is established, under the procedure referred to in paragraph 3, that the economic policies of a Member State are not consistent with the broad guidelines referred to in paragraph 2 or that they risk jeopardising the proper functioning of economic and monetary union, the Council may, acting by a qualified majority on a recommendation from the Commission, make the necessary recommendations to the Member State concerned. The Council may, acting by a qualified majority on a proposal from the Commission, decide to make its recommendations public.

The President of the Council and the Commission shall report to the European Parliament on the results of multilateral surveillance. The President of the Council may be invited to appear before the competent Committee of the European Parliament if the Council has made its recommendations public.

5. The Council, acting in accordance with the procedure referred to in Article 189c, may adopt detailed rules for the multilateral surveillance procedure referred to in paragraphs 3 and 4 of this Article.

Article 104c

1. Member States shall avoid excessive government deficits.

2. The Commission shall monitor the development of the budgetary situation and of the stock of government debt in the Member States with a view to identifying gross errors. In particular it shall examine compliance with budgetary discipline on the basis of the following two criteria:

(a) whether the ratio of the planned or actual government deficit to gross domestic product exceeds a reference value, unless:
  – either the ratio has declined substantially and continuously and reached a level that comes close to the reference value;
  – or, alternatively, the excess over the reference value is only exceptional and temporary and the ratio remains close to the reference value;

(b)   whether the ratio of government debt to gross domestic product exceeds a reference value, unless the ratio is sufficiently diminishing and approaching the reference value at a satisfactory pace.

The reference values are specified in the Protocol on the excessive deficit procedure annexed to this Treaty.

[A15]   Maastricht Treaty: provisions on a common foreign and security policy

Article J

A common foreign and security policy is hereby established which shall be governed by the following provisions.

Article J.1

1. The Union and its Member States shall define and implement a common foreign and security policy, governed by the provisions of this Title and covering all areas of foreign and security policy.
   2. The objectives of the common foreign and security policy shall be:

   − to safeguard the common values, fundamental interests and independence of the Union;
   − to strengthen the security of the Union and its Member States in all ways;
   − to preserve peace and strengthen international security, in accordance with the principles of the United Nations Charter as well as the principles of the Helsinki Final Act and the objectives of the Paris Charter;
   − to promote international co-operation;
   − to develop and consolidate democracy and the rule of law, and respect for human rights and fundamental freedoms.

   3. The Union shall pursue these objectives:

   − by establishing systematic co-operation between Member States in the conduct of policy, in accordance with Article J.2;
   − by gradually implementing, in accordance with Article J.3, joint action in the areas in which the Member States have important interests in common.

4. The Member States shall support the Union's external and security policy actively and unreservedly in a spirit of loyalty and mutual solidarity. They shall refrain from any action which is contrary to the interests of the Union or likely to impair its effectiveness as a cohesive force in international relations. The Council shall ensure that these principles are complied with.

Article J.2

1. Member States shall inform and consult one another within the Council on any matter of foreign and security policy of general interest in order to ensure that their combined influence is exerted as effectively as possible by means of concerted and convergent action.

2. Whenever it deems it necessary, the Council shall define a common position.

Member States shall ensure that their national policies conform to the common positions.

3. Member States shall co-ordinate their action in international organisations and at international conferences. They shall uphold the common positions in such fora.

In international organisations and at international conferences where not all the Member States participate, those which do take part shall uphold the common positions.

Article J.3

The procedure for adopting joint action in matters covered by the foreign and security policy shall be the following:

1. The Council shall decide, on the basis of general guidelines from the European Council, that a matter should be the subject of joint action.

Whenever the Council decides on the principle of joint action, it shall lay down the specific scope, the Union's general and specific objectives in carrying out such action, if necessary its duration, and the means, procedures and conditions for its implementation.

2. The Council shall, when adopting the joint action and at any stage during its development, define those matters on which decisions are to be taken by a qualified majority.

Where the Council is required to act by a qualified majority pursuant to the preceding subparagraph, the votes of its members shall be weighted in accordance with Article 148(2) of the Treaty establishing the European Community **[B19]**, and for their adoption, acts of the Council shall require at least fifty-four votes in favour, cast by at least eight members.

3. If there is a change in circumstances having a substantial effect on a question subject to joint action, the Council shall review the principles and objectives of that action and take the necessary decisions. As long as the Council has not acted, the joint action shall stand.

4. Joint actions shall commit the Member States in the positions they adopt and in the conduct of their activity.

. . .

Article J.7

The Presidency shall consult the European Parliament on the main aspects and the basic choices of the common foreign and security policy and shall ensure that the views of the European Parliament are duly taken into consideration. The European Parliament shall be kept regularly informed by the Presidency and the Commission of the development of the Union's foreign and security policy.

The European Parliament may ask questions of the Council or make recommendations to it. It shall hold an annual debate on progress in implementing the common foreign and security policy.

Article J.8

1. The European Council shall define the principles of and general guidelines for the common foreign and security policy.

2. The Council shall take the decisions necessary for defining and implementing the common foreign and security policy on the basis of the general guidelines adopted by the European Council. It shall ensure the unity, consistency and effectiveness of action by the Union.

The Council shall act unanimously, except for procedural questions and in the case referred to in Article J.3(2).

3. Any Member State or the Commission may refer to the Council any question relating to the common foreign and security policy and may submit proposals to the Council.

4. In cases requiring a rapid decision, the Presidency, of its own motion, or at the request of the Commission or a Member State, shall convene an extraordinary Council meeting within forty-eight hours or, in an emergency, within a shorter period.

5. Without prejudice to Article 151 of the Treaty establishing the European Community, a Political Committee consisting of Political Directors shall monitor the international situation in the areas covered by common foreign and security policy and contribute to the definition of policies by delivering opinions to the Council at the request of the Council or on its own initiative. It shall also monitor the implementation of agreed policies, without prejudice to the responsibility of the Presidency and the Commission.

Article J.9

The Commission shall be fully associated with the work carried out in the common foreign and security policy field.

[A16]   Maastricht Treaty: provisions on co-operation in the fields of justice and home affairs

Article K

Co-operation in the fields of justice and home affairs shall be governed by the following provisions.

Article K.1

For the purpose of achieving the objectives of the Union, in particular the free movement of persons, and without prejudice to the powers of the European Community, Member States shall regard the following areas as matters of common interest:

1. asylum policy;
2. rules governing the crossing by persons of the external borders of the Member States and the exercise of controls thereon;
3. immigration policy and policy regarding nationals of third countries:

(a) conditions of entry and movement by nationals of third countries on the territory of Member States;
(b) conditions of residence by nationals of third countries on the territory of Member States, including family reunion and access to employment;

(c)   combating unauthorised immigration, residence and work by nationals of third countries on the territory of Member States;

4. combating drug addiction in so far as this is not covered by 7 to 9;
5. combating fraud on an international scale in so far as this is not covered by 7 to 9;
6. judicial co-operation in civil matters;
7. judicial co-operation in criminal matters;
8. customs co-operation;
9. police co-operation for the purposes of preventing and combating terrorism, unlawful drug trafficking and other serious forms of international crime, including if necessary certain aspects of customs co-operation, in connection with the organisation of a Union-wide system for exchanging information within a European Police Office (Europol).

Article K.2

1. The matters referred to in Article K.1 shall be dealt with in compliance with the European Convention for the Protection of Human Rights and Fundamental Freedoms of 4 November 1950 and the Convention relating to the Status of Refugees of 28 July 1951 and having regard to the protection afforded by Member States to persons persecuted on political grounds.
2. This Title shall not affect the exercise of the responsibilities incumbent upon Member States with regard to the maintenance of law and order and the safeguarding of internal security.

Article K.3

1. In the areas referred to in Article K.1, Member States shall inform and consult one another within the Council with a view to co-ordinating their action. To that end, they shall establish collaboration between the relevant departments of their administrations.

. . .

Article K.6

The Presidency and the Commission shall regularly inform the European Parliament of discussions in the areas covered by this Title.

The Presidency shall consult the European Parliament on the principal aspects of activities in the areas referred to in this Title and shall ensure that the views of the European Parliament are duly taken into consideration.

The European Parliament may ask questions of the Council or make recommendations to it. Each year, it shall hold a debate on the progress made in implementation of the areas referred to in this Title.

Article K.7

The provisions of this Title shall not prevent the establishment or development of closer co-operation between two or more Member States so far as such co-operation does not conflict with, or impede, that provided for in this Title.

. . .

Article K.9

The Council, acting unanimously on the initiative of the Commission or a Member State, may decide to apply Article 100c of the Treaty establishing the European Community to action in areas referred to in Article K.1(1) to (6), and at the same time determine the relevant voting conditions relating to it. It shall recommend the Member States to adopt that decision in accordance with their respective constitutional requirements.

SECTION TWO

ESTABLISHING THE COMMUNITY DIMENSION

MATERIALS

1   The approach of the Court of Justice under the EC Treaty

[A17]   Case C-60/91 Portugal v Morais [1992] 2 CMLR 533

The European Court of Justice

1. By order of 10 December 1990, received by the court on 13 February 1991, the Tribunal da Relaçao, Lisbon, requested a preliminary ruling pursuant to Article 177 EEC on four questions relating to the interpretation of the Treaty rules on the freedom of movement of persons and services, and of the competition rules, and the interpretation of Council Directive 80/1263 on the introduction of a Community driving licence.

2. The questions have arisen in the context of criminal proceedings brought by the Public Prosecutor against Mr José António Batista Morais, a driving instructor employed by a driving school established in Lisbon, who was charged with giving driving lessons on a motorway situated on the territory of a district adjoining Lisbon. Under Portuguese law it is an offence to give driving lessons in the territory of a district other than the one where the driving school is established.

3. Mr Batista Morais appealed against his conviction by the first instance court, which imposed a fine, basing his appeal on the ground that the national measures were contrary to the above-mentioned Directive 80/1263 in that they do not permit driving instruction to be given on motorways.

4. In these circumstances the Tribunal da Relaçao, Lisbon, decided to stay the proceedings until the Court of Justice gives a preliminary ruling on the following questions:

(a)   May or must Article 7(1) of Decree-Law 6/82 be regarded as infringing the rules on the free movement of persons and services and, in particular, Articles 52, 53, 54(2) and (3)(c), 56 and 57 EEC (on the right of establishment), Articles 60(a), 63(2) and 65 EEC (on the free movement of services) and Article 85(1)(c) (on the rules of competition), and as such is it inapplicable in national law?

(b)   Must the rules on the free movement of persons, services and goods laid down in the Treaty, which relate to the citizens or goods of one state in connection with situations arising in another Member State of the Community, also be applied in cases where barriers to freedom of movement may arise in relation to citizens of only one Member State and within its geographical territory?

(c)   May or must Directive 80/1263, although it concerns driving tests, be interpreted as meaning that driving instruction itself is subject to similar requirements, such as the requirement that it must be provided, as far as possible, on motorways and in different traffic conditions as advised for the purposes of the test?

(d) Finally, may or must the directive in question be interpreted as being in the nature purely and simply of a directive within the meaning of Article 189 EEC inasmuch as it is left to the national authorities to determine the choice of form and methods for its implementation (that is to say, where it needs merely to be implemented) or must it, on the contrary, notwithstanding its designation as a directive, be regarded as a generally applicable and mandatory directive of the kind adopted pursuant to Articles 56, 63 and 87 EEC?

. . .

6. Having regard to considerations of logic in reasoning, it is appropriate to take the second question first, which asks in essence whether the rules of the Treaty relating to the freedom of movement of persons and services apply to barriers affecting nationals of a Member State on its own territory.

7. To reply to this question, it should be observed that, in accordance with the court's established case law, the provisions of the Treaty concerning the freedom of movement of persons and services cannot be applied to activities all the elements of which are confined within a single Member State: see most recently Joined Cases C-330 and C-331/90 *Lopez Brea*.

8. It appears from the facts as found by the national court in the order making the reference that the main proceedings concern a Portuguese national who is employed in Portugal as a driving instructor by a driving school and that the situation in which he finds himself has no element of connection with any of the situations envisaged by Community law.

9. Consequently the reply to the second question should be that the rules of the Treaty concerning the freedom of movement of persons and services do not apply to obstacles affecting nationals of a Member State on its own territory when the situation in which they find themselves has no element of connection with any of the situations envisaged by Community law.

10. In view of the reply to the second question, the first question must be construed as meaning that the national court wishes to ascertain whether Article 85(1) precludes national measures which restrict the activities of a driving school to the territory of the district where it is established.

11. In this connection, it should be observed that, according to established case law, Member States are required by Article 5(2) EEC not to jeopardise, by their national legislation, full and uniform application of Community law and the effect of acts implementing it, and not to take or maintain in force measures likely to obviate the useful effect of the rules of competition applying to enterprises: see Case 231/83 *Cullet*.

12. It is unnecessary to ascertain whether and, if so, to what extent provisions of the type concerned in the main proceedings promote or render compulsory or inevitable any of the practices by undertakings referred to by Article 85 EEC, and it is sufficient to point out that this provision can be applied only in so far as the allegedly anti-competitive practices are capable of affecting trade between Member States.

13. This condition would be fulfilled only if it were shown that the national legislation, like a network of similar agreements concluded in a reference

market, would have the effect of preventing access to the market for new national and foreign competitors: see Case-234/89 *Delimitis*. It must, however, be said that national legislation of the type in question in the main proceedings is not capable of having any such effect.

14. In these circumstances, the reply to the first question must be that Article 85 EEC does not preclude national legislation which confines the activities of a driving school to the territory of the district where it is established.

15. By the third question the national court asks, essentially, whether the above-mentioned Directive 80/1263 requires the Member States to provide for driving tests to be conducted on motorways wherever these are accessible from the test centre and, therefore, whether the Member States must also ensure that driving instruction can be given on motorways.

16. To reply to this question, it should be observed first that Directive 80/1263 is part of a gradual process of harmonisation of national systems for driving tests and, in Annex II, merely lays down certain minimum requirements without attempting to bring about total harmonisation of regulations for driving tests.

17. Secondly, it should be noted that, with regard to the location of the driving test, paragraph 9 of Annex II, which is entitled 'Minimum requirements for driving tests', provides that the part of the test relating to the candidate's behaviour in traffic shall be conducted, wherever possible, on roads outside built-up areas and on motorways as well as in urban traffic.

18. It is clear from the purpose of the directive and the wording of paragraph 9 of Annex II that the Member States have, with regard to determining the location of the driving test, a discretionary power which enables them to take account of the accessibility of certain kinds of roads and considerations arising from the need to ensure a uniform examination throughout the whole of their territory and secure road safety.

19. In these circumstances the reply to the third question should be that Directive 80/1263 does not require the Member States to provide for driving tests to be conducted on motorways wherever these are accessible from test centres and that therefore they also have no obligation to ensure that driving instruction can be given on roads of that kind.

20. In view of the reply to the third question, the fourth does not fall to be answered.

[A18]   Case C-169/91 Council of the City of Stoke-on-Trent, Norwich City Council v B & Q plc [1993] AC 900

Report for the hearing

I   Facts and procedure

1. The House of Lords is seised of two consolidated appeals . . . concerning the applicability of Article 30 of the EEC Treaty to s 47 of the Shops Act 1950.

2. Section 47 aforesaid provides that: 'Every shop shall, save as otherwise provided by this part of this Act, be closed for the serving of customers on Sunday: provided that a shop may be open for the serving of customers on Sunday for the purposes of any transaction mentioned in the Fifth

Schedule to this Act.' The Fifth Schedule . . . contains a list of items which may be sold in shops on Sundays, such as intoxicating liquors, certain food-stuffs, tobacco, newspapers and other products of everyday consumption.

3. After the judgment of the court . . . in Case C-145/88 *Torfaen Borough Council v B & Q plc* [1989] ECR 3851, in which the court held that 'Article 30 of the Treaty must be interpreted as meaning that the prohibition which it lays down does not apply to national rules prohibiting retailers from opening their premises on Sunday where the restrictive effects on Community trade which may result therefrom do not exceed the effects intrinsic to rules of that kind', the respondent local authorities each issued proceedings against the appellant ('B & Q') for a final injunction to enforce compliance with s 47 of the Shops Act 1950 in B & Q's Stoke and Norwich stores . . . [The] High Court held (in the judgment appealed against before the House of Lords) that the local authorities were entitled to final injunctions.

. . .

7. After delivery of the judgment appealed against in the national proceedings, the court in two judgments . . . held that Article 30 must be interpreted as meaning that the prohibition which it lays down does not apply to national legislation prohibiting the employment of staff on Sundays (Case C-312/89 *Conforama* [1991] ECR I-997) or on Sundays after 12 noon (Case C-332/89 *Marchandise* [1991] ECR I-1027).

8. Before the House of Lords it became apparent that the parties are at issue on two specific points, namely:

(a) the interpretation and effect of the judgment of the Court of Justice in *Torfaen* and in particular the nature of the task reserved to the national court in determining whether the effects of national rules remain within the limits of the effects intrinsic to trading rules; and

(b) the possible application of the principles laid down in the *Conforama* and *Marchandise* judgments, cited above, to the United Kingdom legislative situation.

9. the House of Lords requested the court to give a preliminary ruling on the following questions:

'1. Is the effect of the . . . rulings in . . . *Conforama* and . . . *Marchandise* to determine that the prohibition contained in Article 30 . . . does not apply to national rules, such as those in issue in . . . *Torfaen* . . ., which prohibit retailers from opening their premises on Sunday for the serving of customers with certain goods?. . .'

[Second and third questions omitted]

II Written observations submitted to the court

According to B & Q, irrespective of the fact that there are strong arguments for saying that no discernible objective can be attributed to the Sunday trading restrictions in question, those rules are disproportionate since the 'objective' of s 47 of the Shops Act 1950 cannot possibly have sufficient importance to outweigh a reduction in intra-Community trade of around one billion ECUs per annum.

B & Q considers that the importance of the objective may be regarded as less where the restriction is subject to many exceptions. Thus, the exceptions to s 47 of the Shops Act 1950 have the effect that many shops, such as B & Q, are permitted to open on Sunday for the sale of much of their stock. Similarly, the fact that the whole of Scotland is exempt from the restriction is a further indication of the degree of importance attached to the objective (whatever it may be) of s 47. In the same way, the total absence of any analogous restriction for workers in all industrial and commercial sectors other than retailing has a bearing on the importance of the aim.

In any event, it would be difficult to find a measure whose enforcement is given lower priority than s 47. A significant number of local authorities do not enforce it at all; none enforces it fully; those authorities which do attempt to enforce the restrictions do so only against a few, usually the largest traders in the area. The vast majority of retail establishments are left to decide whether to open on Sunday or not.

In B & Q's view, it is also relevant to take into account other negative effects of the law in addition to the restrictions on inter-state trade, such as the loss of employment, particularly part-time employment opportunities, which enforcement of s 47 would entail; and indeed the fact that Sunday has become the most important trading day for non-essential, leisure items, such as garden and DIY products. Other days of the week could not compensate for the loss of such revenue.

B & Q concludes its observations . . . by pointing out that, contrary to the situation in 1950, a very large proportion of shop workers employed on Sundays are now part-time workers. Although part-time workers need to be protected, the measures designed to protect full-time workers (particularly in the context of weekend working) are not appropriate for part-time workers, given that it is at the weekend in particular that part-time jobs are available in the retail sector.

Even if (which is not the case) the objective of the Sunday trading rules were held to extend beyond the protection of shop workers (for example, to the protection of what some regard as the 'traditional' English and Welsh Sunday), all the available evidence suggests that none of the alternative measures, or even the introduction of total deregulation as in Scotland, would adversely affect the present level of achievement to any perceptible degree. This is because, on the one hand, the existence of 'mixed' shops, such as the stores of B & Q, means that even under the existing law many shops are entitled to open on Sunday for the sale of some of their goods and, on the other hand, the Scottish experience shows that even with total deregulation . . . only 15 to 20% of shops choose to open on Sunday . . .

The European Court of Justice

. . .

The first question

. . .

9. In those three judgments [*Conforama, Marchandise* and *Torfaen*] the court found that the various bodies of national legislation concerning the closing of shops on Sundays were not intended to regulate the flow of goods.

10. It is also apparent from those judgments that such legislation may

indeed have adverse repercussions on the volume of sales of certain shops, but that it affects the sale of both domestic and imported products. The marketing of products from other Member States is not therefore made more difficult than the marketing of national products.

11. Furthermore, in the above-mentioned judgments the court recognised that the legislation at issue pursued an aim which was justified under Community law. National rules restricting the opening of shops on Sundays reflected certain choices relating to particular national or regional socio-cultural characteristics. It was for the Member States to make those choices in compliance with the requirements of Community law, in particular the principle of proportionality.

12. As far as that principle is concerned, the court stated in its judgment in the *Torfaen* . . . case that such rules were not prohibited by Article 30 of the Treaty where the restrictive effects on Community trade which might result from them did not exceed the effects intrinsic to such rules and that the question whether the effects of those rules actually remained within that limit was a question of fact to be determined by the national court.

13. In its judgments in . . . *Conforama* and *Marchandise* . . ., however, the court found it necessary to make clear, with regard to similar rules, that the restrictive effects on trade which might result from them did not appear to be excessive in relation to the aim pursued.

14. The court considered that it had all the information necessary for it to rule on the question of the proportionality of such rules and that it had to do so in order to enable national courts to assess their compatibility with Community law in a uniform manner since such an assessment cannot be allowed to vary according to the findings of fact made by individual courts in particular cases.

15. Appraising the proportionality of national rules which pursue a legitimate aim under Community law involves weighing the national interest in attaining that aim against the Community interest in ensuring the free movement of goods. In that regard, in order to verify that the restrictive effects on intra-Community trade of the rules at issue do not exceed what is necessary to achieve the aim in view, it must be considered whether those effects are direct, indirect or purely speculative and whether those effects do not impede the marketing of imported products more than the marketing of national products.

16. It was on the basis of those considerations that in its judgments in the *Conforama* and *Marchandise* cases the court ruled that the restrictive effects on trade of national rules . . . were not excessive in relation to the aim pursued. For the same reasons, the court must make the same finding with regard to national rules prohibiting shops from opening on Sundays.

17. It must therefore be stated in reply to the first question that Article 30 of the Treaty is to be interpreted as meaning that the prohibition which it lays down does not apply to national legislation prohibiting retailers from opening their premises on Sundays . . .

Questions

1. Could the rules in *Stoke on Trent* relating to Sunday trading be described as 'wholly internal to a Member State'? Would it be appropriate to say that the driving school regulations in *Morais* were 'not excessive in relation to the aim pursued'?

2. Does this juxtaposition of the approaches taken in the two cases make any conceptual difference as far as the legal basis for the non-application of Community law is concerned?

[A19]   Case C-159/90 Society for the Protection of Unborn Children Ireland Ltd v Grogan [1991] ECR I-4685

The European Court of Justice (Judgment, 4 October 1991)

1. By order dated 5 March 1990 . . . the High Court of Ireland referred to the court for a preliminary ruling under Article 177 of the EEC Treaty three questions on the interpretation of Community law, in particular Article 60 **[E45]** of the EEC Treaty.

2. The questions arose in proceedings brought by the Society for the Protection of Unborn Children Ireland Ltd ('SPUC') against Stephen Grogan and 14 other officers of students associations in connection with the distribution in Ireland of specific information relating to the identity and location of clinics in another Member State where medical termination of pregnancy is carried out.

3. Abortion has always been prohibited in Ireland, first of all at common law, then by statute. The relevant provisions at present in force are ss 58 and 59 of the Offences Against the Person Act 1861, as reaffirmed in the Health (Family Planning) Act 1979.

4. In 1983 a constitutional amendment approved by referendum inserted in Article 40, s 3, of the Irish Constitution a third subsection worded as follows: 'The State acknowledges the right to life of the unborn and, with due regard to the equal right to life of the mother, guarantees in its laws to respect, and, as far as practicable, by its laws to defend and vindicate that right.'

5. According to the Irish courts (High Court, judgment of 19 December 1986, and Supreme Court, judgment of 16 March 1988, *A-G (ex rel Society for the Protection of Unborn Children (Ireland) Ltd) v Open Door Counselling Ltd and Dublin Wellwoman Centre Ltd* [1988] IR 593) to assist pregnant women in Ireland to travel abroad to obtain abortions, inter alia by informing them of the identity and location of a specific clinic or clinics where abortions are performed and how to contact such clinics, is prohibited under Article 40.3.3 of the Irish Constitution.

6. SPUC, the plaintiff in the main proceedings, is a company incorporated under Irish law whose purpose is to prevent the decriminalisation of abortion and to affirm, defend and promote human life from the moment of conception. In 1989–90 Stephen Grogan and the other defendants in the main proceedings were officers of student associations which issued certain publications for students. Those publications contained information about the availability of legal abortion in the United Kingdom, the identity and location of a number of abortion clinics in that country and how to contact them. It is undisputed that the student associations had no links with clinics in another Member State.

7. In September 1989 SPUC requested the defendants, in their capacity as officers of their respective associations, to undertake not to publish information of the kind described above during the academic year 1989–90. The

defendants did not reply, and SPUC then brought proceedings in the High Court for a declaration that the distribution of such information was unlawful and for an injunction restraining its distribution.

8. By a judgment of 11 October 1989 the High Court decided to refer certain questions to the Court of Justice for a preliminary ruling under Article 177 of the EEC Treaty before ruling on the injunction applied for by the plaintiff. An appeal was brought against that judgment and, on 19 December 1989, the Supreme Court granted the injunction applied for but did not overturn the High Court's decision to refer questions to the Court of Justice for a preliminary ruling. Moreover, each of the parties was given leave to apply to the High Court in order to vary the decision of the Supreme Court in the light of the preliminary ruling to be given by the Court of Justice.

9. As it had already indicated in its judgment of 11 October 1989, the High Court considered that the case raised problems of interpretation of Community law; it therefore stayed the proceedings and referred the following questions to the Court of Justice for a preliminary ruling:

1. Does the organised activity or process of carrying out an abortion or the medical termination of pregnancy come within the definition of 'services' provided for in Article 60 of the Treaty establishing the European Economic Community?

2. In the absence of any measures providing for the approximation of the laws of Member States concerning the organised activity or process of carrying out an abortion or the medical termination of pregnancy, can a Member State prohibit the distribution of specific information about the identity, location and means of communication with a specified clinic or clinics in another Member State where abortions are performed?

3. Is there a right at Community law in a person in Member State A to distribute specific information about the identity, location and means of communication with a specified clinic or clinics in Member State B where abortions are performed, where the provision of abortion is prohibited under both the constitution and the criminal law of Member State A but is lawful under certain conditions in Member State B?

. . .

First question

16. In its first question, the national court essentially seeks to establish whether medical termination of pregnancy, performed in accordance with the law of the State where it is carried out, constitutes a service within the meaning of Article 60 of the EEC Treaty.

17. According to the first paragraph of that provision, services are to be considered to be 'services' within the meaning of the EEC Treaty where they are normally provided for remuneration, in so far as they are not governed by the provisions relating to freedom of movement for goods, capital or persons. Indent (d) of the second paragraph of Article 60 expressly states that activities of the professions fall within the definition of services.

18. It must be held that termination of pregnancy, as lawfully practised in several Member States, is a medical activity which is normally provided for remuneration and may be carried out as part of a professional activity. In any event, the court has already held in the judgment in [*Luisi and Carbone v Ministero del Tesoro*](Joined Cases 286/82 and 26/83 . . . [1984] ECR

377, paragraph 16) that medical activities fall within the scope of Article 60 of the Treaty.

19. SPUC, however, maintains that the provision of abortion cannot be regarded as being a service, on the grounds that it is grossly immoral and involves the destruction of the life of a human being, namely the unborn child.

20. Whatever the merits of those arguments on the moral plane, they cannot influence the answer to the national court's first question. It is not for the court to substitute its assessment for that of the legislature in those Member States where the activities in question are practised legally.

21. Consequently, the answer to the national court's first question must be that medical termination of pregnancy, performed in accordance with the law of the state in which it is carried out, constitutes a service within the meaning of Article 60 of the Treaty.

Second and third questions

22. Having regard to the facts of the case, it must be considered that, in its second and third questions, the national court seeks essentially to establish whether it is contrary to Community law for a Member State in which medical termination of pregnancy is forbidden to prohibit students associations from distributing information about the identity and location of clinics in another Member State where voluntary termination of pregnancy is lawfully carried out and the means of communication with those clinics, where the clinics in question have no involvement in the distribution of the said information.

23. Although the national court's questions refer to Community law in general, the court takes the view that its attention should be focused on the provisions of Article 59 et seq of the EEC Treaty, which deal with the freedom to provide services, and the argument concerning human rights, which has been treated extensively in the observations submitted to the court.

24. As regards, first, the provisions of Article 59 of the Treaty, which prohibit any restriction on the freedom to provide services, it is apparent from the facts of the case that the link between the activity of the students associations of which Mr Grogan and the other defendants are officers and medical termination of pregnancies carried out in clinics in another Member State is too tenuous for the prohibition on the distribution of information to be capable of being regarded as a restriction within the meaning of Article 59 of the Treaty.

25. The situation in which students associations distributing the information at issue in the main proceedings are not in co-operation with the clinics whose addresses they publish can be distinguished from the situation which gave rise to the judgment in . . . Case C-362/88 *GB-INNO-BM v Confédération du Commerce Luxembourgeoise Asbl* [1990] ECR I-667 **[E25]**, in which the court held that a prohibition on the distribution of advertising was capable of constituting a barrier to the free movement of goods and therefore had to be examined in the light of Articles 30, 31 and 36 of the EEC Treaty.

26. The information to which the national court's questions refer is not distributed on behalf of an economic operator established in another Member State. On the contrary, the information constitutes a manifestation of freedom of expression and of the freedom to impart and receive information which is independent of the economic activity carried on by clinics established in another Member State.

27. It follows that, in any event, a prohibition on the distribution of information in circumstances such as those which are the subject of the main proceedings cannot be regarded as a restriction within the meaning of Article 59 of the Treaty.

28. Secondly, it is necessary to consider the argument of the defendants in the main proceedings to the effect that the prohibition in question, inasmuch as it is based on a constitutional amendment approved in 1983, is contrary to Article 62 of the EEC Treaty, which provides that Member States are not to introduce any new restrictions on the freedom to provide services in fact attained at the date when the Treaty entered into force.

29. It is sufficient to observe, as far as that argument is concerned, that Article 62, which is complementary to Article 59, cannot prohibit restrictions which do not fall within the scope of Article 59.

30. Thirdly and lastly, the defendants in the main proceedings maintain that a prohibition such as the one at issue is in breach of fundamental rights, especially of freedom of expression and the freedom to receive and impart information, enshrined in particular in Article 10(1) of the European Convention on Human Rights.

31. According to, inter alia, the judgment of 18 June 1991 in . . . Case C-260/89 *Elliniki Radiophonia Tiléorassi v Dimotiki Étairia Pliroforissis* [1991] ECR I-2925, paragraph 42, where national legislation falls within the field of application of Community law the court, when requested to give a preliminary ruling, must provide the national court with all the elements of interpretation which are necessary in order to enable it to assess the compatibility of that legislation with the fundamental rights – as laid down in particular in the European Convention on Human Rights – the observance of which the court ensures. However, the court has no such jurisdiction with regard to national legislation lying outside the scope of Community law. In view of the facts of the case and of the conclusions which the court has reached above with regard to the scope of Articles 59 and 62 of the Treaty, that would appear to be true of the prohibition at issue before the national court.

32. The reply to the national court's second and third questions must therefore be that it is not contrary to Community law for a Member State in which medical termination of pregnancy is forbidden to prohibit students associations from distributing information about the identity and location of clinics in another Member State where voluntary termination of pregnancy is lawfully carried out and the means of communicating with those clinics, where the clinics in question have no involvement in the distribution of the said information.

[A20]   Case C-379/87 Groener v Minister for Education and the City of Dublin Vocational Educational Committee [1989] ECR 3967

Opinion of Advocate General Darmon

1. The case before the court today following a request for a preliminary ruling submitted by the High Court, Dublin, relates to one of the most sensitive aspects of cultural identity. The importance of the court's reply and its consequences for the Member States and for the diversity of the Community as a whole are so evident that I need not dwell upon them, for at issue here is the power of the state to protect and foster the use of a national language.

2. The facts are as follows. Mrs Groener, the applicant in the main proceedings, who is a Netherlands national, has, since September 1982, been
working as a part-time teacher of art at the College of Marketing and
Design, Dublin. That establishment comes under the authority of the City of
Dublin Vocational Educational Committee, which is a public body responsible for the administration of vocational education subsidised by the State in
the Dublin area. In July 1984, Mrs Groener entered a competition with a
view to obtaining a permanent teaching post. She was successful in the
competition but failed the special examination in Irish. Circular Letter 28/79
of the Irish Minister for Education requires candidates for permanent posts
as assistant lecturer, lecturer or senior lecturer in the City of Dublin or any
post subject to any other Vocational Educational Committee to demonstrate
their knowledge of the Irish language. Such proof may be supplied either by
production of a certificate (*An Ceard-Teastas Gaeilge*) or by passing a special examination in the Irish language. It is not disputed that the post in
question fell within the scope of that circular letter.

3. Mrs Groener challenged the refusal to appoint her before the Irish
courts. She argued that Circular Letter 28/79 was incompatible with Article
48 of the EEC Treaty and Article 3 of Regulation 1612/68 of the Council on
freedom of movement for workers within the Community (hereinafter
referred to as 'the Regulation'), which prohibit discrimination against
Community nationals.

4. Consequently, the High Court, Dublin, submitted a number of questions which, in substance, request this court to give a ruling on whether a
national provision requiring knowledge of one of the official languages of a
Member State for a permanent teaching post is compatible with Article 48 of
the Treaty and Article 3 of the Regulation in circumstances where, according to the national court, knowledge of that language is not actually
necessary to carry out the relevant duties.

5. The disputed administrative measure is applicable without distinction
to Irish nationals and other Community nationals. However, it should be
recalled that, generally speaking, the court not only takes into account
direct discrimination but also endeavours to ascertain whether the legal
appearance of a provision applicable without distinction conceals de facto
discrimination due to the specific circumstances prevailing in the field in
question.

. . .

12. The order making the reference asks three questions which relate,
first, to the possible existence of de facto discrimination, secondly to the
concept of a post the nature of which requires linguistic knowledge and,
finally, to the concept of public policy.

. . .

16. However, it does not seem to me necessary to embark upon a complex analysis to ascertain whether lack of knowledge of the Irish language
may in fact create difficulties in the efficient teaching of the subject concerned, for – and we are now at the heart of the matter – it is a question of
drawing a line between the powers of the Community and those of the
Member States and of considering whether or not a policy of preserving and
fostering a language may be pursued, having regard to the requirements of
Community law. The Regulation attempted to reconcile these apparently

conflicting requirements by excluding conditions relating to linguistic knowledge from the scope of the principle of non-discrimination when the nature of the post to be filled requires such knowledge. May the intention of a state to promote the use of one of its languages be taken into account in this respect?

. . .

18. Certainly, Irish cannot be described as a regional language. Indeed, the Irish Constitution gives it the status of a national language. However, since it is a minority language, such a language cannot be preserved without the adoption of voluntary and obligatory measures. Any minority phenomenon, in whatever field, cannot usually survive if appropriate measures are not taken.

19. The preservation of languages is one of those questions of principle which one cannot dismiss without striking at the very heart of cultural identity. Is it therefore for the Community to decide whether or not a particular language should survive? Is the Community to set Europe's linguistic heritage in its present state for all time? Is it to fossilise it?

20. It seems to me that every state has the right to try to ensure the diversity of its cultural heritage and, consequently, to establish the means to carry out such a policy. Such means concern primarily public education. Likewise, every state has the right to determine the importance it wishes to attribute to its cultural heritage. The fact that Irish is recognised as an official language in the constitution is evidence in this case of the desire of the Irish State to attribute major importance to the preservation of this heritage.

21. Once a constitution (that is to say, all the fundamental values to which a nation solemnly declares that it adheres) recognises the existence of two official languages without limiting their use to specific parts of the national territory or to certain matters, each citizen has the right to be taught in those two languages. The fact that only 33.6% of Irish citizens use the Irish language is no justification for sweeping away that right altogether, for its importance is measured not only by its use but also by the possibility of preserving its use in the future.

. . .

23. Every Irishman has the right – enshrined, as we have seen, in the Irish State's most fundamental legal instrument – to be taught any subject at all, including painting, in Irish, if he so desires. Whatever the official language used in an educational institution, a state is entitled to ensure that any citizen can express himself and be understood there in another language, which is also an official language and which is a repository of and a means of transmitting a common cultural heritage.

24. Consequently, it seems to me that teaching posts fall by their nature within a field essential to the pursuit of a policy of preserving and fostering a language . . .

The European Court of Justice

. . .

18. As is apparent from the documents before the court, although Irish is not spoken by the whole Irish population, the policy followed by Irish

governments for many years has been designed not only to maintain but also to promote the use of Irish as a means of expressing national identity and culture. It is for that reason that Irish courses are compulsory for children receiving primary education and optional for those receiving secondary education. The obligation imposed on lecturers in public vocational education schools to have a certain knowledge of the Irish language is one of the measures adopted by the Irish government in furtherance of that policy.

19. The EEC Treaty does not prohibit the adoption of a policy for the protection and promotion of a language of a Member State which is both the national language and the first official language. However, the implementation of such a policy must not encroach upon a fundamental freedom such as that of the free movement of workers. Therefore, the requirements deriving from measures intended to implement such a policy must not in any circumstances be disproportionate in relation to the aim pursued and the manner in which they are applied must not bring about discrimination against nationals of other Member States.

20. The importance of education for the implementation of such a policy must be recognised. Teachers have an essential role to play, not only through the teaching which they provide but also by their participation in the daily life of the school and the privileged relationship which they have with their pupils. In those circumstances, it is not unreasonable to require them to have some knowledge of the first national language.

21. It follows that the requirement imposed on teachers to have an adequate knowledge of such a language must, provided that the level of knowledge required is not disproportionate in relation to the objective pursued, be regarded as a condition corresponding to the knowledge required by reason of the nature of the post to be filled within the meaning of the last subparagraph of Article 3(1) of Regulation 1612/68 **[D15]**.

[A21]   Case C-168/91 Konstantinidis v Stadt Altensteig

[German law provisions required Greek names to be transliterated into Roman characters according to a system which was phonetically inaccurate.]

Opinion of Advocate General Jacobs (9 December 1992)

A person's right to his name is fundamental in every sense of the word. After all, what are we without our name? It is our name that distinguishes each of us from the rest of humanity. It is our name that gives us a sense of identity, dignity and self-esteem. To strip a person of his rightful name is the ultimate degradation, as is evidenced by the common practice of repressive penal regimes which consists in substituting a number for the prisoner's name. In the case of Mr Konstantinidis the violation of his moral rights, if he is compelled to bear the name 'Hréstos' instead of 'Christos' is particularly great; not only is his ethnic origin disguised, since 'Hréstos' does not look or sound like a Greek name and has a vaguely Slavonic flavour, but in addition his religious sentiments are offended, since the Christian character of his name is destroyed. At the hearing Mr Konstantinidis pointed out that he owes his name to his date of birth (25 December), Christos being the Greek name for the founder of the Christian – not 'Hréstian' religion.

In view of the above considerations I do not think that it would be right to say that the German authorities' treatment of Mr Konstantinidis is necessarily consistent with the European Convention on Human Rights simply because the Convention does not contain express provisions recognising the individual's right to his name or protecting his moral integrity. On the contrary, I consider that it ought to be possible, by means of a broad interpretation of Article 8 of the Convention, to arrive at the view that the Convention does indeed protect the individual's right to oppose unjustified interference with his name.

The more difficult question is to determine whether a person who exercises his right of free movement under Articles 48, 52 or 59 of the Treaty is entitled, as a matter of Community law, to object to treatment which constitutes a breach of his fundamental rights. On that point the court's case law has developed considerably in recent years. The most complete statement of the present position is contained in the judgment in Case C-260/89 *ERT* [1991] ECR I-2925.

. . .

That judgment does not establish clearly, one way or the other, whether Mr Konstantinidis may, as a matter of Community law, invoke the protection of his fundamental rights in the circumstances of the present case. The following points may be noted.

First, it cannot be said that the regulations at issue in this case lie entirely outside the scope of Community law since they are, when applied to migrant workers, capable of having a particularly adverse effect on the nationals of one Member State. Secondly, there are now at least two situations in which Community law requires national legislation to be tested for compliance with fundamental rights: namely (a) when the national legislation implements Community law (paragraph 19 of the *Wachauf* judgment) and (b) when a Treaty provision derogating from the principle of free movement is invoked in order to justify a restriction on free movement (paragraph 43 of the *ERT* judgment). Thus it is clear that if, as I have suggested, the German authorities' treatment of Mr Konstantinidis constitutes discrimination prohibited by Articles 7 and 52 of the Treaty, there can be no question of its being justified on grounds of public policy under Article 56(1) if it infringes his fundamental rights.

But let us suppose that the view is taken that the German authorities' treatment of Mr Konstantinidis is *not* discriminatory. Does that mean that it cannot be contrary to Article 52, even though it infringes Mr Konstantinidis' fundamental rights? The implications of that question are perhaps easier to see if a more drastic example is considered. Suppose that a Member State introduces a draconian penal code under which theft is punishable by amputation of the right hand. A national of another Member State goes to that country in exercise of the rights of free movement conferred on him by Article 48 et seq of the Treaty, steals a loaf of bread and is sentenced to have his right hand cut off. Such a penalty would undoubtedly constitute inhuman and degrading punishment contrary to Article 3 of the European Convention on Human Rights. But would it also be a breach of the individual's rights under Community law, even though it were applied in a non-discriminatory manner? I believe that it would.

In my opinion, a Community national who goes to another Member State as a worker or self-employed person under Articles 48, 52 or 59 of the Treaty is entitled not just to pursue his trade or profession and to enjoy the same living and working conditions as nationals of the host state; he is in addition entitled to assume that, wherever he goes to earn his living in the European Community, he will be treated in accordance with a common code of fundamental values, in particular those laid down in the European Convention on Human Rights. In other words, he is entitled to say '*civis europeus sum*' and to invoke that status in order to oppose any violation of his fundamental rights.

Three arguments might be advanced to counter that proposition: first, that it would be inconsistent with the court's existing case law, according to which Article 52 has generally been understood as nothing more than a prohibition of discrimination against nationals of other Member States . . .; secondly, that it would lead to 'reverse' discrimination against nationals of the host state; thirdly, that it would create an overlap between the jurisdiction of the Court of Justice and that of the European Court of Human Rights, with the possibility of conflicting decisions. None of those arguments is convincing.

As regards the first argument, although most of the cases in which the court has recognised a breach of Article 52 concerned discriminatory measures, I do not think that the case law should be read as establishing that a measure can never be contrary to Article 52 simply because it is non-discriminatory . . . It is perhaps not unreasonable that, as regards technical obstacles to freedom of establishment, a person who moves to another Member State should in general have to comply with the local legislation (eg a rule that restaurateurs should have several years' experience in the catering trade), though I question whether, even on a technical level, a disproportionate restriction or one entirely devoid of justification could be applied against a national of another Member State . . . But when a breach of fundamental rights is in issue, I do not see how the non-discriminatory nature of the measure can take it outside the scope of Article 52. Indeed, the proposition that a Member State may violate the fundamental rights of nationals of other Member States, provided that it treats its own nationals in the same way, is untenable.

As regards the second argument, I do not think that the danger of reverse discrimination can be a valid argument for limiting the scope of the rights conferred by the Treaty on persons who seek their livelihood in another Member State. The notion that the free movement provisions of the Treaty merely prohibit discriminatory measures was abandoned long since in relation to goods (in the *Cassis de Dijon* judgment **[E21]**) and more recently in relation to the provision of services (Case C-76/90 *Säger v Dennemeyer & Co Ltd* [1991] ECR I-4221, paragraph 12). Once it is accepted that the Treaty requires more than the abolition of discrimination, it follows ex hypothesi that a Member State may in certain circumstances be obliged to treat producers or workers from other Member States more favourably than it treats its own producers and workers.

As regards the third argument, the danger of an overlap between the jurisdiction of the Court of Justice and the European Court of Human Rights would not in fact be great. The latter has always stressed that its jurisdiction is subsidiary, in the sense that it is primarily for the national authorities and the national courts to apply the Convention . . . In any event, applicants must first, under Article 26 of the Convention, exhaust the remedies available under domestic law, which includes of course the possibility of a reference for a preliminary ruling under Article 177 of the Treaty. Thus, if the Court of Justice were to extend the circumstances in which the Convention may be invoked under Community law, the result would simply be to increase the likelihood of a remedy being found under domestic law, without the need for an application to the organs established by the Convention.

As for the possibility of conflicting rulings on the interpretation of the Convention, that has existed ever since the Court of Justice recognised that the Convention may be invoked under Community law. Such a possibility does not seem to have caused serious problems. It would in any event be paradoxical if the existence of the Convention and the system established under the Convention were to reduce the protection available in national law or in Community law.

Conclusion

I am accordingly of the opinion that the questions referred . . . should be answered as follows: Where a national of a Member State establishes himself, pursuant to Article 52 of the EEC Treaty, in another Member State which uses an alphabet different from the one used in his own State, Articles 7 and 52 of the Treaty are infringed by rules or practices of the host state which require his name to be entered in a register of civil status, against his wishes, in a transliteration which, as in circumstances such as those of the present case, seriously misrepresents the correct pronunciation of the name.

The European Court of Justice (Judgment, 30 March 1993) (1993) The Times, 2 April

By its two questions the German court sought in substance to establish whether Article 52 of the Treaty was to be interpreted as prohibiting the name of a Greek national, who had established himself in another Member State in order to practise a profession, from being entered in the registers of civil status of that state according to spelling which was inconsistent with the phonetic transcription of his name such that the pronunciation of his name was changed and distorted.

Article 52 was one of the fundamental provisions of the Community. So far as the right of establishment was concerned that Article required nationals of other Member States to be assimilated to nationals of the country concerned by prohibiting any discrimination resulting from national laws, regulations or practices.

It was therefore necessary to examine whether national rules on transcription into Latin characters of the name of a Greek national in the registers of civil status of a Member State where he was established were capable of putting him in a less favourable legal or factual position than that of a national of that Member State in similar circumstances.

Nothing in the Treaty prevented the transcription of a Greek name into Latin characters in the registers of civil status of a Member State which used the Latin alphabet. In those circumstances it was for that Member State to lay down the procedures, whether by legislation or administrative provisions and according to the rules provided by international convention which it had concluded in regard to civil status.

Rules of that kind could not be regarded as incompatible with Article 52 of the Treaty except to the extent to which their application would create such difficulties for a Greek national that, in practice, it would restrict his freedom to exercise his right of establishment under that Article.

That would be the case where the legislation of the State of establishment required a Greek national in the exercise of his profession to use a spelling of his name arising from the transliteration in the registers of civil status, if that spelling was such that the pronunciation of the name was thereby distorted and if that distortion exposed him to a risk of confusion with other persons on the part of his potential clients.

On those grounds the European Court (Sixth Chamber) ruled: Article 52 of the Treaty was to be interpreted as prohibiting a Greek national from being required, by the relevant national legislation, to use, in exercising his profession, spelling of his name such that the pronunciation was distorted and that the distortion resulting therefrom gave rise to a risk of confusion on the part of his potential clients.

Questions

1. If a Member State is entitled to preserve its language to retain identity, why cannot an individual preserve his or her name?

2. Are the *Grogan*, *Groener* and *Konstantinidis* cases consistent in where they draw the line between Community law competence and the legitimate internal affairs of Member States?

2   The principle of subsidiarity following the Maastricht Treaty

[A22]   EC Treaty, Article 3b

The Maastricht Treaty amends the EC Treaty as follows:

Article 3b

The Community shall act within the limits of the powers conferred upon it by this Treaty and of the objectives assigned to it therein.

In areas which do not fall within its exclusive competence, the Community shall take action, in accordance with the principle of subsidiarity, only if and in so far as the objectives of the proposed action cannot be sufficiently achieved by the Member States and can therefore, by reason of the scale or effects of the proposed action, be better achieved by the Community.

Any action by the Community shall not go beyond what is necessary to achieve the objectives of this Treaty.

[A23]   A Toth: 'The principle of subsidiarity in the Maastricht Treaty' (1992) 29 Common Market Law Review 1079

It is arguable that Article B, last paragraph [A3], makes the principle of subsidiarity applicable across the whole Union (ie Maastricht) Treaty. This is, however, subject to two important qualifications. First, by definition the principle applies only to matters brought within Union competence. In matters left within Member State competence, the Union cannot take action, therefore here the principle is irrelevant. Consequently, the principle applies to the common foreign and security policy only to the extent to which this policy has been placed within Union competence, while it cannot apply to justice and home affairs since these matters have been expressly left to inter-governmental co-operation. The second qualification is that since the jurisdiction of the European Court of Justice does not extend to the preamble **[A2]** and Titles I, V and VI **[A3]**, **[A15]**, **[A16]**, the principle is not justiciable before the court except in so far as it has been incorporated in the EEC (henceforth EC) Treaty. For these reasons, it will only be examined in the context of that Treaty.

. . . The first, and most difficult, problem arises from the fact that the principle is stated to apply only 'in areas which do not fall within [the Community's] exclusive competence'. In other words, it applies only in areas which fall within the Community's non-exclusive competence. Given the fact that neither the original EEC Treaty nor the Maastricht Treaty makes any explicit distinction between 'exclusive' and 'non-exclusive' competence and the areas which fall within each, the question arises what exactly is the meaning of these terms and what 'areas' are accordingly subject to the principle of subsidiarity. In order to answer this question, it might be helpful to look briefly at earlier formulations of the principle.

So far as one can ascertain, in Community law the principle of subsidiarity made its first appearance in the Commission's 'Report on European Union' submitted to the Council on 26 June 1975. That Report envisages European Union as a new entity endowed with legal personality and having its own competences. These would be precisely specified in an Act of Constitution, the founding instrument of the Union, to be drawn up in the form of a new Treaty. Union competences would be of three types: exclusive, concurrent and potential. Matters falling within exclusive Union competence would include commercial policy and the Common Customs Tariff. 'Concurrent competence' would cover an extensive border area between Union and Member State competence in which both the Union and the Member States would have the power to act. In this area, the Union would assert its authority only when it felt the need – for example, by dealing only with certain aspects of a matter or by enacting outline legislation. The Member States would remain free to act on all aspect[s] on which the Union had not taken action. 'Potential competence' would include areas which might in due course come within Union competence but which would initially be left with the Member States.

With a view to preventing the proposed European Union from becoming a centralising super-state, the Report states that 'in accordance with the *principe de subsidiarité*, the Union will be given responsibility only for those matters which the Member States are no longer capable of dealing with efficiently'. Nevertheless, the Report adds, 'in deciding on the Union's competence, application of the *principe de subsidiarité* is restricted by the fact that the Union must be given extensive enough competence for its cohesion to be ensured'.

Although the Report is less than clear on this point, it appears from the above passages that it relies on subsidiarity as a principle determining what competences to allocate to the Union *prior to* its coming into existence, rather than one governing the day-to-day division of competences between the Union and its Member States. In other words, the principle is seen as one addressed to those who would draw up the Act of Constitution, the Union's founding instrument, rather than to the Union itself. For this reason, its application is not restricted to matters falling within one type of competence or the other: it applies *in the abstract* to the whole range of competences.

The Commission's Report was not acted upon, and the principle of subsidiarity was not heard of for the next nine years. Then, it resurfaced in 1984 in the Draft Treaty establishing the European Union which was prepared by the European Parliament but never actually entered into force. The principle is referred to twice in the draft. First, in the preamble (last recital) as a general principle determining the allocation of powers between the Union institutions and the Member States. Here, its role is not unlike that assigned to it by the Commission's Report. Secondly, in Article 12 which deals with the Union's competences. This article makes a clear distinction between 'exclusive competence', where the institutions of the Union have sole power to act, and 'concurrent competence', where the Member States may continue to act so long as the Union has not legislated. The principle of subsidiarity applies only where the Union has concurrent competence. In that case,

> the Union shall only act to carry out those tasks which may be undertaken more effectively in common than by the Member States acting separately, in particular those whose execution requires action by the Union because their dimension or effects extend beyond national frontiers.

This provision is a major departure from the Commission's Report in that here the principle is used to determine the day-to-day and matter-by-matter allocation of decision-making powers, although the article is silent on the vital question, who is to make the determination: the Union or the Member States. While the Draft Treaty does not contain a single list of matters falling within exclusive or concurrent Union competence, it does state in clear and unequivocal language in relation to each and every activity, whether it falls within one or the other. It can thus be ascertained, without any ambiguity, that the free movement of persons, services, goods and capital, trade between Member States, competition and commercial policy fall within the Union's exclusive competence, while conjunctural, money and credit policies, the Monetary Union, sectoral policies and a number of other policies termed 'policies for society' fall within its concurrent competence. This clear-cut division of competences makes it possible to identify the areas and subject matters to which the principle of subsidiarity applies.

If one compares the new Article 3b of the EC Treaty and Article 12 of the Draft Treaty, there can be hardly any doubt that the former owes its origin to the latter to a large extent (just as the latter owes its origin to the Federal German Constitution). There is, however, a fundamental philosophical difference between the Draft Treaty and the Commission's 1975 Report on the one hand, and the Maastricht Treaty, on the other. Both former documents envisage European Union as an entirely new creation, a legal person under international law, to be set up by a new Treaty–Constitution, which upon coming into existence would replace the present Communities. Both documents envisage, moreover, the precise allocation of competences between the Union and its Member States according to a well thought-out system, clearly distinguishing between two (or possibly three) types of Union competence: exclusive, concurrent and potential, and specifying the matters falling within each. It is in this context (and only in this context) that subsidiarity must be understood, and can play its full role, as an important constitutional principle. It is a principle which may be used either to determine the allocation of competences *in the Constitution itself*, or to enable matters to be allocated to Union of Member State competence in the daily life of the Union after it has come into existence, or possibly both.

Unfortunately, the Maastricht Treaty is based on a different philosophy. The European Union which it purports to establish is not a new legal entity separate from the Communities. It does not replace the Communities but is superimposed upon them. The Treaty does not allocate competences between the Union and the Member States on a well thought-out, systematic basis and in clear terms. It does not distinguish between exclusive and other competences. As a result, by implication it allows the existing principles governing the division of competences to continue to operate . . . [T]hese principles follow a logic of their own and are different from those contemplated in the 1975 Commission Report and the 1984 Draft Treaty. The slavish transposition into this system of the principle of subsidiarity, originally conceived to serve its purpose under entirely different conditions, is a mistake which is bound to cause insoluble conflicts and problems.

Since (1) Article 3b expressly excludes the application of the principle of subsidiarity from areas falling within exclusive Community competence; (2) the original EEC Treaty does not distinguish between areas falling within exclusive and those falling within non-exclusive Community competence (which may mean concurrent competence or potential competence or both); and (3) according to the case law of the European Court of Justice the Community's competence is necessarily exclusive over all matters pertaining to the pursuit of the common objectives, the inevitable conclusion must be that the principle of subsidiarity as defined in the Maastricht Treaty *cannot* apply to any matter covered by the original EEC Treaty. Otherwise, the situation would arise that in an indeterminate and indeterminable number of matters (since no-one has ever defined the matters falling within the alleged 'non-exclusive' competence of the Community, nor are there any objective criteria whereby to define them) the decision-making power, 'definitively and irreversibly' renounced by the Member States in favour of the Community, would be handed back to the Member States – a major step backwards in the process of European integration. Moreover, the principle as laid down in Article 3b cannot *create* or *confer* competences on the Community and Article 3b therefore cannot serve as a legal basis for a Community act, at least on its own. It can only be used to allocate the exercise of competences which have already been created by other provisions of the Treaty . . .

The last, but by no means the least difficult, problem is: who is to decide, and by what procedure, whether the principle of subsidiarity is applicable in individual cases? Is it the Member States? the Commission? the European Parliament? the Council? the European Council? or – ultimately – the Court of Justice? Should this decision be taken, in each individual case, during the course of the normal decision-making process so that each institution, acting within its own respective sphere of competence, can participate in it? Or should there be a special procedure devised for this purpose? In the absence in the Maastricht Treaty of a clearly defined list of matters which are subject to the principle, and of a decision-making mechanism for its application, these questions are bound to arise in practice and need urgent solution . . .

In this context, two major problems can be foreseen. The first arises from the very wording of Article 3b which seems to create a presumption in favour of Member State competence ('the Community shall take action . . . only if and in so far as the objectives of the proposed action . . . can . . . be better achieved by the Community'). This puts the onus of proof on the Community to justify its action. Therefore, before a decision may be taken on the substance of a given matter, a preliminary decision will have to be taken on the question whether that matter is subject to Community action. Is that preliminary decision to be taken by the Commission (with the result that if it is negative the Commission will not put forward a legislative proposal) or by the Council? In the latter case, what voting rules will the Council apply? Those which are applicable to the substance of the matter or unanimity? If it is unanimity, any single Member State will be able to block Community action by arguing that the objectives of that action can be sufficiently achieved at the national level. Subsidiarity would then become the virtual reincarnation of the ghost of the Luxembourg Compromise, just recently banished from the corridors of power. It would become the principle of pick and choose – each Member State would be able to determine what Community policies to pursue in common according to its own convenience or national interests.

The second problem is whether it is appropriate or advisable to involve the European Court of Justice in deciding disputes arising from the application (or non-application) of the principle of subsidiarity. Most legal experts who have expressed an opinion on this question have come out very strongly against incorporating the principle in the EC Treaty (other than in the preamble) and against thereby making subsidiarity justiciable before the European Court of Justice. Yet, with the principle now forming part of the EC Treaty, its interpretation and application is subject to the jurisdiction of the court in the same way as that of any other Treaty provision. This means that both national and Community legislation will be open to challenge, at both national and Community level, on the grounds that it infringes the principle of subsidiarity. Such challenge may be made by Member States, Community institutions and private individuals, in both direct actions and preliminary ruling procedures according to the normal rules . . .

But the main question is: is the European Court of Justice equipped to decide whether the objectives of a measure can be better achieved at the Community level or at the national level? This is clearly a political decision which only the political institutions can take. In the past, the court has consistently refused to get involved in disputes of this nature by saying that these matters fall within the wide discretionary powers of the Council and the Commission. In reviewing the exercise of those powers, the court has always restricted itself to examining whether a measure contains a manifest error or constitutes a misuse of powers or whether the institutions have not clearly exceeded the bounds of their discretion. But the court has never been willing to enter the actual area of the discretion itself by deciding whether a measure is suitable to achieve a given objective or how that objective can best be achieved. By so doing, the court would interfere with the legislative process by replacing the institutions' discretion with its own views. Not only is this not part of the judicial function, but the court is not equipped in terms of staff and expertise to make complex economic and political judgments of this kind.

It is to be expected that the court will adhere to these principles also in the context of subsidiarity. Thus, while the court will be able to decide that a matter falls within exclusive Community competence and is thus excluded from the principle's scope of application, in the opposite situation the court will not be able or willing to go beyond the possible confirmation of the principle's applicability in general terms. It will not, and cannot, become the ultimate arbiter as to whether the principle of subsidiarity has been properly applied in a particular case. In any event, the court will never be able to take into account the statements of the principle occurring in the preamble and Title I of the Maastricht Treaty since those parts are excluded from the court's jurisdiction in toto.

[A24] Debates of the European Parliament No 3-424/117 (18 November 1992)

Subsidiarity

Giscard D'Estaing (PPE). Mr President, it is this Parliament that secured the incorporation of the principle of subsidiarity in the Maastricht Treaty, where it is now embodied in Article 3b, and the purpose of our question to the Commission, whose President I welcome, is to enable us at this stage to establish clearly under what conditions this article is to be applied. It is therefore not a philosophical debate on the principle of subsidiarity that we are seeking today, but a practical debate on implementation of Article 3b.

Our first question is: what will the legal arrangements, the legal framework, be for implementation? What type of decision will be taken, at what level and when?

In our second question, we are seeking an assurance that Article 3b is going to be applied in a manner that upholds the inter-institutional balance and that, contrary to what some people may have been imagining or fearing, reference to the principle of subsidiarity is not going to change the balance between the three institutions.

Our third question to the Commission is: how is application of the subsidiarity principle to be monitored during the course of the Community decision-making process? At what stages? We suggest that this should be done under the existing procedure, in other words that there should be no new procedure for monitoring subsidiarity, but instead that the checks should be made at the normal stages of the Community decision-making process, so that it does not become any more unwieldy than at present.

Our last question . . . concerns the timing of implementation of these measures. As matters stand, we are preparing for entry into force of the Maastricht Treaty on 1 January [1993] . . . but ratification is getting behind schedule . . . I therefore wish to put this question to the Commission: given that it has been said that [the subsidiarity] principle already informs the earlier texts, are there not some provisions concerning subsidiarity that could actually be brought into force, in spirit at least, as from 1 January 1993, to show that Europe is still moving forward?

Barrera I Costa (ARC).   Mr President, the Rainbow Group considers the principle of subsidiarity an essential cornerstone of European integration. Its proper application would maximise democratic involvement and therefore reduce the democratic deficit and citizens' mistrust of centralised power. However, only by respecting the principle can we preserve the national identities that nobody is willing to lose. The scope of the principle was broad because it covers the criteria for the allocation of competence and powers as well as their exercise. It also lays the emphasis on effectiveness, not in economic or technical terms but in terms of citizens' satisfaction.

Finally, with regard to its field of application, the principle concerns not only the distribution of powers between the Community and Member States but also between the national governments and the regional and local governments within each state. It might be said that the latter point is not pertinent to this debate but this objection is not valid because in the areas where the Community has exclusive powers, it should be entitled to ensure maximum devolution, that is to specify at which level of government Community legislation must be implemented. Furthermore, if the Community assumes a responsibility which, in the Member States, is a matter for regional or local government, the Community should ask for the advice and consent of the regional or local governments in question. Citizens will otherwise feel that the Community is an instrument of centralisation and complaints about the misconduct of the Brussels bureaucracy will still occur.

My conclusion is that the correct application of the principle of subsidiarity requires the intervention of the Committee of the Regions **[B16]** and probably, in the future, the splitting of that body into two committees representing separately the regions and the municipalities.

...

De Giovanni (GUE).   . . . I think a concept as apparently abstract as 'subsidiarity' in fact reflects a problem of our times, that is the problem of the relationship between the centre and the periphery, of the relationship of the various levels of authority between the Community and the states, between the states and the regions. This concept is an attempt to reply to the question: 'Who decides, and what is the balance between the various authorities?'

In substance, the question of subsidiarity raises the question of legitimate authority, and in that sense it is a question to which we must pay utmost attention, a question which has not surprisingly arisen at some of the great moments in history, from the American revolution to the papal encyclicals.

Regarding the Community I have two comments to make. First, subsidiarity must be regarded primarily as an essential principle of the organisation, and not the demolition, of the Community; it concerns the revival, and not the death, of the idea of Europe. There is in effect a risk, that of dogmatically renationalising Community policies as the alleged answer to the crises of the Community. Instead we must work to establish a balance within which the supranational dimension represents that wider dimension of reality that will prove to be interdependent and universal, from the market to the citizens, to the need to affirm that Europe as such has a real political role to play.

My second comment is that subsidiarity relates to procedure, to the rules of legislative procedure. In that sense subsidiarity must serve as an instrument for reinforcing the quality of Community legislation, for useful rather than superfluous legislation, and one that must also, and fundamentally, consider the possibility of a legislative hierarchy.

To conclude, the demand for subsidiarity must not be taken as an opportunity to call the constitutional structure set out in the Treaties in question again . . . rather it must help maintain normal inter-institutional relations without encouraging any abuse of power by the state institutions vis-à-vis the others.

...

Dillen (DR). . . . there is no end to the torrent of words about the principle of subsidiarity. That in itself makes us suspicious. Anything clear does not need one long-winded explanation after another. The interminable torrent of words is only intended to conceal the wretched reality behind the words. That is, the concept itself is more easily watered down by assiduously parading the word 'subsidiarity'.

Matters which a nation can manage properly itself must be decided by the nation and not get to European level. That is where the shoe pinches. What at first sight seems simple and clear, and actually is, if we leave words and actions to common sense, turns, in the hands of Euro-centralists, into an obscure conglomeration in which a cat could not find its own kittens.

One example: first it is said that culture and education are the responsibility of the state, which is only logical. But a few paragraphs further on, Maastricht shows its real hand by revealing its love of meddling in culture and education too.

And who decides in the event of disagreements? The European Court of Justice, itself a European institution which must inevitably be inclined to tip the scales towards European centralism.

We must ensure, before it is too late, that the European nations decide freely in a confederal, not a federal, spirit what must remain a matter for the nation and what may become European.

Ephremedis (CG). . . . the Left Unity Group appreciates that all this talk about subsidiarity aims to cover up the lacunae of the Community's bureaucratic operation, the vacuum of the democractic deficit and the lack of any active presence and participation by citizens and even by the national parliaments in the taking of Community decisions that concern the present and future of the Community's peoples . . . We fear . . . that the deficit is widening, opacity persists, and decisions will be taken without involving the citizens.

As for monitoring the implementation of subsidiarity, we cannot and must not − we have no right to − entrust this to the Commission. Because it will then be the Commission that proposes and disposes; is it also to monitor how subsidiarity is implemented? That possibility must be excluded. Neither can we entrust this to the European Court of Justice, because the issues in question are essentially political ones and ought not to be subject to judicial opinions. Monitoring should be carried out by this Parliament, by the national parliaments, and most of all, by the organised representatives of those directly affected, the working people in our countries . . .

Hänsch (S). . . . The principle of subsidiarity has two enemies: first, the ideology of an abstract unity that confuses unity and uniformity, together with an abstract justice that confuses justice and sameness. Matters that are not the same must not be treated the same.

The second enemy is the indolence that extends from smaller organisations up to our national states, which do not want to regulate their own affairs themselves because they do not want to pay the costs and consequences of what they could regulate themselves. Subsidiarity is also bound up with responsibility and being prepared to bear the consequences of one's own independence. Subsidiarity is bound up with being aware that one can afford a degree of independence only because one is safely ensconced in the larger whole. The other side of subsidiarity is the principle of solidarity, something we must not forget when we talk about subsidiarity . . .

Delors, President of the Commission. . . . The subsidiarity principle is based, as we see it, on a simple idea: in the common interest, a state or federation of states has competence for those things, and only those things, for which individuals, families, businesses and local or regional authorities cannot assume responsibility on their own. This common sense principle has to ensure that decision making is kept as close as possible to the citizen, by limiting action taken at the highest levels of the body politic . . .

One of the key difficulties . . . is that we are not operating in the framework of a purely federal type of constitution. The Treaty of Rome, in common with the new Treaty on European Union, does contain references to competence but it also assigns objectives to the Community without going into detail on how they are to be attained. We must never forget that. So this principle is difficult to codify . . .

I come now to the questions you have asked . . . The first . . . concerns the legal framework for practical implementation. As the Commission sees it, the answer is an inter-institutional agreement, and we have already proposed the main points of such an agreement . . .

The second question is about whether it is appropriate, necessary or possible to draw up lists of competences. The Commission, for its part, advises against drawing up lists of competences because of the very nature of the Treaty . . . We are not a federation, with lists and a constitutional supreme court to rule on them in response to actions brought before it, which all citizens in federal states have the right to do. Secondly, it would be inappropriate in the case of exclusive Community competences, both because . . . there is no agreement among the institutions on the list of exclusive competences and because . . . the Treaty lays down objectives which have to be attained. It would therefore be dangerous to have a fixed list of competences.

The third question was about checking for subsidiarity in advance. In the Commission's opinion, subsidiarity is not a matter that should be considered before a proposal is examined but should be part and parcel of the proposal, which should then be examined as a whole under the existing procedures. If it were otherwise and there had to be an advance check on compliance with the subsidiarity principle, the very spirit of our treaty would be in question. This would, in a manner of speaking, create a new veto that could be exercised by a Member State when it did not like the substance of a proposal, using the subsidiarity principle as a pretext for delaying or perhaps even blocking a decision.

...

The fifth question is about the choice between judicial and political scrutiny of the allocation of competence. It is a difficult question. The Commission cannot prejudge the attitude that the Court of Justice is going to take. Checking how things can be done better by doing less is an essentially political exercise. The Commission's own view is that, as regards the need for action, there should first be political scrutiny, the organisation of which would be facilitated, I repeat, by the drafting and signature of an inter-institutional agreement. As for the Court of Justice, need I remind the House that it already scrutinises proportionality between measures and the objectives they are intended to pursue?

...

Finally, the timing of implementation . . . Everything will depend on the inter-institutional agreement . . . But all I can tell you is that we are already applying it in our proposals. The most recent example, which is very interesting from this viewpoint, is the directive **[A43]** on the restitution of national treasures, which I consider a rather interesting illustration of how Member States can co-operate in pursuing a common resolve and common action without necessarily having to transfer too many powers or create too much bureaucracy at Community level.

Garel Jones, President-in-Office of the Council. . . . There will always be tension between institutions. That is part of the democratic process, but I very much hope that when we have the Maastricht Treaty ratified one of the things it will do . . . is to ensure that this Parliament and our national parliaments work together so that if there is inter-institutional tension it will not occur between this Parliament and national parliaments but will be the right sort of tension which ought to exist between all parliaments, the executive and the Commission. I think that would be right. But I hope this Treaty, and the principle of subsidiarity, will begin to lay the foundations of a partnership between this European Parliament and our national parliaments.

. . . President Delors told us . . . that the Commission is already applying in some areas the principle of subsidiarity. Whilst, of course, it cannot be properly applied throughout the institutions of the Community until we have the inter-institutional agreement and, indeed, until we have the Treaty ratified, we ourselves – I am speaking as a British Minister now – in the United Kingdom have begun to apply the principle too because the scrutiny process that we have in our own parliament involves sending draft European Community legislation to our scrutiny committee and we are already including in the explanatory memorandum that we send to that committee, as is President Delors inside the Commission, a paragraph on subsidiarity, and that, I think, is a good discipline for us.

Finally, so far as questions raised by honourable Members are concerned, Mr Barrera i Costa did me the courtesy of speaking in my own language so I will do him the courtesy of replying to him in his own.

I agree with what [he] says about the need to satisfy the citizen and that the principle of subsidiarity must continue the process of bringing the activities of the Community closer to the citizen himself. On the other hand I do not agree with what he said about regional powers. The principle of subsidiarity ought, I think, to clarify the responsibilities of the Community and the Member States, but the distribution of powers within each state must be decided by that state itself according to its own traditions and its own constitution. An attempt to impose these questions within the Member States by the Treaty of Maastricht would, in my opinion, contradict the very principle of subsidiarity . . .

Barrera i Costa (ARC).   . . . I would like to say to the President-in-Office of the Council that Spanish is not my language because I am a Catalan.
(Mixed reactions) . . .

[A25]   Conclusions of the Presidency, European Council in Edinburgh 11-12 December 1992

Overall approach to the application by the Council of the subsidiarity principle and Article 3b of the EC Treaty.

I   BASIC PRINCIPLES

European Union rests on the principle of subsidiarity, as is made clear in Articles A and B of title I of the Treaty on European Union **[A3]**. This principle contributes to the respect for the national identities of Member States and safeguards their powers. It aims at decisions within the European Union being taken as closely as possible to the citizen.

1. Article 3b of the EC Treaty covers three main elements:

   – a strict limit on Community action (first paragraph);
   – a rule (second paragraph) to answer the question 'Should the Community act?' This applies to areas which do not fall within the Community's exclusive competence;
   – a rule (third paragraph) to answer the question 'What should be the intensity or nature of the Community's action?' This applies whether or not the action is within the Community's exclusive competence.

2. The three paragraphs cover three distinct legal concepts which have historical antecedents in existing Community Treaties or in the case law of the Court of Justice.

   (i) The principle that the Community can only act where given the power to do so – implying that national powers are the rule and the Community's the exception – has always been a basic feature of the Community's legal order (the principle of attribution of powers).
   (ii) The principle that the Community should only take action where an objective can better be attained at the level of the Community than at the level of the individual Member States is present in embryonic or implicit form in some provisions of the ECSC Treaty and the EEC Treaty; the Single European Act spelled out the principle in the

environment field (the principle of subsidiarity in the strict legal sense).

(iii) The principle that the means to be employed by the Community should be proportional to the objective pursued is the subject of a well-established case law of the Court of Justice which, however, has been limited in scope and developed without the support of a specific article in the Treaty (the principle of proportionality or intensity).

3. The Treaty on European Union defines these principles in explicit terms and gives them a new legal significance:

- by setting them out in Article 3b as general principles of Community law;
- by setting out the principle of subsidiarity as a basic principle of the European Union;
- by reflecting the idea of subsidiarity in the drafting of several new Treaty articles.

4. The implementation of Article 3b should respect the following basic principles:

- making the principle of subsidiarity and Article 3b work is an obligation for all the Community institutions, without affecting the balance between them; . . .
- the principle of subsidiarity does not relate to and cannot call into question the powers conferred on the European Community by the Treaty as interpreted by the court. It provides a guide as to how those powers are to be exercised at the Community level, including the application of Article 235 **[A35]**. The application of the principle shall respect the general provisions of the Maastricht Treaty, including the 'maintaining in full of the *acquis communautaire*', and it shall not affect the primacy of Community law nor shall it call into question the principle set out in Article F(3) of the Treaty on European Union, according to which the Union shall provide itself with the means necessary to attain its objectives and carry through its policies;
- subsidiarity is a dynamic concept and should be applied in the light of the objectives set out in the Treaty. It allows Community action to be expanded where circumstances so require, and conversely, to be restricted or discontinued where it is no longer justified;
- where the application of the subsidiarity test excludes Community action, Member States would still be required in the action to comply with the general rules laid down in Article 5 of the Treaty **[A5]**, by taking all appropriate measures to ensure fulfilment of their obligations under the Treaty and by abstaining from any measure which could jeopardise the attainment of the objectives of the Treaty;
- the principle of subsidiarity cannot be regarded as having direct effect; however, interpretation of this principle, as well as review of compliance with it by the Community institutions, are subject to control by the Court of Justice, as far as matters falling within the Treaty establishing the European Community are concerned;
- paragraphs 2 and 3 of Article 3b apply only to the extent that the Treaty gives to the institution concerned the choice whether to act and/or a choice as to the nature and extent of the action. The more

specific the nature of a Treaty requirement, the less scope exists for applying subsidiarity. The Treaty imposes a number of specific obligations upon the Community institutions, for example concerning the implementation and enforcement of Community law, competition policy and the protection of Community funds. These obligations are not affected by Article 3b: in particular the principle of subsidiarity cannot reduce the need for Community measures to contain adequate provision for the Commission and the Member States to ensure that Community law is properly enforced and to fulfil their obligations to safeguard Community expenditures;
- where the Community acts in an area falling under shared powers the type of measures to apply has to be decided on a case by case basis in the light of the relevant provisions of the Treaty.

II   GUIDELINES

In compliance with the basic principles set out above, the following guidelines – specific to each paragraph of Article 3b – should be used in examining whether a proposal for a Community measure conforms to the provisions of Article 3b.

First paragraph (Limit on Community action)

Compliance with the criteria laid down in this paragraph is a condition for any Community action.

In order to apply this paragraph correctly the institutions need to be satisfied that the proposed action is within the limits of the powers conferred by the Treaty and is aimed at meeting one or more of its objectives. The examination of the draft measure should establish the objective to be achieved and whether it can be justified in relation to an objective of the Treaty and that the necessary legal basis for its adoption exists.

Second paragraph (Should the Community act?)

(i) This paragraph does not apply to matters falling within the Community's exclusive competence.

For Community action to be justified the Council must be satisfied that both aspects of the subsidiarity criterion are met: the objectives of the proposed action cannot be sufficiently achieved by Member States' action and they can therefore be better achieved by action on the part of the Community.

(ii) The following guidelines should be used in examining whether the above-mentioned condition is fulfilled:

- the issue under consideration has transnational aspects which cannot be satisfactorily regulated by action by Member States; and/or
- actions by Member States alone or lack of Community action would conflict with the requirements of the Treaty (such as the need to correct distortion of competition or avoid disguised restrictions on trade or strengthen economic and social cohesion) or would otherwise significantly damage Member States' interests; and/or
- the Council must be satisifed that action at Community level would produce clear benefits by reason of its scale or effects compared with action at the level of the Member States.

(iii) The Community should only take action involving harmonisation of national legislation, norms or standards where this is necessary to achieve the objectives of the Treaty.

(iv) The objective of presenting a single position of the Member States vis-à-vis third countries is not in itself a justification for internal Community action in the area concerned.

(v) The reasons for concluding that a Community objective cannot be sufficiently achieved by the Member States but can be better achieved by the Community must be substantiated by qualitative or, wherever possible, quantitative indicators.

Third paragraph (Nature and extent of Community action)

(i) This paragraph applies to all Community action, whether or not within exclusive competence.

(ii) Any burdens, whether financial or administrative, falling upon the Community, national governments, local authorities, economic operators and citizens, should be minimised and should be proportionate to the objective to be achieved.

(iii) Community measures should leave as much scope for national decisions as possible, consistent with securing the aim of the measure and observing the requirements of the Treaty. While respecting Community law, care should be taken to respect well-established national arrangements and the organisation and working of Member States' legal systems. Where appropriate and subject to the need for proper enforcement, Community measures should provide Member States with alternative ways to achieve the objectives of the measures.

(iv) Where it is necessary to set standards at Community level, consideration should be given to setting minimum standards, with freedom for Member States to set higher national standards, not only in the areas where the Treaty so requires (118a, 130t) but also in other areas where this would not conflict with the objectives of the proposed measure or with the Treaty.

(v) The form of action should be as simple as possible, consistent with satisfactory achievement of the objective of the measure and the need for effective enforcement. The Community should legislate only to the extent necessary. Other things being equal, directives should be preferred to regulations and framework directives to detailed measures. Non-binding measures such as recommendations should be preferred where appropriate. Consideration should also be given where appropriate to the use of voluntary codes of conduct.

(vi) Where appropriate under the Treaty, and provided this is sufficient to achieve its objectives, preference in choosing the type of Community action should be given to encouraging co-operation between Member States, co-ordinating national action or to complementing, supplementing or supporting such action.

(vii) Where difficulties are localised and only certain Member States are affected, any necessary Community action should not be extended to other Member States unless this is necessary to achieve an objective of the Treaty.

[A26]   Conclusions of the Presidency, European Council in Edinburgh 11-12 December 1992

[In relation to subsidiarity and the review of pending proposals and existing legislation.]

. . . The Commission has come to the conclusion that certain of its proposals were not fully warranted in terms either of value added by Community action or of comparative efficiency in relation to other possibilities of action in national or international contexts.

In this spirit it recently withdrew three proposals for Directives:

- compulsory indication of nutritional values on the packaging of foodstuffs;
- radio frequencies for land-based telecommunications with aircraft; and
- radio frequencies for remote-processing facilities in road transport.

After the proper contacts, notably with Parliament, it is further considering withdrawing the following proposals:

- . . . conditions in which animals are kept in zoos; . . .
- indirect taxation on transactions in securities; . . .
- VAT on ships' supplies; . . .
- classification of documents of Community institutions . . .

. . . The Commission has concluded, notably following debates in Parliament and the Council, that certain pending proposals tend to go into excessive detail in relation to the objective pursued.

It is accordingly planning to revise a number of them so that they establish general principles to be given more detailed form by the Member States:

- public takeover bids; . . .
- comparative advertising;
- labelling of shoes;
- liability of suppliers of services;
- protection of natural persons in relation to data processed via digital telecommunications networks.

. . . Finally, the Commission can say that, following consultations with interested parties, it intends to abandon certain initiatives that had been planned.

It will not, for instance, be going ahead with proposals on the harmonisation of vehicle number plates or the regulation of gambling.

Similarly, the Commission can see no need to continue preparatory work on the harmonisation of certain technical standards (for instance, on dietary foods, second-hand machinery, structures and equipment for funfairs and theme parks, mechanical fixing and bolts in particular).

In more general terms the Commission is intending to use its monopoly of the right of initiative by declining to accept requests made by the Council at informal meetings that it make proposals for directives. In the same spirit it will be tougher about rejecting amendments proposed by the Council and Parliament that run counter to the proportionality rule or would unnecessarily complicate directives or recommendations that are in fact justified under the need-for-action criterion.

[A27] Hella Pick: 'Hurd declares war on "Eurocrap" ' (The Guardian, 12 November 1992)

The word 'Eurocrap' was coined by a senior British mandarin after a particularly exasperating European Community meeting. Now Douglas Hurd, who prides himself on being a wordsmith, has decided that the time has come to define it. The Foreign Office is selling a learned paper explaining Euromyths, Euroscares and Eurolunacies. All three have a generic link to Eurocrap. Mr Hurd explains that Euromyths 'though entertaining often have no basis in fact'. Euroscares come about through misunderstanding or mis-interpretation of EC legislation. Eurolunacies, however, are real and stem from 'sillinesses among the Community's rules'. Britain's goal is to make them a thing of the past. But, fearful that anti-marketeers may not fully appreciate the government's dedication to the task, the Foreign Office has compiled a list of examples.

First, the Euromyths which sections of the press are fond of propagating: No, the EC is not banning round cheeses. 'This story has no basis in fact whatsoever,' says the Foreign Office. It stems from confusion over hygiene rules that cover the production of soft cheeses. No, the Commission is not forcing Euro-lavatories on British citizens. New rules limiting the amount of water that lavatories may flush are determined by British bylaws, the Foreign Office says. No, the Commission is not forcing fishermen to wear hairnets. Member States are free to take their own decisions and Britain has decided that there is no need for them. Euroscares are legion, the Foreign Office analysis has established. But, accurately interpreted, EC regulations can be harmless. *Appelation contrôlée* food products are not affected. The production of Bath buns need not be confined to Chris Patten's former constituency; York ham need not come only from York; and British farmers need have no worries about their Brussels sprouts. And the EC has not banned the sale of 'ripe pheasants', just prescribed a longer hanging process. Paper boys will not be banned under EC rules to limit the working hours of young people. Firemen will not be bound to change their yellow gear for 'EC-approved blue trousers'.

Curiously, the Foreign Office has come up with few examples of Eurolunacies, though these 'sillinesses' provide much propaganda fodder for Eurorebels. There is the matter of Euro-rules imposing maximum noise levels on lawnmowers, and Eurocucumbers, which have to be the right shade of green and possess a minimum curve. Carrots have to be classified as 'fruit' because the Portuguese mix them with other fruit for jam-making. The Foreign Office explains that this is an example of the Commission's 'old-style vertical' food laws, which are about to be replaced by 'horizontal' rules. No doubt that will end Eurolunacy.

[A28] Foreign Affairs Committee: Appendix 4. Memorandum submitted by Martin Howe

'Subsidiarity': how to make it work

1.1 Introduction

The success or failure of any attempt to secure the effective implementation of the principle of subsidiarity in the workings of the European

Communities will depend upon political, institutional and legal factors.

In a political climate where there is universal acceptance – on the part of all Member States and amongst the Community institutions – of the principle of subsidiarity, and agreement on its meaning, it might matter less whether or not the principle had the backing of legal norms or institutional mechanisms.

It must be doubted how firmly rooted is the apparent enthusiasm for 'subsidiarity' which has recently become widespread within the Community and its institutions. How much of this apparent enthusiasm is lip service provoked by the ratification difficulties faced by the Maastricht Treaty, which will dissipate once the ratification hurdle is surmounted? Still less is there any general acceptance at the political level of what the principle actually means when translated into practice in specific areas of policy.

All this means that a firm legal underpinning of the principle is essential if 'subsidiarity' is not to disappoint the hopes which are now being placed upon it. Furthermore, the prerequisites for making the principle legally effective – agreement on a definition of subsidiarity which is capable of being effectively interpreted – are essential for its effectiveness in the political sphere as well. A well constructed legal underpinning should both give protection in its own right against unwelcome Community intrusions into the life of Member States, and also foster the political climate in which such intrusions are increasingly seen as unacceptable.

The legal effectiveness of any attempt to secure the observance by the Community of the principle of subsidiarity will depend upon three factors:

(1)   Definition: Whether the principle is defined in a way which is (a) satisfactory in concept and (b) of sufficient clarity to permit of predictable interpretation and application.
(2)   The strength of the juridical basis and the width of the field of application of any provisions governing subsidiarity.
(3)   Whether institutional mechanisms exist which will secure the effective observance and enforcement of the principle of subsidiarity; or whether, on the contrary, institutional pressures will lead to it being largely sidelined in practice.

1.2   Defining the principle of subsidiarity

As soon as one starts to look closely at possible definitions of the principle of 'subsidiarity', it becomes clear that the word is used by different people to describe a range of widely different concepts. In its papal historical origins, the word conveys that a central authority should perform only those tasks which cannot be performed effectively at a more immediate or local level. Its meaning according to its historical origins is perhaps less important than present-day political expectations of what 'subsidiarity' is intended to achieve.

Mr Douglas Hurd has described it as the principle of 'minimum interference' by the Community institutions in the affairs of Member States. It is probably this sense which most closely reflects political expectations in the United Kingdom of what the principle is seeking to achieve.

However, the definition most established in Community legislation is what I shall refer to as the 'better attained' test. This asks whether Community-defined objectives are better attained by action at Community or national level. This test is already present in the Rome Treaty in Article 130r(4), which reads: 'The Community shall take action relating to the environment to the extent to which the objectives referred to in paragraph 1 can be attained better at Community level than at the level of the individual Member States.'

New Article 3b of the Rome Treaty, which will be inserted by the Treaty of Maastricht, is very similar to Article 130r(4) – I discuss the wording of Article 3b below in more detail.

The problem with the 'better attained' test is that it merely asks whether it is the Community or Member States who will be better at attaining objectives laid down by the Community. In no way does it question the justifiability of the objectives themselves. It risks reserving to Member States merely the role of implementors of policies laid down by the Community.

The 'better attained' test does not seek to require that attainment or non-attainment of the objectives within one Member State should in any way affect the interests of other Member States. It does not ask whether the objectives concerned are worth pursuing at all having regard to the interference which they may cause in the internal affairs of Member States; and the test does not ask whether or not the subject matter is such that it might be legitimate for Member States to set objectives which might differ from those of the Community.

An example will illustrate this point. One objective of the Rome Treaty (as amended by Maastricht) is to secure 'a high level of social protection'. A measure which, in aid of this objective, required Member States to provide certain specified social benefits to their citizens would not be challengeable under the 'better attained' test. A Member State which disagreed with the necessity of this level of social protection would, by definition, be frustrating the 'better attainment' of the objective. Accordingly, to achieve the objective, a recalcitrant Member State must be compelled by action at Community level.

The fundamental problem with the 'better attained' test arises where the Treaty objective or the objective of the proposed measure is itself internal to the Member States. A test which merely questions what is the right mode of achieving the Community-defined objective, without testing the objective itself in some way, wholly fails to confront this problem.

The basis for a more satisfactory definition of subsidiarity can be found in a publication of the Commission itself [Programme for 1989]: 'The autonomy of decision making at whatever level of personal and collective life should be limited only to the extent dictated by the common interest. This principle has a long tradition in the Community: it is called subsidiarity.'

The introduction of the notion of common interest opens up a way of questioning not merely the mode of attainment of objectives, but the objectives themselves. It is important that common interest is interpreted not merely to mean Treaty objectives, but real interests of other Member States which would be harmed if the action is not taken.

I would advance a tentative general definition of subsidiarity as follows:

The Community shall respect the principle that there should be minimum interference with the autonomy of each Member State and of its citizens. Limitation of or interference with such autonomy is only justified if and to the extent that it is clearly necessary to protect a substantial Community interest, in that there would otherwise be an adverse effect upon the material interests of other Member States.

This definition embodies both the concept of 'minimum interference' and also the need to justify any Community measure by reference to impact on other Member States. It is far closer to the 'everyday' understanding of the meaning of 'subsidiarity' than the 'better attained' test.

Some might think that the above discussion of the definition of subsidiarity is merely lawyers' logic chopping and over-concern with fine print. Nothing could be further from the case. The 'better attained' test, and the definition which I propose above, embody materially different concepts. If adopted as a basis for the implementation of subsidiarity in the European Communities, they will give rise to markedly different practical results.

The 'better attained' test is in fact a very limited definition of subsidiarity which falls a long way short of what subsidiarity is understood to mean in current political expectations. Its adoption as the basis for implementation of 'subsidiarity' in the Community will seriously disappoint those expectations. The 'better attained' definition contains a very restricted form of subsidiarity: subsidiarity only in the mode of achievement of a programme of objectives laid down by the Community. As such, it reserves for Member States the role of agents for the implementation of Community policies.
. . .

1.4   Subsidiarity in specific areas of policy

Agreement of guidelines for the application of the principle to specific areas of policy would . . . be the most vital element in securing the effective implementation of the principle in the Community. Without such agreement, the implementation of the principle could well prove disappointing both at the legal and at the political level.

Competition law and State aids.   This field is of particular interest because of an analysis of the potential application of subsidiarity to this field by the Commissioner responsible, Sir Leon Brittan. As an example of the principle of subsidiarity in operation, Sir Leon points to the division, based principally on turnover limits, between Community and national control of mergers. Mergers which have significant effects at Community level should be analysed and regulated at that level; mergers which only have effects at national level should be left to be regulated at that level.

Sir Leon proposes extending this principle to the control of potentially anti-competitive agreements and cartels by, in effect, delegating responsibility for the enforcement of Community competition law to national authorities and courts in cases where multi-country or Community-wide investigations and actions are not necessary. Sir Leon also refers to his proposal to exempt state aids amounting to less than ECU 50,000 over a three-year period from Commission scrutiny, as an example of subsidiarity in action.

One can have certain reservations about aspects of Sir Leon's case. The fact that the Commission is actively pressing for a radical reduction of the merger turnover threshold, so bringing many more mergers within its own control, suggests that the Commission sees the need for its own intervention with different eyes from more detached observers. The state aids threshold is minuscule and would have to be substantially raised to be taken seriously as an implementation of the principle of subsidiarity. The return of competition law to national authorities is proposed to be delegation merely of the enforcement of Community law and policy, rather than the restoration to Member States of fuller freedom of action in substantive competition law and policy.

These reservations point to the necessity of the Commission not being judge in its own cause when it comes to questions of subsidiarity. But despite these reservations, Sir Leon has identified a principle according to which a dividing line can be worked out between Community and national spheres of action in the competition field.

Social policy.   This is probably the most difficult area to achieve agreement within the Community on how subsidiarity should be applied; or at least to achieve an agreement which reflects Britain's views and interests.

The problem is that, at least on one view, the Treaty objectives in the social policy field themselves offend against the principle of subsidiarity. Article 119 **[D58]** of the Rome Treaty provides for equal pay between the sexes, and has been held to be directly applicable. Article 118a **[D58]** provides for the adoption of measures (by qualified majority voting) in aid of the health and safety of workers. Article 118a is the Treaty provision which is being used to press the United Kingdom to adopt the 48-hour working week.

Health and safety standards, or equal pay at work, within one Member State do not directly affect other Member States. At first sight one would therefore think that measures in the social field would be prime candidates for falling foul of the application of the principle of subsidiarity. This reckons without the view which found expression in the judgment of the European Court in the *Defrenne* case **[D59]** on equal pay:

> The aim of Article 119 is to avoid a situation in which undertakings established in States which have actually implemented the principle of equal pay suffer a competitive disadvantage in intra-Community competition as compared with undertakings established in States which have not yet eliminated discrimination against women workers as regards pay.

The same line of reasoning could, of course, be used to justify all forms of Community social policy which impose costs on businesses. The problem is that once this argument is accepted, it is very difficult to see any dividing line by which the principle of subsidiarity can be applied in the social sphere.

It is very important that the United Kingdom wins agreement that this argument – the 'uniform handicap' argument – is not of itself a sufficient justification under the principle of subsidiarity for the imposition of internal measures within Member States. If such agreement is not won, it is very likely that the principle of subsidiarity will in practice prove of little use as a means of checking intrusive social policy measures.

Environment.   In this field, a form of the subsidiarity principle is already present in the Treaty, in Article 130r(4) quoted above. This is a 'better attained' test, upon whose limitations I have already commented above. Those shortcomings are graphically illustrated by the Community's failure in the environmental field to keep out of environmental matters which are purely internal to Member States.

In the field of the environment it is possible in principle to construct a dividing line between matters which are internal to Member States, and those matters which may impinge upon other Member States. Atmospheric and sea pollution for example are matters which may impinge on other Member States, and therefore for which there is a case for regulation at

Community level. On the other hand, the line of motorways is an internal matter which should not be the concern of the Community.

It is ironic that drinking water standards, which have recently caused so much trouble to the United Kingdom, appear to be essentially an internal matter. This is a matter which is ripe for return to national standards of regulation if the principle of subsidiarity is genuinely applied. Drinking water is not (except in bottled form to which different standards apply) generally traded across national frontiers in the Community.

Single market.   It may be thought at first that there is little scope for the application of the principle of subsidiarity in the field of 'single market' measures, since the essence of such measures is to create a uniform set of rules for goods and services which circulate within the single market. Furthermore, there is reluctance from the United Kingdom's point of view to weaken single market measures, since the single market is viewed as one of the most important benefits of membership of the Community.

None the less, there are aspects of single market measures which could benefit from the application of the principle of subsidiarity.

An absolutist approach to single market measures requires that in order to achieve a uniform market across the Community, all goods (or services) which satisfy a set of standards laid down by the Community should be allowed to circulate freely in all Member States; and all goods (or services) which do not satisfy the Community standards must be banned in all Member States. This leads to the extremely difficult task of devising a uniform set of standards, and has a tendency to lead to the most restrictive forms of national standards being adopted as the Community standards.

This leads, for example, to attempts to ban certain French cheeses from sale in France because their methods of production do not conform to hygiene standards expected in Germany and elsewhere.

A subsidiarist approach to single market measures would lead to far more emphasis being placed on the function of Community-wide standards as acting as a passport to free circulation, rather than those standards being used restrictively in all cases to ban local production and sale of all goods which fail to reach those standards. A purist would argue against this approach by saying that local production and sale of lower-standard goods might compete unfairly with higher-standard goods from elsewhere in the Community.

It is questionable how real is this argument. Such 'uniform handicap' arguments, if accepted, can be used to justify the imposition of all sorts of costs and restrictions – including employee social benefits and Social Charter measures – upon the grounds that if businesses in some Member States carry a cost, then all must be forced to do so.

More emphasis on liberalising measures in the single market area – making achievement of a set of Community standards a passport to free circulation – rather than on restrictive measures, would be consistent with the United Kingdom's general arguments against the imposition of 'social' measures on grounds of alleged distortion of competition. Furthermore, it would reduce the real resentment generated by European Community measures when, for example, well-loved national foodstuffs or other goods are suppressed for failure to meet a set of uniform Euro-standards.

1.5   *Juridical basis and width of application of subsidiarity provisions*

The 'juridical basis' is the legal strength or force of a measure; at one end of the scale a measure can be embodied at Treaty level, so governing the legal validity of subordinate Community measures such as regulations and directives. At the opposite end of the scale of legal strength, a provision could be embodied in a 'gentlemen's agreement' between governments with no legal force in Community law or international law.

There are the following choices for the juridical basis of a provision implementing the principle of subsidiarity.

Treaty text. It is most satisfactory from a legal point of view to embed the principle in the Treaty text. Such a principle in the Treaty text should not only regulate certain subordinate measures taken under the Treaty, but should also explicitly apply as a guide to the interpretation of the Treaty itself and so qualify or limit Treaty objectives which might otherwise be inconsistent with the principle.

Protocol. Legally a protocol is as much a part of a Treaty as the text itself. It is attached to the Treaty at signature and has to go through the same ratification procedure. Attaching a protocol to the Treaty of Maastricht would be only cosmetically different from amending the text: the political attractions of employing a protocol are in the appearance it gives of not 'renegotiating' the text. However, it is inherently unsatisfactory trying to improve a deficient provision in the text by leaving the deficient provision unamended and seeking to rectify it in a protocol. Given the fundamentally flawed nature of the 'better attained' definition of subsidiarity in existing clause 3b, it would be very difficult to achieve satisfactory improvement with a protocol, especially if the protocol sought to be merely 'explanatory'.

Declaration. A declaration is a statement made by Member States about a Treaty. It expresses their view as to how it should be interpreted or applied. The political attraction of using a declaration is that it need not go through the ratification procedures in the same way as the Treaty itself or a protocol. However, in that very fact lies its legal weakness. A declaration does not have the legal force of a Treaty provision and so would only be of persuasive force when the Treaty came to be interpreted by the European Court of Justice. A declaration would be an even less satisfactory method of seeking to strengthen a flawed text than a protocol.

Subordinate measure. An attempt could be made to embody the principle of subsidiarity in a subordinate measure under the Treaties such as a Regulation of the Council of Ministers. However, the Council could not by such a measure impose a binding fetter on its exercise of the powers conferred on it by the Treaty, so such a measure could be overridden if felt politically convenient at the time. It would however be possible to create a Treaty provision which empowers the Council or another body to create detailed guidelines on the application of the principle of subsidiarity and gives force to those guidelines.

Inter-governmental agreement. This would essentially be little different in its legal effects from a Declaration, unless given force in Community law as an addition to or amendment of the Community Treaties.

. . .

Annex: Suggested revised Article 3b

1. The Community shall act within the limits of the powers conferred upon it by this Treaty and of the objectives assigned to it therein.

2. The Community shall respect the principle that there should be minimum interference with the autonomy of each Member State and of its

citizens. Limitation of or interference with such autonomy is only justified if and to the extent that it is clearly necessary in order to protect a substantial Community interest, in that there would otherwise be an adverse effect upon the material interests of other Member States.

3. The provisions of this Treaty, including provisions which may be directly applicable, shall be construed and have effect subject to this principle. Any action by the Community shall not go beyond what is necessary to achieve the objectives of this Treaty, and those objectives shall be pursued only to the extent that such pursuit is compatible with the principle in paragraph 2 of this Article.

[A29]   Editorial: (1993) 30 Common Market Law Review 241

Subsidiarity: backing the right horse?

Notwithstanding the progress made in Edinburgh **[A25]**, **[A26]** in defining the subsidiarity principle, one may wonder whether the Community is following the right track towards further integration. The traditional legal approach to bringing order in new and complicated areas of society is to start by laying down procedures and forms. Traditional societies have developed rituals to shape and stabilise human relations. Roman law largely developed following the principle of ubi remedium, ibi jus. This principle is also applied in modern constitutional law and economic law, for example. In complex new areas of the law procedural law often precedes substantive law. By getting procedures right and initiating mediation, conciliation and adjudication processes, a gradually developing line of precedent is created which will in due time lead to substantive principles. It is this traditional legal approach which has been ignored in the run up to Maastricht. It may be that the successful developments with the formulation of the rules embodying the EMU [Economic and Monetary Union] led people astray. To the surprise of many involved in the drafting of the provisions on the EMU, it proved possible to reach agreement on stringent economic criteria (and procedures!). This may have been facilitated by the fact that monetary policy and economic policy are largely pursued outside the scope of substantive legal norms. That fact may also go some way to explain the public acceptance of such norms at Community level.

In most areas of society, however, the formulation of substantive norms is an esoteric activity which confirms to the citizens of the Community the abstract, Eurocratic and non-democratic character of the Union. The citizens of the Union who voted against Maastricht did not do so because the Union did not get the definition of the subsidiarity principle right. The subsidiarity principle has become a sort of black box, a sorcerer's device to lead the public into believing that everything will be all right. The historical background of the subsidiarity principle may have something to do with this. The principle was adopted by the Catholic Church to delineate the division of power between the different parts of society, ie the State, the Church and private enterprise and industry. The concept of subsidiarity is not a hard and fast rule in constitutional law, as comparative studies have demonstrated. It is like quicksand, and allows only for short respite.

In the longer run, more solid ways have to be resorted to. Such solutions should address the heart of the feeling of discomfort of Europe's citizens, ie the feeling of being left out of the decision-making process. This feeling is accompanied by uneasiness about the dominant forces in the Community, be they large Member States (the FRG in Denmark, in France and even in the UK), multinational enterprises, or more vaguely and ideologically 'the forces of capital'. It is this concern that should be addressed. It can be met by focusing on procedures. This also fits the role of lawyers. Let us look therefore at ideas that involve the citizens of the Community in decision making.

At the same time we should explain to the citizens of the Community that nation States can no longer be relied upon to protect the national backyard. Increased travel, transborder activities such as TV broadcasting, telecommunication connections, greatly increased volumes of imports and exports, have made efforts to keep one's own garden tidy futile at best. More realistically, purely national orientations in law and policy seriously reduce chances of achieving the best overall results. National nimbyism will ultimately ruin the efforts to achieve the closer – and more stable – Union among the peoples of Europe.

In the meantime a few ideas may be offered. One such an idea would be to create the possibility of calling a referendum to decide on the demarcation of Community matters vis-à-vis national matters. There are several ways to trigger a referendum: a certain number of voters may ask for it (as in, for instance, the Italian system), the majority or minority of the Council, the European Parliament or a combination of Council and European Parliament. Why should not the peoples of Europe decide whether they want the Community to enact a ban on advertising for tobacco or a television without frontiers? The institution of a referendum has been criticised. Major objections centre around the difficulty of formulating the right question to put to the voters, and the protection of minorities. It may be possible however to avoid these pitfalls if the conditions for calling the referendum are clearly spelled out. The specifications of the Edinburgh summit on subsidiarity may be useful for this purpose.

Short of a referendum there is the possibility of turning to the European Parliament. Even though there is still considerable hesitation whether the EP has acquired sufficient maturity and democratic standing, it is nevertheless the closest representation of the peoples of Europe. A further strengthening of the position of the EP will then also increase the say of the citizens in deciding whether certain subjects should be taken up by Brussels or at the national level.

Questions

1. How far do the pre-Maastricht cases decided by the court reflect any or all of the above materials relating to subsidiarity?
2. 'Subsidiarity is proportionality applied to competence.' Discuss.

SECTION THREE

THE PRESSURES AND AGENTS FOR CHANGE

MATERIALS

1   The single market and the legislative framework to achieve it

[A30]   Article 8a EEC (renumbered as Article 7a by Maastricht Treaty)

The Community shall adopt measures with the aim of progressively establishing the internal market over a period expiring on 31 December 1992, in accordance with the provisions of this Article and of Articles [7b, 7c], 28, 57(2), 59, 70(1), 84, 99, 100a and 100b and without prejudice to the other provisions of this Treaty.

The internal market shall comprise an area without internal frontiers in which the free movement of goods, persons, services and capital is ensured in accordance with the provisions of this Treaty.

[A31]   Article 100 EEC

The Council shall, acting unanimously on a proposal from the Commission, issue directives for the approximation of such laws, regulations or administrative provisions of the Member States as directly affect the establishment or functioning of the common market.

The European Parliament and the Economic and Social Committee shall be consulted in the case of directives whose implementation would, in one or more Member States, involve the amendment of legislation.

[A32]   Article 100 as amended by Maastricht

The Council shall, acting unanimously on a proposal from the Commission and after consulting the European Parliament and the Economic and Social Committee, issue directives for the approximation of such laws, regulations or administrative provisions of the Member States as directly affect the establishment or functioning of the common market.

[A33]   Article 100a EEC

(1) By way of derogation from Article 100 and save where otherwise provided in this Treaty, the following provisions shall apply for the achievement of the objectives set out in Article 8a. The Council shall, acting by a

qualified majority on a proposal from the Commission in co-operation with the European Parliament and after consulting the Economic and Social Committee, adopt the measures for the approximation of the provisions laid down by law, regulation or administrative action in Member States which have as their object the establishment and functioning of the internal market.

(2) Paragraph 1 shall not apply to fiscal provisions, to those relating to the free movement of persons nor to those relating to the rights and interests of employed persons.

(3) The Commission, in its proposals envisaged in paragraph 1 concerning health, safety, environmental protection and consumer protection, will take as a base a high level of protection . . .

[A34] Article 100a(1) as amended by Maastricht

By way of derogation from Article 100 and save where otherwise provided in this Treaty, the following provisions shall apply for the achievement of the objectives set out in Article 7a. The Council shall, acting in accordance with the procedure referred to in Article 189b and after consulting the Economic and Social Committee, adopt the measures for the approximation of the provisions laid down by law, regulation or administrative action in Member States which have as their object the establishment and functioning of the internal market.

[A35] Article 235 EEC (unaffected by Maastricht Treaty)

If action by the Community should prove necessary to attain, in the course of the operation of the common market, one of the objectives of the Community and this Treaty has not provided the necessary powers, the Council shall, acting unanimously on a proposal from the Commission and after consulting the European Parliament, take the appropriate measures.

[A36] Article 236 EEC (repealed by Maastricht Treaty)

The government of any Member State or the Commission may submit to the Council proposals for the amendment of this Treaty.

If the Council, after consulting the European Parliament and, where appropriate, the Commission, delivers an opinion in favour of calling a conference of representatives of the governments of the Member States, the conference shall be convened by the President of the Council for the purpose of determining by common accord the amendments to be made to this Treaty.

The amendments shall enter into force after being ratified by all the Member States in accordance with their respective constitutional requirements.

Note. The corresponding provision in the Maastricht Treaty is Article N, which provides for the same procedures, with the additional requirement that the European Central Bank shall also be consulted in the case of institutional changes in the monetary area.

[A37]   Case C-169/89 Criminal Proceedings against Gourmetterie Van den Burg [1990] ECR I-2143

The European Court of Justice

1. By judgment of 25 April 1989, . . . the *Hoge Raad der Nederlanden* referred to the court for a preliminary ruling under Article 177 of the EEC Treaty a question concerning the interpretation of Articles 30 and 36 **[E11]** of the Treaty. That question arose in criminal proceedings instituted against a trader in foodstuffs, Gourmetterie Van den Burg.

2. In 1984 inspectors entrusted with ensuring compliance with the Netherlands *Vogelwet* (Law on Birds) confiscated a dead red grouse on the premises of Gourmetterie Van den Burg. The trader was subsequently prosecuted and convicted for infringing the provisions of the law in question, which is designed to protect birds occurring in the wild state in Europe. It appealed against that conviction on the ground that the confiscated red grouse had been lawfully killed in the United Kingdom, in accordance with the combined provisions of Article 6(2) and (3) and Annex III/1.2 of Council Directive 79/409 of 2 April 1979 on the conservation of wild birds (OJ 1979 L103 p 1).

3. The *Hoge Raad*, hearing the case at last instance, found that Article 7 of the *Vogelwet* precluded the bird in question from being bought or sold on the domestic market and that the application of that law hindered trade in a British game bird, lawfully shot and freely marketed in the country of origin. The *Hoge Raad* considered that, in so far as the prohibition laid down in the *Vogelwet* also extends to the importation and keeping of dead red grouse, it was in the nature of a measure having an effect equivalent to a quantitative restriction within the meaning of Article 30 of the Treaty. In its view, the assessment of the appeal depends on the question whether the prohibition in question may be considered justified under Article 36 of the Treaty on grounds of the protection of health and life of animals.

4. The *Hoge Raad* accordingly referred the following question to the court: 'May the prohibition applicable in the Netherlands by virtue of Article 7 of the *Vogelwet* (Law on Birds) on the importation and keeping of red grouse, shot and killed in the United Kingdom without any breach of the law applicable in that country, be regarded as a prohibition which is justified under Article 36 of the EEC Treaty on grounds of protection of health and life of animals, regard being had to the fact that:

in the first place, the exception referred to in Article 6(2) of Directive 79/409 applies to red grouse, which are referred to in Annex III/1 to the directive;

secondly, the purpose of the prohibition laid down in Article 7 of the *Vogelwet* is the preservation of wild birds and in particular the protection of all species of birds occurring in the wild state in Europe, subject to certain exceptions which do not, however, include the red grouse?'

. . .

6. In its question, the national court raises in substance a problem concerning the interpretation of Article 36 of the Treaty, according to which the principle of the free movement of goods does not preclude prohibitions or restrictions on imports which are justified on grounds of the protection of health and life of animals.

7. It is not disputed that the national measure in question constitutes a prohibition on imports and that the red grouse is a species which does not occur within the Netherlands.

8. With regard to Article 36 of the Treaty, the court has consistently held (see, most recently, the judgment of 14 June 1988 in Case 29/87 *Dansk Denkavit v Danish Ministry of Agriculture* [1988] ECR 2982) that a directive providing for full harmonisation of national legislation deprives a Member State of recourse to that article.

9. As regards the degree of harmonisation brought about by Directive 79/409, it should be noted that, although the bird in question may, in accordance with Article 6(2) and (3) of the directive, be hunted within the Member State in which it occurs, the fact remains that Article 14 authorises the Member States to introduce stricter protective measures than those provided for under the directive. The directive has therefore regulated exhaustively the Member States' powers with regard to the conservation of wild birds.

10. It is therefore appropriate to define the scope of the powers conferred on the Member States by Article 14 of the directive. In that regard, reference should be made to the principal criteria on which the Community legislature has relied in the matter.

11. First of all, as the court emphasised in its judgment of 27 April 1988 in Case 252/85 *Commission v France* [1988] ECR 2243, Directive 79/409 grants special protection to migratory species which constitute, according to the third recital in the preamble to the directive, a common heritage of the Community. Secondly, in the case of the most endangered birds, the directive provides that the species listed in Annex I must be the subject of special conservation measures in order to ensure their survival and reproduction.

12. It follows from those general objectives laid down by Directive 79/409 for the protection of birds that the Member States are authorised, pursuant to Article 14 of the directive, to introduce stricter measures to ensure that the aforesaid species are protected even more effectively. With regard to the other bird species covered by Directive 79/409, the Member States are required to bring into force the laws, regulations and administrative provisions necessary to comply with the directive, but are not authorised to adopt stricter protective measures than those provided for under the directive, except as regards species occurring within their territory.

13. Next, it should be noted that the red grouse is neither a migratory species nor a seriously endangered species set out in Annex I to the directive.

14. Furthermore, Council Regulation (EEC) No 3626/82 of 3 December 1982 on the implementation in the Community of the Convention on international trade in endangered species of wild fauna and flora (OJ 1982 L384 p 1) does not refer to the red grouse as an endangered animal within the meaning of that Convention.

15. It follows from the foregoing that Article 14 of the directive does not

empower a Member State to afford a given species which is neither migratory nor endangered stricter protection, by means of a prohibition on importation and marketing, than that provided for by the legislation of the Member State on whose territory the bird in question occurs, where such legislation is in conformity with the provisions of Directive 79/409.

16. The answer to the question submitted for a preliminary ruling must therefore be that Article 36 of the Treaty, read in conjunction with Council Directive 79/409 of 2 April 1979 on the conservation of wild birds, must be interpreted as meaning that a prohibition on importation and marketing cannot be justified in respect of a species of bird which does not occur in the territory of the legislating Member State but is found in another Member State where it may lawfully be hunted under the terms of that directive and under the legislation of that other State, and which is neither migratory nor endangered within the meaning of the directive . . .

2   Problems of choice of legal base

[A38]   Case C-300/89 Commission v Council [1991] ECR I–2867

The European Court of Justice

1. By application lodged at the Court Registry on 28 September 1989, the Commission of the European Communities brought an action under the first paragraph of Article 173 of the EEC Treaty for the annulment of Council Directive 89/428 of 21 June 1989 on procedures for harmonising the programmes for the reduction and eventual elimination of pollution caused by waste from the titanium dioxide industry (OJ L201 p 56).

2. That directive, which was unanimously adopted by the Council on the basis of Article 130s of the EEC Treaty, 'lays down . . . procedures for harmonising the programmes for the reduction and eventual elimination of pollution from existing industrial establishments and is intended to improve the conditions of competition in the titanium dioxide industry' (Article 1). For that purpose, it establishes harmonised levels for the treatment of different kinds of waste from the titanium dioxide industry. Thus, for certain waste from existing establishments using particular processes, a total prohibition is imposed (Articles 3 and 4). On the other hand, for other waste from existing establishments, the directive lays down maximum values for harmful substances (Articles 6 and 9).

3. It is apparent from the documents before the court that the contested measure derived from a proposal for a directive presented by the Commission on 18 April 1983 on the basis of Articles 100 **[A31]** and 235 **[A35]** of the EEC Treaty. Following the entry into force of the Single European Act, the Commission changed the legal basis to Article 100a **[A33]** of the EEC Treaty, which had been inserted by the Single European Act. At its meeting on 24 and 25 November 1988, the Council nevertheless arrived at a common position whereby the directive would be based on Article 130s **[A7]** of the EEC Treaty. Despite the objections voiced by the European Parliament which, having been consulted by the Council pursuant to Article 130s, considered the legal basis proposed by the Commission to

be appropriate, the Council adopted the directive at issue on the basis of Article 130s.

4. Taking the view that Directive 89/428 lacked a valid legal basis, in that it was based on Article 130s but should have been based on Article 100a, the Commission brought the present action for annulment.

5. By order of 21 February 1990, the Parliament was granted leave to intervene in support of the applicant.

6. Reference is made in the Report for the Hearing for a fuller account of the facts of the case, the course of the procedure and the pleas and arguments of the parties, which are mentioned or discussed hereinafter only in so far as is necessary for the reasoning of the court.

7. The Commission, supported by the Parliament, claims that the directive, although contributing to environmental protection, has as its 'main purpose' or 'centre of gravity' the improvement of conditions of competition in the titanium dioxide industry. It is therefore a measure concerning the establishment and functioning of the internal market, within the meaning of Article 100a, and should therefore have been based on the latter enabling provision.

8. The Commission states that the very text of Articles 100a and 130s shows that the requirements of environmental protection form an integral part of the harmonising action to be taken on the basis of Article 100a. It follows, according to the Commission, that Article 100a, which relates to the establishment and functioning of the internal market, constitutes a *lex specialis* in relation to Article 130s, the latter article not being intrinsically directed towards the attainment of that objective.

9. The Council, for its part, contends that Article 130s is the correct legal basis for Directive 89/428. Whilst conceding that that directive is intended also to harmonise conditions of competition in the industrial sector concerned and thus to foster the establishment and functioning of the common market, it considers that the 'centre of gravity' of the contested measure is the elimination of the pollution caused by waste from the titanium dioxide manufacturing process. That objective is one of those referred to in Article 130r, which are pursued by means of measures adopted under Article 130s.

10. It must first be observed that in the context of the organisation of the powers of the Community the choice of the legal basis for a measure may not depend simply on an institution's conviction as to the objective pursued but must be based on objective factors which are amenable to judicial review (see the judgment in Case 45/86 *Commission v Council* [1987] ECR 1493, paragraph 11). Those factors include in particular the aim and content of the measure.

11. As regards the aim pursued, Article 1 of Directive 89/428 indicates that it is intended, on the one hand, to harmonise the programmes for the reduction and ultimate elimination of pollution caused by waste from existing establishments in the titanium dioxide industry and, on the other, to improve the conditions of competition in that industry. It thus pursues the twofold aim to environmental protection and improvement of the conditions of competition.

12. As regards its content, Directive 89/428 prohibits, or, according to strict standards, requires reduction of the discharge of waste from existing establishments in the titanium dioxide industry and lays down time limits for the implementation of the various provisions. By thus imposing obligations concerning the treatment of waste from the titanium dioxide production

process, the directive conduces, at the same time, to the reduction of pollution and to the establishment of greater uniformity of production conditions and therefore of conditions of competition, since the national rules on the treatment of waste which the directive seeks to harmonise have an impact on production costs in the titanium dioxide industry.

13. It follows that, according to its aim and content, as they appear from its actual wording, the directive is concerned, indissociably, with both the protection of the environment and the elimination of disparities in conditions of competition.

14. Article 130s of the Treaty provides that the Council is to decide what action is to be taken by the Community concerning the environment. Article 100a(1), for its part, is concerned with the adoption by the Council of measures for the approximation of the provisions laid down by law, regulation or administrative action in Member States which have as their object the establishment and functioning of the internal market. According to the second paragraph of Article 8a of the EEC Treaty, that market is to comprise 'an area without internal frontiers in which the free movement of goods, persons, services and capital is ensured'. By virtue of Articles 2 and 3 of the Treaty, a pre-condition for such a market is the existence of conditions of competition which are not distorted.

15. In order to give effect to the fundamental freedoms mentioned in Article 8a, harmonising measures are necessary to deal with disparities between the laws of the Member States in areas where such disparities are liable to create or maintain distorted conditions of competition. For that reason, Article 100a empowers the Community to adopt measures for the approximation of the provisions laid down by law, regulation or administrative action in Member States and lays down the procedure to be followed for that purpose.

16. It follows that, in view of its aim and content, the directive at issue displays the features both of action relating to the environment with which Article 130s of the Treaty is concerned and of a harmonising measure which has as its object the establishment and functioning of the internal market, within the meaning of Article 100a of the Treaty.

17. As the court held in Case 165/87 *Commission v Council* [1988] ECR 5545, paragraph 11, where an institution's power is based on two provisions of the Treaty, it is bound to adopt the relevant measures on the basis of the two relevant provisions. However, that ruling is not applicable to the present case.

18. One of the enabling provisions at issue, Article 100a, requires recourse to the co-operation procedure provided for in Article 149(2) of the Treaty, whereas the other, Article 130s, requires the Council to act unanimously after merely consulting the European Parliament. As a result, use of both provisions as a joint legal basis would divest the co-operation procedure of its very substance.

19. Under the co-operation procedure, the Council acts by a qualified majority where it intends accepting the amendments to its common position proposed by the Parliament and included by the Commission in its re-examined proposal, whereas it must secure unanimity if it intends taking a decision after its common position has been rejected by the Parliament or if it intends modifying the Commission's re-examined proposal. That essential element of the co-operation procedure would be undermined if, as a result of simultaneous reference to Articles 100a and 130s, the Council were required, in any event, to act unanimously.

20. The very purpose of the co-operation procedure, which is to increase the involvement of the European Parliament in the legislative process of the Community, would thus be jeopardised. As the court stated in its judgments in Case 138/79 *Roquette Frères v Council* [1980] ECR 3333 and Case 139/79 *Maizena v Council* [1980] ECR 3393, paragraph 34, that participation reflects a fundamental democratic principle that the peoples should take part in the exercise of power through the intermediary of a representative assembly.

21. It follows that in the present case recourse to the dual legal basis of Articles 100a and 130s is excluded and that it is necessary to determine which of those two provisions is the appropriate legal basis.

22. It must be observed in the first place that, pursuant to the second sentence of Article 130r(2) of the Treaty, 'environmental protection requirements shall be a component of the Community's other policies'. That principle implies that a Community measure cannot be covered by Article 130s merely because it also pursues objectives of environmental protection.

23. Secondly, as the court held in its judgments in Cases 91/79 and 92/79 *Commission v Italy* [1980] ECR 1099 (paragraph 8) and 1115 (paragraph 8), provisions which are made necessary by considerations relating to the environment and health may be a burden upon the undertakings to which they apply and, if there is no harmonisation of national provisions on the matter, competition may be appreciably distorted. It follows that action intended to approximate national rules concerning production conditions in a given industrial sector with the aim of eliminating distortions of competition in that sector is conducive to the attainment of the internal market and thus falls within the scope of Article 100a, a provision which is particularly appropriate to the attainment of the internal market.

24. Finally, it must be observed that Article 100a(3) requires the Commission, in its proposals for measures for the approximation of the laws of the Member States which have as their object the establishment and functioning of the internal market, to take as a base a high level of protection in matters of environmental protection. That provision thus expressly indicates that the objectives of environmental protection referred to in Article 130r may be effectively pursued by means of harmonising measures adopted on the basis of Article 100a.

25. In view of all the foregoing considerations, the contested measure should have been based on Article 100a of the EEC Treaty and must therefore be annulled.

. . .

Note. In Case C-155/91 *Commission v Council* [1993] ECR I-939, the above judgment was distinguished in an action brought to challenge the legal basis of Directive 91/156 relating to waste disposal. In the court's view, where the main object of the measure was to ensure the effective management of waste in the Community, and there was only an 'ancillary effect' on the conditions of competition and trade, the act could validly be adopted on the sole basis of Article 130s.

[A39]   Freight Transport Association Ltd v London Boroughs Transport Committee [1991] 3 All ER 915, HL

Background

European Community directives had harmonised the permissible sound levels of vehicles and exhaust systems (in Directive 70/157) and the technical requirements for vehicle brakes (in Directive 71/320). These directives provided that the sale, registration or use of a vehicle could not be prohibited on grounds relating to its brakes, sound level or exhaust system if the vehicle conformed to the requirements set out in the directives. Using powers under the Road Traffic Regulation Act 1984, the predecessor in title to the appellant transport committee imposed a ban on heavy goods vehicles using residential streets in Greater London at night-time without a permit. The grant of this permit was subject to the condition [condition 11] that the vehicle was fitted with an air brake noise suppressor. The group of respondent organisations sought judicial review of the suppressor condition attached to the granting of permits.

Lord Templeman

The Brake Directive has got nothing to do with sound levels and is not concerned with traffic regulation. The Brake Directive harmonises the technical requirements of brake devices used in vehicles throughout the Community and ensures that the brake systems of all vehicles are efficient and safe. For example, every brake device must be capable of bringing a vehicle to a stop within a specified distance depending on the weight and speed of the vehicle. The Brake Directive applies to all braking devices including compressed air brakes but no one reading the directive would be made aware that the operation of compressed air brakes produced any noise at all . . .

Condition 11 does not prohibit the use of a vehicle on grounds relating to its braking devices. Condition 11 regulates traffic and protects the environment by providing that certain roads remain banned to [certain heavy goods] vehicles whose brake sound levels create a nuisance unnecessarily.

The Sound Level Directive harmonises the permissible sound level of vehicles and exhaust systems. The maximum permitted sound level of a vehicle depends on whether the vehicle is intended for passengers or goods, and varies with the engine capacity and the weight of the vehicle . . . The sound level must be tested . . . These tests are irrelevant to brake noise. The braking system is not mentioned, and the only reference to a silencer is reference to a silencer attached to the exhaust system. The Sound Level Directive does not deal with the sound of compressed air brakes and is not concerned with traffic regulation . . .

The distinction between the control of vehicles and the regulation of traffic is fully recognised by Community law. Article 30 of the EEC Treaty provides: 'Quantitative restrictions on imports and all measures having equivalent effect shall . . . be prohibited . . .' Article 130r deals with the environment and so far as relevant directs:

1. Action by the Community relating to the environment shall have the following objectives: (i) to preserve, protect and improve the quality of the environment; (ii) to contribute towards protecting human health; (iii) to

ensure a prudent and rational utilisation of natural resources.
2. Action by the Community relating to the environment shall be based on the principles that preventive action should be taken, that environmental damage should as a priority be rectified at source, and that the polluter should pay. Environmental protection requirements shall be a component of the Community's other policies . . .
4. The Community shall take action relating to the environment to the extent to which the objectives referred to in paragraph 1 can be attained better at Community level than at the level of the individual Member States. Without prejudice to certain measures of a Community nature, the Member States shall finance and implement the other measures . . .

Article 100 provides:

The Council shall, acting unanimously on a proposal from the Commission, issue directives for the approximation of such provisions laid down by law, regulation or administrative action in Member States as directly affect the establishment or functioning of the common market . . .

Pursuant to Article 100 the Council has issued 140 directives prescribing technical requirements and safety and environmental standards for vehicles, their components and spare parts so that national requirements and standards shall not infringe Article 30 or obstruct the free flow of goods and services throughout the Community. But paragraph 4 of Article 130r recognises that London's environmental traffic problems cannot be solved, although they can be ameliorated by Council directives to control every vehicle at all times throughout the Community.

The attainment of the Community object of preserving, protecting and improving the quality of the environment requires action at the level of individual Member States. A vehicle which complies with all the weight, size, sound level and other technical requirements and standards of directives issued by the Council pursuant to Article 100 and is therefore entitled to be used in every Member State throughout the Community is not thereby entitled to be driven on every road, on every day, at every hour throughout the Community. In the interests of the environment the traffic authorities of Santiago de Compostela may ban all or some Community vehicles from medieval streets. The traffic authorities of Greater London may ban all or some Community vehicles from residential streets at night. The ban may be limited to loud vehicles; the ban may be limited to some vehicles which are louder than others. Condition 11 bans some vehicles which are unnecessarily louder than others.

The Commission, which is charged with the duty of proposing directives for adoption by the Council, has recognised that local authorities must regulate local traffic. The Commission has also recognised that the 140 directives dealing with vehicles, including the Brake Directive and the Sound Level Directive, do not deal with brake noise.

. . .

Finally the respondents sought a reference to the Court of Justice of the European Communities for a ruling under Article 177 of the EEC Treaty. It was said that a reference was necessary because the Court of Appeal had held that condition 11 infringed the Brake Directive and Sound Level

Directive . . . My Lords, in my opinion, the Court of Appeal failed to recognise the fundamental distinction between the control of vehicles, necessarily subject to harmonisation by Community legislation, and the regulation of local traffic, which, as I have indicated and as the Commission has recognised, can only be carried out by local authorities . . . I do not attach significance to [the Court of Appeal's] decision on Community law. In my opinion it is clear that the 1985 order and condition 11 are concerned solely with the regulation of local traffic. No plausible grounds have been advanced for a reference to the European Court.

I would allow this appeal.

Question

Would different rules in Member States relating to whether vehicles required noise suppressors (for whatever purpose) be capable of distorting trade?

For a biting criticism of Lord Templeman's judgment, see **[A40]**.

[A40]   S Weatherill: 'Regulating the internal market: result orientation in the House of Lords' (1992) 17 European Law Review 299

Strictly, Lord Templeman should have considered none of these matters, for the legal base of the relevant directives was Article 100, which is pre-SEA. However, even his discussion of post-SEA Community law reads oddly. He explained that the Court of Appeal had failed to appreciate the basic distinction between control of vehicles, achieved by Community harmonisation legislation, and local traffic regulation, a matter for local action. There are problems in making the distinction between vehicle control and traffic regulation, even though it might be fully recognised by Community law. Particularly, there are problems in the House of Lords' location of that distinction in this case. The traffic regulation relates to the state of the vehicle. The two cannot sensibly be separated. Watkins LJ in the High Court observed that '[f]itting a silencer upon an air brake is clearly a technical matter going to the construction of a brake.' It would be different if the matter concerned left-hand driving or a 60 mph speed limit, neither of which has any significant impact on the characteristics of the vehicle, but rather concern the conditions of operation. The problem is that the House of Lords has decided for itself what the functions of the directives are, yet directives are notoriously multi-functional. The House of Lords should have made a reference to Luxembourg to avoid disunity between the courts of different Member States . . .

[A41]   S Weatherill: 'Regulating the internal market: result orientation in the House of Lords' (1992) 17 European Law Review 299

From the economic and political perspective, measures such as that relating to brake noise suppression have several functions as instruments of market regulation. They impinge both on market liberalisation and on environmental protection. To suppose that they can be tied to one policy/one legal base to the exclusion of another is irrational and neglects the reality of modern multi-faceted market regulation. The culprit, then, is the Commission's bizarre range of legislative procedures arising out of the EEC Treaty structure of attributed powers. This haphazard combination of several voting rules and varying institutional roles lacks constitutional respectability. At present debate about the nature of market regulation in the Community is concealed behind arguments about legal base; the judicial forum is entered in order to save political conflict. The legal base cases involve jockeying for position by both the institutions and the Member States, rather than attempts to develop the Community's regulatory structure. Inter-institutional wrangling prompted the litigation concerning the Titanium Dioxide Directive. Both Commission and Parliament have used the legal base to flex their (relatively weak) muscles before the court. Member States have on occasion preferred to assert opposition to Community initiatives through constitutional challenges to the capacity of the institutions to adopt relevant legislation at all; or to adopt it without a unanimous vote. Such problems have been noted as detrimental to the standing of the Social Charter; 'little progress has been made to date on the implementation of the Charter since debate was centred on the legal basis chosen by the Commission rather than on the substance of its proposals'. Exactly this pattern was visible in the negotiations leading up to Maastricht, where arguments about voting rules were every bit as loud as arguments about the desirability of developing substantive policies. As the Community develops a power to make binding legislation despite a dissenting minority, so the appreciation of the importance of jurisdiction in law becomes more acute, because the power to assert a national veto is curtailed. This readily explains the increase in litigation on these points since the Single European Act, which enhanced the status of majority voting. The United Kingdom's insistence at Maastricht on a Social Policy 'opt-out' **[A8]**, **[A9]** should also be assessed from this perspective. That 'solution' will invite more jurisdictional, rather than substantive, argument about whether a proposal is covered by EEC Treaty social policy (in which the United Kingdom participates) or the new 'Maastricht Social Policy', which the United Kingdom can shun. The implication is that there is an outer limit to the *acquis communautaire* beyond which the new Maastricht initiatives alone apply, but, in locating that margin, it seems legally highly dubious that the United Kingdom could rely on the Maastricht agreement-of-11 as an interpretative aid in order to curtail the development of the ever-expanding *acquis communautaire* which binds all 12.

Vital issues of Community government are being ventilated through the judicial process, yet the peculiarities of legal base under the Treaty deprive the court of a coherent framework for decision making. In its 'Opinion on the Draft Agreement relating to the Creation of a EEA' **[A56]** the court described the EEC Treaty as a constitutional charter. This article does not deny the court a role as a constitutional court, but it questions whether it can effectively play such a role on the basis of *this* constitution. It demeans and ultimately weakens the judicial function to rule on provisions as irrational as those presently to be found in the EEC Treaty. The Community's legislative procedure itself needs an overhaul. There should be one legal base. Furthermore, that base must have a stronger democratic input.

Regrettably, the addition of new Titles at Maastricht, such as consumer protection, which are independent of, but which impinge on, the internal market provisions has simply deepened the side issue of legal base.

[A42]   Opinion on the proposal for a Council Directive concerning the protection of purchasers in contracts relating to the utilisation of immovable property on a timeshare basis (OJ 1993 C108/1)

[The text of the Draft Directive was published in OJ 1992 C222/5.]
At its meeting on 24 February 1993 the Economic and Social Committee adopted the following Opinion by a majority vote with one abstention.

1.   *Introduction*

1.1. The legal and economic practice known as timesharing has grown significantly as a form of tourist accommodation over the last few decades, and has become too common a social phenomenon to be ignored by Community legislation.

1.1.1. The Commission's proposal for a Council Directive on timesharing, issued in response to requests by various Member States, is prompted by a number of reasons: the complex problems faced by consumers who decide to purchase a timeshare right; the transnational nature of timesharing; the differences between, and gaps in, national legislations; the ambiguous nature of the information provided by some timeshare vendors; and these vendors' aggressive sales techniques.

1.1.2. The Committee has already called for Community legislation on the sector.

1.2. The proposal is designed to:

(a) make it obligatory for purchasers of timeshare rights to be provided with relevant, detailed information on the contractual commitments entered into by them when they sign a timeshare agreement, so that they know exactly where they stand;

(b) help establish a harmonised legislative framework covering the main aspects of the sector, both for Member States which have legislation on the matter and those which hitherto have had none. Only four Member States have specific laws on timeshares, and these differ considerably:
  – in France, timesharing is considered a personal right, and is covered by the law of obligations,
  – in Greece, it is considered a right of tenancy,
  – in Portugal, it is a real right, and is also covered by the law of obligations,
  – in the United Kingdom, the 'club trustee' system prevails;

(c) provide purchasers with a sufficiently long cooling-off period to allow them to study in full the commitments they have entered into by signing the contract;

(d) provide a longer cooling-off period when the timeshare is in another country, bearing in mind that most timeshare rights held by EC nationals are not in their country of domicile.

1.3. The proposal goes some way towards filling a gap in the timeshare sector, although the Member States themselves are left to adopt provisions on the establishment of legislative and financial guarantees, the form of such guarantees, and the legal nature of timesharing.

1.4. Legislative divergences are likely to increase, as Spain and Italy are also working on legislation.

2.　*General comments*

2.1. The proposal is based on Treaty Article 100a.

2.1.1. This Article concerns the adoption of measures for the approximation of legislative provisions which have as their object the establishment and functioning of the internal market.

2.1.2. Article 100a might not be the best legal basis, since timesharing does not come under the approximation of national legislations which have as their object the establishment and functioning of the internal market. This is because in many cases it does not involve a property or property right that is subject to free movement. It would thus seem more appropriate to regulate the sector by means of a convention on the establishment of uniform legislation.

2.1.3. The preparatory work that preceded the European conventions currently in force, and the slow and complex nature of the process, lead the Committee to accept the legal basis proposed by the Commission.

2.2. The proposal safeguards the consumer's right to information and freedom to negotiate contracts; by granting the purchaser a cooling-off period, it provides a defence mechanism against the snares of aggressive sales promotion techniques.

2.3. It should be stressed that the proposal takes a minimalist approach and fully respects the principle of subsidiarity. The Committee supports this.

2.3.1. Member States are to be free to decide how to regulate other aspects, in particular the legal nature of timeshare rights, thus maintaining their differing legal arrangements.

2.3.2. The proposal does not, however, go far enough in dealing with financial regulations to protect the purchaser, and therefore the Committee suggests that all 'timeshare' operations should be required to be registered in the Member State where the property is situated, should be able to provide financial guarantees, and should work within a code of practice clearly defining the contents of this Directive and other legislation to protect the purchaser.

2.4. The Committee fears that although the proposed legislative framework is the one which is practicable, it may not prevent conflicts between timeshare rightholders and the real owner/manager of the property, or even between rightholders themselves.

2.4.1. The complexity and excessive division of legal powers between the property and rightholders will create serious problems when major repair and maintenance work is done, and also – in extreme cases – if the questions which are not fully addressed in any of the national legislation mentioned above apart from the Portuguese and which are naturally left unresolved by the directive.

. . .

2.5.3. . . . the Committee does not accept that Community legislation should cover immovable property in general . . . [T]he proposal should only apply to areas in which disputes have arisen: buildings and parts of buildings used for tourist or leisure activities.

3.   Specific comments

. . .

3.8. The focus must be on the tourist sector, which is clearly not properly regulated. There is no point in intervening in other areas where harmonisation is not needed.

3.8.1. The directive should therefore mention the purely tourist nature of timesharing. Without this, there would be a risk of legislating on matters where intervention is not justified.

3.8.2. It would also create serious problems in the property sector, which is already facing difficulties that cannot be ignored.

. . .

3.36. [The draft directive] leaves the Member States to decide the deadline for reimbursement. This could lead to divergences in legislation and possibly to discrimination between EC citizens.

3.37. The deadline for reimbursement could therefore be laid down within the actual directive or . . . the Annex. It should not be longer than the cooling-off period . . . Reimbursement should be made without deductions or penalty.

. . .

4.   Conclusions

4.1. Although it is hoped that the present comments will be taken into account, the Commission has addressed the main problems raised by timesharing.

4.2. Subject to the above recommendations, the Committee endorses the proposal.

[A43]   Proposal for a Council Directive on the return of cultural objects unlawfully removed from the territory of a Member State

THE COUNCIL OF THE EUROPEAN COMMUNITIES
Having regard to the Treaty establishing the European Economic Community, and in particular Article 100a thereof,
Having regard to the proposal from the Commission,
In co-operation with the European Parliament,
Having regard to the opinion of the Economic and Social Committee,

Whereas Article 8a of the Treaty provides for the establishment, not later than 1 January 1993, of the internal market, which is to comprise an area without internal frontiers in which the free movement of goods, persons, services and capital is ensured in accordance with the provisions of the Treaty;

Whereas, under the terms and within the limits of Article 36 of the Treaty, Member States will after 1992 retain the right to define their national treasures and to take the necessary measures to protect them; whereas they will, on the other hand, no longer be able to apply checks or formalities at the Community's internal frontiers to ensure the effectiveness of those measures;

Whereas arrangements should therefore be introduced enabling Member States to secure the return to their territory of cultural objects which are classed as national treasures within the meaning of Article 36 of the Treaty and have been removed from their territory in breach of the above-mentioned national measures or of Council Regulation (EEC) 000/91; whereas to facilitate co-operation with regard to return, the scope of the arrangements should be confined to items belonging to common categories of cultural object; whereas the Annex to this directive is consequently not intended to define objects which rank as 'national treasures' within the meaning of Article 36 of the Treaty, but merely categories of object which may be classed as such and may accordingly be covered by the return procedure introduced by this directive;

Whereas the procedure introduced by this directive is a first step in establishing co-operation between Member States in this field in the context of the internal market; whereas the aim is mutual recognition of the relevant national laws; whereas provision should therefore be made, in particular, for the Commission to be assisted by an advisory committee with a view to amending, if necessary, the Annex to this directive in the light of experience,

HAS ADOPTED THIS DIRECTIVE:

. . .

[A44] House of Lords Select Committee on the European Communities, Session 1992-93 6th Report (HL Paper 17): control of national treasures

Part 2: Opinion of the Committee

The United Kingdom interest

12. The United Kingdom interest in the proposals for control of national treasures differs in a number of ways from that of other Member States:

   (i) The number of national heritage objects in private hands is very much larger than the number of national treasures privately owned in any other Member State.
   (ii) The market in objects of cultural value or interest is much larger than in any other Member State. The United Kingdom share of the art exports from all Community Member States could be as high as 75%. The United Kingdom trade is therefore particularly vulnerable

to any uncertainty which could result from the proposals and would carry a disproportionate share of the burden of restitution.

(iii)   There is in the United Kingdom no system of listing national treasures in order to prohibit their export. The view has been taken that a listing of objects in private ownership would (by limiting potential buyers to those resident in the United Kingdom) reduce their market value and so, if not accompanied by compensation, amount to a form of wealth tax.

(iv)   The United Kingdom appears to have a less protective approach to its national treasures in that if they have gone abroad – whether lawfully or unlawfully – little public effort has been made to seek restitution.

The Community interest

13.   All Member States appear to accept that some system to strengthen the powers of the Community as a whole to prevent export of national treasures and to provide for restitution among Member States is needed to compensate for the virtual elimination of border control of goods after 1992. The objective of the negotiations has been to find a balance between on the one hand the wish of all Member States to retain their national treasures and on the other hand the rights of owners freely to dispose of their property and the rights of art dealers to conduct lawful trade.

14.   From what we have been told of the negotiations by the government, a balance acceptable to Member States appears to be emerging. The United Kingdom government has shown that it is ready to accept responsibilities which will undoubtedly impose new burdens on the art market. The southern Member States – often referred to in this context as 'victim states' of cultural depredation – have responded to many of the objections made by the United Kingdom to the Commission's original proposals. In consequence the system which is likely to emerge has been much improved from the standpoint of the United Kingdom. But on the limited evidence before us, we are unable to say that it would not impose unreasonable burdens on the art trade or on owners.

. . .

The Directive

17.   The system of restitution among Member States which would be established by the directive raises more fundamental problems. The Commission in its Preamble describes the proposed procedure as 'a first step in establishing co-operation between Member States in this field in the context of the internal market'. It proposes no harmonisation of national laws controlling export of national treasures but merely mutual recognition, in respect of objects of agreed value and antiquity. There are clear advantages to Member States in establishing habits of assistance in law enforcement. We have previously supported efforts to establish links and obligations of this kind as a necessary corollary of greater freedom of movement across borders. At a practical level, the existence of the possibility of restitution and enforced compensation is likely to be a deterrent to smuggling between Member States. The art market, already alert to the possibility of dealing in stolen goods, will have to become more alert to the

possibility of dealing in illegally exported goods. Owners will therefore be forced into more rigorous compliance with the laws of their own Member States.

18. It may be argued that it is not for Member States to assist one another to enforce their export controls. This would go beyond the mutual assistance in clearly criminal matters which is now extensively practised. The possibility that works of art could be seized and subjected to prolonged litigation would be damaging to the art market, and particularly so to the United Kingdom market which is much more international in character than that of other Member States. Innocent purchasers would be placed at risk. It is inherently likely that the United Kingdom would find itself more often as detective in response to a claim from elsewhere than as claimant to an item of British treasure which had escaped our own controls.

19. At this stage we cannot say that the fears of the market are exaggerated. Much has been achieved in negotiation to ensure that procedures for restitution are not launched without sufficient evidence to facilitate search, to circumscribe the procedures with realistic time limits, and to ensure that purchasers are not placed under the burden of proving that their possession of a national treasure is innocent. No Member State will be laid open against its will as a result of the directive to retroactive claims to treasures which crossed borders many years ago. It is in this context of particular relevance that we were told that although Spain, Italy and Greece and perhaps Portugal as well as the United States, Canada, Australia and New Zealand had ratified and implemented the UNESCO Convention, no Community Member State had so far made use of it. It is in any event clear that progress in the Council has been rapid and that the basic principle of co-operation between Member States in restitution of national treasures appears to be accepted.

20. One important improvement which our negotiators have secured for the United Kingdom is that under the revised wording of Article 1(1) a 'cultural object' may be defined as a national treasure before or after its unlawful removal from the territory of a Member State. The United Kingdom will be entitled to invoke the machinery of restitution of a national heritage object from another Member State without having listed the object before it was taken abroad. The directive is thus capable of operating in a reciprocal fashion without the United Kingdom being required to list its national treasures – a step against which, as explained above, there are powerful arguments.

[A45] Amended proposal for a Council Directive on the protection of individuals with regard to the processing of personal data and on the free movement of such data ((1992) COM 422 final – SYN 287, Brussels, 15 October 1992)

THE COUNCIL OF THE EUROPEAN COMMUNITIES,

Having regard to the Treaty establishing the European Economic Community, and in particular Articles 100a and 113 [common commercial policy with regard to third countries] thereof,

Having regard to the proposal from the Commission,
In co-operation with the European Parliament,
Having regard to the opinion of the Economic and Social Committee,

(1) Whereas the objectives of the Community, as laid down in the Treaty, as amended by the Single European Act, include strengthening an ever closer union among the peoples of Europe, fostering closer relations between the states belonging to the Community, ensuring economic and social progress by common action to eliminate the barriers which divide Europe, encouraging the constant improvement of the living conditions of its peoples, preserving and strengthening peace and liberty and promoting democracy on the basis of the fundamental rights recognised in the constitutions and laws of the Member States and in the European Convention for the Protection of Human Rights and Fundamental Freedoms;

(2) Whereas data-processing systems are designed to serve society; whereas they must respect the fundamental freedoms and rights of individuals, notably the right to privacy, and contribute to economic and social progress, trade expansion and the well-being of individuals;

(3) Whereas the establishment and functioning of an internal market in which, in accordance with Article 8a of the Treaty, the free movement of goods, persons, services and capital is ensured require not only that personal data should be able to flow freely from one Member State to another, but also that the fundamental rights of individuals should be safeguarded;

(4) Whereas increasingly frequent recourse is being had in the Community to the processing of personal data in the various spheres of economic and social activity; whereas the progress made in information technology is making the processing and exchange of such data considerably easier;

(5) Whereas the economic and social integration resulting from the establishment and functioning of the internal market within the meaning of Article 8a of the Treaty will necessarily lead to a substantial increase in cross-border flows of personal data between all those involved in a private or public capacity in economic and social activity in the Member States; whereas the exchange of personal data between undertakings in different Member States is set to increase; whereas the national authorities in the various Member States are being called upon, by virtue of Community law, to collaborate and exchange personal data so as to be able to perform their duties or carry out tasks on behalf of an authority in another Member State within the context of the area without internal frontiers as constituted by the internal market;

(6) Whereas, furthermore, the increase in scientific and technical co-operation and the co-ordinated introduction of new telecommunications networks in the Community necessitate and facilitate cross-border flows of personal data;

(7) Whereas the difference in levels of protection of the rights and freedoms of individuals, notably the right to privacy, with regard to the processing of personal data afforded in the Member States may prevent the transmission of such data from the territory of one Member State to that of another Member State; whereas this difference may therefore constitute an obstacle to the pursuit of a number of economic activities at Community level, distort competition and impede authorities in the discharge of their responsibilities under Community law; whereas this difference in levels of

protection is due to the existence of a wide variety of national laws, regulations and administrative provisions;

(8) Whereas, in order to remove the obstacles to flows of personal data, the level of protection of the rights and freedoms of individuals with regard to the processing of such data must be equivalent in all the Member States; whereas this objective is vital to the internal market but cannot be achieved by the Member States alone, especially in view of the scale of the divergences which currently exist between the relevant laws in the Member States and the need to co-ordinate the laws of the Member States so as to ensure that the cross-border flow of personal data is regulated in a consistent manner that is in keeping with the objective of the internal market as provided for in Article 8a of the Treaty; whereas Community action to approximate those laws is therefore needed;

(9) Whereas the object of the national laws on the processing of personal data is to protect fundamental rights and freedoms, notably the right to privacy, which is recognised both in Article 8 of the European Convention for the Protection of Human Rights and Fundamental Freedoms and in the general principles of Community law; whereas, for that reason, the approximation of those laws must not result in any lessening of the protection they afford but must, on the contrary, seek to ensure a high level of protection in the Community;

(10) Whereas the principles of the protection of the rights and freedoms of individuals, notably the right to privacy, which are contained in this directive, give substance to and amplify those contained in the Council of Europe Convention of 28 January 1981 for the Protection of Individuals with regard to Automatic Processing of Personal Data;

(11) Whereas the protection principles must apply to all processing of personal data by any person whose activities are governed by Community law; whereas processing carried out by a Member State's own authorities, organisations or other bodies in the course of activities which are not governed by Community law should, as is provided for in the Resolution of the representatives of the governments of the Member States of the European Communities meeting within the Council of . . ., be subject to the same protection principles set out in national laws; whereas processing carried out by a natural person for purely private purposes in connection, for example, with correspondence or the maintenance of lists of addresses must be excluded;

(12) Whereas, in order to ensure that individuals are not deprived of the protection to which they are entitled under this directive, any processing of personal data in the Community must be carried out in accordance with the law of one of the Member States; whereas, in this connection, processing carried out by a person who is established in a Member State should be governed by the law of that State; whereas, the fact that processing is carried out by a person established in a third country must not stand in the way of the protection of individuals provided for in this directive; whereas, in that case, the processing should be governed by the law of the Member State in which the means used are located, and there should be guarantees to ensure that the rights and obligations provided for in this directive are respected in practice;

(13) Whereas Member States may more precisely define in the laws they enact or when bringing into force the measures taken under this directive the general circumstances in which processing is lawful; whereas,

however, more precise rules of this kind cannot serve as a basis for supervision by a Member State other than the Member State of residence of the person responsible for the processing, since the obligation on the part of the latter to ensure, in accordance with this directive, the protection of rights and freedoms with regard to the processing of personal data is sufficient, under Community law, to permit the free flow of data;

(14) Whereas the principles of protection must be reflected, on the one hand, in the obligations imposed on persons, public authorities, enterprises or bodies carrying out processing, in particular regarding quality, technical security, notification to the supervisory authority, and the circumstances under which processing is admissible, one such possible circumstance being that the data subject has consented, and, on the other hand, in the rights conferred on individuals, the data on whom are the subject of processing, to be informed that processing is taking place, to consult the data, to demand corrections and even to object to processing;

(15) Whereas any processing of personal data must be lawful and fair to the person concerned; whereas, in particular, the data must be relevant and not excessive in relation to the purposes for which they are processed; whereas such purposes must be explicit and lawful;

(16) Whereas, in order to be lawful, the processing of personal data must be carried out with the consent of the data subject or with a view to the conclusion or performance of a contract, binding on the data subject, or be required by Community law, by national law, by the general interest or by the interest of an individual, provided that the data subject has no legitimate grounds for objection; whereas, in particular, in order to maintain a balance between the interests involved, while guaranteeing effective competition, Member States remain free to determine the circumstances in which personal data may be disclosed to a third party for mailing purposes or research being carried out by an organisation or other association or foundation, of a political nature for example, subject to the provisions allowing a data subject to object to the disclosure of data regarding him, at no cost and without having to state his reasons;

(17) Whereas data which are capable by their nature of infringing fundamental freedoms or privacy should not be processed unless the data subject gives his written consent; whereas, however, processing of these data must be permitted if it is carried out by an association the purpose of which is to help safeguard the exercise of those freedoms; whereas, on grounds of important public interest, notably in relation to the medical profession, exemptions may be granted by law or by decision of the supervisory authority laying down the limits and suitable safeguards for the processing of these types of data;

(18) Whereas the processing of personal data for purposes of journalism should qualify for exemption from the requirements of this directive wherever this is necessary to reconcile the fundamental rights of individuals with freedom of information and notably the right to receive and impart information, as guaranteed in particular in Article 10 of the European Convention for the Protection of Human Rights and Fundamental Freedoms;

(19) Whereas, if the processing of data is to be fair, the data subject must be in a position to learn of the existence of a processing operation and must be given accurate and full information where data are collected from him, and not later than the time when the data are first disclosed to a third party if the data subject was not informed at the time the data were collected;

(20) Whereas any person must be able to exercise the right of access to data relating to him which are being processed, in order to verify the accuracy of the data and the lawfulness of the processing; whereas, therefore, any person should be entitled to object to the processing of the data on legitimate grounds;

(21) Whereas the protection of the rights and freedoms of data subjects with regard to the processing of personal data requires that appropriate technical measures be taken, both at the time of the design of the techniques of processing and at the time of the processing itself, particularly in order to maintain security and thereby to prevent any unauthorised processing;

(22) Whereas the notification procedures are designed to ensure disclosure of the purposes and main features of any processing operation, for the purpose of verification that the operation is in accordance with the national measures taken under this directive; whereas, in order to avoid unsuitable administrative formalities, exemption from the obligation to notify and simplification of the notification required must be provided for by Member States in cases where processing does not adversely affect the rights and freedoms of data subjects provided that it is in accordance with a measure taken by a Member State and specifying its limits;

(23) Whereas ex post facto verification by the competent authorities must, in general, be considered a sufficient measure; whereas, however, Member States must provide for checking by the supervisory authority prior to any processing which poses a particular threat to the rights and freedoms of data subjects by virtue of its nature, scope or purpose, such as processing which has as its object the exclusion of data subjects from a right, a benefit or a contract; whereas Member States should be entitled to replace such prior checking by means of a legislative measure or a decision of the supervisory authority authorising the processing operation and specifying suitable safeguards;

(24) Whereas, if the person carrying out processing fails to respect the rights of data subjects, national legislation must provide for a judicial remedy; whereas any damage which a person may suffer as a result of unlawful processing must be compensated for by the person responsible for the processing, who may be exempted from liability only if he proves that he has taken suitable security measures; whereas dissuasive penalties must be imposed on any person, whether governed by private or public law, who fails to comply with the national measures taken under this directive;

(25) Whereas cross-border flows of personal data are necessary to the expansion of international trade; whereas the protection of individuals guaranteed in the Community by this directive does not stand in the way of transfers of personal data to third countries which ensure an adequate level of protection; whereas the adequacy of the level of protection afforded by a third country must be assessed in the light of all the circumstances surrounding the transfer operation or set of transfer operations;

(26) Whereas, on the other hand, the transfer of personal data to a third country which does not ensure an adequate level of protection must be prohibited; whereas provision should be made for exemptions in certain circumstances where the data subject has given his consent or has been informed or where protection of the public interest so requires; whereas particular measures may be taken to rectify the lack of protection in a third

country in cases where the person responsible for the processing offers appropriate assurances; whereas, moreover, provision must be made for procedures for negotiations between the Community and such third countries;

(27) Whereas Member States may also provide for the use of codes of conduct drawn up by the business circles concerned and approved by the supervisory authority, with a view to adapting the national measures taken under this directive to the specific characteristics of processing in certain sectors;

(28) Whereas Member States must encourage the business circles concerned to draw up Community codes of conduct so as to facilitate the application of this directive; whereas the Commission will support such initiatives and will take them into account when it considers the appropriateness of additional specific measures in respect of certain sectors;

(29) Whereas the establishment in each Member State of an independent supervisory authority is an essential component of the protection of individuals with regard to the processing of personal data; whereas such an authority must have the necessary means to perform its duties, including powers of investigation or intervention and powers in connection with notification procedures; whereas such authority must help to ensure transparency of processing in the Member States within whose jurisdiction it falls; whereas the authorities in the different Member States will need to assist one another in performing their duties;

(30) Whereas, at Community level, a Working Party on the Protection of Individuals with regard to the Processing of Personal Data must be set up and be completely independent in the performance of its functions; whereas, having regard to its specific nature, it must advise the Commission and, in particular, contribute to the uniform application of the national rules adopted pursuant to this directive;

(31) Whereas the adoption of additional measures for applying the principles set out in this directive calls for the conferment of rule-making powers on the Commission and the establishment of an Advisory Committee in accordance with the procedures laid down in Council Decision 87/373;

(32) Whereas the principles set out in this directive regarding the protection of the rights and freedoms of individuals, notably their right to privacy, with regard to the processing of personal data may be supplemented or clarified, in particular as far as certain sectors are concerned, by specific rules based on those principles;

(33) Whereas Member States should be allowed a period of not more than three years from the entry into force of the national measures transposing this directive in which to apply such new national rules gradually to all processing operations already under way;

(34) Whereas this directive does not stand in the way of a Member State's regulating market research activities aimed at consumers residing in its territory in so far as such regulation does not concern the protection of individuals with regard to the processing of personal data, . . .

Question

Is this proposal consistent with the function of Article 100a which it purports to serve?

**[A46]   Case C-295/90 re students' rights: European
Parliament (EC Commission intervening) v EC
Council (United Kingdom and The Netherlands
intervening) [1992] 3 CMLR 281**

The European Court of Justice (Judgment, 7 July 1992)

1. By application received by the Court Registry on 28 September 1990,
the European Parliament seeks the annulment of Council Directive 90/366
of 28 June 1990 on the right of residence for students.

2. The legal basis of the directive is Article 235 EEC, whereas the
Commission had proposed to base it on Article 7(2) [relating to the prohibition of discrimination on grounds of nationality in areas within the scope of
application of the Treaty].

3. The Parliament relies on three grounds in support of its application.

4. It contends primarily that, by failing to choose the proper legal basis,
viz Article 7(2) EEC, the Council disregarded the Parliament's powers in
the legislative process because Article 7(2) provides for the latter's participation in accordance with the co-operation procedure, whereas Article 235
merely requires the Parliament to be consulted.

5. Alternatively, the Parliament contends that the Council has not stated
sufficient reason for having recourse to Article 235 and has therefore
deprived the Parliament of the opportunity to ascertain whether its powers
in the legislative process have been respected.

6. In the further alternative, it contends that the Council ought to have
given reasons for its refusal to adopt certain amendments proposed by the
Parliament.

7. Reference is made to the Report for the Hearing for a fuller account
of the facts of the case, the course of the procedure and the parties' submissions and arguments, which are mentioned or discussed hereinafter
only in so far as is necessary for the reasoning of the court . . .

Legal basis

11. First of all, it should be observed that, as the court has previously
stated, it follows from the very wording of Article 235 that its use as the
legal basis for a measure is justified only where no other provision of the
Treaty gives the Community institutions the necessary power to adopt the
measure in question: see Case 45/86 *Commission v Council* [1987] ECR
1493, at paragraph 13.

12. Therefore it is necessary to determine whether the Council had
power to adopt the contested directive on the basis of Article 7(2), as maintained by the Parliament, the Commission and, at the hearing, the British
government, which altered its original position as a result of Case C-357/89
Raulin [1992] ECR I-1027.

13. According to case law which is now settled, in the framework of the
system of the functions of the Community, the choice of the legal basis for
a measure must be founded upon objective factors which are open to judicial review. Such factors include in particular the purpose and content of
the measure: see Case C-300/89 *Commission v Council* [1991] ECR
I-2867 **[A38]**.

14. The contested directive aims to give effect to and organise the right of residence, limited to the duration of the course of studies, for students who are nationals of a Member State, their spouses and dependent children. Those concerned merely have to prove, by suitable means, that they are enrolled at a recognised institution for the principal purpose of following a vocational training course, that they are covered by sickness insurance and that they will not become a burden on the social assistance system of the host Member State. They receive from the said State a residence document which is valid for a maximum of one year but may be extended. Member States may not derogate from the provisions of the directive except on grounds of public policy, public security or public health. The directive does not give rise to a right to the payment of maintenance grants by the host State.

15. As the court pointed out in paragraph 34 of *Raulin* cited above, the right to equal treatment in relation to the conditions of access to vocational training applies not only to requirements imposed by the educational establishment in question, such as registration fees, but also to any measure liable to hinder the exercise of that right. It is obvious that a student who is admitted to a course may be unable to follow it if he has no right to reside in the Member State where the course is being held. It follows that the principle of non-discrimination in relation to the conditions of access to vocational training which derive from Articles 7 and 128 EEC mean that a national of a Member State who has been admitted to a course of vocational training in another Member State enjoys the right to reside in the latter State for the duration of the course.

16. It follows that the contested directive lays down, in a sphere of application of the Treaty, viz that of vocational training which is referred to by Article 128, measures which prohibit discrimination on the grounds of nationality, as provided for by Article 7(2).

17. At the hearing, however, the Council and the Dutch government argued that the contested directive conferred upon students a freedom of movement which is similar to that of migrant workers and goes beyond a right of residence for the purposes of vocational training and that, consequently, the object and content of the directive exceeded the framework of Article 7 EEC and therefore necessitated recourse to Article 235 as the legal basis.

18. On this point it should be observed that the general principle of Article 7(1) can only be applied subject to special provisions of the Treaty: see Case 8/77 *Sagulo* [1977] ECR 1495, and that Article 7(2) has the object of enabling the Council to take the necessary measures, depending on the rights and interests involved, for the effective elimination of discrimination on grounds of nationality in matters where its power has no foundation in one of the special provisions governing the different spheres of application of the Treaty. However, rules adopted pursuant to Article 7(2) should not necessarily be limited to regulating rights deriving from paragraph (1) of the same Article, but they may also deal with aspects the regulation of which appears necessary for the effective exercise of those rights.

19. Secondly, it should be noted that the different elements of the contested directive are bound up with practical exercise of the right of residence for students for the purpose of vocational training. On this point it should be stressed that the right of residence conferred upon the spouse and dependent children appears to be an essential element for genuine

exercise of the student's right of residence, as expressly stated in the eighth recital of the preamble to the directive.

20. It follows from what has been said that the Council had power to adopt the contested directive under Article 7(2) EEC and that consequently there was no foundation for using Article 235.

21. Therefore the contested directive should be annulled, and it is unnecessary to examine the Parliament's alternative grounds . . .

[A47] H Sevenster: 'Criminal Law and EC Law' (1992) 29 Common Market Law Review 30

5.1 The completion of the internal market

A number of developments in the process of completing the internal market may bear on the problem of differences between criminal law systems. Various authors assume that there are great differences in the maximum punishments and in the infliction of punishments between Member States. Yet, no extensive research has been undertaken into these differences in the implementing legislation, not least because of the enormous amount of work it would involve. Therefore, the extent to which there actually are differences in the penal sanctions for the same infringements of Community law, is dealt with only speculatively. This is also the case for the associated question of whether these differences are such as to cause companies to engage in illegal activities in another country. Assuming then that there are divergences which are significant, what effect does '1992' have?

First, with increasing integration, the 'old' reasons for proposing harmonisation are just as urgent as before. Only the contravention of the principle of *ne bis in idem* may come to an end with the signing by all Member States of the relevant treaty. In my view, the other arguments – uniformity of Community law, problems of enforcement, fraud, unequal treatment and distortion of competition – are as valid as ever, if not more so.

The completion of the internal market means that divergences become more important; if everyone and everything can move freely, this also offers opportunities of engaging in activities for which this freedom was not intended. Apart from uniformity as a matter of principle, the more practical (second) question may play an important role in future. Committing an offence in another Member State in order to escape stricter national legislation, will become simpler. After all, once . . . all trade barriers are removed . . . nothing will prevent a company from moving to the country where it deems the conditions of competition to be most favourable. Among the conditions of competition which the company will consider, may also be the severity of penalties for infringements of (Community) law. Here I refer once more to the bank robber . . ., who had come to the Netherlands because criminal sanctions (and the chance of being caught?) were lowest there. In the United States, there is something called the 'Delaware effect' in company law. This refers to the attraction the state of Delaware holds for companies, because of its very favourable climate in terms of company law. Within the Community, we see a similar effect with respect to taxes . . . Such effects could also occur if (economic) norms were more or less equal, but the penal legislation in Member States showed great divergence. The greater the extent of integration aimed for, the greater the nuisance of lack of uniformity. The importance of equal sanctions for equal offences increases. The same holds good for the prevention of distortion of competition. Moreover, the increasing integration will depend heavily on the enforcement of Community legislation. The problems of EEC fraud and abuse of free movement of goods provisions, so-called 'carousels', will worsen unless Community legislation is brought about. Internal border controls will have disappeared. The necessity of agreements on the controls at the outer borders of the EEC will increase.

Secondly, we may point to the growth of Community law. In imposing penalties on 'unlawful' acts, the term 'unlawful' refers to national law, which is increasingly dominated by EEC legislation. EEC legislation will set norms in more and more areas. The margins for establishing the substance of criminal law by Member States become proportionally smaller. In many areas, Community competence will develop into an exclusive one. Regulations are the more usual instruments in such areas.

. . .

Thirdly, with the completing of the internal market the danger of 'spontaneous harmonisation' presents itself in full force. This refers to the phenomenon that some differences in legislation get ironed out 'automatically', without any agreement among Member States to do this. In the strongly competitive Europe of 1993, no Member State will want to be the only strict one. Companies and governments have been hinting at this problem for some time now. It is particularly evident in discussions on environmental issues. If Member States were indeed to feel that they should 'spontaneously' adapt their (penal) legislation, this 'spontaneous' harmonisation would take the place of the harmonisation via EEC legislation which has not been achieved. Thus, non-action may lead to undesirable results.

Fourthly, it is to be expected that a higher level of integration will increase Member States' obligations towards the Community. Even now one can identify a tendency to point out more and more the obligations and responsibilities of Member States. A central role is played by Article 5 EEC **[A5]**, which in its accepted interpretation encompasses the duty of loyal co-operation between Member States and the Community. It is not surprising to find that this duty to co-operate is of increasing significance as integration increases. The judgment in Case 68/88 *Commission v Greece* [1989] ECR 2965 (obligation for a Member State to prosecute) and the *Zwartveld I* decision **[D60]** (obligation for the Commission to open its files) are omens. On this basis it is quite possible that the obligations of Member States in terms of penal law will be given further substance in future. The responsibility of Member States to guarantee full compliance with Community law can only grow further.

. . .

6.   Harmonisation of criminal law?

At present many far-reaching decisions are being taken in the EC. But there are two (political) obstacles to harmonisation of criminal law in the near future. The first is, paradoxically, the completing of the internal market. All attention and expertise is spent on this task and the proposals for an [Economic and Monetary Union and European Political Union], and those concerned are not particularly eager to see a difficult dossier on criminal law added. The problem may well receive more attention after 1992. Secondly, a new magic word has enriched the vocabulary of EEC discussions and negotiations: subsidiarity. This term applies to the division of competences between the Community and the Member States in such a way that the Community is (exclusively) competent to act if that is 'better' (or 'more efficient') than if Member States acted individually.

. . .

In short, there are no indications that the harmonisation of criminal law is imminent, and the arduous nature of the Schengen Agreement **[A49]** negotiations indicate that Member States fear a loss of sovereignty.

Note. See also **[A16]** on the 'third pillar' of the Maastricht Treaty.

[A48] Council Regulation 302/93 on the establishment of a European Monitoring Centre for Drugs and Drug Addiction (OJ 1993 L36/1)

THE COUNCIL OF THE EUROPEAN COMMUNITIES

Having regard to the Treaty establishing the European Economic Community, and in particular Article 235 thereof,
Having regard to the proposal from the Commission,
Having regard to the opinion of the European Parliament,
Having regard to the opinion of the Economic and Social Committee,

Whereas at its meeting in Dublin on 25 and 26 June 1990, the European Council:

- ratified the 'Guidelines for a European Plan to Combat Drugs' submitted to it by the European Committee to Combat Drugs (Celad), and in particular the recommendation that 'a study be conducted by experts on the existing sources of information, their reliability and their usefulness, and on the need for and possible scope of a European Drugs Monitoring Centre and the financial implications of setting up such a Centre, on the understanding that the brief of this Centre would cover not only the social and health aspects but also other drugs-related aspects, including trafficking and repression';
- stressed that it was the responsibility of each Member State to develop an appropriate drug demand reduction programme and considered that effective action by each Member State, supported by joint action of the Twelve and the Community, should be a main priority over the coming years;

Whereas the findings of the feasibility study on the Centre and the European Plan to Combat Drugs submitted to the Rome European Council on 13 and 14 December 1990 should be borne in mind;

Whereas the European Council, at its meeting in Luxembourg on 28 and 29 June 1991, 'approved the setting up of a European Drugs Monitoring Centre on the understanding that the practical arrangements for its implementation, eg its size, institutional structure and computer systems, are still to be discussed and instructed Celad to continue work to that end and bring it rapidly to a successful conclusion, in liaison with the Commission and the other relevant political bodies';

Whereas the European Council, at its meeting in Maastricht on 9 and 10 December 1991, 'invited the institutions of the Community to employ all means to ensure that the act setting up the European Drugs Centre could be adopted before 30 June 1992';

Whereas the Community concluded, by Decision 90/611, the United Nations Convention against Illicit Traffic in Narcotic Drugs and Psychotropic Substances, hereinafter referred to as the 'Vienna Convention', and deposited a declaration of competence regarding Article 27 thereof;

Whereas the Council adopted Regulation 3677/90 for the implementation by the Community of the system provided for in Article 12 of the aforementioned Vienna Convention for monitoring trade in certain substances;

Whereas the Council adopted Directive 91/308 of 10 June 1991 on prevention of the use of the financial system for the purpose of money laundering, which aims in particular to combat drug trafficking;

Whereas objective, reliable and comparable information concerning drugs, drug addiction and their consequences is required at Community level to help provide the Community and the Member States with an overall view and thus give them added value when, in their respective areas of competence, they take measures or decide on action to combat drugs;

Whereas the drug phenomenon comprises many complex and closely interwoven aspects which cannot easily be dissociated; whereas, therefore, the Centre should be entrusted with the task of furnishing overall information which will help to provide the Community and its Member States with an overall view of the drug and drug addiction phenomenon; whereas this task should not prejudice the allocation of powers between the Community and its Member States with regard to the legislative provisions concerning drug supply and demand;

Whereas the Centre's organisation and working methods must be consistent with the objective nature of the results sought, namely the comparability and compatibility of sources and methods in connection with drug information;

Whereas the information compiled by the Centre will concern priority areas whose content, scope and implementing arrangements should be defined;

Whereas, during the first three-year period, special attention will be given to demand and demand reduction;

Whereas, in their resolution of 16 May 1989 concerning a European network of health data on drug abuse, the Council and the Ministers for Health of the Member States meeting within the Council invited the Commission to take possible initiatives in this area;

Whereas a European information network on drugs and drug addiction should be set up, to be co-ordinated and led at Community level by the European Drugs Monitoring Centre;

Whereas Convention 108 of the Council of Europe for the Protection of

Individuals with regard to Automatic Processing of Personal Data (1981) should be taken into account;

Whereas there already exist national, European and international organisations and bodies supplying information of this kind, and whereas the Centre should be able to carry out its tasks in close co-operation with them;

Whereas the Centre must have legal personality;

Whereas it is necessary to ensure that the Centre carries out its information task and to confer jurisdiction for this purpose on the Court of Justice;

Whereas it is desirable to recognise the possibility of opening the Centre to non-Community countries which share the interest of the Community and the Member States in the attainment of these objectives, under agreements to be concluded between them and the Community;

Whereas this Regulation could, if necessary, be adapted after a three-year period with a view to a decision on the possible extension of the Centre's tasks, taking into account, in particular, the evolution of Community powers;

Whereas, for the adoption of this Regulation the Treaty provides for no powers to act other than those laid down in Article 235,

HAS ADOPTED THIS REGULATION:

Article 1   Objective

1. This Regulation establishes the European Monitoring Centre for Drugs and Drug Addiction (EDMC), hereinafter referred to as 'the Centre'.

2. The Centre's objective is to provide, in the areas referred to in Article 4, the Community and its Member States with objective, reliable and comparable information at European level concerning drugs and drug addiction and their consequences.

3. The statistical, documentary and technical information processed or produced is intended to help provide the Community and the Member States with an overall view of the drug and drug addiction situation when, in their respective areas of competence, they take measures or decide on action.

4. The Centre may not take any measure which in any way goes beyond the sphere of information and the processing thereof.

5. The Centre shall not collect any data making it possible to identify individuals or small groups of individuals. It shall refrain from any transmission of information relating to specific named cases.

. . .

Article 4   Priority areas of activity

The objectives and tasks of the Centre, as defined in Articles 1 and 2, shall be implemented following the order of priorities indicated in the Annex.

. . .

Annex

A. The work of the Centre shall be carried out with due regard to the respective powers of the Community and its Member States in the area of drugs, as those powers are defined by the Treaty.

The information gathered by the Centre shall relate to the following priority areas:
1. demand and reduction of the demand for drugs;
2. national and Community strategies and policies (with special emphasis on international, bilateral and Community policies, action plans, legislation, activities and agreements);
3. international co-operation and geopolitics of supply (with special emphasis on co-operation programmes and information on producer and transit countries);
4. control of trade in narcotic drugs, pyschotropic substances and precursors, as provided for in the relevant present or future international conventions and Community acts;
5. implications of the drugs phenomenon for producer, consumer and transit countries, within areas covered by the Treaty, including money laundering, as laid down by relevant present or future Community acts.

[A49]   Resolution A3-0336/92 of the European Parliament on the entry into force of the Schengen Agreement (OJ 1992 C337/214)

19 November 1992

The European Parliament
. . .

A. whereas the EEC Treaty provides for the free movement of persons, which must be a reality by 31 December 1992; whereas, pursuant to Article 175 of the EEC Treaty, an action may be brought before the Court of Justice if the Council and the Commission fail adequately to implement the free movement of persons laid down in Article 8a and to take the decisions provided for by the EEC Treaty to that end;

B. whereas the EC Member States have ratified the 1951 Geneva Convention and the New York supplementary protocol of 1967;

C. whereas the EC Member States have acceded individually to the European Convention on Human Rights and the European Community ought to do so;

D. whereas nine [Belgium, France, Germany, Greece, Italy, Luxembourg, the Netherlands, Portugal and Spain] of the EC Member States intend to implement the Convention applying the Schengen Agreement, which means that their citizens, and also persons wishing to enter their territory, will be subject to additional rights and duties relating to the free movement of persons and that the citizens of non-Schengen countries will be treated differently from the citizens of other EC Member States;

E. whereas the Convention applying the Schengen Agreement must ultimately be replaced by Community rules, due account being taken of the many reservations about the gaps and imperfections in this convention;

F. whereas numerous working parties are already in the process of drawing up provisions and documents for the implementation of the Convention applying the Schengen Agreement, the buildings for the Schengen Information System in Strasbourg have been constructed, a provisional committee of control for the SIS has already been appointed and this is happening without one iota of democratic control and before all the parliaments of the Schengen Member States have ratified the Convention applying the Schengen Agreement;

G. whereas the many international agreements, international co-operation structures and bodies for international judicial and police co-operation have been instrumental in creating a deficit in terms of human rights and democracy, and whereas the citizens affected can not be adequately informed about their rights and duties in this field;

H. whereas it is necessary to proceed as rapidly as possible from the experimental, constitutive stage to a binding arrangement in which the principles of parliamentary supervision, judicial review and public information are formally sanctioned;

1. considers that the Convention applying the Schengen Agreement must be regarded as an excellent testing ground for Community settlement of the matters dealt with in the agreement and an opportunity to make the European Parliament and national parliaments aware of these matters;

2. considers that the free movement of persons is an essential component of the internal market;

3. reiterates, therefore, its call for the Commission to submit to the Council and Parliament as soon as possible, and in any event within the period of time laid down in Article 175 of the EEC Treaty, appropriate proposals for replacing the provisions of the Convention applying the Schengen Agreement with Community law, and calls on the Council to take the necessary decisions;

...

5. reserves the right, pursuant to Article 175 of the EEC Treaty, to bring an action against the Council and the Commission for failure to act;

6. calls for the harmonisation of visa and asylum policy within the Community and a single, Community-wide interpretation of the provisions of the relevant international conventions;

7. fears that current practice, whereby the free movement of persons, the elimination of controls of individuals at internal borders and the implementation of compensatory measures are arranged through inter-governmental agreements to which not all of the 12 Member States are always party, will result in discrimination between EC citizens on nationality grounds and discrimination against non-EC citizens living in the various Member States;

8. calls on the Commission to work for the application of the principle of equal treatment and freedom of movement to all citizens, including those from third countries, in the Community, as set out in the Convention applying the Schengen Agreement;

9. regrets that the Convention applying the Schengen Agreement makes no reference whatsoever to the European Convention for the Protection of Human Rights and Fundamental Freedoms;.

. . .

13. considers that the provisions on police co-operation in the Convention applying the Schengen Agreement are too vaguely worded and that if putting them into practice is left to bilateral agreements, the result will be legal uncertainty;

. . .

15. considers that the provisions of the Convention applying the Schengen Agreement on mutual judicial assistance, extradition and the transfer of execution of sentences do not take sufficient account of the provisions laid down in the Council of Europe's conventions, and that the latter provisions should therefore be implemented unconditionally;

. . .

17. calls on the Commission to ensure, in collaboration with the European Parliament, that data protection is included among the responsibilities of the European Ombudsman;

18. considers that the provisions of the Convention applying the Schengen Agreement on the transfer of the execution of sentences do not take the prisoners' interests sufficiently into account, as the consent of the sentenced person is not required for such a transfer;

. . .

21. calls for provision to be made for international judicial monitoring of the implementation of the Convention applying the Schengen Agreement, and considers the Court of Justice . . . to be the appropriate judicial body for this purpose;

22. in view of the liberal and widespread use of the notions of public order and national security, calls in particular for the adoption of a uniform interpretation referring to the case law of the Court of Justice;

23. is afraid that the very wide special powers and the general duties of the Executive Committee might give rise to a number of fears and certain difficulties with regard to constitutional law in various countries and that it would hardly be possible for them to have direct effect;

. . .

28. calls on the national parliaments to consider the European Parliament's criticisms of the Convention applying the Schengen Agreement and, inter alia, to demand that their governments provide the necessary guarantees for democratic control of implementation of the Convention – particularly of the activities of the Executive Committee established in Title VII of the Convention – public access to the committee's decisions, and better legal protection and legal aid for citizens affected by implementation of the agreements (by, inter alia, declaring the European Court of Justice competent to give preliminary rulings pursuant to Article 177 of the EEC Treaty);

29. instructs its President to forward this resolution to the Commission,

the Council, the Presidency of the Schengen Group, the governments and parliaments of the Member States and the UN High Commissioner for Refugees.

Question

From **[A47]**, **[A48]** and **[A49]**, does the European Community have any general competence to act in matters of criminal liability or penal sanctions? Compare **[A16]**.

SECTION FOUR

SIGNPOSTS AND DIRECTIONS

MATERIALS

1   The notion of citizenship of the Union

[A50]   EC Treaty Part Two

CITIZENSHIP OF THE UNION

Article 8

1. Citizenship of the Union is hereby established.
Every person holding the nationality of a Member State shall be a citizen of the Union.
2. Citizens of the Union shall enjoy the rights conferred by this Treaty and shall be subject to the duties imposed thereby.

Article 8a

1. Every citizen of the Union shall have the right to move and reside freely within the territory of the Member States, subject to the limitations and conditions laid down in this Treaty and by the measures adopted to give it effect.
2. The Council may adopt provisions with a view to facilitating the exercise of the rights referred to in paragraph 1; save as otherwise provided in this Treaty, the Council shall act unanimously on a proposal from the Commission and after obtaining the assent of the European Parliament.

Article 8b

1. Every citizen of the Union residing in a Member State of which he is not a national shall have the right to vote and to stand as a candidate at municipal elections in the Member State in which he resides, under the same conditions as nationals of that state. This right shall be exercised subject to detailed arrangements to be adopted before 31 December 1994 by the Council, acting unanimously on a proposal from the Commission and after consulting the European Parliament; these arrangements may provide for derogations where warranted by problems specific to a Member State.
2. Without prejudice to Article 138(3) **[B2]** and to the provisions adopted for its implementation, every citizen of the Union residing in a Member State of which he is not a national shall have the right to vote and to stand as a candidate in elections to the European Parliament in the Member State in which he resides, under the same conditions as nationals of that state. This

right shall be exercised subject to detailed arrangements to be adopted before 31 December 1993 by the Council, acting unanimously on a proposal from the Commission and after consulting the European Parliament; these arrangements may provide for derogations where warranted by problems specific to a Member State.

Article 8c

Every citizen of the Union shall, in the territory of a third country in which the Member State of which he is a national is not represented, be entitled to protection by the diplomatic or consular authorities of any Member State, on the same conditions as the nationals of that state. Before 31 December 1993, Member States shall establish the necessary rules among themselves and start the international negotiations required to secure this protection.

Article 8d

Every citizen of the Union shall have the right to petition the European Parliament in accordance with Article 138d **[B2]**.

Every citizen of the Union may apply to the Ombudsman established in accordance with Article 138e **[B2]**.

Article 8e

The Commission shall report to the European Parliament, to the Council and to the Economic and Social Committee before 31 December 1993 and then every three years on the application of the provisions of this Part. This report shall take account of the development of the Union.

On this basis, and without prejudice to the other provisions of this Treaty, the Council, acting unanimously on a proposal from the Commission and after consulting the European Parliament, may adopt provisions to strengthen or to add to the rights laid down in this Part, which it shall recommend to the Member States for adoption in accordance with their respective constitutional requirements.

[A51] Conclusions of the Presidency, European Council in Edinburgh, 11-12 December 1992

. . .The European Council has agreed on the following set of arrangements, which are fully compatible with the Treaty, are designed to meet Danish concerns, and therefore apply exclusively to Denmark and not to other existing or acceding Member States . . .

DECISION OF THE HEADS OF STATE AND GOVERNMENT, MEETING WITHIN THE EUROPEAN COUNCIL, CONCERNING CERTAIN PROBLEMS RAISED BY DENMARK ON THE TREATY ON EUROPEAN UNION

The Heads of State and Government, meeting within the European Council, whose Governments are signatories of the Treaty on European

Union, which involves independent and sovereign States having freely decided, in accordance with the existing Treaties, to exercise in common some of their competences,

- desiring to settle, in conformity with the Treaty on European Union, particular problems existing at the present time specifically for Denmark and raised in its memorandum 'Denmark in Europe' of 30 October 1992,
- having regard to the conclusions of the Edinburgh European Council on subsidiarity and transparency,
- noting the declarations of the Edinburgh European Council relating to Denmark,
- taking cognisance of the unilateral declarations of Denmark made on the same occasion which will be associated with its act of ratification,
- noting that Denmark does not intend to make use of the following provisions in such a way as to prevent closer co-operation and action among Member States compatible with the Treaty and within the framework of the Union and its objectives,

Have agreed on the following decision:

Section A   Citizenship

The provisions of Part Two of the Treaty establishing the European Community relating to citizenship of the Union give nationals of the Member States additional rights and protection as specified in that Part. They do not in any way take the place of national citizenship. The question whether an individual possesses the nationality of a Member State will be settled solely by reference to the national law of the Member State concerned.

Note.   Sections B-E, relating to economic and monetary union, defence policy, justice and home affairs and final provisions, are omitted.

2   The European Community's relationship with other bodies and international rules

[A52]   House of Lords Select Committee on the European Communities, Session 1992-93 3rd Report (HL Paper 10): human rights re-examined

The power of the Communities – or of the Union – to accede to the Convention

84. We have carefully considered the argument that it should be not the three Communities – the European Economic Community, the European Coal and Steel Community and the European Atomic Energy Community – but the Union which would accede to the European Convention, but we do not believe that such an accession would be legally possible. As the Foreign and Commonwealth Office emphasised, the Union has not been set up as an international organisation having international legal personality or treaty-making capacity. Action under the Common Foreign and Security Policy **[A15]** and under the provisions on Co-operation in Justice and Home

Affairs **[A16]** remains inter-governmental action, as we ourselves strongly recommended before and during the Conferences which led to Maastricht. Although we have noted the concerns expressed by some witnesses that the possibility of action in regard to such matters as asylum and immigration could be open to challenge on human rights grounds, we believe that these would be largely met by the inclusion, in Article K2 of the Maastricht Treaty Provisions on Co-operation in the Fields of Justice and Home Affairs of the following requirement:

1. The matters referred to in Article K1 shall be dealt with in compliance with the European Convention of Human Rights and Fundamental Freedoms of 4 November 1950 and the Convention relating to the Status of Refugees of 28 July 1951 and having regard to the protection afforded by Member States to persons persecuted on political grounds.

This new provision strengthens, if it were necessary, the duty of Member States to observe the Convention, regardless of how they act within the Council – whether by consultation or under joint positions or joint action and regardless of whether, pursuant to Article K3, they agree to draw up conventions giving interpretative jurisdiction to the Court of Justice. Any complaints of violation would go directly to the Commission and Court in Strasbourg against the Member States (singly or perhaps sometimes collectively), even if the Community were to accede to the Convention. There would be no need for the individual, as part of the exhaustion of domestic remedies, to show that the European Court of Justice had considered his complaint.

85. It would therefore be the three Communities which would require to have the legal power to accede to the Convention, as the Commission proposes. In 1980 we considered that it would be necessary to amend the EEC Treaty to permit accession. The Commission had suggested in their 1979 Memorandum that the EEC might accede under the terms of Article 235 **[A35]**, but the Foreign and Commonwealth Office expressed 'considerable doubts' as to whether Article 235 could provide the necessary vires for Community accession. Sir Ian Sinclair in evidence said 'I think it is quite clear that certainly the objectives of the Community as spelt out in Articles 2 and 3 of the Treaty of Rome do not encompass, certainly in terms, the protection of fundamental rights'.

86. Article 235 of the EEC Treaty can only be used for Community action with a Community objective. It has been traditional, in construing Article 235, to do so by reference to Articles 2 and 3 of the EEC Treaty **[A1]**, although these Articles do not define Community objectives but set out the tasks and activities of the Community. Although Articles 2 and 3 have been extended by the Maastricht Treaty, they still do not refer in express terms to the protection of human rights. Protection of human rights is certainly not as such a task or an activity of the Community and is unlikely to be brought within those categories. But the word 'objective' is wider. Article 1 of the Single European Act provides the Community with a very wide-ranging objective in the following terms: 'The European Communities and European Political Co-operation shall have as their objective to contribute together to making concrete progress towards European unity.'

The Community is based in a very fundamental sense on the rule of law and the protection of human rights, and we believe that it is a Community objective to ensure that its tasks and activities are carried out in accordance with law and on the basis of individual rights. This may originally have been only an implied objective, but the language used in the Single European Act, where the Member States express their determination to work together to promote democracy on the basis of the fundamental rights recognised in the constitutions and law of the Member States and in the European Convention, transform it in our view into an express objective. It may perhaps best be explained as a 'parallel objective' or an 'ancillary objective' of Community activities as a whole. The terms of Article F of the Maastricht Treaty **[A3]** are also helpful, in requiring the Union (which is founded on the European Communities) to respect fundamental rights, as guaranteed by the European Convention as general principles of Community law.

87. Article 235 also requires that the action proposed should be necessary for the attainment in question. This is ultimately a matter of political judgment by the Member States, and they must – even under the new Treaty – be unanimous. The European Court of Justice has never in fact annulled any measure adopted by the Council under Article 235. In practice, if all the Member States were to be satisfied that the case for Community accession has on balance been made out, we are inclined to the view that the Council could make use of the powers in Article 235 so far as EEC accession is concerned . . .

The relationship between the courts at Strasbourg and Luxembourg

97. The institutional problems in regard to the two European courts fall into two categories – conceptual or constitutional on the one hand and practical or procedural on the other. As regards the first, the proposed constitutional subordination, in regard to one aspect of the law, of the European Court of Justice to the European Court of Human Rights has been discussed (in a personal capacity) by two of the Judges of the European Court of Justice . . . The position has been clarified recently by the opinion of the full European Court in December 1991 on the European Economic Area Agreement **[A56]**. The opinion reads, in part, as follows:

> Where, however, an international agreement provides for its own system of courts, including a court with jurisdiction to settle disputes between the Contracting Parties to the agreement, and, as a result, to interpret its provisions, the decisions of that court will be binding on the Community institutions, including the Court of Justice. Those decisions will also be binding in the event that the Court of Justice is called upon to rule, by way of preliminary ruling or in a direct action, on the interpretation of the international agreement, in so far as that agreement is an integral part of the Community legal order.
>
> An international agreement providing for such a system of courts is in principle compatible with Community law. The Community's competence in the field of international relations and its capacity to conclude international agreements necessarily entails the power to submit to the decisions of a court which is created or designated by such an agreement as regards the interpretation and application of its provisions.

In the longer term, as the Community is enlarged and the volume of European litigation increases, some further specialisation among international or European tribunals is likely. Just as the establishment of the Court of First Instance has relieved the European Court of Justice of the main burden of staff cases and cases on competition, so could the European Court of Human Rights ultimately assume full authority as ultimate arbiter of the European law on human rights questions. We agree with Professor Schermers that 'the autonomy of both courts would be strengthened if each Court would be full master in its own field'.

[A53]   Opinion of the Court of Justice on Convention No 170 of the International Labour Organisation concerning safety in the use of chemicals at work

Opinion 2/91 OJ 1993 C109/1

The ILO was founded in 1919 with the aim of improving the conditions of labour and promoting social justice. Its principal task, through its General Conference, is to adopt proposals in the form of international conventions or recommendations. States which are members of the United Nations may join the ILO. The European Community is not a member of the ILO but has observer status. As a result of a decision taken by the Council of Ministers in 1986, certain procedures were created for the participation of the Community through the medium of the EC Commission in areas coming within the exclusive competence of the Community.

Convention No 170 is designed to protect workers against the harmful effects of using chemicals in the workplace. In the course of its adoption, several Member States contested the Community's exclusive competence to act in the matter and thus the Commission's power to speak for the Community. The Commission therefore exercised its power under Article 228(1), according to which 'The Council, the Commission or a Member State may obtain beforehand the opinion of the Court of Justice as to whether an agreement envisaged is compatible with the provisions of this Treaty. Where the opinion of the Court of Justice is adverse, the agreement may enter into force only in accordance with Article 236.'

Arguments were put to the court on both the admissibility of the request and its substance.

The reasoning of the court

The admissibility of the request for an opinion

(1) . . . According to [the German and Netherlands] governments, the procedure set out in [Article 228] is intended only for the examination of the compatibility with the Treaty of an agreement the conclusion of which is envisaged between the Community and one or more states or an international organisation. The present request, they submit, relates to the Community's competence to conclude a convention which is capable of being ratified only by Member States of the ILO and not by the Community, which is not a member of that international organisation.

(2) Those arguments cannot be accepted.

(3) The court has consistently held . . . that it is possible under the procedure set out in Article 228 . . . to consider all questions concerning the compatibility with the provisions of the Treaty of an agreement envisaged,

and in particular the question whether the Community has the power to enter into that agreement. That interpretation is confirmed by Article 107(2) of the Rules of Procedure of the court.

(4) It follows that the request for an opinion does not concern the Community's capacity, on the international plane, to enter into a convention drawn up under the auspices of the ILO but relates to the scope, judged solely by reference to the rules of Community law, of the competence of the Community and the Member States within the area covered by Convention No 170. It is not for the court to assess any obstacles which the Community may encounter in the exercise of its competence because of constitutional rules of the ILO.

(5) In any event, although, under the ILO Constitution, the Community cannot itself conclude Convention No 170, its external competence may, if necessary, be exercised through the medium of the Member States acting jointly in the Community's interest.

(6) The conditions laid down in the second subparagraph of Article 228(1) of the Treaty have therefore been satisfied and the request is consequently admissible.

The substance

(7) Before examining whether Convention No 170 falls within the scope of the Community's competence and whether the Community's competence is exclusive, the court must point out that, as it stated in particular in . . . Opinion 1/76 [1977] ECR 741, authority to enter into international commitments may not only arise from an express attribution by the Treaty, but may also flow implicitly from its provisions. The court concluded, in particular, that whenever Community law created for the institutions of the Community powers within its internal system for the purpose of attaining a specific objective, the Community had authority to enter into the international commitments necessary for the attainment of that objective even in the absence of an express provision in that connection.

. . .

(9) The exclusive or non-exclusive nature of the Community's competence does not flow solely from the provisions of the Treaty but may also depend on the scope of the measures which have been adopted by the Community institutions for the application of those provisions and which are of such a kind as to deprive the Member States of an area of competence which they were able to exercise previously on a transitional basis. As the court stated . . . in Case 22/70 *Commission v Council* [1971] ECR 263 (the *AETR* judgment), where Community rules have been promulgated for the attainment of the objectives of the Treaty, the Member States cannot, outside the framework of the Community institutions, assume obligations which might affect those rules or alter their scope.

(10) Contrary to the contentions of the German, Spanish and Irish governments, the authority of the decision in that case cannot be restricted to instances where the Community has adopted Community rules within the framework of a common policy. In all the areas corresponding to the objectives of the Treaty, Article 5 requires Member States to facilitate the achievement of the Community's tasks and to abstain from any measure which could jeopardise the attainment of the objectives of the Treaty.

(11) The Community's tasks and the objectives of the Treaty would also be compromised if Member States were able to enter into international commitments containing rules capable of affecting rules already adopted in areas falling outside common policies or of altering their scope.

(12) Finally, an agreement may be concluded in an area where competence is shared between the Community and the Member States. In such a case, negotiation and implementation of the agreement require joint action by the Community and the Member States.

. . .

(13) It is necessary to bear in mind the foregoing when examining the question whether Convention No 170 comes within the Community's sphere of competence and, if so, whether that competence is exclusive in nature.

(14) Convention No 170 concerns safety in the use of chemicals at work. According to the preamble, its essential objective is to prevent or reduce the incidence of chemically induced illnesses and injuries at work by ensuring that all chemicals are evaluated to determine their hazards, by providing employers and workers with the information necessary for their protection and, finally, by establishing principles for protective programmes.

(15) The field covered by Convention No 170 falls within the 'social provisions' of the EEC Treaty which constitute Chapter 1 of Title III on social policy.

(16) Under Article 118a **[D58]** of the Treaty, Member States are required to pay particular attention to encouraging improvements, especially in the working environment, as regards the health and safety of workers, and to set as their objective the harmonisation of conditions in this area, while maintaining the improvements made. In order to help achieve this objective, the Council has the power to adopt minimum requirements by means of directives. It follows from Article 118a(3) that the provisions adopted pursuant to that article are not to prevent any Member State from maintaining or introducing more stringent measures for the protection of working conditions compatible with the Treaty.

(17) The Community thus enjoys an internal legislative competence in the area of social policy. Consequently, Convention No 170, whose subject matter coincides, moreover, with that of several directives adopted under Article 118a, falls within the Community's area of competence.

. . .

(22) A number of directives adopted in the areas covered by Part III of Convention No 170 do, however, contain rules which are more than minimum requirements . . .

(23) Those directives contain provisions which in certain respects constitute measures conferring on workers, in their conditions of work, more extensive protection than that accorded under the provisions contained in Part III of Convention No 170. This is so, in particular, in the case of the very detailed rules on labelling set out in . . . Directive 88/379.

(24) The scope of Convention No 170, however, is wider than that of the directives mentioned. The definition of chemicals . . ., for instance, is broader than that of products covered by the directives. In addition (and in contrast to the provisions contained in the directives), . . . the Convention regulate[s] the transport of chemicals.

(25) Whilst there is no contradiction between these provisions of the Convention and those of the directives mentioned, it must nevertheless be accepted that Part III of Convention No 170 is concerned with an area which is already covered to a large extent by Community rules progressively adopted since 1967 with a view to achieving an ever greater degree of harmonisation and designed, on the one hand, to remove barriers to trade resulting from differences in legislation from one Member State to another and, on the other hand, to provide, at the same time, protection for human health and the environment.

(26) In those circumstances, it must be considered that the commitments arising from Part III of Convention No 170, falling within the area covered by the directives cited above . . ., are of such a kind as to affect the Community rules laid down in those directives and that consequently Member States cannot undertake such commitments outside the framework of the Community institutions.

(27) Part II of Convention No 170 contains general principles relating to its implementation; these are set out in Articles 3, 4 and 5.

(28) In so far as it has been established that the substantive provisions of Convention No 170 come within the Community's sphere of competence, the Community is also competent to undertake commitments for putting those provisions into effect.

(29) Article 3 requires that the most representative organisations of employers and workers should be consulted on the measures to be taken to give effect to the provisions of Convention No 170. Article 4 provides that each Member State must, in the light of national conditions and practice and in consultation with those organisations, formulate, implement and periodically review a coherent policy on safety in the use of chemicals at work.

(30) Admittedly, as Community law stands at present, social policy and in particular co-operation between both sides of industry are matters which fall predominantly within the competence of the Member States.

(31) This matter, has not, however, been withdrawn entirely from the competence of the Community. It should be noted, in particular, that, according to Article 118b of the Treaty, the Commission is required to endeavour to develop the dialogue between management and labour at European level.

(32) Consequently, the question whether international commitments, whose purpose is consultation with representative organisations of employers and workers, fall within the competence of the Member States or of the Community cannot be separated from the objective pursued by such consultation.

. . .

(36) . . . in ruling 1/78 [1978] ECR 2151, the court pointed out that when it appears that the subject matter of an agreement or contract falls in part within the competence of the Community and in part within that of the Member States, it is important to ensure that there is a close association between the institutions of the Community and the Member States both in the process of negotiation and conclusion and in the fulfilment of the obligations entered into. This duty of co-operation, to which attention was drawn in the context of the EAEC Treaty, must also apply in the context of the EEC Treaty since it results from the requirement of unity in the international representation of the Community.

(37) In this case, co-operation between the Community and the Member States is all the more necessary in view of the fact that the former cannot, as international law stands at present, itself conclude an ILO Convention and must do so through the medium of the Member States.

(38) It is therefore for the Community institutions and the Member States to take all the measures necessary so as best to ensure such co-operation both in the procedure of submission to the competent authority and ratification of Convention No 170 and in the implementation of commitments resulting from that Convention.

(39) It follows from all the foregoing considerations that the conclusion of ILO Convention No 170 is a matter which falls within the joint competence of the Member States and the Community.

3   Enlargement of the Community or its application

[A54]   Article 237 EEC (repealed by the Maastricht Treaty)

Any European State may apply to become a member of the Community. It shall address its application to the Council, which shall act unanimoucly after consulting the Commission and after receiving the assent of the European Parliament which shall act by an absolute majority of its component members.

The conditions of admission and the adjustments to this Treaty necessitated thereby shall be the subject of an agreement between the Member States and the applicant State. This agreement shall be submitted for ratification by all the contracting States in accordance with their respective constitutional requirements.

Note.   Article O of the Maastricht Treaty is in corresponding terms.

[A55]   House of Lords Select Committee on the European Communities, Session 1992-93 1st Report (HL Paper 5): enlargement of the Community

139. The enlargement of the Community to which the Member States are, as they always have been, rightly committed, raises many difficult and complex problems. Whilst it is clear to the Committee that much deep and serious thought has been given by governments and the Commission in recent months to those problems and the choices that have to be made, particularly of timing and the adaptation of institutional structures and procedures, it is our belief that the political and public debate needs a greater understanding of these problems and choices. This understanding will doubtless be assisted by the report which the European Council asked the Commission to prepare in advance of the Lisbon Council.

140. The Maastricht Treaty would establish the structure the Community will develop over the immediate future, and into which the new members will be welcomed. It seems to us that the essence of the structure of the

Community will be: (i) the single market and its associated policies so necessary for full freedoms of trade in goods and services, and of capital movements and of persons; (ii) advance towards economic and monetary union, however that may be defined and whatever the speed of the advance may prove to be; (iii) the Common Foreign and Security Policy **[A15]**, with its defence component; (iv) arrangements for full co-operation on certain interior and justice matters; and (v) the principle of subsidiarity which will govern both policy making and its implementation. It should be emphasised that the Community is more than a traditional alliance of nations: it is a peculiar, in the proper sense of that word, Community or Union of diverse Member States, with powers and bonds that make it effective in the world both politically and economically and with benefits to, and obligations on, its members. It is the more effective politically because of its economic strength, based on the freedoms of trade, services and movement of capital and persons. It is not in the interests of any Member State, certainly not of the United Kingdom, to weaken that economic strength. It seems to the Committee that enlargement must not, and need not, threaten the full effectiveness of a Community with this essential structure.

141. We agree with the evidence given us of the powerful potential benefits of enlargement for the future of the Community. The Community's advantages of democracy, stability and prosperity can best be extended to Central and Eastern Europe by integrating those countries, when ready, into the Community. The Community itself will gain from the diverse contributions which new members will bring, particularly in the first place with the [European Free Trade Area] countries, who will also bring financial and industrial strength. The Community will thus carry even more weight in the world. A larger Community will be both more diverse and more outward-looking. The vision is clear; but the reality is that without careful analysis of the ability of each applicant State to fulfil the criteria of membership, and of the effect of each enlargement on the institutional capability and the financial well-being of the Community, both new members and old could be damaged, and the attractiveness of the Community to new applicants removed, and the ability of the Community to carry weight in the world much lessened.

142. We see, however, no reason why substantial enlargement of the Community should not be successfully achieved with careful timing, and necessary adaptation of the Community's institutions and procedures.

143. The interest in membership now shown by EFTA countries reflects many of the considerations which motivated earlier applicants; enjoying broadly similar political, economic and cultural backgrounds and having close commercial and financial links to the Community, they seek access to the decision-making machinery because it directly impinges on their own interests. While it would pose certain problems for the Community to adjust to such a significant increase in membership and while there could be specific difficulties in relation to foreign policy, accession by EFTA countries would fit into the pattern established in previous enlargements and would not fundamentally affect the Community's structure or practices.

144. The Community might have hoped to deal with its far-reaching programme of internal development and with the EFTA applications in isolation from other major policy questions. But these developments have coincided with and to some extent been influenced by the dramatic changes in Europe – the reunification of Germany, the collapse of Communism, the

re-emergence of independent states in Central and Eastern Europe, the break-up of the Soviet Union. This situation confronts the Community and its Member States with an historic opportunity and a challenge: their response will go far to determine the shape of European politics into the next century. The States which have emerged from decades of Soviet military domination and Communist oppression are looking to the Community as an anchor for their fragile democracy, security and independence and as a source of strength for their crippled economies. They see eventual membership as the guarantee that they will not be sucked back into the quagmire from which they have just escaped. They wish to attach themselves to the European values and achievements enshrined in the Community.

145. This poses a dilemma for the Community which must reconcile its obligations to ensure stability and to consolidate democratic renewal in Central and Eastern Europe with the need to protect its own cohesion and effectiveness, without which it could not perform this role. Its response to further bids for membership must balance these two considerations, while taking account of the needs of its own internal development and of the projected accession of EFTA States. It will be possible to separate some of these questions in time: for some potential applicants full membership will not be practicable until well into the next century, but it will be necessary to devise appropriate alternatives or half-way houses if major political objectives are not to be put at risk. Moreover negotiations with the EFTA countries cannot be conducted in disregard of their impact on later negotiations with other applicants.

The attraction of the European Community

146. Some enlargement of the Community is now accepted by all the existing Member States as being both inevitable and desirable. The Community of 12 has proved so successful that there will be pressure for its membership to double or treble over the next 15 to 20 years. The fact that so many countries have either applied to join the Community or have expressed an interest in applying is evidence of their confidence in its strength, and in its value to their peoples. They look at its economic successes and at its political influence in Europe and the world. For the EFTA countries, the initial attraction of the Community was principally economic; the political obligations of membership are now accepted as a consequence, but with full realisation of the value of being able to share in the benefits of CFSP. The Central European countries, on the other hand, were initially attracted by the prospect of political stability and of financial and other assistance. They now accept the economic challenges of Community membership as of long-term benefit to them.

147. Although there is agreement among the existing Member States of the Community that enlargement is desirable, there is as yet uncertainty as to the extent, timing and consequences of this enlargement. It is, for example, widely accepted that enlargement is likely to take place in phases but there are differences as to which countries will be included in each phase. There are differences too over whether the institutional problems attendant on the Community's enlargement should delay membership until these problems have been solved. There is also concern over whether the enlargement of the Community might conflict with its effective functioning. There is as much concern that increased membership of the Community

and greater diversity of the political backgrounds of Member States, including neutral countries and former members of the Warsaw Pact, might blunt the effectiveness of the progress towards a Common Foreign and Security Policy. These problems are discussed in the paragraphs which follow.

Criteria for applications

148. 'European' is not defined in the Community treaties . . . A judgment has to be made as to whether or not a State is 'European' each time a State announces its intention formally to apply to join the Community. There are several factors which provide guidelines for such a judgment: history, geographical position, culture and religion may all provide such guidelines. We have concluded that there can be no firm rules.

149. We believe that there is general acceptance within the existing Community that the following criteria should be applied by the Commission, the European Parliament and the Council in considering applications for membership: (i) the practice of pluralist democratic parliamentary principles; (ii) the demonstration of their respect for human rights; (iii) the existence of a market economy and the ability to meet financial and economic criteria so as not to impede the Community's progress; (iv) the ability broadly to accept the *acquis communautaire* . . .

[A56]   Opinion 1/91 re the draft Treaty on a European Economic Area [1992] 1 CMLR 245

The EEA Agreement between the EC and the EFTA countries is intended to define a more structured framework for co-operation between the two groups. Initial agreement in October 1991 was renegotiated in the light of the court's 1/91 Opinion, extracted below. The revised agreement was approved in Opinion 1/92 and the final EEA Agreement was signed on 2 May 1992. According to Article 1(1) of the agreement, its aim is 'to promote a continuous and balanced strengthening of trade and economic relations between the Contracting Parties with equal conditions of competition, and the respect of the same rules, with a view to creating a homogeneous European Economic Area'. In effect, the agreement entails the acceptance by the EFTA countries of the *acquis communautaire* in the areas covered.

An opinion under Article 228 of the Treaty was first sought from the court on the compatibility of the original agreement with the EEC Treaty, particularly the intended judicial machinery. This contemplated the establishment of an EEA court.

Opinion of the European Court of Justice

13. Before considering the questions raised by the Commission's request for an opinion it is appropriate to compare the aims and context of the agreement, on the one hand, with those of Community law, on the other.

14. The fact that the provisions of the agreement and the corresponding Community provisions are identically worded does not mean that they must necessarily be interpreted identically. An international treaty is to be

interpreted not only on the basis of its wording, but also in the light of its objectives. Article 31 of the Vienna Convention of 23 May 1969 on the law of treaties stipulates in this respect that a treaty is to be interpreted in good faith in accordance with ordinary meaning to be given to its terms in their context and in the light of its object and purpose.

15. With regard to the comparison of the objectives of the provisions of the agreement and those of Community law, it must be observed that the agreement is concerned with the application of rules on free trade and competition in economic and commercial relations between the Contracting Parties.

16. In contrast, as far as the Community is concerned, the rules on free trade and competition, which the agreement seeks to extend to the whole territory of the Contracting Parties, have developed and form part of the Community legal order, the objectives of which go beyond that of the agreement.

17. It follows inter alia from Articles 2, 8a and 102a of the EEC Treaty that that Treaty aims to achieve economic integration leading to the establishment of an internal market and economic and monetary union. Article 1 of the Single European Act makes it clear moreover that the objective of all the Community treaties is to contribute together to making concrete progress towards European unity.

18. It follows from the foregoing that the provisions of the EEC Treaty on free movement and competition, far from being an end in themselves, are only means for attaining those objectives.

19. The context in which the objective of the agreement is situated also differs from that in which the Community aims are pursued.

20. The EEA is to be established on the basis of an international treaty which, essentially, merely creates rights and obligations as between the Contracting Parties and provides for no transfer of sovereign rights to the inter-governmental institutions which it sets up.

21. In contrast, the EEC Treaty, albeit concluded in the form of an international agreement, none the less constitutes the constitutional charter of a Community based on the rule of law. As the Court of Justice has consistently held, the Community treaties established a new legal order for the benefit of which the states have limited their sovereign rights, in ever wider fields, and the subjects of which comprise not only Member States but also their nationals (see, in particular, Case 26/62 *Van Gend en Loos*). The essential characteristics of the Community legal order which has thus been established are in particular its primacy over the law of the Member States and the direct effect of a whole series of provisions which are applicable to their nationals and to the Member States themselves.

22. It follows from those considerations that homogeneity of the rules of law throughout the EEA is not secured by the fact that the provisions of Community law and those of the corresponding provisions of the agreement are identical in their content or wording.

23. It must therefore be considered whether the agreement provides for other means of guaranteeing that homogeneity.

24. Article 6 of the agreement pursues that objective by stipulating that the rules of the agreement must be interpreted in conformity with the case law of the Court of Justice on the corresponding provisions of Community law.

25. However, for two reasons that interpretation mechanism will not enable the desired legal homogeneity to be achieved.

26. First, Article 6 is concerned only with rulings of the Court of Justice given prior to the date of signature of the agreement. Since the case law will evolve, it will be difficult to distinguish the new case law from the old and hence the past from the future.

27. Secondly, although Article 6 of the agreement does not clearly specify whether it refers to the court's case law as a whole, and in particular the case law on the direct effect and primacy of Community law, it appears from Protocol 35 to the agreement that, without recognising the principles of direct effect and primacy which that case law necessarily entails, the Contracting Parties undertake merely to introduce into their respective legal orders a statutory provision to the effect that EEA rules are to prevail over contrary legislative provisions.

28. It follows that compliance with the case law of the Court of Justice, as laid down by Article 6 of the agreement, does not extend to essential elements of that case law which are irreconcilable with the characteristics of the agreement. Consequently, Article 6 as such cannot secure the objective of homogeneity of the law throughout the EEA, either as regards the past or for the future.

29. It follows from the foregoing considerations that the divergences which exist between the aims and context of the agreement, on the one hand, and the aims and context of Community law, on the other, stand in the way of the achievement of the objective of homogeneity in the interpretation and application of the law in the EEA.

30. It is in the light of the contradiction which has just been identified that it must be considered whether the proposed system of courts may undermine the autonomy of the Community legal order in pursuing its own particular objectives.

31. The interpretation of the expression 'Contracting Party' which the EEA Court will have to give in the exercise of its jurisdiction will be considered first . . .

32. . . . it must be observed that the EEA Court has jurisdiction under . . . the agreement with regard to the settlement of disputes between the Contracting Parties and that, according to . . . the agreement, the EEA Joint Committee or a Contracting Party may bring such a dispute before the EEA Court.

33. The expression 'Contracting Parties' is defined in Article 2(c) of the agreement. As far as the Community and its Member States are concerned, it covers the Community and the Member States, or the Community, or the Member States, depending on the case. Which of the three possibilities is to be chosen is to be deduced in each case from the relevant provisions of the agreement and from the respective competences of the Community and the Member States as they follow from the EEC Treaty and the ECSC Treaty.

34. This means that, when a dispute relating to the interpretation or application of one or more provisions of the agreement is brought before it, the EEA Court may be called upon to interpret the expression 'Contracting Party', within the meaning of Article 2(c) . . . in order to determine whether, for the purposes of the provision at issue, the expression 'Contracting Party' means the Community, the Community and the Member States, or simply the Member States. Consequently, the EEA Court will have to rule on the respective competences of the Community and the Member States as regards the matters governed by the provisions of the agreement.

35. It follows that the jurisdiction conferred on the EEA Court under . . . the agreement is likely adversely to affect the allocation of responsibilities defined in the Treaties and, hence, the autonomy of the Community legal order, respect for which must be assured by the Court of Justice pursuant to Article 164 of the EEC Treaty. This exclusive jurisdiction of the Court of Justice is confirmed by Article 219 of the EEC Treaty, under which Member States undertake not to submit a dispute concerning the interpretation or application of that treaty to any method of settlement other than those provided for in the Treaty.

. . .

36. Consequently, to confer that jurisdiction on the EEA Court is incompatible with Community law.

Note. The revised agreement abandoned the notion of an EEA Court. The revisions formed the subject of Opinion 1/92, extracted below.

[A57]   Opinion 1/92 re the draft Treaty on a European Economic Area (No 2) [1992] 2 CMLR 217

The European Court of Justice

12. By comparison with the former version of the agreement, the new provisions on the system for the settlement of disputes differ essentially in the following respects.
13. First, the agreement no longer sets up an EEA Court. The EFTA Court will have jurisdiction only within the framework of EFTA and will have no personal or functional links with the Court of Justice.
14. Secondly, the agreement provides for two procedures, the first being designed to preserve the homogeneous interpretation of the agreement, the other being concerned with the settlement of disputes between Contracting Parties. In the course of that dispute settlement procedure, the Court of Justice may be asked to give a ruling on the interpretation of the relevant rules.
15. Thirdly, under Article 107 and Protocol 34, the EFTA States may authorise their courts to ask the Court of Justice to give a decision and not, as the former version of the agreement had it, to 'express itself' on the interpretation of a provision of the agreement.
16. Fourthly, the agreement no longer contains any provision requiring the Court of Justice to pay due account to decisions of other courts.

. . .

21. In order to achieve the most uniform interpretation possible of the provisions of the agreement and those of Community law whose substance is incorporated in the agreement, Article 105 of the agreement empowers the Joint Committee to keep under constant review the development of the case law of the Court of Justice of the European Communities and of the EFTA Court and to act as to preserve the homogeneous interpretation of the agreement.
22. If that Article were to be interpreted as empowering the Joint

Committee to disregard the binding nature of decisions of the Court of Justice within the Community legal order, the vesting of such a power in the Joint Committee would adversely affect the autonomy of the Community legal order, respect for which must be assured by the court pursuant to Article 164 EEC, and would therefore be incompatible with the Treaty.

23. However, according to the *procès-verbal agréé ad Article 105*, decisions taken by the Joint Committee under the Article are not to affect the case law of the Court of Justice.

24. That principle constitutes an essential safeguard which is indispensable for the autonomy of the Community legal order.

25. Consequently, the power which Article 105 confers on the Joint Committee for the purposes of preserving the homogeneous interpretation of the agreement is compatible with the EEC Treaty only if that principle is laid down in a form binding on the Contracting Parties.

. . .

32. The powers conferred on the court by the [EEC] Treaty may be modified pursuant only to the procedure provided for in Article 236 EEC. However, an international agreement concluded by the Community may confer new powers on the court, provided that in so doing it does not change the nature of the function of the court as conceived in the EEC Treaty.

33. It was in that context that the Opinion of 14 December 1991 accepted that an international agreement concluded by the Community might confer on the court jurisdiction to interpret the provisions of such an agreement, provided that the court's decisions have binding effects. The function of the court as conceived in the EEC Treaty is that of a court whose decisions are binding.

34. Admittedly, the aim of requesting a ruling from the Court of Justice pursuant to Article 111(3) of the agreement is not to entrust the court with the settlement of the dispute, which continues to be the responsibility of the Joint Committee. Nevertheless, the interpretation to be given by the Court of Justice is binding, as is clear from the very wording of the two language versions of the agreement submitted to the court, which use the French expression *se prononcer* and the English 'give a ruling'.

35. It follows that, if the court is called upon to give a ruling pursuant to Article 111(3) of the agreement, the Contracting Parties and the Joint Committee alike will be bound by the court's interpretation of the rules at issue. Consequently, the jurisdiction conferred on the court by that provision for the purposes of interpreting the provisions of the agreement at the request of the Contracting Parties in dispute is compatible with the EEC Treaty . . .

37. As regards the provisions of the agreement under which EFTA states may authorise their courts to request the Court of Justice to decide on the interpretation of a provision of the agreement, it is to be noted that the wording of Article 107 ensures that the answers which the Court of Justice may be called upon to give will be binding. Consequently, that mechanism satisfies the requirements set out in the Opinion of 14 December 1991 and is therefore compatible with Community law.

4 Future paths and attitudes

[A58] Martin Holland: European Community Integration (Pinter Publishers, London, 1993) pp 83–88

Common themes

Despite Spinelli's opinion . . . that the Tindemans Report ['Report on European Union', Supplement of the Bulletin of the EC, 1/76] had 'the consequence that it remained without consequence', there is evidence that both the SEA [Single European Act] and 1991 IGCs inherited many of the themes and aspirations first enunciated in the mid-1970s by Tindemans. What, then, are these common strands in the Community's reform programme?

European Union and a vision for the Community

All three reform proposals have attempted to offer a goal that the Community should strive for. This objective was not in the form of a detailed definition, but rather a working principle within which future policies and institutional arrangements could be framed. As the frenetic and unpredictable nature of change in recent international politics has indicated (for example, the unprecedented events such as the fall of the Berlin Wall in November 1989 and the fragmentation of the Soviet Union in 1991), to be prescriptive as to the shape of the Community for even the 1990s would be conceited, foolish and probably inaccurate.

In their respective individual interpretations, each reform sought to promote a European Union consistent with the commitment to 'an ever closer union among the peoples of Europe'. For Tindemans, like Monnet, the Community was an embryonic federation; European Union was dependent on the mutual development of a series of interrelated factors which could only be built gradually. This evolutionary perspective can be found in both the SEA and the Maastricht Treaty. The Community vision of the SEA 'to transform relations as a whole . . . into a European Union' stipulated the need collectively to ensure 'concrete progress towards European Unity'. But these objectives were neither binding nor hardly revolutionary and mimicked earlier solemn commitments and declarations on European Union that had failed to produce a *saut qualitif*. Although not adopted, the Draft Treaty at least had the unique virtue of clearly and openly stating the 'federal goal' of European Union, though once again the emphasis was placed on the gradual process of constructing a Union. This approach confronted the two seemingly irreconcilable visions of Community development – inter-governmentalism and federalism. Despite being deleted from the final version, the 1991 IGCs made the invaluable contribution of insisting that this fundamental issue of federalism be discussed fully and publicly. If not immutable, by the end of 1991 the Community had made significant progress in designing the central elements of the long-awaited European Union.

A people's Europe

Both the Tindemans Report and the IGC on Political Union addressed the necessity to transform the popular negative image of a Brussels bureaucratic Community into a positive expression of Community citizenship that was visible and applicable to everyday life. The aspirations of Tindemans were expansive and foreshadowed many of the arguments that were to emerge in the second half of the 1980s concerning a European Social Charter to protect fundamental rights. In contrast, the SEA specifically avoided this concern with the place of the individual within the Community and stressed the economic and technological aspects of integration. The IGC had the virtue of placing the idea of European citizenship within a treaty and, therefore, a legal context. This was a necessary, but not sufficient step. The idea of the Community required more than the symbolic trappings of a flag, anthem and periodic popular elections: a new Community political culture had to be nurtured and matured if a people's Europe was to be cultivated out of the purely legal notion of citizenship.

A global role and a common foreign policy

All three reforms isolated the inadequacies of the Community's existing mechanisms for international action and eulogised Europe's potential to regain its historical role as a major global actor. Their respective remedies for these inadequancies were substantially different, however. The SEA was the most conservative in its position although it did introduce two crucial changes. First, an important practical development was the establishment of the [European Political Co-operation] Secretariat (despite the inter-governmental rather than supranational nature of its organisation); and second, EPC was finally brought within the ambit of a treaty (even if a *communautairisation* of the procedure was resisted). In somewhat of an ironic contrast, the Tindemans Report advocated radical change, but had virtually no practical impact. The issues of an obligatory common policy via majority voting, defence co-operation, the joint manufacture of armaments and extending the scope of Community action were largely ignored. Any changes adopted were behavioural and procedural and did not require any formal Treaty revision.

The IGCs represent the compromise position between these two options. The obligation to reach a common position was abandoned, but a procedure for exercising majority decisions was introduced and the existing narrow EPC mechanism was jettisoned for a more comprehensive and effective Common Foreign and Security Policy **[A15]**. While still not yet a single policy, Maastricht represented a qualitative change: there is now a consensus on the necessity to develop a collective European response to foreign security and, ultimately, defence policy, a development that is in keeping with Tindemans' overall prescription.

Policy expansion and cohesion

Paradoxically, Tindemans' radicalism in external relations was, with respect to [Economic and Monetary Union], cautious and deferential to the then existing political obstacles to further integration. He even endorsed a Europe *à deux vitesses*, an inter-governmental anathema to most federalists. Yet despite these reservations, the seeds of the EMU debate were sown in 1975 making the path towards these objectives less difficult by 1991. The Report called for stability in internal and external monetary policy, an embryonic European central bank, closer linking of EC currencies and the free movement of capital throughout the Community. The SEA built upon the economic rather than the monetary recommendations by establishing the principle of the single market for 1992. The IGCs picked up the gauntlet of monetary union directly and committed the Community to full monetary union before the turn of the century, with the complementary development of a central European bank, common currency and external currency stability.

While all three reports placed a premium on aspects of EMU, they all also recognised the need to balance this with an extension of the Community's general policy competence, particularly in terms of regional and social policies, supplementing and reinforcing the belief in a people's Europe. Thus Tindemans prescribed the abolition of internal frontier controls not on the grounds of an economic single market, but on the basis of individual human rights. Policy co-ordination was needed to facilitate this free movement so that European citizens would be treated equally (socially, politically and economically) irrespective of their nationality. This recognition of comprehensive policy cohesion was to appear again in the Draft Treaty. It proposed an innovative reform and possibly the most important contribution to European Union – the inclusion of the principle of subsidiarity in the Treaty. This provided a consistent measure by which the extension of Community competences could be evaluated . . .

Finally, there appeared to be the possibility of constructing Community integration and federal Union according to a general principle acceptable to all. Experience would tell whether this general principle was workable and legally enforceable.

Institutional reform and the democratic deficit

How to revise the institutional structure has been an almost perennial Community preoccupation. However, the basic framework established in 1957 has not come into disrepute, but rather successive reforms have sought to accommodate new bodies and relationships within the context of the existing unicity. Thus the existing *acquis communautaire*, derived from the practical experience of the Treaty of Rome, remains the non-negotiable basis for any institutional reform. The consistent reform elements have been efficiency, supranational authority and most importantly, democracy: as should be apparent by now, on occasions these combined characteristics have been antagonistic, even mutually exclusive.

. . .

The Community's democratic deficit concerns the limited legislative role ascribed to the European Parliament and the lack of direct accountability of key Community institutions, notably the Commission. While all the three reform proposals pay homage to this principle, none has introduced a successful remedy. Understandably perhaps, Tindemans was restrained in his vision of parliamentary powers given that direct elections had yet to take place; he called for Parliament to be given the right of initiative and full competence to discuss any Treaty matter. The SEA introduced the complex co-decisions and co-operation procedures, but failed to provide the Parliament with much more than a negative legislative role, a condition replicated at Maastricht . . . While disappointing the parliamentarians, the proposed involvement of the Parliament in ratifying the appointment of the Commission President moves somewhat closer to removing the democratic deficit vis-à-vis the Community's executive. Lastly, none of the three reform packages could be expected to have an impact on what many commentators see as the fundamental issue relating to the democratic deficit: namely, the Parliament's reduced legitimacy caused by the low turnout at each of the three direct elections held since 1979. The dilemma remains whether to extend Parliament's authority immediately in the hope of stimulating increased legitimacy, or to wait for evidence of popular support before conferring real legislative powers.

Conclusion

The central issue underlying these various procedural and substantive reforms is the conflict over the form of Union being envisaged, a problem that has been an integral part of the Community since its origin. In the contemporary period, this discord has primarily been represented by two of Europe's leading political figures: Jacques Delors, the federalist President of the Commission from 1985-92, and Margaret Thatcher, British Prime Minister from 1979-90 and defender of the inter-governmentalist cause. This dispute goes beyond personalities, however, and represents a serious tension within the Community. While the maximalist supporters of supranationalism (led by Mitterrand and Kohl) are a clear majority within the Twelve, inter-governmental concern is not unique to the United Kingdom; increasingly, other states questioned specific federal initiatives at the 1991 IGCs. Progress since the SEA has significantly enhanced the level of integration, but the fundamental issue of the 'federal goal' of the Community has not been adequately resolved. This negative theme is perhaps the dominant strand connecting each of the three reform processes examined here.

The conclusion should not be overly pessimistic: successive enlargements have tended to strengthen the inter-governmentalists – the United Kingdom, Denmark and Greece – but supranationalism has been resilient and made significant advances which cumulatively have progressively undermined national sovereignty. Writing prior to the decision to convene the IGCs, Nugent listed the various inter-governmental and supranational characteristics contained within the Community: those areas where inter-governmentalism was dominant were over the control of the major areas of policy making; through the decision-making pre-eminence of the Council; via the consensus principle; the limited roles ascribed to the Commission and the Parliament; and the political authority of the European Council. In the light of Maastricht a perceptible movement in favour of supranationalism can be perceived. First, the scope for national policy making has been reduced, most spectacularly in relation to EMU, but also in social areas and in foreign policy: this expansion of Community competence has also been given stronger legal backing through the ability of the Court of Justice to impose penalties. Second, though formally limited to specific Treaty articles, majority voting has begun to have a more pervasive effect on the prevailing political culture within the Council and has replaced the Luxembourg Compromise as the axis on which decision making rests. Third, the new co-operation and co-decision procedures and the retention of the Commission as policy initiator have contributed, in a modest way, to rebuffing inter-governmental advances from the Council. Fourthly, although usually seen as the manifestation of inter-governmentalism, the role of the European Council as specified in the Treaty on European Union can give some comfort to advocates of supranationalism. The commitment to a federal Union can only come through political consensus in the European Council. Thus fully incorporating this body within the constitutional structure of the Community is an essential prerequisite to achieving Union. Despite the difficulties, there is no other path to federalism.

This chapter has shown the consistency in the Community's reform programme and recorded the important changes that have been adopted incrementally in recent years. The supranational dynamic is in the ascendancy, but its eventual success cannot be guaranteed, as the Danish referendum on the Maastricht Treaty underlined. As the history of the Community repeatedly illustrates, the fate of constitutional reform is as dependent on political personalities and public opinion as it is upon a belief in the Community ideal. It is instructive to recall that the current EMU debate is taking place more than three decades since Monnet considered that 'the first steps towards a European currency seemed to be practicable'. There is nothing inevitable about European integration. The Community has survived the inter-governmental rebukes of de Gaulle and Thatcher, but it would be remarkable if a new heir apparent to the inter-governmental crown were not to emerge in the 1990s. Thus the tension between these two opposing visions of the Community are set to remain for the foreseeable future. Indeed, some have argued that the Community derives its own dynamic from this tension and inter-governmental criticism is essential to the development of appropriate and acceptable supranational structures for the 21st century.

To conclude, despite their different legal status and eventual fates as well as their clearly different inter-governmental and federal strands, the symmetry of the Tindemans, SEA and Maastricht attempts to reform the Community is striking. And yet it is sobering to record that the 'overall picture of European Union' as depicted by Tindemans remains the most informative expression of this objective (whether implicitly or explicitly federal). The task still remains:

> . . . arriving at a political consensus on the aims and main features of the Union in terms which give expression to the deep aspirations of our peoples;

> . . . determining the consequences of this choice in the various areas of the Union's internal and external activities;

> . . . strengthening the institutional machinery to enable it to cope with the tasks awaiting it.

[A59] House of Commons Foreign Affairs Committee Session 1992-93, First Report (Interim Report (HC Paper 205): Europe after Maastricht)

Appendix 3: Memorandum submitted by Philip Allott, Trinity College, Cambridge

BRITAIN AND THE EUROPEAN COMMUNITY

An historic error and an historic challenge

1. The reaction of British governments to the European Community has been the confused product of two basic instincts, both deeply rooted in our

historical experience – the instinct of political freedom and the instinct of the balance of power.

2. British governments have been correct in recognising the EC as the latest episode in the unending process of European political organisation and reorganisation. The error they have made is in allowing the balance of power instinct to dominate their contribution to solving the problem of the long-term development of the EC. The challenge they now face is to bring to the solving of that problem their long-matured instinct for political freedom.

3. By a tragic failure of political imagination, Her Majesty's Government have identified the EC as simply posing one more challenge in the long story of our tangled relations with continental Europe, rather than as an opportunity for the United Kingdom to play a major part in creating a new constitutional order for Europe.

4. The instinct for political freedom has even been abused to bolster this 'foreign policy' view of the EC, by suggesting that the challenge of the EC to Britain is a collision between 'Brussels' (that is, foreign civil servants) and British 'sovereignty' (that is, British political freedom). This has led to the view that anything that can be done to limit the power of the EC institutions, other than the Council, is a victory gained for so-called British interests.

5. The same misjudgment leads to the view that the EC Council should be reconceived in such a way that it might become essentially inter-governmental in character, a natural successor to the forms of collective hegemony which Europe has known in previous centuries, especially the 19th century, and which, in the League of Nations and the United Nations, have been extended to cover the whole world in the 20th century. British governments have always treated such things with wary concern but, sometimes also, with great manipulative skill.

6. This instinctive 'Foreign Office' approach to the EC has had to meet and come to terms with an EC reality which cannot be forced into such narrow and old-fashioned categories. And it is this tension which led to the misbegetting of the Maastricht Treaty. It is now threatening to generate one or more of three outcomes – the aborting of the EC as a lively and developing constitutional system, the formal establishment of a Franco–German hegemony in Europe, the formal marginalising of the UK as an EC Member State.

7. Following another hallowed British tradition, the British government of the day would no doubt find some way of presenting any or all of these outcomes as triumphs of British diplomacy.

8. The EC reality which has derailed the instinct-led British governmental response is twofold – the ambitions of France and Germany, and the sheer magnitude and energy of the EC system, its political and economic and legal density.

9. The ambitions of the French and German governments pose a challenge to the United Kingdom which goes far beyond the power play diplomatic challenges which we have learned to live with over long centuries. The EC is a revolutionary challenge, comparable to the challenge posed by the French Revolution. The British official response to the French Revolution was cynical incomprehension. But, at least, official Britain had the intelligence to see that things would never be the same again in Europe. In particular, it was obvious that the Revolution posed not only a foreign policy challenge, in terms of the so-called stability of Europe, but also a

challenge to all social order everywhere. Like Reformation three centuries before, Revolution seemed likely to be socially contagious.

10. Edmund Burke, passionate advocate of evolutionary constitutionalism, diagnosed the weakness of the French Revolution as the product of the illegitimate intrusion of ideas into the otherwise instinctive business of political change. The British government's handling of the long-term development of the EC shows the same rejection of the notion that ideas could or should be at the root of the reordering of Europe.

11. The French and the Germans, in particular, have other perspectives on European history and very different notions of the social role of ideas. For the British, instinct serves the function of ideas. Action, or inaction, speaks louder than words. For the French, ideas are the way of expressing political reality in order to control it. For the Germans, ideas are the way of imagining political reality, and thereby of identifying the possibilities of political action. For the French, ideas represent a possible rationality of society. For the Germans, ideas represent the possibility of power over society. For the British, ideas are merely behavioural facts, useful or dangerous depending on circumstances.

12. So, for the French and the Germans, the idea of European integration is itself a social force of a revolutionary character – the possibility, or the threat, not merely of a new political order but of a new moral order in Europe. They may disagree profoundly among themselves about the nature and purpose of that revolution, in particular as to the reconciling of national and regional identities with the new European order. But it is in the nature of social ideas that they generate opposing ideas. The French have always disagreed among themselves about their own Revolution. (It has been said that French politics since 1789 has been a permanent debate about the merits of the Revolution. The referendum of 20 September 1992 suggests that French politics will hereafter be a permanent debate about the nature and purpose of the EC.) But the British make a serious mistake when they imagine that continental factiousness about social ideas is the same phenomenon as British disdain for ideas.

13. The French and German governments must now be tempted to seek a new bilateral modus vivendi within an EC relaunched on the basis of the Maastricht Treaty. If they were able to work from and beyond Maastricht in this way, and to share their further progress with a number of other continental countries, and if Germany is able, over the next ten years, to achieve in practice the vast potentiality of its economic power, then the prize would be very great – a dynamic and dominating world power, surrounded by a penumbra of colonies and satellites, including the United Kingdom and various countries of eastern and southern Europe, with the European Central Bank in Frankfurt, the European Foreign Ministry in Paris, and the Supreme Headquarters of European Armed Forces in a specially created 'European territory' in Alsace-Lorraine.

14. In 1799 the British Prime Minister told First Consul Napoleon that the best thing for the peace of Europe 'would be the restoration of that line of princes, which for so many centuries maintained the French nation in prosperity at home and in consideration and respect abroad'. To that impudent advice Napoleon replied icily, in a note drafted by Talleyrand, that the British government was not in a strong position to give such advice, seeing that the British monarch was himself the beneficiary of power usurped through revolution.

15. As Her Majesty's Government seek to remove the revolutionary pith from the EC fruit and to restore something more reminiscent of the old European regime, the French and German governments must be inclined to say that neither British diplomacy nor British economic management in the 20th century justify any preaching from Britain about the proper organisation of Europe.

16. The British government's advice to France in 1799 seemed to be proved sound in the short term. The Bourbons were restored. In the long term it was completely wrong. The internal situation of one west European country after another, including Britain, was transformed, in the course of the 19th century, by means of a sort of permanent revolution. Every social system – political, economic, legal – was reconstructed.

17. In the idea of Maastricht II and in the accession of a motley collection of new EC Member States in the future, the British government see the possibility of some sort of counter revolution. But the chances are that such a judgment, based on ancient instincts rather than new ideas, will be fundamentally wrong, once again. With whatever social and ideological pain and struggle, continental Europe has begun to create, and will now continue to create, a new constitutional and economic and moral order in Europe, with or without Britain.

18. One lesson of Maastricht is clear. The people of Europe do not accept the political legitimacy of the executive branches of government conspiring together in the meeting rooms of the EC. National elections are not sufficient to authorise or validate such behaviour.

19. A new constitutional order for 12 nations cannot be cobbled together in secret by civil servants and diplomats, as if they were drafting an arms control treaty. There is no such thing as a 'British interest' for or against so-called federalism, for or against principles of so-called social policy, for or against fixed exchange rates, for or against subsidies for farmers, for or against so-called over-regulation by government.

20. Such things would be a matter of intense debate within the internal political system of each Member State. The fact that they now have to be dealt with at the EC level does not mean that they have suddenly become technical matters, or matters to be resolved by diplomatic bargaining. No executive branch of government, least of all the British government, can claim that whatever view of such matters that it chooses in Cabinet to call a 'British interest' has been sufficiently authorised, or will be sufficiently validated, by general elections to the national parliament or by executive-orchestrated simple majority votes in the national parliament.

21. Maastricht has brought the people of Europe to open rebellion against an EC system which they see as a New Leviathan. That fact gives to the United Kingdom the opportunity for a unique and decisive role in the future development of the EC system.

22. The people's rebellion has been brought to a head by three things.

23. (1) There is a crisis of confidence in the legitimating of government in the democracies of all the advanced industrialised countries. Election campaigns seem to the people to be more and more of a media-led charade. The problems and the issues facing governments have increased intensely in scale and complexity. But elections seem to the people to be less and less a debate about issues, and hence the verdict of the electorate seems less and less to be a significant judgment on past and future policies. As a consequence, some democracies have become de facto oligarchies,

controlled by money and influence. Others have become de facto monarchies, run by permanent official courtiers under the control of autocratic presidents.

24. The crisis of legitimation in the EC thus unfortunately coincides with a much wider crisis of democratic process in general.

25. ... (2) But the EC crisis of legitimation seems much more important because the more or less legitimate government of each Member State is only one government among 12. And the EC is obviously taking into its system all the more important aspects of government.

26. The phoney war against the EC Commission is a diversionary tactic of national executive branches. They should see the moloch in their own eye before they claim to see the leviathan in Brussels. Flattering as it must be to the self-esteem of the EC Commission to suggest otherwise, that body is in no position to realise any megalomaniac ambitions at all. Its independent powers of final decision are extremely limited. Even the nooks and crannies for which it is alleged to have a special fondness – the alcohol content of lawnmowers and the noise levels of beer bottles – are places where it has been sent by the Community treaties or by the Council. The Commission deals with such matters because all modern governments deal with such matters, in thousands of acts of executive branch legislation every year, and it is obviously sensible to have one set of a thousand such things, rather than 12,000 of them.

27. The central problem of the EC system is not the Commission but the Council. The Council has virtually no political legitimacy. It is accountable to no-one. Its relationship to the Commission is irretrievably obscure. It is more of a cabal than a cabinet, more of a permanent diplomatic conference than a senate. And yet it legislates profusely. It deliberates and decides in splendid isolation.

28. ... (3) Putting (1) and (2) together, there is formed an almost universal feeling in Europe that there is something fundamentally wrong with the EC constitutional system. Even those most closely involved in working the system seem, to their credit, to have a dull anguish about the impropriety of it all.

29. To suggest that such problems can be dealt with by a new principle of distribution of power between 'Brussels' and the national capitals (so-called 'subsidiarity') is a cruel deception of the people. Subsidiarity, if it means anything in the EC context, is an anti-competitive arrangement among executive branches (EC and national). By using the Maastricht Treaty to include it as a legal text in the Community treaties, they have, at least, removed the objection that the principle is a violation of the EC's own rules of competition (both Articles 85 and 86 EEC). And, as a masterpiece of cynicism, that text would give to the European Court of Justice the task of deciding turf disputes between the executive branches of the EC and the Member States, by interpretations of the word 'necessary'.

30. A true restructuring of the EC system will involve a fundamental redistribution of power at every level from the EC to the village, including the power not only of national central governments but also the growing power of sub-national governments.

31. Such is the special challenge for Britain. Our instinct for political freedom is the product of a national history which, in one respect, is unique in Europe. For 15 centuries, we have lived the problem of social organisation, developing, through much trial and much error, the social systems and

social ideals which have spread through the nations of Europe and then to nations far beyond Europe.

32. The historic challenge of Europe for Britain is not a diplomatic challenge but a constitutional challenge. The problem of the long-term development of the EC should be taken out of the hands of Foreign Offices and, with great respect, of Foreign Affairs Committees. Their concern should be with the foreign policy of the EC.

33. The appropriate course of action for Britain would then be –

(1) to press for the entry into force of the Maastricht Treaty at the earliest possible time, subject to some sort of a declaration to say that organisational aspects of the Danish problem will be solved within six months of Maastricht's entry into force. The entry into force of the Treaty will be merely a symbolic event. There will be much further political struggle before it enters into force as a practical reality. The idea of Maastricht II is self-delusion. France and Germany could well take the opportunity to ensure that its main provisions would finally formalise Britain's permanent marginalisation in Europe;

(2) to press for the bringing forward of the 1996 Conference on EC Institutional Reform or, at least, to press for the most intensive and most extensive possible debate between now and 1996 about the nature and purpose and, hence, the restructuring of the EC. In the process, the British people might even stumble upon some way to reform our own second-rate and under-performing society.

Further reading

Constantinesco, V, 'Who's afraid of subsidiarity?' (1991) 11 Yearbook of European Law 33.

de Burca, G, 'Fundamental human rights and the reach of EC Law' (1993) 13 OxJLS 283.

Emiliou, N, 'Subsidiarity: an effective barrier against "the enterprises of ambition"?' (1992) 17 European Law Review 383.

Lane, R, 'New Community competences under the Maastricht Treaty' (1993) 30 Common Market Law Review 939.

Loman, A, Mortelmans, K, Post, H, Watson, S, Culture and Community Law before and after Maastricht (Kluwer, 1992).

Michalski, A, and Wallace, H, The European Community: The Challenge of Enlargement (Royal Institute of International Affairs, 1992).

O'Keeffe, D, 'The agreement on the European Economic Area' (1992) 1 Legal Issues of European Integration 1.

Pipkorn, J, 'Legal arrangements in the Treaty of Maastricht for the effectiveness of the economic and monetary union' (1994) 31 Common Market Law Review 263.

Shennan, M, Teaching about Europe (Cassell Council of Europe series, 1991).

Swann, D (ed), The Single European Market and Beyond (Routledge, 1992).

Toth, A, 'Is subsidiarity justiciable?' (1994) 19 European Law Review 268.

Chapter Two

The European Constitution

The creation of a European constitution

A discussion of the European Constitution must commence by looking backwards from the Treaty of Union and the Single European Act to a Europe devastated by war, devastated politically, socially and economically, and with the desire for political, social and economic reconstruction, together with the fervent wish that never again should there be war in Europe. The solution to this lay in some form of inter-state action or in some form of unification or integration. The original Member States (Germany, Belgium, France, Italy, Luxembourg and the Netherlands) first created the European Coal and Steel Community and then gradually concluded that each country could improve its economic progress and lessen somewhat its over-reliance on foreign trade by the creation of a European trading area and that this would give them a firm base on which to establish export markets with the rest of the world. The Treaty of Rome was signed in 1957 and the European Economic Community, an organisation of six independent states, came into existence on 1 January 1958. The aims of the Community, to lay the foundations of an ever closer union among the peoples of Europe, to ensure the economic and social progress of their peoples and the constant improvement in their living and working conditions, to stengthen the unity of their economies and to ensure the progressive abolition of restrictions in international trade were laid down in the Treaty.

Any organisation, including any organisation of states, which comes together with a common purpose, or a series of common purposes, will tend to create a formal, political, structure by which those purposes may be achieved and a general system according to which the members of the organisation agree to be governed.

In one sense, concentrating overtly on economic policies was not as innocuous as it might at first seem, because inherent in the methods and machinery designed to promote economic integration is the surrender, in some part at least, of national sovereignty. Traditionally, states have taken measures to protect their own economies (tariffs, customs duties, import quotas, subsidies for domestic industry and the imposition of taxes on imported goods) and such measures are the antithesis of economic integration. Economic integration may be achieved by free trade areas (whereby Member States eliminate restrictions relating to trade between those states on products originating in such states, leaving individual states free to impose restrictions on products originating from outside the area), customs unions (which take integration a stage further by the adoption by the Member States of a common position with regard to uniform restrictions with regard to products originating outside the union) and common markets (which take the integration even further by eliminating all restrictions to free trade, by permitting free movement of such factors of production as labour and capital, and by harmonising the legislation and administrative practices of the states concerned). See, further, Chapter Five.

There is a logical simplicity underpinning the infrastructure created by the Treaty of Rome. Economic agreement between states is not new but traditionally such co-operation has involved the reservation of national sovereignty in order to defend national interests and this immediately forms a barrier to economic integration and, if used only once by one Member State, may lead to its use by all other Member States. Therefore, the successful working of economic integration depended on the surrender of national sovereignty in favour of common and uniform rules imposed by the constituent states upon themselves.

Traditionally, states enter into agreements by way of treaties and resolve disputes among themselves or by submission to international arbitration and judgment. Traditionally, such treaties are comprehensive and self-contained documents, designed to enact all matters contemplated by the parties involved and requiring amending treaties, agreed to by all parties concerned, should they not fulfil their purpose. A process of economic integration within Europe needed a different sort of treaty and a different sort of constitution. It was accepted that the process would be a continuing and developing one and no one could predict all possible contingencies. Although the main aims (for example, the customs union, the free movement of persons and capital, common policies in agriculture and transport) and many major principles (for example, fulfilment of Community obligations and non-discrimination on grounds of nationality) could be laid down in the founding treaty, the implementation of those aims and, in particular, the harmonisation of national laws in accordance with those aims, could only practicably be undertaken by an 'ongoing mechanism'. There had to be institutions to look after both day-to-day regulation of the system and the long-term developments. It was accepted that policies would need to be developed and that a 'policy initiating' authority would be necessary; it was accepted that secondary rule making would be needed in order to implement the Treaty and that a 'legislature' with the power to make binding decisions would be necessary; it was accepted that there might be divergent interpretations of those rules by the individual states and that an authority (such as a 'supreme court') to make binding decisions on questions of interpretation would be necessary; it was accepted that primary and secondary legislation might need also to be developed by reference to the legal principles which were then common to the Member States; it was accepted that states might want to continue to protect domestic economies and might be slow to implement the rules or, indeed, to fail to implement those rules and that independent machinery to provide continuing supervision of Member States and to make binding declarations as to whether a state had fulfilled or failed to fulfil a Community obligation would be necessary. In other words, it was accepted that the normal functions allocated by constitutions to organs within the state (legislative, executive and judicial) should be applied to the process of economic integration by the creation of Community institutions, with power to carry out the purposes of the Community independently of the Member States, in which the national interests would be represented but would not be permitted to hinder the process of integration. The Treaty of Rome, albeit concluded in the form of an international agreement, nonetheless constituted the constitutional charter of a Community based on the rule of law.

It will be seen that the organs of government normally found in national constitutions are to a considerable extent mirrored within the Community, albeit in different form. These, the European Parliament, the Council, the Commission, the Economic and Social Committee and the Committee of the Regions, are discussed in Section One of this chapter. The Community has power to enact legislation (both constitutional legislation and legislation designed to lay down and implement Community objectives) and this is discussed in Section Two of this chapter. The European Constitution has created a self-contained mechanism to determine the different types of Community dispute which may arise and to ensure that Community law is implemented in a uniform manner. This is the Court of Justice, whose jurisdiction, composition and procedure is discussed in Section Three of this chapter. The European Court of Justice has developed an all-pervasive case law, creating doctrines both of interpretation and substance in order to weld Community law into a cohesive whole. Community case law is discussed in Section Four of this chapter. In most countries with a written constitution there is some authority with power to determine whether legislation is enacted in conformity with that constitution and in most countries there is some authority with power to ensure that acts of administrative authorities are executed in accordance with the powers granted to them. Both the constitutional and administrative jurisdictions are granted to the court and are discussed in Section Five of this chapter.

In addition to what may be termed the 'internal' constitution of the Community, that constitution is also an integral part of the constitutions of the Member States. Community law does not simply impose new benefits and obligations upon Member States but may create benefits and obligations for persons other than the Member States within the domestic legal systems of all Member States. The legal and constitutional implications of such a proposition follow with some logic. There is an 'all or nothing' situation: the Community is based on a principle of solidarity in that Member States cannot act unilaterally and a share in the envisaged prosperity brings with it a duty to comply with obligations; the Community is based on a principle of cohesion in that economic forces are transnational and must be met, both inwardly and outwardly, by a common response; Community law must be implemented in all states and must be the same in all states, otherwise states might revert to national protection of domestic industry and services; all states must provide for this implementation or incorporation in accordance with their national constitutions and by the constitutional organs within the state; since Community law must be the same in all states, the law and administrative practices of those states cannot be different from, or conflict with, Community law and any differences or conflicts must be eliminated in each state; finally, if there is a difference or conflict which has not been eliminated within the state, such conflict must be resolved by the acceptance of the superiority of Community law; a state cannot opt out of any part of Community law which it finds burdensome and either surrenders all of its sovereignty in those areas where the Treaty provides for Community law to be created or surrenders nothing of its sovereignty and is no longer treated as a member of the Community. These issues are discussed in Chapter Three.

The Treaty of Rome referred to the establishment of a common market and the progressive approximation of the 'economic policies of the Member States' and the Treaty contained measures to promote those aims, together with appropriate institutional and legislative machinery. However, the European constitutional scheme of things which the Treaty of Rome created has itself undergone substantial amendment. As was demonstrated in Chapter One, the Member States have become more than a European Economic Community, have taken steps to establish a single market and contemplate the further integration of policies previously reserved to Member States. There has been a further transfer of power from the Member States to the Community, both with regard to the subject matter of the Community's competence and with regard to the roles to be played by the Member States (a diminishing role) and the part to be played by the Community institutions (an ever-increasing role). The process is not yet over [A22]–[A25] and the trends referred to above are reinforced by the Treaty of Union, with the appropriate provisions of that Treaty being included in this chapter in order to demonstrate what effects the next stage of European integration will have on the European Constitution and its citizens (including potential problems posed by the Social Chapter [D65]–[D67]).

SECTION ONE

THE GOVERNMENT OF THE COMMUNITY

1 The European Parliament

The European Parliament does not play the same role as a national Parliament which is normally the principal legislator and to which the government is normally responsible.

The Parliament does not have the legislative powers of national Parliaments (these belong principally to the Commission, which has the sole power of initiative, and the Council, which plays the major role in taking decisions: see below). However, a principal feature of the development of the Community constitution has been the development of the European Parliament from an 'Assembly' (its original title), composed of designated members of national Parliaments, towards a Parliament representative of the electorate and claiming additional roles and powers based on that political legitimacy [B1]. In the legislative field, the Parliament's role was originally simply to be consulted and, although failure to consult the Parliament is a breach of the Treaty provision imposing that obligation, there is no corresponding obligation to take the Parliament's opinion into account. However, the Single European Act introduced the co-operation procedure and this enhanced the powers of the Parliament (see Section Two of this chapter).

The 'government' of the Community is not derived from the European Parliament. There is nothing as yet in the constitutional scheme of things whereby the government consists of ministers chosen from the majority political party (or a coalition) or of ministers appointed with the approval of Parliament. As will be seen, the equivalent of a national government within the Community is provided by a division of function between the Council, composed of ministers from the Member States, and the Commission, appointed by the Member States. The European Parliament exercises advisory and supervisory powers to hear members of the Commission and the Council, to question members of the Commission and has the (not yet used) power to dismiss the Commission by a two-thirds majority. However, since the power of appointment of the Commission is currently exercised by the Member States and since there is no constitutional mechanism to bring the Council to account, there is not the equivalent of the political accountability of the government to the Parliament which is normally found in a national constitution. Any accountability of the Council must be to the individual electorates and parliamentary institutions within the Member States.

It should be noted that the Treaty of Union greatly increases the powers and influence of the European Parliament and the Parliament will assume more (but not yet all the) features of a national Parliament. In particular, the Parliament will have a greater role in the appointment of the Commission and greater control over Community administrative activity. Consequently, there are extracted both the pre-Treaty of Union Treaty provisions and the Treaty provisions in the form as they are replaced by the Treaty of Union [B2].

The European Parliament's principal role is to discuss and to give opinion on major Community problems in committee and in plenary session. By means of debating the programmes and reports of the Commission and Council it adds an element of democratic supervision of those bodies and can achieve publicity for its views which, in turn, may influence the Council and Commission (Articles 139–144). The debates of the Parliament are published and the Parliament publicises its views in a number of ways, principally by issuing reports and briefing papers, and communicates with the general public by means of a periodical, *European Parliament News*. The European Parliament holds an annual session and may meet in extraordinary sesssion at the request of a majority of its members or at the request of the Council or Commission. Members of the Commission may attend all meetings and, at their request, are heard on behalf of the Commission. The European Parliament discusses in open session the annual report submitted to it by the Commission. Finally, the Parliament has certain budgetary powers which allow it to take part in important decisions on Community expenditure. The Parliament has been very determined to protect its powers (or prerogatives) and Parliament examines Community legislation to ensure that its rights have been fully respected (*Parliament v Council* [B50]).

The European Parliament consists of representatives of the peoples of the states and its members are elected every five years by universal suffrage (Articles 137, 138). The number of representatives from each state is allocated roughly on the basis of population but it is noticeable that the smaller states are more fully represented. At the Edinburgh Summit in December 1992 it was agreed to increase the number of representatives, in particular those from the reunited Germany, and there were 567 instead of 518 seats contested in the 1994 Parliamentary elections. In the United Kingdom, elections to the Parliament are governed by the European Assembly Elections Act 1978, as amended. In the 1989 European elections, the Labour Party obtained 45 seats, the Conservative Party obtained 32 seats, and the Scottish National Party, the Democratic Unionist, the Social Democrat and Labour Party and the Official Unionist Party each obtained 1 seat. It must be noted that Members of Parliament do not act and vote on national lines, rather they form political groups [B3], [B4]. In addition, members may form pressure groups to persue particular aims. For example, there is an Intergroup on Animal Welfare which meets regularly with members of national and international associations and both seeks to secure the enactment of legislation, to monitor the application or contravention of that legislation in the Member States and produces a monthly News Bulletin.

The European Parliament has its own officers and executive structure. The President of the Parliament directs all the activities of Parliament and of its bodies under the conditions laid down in the Rules of Procedure [B5]. The President opens, suspends and closes sittings, ensures observance of the Rules of Procedure, maintains order, calls upon speakers, puts matters to the vote and announces the results of votes. Should the President be absent or unable to discharge his or her duties, he or she is replaced by one of the Vice-Presidents. The Quaestors are members responsible for administrative and financial matters directly concerning members, pursuant to guidelines laid down by the Bureau (below). These officers are elected by secret ballot. Nominations may only be made by a political group or by at least 13 members. In the election of the officers, account is taken of the need to ensure an overall representation of Member States and political views. The Bureau of Parliament consists of the President and the 14 Vice-Presidents of

Parliament. The Quaestors are members of the Bureau in an advisory capacity. The Bureau takes financial and organisational decisions on matters concerning members, Parliament and its bodies. The enlarged Bureau consists of the Bureau and the chairmen of the political groups. The non-attached members (ie those who do not belong to a political group) delegate two of their number to attend meetings of the enlarged Bureau, without having the right to vote. The enlarged Bureau takes decisions on questions relating to Parliament's internal organisation and on matters affecting relations with non-Community institutions and organisations. Parliament sets up standing committees whose powers are defined in an annex to the Rules of Procedure [B6] and which, in particular, give opinions on proposed legislation [B26].

2 The Council

The Council of the European Community, the Council of Ministers, is the institution which emphasises the direct interests of the Member States. It has the duty to ensure that the objectives of the Treaty are attained and to ensure the co-ordination of the general economic policies of the Member States by taking the major policy decisions of the Community and by conferring on the Commission powers for the implementation of those decisions. The Council consists of representatives of each Member State in that one Minister from each Member State government is delegated to the Council. The composition of the Council varies, depending on the subject matter to be discussed at a particular Council meeting. Normally, the national ministers take part in meetings held on their respective fields (for example, agriculture ministers discuss agricultural policy, finance ministers discuss budgetary policy and transport ministers discuss transport policy). See [B7] and note Article 146.

The Council has laid down its own Rules of Procedure [B8] and much power lies in the hands of the President of the Council. The Presidency of the Council is held by each Member State in turn for six months in accordance with an order laid down in the Treaty (1992: Portugal, United Kingdom; 1993: Denmark, Belgium; 1994: Greece, Germany; 1995: France, Spain; 1996: Italy, Ireland). Council meetings are chaired by the appropriate minister from the Member State holding the Presidency. The current Presidency-in-Office will co-operate with the previous and following Presidencies in order to provide continuity and to achieve better organisation of the Council's work, but each Presidency (in other words each Member State holding the Presidency) announces a programme which it hopes to achieve during its term of office. Statements are made to the European Parliament on the Presidency programmes. For example, on 5 July 1988, Mr Papoulis, President-in-Office, made a statement to the European Parliament on the programme of the Greek Presidency. In addition to helping to build the Single Market, his priorities included in particular the wish to create a proper European Social Area. In this connection, the Presidency proposed to give impetus to the work of the Council on the important series of measures concerning health and safety at the workplace, to foster the dialogue between management and labour, and to promote a policy to absorb unemployment amongst young people and to provide vocational training for them. It also wished to make progress in such fields as health and social security, equal treatment of men and women, education, culture and demographic policy.

The Council meets when convened by the President on his or her initiative or at the request of a Member State or the Commission. The 80 meetings held during 1987 were devoted to the following topics: agriculture (16), general and foreign affairs (12), economy and finance (8), internal market (6), budget (6), industry (5), transport (4), environment (4), fisheries (3), research (3), consumer protection and information (3), development co-operation (3), energy (2), labour and social affairs (2), education (1), health (1), law and order (1), legal affairs (1). The 77 meetings held during 1988 were devoted to the following topics: agriculture (12), general affairs (12), internal market (8), economic and financial affairs (7), fisheries (5), budget (4), industry (4), transport (4), research (4), environment (3), development co-operation (2), energy (2), labour and social affairs (2), education (2), health (2), consumer protection and information (1), civil protection (1), cultural affairs (1), tourism (1), APC/EEC relations (1), GATT negotiations (1) (35th and 36th Annual Reviews of the Council's work).

As will be seen (in Section Two of this chapter) the Council plays a dominant role in the enactment of Community secondary legislation. The Council is the nearest equivalent to a legislature. Originally, its system of voting possessed characteristics of an international organisation of independent sovereign states, with decisions needing unanimity. However, as the Community has passed the introductory or transitional stages of its development a constant feature of the amending treaties has been the elimination of the requirement for unanimity.

Members of the Council co-operate with the other institutions. They take part in a debates of the European Parliament, speak to the Parliament on Council policy, and reply to questions raised by the Parliament. They also attend plenary sessions of the Economic and Social Committee. The Council has a staff in Brussels of some 2,000 officials. This is the General Secretariat, divided into a Legal Service and seven Directorates General, responsible for specific sectors, such as agriculture and fisheries [B9].

Ministers are busy people and are engaged in the politics and administration of their own Member State. They cannot remain permanently in Council sessions and, in order to achieve an element of permanence and continuity of Community decision making, the Council is assisted by the Committee of Permanent Representatives of the Member States (COREPER) which is responsible for preparing the work of the Council. COREPER co-ordinates the preparatory work for Council decisions by means of meetings of senior civil servants from each Member State, who are, in effect, rather like Ambassadors and diplomats to the Community (Article 151). COREPER, together with a large number of working parties established to discuss specific matters, will draw up agenda for Council meetings, draft legislative texts and attempt to achieve an informal agreement on proposed policies in order to save the time of the Council. It would be normal for each Member State to have in its Embassy or Chancery in Brussels, an Ambassador Extraordinary and Plenipotentiary, together with Minister Counsellors, Counsellors, Secretaries and Attachés from such Ministries as Finance, Inland Revenue, Agriculture, Fisheries, Labour and Social Affairs, Industry, Transport, Justice, Environment, Health, Energy, Education and

Research, Cultural Affairs, Communications, together with a Press Office and Chancery officials.

3 The Commission

The Commission is the institution which emphasises the supranational nature of the Community. It is charged with ensuring the proper functioning and development of the common market by, inter alia, ensuring that the Treaty provisions and the measures taken by the institutions under the Treaty are applied, by formulating recommendations and delivering opinions, by participating in the legislative process by proposing to the Council of Ministers measures likely to advance the development of Community policies (Article 155 **[B10]**). It will be seen (Section Two of this chapter) that, with regard to the enactment of Community secondary legislation, the Commission has the right of initiating such legislation and that the Council may only act on a proposal from the Commission. The Commission is often referred to as the 'guardian of the Treaties' and it will be seen (Section One of Chapter Three) that Member States which fail to obey Treaty obligations may be taken before the European Court of Justice. The Commission publishes an annual report on the activities of the Community and monthly Bulletins on its work, together with Bulletin Supplements on specific matters.

The Commission is composed of at least one (but not more than two) nationals from each Member State. At present there are 17 Commissioners: two from Germany, Spain, France, Italy and the United Kingdom, and one from each of the other Member States. Commissioners are appointed by common accord of the governments of Member States (ie they are not appointees of any particular state) and are chosen on the grounds of general competence and from persons whose independence is beyond doubt. Many of them have had an active political life (often at ministerial rank) in their respective Member States **[B11]**. In the United Kingdom it has become almost a convention that one Commissioner will be of Conservative persuasion and one Labour. In one sense, the Commission is responsible to the European Parliament as this is the only body that can force them collectively to resign. However, as the Commission is not appointed by the Parliament, it does not possess a direct political link to the European peoples and is still subject to the Council. Under the Treaty of Union changes to the institutional equilibrium, the European Parliament will have a greater role in the appointment of the Commission (Articles 156–160: **[B10]**).

Commission decisions are taken on a collegiate basis, even though specific portfolios (such as competition policy, regional policy and budgetary policy) are allocated to each Commissioner **[B11]**, and decisions are taken by a simple majority vote (Article 163). The Commission has an administrative staff which is divided into specific departments (known as Directorates General) **[B12]**, **[B13]**.

4 The Economic and Social Committee and the Committee of the Regions

The Economic and Social Committee is an advisory body **[B14]**. It consists of representatives of various economic and social sectors within the

Community, which is consulted by the Commission or Council in accordance with the Treaty (Articles 193–198). The Committee debates the economic and social policies of the Community **[A42]**, **[B15]** and plays a consultative role in the enactment of secondary legislation, if the Treaty so provides **[B23]**. Its opinions are published in the Official Journal and it publishes Bulletins and Annual Reports. The Treaty of Union establishes a new advisory body called the Committee of the Regions **[B16]**.

MATERIALS

[B1]   Direct elections to the European Parliament

(a)   Treaty of Rome, Article 138 (as enacted)

1. The Assembly shall consist of delegates who shall be designated by the respective Parliaments from among their members in accordance with the procedure laid down by each Member State.

. . .

3. The Assembly shall draw up proposals for elections by direct universal suffrage in accordance with a uniform procedure in all Member States.

The Council shall, acting unanimously, lay down the appropriate provisions, which it shall recommend to Member States for adoption in accordance with their respective constitutional requirements.

(b)   Final Communiqué of the Paris Summit Conference of 9 and 10 December 1974

12. The Heads of Government note that the election of the European Assembly by universal suffrage, one of the objectives laid down in the Treaty, should be achieved as soon as possible. In this connection, they await with interest the proposals of the European Assembly, on which they wish the Council to act in 1976. On this assumption, elections by direct universal suffrage could take place at any time in or after 1978.

Since the European Assembly is composed of representatives of the peoples of the states united within the Community, each people must be represented in an appropriate manner.

The European Assembly will be associated with the achievement of European unity. The Heads of Government will not fail to take into consideration the points of view which, in October 1972, they asked it to express on this subject.

The competence of the European Assembly will be extended, in particular by granting it certain powers in the Community's legislative process.

(c)   Act of 20 September 1976

Act concerning the election of the representatives of the Assembly by direct universal suffrage

Article 1

The representatives in the Assembly of the peoples of the States brought together in the Community shall be elected by direct universal suffrage.

. . .

Article 3

1. Representatives shall be elected for a term of five years.
2. This five-year period shall begin at the opening of the first session following each election.

. . .

Article 7

. . .

2. Pending the entry into force of a uniform electoral procedure and subject to the other provisions of this Act, the electoral procedure shall be governed in each Member State by its national provisions.

(d) Communiqué of the European Council, Copenhagen, April 1978

The Heads of State and of Government note with satisfaction that the legislative procedures in the member countries for the holding of direct general elections to the Assembly are now nearing completion. After examining dates suitable for the election they have reached agreement that the elections to the Assembly shall be held from 7–10 June 1979.

(e)   Speech of Mme Simone Veil, President, Strasbourg, 18 July 1979

Ladies and gentlemen, you have done me a signal honour in electing me President of the European Parliament, and my emotions on taking the chair are deeper than I can put into words. [Today's] sitting is being held in a setting with which many of you are familiar, but it is nonetheless an historic occasion.

. . .

While we cannot forget the substantial achievements of the Assemblies which preceded us, I must now lay full emphasis on the fundamentally new departure that has been made by the European Communities in having their Parliament elected for the first time by direct universal suffrage.

For this is the first time in history, a history in which we have so frequently been divided, pitted one against the other, bent on mutual destruction, that the people of Europe have together elected their delegates to a common assembly representing, in this Chamber today, more than 260 million people. Let there be no doubt, these elections form a milestone on the path of Europe, the most important since the signing of the Treaties.

. . .

Whatever our political beliefs, we are all aware that this historic step, the election of the European Parliament by universal suffrage, has been taken at a crucial time for the people of the Community. All its Member States are faced with three great challenges: the challenge of peace, the challenge of freedom and the challenge of prosperity, and it seems clear that they can only be met through the European dimension.

. . .

We all know that these challenges, which are being felt throughout Europe with equal intensity, can only be effectively met through solidarity. Beside the superpowers, only Europe as a whole is capable of taking the necessary action which is beyond its individual members in isolation. However, in order to take effective action the European Communities must unite and gather strength. The European Parliament, now that it is elected by direct universal suffrage, will in future bear a special responsibility. If the challenges facing Europe are to be met, we need a Europe capable of solidarity, of independence and of co-operation.

...

Because it has been elected by universal suffrage and will derive a new authority from that election, this Parliament will have a special rôle to play in enabling the European Community to attain these objectives and so prove equal to the challenges facing it. The historic election of June 1979 has raised hopes – tremendous hopes – in Europe. Our electors would not forgive us if we failed to take up this heavy but infinitely rewarding responsibility.

...

I should, however, like to stress the extent to which, in my view, this new authority will prompt Parliament to intensify its action on two fronts: first, by performing its function of control more democratically, and secondly, by acting as a more effective motive force in European integration.

The directly elected European Parliament will be able fully to perform its function of democratic control, which is the prime function of any elected Assembly.

...

Parliament must also be an organ of control of general policy within the Community. Let us not be deluded into believing that the strictly institutional limitations on its powers can prevent a Parliament such as ours from speaking out at all times, and in every field of Community action, with the political authority conferred on it by its election.

Our Parliament must also be a motive force in European integration. This is particularly true at a time [when] Europe's prime need is a further measure of solidarity. This new Parliament will make it possible for the views of all Community citizens to be voiced at European level, and will at the same time more effectively impress upon every sector of society the need for a solidarity transcending immediate concerns, however legitimate, which must never be allowed to mask the fundamental interests of the Community.

We are, of course, aware of the existing allocation of powers in the Community, which confers autonomy on each institution. The Treaties attribute the right of initiative to the Commission and legislative power to the Council. The autonomy of each of the institutions, which is so necessary to the proper functioning of the Communities, does not prevent these institutions from essentially working together with one another, and it is within the context of this co-operation that the fresh impetus provided by the newly-acquired legitimacy of this Assembly must be turned into an effective driving force.

[B2]   The European Parliament, Treaty articles

Article 137 *(as replaced by the Treaty of Union)*

The European Parliament, which shall consist of representatives of the peoples of the states brought together in the Community, shall exercise the powers conferred upon it by this Treaty.

Article 138

1. The representatives in the European Parliament of the peoples of the states brought together in the Community shall be elected by direct universal suffrage.

2. The number of representatives elected in each Member State is as follows:

Belgium	24
Denmark	16
Germany	81
Greece	24
Spain	60
France	81
Ireland	15
Italy	81
Luxembourg	6
Netherlands	25
Portugal	24
United Kingdom	81

3. [pre-Treaty of Union] The European Parliament shall draw up proposals for elections by direct universal suffrage in accordance with a uniform procedure in all Member States.

The Council shall, acting unanimously, lay down the appropriate provisions, which it shall recommend to Member States for adoption in accordance with their respective constitutional requirements.

3. [as replaced by the Treaty of Union] The European Parliament shall draw up proposals for elections by direct universal suffrage in accordance with a uniform procedure in all Member States.

The Council shall, acting unanimously after obtaining the assent of the European Parliament, which shall act by a majority of its component members, lay down the appropriate provisions, which it shall recommend to Member States for adoption in accordance with their respective constitutional requirements.

Article 138a (as inserted by the Treaty of Union)

Political parties at European level are important as a factor for integration within the Union. They contribute to forming a European awareness and to expressing the political will of the citizens of the Union.

Article 138b (as inserted by the Treaty of Union)

In so far as provided in this Treaty, the European Parliament shall participate in the process leading up to the adoption of Community acts by exercising its powers under the procedures laid down in Articles 189b and 189c **[B19]** and by giving its assent or delivering advisory opinions.

The European Parliament may, acting by a majority of its members, request the Commission to submit any appropriate proposal on matters on which it considers that a Community act is required for the purpose of implementing this Treaty.

Article 138c (as inserted by the Treaty of Union)

In the course of its duties, the European Parliament may, at the request of a quarter of its members, set up a temporary Committee of Inquiry to investigate, without prejudice to the powers conferred by this Treaty on other institutions or bodies, alleged contraventions or maladministration in the implementation of Community law, except where the alleged facts are being examined before a court and while the case is still subject to legal proceedings.

The temporary Committee of Inquiry shall cease to exist on the submission of its report.

The detailed provisions governing the exercise of the right of inquiry shall be determined by common accord of the European Parliament, the Council and the Commission.

Article 138d (as inserted by the Treaty of Union)

Any citizen of the Union, and any natural or legal person residing or having his registered office in a Member State, shall have the right to address, individually or in association with other citizens or persons, a petition to the European Parliament on a matter which comes within the Community's fields of activity and which affects him directly.

Article 138e (as inserted by the Treaty of Union)

1. The European Parliament shall appoint an Ombudsman empowered to receive complaints from any citizen of the Union or any natural or legal person residing or having his registered office in a Member State concerning instances of maladministration in the activities of the Community institutions or bodies, with the exception of the Court of Justice and the Court of First Instance acting in their judicial role.

In accordance with his duties, the Ombudsman shall conduct inquiries for which he finds grounds, either on his own initiative or on the basis of complaints submitted to him direct or through a member of the European Parliament, except where the alleged facts are or have been the subject of legal proceedings. Where the Ombudsman establishes an instance of maladministration, he shall refer the matter to the institution concerned, which shall have a period of three months in which to inform him of its views. The Ombudsman shall then forward a report to the European Parliament and the institution concerned. The person lodging the complaint shall be informed of the outcome of such inquiries.

The Ombudsman shall submit an annual report to the European Parliament on the outcome of his inquiries.

2. The Ombudsman shall be appointed after each election of the European Parliament for the duration of its term of office. The Ombudsman shall be eligible for reappointment.

The Ombudsman may be dismissed by the Court of Justice at the request of the European Parliament if he no longer fulfils the conditions required for the performance of his duties or if he is guilty of serious misconduct.

3. The Ombudsman shall be completely independent in the performance of his duties. In the performance of those duties he shall neither seek nor take instructions from any body. The Ombudsman may not, during his term

of office, engage in any other occupation, whether gainful or not.

4. The European Parliament shall, after seeking an opinion from the Commission and with the approval of the Council, acting by a qualified majority, lay down the regulations and general conditions governing the performance of the Ombudsman's duties.

Article 139

The European Parliament shall hold an annual session. It shall meet, without requiring to be convened, on the second Tuesday in March.

The European Parliament may meet in extraordinary session at the request of a majority of its members or at the request of the Council or of the Commission.

Article 140

The European Parliament shall elect its President and its officers from among its members.

Members of the Commission may attend all meetings and shall, at their request, be heard on behalf of the Commission.

The Commission shall reply orally or in writing to questions put to it by the European Parliament or by its members **[B5]**.

The Council shall be heard by the European Parliament in accordance with the conditions laid down by the Council in its rules of procedure.

Article 141

Save as otherwise provided in this Treaty, the European Parliament shall act by an absolute majority of the votes cast.

The rules of procedure shall determine the quorum.

Article 142

The European Parliament shall adopt its rules of procedure **[B3]**, **[B5]**, **[B21]**, acting by a majority of its members.

The proceedings of the European Parliament shall be published in the manner laid down in its rules of procedure.

Article 143

The European Parliament shall discuss in open session the annual general report submitted to it by the Commission **[B5]**.

Article 144

If a motion of censure on the activities of the Commission is tabled before it, the European Parliament shall not vote thereon until at least three days after the motion has been tabled and only by open vote **[B5]**.

If the motion of censure is carried by a two-thirds majority of the votes cast, representing a majority of the members of the European Parliament, the members of the Commission shall resign as a body. They shall continue to deal with current business until they are replaced in accordance with Article [158].

[B3] Political groups in the European Parliament, Rules of Procedure

Rule 26 Formation of political groups

1. Members may form themselves into groups according to their political affinities.

2. A political group shall be considered to have been set up after the President has been handed a statement to that effect containing the name of the group, the signatures of its members and the composition of its Bureau.

3. This statement shall be published in the Official Journal of the European Communities.

4. A member may not belong to more than one group.

5. A minimum number of 23 members shall be required to form a political group if all the members come from a single Member State. The corresponding number shall be 18 if the members come from two Member States and 12 if they come from three or more Member States.

Rule 27 Non-attached members

1. Non-attached members shall be those who do not belong to a political group.

2. The non-attached members shall delegate two of their number to attend meetings of the enlarged Bureau, without having the right to vote.

3. The non-attached members shall be provided with administrative facilities and a secretariat, the composition and size of which shall be determined by the enlarged Bureau on a proposal from the Secretary-General, having regard to the number of non-attached members.

4. The speaking time of non-attached members shall be calculated in accordance with Rule 83(2) [B5]. The time thus obtained shall be doubled so as to take account of the great diversity of political views among the non-attached members and enable, as far as possible, each such view to be expressed. Each non-attached member shall be accorded the same speaking time. If he does not wish to use his speaking time he may assign it to another non-attached member. The rules governing the utilisation of speaking time shall be determined by the enlarged Bureau.

5. The allocation of seats on the various committees to non-attached members shall be made in accordance with the provisions of Rule 110 [B6].

Rule 28 Allocation of seats in the Chamber

The enlarged Bureau shall decide how seats in the Chamber are to be allocated among the political groups, the non-attached members and the institutions of the Communities.

[B4]   Political groups in the European Parliament, January 1993

(*Source*: European Parliament News)

	B	DK	G	GR	S	F	IR	I	L	N	P	UK	TOTAL
SOC	8	3	31	8	27	22	1	34	2	8	8	46	198
EPP	7	4	32	10	17	12	4	27	3	10	3	33	162
LDR	4	3	5	–	5	10	2	3	1	4	9	–	46
GRN	3	1	6	–	1	8	–	7	–	2	–	–	28
EDA	–	–	–	1	2	11	6	–	–	–	–	–	20
RBW	1	4	1	–	3	1	1	3	–	–	1	1	16
ER	1	–	3	–	–	10	–	–	–	–	–	–	14
LU	–	–	–	3	–	7	–	–	–	–	3	–	13
IND	–	1	3	2	5	–	1	7	–	1	–	1	21
TOTAL	24	16	81	24	60	81	15	81	6	25	24	81	518

SOC – Socialist Group
EPP – Group of the European People's Party (Christian Democratic Group)
LDR – Liberal Democrat and Reformist Group
GRN – Group of Greens in the European Parliament
EDA – Group of the European Democratic Alliance
RBW – Rainbow Group
ER – Technical Group of the European Right
LU – Left Unity
IND – Non-attached

[B5]   European Parliament, Rules of Procedure

Note.   These rules are taken from the latest published version of the Parliament's rules (1987). In September 1993 proposals (EP Working Document A3–240/93) to amend the rules consequent upon the coming into force of the Treaty of Union were submitted to and approved by the European Parliament.

Rule 29   Annual General Report of the Commission and Annual Legislative Programme

1. The annual general report of the Commission on the activities of the Communities shall be distributed immediately after publication.

2. The various parts of the report shall be referred to the appropriate committees.

3. Committees consulted under paragraph 2 shall not be obliged to submit a report. Any committee may, where it feels it necessary for Parliament to make known its views on certain essential problems raised by the general report, bring these problems up in plenary sitting by resorting to one of the existing procedures.

4. After the presentation of the Annual Programme by the Commission and the debate thereon in Parliament, the enlarged Bureau and the Commission shall agree on an annual legislative programme and a timetable for the submission by the Commission and the examination by Parliament of proposals which the Commission intends to remit to the Council.

Rule 30   Motion of censure on the Commission

1. A motion of censure on the Commission may be handed to the President of Parliament by a political group or one-tenth of the current Members of Parliament.

2. The motion shall be presented in writing, labelled 'motion of censure' and supported by reasons. It shall be printed and distributed in the official languages as soon as it is received, and brought to the notice of the Commission.

3. The President shall announce to members that a motion of censure has been tabled immediately he receives it, and where the motion of censure is received during an adjournment of the session, he shall repeat that announcement at the beginning of the first part-session following receipt of the motion. The debate on the motion shall not be opened until at least 24 hours after its receipt is announced. The vote shall not be taken on the motion until at least 48 hours after the beginning of the debate. Voting shall be by open vote by way of roll call [see Rule 95].

4. The motion of censure shall be adopted only if it secures a two-thirds majority of the votes cast, representing a majority of the current Members of Parliament. The result of the vote shall be notified to the President of the Commission and the President of the Council.

Rule 58 Questions for oral answer with debate

1. Questions may be put to the Commission [or] the Council [by] a committee, a political group or seven or more members in order that they may be placed on the agenda of Parliament and dealt with by the procedure provided for under this Rule.

Such questions, which may also relate to problems of a general nature, shall be submitted in writing to the President, who shall place them before the enlarged Bureau at the next meeting held for the purpose of drawing up the draft agenda.

Subject to the provisions below, during each part-session each political group shall have the right to have not more than one question dealt with by the procedure with debate.

. . .

2. The enlarged Bureau shall decide whether the Commission or the Council is to be consulted. It shall decide whether the question is to be converted into a question for written answer, for oral answer at Question Time, or is to be dealt with by oral procedure without debate under Rule 59 or by the procedure provided for under this Rule.

The decision of the enlarged Bureau shall be notified immediately to the questioner and to the institutions concerned.

A question tabled under this Rule shall be placed on the agenda of the next part-session on the expiry of a three months' period from its date of tabling if within that time no decison has been taken by the enlarged Bureau as to the manner in which it is to be answered.

The procedure for questions under this Rule may be proposed only where notice of the question can be given within the following time limits: if the question is addressed to the Commission, at least one week and if to the Council, at least five weeks before the opening of the sitting on whose agenda it is to appear.

In urgent cases, the President may propose directly to Parliament that a question which could not be placed before the enlarged Bureau under the foregoing conditions be placed on the agenda. Such questions, together with any that could not be notified within the time limit specified above, may be placed on the agenda only with the agreement of the institution to which they are addressed.

...

4. One of the questioners may speak to the question for not more than ten minutes. One member of the institution concerned shall answer. Other Members of Parliament may speak for not more than five minutes, and may do so only once.

One of the questioners may, at his request, comment for not more than five minutes on the answer given.

...

Rule 59   Questions for oral answer without debate

1. Any member may put questions to the Commission [or] the Council [and] ask that they be placed on the agenda of Parliament and dealt with by the procedure provided for under this Rule.

Such questions shall be submitted in writing to the President, who shall place them before the enlarged Bureau at the next meeting held for the purpose of drawing up the draft agenda.

The enlarged Bureau shall decide whether the question is to be converted into a question for written answer, or for oral answer at Question Time, or whether it is to be dealt with by the procedure provided for under this Rule.

The decision of the enlarged Bureau shall be notified immediately to the questioner and to the institutions concerned. If the question is addressed to the Commission such notification shall be made at least one week, and if to the Council, at least five weeks before the opening of the sitting on whose agenda it is to appear.

...

3. Questions shall be clearly worded and relate to specific points, not to problems of a general nature. Parliament shall set aside not more than half a day during each part-session for oral answers to these questions. Questions that remain unanswered during that period shall be carried forward to the next part-session or converted into questions for written answer, as the questioner may choose.

4. The questioner shall read out his question. He may speak to it for not more than ten minutes. A member of the institution concerned shall give a brief answer. Where the question is addressed to the Commission, the questioner may ask one or two supplementary questions, to which the member of this institution shall give a brief answer.

...

Rule 60   Question Time

1. Question Time shall be held at each part-session at such times as may be decided by Parliament on a proposal from the enlarged Bureau.

2. Questions shall be submitted in writing to the President, who shall

decide whether they are admissible; he shall determine the order in which they will be taken, and how they will be grouped.

The questioner shall be notified immediately of the President's decision.

3. During Question Time any member may put oral questions to the Commission or Council, in accordance with the provisions of this Rule.

. . .

5. Questions put to the Council [shall] be taken first on the second day of Question Time.

6. At each part-session, any member may put only one question respectively to the Commission [or Council].

. . .

Rule 61   Debate following Question Time

1. Before the close of Question Time, any political group or at least seven members may request that a debate be held immediately thereafter on the answer given by the Commission [or Council] on a specific matter of general and topical interest.

2. Such a debate may be requested only after the Commission [or Council] has or have replied to all supplementary questions on the specific matter concerned.

. . .

4. The debate shall be limited to one hour, excluding speaking time set aside for the Commission [or Council]. No member may speak for more than five minutes.

5. The order of speaking shall be governed by Rule 84, the first speaker being a spokesman for the political group or the Members who requested the debate.

Rule 62   Questions for written answer

1. Questions for written answer may be put by any Member to the Commission [or to the Council].

These questions shall be brief and relate to specific points falling within the sphere of activities of the Communities; they shall be submitted in writing to the President, who shall communicate them to the institution concerned.

2. Questions to which answers have been given shall be published, together with the answers, in the Official Journal of the European Communities.

3. Questions to which no answer has been given within one month by the Commission, or within two months by the [Council], shall also be published in the Official Journal of the European Communities.

Rule 64   Debates on topical and urgent subjects of major importance

1. A political group or at least 23 members may ask the President in writing for a debate to be held on a topical and urgent subject of major [importance]. The President shall notify Parliament immediately of any request for a debate on a topical and urgent subject of major importance and the request shall be printed and distributed in the official languages.

2. After a meeting with the political group chairmen and a representative of the non-attached members, the President shall draw up a list of subjects to be included on the agenda of the next debate on topical and urgent subjects of major [importance]. The total number of subjects included on the agenda shall not exceed five. The President shall notify Parliament of this list not later than at the resumption of the sitting on the afternoon of the same day. In drawing up this list, the President shall ensure that during a part-session a balance is maintained both between the requests from the political groups and between these requests and those from individual members.

. . .

3. The total speaking time for political groups and non-attached members shall be allocated in accordance with the procedure laid down in Rule 83(2) to (4) within the maximum time for debates on topical and urgent subjects of major importance of three hours per part-session. Any time remaining after taking account of the time required for the introduction of and vote on the motions for resolutions and the time agreed on for statements, if any, by the Commisson and Council, shall be broken down between the political groups and the non-attached members.

4. At the end of the debate there shall be an immediate vote.

. . .

Rule 81   *Public conduct of proceedings*

Debates in Parliament shall be public unless Parliament decides otherwise by a majority of two-thirds of the votes cast.

Rule 82 *Calling speakers and content of speeches*

1. No member may speak unless called upon to do so by the President. Members shall speak from their places and shall address the Chair; the President may invite them to come to the rostrum.

2. If a speaker departs from the subject, the President shall call him to order. If a speaker has already been called to order twice in the same debate, the President may, on the third occasion, forbid him to speak for the remainder of the debate on the same subject.

. . .

4. A speaker may not be interrupted. He may, however, by leave of the President, give way during his speech to allow another Member, the Commission or the Council to put to him a question on a particular point in his speech.

Rule 83 *Allocation of speaking time*

1. The President may, after consulting the chairmen of the political groups, propose to Parliament that speaking time be allocated for a particular debate. Parliament shall decide on this proposal without debate.

2. The President shall allocate speaking time in accordance with the following criteria:

(a)   a first fraction of speaking time shall be divided equally among all the political groups;
(b)   a further fraction shall be divided among the political groups in proportion to the total number of their members;

(c) the non-attached members shall be allocated an overall speaking time based on the fractions allocated to each political group under sub-paragraphs (a) and (b).

3. The speaking time of non-attached members, calculated in accordance with paragraph 2, shall be doubled so as to take account of the great diversity of political views among them and enable, as far as possible, each such view to be expressed.

Each non-attached member shall be accorded the same speaking time. If he does not wish to use his speaking time he may assign it to another non-attached member.

The rules governing the utilisation of speaking time shall be determined by the enlarged Bureau.

4. Where a total speaking time is allocated for several items on the agenda, the political groups shall inform the President of the fraction of their speaking time to be used for each individual item. The President shall ensure that these speaking times are respected.

. . .

Rule 84   List of speakers

1. The names of members who ask leave to speak shall be entered in the list of speakers in the order in which their requests are received.

2. The President shall call upon members to speak, ensuring as far as possible that speakers of different political views and using different languages are heard in turn.

3. On request, however, priority may be given to the rapporteur of the committee responsible and to the chairmen of political groups who wish to speak on their behalf, or to speakers deputising for them.

4. No member may speak more than twice on the same subject, except by leave of the President.

The chairman and the rapporteur of the committees concerned shall, however, be allowed to speak at their request for a period to be decided by the President.

5. Members of the Commission and Council shall be heard at their request.

Rule 93   Right to vote

The right to vote is a personal right. Voting by proxy is prohibited.

Rule 94   Voting

1. Normally Parliament shall vote by show of hands.

2. If the President decides that the result of the show of hands is doubtful, a fresh vote shall be taken by sitting and standing.

3. If the President decides that the result of this last vote is doubtful, the vote shall be taken by roll call.

. . .

Rule 95   Voting by roll call

1. The vote shall be taken by roll call if so requested in writing by at least 23 Members or a political group before voting has begun and in cases where [Rule 94(3) applies].

2. The roll shall be called in alphabetical order, beginning with the name of a member drawn by lot. The President shall be the last to be called to vote.

Voting shall be by word of mouth and shall be expressed by 'Yes', 'No' or 'I abstain'. In calculating whether a motion has been adopted or rejected account shall be taken only of votes cast for and against. The President shall establish the result of the vote and announce it.

Voting shall be recorded in the minutes of proceedings of the sitting in the alphabetical order of members' names.

. . .

Rule 97   Voting by secret ballot

. . .

2. Voting may [be] by secret ballot if requested by at least one-fifth of the current Members of Parliament. Such requests must be made before voting begins.

3. A request for a secret ballot shall take priority over a request for a vote by roll call.

[B6]   Standing Committees of the European Parliament, Rules of Procedure

Rule 109   Setting up of committees

1. Parliament shall set up standing committees whose powers shall be defined in an annex to the Rules of Procedure. Their members shall be elected during the first part-session following the re-election of Parliament and again two and a half years thereafter.

. . .

Rule 110   Composition of committees

1. Committee members shall be elected after nomination to the Bureau by the political groups, the non-attached members or at least 13 members. The Bureau shall submit to Parliament proposals designed to ensure fair representation of Member States and of political views.

2. Amendments to the proposals of the Bureau shall be admissible only if they are tabled by at least 13 members. Parliament shall vote on such amendments by secret ballot.

3. Members shall be deemed to be elected on the basis of the Bureau's proposals, as and where amended pursuant to paragraph 2.

Annex VI   List of standing committees

I. Political Affairs Committee.
II. Committee on Agriculture, Fisheries and Food.
III. Committee on Budgets.
IV. Committee on Economic and Monetary Affairs and Industrial Policy.
V. Committee on Energy, Research and Technology.
VI. Committee on External Economic Relations.
VII. Committee on Legal Affairs and Citizens' Rights.

VIII. Committee on Social Affairs and Employment.
IX. Committee on Regional Policy and Regional Planning.
X. Committee on Transport.
XI. Committee on the Environment, Public Health and Consumer Protection.
XII. Committee on Youth, Culture, Education, Information and Sport.
XIII. Committee on Development and Co-operation.
XIV. Committee on Budgetary Control.
XV. Committee on Institutional Affairs.
XVI. Committee on the Rules of Procedure, the Verification of Credentials and Immunities.
XVII. Committee on Women's Rights.
XVIII. Committee on Petitions.

Annex VI Specific responsibilities of certain committees

I. The Political Affairs Committee is responsible for matters relating to: political and institutional aspects of relations with other international organisations and with third countries (the Committee on Institutional Affairs will give an opinion on this matter); political aspects of international problems; problems concerning human rights in third countries; the preparation of a draft uniform electoral procedure (the Committee on Legal Affairs and Citizens' Rights will give an opinion on the draft report by the Political Affairs Committee on the draft uniform electoral procedure); political aspects of the seat of the Community institutions.

II. The Committee on Agriculture, Fisheries and Food is generally responsible for all matters relating to Articles 38 to 47 of the EEC Treaty: operation and development of the common agricultural policy; establishment, operation and development of a common fisheries policy; and veterinary legislation relating to the control and elimination of diseases in domestic animals. The committee will be required to give its opinion on all matters which, although arising in a different specific field (public health, economic policy, external economic relations, relations with European or other associated countries), may have some bearing on the organisation of the Community's agricultural market or on the organisation of the market in fisheries products, and on matters pertaining to commercial policy with regard to agricultural and fisheries products.

. . .

VII. The Committee on Legal Affairs and Citizens' Rights is responsible for matters relating to: legal aspects of the creation, interpretation and application of Community law; the law of the sea; human rights problems in the Community (the Political Affairs Committee could give an opinion on these matters if it so requests); all matters relating to the definition of the rights of Community citizens as such and the consolidation of legislation covering these rights (the Political Affairs Committee could give an opinion on these matters if it so requests); co-ordination at Community level of national legislation relating to freedom of establishment and freedom to provide services; the submission of actions by Parliament in the Court of Justice; action by Parliament on behalf of the plaintiff or defendant in actions before the Court of Justice; preparing the opinion of the plenary assembly of Parliament which may be needed on an action brought against Parliament.

VIII. The Committee on Social Affairs and Employment is responsible for matters relating to: improving living and working conditions; employment policy, particularly where it affects young people; vocational training, particularly as regards access to the labour market and to retraining in connection with reconversion and occupational mobility; activities of the European Social Fund; free movement of workers; social security of migrant workers; housing policy and low-cost housing schemes; promoting co-operation between the Member States in the field of social policy, with particular emphasis on labour law and the approximation of social legislation; equal pay and equal job and vocational training opportunities for men and women; paid holiday schemes. The committee will also be required to give its opinion on matters relating to the rights of migrant workers.

XI. The Committee on the Environment, Public Health and Consumer Protection is responsible for matters relating to: environment policy and environmental protection measures; pollution of air, earth and water; classification, packing, labelling, transport and use of dangerous substances; fixing new permissible noise levels; treatment and storage of waste (including recycling); international and regional measures and agreements aimed at protecting the environment (for example, the Rhine, the Mediterranean); protecting fauna and its habitat; giving opinions on energy and research programmes affecting the environment; environmental aspects of the Law of the Sea; public health and safety at work; checks on foodstuffs; programmes in the field of health education; veterinary legislation concerning protection against dangers to human health; pharmaceutical products; cosmetic products; medical research programmes; protection of employees at work; consumer protection; protection of consumers against risks to health and safety; protection of consumers' economic interests; improvement of legal protection for consumers (assistance, advice and legal redress); improvement of consumer information and education.

[B7]   The Council, Treaty articles

Article 145

To ensure that the objectives set out in this Treaty are attained, the Council shall, in accordance with the provisions of this Treaty:

- ensure co-ordination of the general economic policies of the Member States;
- have power to take decisions;
- confer on the Commission, in the acts which the Council adopts, powers for the implementation of the rules which the Council lays down. The Council may impose certain requirements in respect of the exercise of these powers. The Council may also reserve the right, in specific cases, to exercise directly implementing powers itself. The procedures referred to above must be consonant with principles and rules to be laid down in advance by the Council, acting unanimously on a proposal from the Commisssion and after obtaining the Opinion of the European Parliament.

Article 146 (pre-Treaty of Union)

The Council shall consist of representatives of the Member States. Each government shall delegate to it one of its members.

The office of President shall be held for a term of six months by each member of the Council in turn, in the following order of Member States:

- for a first cycle of six years: Belgium, Denmark, Germany, Greece, Spain, France, Ireland, Italy, Luxembourg, Netherlands, Portugal, United Kingdom;

- for the following cycle of six years: Denmark, Belgium, Greece, Germany, France, Spain, Italy, Ireland, Netherlands, Luxembourg, United Kingdom, Portugal.

Article 146 (as replaced by the Treaty of Union)

The Council shall consist of a representative of each Member State at ministerial level, authorised to commit the government of that Member State.

The office of President shall be held in turn by each Member State in the Council for a term of six months, in the following order of Member States:

- for a first cycle of six years: Belgium, Denmark, Germany, Greece, Spain, France, Ireland, Italy, Luxembourg, Netherlands, Portugal, United Kingdom;
- for the following cycle of six years: Denmark, Belgium, Greece, Germany, France, Spain, Italy, Ireland, Netherlands, Luxembourg, United Kingdom, Portugal.

Article 147 (as replaced by the Treaty of Union)

The Council shall meet when convened by its President on his own initiative or at the request of one of its members or of the Commission.

[Article 148 is extracted in **[B19]**.]
[Article 149 is extracted in **[B19]**.]

Article 150

When a vote is taken, any member of the Council may also act on behalf of not more than one other member.

Article 151 (as amended by the Treaty of Union)

1. A Committee consisting of the Permanent Representatives of the Member States shall be responsible for preparing the work of the Council and for carrying out the tasks assigned to it by the Council. . . .

3. The Council shall adopt its Rules of Procedure **[B8]**.

Article 152

The Council may request the Commission to undertake any studies the Council considers desirable for the attainment of the common objectives, and to submit to it any appropriate proposals.

[B8]   Council Rules of Procedure

(Adopted by the Council on 24 July 1979 (OJ No L268/1) and amended by the Council on 20 July 1987 (OJ No 291/27).)

Article 1

1. The Council shall meet when convened by its President on his own initiative or at the request of one of its members or of the Commission.

2. The President shall make known the dates which he envisages for meetings of the Council during his period of office as President, seven months before the beginning thereof.

Article 2

1. The President shall draw up the provisional agenda for each meeting. The agenda shall be sent to the other members of the Council and to the Commission at least 14 days before the beginning of the meeting.

2. The provisional agenda shall contain the items in respect of which a request for inclusion on the agenda, together with any documents relating thereto, has been received by the General Secretariat from a member of the Council or from the Commission at least 16 days before the beginning of that meeting.

The provisional agenda shall also indicate the items on which the Presidency, delegations or the Commission may request a vote.

3. Only items in respect of which the documents have been sent to the members of the Council and to the Commission at the latest by the date on which the provisional agenda is sent may be placed on that agenda.

4. The General Secretariat shall transmit to the members of the Council and to the Commission requests for the inclusion of items in the agenda, documents and indications concerning voting relating thereto in respect of which the time limits specified above were not respected.

5. The agenda shall be adopted by the Council at the beginning of each meeting. The inclusion in the agenda of an item other than those appearing on the provisional agenda shall require unanimity in the Council. Items entered in this way may be put to the vote.

6. The provisional agenda shall be divided into Part A and Part B. Items for which the approval of the Council is possible without discussion shall be included in Part A, but this does not exclude the possibility of any member of the Council or of the Commission expressing an opinion at the time of the approval of these items and having statements included in the minutes.

7. However, an 'A' item shall be withdrawn from the agenda, unless the Council decides otherwise, if a position on an 'A' item might lead to further discussion thereof or if a member of the Council or the Commission so requests.

Article 3

1. Meetings of the Council shall not be public, unless the Council unanimously decides otherwise.

2. The Commission shall be invited to take part in meetings of the Council. The Council may, however, decide to deliberate without the presence of the Commission.

3. The members of the Council and of the Commission may be accompanied by officials who assist them. The number of such officials may be laid down by the Council.

. . .

Article 4

Subject to the provisions of Article 5 on the delegation of voting rights, a member of the Council who is prevented from attending a meeting may arrange to be represented.

Article 5

1. The Council shall vote on the initiative of its President.

The President shall, furthermore, be required to open voting proceedings on the invitation of a member of the Council or of the Commission, provided that a majority of the Council's members so decides.

2. The members of the Council shall vote in the alphabetical order of the Member [States], beginning with the member who, according to that order, follows the member holding the office of President.

3. Delegation of the right to vote may only be made to another member of the Council.

Article 6

1. Acts of the Council on an urgent matter may be adopted by a written vote where all the members of the Council agree to that procedure in respect of the matter in question.

2. Furthermore, agreement by the Commission to the use of this procedure shall be required where the written vote is on a matter which the Commission has brought before the Council.

3. A summary of acts adopted by the written procedure shall be drawn up every month.

Article 7

1. Minutes of each meeting shall be drawn up and, when approved, shall be signed by the President-in-Office at the time of such approval and by the Secretary-General.

The minutes shall as a general rule indicate in respect of each item on the agenda:

- the documents submitted to the Council,
- the decisions taken or the conclusions reached by the Council,
- the statements made by the Council and those whose entry has been requested by a member of the Council or the Commission.

2. The draft minutes shall be drawn up by the General Secretariat within 15 days and submitted to the Council for approval.

3. Prior to such approval any member of the Council, or the Commission, may request that more details be inserted in the minutes regarding any item on the agenda.

4. The texts referred to in Article 9 shall be annexed to the minutes.

Article 8

1. Except as otherwise decided unanimously by the Council on grounds of urgency, the Council shall deliberate and take decisions only on the basis of documents and drafts drawn up in the languages specified in the rules in force governing languages.

2. Any member of the Council may oppose discussion if the texts of any proposed amendments are not drawn up in such of the said languages as he may specify.

Article 9

The texts of the acts adopted by the Council shall be signed by the President-in-Office at the time of their adoption and by the Secretary-General.

. . .

Article 16

1. The Committee consisting of the Permanent Representatives of the Member States [shall] prepare the work of the Council and shall carry out the tasks assigned to it by the Council.

2. It may set up working parties and instruct them to carry out such preparatory work or studies as it shall define.

3. Unless the Council decides otherwise, the Commission shall be invited to be represented in the work of the Committee and of the working parties.

4. The Committee shall be presided over by the delegate of that Member State whose representative is President of the Council. The same shall apply to the working parties, unless the Committee decides otherwise.

Article 17

1. The Council shall be assisted by a General Secretariat under the direction of a Secretary-General. The Secretary-General shall be appointed by the Council acting unanimously.

2. The Council shall determine the organisation of the General Secretariat.

Under its authority the Secretary-General shall take all the measures necessary to ensure the smooth running of the General Secretariat.

. . .

Article 18

Without prejudice to other applicable provisions, the deliberations of the Council shall be covered by the obligation of professional secrecy, except in so far as the Council decides otherwise.

The Council may authorise the production of a copy or an extract from its minutes for use in legal proceedings.

Article 19

1. Subject to special procedures, the Council may be represented by its President or by any other of its members before the European Parliament or its Committees.

2. The Council may also present its views to the European Parliament by means of a written statement.

[B9] Council Directorate General B: Agriculture and Fisheries

Directorate I: agricultural policy (including international aspects), organisation of the markets in agricultural products and harmonisation of veterinary and zootechnical legislation (plant products, cereals, fruit and vegetables, protein products, textile fibres, tobacco, wine, sugar, beef, veal and sheep meat, milk and milk products, pig meat, eggs and poultry).
Directorate II: agricultural structures policy, agri-monetary and agri-financial questions, harmonisation of legislation on agriculture and food.
Directorate III: fisheries policy (including external relations), general questions, structural policy, market organisation, Mediterranean, relations with countries in Africa, the Indian Ocean and Latin America, Antarctica, resource management and conservation policy, monitoring of fishery activities, relations with countries in Northern and Eastern Europe and North America, North Atlantic and Baltic Sea international organisations, research.

[B10] The Commission, Treaty articles

Article 155

In order to ensure the proper functioning and development of the common market, the Commission shall:

- ensure that the provisions of this Treaty and the measures taken by the institutions pursuant thereto are applied;
- formulate recommendations or deliver opinions on matters dealt with in this Treaty, if it expressly so provides or if the Commission considers it necessary;
- have its own power of decision and participate in the shaping of measures taken by the Council and by the European Parliament in the manner provided for in this Treaty;
- exercise the powers conferred on it by the Council for the implementation of the rules laid down by the latter.

Article 156 (as replaced by the Treaty of Union)

The Commission shall publish annually, not later than one month before the opening of the session of the European Parliament, a general report on the activities of the Community.

Article 157 (as replaced by the Treaty of Union)

1. The Commission shall consist of 17 members, who shall be chosen on the grounds of their general competence and whose independence is beyond doubt.
The number of members of the Commission may be altered by the Council acting unanimously.
Only nationals of Member States may be members of the Commission.
The Commission must include at least one national of each of the Member States, but may not include more than two members having the nationality of the same state.

2. The members of the Commission shall, in the general interest of the Community, be completely independent in the performance of their duties.

In the performance of these duties, they shall neither seek nor take instructions from any government or from any other body.

They shall refrain from any action incompatible with their duties.

Each Member State undertakes to respect this principle and not to seek to influence the members of the Commission in the performance of their tasks.

The members of the Commission may not, during their term of office, engage in any other occupation, whether gainful or not. When entering upon their duties they shall give a solemn undertaking that, both during and after their term of office, they will respect the obligations arising therefrom and in particular their duty to behave with integrity and discretion as regards the acceptance, after they have ceased to hold office, of certain appointments or benefits. In the event of any breach of these obligations, the Court of Justice may, on application by the Council or the Commission, rule that the member concerned be, according to the circumstances, either compulsorily retired in accordance with Article 160 or deprived of his rights to a pension or other benefits in its stead.

Article 158 (pre-Treaty of Union)

The members of the Commission shall be appointed by common accord of the governments of the Member States.

Their term of office shall be four years. It shall be renewable.

Article 158 (as replaced by the Treaty of Union)

1. The members of the Commission shall be appointed, in accordance with the procedure referred to in paragraph 2, for a period of five years, subject, if need be, to Article 144.

Their term of office shall be renewable.

2. The governments of the Member States shall nominate by common accord, after consulting the European Parliament, the person they intend to appoint as President of the Commission.

The governments of the Member States shall, in consultation with the nominee for President, nominate the other persons whom they intend to appoint as members of the Commission.

The President and the other members of the Commission thus nominated shall be subject as a body to a vote of approval by the European Parliament. After approval by the European Parliament, the President and the other members of the Commission shall be appointed by common accord of the governments of the Member States.

3. Paragraphs 1 and 2 shall be applied for the first time to the President and the other members of the Commission whose term of office begins on 7 January 1995.

The President and the other members of the Commission whose term of office begins on 7 January 1993 shall be appointed by common accord of the governments of the Member States. Their term of office shall expire on 6 January 1995.

Article 159 (as replaced by the Treaty of Union)

Apart from normal replacement, or death, the duties of a member of the Commission shall end when he resigns or is compulsorily retired.

The vacancy thus caused shall be filled for the remainder of the member's term of office by a new member appointed by common accord of the governments of the Member [States].

Save in the case of compulsory retirement under Article 160, members of the Commission shall remain in office until they have been replaced.

Article 160 (as replaced by the Treaty of Union)

If any member of the Commission no longer fulfils the conditions required for the performance of his duties or if he has been guilty of serious misconduct, the Court of Justice may, on application by the Council or the Commission, compulsorily retire him.

. . .

Article 162 (as replaced by the Treaty of Union)

1. The Council and the Commission shall consult each other and shall settle by common accord their methods of co-operation.

. . .

Article 163 (as replaced by the Treaty of Union)

The Commission shall act by a majority of the number of members provided for in Article 157.

A meeting of the Commission shall be valid only if the number of members laid down in its rules of procedure is present.

[B11]   Members of the Commission (6 January 1989 to 5 January 1993)

The representatives of the governments of the Member States adopted a decision appointing the members of the Commission for the period from 6 January 1989 to 5 January 1993 on 8 December 1988 (OJ L351, 21 December 1988). Mr Jaques Delors was appointed President of the Commission.

Mr Frans Andriessen (Doctor of Law of the University of Utrecht, Director of the Catholic Subsidised Housing Institute, Member of the States-General, Minister for Finance, Member of the European Commission with responsibility for relations with Parliament and competition). Portfolios: External relations and trade policy, Co-operation with other European countries.

Mr Martin Bangemann (Member of the Bundestag (German Parliament), Member of the European Parliament, Vice-Chairman of the Liberal and Democratic Group in the European Parliament, Federal Minister for Economic Affairs). Portfolios: Internal market and industrial affairs, Relations with the European Parliament.

Sir Leon Brittan (Barrister, Member of Parliament, Minister of State at the

Home Office, Chief Secretary to the Treasury, Secretary of State for the Home Department, Secretary of State for Trade and Industry). Portfolios: Competition, Financial institutions.

Mr António Cardoso e Cunha (Chemical engineer and businessman, Secretary of State for Foreign Trade and for Manufacturing Industry, Minister for Agriculture and Fisheries, Member of Parliament, Member of the European Commission with responsibility for fisheries). Portfolios: Personnel, administration and translation, Energy and Euratom Supply Agency, Small business, distributive trades and tourism, Co-operatives.

Mr Henning Christophersen (Economist, Member of the Folketing (Danish Parliament), Minister for Foreign Affairs, Minister for Finance, Deputy Prime Minister, Vice-President of the European Commission with responsibility for the Community budget, financial control and personnel administration). Portfolios: Economic and financial affairs, Co-ordination of Structural Funds, Statistical Office.

Mr Jaques Delors (Senior executive at the Banque de France, Lecturer Ecole nationale d'administration, Adviser to the Prime Minister, Member of the European Parliament, Chairman of the European Parliament's Committee on Economic and Monetary Affairs, Minister for Economic and Financial Affairs, President of the European Commission). Portfolios: Secretariat-General, Forward Studies Unit, Inspectorates-General, Legal Services, Monetary affairs, Spokesman's Service, Joint Interpreting and Conference Service, Security Office.

Mr Jean Dondelinger (Lawyer, International Economic Relations Department of the Luxembourg Ministry of Foreign Affairs, Ambassador and Permanent Representative of Luxembourg to the European Community, Secretary-General of the Ministry of Foreign Affairs). Portfolios: Audiovisual and cultural affairs, Information and Communication, A People's Europe, Office for Official Publications.

Mr Ray MacSharry (Member of the Dáil Éireann (Parliament of Ireland), Minister of State of the Department of Finance and the Public Service, Minister for Agriculture, Governor European Investment Bank, Tánaiste (Deputy Prime Minister), Minister for Finance, Member of the European Parliament). Portfolios: Agriculture, Rural development.

Mr Manuel Marín González (Doctor of Law, University of Madrid, Certificate in Advanced European Studies from the College of Europe, Bruges, Member of the Cortes (Spanish Parliament), Deputy Chairman of the Confederation of Socialist Parties in the European Community, Secretary of State for Relations with the European Community). Portfolios: Co-operation and development, Fisheries.

Mr Abel Matutes Juan (Professor of Law and Public Finance at the University of Barcelona, Member of Parliament for the Balearic Islands, Member of the European Commission with responsibility for small business, credit, investments and financial engineering). Portfolios: Mediterranean policy, relations with Latin America and Asia, North–South relations.

Mr Bruce Millan (Chartered accountant, Member of Parliament, Parliamentary Under Secretary of State at the Ministry of Defence, Minister of State (Industry and Economic Department), Scottish Office, Secretary of State for Scotland, Opposition spokesman on Scottish affairs). Portfolio: Regional policy.

Mr Filippo Maria Pandolfi (Member of the Italian Chamber of Deputies,

Minister for Finance, Minister for Industry, Minister for Agriculture). Portfolios: Science, research and development, Telecommunications, information technology and innovation, Joint Research Centre.

Ms Vasso Papandreou (Economist with degrees from Athens, London and Reading, Tutor in economics at Exeter University, Lecturer at the Athens School of Economics, Member of the Board of Directors of the Commercial Bank of Greece, Member of the Greek Parliament, Deputy Minister for Industry, Energy and Technology, and Trade). Portfolios: Employment, industrial relations and social affairs, Human resources, education, training and youth, relations with the Economic and Social Committee.

Mr Carlo Ripa di Meana (Journalist and publisher, Member of the Board of La Scala in Milan, prominent member of the Italian Socialist Party, Member of the European Parliament, Member of the European Parliament's Committee on Political Affairs and Transport, Member of the European Commission with responsibility for institutional matters, a people's Europe, information and communication, cultural affairs and tourism). Portfolios: Environment, Nuclear safety, Civil protection.

Mr Peter Schmidhuber (Lawyer, employed in the Bavarian State Ministries of Finance, Economic Affairs and Transport, Member of the Bundestag (German Parliament), Member of the Bavarian Parliament, Bavarian State Minister for Federal Affairs, Member of the Bundesrat (Upper House of Parliament), Member of the European Commission with responsibility for economic affairs, regional policy and the Statistical Office). Portfolios: Budget, financial control.

Mrs Christiane Scrivener (Businesswoman, graduate of the Harvard Business School, Secretary of State for Consumer Affairs, Member of the European Parliament). Portfolios: Taxation and customs union, matters relating to the overall tax burden.

Mr Karel Van Miert (Lecturer in international and social law at the Free University of Brussels, Deputy Chairman of the Confederation of Socialist Parties in the European Community, Member of the European Parliament, Member of the Belgian Chamber of Representatives). Portfolios: Transport, Credit and investments, Protection and promotion of consumer interests.

[B12]   List of Commission Directorates General

DG I – External Relations.
DG II – Economic and Financial Affairs.
DG III – Internal Market and Industrial Affairs.
DG IV – Competition.
DG V – Employment, Industrial Relations and Social Affairs.
DG VI – Agriculture.
DG VII – Transport.
DG VIII – Development.
DG IX – Personnel and Administration.
DG X – Audiovisual Media, Information, Communications and Culture.
DG XI – Environment, Nuclear Safety and Civil Protection.
DG XII – Science, Research and Development.
DG XIII – Telecommunications, Information Industries and Innovation.
DG XIV – Fisheries.

DG XV – Financial Institutions and Company Law.
DG XVI – Regional Policy.
DG XVII – Energy.
DG XVIII – Credit and Investments.
DG XIX – Budgets.
DG XX – Financial Control.
DG XXI – Customs and Indirect Taxation.
DG XXII – Co-ordination of Structural Policies.
DG XXIII – Enterprise Policy, Distributive Trades, Tourism and Co-operatives.

[B13]   Responsibilities of certain Directorates General

(a)   Directorate General XI: Environment, Nuclear Safety and Civil Protection

Directorate A is responsible for nuclear safety, industry and the environment and civil protection (radiation protection, environmental monitoring and inspection; environmental control of products, industrial installations and biotechnology; emissions from industrial installations and products; waste management policy; civil protection).

Directorate B is responsible for environment quality and natural resources (water protection, coastal zones, environment and tourism; nature protection and soil conservation, environment and agriculture; urban environment, air quality, transport and noise; global environment, climate change, geosphere and biosphere).

Directorate C is responsible for environmental instruments and international affairs (international affairs; management and co-ordination of financial instruments in the environment field, programming and emergency aid; economic aspects; communication and training, environment and education).

(b)   Directorate General XII: Science, Research and Development

Directorate A is responsible for scientific and technological policy (framework programme: overall formulation of scientific and technological policy; co-ordination of scientific and technological policies of Member States; Researchers' Europe and integration with other Community policies; inter-institutional relations).

Directorate B is responsible for means of action (budget policy and management, financial co-ordination and Court of Auditors; research and technological development contract policy and management; personnel, data processing and co-ordination).

Directorate C is responsible for technological research (development and application of advanced technology; production and materials technologies; materials research; technical research (steel); mineral raw materials; Community Bureau of Reference (metrology and reference materials)).

Directorate D is responsible for nuclear safety research (nuclear plant safety; radioactive waste and fuel cycle; radiation protection, radiation biology and health effects, radiation risk evaluation and radioecology).

Directorate E is responsible for environment and non-nuclear energy sources (environment and waste recycling; climatology and natural hazards; renewable energy resources; geothermal energy; rational energy use and energy systems analysis; advanced fuel technology).

Directorate F is responsible for biology (CUBE (Concertation Unit for Biotechnology in Europe); biotechnology; agro-industrial research; biomass; renewable raw materials (timber); medical research).

Directorate G is responsible for scientific and technical co-operation with non-member countries (scientific and technical co-operation with the EFTA countries; Eureka; bilateral and multilateral scientific and technical co-operation with industrialised countries (other than EFTA); scientific and technical co-operation with developing countries).

Directorate H is responsible for science and technology policy support (development of scientific and technical co-operation and exchanges, support for researchers and training; strategic analysis of science and technology; science and technology forecasting; evaluation of research and development programmes; Espace).

[B14] The Economic and Social Committee, Treaty articles as enacted

Article 193

An Economic and Social Committee is hereby established. It shall have advisory status.

The Committee shall consist of representatives of the various categories of economic and social activity, in particular, representatives of producers, farmers, carriers, workers, dealers, craftsmen, professional occupations and representatives of the general public.

Article 194

The number of members of the Committee shall be as follows:

Belgium	12
Denmark	9
Germany	24
Greece	12
Spain	21
France	24
Ireland	9
Italy	24
Luxembourg	6
Netherlands	12
Portugal	12
United Kingdom	24

The members of the Committee shall be appointed by the Council, acting unanimously, for four years. Their appointments shall be renewable.

The members of the Committee shall be appointed in their personal capacity and may not be bound by any mandatory instructions.

Article 195

1. For the appointment of the members of the Committee, each Member State shall provide the Council with a list containing twice as many candidates as there are seats allotted to its nationals.

The composition of the Committee shall take account of the need to ensure adequate representation of the various categories of economic and social activity.

2. The Council shall consult the Commission. It may obtain the opinion of European bodies which are representative of the various economic and social sectors to which the activities of the Community are of concern.

Article 196

The Committee shall elect its chairman and officers from among its members for a term of two years.

It shall adopt its rules of procedure and shall submit them to the Council for its approval, which must be unanimous.

The Committee shall be convened by its chairman at the request of the Council or of the Commission.

Article 197

The Committee shall include specialised sections for the principal fields covered by this Treaty.

In particular, it shall contain an agricultural section and a transport section, which are the subject of special provisions in the Titles relating to agriculture and transport.

These specialised sections shall operate within the general terms of reference of the Committee. They may not be consulted independently of the Committee.

Sub-committees may also be established within the Committee to prepare on specific questions or in special fields, draft opinions to be submitted to the Committee for its consideration.

The rules of procedure shall lay down the methods of composition and the terms of reference of the specialised sections and of the sub-committees.

Article 198

The Committee must be consulted by the Council or by the Commission where this Treaty so provides. The Committee may be consulted by these institutions in all cases in which they consider it appropriate.

The Council or the Commission shall, if it considers it necessary, set the Committee, for the submission of its opinion, a time limit which may not be less than ten days from the date on which the chairman receives notification to this effect. Upon expiry of the time limit, the absence of an opinion shall not prevent further action.

The opinion of the Committee and that of the specialised section, together with a record of the proceedings, shall be forwarded to the Council and to the Commission.

[B15]   A session of the Economic and Social Committee (Bulletin of the European Communities, 1/2, 1992)

The Economic and Social Committee held its 294th plenary session in Brussels on 26 and 27 February, chaired by Mr Geuenich, and attended by

Mr Delors, President of the Commission, and Miss Papandreou, Member of the Commission.

Mr Delors presented the Commission's programme for 1992 and the second package of structural and financial measures (Delors II package). Completing the single market and implementing the Maastricht decisions meant that 1992 would be a crucial year for the Community's development, with the creation of a common foreign and security policy, the setting up of the Committee of the Regions, the improvement of transparency in the allocation of responsibilities through the operation of the subsidiarity principle, the definition of the criteria for enlargement in the context of a greater Europe, the reaffirmation of the importance of the economic and social cohesion [and] progress on the social dimension in 11 Member States. The Commission's programme accordingly revolved round four main priorities: the strengthening of economic and social cohesion, adoption of the changes needed in the common agricultural policy, creation of a favourable environment for competitiveness and expansion of the Community's external responsibilities.

. . .

The debate brought into focus the concerns of the various groups: continuing unemployment, an 11-member 'social' Europe, a discouraging economic climate, the expectations of environmentalists, Community participation at the Rio de Janeiro Conference, the future of the GATT negotiations, hostility towards the idea of a European tax, the reluctance of providers of services to accept responsibility, and the utilisation of the various Community funds. Mr Delors said the Commission would be pressing the Council to adopt its social proposals and to prepare for application of the protocol signed by 11 Member States. He said the Committee was irreplaceable because it represented all economic and social interests.

. . .

The Committee debated and adopted opinions on the following: the Annual Economic Report; the scheme for the exchange of national officials; the promotion of employee participation in profits and enterprise results; economic and social cohesion; the integrated systems for the management and supervision of certain Community aid schemes; the common organisation of the market in cereals; the common organisation of the market in tobacco; the common organisation of the market in milk and milk products; the common organisation of the market in beef and veal and sheepmeat; agricultural production methods compatible with the requirements of the protection of the environment and the maintenance of the countryside.

The Committee adopted opinions on the following without debate: the free movement of doctors and the mutual recognition of their diplomas, certificates and other evidence of formal qualifications; the approximation of the laws of the Member States relating to wheeled agricultural or forestry tractors; copyright and neighbouring rights applicable to satellite broadcasting and cable retransmission; the application of social security schemes to employed persons, to self-employed persons and to members of their families moving within the Community; the harmonisation of programmes for the reduction and eventual elimination of pollution caused by waste from the titanium dioxide industry; inter-branch organisations and agreements in the tobacco sector; the trans-European mobility scheme for university studies (Tempus); the national treatment instrument.

[B16]   The Committee of the Regions, Treaty articles inserted by the Treaty of Union

Article 198a

A Committee consisting of representatives of regional and local bodies, hereinafter referred to as 'the Committee of the Regions', is hereby established with advisory status.

The number of members of the Committee of the Regions shall be as follows:

Belgium	12
Denmark	9
Germany	24
Greece	12
Spain	21
France	24
Ireland	9
Italy	24
Luxembourg	6
Netherlands	12
Portugal	12
United Kingdom	24

The members of the Committee and an equal number of alternate members shall be appointed for four years by the Council acting unanimously on proposals from the respective Member States. Their term of office shall be renewable.

The members of the Committee may not be bound by any mandatory instructions. They shall be completely independent in the performance of their duties, in the general interest of the Community.

Article 198b

The Committee of the Regions shall elect its chairman and officers from among its members for a term of two years. It shall adopt its rules of procedure and shall submit them for approval to the Council, acting unanimously.

The Committee shall be convened by its chairman at the request of the Council or of the Commission. It may also meet on its own initiative.

Article 198c

The Committee of the Regions shall be consulted by the Council or by the Commission where this Treaty so provides and in all other cases in which one of these two institutions considers it appropriate.

The Council or the Commission shall, if it considers it necessary, set the Committee, for the submission of its opinion, a time limit which may not be less than one month from the date on which the chairman receives notification to this effect. Upon expiry of the time limit, the absence of an opinion shall not prevent further action.

Where the Economic and Social Committee is consulted pursuant to Article 198 **[B14]**, the Committee of the Regions shall be informed by the Council or the Commission of the request for an opinion. Where it considers that specific regional interests are involved, the Committee of the

Regions may issue an opinion on the matter.

It may issue an opinion on its own initiative in cases in which it considers such action appropriate.

The opinion of the Committee, together with a record of the proceedings, shall be forwarded to the Council and to the Commission.

SECTION TWO

COMMUNITY LEGISLATION

1 Community competence to legislate

There are two principal forms of Community legislation.

First, there is the 'primary legislation' created directly by the Member States. It comprises the Community law contained in the treaties establishing and developing the European Communities. Examples are the Treaty of Rome, the Merger Treaty, the Single European Act, the Accession Treaties making provisions for the accession to the Community of new Member States. In addition to the main text of a treaty there may be additional annexes and protocols which have the same legal force as their parent treaty. The treaties lay down the basic aims of the Community, establish the institutions and their powers, formulate the policies of the Community.

Secondly, there is the 'secondary legislation' of the Community, the legal rules created by the Community institutions under the authority of the treaties.

Community secondary legislation can only be enacted if there is a treaty provision authorising this. The Treaty does not confer general powers but enacts, in the respective articles, individual powers to act. However, it may be noted that if 'action by the Community should prove necessary to attain, in the course of the operations of the common market, one of the objectives of the Community and this Treaty has not provided the necessary powers, the Council shall, acting unanimously on a proposal from the Commission and after consulting the Assembly, take the appropriate measures' (Article 235: see, further, *Commission v Council* [B58]). Furthermore, as was seen in Chapter One, the Single European Act and the Treaty of Union greatly extend the areas of competence reserved for Community legislative action. Whether there is authority to enact secondary legislation, therefore, depends on the existence of a provision of a treaty. Any question as to whether the Community has authority to act at all and to the exclusion of the Member States, as to which institution has authority to act on behalf of the Community and as to whether that institution has acted in accordance with the correct procedures laid down may be referred to the Court of Justice (see Section Five of this chapter).

2 Secondary legislative measures

The principal secondary legislative measures are regulations and directives. Extracts from regulations and directives are given at appropriate places in this work (see, for example, [D9], [D14], [D29], [E59], [E78]).

In many cases, it is possible for secondary legislation to be drafted in such a way that its content can be translated directly and automatically into the domestic legal systems of each and every one of the Member States in order that Community law is identical in each Member State. The measure used here is the regulation. A regulation has 'general application', is 'binding in its entirety' in that a Member State cannot opt out of any provision in a regulation of which that state disapproves, and is 'directly applicable' in all Member States in that there is no need whatsoever for Member States to implement a regulation or transpose a regulation into its own domestic legal system. A regulation, therefore, is legislation created for each Member State by the Community and, as will be seen in Chapter Three, replaces any existing and conflicting rule created by the domestic legal system of a Member State. It is as though the exact words of a regulation automatically become part of the law of each Member State in a uniform manner and at the same time with no further action being required by the Member State. Member States do not need to ratify a regulation as a regulation is, in effect, deemed to have been ratified, irrespective of the fact that any rules contained therein are not enacted by any of the national Parliaments. The consequence of this is that a regulation may confer rights and obligations within a Member State on the Member State, any organisation of that state, all organisations and all individuals within that state. Regulations adopted by the Council must be published in the Official Journal of the European Communities by the Council's Secretary-General. On publication, see *Decker* [B17]. The Official Journal is published in each of the official languages of the Community.

On other occasions, it may be that the content of secondary legislation cannot be translated directly into the legal systems of the Member States in a uniform manner because different Member States may have different legislative and administrative mechanisms in their own systems for dealing with the relevant subject matter (eg statute, delegated legislation or Royal or Presidential Decree). The measure used here is the directive. A directive is actually addressed, usually through its final article, to a Member State or to some or all Member States. A directive is binding, as to the result to be achieved, upon each Member State to which it is addressed, but leaves to the national authorities the choice of form and methods. A directive, being addressed to Member States rather than directly applicable in Member States, is an instruction to each Member State to bring its legal system into exact conformity with the objectives specified in the directive (and within a specified time limit). It will usually impose this obligation by stating that 'Member States shall take the measures necessary to' achieve the purpose(s) intended and conveyed therein (see, for example, [C2], [D9]). Although not expressly stated, the obvious implication is that the purposes of a directive must be achieved in their entirety. The specified time limit may be months or years and this permits each Member State to proceed at its own speed to repeal existing domestic laws, regulations and administrative practices and to enact new domestic laws, regulations and administrative practices. A directive differs from a regulation in that what creates its normative force is not (as it is with a regulation) the adoption by the Community institution of the directive but the entry into force of the national implementing measures (Act of Parliament or Ministerial or Royal Decree). Therefore the rule becomes 'law' in a Member State when that Member State implements the directive (provided that it does so within the prescribed time limit). If a Member State fails to fulfil the instruction, the omission may be rectified by the Commission (or another Member State) bringing an action before the Court of Justice (see Chapter Three, Section One) or by an individual in the national courts of the Member State under the principle of 'direct effect', created by the European Court of Justice, although it must be mentioned here that the principle of direct effect only has the result of imposing an obligation on the Member State (or one of its organs) and not on private organisations or individuals (see Chapter Three, Section Three). Although at one time it might have been possible to argue that a directive is a less burdensome legislative tool and to allow a degree of divergence of implementation within the Member States as to detail, provided that the overall general purpose was achieved, and it was possible to query whether the 'result to be achieved' could include the imposition of detailed rules in their entirety within each Member State to which a directive was addressed, it has to be accepted now that, in their wording, many directives appear little different from regulations (cf Directive 68/360 [D9] and Regulation 1612/68 [D14]) and both the Commission and the European Court of Justice have insisted that the obligation to implement a directive, where the wording of the directive so requires, be achieved to the very last letter (*Von Colson* [C29], *Marleasing* [C31]).

As an example of national implementing measures to give effect to the White Paper of the Commission on the completion of the internal market, one may take Council Directive 89/108 of 21 December 1988 on the approximation of the laws of the Member States relating to quick frozen foodstuffs for human consumption (OJ L40, 11 February 1989). This was, for example, implemented in Belgium by an Arrêté Royal/Koninklijk Bestuit, published in the Moniteur Belge/Belgisch Staatsblad, in Spain by a Real Decreto, published in the Boletín Oficial del Estado, in France by a Décret, published in the Journal Officiel, in Luxembourg by a Règlement Grand Ducal, published in the Duchy's Mémorial, in Portugal by a Decreto-Lei, published in the Diário de República, and in the United Kingdom by the Quick-Frozen Foodstuffs Regulations 1990 (SI 1990 No 2615) and the Quick-Frozen Foodstuffs Regulations (Northern Ireland) 1990 (Statutory Rules of Northern Ireland No 455), published by HMSO.

Sometimes the Community will wish to make a legally binding rule which only affects one or a limited number of Member States or an identifiable organisation or even one individual. Sometimes the Community will wish to require a Member State to take a course of action which does not directly concern individuals and which does not have to become in any direct way the law of the Member State. Sometimes the Community makes what are more akin to administrative decisions (in particular in the organisation of agricultural and competition matters). The measure here is called a decision (see, for example, [B18], [C4], [C5], [E76] and [E81]). A decision is binding on the addressee of the decision.

The Council must decide unanimously whether directives and decisions should be published for the purposes of information in the Official Journal of the European Communities. As a matter of normal practice, directives are usually published in the Official Journal, which is published in each of the official languages of the Community.

3   The Community legislator

As was stated in Section One of this chapter, the nearest equivalent within the Community to a national legislature is the Council. In practice, the Council, being in legal form simply a small group of representatives from each Member State, cannot possibly undertake the vast amount of labour involved, or possess the complete expertise needed, in the enactment of secondary legislation. Consequently, the Council works through working parties composed of the administrative staff of the Council and the Committee of Permanent Representatives (see Section One of this chapter).

COREPER will co-ordinate the work needed to prepare the Council for the formal adoption of secondary legislation and, in practice, unanimity achieved within COREPER will often result in speedy adoption by the Council.

In essence, the Community 'legislator' represents a balance of power between the representatives of the Member States (the Council of Ministers) and the representative of the Community (the Commission). The balance is laid down in the Treaty [B19] and is achieved by the fact that the final decision belongs to the Council, and Treaty provisions will expressly state that regulations, directives and decisions are to be made, issued and taken by the Council, but the Council can only act upon a proposal from the Commission (see eg Articles [7], 49, 51 and 100a) and if the Council acts on a proposal from the Commission unanimity is required for an act constituting an amendment to that proposal (Article 149.1: re-enacted as Article 189a.1 by the Treaty of Union). There is a further balance between the desire to allow Member States to protect their national interests and the desire to limit the right of Member States to veto matters on which there is overwhelming agreement by the majority of Member States. This is achieved by provisions which provide for decisions to be taken by the Council by a simple majority of states (Article 148.1), by unanimity (see eg Articles 51, 100 and 235 (above)) and by a 'qualified majority', designed to achieve some measure of weighting according to the population of the state (Article 148.2). A feature of the development of the Community has been a gradual change from the requirement of unanimity to the requirement of qualified majority. The Single European Act took this even further by amending a number of important provisions of the EEC Treaty which required unanimity so that, in the interests of 'unblocking' and speeding up the Community decision-making process, the requirement now is only that of a qualified majority and by making legislative decision making in several of the new areas of Community competence (including the key Article 100a relating to the internal market: see [E38]–[E44]) subject to qualified majority voting. This process is taken further by the Treaty of Union. In 1966, the Council attempted to lay down a procedure, which has no constitutional validity, whereby a Member State's particular interests might be recognised (the Luxembourg Accords [B20]).

There is no single legislative procedure that is applied unwaveringly to the creation of all secondary legislation.

In all cases the Council, as has been seen, can only act following a proposal from the Commission. The Commission may initiate a proposal of its own motion or it may be required by the Council to draw up a proposal. The proposal will be drafted within the appropriate Commission Directorate(s) General and the final text, if approved by the Commission, will be submitted to the Council for formal adoption.

However, other Community institutions may, in varying degrees and in accordance with the specific wording of the provision authorising legislative activity, also have a role to play. In addition to the Council and the Commission, a role may be played by the European Parliament and by the Economic and Social Committee. The Council may be required to consult the European Parliament (eg Article 100), may be required to act in co-operation with the European Parliament (eg Articles [7] and 100a), or there may be no obligation to involve the European Parliament (eg Article 51). The Council may be required to consult the Economic and Social Committee (eg Article 49) or there may be no obligation to involve the

Economic and Social Committee (eg Article 51). If the Treaty requires the Council to act 'in co-operation with' the Parliament, a special 'co-operation procedure' must be followed. The co-operation procedure is applied to several important Treaty provisions (eg Articles [7] and 100a) and is described in Article 149.2 (re-enacted as Article 189c by the Treaty of Union). Essentially, the procedure strengthens the role of the European Parliament but, in the last resort, the Council's ultimate powers are not reduced. An example of the various stages involved in the co-operation procedure between the Commission, Council and European Parliament, together with the participation of the Economic and Social Committee, is given in **[B22]–[B28]**. Under the Treaty of Union, a new form of legislative procedure is introduced. This involves the establishment of a Conciliation Committee composed of an equal number of members of the Council, or their representatives, and of the European Parliament. The co-decision procedure applies mainly to policies where qualified majority voting is provided for. The Parliament will have a rejection power but not one of legislative initiative (Article 189b **[B19]**).

It must be emphasised that if there is a requirement to consult the European Parliament or Economic and Social Committee or if there is a requirement to act in co-operation with the European Parliament and the Council fails to carry out such an obligation, the secondary legislation in question may be annulled by the Court of Justice (see Section Five of this chapter).

MATERIALS

[B17] Case 99/78 Weingut Gustav Decker KG v Hauptzollamt Landau [1979] ECR 101

The European Court of Justice (at pp 109–110)

3. [The Court cited Article 191 **[B19]**].

The Official Journal is published by the Office for Official Publications of the European Communities, situated in Luxembourg, which has received formal instructions from the Council intended to ensure that the date of publication borne by each issue of the Official Journal corresponds to the date on which that issue is in fact available to the public in all the languages at the said Office.

These provisions give rise to a presumption that the date of publication is in fact the date appearing on each issue of the Official Journal.

However, should evidence be produced that the date on which an issue was in fact available does not correspond to the date which appears on that issue, regard must be had to the date of actual publication.

A fundamental principle in the Community legal order requires that a measure adopted by the public authorities shall not be applicable to those concerned before they have the opportunity to make themselves acquainted with it.

4. [It] is important that the date on which a regulation is to be regarded as published should not vary according to the availability of the Official Journal of the Communities in the territory of each Member State.

The unity and uniform application of Community law require that, save as otherwise expressly provided, a regulation should enter into force on the same date in all the Member States, regardless of any delays which may arise in spite of efforts to ensure rapid distribution of the Official Journal throughout the Community.

5. Therefore [Article 191] must be interpreted to mean that, in the absence of evidence to the contrary, a regulation is to be regarded as published throughout the Community on the date borne by the issue of the Official Journal containing the text of that regulation.

[B18] Commission decision on import licences in respect of beef and veal products originating in Botswana, Kenya, Madagascar, Swaziland, Zimbabwe and Namibia (Decision 92/89: OJ L32/35, 8 February 1992)

Article 1

The following Member States shall issue on 21 December 1991 import licences concerning beef and veal products, expressed in terms of boned meat, originating in certain African, Caribbean and Pacific States, in respect of the quantities and the countries of origin stated:

Belgium:
– 20.48 tonnes originating in Madagascar;
Greece:
– 17.00 tonnes originating in Madagascar;
Germany:
– 40.00 tonnes originating in Botswana;
– 2.10 tonnes originating in Swaziland;
United Kingdom:
– 100.00 tonnes originating in Botswana.

Article 2

Applications for licences may be submitted [during] the first ten days of January 1992 in respect of the following quantities of boned beef and veal:
– Botswana: 18,776.00 tonnes
– Kenya: 142.00 tonnes
– Madagascar: 7,541.52 tonnes
– Swaziland: 3,360.90 tonnes
– Zimbabwe: 9,100.00 tonnes
– Namibia: 10,500.00 tonnes

Article 3

This decision is addressed to the Member States.

[B19]   Secondary legislation, Treaty articles

Article 7(1) (re-numbered as 6(1) by the Treaty of Union)

Within the scope of application of this Treaty, and without prejudice to any special provisions contained therein, any discrimination on grounds of nationality shall be prohibited.

Article 7(2) (as enacted)

The Council may, on a proposal from the Commission and after consulting the Assembly, adopt, by a qualified majority, rules designed to prohibit such discrimination.

Article 7(2) (as amended by the Single European Act)

The Council may, on a proposal from the Commission and in co-operation with the European Parliament, adopt, by a qualified majority, rules designed to prohibit such discrimination.

Article 6b(2) (as re-numbered and amended by the Treaty of Union)

The Council, acting in accordance with the procedure referred to in Article 189c, may adopt rules designed to prohibit such discrimination.

Article 49 (as enacted)

As soon as this Treaty enters into force, the Council shall, acting on a proposal from the Commission and after consulting the Economic and Social

Committee, issue directives or make regulations setting out the measures required to bring about, by progressive stages, freedom of movement for workers.

. . .

Article 49 (as amended by the Single European Act)

As soon as this Treaty enters into force, the Council shall, acting by a quali- fied majority on a proposal from the Commission, in co-operation with the European Parliament and after consulting the Economic and Social Committee, issue directives or make regulations setting out the measures required to bring about, by progressive stages, freedom of movement for workers.

. . .

Article 49 (as amended by the Treaty of Union)

As soon as this Treaty enters into force, the Council shall, acting in accor- dance with the procedure referred to in Article 189b and after consulting the Economic and Social Committee, issue directives or make regulations set- ting out the measures required to bring about, by progressive stages, freedom of movement for workers . . .

Article 51

The Council shall, acting unanimously on a proposal from the Commission, adopt such measures in the field of social security as are necessary to pro- vide freedom of movement for workers.

. . .

Article 59(1)

Within the framework of the provisions set out below, restrictions on free- dom to provide services within the Community shall be progressively abolished during the transitional period in respect of nationals of Member States who are established in a state of the Community other than that of the person for whom the services are intended.

Article 59(2) (as enacted)

The Council may, acting unanimously on a proposal from the Commission, extend the provisions of this Chapter to nationals of a third country who provide services and who are established within the Community.

Article 59(2) (as amended by the Single European Act)

The Council may, acting by a qualified majority on a proposal from the Commission, extend the provisions of this Chapter to nationals of a third country who provide services and who are established within the Community.

Article 100 (as enacted)

The Council shall, acting unanimously on a proposal from the Commission, issue directives for the approximation of such provisions laid down by law, regulation or administrative action in Member States as directly affect the establishment or functioning of the common market.

The Assembly and the Economic and Social Committee shall be consulted in the case of directives whose implementation would, in one or more Member States, involve the amendment of legislation.

Article 100 (as amended by the Single European Act)

The Council shall, acting unanimously on a proposal from the Commission, issue directives for the approximation of such provisions laid down by law, regulation or administrative action in Member States as directly affect the establishment or functioning of the common market.

The European Parliament and the Economic and Social Committee shall be consulted in the case of directives whose implementation would, in one or more Member States, involve the amendment of legislation.

Article 100a (as inserted by the Single European Act)

1. By way of derogation from Article 100 and save where otherwise provided in this Treaty, the following provisions shall apply for the achievement of the objectives set out in Article 8a. The Council shall, acting by a qualified majority on a proposal from the Commission in co-operation with the European Parliament and after consulting the Economic and Social Committee, adopt the measures for the approximation of the provisions laid down by law, regulation or administrative action in Member States which have as their object the establishment and functioning of the internal market.

Article 148

1. Save as otherwise provided in this Treaty, the Council shall act by a majority of its members.

2. Where the Council is required to act by a qualified majority, the votes of its members shall be weighted as follows:

Belgium	5
Denmark	3
Germany	10
Greece	5
Spain	8
France	10
Ireland	3
Italy	10
Luxembourg	2
Netherlands	5
Portugal	5
United Kingdom	10

For their adoption, acts of the Council shall require at least:

- 54 votes in favour where this Treaty requires them to be adopted on a proposal from the Commission,
- 54 votes in favour, cast by at least eight members, in other cases.

3. Abstentions by members present in person or represented shall not prevent the adoption by the Council of acts which require unanimity.

Article 149

Note. Article 149 is repealed by the Treaty of Union and re-enacted in new Articles 189a and 189c (below).

1. Where, in pursuance of this Treaty, the Council acts on a proposal from the Commisssion, unanimity shall be required for an act constituting an amendment to that proposal.

[The co-operation procedure]

2. Where, in pursuance of this Treaty, the Council acts in co-operation with the European Parliament, the following procedure shall apply:

(a) The Council, acting by a qualified majority under the conditions of paragraph 1, on a proposal from the Commission and after obtaining the opinion of the European Parliament, shall adopt a common position.

(b) The Council's common position shall be communicated to the European Parliament. The Council and the Commission shall inform the European Parliament fully of the reasons which led the Council to adopt its common position and also of the Commission's position.

If, within three months of such communication, the European Parliament approves this common position or has not taken a decision within that period, the Council shall definitively adopt the act in question in accordance with the common position.

(c) The European Parliament may, within the period of three months referred to in point (b), by an absolute majority of its component members, propose amendments to the Council's common position. The European Parliament may also, by the same majority, reject the Council's common position. The result of the proceedings shall be transmitted to the Council and the Commission.

If the European Parliament has rejected the Council's common position, unanimity shall be required for the Council to act on a second reading.

(d) The Commission shall, within a period of one month, re-examine the proposal on the basis of which the Council adopted its common position, by taking into account the amendments proposed by the European Parliament.

The Commission shall forward to the Council, at the same time as its re-examined proposal, the amendments of the European Parliament which it has not accepted, and shall express its opinion on them. The Council may adopt these amendments unanimously.

(e) The Council, acting by a qualified majority, shall adopt the proposal as re-examined by the Commission.

Unanimity shall be required for the Council to amend the proposal as re-examined by the Commission.

(f) In the cases referred to in points (c), (d) and (e), the Council shall be required to act within a period of three months. If no decision is taken within this period, the Commission proposal shall be deemed not to have been adopted.

(g) The periods referred to in points (b) and (f) may be extended by a maximum of one month by common accord between the Council and the European Parliament.

3. As long as the Council has not acted, the Commission may alter its proposal at any time during the procedures mentioned in paragraphs 1 and 2.

Article 189 (as enacted)

In order the carry out their task the Council and the Commission shall, in accordance with the provisions of this Treaty, make regulations, issue directives, take decisions, make recommendations or deliver opinions.

A regulation shall have general application. It shall be binding in its entirety and directly applicable in all Member States.

A directive shall be binding, as to the result to be achieved, upon each Member State to which it is addressed, but shall leave to the national authorities the choice of form and methods.

A decision shall be binding in its entirety upon those to whom it is addressed.

Recommendations and opinions shall have no binding force.

Article 189(1) (as amended by the Treaty of Union)

In order the carry out their task and in accordance with the provisions of this Treaty, the European Parliament acting jointly with the Council, the Council and the Commission shall make regulations and issue directives, take decisions, make recommendations or deliver opinions.

Article 189a (as inserted by the Treaty of Union)

1. Where, in pursuance of this Treaty, the Council acts on a proposal from the Commission, unanimity shall be required for an act constituting an amendment to that proposal, subject to Article 189b(4) and (5).

2. As long as the Council has not acted, the Commission may alter its proposal at any time during the procedures leading to the adoption of a Community act.

Article 189b (as inserted by the Treaty of Union)

1. Where reference is made in this Treaty to this Article [see, eg, Article 129a(2): **[A6]**] for the adoption of an act, the following procedure shall apply.

2. The Commission shall submit a proposal to the European Parliament and the Council.

The Council, acting by a qualified majority after obtaining the opinion of the European Parliament, shall adopt a common position. The common position shall be communicated to the European Parliament. The Council shall inform the European Parliament fully of the reasons which led it to adopt its common position. The Commission shall inform the European Parliament fully of its position.

If, within three months of such communication, the European Parliament:

(a)   approves the common position, the Council shall definitively adopt the act in question in accordance with that common position;

(b)   has not taken a decision, the Council shall adopt the act in question in accordance with its common position;

(c)   indicates, by an absolute majority of its component members, that it intends to reject the common position, it shall immediately inform the

Council. The Council may convene a meeting of the Conciliation Committee referred to in paragraph 4 to explain further its position. The European Parliament shall thereafter either confirm, by an absolute majority of its component members, its rejection of the common position, in which event the proposed act shall be deemed not to have been adopted, or propose amendments in accordance with subparagraph (d) of this paragraph;

(d)   proposes amendments to the common position by an absolute majority of its component members, the amended text shall be forwarded to the Council and to the Commission, which shall deliver an opinion on those amendments.

3. If, within three months of the matter being referred to it, the Council, acting by a qualified majority, approves all the amendments of the European Parliament, it shall amend its common position accordingly and adopt the act in question; however, the Council shall act unanimously on the amendments on which the Commission has delivered a negative opinion. If the Council does not approve the act in question, the President of the Council, in agreement with the President of the European Parliament, shall forthwith convene a meeting of the Conciliation Committee.

4. The Conciliation Committee, which shall be composed of the members of the Council or their representatives and an equal number of representatives of the European Parliament, shall have the task of reaching agreement on a joint text, by a qualified majority of the members of the Council or their representatives and by a majority of the representatives of the European Parliament. The Commission shall take part in the Conciliation Committee's proceedings and shall take all the necessary initiatives with a view to reconciling the positions of the European Parliament and the Council.

5. If, within six weeks of its being convened, the Conciliation Committee approves a joint text, the European Parliament, acting by an absolute majority of the votes cast, and the Council, acting by a qualified majority, shall have a period of six weeks from that approval in which to adopt the act in question in accordance with the joint text. If one of the two institutions fails to approve the proposed act, it shall be deemed not to have been adopted.

6. Where the Conciliation Committee does not approve a joint text, the proposed act shall be deemed not to have been adopted unless the Council, acting by a qualified majority within six weeks of expiry of the period granted to the Conciliation Committee, confirms the common position to which it agreed before the conciliation procedure was initiated, possibly with amendments proposed by the European Parliament. In this case, the act in question shall be finally adopted unless the European Parliament, within six weeks of the date of confirmation by the Council, rejects the text by an absolute majority of its component members, in which case the proposed act shall be deemed not to have been adopted.

7. The periods of three months and six weeks referred to in this Article may be extended by a maximum of one month and two weeks respectively by common accord of the European Parliament and the Council. The period of three months referred to in paragraph 2 shall be automatically extended by two months where paragraph 2(c) applies.

8. The scope of the procedure under under this article may be widened [on] the basis of a report to be submitted to the Council by the Commission by 1996 at the latest.

Article 189c (as inserted by the Treaty of Union)

Where reference is made in this Treaty to this Article for the adoption of an act [see eg Article 130s: **[A6]**], the following procedure shall apply:

(a)   The Council, acting by a qualified majority on a proposal from the Commission and after obtaining the opinion of the European Parliament, shall adopt a common position.

(b)   The Council's common position shall be communicated to the European Parliament. The Council and the Commission shall inform the European Parliament fully of the reasons which led the Council to adopt its common position and also of the Commission's position.

   If, within three months of such communication, the European Parliament approves this common position or has not taken a decision within that period, the Council shall definitively adopt the act in question in accordance with the common position.

(c)   The European Parliament may, within the period of three months referred to in subparagraph (b), by an absolute majority of its component members, propose amendments to the Council's common position. The European Parliament may also, by the same majority, reject the Council's common position. The result of the proceedings shall be transmitted to the Council and the Commission.

   If the European Parliament has rejected the Council's common position, unanimity shall be required for the Council to act on a second reading.

(d)   The Commission shall, within a period of one month, re-examine the proposal on the basis of which the Council adopted its common position, by taking into account the amendments proposed by the European Parliament.

   The Commission shall forward to the Council, at the same time as its re-examined proposal, the amendments of the European Parliament which it has not accepted, and shall express its opinion on them. The Council may adopt these amendments unanimously.

(e)   The Council, acting by a qualified majority, shall adopt the proposal as re-examined by the Commission.

   Unanimity shall be required for the Council to amend the proposal as re-examined by the Commission.

(f)   In the cases referred to in subparagraphs (c), (d) and (e), the Council shall be required to act within a period of three months. If no decision is taken within this period, the Commission proposal shall be deemed not to have been adopted.

(g)   The periods referred to in subparagraphs (b) and (f) may be extended by a maximum of one month by common accord between the Council and the European Parliament.

Article 190 (as enacted)

Regulations, directives and decisions of the Council and of the Commission shall state the reasons on which they are based and shall refer to any proposals or opinions which were required to be obtained pursuant to this Treaty.

Article 191 (as enacted)

Regulations shall be published in the Official Journal of the Community. They shall enter into force on the date specified in them or, in the absence thereof, on the twentieth day following their publication.

Directives and decisions shall be notified to those to whom they are addressed and shall take effect upon such notification.

[B20] The Luxembourg Accords (Extraordinary Council session of 28 and 29 January 1966)

. . .

(b) Majority voting procedure

I. Where, in the case of decisions which may be taken by majority vote on a proposal of the Commission, very important interests of one or more partners are at stake, the Members of the Council will endeavour, within a reasonable time, to reach solutions which can be adopted by all the Members of the Council while respecting their mutual interests and those of the Community, in accordance with Article 2 of the Treaty.

[B21] The legislative process – European Parliament Rules of Procedure

Note. These rules are taken from the latest published version of the Parliament's rules (1987). In September 1993 proposals (EP Working Document A3-240/93) to amend the rules consequent upon the coming into force of the Treaty of Union were submitted to and approved by the European Parliament.

CONSULTATION PROCEDURE: ACTS REQUIRING ONE READING

Rule 36 Consultation of Parliament

1. Requests from the Council or Commission for an opinion or for advice shall be printed and distributed. The President shall refer such requests to the appropriate committee for consideration.

2. A list of these requests for an opinion or for advice shall be published in the Bulletin of Parliament, together with the name of the committee responsible and a description of the chosen legal base for the draft measure.

3. The committee responsible shall examine the validity and appropriateness of the chosen legal base for any draft measure on which Parliament is consulted. Where it disputes the validity or appropriateness of the legal base it may, before dealing with the substance of the proposal and after consultation with the committee responsible for legal affairs, refer the matter to Parliament, reporting orally or in writing.

. . .

5. Parliament shall first vote on the amendments to the proposal with which the report of the committee responsible is concerned, then on the proposal, amended or otherwise, then on the amendments to the draft legislative resolution, then on the draft legislative resolution as a whole, which shall only contain a statement as to whether Parliament approves, rejects or proposes amendments to the Commission's proposal and any procedural requests.

The consultation procedure is concluded if the draft legislative resolution is adopted.

. . .

7. The text of the proposal as approved by Parliament and its accompanying resolution shall be forwarded to the Council and Commission by the President as Parliament's opinion.

. . .

Rule 39   *Rejection of a Commission proposal*

1. If a Commission proposal fails to secure a majority of the votes cast, the President shall, before Parliament votes on the draft legislative resolution, request the Commission to withdraw the proposal.

2. If the Commission does so, the President shall hold the consultation procedure on the proposal to be superfluous and shall inform the Council accordingly.

3. If the Commission does not withdraw its proposal, Parliament shall refer the matter back to the committee responsible without voting on the draft legislative resolution.

. . .

Rule 40   *Amendment of a Commission proposal*

1. Where the Commission proposal as a whole is approved, but on the basis of amendments which have also been adopted, the vote on the draft legislative resolution shall be postponed until the Commission has stated its proposal on each of Parliament's amendments.

. . .

2. Where the Commission announces that it does not intend to adopt all Parliament's amendments, the rapporteur of the committee responsible or, failing him, the chairman of that committee shall make a formal proposal to Parliament as to whether the vote on the draft legislative resolution should proceed.

. . .

Should Parliament decide to postpone the vote, the matter shall be deemed to be referred back to the committee responsible for reconsideration.

. . .

PARLIAMENTARY ACTION IN THE EVENT OF FAILURE BY THE COUNCIL OR THE COMMISSION TO ABIDE BY PARLIAMENT'S OPINION

Rule 41 Follow-up to Parliament's opinion

1. In the period following the adoption by Parliament of its opinion on a proposal by the Commission, the chairman and the rapporteur of the committee responsible shall monitor the progress of the proposal in the course of the procedure leading to its adoption by the Council to ensure that the undertakings made by the Commission to Parliament with respect to its amendments are properly observed.

2. The Council or, if necessary, the Commission shall during this period and at least once every three months, furnish all necessary information to the committee responsible.

3. The committee responsible shall, in particular, bring to Parliament's attention any potential or actual breach of undertakings made by the Commission to Parliament.

4. The committee responsible may, if it deems it necessary, at any stage of the follow-up procedure table a motion for a resolution under this Rule inviting Parliament:

– to call upon the Commission to withdraw its proposal, or
– to call upon the Council to open a conciliation procedure with the Parliament, pursuant to Rule 43, or
– to call upon the Council to reconsult Parliament pursuant to Rule 42, or
– to decide to take such other action that it deems appropriate.

. . .

Rule 42 Renewed consultation

The President shall, at the request of the committee responsible, call on the Council to reconsult Parliament:

– where the Commission withdraws its initial proposal after Parliament has delivered its opinion in order to replace it with another text, or
– where the Commission or the Council substantially amend or intend to amend the proposal on which Parliament originally delivered an opinion, or
– where, through the passage of time or changes in circumstances, the nature of the problem with which the proposal is concerned substantially changes.

The President shall also request reconsultation in the circumstances defined in this Rule where Parliament so decides on a proposal from a political group or at least 23 members.

Rule 43 Conciliation procedure

1. Where, in the case of certain important Community decisions, the Council intends to depart from the opinion of Parliament, a procedure for conciliation with the Council, with the active participation of the Commission, may be opened by Parliament when delivering its opinion.

2. This procedure shall be initiated by Parliament, either at its own or at the Council's initiative.

3. The delegation which consults with the Council shall consist of a

number of members corresponding to the number of members of the Council; it shall reflect the political composition of Parliament, care being taken to ensure balanced representation of political tendencies; in principle it shall include the chairmen and the rapporteurs of the committees concerned.

. . .

4. The committee responsible shall report on the results of the conciliation. This report shall be debated and voted on by Parliament.

CO-OPERATION PROCEDURE: ACTS REQUIRING TWO READINGS

Rule 44   First and second reading

1. For acts requiring two readings in accordance with the co-operation procedure laid down in Article 149(2) **[B19]**, the procedure for the first reading shall be identical to the procedure set out in Rules 36 to 43.
2. For the second reading, the provisions in Rules 44 to 52 shall apply.

. . .

Rule 45   Communication of the common position of the Council

1. Communication of the common position of the [Council] takes place when it is announced by the President in Parliament. On the day of the announcement, the President must have received the documents containing the common position itself, the reasons which led the Council to adopt its common position and the Commission's position, duly translated into the official languages of the Community.

. . .

2. A list of such communications shall be published in the Bulletin of Parliament together with the name of the committee responsible.

Rule 46   Time limits

1. The President shall, on a request from the chairman or the rapporteur of the committee responsible, ask the Council's agreement to extend the period of three months following either the communication of the common position to Parliament or the presentation of the Commission's re-examined proposal by a maximum of one month.
2. The President may, after consulting the chairman and the rapporteur of the committee responsible, on behalf of Parliament agree, on a request from the Council, to extend the period of three months following the communication of the common position to Parliament or the presentation of the Commission's re-examined proposal by a maximum of one month.

Rule 47   Referral to and procedure in the committee responsible

1. On the day of its communication to Parliament pursuant to Rule 45(1), the common position shall be deemed to have been referred automatically to the committee responsible and to the committees asked for their opinion at first reading.

. . .

4. The provisions for Parliament's second reading in Rules 50(1) and 51(2) shall apply to the proceedings in the committee responsible; only members or permanent substitutes of that committee may table amendments. The committee shall decide by a majority of the votes cast.

5. The committee responsible may request a dialogue with the Council in order to reach a compromise.

6. The committee responsible shall submit a Recommendation on the Second Reading as to the decision which Parliament should take with respect to the common position adopted by the Council. The Recommendation shall include a short justification for the decision proposed.

Rule 48 Conclusion of the co-operation procedure

1. The Council's common position and, where available, the Recommendation on the Second Reading of the committee responsible shall automatically be placed on the draft agenda for the part-session whose Wednesday falls before and closest to the day of expiry of the period of three months or, if extended in accordance with Rule 46, of four months, unless the matter has been dealt with at an earlier part-session.

2. The co-operation procedure is concluded by Parliament approving, rejecting or amending the common position within the time limits and in accordance with the conditions laid down by the Single Act.

Rule 49 Approval without amendment of the common position of the Council

Where no motion to reject the common position, and no amendments to the common position, are adopted under Rules 50 and 51 within the time limits specified by the Single Act, the President shall declare the common position adopted without a vote, unless Parliament has marked its approval of the common position by a majority of the votes cast.

Rule 50 Rejection of the common position of the Council

1. Any member may, in writing and before a deadline fixed by the President, table a proposal to reject the common position of the Council. Such a proposal shall require for its adoption the votes of a majority of the current Members of Parliament.

. . .

2. Notwithstanding a vote by Parliament against the initial proposal to reject the common position, Parliament may, on the recommendation of the rapporteur, consider a further proposal for rejection after voting on the amendments and hearing a statement from the Commission pursuant to Rule 51(4).

3. If the common position of the Council is rejected, the President shall request the Commision to withdraw its proposal.

4. If the Commission does so, the President shall hold the co-operation procedure on the proposal to be superfluous and shall inform the Council accordingly.

Rule 51   Amendments to the common position of the Council

1. A committee, a political group or at least 23 members may table amendments to the Council's common position for consideration in Parliament.

2. An amendment to the common position shall be admissible only [if]:

(a)   it seeks to restore wholly or partly the position adopted by Parliament in its first reading; or

(b)   it is a compromise amendment representing an agreement between the Council and Parliament.

The President's discretion to declare an amendment admissible or inadmissible cannot be questioned.

3. An amendment shall be adopted only if it secures the votes of a majority of the current Members of Parliament.

4. If one or more of the amendments are adopted, the rapporteur of the committee responsible or, failing him, the chairman of that committee shall ask the Commission whether it proposes to include such amendments in its re-examined proposal.

Rule 52   The consequences of the Commission failing to accept Parliament's amendments in its re-examined proposal

1. The enlarged Bureau shall place the Commission's re-examined proposal on the draft agenda for the part-session following its adoption and the Parliament shall request the Commission to inform Parliament of the reasons which led the Commission to fail to accept Parliament's amendments.

2. Parliament may, by a majority of its current members, request the Commission to withdraw its proposal.

Rule 54   The consequences of the Council failing to act following approval of its common position

If, within three months or, with the agreement of the Council, up to four months following the communication of the common position, Parliament has neither rejected nor amended that position and where the Council fails to adopt the proposed legislation in accordance with the common position, the President may, on behalf of Parliament and after consulting the committee responsible for legal affairs, bring an action against the Council in the Court of Justice under Article [175: **[B29]**].

[B22]   Commission proposal for a Directive on Toy Safety

[On 22 October 1986, the Commission submitted a proposal to the Council for a directive on the approximation of the laws of the Member States concerning the safety of toys (COM(86) 541 final: OJ C282/4, 8 November 1986). The recital of reasons for the draft directive were:]

Whereas the laws, regulations and administrative provisions in force in Member States relating to the safety characteristics of toys differ in scope and content; whereas such disparities are liable to create barriers to trade and unequal conditions of competition within the Community without necessarily affording consumers in the common market, especially children, effective protection against the hazards arising from the products in question;

Whereas these obstacles to the attainment of an internal market in which only sufficiently safe products would be sold should be removed; whereas for this purpose the marketing and free movement of toys should be made subject to uniform rules based on the objectives regarding protection of consumer health and safety as set out in the Council resolution of 6 May 1985 on a new impetus for consumer protection policy;

Whereas total harmonisation in this area is necessary since children's health and safety cannot be allowed to remain subject to different standards of protection in the various Member States;

. . .

Whereas, in view of the size and mobility of the toy market and the diversity of the products concerned, the scope of this Directive should be determined on the basis of a sufficiently broad definition of 'toys'; whereas nevertheless it should be specified that some products are not to be regarded as toys for the purposes of this Directive either because they are not in fact intended for children or because they call for supervision or special conditions of use;

Whereas toys placed on the market should not jeopardise the safety and/or health either of children using the toys or of third parties, domestic animals or property;

. . .

Whereas compliance with the essential requirements is likely to guarantee consumer health and safety; whereas all toys placed on the market must comply with these requirements and, if they do, no obstacle must be put in the way of their free movement;

Whereas toys may be presumed to comply with these essential requirements where they are in conformity with the European standards or harmonisation documents adopted by the European Committte for Standardisation (CEN) and the European Committee for Electrotechinal Standardisation (CENELEC) at the request of the Commission . . .;

Whereas toys that conform to a model approved by an inspection body may also be regarded as complying with the essential requirements; whereas such conformity must be certified by the affixing of a European mark; whereas manufacturers who decide to manufacture toys in conformity with standards must have the choice either of submitting a model for approval or of informing an inspection body of their intention;

. . .

Whereas Member States must appoint inspection bodies for application of the system introduced for toys;

. . .

Whereas for some categories of toys that are particularly dangerous or intended for very young children warnings or details of precautions to be taken must also be [given].

[B23] Opinion of the Economic and Social Committee (OJ C232/22, 31 August 1987)

On 20 November 1986 the Council decided to consult the Economic and Social Committee, under Article 198 of the [Treaty]. The Committee instructed its Section for Protection of the Environment, Public Health and Consumer Affairs to prepare its work on the matter. [At] its 247th plenary session (meeting of 1 July 1987) the Economic and Social Committee adopted unanimously the following opinion:

1. General comments

1.1. It is now 12 years since the Commission first set out to produce Community legislation on the safety of toys. Different draft directives were considered by [the European Parliament and the Economic and Social Committee], but were consequently withdrawn by the Commission. In the present case, the Commission's document is based on these earlier proposals. While the inclusion of elements from these earlier proposals is a good thing, there is a consequent unwieldiness, particularly as regards administration.

1.2. Introduction

[1.2.3.] The draft directive aims to bring the diversity in legislation on toy safety into a harmonised whole within the internal market, with a common approach to safety and common rules to achieve and maintain it.

1.2.4. The Committee sees toy safety within the context of the more generally applicable directive on product liability and it points to the need for greater public awareness both of responsibility for product liability and of the means of obtaining compensation for injury. It regards therefore this draft directive on toy safety both as a step forward and as an in-depth contribution to the wider-ranging forthcoming draft directive on the general duty to trade safely.

1.2.5. The Committee agrees that the starting point is the premise that all toys must be safe, that children – because of their age and inexperience – are vulnerable in cases of danger and must have a right to special protection.

1.2.6. The Committee recognises that there is a price to be paid for safety, by society as a whole, not only in terms of money but also in terms of the acceptance of additional controls of various kinds, of the restriction of freedom, of the demands of responsibility for vigilance and [supervision].

2. Specific comments

[2.1. Article 2]

2.2.1. The Committee suggests that the reference to 'domestic animals' should be deleted from the present draft directive and dealt with more appropriately elsewhere. [This was done.]

3.1. Annex I [Products not regarded as toys]

3.1.1. The Committee has serious doubts about many of the exemptions listed in Annex [I].

[Equipment intended to be used collectively in playgrounds was to be exempted.]

3.1.2. The Committee, concerned about the general safety of children and young people, questions where protection lies in respect of items connected with playgrounds, sports and leisure activities if it did not come under the heading of the Toy Directive.

[The exemption was maintained in the adopted directive.]

[Folk dolls and decorative dolls and other similar articles for collectors were to be exempted.]

3.1.3. It notes that the items listed [should] be seen in the light of the definition of a toy in Article 1. Nevertheless, it points to possible problems of interpretation: that children themselves might regard items on the list as toys, such as folk [dolls]. There is a thin dividing line in some categories, for example scale models for children and those for adults.

[The final version exempted 'Folk dolls and decorative dolls and similar articles for adult collectors'.]

[B24] The first reading in the European Parliament (Debates of the European Parliament, 8 July 1987, No 2-354/199)

President. The next item is the report (Doc A2-87/87) by Mrs Oppenheim on behalf of the Committee on Economic and Monetary Affairs and Industrial Policy on the [proposal] from the Commission to the Council [for] a directive on the approximation of the laws of the Member States concerning the safety of toys.

Oppenheim (ED), rapporteur. (DA) Mr President, [this] proposal follows the so-called new method, adopted in May 1985, on the harmonisation of technical conditions and standards. It is the first time moreover that this new method has been applied to consumer goods [and] it is worth noting that this proposal belongs to a group of proposals which are covered by Article [100a: **[E38]**, **[E39]**] and thus conform to the new provisions.

The Commission has thus specified Article 100a as the legal basis, pointing out that the main aim of the directive is to secure the free movement of goods. The Committee on Economic and Monetary Affairs agrees with this legal basis.

. . .

The Committee on Economic and Monetary Affairs was looking forward to this initiative from the Commission and has had detailed discussions on the proposal. However the committee proposes that the directive be simplified so that it is easier to apply in [practice]. The most important changes concern the quality of the products themselves and arrangements for subsequent inspection. On the first point the committee considers that affixing the EC mark to the toy is sufficient, provided the product complies with the standards. The 'standards' in this instance should be understood to mean the European standards or harmonisation documents adopted by the European Committee for Standardisation (CEN) or the European Committee for Electrotechnical Standardisation (CENELEC). Products which do not fall immediately within this group and comply with these standards would be subjected to a more detailed approval procedure as described in the draft directive.

. . .

The inspection arrangements should be [simplified] not just for administrative reasons, nor to relax the safety requirements, but in order that the directive can become an effective working tool.

. . .

Apart from the amendments proposed by the committee, to which the Commission has reacted positively, a number of other motions for amendments have also been tabled. Some were tabled by my colleague, Mr Metten. Similar amendments were discussed in committee, but were not adopted.

. . .

Varfis, Member of the Commission.   (GR) Mr President, to begin with I should like, on behalf of the Commission, to thank the European Parliament for its concern about the safety of toys. You are aware that the Commission attaches great importance to this proposal for a directive, both in the context of achieving the internal market and in the framework of the new approach for the protection of consumers and of children in particular. [The] Commission has already submitted two directives, in 1980 and 1983, [and] this third directive is the first in the framework of the new approach.

The Commission is already familiar of course with the views of Parliament because of the discussions on the earlier proposals. I can tell you that the Commission accepts nearly all of the amendments which have been proposed. Basically these amendments are intended to simplify the procedures. The complexity of our proposals was rooted in a desire to afford children the best possible protection. But we accept that Parliament's simplified procedures will allow the directive to have enough muscle and not detract from its objectives.

. . .

To be specific the Commission can accept [15 amendments] because we believe that these enhance the proposals. As regards the other amendments the Commission's position is categorical. [Regarding] the chemical safety of [toys] I can tell you that the Commission has already passed on two mandates for drawing up of standards to the CEN standardisation committee, one referring to methods of analysis and the other to clarification of the principle on non-toxicity in various types of toys and materials.

. . .

Metten (S).   (NL) Mr President [the] scope of application of the proposed directive is restricted in an unsatisfactory way in that the directive does not apply to toys used in playgrounds. An important argument for including them can be seen in my own country where there alone there are some 46,000 accidents every year in playgrounds where the child needs medical treatment, and 15,000 of these need hospital treatment.

. . .

Oppenheim (ED), rapporteur. (DA) Mr President [I] think that I should comment on the Commission's remarks regarding the motions for amendment. It is my [opinion] that the motions which the Commission cannot support are not so crucial that the report should be referred back to the committee for re-examination. I should like to take this opportunity of stressing my regret that the Commission could not support all the committee's proposals, but I view the Commission's comments as a harbinger of the spirit in which the further work on the directive will proceed.

[B25] Legislative resolution of the European Parliament

LEGISLATIVE RESOLUTION embodying the opinion of the European Parliament on the proposal from the Commission of the European Communities to the Council for a directive on the approximation of the laws of the Member States concerning the safety of toys.

The European Parliament

- having regard to the proposal from the Commission to the Council,
- having been consulted by the Council pursuant to Article 100a of the EEC Treaty,

. . .

- having regard to the report of the Committee on Economic and Monetary Affairs and Industrial Policy and the opinion of the Committee on the Environment, Public Health and Consumer Protection,
- having regard to the result of the vote on the Commission's proposal,

A. having regard to the stage reached in discussions on previous Commission proposals . . .,

B. appreciating the fact that the Commission has at long last complied with the request made by the parliamentary committee responsible in October 1984 that it submit a new proposal for a directive that took account of Parliament's earlier calls for efficiency and simplification,

C. whereas Community rules governing the safety of toys are necessary in order not only to abolish technical barriers to trade but also to promote the free movement of goods and protect consumers,

D. whereas regulations governing the safety of toys obviously cannot replace but can only supplement and back up the responsibility of parents, supervisors and teachers,

E. whereas out of consideration for manufacturers and consumers alike as well as for the market as a whole, provisions must be adopted and implemented now so as to dispel any uncertainty on the part of the parties concerned,

1. Is of the view that the provisions of the proposal for a directive as they now stand take as much account as possible of all the parties concerned;

2. Nevertheless believes that the rules can be simplified and streamlined without losing sight of the overall objective;

3. Therefore tables amendments to the proposal for a directive;

4. Calls on the Commission to incorporate Parliament's amendments in

its proposal and on the Council to adopt the amended version;

5. Calls on the Commission to state its position on Parliament's amendments;

6. Instructs its President to forward to the Council and Commission, as Parliament's opinion, the Commission's proposal as voted by Parliament together with this legislative resolution.

Note. On 6 October 1987, following the opinion of the European Parliament of 9 July 1987, the Commission forwarded to the Council an amended proposal (COM(87) 467 final: OJ C343, 21 December 1987). As indicated in the first reading debate **[B24]** the Commission incorporated certain of the Parliament's amendments. The original Articles 11–14 contained detailed provisions relating to conformity to standards, but the Parliament considered these too complicated and recommended their deletion. The Commission deleted the offending articles. One article enjoined Member States to carry out sample checks on toys which are on the market so as to verify their conformity with the provisions of the directive. The Parliament wanted the inspection bodies to have on request access to the places of manufacture or storage and to the necessary documents. The final verson of the directive stated 'The authority responsible for inspection shall obtain access, on request, to the place of manufacture or storage and to the [necessary] information'. On 18 December 1987, the Council held a Council Meeting on Consumer Protection and adopted a common position on the directive. This was sent to the Parliament.

[B26]   Recommendation to the Parliament on the Council's common position (PE Doc A2-311/87, 23 February 1988)

Recommendation drawn up for the Committee on Economic and Monetary Affairs and Industrial Policy on the Council's common position on the proposal for a directive on the approximation of the laws of the Member States concerning the safety of toys (Doc C2-272/87).

At its sitting of 9 July 1987 the European Parliament delivered its opinion, at first reading, on the Commission's [proposal]. At the sitting of 20 January 1988 the President of Parliament announced receipt of the common position (Doc C2-272/87), which he forwarded to the Committee on Economic and Monetary Affairs and Industrial Policy as the committee responsible and to the Committee on the Environment, Public Health and Consumer Protection for its opinion. The Committee on Economic and Monetary Affairs and Industrial Policy considered the common position at its meeting of 16–17 February 1988 and adopted the recommendation by 15 votes to 4 with 1 abstention. [The] recommendation was tabled on 23 February 1988.

. . .

The Committee on Economic and Monetary Affairs and Industrial Policy, having regard to the common position of the Council as referred to the Committee (Doc C2-272/87), recommends that the European Parliament amend the common position as follows.

...

[There followed a list of amendments proposed by the European Parliament to the common position of the Council and an Explanatory Statement:]

The amended Commission proposal incorporates nearly all Parliament's amendments from the first reading in July 1987. The proposal for a directive has thus been simplified and made easier to administer without losing sight of its objective.

...

It seems inappropriate from the point of view of both manufacturer and consumer for warnings and indications of precautions to be given in all official Community languages. Neither the Commission nor the Council has accepted Parliament's previous amendments on the use of symbols as an alternative to texts. [The] objective must be for all manufacturers to use a symbol that is easy and cheap to affix to toys and that is clearly understood by consumers. When a particular symbol has been devised and approved by the Member States, a manufacturer cannot maintain that fixing a text in [nine] languages puts him in a worse situation than other [manufacturers]. It is therefore obvious that there is a considerable saving in the labelling of toys and manufacture of packaging if a manufacturer can use a single symbol instead of printing a warning in nine different languages.

...

Lastly, Parliament maintains its amendments to the effect that equipment to be used in [playgrounds] are toys for the purposes of the directive and must therefore fulfil the safety requirements contained in it.

[B27] The second reading in the European Parliament (Debates of the European Parliament, 8 March 1988, No 2-363/25-27)

President. The next item is the recommendation for a second reading (Doc A2-311/87), by the Committee on Economic and Monetary Affairs and Industrial Policy, on the common position of the Council on the proposal for a directive on the approximation of the laws of the Member States relating to the safety of toys (Doc C2-272/87).

Oppenheim (ED), rapporteur. (DA) Mr President, [now we have] before us what is, in the committee's opinion, a usable proposal for safety rules on toys. The Commission originally, when we dealt with the matter last, put forward a proposal which Parliament's Committee on Economic and Monetary Affairs found fairly technical. We favoured simplification and felt that harmonisation and similar measures should be left to the standardisation organisations; also we wanted to make it easier to understand.

A proposal was subsequently drafted which took account of many of the committee's amendments from the first reading, and the Council also put forward some amendments which would make the whole thing simpler and more straightforward. There remain at present one or two amendments which Parliament would like to see retained. The aim of one of them is to promote the use of symbols, corresponding to the warnings and safety rules, devised by the international standardisation organisations. A second amendment would require the standardisation organisations to set maximum values for heavy metals. And finally Parliament has tightened up the proposal somewhat by calling for playground [equipment] to be regarded as toys and therefore to be covered by the safety requirements which the directive is to lay down.

. . .

Last but not least, it is a draft directive which also benefits the People's Europe, since we have to a large extent taken account of the interests of the consumers. This is a large field; many toys are produced, and all the parties involved now have firm guidelines on what safety requirements are to be applied. Generally speaking, there will also be substantial advantages for the consumers.

With these comments, I urge my colleagues in the vote tomorrow to be unanimous in their support of the committee's amendments.

Metten (S). (NL) Mr President, this was one of the proposals of the Commission, one of the first to be debated in this Parliament in accordance with the Single European Act. At first reading the Committee on Economic and Monetary Affairs and Industrial Policy presented a large number of amendments, and I have to note that a high proportion of them were taken on board by the Commission and the Council.

[Some] amendments were concerned principally with the extension of the scope of the directive. We have to note that the Council had much more difficulty with those, and that is also the reason why the Committee on Economic and Monetary Affairs and Industrial Policy, with the support of my group, has resubmitted a number of those amendments.

I would mention in particular an amendment concerned with the extension of the scope of the directive to toys on playgrounds. The intention of the directive is to increase the safety of the child. A detailed study has shown that a great many avoidable accidents happen on playgrounds in particular, due to the design or unsafe characteristics of those toys. I think that that is an important argument in favour of drawing toys on playgrounds within the scope of the directive. I would therefore strongly recommend that amendment in particular.

Hammerich (ARC). (DA) Mr President, we have tabled the joint motion for rejection because it is a maximum directive, in other words, the individual country cannot impose stricter rules for toys than those laid down in the directive. A directive concerned with health and safety should be a minimum [directive]. Besides the directive is a bad one. It only covers eight chemical substances, whereas the toy industry uses getting on for 10,000 substances. It does not cover materials such as paint, glue, dyes and plasticine, which often contain carcinogenic substances and organic solvents.

. . .

Varfis, Member of the Commission. (GR) Mr President, on behalf of the Commission I would like to thank Parliament for its support on the very important subject of toy safety.

In July 1987 Parliament published a [resolution **[B25]**] expressing the opinion that the provisions of the proposed directive presented by the

Commission in October 1986 take the greatest possible account of all interested parties. At the same time, Parliament proposed amendments which aimed to simplify the rules embodied in the directive. The Commission accepted in essence nearly all the proposed basic amendments [and] submitted it to the Council on the basis of Article [149 **[B19]**]. In December [the] Council unanimously adopted a common position on the basis of the amended proposal. The Commission then conveyed this common position to the European Parliament, and explained why it had rejected some of the amendments. After that, Parliament's Committee on Economic and Monetary Affairs and Industrial Policy resubmitted five of those amendments, and I will now briefly explain the Commisson's attitude to each of them.

As for the first amendment, which concerns the use of symbols designed by the international standards organisations to express warnings and indicate the requisite precautions during the use of toys, warnings and precautions envisaged by the directive, I would like to stress that the text of the common position does not preclude the use of such [symbols]. We believe that the proposed amendment, if embodied in the directive, could create some confusion from the legal standpoint, and that it is therefore preferable not to amend our common position in this respect.

. . .

As for the second amendment, which aims to include in the directive's field of application equipment intended for collective use at sports fields, I would like to remind you that the proposed directive simply aims to ensure the safety of toys, ie it does not aspire to cover all aspects of children's safety. Nevertheless, the Commission is aware of the danger of accidents, for example in adventure playgrounds, and believes that this subject of children's safety in playgrounds will have to be followed up outside the scope of the present directive, which relates exclusively to toys.

. . .

In conclusion, I would like to pay tribute to the co-operation between the European Parliament and the Commission, which was fruitful and useful in relation to this most important subject of toy safety and, Mr President, on behalf of the Commission I would like once again to thank Parliament for its contribution and support.

[Parliament amended the common position.]

[B28]   The Council's reaction

[On 3 May 1988, the Council unanimously adopted the directive (Directive 88/378/EEC: OJ L187/1, 16 July 1988). As originally drafted, Annex IV set out the warnings and indications of precautions to be taken for certain toys. Member States could require that these or other warnings and precautions be given in their own national language or languages when the toys were placed on the market. Parliament, at the second reading, proposed an additional sentence: 'The warnings and precautions [may] be represented by symbols (pictograms) drawn up by the international standards organisations'. This was adopted by the Council. However, with regard to the exemption of equipment intended to be used collectively in playgrounds from the meaning of 'toys', deleted by Parliament at the first reading, reinstated by the Commission and adopted as part of the common position, deleted by Parliament at the second reading, the Council stood firm and the exemption stood.]

SECTION THREE

THE EUROPEAN COURT OF JUSTICE

1   Introduction

The European Constitution has created a self-contained mechanism to determine the different types of Community disputes which may arise and to ensure that Community law is implemented in all spheres where this is necessary in a uniform manner. The Court of Justice (together with the Court of First Instance, below) is the only judicial authority established by the Community Constitution (but note potential problems raised by the Social Chapter: [D65]–[D67]).

The court's jurisdiction, composition and procedures are determined by the Treaty (and it should be noted that under the Treaty of Union there are some significant amendments of the court's jurisdiction and organisation) [B29], the Statute of the Court of Justice, on which much of this account is based, and the court's Rules of Procedure [B30].

2   Jurisdiction

The Court of Justice has been allocated a wider variety of jurisdictions than is normally given to a court.

First of all, the court has the characteristics of an international court in that it hears and determines disputes between Community institutions and Member States and between Member States and Member States. If the Commission considers that a Member State has failed to fulfil an obligation under the Treaty, the Commission will deliver a reasoned opinion on the matter, after giving the state concerned the opportunity to submit its observations. If the state concerned does not comply with the opinion within the period laid down by the Commission, the Commission may bring the matter before the court. A Member State which considers that another Member State has failed to fulfil an obligation under the Treaty may bring the matter before the court, after bringing the matter before the Commission. If the court finds that a Member State has failed to fulfil the obligation, the state is required to take the necessary measures to comply with the judgment of the court (Articles 169, 170, 171. See, further, Chapter Three, Section One).

Secondly, the court has the characteristics of a constitutional court and an administrative court in that it has jurisdiction to pronounce upon the legality of acts of Community institutions and their compatibility with Treaty provisions and other legal rules and to give compensation for damage caused by Community institutions and their servants (Articles 173, 174. See, further, Section Five of this chapter). Should a specified institution, in infringement of the Treaty, fail to act, the Member States and the other institutions of the Community may bring an action before the Court of Justice to have the infringement established. Any natural or legal person may also complain to the court that an institution of the Community has failed to address to that person certain acts (Article 175). The institution whose act has been declared void or whose failure to act has been declared contrary to the Treaty will be required to take the necessary measures to comply with the court (Article 176). The Court of Justice has jurisdiction in disputes relating to compensation for damage caused by Community institutions and servants (Article 178).

Thirdly, the Court of Justice possesses the characteristics of both an international court and a constitutional court in that it has jurisdiction to give preliminary rulings concerning the interpretation of the Treaty and the validity and interpretation of acts of the institutions of the Community. If such a question is raised before any court or tribunal of a Member State, that court or tribunal may, if it considers that a decision on the question is necessary to enable it to give judgment, request the court to give a ruling on the question. If any such question is raised in a case pending before a court or tribunal of a Member State, against whose decisions there is no judicial remedy under national law, that court or tribunal must bring the matter before the Court of Justice (Article 177. See, further, Chapter Three, Section Two).

Fourthly, the Court of Justice, or rather the Court of First Instance, has the characteristics of an internal labour court in that it has jurisdiction in any dispute between the Community and its servants (see, for example, *Sabbatini* **[B61]**, *Gutmann* **[B64]**) (Article 179).

Finally, the Court of Justice has the characteristics of a criminal court, in that certain regulations made under the Treaty, may give it unlimited jurisdiction with regard to the penalties provided for in such regulations (Article 172).

3   Composition

The Court of Justice consists of 13 Judges. The Court is assisted by six Advocates General (below). The Court of Justice sits either in plenary session or in Chambers (Articles 165–167).

The duty of the Advocates General is to make, acting with complete impartiality and independence and in open court, reasoned submissions on cases brought before the Court of Justice, in order to assist the court in the performance of the court's various tasks. The principal duty of the Advocate General is to act independently of the court in a case before it. The Advocate General will study the facts of the case, the contentions of the parties, the relevant Treaty and secondary legislative provisions, the previous decisions of the Court of Justice, and, of highest importance, relevant legal rules from the legal systems of the Member States and from international law, in order to propose a solution to the given litigation. The court is not bound to follow the advice of the Advocate General but it usually does so. Given the sometimes terse or laconic method of declaring judgments, the court preferring to limit its statement to a resolution of the case in hand – and no more, the more detailed exposition of the Advocate General is often the more instructive. Examples of submissions of Advocates General may be found in *Bela-Mühle* **[B36]**, *Transocean Marine Paint Association* **[B38]**, *Marleasing* **[C31]**, *Johnston* **[C32]**, *Re Import of Waste* **[E28]**, *Cullet* **[E31]** and *Wood Pulp* **[E58]**.

The Court of Justice appoints its Registrar, who is responsible for the court register. There is kept in the Registry a register in which all pleadings and supporting documents are entered in the order in which they are lodged. The Registrar is responsible, under the authority of the President, for the acceptance, transmission and custody of documents and for effecting service. The Registrar assists the Court of Justice, the Chambers (below), the

President and the Judges in all their official functions. Subject to certain exceptions, the Registrar attends the sittings of the court and of the Chambers.

The court has established a translating service staffed by experts with adequate legal training and a thorough knowledge of several official languages of the court (see below).

4 The Court of First Instance

A court, called the Court of First Instance of the European Communities, was established in 1988. The Court of First Instance consists of 12 members, who elect their President from among their number for a term of three years. The members of the Court of First Instance may be called upon to perform the task of Advocate General (performing the same functions as before the Court of Justice) but a member called upon to perform the task of Advocate General in a case can not take part in the judgment of the case. The Court of First Instance normally sits in chambers of three or five Judges.

The Court of First Instance exercises, at first instance, the jurisdiction conferred on the Court of Justice in two principal areas: first, the disputes between the Community and its servants and, second, actions for annulment or failure to act, together with actions for damages, brought against an institution of the Community by natural or legal persons in cases which relate to the implementation of the competition rules applicable to undertakings (see eg *Hercules* [E51] and *Flat Glass* [E69]).

An appeal from the Court of First Instance may be brought before the Court of Justice, within two months of the notification of the decision appealed against. An appeal to the Court of Justice is limited to points of law only. The appeal lies on the grounds of lack of competence of the Court of First Instance, a breach of procedure before the Court of First Instance which adversely affects the interests of the appellant, and any infringement of Community law by the Court of First Instance. If the appeal is well founded, the Court of Justice will quash the decision of the Court of First Instance. It may either give final judgment in the matter itself or refer the case back to the Court of First Instance for judgment. If a case is referred back to the Court of First Instance, that court is bound by the decision of the Court of Justice on points of law.

5 General procedure

The procedure before the Court of Justice is determined by the Statute of the Court of Justice and its Rules of Procedure [B30]. The procedure consists of two parts, namely the written procedure and the oral procedure.

The written procedure consists of the communication to the parties and to the institutions of the Community whose decisions are in dispute, of applications, statements of case, defences and observations, and of replies, if any, as well as of all papers and documents in support or of certified copies of them. A case must be brought before the Court of Justice by a written application addressed to the Registrar. As soon as an application originating proceedings has been lodged, the President will assign the case to one of the Chambers for any preparatory inquiries and will designate a Judge from that Chamber to act as rapporteur. In essence the role of the Judge Rapporteur is to oversee the case from the beginning until the case comes to be determined by the Court of Justice or Chamber. One Advocate General is designated as the First Advocate General and the First Advocate General assigns each case to an Advocate General as soon as the Judge Rapporteur has been designated by the President.

The Court of Justice may require the parties to produce all documents and to supply all information which the court considers desirable. The court may also require the Member States and institutions not being parties to the case to supply all information which the court considers necessary for the proceedings. The court, and note that it is the court rather than the parties or their legal advisers, may at any time entrust any individual, body, authority, committee or other organisation it chooses with the task of giving an expert opinion (see eg *Wood Pulp* [E50]) and may determine that witnesses be heard in accordance with the rules of procedure, which, in particular, emphasise that the nature and content of a witness's testimony is for the court to decide. The court may order that a witness or expert be heard by the judicial authority of his or her place of permanent residence.

The dates and times of the sittings of the court are fixed by the President and the dates and times of the sitting of the Chambers are fixed by their respective Presidents.

The oral procedure consists of the reading of the report presented by the Judge Rapporteur, which summarises the facts and arguments of the parties (see eg *Stoke-on-Trent* [A18], *Gallaher* [E40]), the hearing by the court of agents, advisers and lawyers, together with the submissions of the Advocate General, as well as the hearing, if any, of witnesses and experts. The hearing is in public, unless the court, of its own motion or on application of the parties, decides otherwise for serious reasons. During the hearing the court may examine the experts, the witnesses and the parties themselves. The latter, however, may address the court only through their representatives.

The Court of Justice (and the Chambers) deliberate in closed session.

The deliberations of the court are and remain secret. Only those Judges who were present at the oral proceedings may take part in the deliberation on that case. At the deliberation each Judge taking part will state his or her opinion and the reasons for that opinion. The conclusions reached by the majority of the Judges after final discussion determine the decision of the court. Votes are cast in strict order of precedence, the most junior Judge voting first and the most senior Judge voting last. Decisions of the court are valid only when an uneven number of its members sit in the deliberation. Decisions of the full court are valid if seven members sit and decisions of Chambers are valid only if three Judges sit.

6　Legal representation and legal aid

The states and the Community institutions are represented before the Court of Justice by an agent appointed for each case. The agent may be assisted by an adviser or by a lawyer entitled to practise before a court of a Member State. Other parties must be represented by a lawyer entitled to practise before a court of a Member State. University teachers being nationals of a Member State whose law accords them a right of audience have the same rights before the court as are accorded to lawyers entitled to practise before a court of a Member State.

A party who is wholly or in part unable to meet the costs of the proceedings may at any time apply for legal aid. The application must be accompanied by evidence of the applicant's need of assistance, and in particular by a document from the competent national authority (such as the Ministry of Justice or the national lawyers' association which administers legal aid) certifying the applicant's lack of means. If the application is made prior to the proceedings which the applicant wishes to commence, it must briefly state the subject of such proceedings. The application need not be made through a lawyer. The President designates a Judge to act as rapporteur. The Chamber to which the latter belongs will, after considering the written observations of the opposite party and after hearing the Advocate General, decide whether legal aid should be granted in full or in part, or whether it should be refused. The Chamber considers, in particular, whether there is manifestly no cause of action. The Chamber makes its decision without giving reasons and no appeal lies from that decision. The Chamber may at any time, either of its own motion or on application, withdraw legal aid if the circumstances which led to its being granted alter during the proceedings.

7   The language of the case

In a case before the Court of Justice, the language of the case may be Danish, Dutch, English, French, German, Greek, Irish, Italian, Portuguese or Spanish. The language of a case is normally chosen by the applicant, except that:

(1) if the defendant is a Member State or a natural or legal person having the nationality of a Member State, the language of the case will be the official language of that state. If that state has more than one official language (eg Belgium) the applicant may chose between them;
(2) at the joint request of the parties the court may authorise another of the languages mentioned in head (1) to be used as the language of the case for all or part of the proceedings;
(3) at the request of one of the parties, and after the opposite party and the Advocate General have been heard, the court may, by way of derogation from heads (1) and (2), authorise another of the languages mentioned in head (1) to be used as the language of the case for all or part of the proceedings. Such a request may not be submitted by an institution of the European Community.

If there is a request for a preliminary ruling under Article 177 (see Chapter Three, Section Two), the language of the case will be the language of the national court or tribunal which refers the matter to the Court of Justice.

The language of the case must be used in the written and oral pleadings of the parties and in supporting documents, and also in the minutes and decisions of the court. Any supporting documents expressed in another language must be accompanied by a translation into the language of the case. Notwithstanding the above, a Member State is entitled to use its official language when intervening in a case before the court (see below) or when taking part in any reference for a preliminary ruling. This latter provision applies both to written statements and to oral addresses and the Registrar will ensure that any such statement or address is translated into the language of the case. If a witness or expert states that he or she is unable adequately to express him or herself in one of the languages referred to above, the Court of Justice or a Chamber may authorise the person to give his or her evidence in another language. The Registrar will arrange for translation into the language of the case.

The President of the Court and the Presidents of Chambers in conducting oral proceedings, the Judge Rapporteur both in his or her preliminary report and in his or her report for the hearing, Judges and Advocates General in putting questions and Advocates General in delivering their opinions may use one of the languages referred to above other than the language of the case. The Registrar will arrange for translation into the language of the case.

8   Special procedures

There are a number of special procedures and these relate to intervention by third parties, preliminary rulings and other references for interpretation, and suspension of acts and other interim measures.

An important factor in the development of a coherent and consistent Community law has been the fact that litigation is not limited to the parties concerned. There are two particular procedural features, namely intervention in a case and procedures relating to a reference for a preliminary ruling.

Member States and institutions of the Community may intervene in cases before the Court of Justice in which they are not parties. Although the Commission or the Council (and sometimes both) are so very often either plaintiff or defendant in direct actions before the court, this is none the less an important right. The right is of course most valuable for the Member States who may find that a dispute between, for example, the Commission and another Member State could very well affect their own interest either immediately or in the future. Examples of cases where Member States have intervened are *Piraiki* [B55], *Commission v Council* [B58] and *France v Commission* [E86]. Notice is given in the Offical Journal of the date of registration of all applications initiating proceedings before the court and an application to intervene must be made within three months of the publication of that notice. The application is served on the parties and the President gives the parties an opportunity to submit their written or oral observations before deciding on the application. If the intervention is allowed, the intervener has the right to receive a copy of every document served on the parties (except for secret or confidential documents).

The intervener must accept the case as the intervener finds it at the time of the intervention. The President lays down a period within which the intervener may submit a statement in intervention and that statement must contain the legal and factual argument relied on by the intervener, together with the nature of any evidence offered. After the statement in intervention has been lodged, the President will lay down a time limit within which the parties may reply to that statement.

If there is a reference for a preliminary ruling under Article 177 (see, further, Chapter Three, Section Two), the decision of the court or tribunal of a Member State which suspends its proceedings and refers a case to the Court of Justice must be notified to the court by the national court or tribunal concerned. The decision must then be notified by the Registrar of the court to the parties, to the Member States and to the Commission, and also to the Council if the act the validity or interpretation of which is in dispute originates from the Council. Within two months of this notification, the parties, the Member States, the Commission and, where appropriate, the Council, are entitled to submit written observations to the court. The procedure is governed by the normal procedural rules, subject to necessary adaptations. The decisions of national courts or tribunals which make a request for a preliminary ruling are communicated to the Member States in the original version, accompanied by a translation into the official language of the state to which they are addressed. If a question referred to the court for a preliminary ruling is manifestly identical to a question on which the court has already ruled, the court may, after informing the court or tribunal which referred the question to it, hearing any observations submitted by the parties, Member States, the Commission or the Council, and hearing the Advocate General, give its decision by reasoned order in which reference is made to its previous judgment. The procedure before the court in the case of a reference for a preliminary ruling will normally also include an oral part. It is up to the national court or tribunal to decide as to the costs of the reference. In special circumstances the court may grant, as legal aid, assistance for the purpose of facilitating the representation or attendance of a party.

Actions brought before the Court of Justice do not have suspensory effect. The court may, however, if it considers that circumstances so require, order that application of a contested act be suspended, and may prescribe any necessary interim measures (Articles 185, 186). An application to suspend the operation of any measure adopted by an institution is admissible only if the applicant is challenging that measure in proceedings before the court. An application for the adoption of any other interim measure will be admissible only if it is made by a party to a case before the court and relates to that case. An application to suspend and an application for any other interim measure must state the subject matter of the proceedings, the circumstances giving rise to urgency and the pleas of fact and law establishing a prima facie case for the interim measures applied for. The application must be served on the opposite party, and the President will prescribe a short period within which that party may submit written or oral observations. The President may order a preparatory inquiry. The President may grant the application even before the observations of the opposite party have been submitted. The President will either decide the application himself or refer it to the Court of Justice. The decision on the application takes the form of a reasoned order, from which no appeal lies (see *Commission v Germany* **[C7]**, **[C8]**). The order is immediately served on the parties. The enforcement of the order may be made conditional on the lodging by the applicant of security, of an amount and nature to be fixed in the light of the circumstances. Unless the order fixes the date on which the interim measure is to lapse, the measure lapses when final judgment is delivered. The order can only have an interim effect, and is without prejudice to the decision of the court on the substance of the case.

MATERIALS

[B29]   The Court of Justice, Treaty articles

Article 164

The Court of Justice shall ensure that in the interpretation and application of this Treaty the law is observed.

Article 165 (pre-Treaty of Union)

The Court of Justice shall consist of 13 Judges.

The Court of Justice shall sit in plenary session. It may, however, form Chambers, each consisting of three or five Judges, either to undertake certain preparatory inquiries or to adjudicate on particular categories of cases in accordance with rules laid down for these purposes.

Whenever the Court of Justice hears cases brought before it by a Member State or by one of the institutions of the Community or, to the extent that the Chambers of the court do not have the requisite jurisdiction under the Rules of Procedure, has to give preliminary rulings on questions submitted to it pursuant to Article 177, it shall sit in plenary session.

Should the Court of Justice so request, the Council may, acting unanimously, increase the number of Judges and make the necessary adjustments to the second and third paragraphs of this Article and to the second paragraph of Article 167.

Article 165 (as replaced by the Treaty of Union)

The Court of Justice shall consist of 13 Judges.

The Court of Justice shall sit in plenary session. It may, however, form Chambers, each consisting of three or five Judges, either to undertake certain preparatory inquiries or to adjudicate on particular categories of cases in accordance with rules laid down for these purposes.

The Court of Justice shall sit in plenary session when a Member State or a Community institution that is a party to the proceedings so requests.

Should the Court of Justice so request, the Council may, acting unanimously, increase the number of Judges and make the necessary adjustments to the second and third paragraphs of this Article and to the second paragraph of Article 167.

Article 166

The Court of Justice shall be assisted by six Advocates General.

It shall be the duty of the Advocate General, acting with complete impartiality and independence, to make, in open court, reasoned submissions on cases brought before the Court of Justice, in order to assist the court in the performance of the task assigned to it in Article 164.

Should the Court of Justice so request, the Council may, acting unanimously, increase the number of Advocates General and make the necessary adjustments to the third paragraph of Article 167.

Article 167

The Judges and Advocates General shall be chosen from persons whose independence is beyond doubt and who possess the qualifications required for appointment to the highest judicial offices in their respective countries or who are jurisconsults of recognised competence; they shall be appointed by common accord of the governments of the Member States for a term of six years.

Every three years there shall be a partial replacement of the Judges. Seven and six Judges shall be replaced alternately.

Every three years there shall be a partial replacement of the Advocates General. Three Advocates General shall be replaced on each occasion.

Retiring Judges and Advocates General shall be eligible for reappointment.

The Judges shall elect the President of the Court of Justice from among their number for a term of three years. He may be re-elected.

Article 168

The Court of Justice shall appoint its Registrar and lay down the rules governing his service.

Article 168a (pre-Treaty of Union)

1. At the request of the Court of Justice and after consulting the Commission and the European Parliament, the Council may, acting unanimously, attach to the Court of Justice a court with jurisdiction to hear and determine at first instance, subject to a right of appeal to the Court of Justice on points of law only and in accordance with the conditions laid down by the Statute, certain classes of action or proceeding brought by natural or legal persons. That court shall not be competent to hear and determine actions brought by Member States or by Community institutions or questions referred for a preliminary ruling under Article 177.

2. The Council, following the procedure laid down in paragraph 1, shall determine the composition of that court and adopt the necessary adjustments and additional provisions to the Statute of the Court of Justice. Unless the Council decides otherwise, the provisions of this Treaty relating to the Court of Justice, in particular the provisions of the Protocol on the Statute of the Court of Justice, shall apply to that court.

3. The members of that court shall be chosen from persons whose independence is beyond doubt and who possess the ability required for appointment to judicial office; they shall be appointed by common accord of the governments of the Member States for a term of six years. The membership shall be partially renewed every three years. Retiring members shall be eligible for reappointment.

4. That court shall establish its rules of procedure in agreement with the Court of Justice. Those rules shall require the unanimous approval of the Council.

Article 168a (as replaced by the Treaty of Union)

1. A Court of First Instance shall be attached to the Court of Justice with jurisdiction to hear and determine at first instance, subject to a right of appeal to the Court of Justice on points of law only and in accordance with

the conditions laid down by the Statute, certain classes of action or proceeding defined in accordance with the conditions laid down in paragraph 2. The Court of First Instance shall not be competent to hear and determine questions referred for a preliminary ruling under Article 177.

2. At the request of the Court of Justice and after consulting the European Parliament and the Commission, the Council, acting unanimously, shall determine the classes of action or proceeding referred to in paragraph 1 and the composition of the Court of First Instance and shall adopt the necessary adjustments and additional provisions to the Statute of the Court of Justice. Unless the Council decides otherwise, the provisions of this Treaty relating to the Court of Justice, in particular the provisions of the Protocol on the Statute of the Court of Justice, shall apply to the Court of First Instance.

3. The members of the Court of First Instance shall be chosen from persons whose independence is beyond doubt and who possess the ability required for appointment to judicial office; they shall be appointed by common accord of the governments of the Member States for a term of six years. The membership shall be partially renewed every three years. Retiring members shall be eligible for reappointment.

4. The Court of First Instance shall establish its rules of procedure in agreement with the Court of Justice. Those rules shall require the unanimous approval of the Council.

Article 169

If the Commission considers that a Member State has failed to fulfil an obligation under this Treaty, it shall deliver a reasoned opinion on the matter, after giving the state concerned the opportunity to submit its observations.

If the state concerned does not comply with the opinion within the period laid down by the Commission, the latter may bring the matter before the Court of Justice.

Article 170

A Member State which considers that another Member State has failed to fulfil an obligation under this Treaty may bring the matter before the Court of Justice.

Before a Member State brings an action against another Member State for an alleged infringement of an obligation under this Treaty, it shall bring the matter before the Commission.

The Commission shall deliver a reasoned opinion after each of the states concerned has been given the opportunity to submit its own case and its observations on the other party's case both orally and in writing.

If the Commission has not delivered an opinion within three months of the date on which the matter was brought before it, the absence of such opinion shall not prevent the matter from being brought before the Court of Justice.

Article 171 (pre-Treaty of Union)

If the [court] finds that a Member State has failed to fulfil an obligation under this Treaty, the state shall be required to take the necessary measures to comply with the judgment of the Court of Justice.

Article 171 (as replaced by the Treaty of Union)

1. If the Court of Justice finds that a Member State has failed to fulfil an obligation under this Treaty, the state shall be required to take the necessary measures to comply with the judgment of the Court of Justice.

2. If the Commission considers that the Member State concerned has not taken such measures it shall, after giving that state the opportunity to submit its observations, issue a reasoned opinion specifying the points on which the Member State concerned has not complied with the judgment of the Court of Justice.

If the Member State concerned fails to take the necessary measures to comply with the Court's judgment within the time limit laid down by the Commission, the latter may bring the case before the Court of Justice. In so doing it shall specify the amount of the lump sum or penalty payment to be paid by the Member State concerned which it considers appropriate in the circumstances.

If the Court of Justice finds that the Member State concerned has not complied with its judgment it may impose a lump sum or penalty payment on it.

This procedure shall be without prejudice to Article 170.

Article 172 (pre-Treaty of Union)

Regulations made by the Council pursuant to the provisions of this Treaty, may give the Court of Justice unlimited jurisdiction with regard to the penalties provided for in such regulations.

Article 172 (as replaced by the Treaty of Union)

Regulations adopted jointly by the European Parliament and the Council, and by the Council, pursuant to the provisions of this Treaty, may give the Court of Justice unlimited jurisdiction with regard to the penalties provided for in such regulations.

Article 173 (pre-Treaty of Union)

The Court of Justice shall review the legality of acts of the Council and the Commission other than recommendations or opinions. It shall for this purpose have jurisdiction in actions brought by a Member State, the Council or the Commission on grounds of lack of competence, infringement of an essential procedural requirement, infringement of this Treaty or of any rule of law relating to its application, or misuse of powers.

Any natural or legal person may, under the same conditions, institute proceedings against a decision addressed to that person or against a decision which, although in the form of a regulation or a decision addressed to another person, is of direct and individual concern to the former.

The proceedings provided for in this article shall be instituted within two months of the publication of the measure, or of its notification to the plaintiff, or, in the absence thereof, of the day on which it came to the knowledge of the latter, as the case may be.

Article 173 (as replaced by the Treaty of Union)

The Court of Justice shall review the legality of acts adopted jointly by the European Parliament and the Council, of acts of the Council, of the

Commission and of the ECB [European Central Bank], other than recommendations and opinions, and of acts of the European Parliament intended to produce legal effects vis-à-vis third parties.

It shall for this purpose have jurisdiction in actions brought by a Member State, the Council or the Commission on grounds of lack of competence, infringement of an essential procedural requirement, infringement of this Treaty or of any rule of law relating to its application, or misuse of powers.

The court shall have jurisdiction under the same conditions in actions brought by the European Parliament and by the ECB for the purpose of protecting their prerogatives.

Any natural or legal person may, under the same conditions, institute proceedings against a decision addressed to that person or against a decision which, although in the form of a regulation or a decision addressed to another person, is of direct and individual concern to the former.

The proceedings provided for in this article shall be instituted within two months of the publication of the measure, or of its notification to the plaintiff, or, in the absence thereof, of the day on which it came to the knowledge of the latter, as the case may be.

Article 174

If the action is well founded, the Court of Justice shall declare the act concerned to be void.

In the case of a regulation, however, the Court of Justice shall, if it considers this necessary, state which of the effects of the regulation which it has declared void shall be considered as definitive.

Article 175 (pre-Treaty of Union)

Should the Council or the Commission, in infringement of this Treaty, fail to act, the Member States and the other institutions of the Community may bring an action before the Court of Justice to have the infringement established.

The action shall be admissible only if the institution concerned has first been called upon to act. If, within two months of being so called upon, the institution concerned has not defined its position, the action may be brought within a further period of two months.

Any natural or legal person may, under the conditions laid down in the preceding paragraphs, complain to the Court of Justice that an institution of the Community has failed to address to that person any act other than a recommendation or an opinion.

Article 175 (as replaced by the Treaty of Union)

Should the European Parliament, the Council or the Commission, in infringement of this Treaty, fail to act, the Member States and the other institutions of the Community may bring an action before the Court of Justice to have the infringement established.

The action shall be admissible only if the institution concerned has first been called upon to act. If, within two months of being so called upon, the institution concerned has not defined its position, the action may be brought within a further period of two months.

Any natural or legal person may, under the conditions laid down in the preceding paragraphs, complain to the Court of Justice that an institution of the Community has failed to address to that person any act other than a recommendation or an opinion.

The Court of Justice shall have jurisdiction, under the same conditions, in actions or proceedings brought by the ECB in the areas falling within the latter's field of competence and in actions or proceedings brought against the latter.

Article 176 (pre-Treaty of Union)

The institution whose act has been declared void or whose failure to act has been declared contrary to this Treaty shall be required to take the necessary measures to comply with the judgment of the Court of Justice.

This obligation shall not affect any obligation which may result from the application of the second paragraph of Article 215.

Article 176 (as replaced by the Treaty of Union)

The institution or institutions whose act has been declared void or whose failure to act has been declared contrary to this Treaty shall be required to take the necessary measures to comply with the judgment of the Court of Justice.

This obligation shall not affect any obligation which may result from the application of the second paragraph of Article 215.

This Article shall also apply to the ECB.

Article 177 (pre-Treaty of Union)

The Court of Justice shall have jurisdiction to give preliminary rulings concerning:

(a) the interpretation of this Treaty;
(b) the validity and interpretation of acts of the institutions of the Community;
(c) the interpretation of the statutes of bodies established by an act of the Council, where those statutes so provide.

Where such a question is raised before any court or tribunal of a Member State, that court or tribunal may, if it considers that a decision on the question is necessary to enable it to give judgment, request the Court of Justice to give a ruling thereon.

Where any such question is raised in a case pending before a court or tribunal of a Member State, against whose decisions there is no judicial remedy under national law, that court or tribunal shall bring the matter before the Court of Justice.

Article 177 (as replaced by the Treaty of Union)

The Court of Justice shall have jurisdiction to give preliminary rulings concerning:

(a) the interpretation of this Treaty;
(b) the validity and interpretation of acts of the institutions of the Community and of the ECB;
(c) the interpretation of the statutes of bodies established by an act of the Council, where those statutes so provide.

Where such a question is raised before any court or tribunal of a Member State, that court or tribunal may, if it considers that a decision on the question is necessary to enable it to give judgment, request the Court of Justice to give a ruling thereon.

Where any such question is raised in a case pending before a court or tribunal of a Member State against whose decisions there is no judicial remedy under national law, that court or tribunal shall bring the matter before the Court of Justice.

Article 178

The Court of Justice shall have jurisdiction in disputes relating to compensation for damage provided for in the second paragraph of Article 215.

Article 179

The Court of Justice shall have jurisdiction in any dispute between the Community and its servants within the limits and under the conditions laid down in the Staff Regulations or the Conditions of Employment.

. . .

Article 183

Save where jurisdiction is conferred on the Court of Justice by this Treaty, disputes to which the Community is a party shall not on that ground be excluded from the jurisdiction of the courts or tribunals of the Member States.

Article 184 (pre-Treaty of Union)

Notwithstanding the expiry of the period laid down in the third paragraph of Article 173, any party may, in proceedings in which a regulation of the Council or of the Commission is in issue, plead the grounds specified in the first paragraph of Article 173, in order to invoke before the Court of Justice the inapplicability of that regulation.

Article 184 (as replaced by the Treaty of Union)

Notwithstanding the expiry of the period laid down in the fifth paragraph of Article 173, any party may, in proceedings in which a regulation adopted jointly by the European Parliament and the Council, or a regulation of the Council, of the Commission, or of the ECB is at issue, plead the grounds specified in the second paragraph of Article 173 in order to invoke before the Court of Justice the inapplicability of that regulation.

Article 185

Actions brought before the Court of Justice shall not have suspensory effect. The Court of Justice may, however, if it considers that circumstances so require, order that application of the contested act be suspended.

Article 186

The Court of Justice may in any cases before it prescribe any necessary interim measures.

[B30]   Rules of Procedure of the Court of Justice (OJ L176/7, 4 July 1991)

TITLE II – PROCEDURE

CHAPTER 1 – WRITTEN PROCEDURE

Article 37

1. The original of every pleading must be signed by the party's agent or lawyer.

The original, accompanied by all annexes referred to therein, shall be lodged together with five copies for the court and a copy for every other party to the proceedings. Copies shall be certified by the party lodging them.

2. Institutions shall in addition produce, within time limits laid down by the court, translations of all pleadings into the other [official languages]. The second subparagraph of paragraph (1) of this article shall apply.

3. All pleadings shall bear a date. In the reckoning of time limits for taking steps in proceedings, only the date of lodgment at the Registry shall be taken into account.

4. To every pleading there shall be annexed a file containing the documents relied on in support of it, together with a schedule listing them.

5. Where in view of the length of a document only extracts from it are annexed to the pleading, the whole document or a full copy of it shall be lodged at the Registry.

Article 38

1. An application [to the court] shall state:

(a)   the name and address of the applicant;
(b)   the designation of the party against whom the application is made;
(c)   the subject matter of the proceedings and a summary of the pleas in law on which the application is based;
(d)   the form of order sought by the applicant;
(e)   where appropriate, the nature of any evidence offered in support.

. . .

Article 39

The application shall be served on the defendant.

. . .

Article 40

1. Within one month after service on him of the application, the defendant shall lodge a defence, stating:

(a)   the name and address of the defendant;
(b)   the arguments of fact and law relied on;
(c)   the form of order sought by the defendant;
(d)   the nature of any evidence offered by him.

. . .

2. The time limit laid down in paragraph (1) of this Article may be extended by the President on a reasoned application by the defendant.

Article 41

1. The application initiating the proceedings and the defence may be supplemented by a reply from the applicant or by a rejoinder from the defendant.
2. The President shall fix the time limits within which these pleadings are to be lodged.

Article 42

1. In reply or rejoinder a party may offer further evidence. The party must, however, give reasons for the delay in offering it.
2. No new plea in law may be introduced in the course of proceedings unless it is based on matters of law or of fact which come to light in the course of the procedure.

If in the course of the procedure one of the parties puts forward a new plea in law which is so based, the President may, even after the expiry of the normal procedural time limits, acting on a report of the Judge Rapporteur and after hearing the Advocate General, allow the other party time to answer on that plea.

The decision on the admissibility of the plea shall be reserved for the final judgment.

Article 43

The court may, at any time, after hearing the parties and the Advocate General [order] that two or more cases concerning the same subject matter shall, on account of the connection between them, be joined for the purposes of the written or oral procedure or of the final judgment. The cases may subsequently be disjoined.

Article 44

1. After the rejoinder provided for in Article 41(1) of these Rules has been lodged, the President shall fix a date on which the Judge Rapporteur is to present his preliminary report to the court. The report shall contain recommendations as to whether a preparatory inquiry or any other preparatory step should be undertaken and whether the case should be referred to the Chamber to which it has been assigned . . . .

The court shall decide, after hearing the Advocate General, what action to take upon the recommendations of the Judge Rapporteur.

The same procedure shall apply:

(a) where no reply or no rejoinder has been lodged within the time limit fixed in accordance with Article 41(2) of these Rules;
(b) where the party concerned waives his right to lodge a reply or rejoinder.

2. Where the court orders a preparatory inquiry and does not undertake it itself, it shall assign the inquiry to the Chamber.

Where the court decides to open the oral procedure without an inquiry, the President shall fix the opening date.

Article 44a

Without prejudice to any special provisions laid down in these Rules, and except in the specific cases in which, after the pleadings referred to in Article 40(1) and, as the case may be, in Article 41(1) have been lodged, the court, acting on a report from the Judge Rapporteur, after hearing the Advocate General and with the express consent of the parties, decides otherwise, the procedure before the court shall also include an oral part.

CHAPTER 2 – PREPARATORY INQUIRIES

Section 1 – Measures of inquiry

Article 45

1. The court, after hearing the Advocate General, shall prescribe the measures of inquiry that it considers appropriate by means of an order setting out the facts to be proved. Before the court decides on the measures of inquiry referred to in paragraph (2)(c), (d) and (e) the parties shall be heard. The order shall be served on the parties.
   2. [The] following measures of inquiry may be adopted:

(a) the personal appearance of the parties;
(b) a request for information and production of documents;
(c) oral testimony;
(d) the commissioning of an expert's report;
(e) an inspection of the place or thing in question.

3. The measures of inquiry which the court has ordered may be conducted by the court itself, or be assigned to the Judge Rapporteur.
   The Advocate General shall take part in the measures of inquiry.
   4. Evidence may be submitted in rebuttal and previous evidence may be amplified.

Article 46

. . .

3. The parties shall be entitled to attend the measures of inquiry.

Section 2 – The summoning and examination of witnesses and experts

Article 47

1. The court may, either of its own motion or [on] an application by a party, and after hearing the Advocate General, order that certain facts be proved by witnesses. The order of the court shall set out the facts to be established.
   The court may summon a witness of its own motion or on application by a party or at the instance of the Advocate General.
   An application by a party for the examination of a witness shall state precisely about what facts and for what reasons the witness should be examined.
   2. The witness shall be summoned by an order of the court containing the following information:

(a) the surname, forenames, description and address of the witness;
(b) an indication of the facts about which the witness is to be examined;
(c) where appropriate, particulars of the arrangements made by the court for reimbursement of expenses incurred by the witness, and of the penalties which may be imposed on defaulting witnesses.

The order shall be served on the parties and the witnesses.

. . .

4. After the identity of the witness has been established, the President shall inform him that he will be required to vouch the truth of his evidence in the manner laid down in these Rules.

The witness shall give his evidence to the court, the parties having been given notice to attend. After the witness has given his main evidence the President may, at the request of a party or of his own motion, put questions to him.

The other Judges and the Advocate General may do likewise.

Subject to the control of the President, questions may be put to witnesses by the representatives of the parties.

5. After giving his evidence, the witness shall take the following oath:

I swear that I have spoken the truth, the whole truth and nothing but the truth.

The court may, after hearing the parties, exempt a witness from taking the oath.

6. The Registrar shall draw up minutes in which the evidence of each witness is reproduced.

The minutes shall be signed by the President or by the Judge Rapporteur responsible for conducting the examination of the witness, and by the Registrar. Before the minutes are thus signed, witnesses must be given an opportunity to check the content of the minutes and to sign them.

The minutes shall constitute an official record.

Article 48

1. Witnesses who have been duly summoned shall obey the summons and attend for examination.

2. If a witness who has been duly summoned fails to appear before the court, the court may impose upon him a pecuniary penalty [and] may order that a further summons be served on the witness at his own expense.

The same penalty may be imposed upon a witness who, without good reason, refuses to give evidence or to take the oath or where appropriate to make a solemn affirmation equivalent thereto.

. . .

Article 49

1. The court may order that an expert's report be obtained. The order appointing the expert shall define his task and set a time limit within which he is to make his report.

. . .

4. The expert may give his opinion only on points which have been expressly referred to him.

5. After the expert has made his report, the court may order that he be examined, the parties having been given notice to attend.

Subject to the control of the President, questions may be put to the expert by the representatives of the parties.

. . .

Article 53

1. The Registrar shall draw up minutes of every hearing. The minutes shall be signed by the President and by the Registrar and shall constitute an official record.

2. The parties may inspect the minutes and any expert's report at the Registry and obtain copies at their own expense.

. . .

CHAPTER 3 – ORAL PROCEDURE

Article 56

1. The proceedings shall be opened and directed by the President, who shall be responsible for the proper conduct of the hearing.

2. The oral proceedings in cases heard *in camera* shall not be published.

Article 57

The President may in the course of the hearing put questions to the agents, advisers or lawyers of the parties.

The other Judges and the Advocate General may do likewise.

Article 58

A party may address the court only through his agent, adviser or lawyer.

Article 59

1. The Advocate General shall deliver his opinion orally at the end of the oral procedure.

2. After the Advocate General has delivered his opinion, the President shall declare the oral procedure closed.

Article 60

The court may at any time, in accordance with Article 45(1), after hearing the Advocate General, order any measure of inquiry to be taken or that a previous inquiry be repeated or expanded. The court may direct the Chamber or the Judge Rapporteur to carry out the measures so ordered.

Article 61

The court may after hearing the Advocate General order the reopening of the oral procedure.

Article 62

1. The Registrar shall draw up minutes of every hearing. The minutes shall be signed by the President and by the Registrar and shall constitute an official record.

2. The parties may inspect the minutes at the Registry and obtain copies at their own expense.

CHAPTER 4 – JUDGMENTS

Article 63

The judgment shall contain:

- a statement that it is the judgment of the court,
- the date of its delivery,
- the names of the President and of the Judges taking part in it,
- the name of the Advocate General,
- the name of the Registrar,
- the description of the parties,
- the names of the agents, advisers and lawyers of the parties,
- a statement of the forms of order sought by the parties,
- a statement that the Advocate General has been heard,
- a summary of the facts,
- the grounds for the decision,
- the operative part of the judgment, including the decision as to costs.

Article 64

1. The judgment shall be delivered in open court; the parties shall be given notice to attend to hear it.
2. The original of the judgment, signed by the President, by the Judges who took part in the deliberations and by the Registrar, shall be sealed and deposited at the Registry; the parties shall be served with certified copies of the judgment.
3. The Registrar shall record on the original of the judgment the date on which it was delivered.

Article 65

The judgment shall be binding from the date of its delivery.

CHAPTER 9 – TIME LIMITS

Article 81

1. The period of time allowed for commencing proceedings against a measure adopted by an institution shall run from the day following the receipt by the person concerned of notification of the measure or, where the measure is published, from the 15th day after publication thereof in the *Official Journal of the European Communities*.
2. The extensions, on account of distance, of prescribed time limits shall be provided for in a decision of the court which shall be published in the *Official Journal of the European Communities*.

Article 82

Any time limit prescribed pursuant to these Rules may be extended by whoever prescribed it.

ANNEX II DECISION ON EXTENSION OF TIME LIMITS ON
ACCOUNT OF DISTANCE

In order to take account of distance, procedural time limits for all parties save those habitually resident in the Grand Duchy of Luxembourg shall be extended as follows:

- for the Kingdom of Belgium: two days,
- for the Federal Republic of Germany, the European territory of the French Republic and the European territory of the Kingdom of the Netherlands: six days,
- for the European territory of the Kingdom of Denmark, for the Hellenic Republic, for Ireland, for the Italian Republic, for the Kingdom of Spain, for the Portuguese Republic (with the exception of the Azores and Madeira) and for the United Kingdom: ten days,
- for other European countries and territories: two weeks,
- for the autonomous regions of the Azores and Madeira of the Portuguese Republic: three weeks,
- for other countries, departments and territories: one month.

SECTION FOUR

COMMUNITY CASE LAW

1   Introduction

In Section Three of this chapter it was seen that the European Constitution has created a self-contained mechanism to determine the different types of Community disputes which may arise and to ensure that Community law is implemented in all spheres where this is necessary in a uniform manner.

The European Court of Justice has been allocated a wider variety of juris-dictions than is normally given to a court, principal of which is the seemingly innocuous statement (Article 164 **[B29]**) that the 'Court of Justice shall ensure that in the interpretation and application of this Treaty the law is observed'. The 'law' is derived ostensibly from a number of written sources, the primary and secondary legislation discussed in Section Three of this chapter, but the need to interpret that legislation has over the years resulted in the growing dominance of the Court of Justice as a legislator and a Treaty developer in its own right. Of paramount importance is the creation, by its case law, of doctrines of both interpretation and of substance which pervade all aspects of the Community activity described in this work and which have welded that activity into something approaching a cohesive and coherent whole. In particular, the Court of Justice has acted to ensure that the spirit of Community objectives is paramount and, sometimes with apparent disre-gard for the literal wording of Treaty provisions and secondary legislation, has used those words to create the new legal order for the Community.

2   Interpretation

Community legislation, both primary and secondary, is drafted in several ways, ranging from very wide (some might say deliberately vague) statements of principle to extremely detailed and minute and technical rules. In addi-tion Community legislation is drafted in the various languages of the Community and may utilise, in diverse and sundry places, legal concepts which may be identical in each Member State or which may exist in some Member States and not in others. The Court of Justice, therefore, has faced problems of interpretation similar to those faced by the courts of Member States, but accentuated by the fact that the court is the court of last instance for both the Community institutions and the Member States. The Court of Justice does not decline jurisdiction on the ground that the formal written sources do not provide an exact set of solutions for the legal problem at hand, since the court has a positive duty to ensure that the law is observed. As was argued early on, if a case involves a problem of law well known in the case law and legal theory of all the countries of the Community but for whose solution the Treaty does not contain any rules the Court, on pain of perpetrating a denial of justice, is therefore obliged to resolve the problem by drawing on the rules recognised by the legislation, legal theory and case-law of the member countries (*Algera v Common Assembly*, Case 7/56 [1957] ECR 39, at p 55).

When interpreting statutory rules, the Court of Justice has followed interpretative techniques common to all legal systems. The starting point will, as with the national courts, be the literal interpretation of clearly defined Treaty and secondary legislative provisions and if the meaning of the words is clear, the statutory provision will be applied, unless so to do would achieve a result clearly absurd in relation to the objectives of the Treaty. As in municipal systems of law, the court uses clearly defined provisions as an aid to interpretation of provisions not so clearly defined, such as using one article to explain the meaning of another (*Commission v Council* [B58], *Commission v Ireland* [E14] and *Continental Can* [E64]), using the recitals which state the reasons for enacting secondary legislation as a guide to interpreting that legislation (*Marleasing* [C31]) and using the superior legal force of a Treaty provision to interpret secondary legislation (*Reyners* [D56]). Very often the spirit and purpose of the written provisions will be used to lay down certain presumptions or canons of interpretation, such as the fact that a provision creating what are called fundamental freedoms, such as free movement of goods or persons, must be interpreted broadly, whereas any statutory derogations from such fundamental freedoms must be interpreted narrowly (*Piraiki* [B55]; *Levin* [D5]; *Commission v Ireland* [E22]; *Centrafarm* [E36] and *Commission v Greece* [E46]).

These interpretative techniques, however, take on a new dimension when the primary sources are conceived, drafted and enacted in several languages by persons versed in different legal systems and when those sources have to be interpreted by judges who are masters of different legal systems. There has to be a considerable element of comparative study in order to obtain an interpretation in accordance with the overriding purpose of achieving uniformity of application within the Community's internal legal order and the several legal orders of all the Member States. The treaties did not, and indeed could not, create a completely original legal system which derived absolutely no rules and concepts from the legal systems of the Member States. Those states had, long before the Community was envisaged, their own legal systems. Therefore, the interpretation of Treaty provisions and secondary legislation may well be aided by a comparative study and analysis of the vocabulary used in the written texts, together with further and similar analysis of the national legal systems from which that vocabulary may have been taken (*Wörsdorfer* [C20]; *Lebon* [D25]).

The Court of Justice has, however, realised that the process of legal and linguistic semantics can be taken too far and has realised that the difficulties of providing an exact meaning to a word, phrase or principle are multiplied many-fold when working in more than one language and with more than one national legal system, and that this is increased even more by the increase in the number of languages and legal systems consequent upon the enlargement of Community membership. On many occasions, the court has been well advised by its Advocates General to think and determine in terms of principle, of the objectives and purposes of the treaties, and of the creation and development of Community legal terms and concepts which can transcend those of national legal systems (*de Geus* [B31], and see Cases C-90, 91/90 *Jean Neu v Secrétaire d'Etat à l'Agriculture* [1991] ECR I-3617).

Sometimes the court has relied very heavily upon the legal system of one Member State (*Transocean* [B38]) but, in the main, the court aided by its Advocates General have searched for principles of Community law from all the national legal systems of the Member States (and other states: *Wood Pulp* [E50]), together with principles from international law (*Van Duyn* [D43],

Wood Pulp [E58]). Perhaps the court has attempted to find and use principles well known and accepted by the legal systems of the Member States in order to encourage the observance of Community law by the Member States. The Court, when making its judgments, calls to a very large extent upon national municipal laws in order to extract from them the rules of law relative to the application of the Treaty, but it is not content to draw its sources from a more or less arithmetical average of the various national solutions and will choose from each of the member countries those principles which, having regard to the objective of the treaty, appear the best, or, if one wishes to use such a word, the most progressive. 'That is the spirit which has hitherto guided the Court' (Case 14/61 *Hoogovens v High Authority* [1962] ECR 253, at pp 283–284, per Advocate General Lagrange).

This attitude has been of great importance in cases for preliminary rulings where there is a need for fruitful collaboration between the Court of Justice and the national courts which both refer questions to and receive replies from the court (see, further, Chapter Three, Section Two). By drawing upon principles already established in the Member States the court can at the same time guarantee that it will be employing methods of solving legal disputes that have already been proved in municipal law. Such principles are more likely to meet with municipal approval than the imposition of unknown and revolutionary solutions and all Member States may find themselves making a positive contribution to Community law, which will then merge back into the several national legal systems, and yet, at the same time, the court by choosing the most appropriate or 'progressive' national solution(s) for the application of the Community objectives can develop supranational concepts where these are considered necessary (*Hoekstra* [D4]; *Levin* [D5]; cf *Henn* [E29] ('public morality')).

3   Community case law

Whether the Court of Justice has the power to make decisions which can form a source of Community law is not expressly stated in the Treaty.

The 'interpretation' function of the Court of Justice has resulted, naturally, in decisions interpreting many specific written provisions. Two features stand out. First, as mentioned above, the court has developed Community concepts when called upon to interpret words and phrases and, in so doing, the court has undertaken at least a supplementary legislative function. Secondly, it would be very natural for a judicial body which interpreted a word or a phrase one way when the matter first came before the court to accept that its original interpretation was correct when the matter was again raised and to repeat its earlier decision and the reasons therefor. In this way legal certainty is reinforced and the court's decisions can provide a guide to the results of litigation before the court and, in particular, can be applied by each and every national court. The Advocates General in their submissions to the court very early on offered to the court a suggested solution to the case in hand by referring to previous decisions, sometimes indicating that the court had already followed a consistent trend (*Bela-Mühle* [B36]), sometimes showing that a number of alternatives could be chosen by the court. The court in the early days did not act very overtly, preferring to refer to its earlier decisions by implication by simply repeating earlier words, phrases (and sometimes quite lengthy pasages) without assigning any express citation to the earlier decision (cf *Commission v Italy* **[C9]** and *Commission v United Kingdom* **[C10]** and *Commission v Germany* **[E32]** and *Bellon* **[E33]**). As the court developed, the court started actively to cite previous decisions, sometimes by using such phrases as 'as the Court has already stated' or 'according to consistent case law' (*IBM* **[B48]**, *Belgium v Commission* **[E92]** and *Boussac* **[E94]**). Later the court started to cite previous decisions rather in the manner used by common law jurisdictions (*Commission v Council* **[B58]**; *Bettray* **[D8]**; *Bellon* **[E33]**; *Gouda* **[E47]**). Therefore, the court has, on many occasions, built up a settled case law which since it will be followed in practice, even if not in legal theory, becomes a source of law in its own right because it is possible to predict the answer which will be handed down (see the 'social advantage formula' cases: **[D18]**–**[D24]**). The court has even gone so far as to state, with regard to the obligation of a national court to refer a question for a preliminary ruling, that 'the authority of an interpretation already given by the Court may deprive the obligation of its purpose and thus empty it of its substance' (*Cilfit* **[C19]**). The court has not, however, erected a system of binding precedent which must be followed slavishly or unquestioningly in such a way that its rigidity might hinder the development of Community law and the objectives of the Treaty as they may change.

The powers to 'interpret' and to 'apply' the law which have been given to the Court of Justice by the Treaty both lead to the assumption by the court of the power to make binding judgments, not simply on the particular case brought before the court but to make judgments of general application which are binding on the Member States and the Community institutions. There has been a gradual merging of a function of interpretation, pure and simple, through to a function of creating rules of interpretation binding the institutions (for example decisions to annul Community legislative and administrative acts are accepted as binding) and the Member States (for example decisions that provisions of a directive may have legal effects within a Member State and grant rights to individuals against that state have been accepted by the Member States), and especially their national courts when those courts receive a reply to a question referred for a preliminary ruling, through presumptions of interpretation to fill in gaps, through to an assumed power to create legal rules and principles whenever the court deems this necessary to fulfil the purposes of Community integration (see, especially, the 'rule of reason' in *Cassis de Dijon* **[E21]** and *Commission v Denmark* **[E26]**).

Outstanding amongst the creations of the court's case law have been answers to fundamental questions which were very much not answered by express Treaty provisions. The court has created constitutional doctrines and glosses which emphasise the autonomy of Community law and its supremacy over and within each Member State and which, quite simply, cannot be found in any express way within the Treaty. Doctrines such as the supremacy of a Community law and the granting of rights to individuals, in the absence of fulfilment of Community obligations by Member States, by virtue of Community law itself have been based on the presumed (very presumed) intentions of the Treaty makers. These doctrines relate to the relationship between Community law and the Member States and it is more convenient to discuss these in Chapter Three.

What will be discussed in this section of this chapter is the creation by the court of what are known as general principles of law. These are principles which supplement the formal written sources of law when those sources are

silent and which pervade this work and, in keeping with the notion of a constitution, has created something akin to a series of fundamental freedoms
against which may be measured the actions of the Community institutions
and the Member States. These general principles of law have been taken
from the legal systems of the Member States to assist in the process of the
creation of an autonomous and separate legal order of Community law. The
use of judge-made principles in public law has, of course, been known for
many years but they may take on a special significance in countries with written constitutions and a heavily codified legal system. General principles of
law have achieved their legitimacy and normative force within the
Community legal order by virtue of the fact that the Court of Justice has
based them, sometimes very indirectly, upon Treaty provisions, albeit somewhat vague provisions. 'The Court of Justice shall ensure that in the
interpretation and application of the Treaty the law is observed'; 'infringement of this Treaty or of any rule of law relating to its application'; 'in
accordance with the general principles common to the laws of the Member
states' (Articles 164, 173(2), 215(2), respectively). The silence of the Treaty
but for oblique references to some other 'law' has, argued the court, imposed upon the court itself the obligation to supplement the written law by a
form of equity, albeit used in terms more familiar to the public lawyer. From
the case law a number of principles may be discerned.

(a)　Equality
The principle of equality is sometimes written into the Community constitution by means of Treaty and secondary legislative provisions. For example,
Article 7 (now 6) states that within the scope of application of the Treaty
'any discrimination on grounds of nationality shall be prohibited'.
Examples of this principle are *Airola* **[B32]**; *Sotgiu* **[D16]**; *Sabbatini* **[B61]**;
Cowan **[D68]**; *Driancourt* **[E20]**. Similarly, Article 40(3) of the Treaty provides that the common organisation of agricultural markets 'shall exclude
any discrimination between producers or consumers within the
Community'. In Cases 117/76, 16/77 *Albert Ruckdeschel & Co and others v
Hauptzollamt Hamberg-St Annen* [1977] ECR 1753, the court held that the
specific prohibition of discrimination laid down in that provision 'is merely
a specific enunciation of the general principle of equality which is one of
the fundamental principles of Community law. This principle requires that
similar situations shall not be treated differently unless differentiation is objectively justified'. In Cases 63 to 69/72 *Wilhelm Werhahn Hansamühle and
others v Council of the EEC* [1973] ECR 1229, the court held that since a claim
for non-contractual liability was founded on a legislative act involving
choices of economic policy, there was ordinarily no liability on the part of
the Community for damages which individuals may have suffered by reason
of this act, but added 'unless there is sufficiently flagrant infringement of a
superior rule of law protecting the individual' such as infringement of the
rule against discrimination and the principle of proportionality expressed
in Article 40(3) of the Treaty. Furthermore, Article 119 envisages equality
between men and women in matters of equal pay for equal work (see
[D60]–[D64]).

(b)　Legal certainty
This principle means that an individual or organisation must be in a position to know where he, she or it stands with regard to Community rights and
obligations. The principle has been invoked by the court in condemning

Member States for failure to implement directives in a manner which enables persons concerned to know their rights and obligations (*Commission v Denmark* **[C6]**), in giving replies to preliminary rulings (*Maïseries de Beauce* **[C15]**; *Rheinmühlen* **[C18]**), and to limit the temporal effect of the court's decisions (*Defrenne* **[C23]**). See, also, *Wood Pulp* **[E50]**, *Delimitis* **[E61]** and *Boussac* **[E94]**. The court has on numerous occasions stated that a general principle of legal certainty comprises the idea that a person should not be deprived of rights which that person was led to believe would be conferred, the principle of legitimate expectation (*Commission v Council* **[B33]**; *Merkur* **[B34]**; *Töpfer* **[B60]**), and that rights should not be interfered with restrospectively, the principle of non-retroactivity (*Amylum* **[B35]**). In Case 70/83 *Gerda Kloppenburg v Fianzamt Leer* [1984] ECR 1075, the court was concerned to inquire whether the legal position of an individual had been altered with retroactive effect by a later directive extending the period for transposing an earlier directive into national law in favour of those Member States which were unable to complete, within the period initially prescribed, the legislative procedure for amending their legislation on value added tax. The court emphasised that Community legislation must be unequivocal and its application must be predictable for those who are subject to it and that postponement of the date of entry into force of a measure of general application is in itself liable to undermine that principle. (The court found, on an examination of the later directive, that that directive did not have retroactive effect.) The principle that penal provisions may not have retroactive effect is one which is common to all the legal orders of the Member States, is enshrined in the European Convention on Human Rights as a fundamental right, and takes its place among the general principles of law whose observance is ensured by the Court of Justice (Case 63/83 *R v Kent Kirk* [1984] ECR 2689).

(c) Proportionality
This principle means that, given that a power to act exists and given that there is a choice of methods whereby to exercise that power, the method chosen must be suitable or appropriate to achieve the purpose of the power and the method chosen must not go further than is necessary in order to achieve that purpose. There must be given a preference to that method which restricts the least those freedoms guaranteed by Community law. It may be necessary to consider all available methods and to measure these against the method actually chosen (*Bela-Mühle* **[B36]**). The principle is also applied to any sanctions imposed and the reaction of authority to the violation of a rule must be proportionate. In Case 181/84 *R v Intervention Board for Agricultural Produce, ex p ED & F Man (Sugar) Ltd* [1985] ECR 2889, there was a scheme whereby companies could apply for permission to export sugar to third countries. Companies had to give a security to ensure that they actually exported the sugar and make a formal application for an export licence to the Commission. A regulation provided that if the application were late the whole security would be forfeit. Man applied for a licence and the application by telex was three to four hours late as the employee who normally sent such telexes was absent from work that day. The Commission declared that the £1,670,370 security should be forfeit. It was held that although the Commission, in the interests of sound administration, was entitled to impose a time limit for applications, the penalty imposed, namely, the automatic forfeiture of the entire security, in the event of an infringement significantly

less serious than the failure to fulfil the primary obligation to export, which the security was intended to guarantee, must be considered too drastic a penalty. The principle has been used in particular by applicants as a ground for an action to annul Community legislative and administrative action (*Bela-Mühle* [B36]) and to found actions for non-contractual liability (*Rau* [B37]). The principle may be used against Member States. For example, where Community law permits Member States to make derogations from normally guaranteed freedoms, those derogations are subject to the principle and the principle has been applied with regard to free movement of persons (*Rutuli* [D45]; *Watson* [D10]; *Pieck* [D11]) and goods (*Cassis de Dijon* [E21]; *Boscher* [E27]; *Commission v Germany* [E32]) and services (*Commission v Greece* [E46]).

(d)   Procedural rights and remedies

A basic principle of public law is that of a fair administrative process. This may be statutory in that detailed procedural rules are laid down by the Community legislator. If, however, the statute is silent or inadequate then the general principle of a fair hearing and the adequacy of legal remedies is applied both to Community institutions (*Transocean* [B38]; *Hoffman* [B39]; cf *Boussac* [E94]) and to Member States (*Heylens* [D33]; *Johnston* [C32]; *Santillo* [D49]).

(e)   The protection of human rights

In most written constitutions it is normal to find a comprehensive statement of the rights and duties of the citizen. Such declarations of the rights of man arose in the 17th and 18th centuries and in modern times, especially following the violation of such rights during the Second World War, the states of Europe incorporated express declarations into their written constitutions and ratified international conventions, such as the European Convention for the Protection of Human Rights and Fundamental Freedoms. The European Constitution, as established by the Treaty of Rome, does not possess an express Bill of Rights and phrases such as 'human rights' and 'fundamental freedoms' are not contained therein. However, as the European Constitution developed from one governing an economic Community to one governing a European Union references to human rights in Community documents emerged [B40], [B41] (and note [D66]). In the meantime, the Court of Justice took analogous provisions in the Treaty, the principles common to Member States and the European Convention and incorporated the principle that the protection of human rights was indeed a part of Community law (which in turn was part of the law of the individual Member States) (*Grogan* [A19]; *Konstantidis* [A21]; *Internationale* [B42], *Stauder* [B43]; *Nold* [B44]; *Cinétèque* [E24]; *Dimotiki* [E89]). Principles such as non-discrimination on grounds of nationality (*Cowan* [D68]) or sex (*Defrenne* [C23]), rights to religion (*Prais* [B45]) and to property (*Hauer* [B46]), and free movement (*Rutili* [D45]) have all been consecrated by the Court of Justice.

MATERIALS

[B31] Case 13/61 Kledingverkoopbedrijf de Geus en Uitdenbogerd v Robert Bosch GmbH [1962] ECR 45

[The case concerned the meaning of the words (in Article 85 **[E49]**) 'which are likely to affect trade between Member States'. It was argued by Bosch that a sole-agency agreement between Bosch and van Rijn did not 'affect' trade, as had been contended by de Geus, since its effect would be to increase trade in refrigerators between Member States.]

Submissions of Advocate General Lagrange (at p 70)

It is clear that in French the word 'affecter' means 'to influence', 'to have an effect on'; the effect might be good or bad; the word does not necessarily carry a pejorative meaning. However, perceptible nuances exist in the terms employed in the other languages. In Italian 'pregiudicare' is perhaps scarcely more pejorative than 'affecter'; in German 'beeinträchtigen' seems to connote a more unfavourable effect, while in the Dutch text we find 'ongunstig beinvloeden' which means to exercise an unfavourable influence. As you know all four languages are authentic. [In] such a case, just as when obscurities or contradictions arise in the interpretation of a text in municipal law, [it is necessary to refer] to its 'context' or [to the 'spirit' of the text].

[B32] Case 21/74 Jeanne Airola v Commission of the European Communities [1975] ECR 221

[The applicant was born in Belgium and married an Italian national. According to Italian law an alien who became the wife of an Italian citizen acquired Italian nationality. According to Belgian law a person in the situation of the applicant could make a declaration of retention of her Belgian nationality and this she did. She then entered the Community service and later sought the annulment of a decision by which the Commission withdrew the decision granting her the expatriation allowance provided for under the Staff Regulations of Community Officials.]

The European Court of Justice (at pp 227–229)

3. She contends that the condition laid down in Article 4(a) of Annex VII of the Staff Regulations, whereby an expatriation allowance shall be paid to officials who, in the words of the Article, 'are not and have never been nationals of the State in whose European territory the place where they are employed is situated' does not apply if, owing to circumstances outside her control and solely as the result of national laws, the individual concerned acquires dual nationality.

4. In the case of a female official who is granted the nationality of her husband as a result of her marriage with a national of another state, the

application of that condition results in discrimination, since under no national legislation does the male official acquire the nationality of his wife.

5. On the question of nationality, the provisions of national legislations are not uniform; some laws, particularly those of recent date, provide that a foreign wife does not automatically acquire the nationality of her husband, whereas, under other legislations, it is still provided that, as was once the common rule, the nationality of a married woman depends upon that of her husband.

6. In accordance with the general pattern of Article 4 of Annex VII this provision adopts the official's habitual residence before he entered the service as the paramount consideration in determining entitlement to an expatriation allowance.

7. The official's nationality is regarded as being only a subsidiary consideration, ie as serving to define the effect of the length of such residence outside the territory in which the place where he is employed is situated.

8. The object of the expatriation allowance is to compensate officials for the extra expense and inconvenience of taking up employment with the Communities and being thereby obliged to change their residence.

9. Though 'expatriation' is a subjective state conditioned by the official's assimilation into new surroundings, the Staff Regulations of Officials cannot treat officials differently in this respect according to whether they are of the male or of the female sex since, in either case, payment of the expatriation allowance must be determined by considerations which are uniform and disregard the difference in sex.

10. The concept of 'nationals' contained in Article 4(a) must therefore be interpreted in such a way as to avoid any unwarranted difference of treatment as between male and female officials who are, in fact, placed in comparable situations.

11. Such unwarranted difference of treatment between female officials and officials of the male sex would result from an interpretation of the concept of 'nationals' referred to above as also embracing the nationality which was imposed by law on an official of the female sex by virtue of her marriage, and which she was unable to renounce.

12. It is therefore necessary to define the concept of an official's present or previous nationality under Article 4(a) of Annex VII as excluding nationality imposed by law on a female official upon her marriage with a national of another state, when she has no possibility of renouncing it.

13. In the present case the applicant, on her marriage, had the nationality of her husband conferred on her without the right to renounce it but by an express declaration she retained her Belgian nationality of origin.

14. Consequently, in applying the provision in question, the applicant's Italian nationality has not to be taken into account.

15. The applicant, accordingly, fulfils the condition of Article 4(a) of Annex VII of the Staff Regulations.

16. The decision [by] which the Commission withdrew its original decision to pay the applicant the expatriation allowance provided for by the Staff Regulations of Officials must, therefore, be annulled.

[B33]   Case 81/72 Commission of the European Communities v Council of the European Communities [1973] ECR 575

[The Council were under a duty to review the remuneration of Community officials in the light of a report from the Commission. As a matter of practice the Council and Commission worked with the collaboration of the organisations representing the staff. The Council made a decision to apply, as an experiment and for a period of three years, a system of adjusting remuneration, based on two indices (a lower and an upper index) which were related to salaries in the public service in other Member States. The Commission's report indicated that the lower index was 3.6% and the upper index was 3.9%. With the wisdom of Solomon, the Commission proposed an increase of 3.75%. However, the Council adopted a regulation limiting the increase to 2.5%.]

The European Court of Justice (at pp 583–586)

8. There is no doubt that in deciding on [the decision], the Council had gone beyond the stage of preparatory consideration and had entered on the phase of decision making.

. . .

Both the antecedents and the terms of the decision taken make it clear that the Council intended to bind itself to observe fixed criteria, in the working out of subsequent measures relative to the periodic determination of remunerations.

. . .

9. It appears, therefore, that by its [decision], the Council acting within the framework of the powers relating to the remunerations of [staff] assumed obligations which it has bound itself to observe for the period it has defined.

. . .

13. [It] follows that in fixing the increases [below] the level established by the lower index calculated in conformity with the [decision], the Council has violated the rule relating to the protection of legitimate confidence [legitimate expectation] in the implementation of [the] Staff Regulations.

[B34]   Case 97/76 Merkur Außenhandel GmbH & Co KG v Commission of the European Communities [1977] ECR 1063

[Merkur sought compensation for the injury which it claimed to have suffered as a result of a Regulation (EEC) 1497/76, the effect of which was to modify certain monetary compensatory amounts (see below). Merkur claimed that as a result of this modification it was prevented from performing in full contracts of sale, entered into before the entry into force of the regulation, for the delivery to two Danish companies and one English company of certain tapioca products, and it had to undertake to deliver alternative products under more onerous conditions in return for partial termination of the original contracts. By omitting to provide in the regulation for adequate transitional measures to protect the legitimate expectations of the traders concerned, without the omission being justified by an overriding matter of public interest, the Commission flagrantly violated a superior rule of law, thus incurring the civil liability of the Community. The system of compensatory amounts was intended principally to safeguard the level of prices in the Member States concerned against the disturbance which might be caused by monetary instability and might jeopardise a normal trend of business in agriculture. The aim of the system of compensatory amounts was, in particular, to obviate the difficulties which monetary instability might create for the proper functioning of the common organisations of the market, rather than to protect the individual interests of traders.]

The European Court of Justice (at pp 1078–1080)

5. [Regulation 1497/76 is] a legislative measure adopted by the Community in the area of economic policy in the higher interest of the proper functioning of [market] organisations.

In those circumstances, although the possibility of protecting the legitimate interests of the trader cannot be excluded, nevertheless the Community could only be rendered liable for the damage suffered by such traders as a result of the adoption of legislative measures governing the [compensatory amounts] system if in the absence of any overriding public interest the Commission were to abolish or modify the compensatory amounts applicable in a specific sector with immediate effect and without warning and in the absence of any appropriate transitional measures and if such abolition or modification was not foreseeable by a prudent trader.

6. It is clear that in this instance [Regulation 1497/76] did not take effect immediately and without warning, since its entry into force had been fixed for the 15th day after its publication in the Official Journal of the European Communities.

Furthermore, [an announcement in the trade press] of 19 June 1976 informed the interested parties that the Commission was intending to adopt a regulation to subject to the same tariff classification as tapioca any product composed of more than 50% of tapioca.

[Merkur] acknowledges that it became aware of that announcement on 22 June 1976.

7. In the light of those circumstances the Commission cannot be said to have adopted the measure in dispute with immediate effect and without warning in violation of the principle of the protection of the legitimate expectation of the parties concerned.

It is also unjustified to allege that the Commission failed to adopt appropriate transitional measures to accompany the entry into force of the regulation at issue, enabling the interested parties and in particular [Merkur] to avoid the risk of an unforeseeable modification of the compensatory amounts.

On that point [Merkur] maintains that the Commission could at least have authorised performance in full of the contracts concluded finally and irrevocably before the entry into force of the regulation or before the trader became aware of the proposals for its adoption.

8. In the present case the 'respect for existing contracts' referred to by [Merkur] would amount to granting to the contracts concluded a guarantee equivalent to that which they normally obtain from fixing the compensatory amount in advance.

The Community rules on monetary compensatory amounts applicable here made no provision for such amounts to be fixed in advance.

Although in certain cases concerning monetary compensatory amounts which cannot be fixed in advance the Commission has made provision for transitional measures out of a desire to respect existing contracts, nevertheless, the cases in which such measures have been adopted differ widely from the present and relate, in particular, to cases in which the compensatory amounts in question were levied rather than granted on imports and exports and thus constituted an increased burden on the trader.

9. At all events, the adoption of transitional measures on the basis of the principle referred to by [Merkur] could only have been envisaged by the Commission if it appeared that the modification of the monetary compensatory amounts in question could not have been foreseen by a prudent trader.

On the other hand, the very fact that the regulation relating to those amounts had not provided for them to be fixed in advance, although that possibility existed in relation to [certain] compensatory amounts, should have warned a prudent trader that the Commission intended the system of monetary compensatory amounts to be very flexible.

Thus, in the light of the structure of the Community rules applicable and taking into account the nature and aims of the machinery for monetary compensatory amounts, in particular, where such amounts are granted rather than levied on exports, it seems impossible that a modification of the monetary compensatory amounts could be regarded as unforeseeable by a prudent trader.

That such a modification was not unforeseeable in this instance is all the more clear from the express provision for it in the contract [concluded] on 20 May 1976 with the Danish company [in] which the vendor reserved the right to supply a similar product should the monetary compensatory amounts in force when the contract was concluded be modified or abolished.

. . .

11. The result of all the foregoing is that the conditions fixed for the entry into force of Regulation (EEC) 1497/76 do not amount to a flagrant violation of a superior rule of law for the protection of the individual sufficient to incur the liability of the Community under [Article 215(2)] of the Treaty.

[B35] Case 108/81 GR Amylum v Council of the European Communities [1982] ECR 3017

[Regulation 1293/79 laid down a system of quotas and levies relating to the production of isoglucose for the period running from 1 July 1979 to 30 June 1980. In Case 138/79 *Roquette Frères SA v Council of the European Communities* [1980] ECR 3333 and Case 139/79 *Maizena GmbH v Council of the European Communities* [1980] ECR 3393, Regulation 1293/79 was in fact declared void by the Court of Justice, on 29 October 1980, because it was adopted in the absence of the opinion of the Parliament, required by Article 43 of the Treaty. Regulation 387/81 reinstated, in respect of the same period, that is to say with retroactive effect, the system of quotas laid down by Regulation 1293/79 in respect of the period running from 1 July 1979 to 30 June 1980. Amylum brought an action to annul Regulation 387/81, claiming that Regulation 387/81 offended against the principle that Community measures should not have retroactive effect.]

The European Court of Justice (at pp 3130–3134)

4. As the court has already held, in particular in [Case] 98/78 *Racke* [1979] ECR 69 and Case 99/78 *Decker* [1979] ECR 101, although in general the principle of legal certainty, as the applicant states, precludes a Community measure from taking effect from a point in time before its publication, it may exceptionally be otherwise where the purpose to be achieved so demands and where the legitimate expectations of those concerned are duly respected.

5. As regards the first of those two conditions it is well to call to mind certain matters of fact or law which are moreover well known to the parties. During the period of application of the contested regulation sugar producers were, in particular, subject to quotas and production levies. Isoglucose is a product which may be substituted for sugar and is in direct competition with it. Any Community decision concerning one of those products necessarily has repercussions on the other. Having regard to that situation, although by judgments of 29 October 1980 the court declared Regulation 1293/79 void for infringement of an essential procedural requirement, namely the absence of the Parliament's opinion, the court nevertheless considered that it was a matter for the Council, in view of the fact that isoglucose production was contributing to an increase in sugar surpluses and that it was open to it to impose restrictive measures on that production, to [take] measures in the context of the agricultural policy as it judged to be useful, regard being had to the similarity and interdependence of the two markets and the specific nature of the isoglucose market.

6. If, following the declaration of the nullity of Regulation 1293/79, the Council had adopted no measure restrictive of isoglucose production – in the present case the reinstatement with effect from 1 July 1979 of the quotas allocated and the levies imposed on the producers – the objective which it was pursuing, namely the stabilisation, in the general interest, of the sugar market, could not have been achieved or could only have been achieved to the detriment of sugar producers, who alone would have had to finance the costs of Community surpluses, or even to the detriment of the Community as a whole, whilst isoglucose producers whose production competed with that of sugar undertakings would have escaped all restraints.

7. The court is unable to uphold the argument put forward by the applicant that the application of Regulation 1293/79, until it was declared void by the court, had held isoglucose producers to observe the quotas which it laid down and thus rendered superfluous their reinstatement by the contested regulation. In fact, in addition to the legal basis which the contested regulation gave to the system of quotas during the period in question from 1 July 1979 to 30 June 1980, the maintenance of levies during that period, which was necessary to attain the objectives of public interest pursued by the

Council, made it necessary to fix the quotas upon which the amount of those levies depended.

8. Thus the Council was lawfully entitled to consider that the objective to be achieved in the general interest, namely the stabilisation of the Community market in sweeteners without arbitrary discrimination between traders, required the contested provisions to be retroactive in nature and thus the first of the conditions which the court lays down for the applicability rationae temporis of a Community measure to a date prior to the date of its publication may be regarded as satisfied.

9. To ascertain whether the second of the [two] conditions set out above is satisfied it is necessary to inquire whether the action of the Council in publishing on 17 February 1981 Regulation 387/81 has frustrated a legitimate expectation on the part of the applicants to the effect that the production of isoglucose would not be regulated during the period from 1 July 1979 to 30 June 1980.

. . .

10. It should first be pointed out that the contested provisions of Regulation 387/81 do not include any new measures and merely reproduce the provisions of [Regulation] 1293/79 declared void by the court on 29 October 1980.

11. In view of the fact that [Regulation] 1293/79 [retained] its full effect within the Community legal order untill it was declared void, so that the national authorities responsible for its implementation were required to subject the production of isoglucose to the restrictive system which it laid down, such a legitimate expectation could only be founded on the unforeseeability of the reinstatement with retroactive effect of the measures contained in Regulation 1293/79 declared void by the court.

12. In the present case the applicant cannot show any legitimate expectation worthy of protection.

13. In the first place the traders concerned by the rules in question are limited in number and are reasonably well aware of the interdependence of the markets in liquid sugar and isoglucose, of the situation of the Community market in sweeteners and therefore of the consequences which, following the declaration that Regulation 1293/79 was void, the imposition on the production of sugar in respect of the period from 1 July 1979 to 30 June 1980 of stabilisation measures from which the production of isoglucose would have been entirely exempt might have had.

14. Secondly by adopting successively regulations [extending] the effects of the previous one in respect of the period from 1 July 1980 to 30 June 1981 the Council had clearly manifested its intention of regulating the production of all sweeteners in the Community and to that end of subjecting the production of isoglucose to a restrictive system based on a system of quotas and production levies.

15. Thirdly it could not have escaped the notice of the applicant that in both judgments of the court of 29 October 1980 which declared void Regulation 1293/79 (which also fixed its own production quota), the court rejected the grounds on which the applicant companies Roquette and Maizena were contesting the substantive validity of that regulation and was at pains, at the same time [to state] that such nullity was without prejudice to 'the Council's power following the present judgment to take all appropriate measures pursuant to [Article 176(1)] of the Treaty'.

16. Finally, from the publication of the Commission's proposal in the Official Journal of 20 December 1980 [the] applicant knew that the Commission had, as early as 3 December 1980, submitted to the Council a proposal for a regulation [in] order to reinstate, for the period from 1 July 1979 to 30 June 1980, the system of quotas and levies in the form in which that system had been laid down by Regulation 1293/77 and in which it was to be reinstated by the contested provisions of Regulation 387/81.

17. In so challenging the retroactivity of those provisions the applicant further claims that they disturb the institutional equilibrium of the Communities. That claim cannot be upheld. On the one hand, there is no provision of the Treaty which precluded the Parliament from being called upon to express its views on a retroactive reinstatement of Regulation 1293/79 although it had not given its opinion on that regulation. On the other hand, the fact that the court, in declaring that regulation void, did not think to make use of the power given to it by [Article 174(2)] to state which of the effects of the regulation which it had declared void should be considered definitive, gives no ground for regarding the retroactive effect given to the contested provisions of Regulation 387/81, adopted by the Council in the context of [Article 176(1)], as a trespass on the prerogatives of the court.

[B36]   Case 114/76 Bela-Mühle Josef Bergmann KG v Grows-Farm GmbH & Co KG [1977] ECR 1211

[This case concerned the validity of a regulation (Regulation 563/76) on the compulsory purchase of skimmed milk powder held by intervention agencies. The regulation was made at a time when the stocks of skimmed milk powder bought in by the intervention agencies had reached considerable proportions and were continuing to increase (creating a skimmed milk powder mountain), despite the measures adopted by the Community institutions to curb the tendency towards over-production of milk and to increase the sale of skimmed milk powder. The system established by the regulation was designed to reduce stocks through the increased use in feeding stuffs of the protein contained in skimmed milk powder, by making the grant of the aids provided for certain vegetable protein products as well as the free circulation in the Community of certain imported animal feed products subject to the obligation to purchase specified quantities of skimmed milk powder. In order to ensure that this obligation was fulfilled, the grant of aid and free circulation were subject to the provision of a security or the production, on the prescribed form, of evidence of the purchase and of the denaturing of the prescribed quantities of skimmed milk powder. Bela-Mühle, a producer of concentrated feeding stuffs, brought an action against Grows-Farm, the proprietor of a battery hen unit, concerning the performance of a contract for delivery of feeding stuffs concluded between them. In addition to the price agreed under the contract, the supplier asked for payment of a sum equivalent to the charge arising under Regulation 563/76, the validity of which was contested by Grows-Farm on the grounds that Regulation 563/76 conflicted with the objectives of the common agricultural policy as defined in Article 39 of the Treaty, the prohibition against discrimination laid down by Article 40(3) of the Treaty and the principle of proportionality.]

Opinion of Advocate General Capotorti (at pp 1232–1234)

[The question] calling for a reply is whether in the present case the principle of proportionality has been complied with. The difference in concept between that principle and the principle of non-discrimination may be described in these terms: non-discrimination is concerned with the relationship between various groups of persons and takes the form of equality of treatment by bodies vested with public authority, whereas the principle of proportionality means that the burdens imposed on the persons concerned must not exceed the steps required in order to meet the public interest involved. If, therefore, a measure imposes on certain categories of persons a burden which is in excess of what is necessary – which must be appraised in the light of the actual economic and social conditions and having regard to the means available – it violates the principle of proportionality.

The need to have regard to that principle in reviewing the validity of Community measures which impose burdens and restrictions on those affected by them first found expression in the case law of the court in Case 19/61 *Mannesmann AG v High Authority* [1962] ECR 357. On that occasion the court held that 'the High Authority, in working out and applying the financial arrangements which it has established to safeguard the stability of the market, has indeed a duty to take account of the actual economic circumstances in which these arrangements have to be applied, so that the aims pursued may be attained under the most favourable conditions and with the smallest possible sacrifices by the undertakings affected'.

In Case 25/70 *Einfuhr- und Vorratsstelle für Getreide und Futtermittel v Köster* [1970] ECR 1161, the court was called upon to decide whether the Commission, in making, in one of its regulations, the grant of a licence subject to the obligation to export and to the lodging of a forfeitable deposit, had not contravened the principle that the means must be proportionate to the end. The [court] laid down that this principle, which represents a fundamental right, is one of the general principles of law protected by the Court of Justice. The burdens arising under the regulation in question were therefore examined in order to establish whether they were necessary and appropriate to the attainment of the aim in view. The court also took into account the amount of the deposit required in order to determine whether it was in proportion to the total value of the goods and of the other trading costs on the basis that if there had been a disproportion, it would have given rise to a breach of a fundamental right.

. . .

The court had to deal with another question relating to proportionality in Case 5/73 *Balkan – Import-Export v Hauptzollamt Berlin-Packhof* [1973] ECR 1091, in connection with the levying of compensatory amounts in the milk and milk products [sector]. On that occasion, the court emphasised that, in exercising their powers, the Community institutions must ensure that the amounts which traders are charged are no greater than is required to achieve the aim which the authorities are to accomplish.

. . .

In Case 95/75 *Effem GmbH v Hauptzollamt Lüneburg* [1976] ECR 361, it was held that the provisions relating to an export levy to be applied to cereals were infringed in circumstances where the levy was fixed at a standard rate without taking account of the quantity of raw materials contained in the finished product. In contrast to the Advocate General, the court did not in that case expressly refer to the principle of proportionality but I feel justified in saying that the decision was based on that principle.

Finally, I would point out that the court has referred to proportionality as a criterion in a whole series of judgments relating to the freedom of movement and of establishment and of freedom to provide services which the Treaty confers on individuals. In those cases, however, the principle of proportionality was applied as a measure of the legality of national provisions and measures restricting those rights.

I turn now to the present case. The burden imposed by Regulation 563/76 on producers and importers of seeds for use in feeding stuffs which, as we have seen, may be passed on to breeders who purchase animal feed, can be calculated by taking two factors into account: the price fixed for the compulsory purchase of milk powder and the actual value of that product compared with the price of other substances having the same nutritional value. Under [the scheme] the price at which the intervention agencies sold skimmed milk powder for use in animal feed was 52.16 [units of account for each 100 kilogrammes]. According to a working document of the Commission [the] market value of that type of milk at the time, having regard to its protein value compared with that of other feeding stuffs, may be reckoned to be in the region of 15 [units of account for each 100 kilogrammes]. As for the price of substitute products it must be borne in mind that [the] Commission admitted that the nutritive value of broken soya beans is, weight for weight, substantially the same as that of skimmed milk powder and [that] during the period when Regulation 563/76 applied, the price of broken soya beans was, on average, a little over 17 [units of account for each 100 kilogrammes].

Breeders were in consequence obliged to purchase milk powder for animal feed at a price which was more than three times its actual market value [see paragraph 7 of the judgment]. The burden represented by the difference between the imposed price and the market value [about 35 units of account for each 100 kilogrammes] amounted to a kind of tax levied on the afore-mentioned categories to meet the need to dispose of surplus milk powder stocks.

In fact, according to a report of the Federal German Minister for Agriculture, quoted by the Council, the increase in costs incurred by the breeders as a result of the obligation to purchase milk powder amounted to 2.81% in the case of feeding stuffs for use by poultry and to 1.34% in the case of feeding stuffs for use by pigs. The question therefore arises whether that need could have been satisfied by imposing a less onerous burden on those categories.

Two answers can be given to that question. The first and rather obvious one is that the sacrifice would certainly have been more evenly distributed if it had [been] shared by all citizens of the Community by making the Community budget bear the whole of the cost. In this connection it must be borne in mind that even if the Community had sold the milk powder for animal feed at the imposed price of 52.16 [units of account for each 100 kilogrammes], it still lost, in 1976, 38 [units of account for each 100 kilogrammes], which is the figure representing the difference between the intervention price and the selling price. It is worth noting that this possibility was the solution adopted later by the Community after the expiry of Regulation 563/76 [since under Regulation 2706/76] the selling price of denatured milk powder for animal feed was drastically reduced from 52 to 17 [units of account] to enable it to be competitive on the market. The second answer may be based on the fact that the costs of processing liquid skimmed milk into milk powder and of subsequent denaturing are higher than the market price of this milk for use in animal feed, namely prices of from 17 to 19 [units of account for each 100 kilogrammes] compared with the price of 15 [units of account]. If, therefore, continued encouragement had not been given to the processing of liquid milk into a milk powder which, in so far as it was for use in animal feed, had a market value less than the mere costs of processing and if an attempt had, instead, been made to reduce the extent of such processing, devoting the liquid milk to different uses, and actually destroying a part of it, it would have been possible, at less total cost, to prevent the growth of surplus stocks of milk powder. In those circumstances the extent of the burden on producers and importers of feeding stuffs and upon cattle raisers could have been less. At the hearing, the Commission objected that destruction of huge quantities of liquid milk might have created problems from the ecological standpoint. I do not find that argument very convincing. In any event, it cannot, in my view, bo donicd that, on the basis of a solution of this kind, designed to slow down production of milk powder and, in consequence, sales to the intervention agencies, the essential objective pursued by means of the system introduced by Regulation 563/76, namely, the reduction of milk powder stocks held by those agencies, could have been attained by means which were less burdensome.

Finally, the fact that, compared with the advantage sought for the Community, that system made demands which were too heavy on certain categories of producers and consumers leads me to conclude that the said regulation breached the general principle of proportionality.

The European Court of Justice (at pp 1220–1221)

6. Under Article 39, the objectives of the common agricultural policy are to be the rational development of agricultural production, the assurance of a fair standard of living for the whole of the agricultural community, the stabilisation of markets and the availability of supplies to consumers at reasonable prices. Although Article 39 thus enables the common agricultural policy to be defined in terms of a wide choice of measures involving guidance or intervention, the fact nevertheless remains that [Article 40(3)] provides that the common organisation of the agricultural markets shall be limited to pursuit of the objectives set out in Article 39. Furthermore, [Article 40(3)] lays down that the common organisation of the markets 'shall exclude any discrimination between producers or consumers within the Community'. Thus the statement of the objectives contained in Article 39, taken together with the rules in [Article 40(3)], supplies both positive and negative criteria by which the legality of the measures adopted in this matter may be appraised.

7. The arrangements made by Regulation [563/76] constituted a temporary measure intended to counteract the consequences of a chronic

imbalance in the common organisation of the market in milk and milk prod-ucts. A feature of these arrangements was the imposition not only on producers of milk and milk products but also, and more especially, on pro-ducers in other agricultural sectors of a financial burden which took the form, first, of the compulsory purchase of certain quantities of an animal feed product and, secondly, of the fixing of a purchase price for that prod-uct at a level three times higher than that of the substances which it replaced. The obligation to purchase at such a disproportionate price con-stituted a discriminatory distribution of the burden of costs between the various agricultural sectors. Nor, moreover, was such an obligation neces-sary in order to attain the objective in view, namely, the disposal of stocks of skimmed milk powder. It could not therefore be justified for the purposes of attaining the objectives of the common agricultural policy.

8. In consequence, the answer must be that [Regulation 536/76] is null and void.

[B37]   Cases 279, 280, 285, 286/84 Walter Rau Lebensmittelwerke v Commission of the European Communities [1987] ECR 1069

[Rau claimed that they had suffered damage as a result of the 'Christmas butter' scheme. A regulation stated that the essential aims of the scheme were to increase the consumption of butter not merely in order to make an overall reduction in butter stocks but also to avoid prolonging the period of storage of older butter which, beyond a certain period, becomes unfit for human consumption and must be further processed. The regulation estab-lished a scheme to sell butter at reduced prices over the Christmas period. Rau claimed that they suffered not just because the butter in question was bought in preference to fresh butter but also in preference to margarine, sales of which dropped noticeably during and after the Christmas butter scheme.]

The European Court of Justice (at pp 1125–1126)

34. It is settled case law that in order to establish whether a provision of Community law complies with the principle of proportionality, it must be as-certained whether the means which it employs are suitable for the purpose of achieving the desired objective and whether they do not go beyond what is necessary to achieve it. Furthermore, as the court stated in [Case 138/78 *Stölting v Hauptzollamt Hamburg-Jonas* [1979] ECR 713], if a measure is patently unsuited to the objective which the competent institution seeks to pursue this may affect its legality; however the [Commission] must be recog-nised as having a discretionary power in regard to the common agricultural policy which reflects the responsibilities which the Treaty imposes on them.

35. [It] can be seen [that] the essential aims of the [regulation] were to increase the consumption of butter not merely in order to make an overall reduction in butter stocks but also to avoid prolonging the period of storage of older butter which, beyond a certain period, becomes unfit for human consumption and must be further processed. It can be seen [that the] con-tested scheme actually led to additional sales of approximately 40,000 tonnnes of butter in the Community, thus avoiding the storage of that

quantity, and [there] was consequently a better rotation and a certain renewal of butter stocks.

. . .

36. [It] does not appear either from the documents on the file or from the arguments made before the court that the Commission committed a manifest error of assessment in considering that it did not have any other possible way of achieving the desired objectives by more efficient and less onerous means under conditions which were legally, economically and psychologically acceptable.

37. In those circumstances, and although it must be admitted, as the Commission itself admits, that schemes such as the Christmas butter scheme are of limited effectiveness and are very costly from the point of view of Community finances, it does not appear that the contested measure was unsuitable for the purpose of achieving the desired aims or that it went further than was necessary to achieve them. Therefore, the submission alleging breach of the principle of proportionality must be rejected.

[B38]   Case 17/74 Transocean Marine Paint Association v Commission of the European Communities [1974] ECR 1063

[In purported exercise of its powers with regard to the granting of the renewal of an exemption from rules relating to competition policy (see **[E59]-[E63]**), the Commission, inter alia, imposed a condition on the Association with regard to the provision to the Commission of certain information. The Association was composed of members established within the Community and members not so established and the condition was imposed on the Association as a whole. The Association claimed that the condition was too great a burden and might be impossible to perform with regard to its non-EEC members, some of whose laws would not permit the disclosure of such information. Failure to provide the information could be punished by fines imposed on the EEC members for a situation which was not their fault. There were fears that the EEC members might be dropped from the Association by the non-EEC members because of the condition. During the discussions which took place before the condition was imposed, the Commission had in writing given advance warning that it would want some information to be communicated to it and the Association had agreed and indeed their Board of Directors had been quite prepared to discuss the form of words whereby the Commission and the Association would agree what information was necessary. The Association claimed that they were not given the opportunity to state their case, to give their view as to what information should be communicated to the Commission and what dangers a too burdensome condition might await the EEC members of the Association. The Association argued that the Commission were under an obligation to inform them of its intentions with regard to the renewal of the exemption, especially those of its intentions which might penalise the Association, and to give the Association an opportunity to make representations on its behalf. They first of all argued that the written rules of procedure laid down in a regulation implementing basic guidelines relating

to competition had been breached by the Commission. In addition, in anticipation of a ruling that the formal written statutory provisions did not impose
on the Commission the duty to give a hearing to the Association before attaching conditions to an exemption, the Association pointed to another
source of law imposing legal obligations on the Commission and claimed
that the Commission had violated general principles of administrative procedure.]

Opinion of Advocate General Warner (at pp 1088–1089)

My Lords, [there] is a rule embedded in the law of some of our countries
that an administrative authority, before wielding a statutory power to the
detriment of a particular person, must in general hear what that person has
to say about the matter, even if the statute does not expressly require it.
'Audi alteram partem'. [In] the law of England the rule is centuries old, firmly
established and of daily application. It is considered to be a 'rule of natural
justice', a somewhat flamboyant and sometimes criticised phrase. [The]
most often cited expression of the rule is in the judgment of Byles J, in
Cooper v Wandsworth Board of Works (1863) 14 CBNS 180, where he said
that 'although there are no positive words in a statute requiring that the
party shall be heard, yet the justice of the common law will supply the omission of the legislature'. In England today there is no scope for controversy
about the existence of the rule. [I] know, my Lords, of no exception to the
rule, acknowledged in English law, which could have deprived the
[Association] in the circumstances of the present case of the right to be
heard before being subjected to an obligation such as that [at issue].

There can be no doubt that the rule forms part also of the law of
Scotland (consider *Malloch v Aberdeen Corporation* [1971] 1 WLR 1578)
and of the laws of Denmark (see Andersen, *Dansk Forvaltningsret . . .*), of
Germany (see Forsthoff, *Lehrbuch des Verwaltungsrechts . . .*) and of
Ireland (see Kelly, *Fundamental Rights in the Irish Law and Constitution
. . .*). [It] appears that the principle here in question is of fairly recent origin
in French law and that its scope is not yet settled. The decisions of the
Conseil d'Etat evince three different approaches: the narrowest being to
apply it only when the decision of the administrative authority concerned is
in the nature of a sanction; a slightly wider approach which would apply it in
any case where the decision of that authority is based on the character or
on the behaviour of the person to be affected; and a third approach which
is virtually as wide as that of the English common law. [The] position in
Belgium and in Luxembourg is similar, though the Conseils d'Etat of those
countries seem to have been less hesitant in developing the principle than
that of France. [In] Italy the Consiglio di Stato has held that there is no general principle of law requiring an administrative authority to inform those
concerned of its proposals so as to enable them to comment [and] it seems
that the law of the Netherlands is similar, in this respect, to that of Italy.

[My] Lords, that review, which I have sought to keep short, of the laws of
the Member States, must, I think, on balance, lead to the conclusion that
the right to be heard forms part of those rights which 'the law' referred to in
Article 164 of the Treaty upholds, and of which, accordingly, it is the duty of
this court to ensure the observance.

I would therefore reject the contention of the Commission that it was
under no duty to inform the [Association] of what it had in mind before imposing on them the obligation [to provide the information].

The European Court of Justice (at pp 1079–1080)

15. It is clear [that the relevant regulation implementing Regulation 17/62 **[E59]**] applies the general rule that a person whose interests are perceptibly affected by a decision taken by a public authority must be given the opportunity to make his point of view known. This rule requires that an undertaking be clearly informed, in good time, of the essence of [the] conditions to which the Commission intends to subject an exemption and it must have the opportunity to submit its observations to the Commission. This is especially so in the case of conditions which, as in this case, impose considerable obligations having far-reaching effects.

[B39]   Case 85/76 Hoffman-La Roche & Co AG v Commission of the European Communities [1979] ECR 461

[The applicants complained that, in taking a decision against them, the Commission had taken into account various documents and other evidence, which the Commission had refused to let them inspect because of the duty to respect professional secrecy (see, further, **[E59][E63]**).]

The European Court of Justice (at pp 511–512)

9. Observance of the right to be heard is in all proceedings in which sanctions, in particular fines or penalty payments, may be imposed a fundamental principle of Community law which must be respected even if the proceedings in question are administrative proceedings.

Article 19(1) of [Regulation 17: **[E59]**] obliges the Commission before taking a decision in connection with fines, to give the persons concerned the opportunity of putting forward their point of view with regard to the complaints made against them.

Similarly Article 4 of [Regulation 99/63, governing the hearing provided for by Article 19] provides that the Commission shall in its decision deal only with those objections raised against undertakings and associations of undertakings in respect of which they have been afforded the opportunity of making known their views.

. . .

11. Thus it emerges from the provisions quoted above and also from the general principle to which they give effect that in order to respect the principle of the right to be heard the undertakings concerned must have been afforded the opportunity during the administrative procedure to make known their views on the truth and [the] relevance of the facts and circumstances alleged and on the documents used by the Commission to support its claim that there has been an infringement of [Article 86 of the Treaty: **[E49]**].

[B40]   Joint Declaration by the European Parliament, the Council and the Commission (OJ C103/1, 27 April 1977)

THE EUROPEAN PARLIAMENT, THE COUNCIL AND THE COMMISSION,

Whereas the Treaties establishing the European Communities are based on the principle of respect for the law;

Whereas, as the Court of Justice has recognised, that law comprises, over and above the rules embodied in the treaties and secondary Community legislation, the general principles of law and in particular the fundamental rights, principles and rights on which the constitutional law of the Member States is based;

Whereas, in particular, all the Member States are Contracting Parties to the European Convention for the Protection of Human Rights and Fundamental Freedoms signed in Rome on 4 November 1950,

HAVE ADOPTED THE FOLLOWING DECLARATION :

1. The European Parliament, the Council and the Commission stress the prime importance they attach to the protection of fundamental rights, as derived in particular from the constitutions of the Member States and the European Convention for the Protection of Human Rights and Fundamental Freedoms.
2. In the exercise of their powers and in pursuance of the aims of the European Communities they respect and will continue to respect these rights.

[B41]   Single European Act, preamble (1986, Cmnd 9758)

Determined to work together to promote democracy on the basis of the fundamental rights recognised in the constitutions and laws of the Member States, in the Convention for the Protection of Human Rights and Fundamental Freedoms and the European Social Charter, notably freedom, equality and social justice, . . .

[B42]   Case 11/70 Internationale Handelsgesellschaft mbH v Einfuhr- und Vorratsstelle für Getreide und Futtermittel [1970] ECR 1125

[Internationale Handelsgesellschaft, an export-import undertaking based in Frankfurt-am-Main in Germany, obtained a licence to export maize. Under a regulation, the issue of the licence was conditional upon the lodging by the undertaking of a deposit guaranteeing that the exportation would be effected during the period of validity of the licence (the 'system of deposits').

Since the exportation was only partially completed during the period of validity of the licence, the appropriate German administrative authority, again in
accordance with the provisions of a regulation, declared that a considerable
portion of the deposit should be forfeited. The Verwaltungsgericht (administrative court) of Frankfurt-am-Main referred to the European Court of
Justice certain questions on the validity of the system of deposits.
According to the Verwaltungsgericht, the system of deposits was contrary
to certain principles of German constitutional law, such as freedom of
action in trading, economic liberty and the principle of proportionality, and
that that national constitutional law ought to be protected within the framework of Community law, with the result that the primacy of supranational
law must yield before the principles of the German Constitution.]

The European Court of Justice (at p 1134)

3. Recourse to the legal rules or concepts of national law in order to
judge the validity of measures adopted by the institutions of the Community
would have an adverse effect on the uniformity and efficacy of Community
law. The validity of such measures can only be judged in the light of
Community law. In fact, the law stemming from the Treaty, an independent
source of law, cannot because of its very nature be overridden by rules of
national law, however framed, without being deprived of its character as
Community law and without the legal basis of the Community itself being
called in question. Therefore the validity of a Community measure or its effect within a Member State cannot be affected by allegations that it runs
counter to either fundamental rights as formulated by the constitution of
that state or the principles of a national constitutional structure.

4. However, an examination should be made as to whether or not any
analogous guarantee inherent in Community law has been disregarded. In
fact, respect for fundamental rights forms an integral part of the general
principles of law protected by the Court of Justice. The protection of such
rights, whilst inspired by the constitutional traditions common to the
Member States, must be ensured within the framework of the structure and
objectives of the Community. It must therefore be ascertained, in the light
of the doubts expressed by the Verwaltungsgericht, whether the system of
deposits has infringed rights of a fundamental nature, respect for which
must be ensured in the Community legal system.

[The court was prepared, in particular, to examine the detailed rules of
the system of deposits and to consider whether those rules might be contested in the light of the allegation that the obligations of the system of
deposits constituted a breach of the principle of proportionality in that it was
an excessive intervention with the constitutional freedom of disposition in
trade, as the objective of the system could have been attained by methods
of intervention having less serious financial consequences. Having made
its examination, the Court of Justice held that the costs involved in the system did not constitute an amount disproportionate to the total value of the
goods in question and that the burdens resulting from the system were not
excessive, being the normal consequences of a system of organisation of
the markets (conceived to meet the general interest of ensuring a fair standard of living for the agricultural community while ensuring that supplies
reached customers at reasonable prices). The system of deposits constituted an appropriate (ie not disproportionate) method for the purpose of

carrying out the common organisation of the agricultural markets and the fact that the system of deposits involved the lodging of a guaranteed deposit did not violate any right of a fundamental nature.]

[B43]   Case 29/69 Erich Stauder v City of Ulm, Sozialamt [1969] ECR 419

[A Commission decision authorised the Member States to make butter available at a reduced price to beneficiaries under certain social welfare schemes and whose income did not enable them to buy butter at normal prices. Article 4 of the decision, in its German version only, provided that Member States were to take the necessary measures to ensure that persons benefiting from the cheap butter scheme might only receive butter in exchange for a coupon issued in their names. The system used by Germany to implement this article was the issue of cards with a detachable coupon with a stub which had, in order to be valid, to bear the name and address of the beneficiary. Stauder was entitled to buy reduced price butter but he considered it illegal to make the appearance of the name of the beneficiary on the stub a condition for buying the butter. He brought an action before the Verwaltungsgericht, Stuttgart (Administrative Court of Stuttgart) against the City of Ulm and the Verwaltungsgericht referred for decision by the European Court of Justice the question whether the requirement in Article 4 of the decision that the sale of butter at reduced prices to beneficiaries was to be subject to the condition that the name of the beneficiary was to be divulged to retailers could be considered compatible with the general principles of Community law.]

The European Court of Justice (at pp 424–425)

2. The above-mentioned decision is addressed to all the Member States and authorises them, with a view to stimulating the sale of surplus quantities of butter on the Common Market, to make butter available at a lower price than normal to certain categories of consumers who are in receipt of certain social assistance. This authorisation is subject to certain conditions designed, inter alia, to ensure that the product, when marketed in this way, is not prevented from reaching its proper destination. To that end Article 4 of [the decision] stipulates in two of its versions, one being the German version, that the states must take all necessary measures to ensure that beneficiaries can only purchase the product in question on presentation of a 'coupon indicating their names', whilst in the other versions, however, it is only stated that a 'coupon referring to the person concerned' must be shown, thus making it possible to employ other methods of checking in addition to naming the beneficiary. It is therefore necessary in the first place to ascertain exactly what methods the provision at issue prescribes.

3. When a single decision is addressed to all the Member States the necessity for uniform application and accordingly for uniform interpretation makes it impossible to consider one version of the text in isolation but requires that it be interpreted on the basis of both the real intention of its author and the aim he seeks to achieve, in the light in particular of the versions in all four languages.

4. In a case like the present one, the most liberal interpretation must

prevail, provided that it is sufficient to achieve the objectives pursued by the decision in question. It cannot, moreover, be accepted that the authors of the decision intended to impose stricter obligations in some Member States than in others.

5. This interpretation is, moreover, confirmed by the Commission's declaration that an amendment designed to remove the requirement that a name shall appear on the coupon was proposed by [the committee] to which the draft of [the decision] was submitted for its opinion. The last recital of the preamble to this decision shows that the Commission intended to adopt the proposed amendment.

6. It follows that the provision in question must be interpreted as not requiring – although it does not prohibit – the identification of beneficiaries by name. The Commission was thus able to publish [later on] an amending decision to this effect. Each of the Member States is accordingly now able to choose from a number of methods by which the coupons may refer to the person concerned.

7. Interpreted in this way the provision at issue contains nothing capable of prejudicing the fundamental human rights enshrined in the general principles of Community law and protected by the court.

[B44]   Case 4/73 J Nold, Kohlen- und Baustoffgroßhandlung v Commission of the European Communities [1974] ECR 491

[Nold was a company carrying out a wholesale coal and constructions materials business in Germany. In 1969 the Commission, by a decision, authorised the merger of the mining companies of the Ruhr Basin by the transfer of colliery assets to a single company, Ruhrkohle, and obliged Ruhrkohle to submit to the Commission any amendment to its terms of business. The Commission later, by a second decision, authorised new trading rules which, in particular, fixed the conditions required for acquisition of the status of a direct wholesaler of coal, whereby the entitlement of a wholesaler to buy coal direct was subject to the conclusion of a fixed two-year contract stipulating the purchase of at least 6,000 metric tons of coal a year from Ruhrkhole for the supply of domestic and small consumers, a quantity which greatly exceeded Nold's previous two years' annual sales of coal. Nold claimed that from the date the second decision came into force it could no longer meet such a condition as in the previous two years Nold had been unable to reach the minimum quota henceforth required and therefore that decision meant that Nold could no longer be considered as a direct wholesaler in the coal trade. The decision had the effect of withdrawing Nold's status as a direct wholesaler and Nold claimed that it was therefore the victim of discrimination. Nold also claimed that both the terms of business of Ruhrkhole and their application violated certain fundamental rights enshrined by both the national constitutions of some Member States and by international conventions and, consequently, 'received' into Community law. In particular there was, claimed Nold, a violation of the right of free development of the personality, the free choice and pursuit of employment and the right of property ownership, the protection of which was ensured in particular by Article 14 of the Grundgesetz (the Constitution of the Federal Republic of Germany) and the Constitution of the Land of Hesse (the region in Germany where Nold's business was situated). It was argued that Nold's exclusion from the coal trade was equivalent to expropriation because it deprived Nold of 'actual possession'. The following rights are also at issue in this case: namely the right to free development of the personality, the right to freedom of economic action and the principle of proportionality. The Commission argued that there could be discrimination only if dealers in a similar position to that of Nold were treated differently in respect of the ability to purchase coal directly from the producer but that, in this situation, this was not the case, as the criteria adopted were equally valid for all dealers in the Community. The Commission also argued that with regard to the question of fundamental rights, the protection of property ownership constituted without any doubt one of the guarantees recognised by Community law which, in this connection, was based on the constitutional traditions of Member States and on acts of public international law, such as the Convention for the Protection of Human Rights and Fundamental Freedoms. However, as the concept of effective protection of the right of property ownership varied from one Member State to another, its practical application had to take account of that national norm which affords the greatest protection and that the right of a wholesaler to qualify for direct supplies was not a right covered by the guarantee of property ownership and, in any case, the Community had not interfered with any such right.]

The European Court of Justice (at pp 506–508)

[On the question of discrimination]

8. It is objected that the Commission allowed [Ruhrkohle] arbitrarily to fix [the terms of business so] that, having regard to the quantity and nature of its annual sales, [Nold] has lost its entitlement to direct supplies and is relegated to the position of having to deal through an intermediary, with all the commercial disadvantages which this involves.

[Nold] considers it to be discriminatory that, unlike other undertakings, it should lose its entitlement to direct supplies from the producer and should thereby be in a more unfavourable position than other dealers who continue to enjoy this advantage.

. . .

9. In the reasoning given in its decision the Commission emphasised that it was aware that the introduction of the new terms of business would mean that a number of dealers would lose their entitlement to buy direct from the producer, due to their inability to undertake [those terms].

It justifies this measure by the need for [Ruhrkohle], in view of the major decline in coal sales, to rationalise its marketing system in such a way as to limit direct business association to dealers operating on a sufficient scale.

The requirement that dealers contract for an annual minimum quantity is in fact intended to ensure that the collieries can market their products on a regular basis and in quantities suited to their production capacity.

10. It emerges from the explanations given by the Commission [that] the imposition of the criteria indicated above can be justified on the grounds not only of the technical conditions appertaining to coal mining but also of the

particular economic difficulties created by the recession in coal production.

It therefore appears that these criteria, established by an administrative act of general application, cannot be considered discriminatory.

. . .

As regards the application of these criteria, it is not alleged that [Nold] is treated differently from other undertakings which, having failed to meet the requirements laid down under the new rules, have likewise lost the advantage of their entitlement to purchase direct from the producer.

11. These submissions must therefore be dismissed.

[On the question of the alleged violation of fundamental rights]

12. [Nold] asserts finally that certain of its fundamental rights have been violated, in that the restrictions introduced by the new trading rules authorised by the Commission have the effect, by depriving it of direct supplies, of jeopardising both the profitability of the undertaking and the free development of its business activity, to the point of endangering its very existence.

In this way, the decision is said to violate, in respect of [Nold], a right akin to a proprietary right, as well as its right to the free pursuit of business activity, as protected by the Grundgesetz of the Federal Republic of Germany and by the constitutions of other Member States and various international treaties, including in particular the Convention for the Protection of Human Rights and Fundamental Freedoms of 4 November 1950 and the Protocol to that Convention of 20 March 1952.

13. As the court has already stated, fundamental rights form an integral part of the general principles of law, the observance of which it ensures.

In safeguarding these rights, the court is bound to draw inspiration from constitutional traditions common to the Member States, and it cannot therefore uphold measures which are incompatible with fundamental rights recognised and protected by the constitutions of those states.

Similarly, international treaties for the protection of human rights on which the Member States have collaborated or of which they are signatories, can supply guidelines which should be followed within the framework of Community law.

The submissions of [Nold] must be examined in the light of these principles.

14. If rights of ownership are protected by the constitutional laws of all the Member States and if similar guarantees are given in respect of their right freely to choose and practice their trade or profession, the rights thereby guaranteed, far from constituting unfettered prerogatives, must be viewed in the light of the social function of the property and activities protected thereunder.

For this reason, rights of this nature are protected by law subject always to limitations laid down in accordance with the public interest.

Within the Community legal order it likewise seems legitimate that these rights should, if necessary, be subject to certain limits justified by the overall objectives pursued by the Community, on condition that the substance of these rights is left untouched.

As regards the guarantees accorded to a particular undertaking, they can in no respect be extended to protect mere commercial interests or opportunities, the uncertainties of which are part of the very essence of economic activity.

15. The disadvantages claimed by [Nold] are in fact the result of economic change and not of the contested decision.

It was for [Nold], confronted by the economic changes brought about by the recession in coal production, to acknowledge the situation and itself carry out the necessary adaptations.

16. This submission must be dismissed for all the reasons outlined above.

17. The action must accordingly be dismissed.

[B45]   Case 130/75 Vivien Prais v Council of the European Communities [1976] ECR 1589

[Vivien Prais was a candidate for a competitive entrance examination for a post as linguistic expert (translator) for the Council. The date fixed by the Council for the written test in that competition, which needed to take place simultaneously in Brussels and London, was 16 May 1975. On 25 April, she informed the Council by letter that, being of Jewish religion, she would be unable to undergo the test on 16 May, since that day was the first day of the Jewish feast of Shavuot (Pentecost), during which it is not permitted to travel or to write. She asked the Council to fix another day for the test. On 5 May 1975, the Council replied to her that it could not fix another date, since it was essential that all candidates should be examined on tests passed on the same day.]

The European Court of Justice (at pp 1597–1599)

6. The plaintiff claims firstly that the refusal of her request had as a result that by reason of her religious convictions she was prevented from taking part in the competition, in contravention of [Article 27(2)] of the Staff Regulations, which provides that officials shall be selected without reference to race, creed or sex.

7. In addition the plaintiff claims that religious discrimination is prohibited by Community law as being contrary to the fundamental rights of the individual, respect for which the court is bound to ensure.

8. The plaintiff also relies on [Article 9(2)] of the European Convention for the Protection of Human Rights and Fundamental Freedoms [which] provides as follows: 'Freedom to manifest one's religion or beliefs shall be subject only to such limitations as are prescribed by law and are necessary in a democratic society in the interests of public safety, for the protection of public order, health or morals, or for the protection of the rights and freedoms of others.' Since the European Convention has been ratified by all the Member States the rights enshrined in it are, according to the plaintiff, to be regarded as included in the fundamental rights to be protected by Community law.

9. The plaintiff claims that Article 27 of the Staff Regulations is to be interpreted in such a manner that the [Council] should so arrange the dates of tests for competitions to enter its service as to enable every candidate to take part in the tests, whatever his religious circumstances. Alternatively the right of freedom of religion guaranteed by the European Convention so requires.

10. The [Council] does not deny that Article 27 of the Staff Regulations requires that officials shall be selected without reference to race, creed or sex, nor does it seek to suggest that the right of freedom of religion as embodied in the European Convention does not form part of the fundamental rights recognised in Community law, but says that neither the Staff Regulations nor the European Convention are to be understood as according to the plaintiff the rights she claims.

11. The [Council] submits that such an obligation would force it to set up an elaborate administrative machinery. Article 27 does not limit its application to any particular creeds by enumerating them, and it would be necessary to ascertain the details of all religions practised in any Member State in order to avoid fixing for a test a date or a time which might offend against the tenets of any such religion and make it impossible for a candidate of that religious persuasion to take part in the test.

12. The Staff Regulations envisage that when a vacant post is being filled, and it is decided not to fill it by promotion or transfer, the selection of the candidate to be appointed shall, in general, be made by following the procedure of competition which may be on the basis of qualifications or of tests or of both qualifications and tests.

13. When the competition is on the basis of tests, the principle of equality necessitates that the tests shall be on the same conditions for all candidates and in the case of written tests the practical difficulties of comparison require that the written tests for all [the] candidates should be the same.

14. It is therefore of great importance that the date of the written tests should be the same for all candidates.

15. The interest of participants not to have a date fixed for the test which is unsuitable must be balanced against this necessity.

16. If a candidate informs the appointing authority that religious reasons make certain dates impossible for him the appointing authority should take this into account in fixing the date for written tests, and endeavour to avoid such dates.

17. On the other hand if the candidate does not inform the appointing authority in good time of his difficulties, the appointing authority would be justified in refusing to afford an alternative date, particularly if there are other candidates who have been convoked for the test.

18. If it is desirable that an appointing authority informs itself in a general way of dates which might be unsuitable for religious reasons, and seeks to avoid fixing such dates for tests, nevertheless, for the reasons indicated above, neither the Staff Regulations nor the fundamental rights already referred to can be considered as imposing on the appointing authority a duty to avoid a conflict with a religious requirement of which the authority has not been informed.

19. In so far as the [Council], if informed of the difficulty in good time, would have been obliged to take reasonable steps to avoid fixing for a test a date which would make it impossible for a person of a particular religious persuasion to undergo the test, it can be said that the [Council] in the present case was not informed of the unsuitability of certain days until the date for the test had been fixed, and the [Council] was in its discretion entitled to refuse to fix a different date when the other candidates had already been convoked.

20. For these reasons the plaintiff's claim should be rejected.

[B46]   Case 44/79 Liselotte Hauer v Land Rheinland-Pfalz [1979] ECR 3727

[A regulation, in order to adjust the Community wine-growing potential to market requirements, inter alia, imposed for a period of three years a prohibition on all new planting of vines. Mrs Hauer was refused permission to undertake the planting of new vines on her land by the regional authority and claimed that this refusal was contrary to the right to property which she claimed was guaranteed by national and Community law.]

The European Court of Justice (at pp 3745–3747)

17. The right to property is guaranteed in the Community legal order in accordance with the ideas common to the constitutions of the Member States, which are also reflected in the first Protocol to the European Convention for the Protection of Human Rights.

18. Article 1 of that Protocol provides as follows:

Every natural or legal person is entitled to the peaceful enjoyment of his possessions. No one shall be deprived of his possessions except in the public interest and subject to the conditions provided for by law and by the general principles of international law.

The preceding provisions shall not, however, in any way impair the right of a State to enforce such laws as it deems necessary to control the use of property in accordance with the general interest or to secure the payment of taxes or other contributions or penalties.

19. Having declared that persons are entitled to the peaceful enjoyment of their property, that provision envisages two ways in which the rights of a property owner may be [impaired]. In this case it is incontestable that the prohibition on new planting cannot be considered to be an act depriving the owner of his property, since he remains free to dispose of it or to put it to other uses which are not prohibited. On the other [hand], the second paragraph of Article 1 of the Protocol provides an important indication in so far as it recognises the right of a state 'to enforce such laws as it deems necessary to control the use of property in accordance with the general interest'. Thus the Protocol accepts in principle the legality of restrictions upon the use of property, whilst at the same time limiting those restrictions to the extent to which they are deemed 'necessary' by a state for the protection of the 'general interest'.

20. [It] is necessary to consider [the] indications provided by the constitutional rules and practices of the nine Member States. One of the first points to emerge in this regard is that those rules and practices permit the legislature to control the use of private property in accordance with the general interest. Thus some constitutions [Germany, Italy and Ireland] refer to the obligations arising out of the ownership of [property], to its social [function], to the subordination of its use to the common [good], or of social justice. [In] all the Member States, numerous legislative measures have given concrete expression to that social function of the right to property. Thus in all the Member States there is legislation on agriculture and forestry, the water supply, the protection of the environment and town and country planning, which imposes restrictions, sometimes appreciable, on the use of real property.

21. More particularly, all the wine-producing countries [have] restrictive legislation, albeit of differing severity, concerning the planting of vines, the selection of varieties and the methods of cultivation. In none of the countries concerned are those provisions considered to be incompatible in principle with the regard due to the right to property.

22. Thus it may be stated, taking into account the constitutional precepts common to the Member States and consistent legislative practices, in widely varying spheres, that the fact that [the regulation] imposed restrictions on the new planting of vines cannot be challenged in principle. It is a type of restriction which is known and accepted as lawful, in identical or similar forms, in the constitutional structure of all the Member States.

SECTION FIVE

JUDICIAL CONTROL OF LEGISLATIVE AND ADMINISTRATIVE ACTION

1   Introduction

It has been seen that the European Constitution is based on the Treaty, whereby individual Member States have created a new legal order and have undertaken to be governed, at least in part, by Community institutions. There are two logical corollaries to this. First, the Community has jurisdiction to act to the exclusion of Member States and, second, the Member States remain competent to act where they have not granted jurisdiction to the Community (see, on 'subsidiarity', Chapter One). The drawing up of the respective competences of the Community and the Member States lies with the Member States who agree and ratify the primary legislation of the Treaties and who, through the Council, take final decisions as to the adoption of secondary legislation. Although the developing nature of the Community has seen a continuing devolution of national competence in favour of the Community institutions (and this will be continued even further under the Treaty of Union) and the Community institutions themselves have endeavoured to have assigned to themselves as much power as the Member States will allow, the normal constitutional tensions within a national state are mirrored within the Community by the desire to ensure both political and legal accountability of institutions to Member States and a corresponding accountability of institutions to each other. Consequently, the Treaty provides that the tasks entrusted to the Community are to be carried out principally by the European Parliament, the Council, the Commission, and the Court of Justice and that each institution must 'act within the limits of the powers conferred upon it by this Treaty' (Article 4). Community acts, therefore, both legislative and administrative, must be adopted in accordance with the Treaty and its secondary legislation. The Treaty, therefore, uses phrases such as 'pursuant to this Treaty', 'in accordance with the provisions of this Treaty' and 'as provided in this Treaty'.

The imposition of constitutional restraints upon institutions is a normal feature of a national system of government based on a written constitution and within many of the Member States the provisions of the written constitution are the highest form of law and take precedence over the legislation of the legislature and administration and the administrative acts of national institutions are subject to both constitutional laws and ordinary legislation. In countries which have a written constitution it is normal to have some form of independent or judicial authority to examine and declare upon the constitutionality of acts of the legislature (to determine whether a statute contravenes or is in conformity with the constitution). Several of the original Member States, for example France, Germany and Italy, had constitutional courts or councils to perform the constitutionality function. Furthermore, it is normal, whether or not there is a written constitution, to have some form of independent or judicial authority to exercise an administrative law function designed to ensure that the administration's acts are executed in accordance with the legal powers granted to them. It was, therefore, entirely in keeping with general principles of constitutional law that the designers of the Treaty created both a constitutionality jurisdiction and an administrative law jurisdiction and, in order to ensure that both jurisdictions should act with one mind to produce a cohesive interpretation and application of the Treaty, granted both jurisdictions to the European Court of Justice under Article 173 **[B29]**.

2   Community acts

What is a Community act which is susceptible to review? Article 189 **[B19]** provides that Community institutions may make regulations, issue directives, take decisions, make recommendations or deliver opinions. An act is, prima facie, a regulation, directive or decision. This will include instruments ranging from the most far-reaching regulations to simple letters containing a decision against one person. The court has, however, emphasised that it is not the title of regulation or directive which governs exhaustively the definition of a Community act but rather its capability of producing legal effects (*Commission v Council* **[B47]**; *IBM* **[B48]**), including a binding act of the European Parliament (*Les Verts* **[B49]**).

In Cases 8-11/66 *Société Anonyme Cimenteries CBR Cementbedrijven NV (and others) v Commission of the EEC* [1967] ECR 75, a regulation empowered the Commission to impose fines on undertakings which intentionally or negligently infringed provisions on competition. Certain undertakings were exempted from the system of fines. The Commission took a decision to withdraw the benefit of the exemption in certain circumstances, with the result that the undertakings ceased to be protected and came under the contrary rules which therefore exposed them to the risk of fines. The court held that the Commission's measure deprived the undertakings of the advantages of a legal system and exposed them to a grave financial risk and that, since the 'measure' affected the interests of the undertakings by bringing about a distinct change in their legal position and by producing unequivocal legal effects touching the interests of the undertakings concerned and which was binding on them, the 'measure' thus constituted not a mere opinion but a decision (see, also, Case C-50/90 *Sunzest v Commission of the European Communities* [1991] ECR I-2917). In Case 26/76 *Metro-SB-Großmärkte GmbH & Co KG v Commission of the EEC* [1977] ECR 1875, it was held that a letter merely confirming a decision does not alter a person's legal position resulting from the decision itself – it is the decision which has legal effect (see, further, **[E54]**).

3   Who can bring an action

A Member State, the Council or the Commission, by virtue of Article 173, has an automatic right to bring an action. There is, therefore, no problem at all here. The omission of the European Parliament from the original list in Article 173, despite the Parliament being a Community institution, caused some problems because there was no identifiable way in which the infringement of the Parliament's rights or prerogatives could be challenged directly by the Parliament. In Case 302/87 *European Parliament v Council* [1988] ECR 5615, the court referred to the indirect protection of the Parliament's rights or prerogatives by the Commission, but when this was shown not to be completely effective the court, despite the wording of the Treaty (as enacted), granted to the Parliament a limited right to bring an action (*Parliament v Council* [B50]) and this judicial amendment of the Treaty is given legitimacy by the Treaty of Union [B29].

Problems have, however, arisen with regard to Article 173(2) (re-enacted as Article 173(4): [B29]), which, on analysis, permits a natural or legal person to bring an action for the annulment of: (1) a decision addressed to that natural or legal person; or (2) a decision which, although in the form of a regulation, is of direct and individual concern to that natural or legal person; or (3) a decision which, although in the form of a decision addressed to another person, is of direct and individual concern to that natural or legal person. First, a decision addressed to a natural or legal person. There are many examples of a decision addressed to a natural or legal person, which, according to Article 189, binds or has legal consequences for that person. In keeping with the general principles of administrative law an addressee of a decision has an automatic right to challenge that decision (*Sabbatini* [B61], *Gutmann* [B64], *BP v Commission* [E73] and *British Aerospace* [E95]). Secondly, a decision which, although in the form of a regulation, is of direct and individual concern to a natural or legal person. The purpose of this provision is to prevent the Community institutions from being able, merely by choosing to categorise or entitle a Community measure (to use a neutral word) as a 'regulation', to exclude an application by an individual against what is in reality a decision which concerns a natural or legal person directly and individually. The provision is a device to prevent the Community institutions from by-passing the right of a person to bring an action for annulment simply by calling a measure a 'regulation'. The court has emphasised that the choice of form of a measure cannot change the actual nature of the measure itself and in each case it is therefore necessary to examine whether a contested measure is a regulation or a decision. The typical case is that in which a regulation refers to a fixed and known number of manufacturers or traders identified by reason of an individual course of action, where, had the Community institution used the form of a decision addressed to that fixed and known number of persons (or of individual decisions addressed to each of that fixed and known number of persons), the aim of the Community action would have had the identical results as those achieved by means of utilising a regulation. Third, a decision which, although in the form of a decision addressed to another person, is of direct and individual concern to a natural or legal person. This is again a device to ensure that a person who is in the same position as the actual addressee of the decision and upon whom legal effects will be made by the decision will be permitted to challenge that decision. It may be noted that a decision addressed to another person will include a decision addressed to a Member State (*Plaumann* [B54]).

Therefore, for a natural or legal person to bring an action for annulment the measure which it is desired to challenge must be a decision and the person must either be the addressee of that decision or be directly or individually concerned by it. In practice, the question as to whether a measure is a decision is resolved by examining the same factors as are examined in resolving the question of individual concern and many of the cases merge the two questions.

In determining whether a measure is a regulation or a decision the Court of Justice has used the words of Article 189 to accord to a regulation the

status of a legislative instrument, emphasising the criterion of general application, and to a decision the status of an administrative instrument,
emphasising the limited range of persons affected thereby (*Producteurs de
fruits* [**B51**], *Koninklijke Scholten Honig* [**B52**], *Salerno* [**B53**]). In Case 41-44/70
NV International Fruit Company and others v Commission of the EEC [1971] ECR
411, the applicants sought to annul a measure adopted by the Commission
refusing to grant them licences to import dessert apples from third countries. A regulation (Regulation 'X') was made adopting measures applicable
to the import of dessert apples. Within this framework there was a system of
import licences and the administration of this scheme was specified in another regulation (Regulation 'Y'), adopted with a view to the current state of
the market and to the quantities of dessert apples for which applications for
import licences had been made in a specified and specific week. This system
was continued until 22 May 1970 (the specified date) by a third regulation
(Regulation 'Z'). The Court of Justice held that it followed that when
Regulation 'Y' was adopted, the number of applicants which could be affected by it was fixed. No new applications could be added; to what extent
(in percentage terms) the applications could be granted depended on the
total quantity in respect of which applications had been submitted; and the
Commission decided on the subsequent fate of each application which had
been lodged because they had provided that the system introduced by
Regulation 'Y' should by virtue of Regulation 'Z' be maintained until the
specified date. It was held that Regulation 'Y' was not a provision of general
application but must be regarded as a conglomeration of individual decisions taken by the Commission under the guise of a regulation pursuant to
Regulation 'X'. Since each of which decisions affected the legal position of
each author of an application for a licence, the decisions were of individual
concern to the applicants. In Case 112/77 *August Töpfer & Co GmbH v
Commission of the EEC* [1978] ECR 1019, it was held that the natural or legal
persons to whom a provision referred were identifiable. Consequently, although this provision was in a regulation, it amounted in substance to a
decision of just the same direct and individual concern to holders of export
licences, such as the applicant, as if it had been addresssed to them.

   The concept of direct concern relates to the effect of the measure in question on the natural or legal person. In the case of a genuine decision
addressed to such a person, that measure is binding on the addressee
(Article 189). If a decision in the form of a regulation or a decision addressed to another person can be shown to have the same immediate
binding effects as if it were a decision addressed to the person then it may be
said directly to concern that person. There must be some element of automatic application of the measure against the person rather than a mere
discretion to apply the measure to the person (*Les Verts* [**B49**], *Plaumann*
[**B54**], *Piraiki* [**B55**]).

   Since the facility to permit natural or legal persons to bring an action for
annulment with regard to a decision not addressed to them is a device to
prevent the by-passing of the court's jurisdiction by the creation of disguised
measures, the court has taken as its starting point the general approach that
such actions can be brought only in circumstances which would not jeopardise the system of the Treaty which only permits an application for
annulment to be brought by a natural or legal person in limited circumstances. If in reality there is a disguised measure the person should not be
unprotected. Conversely, if the measure is genuine the person has no rights.

In many cases, an applicant maintains that a measure affects it legally by reason of a factual situation whereby it is differentiated from all other persons and which distinguishes it individually in the same way as the person to whom a decision is addressed and the court has accepted that this is an important, although not exclusive, criterion (*Koninklijke Scholten Honig* [B52], *Plaumann* [B54]), but one which must be determined on the facts (*Société CAM* [B56]), some of which may be only of specific rather than general application (*Allied Corporation* [B57]). In *Metro-SB-Großmärkte GmbH & Co KG v Commission* [E54], it was held that the contested decision was adopted in particular as a result of a complaint submitted by Metro and that, therefore, the applicant must be considered to be directly and individually concerned. In Case 264/82 *Timex Corporation v Council and Commission* [1985] ECR 849, it was submitted that a regulation was a decision of direct and individual concern to Timex because the regulation was adopted as a result of a complaint lodged by Timex and the regulation therefore constituted the culmination of the administrative proceeding initiated at Timex's request. It was held that it was necessary to consider the part played by Timex in anti-dumping proceedings and it was found that the complaint which led to the opening of the investigation procedure owed its origin to the complaints originally made by Timex. Since the contested regulation was based on Timex's own situation, the measure was, therefore, a decision of direct and individual concern to Timex.

If an applicant is affected simply because it belongs to a class which has been objectively defined by measures which might affect more than a restrictively defined class, this may not be sufficient so as to differentiate the applicant from all other persons and therefore distinguish the applicant individually just as in the case of the person addressed. In Case 42/71 *Nordgetreide GmbH & Co. KG v Commission of the EEC* [1972] ECR 105, the applicant made a request to include in a regulation, relating to compensatory amounts, certain products of concern to them. The Commission refused to accede to the request and the applicants sought the annulment of the communication in which the Commission refused to accede to the request. It was held that, since inclusion of the products would have had the effect of applying the system of compensatory amounts to all exports and, furthermore, to all imports of the products involved to the advantage or the disadvantage, as the case may be, of any and every exporter and importer, such a provision would have affected the applicant only in so far as the applicant belonged to a category viewed in the abstract and in its entirety and not as the person to whom the act of direct and individual concern to him was addressed. Therefore, the applicants had no locus standi to bring an action for annulment. In particular, the nature of a measure as a regulation is not called in question by the possibility of determining more or less precisely the number or even the identity of the persons to whom it applies at a given moment as long as it is established that it is applied by virtue of an objective legal or factual situation defined by the measure in relation to the objective of the latter (*Producteurs de fruit* [B51], *Koninklijke Scholten Honig* [B52], *Piraiki* [B55]).

4   Time limits

The proceedings to annul a Community act must be instituted within two months of the publication of the measure, or of its notification to the plaintiff, or, in the absence thereof, of the day on which it came to the knowledge of the latter, as the case may be. In the case of regulations, they will be published in the Official Journal of the European Communities. They enter into force on the date specified in them or, in the absence thereof, on the 20th day following their publication. Decisions are notified to those to whom they are addressed and take effect upon such notification (Article 173(3) (re-enacted as Article 173(5), 191 **[B19]**).

5 Grounds

The grounds on which an action for annulment may be brought are specified in the Treaty as: (1) lack of competence; (2) infringement of an essential procedural requirement; (3) infringement of the Treaty or of any rule of law relating to its application; or (4) misuse of powers (Article 173(1) (re-enacted as Article 173(2))).

Lack of competence, in essence, means that the Community act in question was adopted either by an institution which did not have jurisdiction to adopt such an act in that another institution should have acted or that no institution should have acted or that the Community act was not within the subject matter within the institution's competence. Cases are rare and have usually related to conflicts as to competence between the Community institutions and the use of Article 235 of the Treaty (*Commission v Council* **[B58]**). In Case C-295/90 *European Parliament v Council of the European Communities* 7 July 1992, it was held that the Council was not justified in basing a directive on Article 235 of the Treaty when it was competent to adopt the contested directive under Article 7(2) of the Treaty.

An infringement of an essential procedural requirement may relate to a breach of a written rule of procedure or a breach of a rule of procedure enshrined in a general principle of law (such as a breach of the rule to a fair hearing). The usual example of the former is the rule that regulations, directives and decisions of the Council and of the Commission must state the reasons on which they are based and refer to any proposals or opinions which were required to be obtained pursuant to the Treaty (Article 190) (*Germany v Commission* **[B59]**; cf *Automec* **[E62]**). In Case 69/83 *Charles Lux v Court of Auditors of the European Communities* [1984] ECR 2447, the Court of Justice held that the purpose of the duty to state the reasons on which a decision is based is both to permit the person concerned to determine whether a decision contains a defect allowing its legality to be challenged and to enable it to be reviewed by the court. In Cases 103, 145/77 *Royal Scholten-Honig (Holdings) Ltd v Intervention Board for Agricultural Produce* [1978] ECR 2037, the Court of Justice held that the statement of reasons on which one provision in a regulation is based, must nevertheless be examined and assessed in the context of the whole of the rules of which the regulation forms an integral part. Other statutory provisions may provide for reasons (*Gutmann* **[B64]**). Another essential statutory procedural rule relates to the frequent stipulations in the Treaty that during the legislative process the European Parliament or Economic and Social Committee must be consulted (see Section Two of this chapter). A breach of this obligation will be fatal (Case 138/79 *Roquette Frères v Council* [1980] ECR 3333). As was seen in Section Four of this chapter, the court has developed general principles of law and these include the procedural requirement of a fair hearing (*Transocean* **[B38]**; *Hoffman* **[B39]**).

An 'infringement of the Treaty' is to some extent tautological in that lack of competence and breach of a Treaty rule of procedure will also be infringements of the Treaty. More important in the development of Community law is the use of the phrase 'of any rule of law relating to' the application of the Treaty. In particular, the development of general principles of law (discussed in Section Four of this chapter) has been utilised to challenge Community acts which breach the principle of legitimate expectation (*Merkur* [B34], *Amylum* [B35], *Töpfer* [B60]), of proportionality (*Bela-Mühle* [B36], *Rau* [B37]) and of non-discrimination (*Airola* [B32], *Sabbatini* [B61]). See also *France v Commission* [E86]. Consequently, in Cases 75, 117/82 *C Razzouk and A Beydoun v Commission of the European Communities* [1984] ECR 1509, it was held that the principle of equal treatment of both sexes formed part of the fundamental rights the observance of which the court has a duty to ensure. Since a decision of the Commission was based on the provisions of the Community Staff Regulations, and these were inapplicable in so far as they treated surviving spouses of officials unequally according to the sex of the person concerned, that Commission decision had to be annulled.

Misuse of powers reflects the general principle of administrative law known to the public law of most Member States that a power, an admitted power, which is granted for one purpose may not be used for a purpose unconnected with the purpose for which the power was granted. The ground is rarely successful because Community institutions possess many specific powers on which to base their decisions, because the court has often granted an institution a wide measure of discretion in what it does (*Agence Européenne* [B62]), and because it is very difficult to prove by objective evidence. Consequently, in Case 69/83 *Charles Lux v Court of Auditors of the European Communities* [1984] ECR 2447, Lux maintained that a decision changing his posting constituted a disguised disciplinary measure in as much as earlier the President of the Court of Auditors allegedly made it clear to him that he might be transferred to another department unless he withdrew two actions which he had brought before the Court of Justice. The court held that a decision may amount to a misuse of power only if it appears on the basis of objective, relevant and consistent evidence, to have been taken for purposes other than those stated. The court held that, since it was clear from the file on the case and, in particular, from the statements made at the hearing that the applicant had been unable to demonstrate convincingly that the President of the Court of Auditors intended to take disciplinary action against him, Lux had been unable to adduce sufficient evidence that the appointing authority pursued any objective other than a legitimate objective. Consequently, the application failed. Examples of successful actions are *Giuffrida* [B63] and *Gutmann* [B64].

6   The plea of illegality

Article 184 [B29] provides that notwithstanding the expiry of the normal two months' time limit, any party may, in proceedings in which a regulation is in issue, plead the normal grounds for review in order to invoke before the European Court of Justice the inapplicability of that regulation. The intention of Article 184 is not to allow a party to contest at will the applicability of any regulation in support of an application. The regulation of which the legality is called in question must be applicable, directly or indirectly, to the issue with which the application is concerned (Case 32/65 *Government of the Italian Republic v Council and Commission* [1966] ECR 389. In Cases 87, 130/77, 22/83, 9, 10/84 *Vittorio Salerno and others v Commission and Council* [1985] ECR 2523, it was held that the sole purpose of Article 184 is to protect parties against the application of an unlawful regulation where the regulation itself can no longer be challenged owing to the expiry of the period laid down in Article 173. However, in allowing a party to plead the inapplicability of a regulation, Article 184 does not create an independent right of action; such a plea may only be raised indirectly in proceedings against the implementing measure, the validity of the regulation being challenged in so far as it constitutes the legal basis of that measure.

MATERIALS

[B47]   Case 22/70 Commission of the European Communities v Council of the European Communities [1971] ECR 263

[The Commission sought the annulment of the 'proceedings' of the Council relating to the negotiation and conclusion by the Member States of the Community of a European Agreement concerning the work of crews of vehicles engaged in international transport. It was held that since the 'proceedings' were designed to lay down a course of action binding on both the institutions and the Member States, the 'proceedings' had definite legal effects both on relations between the Community and Member States and on the relationship between institutions.]

The European Court of Justice (at pp 276–277)

34. The Council considers that the proceedings [do] not constitute an act, within the meaning of the first sentence of the first paragraph of Article 173, the legality of which is open to review.

35. Neither by their form nor by their subject matter or content, it is argued, were these proceedings a regulation, a decision or a directive within the meaning of Article 189.

36. They were really nothing more than a co-ordination of policies amongst Member States within the framework of the Council, and as such created no rights, imposed no obligations and did not modify any legal position.

37. This is said to be the case more particularly because in the event of a dispute between the institutions admissibility has to be appraised with particular rigour.

. . .

39. Since the only matters excluded from the scope of the action for annulment open to the Member States and the institutions are 'recommendations' or 'opinions' – which by the final paragraph of Article 189 are declared to have no binding force – Article 173 treats as acts open to review by the court all measures adopted by the institutions which are intended to have legal force.

40. The objective of this review is to ensure, as required by Article 164, observance of the law in the interpretation and application of the Treaty.

41. It would be inconsistent with this objective to interpret the conditions under which the action is admissible so restrictively as to limit the availability of this procedure merely to the categories of measures referred to by Article 189.

42. An action for annulment must therefore be available in the case of all measures adopted by the institutions, whatever their nature or form, which are intended to have legal effects.

[B48]　Case 60/81 International Business Machines v Commission of the European Communities [1981] ECR 2639

The European Court of Justice (at pp 2651–2652)

9. [According] to the consistent case law of the court, any measure the legal effects of which are binding on, and capable of affecting the interests of, the applicant by bringing about a distinct change in his legal position is an act or decision which may be the subject of an action under Article 173 for a declaration that it is void. However, the form in which such acts or decisions are cast is, in principle, immaterial as regards the question whether they are open to challenge under that article.

10. In the case of acts or decisions adopted by a procedure involving several stages, in particular where they are the culmination of an internal procedure, it is clear from the case law that in principle an act is open to review only if it is a measure definitively laying down the position of the Commission or the Council on the conclusion of that procedure, and not a provisional measure intended to pave the way for the final decision.

[B49]　Case 294/83 Parti écologiste 'Les Verts' v European Parliament [1986] ECR 1339

[The political party 'Les Verts' brought an action to annul decisions by the Bureau and the enlarged Bureau of the European Parliament, allocating the appropriations to finance the information campaign for the European Parliament elections.]

The European Court of Justice (at pp 1366–1367)

25. An interpretation of Article 173 which excluded measures adopted by the European Parliament from those which could be contested would lead to a result contrary both to the spirit of the Treaty as expressed in Article 164 and to its system. Measures adopted by the European Parliament in the context of the EEC Treaty could encroach on the powers of the Member States or of the other institutions, or exceed the limits which have been set to the Parliament's powers, without its being possible to refer them for review by the court. It must therefore be concluded than an action for annulment may lie against measures adopted by the European Parliament intended to have legal effects vis-à-vis third parties.

. . .

27. The two contested measures both concern [the] appropriations entered in the budget of the European Parliament to cover the cost of preparations for the 1984 European elections. They deal with the allocation of those appropriations to third parties for expenses relating to activities to take place outside the European Parliament. In that regard they govern the rights and obligations both of political groupings which were already represented in the European Parliament in 1979 and of those which were to take part in the 1984 elections. They determine the proportion of the appropriations to be received by each of the groupings, either on the basis of the

number of seats obtained in 1979 or on the basis of the number of votes obtained in 1984. For that reason, the measures in question were designed to produce legal effects vis-à-vis third parties and may therefore be the subject of an action under Article 173 of the Treaty.

. . .

31. [The] contested measures are of direct concern to the applicant association. They constitute a complete set of rules which are sufficient in themselves and which require no implementing provisions, since the calculation of the share of the appropriations to be granted to each of the political groupings concerned is automatic and leaves no room for any discretion.

[B50]   Case C-70/88 European Parliament v Council of the European Communities [1990] ECR I-2041

[The Council, basing its action on Article 31 of the Euratom Treaty, which provides that the Council shall 'consult' the European Parliament, made a regulation laying down maximum permitted levels of radioactive contamination for foodstuffs and of feeding stuffs following a nuclear accident or any other case of radiological emergency. During the legislative proceedings, the European Parliament, which was in fact consulted by the Council in accordance with Article 31, stated that it did not agree with the legal basis adopted by the Commission and asked the Commission to submit to it a new proposal based on Article 100a of the EEC Treaty, which, significantly, provides that the Council must act 'in co-operation with the European Parliament' (ie follow the co-operation procedure under the pre-Treaty of Union Article 149.2 **[B19]**). Since the Commission did not comply with that request, the Council adopted the regulation on the basis of Article 31. The Parliament brought an action under Article 146 of the Euratom Treaty and Article 173 of the EEC Treaty to annul the Regulation. The Council claimed that the question of the European Parliament's capacity to bring an action for annulment had been clearly decided by the court in its judgment in Case 302/87 *European Parliament v Council* [1988] ECR 5615 and that the present action was therefore inadmissible. Note that the court's decision is legitimised by the Treaty of Union **[B29]**.]

The European Court of Justice (at pp 2070–2074)

6. The European Parliament asked the court to dismiss [the Council's] objection. It claimed that a new factor distinguished the present case from Case 302/87. According to the Parliament, in order to justify its refusal in that case to recognise the European Parliament's capacity to bring an action for annulment the court pointed out that it was the responsibility of the Commission under Article 155 of the EEC Treaty to ensure that the Parliament's prerogatives were respected and to bring any actions for annulment which might be necessary for that purpose. However, the present case shows that the Commission cannot fulfil that responsibility since it chose a legal basis for its proposal which was different from the legal basis which the Parliament considered appropriate. Consequently, the Parliament cannot rely on the Commission to defend its prerogatives by bringing an action for annulment.

7. The European Parliament added that the Council's adoption of the contested measure cannot be regarded as an implied refusal to act which would enable the Parliament to bring an action for failure to act. Moreover, the defence of its prerogatives by actions brought by individuals would be completely fortuitous and therefore ineffective.

8. Therefore, according to the Parliament, there is a legal vacuum which the court must fill by recognising that the European Parliament has capacity to bring an action for annulment, but only to the extent necessary to safeguard its own prerogatives.

. . .

12. As is evident from the judgment in Case 302/87 [the] Parliament does not have the right to bring an action for annulment under Article 173 of the EEC Treaty or under Article 146 of the Euratom Treaty [in their pre-Treaty of Union form], which are identical in content.

13. First of all, in the first paragraph of Article 173 or Article 146 [in their pre-Treaty of Union form], the Parliament is not included among the institutions which, like the Member States, can bring an action for annulment against any measure of another institution.

14. Furthermore, since the Parliament is not a legal person it cannot bring an action before the court under [Article 173(2) or 146(2) (in their pre-Treaty of Union form), respectively], the scheme of which would, in any event, be inappropriate to an action for annulment brought by the Parliament.

15. In the judgment in Case 302/87, after having stated the reasons why the Parliament did not have capacity to bring an action under Article 173 of the EEC Treaty, the court pointed out that various legal remedies were available to ensure that the Parliament's prerogatives were defended. As was observed in that judgment, not only does the Parliament have the right to bring an action for failure to act, but the Treaties provide means for submitting for review by the court acts of the Council or the Commission adopted in disregard of the Parliament's prerogatives.

16. However, the circumstances and arguments adduced in the present case show that the various legal remedies provided for both in the Euratom Treaty and in the EEC Treaty, however effective and diverse they may be, may prove to be ineffective or uncertain.

17. First, an action for failure to act cannot be used to challenge the legal basis of a measure which has already been adopted.

18. Secondly, the submission of a reference for a preliminary ruling on the validity of such an act or the bringing of an action by Member States or individuals for the annulment of the act are mere contingencies, and the Parliament cannot be sure that they will materialise.

19. Finally, while the Commission is required to ensure that the Parliament's prerogatives are respected, that duty cannot go so far as to oblige it to adopt the Parliament's position and bring an action for annulment which the Commission itself considers unfounded.

20. It follows from the foregoing that the existence of those various legal remedies is not sufficient to guarantee, with certainty and in all circumstances, that a measure adopted by the Council or the Commission in disregard of the Parliament's prerogatives will be reviewed.

21. Those prerogatives are one of the elements of the institutional balance created by the Treaties. The Treaties set up a system for distributing

powers among the different Community institutions, assigning to each institution its own role in the institutional structure of the Community and the accomplishment of the tasks entrusted to the Community.

22. Observance of the institutional balance means that each of the institutions must exercise its powers with due regard for the powers of the other institutions. It also requires that it should be possible to penalise any breach of that rule which may occur.

23. The court, which under the Treaties has the task of ensuring that in the interpretation and application of the Treaties the law is observed, must therefore be able to maintain the institutional balance and, consequently, review the observance of the Parliament's prerogatives when called upon to do so by the Parliament, by means of a legal remedy which is suited to the purpose which the Parliament seeks to achieve.

24. In carrying out that task the court cannot, of course, include the Parliament among the institutions which may bring an action under Article 173 of the EEC Treaty or Article 146 of the Euratom Treaty without being required to demonstrate an interest in bringing an action.

25. However, it is the court's duty to ensure that the provisions of the Treaties concerning the institutional balance are fully applied and to see to it that the Parliament's prerogatives, like those of the other institutions, cannot be breached without it having available a legal remedy, among those laid down in the Treaties, which may be exercised in a certain and effective manner.

26. The absence in the Treaties of any provision giving the Parliament the right to bring an action for annulment may constitute a procedural gap, but it cannot prevail over the fundamental interest in the maintenance and observance of the institutional balance laid down in the Treaties establishing the European Communities.

27. Consequently, an action for annulment brought by the Parliament against an act of the Council or the Commission is admissible provided that the action seeks only to safeguard its prerogatives and that it is founded only on submissions alleging their infringement. Provided that condition is met, the Parliament's action for annulment is subject to the rules laid down in the treaties for actions for annulment brought by the other institutions.

28. In accordance with the Treaties, the Parliament's prerogatives include participation in the drafting of legislative measures, in particular participation in the co-operation procedure laid down in the EEC Treaty.

29. In the present case, the Parliament claims that the contested regulation is based on Article 31 of the Euratom Treaty, which provides only that the Parliament is to be consulted, whereas it ought to have been based on Article 100a of the EEC Treaty, which requires implementation of the procedure for co-operation with the Parliament.

30. The Parliament infers from that that the Council's choice of legal basis for the contested regulation led to a breach of its prerogatives by denying it the possibility which the co-operation procedure offers, of participating in the drafting of the measure more closely and actively than it could in the consultation procedure.

31. Since the Parliament claims that its prerogatives were breached as a result of the choice of legal basis for the contested measure, it follows from all the foregoing that the present action is admissible. The Council's objection of inadmissibility must therefore be dismissed and the proceedings must be continued with regard to the substance of the case.

[B51] Cases 16, 17/62 Confédération nationale des producteurs de fruits et légumes v Council of the European Economic Community [1962] ECR 471

[The applicants, associations of producers of fruit and vegetables, contested Council Regulation 23 (on the progressive establishment of a common organisation of the market in fruit and vegetables), Article 9, permitting Member States to dispense with recourse to the provisions of Article 44 of the Treaty because such a dispensation would occasion the most serious loss to French fruit and vegetable producers. Note that the court refers to Article 173(2) in its pre-Treaty of Union form.]

The European Court of Justice (at pp 477–480)

1. [It follows from Article 173(2) that a natural or legal] person is not entitled to make an application for annulment of regulations adopted by the Council or the Commission.

. . .

The court is unable in particular to adopt the interpretation suggested by one of the [applicants], according to which the term 'decision', as used in [Article 173(2)], could also cover regulations. Such a wide interpretation conflicts with the fact that Article 189 makes a clear distinction between the concept of a 'decision' and that of a 'regulation'. It is inconceivable that the term 'decision' would be used in Article 173 in a different sense from the technical sense as defined in Article 189. It follows from the foregoing considerations that the present applications should be dismissed as inadmissible if the measure in dispute constitutes a regulation.

In examining this question, the court cannot restrict itself to considering the official title of the measure, but must first take into account its object and content.

2. Under the terms of Article 189 of the EEC Treaty, a regulation shall have general application and shall be directly applicable in all Member States, whereas a decision shall be binding only upon those to whom it is addressed. The criterion for the distinction must be sought in the general 'application' or otherwise of the measure in question.

The essential characteristics of a decision arise from the limitation of the persons to whom it is addressed, whereas a regulation, being essentially of a legislative nature, is applicable not to a limited number of persons, defined or identifiable, but to categories of persons viewed abstractly and in their entirety. Consequently, in order to determine in doubtful cases whether one is concerned with a decision or a regulation, it is necessary to ascertain whether the measure in question is of individual concern to specific individuals.

In these circumstances, if a measure entitled by its author a regulation contains provisions which are capable of being not only of direct but also of individual concern to certain natural or legal persons, it must be admitted, without prejudice to the question whether that measure considered in its entirety can be correctly called a regulation, that in any case those provisions do not have the character of a regulation and may therefore be impugned by those persons under the terms of [Article 173(2)].

3. In this case the measure in dispute was entitled by its author a

'regulation'. However, the applicants maintain that the disputed provision is in fact a 'decision in the form of a regulation'. It is possible without doubt for a decision also to have a very wide field of application. However, a measure which is applicable to objectively determined situations and which involves immediate legal consequences in all Member States for categories of persons viewed in a general and abstract manner cannot be considered as constituting a decision, unless it can be proved that it is of individual concern to certain persons within the meaning of [Article 173(2)].

In this particular case, the disputed provision involves immediate legal consequences in all Member States for categories of persons viewed in a general and abstract manner. In fact, Article 9 of the measure in [dispute] abolishes, for certain products and subject to certain time limits, quantitative restrictions on imports and measures having equivalent effect. It involves in addition the requirement that Member States shall dispense with recourse to the provisions of Article 44 of the Treaty, in particular with regard to the right temporarily to suspend or reduce imports. Consequently, the said Article eliminates the restrictions on the freedom of traders to export or import within the Community.

It remains to be considered whether the disputed provision is of individual concern to the applicants.

Although this provision, by obliging Member States to put an end to or to dispense with various measures capable of favouring agricultural producers, affects in so doing their interests and the interests of the members of the applicant associations, it must be stated nevertheless that those members are concerned by the said provision in the same way as all other agricultural producers of the Community.

Moreover, one cannot accept the principle that an association, in its capacity as the representative of a category of businessmen, could be individually concerned by a measure affecting the general interests of that category.

Such a principle would result in the grouping, under the heading of a single legal person, of the interests properly attributed to the members of a category, who have been affected as individuals by genuine regulations, and would derogate from the system of the Treaty which allows applications for annulment by private individuals only of decisions which have been addressed to them, or of acts which affect them in a similar manner.

In these circumstances, it cannot be admitted that the provision in dispute is of individual concern to the applicants. It follows that the [Council] was correct in designating the provision in question as a regulation.

[B52]   Case 101/76 Koninklijke Scholten Honig v Council and Commission of the European Communities [1977] ECR 797

[The case concerned a sweetening agent known as glucose with a high fructose content (and referred to below as 'isoglucose'). Isoglucose is a product which is manufactured from any type of starch but most often from maize. The manufacture of isoglucose became profitable as a result of the rise in the price of sugar and the shortage of sugar and the sugar industry considered that the manufacture of isoglucose might well constitute a threat to that industry. Only a small number of companies and their subsidiaries manufactured isoglucose and, although other companies were interested in its manufacture, for technical reasons other companies would not be able to manufacture isoglucose for two years. The sugar industry brought the matter before the Community authorities, which, by means of two regulations, reduced the amount of the production refund for starch used in the manufacture of isoglucose for the 1976–1977 marketing year and provided for it to be completely abolished for the 1977–1978 marketing year. The applicants brought an action for the annulment of the two regulations and were met with the objection that they could not bring such an action against a 'regulation'.

The applicants argued that there was in the whole Community only a restricted number of manufacturers of isoglucose and, having regard to the necessary economic and technological investment needed, it was impossible to increase their present number rapidly. Furthermore, the knowledge necessary for this purpose was protected by patents. There were only four undertakings manufacturing isoglucose. The applicants maintained that the regulations affected them legally by reason of a factual situation whereby they were differentiated from all other persons and were distinguished individually in the same way as the person to whom a decision is addressed. The fact that at the date on which the Council and the Commission adopted the measure there was in the Community only a very limited number of known undertakings engaged in the manufacture of isoglucose strengthened their argument that the measure adopted affected them and the other undertakings in question individually. When the Council and the Commission adopted the measure they knew or at least were perfectly able to know which undertakings were manufacturing isoglucose in the Community. The regulations had made an exception to the general rules relating to the starch sector of industry with regard to a single product, namely, isoglucose. Since it had distinguished a single end product individually the Council had by that very fact distinguished the manufacturers of isoglucose individually. Within the context of the market in starch, the legal situation of the manufacturers of isoglucose was altered in relation to that of the rest of the industry. The regulations entailed legal consequences solely and exclusively for manufacturers of isoglucose.

The Council argued (and note paragraph 23 of the Court of Justice's decision) that the number, however limited, of traders concerned by Community rules could not serve as a criterion for the purpose of the assessment of the nature of the measure (ie whether it was a regulation or a decision). It was unimportant for this purpose that at the date on which a measure is adopted or subsequently it was possible to determine the number or even the identity of the persons to whom it applied. The applicants were affected because they belonged to a class which had been objectively defined by measures applying to the products which it manufactured. Although manufacturing isoglucose was very specialised and carried out by a small number of companies, it might at any time be carried out by any person and was therefore not such as to differentiate the applicants from all other persons and to distinguish the applicants individually just as in the case of the person addressed. The regulations aimed to regulate production refunds affecting certain products in the cereals and rice sectors and, consequently, potential traders carrying on their activity in these fields. The fact that advanced technology was required in order to manufacture isoglucose and the fact that this process was patented and that inevitably some time would elapse before other undertakings could manufacture that product were not relevant in order to prove in any way an individual interest in the case and therefore the existence of a group of decisions within the contested regulation. Finally (and note paragraph 25 of the court's decision), if the applicants were to succeed, the concept of a decision would be made so wide as to jeopardise the system of the Treaty, which only permitted an application for annulment to be brought by any person against an individual decision which affected him as the person to whom it was addressed or against a measure which affected that person as in the case of such persons. The applicants were only 'concerned' by the regulations because they manufactured products to which the measures applied. At most it was possible to say that the applicants were 'passively' concerned as are, in the great majority of cases, the natural or legal persons to whom a body of legislation applies.]

The European Court of Justice (at pp 807–808)

20. A regulation which provides for the reduction of a production refund for a whole marketing year with regard to a certain product processed from cereals and rice and for its complete abolition from the following marketing year is by its nature a measure of general application within the meaning of Article [189].

21. It in fact applies to objectively determined situations and produces legal effects with regard to categories of persons regarded generally and in the abstract.

22. It only affects the applicant by virtue of its capacity as a producer of [isoglucose] without any other specification.

23. Moreover, the nature of a measure as a regulation is not called in question by the possibility of determining more or less precisely the number or even the identity of the persons to whom it applies at a given moment as long as it is established that it is applied by virtue of an objective legal or factual situation defined by the measure in relation to the objective of the latter.

24. Moreover, the fact that a legal provision may have different actual effects for the various persons to whom it applies is not inconsistent with its nature as a regulation when that situation is objectively defined.

25. To refuse to acknowledge that rules on production refunds amounted to a regulation only because they concerned a specific product and to take the view that such rules affected the manufacturers of that product by virtue of circumstances which differentiated them from all other persons would enlarge the concept of a decision to such an extent as to jeopardise the system of the Treaty which only permits an application for annulment to be brought by any person against an individual decision which affects him as the person to whom it is addressed or against a measure which affects him as in the case of such a person.

[B53]   Cases 87, 130/77, 22/83, 9, 10/84 Vittorio Salerno and others v Commission and Council of the European Communities [1985] ECR 2523

The European Court of Justice (at pp 2534–2535)

28. [The application for annulment] is only admissible if [the regulation] is to be regarded as a decision which, although adopted in the guise of a regulation, is of direct and individual concern to the [applicants].

29. [The] test for distinguishing between a regulation and a decision is to ascertain whether or not the measure in question has general application.

30. It is not disputed that Regulation 3332/82 was adopted for the sole purpose of recruiting the 56 members of the [European Association for Co-operation] headquarters staff who occupied posts on 1 January 1982 and who were still employed there on 15 December [1982]. When the regulation was adopted, the number and the identity of those who could be affected by it were definitively determined. The regulation is thus not of general application but must be regarded as a series of decisions adopted by the Council concerning each of the 56 members of [the] headquarters staff individually.

31. With regard to the question whether the regulation at issue is of direct concern to the applicants, it should be borne in mind that Article 3 of the regulation provides that the headquarters staff recruited by virtue of the regulation are to be appointed to the appropriate grade and step indicated in the table of equivalence in the annex to the regulation. It is clear from that provision that the appointing authority has no discretion with regard to the grading of the persons concerned.

32. In those circumstances, Regulation 3332/82 is of direct and individual concern to the applicants and therefore their actions are admissible.

[B54]   Case 25/62 Plaumann & Co v Commission of the European Economic Community [1963] ECR 95

[Plaumann sought the annulment of a decision of the Commission refusing to authorise the Federal Republic of Germany to suspend certain customs duties applicable to fresh clementines imported from third countries. The Commission argued that the words 'other person' in Article 173(2) (in its pre-Treaty of Union form) did not refer to Member States, in their capacity as sovereign authorities, and that individuals could not therefore bring an action for annulment against any decisions of the Commission or of the Council which were addressed to Member States. The Commission also argued that the decision was, by its very nature, a regulation in the form of an individual decision and therefore an action for annulment of the decision was no more available to individuals than in the case of legislative measures of general application. The Commisson also argued that the contested decision was not of direct and individual concern to Plaumann.]

The European Court of Justice (at pp 106–107)

[Article 173(2)] does allow an individual to bring an action against decisions addressed to 'another person' which are of direct and individual concern to the former, but this Article neither defines nor limits the scope of these words. The words and the natural meaning of this provision justify the broadest interpretation. Moreover provisions of the Treaty regarding the right of interested parties to bring an action must not be interpreted restrictively. Therefore, the Treaty being silent on the point, a limitation in this respect may not be presumed. It follows that the [Commission's] argument cannot be regarded as well [founded].

It follows however from Articles 189 and 191 of the EEC Treaty that decisions are characterised by the limited number of persons to whom they are addressed. In order to determine whether or not a measure constitutes a decision one must enquire whether that measure concerns specific persons. The contested decision was addressed to the government of the Federal Republic of Germany and refuses to grant it authorisation for the partial suspension of customs duties on certain products imported from third countries. Therefore the contested measure must be regarded as a decision referring to a particular person and binding that person alone.

. . .

It is appropriate in the first place to examine whether the second requirement of admissibility is fulfilled because, if the applicant is not individually concerned by the decision, it becomes unnecessary to enquire whether he is directly concerned.

Persons other than those to whom a decision is addressed may only claim to be individually concerned if that decision affects them by reason of certain attributes which are peculiar to them or by reason of circumstances in which they are differentiated from all other persons and by virtue of these factors distinguishes them individually just as in the case of the person addressed. In the present case the applicant is affected by the disputed decision as an importer of clementines, that is to say, by reason of a commercial activity which may at any time be practised by any person and is not therefore such as to distinguish the applicant in relation to the contested decision as in the case of the addressee. For these reasons the present action for annulment must be declared inadmissible.

[B55]   Case 11/82 AE Piraiki-Patraiki and others v Commission of the European Communities [1985] ECR 207

[Under the Act of Accession whereby the Hellenic Republic joined the Community, Article 130, an existing Member State could apply for authorisation to take protective measures with regard to the Hellenic Republic if 'difficulties arise which are serious and liable to persist in any sector of the economy or which could bring about serious deterioration in the economic situation of a given area'. The measures authorised could involve derogations from the rules of the EEC Treaty to such an extent and for such periods as were strictly necessary in order to attain the above objectives. Following representations by France, which wanted to protect the French cotton industry, the Commission made a decision, adopted under Article 130, which authorised France to impose a quota system on imports into France of cotton yarn from Greece during the months of November and

December 1981 and January 1982. Seven Greek cotton undertakings brought an action to annul that decision. The Commission raised an objection of inadmissibility and the government of the French Republic, intervening, joined in that objection.]

The European Court of Justice (at pp 241–247)

[A decision addressed to another person]

3. The Commission and the government of the French Republic point out that the decision in question is addressed to the French Republic and the Hellenic Republic. They argue that it is an economic decision of a general nature, affecting a whole sector of the economy rather than individuals. Although the applicants are touched by the effects of the protective measures authorised, the decision in question is not of direct or individual concern to them.

. . .

5. It is common ground [that] the contested decision is not addressed to the applicants. It is therefore necessary, without going into the legal nature of the decision, to consider whether the decision is nevertheless of direct and individual concern to the applicants.

[Direct concern]

6. With regard to the question of direct concern, the Commission and the government of the French Republic argue that the applicants are not directly affected by the decision at issue since that decision merely authorises the French Republic to institute a quota system on imports of cotton yarn from Greece, and thus leaves the Member State which requested the authorisation free to make use of it or not. The decision therefore does not itself establish a system limiting imports but, in order for it to have practical effect, requires implementing measures on the part of the French authorities.

7. It is true that without implementing measures adopted at the national level the Commission decision could not have affected the applicants. In this case, however, that fact does not in itself prevent the decision from being of direct concern to the applicants if other factors justify the conclusion that they have a direct interest in bringing the action.

8. In that respect it should be pointed out that, as the Commission itself admitted during the written procedure, even before being authorised to do so by the Commission the French Republic applied a very restrictive system of licences for imports of cotton yarn of Greek origin. It should moreover be observed that the request for protective measures not only came from the French authorities but sought to obtain the Commission's authorisation for a system of import quotas more strict than that which was finally granted.

9. In those circumstances the possibility that the French Republic might decide not to make use of the authorisation granted to it by the Commission decision was entirely theoretical, since there could be no doubt as to the intention of the French authorities to apply the decision.

10. It must therefore be accepted that the decision at issue was of direct concern to the applicants.

[Individual concern – general]

11. With regard to the question whether the applicants are also individually concerned, it should first be pointed out, as the court stated in [*Plaumann* **[B54]**], that 'persons other than those to whom a decision is addressed may only claim to be individually concerned if that decision affects them by reason of certain attributes which are peculiar to them or by reason of circumstances in which they are differentiated from all other persons and by virtue of these factors distinguishes them individually just as in the case of the person addressed'.

[Individual concern – one]

12. The applicants argue that they fulfil the conditions set out above since they are the main Greek undertakings which produce and export cotton yarn to France. They argue that they therefore belong to a class of traders individually identifiable on the basis of criteria having to do with the product in question, the business activities carried on and the length of time during which they have been carried on. In that regard the applicants emphasise that the production and export to France of cotton yarn of Greek origin requires an industrial and commercial organisation which cannot be established from one day to the next, and certainly not during the short period of application of the decision in question.

13. That proposition cannot be accepted. It must first be pointed out that the applicants are affected by the decision at issue only in their capacity as exporters to France of cotton yarn of Greek origin. The decision is not intended to limit the production of those products in any way, nor does it have such a result.

14. As for the exportation of those products to France, that is clearly a commercial activity which can be carried on at any time by any undertaking whatever. It follows that the decision at issue concerns the applicants in the same way as any other trader actually or potentially finding himself in the same position. The mere fact that the applicants export goods to France is not therefore sufficient to establish that they are individually concerned by the contested decision.

[Individual concern – two]

15. The applicants argue however that their situation may be distinguished from that of any other exporter to France of cotton yarn of Greek origin inasmuch as they had entered into a series of contracts of sale with French customers, to be performed during the period of application of the decision and covering quantities of cotton yarn in excess of the quotas authorised by the Commission. The applicants state that those contracts could not be carried out because of the quota system applied by the French authorities. They take the view that in those circumstances their individual interests were affected by the decision in question.

16. According to the applicants the Commission was in a position, and even under an obligation, to identify the traders who, like the applicants, were individually concerned by its decision. In failing to obtain information in that regard it did not comply with the conditions of application of Article 130 of the Act of Accession, since in the applicants' view that provision obliges the Commission, before making a decision, to ascertain which

traders, in this case Greek traders, would be individually concerned by the protective measures authorised.

17. It should first be observed that if that argument were held to be well founded, it would only avail those applicants who could show that before the date of the contested decision they had entered into contracts with French customers for the delivery of cotton yarn from Greece during the period of application of that decision.

18. Since [two traders did not provide] evidence in that respect, the application must be declared inadmissible in so far as they are concerned.

19. With regard to the other applicants, it must be held that the fact that, before the adoption of the decision at issue, they had entered into contracts which were to be carried out during the months to which the decision applied constitutes a circumstance which distinguishes them from any other person concerned by the decision, in so far as the execution of their contracts was wholly or partly prevented by the adoption of the decision.

[Individual concern – three]

20. The Commission, however, challenges the assertion that that circumstance is sufficient in itself for the applicants to be regarded as individually concerned. It argues that in any event when it adopted the decision it was unaware of the number of contracts already entered into for the period covered by that decision and that, in contrast to the cases considered in previous decisions of the court, it had no way of obtaining information in that regard, since the contracts in question were governed by private law and there was no obligation to declare them to Community or national authorities.

21. In that respect it must be observed that the reply to be given to the question whether and to what extent the Commission was aware, or could have made itself aware, which Greek exporters had entered into contracts covering the period of application of the contested decision depends on the interpretation given to Article 130 of the Act of Accession, and in particular on the question whether the Commission, before authorising a protective measure under that provision, is obliged to make appropriate enquiries as to the economic effects of the decision to be taken and the undertakings which would be affected by it. Since arguments related to that problem were raised in support of the assertion that the decision at issue is unlawful, the admissibility of the application from that point of view must be considered in conjunction with the substance of the case.

22. The applicants argue first that in the adoption of the contested decision the conditions laid down in Article 130 of the Act of Accession were not met. In that regard the applicants make three distinct submissions. In the first place they maintain that the product covered by the decision at issue does not constitute a 'sector of the economy' as envisaged by Article 130. In their second submission they argue that the sectoral or regional difficulties referred to in that article did not exist in this case. In their third submisson they assert that the content of the decision in question was not restricted to the measures strictly necessary, contrary to Article 130(3).

23. Taking into account what has already been said with regard to the admissibility of the action, this last submission should be considered first.

24. It should be borne in mind in this regard that under Article 130(1) of the Act of Accession a Member State may apply for authorisation to take

protective measures with regard to the Hellenic Republic 'if . . . difficulties arise which are serious and liable to persist in any sector of the economy or which could bring about serious deterioration in the economic situation of a given area'.

25. Article 130(3) provides that: 'the measures authorised [may] involve derogations from the rules of the EEC Treaty and of this Act to such an extent and for such periods as are strictly necessary in order to attain the objectives referred to in paragraph (1). Priority shall be given to such measures as will least disturb the functioning of the common market'.

26. That requirement may be explained by the fact that a provision permitting the authorisation of protective measures with regard to a Member State which derogate, even temporarily and in respect of certain products only, from the rules relating to the free movement of goods must, like any provision of that nature, be interpreted strictly.

27. The applicants argue that the decision at issue has a serious impact on the Greek traders concerned, even though there is not the slightest indication in the statement of the reasons on which that decision is based that the Commission took into account the very serious effects which its decision would have for those traders.

28. It must be observed that in order to ascertain whether the measure whose authorisation is being considered meets the conditions laid down in Article 130(3) the Commission must also take into account the situation in the Member State with regard to which the protective measure is requested. In particular, in so far as the circumstances of the case permit, the Commission must inquire into the negative effects which its decision might have on the economy of that Member State as well as on the undertakings concerned. In that connection it must also consider, in so far as is possible, the contracts which those undertakings, relying on the continuation of free trade within the Community, have already entered into and whose execution will be wholly or partially prevented by the decision authorising the protective measure.

29. In that regard the Commission objects that it would be impossible for it, during the brief period within which it must act, to make itself aware of the exact number of contracts meeting that description.

30. That argument cannot be accepted in the light of the circumstances of this case. Before adopting the contested decision the Commission had sufficient time to obtain the necessary information. As the Commission admitted at the hearing, moreover, it had arranged a meeting with representatives of the Greek government and of the trade interests concerned, which even included certain of the applicants.

31. In those circumstances it must be concluded that the Commission was in a position to obtain sufficiently exact information on the contracts already entered into which were to be performed during the period of application of the decision at issue. It follows that the undertakings which were party to contracts meeting that description must be considered as individually concerned for the purposes of the admissibility of this action, as members of a limited class of traders identified or identifiable by the Commission and by reason of those contracts particularly affected by the decision at issue.

32. The objection of inadmissibility raised by the Commission and supported by the government of the French Republic must therefore be dismissed, except as regards the two applicants referred to above in paragraph 18.

[Grounds]

33. With regard to the substance of the case, it appears from the text of the decision in question that the Commission did to a certain extent comply with the requirements laid down by Article 130(3). It did authorise quotas less strict than those requested by the French Republic. In Article 3 of the decision, moreover, it included a clause exempting shipments sent from Greece before the notification of the decision.

34. Having regard to the particular circumstances of this case it does not however appear that the Commission took sufficient account of the interests of other Greek traders also affected by its decision. In a case such as this, where the request for protective measures was made at the time when the Member State requesting them was already applying an unauthorised system of import quotas for the products in question, the Commission should have been more prudent in its attitude and should have shown greater concern for the situation of the Greek undertakings; it should in particular have taken into account, with a view to their possible exemption in whole or in part from the application of the decision, contracts entered into in good faith before the date of that decision and to be performed during the months covered by the protective measures.

35. It follows from the foregoing that in taking into consideration only those contracts under which shipments had already been sent from Greece and not those which met the description set out above, although nothing prevented it from doing so, the Commission did not entirely comply with the provisions of Article 130(3).

[B56]   Case 100/74 Société CAM SA v Commission of the European Communities [1975] ECR 1393

[Under the scheme for the common organisation of the market in cereals, exporters of certain cereals were authorised to request advance fixing of certain refunds to which they were entitled. The refunds thus fixed in advance, at the amount in force on the day of the application, were nevertheless subject to monthly adjustments which had repercussions on the amount of the refunds even in cases where they were fixed in advance. The Council adopted a regulation whereby different export refunds were granted according to the date of the application for advanced fixing.]

The European Court of Justice (at pp 1402–1403)

14. The contested measure, by denying to a class of traders the benefit of an increase in the amount of refunds for specific exports which was on the contrary granted to those whose applications for advance fixing were made at a later date, directly concerns the said traders.

15. On the other hand it applies to a fixed and known number of cereal exporters as well as, in respect of each of them, to the amount of the transactions for which advance fixing had been requested.

. . .

18. By adopting these distinguishing criteria the contested measure affects a fixed number of traders identified by reason of the individual

course of action which they pursued or are regarded as having pursued during a particular period.

19. Such a measure, even if it is one of a number of provisions having a legislative function, individually concerns the persons to whom it applies in that it affects their legal position because of a factual situation which differentiates them from all other persons and distinguishes them individually just as in the case of the person addressed.

[B57]   Cases 239, 275/82 Allied Corporation and others v Commission of the European Communities [1984] ECR 1005

The European Court of Justice (at p 1030)

11. [Regulation 3017/79, Article 13(1), provides that 'anti-dumping duties], whether provisional or definitive, shall be imposed by regulation'. Although it is true that, in the light of the criteria set out in [Article 173(2)], such measures are, in fact, as regards their nature and their scope, of a legislative character, inasmuch as they apply to all the traders concerned, taken as a whole, the provisions may none the less be of direct and individual concern to those producers and exporters who are charged [with] anti-dumping. It is clear from [Regulation 3017/79, Article 2] that anti-dumping duties may be imposed only on the basis of the findings resulting from investigations concerning the production prices and export prices of undertakings which have been individually identified.

12. It is thus clear that measures imposing anti-dumping duties are liable to be of direct and individual concern to those producers and exporters who are able to establish that they were identified in the measures adopted by the Commission or Council or were concerned by the preliminary investigations.

[B58]   Case 242/87 Commission of the European Communities v Council of the European Communities [1989] ECR 1425

[The Commission brought an action for the annulment of Council Decision 87/327, adopting the European Community action scheme for the mobility of university students (Erasmus). The Council decision purported to have as its legal basis both Articles 128 and 235 of the EEC Treaty and also Council Decision 63/266, laying down general principles for implementing a common vocational training policy. The Commission submitted, inter alia, that this was an infringement of the Treaty, because the Council added to the legal basis proposed by the Commission, namely Article 128, a further legal basis, namely, Article 235. Germany, the United Kingdom and France intervened in support of the Council. Cf **[A38]** and **[A46]**.]

The European Court of Justice (at pp 1452–1459)

Legal basis

6. As the court has already stated, it follows from the very wording of Article 235 that its use as the legal basis for a measure is justified only where no other provision of the Treaty gives the Community institutions the necessary power to adopt the measure in question ([Case 45/86] *Commission v Council* [1987] ECR 1493).

7. The Commission maintains that the Council had the power to adopt the contested decision on the sole basis of Article 128 of the Treaty and Decision 63/266. According to the Council and the intervening governments, the additional reference to Article 235 was necessary, first, because the measures planned under the Erasmus programme go beyond the powers conferred on the Council by Article 128 in the area of vocational training and, secondly, because the subject matter of that programme exceeds the scope of vocational training within the meaning of that article. It is therefore necessary to examine the various arguments put forward to justify recourse to Article 235 with those two points in mind.

(a) The powers of the Council in the area of vocational training

8. Whereas the Commission considers that Article 128 [constitutes] the proper legal basis for the adoption of operational measures for implementing the common vocational training policy, the Council and the intervening governments maintain that that provision of the Treaty allows for the development of that policy at an embryonic stage only. They believe that the provision in question is of a programmatic rather than instrumental character and provides for a division of powers between the Member States and the Community institutions. They assert that while it is for the Council to define the criteria with which the Member States are obliged to comply when implementing the vocational training policy, it is not within the Council's power, on the basis of that same provision, to specify Community action of the kind planned in the Erasmus programme.

9. In the face of those divergent views, it should be recalled that Article 128 provides that 'the Council shall, acting on a proposal from the Commission and after consulting the Economic and Social Committee, lay down general principles for implementing a common vocational training policy capable of contributing to the harmonious development both of the national economies and of the common market'. As the Commission has rightly pointed out, the fact that the implementation of a common vocational training policy is provided for precludes any interpretation of that provision which would mean denying the Community the means of action needed to carry out that common policy effectively.

10. The court has already noted, in [Gravier **[D69]**], that the common vocational training policy referred to in Article 128 [is] gradually being established. The above-mentioned Decision 63/266, which constitutes the point of departure for that process of gradual implementation, is based on the idea that the task of implementing the general principles of the common vocational training policy [is] one for the Member States and the Community institutions working in co-operation.

11. From an interpretation of Article 128 based on that conception it follows that the Council is entitled to adopt legal measures providing for Community action in the sphere of vocational training and imposing

corresponding obligations of co-operation on the Member States. Such an interpretation is in accordance with the wording of Article 128 and also ensures the effectiveness of that provision.

12. That interpretation cannot be invalidated by the fact that Article 128 does not provide for the involvement of the European Parliament and does not contain any specific requirements concerning the majority required for a decision by the Council, whereas other provisions of the Treaty lay down stricter procedural requirements for the adoption of measures concerning the implementation of a common policy or even the co-ordination of national policies or provisions.

13. Under the system governing Community powers, the powers of the institutions and the conditions on their exercise derive from various specific provisions of the Treaty, and the differences between those provisions, particularly as regards the involvement of the European Parliament, are not always based on consistent criteria.

14. It must, however, be added that among the provisions of the Treaty relied upon in support of the Council's position, Article 57 **[D30]** is certainly relevant in defining the scope of Article 128. Article 57 provides specifically for the adoption of directives for the mutual recognition of diplomas, certificates and other evidence of formal qualifications and for the co-ordination of national provisions concerning the taking up and pursuit of activities as self-employed persons. It follows that that type of measure, even if it concerns the area of vocational training, does not fall under Article 128.

15. However, the scope of that provision as a general basis for the adoption of measures relating to vocational training policy cannot be limited by the fact that specific action in the sphere of vocational training is envisaged in particular in Article 41 of the Treaty in the context of the common agricultural policy and in Article 125 in connection with aid granted by the European Social Fund.

. . .

19. In the light of the foregoing, it must be held that the measures envisaged under the Erasmus programme do not exceed the limits of the powers conferred on the Council by Article 128 of the Treaty in the area of vocational training. The decision in question provides for Community information projects and promotional activity and imposes on Member States obligations of co-operation.

20. Although it is true that Action 3 of the programme concerns 'measures to promote mobility through the academic recognition of diplomas and periods of study', examination of the various measures provided for in this part of the programme shows that they are designed merely to prepare for and encourage the recognition envisaged; that recognition itself is not the subject matter of the action. The nature of the action is thus sufficient to show that it does not fall under the exclusive scope of application of Article [57].

21. It follows from the foregoing that the Council was empowered to enact the contested measure on the basis of Article [128], subject to examination of the question whether that measure exceeded the scope of vocational training.

(b)   The scope of vocational training

22. While the Commission considers that the programme in question

concerns vocational training alone, the Council and the intervening governments believe that it goes beyond that field in several respects.

23. They claim in the first place that the Erasmus programme is applicable to all university studies, a large part of which do not constitute vocational training.

24. As the court has consistently held (see primarily [*Gravier* **[D69]**]), any form of education which prepares for a qualification for a particular profession, trade or employment or which provides the necessary skills for such a profession, trade or employment is vocational training, whatever the age and level of training of the pupils or students, even if the training programme includes an element of general education.

25. In [Case 24/86 *Blaizot* [1988] ECR 379], the court has already stated that, in general, university studies fulfil those criteria and the only exceptions are certain courses of study which, because of their particular nature, are intended for persons wishing to improve their general knowledge rather than prepare themselves for an occupation.

26. It also follows from that judgment that studies do not cease to constitute vocational training where they do not directly provide the required qualification for a particular profession but provide specific training and skills, or in the case of university education, they are divided into different stages which must be regarded as a single unit, where it is not possible to make a distinction between one stage which does not constitute vocational training and a second which [does].

27. It follows that in general the studies to which the contested programme applies fall within the sphere of vocational training, and only in exceptional cases will the action planned under the programme be found to be applicable to university studies which, because of their particular character, are outside that sphere. The mere possibility of the latter cannot justify the conclusion that the contested programme goes beyond the scope of vocational training and that therefore the Council was not empowered to adopt it pursuant to Article [128].

28. It was maintained, secondly, that certain objectives of the contested programme, in particular that of '[strengthening] the interaction between citizens in different Member States with a view to consolidating the concept of a people's Europe' (Article 2(iv) of the contested decision) exceeded the scope of vocational training.

29. In that regard it must be pointed out, first, that the court has already held that there is a special link between the common vocational training policy and the free movement of persons (see [*Gravier*]) and, secondly, that the perfectly legitimate aim that the development of a common policy should be in keeping with the general objectives of the Community, such as the achievement of a people's Europe, cannot lead to a change in the proper legal basis of measures which fall objectively under the common policy in question.

30. Thirdly, it was asserted that the contested decision affected the organisation of education inasmuch as it is intended to set up a European network for university co-operation (Action 1 of the programme).

31. The court has already held in [*Casagrande* **[D28]**] that although educational and training policy is not as such included in the spheres which the Treaty has entrusted to the Community institutions, it does not follow that the exercise of powers transferred to the Community is in some way limited if it is of such a nature as to affect the measures taken in the execution of a policy such as that of education and training.

32. According to the terms of Action 1, set out in the annex to the contested decision, the European university network will be composed of those universities which have chosen to conclude certain agreements for exchanges of students and teachers. Although it is true that it is for the Community to set up the network, universities may only participate on the basis of the provisions governing their status and organisation, which are not affected by the programme in question. Consequently that argument cannot be accepted.

33. It was also maintained that recourse to Article 235 [was] necessary because the programme in question included some aspects falling within the sphere of research.

34. It is clear that scientific research is characteristically one of the proper functions of a university. Not only does a proportion of university staff devote its time exclusively to research but research constitutes in principle an essential element in the work of most university teachers and of some students, for example those studying for a doctorate or similar qualification.

35. Any interpretation of the contested decision to the effect that it did not concern the scientific research work of universities would lead to a considerable limitation on the scope of certain objectives of the Erasmus programme, in particular that of '[promoting] broad and intensive co-operation between universities in all Member States' and that of '[harnessing] the full intellectual potential of the universities in the Community by means of increased mobility of teaching staff, thereby improving the quality of the education and training provided by the universities with a view to securing the competitiveness of the Community in the world market' (Article 2(ii) and (iii)).

36. Consequently, in the absence of any express reservation in the contested decision as regards scientific research, it must be held that at least some of the initiatives planned are aimed at the spheres of both research and vocational training. That is especially true of Action 1 ('Establishment and operation of a European university network'), which provides in particular for 'support for teaching staff and university administrators to visit other Member States, to enable them to prepare programmes of integrated study with universities of these Member States and to exchange experience on the latest developments in their area of expertise', and support to encourage greater mobility for teaching staff (paragraphs 3 and 4). Moreover, Article 130g of the Treaty, added by the Single European Act, sets out, among other activities to be carried out by the Community in pursuing the objectives laid down in the new Title of the Treaty on research and technological development, the stimulation of training and mobility of researchers in the Community.

37. It follows that inasmuch as the contested decision concerns not only the sphere of vocational training but also that of scientific research, the Council did not have the power to adopt it pursuant to Article 128 alone and thus was bound, before the Single European Act entered into force, to base the decision on Article 235 as well. The Commission's [submission] that the legal basis chosen was unlawful must therefore be rejected.

[B59]   Case 24/62 Government of the Federal Republic of Germany v Commission of the European Economic Community [1963] ECR 63

The European Court of Justice (at pp 69–70)

In imposing upon the Commission the obligation to state reasons for its decisions, Article 190 is not taking mere formal considerations into account but seeks to give an opportunity to the parties of defending their rights, to the court of exercising its supervisory functions and to Member States and to all interested nationals of ascertaining the circumstances in which the Commission has applied the Treaty. To attain these objectives, it is sufficient for the decision to set out, in a concise but clear and relevant manner, the principal issues of law and of fact upon which it is based and which are necessary in order that the reasoning which has led the Commission to its decision may be understood. Apart from general considerations, which apply without distinction to other cases, or which are confined to repeating the wording of the Treaty, the Commission has been content to rely upon 'the information collected', without specifying any of it, in order to reach a conclusion 'that the production of the wines in question is amply sufficient'.

This elliptical reasoning is all the more objectionable because the Commission gave no indication [of] the evolution and size of the [wine] surpluses, but only repeated, without expanding the reasons for it, the same statement 'that there was no indication that the existing market situation within the Community did not allow these branches of the industry in the German Federal Republic a supply which is adequate in quantity and in quality'.

[It] follows from these factors that the inadequacy, the vagueness and the inconsistency of the statement of reasons for the decision, both in respect of the refusal of the quota requested and of the concession of the quota granted, do not satisfy the requirements of Article 190.

[B60]   Case 112/77 August Töpfer & Co GmbH v Commission of the European Communities [1978] ECR 1019

[Topfer claimed, unsuccessfully, in proceedings to annul a regulation, that the regulation at issue contained a breach of the principle of the protection of legitimate expectation.]

The European Court of Justice (at p 1033)

19. The submission that there has been a breach of this principle is admissible in the context of proceedings instituted under Article 173, since the principle in question forms part of the Community legal order with the result that any failure to comply with it is 'an infringement of this Treaty or of any rule of law relating to its application' within the meaning of [Article 173].

[B61]   Case 20/71 Luisa Sabbatini (née Bertoni) v European Parliament [1972] ECR 345

[Mrs Sabbatini sought the annulment of certain decisions by which, following her marriage, the administration of the European Parliament, acting under Article 4(3) of Annex VII to the Staff Regulations, withdrew the expatriation allowance which she had previously received.]

The European Court of Justice (at pp 350–351)

3. [The] applicant claims that Article 4(3) of Annex [VII], on which the contested decisions are founded, is illegal because it is contrary to a general principle of law prohibiting any discrimination on grounds of sex and, more particularly, because it is contrary to Article 119 of the EEC Treaty relating to the principle of equal pay for male and female workers.

4. Under Article 4(3) of Annex VII an official 'who marries a person who at the date of marriage does not qualify for the allowance shall forfeit the right to expatriation allowance unless that official thereby becomes a head of household'.

5. Although this provision does not of itself create any difference of treatment as between the sexes, it must however be examined in conjunction with Article 1(3) of the same Annex, which provides that the term 'head of household' normally refers to a married male official, whereas a married female official is considered to be head of household only in exceptional circumstances, in particular in cases of invalidity or serious illness of the husband.

6. It is thus clear that the provision the validity of which is contested does in fact create a difference of treatment as between male and female officials inasmuch as it renders the retention of the expatriation allowance conditional upon the acquisition of the status of head of household within the meaning of the Staff Regulations.

7. It is therefore necessary to examine whether this difference of treatment is such as to affect the validity of the contested provision of the Staff Regulations.

8. The purpose of the expatriation allowance is to compensate for the special expenses and disadvantages resulting from entry into the service of the Communities for those officials who [are] thereby obliged to change their place of residence.

9. Article 4, taken as a whole, indicates that the expatriation allowance is paid to married officials not only in consideration of the personal situation of the recipient, but also of the family situation created by the marriage.

10. Thus Article 4(3) takes into account the new family situation entered upon by the official when he or she marries a person who does not satisfy the conditions for the grant of the expatriation allowance.

11. The withdrawal of the allowance following the marriage of the recipient might be justified in cases in which this change in the family situation is such as to bring to an end the state of 'expatriation' which is the justification for the benefit in question.

12. In this respect, the Staff Regulations cannot however treat officials differently according to whether they are male or female, since termination of the status of expatriate must be dependent for both male and female officials on uniform criteria, irrespective of sex.

13. Consequently, by rendering the retention of the allowance subject to the acquisition of the status of 'head of household' [the] Staff Regulations have created an arbitrary difference of treatment between officials.

14. Consequently, the decisions taken with regard to the applicant are devoid of any legal basis and must be [annulled].

[B62]   Case 56/77 Agence Européenne d'Interims SA v Commission of the European Communities [1978] ECR 2215

[There was an application to annul a decision of the Commission by which the Commission rejected the applicant's offer to make temporary staff available.]

The European Court of Justice (at pp 2233–2236)

20. Although the court has jurisdiction to review the judgment of the departments of the Commission to decide whether there is any misuse of powers or a serious and manifest error of judgment it must, however, respect the discretion given to the competent authorities [in] assessing the factors to be taken into account in the interests of the department for the purpose of deciding to enter into a contract for the supply of temporary staff to an institution.

. . .

24. Provided that the Commission has assessed the tenders fairly on the same basis and according to the same criteria the choice of methods which it has employed to compare the tenders cannot be questioned.

. . .

36. [The] Commission had to judge the tenders on the basis of an assessment of its future needs and in particular of the number of hours of use of the temporary staff and the allocation of these according to occupations and only the Commission is in a position to make this assessment.

[B63]   Case 105/75 Franco Giuffrida v Council of the European Communities [1976] ECR 1395

[Giuffrida, an official of the European Council, sought the annulment of the Council's decision appointing one Martino to the post of principal administrator at the Directorate General for Regional Policy, on the ground that the Council's decision was adopted following an internal competition which was organised for the sole purpose of appointing to the vacant post the candidate who was in fact successful and that this was both contrary to the provisions of the Staff Regulations and also a misuse of powers. By Article 27(1) of the Staff Regulations, 'recruitment shall be directed to securing for the institution the services of officials of the highest standard of ability, efficiency and integrity', and by Article 29, laying down the necessary recruitment procedures (including internal competitions), vacant posts may be filled by officials chosen on the basis of objective criteria and only in the interests of the service.]

The European Court of Justice (at pp 1403–1404)

10. It is clear [that the internal competition] was organised by the appointing authority for the sole purpose of remedying the anomalous administrative status of a specific official and of appointing that same official to the post declared vacant.

11. The pursuit of such a specific objective is contrary to the aims of any recruitment procedure, including the internal competititon procedure, and thus constitutes a misuse of powers.

12. The existence of misuse of powers in this instance is moreover confirmed by the fact that one of the conditions for admission to the competition was that the successful candidate must have held the secretariat for meetings of Council working parties or committees on regional policy for at least four years.

13. It is not disputed that such a restrictive condition corresponds exactly to the duties performed by [Martino] in his previous post.

14. Furthermore, none of the information provided by the [Council] shows why it was necessary in the interests of the service to lay down such a specific condition as regards the duration of the duties referred to.

15. Furthermore, in a memorandum [which] was drawn up after agreement with the staff representatives, the Secretary-General of the Council had given the Directorate for Administration certain directives in relation to internal [competitions].

16. The memorandum provided, in particular, that 'in order to ensure the equal treatment of all officials internal competitions will take place on the basis of qualifications and tests offering the same guarantees of selection as open competitions although adapted to the internal nature of the competition and the types of post to be filled'.

17. Whether or not the memorandum in question was at that time in the nature of a decision, the fact remains that, in the interests of proper administration and in so far as an internal competition may result in transfer or promotion into a higher [category], the appointing authority should have regarded itself as under a moral obligation to comply with it and, therefore, to organise the competition in question on the basis not only of qualifications but of tests also.

18. On these grounds it must be concluded that the decision to make the appointment in question involves a misuse of powers and must therefore be annulled.

[B64]   Cases 18, 35/65 Max Gutmann v Commission of the European Atomic Energy Community [1966] ECR 103

[Gutmann was an official of the staff of Euratom, responsible, as Head of Division, for the Press and Public Relations Department of the Nuclear Research Centre. In May 1964, the Centre Director investigated Gutmann's conduct and, in July 1964, Gutmann was reprimanded. Gutmann made no complaint against this minor disciplinary measure. The Commission further pursued Gutmann's conduct. He was interviewed on 25 September 1964 by the head of the Commission's security department. On the same day the Director told Gutmann that he was being temporarily suspended on full pay. The Director also ordered that Gutmann's office be sealed off and that he be forbidden access to the Research Centre. During this temporary suspension from duty the Commission decided not to allow him to continue as Head of Division and on 9 December the Commission ordered his transfer to Brussels, appointing him Principal Administrator in the library of the Information Services Directorate. He complained about both decisions (suspension and transfer). On 18 February 1965, he received a letter, dated 5 February, rejecting his complaint.]

The European Court of Justice (at pp 116–119)

[On the adequacy of the reasons]

A distinction must be drawn with regard to the decision of 5 February between the factors relating to suspension and those relating to transfer. In so far as this decision concerns the decision of 25 September 1964 to suspend the applicant it must be deemed to incorporate the statement of reasons given in the latter. Since a decision to suspend an official is an act adversely affecting him it must, in accordance with Article 25 [of the Staff Regulations], state the reasons on which it is based.

This statement of reasons must comply with the requirements of [Article] 88 of the Staff Regulations which do not permit the appointing authority to suspend an official unless serious misconduct is alleged, whether this amounts to failure to carry out his official duties or to a breach of law.

The decision of 25 September 1964 is limited to a statement that 'the inquiry carried out has revealed in Mr Gutmann's relationships with his staff and in the general management of his department, conduct inconsistent with his duties as Head of a Division' and that 'he must be suspended from his duties in order to allow these facts to be elucidated'.

This brief and vague statement of reasons contains no precise indication capable of amounting to an allegation of serious misconduct. Nothing therein makes it possible to deduce the nature and gravity of the 'conduct' described. The complaints concerning 'Mr Gutmann's relationships with his staff' are not explained even briefly in such a way as to enable the court to carry out its review, in particular as regards the degree of seriousness of the [misconduct].

It is therefore appropriate to annul the decision of 5 February 1965 rejecting the applicant's complaint in so far as it confirms the decision of 25 September 1964 suspending [him].

[On the allegation of misuse of powers]

The decision of 5 February 1965 rejecting his complaint has also to be examined in so far as it confirms the decision of 9 December 1964 to transfer him, of which he was notified on 22 December 1964.

As the transfer decision of 9 December 1964 was based on the interests of the service there was no need to state the reasons therefor. If such a decision is indeed taken on that basis, it cannot constitute an act adversely affecting an official and falls within the discretionary powers of the administration, which may arrange its departments and move its staff as required for the performance of the tasks assigned to it.

On the other hand, such a decision may amount to a misuse of powers if it appears, on the basis of objective, relevant and consistent facts, to have been taken for purposes other than those stated.

The documents produced show that after various irregularities had been found in the applicant's conduct he was reprimanded on 3 July 1964.

By a decision of the Director General of the [Research Centre] dated 25 September 1964 the applicant was suspended from duty, banned from the Centre and his office was sealed off, on the ground that a fresh inquiry had 'brought to light' in Mr Gutmann's relationship with his subordinates and in the management of his department conduct inconsistent with his duties. Approving this step on 30 September 1964, the Commission ordered an inquiry based on certain irregularities 'which have been established' and a 'complaint lodged by a Head of Division'.

As a consequence of these serious charges, which were stated to have been 'established', and of the special measures, the Commission decided on 9 December 1964 to transfer Mr Gutmann [to] Brussels 'in the interests of the service' and published on the same day the vacancy notice for a post of Principal Administrator in the library.

However, despite the statement on 3 July 1964 to the effect that the possibility of a transfer would depend on 'fresh lapses' being 'found to have occurred' (letter from the Deputy Director of the [Centre to the Director General]) and the statement of 30 September 1964 to the effect that 'certain irregularities' had been 'established', this complaint was no longer quoted in support of the transfer when [the Director General] sent the applicant the letter of 5 February 1965 informing him of the grounds for the Commission's rejection of his complaints against the decision to transfer him.

The applicant was in fact told that his complaint had been rejected on the ground that, first, since July 1964 the Commission 'had been considering the possibility of a transfer' and secondly, that the decision reprimanding him 'had contributed to undermining your reputation' as Head of Division, and finally that 'the nature of [your] relationship with [your] staff was making the atmosphere in [your] department intolerable'. So, having first decided to treat the transfer as not arising out of the reprimand, the Commission then proceeded to adopt the measure in connection with the reprimand.

Whilst making the adoption of this measure subject to a finding of fresh misconduct, it seems later to have set this condition aside. Instead it relied on a complaint with regard to the applicant's difficult relationships with his staff. Whilst these relationships can only have been unfavourably influenced by the effects of disciplinary action against a Head of Division for highly reprehensible conduct, those effects were nevertheless discernable when, on 3 July 1964, the Deputy Director of the [Centre] took the view that they were not sufficient to justify a transfer.

The publicity which was in fact – though doubtless unintentionally – given to the applicant's reprimand, to the sealing off of his office and to the other special precautions taken by the Commission, which became common knowledge, could not but worsen the relationship between the applicant and his staff.

Reports on the applicant described him, some months before the events in question, as fulfilling his duties with 'perfect tact' and maintaining 'good' relationships with his staff. The immediate contradiction between the grounds given in the letter of 19 February 1965 and his reports is [obvious].

The variations and discrepancies described above, together with circumstances such as the timing of the publication of the vacancy notice simultaneously with the transfer of the applicant to the vacant post, the long period of inactivity, not seriously contested, forced on the applicant after taking up his new post and the general circumstances of the case, together amount to a series of objective facts leading to the conclusion that in transferring Mr Gutmann the administration was not exercising its powers for the purpose prescribed for such a measure by the Staff Regulations.

Accordingly the decision of 5 February 1965 rejecting the applicant's complaint must be annulled on the ground of misuse of powers in so far as it confirms the decision of 9 December 1964 to transfer him.

Further reading

Brittan, L, 'Institutional Development of the European Community' [1992] Public Law 567.
Brown, L, and Jacobs, F, *The Court of Justice of the European Communities* (3rd edn, 1989).
Capelletti, M, 'Is the Court of Justice "Running Wild" ' (1987) 12 ELR 3.
Dauses, M, 'The Protection of Fundamental Rights in the Community Legal Order' (1985) 10 ELR 398.
European Commission, 'Accession of the Communities to the European Convention on Human Rights', EC Bull Supp 2/79.
European Commission, 'European Union', EC Bull Supp 1/76.
European Commission, 'The Protection of Fundamental Rights in the European Community', EC Bull Supp 5/76.
Grief, N, 'The Domestic Impact of the European Convention on Human Rights as Mediated Through Community Law' [1992] Public Law 555.
Hartley, T, *The Foundations of European Community Law* (3rd edn, 1994).
Lasok, K, *The European Court of Justice: Practice and Procedure* (1984).
Lasok, D, and Bridge, J, *Law and Institutions of the European Communities* (5th edn, 1991).
Lauwaars, R, 'The European Council' (1977) 14 CMLR 25.
Millet, T, *The Court of First Instance of the European Communities* (1990).
Noel, N, 'The Commission's Power of Initiative' (1973) 10 CMLR 123.
Rasmussen, H, *On Law and Policy in the European Court of Justice* (1986).
Schmitthoff, C, 'The Doctrines of Proportionality and Non-Discrimination' (1977) 2 ELR 329.
Usher, J, 'The Influence of National Concepts on Decisions of the European Court' (1976) 1 ELR 359.
Wyatt, D, and Dashwood, A, *European Community Law* (3rd edn, 1993).
Agricola Commerciale Olio Srl and Others v Commission of the EEC 232/81 [1984] ECR 3881.
Aktien -Zuckerfabrik Schöppenstedt v Council of the EEC 5/71 [1971] ECR 975.
Alfons Lütticke GmbH v Commission of the EEC 4/69 [1971] ECR 325.
Compagnie d'Approvisionnement, de Transport et de Crédit SA v Commission of the EEC 9, 11/711 [1972] ECR 391.
Compagnie Continentale France v Council of the EEC 169/73 [1975] ECR 117.

Control Data Belgium NV SA v Commission of the EEC 294/81 [1983] ECR 911.
Fabrique de Fer Charleroi (and others) v Commission of the EEC 351, 360/85 [1987] ECR 3639.
Fédération Charbonnière de Belgique (Fedechar) v High Authority of the ECSC 8/55 [1956] ECR 292.
Government of the Kingdom of the Netherlands v High Authority of the ECSC 6/54 [1955] ECR 103.
Josette Pecastaing v Belgian State 98/79 [1980] ECR 691.
Meroni & Co, Industrie Metallurgiche, Spa v High Authority of the ECSC 9/56 [1958] ECR 133.
Milchwerke Heinz Wöhrmann & Sohn KG and Alfons Lütticke GmbH v Commission of the EEC 31, 33/62 [1962] ECR 501.
Nicholas William, Lord Bethel v Commission of the EEC 246/81 [1982] 2277.
Società Eridania Zuccherifici Nazionali v Commission of the EEC 10, 18/68 [1969] ECR 459.
Société des Usines de Beauport v Council of the EEC 103-109/78 [1979] EDCR 17.
Société pour l'exportation des Sucres SA v Commission of the EEC 88/76 [1977] ECR 709.
Spijker Kwasten BV v Commission of the EEC 231/82 [1983] ECR 2559.
Stanley George Adams v Commission of the EEC 145/83 [1985] ECR 3539.
Unione Nazionale Importatori e Commercianti Motoveicoli Esteri (UNICME) and others v Council 123/77 [1978] ECR 845.
Universität Hamburg v Hauptzollamt Hamburg-Kehrwieder 216/82 [1983] ECR 2711.
Werner A Bock KG v Commission of the EEC 62/70 [1971] ECR 897.
Zuckerfabrik Watenstedt GmbH v Council of the EEC 6/68 [1968] ECR 409.

Chapter Three

Community Law and the Member States

The supremacy of Community law

A number of crucial questions follow the discussion of the European Constitution in Chapter Two with regard to the relationship between the Member States and the primary and secondary legislation created by the Member States and the Community institutions, respectively, and these lead, inevitably, to the proposition of the supremacy of Community law over the laws of the Member States. First, what is the effect of the treaties on the legal systems of the Member States? Secondly, with regard to regulations, what is the meaning of 'shall have general application . . . be binding in its entirety and directly applicable in all Member States'? Thirdly, what if a Member State does not comply with a Treaty obligation imposed on it, in particular if a Member State does not implement (or partially or imperfectly implements) a directive? The answers are not expressly provided for in the EEC Treaty and come from the decisions of the European Court of Justice interpreting the relevant provisions and inferring, deducing and applying an inevitable logical corollary to each provision. This logical corollary has, it is suggested, not simply been demonstrated with regard to disputes between Community institutions and Member States (or between Member States and Member States) being resolved by some form of international arbitration. More significantly, the logical corollary has been directed to ensuring that the citizens of, or living or working in, Member States are themselves, by the supremacy of Community law, the recipients of the rights granted and the obligations imposed by the Community in the achievement of the objectives of the Treaty.

The issue of the legal status of the EEC Treaty in relation to the internal laws of a Member State was first raised in *van Gend* **[C22]**, where the court deduced from the objectives of the Treaty, which is to establish a common market, from the preamble to the Treaty, which refers not only to governments but to peoples, and more specifically by the establishment of institutions endowed with sovereign rights, that the Treaty is more than an agreement which merely creates mutual obligations between the contracting states. The conclusion to be drawn from this was the court's historic and often repeated statement that 'the Community constitutes a new legal order of international law for the benefit of which the states have limited their sovereign rights, albeit within limited fields, and the subjects of which comprise not only Member States but also their nationals'. This was repeated and amplified in *Costa* **[C13]**. Finally, the 'EEC Treaty has established its own system of law, integrated into the legal systems of the Member States, and which must be applied by their courts. It would be contrary to the nature of such a system to allow Member States to introduce or to retain measures capable of prejudicing the practical effectiveness of the Treaty. The binding force of the Treaty and of measures taken in application of it must not differ from one state to another as a result of internal measures, lest the functioning of the Community system should be impeded and the achievement of the aims of the Treaty placed in peril' (Case 14/68 *Walt Wilhelm and others v Bundeskartellamt* [1969] ECR 1).

With regard to regulations, the court has constantly emphasised the wording of Article 189 **[B19]**. The inevitable logical corollary of the phrase 'shall have general application' is that regulations are general legislative acts of the Community and instruments for securing the uniformity of Community law. The inevitable logical corollary of the phrase 'be binding in its entirety' means that there is a fundamental rule requiring the uniform application of regulations throughout the Community and that a Member State cannot disregard any part of a regulation or subject a regulation to implementing provisions other than those which might be required by the regulation itself. The inevitable logical corollary of the phrase 'directly applicable in all Member States' means that the legal effects occur without any further legislative activity by Member States or their institutions and, indeed, the Court of Justice has specifically stated that enactment of the words of a regulation (eg in a statute or a decree) is unlawful in that this might distort the uniformity of the effect of the words in all Member States. Regulations apply not only to, but also in, the Member States and regulations become part of the legal system applicable within the national territory of the Member State. It is as though the exact words (and all the exact words) of the regulation enter the legal system of each Member State automatically and contemporaneously. Furthermore, the court has constantly referred to Article 189, by which directives and decisions are binding in their entirety on those to whom they are addressed and has prefaced many rulings by such phrases as 'it would be incompatible with the binding effect attributed to decisions' (*Grad* **[C25]**) and 'it would be incompatible with the binding effect which Article 189 ascribes to directives' (*Ratti* **[C26]**).

The proposition that Community law becomes an integral part of the legal systems of all Member States and takes precedence within those states has been consistently followed, the Court of Justice not permitting any exceptions to its stated position, and leads to the legal and constitutional consequence that any provision of national law which conflicts with Community law is invalid. Therefore, any conflict must be resolved by the national legal system withdrawing its rule so that the Community provision is the only one in existence within the Member State.

Member States are under a duty to fulfil Treaty obligations and the Commission (or, more rarely, another state) may bring a defaulting Member State before the Court of Justice (below). The court has emphasised that in permitting Member States to profit from the advantages of the Community, the Treaty imposes on them also the obligations to respect its rules and any failure in the duty of solidarity accepted by Member States by the fact of their adherence to the Community strikes at the fundamental basis of the Community legal order. The court has emphasised that rules of Community law must be fully and uniformly applied in all the Member States from the date of their entry into force and for so long as they continue in force.

Obligations are thus imposed on not only the governments and legislatures of Member States but also on their courts to apply Community law in its entirety and, if necessary, accordingly set aside any provision of national law which may conflict with it, whether prior or subsequent to the Community rule. The constitutional obligation to comply with Community law and the enforcement of such obligations by the Commission is discussed in Section One of this chapter.

Article 177 [B29] provides that any court or tribunal of a Member State is entitled or in certain situations obliged to make a reference to the Court of Justice whenever it considers that a preliminary ruling on a question of interpretation or validity relating to Community law is necessary to enable it to give judgment. There is an obligation to comply with the reply received from the Court of Justice and the effectiveness of Article 177 would be impaired if the national court were prevented from applying Community law in accordance with the decision of the court. The reference procedure under Article 177 is discussed in Section Two of this chapter.

However, the question has arisen on many occasions as to the position of the individual (person or company) who points to the fact that a national legal system has not been adjusted in order to comply with a Community obligation which grants that individual Community rights and that there are two rules, one emanating from the national legal system and one emanating from the Community, when it is the latter which is more favourable to the individual. The protection of Community rights granted to individuals, by means of the principle of direct effect, by positive interpretation by the national courts, and by the quest for adequate judicial remedies (including damages), is discussed in Section Three of this chapter.

The supremacy of Community law is, therefore, imposed on all Member States' legislative, administrative and judicial organs. Furthermore, the law stemming from the Treaty, an independent source of law, cannot because of its very nature be overridden by rules of national law, however framed, without being deprived of its character as Community law and without the legal basis of the Community itself being called in question. Therefore the validity of a Community measure or its effect within a Member State cannot be affected by allegations that it runs counter to either fundamental rights as formulated by the constitution of that state or the principles of a national constitutional structure. All Member States have, therefore, had to incorporate the principle of the supremacy of Community law into their own internal domestic legal and constitutional systems. How this has occurred in two Member States, the United Kingdom and France, is discussed in Sections Four and Five of this chapter, respectively.

SECTION ONE

ENFORCING COMMUNITY OBLIGATIONS

Community obligations are imposed on the Member States in a number of ways, principally by Treaty provisions, regulations, directives and decisions. Member States are enjoined to take all appropriate measures, whether general or particular, to ensure fulfilment of the obligations arising out of the Treaty or resulting from action taken by the institutions of the Community; they must facilitate the achievement of the Community's tasks; they must abstain from any measure which could jeopardise the attainment of the objectives of the Treaty (Article 5). Regulations have general application and are binding in their entirety and directly applicable in all Member States; directives are binding, as to the result to be achieved, upon each Member State to which they are addressed; decisions are binding in their entirety upon those Member States to whom they are addressed (Article 189).

In order to ensure the proper functioning and development of the common market, the Commission is under a duty to ensure that the provisions of the Treaty and the measures taken by the institutions pursuant thereto are applied (Article 155) and the European Court of Justice is enjoined to ensure that in the interpretation and application of the Treaty the law is observed (Article 164). The Commission and the Court of Justice, therefore, have, as one of their roles, the enforcement of Community obligations, either at the instance of the Commission (the usual case) or at the instance of another Member State.

If the Commission considers that a Member State has failed to fulfil an obligation under the Treaty, it must give the state concerned the opportunity to submit its observations and then deliver a reasoned opinion on the matter. If the state concerned does not comply with that opinion within the period laid down by the Commission, the Commission may bring the matter before the Court of Justice. Any Member State which considers that another Member State has failed to fulfil an obligation under the Treaty may bring the matter before the Court of Justice, but, before the accusing Member State brings an action against another Member State for an alleged infringement of such an obligation, it must bring the matter before the Commission. In such a case, the Commission must deliver a reasoned opinion after each of the states concerned has been given the opportunity to submit its own case and its observations on the other party's case (both orally and in writing) (Articles 169 and 170 **[B29]**. See eg Case C-247/89 *Commission of the European Communities v Republic of Portugal* [1991] ECR I-3659).

The role of the Commission may be evidenced by one of the Commission's reports on monitoring the application of Community law **[C1]**. There are a number of means whereby allegations of a breach of a Community obligation may be brought to the Commission's notice, including complaints from members of the public and organisations and pressure groups (for example those concerned with equal opportunities, animal welfare and environmental protection), questions in the European Parliament and the Commission's own monitoring system. The Commission regards the formal complaint as a valuable instrument in ensuring efficient monitoring of the effective implementation of Community law. Examples include letters in which the writers complained about charges for transferring money from one Community country to another, complaints and protests at red tape encountered when crossing borders, involving inspection of goods or identity checks and, in particular, the environment (protection of the countryside and water and atmospheric pollution). The Commission has noted that complaints regarding the environment are lodged with it not only by private individuals and environmental protection associations but also by political parties, political groupings in national parliaments and municipal authorities. Sometimes, the Commission will ask members of the public for complaints on a specific topic.

The enforcement of Community law is carried out at both Community level and within the Member States. The primary responsibility for enforcing Community law lies with each Member State and some Community measures impose very stringent duties upon the Member State, together with policing powers being granted to the Commission. A good example is a directive on animal transport [C2]. Sometimes Member States are enjoined to give the Commission information and if they fail to give the correct information the Commission may take action (*Commission v Ireland* [C3]). Often, there is an obligation to inform the Commission of action Member States have taken to implement a directive (see Directive 64/221 [D42]). Sometimes a specific obligation is imposed on one or more Member States to draw up plans to achieve Community policies, together with provision for the examination of such plans by the Commission [C4], [C5].

The first stage in the process following a complaint, parliamentary question or an investigation by the Commission's staff is the administrative or pre-hearing stage. The Commission must give the state concerned the opportunity to submit its observations and the Commission must deliver a reasoned opinion on the failure, containing a formal statement of the existence of a breach of obligation. As far as investigations are concerned, the Commission tries to settle as many cases as possible at the pre-hearing stage. With this end in view, the practice has arisen of holding package meetings, at regular intervals, in each Member State with representatives of the government departments concerned. At such meetings, all the cases involving a Member State are discussed. Pragmatic solutions in keeping with Community law can thus be sought jointly as early as the complaint stage.

There must be a failure to fulfil an obligation under the Treaty and failures may be the result of a positive breach (eg introducing legislative or administrative measures contrary to Community law) or a negative breach (eg failing to transpose the provisions of a directive into national law, maintaining in force existing national provisions contrary to the results to be achieved by a directive, failing to obey a decision or failing to give the Commission sufficient information required by a regulation or directive). Examples of 'failures' in other Sections of this work are *Commission v Germany* [D27], [E32], *Commission v Belgium* [E10], *Commission v Greece* [E7], [E46], *Commission v Ireland* [E14], *Commission v United Kingdom* [E9] and *Commission v France* [E16]. The transposition of Community legislation into national law does not necessarily require the provisions of that Community legislation to be enacted in precisely the same words in an express and specific enactment. A general legal context may be sufficient if it is sufficiently clear and precise in order to ensure effectively the full application of the directive (Case 29/84 *Commission of the European Communities v Federal Republic of Germany* [1985] ECR 1661). However, a faithful and exact transposition of the words of a directive may be imperative in certain situations, expecially those where there is an element of technical language. For example, a faithful transposition was held to become particularly important in a case concerning Directive 79/409 on the conservation of wild birds, where it was held that the fact that the list of birds in articles of the Netherlands legislation on the protection of wild birds was not identical to the list of birds referred to and contained in the directive constituted an inadequate transposition of the directive into Netherlands law (Case 236/85 *Commission of the European Communities v Kingdom of the Netherlands* [1987] ECR 3989). On implementing a directive and the principle of legal certainty, see *Commission v Denmark* **[C6]**. The Court of Justice has consistently held that mere administrative practices, which by their nature are alterable at will by the authorities and are not given the appropriate publicity, cannot be regarded as constituting the proper fulfilment of obligations under the Treaty (Case 168/85 *Commission of the European Communities v Italian Republic* [1986] ECR 2945).

The failure must be on the part of the Member State and this includes all those arms of the state which have, within the state, the jurisdiction to fulfil the obligation (legislature, administration both central and local, judiciary and whatever organ is entrusted with the power to make constitutional rules). In Case 77/69 *Commission of the European Communities v Kingdom of Belgium* [1970] ECR 237, Belgium did not dispute the existence of discriminatory tax rules between home-grown and imported wood contrary to Article 95 **[E4]–[E10]** and, following some prompting by the Commission, showed itself willing to take the necessary measures to eliminate the discriminatory provisions complained of by the Commission. A draft law was put before the Belgian Parliament but Parliament was dissolved. Provisions were later adopted in order to revive the draft law and the Belgian government argued that this delay in enacting the law amounted to a 'force majeure' beyond its control. However, the court held that the obligations arising from Article 95 'devolve upon States as such and the liability of a Member State under Article 169 arises whatever the agency of the State whose action or inaction is the cause of the failure to fulfil its obligations, even in the case of a constitutionally independent institution'.

It may happen that the Commission considers that an alleged failure to comply with an obligation will cause irreparable harm during the time it takes to determine an Article 169 application. In such a case the Commission may apply for a protective or interim measure (see *Commission v Germany* **[C7]**, **[C8]**).

If the state concerned does not comply with the opinion within the period laid down by the Commission, the Commission may bring the matter before the Court of Justice for the judicial stage of the process. In making use of Article 169, the Commission enjoys a wide discretionary power ('if the Commission considers . . . the latter may'). The action for a declaration that a state has failed to fulfil an obligation does not have to be brought within a pre-determined period, since, by reason of its nature and its purpose, this procedure involves a power on the part of the Commission to consider the most appropriate means and time limits for the purpose of putting an end to any contravention of the Treaty. Furthermore, the fact that the Commission only commenced its action after a lengthy period of time cannot have the effect of regularising a continuing contravention (Case 7/71 *Commission of the European Communities v French Republic* [1971] ECR 1003). The width of the Commission's powers can be illustrated by Case 416/85 *Commission of the European Communities v United Kingdom of Great Britain and Northern Ireland* [1988] ECR 3127. The United Kingdom argued that the

Commission's action in bringing Article 169 proceedings was intended in fact to attain by means of judicial proceedings an objective which could only be achieved by a decision of the Community legislature. The Commission's intention in bringing the proceedings was to by-pass a procedural require-ment under which it was for the Council, acting unanimously, to take a course of action relating to value added tax on certain groups of goods and services. The United Kingdom argued that it was not the task of the court 'to substitute itself for' those political procedures. The court held that such an argument could not be upheld, since in the context of the balance of powers between the institutions, it is not for the court to consider what objectives are pursued in an action brought under Article 169. Its role is to decide whether or not the Member State in question has failed to fulfil its obliga-tion as alleged and an action against a Member State for failure to fulfil its obligations, 'the bringing of which is a matter for the Commission in its en-tire discretion', is objective in nature.

The Court of Justice has taken a logically strict view of breaches of obliga-tions. The court has not permitted a Member State to apply Community law in an incomplete or selective manner, especially since a Member State which omits to take, within the requisite time limits and simultaneously with the other Member States, the measures which it ought to take, undermines the efficacy of the provisions decided upon in common, while at the same time taking an undue advantage to the detriment of its partners. For a state uni-laterally to break, according to its own conception of national interest, the equilibrium between advantages and obligations flowing from its adherence to the Community brings into question the equality of Member States before Community law and any failure in the duty of solidarity accepted by Member States by the fact of their adherence to the Community strikes at the funda-mental basis of the Community legal order (*Commission v Italy* **[C9]**; *Commission v United Kingdom* **[C10]**). In Cases 90, 91/63 *Commission of the European Communities v Grand Duchy of Luxembourg and Kingdom of Belgium* [1964] ECR 625, the defendants argued that the Community itself had in-fringed the Treaty and was thus responsible for the continuance of the alleged infringement of the Treaty and that, since international law allows a party injured by the failure of another party to perform its obligations, to withhold performance of its own, the Commission had lost the right to plead infringement of the Treaty by Belgium and Luxembourg. However, the court held that this relationship between the obligations of parties could not be recognised under Community law. The Treaty was not limited to creating reciprocal obligations between the different natural and legal persons to whom it is applicable, but established a new legal order which governs the powers, rights and obligations of these persons, as well as the necessary pro-cedures for taking cognisance of and penalising any breach of it. Therefore, the basic concept of the Treaty requires that Member States shall not take the law into their own hands. In the same way, practical difficulties which ap-pear at the stage when a Community measure has to be put into effect cannot permit a Member State unilaterally to opt out of observing its obliga-tions (*Commission v Ireland* **[C3]**). The defendant state cannot rely upon domestic difficulties or provisions of its national legal system, even its consti-tutional system, for the purpose of justifying a failure to comply with obligations resulting from Community directives (Case 100/77 *Commission of the European Communities v Italian Republic* [1978] ECR 879).

If the court finds that a Member State has failed to fulfil an obligation under the Treaty, the state is required to take the necessary measures to comply with the judgment of the Court of Justice (Article 171 **[B29]**). However, there are many examples of a Member State ignoring such decisions, with the result that a second case is initiated against the recalcitrant Member State (see *Commission v Italy* **[C11]** and the situation described in *SA Rothmans* **[C61]**). In *Commission v Greece* **[D57]**, the court held that by prohibiting nationals of other Member States from establishing coaching establishments and private music and dancing schools, and from giving private lessons at home, Greece had failed to fulfil its obligations under the free movement of persons provisions. By failing to take the necessary steps to comply with that judgment, Greece had failed to fulfil its obligations under Article 171 (Case C-328/90 *Commission of the European Communities v Hellenic Republic* [1992] ECR I-425). The Commission has, on a number of occasions, lamented the lack of real sanctions **[C1]** and extra 'teeth' will be granted to the Commission and the court under the Treaty of Union, whereby a new Article 171 is substituted **[B29]**.

MATERIALS

[C1]   Sixth Annual Report to the European Parliament on Commission monitoring of the application of Community Law, 1988 (OJ C330, 30 December 1989)

Introduction

1. The sixth annual report on the application of Community law by the Member States deals with the monitoring of the application of Community law during [1988].

. . .

4. The summaries and tables in the Sixth Annual Report call for the following comments:

(a)   As regards the means of detecting infringements:
    (i)   Complaints are a primary source of information for the Commission. The number of complaints registered continues to grow significantly (1,137 in 1988), thus showing that citizens are assuming an increasingly active role in the effective creation of a Community based on law. The Commission makes every effort [to] give a decision as quickly as [possible];
    (ii)   As regards cases detected by the Commission's own enquiries there is an increase (307), contrary to the situation noted in 1987. A number of such cases originate from parliamentary questions or [petitions];

(b)   The number of letters of formal notice has fallen slightly in comparison with the previous year. The internal market and industrial affairs, agriculture and the environment are the main areas in which infringement procedures have been commenced. In comparison with 1987 there is a sharp increase in relation to agriculture but a fall in the number of cases concerned with the environment, employment and social [affairs];

(c)   The number of reasoned opinions, on the other hand, has increased in 1988 thus continuing the increase noted in 1987. The sectors to which this increase relates are chiefly the environment, transport and agriculture. There has been a fall in the number of cases concerned with the customs union, taxation and the internal market and industrial [affairs];

(d)   The number of actions brought before the Court of Justice has increased slightly in comparison with [1987];

(e)   The number of judgments of the Court of Justice which have not yet been complied with rose considerably, thus aggravating the trend criticised in [1987].

5. These facts call for the following comments:

(a)   Letters of formal notice:
    (i)   The largest number of letters of formal notice relates to the internal market and industrial affairs. This is due to the Commission's intensified monitoring of the observance of Articles 30 to 36 of the EEC Treaty and of implementation of the directives concerned with the achievement of the single market;
    (ii)   Agriculture comes second. The relative increase noted in comparison with 1987 arises particularly from delay in the adoption of national measures implementing harmonisation directives (plant health sector, seeds and plants, animal feeding-stuffs and veterinary law);
    (iii)   Next comes the environment. The considerable fall in the number of letters of formal notice no doubt reflects the fact that the Member States are paying greater attention to observance of their obligations in this field;
    (iv)   Social questions have also seen a substantial fall in the number of letters of formal notice. This is due to [the] better application by the Member States of the directives concerning equality between men and women, those relating to safety and protection of health in the work place and provisions on non-discrimination in access to public employment;

(b)   Reasoned opinions:
    (i)   The environment is the sector giving rise to the largest number of reasoned opinions. This is partly due to the continuation of the numerous infringement procedures initiated in the previous years. It must not, however, obscure the fact that a large number of cases have been terminated because they have been regularised. It must be emphasised that public opinion has played a major part in safeguarding the environment. Thus, the pressure exerted in relation to [one] case encouraged the implementation of the directive on the cross-frontier transport of dangerous waste in Italian law, and consequently the regularisation of the existing situation of [infringement];

(c)   The increase in the number of actions brought before the Court of Justice relates particularly to the environment and social [questions].

6. In conclusion, the Commission wishes to draw the attention of the European Parliament to the following points:

(a)   The objectives to be attained before the end of 1992 require increased attention to the implementation of Community law by the Member States and particularly the directives. Among the directives relating to the single market which are already in force, there are few that have been incorporated into the law of all the Member States. The Commission's action pursuant to Article 169 of the EEC Treaty is essential in this connection. But it must be supplemented by a constant effort to increase public awareness. The Commission is making this effort. A development of the relations between the European Parliament and the national parliaments could contribute to increasing the awareness of the latter where the intervention of the national legislature is necessary;

(b)   In view of the importance of its task, the Commission attaches great value to parliamentary questions, petitions and complaints by the public. These initiatives enable the Commission to exercise more extensive control and for this reason the Commission makes a point of examining them as quickly as possible;

(c) The Commission expresses its concern regarding the judgments of the Court of Justice that have not yet been complied with, although it is certain that cases of a lack of political will are rather rare. It is nevertheless true that this situation undermines the fundamental principle of a Community based on law. The rules must be observed without exception or ambiguity. As regards remedies, the only one available under the system created by the Treaty is a power on the part of the Court of Justice to find that the necessary measures to comply with its judgment have not been taken (Article 171 of the EEC Treaty). In the absence of any further legal means of strengthening the authority of the court's judgments, the grave problem of failure to comply with its judgments can be dealt with only by political action: making both governments and individuals more aware of the situation, increased measures of publicity [and] information and encouragement of references for preliminary [rulings];

(d) In this context and also more generally, the Commission draws the attention of the European Parliament to its practice of giving suitable publicity to cases where infringements are found, and to their regularisation, so as to inform the public of their rights and encourage any indirect checks on the observance of Community law by means of actions before national courts, which may in appropriate cases refer questions for preliminary [rulings].

[C2] Council Directive on the protection of animals during transport (Directive 91/628: OJ L340/17, 11 December 1991)

Article 3

1. Member States shall ensure that:

(a) the transport of animals within, to and from each Member State shall be effected in accordance with this Directive . . .

(b) no animal shall be transported unless it is fit for the intended journey and unless suitable provisions have been made for its care during the journey and on arrival at the place of destination. Animals that are ill or injured shall not be considered fit for transport. However, this provision shall not apply to:
 (i) animals that are slightly injured or ill whose transport would not cause unnecessary suffering;
 (ii) animals that are transported for scientific research purposes approved by the competent authority;

(c) animals that fall ill or are injured during transport shall receive first-aid treatment as soon as possible; they shall be given appropriate veterinary treatment and if necessary undergo emergency slaughter in a way which does not cause them any unnecessary suffering.

. . .

Article 5

Member States shall ensure that:

1. any natural or legal person transporting animals for profit:

(a)   is registered in a manner enabling the competent authority to check that the requirements of this directive are complied with;

(b)   transports animals covered by this directive using means of transport meeting the requirements laid down in the Annex;

(c)   does not transport any animal, or cause any animal to be transported, in a way which may cause injury or unnecessary suffering to that animal;

2. the person in charge of the animal transport undertaking:

(a)   entrusts the transport to staff who possess the necessary knowledge to administer any appropriate care to the animals transported;

(b)   draws up, for journeys exceeding 24 hours from the place of departure and taking account of the place of destination, an itinerary – including any staging and transfer points – whereby it can be ensured that the animals are rested, fed and watered and, if necessary, unloaded and given accommodation in accordance with the requirements of this directive for the type of animal to be transported;

. . .

3. the staging points, agreed upon in advance by the person in charge referred to at 2, are regularly checked by the competent authority.

. . .

Article 9

1. If it is found in the course of transport that the provisions of this directive are not being or have not been complied with, the competent authority of the place at which such a finding is made shall require the person in charge of the means of transport to take any action which the competent authority considers necessary in order to safeguard the welfare of the animals concerned.

. . .

Article 10

Commission experts may, to the extent necessary for [application] of this directive, carry out on-the-spot checks in collaboration with the competent authorities of the Member States. The Member State in whose territory the inspections are carried out shall provide the experts with any assistance required for the accomplishment of their task. The Commission shall inform the Member States of the results of these checks.

. . .

Article 18

1. Member States shall take the appropriate specific measures to penalise any infringement of this directive by natural or legal persons.

2. In the event of repeated infringements of this directive or of an infringement resulting in severe suffering to animals, a Member State may, without prejudice to the other sanctions imposed, take the measures necessary to correct the shortcomings noted.

[C3]   Case C-39/88 Commission of the European Communities v Ireland [1990] ECR I-4271

[The Commission complained that Ireland had failed to notify to the Commission certain prices relating to the market in fish in order to fix an annual guide price for fish. A regulation required Member States to notify the Commission of the prices recorded for fish on representative wholesale markets or in representative ports. The average price on the market day, the total quantities landed and marketed and the total quantity withdrawn from the market had to be sent to the Commission by telex on the 10th and 25th day of each month and each market day if there was a threat of crisis or market disturbance.]

The European Court of Justice (at pp 4282–4283)

8. Ireland acknowledges that it failed to comply with the [obligation]. However, it points out that it has always provided the information required on an annual basis and that this rate of frequency should be adequate to enable the Commission to fix annually the guide [price]. The Irish government stresses in this regard that [a regulation] which is intended to replace [the original regulation] has appreciably reduced the obligations imposed on Member States. Under that new regulation, Member States are in fact required to notify only the average monthly price of the [products].

9. In this connection, it should first be pointed out that the scope and binding nature of a regulation cannot be affected, during the period of its validity, by the adoption of a subsequent regulation which has the same objectives and which imposes less stringent requirements on Member States.

10. Ireland also submits that, as it has already pointed out on several occasions during the discussions on the regulations in question, it is not possible for it to deploy its limited number of fisheries inspectors at the representative ports for the purpose of gathering the pricing information in question and submitting it to the Commission on a bi-monthly basis. Those inspectors are required to monitor some 900 ports and landing places in addition to the representative ports.

11. That submission cannot be accepted. It is well established in the case law of the court [that] a Member State may not plead internal circumstances in order to justify a failure to comply with obligations and time limits resulting from Community law. Moreover, it has been held on several occasions (see [*Commission v Italy* [C9] and *Commission v United Kingdom* [C10]]) that practical difficulties which appear at the stage when a Community measure is put into effect cannot permit a Member State unilaterally to opt out of fulfilling its obligations.

12. In those circumstances, it must be held that by its omission to notify certain prices relating to the market in fish, Ireland has failed to fulfil its obligations under [the regulation].

[C4]   Council Decision introducing a Community financial measure for the eradication of brucellosis in sheep and goats (Decision 90/242: OJ L140/123, 1 June 1990)

Whereas the continued presence of brucellosis in sheep and goats, particularly in the Member States in the Mediterranean basin, is a severe threat to human and animal health;

Whereas the continued presence of this disease constitutes a barrier to the free movement of sheep and goats;

Whereas the eradication of this disease constitutes an essential prerequisite for the establishment – with regard to trade in sheep and goats and their products and by-products – of the internal market in sheep and goats as well as for increasing the productivity of breeding and, consequently, improving the standard of living of persons engaged in this sector;

Whereas the Member States concerned are to present a plan for the eradication of brucellosis in sheep and goats;

Whereas it is, moreover, necessary to lay down the conditions in which slaughter, isolation, cleaning and disinfection should take place and the use which should be made of certain animal products;

Whereas Community financial aid will be in the form of a reimbursement to Member States of a part of the slaughter premium compensating owners of infected sheep and goats for the rapid disposal of such animals;

. . .

Article 1

The French Republic, the Hellenic Republic, the Italian Republic, the Kingdom of Spain and the Portuguese Republic shall, within three months of notification of this Decision, present plans for the eradication of brucellosis (Brucella melitensis) in sheep and goats.

. . .

Article 3

The plans referred to in Article 1 must:
    1. indicate the central authorities which are to implement and co-ordinate the plan;
    2. ensure that the presence and suspected presence of brucellosis are compulsorily and immediately notifiable to the competent authority;
    3. provide for a registration of holdings engaged in sheep and goat farming;
    4. be so devised that, on completion of the plan, the holdings are classified as officially brucellosis-free or brucellosis-free;
    5. ban the therapeutic treatment of brucellosis;
    . . .

8. indicate the national budgetary allocations for the eradication of ovine and caprine brucellosis and the breakdown by item of these allocations and in particular the estimated [costs] for slaughter compensation as well as estimated total costs on an annual basis for carrying out the operations;

9. establish an identification system which makes it possible to monitor movements of sheep and goats;

10. provide for immediate and adequate compensation for the owners of sheep and goats which have been slaughtered because they have reacted positively to an official brucellosis test or because they were suspected by the competent authority of being infected;

11. ensure that, where a holding contains an animal suspected of having brucellosis, the competent authority carry out investigations as soon as possible to confirm or rule out the presence of the disease.

. . .

13. ensure that, where the presence of brucellosis is officially confirmed on a holding, the competent authority shall take appropriate measures to prevent any spread of the disease.

. . .

Article 6

The Commission shall examine the plans drawn up by the authorities of the Member States concerned in order to ascertain whether they meet the conditions for their approval or whether they should be amended in any way.

. . .

Article 7

The measure provided for in this Decision shall qualify for financial aid from the Community.

[C5] Commission decision approving the plan for the eradication of brucellosis in sheep and goats presented by the Republic of Portugal (Decision 91/217: OJ L97/23, 18 April 1991)

Whereas by letter dated 25 September 1990 the Republic of Portugal notified the Commission of a three-year plan for the eradication of brucellosis in sheep and goats;

Whereas, after examination, the plan was found to comply with Decision 90/242/EEC **[C4]**;

. . .

Article 1

The plan for the eradication of brucellosis in sheep and goats presented by Portugal is hereby approved.

Article 2

Portugal shall bring into force by 1 March 1991 the laws, regulations and administrative provisions for implementing the plan referred to in Article 1.

Article 3

This Decision is addressed to the Portuguese Republic.

[C6]   Case 143/83 Commission of the European Communities v Denmark [1985] ECR 427

[The principle of equal pay for men and women means 'for the same work or for work to which equal value is attributed' the elimination of all discrimination on grounds of sex with regard to all aspects and conditions of remuneration (Directive 75/117, see further **[D60]–[D64]**). In purported implementation of the directive, Denmark enacted a law which provided: 'Every person who employs men and women to work at the same place of work must pay them the same salary for the same work under this law if he is not already required to do so pursuant to a collective agreement.' There was, therefore, no express reference to the phrase 'or for work to which equal value is attributed' and it was held that this meant that Denmark had not correctly implemented the directive.]

The European Court of Justice (at pp 434–436)

5. The Commission considers that the Danish legislation does not fulfil all the obligations resulting from Directive 75/117 inasmuch [as] it requires employers to pay men and women the same salary exclusively for the same work but not for work to which equal value is [attributed].

8. It is true that Member States may leave the implementation of the principle of equal pay in the first instance to representatives of management and labour. That possibility does not, however, discharge them from the obligation of ensuring, by appropriate legislative and administrative provisions, that all workers in the Community are afforded the full protection provided for in the directive. That state guarantee must cover all cases where effective protection is not ensured by other means, for whatever reason, and in particular cases where the workers in question are not union members, where the sector in question is not covered by a collective agreement or where such an agreement does not fully guarantee the principle of equal pay.

9. In that respect the Danish law in question does not exhibit the clarity and precision necessary for the protection of the workers concerned. Even accepting the assertions of the Danish government that the principle of equal pay for men and women, in the broad sense required by the directive, is implemented in collective agreements, it has not been shown that the same implementation of that principle is guaranteed for workers whose rights are not defined in such agreements.

10. Since those workers are not unionised and work in small or medium-sized businesses, particular care must be taken to guarantee their rights under the directive. The principles of legal certainty and the protection of individuals thus require an unequivocal wording which would give the persons concerned a clear and precise understanding of their rights and obligations and would enable the courts to ensure that those rights and obligations are observed.

11. In this case it appears that the wording of the Danish law does not

fulfil those conditions inasmuch as it sets out the principle of equal pay without speaking of work of equal value, thus restricting the scope of the principle. The fact that in the preamble to the draft law the government stated that the expression 'same work' was interpreted in Denmark in so broad a sense that the addition of the expression 'work to which equal value is attributed' would not entail any real extension is not sufficient to ensure that the persons concerned are adequately informed.

12. The relevance of those considerations is not affected by the fact that during the preparatory work which led to the adoption of Directive 75/117 the Danish government entered a declaration in the Council minutes to the effect that 'Denmark is of the view that the expression "same work" can continue to be used in the context of Danish labour law'.

13. The court has consistently held that such unilateral declarations cannot be relied upon for the interpretation of Community measures, since the objective scope of rules laid down by the common institutions cannot be modified by reservations or objections which Member States may have made at the time the rules were being formulated.

[C7] Case C-195/90R Commission of the European Communities v Federal Republic of Germany [1990] ECR I-2715

(Order of the President of the Court)
[The Federal Republic of Germany enacted a law on 30 April 1990. The law was due to enter into force on 1 July 1990. Article 1 of the law introduced a new road tax, payable with certain exceptions, on all heavy goods vehicles whose licensed fully loaded weight exceeded 18 tonnes, regardless of their places of registration, which used Federal roads and motorways outside built-up areas. The annual amount of the tax varied, according to the total loaded weight of the vehicle, from DM 1,000 to DM 9,000. This annual value would be applied pro rata according to the time spent using the roads and motorways. Article 2 of the law amended the Law on Motor Vehicle Tax and introduced for a limited period a reduced rate of motor vehicle tax payable on all vehicles according to a scale varying according to the vehicle's total weight up to a maximum of DM 3,500 per vehicle per annum. The Commission brought an action under Article 169 for a declaration that, by enacting the law, Germany had failed to fulfil its obligations under Articles 76, 95 and 5 of the EEC Treaty. The Commission also sought an interim order under Article 186 **[B29]** that Germany should take the necessary measures to suspend the operation of the law until the court had reached a decision in the main proceedings and expressly requested the court to make an order granting the application as a protective measure pending delivery of the final order in the proceedings for interim measures, even before Germany had submitted its observations on the application for interim relief.]

The President (at pp 2716–2720)

9. It is apparent [that] on 21 March 1989 a draft of the [law] was forwarded to the Commission for consultation pursuant to [Council] Decision of 21 March 1962 instituting a procedure for prior examination and consultation

in respect of certain laws, regulations and administrative provisions concerning transport proposed in Member [States].

10. The opinion delivered by the Commission on 15 June 1989 pursuant to the said decision points out that the proposed reduction in the motor vehicle tax would benefit only German carriers, since the carriers of other Member States are, as a result of bilateral agreements, exempt from that tax and the proposed reduction in the rate of [tax] would be practically equivalent to the amount of the road tax contemplated. The introduction of the latter tax would thus in fact not constitute a burden upon German carriers but solely on carriers of other Member States who would be required to pay the road tax without having the benefit of a reduction in the motor vehicle tax.

11. The Commission concludes in its opinion that the provisions contemplated by [Germany] infringe the 'standstill' obligation under Article 76 of the EEC Treaty, according to which, until a common transport policy [has] been established, no Member State may, without the unanimous approval of the Council, make the various provisions governing the subject when the Treaty enters into force less favourable in their direct or indirect effect on carriers of other Member States as compared with carriers who are nationals of that state. According to the opinion, the provisions contemplated were, in addition, contrary in particular to Article 95 **[E4]–[E10]** of the EEC Treaty.

12. The draft law was adopted on 6 April 1990 whereupon the Commission sent formal notice to [Germany] on 11 April 1990 followed, on 1 June 1990, by the reasoned opinion provided for in Article 169(1) of the EEC Treaty.

13. In its replies of 30 April and 22 June 1990 to the formal notice and the reasoned opinion, [Germany] states that the object of the [law] is, first, to bring the motor vehicle tax, which is very high on heavy vehicles, into line with the European average and thus to harmonise the conditions of competition and, secondly, to increase the insufficient contribution made by foreign heavy goods vehicles to the cost of the German road infrastructure. The measures adopted are not contrary to Article 76 of the EEC Treaty, which does not lay down a standstill obligation but is a special provision prohibiting discrimination: neither the new road tax nor the reduction in motor vehicle tax is in itself discriminatory.

14. [Germany] states in the said replies that the road tax is in accordance with the guidelines proposed by the Commission itself in its proposal of 8 January 1988 for a Council directive on the charging of transport infrastructure costs to heavy goods vehicles and that the [law] is of limited duration and is to expire in 1993 if a harmonised system of taxation has been adopted by then.

15. [The] Commission alleges inter alia in relation to the need for urgency that the unilateral introduction of the road tax envisaged would constitute an unacceptable undermining of *ordre public* in the Community and would seriously disrupt the equilibrium of the transport market by threatening the survival of a considerable number of small and medium-sized transport undertakings established in the other Member States.

16. The Commission further states [that] there is a danger of the introduction of the road tax provoking retaliatory measures on the part of the other Member States which would further aggravate the disturbance of the market and render illusory any progress towards achieving a common policy.

17. Pursuant to Article 84(2) of the Rules of Procedure, the President may grant an application for interim measures even before the observations of the opposite party have been [submitted].

18. At the present stage of the proceedings when [Germany] has not yet been able to submit its full observations on the Commission's application for interim measures, it is not possible to decide whether the submissions of fact and law put forward by the Commission suffice to justify the grant of the interim measures which the Commission seeks.

19. However, the Commission's submissions are not prima facie without foundation and it cannot be excluded that the circumstances cited by the Commission establish the requisite urgency for the grant of the interim measures sought.

20. In those circumstances and in view of the particular circumstances of the proceedings, especially the imminence of the entry into force of the [law], it appears necessary, in the interests of the proper administration of justice, that the status quo should be maintained for carriers of other Member States pending a decision on the application for interim measures. It should therefore be ordered, as a protective measure, that [Germany] suspend the charging of the road tax provided for in the [law] in respect of vehicles registered in other Member States pending delivery of the final order in these proceedings for interim measures.

[C8] Case C-195/90R Commission of the European Communities v Federal Republic of Germany [1990] ECR I-3351

(Order of the Court)
[The President of the Court of Justice referred the final decision in the proceedings for interim measures to the court. Belgium, Denmark, France, Luxembourg and the Netherlands were given leave to intervene in the proceedings in support of the Commission.]

The European Court of Justice (at pp 3357–3363)

19. According to Article 83(2) of the Rules of Procedure, a decision ordering an interim measure may be made only where there are circumstances giving rise to urgency and factual and legal grounds establishing a prima facie case for the interim measure applied for.

20. As factual and legal grounds establishing a prima facie case for the interim measure applied for, the Commission and the Member States intervening in its support make three submissions, concerning the infringement of Article 76 of the EEC Treaty, of Article 95 of the EEC Treaty, and of the combined provisions of Articles 5 and 8a of the EEC Treaty respectively.

21. The Commission maintains that [Germany] has infringed Article 76 of the EEC Treaty by adopting measures discriminating against carriers of other Member States and not observing the standstill clause laid down therein.

22. The German law is, in the Commision's view, also contrary to Article 95 of the EEC Treaty in so far as carriers of other Member States are subject to heavier taxation than German carriers and such taxation which will

lead to an increase in transport prices, will inevitably have repercussions on the price of imported products.

23. The Commission also alleges that [Germany] has infringed Article 5 of the EEC Treaty, which requires abstention from any unilateral measures which could jeopardise the common policy on taxation of means of transport for the use of the road infrastructure by heavy goods vehicles, and has thereby created obstacles to the establishment of an area without internal frontiers as provided for by Article 8a of the Treaty.

24. [Germany] denies having infringed Article 76 of the EEC Treaty and contends that the road tax for heavy goods vehicles, even in conjunction with the reduction in the motor vehicle tax, is not discriminatory. The [law] has two objectives, namely to harmonise the conditions of competition between German carriers and those of other Member States and to establish an adequate contribution to the costs of the road infrastructure in order both to relieve road congestion and to protect the environment. As regards the first objective, [Germany] states that carriers of other Member States do not receive any reduction in the motor vehicle tax because they are exempt from such tax under agreements made between the states in which they are established and [Germany]. In those circumstances, the [law] is not contrary to the standstill obligation laid down in Article 76 of the EEC Treaty.

25. As regards the infringement of Article 95 of the EEC Treaty, [Germany] stresses the non-discriminatory nature of the tax and maintains that it is indirect taxation within the meaning of Article 99 of the EEC Treaty which must be harmonised pursuant to the rules provided for by the Treaty.

26. According to [Germany], Article 5 of the EEC Treaty does not lay down a general standstill obligation and, so long as no common transport policy has been [established], the Member States remain, in principle, competent in this area.

27. It should be observed, as regards the Commission's first submission, that the Commission has adduced weighty factors in support of its argument that Article 76 of the EEC Treaty must be interpreted as prohibiting any unilateral national measure having the direct or indirect effect [in] relation to the conditions under which international transport is carried out from or to the territory of a Member State or crossing the territory of one or more Member States.

28. Such may in particular be the case of a new road tax for heavy goods vehicles introduced by a Member State where the burden on national carriers is largely offset by a reduction in the motor vehicle tax to which the carriers of other Member States are not subject pursuant to bilateral agreements concluded between the state where such carriers are established and the state which has imposed the tax.

29. As regards the German government's argument that the [law] encourages the transfer of road traffic to the railways or inland waterways, it is to be observed that although the protection of the environment constitutes, according to the case law of the court, one of the essential objectives of the Community (see [*Commission v Denmark* **[E26]**]), the importance of which has moreover been confirmed by the Single European Act, it does not necessarily follow that a Member State may, by invoking that objective, evade its obligations under Article 76 of the EEC Treaty. It appears moreover from consideration of the statement of grounds in the [law] that the [law] is mainly intended to harmonise the conditions of competition for German

carriers while the relief of road congestion and the protection of the environment are merely subsidiary aims.

30. Without it being necessary at this stage to consider the other submissions put forward, it is to be observed that the submission relating to infringement of Article 76 of the EEC Treaty constitutes, prima facie, a sufficient basis for the grant of the interim measure applied for.

31. As regards the condition of urgency, it is to be borne in mind that the court has consistently held that the urgency of an application for interim [measures] must be assessed in relation to the necessity for an order granting interim relief in order to prevent serious and irreparable damage by the immediate application of the measure the subject of the main proceedings.

32. On that issue the Commission, backed by the Member States intervening in its support, alleges that there is a risk of the application of the tax at issue causing irreparable damage at least to certain carriers of the other Member States. The damage to those carriers consists, in the Commission's view, in an increase in transport costs which would force them to increase their tariffs – and risk losing customers – or else reduce their profit margins – and risk having to cease trading. The Commission maintains generally that the unilateral introduction of the road tax by [Germany] constitutes an unacceptable undermining of *ordre public* in the Community. Since there is a danger of the introduction of the tax provoking retaliatory measures on the part of the other Member States, it would render illusory any progress towards achieving the common transport policy.

33. [Germany] denies that there would be any irreparable damage to the *ordre public* in the Community and to traders on the transport market as claimed by the Commission.

34. The German tax is neutral as regards competition and brings the German tax system closer into line with those in the majority of Member States and pursues the object of establishing a transport policy based on the principle of territoriality. In those circumstances it cannot be said to jeopardise achievement of the common transport policy.

35. Furthermore, in view of the slight effect it would have on transport costs, the new tax could not affect the competitive position of carriers of other Member States. On the other hand, the danger of deterioration in their competitive position is greater for German carriers who are subject to heavier taxes than their counterparts in other Member States.

36. [Germany] adds that in balancing the interests in question, priority should be given to the requirements of protecting the environment and alleviating congestion on the German road network.

37. It adds that in any event, even if the court were to uphold the main application and find that [Germany] had failed to fulfil its Community obligations by creating the tax at issue, it would be possible to make good any damage suffered by transport undertakings of other Member States. The damage which [Germany] would suffer as a result of an order suspending the operation of the [law] would, on the other hand, be irreparable.

38. It should be noted that, although, in principle, pecuniary damage is not to be regarded as irreparable, the position may be different in exceptional circumstances where pecuniary compensation cannot restore the injured person to the position prior to the occurrence of the damage.

39. That possibility cannot be ruled out in the present case. In view of the often very slender profit margins of many medium-sized transport

[undertakings], there is a danger of the effect of the tax in question on the profitability of carriers of other Member States forcing many of them to stop trading. Furthermore, the application of the tax at issue is likely to bring about irremediable changes in the respective market shares of German carriers and of carriers of other Member States. Such an abrupt and substantial change, caused by a unilateral national measure, in the conditions at present existing on the road transport market in the Community, which could not be exactly re-established later if the measures in question are held to be contrary to the Treaty, would also make the development and completion of the common transport [policy] more difficult.

40. It must therefore be held that the Commission, supported by the interveners, has established the existence of a risk of serious and irreparable damage.

41. [Germany] maintains that the grant of the interim measure applied for would cause it irreparable damage consisting in the loss of revenue from the taxes which are not levied during the main proceedings and the risk to the threat of the economic survival of German carriers.

42. In that respect it should be pointed out that the damage alleged by [Germany] is only the detrimental consequence of a situation existing before the introduction of the new tax. Moreover it has not been shown that the measures which have been introduced were made necessary by a significant change in the factual situation likely to increase substantially the magnitude of the existing damage and to justify a different reaction from the German authorities. Finally there seems little likelihood of any serious risk of the damage increasing to any considerable extent in the time up to the adoption of the decision in the main proceedings.

43. As regards, in particular, the damage arising from uncollected taxes which it will be impossible to recover subsequently, it suffices to observe that no such tax existed in the past and therefore there can be no question of the loss of revenue seriously affecting the public finances of [Germany].

44. As regards the threat to the economic survival of German carriers as a result of the deterioration in their competitive position, there is, at first sight, nothing to suggest that, in the absence of any substantial change in the market situation in relation to circumstances which have prevailed for a long period, such a risk will materialise in the coming months.

45. Regarding the argument that the environment will be affected, Germany has failed to substantiate its contention that imposition of the contested tax on carriers of other Member States would lead to a transfer of road traffic to the railways and inland waterways rather than the transfer of the market share of carriers of other Member States to German carriers.

46. In those circumstances it must be held that the condition of urgency has been satisfied.

47. It should therefore be ordered, as an interim measure, that [Germany] suspend the charging of the road tax provided for in the [law] in respect of vehicles registered in other Member States pending the delivery of the judgment in the main proceedings brought by the Commission.

[C9]   Case 39/72 Commission of the European Communities v Italian Republic [1973] ECR 101

[With a view to reducing the surpluses of milk and milk products, the Council introduced a system of premiums to encourage the slaughtering of dairy cows and the withholding of milk and milk products from the market. This was enacted by Council Regulation 1975/69 and by Commission Regulation 2195/69. The Italian government implemented the system of slaughtering premiums very late and did not implement the system for paying non-marketing premiums.]

The European Court of Justice (at pp 113–116)

With regard to the premiums for slaughtering

14. The regulations [have] provided precise time limits for the carrying into effect of the system of premiums for slaughtering. The efficacy of the agreed measures depended upon the observation of these time limits, since the measures could only attain their object completely if they were carried out simultaneously in all the Member States at the time determined in consequence of the economic policy the Council was pursuing. [It] consequently appears that the delay on the part of the Italian Republic in performing the obligations imposed on it by the introduction of the system of premiums for slaughtering [constitutes] a default in its obligations.

As to the premiums for non-marketing

19. The default in putting into operation the provisions of Regulations 1975/69 and 2195/69 with regard to premiums for non-marketing is due to a deliberate refusal by the Italian authorities.

The defendant justifies this refusal by the difficulty of providing an effective and serious inspection and control of the quantities of milk which are not marketed but destined for other use, taking into account both the special characteristics of Italian agriculture and the lack of adequate administration at a lower level.

In any case, according to the Italian government, measures intended to restrict the production of milk were inappropriate to the needs of the Italian economy, which is characterised by insufficient food production.

During the debate stages of Regulation 1975/69 [the] Italian delegation made these difficulties known and expressed clear reservations at that time with regard to the carrying out of the regulation.

In these circumstances, complaint ought not to be made against the Italian Republic for having refused to put into effect on its national territory provisions passed in spite of the oppostion which it has manifested.

20. According to [Article 43(2)] of the Treaty, on which Regulation 1975/69 is founded, regulations are validly enacted by the Council as soon as the conditions contained in the article are fulfilled.

Under the terms of Article 189, the regulation is binding 'in its entirety' for Member States.

In consequence, it cannot be accepted that a Member State should apply in an incomplete or selective manner provisions of a Community regulation so as to render abortive certain aspects of Community legislation which it has opposed or which it considers contrary to its national interests.

21. In particular, as regards the putting into effect of a measure of economic policy intended to eliminate surpluses of certain products, the Member State which omits to take, within the requisite time limits and simultaneously with the other Member States, the measures which it ought to take, undermines the efficacy of the provision decided upon in common,

while at the same time taking an undue advantage to the detriment of its partners in view of the free circulation of goods.

22. As regards the defence based on the preparatory work on Regulation 1975/69, the objective scope of rules laid down by the common institutions cannot be modified by reservations or objections which Member States have made at the time the rules were being formulated.

In the same way, practical difficulties which appear at the stage when a Community measure has to be put into effect cannot permit a Member State unilaterally to opt out of observing its obligations.

The Community institutional system provides the Member State concerned with the necessary means to secure that its difficulties should be reasonably considered within the framework and principles of the Common Market and the legitimate interests of other Member States.

23. In this respect, an examination of the regulations in question and their modifying instruments reveals that in many respects the Community legislator has taken into consideration, by means of special clauses, the particular difficulties of the Italian Republic.

In these circumstances, any practical difficulties of implementation cannot be accepted as a justification.

24. In permitting Member States to profit from the advantages of the Community, the Treaty imposes on them also the obligation to respect its rules.

For a state unilaterally to break, according to its own conception of national interest, the equilibrium between advantages and obligations flowing from its adherence to the Community brings into question the equality of Member States before Community law and creates discriminations at the expense of their nationals, and above all of the nationals of the state itself which places itself outside the Community rules.

25. This failure in the duty of solidarity accepted by Member States by the fact of their adherence to the Community strikes at the fundamental basis of the Community legal order.

It appears therefore that, in deliberately refusing to give effect on its territory to one of the systems provided for by Regulations 1975/69 and 2195/69, the Italian Republic has failed in a conspicuous manner to fulfil the obligations which it has assumed by virtue of its adherence to the European Economic Community.

[C10]   Case 128/78 Commission of the European Communities v United Kingdom [1979] ECR 419

[A Regulation (1463/70) provided for the installation and use of mechanical recording equipment, tachographs, on vehicles used for the carriage of passengers and goods on roads. The tachograph would record such details as length of driving periods and rest periods. The regulation was to come into force with regard to the United Kingdom on 1 January 1976. The United Kingdom decided to introduce a voluntary scheme of recording and expressed its intention not to implement the regulation fully for reasons based on economic, industrial and practical considerations (in that it would not be practical to take the necessary measures within the prescribed period) and also on the practical consequences of attempting to enforce compulsory measures (when important sections of the industry concerned were demonstrating a deep-seated resentment, especially by the trade unions, against the measures proposed – the tachograph was being referred to as 'the spy in the cab' – could not be ignored). The United Kingdom argued that there was a serious risk that labour would be withdrawn from a critical transport sector of the national economy and that the stability of the economy would, or at least might well, be jeopardised. Furthermore, a voluntary scheme would be sufficient to meet the objectives of promoting road safety, of social progress for workers and of the harmonisation of conditions of competition. Note how the court repeats its statements in *Commission v Italy* **[C9]**.]

The European Court of Justice (at pp 428–429)

9. Article 189 of the Treaty provides that a regulation shall be binding 'in its entirety' in the Member States. As the court has already stated in [*Commission v Italy* **[C9]**] it cannot therefore be accepted that a Member State should apply in an incomplete or selective manner provisions of a Community regulation so as to render abortive certain aspects of Community legislation which it has opposed or which it considers contrary to its national interests. In particular, as regards the putting into effect of a general rule intended to eliminate certain abuses to which workers are subject and which in addition involve a threat to road safety, a Member State which omits to take, within the requisite period and simultaneously with the other Member States, the measures which it ought to take, undermines Community solidarity by imposing, in particular as regards intra-Community transport, on the other Member States the necessity of remedying [its] own omissions, while at the same time taking an undue advantage to the detriment of its partners.

10. As the court said in the same judgment, practical difficulties which appear at the stage when a Community measure is put into effect cannot permit a Member State unilaterally to opt out of fulfilling its obligations. The Community institutional system provides the Member State concerned with the necessary means to ensure that its difficulties be given due consideration, subject to compliance with the principles of the common market and the legitimate interests of the other Member States.

11. In these circumstances, the possible difficulties of implementation alleged by the defendant cannot be accepted as a justification.

12. Further, as the court said in the case mentioned above, in permitting Member States to profit from the advantages of the Community, the Treaty imposes on them also the obligation to respect its rules. For a state unilaterally to break, according to its own conception of national interest, the equilibrium between the advantages and obligations flowing from its adherence to the Community brings into question the equality of Member States before Community law and creates discrimination at the expense of their nationals. This failure in the duty of solidarity accepted by Member States by the fact of their adherence to the Community strikes at the very root of the Community legal order.

13. It appears therefore that, in deliberately refusing to give effect on its territory to the provisions of Regulation 1463/70, the United Kingdom has markedly failed to fulfil the obligation which it has assumed by virtue of its membership of the European Economic Community.

[C11]   Case 48/71 Commmission of the European Communities v Italian Republic [1972] ECR 527

[The Commission brought an application for a declaration that Italy, by not complying with the judgment given on 10 December 1968 (Case 7/68 *Commission of the European Communities v Italian Republic* [1968] ECR 423), had failed to fulfil the obligations imposed on it by Article 171 **[B29]**. In that earlier judgment the court had declared that Italy, by continuing to levy after 1 January 1962 the progressive tax laid down by Italian legislation on the export to other Member States of articles of an artistic, historic, archaeological or ethnographic interest, had failed to fulfil the obligations imposed on it by Article 16 of the Treaty.]

The European Court of Justice (at pp 531–532)

3. The Italian Republic, while recognising that it is bound to take measures to comply with this judgment, cites the difficulties which it met in regard to parliamentary procedure aimed at abolishing the tax and reforming the system of protection of the national artistic heritage. These measures must necessarily be adopted in the form and according to the procedures provided for by its constitutional law. Since the levying of the tax can cease only on its formal repeal and since the delays in effecting this repeal are due to circumstances outside the control of the competent authorities, there are no grounds for finding a failure to comply with the obligations under Article [171].

4. The Commission maintains that the national provisions could have been repealed by more expeditious means.

5. Without having to examine the validity of such arguments, it suffices for the court to observe that by judgment of 10 December 1968 it answered in the affirmative the question in dispute between the Italian government and the Commission: whether or not the tax in question was to be regarded as a tax having an effect equivalent to a customs duty on exports within the meaning of Article 16 of the Treaty. Further [in] Case 18/71 *Eunomia di Porroe C v Italian Ministry of Education* [[1971] ECR 811], the court expressly found that the prohibition contained in Article 16 produces direct effects in the national law of all Member States.

6. Since it is a question of a directly applicable Community rule, the argument that the infringement can be terminated only by the adoption of measures constitutionally appropriate to repeal the provision establishing the tax would amount to saying that the application of the Community rule is subject to the law of each Member State and more precisely that this application is impossible where it is contrary to a national law.

7. In the present case the effect of Community law, declared as res judicata in respect of the Italian Republic, is a prohibition having the [force] of law on the competent national authorities against applying a national rule recognised as incompatible with the Treaty and, if the circumstances so require, an obligation on them to take all appropriate measures to enable Community law to be fully applied.

8. The attainment of the objectives of the Community requires that the rules of Community law established by the Treaty itself or arising from procedures which it has instituted are fully applicable at the same time and with identical effects over the whole territory of the Community without the

Member States being able to place any obstacles in the way.

9. The grant made by Member States to the Community of rights and powers in accordance with the provisions of the Treaty involves a definitive limitation on their sovereign rights and no provisions whatsoever of national law may be invoked to override this limitation.

10. It is therefore necessary to find that in not complying with the judgment of the court of 10 December 1968 in Case 7/68 the Italian Republic has failed to fulfil the obligations imposed on it by Article [171].

SECTION TWO

THE REFERENCE PROCEDURE

1 Introduction

The supranational characteristic of Community law means that Community law is part of the internal legal order of all Member States. Therefore, a Community judicial function is carried on by all the courts and tribunals of the Member States before whom arises a question of Community law. Criminal law courts may hear cases in which both prosecution and defence raise questions of Community law; actions for judicial review of administrative action by a Member State's public authorities may be raised in administrative courts; civil courts may have submitted to them actions for damages for loss allegedly caused by the non-implementation of a Community obligation; substantive rights granted in social security and employment protection situations by Community provisions may be enforced before social security and labour courts and tribunals. Within the Member State, litigants may, therefore, come before their own domestic legal systems. National courts and tribunals will determine the facts and upon them is imposed the duty to make judicial determinations. However, during such litigation there may arise a question of interpretation of Community law which it is necessary to resolve before making a final determination. In view of the principle that Community law must be applied uniformly throughout the Community (including the national legal systems), the definitive task of interpreting Community law is taken from the national courts and granted to the Court of Justice by Article 177 **[B29]**. Furthermore, the Court of Justice has emphasised that there is a corresponding constitutional obligation to abide by that court's decisions.

2 The provisions which may be referred to the Court of Justice

Article 177 refers to the jurisdiction of the European Court of Justice to give preliminary rulings concerning the interpretation of the Treaty, the validity and interpretation of acts of the institutions of the Community and the interpretation of the statutes of bodies established by an act of the Council, where those statutes so provide. The court is principally concerned with interpretation of provisions of the Treaty and other acts of the Community, but has taken a wider view of its role under Article 177 than the words of that Article might indicate (*SPI* **[C12]**). Instances of interpretation abound throughout this work and some of the fundamental rules of Community law have their origin in replies to requests for preliminary rulings as to interpretation (see eg *Costa* **[C13]**, *van Gend* **[C22]**, *Marshall* **[C27]**, *Francovich* **[C33]**, *Watson* **[D10]**, *van Duyn* **[D43]**, *Van Tiggele* **[E17]**, *Blesgen* **[E18]**, *Cassis de Dijon* **[E21]**). Only the Court of Justice can declare Community acts invalid because to permit national courts to do so could lead to a divergent case law negating the principle of legal certainty (*Foto-Frost* **[C14]**). On the use of Article 177 to determine the validity of Community acts and the consequences which flow from a declaration of invalidity within the framework of an Article 177 reference, see *Maïseries de Beauce* **[C15]**. In a request for a preliminary ruling on the validity of certain articles of a regulation on denaturing of sugar, the Court of Justice emphasised that the Commission enjoys a significant freedom of evaluation, which must be exercised in the light of the objectives of the economic policy laid down by a regulation within the framework of the common agricultural policy. When examining the lawfulness of the exercise of such freedom, the court cannot substitute their own evaluation of the matter for that of the competent authority but must restrict themselves to examining whether the evaluation of the competent authority contains a patent error or constitutes a misuse of power (Case 57/72 *Westzucker GmbH v Einfuhr- und Vorratsstelle für Zucker* [1973] ECR 321.)

One corollary of the wording of Article 177 is that the court's jurisdiction is confined to Community law and not the national law of the Member States (*Costa* **[C13]**, *Simmenthal* **[C16]**, *van Gend* **[C22]**), but if national law has incorporated a Community provision, that Community provision must be interpreted by the Court of Justice and not by the national court (*Dzodzi* **[C17]**). In Case 77/72 *Carmine Capolongo v Azienda Agricola Maya* [1973] ECR 611, the court was asked to determine, by way of a preliminary ruling, whether the collection of a financial charge levied on the packaging of goods and collected on the basis of a percentage calculated in relation to the value of the product imported from other Member States constituted an infringement of Article 13(2) of the Treaty. The court held that, in the absence of accurate information relating to the objectives, nature and methods of collection of the charge in dispute, the court, having to limit itself to giving an interpretation of the provisions of Community law in question, could not consider legal acts and provisions of national law. It is then for the national courts to receive the interpretation of the court and to apply it (for examples, see *Factortame (2)* **[C49]**, *Santillo* **[D49]**).

3   The meaning of 'court or tribunal'

The Court of Justice can only be requested to give a preliminary ruling by a court or tribunal which is called upon to give judgment in proceedings intended to lead to a decision of a judicial nature. Consequently, in Case 138/80 *Jules Borker* [1980] ECR 1975, the court held that the Conseil de l'Ordre des Avocats à la Cour de Paris (an organisation somewhat akin to the local Bar Council) could not request a preliminary ruling because it did not have before it a case which it was under a legal duty to try. In practice, this requirement has caused little difficulty and the court has received requests for preliminary rulings from a wide variety of judicial bodies. In Case 61/65 *G Vaassen (née Göbbels) v Management of the Beambtenfonds voor het Mijnbedrijf* [1966] ECR 261, in deciding that a Scheidsgerecht (a permanent body charged with the settlement of disputes relating to entitlement to social security) must be considered a court or tribunal, the Court of Justice took note of the fact that persons insured under the social security scheme were bound to take any disputes between themselves and their insurer to the Scheidsgerecht as the proper judicial body and that the Scheidsgerecht was bound by rules of adversary procedure similar to those used by the ordinary courts of law.

4   The power or obligation to refer

A court or tribunal against whose decisions there is a judicial remedy under national law, has a power or faculty, if it considers that a decision on any question of interpretation or validity is necessary to enable it to give judgment, to request the Court of Justice to give a ruling on such a question. Although the use of the phrase 'if it considers' does not impose an express obligation on such a court or tribunal to request a preliminary ruling there may arise difficulties in the implementation of a uniform Community law by courts or tribunals which are not the highest judicial bodies in their respective Member States in that a case may not be heard by the highest court. On the question of lower courts requesting a preliminary ruling, see *Rheinmühlen* [C18]). As a matter of practice, courts and tribunals of quite minor rank in the judicial hierarchy of their respective Member States have requested preliminary rulings and fundamental rules of Community law have been proscribed in reply (*Costa* [C13], *Drake* [C36], *Francovich* [C33], *Royer* [D46], *Cowan* [D68]). In seeking a preliminary ruling the national court must consider such a ruling to be 'necessary' to enable it to give judgment (see *Plymouth Justices* [C41]). In Case C-369/90 *Micheletti v Delegación del Gobierno en Cantabria* 7 July 1992, the Spanish court was faced with the problem that an article of the Spanish Civil Code stated that in cases of dual nationality, neither of which was Spanish, precedence had to be accorded to that corresponding to the habitual residence of the person concerned prior to his entry into Spain. Micheletti held dual nationality (Argentinian and Italian) and the effect of the Spanish law was prima facie that Micheletti was Argentinian and the Spanish authorities refused Micheletti a card identifying him as a Community national for the purposes of working in Spain. The case could, therefore, only be determined after a preliminary ruling.

If a question of interpretation or validity is raised in a case pending before a court or tribunal of a Member State, against whose decisions there is no judicial remedy, such as an appeal or an action to quash a decision, under national law, that court or tribunal must bring the matter before the Court of Justice. Although, in one sense, this is a 'constitutional obligation', it is directed at a specific branch of the state, the judiciary. The reference procedure relies very much, as a method of creating a unified system of Community law, on the willingness of courts and tribunals to refer. The court has emphasised that there is an 'obligation' (*Cilfit* [C19]) to refer a matter to the Court of Justice which is based on co-operation, and is established with a view to ensuring the proper application and uniform interpretation of Community law in all Member States, by a partnership between national courts, in their capacity as courts responsible for the application of Community law, and the Court of Justice. Problems have arisen by the operation of the so-called *acte clair* principle whereby a national court considers that a question of Community law raised before it is so clear or obvious that a reference is not necessary (see eg *Semoules* [C51], *Cohn-Bendit* [C55]). Courts or tribunals are not obliged to refer questions concerning the interpretation of Community law if that question is not relevant (ie if the answer to that question, regardless of what it may be, can in no way affect the outcome of the case) and the correct application of Community law may sometimes be so obvious as to leave no scope for any reasonable doubt as to the manner in which the question raised is to be answered. Before coming to the conclusion that the question is irrelevant or perfectly clear, the national court or tribunal must be convinced that the matter is equally obvious to the courts of the other Member States and to the Court of Justice. Community legislation is drafted in several languages and an interpretation of a Community provision may involve a comparison of the different language versions (*de Geus* [B31], *Wörsdorfer* [C20], *Marleasing* [C31]) and legal concepts do not necessarily have the same meaning in Community law and in the law of the various Member States (*Hoekstra* [D4]). Whether a court or tribunal should decline to refer must be assessed in the light of the specific characteristics of Community law, the particular difficulties to which its interpretation gives rise and the risk of divergences in judicial decisions within the Community (*Cilfit* [C19], and see the observations in *Samex* [C39] and *Henn* [C40]).

5   The decision to refer

The decision to refer is that of the national court (*Cilfit* [C19]). The fact that the parties to the main action fail to raise a point of Community law before the national court does not preclude the national court from bringing the matter before the Court of Justice. The procedure is not restricted exclusively to cases where one or other of the parties to the main action has taken the initiative of raising a point concerning the interpretation or the validity of Community law, but also extends to cases where a question of this kind is raised by the national court or tribunal itself which considers that a decision on the question by the Court of Justice is 'necessary to enable it to give judgment' (Case 126/80 *Maria Salonia v Giorgio Poidomani and Franca Baglieri (née Giglio)* [1981] ECR 1563). The division of powers effected by Article 177 is mandatory. It cannot be altered, nor can the exercise of these powers be impeded, in particular by agreements between private citizens tending to compel the courts of the Member State to request a preliminary ruling by depriving them of the independent exercise of the discretion which they are given by Article 177 (Case 93/78 *Lothar Mattheus v Doego Fruchtimport und Tiefkühlkost* [1978] ECR 2203). It is not for the Court of Justice to assess whether questions referred to it are relevant to the nature and subject matter of the action before the national court, since such assessment comes within the jurisdiction of the national court (Case 52/77 *Leonce Cayrol v Giovanni Rivoira* [1977] ECR 2261) but the Court of Justice has the role to extract from all the information provided by the national court those points of Community law which require attention (*Maïseries de Beauce* [C15]). There is a distinct separation of functions between national courts and the Court of Justice which is not allowed to criticise the reasons for that reference. Consequently, a request from a national court may be rejected only if it is quite obvious that the interpretation of Community law or the examination of the validity of a rule of Community law sought by the national court bears no relation to the actual nature of the case or to the subject matter of the main action (Case 126/80 *Maria Salonia v Giorgio Poidomani and Franca Baglieri (née Giglio)* [1981] ECR 1563). (For an example of rejection, see *Foglia* [C21].)

MATERIALS

[C12]   Cases 267–269/81 Amministrazione delle Finanze dello Stato v Società Petrolifera Italiana SpA (SPI) [1983] ECR 801

[A national court requested a preliminary ruling on the effect within the Community of the General Agreement on Tariffs and Trades (GATT) and of the Tariff Protocols concluded by the Community in order to establish the compatibility of an Italian law, imposing a tax, with the GATT provisions.]

The European Court of Justice (at p 828)

14. [It] is important that the provisions of GATT should, like the provisions of all other agreements binding the Community, receive uniform application throughout the Community. Any difference in the interpretation and application of provisions binding the Community as regards non-member countries would not only jeopardise the unity of the commercial policy, which according to Article 113 of the Treaty must be based on uniform principles, but also create distortions of trade within the Community, as a result of differences in the manner in which the agreements in force between the Community and non-member countries were applied in the various Member States.

15. It follows that the jurisdiction conferred upon the court in order to ensure the uniform interpretation of Community law must include a determination of the scope and effect of the rules of GATT within the Community and also of the effect of the tariff protocols concluded in the framework of GATT.

[C13]   Case 6/64 Flaminio Costa v ENEL [1964] ECR 585

[Costa claimed, before the Giudice Conciliatore (an Italian court), that he was not obliged to pay his electricity bill on the ground that the Italian law nationalising the electricity industry was contrary to certain provisions of the Treaty of Rome and was unconstitutional. The Giudice sought a preliminary ruling on the interpretation of those provisions. The Italian government argued that the reference was 'absolutely inadmissible' as the Giudice merely had to apply the national law which governed the question before it.]

The European Court of Justice (at pp 592–599)

On the application of Article 177

On the submission regarding the wording of the question.   The complaint is made that the intention behind the question posed was to obtain, by means of Article 177, a ruling on the compatibility of a national law with the Treaty.

By the terms of this Article, however, national courts against whose decisions, as in the present case, there is no judicial remedy, must refer the matter to the Court of Justice so that a preliminary ruling may be given upon the 'interpretation of the Treaty' whenever a question of interpretation is raised before them. This provision gives the court no jurisdiction either to apply the Treaty to a specific case or to decide upon the validity of a provision of domestic law in relation to the Treaty, as it would be possible for it to do under Article 169.

Nevertheless, the court has power to extract from a question imperfectly formulated by the national court those questions which alone pertain to the interpretation of the Treaty. Consequently a decision should be given by the court not upon the validity of an Italian law in relation to the Treaty, but only upon the interpretation of the above-mentioned articles in the context of the points of law stated by the Giudice Conciliatore.

On the submission that an interpretation is not necessary. The complaint is made that the Milan court has requested an interpretation of the Treaty which was not necessary for the solution of the dispute before it.

Since, however, Article 177 is based upon a clear separation of functions between national courts and the Court of Justice, it cannot empower the latter either to investigate the facts of the case or to criticise the grounds and purpose of the request for interpretation.

On the submission that the court was obliged to apply the national law. The Italian government submits that the request of the Giudice Conciliatore is 'absolutely inadmissible', inasmuch as a national court which is obliged to apply a national law cannot avail itself of Article 177.

By contrast with ordinary international treaties, the EEC Treaty has created its own legal system which, on the entry into force of the Treaty, became an integral part of the legal systems of the Member States and which their courts are bound to apply.

By creating a Community of unlimited duration, having its own institutions, its own personality, its own legal capacity and capacity of representation on the international plane and, more particularly, real powers stemming from a limitation of sovereignty or a transfer of powers from the states to the Community, the Member States have limited their sovereign rights, albeit within limited fields, and have thus created a body of law which binds both their nationals and themselves.

The integration into the laws of each Member State of provisions which derive from the Community, and more generally the terms and the spirit of the Treaty, make it impossible for the states, as a corollary, to accord precedence to a unilateral and subsequent measure over a legal system accepted by them on a basis of reciprocity. Such a measure cannot therefore be inconsistent with that legal system. The executive force of Community law cannot vary from one state to another in deference to subsequent domestic laws, without jeopardising the attainment of the objectives of the Treaty set out in Article 5(2) and giving rise to the discrimination prohibited by Article 7.

The obligations undertaken under the Treaty establishing the Community would not be unconditional, but merely contingent, if they could be called in question by subsequent legislative acts of the [signatories].

The precedence of Community law is confirmed by Article 189, whereby a regulation 'shall be binding' and 'directly applicable in all Member States'. This provision, which is subject to no reservation, would be quite meaningless if a state could unilaterally nullify its effects by means of a legislative measure which could prevail over Community law.

320 *Community Law and the Member States*

It follows from all these observations that the law stemming from the Treaty, an independent source of law, could not, because of its special and original nature, be overridden by domestic legal provisions, however framed, without being deprived of its character as Community law and without the legal basis of the Community itself being called into question.

The transfer by the states from their domestic legal system to the Community legal system of the rights and obligations arising under the Treaty carries with it a permanent limitation of their sovereign rights, against which a subsequent unilateral act incompatible with the concept of the Community cannot prevail. Consequently Article 177 is to be applied regardless of any domestic law, whenever questions relating to the interpretation of the Treaty arise.

[C14]   Case 314/85 Foto-Frost v Hauptzollamt Lübeck-Ost [1987] ECR 4199

The European Court of Justice (at pp 4230–4232)

11. [The national court] asks whether it itself is competent to declare invalid a Commission decision. [It] casts doubts on the validity of that decision. [However], it considers that in view of the division of jurisdiction between the Court of Justice and the national courts set out in Article 177 of the EEC Treaty only the Court of Justice is competent to declare invalid acts of the Community institutions.

13. In enabling national courts, against those decisions where there is a judicial remedy under national law, to refer to the court for a preliminary ruling questions on interpretation or validity, Article 177 did not settle the question whether those courts themselves may declare that acts of Community institutions are invalid.

14. Those courts may consider the validity of a Community act and, if they consider that the grounds put forward before them by the parties in support of invalidity are unfounded, they may reject them, concluding that the measure is completely valid. By taking that action they are not calling into question the existence of the Community measure.

15. On the other hand, those courts do not have the power to declare acts of the Community institutions invalid. As the court emphasised in [Case] 66/80 *International Chemical Corporation v Amministrazione delle Finanze dello Stats* [1981] ECR 1191, the main purpose of the powers accorded to the court by Article 177 is to ensure that Community law is applied uniformly by national courts. That requirement of uniformity is particularly imperative when the validity of a Community act is in question. Divergences between courts in the Member States as to the validity of Community acts would be liable to place in jeopardy the very unity of the Community legal order and detract from the fundamental requirement of legal certainty.

16. The same conclusion is dictated by consideration of the necessary coherence of the system of judicial protection established by the Treaty. In that regard it must be observed that requests for preliminary rulings, like actions for annulment, constitute means for reviewing the legality of acts of the Community institutions. As the court pointed out in [*Les Verts* **[B49]**], 'in Articles 173 and 184, on the one hand, and in Article 177, on the other, the Treaty established a complete system of legal remedies and procedures

designed to permit the Court of Justice to review the legality of measures adopted by the institutions'.

17. Since Article 173 gives the court exclusive jurisdiction to declare void an act of a Community institution, the coherence of the system requires that where the validity of a Community act is challenged before a national court the power to declare the act invalid must also be reserved to the Court of Justice.

18. It must also be emphasised that the Court of Justice is in the best position to decide on the validity of Community acts. [Community] institutions whose acts are challenged are entitled to participate in the proceedings in order to defend the validity of the acts in question. Furthermore, [the] Court may require the Member States and institutions which are not participating in the proceedings to supply all information which it considers necessary for the purposes of the case before it.

19. It should be added that the rule that national courts may not themselves declare Community acts invalid may have to be qualified in certain circumstances in the case of proceedings relating to an application for interim measures; however, that case is not referred to in the national court's question.

20. The answer to the [question] must therefore be that the national courts have no jurisdiction themselves to declare that acts of Community institutions are invalid.

[C15] Case 109/79 Sàrl Maïseries de Beauce v Office National Interprofessionnel des Céréales (ONIC) [1980] ECR 2883

The European Court of Justice (at p 2903)

15. Although, within the framework of the distribution of tasks between the national courts and the Court of Justice for the implementation of Article 177 of the Treaty, it is for the national courts to decide the relevance of the questions which are referred to the Court of Justice, it is however reserved to the Court of Justice to extract from all the information provided by the national court those points of Community law which, having regard to the subject matter of the dispute, require interpretation, or whose validity requires appraisal.

[Following a request for a preliminary ruling, the Court of Justice replied that in adopting, in successive regulations, a system for the calculation of monetary compensatory amounts on products processed from maize whose price depended on that of maize which resulted in establishing, for the various products obtained by processing a given quantity of maize in a specific manufacturing process, monetary compensatory amounts the sum of which amounted to a figure clearly in excess of that of the monetary compensatory amount fixed for that given quantity of maize, the Commission had infringed both a regulation and Article 40(3) of the Treaty.]

The European Court of Justice (at pp 2913–2914)

44. Although the Treaty does not expressly lay down the consequences which flow from a declaration of invalidity within the framework of a

reference to the court for a preliminary ruling, Articles 174 and 176 contain clear rules as to the effects of the annulment of a regulation within the framework of a direct action. Thus Article 176 provides that the institution whose act has been declared void shall be required to take the necessary measures to comply with the judgment of the Court of [Justice].

45. In this case it is necessary to apply by analogy [Article 174(2) **[B29]**], whereby the Court of Justice may state which of the effects of the regulation which it has declared void shall be considered as definitive, for the same reasons of legal certainty as those which form the basis of that provision. On the one hand the invalidity of the regulation in this case might give rise to the recovery of sums paid but not owed by the undertakings concerned in countries with depreciated currencies and by the national authorities in question in countries with hard currencies which, in view of the lack of uniformity of the relevant national legislation, would be capable of causing considerable differences in treatment, thereby causing further distortion in competition. On the other hand, it is impossible to appraise the economic disadvantages resulting from the invalidity of the fixing of the monetary compensatory amounts under the system of calculation adopted by the Commission without making assessments which that institution alone is required to [make].

46. For these reasons it must be held that the fact that the fixing of the monetary compensatory amounts which result from the system of calculating those compensatory amounts on products processed from maize [has] been found invalid does not enable the charging or payment of monetary compensatory amounts by the national authorities on the basis of that regulation to be challenged as regards the period prior to the date of this judgment.

[C16]   Case 106/77 Amministrazione delle Finanze dello Stato v Simmenthal SpA [1978] ECR 629

[The Pretore di Susa referred to the Court of Justice for a preliminary ruling questions designed to enable him to determine whether veterinary and public health fees levied on imports of beef and veal under an Italian statute (Law 1239) were compatible with certain Treaty provisions and regulations. In Case 35/76 *Simmenthal v Italian Minister for Finance* [1976] ECR 1871, the Court of Justice gave their reply and the Pretore, having regard to that reply, held that the levying of the fees in question was incompatible with Community law and ordered the Amministrazione delle Finanze dello Stato (Italian Finance Administration) to repay the fees unlawfully charged, together with interest. The Amministrazione appealed against that order. During the oral procedure before the court, the agent of the Italian government informed the court of a judgment of the Italian Constitutional Court which declared that certain of the provisions of Law 1239, including those at issue in the action pending before the Pretore di Susa, were unconstitutional.]

The European Court of Justice (at pp 642–643)

9. It was suggested that since the disputed provisions have been set aside by the declaration that they are unconstitutional, the questions raised

by the Pretore no longer have relevance so that it is no longer necessary to answer them.

10. On this issue it should be borne in mind that in accordance with its unvarying practice the Court of Justice considers a reference for a preliminary ruling, pursuant to Article 177 of the Treaty, as having been validly brought before it so long as the reference has not been withdrawn by the court from which it emanates or has not been quashed on appeal by a superior court.

11. The judgment [of the Italian Constitutional Court], which was delivered in proceedings in no way connected with the action giving rise to the reference to this court, cannot have such a result and the court cannot determine its effect on third parties.

12. The preliminary objection raised by the Italian government must therefore be overruled.

[C17]   Cases C-297/88, C-197/89 Massam Dzodzi v Belgian State [1990] ECR I-3763

[Massam Dzodzi entered Belgium and married a Belgian national, Mr Herman. As the spouse of a Belgian national, she then applied to the administrative authorities for permission to remain in Belgium by virtue of a right which she maintained was conferred by Community law. There was no response to her application. The couple then went to Togo and resided there for a few months, but without informing the Belgian authorities. Mr Herman died, shortly after returning to Belgium. Further applications by Massam Dzodzi for the issue of a permit for an extended period of residence in Belgium were rejected. Massam Dzodzi was ordered to leave Belgium. A Belgian statute of 1980 on immigration treated the foreign spouse of a Belgian national, whatever his or her nationality, as an 'alien from the European Community' (Article 40). 'Aliens from the European Community shall have the right of residence on the terms and for the duration determined by the law in accordance with the regulations and directives of the European Communities. The right of residence shall be evidenced by a permit issued in the circumstances and according to the procedures specified by the King in accordance with the said regulations and directives. The decision whether or not to issue a residence permit shall be taken as soon as possible and not later than six months from the date of the application' (Article 42). Various questions were submitted by Belgian courts.]

The European Court of Justice (at pp 3792–3795)

29. The Belgian State and the Commission contend that it is only the application of domestic Belgian law which is at issue, and the Commission argues in particular that a provision of the kind contained in Article 40 of the national law has no effect on the determination of the field of application of Community law. The Belgian State asks the court to rule that it has no jurisdiction to answer these questions.

30. In contrast, Mrs Dzodzi argues that, owing to Article 40 of the national law, the dispute before the national courts puts Community provisions in contention. It is for the court to rule on questions of interpretation

raised in such disputes in order to avoid divergence developing between the case law on the interpretation of Community provisions of the Court of Justice and that of national courts.

[The Court of Justice cited Article 177.]

33. The procedure provided for in Article 177 of the Treaty is therefore an instrument for co-operation between the Court of Justice and the national courts, whereby the Court of Justice provides the national courts with the criteria for the interpretation of Community law which they need in order to dispose of the disputes which they are called upon to resolve.

34. It follows that it is solely for the national courts before which the dispute has been brought, and which must bear the responsibility for the subsequent judicial decision, to determine in the light of the special features of each case both the need for a preliminary ruling in order to enable them to deliver judgment and the relevance of the questions which they submit to the court.

35. Accordingly, since the questions submitted by the national courts concern the interpretation of a provision of Community law, the court is, in principle, obliged to give a ruling.

36. It does not appear either from the wording of Article 177 or from the aim of the procedure introduced by that article that the authors of the Treaty intended to exclude from the jurisdiction of the court requests for a preliminary ruling on a Community provision in the specific case where the national law of a Member State refers to the content of that provision in order to determine rules applicable to a situation which is purely internal to that state.

37. On the contrary, it is manifestly in the interests of the Community legal order that, in order to forestall future differences of interpretation, every Community provision should be given a uniform interpretation irrespective of the circumstances in which it is to be applied.

38. Since the jurisdiction of the court under Article 177 is designed to ensure uniform interpretation in all Member States of the provisions of Community law, the court merely deduces from the letter and spirit of those provisions the meaning of the Community rules at issue. Thereafter it is for the national courts alone to apply the Community provisions thus interpreted in the light of the factual and legal circumstances of the case before them.

39. Consequently, in accordance with the division of judicial tasks between the national courts and the Court of Justice pursuant to Article 177, the court gives its preliminary ruling without, in principle, having to look into the circumstances in which the national courts were prompted to submit the questions and envisage applying the provision of Community law which they have asked the court to interpret.

40. The matter would be different only if it were apparent either that the procedure provided for in Article 177 had been diverted from its true purpose and sought in fact to lead the court to give a ruling by means of a contrived dispute, or that the provision of Community law referred to the court for interpretation was manifestly incapable of applying.

41. Where Community law is made applicable by national provisions, it is for the national court alone to assess the precise scope of that reference to Community law. If it takes the view that the content of a provision of Community law is applicable, by virtue of that reference, to the purely internal situation underlying the dispute brought before it, the national court is

entitled to request the court for a preliminary ruling on the terms laid down by the provisions of Article 177 as a whole, as they have been interpreted in the case law of the Court of Justice.

42. Nevertheless, the jurisdiction of the court is confined to considering provisions of Community law only. In its reply to the national court, the Court of Justice cannot take account of the general scheme of the provisions of domestic law which, while referring to Community law, define the extent of that reference. Consideration of the limits which the national legislature may have placed on the application of Community law to purely internal situations, to which it is applicable only through the operation of the national legislation, is a matter for domestic law and hence falls within the exclusive jurisdiction of the courts of the Member State.

43. In the present case it must be observed that the questions set out above do not relate to provisions of Belgian domestic law but exclusively to provisions [relating to free movement of persons **[D50]**]. Accordingly, for those reasons and within the limits defined above, the court has jurisdiction to rule on those questions.

[C18]   Case 166/73 Rheinmühlen-Düsseldorf v Einfuhr- und Vorratsstelle für Getreide und Futtermittel [1974] ECR 33

[The national court referred for a preliminary ruling the question whether Article 177(2) gives 'to a court or tribunal against whose decisions there is a judicial remedy under national law a completely unfettered right to refer questions to the Court of Justice' or 'does it leave unaffected rules of domestic law to the contrary whereby a court is bound on points of law by the judgments of the courts superior to it'?]

Opinion of Advocate General Warner (at pp 43–47)

One's immediate inclination is to answer [the question] in such a way as to avoid impairing the general principle that a lower court should respect and be loyal to the decisions of courts that are superior to it.

. . .

I have, however, come to the conclusion that to hold, as I would, that Article 177 does confer on every lower court in every Member State a power to refer questions of Community law to this court that cannot be fettered by any rule or provision of national law does not really involve a breach of that principle. The lower court [is] not seeking directly to substitute its own view for that of the superior national court. It is seeking the view of this court on what it conceives to be a doubtful question of Community law, consistently with the principle enshrined in Article 177 that, on such a question, no national court, however high, may rule definitively. Moreover, as the Commission points out in its observations, the question referred by the lower court to this court in such a case may not be the same as that decided by the superior court: it may merely overlap it. But whether it is the same, or merely overlaps it, the ruling of this court upon it, assuming it really to be a question of Community law, must in the end, prevail over that of any national court.

My Lords, I can see no logical stopping point between, on the one hand, holding that no fetter can be placed by national law on the power of a lower court in any Member State to refer questions of Community law to this court and, on the other hand, holding that each Member State is free to qualify Article 177, in its application to that state's own courts and tribunals, in any way that it considers reasonable – free, in other words, to write its own chosen provisos into Article 177. To say that that Article must yield to the general principle of respect by lower courts for the decisions of higher courts would in practice mean that it must yield to a whole variety of rules differing in their detailed content from Member State to Member State.

There are to my mind three obvious objections to the adoption of the view that Member States are, in effect, free to enact their own provisos to Article 177. First, and most obviously, it involves empowering the Member States to qualify by national legislation the terms of the Treaty. Secondly, it opens the way for the Treaty to apply differently in different Member States. One Member State might circumscribe the discretion of its lower courts to refer questions to this court more tightly than another. This, clearly, could injure both the uniform application of Community law and its balanced development. Thirdly, it means that, in deciding upon the admissibility of particular references, this court must be faced with an impossible choice. It must either embark upon the interpretation and application of provisions of national law, including procedural ones – which is not its role – or it must ignore those provisions and thus allow to subsist a situation in which a reference may be admissible in Community law but inadmissible in national law.

. . .

My Lords, in taking the view I do, I am comforted by two considerations. The first is that there is no universal rule that a judicial decision must necessarily be open to appeal. The second is that a decision of a lower court to refer a case to this court can have no final effect on the rights of the parties: those rights will be determined by the national courts in the normal way, and with all normal procedural safeguards, once this court has ruled on the reference.

I am therefore of the opinion that the [question posed should] be answered as follows: 'The second paragraph of Article 177 of the EEC Treaty confers on a court or tribunal against whose decisions there is a judicial remedy under national law a discretion that is exercisable at any stage of proceedings before it and that cannot be fettered by any rule or provision of national law.'

The European Court of Justice (at pp 38–39)

2. Article 177 is essential for the preservation of the Community character of the law established by the Treaty and has the object of ensuring that in all circumstances this law is the same in all states of the Community.

Whilst it [aims] to avoid divergences in the interpretation of Community law which the national courts have to apply, it likewise tends to ensure this application by making available to the national judge a means of eliminating difficulties which may be occasioned by the requirement of giving Community law its full effect within the framework of the judicial systems of the Member States.

Consequently any gap in the system so organised could undermine the effectiveness of the provisions of the Treaty and of the secondary Community law.

The provisions of Article 177, which enable every national court or tribunal without distinction to refer a case to the court for a preliminary ruling when it considers that a decision on the question is necessary to enable it to give judgment, must be seen in this light.

3. The provisions of Article 177 are absolutely binding on the national judge and, in so far as [Article 177(2)] is concerned, enable him to refer a case to the Court of Justice for a preliminary ruling on interpretation or validity.

This article gives national courts the power and, where appropriate, imposes on them the obligation to refer a case for a preliminary ruling, as soon as the judge perceives either of his own motion or at the request of the parties that the litigation depends on a point referred to in [Article 177(1)].

4. It follows that national courts have the widest discretion in referring matters to the Court of Justice if they consider that a case pending before them raises questions involving interpretation, or consideration of the validity, of provisions of Community law, necessitating a decision on their part.

It follows from these factors that a rule of national law whereby a court is bound on points of law by the rulings of a superior court cannot deprive the inferior courts of their power to refer to the court questions of interpretation of Community law involving such rulings.

It would be otherwise if the questions put by the inferior court were substantially the same as questions already put by the superior court.

On the other hand the inferior court must be free, if it considers that the ruling on law made by the superior court could lead it to give a judgment contrary to Community law, to refer to the court questions which concern it.

If inferior courts were bound without being able to refer matters to the court, the jurisdiction of the latter to give preliminary rulings and the application of Community law at all levels of the judicial systems of the Member States would be compromised.

5. The reply must therefore be that the existence of a rule of domestic law whereby a court is bound on points of law by the rulings of the court superior to it cannot of itself take away the power provided for by Article 177 of referring cases to the court.

[On the application of this case by the Court of Appeal, see *Plymouth Justices* **[C41]**.]

[C19] Case 283/81 Srl CILFIT and Lanificio di Gavardo Spa v Ministry of Health [1982] ECR 3415

[There was a dispute between wool importers and the Italian Ministry of Health concerning the payment of a fixed health inspection levy in respect of wool imported from outside the Community. Although Member States were prohibited, by a regulation, from levying charges equivalent to a customs duty on imported 'animal products', the Ministry contended that 'wool' was not within that description and was, therefore, not covered by the prohibition. The Ministry of Health inferred that the answer to any question concerning the interpretation of the regulation was so obvious as to rule out the possibility of there being any interpretative doubt and that this application of the *acte clair* principle obviated the need to refer the matter to the Court of Justice for a preliminary ruling. The wool importers, however, when the case reached the Corte Suprema di Cassazione (the highest civil court in Italy, against whose decisions there was no judicial remedy) argued that, since the question concerning the interpretation of a regulation had been raised before a court against whose decisions there was no judicial remedy, that court could not, according to the terms of Article 177(3), escape the obligation to bring the matter before the Court of Justice. The Corte Suprema di Cassazione referred to the Court of Justice the following question for a preliminary ruling:

> Does [Article 177(3)] lay down an obligation so to submit the case which precludes the national court from determining whether the question raised is justified or does it, and if so within what limits, make that obligation conditional on the prior finding of a reasonable interpretative doubt?]

The European Court of Justice (at pp 3428–3431)

5. In order to answer that question it is necessary to take account of the system established by Article 177, which confers jurisdiction on the Court of Justice to give preliminary rulings on, inter alia, the interpretation of the Treaty and the measures adopted by the institutions of the Community.

6. [The court cited Article 177.]

7. That obligation to refer a matter to the Court of Justice is based on co-operation, established with a view to ensuring the proper application and uniform interpretation of Community law in [all] Member States, between national courts, in their capacity as courts responsible for the application of Community law, and the Court of Justice. More particularly, [Article 177(3)] seeks to prevent the occurrence within the Community of divergences in judicial decisions on questions of Community law. The scope of that obligation must therefore be assessed, in view of those objectives, by reference to the powers of the national courts, on the one hand, and those of the Court of Justice, on the other, where such a question of interpretation is raised within the meaning of Article 177.

8. In this connection, it is necessary to define the meaning for the purposes of Community law of the expression 'where any such question is raised' in order to determine the circumstances in which a national court or tribunal against whose decisions there is no judicial remedy under national law is obliged to bring a matter before the Court of Justice.

9. In this regard, it must in the first place be pointed out that Article 177 does not constitute a means of redress available to the parties to a case pending before a national court or tribunal. Therefore the mere fact that a party contends that the dispute gives rise to a question concerning the interpretation of Community law does not mean that the court or tribunal concerned is compelled to consider that a question has been raised within the meaning of Article 177. On the other hand, a national court or tribunal may, in an appropriate case, refer a matter to the Court of Justice of its own motion.

10. Secondly, it follows from the relationship between the second and

third paragraphs of Article 177 that the courts or tribunals referred to in the third paragraph have the same discretion as any other national court or tribunal to ascertain whether a decision on a question of Community law is necessary to enable them to give judgment. Accordingly, those courts or tribunals are not obliged to refer to the Court of Justice a question concerning the interpretation of Community law raised before them if that question is not relevant, that is to say, if the answer to that question, regardless of what it may be, can in no way affect the outcome of the case.

11. If however, those courts or tribunals consider that recourse to Community law is necessary to enable them to decide a case, Article 177 imposes an obligation on them to refer to the Court of Justice any question of interpretation which may arise.

12. The question submitted by the Corte di Cassazione seeks to ascertain whether, in certain circumstances, the obligation laid down by [Article 177(3)] might none the less be subject to certain restrictions.

13. It must be remembered in this connection that in its judgment [in Cases 28 to 30/62 *Da Costa v Nederlandse Belastingadministratie* [1963] ECR 31] the court ruled that:

> Although the third paragraph of Article 177 unreservedly requires courts or tribunals of a Member State against whose decisions there is no judicial remedy under national law [to] refer to the Court every question of interpretation raised before them, the authority of an interpretation [already] given by the Court may deprive the obligation of its purpose and thus empty it of its substance. Such is the case especially when the question raised is materially identical with a question which has already been the subject of a preliminary ruling in a similar case.

14. The same effect, as regards the limits set to the obligation laid down by [Article 177(3)], may be produced where previous decisions of the court have already dealt with the point of law in question, irrespective of the nature of the proceedings which led to those decisions, even though the questions at issue are not strictly identical.

15. However, it must not be forgotten that in all such circumstances national courts and tribunals, including those referred to in [Article 177(3)], remain entirely at liberty to bring a matter before the Court of Justice if they consider it appropriate to do so.

16. Finally, the correct application of Community law may be so obvious as to leave no scope for any reasonable doubt as to the manner in which the question raised is to be resolved. Before it comes to the conclusion that such is the case, the national court or tribunal must be convinced that the matter is equally obvious to the courts of the other Member States and to the Court of Justice. Only if those conditions are satisfied, may the national court or tribunal refrain from submitting the question to the Court of Justice and take upon itself the responsibility for resolving it.

17. However, the existence of such a possibility must be assessed on the basis of the characteristic features of Community law and the particular difficulties to which its interpretation gives rise.

18. To begin with, it must be borne in mind that Community legislation is drafted in several languages and that the different language versions are all equally authentic. An interpretation of a provision of Community law thus involves a comparison of the different language versions.

19. It must also be borne in mind, even where the different language

versions are entirely in accord with one another, that Community law uses terminology which is peculiar to it. Furthermore, it must be emphasised that legal concepts do not necessarily have the same meaning in Community law and in the law of the various Member States.

20. Finally, every provision of Community law must be placed in its context and interpreted in the light of the provisions of Community law as a whole, regard being had to the objectives thereof and to its state of evolution at the date on which the provision in question is to be applied.

21. In the light of all those considerations, the answer to the question submitted by the Corte Suprema di Cassazione must be that [Article 177(3)] is to be interpreted as meaning that a court or tribunal against whose decisions there is no judicial remedy under national law is required, where a question of Community law is raised before it, to comply with its obligation to bring the matter before the Court of Justice, unless it has established that the question raised is irrelevant or that the Community provision in question has already been interpreted by the court or that the correct application of Community law is so obvious as to leave no scope for any reasonable doubt. The existence of such a possibility must be assessed in the light of the specific characteristics of Community law, the particular difficulties to which its interpretation gives rise and the risk of divergences in judicial decisions within the Community.

[On the application of this case by the House of Lords, see *Factortame (1)* **[C47]**.]

[C20]   Case 9/79 Marianne Wörsdorfer (née Koschniske) v Raad van Arbeid [1979] ECR 2717

[Mrs Wörsdorfer was an employed person who ceased working because of illness and received a pension for incapacity for work in the Netherlands. Because of the incapacity pension, she was entitled (under Community law) to receive family allowances for her three children living with her in Germany under the legislation of the Member State responsible for the pension (ie the Netherlands). It was later found that her husband was engaged in a professional or trade activity in Germany and drawing child allowance under German legislation. Community law provided rules to prevent double payments in that entitlement to family allowances from Member State 'A' is to be suspended when, for the same member of the family, the pensioner or his spouse exercises a professional or trade activity in Member State 'B' which grants entitlement to family allowances from State 'B' and it is in State 'B' that the children reside. The question was whether 'his spouse' could include Mrs Wörsdorfer's husband because of the Dutch version of the appropriate Regulation 574/72 on social security. The Dutch version used a word 'echtgenote' which applied only to a person of the female sex (ie a female partner).]

The European Court of Justice (at p 2724)

6. However, the need for a uniform interpretation of Community regulations makes it impossible for that passage to be considered in isolation and requires that it should be interpreted and applied in the light of the versions existing in the other official languages.

7. A comparison with the other versions of the provision in question reveals that, in all the other versions, a word has been used which includes equally male and female workers (ægtefaellen, Ehegatte, spouse, conjoint, coniuge).

8. This interpretation is borne out on the one hand by the purpose of the provision which is to avoid the overlapping of family allowances for the same children, and, on the other hand, the principle of equal treatment for male and female workers in the field of social security.

[C21] Case 104/79 Pasquale Foglia v Mariella Novello [1980] ECR 745

[Foglia was a wine dealer in Italy and sent some cases of Italian liqueur wines to Novello in France. The contract of sale between Foglia and Novello provided that Novello should not be liable for any duties which were claimed by the Italian or French authorities contrary to the provisions on the free movement of goods between the two countries or which were at least not due. Foglia adopted a similar clause in a contract with a firm called Danzas, to which he entrusted the transport of the cases of liqueur wine. That clause provided that Foglia should not be liable for such unlawful charges or charges which were not due. The subject matter of the dispute was restricted exclusively to the sum paid as a consumption tax when the wines were imported into France. The tax was paid by Danzas to the French authorities. The bill for transport which Danzas submitted to Foglia, and which was settled, included the amount of tax. Novello refused to reimburse the latter amount to Foglia, in reliance on the clause on unlawful charges or charges which were not due expressly included in the contract of sale. In the view of the Italian court the defence advanced by Novello entailed calling in question the validity of French legislation concerning the consumption tax on liqueur wines in relation to Article 95 **[E4]**.]

The European Court of Justice (at pp 759–760)

10. It thus appears that the parties to the main action are concerned to obtain a ruling that the French tax system is invalid for liqueur wines by the expedient of proceedings before an Italian court between two private individuals who are in agreement as to the result to be attained and who have inserted a clause in their contract in order to induce the Italian court to give a ruling on the point. The artificial nature of this expedient is underlined by the fact that Danzas did not exercise its rights under French law to institute proceedings over the consumption tax although it undoubtedly had an interest in doing so in view of the clause in the contract by which it was also bound and moreover of the fact that Foglia paid without protest that undertaking's bill which included a sum paid in respect of that tax.

11. The duty of the Court of Justice under Article 177 of the EEC Treaty is to supply all courts in the Community with the information on the interpretation of Community law which is necessary to enable them to settle genuine disputes which are brought before them. A situation in which the court was obliged by the expedient of arrangements like those described above to give rulings would jeopardise the whole system of legal remedies available to private individuals to enable them to protect themselves against tax provisions which are contrary to the Treaty.

12. This means that the questions asked by the national court, having regard to the circumstances of this case, do not fall within the framework of the duties of the Court of Justice under Article 177 of the Treaty.

13. The Court of Justice accordingly has no jurisdiction to give a ruling on the questions asked by the national court.

SECTION THREE

INDIVIDUAL PROTECTION

In *van Gend* [C22] the Court of Justice was faced with a claim by an individual seeking redress of a grievance caused by a Member State. It was argued that such matters were best dealt with by the traditional international law methods of arbitration which were incorporated into the Community constitution by the provisions for actions to be taken by the Commission discussed in Section One of this chapter. The Court of Justice said otherwise:

> The objective of the EEC Treaty, which is to establish a Common Market, the functioning of which is of direct concern to interested parties in the Community, implies that this Treaty is more than an agreement which merely creates mutual obligations between the contracting states. This view is confirmed by the preamble to the Treaty which refers not only to governments but to peoples. [Independently] of the legislation of Member States, Community law therefore not only imposes obligations on individuals but is also intended to confer upon them rights which become part of their legal heritage. These rights arise not only where they are expressly granted by the Treaty, but also by reasons of obligations which the Treaty imposes in a clearly defined way upon individuals as well as upon the Member States and upon the institutions of the Community.

The court has continued to emphasise that the subjects of Community law include individuals and organisations who may be affected by the law of a Community which is not merely an economic union of Member States, but is at the same time intended to ensure social progress and seek the constant improvement of the living and working conditions of their people, as is emphasised by the Preamble to the Treaty (*Defrenne* [C23]). The individuals and organisations which are affected by the substantive law discussed in Chapters Four and Five vary enormously. There are individuals seeking the rights granted by Community law of entry and residence, of equality in the labour market, together with their families and their employers and there are business organisations (farmers, manufacturers, importers and exporters, and those engaged in a multiplicity of service industries) seeking the economic freedoms the Community was established to guarantee. The one thing all these people have in common is the wish to exercise the rights created by Community law. These rights are created by the Treaty and the secondary legislation discussed in Section Two of Chapter Two and these rights depend for their effectiveness on the transposition of such rights into the national domestic legal systems of all the Member States by national legislation, regulation or administrative practice.

Member States are enjoined, inter alia, by Article 5 of the Treaty to take all appropriate measures, whether general or particular, to ensure fulfilment of the obligations arising out of the Treaty or secondary legislation, to facilitate the achievement of the Community's tasks and to abstain from any measure which could jeopardise the attainment of the objectives of the Treaty. If a Member State adheres to Article 5 (and the other Treaty and secondary legislative provisions which impose obligations on the Member States) then the rights created by Community law are guaranteed. However, if the governments and legislatures of Member States do not fulfil their Community obligations, the rights granted to individuals and organisations become merely illusory and there is no effective enjoyment of such rights if a national legislative, regulatory or administrative rule or practice hinders or, indeed, prevents the exercise of such a right. One manner of ensuring that Member States fulfil Community obligations is that provided for by the Treaty provisions discussed in Section One of this chapter. However, this has serious disadvantages to the individual. It is dependent on the Commission (or another Member State) for its initiation, there are many examples of Member States not obeying the declarations of failure by the Court of Justice, and, probably of greatest importance to the citizen or the business-man, the process of prosecution by the Commission and the judgment of the court takes an inordinately long time. What the Court of Justice has done, therefore, has been to take Article 5 of the Treaty to its logical conclu-sion and hold that if the government, legislature or administration of a Member State fails in its Community obligations, the omissions of such ema-nations of the Member States should be remedied by the judicial organs of the state. After all, litigation designed to enforce rights in national law is de-termined by courts and tribunals and there should be no difference between the enforcement and protection of rights derived from national law and the enforcement and protection of such rights as are derived from Community law. Consequently, Community provisions which are a direct source of rights and duties for all those affected thereby, whether Member States or individu-als, also concerns the national courts. Their task, as an organ of a Member State, is to protect, in a case within its jurisdiction, the rights conferred upon individuals by Community law (*Simmenthal* [C24]).

How the Court of Justice has secured the protection of rights for individu-als and organisations will now be explained. It must be noted that the process has been a gradual but a logical and inexorable one and parallels the development of general principles of law and the protection of human rights discussed in Section Four of Chapter Two. Consequently, the cases are extracted very fully in order that the step-by-step approach and the develop-ing strands are appreciated. The court has started with the proposition that rights conferred by Community law must be protected and enjoyed by those on whom the rights are conferred. The supremacy of Community law means that such rights must be uniformly enjoyed in their entirety within each Member State. If a Member State has not transposed into its own legal sys-tem those rights, the solidarity of Community achievement is jeopardised and if the cohesion of Community law is jeopardised so is the Community. As an inescapable corollary of membership of the Community, therefore, each Member State will be deemed to have complied with Community oblig-ations as from the moment that such obligations have binding force. The court has asked 'what would have been the legal situation within the Member State had Community law been fully implemented by the Member State (a form of equity deeming that to have been done which was left un-done)'. This has been achieved in what may be described as three stages of development which have occurred in roughly chronological order.

The first stage was, and is, the application of the principle of direct effect (sometimes called direct applicability by the court). It is based upon the rationale that a Member State which has not adapted its national law to meet Community obligations may not rely, as against individuals, on its own fail-ure to perform those obligations. In *van Gend* [C22] it was held that the fact of the existence of Article 169 proceedings to bring before the court a state which has not fulfilled its obligations does not mean that individuals cannot plead these obligations, should the occasion arise, before a national court, and that, in this case, a Treaty provision could be characterised as producing direct effects and creating individual rights which national courts must protect. This was followed by *Defrenne* [C23] (see, also *Reyners* [D31], [D56], *von Kempis* [C54] and *Automec* [E62]). Regulations were also held capable of producing direct effects (*Simmenthal* [C24]) and, although it may not have been the original intention of the Community legal scheme of things, decisions (*Grad* [C25]) and directives (*Ratti* [C26], *van Duyn* [D43]) have also been held capable of producing direct effects. However, a directive only imposes obligations on the 'state' (see below) and may not of itself impose obligations on an individual and a provision of a directive may not be relied upon as such against such a person (*Marshall* [C27], *Kolpinghuis* [C30]). On the meaning of the 'state', see *Marshall* [C27], *Fratelli* [C28], *Marleasing* [C31], *Johnston* [C32] and *Foster* [C42].

By this stage in the development of individual protection the cumulative wisdom of the Court of Justice on the direct effect of directives could be summed up (as the court so stated in Case 8/81 *Becker v Finanzamt Münster-Innenstadt* 8/81 [1982] ECR 53) as being that:

> according to the case law of the Court, where the Community institutions have, by means of a directive, placed Member States under a duty to adopt a certain course of action, the effectiveness of such a measure would be diminished if individuals and national courts were precluded from taking it into consideration as an element of Community law. Consequently, a Member State which has not adopted the implementing measures required by the Directive within the prescribed period may not plead, as against individuals, its own failure to perform the obligations which the Directive entails. Thus wherever the provisions of a Directive appear, as far as their subject matter is concerned to be unconditional and sufficiently precise, those provisions may, in the absence of implementing measures adopted within the prescribed period, be relied upon as against any national provision which is incompatible with the Directive or in so far as the provisions define rights which individuals are able to asssert against the State.

With regard to rights intended to be conferred through the medium of directives, there are two sets of circumstances where an individual may be remedy-less and where an individual's enjoyment of those rights is not protected. First, the provisions of Community law expressed in a directive can only relate to rights which may be asserted against the state and not against non-state bodies or individuals. Note that this restriction does not apply to regulations, which may be enforced against both state and non-state bodies or individuals. Should, therefore, the restriction relating to directives be obviated by a more common use of regulations? Secondly, for there to be direct effect the provisions of a directive must be unconditional and sufficiently precise. The 'direct effect test' succeeded in *van Gend* [C22], *Grad* [C25], *Marshall* [C27] and *Fratelli* [C28] but not in *von Colson* [C29] or *Francovich* [C33].

The second stage in the development of effective protection of Community conferred rights may be termed the doctrine of positive interpretation. *Von Colson* [C29] concerned a directive designed to ensure equal treatment in matters of employment and there was, at least, implicitly raised the question of effective enjoyment of a right conferred by Community law, in that there was a failure on the part of Germany to transpose a directive into national law sufficiently effectively so as to give the plaintiffs a real remedy against sex discrimination with regard to access to employment, that failure to fulfil an obligation was not pursued by the Commission under Article 169, and the directive did not lay down any unconditional and sufficiently precise obligation to require the Member State to adopt a sanction for the breach of the principle of equal treatment. The Court of Justice held that it was impossible to establish real equality of opportunity without an appropriate system of sanctions (see, also, *Kolpinghuis* **[C30]**, *Johnston* **[C32]**). The obligation to interpret national law in conformity with a directive was taken further in *Marleasing* **[C31]**, where it was argued by the Advocate General that there was no reason to restrict the requirement that an interpretation must be in conformity with a directive to the situation of a national law specifically introduced in order to implement the directive and the court held that it followed from Article 5 that, in applying national law, whether the provisions in question were adopted before or after the directive, the national court called upon to interpret it is required to do so, as far as possible, in the light of the wording and the purpose of the directive in order to achieve the result pursued by the directive.

The third stage of the development of individual protection may be called the doctrine of the right to a remedy. This had already be emphasised in *von Colson* **[C29]**. In *Johnston* **[C32]** the Advocate General argued that, by removing measures taken by the Member States from the ambit of Community law, this would in fact allow the national authorities to create a 'no-go area for the law' as and when they saw fit, thus calling in question the very foundations of that legal order. The Court of Justice agreed. In *Heylens* **[D33]** the court held that, since free access to employment is a fundamental right which the Treaty confers individually on each worker in the Community, the existence of a remedy of a judicial nature against any decision of a national authority refusing the benefit of that right is essential in order to secure for the individual effective protection for his rights. In Case 208/90 *Emmott* [1991] ECR I-4269, the Court of Justice referred to the principle of legal certainty (discussed in Section Four of Chapter Two) and emphasised that so

> long as a directive has not been properly transposed into national law, individuals are unable to ascertain the full extent of their rights. That state of uncertainty for individuals subsists even after [a] judgment finding that the Member State in question has not fulfilled its obligations under the directive and even if the Court has held that a particular provision or provisions of the directive are sufficiently precise and unconditional to be relied upon before a national court. Only the proper transposition of the directive will bring that state of uncertainty to an end and it is only upon that transposition that the legal certainty which must exist if individuals are to be required to assert their rights is created. [Until such time as a] directive has been properly transposed, a defaulting Member State may not rely on an individual's delay in initiating preceedings against it in order to protect rights conferred upon him by the provisions of the directive and a period laid down by national law within which proceedings must be initiated cannot begin to run before that time.

The right to an effective remedy, in this case adequate interlocutory relief, was also maintained in *Factortame* **[C48]**, **[C49]** and adequacy of financial compensation was considered fundamental in the second *Marshall* case

[D63]. Is there a comparable approach in *Antonissen* **[D13]** and *Cowan* **[D68]**?

One judicial remedy which is common to the public or administrative law legal systems of the Member States is that of awarding damages for wrongful acts of the state and its agents and with regard to damage caused by the Community institutions there is a scheme of non-contractual liability (see, for example, *Rau* **[B37]**). Therefore, the question had to be raised whether an individual who suffers damage as a result of the failure of a Member State to implement a directive may claim damages for any pecuniary loss the person may have suffered as a result of that failure to meet a Member State's obligation. If the intention of Community legislation by way of directives is to confer rights on individuals then, in one sense, direct effect is irrelevant. The fact that a provision of a directive is not unconditional or sufficiently precise has the result that the directive cannot be directly effective and asserted against the Member States – it does not negate the intention to confer those rights. Furthermore, should the Commission (or another Member State) bring an action under Article 169 (or 170) of the Treaty and the Court of Justice finds against the Member State, a further obligation is imposed on the defaulting Member State by Article 171. In these cases the obligation is to take the necessary measures to carry out the obligations to the full and it may happen that until those obligations are in fact carried out, individuals who should have benefited from a correct implementation by the Member State have been caused pecuniary loss by that failure. This issue was faced in *Francovich* **[C33]**, where the court held that the full effectiveness of Community provisions would be jeopardised and the protection of the rights they recognise would be weakened if individuals did not have the possibility to obtain compensation when their rights are infringed by a breach of Community law attributable to a Member State. It followed that the principle of the liability of the state for damage caused to individuals by breaches of Community law for which it is responsible is inherent in the scheme of the Treaty.

MATERIALS

[C22]   Case 26/62 NV Algemene Transport–en Expeditie Onderneming van Gend & Loos v Nederlandse administratie der belastingen [1963] ECR 1

[On 9 September 1960, van Gend imported into the Netherlands from Germany a quantity of ureaformaldehyde, a product which was classified under the current Netherlands import duties regulations (which had come into force on 1 March 1960) as being subject to an import duty of 8% (which was duly imposed). Van Gend complained that on 1 January 1958 (the date on which the Treaty of Rome came into force) the product had been classified under the Netherlands import duties regulations then in force as being subject only to an import duty of 3%; that the current classification of the product as being subject to an import duty was an increase in the import duty on the product after the coming into force of the Treaty of Rome; and that the Netherlands government, in so reclassifying the product, had infringed Article 12 **[E2]**. The Nederlandse administratie der belastingen (Netherlands Inland Revenue Administration) replied that, as a matter of fact, the product in question had, on 1 January 1958, not been charged with a duty of 3% but with a duty of 10%, so that there had not been any increase. Van Gend appealed to the Tariefcommissie (Netherlands revenue tribunal) which, without giving a formal decision on whether the product was subject to a 3%, 8% or 10% duty, decided that it was necessary to determine, as a preliminary question, whether van Gend was entitled to rely on Article 12.]

The European Court of Justice (at pp 10–13)

A – Jurisdiction of the court

The government of the Netherlands and the Belgian government challenge the jurisdiction of the court on the ground that the reference relates not to the interpretation but to the application of the Treaty in the context of the constitutional law of the Netherlands, and that in particular the court has no jurisdiction to decide, should the occasion arise, whether the provisions of the EEC Treaty prevail over Netherlands legislation or over other agreements entered into by the Netherlands and incorporated into Dutch national law. The solution of such a problem, it is claimed, falls within the exclusive jurisdiction of the national courts, subject to an application in accordance with the provisions laid down by Articles 169 and 170 of the Treaty.

However in this case the court is not asked to adjudicate upon the application of the Treaty according to the principles of the national law of the Netherlands, which remains the concern of the national courts, but is asked, in conformity with [Article 177(1)(a)] of the Treaty, only to interpret the scope of Article 12 of the said Treaty within the context of Community law and with reference to its effect on individuals. This argument has therefore no legal foundation.

The Belgian government further argues that the court has no jurisdiction on the ground that no answer which the court could give to the first question of the Tariefcommissie would have any bearing on the result of the proceedings brought in that court.

However, in order to confer jurisdiction on the court in the present case it is necessary only that the question raised should clearly be concerned with the interpretation of the Treaty. The considerations which may have led a national court or tribunal to its choice of questions as well as the relevance which it attributes to such questions in the context of a case before it are excluded from review by the Court of Justice.

It appears from the wording of the questions referred that they relate to the interpretation of the Treaty. The court therefore has the jurisdiction to answer them.

This argument, too, is therefore unfounded.

B – On the substance of the case

The first question of the Tariefcommissie is whether Article 12 of the Treaty has direct application in national law in the sense that nationals of Member States may on the basis of this Article lay claim to rights which the national court must protect.

To ascertain whether the provisions of an international treaty extend so far in their effects it is necessary to consider the spirit, the general scheme and the wording of those provisions.

The objective of the EEC Treaty, which is to establish a common market, the functioning of which is of direct concern to interested parties in the Community, implies that this Treaty is more than an agreement which merely creates mutual obligations between the contracting states. This view is confirmed by the preamble to the Treaty which refers not only to governments but to peoples. It is also confirmed more specifically by the establishment of institutions endowed with sovereign rights, the exercise of which affects Member States and also their citizens. Furthermore, it must be noted that the nationals of the states brought together in the Community are called upon to co-operate in the functioning of this Community through the intermediary of the European Parliament and the Economic and Social Committee [see Chapter Two, Section Two].

In addition the task assigned to the Court of Justice under Article 177, the object of which is to secure uniform interpretation of the Treaty by national courts and tribunals, confirms that the states have acknowledged that Community law has an authority which can be invoked by their nationals before those courts and tribunals.

The conclusion to be drawn from this is that the Community constitutes a new legal order of international law for the benefit of which the states have limited their sovereign rights, albeit within limited fields, and the subjects of which comprise not only Member States but also their nationals. Independently of the legislation of Member States, Community law therefore not only imposes obligations on individuals but is also intended to confer upon them rights which become part of their legal heritage. These rights arise not only where they are expressly granted by the Treaty, but also by reason of obligations which the Treaty imposes in a clearly defined way upon individuals as well as upon the Member States and upon the institutions of the Community.

With regard to the general scheme of the Treaty as it relates to customs duties and charges having equivalent effect it must be emphasised that

Article 9, which bases the Community upon a customs union, includes as an essential provision the prohibition of these customs duties and charges. This provision is found at the beginning of the part of the Treaty which defines the 'Foundations of the Community'. It is applied and explained by Article 12.

The wording of Article 12 contains a clear and unconditional prohibition which is not a positive but a negative obligation. This obligation, moreover, is not qualified by any reservation on the part of states which would make its implementation conditional upon a positive legislative measure enacted under national law. The very nature of this prohibition makes it ideally adapted to produce direct effects in the legal relationship between Member States and their subjects.

The implementation of Article 12 does not require any legislative intervention on the part of the states. The fact that under this Article it is the Member States who are made the subject of the negative obligation does not imply that their nationals cannot benefit from this obligation.

In addition the argument based on Articles 169 and 170 of the Treaty put forward by the three governments which have submitted observations to the court in their statements of case is misconceived. The fact that these Articles of the Treaty enable the Commission and the Member States to bring before the court a state which has not fulfilled its obligations does not mean that individuals cannot plead these obligations, should the occasion arise, before a national court, any more than the fact that the Treaty places at the disposal of the Commission ways of ensuring that obligations imposed upon those subject to the Treaty are observed, precludes the possibility, in actions between individuals before a national court, of pleading infringements of these obligations.

A restriction of the guarantees against an infringement of Article 12 by Member States to the procedures under Article 169 and 170 would remove all direct legal protection of the individual rights of their nationals. There is the risk that recourse to the procedure under these Articles would be ineffective if it were to occur after the implementation of a national decision taken contrary to the provisions of the Treaty.

The vigilance of individuals concerned to protect their rights amounts to an effective supervision in addition to the supervision entrusted by Articles 169 and 170 to the diligence of the Commission and of the Member States.

It follows from the foregoing considerations that, according to the spirit, the general scheme and the wording of the Treaty, Article 12 must be interpreted as producing direct effects and creating individual rights which national courts must protect.

[C23]   Case 43/75 Gabrielle Defrenne v Société Anonyme Belge de Navigation Aérienne Sabena [1976] ECR 455

[There was an action, before the Cour du travail (an industrial court), Brussels, between Miss Defrenne, an air hostess, and her employer, Sabena, concerning compensation claimed by her on the ground that she suffered, as a female worker, discrimination in terms of pay as compared with male colleagues who were doing the same work as 'cabin steward'. It was agreed that the work of an air hostess was identical to that of a cabin steward and in these circumstances the existence of discrimination in pay to the detriment of the air hostess during the period was not disputed. The dispute brought into focus the provisions of Article 119 of the Treaty, by which each 'Member State shall during the first stage ensure and maintain the application of the principle that men and women should receive equal pay for equal work' (ie a positive obligation as opposed to the negative obligation in *van Gend* [C22]). Therefore, the application of the principle of equal pay was to be uniformly ensured by the end of the first stage of the transitional period at the latest (ie by 1 January 1962). However, there were important differences and discrepancies between the various states in the implementation of the principle and, although, in certain Member States, the principle had already largely beeen put into practice before the entry into force of the Treaty, either by means of express constitutional and leg- islative provisions or by social practice, established by collective labour agreements, in other states its full implementation had suffered prolonged delays. The Commission failed to initiate proceedings under Article 169. The Cour du travail referred to the Court of Justice the question whether Article 119 introduced directly into the national law of each Member State of the European Community the principle that men and women should re- ceive equal pay for equal work and did it therefore, independently of any national provision, entitle workers to institute proceedings before national courts in order to ensure its observance?]

The European Court of Justice (at pp 471–476)

7. The question of the direct effect of Article 119 must be considered in the light of the nature of the principle of equal pay, the aim of this provision and its place in the scheme of the Treaty.

8. Article 119 pursues a double aim.

9. First, in the light of the different stages of the development of social legislation in the various Member States, the aim of Article 119 is to avoid a situation in which undertakings established in states which have actually implemented the principle of equal pay suffer a competitive disadvantage in intra-Community competition as compared with undertakings established in states which have not yet eliminated discrimination against women workers as regards pay.

10. Secondly, this provision forms part of the social objectives of the Community, which is not merely an economic union, but is at the same time intended, by common action, to ensure social progress and seek the con- stant improvement of the living and working conditions of their peoples, as is emphasised by the Preamble to the Treaty.

. . .

12. This double aim, which is at once economic and social, shows that the principle of equal pay forms part of the foundations of the Community.

13. Furthermore, this explains why the Treaty has provided for the com- plete implementation of this principle by the end of the first stage of the transitional period.

14. Therefore, in interpreting this provision, it is impossible to base any argument on the dilatoriness and resistance which have delayed the actual implementation of this basic principle in certain Member States.

. . .

18. For the purposes of the implementation of these provisions a distinction must be drawn within the whole area of application of Article 119 between, first, direct and overt discrimination which may be identified solely with the aid of the criteria based on equal work and equal pay referred to by the article in question and, secondly, indirect and disguised discrimination which can only be identified by reference to more explicit implementing provisions of a Community or national character.

. . .

21. Among the forms of direct discrimination which may be identified solely by reference to the criteria laid down by Article 119 must be included in particular those which have their origin in legislative provisions or in collective labour agreements and which may be detected on the basis of a purely legal analysis of the situation.
22. This applies even more in cases where men and women receive unequal pay for equal work carried out in the same establishment or service, whether public or private.
23. As is shown by the very findings of the judgment making the reference, in such a situation the court is in a position to establish all the facts which enable it to decide whether a woman worker is receiving lower pay than a male worker performing the same tasks.
24. In such situations, at least, Article 119 is directly applicable and may thus give rise to individual rights which the courts must protect.

. . .

28. [It] is impossible to put forward an argument against its direct effect based on the use in this article of the word 'principle', since, in the language of the Treaty, this term is specifically used in order to indicate the fundamental nature of certain provisions, as is shown, for example, by the heading of the first part of the Treaty which is devoted to 'Principles' and by Article 113, according to which the commercial policy of the Community is to be based on 'uniform principles'.
29. If this concept were to be attenuated to the point of reducing it to the level of a vague declaration, the very foundations of the Community and the coherence of its external relations would be indirectly affected.
30. It is also impossible to put forward arguments based on the fact that Article 119 only refers expressly to 'Member States'.
31. Indeed, as the court has already found in other contexts, the fact that certain provisions of the Treaty are formally addressed to the Member States does not prevent rights from being conferred at the same time on any individual who has an interest in the performance of the duties thus laid down.
32. The very wording of Article 119 shows that it imposes on states a duty to bring about a specific result to be mandatorily achieved within a fixed period.
33. The effectiveness of this provision cannot be affected by the fact that the duty imposed by the Treaty has not been discharged by certain Member States and that the joint institutions have not reacted sufficiently energetically against this failure to act.

. . .

39. In fact, since Article 119 is mandatory in nature, the prohibition on discrimination between men and women applies not only to the action of public authorities, but also extends to all agreements which are intended to regulate paid labour collectively, as well as to contracts between individuals.

40. The reply to the [question] must therefore be that the principle of equal pay contained in Article 119 may be relied upon before the national courts and that these courts have a duty to ensure the protection of the rights which this provision vests in individuals, in particular as regards those types of discrimination arising directly from legislative provisions or collective labour agreements, as well as in cases in which men and women receive unequal pay for equal work which is carried out in the same establishment or service, whether private or public.

[Having decided that the application of the principle that men and women should receive equal pay was to be fully secured and irreversible at the end of the first stage of the transitional period, that is, by 1 January 1962, in the case of the original Member States, and by 1 January 1973, in the case of the three new Member States, the Court of Justice was faced with a dilemma. On the one hand, individuals who had suffered discrimination by reason of the failure of the Member States to implement fully the principle of equal pay, a failure compounded by the failure of the Commission to take proceedings against the recalcitrant states, should logically and in the interests of justice have been permitted to benefit from claims backdated to cover the whole period during which discrimination had been allowed to affect them adversely. On the other hand, their employers had acted in accordance with the national legal rules, albeit discriminatory rules incompatible with Article 119.]

The European Court of Justice (at pp 480–481)

69. The governments of Ireland and the United Kingdom have drawn the court's attention to the possible economic consequences of attributing direct effect to the provisions of Article 119, on the ground that such a decision might, in many branches of economic life, result in the introduction of claims dating back to the time at which such effect came into existence.

70. In view of the large number of people concerned such claims, which undertakings could not have foreseen, might seriously affect the financial situation of such undertakings and even drive some of them to bankruptcy.

71. Although the practical consequences of any judicial decision must be carefully taken into account, it would be impossible to go so far as to diminish the objectivity of the law and compromise its future application on the ground of the possible repercussions which might result, as regards the past, from such a judicial decision.

72. However, in the light of the conduct of several of the Member States and the views adopted by the Commission and repeatedly brought to the notice of the circles concerned, it is appropriate to take exceptionally into account the fact that, over a prolonged period, the parties concerned have been led to continue with practices which were contrary to Article 119, although not yet prohibited under their national law.

73. The fact that, in spite of the warnings given, the Commission did not initiate proceedings under Article 169 against the Member States

concerned on grounds of failure to fulfil an obligation was likely to consolidate the incorrect impression as to the effects of Article 119.

74. In these circumstances, it is appropriate to determine that, as the general level at which pay would have been fixed cannot be known, important considerations of legal certainty affecting all the interests involved, both public and private, make it impossible [to] reopen the question as regards the past.

75. Therefore, the direct effect of Article 119 cannot be relied on in order to support claims concerning pay periods prior to the date of this judgment, except as regards those workers who have already brought legal proceedings or made an equivalent claim.

[The principle of direct effect, therefore, may, in admittedly exceptional cases, be emasculated by the principle of legal certainty (see, also, *Ten Oever* [D64]). Should, therefore, if a similar situation were to arise, individuals be encouraged to bring actions against a defaulting Member State under the principle enunciated in *Francovich* [C33]? (Note also the discussion in [D65].)].

[C24]   Case 106/77 Amministrazione delle Finanze dello Stato v Simmenthal SpA [1978] ECR 629

[For the facts, see [C16]. The Pretore di Susa, during the appeal of the Amministrazione delle Finanze dello Stato (Italian Finance Administration) referred a question to the Court of Justice.]

The European Court of Justice (at pp 643–644)

13. The main purpose of the [question] is to ascertain what consequences flow from the direct applicability of a provision of Community law in the event of incompatibility with a subsequent legislative provision of a Member State.

14. Direct applicability in such circumstances means that rules of Community law must be fully and uniformly applied in all the Member States from the date of their entry into force and for so long as they continue in force.

15. These provisions are therefore a direct source of rights and duties for all those affected thereby, whether Member States or individuals, who are parties to legal relationships under Community law.

16. This consequence also concerns any national court whose task it is as an organ of a Member State to protect, in a case within its jurisdiction, the rights conferred upon individuals by Community law.

17. Furthermore, in accordance with the principle of the precedence of Community law, the relationship between provisions of the Treaty and directly applicable measures of the institutions on the one hand and the national law of the Member States on the other is such that those provisions and measures not only by their entry into force render automatically inapplicable any conflicting provision of current national law but – in so far as they are an integral part of, and take precedence in, the legal order applicable in the territory of each of the Member States – also preclude the valid adoption of new national legislative measures to the extent to which they would be incompatible with Community provisions.

18. Indeed any recognition that national legislative measures which encroach upon the field within which the Community exercises its legislative power or which are otherwise incompatible with the provisions of Community law had any legal effect would amount to a corresponding denial of the effectiveness of obligations undertaken unconditionally and irrevocably by Member States pursuant to the Treaty and would thus imperil the very foundations of the Community.

. . .

21. It follows from the foregoing that every national court must, in a case within its jurisdiction, apply Community law in its entirety and protect rights which the latter confers on individuals and must accordingly set aside any provision of national law which may conflict with it, whether prior or subsequent to the Community rule.

22. Accordingly any provision of a national legal system and any legislative, administrative or judicial practice which might impair the effectiveness of Community law by withholding from the national court having jurisdiction to apply such law the power to do everything necessary at the moment of its application to set aside national legislative provisions which might prevent Community rules from having full force and effect are incompatible with those requirements which are the very essence of Community law.

23. This would be the case in the event of a conflict between a provision of Community law and a subsequent national law if the solution of the conflict were to be reserved for an authority with a discretion of its own, other than the court called upon to apply Community law, even if such an impediment to the full effectiveness of Community law were only temporary.

24. The [question] should therefore be answered to the effect that a national court which is called upon, within the limits of its jurisdiction, to apply provisions of Community law is under a duty to give full effect to those provisions, if necessary refusing of its own motion to apply any conflicting provision of national legislation, even if adopted subsequently, and it is not necessary for the court to request or await the prior setting aside of such provisions by legislative or other constitutional means.

[C25]   Case 9/70 Franz Grad v Finanzamt Traunstein [1970] ECR 825

[A German court asked the Court of Justice for a preliminary ruling on whether an article of a decision in conjunction with an article of a directive produced direct effects in the legal relationship between the Member States and those subject to their jurisdiction in such a way that these provisions created rights for individuals which the national courts must protect. A decision is binding in its entirety upon those to whom it is addressed and a directive is binding, as to the result to be achieved, upon each Member State to which it is addressed, but leaves to the national authorities the choice of form and methods (Article 189 **[B19]**).]

The European Court of Justice (at pp 837–839)

4. The German government in its observations defends the view that by distinguishing between the effects of regulations on the one hand and of

decisions and directives on the other, Article 189 precludes the possibility of decisions and directives producing the effects mentioned in the question, which are reserved to regulations.

5. However, although it is true that by virtue of Article 189, regulations are directly applicable and therefore by virtue of their nature capable of producing direct effects, it does not follow from this that other categories of legal measures mentioned in that article can never produce similar effects. In particular, the provision according to which decisions are binding in their entirety on those to whom they are addressed enables the question to be put whether the obligation created by the decision can only be invoked by the Community institutions against the addressee or whether such a right may possibly be exercised by all those who have an interest in the fulfilment of this obligation. It would be incompatible with the binding effect attributed to decisions by Article 189 to exclude in principle the possibility that persons affected may invoke the obligation imposed by a decision. Particularly in cases where, for example, the Community authorities by means of a decision have imposed an obligation on a Member State or all the Member States to act in a certain way, the effectiveness (l'effet utile) of such a measure would be weakened if the nationals of that state could not invoke it in the courts and the national courts could not take it into consideration as part of Community law. Although the effects of a decision may not be identical with those of a provision contained in a regulation, this difference does not exclude the possibility that the end result, namely the right of the individual to invoke the measure before the courts, may be the same as that of a directly applicable provision of a regulation.

6. Article 177, whereby the national courts are empowered to refer to the court all questions regarding the validity and interpretation of all acts of the institutions without distinction, also implies that individuals may invoke such acts before the national courts. Therefore, in each particular case, it must be ascertained whether the nature, background and wording of the provision in question are capable of producing direct effects in the legal relationships between the addressee of the act and third parties.

[7.–9. The Court of Justice analysed the decision and held that the obligation contained therein] is unconditional and sufficiently clear and precise to be capable of producing direct effects in the legal relationships between the Member States and those subject to their jurisdiction.

[C26]   Case 148/78 Pubblico Ministero v Tullio Ratti
[1979] ECR 1629

[Dangerous substances contained in certain solvents, paints and varnishes were subject to different rules as regards labelling and packaging in different Member States. The Council determined that the differences constituted a barrier to trade and to the free movement of goods and, in order to eliminate the differences, enacted Directive 73/173 (relating to solvents and to be implemented by 8 December 1974) and Directive 77/728 (relating to paints and varnishes and to be implemented by 9 November 1979). In particular, the directives made rules relating to the packaging and labelling of solvents, paints and varnishes, with regard to the information to be specified as to any harmful substances contained therein. Ratti was the legal representative of an Italian company which had already started to comply with the labelling provisions in anticipation of the implementation of the directives in Italy and in view of the fact that other Member States had already implemented them. However, Italy had not implemented either directive and the relevant Italian statute differed from the directives (in some cases being less stringent and in others being more stringent) and laid down criminal penalties for persons failing to comply with it. Ratti was prosecuted in May 1978 and stated, by way of defence, that the directives, rather than the Italian statute, should be applied by the courts in Italy. The criminal court referred, inter alia, two questions: first, does Directive 73/173 'constitute directly applicable legislation conferring upon individuals personal rights which the national courts must protect?'; fifth, is Directive 77/728 'immediately and directly applicable with regard to the obligations imposed on Member States to refrain from action from the date of notification of that Directive in a case where a person, acting upon a legitimate expectation, has complied with the provisions of that Directive before expiry of the period within which the Member State must comply with the said Directive?' Note how the court follows *Grad* **[C25]**.]

The European Court of Justice (at pp 1641–1646)

[18., 19. The first question raises the general problem of the legal nature of the provisions of a directive adopted under Article 189 of the Treaty. In this regard, the settled case law of the court lays down that, whilst under Article 189 regulations are] directly applicable and, consequently, by their nature capable of producing direct effects, that does not mean that other categories of acts covered by that Article can never produce similar effects.

20. It would be incompatible with the binding effect which Article 189 ascribes to directives to exclude on principle the possibility of the obligations imposed by them being relied on by persons concerned.

21. Particularly in cases in which the Community authorities have, by means of directive, placed Member States under a duty to adopt a certain course of action, the effectiveness of such an act would be weakened if persons were prevented from relying on it in legal proceedings and national courts prevented from taking it into consideration as an element of Community law.

22. Consequently a Member State which has not adopted the implementing measures required by the directive in the prescribed periods may not rely, as against individuals, on its own failure to perform the obligations which the directive entails.

23. It follows that a national court requested by a person who has complied with the provisions of a directive not to apply a national provision incompatible with the directive not incorporated into the internal legal order of a defaulting Member State, must uphold that request if the obligation [is] unconditional and sufficiently precise.

24. Therefore the answer to the first question must be that after the expiration of the period fixed for the implementation of a directive a Member State may not apply its internal law – even if it is provided with penal sanctions – which has not yet been adapted in compliance with the directive, to a person who has complied with the requirements of the directive.

. . .

43. It follows that, for the reasons expounded in the grounds of the answer to the national court's first question, it is only at the end of the prescribed period and in the event of the Member State's default that the directive [will] be able to have the effects described in the answer to the first question.

44. Until that date is reached the Member States remain free in that field.

45. If one Member State has incorporated the provisions of a directive into its internal legal order before the end of the period prescribed therein, that fact cannot produce any effect with regard to the other Member States.

46. In conclusion, since a directive by its nature imposes obligations only on Member States, it is not possible for an individual to plead the principle of 'legitimate expectation' before the expiry of the period prescribed for its implementation.

47. Therefore the answer to the fifth question must be that Directive 77/728 [cannot] bring about with respect to any individual who has complied with the provisions of the said directive before the expiration of the adaptation period prescribed for the Member State any effect capable of being taken into consideration by national courts.

[C27]   Case 152/84 MH Marshall v Southampton and South West Hampshire Area Health Authority (Teaching) [1986] ECR 723

[Miss Marshall worked for the Area Health Authority ('AHA'), which had a policy that the normal retirement age of its employees was the age at which the state retirement pension became payable (60 for a woman and 65 for a man). The AHA waived this policy for Miss Marshall for two years but when she was 62 the AHA dismissed her (although she wished to continue working until she was 65), the sole reason being that she was a woman who had passed the retirement age. The AHA would not have ordinarily dismissed a man until he had attained the age of 65. In view of the fact that she had suffered financial loss consisting of the difference between her earnings as an employee and the pension which she received on retirement and since she had lost the satisfaction derived from her work, Miss Marshall instituted proceedings against the AHA before an industrial tribunal and, on appeal, to the Court of Appeal, on the grounds of discriminatory treatment by the AHA on the ground of her sex, claiming that this was unlawful discrimination contrary to Directive 76/207 (the 'Equal Treatment Directive': below). The Court of Appeal referred the following questions to the Court of Justice:

1. Whether the [authority's] dismissal of [Miss Marshall] after she had passed her sixtieth birthday pursuant to the policy [followed by the authority] and on the grounds only that she was a woman who had passed the normal retiring age applicable to women was an act of discrimination prohibited by the Equal Treatment Directive;

2. If the answer to 1 above is in the affirmative, whether or not the Equal Treatment Directive can be relied upon by [Miss Marshall] in the circumstances of the present case in national courts or [tribunals].

The relevant provisions of the directive are as follows:

Article 1(1)

The purpose of this directive is to put into effect in the Member States the principle of equal treatment for men and women as regards access to employment, including promotion, and to vocational training and as regards working conditions and, on the conditions referred to in paragraph 2, social security. This principle is hereinafter referred to as 'the principle of equal treatment'.

Article 2(1)

[The] principle of equal treatment shall mean that there shall be no discrimination whatsoever on grounds of sex either directly or indirectly by reference in particular to marital or family status.

Article 5(1)

Application of the principle of equal treatment with regard to working conditions, including the conditions governing dismissal, means that men and women shall be guaranteed the same conditions without discrimination on grounds of sex.

Article 5(2)

To this end, Member States shall take the measures necessary to ensure that:

(a) any laws, regulations and administrative provisions contrary to the principle of equal treatment shall be abolished;
(b) any provisions contrary to the principle of equal treatment which are included in collective agreements, individual contracts of employment, internal rules of undertakings or in rules governing the independent occupations and professions shall be, or may be declared, null and void or may be amended;
(c) those laws, regulations and administrative provisions contrary to the principle of equal treatment when the concern for protection which originally inspired them is no longer well founded shall be revised; and that where similar provisions are included in collective agreements labour and management shall be requested to undertake the desired revision.]

The European Court of Justice (at pp 743–750)

[Is there discrimination?]

21. By the first question the Court of Appeal seeks to ascertain whether or not Article 5(1) of [Directive 76/207] must be interpreted as meaning that a general policy concerning dismissal, followed by a state authority, involving the dismissal of a woman solely because she has attained or passed the qualifying age for a state pension, which age is different under national legislation for men and for women, constitutes discrimination on grounds of sex, contrary to that directive.

22. [Miss Marshall] and the Commission consider that the first question must be answered in the affirmative.

23. According to [Miss Marshall], the said age limit falls within the term

'working conditions' within the meaning of Articles 1(1) and 5(1) of [Directive 76/207]. A wide interpretation of that term is, in her opinion, justi-fied in view of the objective of the EEC Treaty to provide for 'the constant improving of the living and working conditions of [the Member States'] peo-ples' and in view of the wording of the prohibition of discrimination laid down in the above-mentioned articles of [Directive 76/207] and in Article 7(1) of [Regulation (EEC) 1612/68 **[D14]**].

. . .

26. The Commission emphasises that neither the [authority's] employ-ment policy nor the state social security scheme makes retirement compulsory upon a person's reaching pensionable age. On the contrary, the provisions of national legislation take into account the case of continued employment beyond the normal pensionable age. In those circumstances, it would be difficult to justify the dismissal of a woman for reasons based on her sex and age.

27. The Commission also refers to the fact that the court has recognised that equality of treatment for men and women constitutes a fundamental principle of Community law.

. . .

38. Consequently, the answer to the first question referred to the [court] must be that Article 5(1) of [Directive 76/207] must be interpreted as mean-ing that a general policy concerning dismissal involving the dismissal of a woman solely because she has attained the qualifying age for a state pen-sion, which age is different under national legislation for men [and] women, constitutes discrimination on grounds of sex, contrary to that directive.

[Is the directive capable of direct effect?]

39. Since the first question has been answered in the affirmative, it is necessary to consider whether Article 5(1) of [Directive 76/207] may be re-lied upon by an individual before national courts and tribunals.

40. [Miss Marshall] and the Commission consider that that question must be answered in the affirmative. They contend in particular, with regard to Articles 2(1) and 5(1) of [Directive 76/207], that those provisions are suf-ficiently clear to enable national courts to apply them without legislative intervention by the Member States, at least so far as overt discrimination is concerned.

41. In support of that view, [Miss Marshall] points out that directives are capable of conferring rights on individuals which may be relied upon di-rectly before the courts of the Member States; national courts are obliged by virtue of the binding nature of a directive, in conjunction with Article 5 of the EEC Treaty, to give effect to the provisions of directives where possi-ble, in particular when construing or applying relevant provisions of national law ([*von Colson* **[C29]**]). Where there is any inconsistency between national law and Community law which cannot be removed by means of such a construction, [Miss Marshall] submits that a national court is obliged to declare that the provision of national law which is inconsistent with the directive is inapplicable.

. . .

43. The [authority] and the United Kingdom propose, conversely, that the second question should be answered in the negative. They admit that a directive may, in certain specific circumstances, have direct effect as against a Member State in so far as the latter may not rely on its failure to perform its obligations under the directive. However, they maintain that a directive can never impose obligations directly on individuals and that it can only have direct effect against a Member State *qua* public authority and not against a Member State *qua* employer. As an employer a state is no different from a private employer. It would not therefore be proper to put persons employed by the state in a better position than those who are employed by a private employer.

44. With regard to the legal position of the [authority's] employees the United Kingdom states that they are in the same position as the employees of a private employer.

Although according to United Kingdom constitutional law the health [authorities] are Crown bodies and their employees are Crown servants, nevertheless the administration of the National Health Service by the health authorities is regarded as being separate from the government's central administration and its employees are not regarded as civil servants.

45. Finally, both the [authority] and the United Kingdom take the view that the provisions of [Directive 76/207] are neither unconditional nor sufficiently clear and precise to give rise to direct effect. The directive provides for a number of possible exceptions, the details of which are to be laid down by the Member States. Furthermore, the wording of Article 5 is quite imprecise and requires the adoption of measures for its implementation.

. . .

48. With regard to the argument that a directive may not be relied upon against an individual, it must be emphasised that according to Article 189 of the EEC Treaty the binding nature of a directive, which constitutes the basis for the possibility of relying on the directive before a national court, exists only in relation to 'each Member State to which it is addressed'. It follows that a directive may not of itself impose obligations on an individual and that a provision of a directive may not be relied upon as such against such a person. It must therefore be examined whether, in this case, the [authority] must be regarded as having acted as an individual.

49. In that respect it must be pointed out that where a person involved in legal proceedings is able to rely on a directive as against the state he may do so regardless of the capacity in which the latter is acting, whether employer or public authority. In either case it is necessary to prevent the state from taking advantage of its own failure to comply with Community law.

50. It is for the national court to apply those considerations to the circumstances of each case: the Court of Appeal has, however, stated in the order for reference that [the] Southampton and South West Hampshire Area Health Authority (Teaching) is a public authority.

51. The argument submitted by the United Kingdom that the possibility of relying on provisions of the directive against the [authority] *qua* organ of the state would give rise to an arbitrary and unfair distinction between the rights of state employees and those of private employees does not justify any other conclusion. Such a distinction may easily be avoided if the Member State concerned has correctly implemented the directive in national law.

52. Finally, with regard to the question whether the provision contained in Article 5(1) of [Directive 76/207], which implements the principle of equality of treatment set out in Article 2(1) of the directive, may be considered, as far as its contents are concerned, to be unconditional and sufficiently precise to be relied upon by an individual as against the state, it must be stated that the provision, taken by itself, prohibits any discrimination on grounds of sex with regard to working conditions, including the conditions governing dismissal, in a general manner and in unequivocal terms. The provision is therefore sufficiently precise to be relied on by an individual and to be applied by the national courts.

. . .

55. It follows that Article 5 of [Directive 76/207] does not confer on the Member States the right to limit the application of the principle of equality of treatment in its field of operation or to subject it to conditions and that that provision is sufficiently precise and unconditional to be capable of being relied upon by an individual before a national court in order to avoid the application of any national provision which does not conform to Article 5(1).

56. Consequently, the answer to the second question must be that Article 5(1) of [Directive 76/207], which prohibits any discrimination on grounds of sex with regard to working conditions, including the conditions governing dismissal, may be relied upon as against a state authority acting in its capacity as employer, in order to avoid the application of any national provision which does not conform to Article 5(1) [see, further, **[D63]**].

[C28]   Case 103/88 Fratelli Costanzo v Comune di Milano [1989] ECR 1839

[Directive 71/305, on the co-ordination of procedures for the award of public works contracts, Article 29(5), provided that, if for a given contract, tenders were obviously abnormally low in relation to the transaction, the authority awarding such contracts must examine the details of the tenders before deciding to whom it should award the contract and take that examination into account. In purported implementation of the directive, the Italian government made a decree that, in order to speed up the procedure for the award of public works contracts, for a period of two years it would define its own terms on which a contract should be considered abnormal and contracts coming within this definition would be excluded from the tendering procedure. In preparation for the 1990 football World Cup, held in Italy, the Comune di Milano issued a call for tenders for alteration works on a football stadium. On the basis of the Italian decree, the Giunta Municipale (the executive authority of Milan) decided to exclude the bid of Fratelli Costanzo from the tendering procedure and to award the contract to another. Costanzo challenged that decision before the Tribunale amministrativo regionale per la Lombardia (the regional administrative court) claiming, inter alia, that the decision was illegal on the ground that it was based on a decree which was itself incompatible with Article 29(5) of Directive 71/305. One question referred by the administrative court was:

If the Court of Justice rules that the [decree conflicts] with Article 29(5) of [Directive 71/305], was the municipal authority empowered, or obliged, to disregard the domestic provisions which conflicted with the aforesaid Community provision (consulting the central authorities if necessary), or does that power or obligation vest solely in the national courts?]

The European Court of Justice (at pp 1870–1871)

28. In the [question] the national court asks whether administrative authorities including municipal authorities are under the same obligation as a national court to apply the provisions of Article 29(5) of [Directive 71/305] and to refrain from applying provisions of national law which conflict with them.

29. In [*Marshall* **[C27]**], the court held that wherever the provisions of a directive appear, as far as their subject matter is concerned, to be unconditional and sufficiently precise, those provisions may be relied upon by an individual against the state where that state has failed to implement the directive in national law by the end of the period prescribed or where it has failed to implement the directive correctly.

30. It is important to note that the reason for which an individual may, in the circumstances described above, rely on the provisions of a directive in proceedings before the national courts is that the obligations arising under those provisions are binding upon all the authorities of the Member States.

31. It would, moreover, be contradictory to rule that an individual may rely upon the provisions of a directive which fulfil the conditions defined above in proceedings before the national courts seeking an order against the administrative authorities, and yet to hold that those authorities are under no obligation to apply the provisions of the directive and refrain from applying provisions of national law which conflict with them. It follows that when the conditions under which the court has held that individuals may rely on the provisions of a directive before the national courts are met, all organs of the administration, including decentralised authorities such as municipalities, are obliged to apply those provisions.

32. With specific regard to Article 29(5) of Directive 71/305, it is apparent [that] it is unconditional and sufficiently precise to be relied upon by an individual against the state. An individual may therefore plead that provision before the national courts and, as is clear from the foregoing, all organs of the administration, including decentralised authorities such as municipalities, are obliged to apply it.

33. The answer to the [question] must therefore be that administrative authorities, including municipal authorities, are under the same obligation as a national court to apply the provisions of Article 29(5) of [Directive 71/305] and to refrain from applying provisions of national law which conflict with them.

[C29] Case 14/83 Sabine von Colson and Elizabeth Kamann v Land Nordrhein-Westfalen [1984] ECR 1891

[The plaintiffs brought an action before the Arbeitsgericht (labour court), claiming that they had been discriminated against because of their sex. They had applied for vacant posts as social workers in a prison and were placed at the top of the list of candidates by the social workers' committee.

354 Community Law and the Member States

However, the prison catered exclusively for male prisoners and the recruiting authority refused to engage the plaintiffs for reasons relating to their sex. The officials responsible for recruitment justified their refusal to engage the plaintiffs by citing the problems and risks connected with the appointment of female candidates and for those reasons appointed instead male candidates who were however less well qualified. The plaintiffs sought a declaration that it was solely because of their sex that they had not been appointed. Consequently, they claimed that the defendant Land, which administered the prison service, should be ordered to offer them a contract of employment in the prison or, in the alternative, to pay them damages amounting to six months' salary. Sabine von Colson claimed the reimbursement of travelling expenses amounting to DM 7.20 incurred by her in pursuing her application for the post. The Arbeitsgericht held that there had indeed been discrimination but the question arose as to the remedy which could, under German law, be awarded. Section 611A of the German Civil Code (which purported to implement Directive 76/207 (below)) provided that:

1. An employer must not discriminate against a worker on grounds of sex, in connection with an agreement or a measure, in particular in the course of the establishment of an employment relationship.
2. If an employment relationship has not been established because of a breach of the prohibition of discrimination in subparagraph (1) attributable to the employer, he is liable to pay damages in respect of the loss incurred by the worker as a result of his reliance on the expectation that the establishment of the employment relationship would not be precluded by such a breach.

The Arbeitsgericht held that under German law it was not able to allow the claimed remedies, with the exception of the reimbursement of the travelling expenses incurred by Sabine von Colson in pursuing her application for the post. It was obviously in the mind of the Arbeitsgericht whether the nature of the redress available to victims under the Civil Code was compatible with Directive 76/207, relating to equal treatment for men and women, in particular with regard to access to employment. That directive provided, inter alia, that Member States are under a duty to enable 'all persons who consider themselves wronged by failure to apply to them the principle of equal treatment [to] pursue their claims by judicial process after possible recourse to other competent authorities' (Article 6).]

The European Court of Justice (at pp 1904–1909)

[Question 1]

8. In its first question the Arbeitsgericht asks essentially whether Directive 76/207 requires discrimination on grounds of sex in the matter of access to employment to be penalised by an obligation, imposed on an employer who is guilty of discrimination, to conclude a contract of employment with the candidate who was the victim of discrimination.

9. According to the Arbeitsgericht, it is clear from the recitals in the preamble to and from the actual provisions of the directive that the directive requires Member States to adopt legal provisions which provide effective sanctions. In its view only compensation in kind, entailing the appointment of the persons who were the victims of discrimination, is effective.

. . .

11. The government of [Germany] is aware of the need for an effective transposition of the directive but stresses the fact that, under [Article 189(3) **[B19]**, each Member State has a margin of discretion as regards the legal consequences which must result from a breach of the principle of equal treatment. The German government submits, moreover, that it is possible for the German courts to work out, on the basis of private national law and in conformity with the substance of the directive, adequate solutions which satisfy both the principle of equal treatment and the interests of all the parties. Finally an appreciable legal consequence is in its view sufficient to ensure compliance with the principle of equal treatment and that consequence should follow only if the victim of discrimination was better qualified for the post than the other candidates; it should not apply where the candidates' qualifications were equal.

12. The Danish government considers that the directive deliberately left to Member States the choice of sanctions, in accordance with their national circumstances and legal systems. Member States should penalise breaches of the principle of equal treatment in the same way as they penalise similar breaches of national rules in related areas not governed by Community law.

13. The United Kingdom is also of the opinion that it is for Member States to choose the measures which they consider appropriate to ensure the fulfilment of their obligations under the directive. The directive gives no indication as to the measures which Member States should adopt and the questions referred to the court themselves clearly illustrate the difficulties encountered in laying down appropriate measures.

14. The Commission considers that although the directive is intended to leave to Member States the choice and the determination of the sanctions, the transposition of the directive must nevertheless produce effective results. The principle of the effective transposition of the directive requires that the sanctions must be of such a nature as to constitute appropriate compensation for the candidate discriminated against and for the employer a means of pressure which it would be unwise to disregard and which would prompt him to respect the principle of equal treatment. A national measure which provides for compensation only for losses actually incurred through reliance on an expectation [is] not sufficient to ensure compliance with that principle.

15. [Although Article 189] leaves Member States to choose the ways and means of ensuring that the directive is implemented, that freedom does not affect the obligation imposed on all the Member States to which the directive is addressed, to adopt, in their national legal systems, all the measures necessary to ensure that the directive is fully effective, in accordance with the objective which it pursues.

16. It is therefore necessary to examine Directive 76/207 in order to determine whether it requires Member States to provide for specific legal consequences or sanctions in respect of a breach of the principle of equal treatment regarding access to employment.

17. The object of that directive is to implement in the Member States the principle of equal treatment for men and women, in particular by giving male and female real equality of opportunity as regards access to [employment].

18. Article 6 requires Member States to introduce into their national legal systems such measures as are necessary to enable all persons who consider themselves wronged by discrimination 'to pursue their claims by judicial process'. It follows from the provision that Member States are required to adopt measures which are sufficiently effective to achieve the objective of the directive and to ensure that those measures may in fact be relied on before the national courts by the persons concerned. Such measures may include, for example, provisions requiring the employer to offer a post to the candidate discriminated against or giving the candidate adequate financial compensation, backed up where necessary by a system of fines. However, the directive does not prescribe a specific sanction; it leaves Member States free to choose between the different solutions suitable for achieving its objective.

19. The reply to the first question should therefore be that Directive 76/207 does not require discrimination on grounds of sex regarding access to employment to be made the subject of a sanction by way of an obligation imposed upon the employer who is the author of the discrimination to conclude a contract of employment with the candidate discriminated [against].

[Questions 5 and 6]

21. In its fifth question the Arbeitsgericht essentially asks whether it is possible to infer from the directive any sanction in the event of discrimination other than the right to the conclusion of a contract of employment. Question 6 asks whether the directive, as properly interpreted, may be relied on before national courts by persons who have suffered injury.

22. It is impossible to establish real equality of opportunity without an appropriate system of sanctions. That follows not only from the actual purpose of the directive but more specifically from Article 6 thereof which, by granting applicants for a post who have been discriminated against recourse to the courts, acknowledges that those candidates have rights of which they may avail themselves before the courts.

23. Although, as has been stated in [reply] to Question 1, full implementation of the directive does not require any specific form of sanction for unlawful discrimination, it does entail that that sanction be such as to guarantee real and effective judicial protection. Moreover it must also have a real deterrent effect on the employer. It follows that where a Member State chooses to penalise the breach of the prohibition of discrimination by the award of compensation, that compensation must in any event be adequate in relation to the damage sustained.

24. In consquence it appears that national provisions limiting the right to compensation of persons who have been discriminated against as regards access to employment to a purely nominal amount, such as, for example, the reimbursement of expenses incurred by them in submitting their application, would not satisfy the requirements of an effective transposition of the directive.

25. The nature of the sanctions provided for in the Federal Republic of Germany in respect of discrimination regarding access to employment and in particular the question whether the rule in Paragraph 611A(2) of the [German Civil Code: above] excludes the possibility of compensation on the basis of the general rules of law were the subject of lengthy discussion before the court. The German government maintained in the oral procedure

that that provision did not necessarily exclude the application of the general rules of law regarding compensation. It is for the national court alone to rule on that question concerning the interpretation of its national law.

26. However, the Member States' obligation arising from a directive to achieve the result envisaged by the directive and their duty under Article 5 of the Treaty to take all appropriate measures, whether general or particular, to ensure the fulfilment of that obligation, is binding on all the authorities of Member States including, for matters within their jurisdiction, the courts. It follows that, in applying the national law and in particular the provisions of a national law specifically introduced in order to implement Directive 76/207, national courts are required to interpret their national law in the light of the wording and the purpose of the directive in order to achieve the result referred to in [Article 189(3)].

27. On the other hand, as the above considerations show, the directive does not include any unconditional and sufficiently precise obligation as regards sanctions for discrimination which, in the absence of implementing measures adopted in good time may be relied on by individuals in order to obtain specific compensation under the directive, where that is not provided for or permitted under national law.

28. It should, however, be pointed out to the national court that although [Directive 76/207], for the purpose of imposing a sanction for the breach of the prohibition of discrimination, leaves the Member States free to choose between the different solutions suitable for achieving its objective, it nevertheless requires that if a Member State chooses to penalise breaches of that prohibition by the award of compensation, then in order to ensure that it is effective and that it has a deterrent effect, that compensation must in any event be adequate in relation to the damage sustained and must therefore amount to more than purely nominal compensation such as, for example, the reimbursement only of the expenses incurred in connection with the application. It is for the national court to interpret and apply the legislation adopted for the implementation of the directive in conformity with the requirements of Community law, in so far as it is given discretion to do so under national law.

[C30] Case 80/86 Criminal proceedings against Kolpinghuis Nijmegen BV [1987] ECR 3969

[Kolpinghuis Nijmegen, a company, were found to have stocked for sale and delivery at its business at Nijmegen a beverage which was called 'mineral water' but which consisted in fact of tap water and carbon dioxide. The' company was charged with infringing a regulation of the municipality of Nijmegen which prohibited the stocking for sale and delivery of goods intended for trade and human consumption which were of unsound composition. Before the criminal court, the public prosecutor relied, inter alia, upon Directive 80/777 (on the approximation of the laws of the Member States relating to the exploitation and marketing of natural mineral waters). This directive, in particular, provided that the Member States were to take the measures necessary to ensure that only waters extracted from the ground of a Member State and recognised by the responsible authority of that Member State as natural mineral water satisfying the provisions contained in the directive could be marketed as natural mineral waters. That provision of the directive ought to have been implemented by 17 July 1984, but the Netherlands legislation was amended only with effect from 8 August 1985, whereas the offences with which the accused was charged took place on 7 August 1984. The criminal court submitted to the Court of Justice the following questions:

(1) Can an authority of a Member State (in this case the prosecuting body) rely as against nationals of that Member State on a provision of a directive in a case which is not covered by the State's own legislation or implementing provisions?

(2) Is a national court obliged, where a directive has not been implemented, to give direct effect to provisions of the directive which lend themselves to such treatment even where the individual concerned does not seek to derive any rights from those provisions?

(3) Where a national court is required to interpret a national rule, should or may that court be guided in its interpretation by the provisions of an applicable directive?

Note how the court refers to general principles of law (discussed in Chapter Two, Section Four).]

The European Court of Justice (at pp 3985–3987)

The first two questions

6. The first two questions concern the possibility whether the provisions of a directive which has not yet been implemented in national law in the Member State in question may be applied as such.

7. In this regard it should be recalled that, according to the established case law of the [court], wherever the provisions of a directive appear, as far as their subject matter is concerned, to be unconditional and sufficiently precise, those provisions may be relied upon by an individual against the state where that state fails to implement the directive in national law by the end of the period prescribed or where it fails to implement the directive correctly.

8. That view is based on the consideration that it would be incompatible with the binding nature which Article 189 confers on the directive to hold as a matter of principle that the obligation imposed thereby cannot be relied on by those concerned. From that the court deduced that a Member State which has not adopted the implementing measures required by the directive within the prescribed period may not plead, as against individuals, its own failure to perform the obligations which the directive entails.

9. In [*Marshall* [C27]], the court emphasised, however, that according to Article 189 of the EEC Treaty the binding nature of a directive, which constitutes the basis for the possibility of relying on the directive before a national court, exists only in relation to 'each Member State to which it is addressed'. It follows that a directive may not of itself impose obligations on an individual and that a provision of a directive may not be relied upon as such against such a person before a national court.

10. The answer to the first two questions should therefore be that a national authority may not rely, as against an individual, upon a provision of a directive whose necessary implementation in national law has not yet taken place.

The third question

11. The third question is designed to ascertain how far the national court may or must take account of a directive as an aid to the interpretation of a rule of national law.

12. As the court stated in [*von Colson* **[C29]**], the Member States' obligation arising from a directive to achieve the result envisaged by the directive and their duty under Article 5 of the Treaty to take all appropriate measures, whether general or particular, to ensure the fulfilment of that obligation, is binding on all the authorities of Member States including, for matters within their jurisdiction, the courts. It follows that, in applying the national law and in particular the provisions of a national law specifically introduced in order to implement the directive, national courts are required to interpret their national law in the light of the wording and the purpose of the directive in order to achieve the result referred to in the third paragraph of Article 189 of the Treaty.

13. However, that obligation on the national court to refer to the content of the directive when interpreting the relevant rules of its national law is limited by the general principles of law which form part of Community law and in particular the principles of legal certainty and non-retroactivity. Thus the court ruled [in] Case 14/86 *Pretore di Salò v X* [1987] ECR 2545 that a directive cannot, of itself and independently of a national law adopted by a Member State for its implementation, have the effect of determining or aggravating the liability in criminal law of persons who act in contravention of the provisions of that directive.

14. The answer to the third question should therefore be that in applying its national legislation a court of a Member State is required to interpret that legislation in the light of the wording and the purpose of the directive in order to achieve the result referred to in the third paragraph of Article 189 of the Treaty, but a directive cannot, of itself and independently of a law adopted for its implementation, have the effect of determining or aggravating the liability in criminal law of persons who act in contravention of the provisions of that directive.

[C31]   Case C-106/89 Marleasing SA v La Comercial Internacional de Alimentación SA [1990] ECR I-4135

[The Juzgado de Primera Instancia e Instrucción, Oviedo, referred to the Court of Justice a request for a preliminary ruling on the interpretation of Article 11 of Directive 68/151 (on the co-ordination of safeguards which, for the protection of the interests of members and others, are required by Member States of companies, with a view to making such safeguards equivalent throughout the Community). There was litigation before the Spanish court between Marleasing, the plaintiff, and several defendants, including La Comercial, established in the form of a public limited company by three persons, including Barviesa. Marleasing, an important creditor of Barviesa, argued that La Comercial had in fact been set up by Barviesa alone and that the two other founders were men of straw. In its view, La Comercial was created for the sole purpose of putting Barviesa's assets beyond the reach of its creditors. Marleasing's primary claim was based on certain articles of the Spanish Civil Code, according to which contracts without cause or whose cause is unlawful have no legal effect. Marleasing sought a declaration that the contract establishing La Comercial and the instrument incorporating La Comercial were void on the ground that the establishment of La Comercial lacked cause, was a sham transaction and was carried out in order to defraud the creditors of Barviesa. La Comercial argued that the action should be dismissed on the ground, inter alia, that Article 11 of Directive 68/151, which listed exhaustively the grounds on which the nullity of a company might be ordered, did not include lack of cause amongst them. La Comercial argued that the grounds of nullity listed in Article 11 were exhaustive, since Article 11 stated that apart 'from the foregoing grounds of nullity, a company shall not be subject to any cause of non-existence, nullity absolute, nullity relative or declaration of nullity'.

Note, first, how the Advocate General builds up a proposition developing the law and applies that proposition to the facts and, secondly, how the court follows the Advocate General.]

Opinion of Advocate General Van Gerven (at pp 4145–4154)

A provision of a directive may not be relied upon as such against an individual

5. In [Case 8/81 *Becker v Finanzamt Münster-Innenstadt* [1982] ECR 53] the court stated that where a provision of a directive is unconditional and sufficiently precise, it may be relied upon by an individual against a Member State which has failed to transpose the directive into national law within the prescribed period. In [*Marshall* **[C27]**] the court added that that possibility exists only in relation to the Member State concerned and state bodies. It follows from that finding 'that a directive may not of itself impose obligations on an individual and that a provision of a directive may not be relied upon as such against such a [person]'.

6. In this case La Comercial relies, in its defence against Marleasing's main contention, on a provision of a directive, [which] had not yet been transposed into Spanish law at the date of the order for reference. The prohibition laid down in that article on a declaration of nullity of a company on grounds other than those listed therein is without the slightest doubt unconditional and sufficiently precise to be regarded on principle as directly applicable. In the light of the established case law of the court, however, that provision cannot be relied upon by La Comercial against Marleasing in the main proceedings. There is no evidence whatsoever that Marleasing is acting as a state body or public authority, not even in the broad sense in which the court has interpreted those terms again today [see *Foster* **[C42]**].

The obligation to interpret national law in conformity with the directive

7. Although a provision of a directive may not be relied upon against an individual, national courts are still required, as the Court of Justice stated in [*von Colson* **[C29]**], 'in applying the national law and in particular the provisions of a national law specifically introduced in order to implement [the] directive [to] interpret their national law in the light of the wording and the purpose of the directive in order to achieve the result referred to [in] Article 189'. That obligation on the part of the national courts to interpret their national law in conformity with a directive, which has been reaffirmed on several occasions ([*Johnston* **[C32]**, *Kolpinghuis* **[C30]**]), does not mean

that a provision in a directive has direct effect in any way as between individuals. On the contrary, it is the national provisions themselves which, interpreted in a manner consistent with the directive, have direct effect.

8. The obligation to interpret a provision of national law in conformity with a directive arises whenever the provision in question is to any extent open to interpretation. In those circumstances the national court must, having regard to the usual methods of interpretation in its legal system, give precedence to the method which enables it to construe the national provision concerned in a manner consistent with the [directive].

The obligation to give an interpretation in conformity with a directive is, it is true, restricted by Community law itself, of which the directive forms part, and in particular by the principles of legal certainty and non-retroactivity which also form part of Community law. In cases involving criminal proceedings, for example, such an interpretation cannot result in criminal liability unless such liability has been introduced by the national legislation implementing the directive ([*Kolpinghuis* **[C30]**]). Nor, similarly, can a directive of itself – that is to say in the absence of national implementing legislation – introduce a civil penalty, such as nullity, in national law. However, that is not the issue here: this case is concerned with a provision of a directive which excludes certain grounds of nullity.

9. The question whether an interpretation is in conformity with a directive usually arises in relation to provisions of national law which are specifically intended to implement the directive concerned. That was the case in [*von Colson* **[C29]**].

However, there is no reason to restrict the requirement that an interpretation must be in conformity with a directive to that situation. That follows, in my view, from the reasoning used by the court to underpin that requirement. It is based on the consideration that judicial authorities, like the other public authorities of the Member States, are required, in the light of Article 5 of the EEC Treaty, to seek to achieve the result pursued by the directive by all appropriate measures within their power. Furthermore, as part of Community law, the directive concerned in principle takes precedence over all provisions of national law. That is true in particular in the case of national provisions which, as in this case, relate to the branch of the law covered by the directive, even though they predate the directive and were thus not enacted for its [implementation].

10. Let us apply the foregoing principles to the question under consideration. [It] follows, in my view, from the reasoning set out in the preceding paragraphs that the requirement that an interpretation must be consistent with a directive precludes the application to public limited companies of the provisions on nullity under ordinary law in such a way as to permit a declaration of nullity of such a company on grounds other than those exhaustively listed in Article 11 of the [directive].

. . .

13. [In] so far as Marleasing's claim seeks a declaration of nullity of La Comercial as such, it does fall within the scope of Articles 11 and 12 of the [directive]. In so far as the national court is under an obligation to take those provisions into consideration when interpreting its own national [law], it must deal with the question whether the ground of nullity referred to in Article 11(2)(b) of the directive covers the case of a company purportedly set up with the aim of placing the founders' creditors at a disadvantage.

This, therefore, is a question involving the interpretation of the directive itself (an interpretation which, in turn, must be taken into consideration in the interpretation of national [law]).

14. Hence the question raised by way of a reference for a preliminary ruling is, essentially, how Article 11(2)(b) is to be interpreted. In the light of the facts central to the dispute in the main proceedings, this case turns on the meaning of the phrase 'the objects of the [company]'.

15. [That] task is all the more delicate in view of the divergences on that point between the different language versions of Article 11(2)(b). According to the Dutch version of that provision, a declaration of nullity of a company may be made where its '*werkelijke doel*' (actual objects) are unlawful or contrary to public policy. Must the phrase '*doel van de vennootschap*' (in the French version: *objet de la société*) be understood as meaning exclusively the company's objects as described in its instrument of incorporation or its statutes, or must it be understood as referring also to the activity actually carried on by the company or even the aim actually pursued by means of the company (in the sense of '*le but de la société*'). Only in the latter case can the national court take the view, without interpreting its national law in a manner inconsistent with the directive, that a declaration of nullity of a company can be made if it was incorporated for the (sole) purpose of placing the founders' creditors at a disadvantage, as Marleasing contends in the main [proceedings].

16. [It] is clear from the rules on nullity in the [directive] and also from the other rules set out therein concerning the disclosure and validity of commitments entered into by a company that the objective of 'protecting the interests of third parties' (second recital in the preamble to the directive) must be reinforced in an expanded market as regards companies which have no safeguards they can offer to third parties other than their assets (first and third recitals in the preamble). The rules on nullity themselves, reflecting the need 'to limit the cases in which nullity can arise and the retroactive effect of a declaration of nullity', are designed 'in order to ensure certainty in the law as regards relations between the company and third parties, and also between members' (sixth recital in the preamble).

In those circumstances, it seems clear to me that each ground of nullity, even taken on its own, must be given a narrow interpretation with a view to protecting the interests of third parties – that is to say the company's creditors – and that a declaration of nullity as a result of infringements arising from the contractual relationship between the members of the company or between the members and the company is a penalty which must be avoided as far as possible. That does not rule out either the possibility or desirability of penalising such infringements in a different manner which does not jeopardise the existence of the company and is less detrimental to its creditors.

Accordingly, I consider that the phrase 'the objects of the company' in Article 11(2)(b) of the directive must be understood as meaning the company's objects as described and disclosed in the instrument of incorporation or the statutes. [Only] where the objects, in that sense, 'are unlawful or contrary to public policy' can a declaration of nullity of the company be made. An aim for which the company was incorporated but which is not stated in the instrument of incorporation or the statutes, for example to defraud the members' creditors, cannot have that consequence.

. . .

19. [As] stated earlier (paragraph 12), the [directive] does not affect other penalties provided for by national law in those circumstances, and the creditors retain, for instance, the possibility of bringing an action to set aside in their interests any capital contribution made in disregard of their rights. Such an action will usually be more effective in protecting their interests than a declaration of nullity of the company [itself].

The European Court of Justice (at pp 4158–4160)

4. The national court observed that in accordance with [the Accession Treaty whereby Spain joined the Community], the Kingdom of Spain was under an obligation to bring the directive into effect as from the date of accession, but that that had still not been done at the date of the order for reference. Taking the view, therefore, that the dispute raised a problem concerning the interpretation of Community law, the national court referred the following question to the Court:

Is Article 11 of [Directive 68/151] which has not been implemented in national law, directly applicable so as to preclude a declaration of nullity of a public limited company on a ground other than those set out in the said Article?

...

6. With regard to the question whether an individual may rely on the directive against a national law, it should be observed that, as the court has consistently held, a directive may not of itself impose obligations on an individual and, consequently, a provision of a directive may not be relied upon as such against such a person ([*Marshall* **[C27]**]).

7. However, it is apparent [that] the national court seeks in substance to ascertain whether a national court hearing a case which falls within the scope of Directive 68/151 is required to interpret its national law in the light of the wording and the purpose of that directive in order to preclude a declaration of nullity of a public limited company on a ground other than those listed in Article 11 of the directive.

8. In order to reply to that question, it should be observed that, as the court pointed out in [*von Colson* **[C29]**], the Member States' obligation arising from a directive to achieve the result envisaged by the directive and their duty under Article 5 [EEC] to take all appropriate measures, whether general or particular, to ensure the fulfilment of that obligation, is binding on all the authorities of Member States including, for matters within their jurisdiction, the courts. It follows that, in applying national law, whether the provisions in question were adopted before or after the directive, the national court called upon to interpret it is required to do so, as far as possible, in the light of the wording and the purpose of the directive in order to achieve the result pursued by the latter and thereby comply with [Article 189(3)].

9. It follows that the requirement that national law must be interpreted in conformity with Article 11 of Directive 68/151 precludes the interpretation of provisions of national law relating to public limited companies in such a manner that the nullity of a public limited company may be ordered on grounds other than those exhaustively listed in Article 11 of the directive in question.

10. With regard to the interpretation to be given to Article 11 of the directive, in particular Article 11(2)(b), it should be observed that that provision

prohibits the laws of Member States from providing for a judicial declaration of nullity on grounds other than those exhaustively listed in the directive, amongst which is the ground that the objects of the company are unlawful or contrary to public policy.

11. According to the Commission, the expression 'objects of the company' must be interpreted as referring exclusively to the objects of the company as described in the instrument of incorporation or the articles of association. It follows, in the Commission's view, that a declaration of nullity of a company cannot be made on the basis of the activity actually pursued by it, for instance defrauding the founder's creditors.

12. That argument must be upheld. As is clear from the preamble to Directive 68/151, its purpose was to limit the cases in which nullity can arise and the retroactive effect of a declaration of nullity in order to ensure 'certainty in the law as regards relations between the company and third parties, and also between members' (sixth recital). Furthermore, the protection of third parties 'must be ensured by provisions which restrict to the greatest possible extent the grounds on which obligations entered into in the name of the company are not valid'. It follows, therefore, that each ground of nullity provided for in Article 11 of the directive must be interpreted strictly. In those circumstances the words 'objects of the company' must be understood as referring to the objects of the company as described in the instrument of incorporation or the articles of association.

13. The answer to the question submitted must therefore be that a national court hearing a case which falls within the scope of Directive 68/151 is required to interpret its national law in the light of the wording and purpose of that directive in order to preclude a declaration of nullity of a public limited company on a ground other than those listed in Article 11 of the directive.

[C32]   Case 222/84 Marguerite Johnston v Chief Constable of the Royal Ulster Constabulary [1986] ECR 1651

[Within Northern Ireland, the United Kingdom measures taken to implement the provisions of Directive 76/207 (the directive which lays down rules to eliminate sex discrimination and seeks to implement the principle of equal treatment as between men and women with regard to access to employment) were contained in the Sex Discrimination (Northern Ireland) Order 1976 (SI 1976 No 1042). Article 53(1) of the order provided that none of its provisions prohibiting discrimination 'shall render unlawful an act done for the purpose of safeguarding national security or of protecting public safety or public order' and Article 53(2) provided that a 'certificate signed by or on behalf of the Secretary of State and certifying that an act specified in the certificate was done for the purposes mentioned in paragraph (1) shall be conclusive evidence that it was done for that purpose'.

Because of the large number of police officers assassinated in Northern Ireland over a number of years, the Chief Constable of the Royal Ulster Constabulary (the 'RUC') considered that he could not maintain the normal practice whereby police officers do not as a general rule carry firearms in the performance of their duties (a practice where no distinction was made between men and women). The Chief Constable decided that, in the RUC and the RUC Reserve, men should carry firearms in the regular course of their duties but that women would not be equipped with firearms and would not receive training in the handling and use of firearms. He also decided, in 1980, that the number of women in the RUC was sufficient for the particular tasks generally assigned to women officers. He took the view that general police duties, frequently involving operations requiring the carrying of firearms, should no longer be assigned to women and decided not to offer or renew any more contracts for women in the RUC full-time Reserve, except where they had to perform duties assigned only to women officers. Mrs Johnston had been a member of the RUC full-time Reserve from 1974 to 1980 and had efficiently performed the general duties of a uniformed police officer (acting as station duty officer, taking part in mobile patrols, driving patrol vehicles and assisting in searching persons brought to the police station). She was not armed when carrying out those duties and was ordinarily accompanied in duties outside the police station by an armed male officer. In 1980 the Chief Constable refused to renew her contract because of his new policy (above) with regard to female members of the RUC full-time Reserve. Mrs Johnston brought an action before an industrial tribunal challenging the decision to refuse to renew her contract and to give her training in the handling of firearms. In the proceedings before the industrial tribunal the Chief Constable produced a certificate issued by the Secretary of State for Northern Ireland in which the Secretary of State certified, in accordance with Article 53 (above) that 'the act consisting of the refusal of the Royal Ulster Constabulary to offer further full-time employment to [Mrs Johnston] in the Royal Ulster Constabulary Reserve was done for the purpose of: (a) safeguarding national security; and (b) protecting public safety and public order'.

Article 6 of Directive 76/207 provides that 'Member States shall introduce into their national legal systems such measures as are necessary to enable all persons who consider themselves wronged by failure to apply to them the principle of equal treatment [to] pursue their claims by judicial process after possible recourse to other competent authorities.' Mrs Johnston argued, inter alia, that Article 53(2) of the Northern Ireland Order (above) was contrary to Article 6 inasmuch as it prevented the industrial tribunal (and any higher appellate court) from exercising any effective judicial control over compliance with the provisions of the directive and with the national legislation intended to put into effect that directive.]

Opinion of Advocate General Darmon (at pp 1656–1658)

The right to obtain a judicial determination

3. Although the principle of legality is the cornerstone of the rule of law, it does not exclude consideration of the demands of public order. Indeed, they must be accommodated in order to ensure the survival of the state, whilst at the same time arbitrary action must be prevented. Review by the courts is a fundamental safeguard against such action; the right to challenge a measure before the courts is inherent in the rule of law.

Formed of states based on the rule of law, the European Community is necessarily a Community of law. It was created and works on the understanding that all Member States will show equal respect for the Community legal order.

Consequently, and subject to review by the courts, the Community legal order expressly incorporates the concept of public order so as to reconcile the proper functioning of the common market with the necessity for the Member States to cope with emergencies which threaten their vital [interests].

4. The Treaty, like the case law of the Court of Justice, therefore lays down the fundamental rule – a corollary of the principle of legality – that, whilst the demands of public order may be allowed to modify the scope of judicial review, they cannot override the actual right to obtain a judicial determination.

Therefore, a provision of national law, purportedly based on considerations of public order, which excluded the very possibility of such review, would, in my opinion, be incompatible with the Community legal order. By removing measures taken by the Member States from the ambit of Community law – primary, secondary or such as implemented by national laws – such a provision would in fact allow the national authorities to create a 'no-go area for the law' as and when they saw fit, thus calling in question the very foundations of that legal order.

[The Advocate General cited Article 6 (above).]

In its judgment in [*von Colson* **[C29]**] the court held that 'by granting applicants for a post who have been discriminated against recourse to the courts, [Article 6] acknowledges that those candidates have rights of which they may avail themselves before the [courts]'.

The court went on to conclude that as an authority of a Member State a national court which is confronted by a provision of national legislation compromising the effectiveness of an obligation arising under a directive (in that case Directive 76/207) and which has a 'duty under Article 5 of the Treaty to take all appropriate measures, whether general or particular, to ensure the fulfilment of that obligation' [must] 'interpret and apply the legislation [in] conformity with the requirements of Community [law]'.

It follows that a national court cannot, without infringing Article 5 of the Treaty and the directive, hold itself bound by a provision of national law which purports to exclude on the grounds of public order all judicial review of the implementation of Community legislation.

That duty of the national court is even more categorical where, as in this case, it is acting as an ordinary court responsible for applying Community law, in which regard it must be borne in mind that the provisions of Article 6, which are unconditional and sufficiently clear, unquestionably have direct effect. Consequently, the right of recourse to the courts for which Article 6 provides may be invoked by individuals in order to challenge any conflicting provision of national law; in this regard, the authority of the Chief Constable cannot be separated from that of the state which confers it upon him.

[The Advocate General cited *Simmenthal* **[C24]**, paragraph 22.]

I therefore consider that a Member State may not be allowed for reasons of public order to exclude all review by the courts of the legality of a national measure with regard to the provisions of Community law. Consequently, in such a situation a national court must [again referring to *Simmenthal*] 'give full effect to those provisions, if necessary refusing of its own motion to apply any conflicting provision of national [legislation]'.

The European Court of Justice (at pp 1681–1691)

The right to an effective judicial remedy

13. It is therefore necessary to examine [whether] Community law, and more particularly Directive 76/207, requires the Member States to ensure that their national courts and tribunals exercise effective control over compliance with the provisions of the directive and with the national legislation intended to put it into effect.

14. In Mrs Johnston's view, a provision such as [Article 53(2)] is contrary to Article 6 of the directive inasmuch as it prevents the competent national court or tribunal from exercising any judicial control.

15. The United Kingdom observes that Article 6 of the directive does not require the Member States to submit to judicial review every question which may arise in the application of the directive, even where national security and public safety are involved. Rules of evidence such as the rule laid down in [Article 53(2)] are quite common in national procedural law. Their justification is that matters of national security and public safety can be satisfactorily assessed only by the competent political authority, namely the minister who issues the certificate in question.

16. The Commission takes the view that to treat the certificate of a minister as having an effect such as that provided for in [Article 53(2)] is tantamount to refusing all judicial control or review and is therefore contrary to a fundamental principle of Community law and to Article 6 of the directive.

17. As far as this issue is concerned, it must be borne in mind first of all that Article 6 of the directive requires Member States to introduce into their internal legal systems such measures as are needed to enable all persons who consider themselves wronged by discrimination 'to pursue their claims by judicial process'. It follows from that provision that the Member States must take measures which are sufficiently effective to achieve the aim of the directive and that they must ensure that the rights thus conferred may be effectively relied upon before the national courts by the persons concerned.

18. The requirement of judicial control stipulated by that article reflects a general principle of law which underlies the constitutional traditions common to the Member States. That principle is also laid down in Articles 6 and 13 of the European Convention for the Protection of Human Rights and Fundamental [Freedoms]. As the European Parliament, Council and Commission recognised in their Joint Declaration **[B40]** [and] as the court has recognised in its decisions, the principles on which that Convention is based must be taken into consideration in Community law.

19. By virtue of Article 6 of Directive 76/207, interpreted in the light of the general principle stated above, all persons have the right to obtain an effective remedy in a competent court against measures which they consider to be contrary to the principle of equal treatment for men and women laid down in the directive. It is for the Member States to ensure effective judicial control as regards compliance with the applicable provisions of Community law and of national legislation intended to give effect to the rights for which the directive provides.

20. A provision which, like [Article 53(2)], requires a certificate such as the one in question in the present case to be treated as conclusive

evidence that the conditions for derogating from the principle of equal treatment are fulfilled allows the competent authority to deprive an individual of the possibility of asserting by judicial process the rights conferred by the directive. Such a provision is therefore contrary to the principle of effective judicial control laid down in Article 6 of the directive.

21. The answer to [the question] put by the industrial tribunal must therefore be that the principle of effective judicial control laid down in Article 6 of [Directive 76/207] does not allow a certificate issued by a national authority stating that the conditions for derogating from the principle of equal treatment for men and women for the purpose of protecting public safety are satisfied to be treated as conclusive evidence so as to exclude the exercise of any power of review by the courts.

. . .

[On the role of the national court]

39. By reason of the division of jurisdiction provided for in Article 177 of the EEC Treaty, it is for the national court to say whether the reasons on which the Chief Constable based his decision are in fact well founded and justify the specific measure taken in Mrs Johnston's case. It is also for the national court to ensure that the principle of proportionality is observed and to determine whether the refusal to renew Mrs Johnston's contract could not be avoided by allocating to women duties which, without jeopardising the aims pursued, can be performed without firearms.

. . .

[On the question of interpretation]

53. [It] should be observed [that], as the court has already stated in [*von Colson* [C29]], the Member States' obligation under a directive to achieve the result envisaged by that directive and their duty under Article 5 of the Treaty [is] binding on all the authorities of Member States including, for matters within their jurisdiction, the courts. It follows that, in applying national law, and in particular the provisions of national legislation specifically introduced in order to implement Directive 76/207, national courts are required to interpret their national law in the light of the wording and purpose of the directive in order to achieve the result referred to in [Article 189(3)]. It is therefore for the industrial tribunal to interpret the provisions of the [Northern Ireland] Order, and in particular Article 53(1) thereof, in the light of the provisions of the directive [in] order to give it its full effect.

[On the meaning of the 'state']

56. The court also held in [*Marshall* [C27]] that individuals may rely on the directive as against an organ of the state whether it acts *qua* employer or *qua* public authority. As regards an authority like the Chief Constable, it must be observed that [the] Chief Constable is an official responsible for the direction of the police service. Whatever its relations may be with other organs of the state, such a public authority, charged by the state with the maintenance of public order and safety, does not act as a private individual. It may not take advantage of the failure of the state, of which it is an emanation, to comply with Community law.

[C33]   Cases C-6, 9/90 Francovich, Bonifaci (and others) v Republic of Italy 19 November 1991 (not yet reported: translation of transcript: not authentic)

[Directive 80/987 was adopted in order to provide employed workers with a Community minimum level of protection in the event of the insolvency of their employer and, in particular, it provided for specific guarantees of payments of workers' outstanding claims relating to remuneration and the establishment of bodies (guarantee institutions) liable to meet those claims. Member States were obliged to bring into force laws, regulations and administrative measures to implement the directive within a prescribed period which expired on 23 October 1983. As the Republic of Italy, once again, did not fulfil the obligation, the Commission finally brought an action under Article 169 and the Court of Justice once again found that the Republic of Italy had failed to comply with a Treaty obligation (Case 22/87 *Commission of the European Communities v Republic of Italy* [1989] ECR 143). Francovich had been employed by a company in Vicenza and had only received part payment of his salary at sporadic intervals. He sued the company before the Pretura di Vicenza which found the company liable for the sum of some 6m lire. The Vicenza court was unable to enforce judgment against the company and Francovich, therefore, relied on his entitlement provided for by Directive 80/987 to obtain the guarantee payment. Bonifaci and other workers brought an action before the Pretura di Bassano del Grappa, stating that they had been employed by a company which had been declared bankrupt on 5 April 1985. When the employment relationship came to an end, the plaintiffs were owed more than 253m lire which was included in the liabilities of the bankrupt company. More than five years after the bankruptcy they had received no payment and the official dealing with the bankruptcy stated that payment of even part of the sum owed was utterly improbable. Consequently, the plaintiffs brought proceedings against the Republic of Italy requesting, in the light of the obligation imposed on the Republic to implement Directive 80/987 as from 23 October 1983, that the Republic be ordered to pay the claimed payments of unpaid remuneration, at least for the last three months, or failing that, that the Republic be ordered to pay them monetary compensation. Both national courts referred, inter alia, to the Court of Justice the following question, identical in both cases, for a preliminary ruling:

    1. By virtue of the Community law in force, can an individual who has suffered harm as a result of the failure by the State to implement Directive 80/987, which failure has been established by a judgment of the Court of Justice, call for the implementation by the State of those provisions contained in the directive which are sufficiently precise and unconditional by invoking directly, against the Member State in default, the Community rules in order to obtain the guarantees which that Member State has to ensure, and, in any event, to claim compensation for the damage suffered in respect of provisions which do not have that character?]

The European Court of Justice

    9. The [question] referred by the national court raises two problems, which it will be convenient to examine separately. On the one hand, the

question concerns the direct effect of those provisions of the directive which define the rights of workers and, on the other hand, the question concerns the existence and extent of the liability of the state for damages arising out of the breach of obligations imposed on it under Community law.

On the direct effect of the provisions of the directive which define the rights of workers

10. The first part of the first question referred by the national court seeks to ascertain whether the provisions of the directive which define the rights of workers must be interpreted in the sense that the parties may rely on these rights against Member States before a national court when no steps have been taken to implement these provisions within the prescribed period.

11. According to established case law, a Member State which has not adopted the implementing measures required by the directive within the prescribed period may not plead, as against individuals, its own failure to perform the obligations which the directive entails. Thus wherever the provisions of a directive appear, as far as their subject matter is concerned, to be unconditional and sufficiently precise, those provisions may, in the absence of implementing measures adopted within the prescribed period, be relied upon as against any national provision which is incompatible with the directive or in so far as the provisions define rights which individuals are able to assert against the [state].

12. It is therefore necessary to examine whether the provisions of Directive 80/987 which define the rights of workers are unconditional and sufficiently precise. This examination must cover three aspects, namely, the determination of the beneficiaries of the guarantee which is envisaged, the content of that guarantee, and, finally, the identity of the body liable for the guarantee. In this respect there is posed in particular the question whether the Member State can be held liable under the guarantee on the grounds that it has not taken, within the prescribed period, the necessary measures for the transposition of the directive into national law.

[(a)   The determination of the beneficiaries of the guarantee which is envisaged]

13. First, as far as the question of the beneficiaries of the guarantee is concerned, it must be noted that according to Article 1(1), the directive applies to claims of employed workers arising from contracts of employment or employment relationships and existing against employers who are in a state of insolvency within the meaning of Article 2(1), which provision specifies the situations in which an employer must be deemed to be in a state of insolvency. Article 2(2) refers to national law for the definition of the terms 'employed worker' and 'employer'. Finally Article 1(2) provides that Member States may, exceptionally and under certain conditions, exclude from the scope of the directive certain categories of workers listed in the annex to the directive.

14. These conditions are sufficiently precise and unconditional to allow a national judge to determine whether a person must or must not be considered as a beneficiary under the directive. In fact, the judge has only to verify, on the one hand, whether the person concerned has the status of employed worker by virtue of national law and whether he is not excluded from the scope of the directive under Article 1(2) and Annex I [and] then, on

the other hand, whether there is found to exist one of the situations of a state of insolvency listed in Article 2 of the directive.

[(b) The content of the guarantee]
15. In so far as it concerns, next, the content of the guarantee, Article 3 of the directive provides that there must be ensured the payment of the outstanding claims resulting from contracts of employment or employment relationships relating to remuneration for the period prior to a date determined by the Member State. In this respect, the Member State may choose between three possibilities, namely, (a) the date of the onset of the employer's insolvency; (b) that of the notice of dismissal of the employed worker concerned issued because of the employer's insolvency; (c) that of the onset of the employer's insolvency or that of the ending of the contract of employment or the employment relationship of the employed worker concerned, occasioned by the employer's insolvency.

16. Because of this choice, Member States have the option, by virtue of Article 4(1) and (2), to limit the liability to pay to periods of three months or eight weeks, as the case may be, calculated according to the methods detailed in the said article. Finally, Article 4(3) provides that the Member States may fix a ceiling for the guaranteed payment in order to avoid the payment of sums going beyond the social objectives of the directive. When they exercise this option, the Member States must inform the Commission of the methods according to which they have fixed this ceiling. Furthermore, Article 10 provides that the directive can not affect the option of Member States to take the measures necessary to avoid abuses or, in particular, to refuse or reduce the liability to make payments in certain circumstances.

17. Article 3 of the directive thus leaves a choice to the Member States to determine the date from which the guarantee of payment of claims must be ensured. Nevertheless, as it already follows impliedly from the case law of the [court], the option for the Member State, to choose between a multiplicity of possible methods in order to achieve the result required by a directive does not exclude the possibility, for individuals, of relying before the national courts on rights whose content can be determined with sufficient precision by reference to the provisions of the directive alone.

18. In the present case the result which the directive in question requires is the guarantee of payment to employed workers of the outstanding claims in the event of the insolvency of the employer. The fact that Articles 3 and 4(1) and (2) permit Member States a certain margin of discretion with regard to the methods of fixing this guarantee and the limitation of its amount does not affect the precise and unconditional character of the result required.

19. In fact, as the Commission and the plaintiffs have noted, it is possible to determine the minimum guarantee provided for by the directive based on the date the choice of which will entail the least burden for the guarantee institution. This date is the date of the onset of the employer's insolvency, given that the two other dates, namely, that of the notice of dismissal of the employed worker and that of the ending of the contract of employment or the employment relationship, are, according to the conditions imposed by Article 3, necessarily later than the onset of the employer's insolvency and therefore produce a longer period during which the payment of claims must be ensured.

20. As far as the option, provided by Article 4(2), to limit this guarantee is concerned, it should be noted that such an option does not prevent the determination of the minimum guarantee. In fact, it follows from the wording of this article that the Member States have the option to limit the guarantees accorded to employed workers to certain periods prior to the date provided in Article 3. These periods are fixed by reference to each one of the three dates listed in Article 3 with the result that it is possible, in any event, to determine how far the Member State would have been able to reduce the guarantee provided by the directive according to the date it would have chosen if it had implemented the directive.

21. With regard to Article 4(3), according to which Member States may fix a ceiling for the guarantee of payment in order to avoid the payment of sums going beyond the social objectives of the directive, and Article 10, which states that the directive can not affect the option of the Member States to take the measures necessary to avoid abuses, it should be noted that a Member State which has failed to fulfil its obligation to implement a directive, cannot frustrate the rights arising under the directive for the benefit of individuals by relying on the option to limit the amount of the guarantee which it would have been able to exercise if it had taken the necessary steps to implement the [directive].

22. It must therefore be stated that the provisions in question are unconditional and sufficiently precise in so far as they concern content of the guarantee.

[(c)   The identity of the body liable for the guarantee]
23. Finally, with regard to the identity of the body liable for the guarantee, Article 5 of the directive provides:

> Member States shall lay down rules for the organisation, financing and operation of the guarantee institutions, observing in particular the following principles:
> (a)   the assets of the institutions must be independent of the employers' operating capital and be established in such a way that they cannot be seized during the course of proceedings for insolvency;
> (b)   employers must contribute to financing, at least to the extent that this is not fully covered by the public authorities;
> (c)   the payment obligation of the institutions must exist independently of the obligations to contribute to financing.

24. It was submitted that, because the directive provides for the possibility of complete financing of guarantee institutions by the public authorities, it would be unacceptable for a Member State to frustrate the effects of the directive by alleging that it could have made other persons to bear part or all of the financial obligation imposed on it.

25. This argument cannot be accepted. It follows from the wording of the directive that the Member State is obliged to organise the whole of the appropriate guarantee institutional system. By virtue of Article 5, the Member State enjoys a wide margin of discretion with regard to the organisation, the functioning and the financing of the guarantee institutions. It must be emphasised that the fact, raised by the Commission, that the directive envisages as a possibility, among others, that such a system would be completely financed by the public authorities cannot mean that the state

may be identified as the body liable for the outstanding claims. The obligation to make payment is imposed on the guarantee institutions and it is only in exercising its power to organise the guarantee system that the state may provide for the complete financing of the guarantee institutions by the public authorities. In that situation the state would assume an obligation which was not in principle its own.

26. It follows that, even if the provisions in question of the directive are sufficiently precise and unconditional with regard to the determination of the beneficiaries of the guarantee and the content of that guarantee, these elements are not sufficient to allow individuals to rely on those provisions before the national courts. In effect, on the one hand, these provisions do not precisely identify the body liable for the guarantee and, on the other hand, the state cannot be considered as the liable body merely because it has not, within the prescribed period, taken steps to implement the directive.

27. It must therefore be stated in reply to the first part of the [question] that the provisions of Directive 80/987 which define the rights of workers must be interpreted as meaning that the parties cannot rely on those rights against the Member State before the national courts, when the state has failed to take the necessary measures to implement the directive within the prescribed period.

On the liability of the state for damages arising out of the breach of obligations imposed the state by virtue of Community law

28. By the second part of the [question] the national court seeks to ascertain whether a Member State is under an obligation to make good damage caused to individuals arising out of the failure to implement Directive 80/987.

29. The national court thus poses the problem of the existence and the extent of the liability of the state for damages arising out of the breach of obligations imposed on it by virtue of Community law.

30. This problem must be examined in the light of the general scheme and fundamental principles of the Treaty.

(a) On the principle of the liability of the state

31. It must be recalled first of all that the EEC Treaty has created its own legal order, integrated into the legal systems of the Member States and which is binding on their courts, whose subjects are not only the Member States, but equally their nationals, and that, although it creates obligations on individuals, Community law also creates rights which form part of their legal heritage; these rights arise not only when explicit reference is made to them by the Treaty, but also by reason of the obligations which the Treaty clearly imposes as much on individuals as on Member States and on Community institutions (see [*van Gend* **[C22]**, *Costa* **[C13]**]).

32. It should equally be recalled that, just as it follows from established case law, it falls to the national courts, entrusted to apply, within the framework of their jurisdiction, the provisions of Community law, to ensure the full effect of those legal norms and to protect the rights which they confer on individuals (see in particular [*Simmenthal* **[C24]**, *Factortame* **[C48]**]).

33. It should be stated that the full effectiveness of Community provisions would be jeopardised and the protection of the rights they recognise would be weakened if individuals did not have the possibility to obtain compensation when their rights are infringed by a breach of Community law attributable to a Member State.

34. The possibility of obtaining compensation from the Member State is particularly essential when, as in the present case, the full effect of Community legal norms is conditional on the state taking certain actions and, in consequence, individuals cannot, in the absence of such action being taken, rely before the national courts on the rights which are accorded to them by Community law.

35. It follows that the principle of the liability of the state for damage caused to individuals by breaches of Community law for which it is responsible is inherent in the scheme of the Treaty.

36. The obligation, for Member States, to make good such damage also finds its basis in Article 5 of the Treaty, by virtue of which the Member States are bound to take all appropriate measures, whether general or particular, to ensure fulfilment of the obligations arising by virtue of Community law. Amongst these obligations is found the obligation to obviate the unlawful consequences of a breach of Community [law].

37. It follows from the foregoing that Community law lays down the principle according to which the Member States are obliged to make good the damage caused to individuals by breaches of Community law for which they are responsible.

(b)   On conditions of the liability of the state

38. If the liability of the state is thus imposed by Community law, the conditions in which Community law opens up a right to compensation depend on the nature of the breach of Community law which is the origin of the damage caused.

39. When, as in the present case, a Member State fails to fulfil the obligation imposed on it by virtue of Article [189(3)] to take all the necessary measures to achieve the result required by a directive, the full effectiveness of this provision of Community law imposes a right to compensation as soon as three conditions are satisfied.

40. The first of these conditions is that the result required by the directive includes the conferring of rights for the benefit of individuals. The second condition is that the content of these rights can be identified by reference to the provisions of the directive. Finally, the third condition is the existence of a causal link between the breach of the obligation imposed on the state and the damage suffered by the injured persons.

41. These conditions are sufficient to give rise to the benefit of individuals to obtain compensation, which is based directly on Community law.

42. Subject to this, it is within the framework of the national law on liability that there is imposed on the state the duty to make good the consequences of the damage caused. Accordingly, in the absence of Community rules on this matter, it is for the domestic legal system of each Member State to designate the courts having jurisdiction and to determine the procedural rules governing legal actions intended to ensure the complete protection of the rights which parties may enjoy under Community [law].

43. It must also be noted that the conditions, both as to substance and form, laid down by the various national laws relating to compensation for damage must be no less favourable than those which concern similar claims under national law and they must not be arranged so as to render the recovery of damages impossible in practice or excessively [difficult].

44. In this case, the breach of Community law on the part of a Member

State by reason of the non-implementation of Directive 80/987 within the prescribed period has been established by a judgment of the court. The result required by this directive includes the conferring on employed workers of the right to a guarantee for the payment of their outstanding claims relating to remuneration. Thus, it follows from the examination of the first part of the first question that the content of this right can be determined by reference to the provisions of the directive.

45. In these conditions, it is for the national courts to ensure within the framework of national law on liability, the right of employed workers to obtain compensation for the damage they have suffered by reason of the non-implementation of the directive.

47. The reply to the national court must therefore be that a Member State is liable to make good the damage resulting for individuals from the non-implementation of Directive 80/987.

[**Stop press**: *Francovich* is reported at [1991] ECR I-5357.]

SECTION FOUR

THE INCORPORATION OF COMMUNITY LAW (THE UNITED KINGDOM)

The United Kingdom had not played any positive part in the creation of the European Economic Community, but, fearing that the creation of the Community might have harmful effects, by the elimination of trade barriers within the Community and the creation by that Community of trade barriers against other countries, helped to create the European Free Trade Area in conjunction with Austria, Denmark, Norway, Portugal, Sweden and Switzerland. Gradually several of the seven decided to seek entry to the European Economic Community. As the United Kingdom White Paper (1971, Cmnd 4715) put it: 'It is generally agreed that for advanced industrial countries the most favourable environment is one where markets are large and are free from barriers to [trade]. In particular, the development and exploitation of modern industrial technology, upon which so much of our employment and income increasingly depends, requires greater resources for research and development and wider markets than any one Western European nation can provide'. The United Kingdom, Ireland and Denmark joined the Community on 1 January 1973. The United Kingdom Constitution was to be changed by a rather abrupt and dramatic process, because (as was seen in Chapter Two) the aims of economic integration had resulted in the Treaty of Rome itself containing constitutional and legal implications which had had (and would continue to have) resounding effects of the constitutions of all Member States. By the time the United Kingdom became a Member State, the principle of supremacy of Community law had become an accepted fundamental constitutional part of Community law **[C34]**.

The incorporation of Community law (as it had been created and developed by and within the original Member States) presented three specific problems to the United Kingdom Constitution. The first was the traditional approach of United Kingdom constitutional law that treaties do not automatically become part of United Kingdom law upon their making or even ratification. The second was that the United Kingdom had to provide for the incorporation of an already well developed system of Community law which had provided for the rule-making capacity of the Treaties and of the secondary legislation created by Community institutions, the provisions for preliminary rulings, the principles of direct applicability and direct effect and, above all, the limited cessation of national sovereignty in favour of the supremacy of Community law. The third related to the traditional view, sometimes referred to as Parliamentary Supremacy, whereby any Act of Parliament may alter previous Acts of Parliament, with the consequence that no current Parliament may bind its successors as to the content of future Acts of Parliament.

The constitutional mechanism utilised was, as it had to be in a country without a written constitution, an Act of Parliament, the European Communities Act 1972 **[C35]**. This provides for the fulfilment of all 'Community obligations', which are obligations arising by or under 'the treaties'. The Act recognised the rule-making capacity of both the treaties and secondary legislation within the United Kingdom and incorporates the supremacy of Community law (past, present or future) over domestic law, but does not purport to bind the United Kingdom to everlasting membership of the Community. Existing legislation which was incompatible with Community obligations was repealed. Incorporation of the ever developing Community law within the United Kingdom could, of course, be achieved by a series of Acts of Parliament similar to the European Communities Act. However, incorporation is achieved in practical and pragmatic terms in two ways.

First, by giving power to amend existing legislation (or to create new legislation) by means of statutory instruments. This means that the government can act quickly and without the need to pass an Act of Parliament every time legislative action is necessary to fulfil a Treaty obligation. This power may even be used to amend an existing Act of Parliament. However, in order to implement certain matters, the measure used must be an Act of Parliament. The United Kingdom has, on a number of occasions, been declared to have failed to fulfil a Community obligation and has responded by amending United Kingdom legislation (see *Invalid care allowance* [C36] and *Pickstone* [C43]). An interesting constitutional innovation is provided by the Consumer Protection Act 1987 [C37]. When the President of the Court of Justice ordered an interim measure, the United Kingdom complied (*Factortame* [C47]).

Secondly, the courts are expressly directed to interpret Community law in accordance with the principles laid down by and any relevant decisions of the Court of Justice and, of course, the most significant of such principles are the uniform application of Community law and the supremacy of Community law over domestic law. Where there is a conflict between a Community rule and a United Kingdom rule, a United Kingdom court must interpret the United Kingdom rule in accordance with Community law.

The European Communities Act has permitted the United Kingdom courts to react to the legislation and case law of the Community as and when that legislation was enacted and that case law developed. It is perhaps fortunate that the problems of incorporation of Community law have been posed in a sequence of situations which has permitted a pragmatic and gradualist series of solutions. An early example of a straightforward case of using primary and secondary Community legislation to produce a conclusion not readily apparent on the face of national legislation is provided by Social Security Decision *R(A) 2/78* [C38].

Perhaps the strangeness of drafting of Community legislation and the method of case law interpretation has, after a shaky start, made the courts very aware of the need to seek preliminary rulings (*Samex* [C39], *Henn* [C40], *Conegate* [E30]). In *Plymouth Justices* [C41], the Court of Appeal took note of *Rheinmühlen* [C18] in discussing the role of a magistrates' court and a request for a preliminary ruling. In *Factortame* [C47], the House of Lords based their decision to refer questions for a preliminary ruling on *Cilfit* [C19]. On the reception by the United Kingdom courts of replies by the Court of Justice, see *Foster* [C42], *Factortame* [C49] and *Santillo* [D49]. The United Kingdom courts have readily accepted the developing doctrines of individual protection discussed in Section Three of this chapter. In *Pickstone* [C43], the House of Lords referred to the principle of interpretation laid down in *von Colson* [C29]. *Bourgoin* [C44] was determined on the then perceived interpretation on non-contractual liability of Community institutions, but, following *Francovich* [C33], was severely doubted in *Kirklees* [C46].

Finally, the House of Lords was prepared to 'disapply' an Act of Parliament in order to give effective enjoyment of the remedy of interim relief in *Factortame* **[C47]**, **[C48]**, **[C49]**.

If, however, there is still a conflict between a rule emanating from the Community and a rule emanating from Westminster or Whitehall and that conflict is not settled by the formal amendment of the United Kingdom rule, we come to the problem posed by the constitutional practice of the Supremacy of Parliament. If it appears that the United Kingdom has deliberately legislated (or failed to legislate) contrary to Community law, the United Kingdom courts are faced with answering the constitutional impasse, thus created. The status of the European Communities Act within the United Kingdom is that of an ordinary Act of Parliament (albeit a rather important one) and the status of the Community law thereby incorporated could be regarded as a form of delegated legislation (albeit of a very special kind). If the United Kingdom were to take the unlikely step of withdrawing from the Community by repealing the European Communities Act, then the courts would follow their traditional role and accept the repealing legislation. The real question is whether and to what extent a deliberate enactment of a rule conflicting with Community law would be interpreted as an implied repeal of not only that subject matter which was in direct conflict but also, in view of the doctrine of supremacy of Community law, of that doctrine itself. That lies in the future.

MATERIALS

[C34]   Commission Opinion of 19 January 1972

Commission Opinion of 19 January 1972 on the application for Accession to the European Communities by the Kingdom of Denmark, Ireland, the Kingdom of Norway, and the United Kingdom of Great Britain and Northern Ireland.

[Whereas] in joining the Communities the applicant states accept without reserve the Treaties and their political objectives, all decisions taken since their entry into force, and the action that has been agreed in respect of the development and reinforcement of the Communities;

whereas it is an essential feature of the legal system set up by the Treaties establishing the Communities that certain of their provisions and certain acts of the Community institutions are directly applicable, that Community law takes precedence over any national provisions conflicting with it, and that procedures exist for ensuring the uniform interpretation of this law; and whereas accession to the Communities entails recognition of the binding force of those rules, observance of which is indispensable to guarantee the effectiveness and unity of Community [law].

[C35]   The European Communities Act 1972
[as amended]

PART I

2.–(1) All such rights, powers, liabilities, obligations and restrictions from time to time created or arising by or under the Treaties, and all such remedies and procedures from time to time provided for by or under the Treaties, as in accordance with the Treaties are without further enactment to be given legal effect or used in the United Kingdom, shall be recognised and available in law, and be enforced, allowed and followed accordingly; and the expression 'enforceable Community right' and similar expressions shall be read as referring to one to which this subsection applies.

(2) Subject to Schedule 2 to this Act, at any time after its passing Her Majesty may by Order in Council, and any designated Minister or department may by regulations, make provision –

(a)   for the purpose of implementing any Community obligation of the United Kingdom, or enabling any [rights] enjoyed or to be enjoyed by the United Kingdom under or by virtue of the Treaties to be exercised; or

(b)   for the purpose of dealing with matters arising out of or related to any such obligation or rights or the coming into force, or the operation from time to time, of subsection (1) above;

and in the exercise of any statutory power or duty, including any power to give directions or to legislate by means of orders, rules, regulations or other subordinate instrument, the person entrusted with the power or duty may have regard to the objects of the Communities and to any such obligation or rights as aforesaid.

. . .

(4) The provision that may be made under subsection (2) above includes, subject to Schedule 2 to this Act, any such provision (of any such extent) as might be made by Act of Parliament, and any enactment passed or to be passed, other than one contained in this Part of this Act, shall be construed and have effect subject to the foregoing provisions of this section; but, except as may be provided by any Act passed after this Act, Schedule 2 shall have effect in connection with the powers conferred by this and the following sections of this Act to make Orders in Council and regulations.

3.–(1) For the purposes of all legal proceedings any question as to the meaning or effect of any of the Treaties, or as to the validity, meaning or effect of any Community instrument, shall be treated as a question of law (and, if not referred to the European Court, be for determination as such in accordance with the principles laid down by and any relevant decision of the European Court or any court attached thereto).

(2) Judicial notice shall be taken of the Treaties, of the Official Journal of the Communities and of any decision of, or expression of opinion by, the European Court or any court attached thereto on any such question as aforesaid; and the Official Journal shall be admissible as evidence of any instrument or other act thereby communicated of any of the Communities or of any Community institution.

(3) Evidence of any instrument issued by a Community institution, including any judgment or order of the European Court or any court attached thereto, or of any document in the custody of a Community institution, or any entry in or extract from such a document, may be [given] by an official of that institution; and any document purporting to be such a copy shall be received in evidence without proof of the official position or handwriting of the person signing the certificate.

PART II

4.–(1) The enactments mentioned in Schedule 3 to this Act (being enactments that are superseded or to be superseded by reason of Community obligations and of the provision made by this Act in relation thereto or are not compatible with Community obligations) are hereby repealed [and] in the enactments mentioned in Schedule 4 to this Act there shall [be] made the amendments provided for by that Schedule.

. . .

SCHEDULE 2

1.–(1) The powers conferred by section 2(2) of this Act to make provision for the purposes mentioned in section 2(2)(a) and (b) shall not include power –

(a) to make any provision imposing or increasing taxation; or

(b) to make any provision taking effect from a date earlier than that of the making of the instrument containing the provision; or

(c) to confer any power to legislate by means of orders, rules, regulations or other subordinate instrument, other than rules of procedure for any court or tribunal; or

(d) to create any new criminal offence punishable [by more than specified limits].

. . .

2.–(1) [Where] a provision contained in any section of this Act confers power to make regulations (otherwise than by modification or extension of an existing power), the power shall be exercisable by statutory instrument.

(2) Any statutory instrument containing an Order in Council or regulations made in the exercise of a power so conferred, if made without a draft having been approved by resolution of each House of Parliament, shall be subject to annulment in pursuance of a resolution of either House.

[C36] Invalid care allowance

(a) Social Security Act 1975, s 37 (as enacted)

Invalid care allowance

37.–(1) Subject to the provisions of this section, a person shall be entitled to an invalid care allowance for any day on which he is engaged in caring for a severely disabled person if –

(a) he is regularly and substantially engaged in caring for that person; and
(b) he is not gainfully employed;

. . .

(3) A person shall not be entitled to an allowance under this section if he is under the age of 16 or receiving full-time education; and a woman shall not be entitled to any such allowance if –

(a) she is married and either -
    (i)   she is residing with her husband, or
    (ii) he is contributing to her maintenance at a weekly rate not less than the weekly rate of such an allowance; or
(b) she is cohabiting with a man as his wife.

(b) Directive 79/7 (equal treatment for men and women in matters of social security)

Article 1

The purpose of this directive is the progressive implementation, in the field of social security and other elements of social protection provided for in Article 3, of the principle of equal treatment for men and women in matters of social security, hereinafter referred to as 'the principle of equal treatment'.

Article 2

This directive shall apply to the working population – including self-employed persons, workers and self-employed persons whose activity is interrupted by illness, accident or involuntary unemployment and persons seeking employment – and to retired or invalided workers and self-employed persons.

Article 3

1. This directive shall apply to:

(a)　statutory schemes which provide protection against the following risks:
  - sickness,
  - invalidity,
  - old age,
  - accidents at work and occupational diseases,
  - unemployment.

. . .

Article 4

1. The principle of equal treatment means that there shall be no discrimination whatsoever on the ground of sex either directly, or indirectly by reference in particular to marital or family status, in particular as concerns:
  - the scope of the schemes and the conditions of access thereto,
  - the obligation to contribute and the calculation of contributions,
  - the calculation of benefits including increases due in respect of a spouse and for dependants and the conditions governing the duration and retention of entitlement to benefits.

2. The principle of equal treatment shall be without prejudice to the provisions relating to the protection of women on grounds of maternity.

(c)　Statement of the Secretary of State for Social Services (HC Deb, vol 100, cols 21–22, 23 June 1986)

Invalid care allowance is intended to help people who care for severely disabled people at home. It is a non-contributory benefit and depends on the claimant caring for the disabled person for at least 35 hours a week. It was introduced by the then Labour government in 1976 for men and single women who had given up their sole means of livelihood to look after a severely disabled relative. But the legislation specifically excluded married women from benefit. [A] case concerning their exclusion is now before the European Court of Justice. [The] government have therefore reviewed the exclusion and have decided that, irrespective of the European Court decision, the allowance should be extended to married women on the same terms as married men and single persons. Accordingly, the government will very shortly introduce an amendment to the Social Security Bill to achieve this.

(d)　Case 150/85 Drake v Chief Adjudication Officer [1986] ECR 1995

[Mrs Drake claimed invalid care allowance as she had given up work to look after her disabled mother. Her claim was refused since she was married and living with her husband. Two questions were referred to the European Court of Justice on the interpretation of Directive 79/7 (above). First, whether invalid care allowance came within the scope of the directive and, secondly, whether the condition that a married woman residing with her husband was not entitled to the allowance was discriminatory in view of the fact that married men did not have to meet a corresponding condition. The court answered the first question in the affirmative.]

The European Court of Justice (at pp 2010–2011)

27. Since question 1 has been answered in the affirmative, it is necessary to examine question 2, which concerns the issue whether discrimination on grounds of sex contrary to Article 4(1) of Directive 79/7 arises where legislation provides that a benefit which forms part of [the statutory scheme] referred to in Article 3(1) of the directive is not payable to a married woman who lives with or is maintained by her husband, although it is paid in corresponding circumstances to a married man.

28. Mrs Drake, the Commission and the Adjudication Officer all suggest that that question should be answered in the affirmative.

29. Mrs Drake and the Commission argue that the exclusion of married women from such a benefit, where married men residing with their wives are not excluded, constitutes a clear example of direct discrimination on grounds of sex.

30. The Adjudication Officer himself has recognised that the provision governing the benefit in question places certain categories of women (married women living with their husbands and women who live with a man as husband and wife) at a disadvantage by precluding them from obtaining that benefit.

31. It should be noted that Article 4(1) of Directive 79/7 provides that the implementation of the principle of equal treatment, with regard in particular to the scope of schemes and the conditions of access to them, means that there should be no discrimination whatsoever on grounds of sex.

32. That provision embodies the aim of the directive, set out in Article 1, that is to say the implementation, in the field of social security and between men and women, of the principle of equal treatment, a principle which the court has frequently described as fundamental.

33. It follows from the foregoing that a national provision such as that at issue before the Chief Social Security Commissioner is contrary to the aim, as stated above, of the directive, which under Article 189 of the Treaty is binding on the Member States as to the result to be achieved.

34. The answer to Question 2 must therefore be that discrimination on grounds of sex contrary to Article 4(1) of Directive 79/7 arises where legislation provides that a benefit which forms part of one of the statutory schemes referred to in Article 3(1) of that directive is not payable to a married woman who lives with or is maintained by her husband, although it is paid in corresponding circumstances to a married man.

(e) Statement of Baroness Trumpington (HL Deb, vol 478, cols 852–853)

[This] amendment fulfils the promise made in another place on 23 June by my right honourable friend the Secretary of State, and which I repeated in your Lordships' House. That promise was to bring forward in the Social

384 Community Law and the Member States

Security Bill legislation which would extend invalid care allowance to married women, and those living with a man as his wife, on equal terms with men and single women. The amendment [will] remove the discrimination against married women which the previous Labour government wrote into the Social Security Act 1975. It does so with retrospective effect from the date on which the directive came into force. As your Lordships will be aware, when we announced our decision on 23 June we did not know what the European Court would decide the following day and, in particular, what the court judgment would say about arrears. In the event, it was silent on the point. We concluded, however, that whatever the legal position about our obligation to pay arrears back to 22 December 1984, we would none the less do so. We have already received some 20,000 claims from married women, and the number is growing daily. We expect to have received an estimated 70,000 by the end of the year. We have decided that in the interests of fairness any married woman whose claim is received by 31 December 1986 will be able to have arrears back to 22 December 1984, if she satisfies all the conditions at that date.

(f) Social Security Act 1986

Invalid care allowance for women

37.–(1) Section 37(3) of the Social Security Act 1975 shall have effect, and shall be treated as having had effect from 22 December 1984, as if the words from 'and a woman' to the end were omitted.

[C37] Consumer Protection Act 1987

PART I

PRODUCT LIABILITY

1.–(1) This Part shall have effect for the purpose of making such provision as is necessary in order to comply with the product liability Directive and shall be construed accordingly.

(2) In this Part ['the] product liability Directive' means the Directive of the Council of the European Communities, dated 25th July 1985 (No 85/374/EEC), on the approximation of the laws, regulations and administrative provisions of the Member States concerning liability for defective products.

[C38] Social Security Commissioner Decision R(A) 2/78

[The claimant claimed attendance allowance (a benefit for disabled persons) and satisfied the disability conditions, but was refused the benefit because she did not satisfy the 'residence conditions' (below). The claimant was a citizen of the Irish Republic and her husband had at some time been an employed person in England. On his death, she returned to England on 18 October 1975.]

The Social Security Commissioner (at paras 5–11)

5. The residence conditions for an award of the attendance allowance [are] as follows:

(c) that [she] has been present in Great Britain for a period of, or periods amounting in the aggregate to, not less than 26 weeks in the 12 months immediately preceding [the day in respect of which the allowance is claimed]; and

(d) in the case of a person who is a British subject whose place of birth is not in the United [Kingdom], that [she] has been present in Great Britain for a period of, or periods amounting in the aggregate to, not less than 52 weeks in the period of 2 years immediately preceding that day; and

(e) in the case of a person who is [not] a British [subject], that [she] has been present in Great Britain for a period of, or periods amounting in the aggregate to, not less than 156 weeks in the period of 4 years immediately preceding that [day].

6. It is clear that the claimant did not satisfy condition (e) above at any relevant time before her death. [The] matter is however materially affected by the EEC Regulation [1408/71].

7. Article 2(1) of the EEC Regulation provides that it applies to workers who are or have been subject to the legislation of one or more Member States and who are nationals of one of the Member States and also to the members of their families and their survivors. It is not in dispute that the claimant's late husband was, but the claimant herself was not, such a worker. She was, however, a survivor of such a worker at the material time so that the Regulation applied to her.

8. Article 3(1) of the EEC Regulation provides [that persons] resident in the territory of one of the Member States [and] to whom this Regulation applies shall be subject to the same obligations and enjoy the same benefits under the legislation of any Member State as the nationals of that [state].

There is no doubt that the claimant as the survivor of a worker to whom the Regulation applies is herself a person to whom it applies. In the result the claimant as an Irish national is, in relation to the attendance allowance, placed in the same position as if she were a British national and condition (e) of the residence conditions [does] not apply to her.

9. Article 3(1) does not however in terms enable the claimant to avoid having to satisfy condition (d) of the residence conditions, which applies to British subjects whose place of birth is not in the United Kingdom, since it does not in terms enable the claimant to be treated as having been born in the United [Kingdom].

10. [The] EEC Regulation according to its preamble is enacted with particular reference [to] Article 7 of the Treaty of Rome **[B19]**, which provides that within the scope of the application of the Treaty any discrimination on grounds of nationality shall be prohibited. The Advocate General [has] on more than one occasion expressed the opinion that this provision of the Treaty is directly applicable and although the European Court has so far avoided committing itself on this point, they have decided nothing to the contrary and I ought to accept the Advocate General's opinion on the point especially as other Articles of the Treaty prohibiting discrimination (eg Article 48 [in *Van Duyn* **[D43]**]) have been held to have direct effect. The European Court has further held in relation to [Article 48] that the prohibition of discrimination embraces not only overt discrimination by reason of nationality but also covert forms of discrimination, such as some residence conditions. [It] appears to me [that] discrimination on the ground of place of

birth must almost necessarily operate as a covert form of discrimination on grounds of nationality. In the result I hold that Article 3(1) read in the light of the rules against discrimination must be taken as having the effect of placing the claimant in the same position as if she had been born in Great [Britain].

11. It follows that if the claimant is placed in the same position as if she had been born in Great Britain she is not required to comply with residence condition [(d)]. I consider however that she has to satisfy condition (c) which applies to all British subjects born in the United Kingdom. This requires physical presence in Great Britain for 26 weeks out of the 12 months immediately preceding the day for which benefit is claimed. In relation at any rate to a non-contributory benefit this seems to me to constitute an objective test that does not amount to covert discrimination on the ground of nationality. The claimant did not satisfy condition (c) until 16 April 1976, 26 weeks after her last return to this country, and the attendance allowance is payable from 19 April 1976 the Monday following the expiration of those 26 [weeks].

[C39]   Customs and Excise Commissioners v Samex ApS [1983] 1 All ER 1042

Bingham J (at pp 1055–1056)

Sitting as a judge in a national court, asked to decide questions of Community law, I am very conscious of the advantages enjoyed by the Court of Justice. It has a panoramic view of the Community and its institutions, a detailed knowledge of the Treaties and of much subordinate legislation made under them, and an intimate familiarity with the functioning of the Community market which no national judge denied the collective experience of the Court of Justice could hope to achieve. Where questions of administrative intention and practice arise the Court of Justice can receive submissions from the Community institutions, as also where relations between the Community and non-member states are in issue. Where the interests of Member States are affected they can intervene to make their views known. [Where] comparison falls to be made between Community texts in different languages, all texts being equally authentic, the multinational Court of Justice is equipped to carry out the task in a way which no national judge, whatever his linguistic skills, could rival. The interpretation of Community instruments involves [often] not the process familiar to common lawyers of laboriously extracting the meaning from words used but the more creative process of supplying flesh to a spare and loosely constructed skeleton. The choice between alternative submissions may turn not on purely legal considerations, but on a broader view of what the orderly development of the Community requires. These are matters which the Court of Justice is very much better placed to assess and determine than a national court.

[C40]   R v Henn [1980] 2 All ER 166, HL

[The decision of the Court of Justice in *Henn* **[E29]** was returned to the House of Lords.]

Lord Diplock (at pp 196–197)

In the Court of Appeal considerable doubt was expressed by that court whether an absolute prohibition on the import of a particular description of goods could amount to a quantitative restriction or a measure having equivalent effect, so as to fall within the ambit of Article 30 at all. That such doubt should be expressed shows the danger of an English court applying English canons of statutory construction to the interpretation of the EEC Treaty or, for that matter, of regulations or directives. What is meant by quantitative restrictions and measures having equivalent effect in Article 30 of the Treaty has been the subject of a whole series of decisions of the European Court to which the attention of the Court of Appeal ought to have been drawn. [There] is in fact a well-established body of case law of the European Court as to what amounts to a quantitative restriction or a measure having equivalent effect, within the meaning of Article 30. So far from supporting the doubts expressed by the Court of Appeal whether an absolute prohibition of import of goods of a particular description could amount to a measure having equivalent effect to a quantitative restriction [within] Article 30, these decisions of the European Court make it clear beyond a peradventure that it does. [In] the light of this established case law of the European Court, it appeared to me to be so free from any doubt that an absolute prohibition of importation of goods of a particular description from other Member States fell within Article 30 that I should not have been disposed to regard the instant case as involving any matter of interpretation of that article that was open to question. But the strong inclination expressed by the Court of Appeal to adopt the contrary view shows that there is involved a question of interpretation on which judicial minds can differ. It serves as a timely warning to English judges not to be too ready to hold that because the meaning of the English text (which is one of six of equal authority) seems plain to them no question of interpretation can be involved. It was for this reason that your Lordships thought it proper to submit to the European Court for a preliminary ruling the question as to the interpretation of Article 30 which is set out hereafter; it was not through any doubts on your Lordships' part as to the answer that would be received.

[C41]   R v Plymouth Justices [1982] 2 All ER 175

[The master of a French fishing boat was prosecuted before the Plymouth magistrates' court for infringing Regulation 2527/80, Article 7, which provided that no 'device shall be used by means of which the mesh in any part of a fishing net is obstructed or otherwise effectively [diminished]' and also for infringing the Fishing Nets (No 2) Order 1980 (SI 1980 No 1994), art 8, which implemented Regulation 2527/80 by prohibiting the attachment to specified types of fishing net of 'a device having the effect of obstructing or diminishing the mesh in contravention of' [art 7]. The fishing boat was caught using one of the specified types of net with a second piece of net attached to it. The master denied that the second piece of net necessarily had the effect of obstructing or diminishing the original net's mesh. The master contended that, first, Regulation 2527/80 did not apply to the facts of the case and, secondly, that only the Community could legislate on fishing conservation matters and that the United Kingdom had no power to make the Fishing Nets (No 2) Order. The magistrates considered it advisable to refer several questions of interpretation to the Court of Justice and the prosecution sought judicial review of their decision in the High Court.]

Lord Lane CJ (at pp 178–182)

There is no dispute that in the appropriate circumstances a magistrates' court has jurisdiction to refer questions to the European Court under Article 177 of the EEC Treaty. [The] magistrates' court is a 'court or tribunal' falling within [Article 177(2)] which has a discretion to refer a question if it considers it 'necessary to enable it to give judgment'. The position of the magistrates' court is to be contrasted with that of a court against whose decision there is no judicial remedy who must refer such a matter to the European Court.

. . .

The argument of counsel for the applicant was confined to the wording of Article 177 of the EEC Treaty. He submits that at the stage which the case had reached before the magistrates' court the justices had no jurisdiction to refer the questions to the Court of Justice. Before they can do so they must consider that a decision on the questions is necessary to enable them to give judgment. At the time they made the decision in this case they were not in a position to reach such a conclusion because there was still an issue as to fact to be resolved, this being that the respondent had not admitted that the second piece of net had the effect of obstructing or diminishing the original net. It was a matter on which he was entitled to call evidence and until he had been given an opportunity to do so and the justices had decided whether this had been proved, it could not be said whether it was necessary to have the opinion of the European Court or not. It was at that stage still possible that the magistrates would not be satisfied that the second piece of net had the effect alleged and if they were not, a reference would serve no purpose.

In support of his contentions counsel for the applicant relied strongly on the judgments of the Court of Appeal in *HP Bulmer Ltd v J Bollinger SA* [1974] 2 All ER 1226, [1974] Ch 401. In that case Lord Denning MR and Stephenson LJ laid down guidance as to the practice to be adopted with regard to referring questions to the European Court. Lord Denning MR said ([1974] 2 All ER 1226, at p 1234, [1974] 1 Ch 401, at p 421):

> An English court can only refer the matter to the European Court 'if it considers that a decision on the question is necessary to enable it to give judgment'. Note the words 'if it considers'. That is, 'if the English court considers'. On this point again the opinion of the English courts is final, just as it is on the matter of discretion. An English judge can say either 'I consider it necessary', or 'I do not consider it necessary'. His discretion in that respect is final. [If] the English judge considers it necessary to refer the matter, no one can gainsay it save the Court of Appeal.

Later Lord Denning MR said ([1974] 2 All ER 1226, at pp 1234–1235, [1974] Ch 401, at pp 422–423):

> The English Court has to consider whether 'a decision on the question is necessary to enable it to give judgment'. That means judgment in the very case which is before the court. The judge must have got to the

stage when he says to himself: 'This clause of the treaty is capable of two or more meanings. If it means this, I give judgment for the plaintiff. If it means that, I give judgment for the defendant.' In short, the point must be such that, whichever way the point is decided, it is conclusive of the case. Nothing more remains but to give judgment. [It] is to be noticed, too, that the word is 'necessary'. This is much stronger than 'desirable' or 'convenient'. There are some cases where the point, if decided one way, would shorten the trial greatly. But, if decided the other way, it would mean that the trial would have to go its full length. In such a case it might be 'convenient' or 'desirable' to take it as a preliminary point because it might save much time and expense. But it would not be 'necessary' at that stage. When the facts were investigated, it might turn out to have been quite unnecessary. The case would be determined on another ground altogether. As a rule you cannot tell whether it is necessary to decide a point until all the facts are ascertained. So in general it is best to decide the facts first.

. . .

Taking the argument of counsel for the applicant to its logical conclusion, it means that no court or tribunal can refer questions to the European Court under Article 177 unless all the facts have been admitted or found on all the issues in the case. It must be a situation where, subject to argument as to the effect of the answers given by the European Court, it is in a position to give final judgment. In the case of a criminal trial this means that it has no jurisdiction to refer on a submission being made that there is no case to answer unless all the facts have been admitted. This involves giving an extremely narrow interpretation to the word 'necessary' in Article 177.

Such an interpretation is not in accord with the general approach to Article 177 adopted by the European Court. For example in the course of its judgment in [*Rheinmühlen* **[C18]**] it is stated:

Article 177 is essential for the preservation of the Community character of the law established by the Treaty and has the object of ensuring that in all circumstances this law is the same in all States of the Community. Whilst it thus aims to avoid divergences in the interpretation of Community law which the national courts have to apply, it likewise tends to ensure this application by making available to the national judge a means of eliminating difficulties which may be occasioned by the requirement of giving Community law its full effect within the framework of the judicial systems of the Member States. [This] Article gives national courts the power and, where appropriate, imposes on them an obligation to refer a case for a preliminary ruling, as soon as the judge perceives either of his own motion or at the request of the parties that the litigation depends on a point referred to in the first paragraph of Article 177. It follows that national courts have the widest discretion in referring matters to the Court of Justice if they consider that a case pending before them raises questions involving interpretation, or consideration of the validity, of provisions of Community law, necessitating a decision on their part.

[Having] regard to these authorities, it is not right to say that the magistrates' court in this case had no jurisdiction to agree to refer questions to the European Court at the stage at which the case which was then before them had reached. The validity of the regulations was the substantive issue before the court. As counsel for the respondent correctly pointed out, in a criminal case a defendant was entitled to have a decision whether there was a case to answer before he was called on to lead evidence in support of his defence. To rule on the submission, a decision on the questions of Community law raised by the respondent was necessary, since if the decision was in the respondent's favour he would be acquitted and if it was not, he would have to decide whether to contest further the one issue of fact which remained.

Although it is the decision of a magistrates' court which is under consideration, the test is no more stringent in the case of a magistrates' court than it is in the case of the High Court. If the justices take the view that a decision on the question is required in order to do justice, then, as long as they have not misdirected themselves in law or acted unreasonably, this court cannot interfere. Applying that approach, there is no material indicating that the Plymouth justices misdirected themselves in any way or acted unreasonably.

. . .

Counsel on behalf of the applicant did not advance an alternative argument suggesting that the justices, even if they had jurisdiction, had exercised their discretion improperly in deciding to refer. This is understandable on the facts of this case. We wish to add that in the ordinary case, it would be highly undesirable for the justices to decide to refer until all the evidence had been called and until they could be satisfied there was no question of the respondent being acquitted on the facts. In the normal way it is the obvious precaution to take to avoid the expense and delay of a reference to the European Court. It may involve the justices themselves taking a decision on the issue as to Community law without the advantage of the guidance of the European Court. However this should not be regarded as unfairly prejudicing the respondent, since his position would be exactly the same as in the case where the magistrates had to make a ruling on domestic law. In such a case it would only be after the conclusion of the hearing that the defendant could exercise his right [to] apply to this court for judicial review.

It is for the same reason that in the ordinary way justices should exercise considerable caution before referring even after they have heard all the evidence. If they come to a wrong decision on Community law, a higher court can make the reference and frequently the higher court would be the more suitable forum to do so. The higher court is as a rule in a better position to assess whether any reference is desirable. On references the form of the question referred is of importance and the higher court will normally be in a better position to assess the appropriateness of the question and to assist in formulating it clearly. Leaving it to the higher court will often also avoid delay.

[C42]   Foster v British Gas plc [1991] 2 All ER 705, HL

[In Case C-188/89 *Foster v British Gas* [1990] ECR 3313, the Court of Justice stated that it had held 'in a series of cases that unconditional and sufficiently precise provisions of a directive could be relied on against organisations or bodies which were subject to the authority or control of the state or had special powers beyond those which result from the normal rules applicable to relations between individuals'. More particularly, 'a body, whatever its legal form, which has been made responsible, pursuant to a measure adopted by the State, for providing a public service under the control of the State and which has for that purpose special powers beyond those which result from the normal rules applicable in relations between individuals is included in any event among the bodies against which the provisions of a directive capable of having direct effect may be relied on'. *Foster* was returned to the House of Lords.]

Lord Templeman (at pp 709–711)

Accordingly, it falls to this House now to determine whether the BGC [British Gas Corporation] was a body which was made responsible, pursuant to a measure adopted by the state, for providing a public service under the control of the state and had for that purpose special powers beyond those which result from the normal rules applicable in relations between individuals.

By the Gas Act 1972, [since] repealed by the Gas Act 1986 and orders made thereunder, the BGC was established as a body corporate. The Secretary of State was authorised to make regulations with regard to the appointment and tenure and vacation of office by members of the corporation. [Section 2(1)] provided '[It] shall be the duty of the Corporation to develop and maintain an efficient, co-ordinated and economical system of gas supply for Great Britain, and to satisfy, so far as it is economical to do so, all reasonable demands for gas in Great [Britain].'

Thus the BGC was a body which was made responsible, pursuant to a measure adopted by the state, for providing a public service.

By [s 4(3)] the BGC was directed to report to the minister, who was authorised [to] 'give to the Corporation such directions as he considers appropriate for securing that the management of the activities of the Corporation and their subsidiaries is organised in the most efficient manner; and it shall be the duty of the Corporation to give effect to any such directions'.

By [s 7(1)] the Secretary of State was authorised [to] 'give to the Corporation directions of a general character as to the exercise and performance by the Corporation of their functions [in] relation to matters which appear to him to affect the national interest, and the Corporation shall give effect to any such directions'.

By [s] 8 the BGC was ordered to make an annual report to the minister, if so directed by the minister, in such form as might be specified in the direction on the exercise and performance by the corporation of its functions during the year and on its policy and programmes. Under Part II of the 1972 Act the Secretary of State was given general control over the finances of the corporation and, in particular, was authorised to direct the corporation to pay over to him so much of excess revenue of the corporation as appeared to him surplus to the corporation's requirements.

In my opinion by these provisions the BGC performed its public service of providing a gas supply under the control of the state. The corporation was not independent: its members were appointed by the state, the corporation was responsible to the minister acting on behalf of the state and the corporation was subject to directions given by the Secretary of State.

By [s] 29(1) of the 1972 Act '[No] person other than the Corporation shall [supply] gas to any premises except with the consent of the Corporation and in accordance with such conditions as may be attached to that consent.'

This section conferred on the BGC 'special powers beyond those which result from the normal rules applicable in relations between individuals'.

Accordingly, the BGC was, in my opinion, a body which was made responsible, pursuant to a measure adopted by the state, for providing a public service under the control of the state and had, for that purpose, special powers beyond those which resulted from the normal rules applicable in relations between individuals and therefore the BGC cannot take advantage of the failure of the state to comply with the equal treatment directive.

. . .

Applying [the plain words of the Court of Justice] it seems to me that the 1972 Act created a body, the BGC, which provided a public service, the supply of gas, to citizens of the state generally under the control of the state, which could dictate its policies and retain its surplus revenue; the BGC was equipped with a special monopoly power which was created and could only have been created by the legislature. The BGC is therefore a body against which the relevant provisions of the equal treatment directive may be enforced.

[C43]   Pickstone v Freemans plc [1989] AC 66

[In Case 61/81 *Commission of the European Communities v United Kingdom* [1982] ECR 2601, the Court of Justice held that the United Kingdom Equal Pay Act 1970 was deficient in that it did not implement a directive (Directive 75/117, referred to as the Equal Pay Directive). The United Kingdom government took steps to correct the defect in its equal pay legislation identified in the judgment of the Court of Justice and made the Equal Pay (Amendment) Regulations 1983 (SI 1983 No 1794), under the European Communities Act 1972, Sched 2 **[C35]**.]

Lord Templeman (at pp 121–123)

The draft of the Regulations of 1983 was not subject to any process of amendment by Parliament. In these circumstances the explanations of the government and the criticisms voiced by Members of Parliament in the debates which led to approval of the draft regulations provide some indications of the intentions of Parliament. The debate on the draft regulations in the House of Commons [was] initiated by the Under Secretary of State for Employment, who [said] 'The Equal Pay Act allows a woman to claim equal pay with a man [if] she is doing the same or broadly similar work, or if her job and his have been rated equal through job evaluation in effort, skill and decision. However, if a woman is doing different work from a comparable man, or if the jobs are not covered by a job evaluation study, the woman has at present no right to make a claim for equal pay. This is the gap identified by the European Court, which we are closing.' [Thus] it is clear that the construction which I have placed upon the regulations corresponds to the intentions of the government in introducing the regulations.

[Lord Templeman referred to *von Colson* **[C29]**]. In *Duke v GEC Reliance Systems Ltd* [1988] AC 618 this House declined to distort the construction of an Act of Parliament which was not drafted to give effect to a directive and which was not capable of complying with the directive as subsequently construed by the European Court of Justice. In the present case I can see no difficulty in construing the Regulations of 1983 in a way which gives effect to the declared intention of the government of the United Kingdom responsible for drafting the regulations and is consistent with the objects of the EEC Treaty, the provisions of the Equal Pay Directive and the rulings of the European Court of Justice.

[C44] Bourgoin SA v Ministry of Agriculture [1985] 3 All ER 585, CA

[The Ministry of Agriculture imposed an embargo on the importation into the United Kingdom of turkeys and turkey parts which had an origin in France. The Court of Justice declared that the United Kingdom had failed to fulfil its obligations under Article 30 **[E11]** (see Case 40/82 *Commission v United Kingdom* [1982] ECR 2793). Following the court's decision, French turkey producers and distributors brought an action against the Ministry of Agriculture claiming damages for the loss caused by the original withdrawal of the licences for the import of turkeys and turkey pieces and other poultry products into England. The Court of Appeal in a majority decision held that this claim disclosed no cause of action.]

Parker LJ (at pp 626–630)

So far as Community law is concerned there is nothing in the decisions of the European Court which positively or specifically requires that for a breach by a Member State of Article 30 a remedy in damages must be available to an individual who suffers damage by the breach. Indeed the decisions of the European Court point forcefully to the conclusion that a remedy in damages is not required by Community law for breach by a Member State of an article having direct effect where such breach consists in the imposition of a legislative or quasi-legislative measure involving the exercise of judgment unless the breach is of a particularly serious character.

The origin of the principle that an article of the EEC Treaty having direct effect creates individual rights in the subjects of Member States as against such Member States themselves and as between individuals was the decision of the European Court in [*van Gend* **[C22]**. That decision] goes no further than establishing that where an article has direct effect, albeit it creates in express terms only a negative obligation on Member States, individual rights are thereby created which must be protected by national courts. The precise nature of the right is not defined any more than the remedy to be afforded.

. . .

[In] Case 143/77 *Koninklijke Scholten Honig NV v EC Council and Commission* [1979] ECR 3583 [the] following passage appears in the judgment of the court (at pp 3625–3626):

A finding that a legal situation resulting from legislative measures by the Community is illegal is insufficient by itself to involve it in liability. The Court has [a] consistent case-law in accordance with which the Community does not incur liability on account of a legislative measure which involves choices of economic policy unless a sufficiently serious breach of a superior rule of law for the protection of the individual has occurred. Having regard to the principles in the legal systems of the Member States, governing the liability of public authorities for damage caused to individuals by legislative measures, the Court has stated that in the context of Community legislation in which one of the chief features is the exercise of a wide discretion essential for the implementation of the Common Agricultural Policy, the liability of the Community can arise only exceptionally in cases in which the institution concerned has manifestly and gravely disregarded the limits on the exercise of its [powers].

[If] the position is that the Council is not liable in damages for a mere breach of an article conferring individual rights, where that breach consists in legislative act, but that the United Kingdom government is so liable, a strange situation might arise. If that government, acting in pursuance of an invalid Council regulation, sought by legislative action to implement it, it would be liable in damages whilst the Council, despite the express provisions of Article 215 and the fact that the United Kingdom government is obliged to implement regulations, would not. This would be the stranger in that the non-liability of the Council has been arrived at having regard to the principles in the legal systems of Member States governing the liability of public authorities for damage caused to individuals by legislative measures.

. . .

Article 30 creates rights in individuals and obligations on the United Kingdom and these must therefore be enforced and allowed. The EEC Treaty, however, does not create procedures or remedies. It provides only, by virtue of decisions of the European Court, that the national courts shall afford no less favourable remedies than those available in respect of the breach of a similar type in national law and must not so adapt procedures as to make enforcement of the right impossible. The plaintiffs seek to go further and say that the remedies provided must be dissuasive of further breaches. If this means any more than that remedies must effectively protect the individual rights, I do not accept it. If it means merely that the rights must be effectively protected, it is I think plainly right.

In the absence of authority compelling me to reach a different conclusion I would have no hesitation in holding that a breach of Article 30 by the imposition of a prohibition or restriction on imports affords in English law a right to judicial review by anyone with sufficient interest, a declaration as to the invalidity of the measure constituting the breach and possibly a mandamus to the relevant officials to permit the landing of the goods concerned. Indeed this is common ground, for such rights and remedies would be available for a similar domestic wrong.

Suppose, for example, an English statute provided that a minister might, or even should, by order prohibit the landing of any goods in so far as might be necessary for the protection of animal life and an order was made prohibiting X from importing, for example, certain feeding stuffs from a particular source on the basis of evidence that feeding stuffs from that source were, or were likely to be, bearers of a disease fatal to livestock. The producer and importer could undoubtedy challenge the order and if successful obtain a declaration. They might even, if the goods were detained by customs officers, obtain a mandamus ordering their immediate release.

They would, however, in English law not be able to obtain damages. The foregoing remedies would, as I think, afford them adequate protection. If the power were abused it would, however, be a different matter. If the minister knew perfectly well that there was nothing wrong with the feeding stuffs and had made the order in fact not to protect animal life but to further the interests of a company making feeding stuffs in which he held shares, the position would, or might, be different. There would then be an abuse of power, for which damages would lie. For a similar breach of Article 30 damages would therefore also lie.

[C45]   The Bourgoin settlement (HC Deb, vol 102, col 116, 22 July 1986, written answer)

Mr Hunter asked the Minister of Agriculture Fisheries and Food whether there have been any developments in the case of *Bourgoin SA and Others v The Minister*.

Mr Jopling: A negotiated settlement of this case has been reached. Parliamentary approval for the relevant payment will be sought in a Supplementary Supply [Estimate]. Pending that approval, this urgent payment of about £3.5m to cover damages, interest and costs will be met by a repayable advance from the Contingencies Fund.

[C46]   Kirklees Metropolitan Borough Council v Wickes Building Supplies Ltd [1992] 3 All ER 717, HL

[Under the Shops Act 1950, s 47, specified Sunday trading is prohibited. It was contended by many traders that s 47 was contrary to Article 30 of the Treaty and this resulted in much, and rather unsatisfactory, litigation before the Court of Justice. Kirklees Council sought an interlocutory injunction to restrain Wickes from trading on Sundays until their prosecution of Wickes under s 47 came to trial. The Court of Appeal required the council to give an undertaking as to damages as a condition of the grant of an injunction in that Wickes ought to be protected by such an undertaking pending the decision of the Court of Justice which would establish Wickes' right to trade on Sundays should the Court of Justice in the Stoke-on-Trent case **[A18]** hold that s 47 was invalid in that it was contrary to Article 30 of the Treaty. Wickes argued that such an undertaking was required to give immediate effect to Community law. The House of Lords held that this submission was misconceived.]

Lord Goff (at pp 734–735)

I approach the matter as follows. In *Bourgoin* **[C44]** [it] was held by the Court of Appeal [that] a breach of Article 30 would not of itself give rise to a claim in damages by the injured party. However, since the decision of the European Court in *Francovich* **[C33]** [there] must now be doubt whether the *Bourgoin* case was correctly decided. It is true that *Francovich*'s case was concerned with the situation where a Member State fails to implement an EEC directive, the court holding that in such a case the Member State is obliged to make good damage suffered by individuals as a result of its failure so to do. But the court in its judgment spoke in more general terms. [His Lordship quoted paragraphs 34 to 37 of the judgment in *Francovich* and continued:] It is not necessary for the purposes of the present case for your Lordships' House to decide whether the *Bourgoin* case was correctly decided, and indeed no argument was addressed to your Lordships on that question. But, having regard to the passage from the judgment of the European Court in *Francovich*'s case which I have just quoted, it is in my opinion right that in the present case your Lordships should proceed on the basis that if, on the reference to it in the *Stoke-on-Trent* [case], the court should hold that s 47 of the Shops Act 1950 is invalid as being in conflict with Article 30 of the EEC Treaty, the United Kingdom may be obliged to make good damage caused to individuals by the breach of Article 30 for which it is responsible.

It does not however follow that, in the present case, the council should be obliged to give an undertaking in damages as a condition of the grant of an injunction restraining Wickes from acting in breach of s 47. This is because the obligation (if any) on the United Kingdom to make good any damage suffered by Wickes will arise irrespective of any undertaking in damages given by the council. In the circumstances, such an undertaking would be superfluous. But there are two other subsidiary matters which reinforce the conclusion that the council should not be required to give such an undertaking. The first is that the effect of such an undertaking would be to impose an obligation on the council to indemnify Wickes against damage suffered by it, in the event of s 47 being held to be invalid as inconsistent with Article 30, irrespective of whether in such circumstances Wickes has a right to damages, ie irrespective of whether the *Bourgoin* case is wrongly decided. In other words, that question is pre-empted by the requirement of such an undertaking from the council. The second is that if, following *Francovich*'s case, there was held to be a right to damages in such circumstances, the effect of requiring an undertaking from the council would be to impose liability in damages on the council instead of on the United Kingdom which, as I understand the position, would properly be the party so liable. That it is the Member State which is liable in such circumstances appears from the passage from the judgment in *Francovich*'s case which I have quoted. This is no doubt because it is the government which would, on the hypothesis that s 47 was invalid because it was inconsistent with Article 30, have failed to take the necessary steps to ensure that s 47 was amended or repealed as necessary. If so, it would be wrong that the council, because it has performed its statutory duty under the national law to enforce s 47, was to find itself under a liability in damages as a result of performing that duty.

For these reasons, I am of the opinion that Wickes' argument that the council should be required to give an undertaking in damages has no justification in Community law.

[C47]   Factortame Ltd v Secretary of State for Transport [1989] 2 All ER 692, HL

[Proceedings were brought against the Secretary of State for Transport by Factortame and other companies, incorporated under United Kingdom law, and also by the directors and shareholders of those companies, most of which were Spanish nationals. The companies were the owners or operators of 95 fishing vessels which were registered in the register of British vessels under the Merchant Shipping Act 1894. Fifty-three of those vessels were originally registered in Spain and flew the Spanish flag but were later registered in the British register. The remaining 42 vessels had always been registered in the United Kingdom, but were purchased by the companies in question. The United Kingdom amended the 1894 legislation in order to put a stop to the practice known as 'quota-hopping', whereby, according to the United Kingdom, its fishing quotas were 'plundered' by vessels flying the British flag but lacking any genuine link with the United Kingdom. Consequently, Parliament enacted the Merchant Shipping Act 1988, Part II, which, together with the Merchant Shipping (Registration of Fishing Vessels) Regulations 1988 (SI 1988 No 1926), radically altered the registration system of British fishing vessels. The 1988 Act provided for the establishment of a new register in which all British fishing vessels were to be registered, including those which were already registered in the old register maintained under the 1894 Act. However, only fishing vessels fulfilling the conditions laid down in s 14 of the 1988 Act could be registered in the new register.

Section 14(1) provided that, subject to dispensations to be determined by the Secretary of State for Transport, a fishing vessel was eligible to be registered in the new register only if '(a) the vessel is British-owned; (b) the vessel is managed, and its operations are directed and controlled, from within the United Kingdom; and (c) any charterer, manager or operator of the vessel is a qualified person or company'.

Section 14(2) provided that a fishing vessel is deemed to be British-owned if the legal title is vested wholly in one or more qualified persons or companies and if the vessel is beneficially owned by one or more qualified companies or, as to not less than 75%, by one or more qualified persons.

Section 14(7) provided that a 'qualified person' means a person who is a British citizen resident and domiciled in the United Kingdom and 'qualified company' means a company incorporated in the United Kingdom and having as its principal place of business there, at least 75% of its shares being owned by one or more qualified persons or companies and at least 75% of its directors being qualified persons.

The 1988 Act and the 1988 Regulations entered into force on 1 December 1988, but the validity of registrations effected under the previous Act was extended for a transitional period until 31 March 1989. On 4 August 1989 the Commission brought an action before the Court of Justice under Article 169 (see Section One of this chapter) for a declaration that, by imposing the nationality requirements laid down in s 14 (above), the United Kingdom had failed to fulfil its obligations under Articles 7 and 52 of the EEC Treaty. The Commission also applied to the Court of Justice for an interim order requiring the United Kingdom to suspend the application of the nationality requirements as regards the nationals of other Member

States and in respect of fishing vessels which until 31 March 1989 were carrying on a fishing activity under the British flag and under a British fishing licence. The President of the Court granted that application. Complying with that order, the United Kingdom made an Order in Council amending s 14 of the 1988 Act (see the Merchant Shipping Act 1988 (Amendment) Order 1989 (SI 1989 No 2006)).

At the time of the institution of the proceedings against the Secretary of State for Transport, the 95 fishing vessels of the companies in question failed to satisfy one or more of the conditions for registration under s 14 of the 1988 Act and thus could not be registered in the new register. Since those vessels were to be deprived of the right to engage in fishing as from 1 April 1989, the companies in question, by means of an application for judicial review, challenged the compatibility of Part II of the 1988 Act with Community law. They also applied for the grant of interim relief until such time as final judgment was given on their application for judicial review. On 10 March 1989 the Divisional Court of the Queen's Bench Division decided to stay the proceedings and to make a reference under Article 177 (see Section Two of this chapter) for a preliminary ruling on the issues of Community law raised in the proceedings and ordered that, by way of interim relief, the application of Part II of the 1988 Act and the 1988 Regulations should be suspended as regards the applicants. On 13 March 1989 the Secretary of State for Transport appealed against the Divisional Court's order granting interim relief. On 22 March 1989 the Court of Appeal held that under United Kingdom law the courts had no power to suspend, by way of interim relief, the application of Acts of Parliament. It therefore set aside the order of the Divisional Court. The case came before the House of Lords.]

Lord Bridge (at pp 696–710)

The applicants sought by application for judicial review to challenge the legality of the relevant 1988 legislation on the ground that it contravened the provisions of the EEC Treaty and other rules of law given effect thereunder by the European Communities Act 1972 by depriving the applicants of rights of the kind referred to in s 2(1) of the 1972 Act **[C35]** as enforceable Community rights. It will be convenient to use the expression 'Community law' as embracing the EEC Treaty, subordinate legislation of institutions of the European Economic Community (the EEC) and the jurisprudence developed by the Court of Justice of the European Communities and to use the expression 'directly enforceable Community rights' as referring to those rights in Community law which have direct effect in the national law of Member States of the EEC. The defence of the Secretary of State to the applicants' challenge was and is, first, that Community law does not in any way restrict a Member State's right to decide who is entitled to be a national of that state or what vessels are entitled to fly its flag and, second, that, in any event, the new legislation is in conformity with Community law and, indeed, is designed to achieve the Community purposes enshrined in the common fisheries policy.

. . .

It is estimated that the preliminary ruling requested by the Divisional Court from the European Court will not be given for two years from the date when the reference is made. The applicants claim that unless they are protected during this period by an interim order which has the effect of enabling them to continue to operate their 95 vessels as if they were duly registered British fishing vessels (which would be necessary to enable them to continue to hold licences to fish against the British quota of controlled stocks of fish) they will suffer irreparable damage. The vessels are not eligible to resume the Spanish flag and fish against the Spanish quota. To lay the vessels up pending the ruling of the European Court would be prohibitively expensive. The only practical alternative would be to sell the vessels or the Spanish holdings in the companies owning the vessels in what would be a glutted market at disastrously low prices. In addition many of the individual applicants are actively engaged in the operation and management of the vessels and would lose their livelihood. No doubt has been cast on the factual accuracy of these claims and I approach the question of interim relief on the footing that they are well founded. Moreover, as the law presently stands on the authority of *Bourgoin* **[C44]** the applicants would have no remedy in damages for losses suffered pending the ruling of the European Court.

. . .

The familiar situation in English law in which the question arises whether or not an interim injunction should be made to protect some threatened right of the plaintiff or applicant for judicial review is one in which the facts on which the right depends are in dispute and the court cannot proceed immediately to the trial which will resolve that dispute. In this situation the court has a discretion to grant or withhold interim relief which it exercises in accordance with the principles laid down by your Lordships' House in *American Cyanamid Co v Ethicon Ltd* [1975] 1 All ER 504, [1975] AC 396. In deciding on a balance of convenience whether or not to make an interim injunction the court is essentially engaged in an exercise of holding the ring.

. . .

[Lord Bridge examined the 'familiar' situation and concluded that the present case was fundamentally different from that familiar situation.]

But an order granting the applicants the interim relief which they seek will only serve their purpose if it declares that which Parliament had enacted to be the law from 1 December 1988, and to take effect in relation to vessels previously registered under the 1894 Act from 31 March 1989, not to be the law until some uncertain future date. Effective relief can only be given if it requires the Secretary of State to treat the applicants' vessels as entitled to registration under Part II of the 1988 Act in direct contravention of its provisions. Any such order, unlike any form of order for interim relief known to the law, would irreversibly determine in the applicants' favour for a period of some two years rights which are necessarily uncertain until the preliminary ruling of the European Court has been given. If the applicants fail to establish the rights they claim before the European Court, the effect of the interim relief granted would be to have conferred on them rights directly contrary to Parliament's sovereign will and correspondingly to have deprived British fishing vessels, as defined by Parliament, of the enjoyment of a substantial proportion of the United Kingdom's quota of stocks of fish protected by the common fisheries policy. I am clearly of opinion that, as a matter of English law, the court has no power to make an order which has these consequences.

It follows that this appeal must fall to be dismissed unless there is, as the applicants contend, some overriding principle derived from the jurisprudence of the European Court which compels national courts of Member States, whatever their own law may provide, to assert, and in appropriate cases to exercise, a power to provide an effective interlocutory remedy to protect putative rights in Community law once those rights have been claimed and are seen to be seriously arguable, notwithstanding that the existence of the rights is in dispute and will not be established unless and until the European Court so rules.

. . .

I turn finally to consider the submission made on behalf of the applicants that, irrespective of the position under national law, there is an overriding principle of Community law which imposes an obligation on the national court to secure effective interim protection of rights having direct effect under Community law where a seriously arguable claim is advanced to be entitled to such rights and where the rights claimed will in substance be rendered nugatory or will be irremediably impaired if not effectively protected during any interim period which must elapse pending determination of a dispute as to the existence of those rights. The basic propositions of Community law on which the applicants rely in support of this submission may be quite shortly summarised. Directly enforceable Community rights are part of the legal heritage of every citizen of a Member State of the EEC. They arise from the EEC Treaty itself and not from any judgment of the European Court declaring their existence. Such rights are automatically available and must be given unrestricted retroactive effect. The persons entitled to the enjoyment of such rights are entitled to direct and immediate protection against possible infringement of them. The duty to provide such protection rests with the national court. The remedy to be provided against infringement must be effective, not merely symbolic or illusory. The rules of national law which render the exercise of directly enforceable Community rights excessively difficult or virtually impossible must be overridden.

Counsel for the applicants [traced] the progressive development of these principles of the jurisprudence of the European Court through a long series of reported decisions on which he relies. I must confess that at the conclusion of his argument I was strongly inclined to the view that, if English law could provide no effective remedy to secure the interim protection of the rights claimed by the applicants, it was nevertheless our duty under Community law to devise such a remedy. But the Solicitor General [has] persuaded me that none of the authorities on which counsel for the applicants relies can properly be treated as determinative of the difficult question, which arises for the first time in the instant case, of providing interim protection of putative and disputed rights in Community law before their existence has been established. This is because the relevant decisions of the European Court, from which the propositions of Community law asserted by counsel for the applicants are derived, were all made by reference to rights which the European Court was itself then affirming or by reference to the protection of rights the existence of which had already been established by previous decisions of the European Court.

. . .

In [the] application of the principles laid down by the European Court in [*Cilfit* **[C19]**], I do not think that it is open to your Lordships' House to decide one way or the other whether, in relation to the grant of interim protection in the circumstances of the instant case, Community law overrides English law and either empowers or obliges an English court to make an interim order protecting the putative rights claimed by the applicants. It follows, I think, that your Lordships are obliged under Article 177 of the Treaty to seek a preliminary ruling from the European Court. I would propose that the questions to be referred should read as follows:

1. Where: (i) a party before the national court claims to be entitled to rights under Community law having direct effect in national law (the rights claimed), (ii) a national measure in clear terms will, if applied, automatically deprive that party of the rights claimed, (iii) there are serious arguments both for and against the existence of the rights claimed and the national court has sought a preliminary ruling under Article 177 whether or not the rights claimed exist, (iv) the national law presumes the national measure in question to be compatible with Community law unless and until it is declared incompatible, (v) the national court has no power to give interim protection to the rights claimed by suspending the application of the national measure pending the preliminary ruling, (vi) if the preliminary ruling is in the event in favour of the rights claimed, the party entitled to those rights is likely to have suffered irremediable damage unless given such interim protection, does Community law either (a) oblige the national court to grant such interim protection of the rights claimed; or (b) give the court power to grant such interim protection of the rights claimed?

2. If question 1(a) is answered in the negative and question 1(b) in the affirmative, what are the criteria to be applied in deciding whether or not to grant such interim protection of the rights claimed?

[C48] Case C-213/89 R v Secretary of State for Transport, ex p Factortame (No 2) [1990] ECR I-2433

Submissions of Advocate General Tesauro (at pp 2455–2461)

15. It is therefore firmly established, in the light of the court's well-settled case law, which has moreover been pertinently cited by the House of Lords, that national courts are required to afford complete and effective judicial protection to individuals on whom enforceable legal rights are conferred under a directly effective Community provision, on condition that the Community provision governs the matter in question from the moment of its entry into force, and that from this it follows that any national provision or practice which precludes those courts from giving 'full effect' to the Community provision is incompatible with Community law.

. . .

16. The problem which the national court has raised is a general one [and] does not concern solely the English legal system, nor does it relate solely to the relationship between a national law and a Community provision, but rather it relates to the requirement for, and the very existence of, the interim protection of a right which is not certain but whose existence is in the course of being determined in a situation where there is a conflict

between legal rules of differing rank. [The] problem arises from the fact that in a structured and intricate context which a modern system of judicial protection demands there is a lack of contemporaneity between the two points in time which mark the course of the law, namely the point when the right comes into existence and the point (later on) when the existence of the right is (definitively) established.

17. To compensate for the fact that these two points in time do not coincide there is a first and general remedy. It is indeed true that only the definitive establishment of the existence of the right confers on the right fullness and certainty of content in the sense of placing the right itself, and the means whereby it may be exercised, finally beyond dispute (res judicata in the substantive sense); but it is also true that that effect is carried back to the point in time when the right was invoked by initiating the procedure for judicial review. The effect of the establishment of the existence of the right, inappropriately but significantly described as retroactive effect, is merely the consequence of the function of the [provision giving rise] to an enforceable legal right from the moment when the provision enters into force and for so long as it continues in force. The only possible delay is that which may occur before the right becomes fully effective and operational in cases where application to a court is needed in order to establish the existence of the right, and in particular in cases of prior review of the validity of the provision which is alleged to be applicable.

. . .

24. If attention is now turned to the relationship between national provisions and Community provisions, there is no doubt that, by means of preliminary rulings given by the Court of Justice and the 'direct' competence of national courts, machinery has been introduced which esssentially consists of the review of the validity (or of compatibility, if this is preferred) of a national provision in relation to a Community provision, given that the national courts have jurisdiction to rule definitively that the former is incompatible with the latter. And if therefore the national courts may, indeed must, disapply a national law which conflicts with a Community provision having direct effect, once a definitive finding has been made to that effect (or, at any rate, must achieve that substantive result), they must also be able to disapply that law provisionally, provided that the preconditions are satisfied, where the incompatibility is not entirely certain or 'established' but may call for a preliminary ruling by the Court of Justice. Otherwise, that judicial protection of the rights conferred on individuals by the Community provision which, as has been affirmed by the court on numerous occasions and also specifically pointed out by the House of Lords, is the subject of a precise obligation on the part of the national courts, might be nullified.

25. This brings me back to the concrete case submitted for the consideration of the court by way of the questions referred to it by the House of Lords. The right of the appellants in the main proceedings, which is denied by the national statute, is claimed on the basis of certain Treaty provisions having direct effect, that is to say provisions which prevail over domestic law but whose interpretation in the sense contended for is not free from doubt and, consequently, requires a preliminary ruling by the court. In the meantime, the national court finds a bar to interim protection of the rights claimed in the presumption of validity which attaches to the statute until a final determination is made.

Inasmuch as the English court, as is undisputed and as it has itself underlined, can and must give precedence, once the final determination is made, by virtue of the review which can be carried out of the compatibility of the English statute with Community law, to the 'certain' Community rule having direct effect, it must also be able, where the necessary preconditions are satisfied, to grant interim protection to the rights claimed on the bases of 'uncertain' Community rules and denied by the provisions of national law.

The European Court of Justice (at pp 2473–2474)

17. It is clear from the information before the court, and in particular from the judgment making the reference and, as described above, the course taken by the proceedings in the national courts before which the case came at first and second instance, that the preliminary question raised by the House of Lords seeks essentially to ascertain whether a national court which, in a case before it concerning Community law, considers that the sole obstacle which precludes it from granting interim relief is a rule of national law must disapply that rule.

18. For the purpose of replying to that question, it is necessary to point out that in its judgment in [*Simmenthal* **[C24]**] the court held that directly applicable rules of Community law 'must be fully and uniformly applied in all the Member States from the date of their entry into force and for so long as they continue in force [and that] in accordance with the principle of the precedence of Community law, the relationship between provisions of the Treaty and directly applicable measures of the institutions on the one hand and the national law of the Member States on the other is such that those provisions and measures [by] their entry into force render automatically inapplicable any conflicting provision [of] national [law]'.

19. In accordance with the case law of the court, it is for the national courts, in application of the principle of co-operation laid down in Article 5 of the EEC Treaty, to ensure the legal protection which persons derive from the direct effect of provisions of Community law (see, most recently, the judgments [in] Case 811/79 *Amministrazione delle Finanze dello Stato v Ariete SpA* [1980] ECR 2545 and Case 826/79 *Amministrazione delle Finanze dello Stato v MIRECO* [1980] ECR 2559).

20. The court has also held that any provision of a national legal system and any legislative, administrative or judicial practice which might impair the effectiveness of Community law by withholding from the national court having jurisdiction to apply such law the power to do everything necessary at the moment of its application to set aside national legislative provisions which might prevent, even temporarily, Community rules from having full force and effect are incompatible with those requirements, which are the very essence of Community law (see [*Simmenthal* **[C24]**]).

21. It must be added that the full effectiveness of Community law would be just as much impaired if a rule of national law could prevent a court seised of a dispute governed by Community law from granting interim relief in order to ensure the full effectiveness of the judgment to be given on the existence of the rights claimed under Community law. It follows that a court which in those circumstances would grant interim relief, if it were not for a rule of national law, is obliged to set aside that rule.

22. That interpretation is reinforced by the system established by Article

177 of the EEC Treaty whose effectiveness would be impaired if a national court, having stayed proceedings pending the reply by the Court of Justice to the question referred to it for a preliminary ruling, were not able to grant interim relief until it delivered its judgment following the reply given by the Court of Justice.

23. Consequently, the reply to the question raised should be that Community law must be interpreted as meaning that a national court which, in a case before it concerning Community law, considers that the sole obstacle which precludes it from granting interim relief is a rule of national law must set aside that rule.

[C49]   Factortame Ltd v Secretary of State for Transport (No 2) [1991] 1 All ER 70, HL

Lord Bridge (at pp 107–109)

My Lords, when this appeal first came before the House in 1989 (see *Factortame Ltd v Secretary of State for Transport* [C47]) your Lordships held that, as a matter of English law, the courts had no jurisdiction to grant interim relief in terms which would involve either overturning an English statute in advance of any decision by the Court of Justice of the European Communities that the statute infringed Community law or granting an injunction against the Crown. It then became necessary to seek a preliminary ruling from the Court of Justice as to whether Community law itself invested us with such jurisdiction. [It] will be remembered that, on that occasion, the House never directed its attention to the question how, if there were jurisdiction to grant the relief sought, discretion ought to be exercised in deciding whether or not relief should be granted.

In June 1990 we received the judgment of the Court of Justice [C48] replying to the questions we had posed and affirming that we had jurisdiction, in the circumstances postulated, to grant interim relief for the protection of directly enforceable rights under Community law and that no limitation on our jurisdiction imposed by any rule of national law could stand as the sole obstacle to preclude the grant of such relief. In the light of this judgment we were able to conclude the hearing of the appeal in July and unanimously decided that relief should be granted in terms of the orders which the House then made, indicating that we would give our reasons for the decision later.

. . .

Some public comments on the decision of the Court of Justice, affirming the jurisdiction of the courts of Member States to override national legislation if necessary to enable interim relief to be granted in protection of rights under Community law, have suggested that this was a novel and dangerous invasion by a Community institution of the sovereignty of the United Kingdom Parliament. But such comments are based on a misconception. If the supremacy within the European Community of Community law over the national law of Member States was not always inherent in the EEC Treaty it was certainly well established in the jurisprudence of the Court of Justice long before the United Kingdom joined the Community. Thus, whatever limitation of its sovereignty Parliament accepted when it enacted the European

Communities Act 1972 **[C35]** was entirely voluntary. Under the terms of the 1972 Act it has always been clear that it was the duty of a United Kingdom court, when delivering final judgment, to override any rule of national law found to be in conflict with any directly enforceable rule of Community law. Similarly, when decisions of the Court of Justice have exposed areas of United Kingdom statute law which failed to implement Council directives, Parliament has always loyally accepted the obligation to make appropriate and prompt amendments. Thus there is nothing in any way novel in according supremacy to rules of Community law in those areas to which they apply and to insist that, in the protection of rights under Community law, national courts must not be inhibited by rules of national law from granting interim relief in appropriate cases is no more than a logical recognition of that supremacy.

Although affirming our jurisdiction, the judgment of the Court of Justice does not fetter our discretion to determine whether an appropriate case for the grant of interim relief has been made out. [A] decision to grant or withhold interim relief in the protection of disputed rights at a time when the merits of the dispute cannot be finally resolved must always involve an element of risk. If, in the end, the claimant succeeds in a case where interim relief has been refused, he will have suffered an injustice. If, in the end, he fails in a case where interim relief has been granted, injustice will have been done to the other party. The objective which underlies the principles by which the discretion is to be guided must always be to ensure that the court shall choose the course which, in [the] circumstances, appears to offer the best prospect that eventual injustice will be avoided or minimised. Questions as to the adequacy of an alternative remedy in damages to the party claiming injunctive relief and of a cross-undertaking in damages to the party against whom the relief is sought play a primary role in assisting the court to determine which course offers the best prospect that injustice may be avoided or minimised. But where, as here, no alternative remedy will be available to either party if the final decision does not accord with the interim decision, choosing the course which will minimise the risk presents exceptional difficulty.

If the applicants were to succeed after a refusal of interim relief, the irreparable damage they would have suffered would be very great. That is now beyond dispute. On the other hand, if they failed after a grant of interim relief, there would have been a substantial detriment to the public interest resulting from the diversion of a very significant part of the British quota of controlled stocks of fish from those who ought in law to enjoy it to others having no right to it. In either case, if the final decision did not accord with the interim decision, there would have been an undoubted injustice. But the injustices are so different in kind that I find it very difficult to weigh the one against the other.

[Unlike] the ordinary case in which the court must decide whether or not to grant interlocutory relief at a time when disputed issues of fact remain unresolved, here the relevant facts are all ascertained and the only unresolved issues are issues of law, albeit of Community law. Now, although the final decision of such issues is the exclusive prerogative of the Court of Justice, that does not mean that an English court may not reach an informed opinion as to how such issues are likely to be resolved.

. . .

[Lords Bridge, Goff and Jauncey referred to two decisions of the Court of Justice on analogous issues: Case C-3/87 *R v Ministry of Agriculture Fisheries and Food, ex parte Agegate Ltd* [1989] ECR 4459 and Case 216/87 *R v Ministry of Agriculture Fisheries and Food, ex parte Jaderow Ltd* [1989] ECR 4509 and the interim decision of the President of the Court of Justice. Their Lordships were prepared to put their collective shirts on the firm favourite, namely, that the applicants had a sufficiently strong case to justify the granting of interim relief. The House of Lords, therefore, ordered that, pending final judgment the Secretary of State (whether by himself, his servants or agents, or otherwise howsoever) be restrained from withholding or withdrawing registration in the register of British fishing vessels maintained by him in respect of certain specified vessels which might be accorded protection and be granted fishing rights by Community law by the forthcoming decision of the Court of Justice. The answers to 'what happened?' may be found in Case C-221/89 *R v Secretary of State for Transport, ex parte Factortame (No 3)* [1991] ECR I-3905 and Case C-279/89 *Commission of the European Communities v United Kingdom* [1993] 1 CMLR 564.]

SECTION FIVE

THE INCORPORATION OF COMMUNITY LAW (FRANCE)

The incorporation of Community law into the French domestic legal system has, naturally, had to operate within the constitution and the constitutional traditions of France. The French Constitution is a written one and the current 1958 Constitution, which came into force after the creation of the European Economic Community, made provision for the superiority of treaties over French statutes (Article 55 [C50]). The word 'statute' is used to translate the French word '*loi*', which is legislation enacted by the French Parliament. An important constitutional tradition, dating from the French Revolution and based on the separation of powers, has been that *loi* is the expression of the sovereignty of the people, through Parliament or by way of referendum, and that the judiciary cannot challenge the legality or constitutionality of a statute. The function of measuring the compatibility of a statute with the provisions of the constitution is performed by the Conseil constitutionnel, established by the 1958 Constitution, which has on numerous occasions declared statutes to be void on the ground that they contravened the constitution. An important feature of the French legal system is the division between the 'administrative courts', which hear actions brought against the administration, and the 'ordinary courts', which hear other cases (both civil and criminal). The highest administrative court is the Conseil d'Etat and the highest ordinary court is the Cour de Cassation. Arguments are addressed to those courts, in the manner of the Advocate General before the Court of Justice, by the 'Commissaire du Gouvernement' and the 'Procureur Général', respectively.

When cases containing a Community law element started to come before the French courts, both the administrative and ordinary courts were faced with the problems posed by legal arguments based on the non-conformity of statutes with primary and secondary Community legislation and the traditional view that to incorporate the principles of the supremacy of Community law and of direct effect in a way which would necessitate French statutes being subordinated to the superiority of Community law would be tantamount to pronouncing upon the validity of those statutes. In 1968 in *Syndicat Général de Fabricants de Semoules de France* [C51], the Conseil d'Etat refused to accord superiority to a treaty over a statute enacted subsequent to that treaty on the ground that to do so would be to adjudicate on the constitutionality of that statute and that the courts had no such jurisdiction. The decision was harshly criticised in the periodical literature [C52]. There was, according to the commentators, a fundamental difference between the control of constitutionality exercised by the Conseil constitutionnel and the role of a court in deciding whether to apply a statute to a concrete situation in the circumstances where the provisions of a prior treaty were incompatible with that statute. The views of the commentators were given constitutional legitimacy by the Conseil constitutionnel. In 1975, the Conseil constitutionnel held that, when exercising its constitutionality jurisdiction, it did not have jurisdiction to investigate the conformity of a statute to the provisions of a treaty or international agreement, that a statute which is contrary to a treaty will not, by reason of that fact alone, be contrary to the constitution and that, by implication, the creators of the 1958 Constitution, by enacting Article 55, enjoined the courts (both administrative and ordinary) to enforce Article 55 and accord to Community law its supremacy over statutes. The Conseil constitutionnel's decision offered a constitutional basis for a reversal of *Semoules*.

On the other hand, the reaction of the ordinary (ie non-administrative) courts to the problems posed by the reception into French internal law of the legal consequences emanating from the Treaty of Rome had been of a very positive nature. In *Torrekens*, a question of interpretation of a regulation on social security for migrant workers arose and a lower court referred that question to the Administrative Commission, established by the regulation to co-ordinate matters of social security. This judgment was quashed by the Cour de Cassation on one ground only, namely, that the lower court had violated not a rule of French judicial procedure but Article 177 of the Treaty. The Cour de Cassation was prepared to treat a breach of Article 177 as engendering the same consequences (ie the decision would be quashed) as a breach of French national law. The major response to the ever-growing insistence of the Court of Justice that Community law emanated directly from the Treaty, to the exclusion of national constitutions, came in *Société Cafés Jacques Vabre* **[C53]**, where the Cour de Cassation overtly took up the solution suggested by the Conseil constitutionnel to the problem on which the Conseil d'Etat had floundered in *Semoules*. A few months later, the Cour de Cassation went one stage further. In *Von Kempis v Geldof* **[C54]**, the Cour de Cassation based a decision directly and exclusively on Article 52 of the Treaty, without any express reference to the constitutional mechanism whereby that article took precedence over French internal law.

The Conseil d'Etat had not completely turned a blind eye towards Community law. Within its self-imposed limitations, the Conseil d'Etat carried out certain obligations imposed by Community law. There was, after an uncertain start, a general pattern of willingness to refer questions of interpretation to the Court of Justice, although interspersed with some examples of over-reliance on the *acte clair* doctrine (*Semoules* **[C51]**, *Cohn-Bendit* **[C55]**, *Mantout* **[C57]**). The Conseil d'Etat also was prepared to extend its well-established case law relating to the responsibility of the state to pay damages in situations where that responsibility arose from breach of a Community obligation. In *Ministre du commerce extérieur v Société Alivar*, Alivar, a company registered in Italy, had made contracts with companies in France with a view to exporting potatoes of a specified category from France to Italy. However, the contracts could not be performed because France made the export of potatoes of that category to other Member States conditional upon submission of an export declaration previously endorsed by the French authorities, who had refused to issue this declaration to Alivar. In Case 68/76 *Commission v France* [1977] ECR 515, the Court of Justice declared that the French Republic, in making the exportation subject to the presentation of a duly authorised declaration, had failed to comply with an obligation imposed on it by Article 34 of the Treaty. Alivar brought an action for damages against the French state and the Conseil d'Etat confirmed a judgment ordering the state to make reparation for the loss suffered by Alivar (cf *Bourgoin* **[C44]** and *Kirklees* **[C46]**).

However, the Conseil d'Etat, having already failed to resolve the problems arising from the apparent incompatibility of statutes with the supremacy of Community law, handed down a number of very 'non-European' decisions, directly resulting from the constitutional impasse which it had created. In *Cohn-Bendit* **[C55]**, the Conseil disregarded the doctrine of direct effect of directives and with regard to the consequences of the principle of direct effect of Community provisions upon 'regulatory measures' (ie legislation made not by a statute but emanating from an enabling statute), the Conseil d'Etat, in several decisions, raised a defensive screen (a *loi écran*), whereby an action to challenge a regulatory measure on the ground that it was incompatible with Community law was treated as an action against the enabling statute itself, and such a challenge could not be entertained. In 1985, the Conseil d'Etat refused to admit an action based on the conflict between a decree founded on a statute regulating the management of the tobacco monopoly and the binding authority of the Court of Justice (*International Sales* [C56]) and in 1986 the Conseil d'Etat again refused an individual the protection afforded by the doctrine of direct effect (*Mantout* [C57]).

There was by now a difference between the Cour de Cassation and the Conseil d'Etat in their several receptions of judgments of the Court of Justice and several series of cases illustrated the fact that whether the European Community law dimension would be afforded to litigants depended on which court was chosen to initiate the litigation.

It was, therefore, necessary to diminish the force of the theory of the *loi écran*. This could be achieved by ascertaining whether, in fact, an enabling statute so bound those entrusted with regulatory powers that they could only act according to the statute and were forced to make substantive rules almost as if those rules were specified in the statute (where any challenge to the rules, whether laid down by regulation, decree or decision, was necessarily an indirect attack on the statute) or whether the enabling statute did not so provide. This new approach states that when the statute which is enacted subsequent to a treaty is simply a wide, general enabling statute (*loi cadre*) which only has as its purpose the simple granting of a power to the administration to make regulatory measures or decisions and which gives those entrusted with regulatory powers a wide perspective within which to make the substantive rules, without determining the exact and detailed manner in which that power is to be exercised, a challenge to the rules is not an indirect challenge to the enabling statute and the Conseil d'Etat is entitled to examine the conformity of the regulatory measure or decision to Community law. Examples of this process are found in cases involving the protection of wildlife. Organisations devoted to the protection of the wild life of France have been particularly active in utilising directives as a weapon against regulatory measures favouring the 'hunting, shooting and fishing lobbies'. The Conseil d'Etat has a good record in annulling regulations and decisions which are contrary to directives relating to conservation, especially Directive 79/409, relating to the conservation of wild birds (*ROALC* [C58]).

Finally, it was necessary to overrule the established case law, dating from *Semoules*. In 1988, a decision was made by the Conseil constitutionnel, this time acting as an electoral court to determine disputed Parliamentary elections, to the effect that in its capacity as an electoral court relating to Parliamentary elections it was of the same hierarchical status as the Conseil d'Etat, when that body acted as an electoral court in European Parliament elections. Therefore, what the Conseil constitutionnel had power under the constitution to do the Conseil d'Etat could also do. Furthermore, it held that, in its capacity as an electoral court, it had jurisdiction to determine the conformity of a statute to a treaty. This decision, therefore, gave an indication to the Conseil d'Etat that if the Conseil d'Etat, acting in its electoral capacity (below), had to resolve a conflict between an electoral statute and the provisions of a treaty, the Conseil d'Etat should not decline jurisdiction and should investigate the matter: if it found conformity, it should say so and apply the statute; if it found a real conflict, it should apply the treaty and not apply the statute. This was accepted in *Nicolo* **[C59]**, when the Conseil d'Etat acting as an electoral court to determine European Parliamentary election disputes reversed the traditional case law dating from *Semoules*. This was hailed as one of the most significant cases in France (and therefore in Europe). The traditional case law of the Conseil d'Etat was seen as being increasingly at variance with France's obligations under the Treaty of Rome and it was a useful decision to make during the French Presidency of the Council of Ministers and at a time of strident calls for ever-closer European integration. However, in *Nicolo*, the Conseil d'Etat was not called upon to take the really decisive step of disregarding a statute on the ground that the statute was contrary to Community law.

It only remained to be seen whether the decision of the Conseil d'Etat acting as an electoral court would be followed by the Conseil d'Etat acting as an administrative court making decisions as to the legality of administrative action, when that administrative action is challenged in circumstances where there is put in issue the status of a statute as being incompatible with the Treaty and Community secondary legislation. This event occurred, with regard to a regulation, a year later in *Boisdet* **[C60]** and, finally, the Conseil d'Etat was presented with a situation where it had to face the relationship between a national statute and the direct effect of a directive. Shedding its psychological blockages which had hindered its acceptance of the supremacy of Community law for so long, the Conseil d'Etat handed down the long-awaited judgment (*SA Rothmans* **[C61]**), continuing the saga of the French state tobacco monopoly referred to in *International Sales* **[C56]** but this time in the post-*Nicolo* context.

MATERIALS

[C50] Article 55 of the 1958 French Constitution

Treaties and agreements duly ratified or approved possess, henceforth from the date of their publication, a legal authority superior to that of statutes, provided that in the case of each measure the agreement or treaty is implemented by the other parties.

[C51] Syndicat Général de Fabricants de Semoules de France (Conseil d'Etat, 1 March 1968)

[The Syndicat brought an action to annul a decision of the French Ministry of Agriculture which, first, authorised the importation from Algeria, after that country's independence from France, of a large quantity of semolina and, secondly, determined that those imports would not be subject to the levy imposed by Regulation 19, which laid down measures relating to the common agricultural policy for cereals, inter alia, imposing levies on imported cereals in order to maintain preference for Member States against non-Member States. The Syndicat objected to the Ministry of Agriculture decision, maintaining that the levy ought to be imposed on the imported semolina by virtue of Regulation 19. During the pre-independence period and for some time thereafter, Franco-Algerian economic (and other) relations were governed by *ordonnances* made by the French President under special enabling powers. The Ministry of Agriculture decision was based on an *ordonnance* which had been made on 19 September 1962 and provided that, as a transitional measure, goods imported from Algeria remained subject to the customs regime which had been applicable before independence under the Customs Code. This transitional measure meant that Algeria was still part of the customs territory of France and, consequently, products which originated in the customs territory were subject to neither customs duties nor to quantitative restrictions. On 15 January 1963, the French Parliament enacted a statute which provided that the *ordonnance* (and other *ordonnances* made by the President under the special enabling powers) possessed and maintained, as from the date of its publication, the force of statute. The legislature had thus provided, by a mechanism possessing the status of a statute, that goods imported from Algeria were to be treated as French products and could be transported to metropolitan France without restriction. It maintained the status quo with regard to Algeria, which before independence according to the Treaty of Rome, Article 227, as enacted, was treated as an integral part of France. However, Algeria became independent and Regulation 19 was, naturally, silent as to the effect of its application to a territory which was no longer a part of a Member State. The question of interpretation of Regulation 19 and the Treaty of Rome as to whether the levy imposed by Regulation 19 should apply to imports from Algeria subsequent to the date of independence was clearly a matter calling for resolution by the Court of Justice on an Article 177 reference.]

Submissions of the Commissaire du Gouvernement:

[The Commissaire du Gouvernement argued that an Article 177 reference was only 'necessary' for the solution of an issue and, in her opinion, there was no need to seek such a reference. This was abundantly clear: the decision of the Ministry of Agriculture was based on the *ordonnance* and the Conseil d'Etat had no power to control the conformity of the *ordonnance* with the Treaty. She argued that, although Article 55 **[C50]** itself affirmed the superiority of international agreements over national statutes, the administrative courts could not control any violation of this superiority by Parliament without changing the constitutional position of the courts, that to apply Article 55 to give the Treaty precedence over the *ordonnance* would be to question the constitutionality of the *ordonnance*, and the 1958 Constitution did not permit this.]

The contested decision is based on the provisions of a French statute and it is not for you to set aside its application in favour of the provisions of the Community Regulations and the [Treaty. You] cannot, in my opinion, construe the conformity of the *ordonnance* with the [Treaty. An administrative court] can neither criticise nor misconstrue a statute. That consideration has always led the court to refuse to examine actions based on the unconstitutionality of a statute [and there is] an abundant case law which [has refused to entertain applications based on] grounds alleging that a statute violates the constitution and grounds based on a violation of the constitution against a decision implementing a statute. [What] is true for the control of a statute as against the superior rules in the constitution is equally applicable as against any written provision which is expressly described, such as an international treaty, as having a status superior to that of a statute. [You] should dismiss actions based on the violation of the Community regulation as soon as the contested decision is legally justified in the light of the *ordonnance* of 19 September 1962.

The Conseil d'Etat

Whereas [the] *ordonnance* of 19 September 1962 relating to the customs régime for trade between Algeria and France, which was adopted by virtue of the powers conferred on the President of the Republic by the statute of 13 April 1962, provides: 'Until the date on which [a proposed statute] comes into force, goods coming from Algeria will continue to be governed [by] the customs régime which was [previously applicable];

[Whereas] these provisions, which have the status of a statute according to [the] statute of 15 January 1963, have maintained, as a transitional measure as far as it concerns the entry into France of goods coming from Algeria, the customs régime in force before Algeria became independent; that, under this régime, the entry into France of cereal products coming from Algeria, which was then included in the customs territory of France, were not subject to customs duties, and would not have been subject to the levy which [a French decree] substituted for those duties by way of implementing Regulation [19;] that, consequently, the above-mentioned provisions of the *ordonnance* of 19 September 1962 prevent the application of the [levy;] that, consequently, the plaintiff Syndicat cannot legally maintain that in taking the contested decisions, the Minister of Agriculture has exceeded his powers.'

[C52]   Comment by M Lagrange (Dalloz, 1968, p 285)

[There] exists an important difference between the usual situation of controlling the constitutionality of statutes and the special situation of investigating the conformity of a statute to an international treaty. The normal situation in effect concerns the verification of the provisions of a legislative enactment to the constitution and presupposes the interpretation not only of the statute but also of the constitution. It is otherwise when Article 55 is under consideration because in that case the court has not to compare a statute with the constitution but with a treaty, and courts have no power to interpret treaties; in such a case the court is limited to recording, should the occasion arise, the inconsistency between the internal statute and the treaty; in doing this, the court applies Article 55 in giving precedence to that one of the two sets of provisions which enjoys a superior authority; in no way does the court interpret the constitution to see if the statute conforms to the constitution or not.

[C53]   Administration des Douanes v Société Cafés Jacques Vabre (Cour de Cassation, 24 May 1975)

[Vabre had bought coffee from coffee merchants in Holland and the coffee was subjected to an internal consumption tax under the French Customs Code, Article 265. Vabre complained that coffee manufactured in Holland and sold in France was subject to a much higher tax than that imposed on coffee manufactured in France and sold in France and that this was contrary to Article 95 **[E4]–[E10]**. Vabre brought an action for the repayment of the unlawful tax paid by them and were successful before a lower court. However, the Customs Administration maintained, inter alia, that the courts had no jurisdiction to hear such an application in that the claim for repayment of tax was governed by Article 265 of the Customs Code, which was inserted into the Customs Code by and, therefore, derived from a statute of 14 December 1966, was of a legal nature, therefore, equivalent to that of a statute, which was naturally enacted subsequent to Article 95, and that the statute should prevail and be applied. They brought an action before the Cour de Cassation to quash the decision of the lower court. The Customs Administration based their argument on the decision of the Conseil d'Etat in *Semoules* **[C51]** (ie they argued that giving preference to the Treaty over a statute, in accordance with Article 55, inescapably meant that at the same time the court was passing judgment on the constitutionality of that statute).]

Submissions of the Procureur Général

Happily, I need not present to you a long argument to show that it is not a question of [the Cour de Cassation] determining the constitutionality of a statute. [According] to the decision of the Conseil constitutionnel [referred to in the text], a court, when faced with a claim of incompatibility between a treaty and a subsequently enacted statute, does not review the constitutionality of the statute but simply investigates the compatibility of the statute and the treaty, which when duly ratified or approved, becomes part of French internal law and the constitution merely happens to state the rule which allows the court to resolve the conflict by giving to the treaty an authority superior to that of statute. Such is the decision of the Conseil constitutionnel and that decision [actually] binds all public authorities, including the courts. [I] can therefore submit that the conflict between a treaty and a subsequently enacted statute does not involve a question of constitutionality of this statute.

[Today] international law, as contained in the treaties, has considerably developed and relates to trade, industry, telecommunications, culture, public health, industrial law, human rights and fundamental feedoms. [There] developed irresistibly the idea that there can be no international relations if international agreements can be thwarted by unilateral decisions of the contracting parties and a fundamental principle of international law is now the duty of the state to respect its international obligations. [Thus], for the first time in France the 1946 Constitution [expressly] consecrated, and in a general way, incorporated the principle of the primacy of international treaties over internal law.

An analysis [of the 1946 and 1958 Constitutions] in conformity with the international ethic desired by the makers of the Constitutions of 1946 and 1958, leads to the inescapable conclusion that the concept of superiority of treaties over statutes can only have any real meaning in relation to statutes subsequent to the treaty and it is clear that the international legal order can only be achieved and developed if states loyally apply the treaties which they have signed, ratified and published.

Finally, let me thus commence an examination of the true problem, that is to say the conflict between the Treaty establishing the European Economic Community and a subsequently enacted statute which is contrary to its provisions. [Since] I hope that I have succeeded [in] demonstrating the superiority of the legal norms of international treaties over the internal legal order, it behoves me now to develop my analysis of the same conflict – but now with the Treaty establishing the European Economic Community, whose ideals and objectives go far beyond the classical concept of treaties. [He cited the Preamble to that Treaty, Articles 5 and 189, and the decision of the Court of Justice in *Costa* **[C13]** and continued:] the force of Community law cannot differ from one Member State to another in favour of internal laws subsequently enacted without endangering the realisation of the aims of the Treaty.

It would be possible for you to give to Article 95 of the Treaty of Rome a precedence over the subsequently enacted statute by basing your decision on Article 55 of our constitution but personally I would ask you not to mention that article expressly in order to base your decision only on the legal order instituted by the Treaty of Rome. In effect to the extent that you restrict the derivation of the primacy within the French internal law of Community law as that of Article 55 of our constitution, you will explain and justify the primacy of Community law, as far as it concerns France, but this reasoning would permit it to be accepted that it is our constitution, and our constitution alone, that is based on the position of Community law in our internal domestic legal system. [These] are the reasons for which I request you not to base your decision on Article 55 of our constitution: you would thus recognise that the transfer operated by the Member States of their internal domestic legal systems to the benefit of the Community legal order, within the limits of the rights and obligations corresponding to the provisions of the Treaty, entails a definitive limitation of the Member States' sovereign rights against which a subsequent unilateral act which is incompatible with the concept of the Community cannot prevail. [In] this great difficult and delicate task of building Europe, difficult because the task often confronts national economic differences which must be abolished, delicate because all the institutions of France are involved, namely, Parliament, Government, the Conseil constitutionnel, the Conseil d'Etat, the Cour de Cassation, it is indisputable that all the decisions of the several constitutional organs should be in conformity with the objectives of the Treaty of Rome.

The Cour de Cassation

[Out of an abundance of caution, the Cour de Cassation took both a 'Constitutional perspective', based on Article 55, and a 'European Community perspective', based on the 'new legal order', as exemplified in *Costa* **[C13]**.]

Whereas, it is alleged that the judgment [of the lower court] declared to be illegal the internal consumption tax laid down by Article 265 of the Customs Code because of its incompatibility with the provisions of Article 95 of the Treaty of 25 March 1957, on the ground that that Treaty, by reason of Article 55 of the constitution, possesses an authority superior to that of French internal law, even a statute enacted subsequently, and, furthermore, even though a fiscal court has jurisdiction to control the legality of subordinate legislation laying down a tax which is challenged, the court could not, without exceeding its jurisdiction, refuse to apply a statute under the pretext that it was clothed with an unconstitutional character; that the totality of the provisions of Article 265 of the Customs Code was enacted by the statute of 14 December 1966 which conferred on those provisions the absolute authority which attaches to statutes and which is binding on all courts in France;

However, whereas the Treaty of 25 March 1957, which, by virtue of the above-mentioned article of the constitution, possesses an authority superior to that of statutes, instituted a separate and new legal order integrated with that of Member States; that by reason of this, the legal order which it has created is directly applicable to the nationals of those states and is binding on their courts; that, because of this, it was a perfectly legally correct decision and without exceeding its powers, that the [lower court] decided that Article 95 of the Treaty of Rome must be applied to the case, to the exclusion of Article 265 of the Customs Code, even though the latter legislative provision was enacted later; from which it follows that the action is dismissed.

[C54] Von Kempis v Geldof (Cour de Cassation, 15 December 1975)

[French law imposed the requirement to obtain official permission before becoming a farmer in France. It was claimed that this was contrary to Article 52 of the Treaty. It will be seen that, without any express reference thereto, the Cour de Cassation followed the decision of the Court of Justice in *Reyners* **[D31]**, **[D56]**, which had been brought to their attention by the Procureur Général.]

The Cour de Cassation

Having regard to Article 52 of the Treaty of 25 March 1957 establishing the European Economic Community;

Whereas, according to the provisions of this Article, restrictions on the freedom of establishment of the nationals of a Member State within the territory of another Member State are to be abolished progressively during the course of the transitional period; that the freedom of establishment includes access to and the pursuit of activities as a self-employed person, as well as the formulation and management of business undertakings, in accordance with the conditions laid down by the legislation of the country of establishment for its own nationals;

Whereas, it appears [from the judgment of the lower court] that, on 2 March 1972 Clave Bouhaben von Kempis, of German nationality, owner of an agricultural holding leased to M and Mme Geldorf, gave notice to quit to these tenants, in order himself to take over the agricultural holding, as from 1 November 1972, the date of expiry of the lease;

Whereas, in annulling the notice to quit the [lower court] stated that no [legal rule] existed either in national internal law or at Community level in order to regulate the right of establishment of farmers who are nationals of the Member States of the European Economic Community and that [amending legislation in 1969] did not have the effect of making inapplicable to such nationals the provisions of [existing French law] according to which an alien who wishes to maintain an agricultural undertaking in France must be specifically authorised so to do;

Whereas, by giving such a judgment, when, since the end of the transitional period which took place on 1 January 1970, Article 52 of the Treaty of 25 March 1957, which is directly applicable to nationals of the Member States of the European Economic Community and which is binding upon the courts of those Member States, prohibits any restriction on the freedom of establishment of these nationals in France and that consequently the provisions of French internal law, which imposed [the need for an] administrative authorisation for those nationals who wished to maintain an agricultural undertaking in France, have ceased to be applicable to such nationals, the [lower court] has acted contrary to [Article 52 and the lower court's judgment was quashed].

[C55]   Ministre de l'Intérieur v Cohn-Bendit (Conseil d'Etat, 22 December 1978)

[On 24 May 1968, the Minister of the Interior made an expulsion order against Daniel Cohn-Bendit and, on 2 February 1976, refused to cancel that order. Cohn-Bendit brought an action before a lower court, seeking the annulment of that refusal, and that court suspended the proceedings, on 21 December 1977, and referred two questions for a preliminary ruling by the Court of Justice on the interpretation of the appropriate Community law. The Minister of the Interior sought the annulment of that judgment before the Conseil d'Etat, which did not appear to have cognisance of *van Duyn* **[D43]** or *Rutili* **[D45]**.]

The Conseil d'Etat

Whereas according to Article 56 of the [Treaty] there is no provision in that article to empower a Community institution to make regulations relating to public order directly applicable within the Member States and the co-ordination of the legislative or regulatory provisions laying down a special régime for foreign nationals on the grounds of public order, public security and public health, is made necessarily the object of a Council Directive [Directive 64/221 **[D42]**];

[Whereas] it appears clearly from the provisions of Article 189 of the [Treaty] that if directives bind Member States 'with regard to the result to be achieved' and if, in order to achieve the results which they define, the national authorities of Member States are under an obligation to adapt their legislative and regulatory provisions to the directives which are addressed to them, these authorities remain the only competent authorities to determine the form to give to the implementation of these directives and to determine themselves, under the control of the national judicial authorities, their own method for producing their effect in internal national law;

[Whereas] directives cannot be invoked by persons within the jurisdiction of those Member States in order to support a legal action undertaken against an administrative act taken with regard to an individual;

[Whereas] it follows from the foregoing that M Cohn-Bendit cannot hope to succeed in his argument, in order to request the [lower court] to annul the decision of the Minister of the Interior dated 2 February 1976, that this decision misconstrues the provisions of [Directive 64/221];

[Whereas], therefore, in default of any legal argument directed against the regulations made by the French government in order to implement [directives], the answer to M Cohn-Bendit's action before the court cannot in any case be made subject to the interpretation of [Directive 64/221];

[Consequently it follows that] the Minister of the Interior has succeeded in his argument that the [lower court], by its judgment dated 21 December 1977, was wrong to submit to the Court of Justice of the European Communities questions for a preliminary ruling as to the interpretation of this directive and to stay proceedings until the reply of the court.

[C56] Société International Sales and Import Corporation (Conseil d'Etat, 13 December 1985)

[The International Sales and Import Corporation requested the Conseil d'Etat to annul a decision, dated 27 July 1977, of the Minister of Finance, informing the French Association of Cigarette Suppliers of his refusal to alter the price of tobacco products in an attempt to counter inflation, together with a request to annul the refusal of the minister to accede to a request for the payment of a large sum by way of reparation for the losses incurred by the company because of the refusal of the minister to vary the price of tobacco products. France has had a state monopoly for manufactured tobacco for many years. The general legislation on price control dated from an *ordonnance* of 1945, which provided (Article 60) that the provisions of the *ordonnance* forming the normal price code did not apply to decisions relating to monopoly products. With regard to the monopoly of manufactured tobacco, a statute of 24 May 1976 provided (Article 3) that the 'manufacture and retail sale of manufactured tobacco are reserved to the State' and (Article 6) that 'the retail price of each product is uniform throughout France. It is fixed according to the conditions determined by a decree'. A decree of 31 December 1976 provided (Article 10) that 'the retail prices of tobacco are fixed by an order of the Minister of the Economy and Finance'.

However, Directive 72/464 (on taxes other than turnover taxes which affect the consumption of manufactured tobacco), Article 5(1), provided that 'Manufacturers and importers shall be free to determine the maximum retail selling price for each of their products. This provision may not, however, hinder implementation of the national systems of legislation regarding the control of price levels or the observance of imposed prices'. The Commission received a number of complaints that the French authorities were using their powers under the 1976 statute to enhance the market position of the state tobacco monopoly and to the detriment of companies wishing to import to and sell within France. The Commission, exasperated with the French official attitude, brought enforcement proceedings under Article 169. The Court of Justice held (Case 90/82 *Commission v French Republic* [1983] ECR 2011, 21 June 1983) that the second sentence of Article 5(1) should be interpreted as referring only to national legislation of a general nature intended to check increases in prices. The power reserved to the government by the French legislation on the fixing of prices for manufactured tobacco was incompatible with Community law to the extent to which that power, by altering the selling price determined by the manufacturer or importer, allowed the comparative relationship between imported tobacco and tobacco distributed by the national monopoly to be adversely affected. The exercise of that power was also contrary to Articles 30 and 37 **[E11]**, **[E83]**. Consequently, 'the French Republic, by fixing the retail selling price of manufactured tobacco at a different level from that determined by the manufacturers or importers, has failed to fulfil its obligations under the EEC Treaty'. Despite this extremely clear condemnation of the French Republic, the Conseil d'Etat refused to admit the plaintiffs' request to annul the decision of the minister.]

The Conseil d'Etat

Whereas, in deciding, by a decree [of 31 December 1976, Article 6], made to implement the [statute of 24 May 1976], that the prices of the retail sale of tobacco are fixed by an order of the Minister of Finance, the government is bound to follow the principles enacted by the legislator and, especially, the maintenance of the monopoly of retail sale and the rule of a uniform price for each product throughout the land;

Whereas, in the first place, the plaintiff company maintains that the Court of Justice of the European Communities, by its judgment [in Case 90/82 (above)] that 'the French Republic, by fixing the retail selling price of manufactured tobacco at a different level from that determined by the manufacturers or importers, has failed to fulfil its obligations under the EEC Treaty', intended to attack the very principle of attributing to the administrative authority the power to determine the retail price of manufactured tobacco;

Whereas, it follows, from what has been stated above, that the power of regulating the tobacco industry, whose terms were determined by the decree of 31 December [1976], finds its legal basis in the principles laid down by the legislature; therefore, the ground raised against the validity of this decree is aimed, in reality, to force the court to make a judgment as to the conformity of the above-mentioned statute of 24 May 1976 with the Treaty of the European Economic Community and with [Directive 72/464], and that, in consequence, the action is inadmissible.

[C57] Société à Responsabilité Limitée Cabinet Mantout (Conseil d'Etat, 16 June 1986)

[The Sixth Council Directive (77/388) on the harmonisation of the laws of the Member States on VAT provided (Article 13) for a number of exemptions from liability to pay VAT, and (Article 1) Member States were under an obligation to implement the directive as from 1 January 1978 (the date of implementation was later postponed to 1 January 1979 by the Ninth Council Directive (78/583)). Mantout requested the Conseil d'Etat to annul the judgment of a lower court which had rejected both its request for a rebate of VAT imposed on the company for the period 1 February to 30 June 1978 and its request for a preliminary ruling to the Court of Justice with regard to the date on which the Sixth Directive took effect in France. Mantout argued that, in the absence of the implementation of the Sixth Directive by France, it should be able to rely on the directly effective provisions of that directive which had in particular provided that from 1 January 1978 specified insurance and reinsurance operations must be exempted from VAT. There was already at the time of the company's action a considerable case law of the Court of Justice which supported the company's argument as to the direct effect of the Sixth Directive (see Case 8/81 *Becker v Finanzamt Münster-Innenstadt* [1982] ECR 53, Case 255/81 *Grendel v Finanzamt für Körperschaften* [1982] ECR 2301, and, a case on almost identical facts to that of the company, Case 70/83 *Kloppenburg v Finanzamt Leer* [1984] ECR 1075). The Conseil d'Etat decided otherwise.]

The Conseil d'Etat

Whereas it appears clearly from the provisions of Article 189 of the Treaty of Rome that, if Council Directives bind Member States 'with regard to the results to be attained' and if, in order to attain the results which directives define, the national authorities are bound to adapt the legislation of Member States to the directives which are addressed to them, these authorities remain the only competent authorities to determine their own methods of permitting directives to become operative in internal law; that therefore, whatever other further matters they contain with regard to

Member States, directives cannot be invoked by persons within the jurisdiction of those states in support of a legal action relating to fiscal matters; that it is settled law that the measures to implement the Sixth Directive so that it becomes operative within French internal law have not yet been taken during the taxation period which is the subject of the litigation; that, in these circumstances, the said directive has, in every respect, no bearing on the application of previously enacted legislative provisions, especially [the] general code of taxation; that, as a result, irrespective of any preliminary ruling, the request to transmit the case to the Court of Justice has no purpose; whereas, it follows from what has been stated above, the company has not proved its case that it was contrary to law that, by the challenged judgment, the [lower court] had rejected the company's submissions aimed at obtaining a rebate of the VAT.

[C58]   Rassemblement des opposants à la chasse (ROALC) (Conseil d'Etat, 7 October 1988)

[ROALC brought an action to annul an order of the Minister of the Environment which had laid down that, in the case of wild fowl, the permitted hunting period in the Département of the Loire should be from Saturday 15 August (at 9 am) until the commencement of the universal hunting period, but only on specified dates and on specified waters. The Conseil d'Etat considered the wording of both Directive 79/409, Article 7(4) (below), and the ministerial order and heard in argument much factual evidence on the problem posed by their reconciliation. The essence of the directive with regard to migratory birds is to ensure their protection, but such protection involves an element of discretionary power within each Member State and leaves to national authorities the task of adapting their hunting laws to the objectives laid down in the directive. This is because of the nature of the problem in that all Member States are not visited or inhabited by the same species of birds, Member States do not have comparable numbers of birds of such and such a species, and there cannot be an absolute harmonised calendar of hunting since different species nest at different times in different areas of different Member States. In the present case, the minister had acted under a general decree enabling him to lay down detailed decisions regulating the hunting calendar for 1987–1988. An important question is whether determining the dates of the commencement of the hunting season comes within the concept of 'results to be achieved' (which binds the Member State) or 'choice of manner and form' (where there is an undoubted discretion). The Conseil d'Etat interpreted the 'aims defined by the appropriate Directive' as meaning that the protection of wild birds was to be achieved by having hunting seasons and non-hunting seasons. Therefore, the determination of the opening date for hunting wild fowl came within the concept of 'results to be achieved', which were laid down by Community law, to the exclusion of national law. The Conseil d'Etat based their decision on the very factual evidence presented by the Commissaire du Gouvernement, who produced much statistical evidence on the habits of different birds and showed, in particular, that the young of many species simply could not fly by mid-July and some even by the beginning of August.]

The Conseil d'Etat

Whereas it clearly appears from the provisions of Article 189 of the Treaty of 25 March 1957 that directives of the Council of the European Economic Community bind Member States 'with regard to the results to be achieved'; that if, in order to achieve the result which is defined by the directives, the national authorities, which are bound to adapt the legislative and regulatory rules of Member States to the directives which are addressed to them, remain solely competent to determine the form of implementation of the directives and to determine themselves, under the control of the national legal system, their own methods in order to produce the effects of the directives in national domestic law, these authorities cannot legally lay down regulatory provisions which would be contrary to the aims defined by the appropriate directives;

Whereas, according to the provisions of Article 7(4) of Council Directive 79/409 of 2 April 1979, relating to the preservation of wild [birds], Member States should ensure that species of birds to which was applied legislation on hunting should not be hunted or shot during their nesting or rearing season nor during the various stages of reproduction and dependence. In the case of migratory species, Member States should ensure, in particular, that the species of birds to which hunting regulations apply are not hunted during their period of reproduction or during their return to their rearing grounds;

Whereas the order made by the Minister of the Environment on 2 July 1987 which laid down that, in the case of wild [fowl], the permitted hunting period in the Département of the Loire should be from Saturday 15 August (at 9 am) until the commencement of the universal hunting period [on specified dates and on specified waters];

Whereas, it appears from the evidence presented to the court, that the decision determining the opening of the hunting season for wild fowl in the Départment of the Loire means that the hunting is authorised for a time and in places where the relevant birds have not finished their period of reproduction and rearing; that, therefore, the ministerial order was taken in defiance of the aims defined by the above-mentioned directive and, consequently, the order [of the Minister of the Environment] is annulled.

[C59]   Nicolo (Conseil d'Etat, 20 October 1989)

[The case concerned the elections for the European Parliament which took place in France in 1989 under the auspices of a statute of 7 July 1977 (the electoral statute) which gave jurisdiction to hear election disputes to the Conseil d'Etat. M Nicolo's argument was that the elections could not have legally taken place in the French overseas departments and territories (the DOMTOM) and that no one from the DOMTOM could be a candidate in the elections. This was based on the somewhat tenuous arguments that, first, the DOMTOM were exluded by the electoral statute which only envisaged the European territorial area of France, and, secondly, if that were not so, that the electoral statute was contrary to the Treaty of Rome. Both arguments were rather summarily and easily dismissed by the Commissaire du Gouvernement. With regard to the first argument, he answered that Article 4 of the electoral statute provided that the 'territory of the Republic shall form a single electoral constituency' and the constitution stated that the DOMTOM form an integral part of an indivisible republic. By virtue of the electoral code, anyone eligible as an elector in the DOMTOM could take part in the European Parliament elections; and, furthermore, Article 5 of the electoral statute applied to the elections for the European Parliament certain provisions of the electoral code by which any elector could be a candidate. With regard to the second argument, he submitted that the Treaty of Rome, Article 227(1), provided that that Treaty 'shall apply to the French Republic' and that included the DOMTOM. Both arguments, submitted the Commissaire du Gouvernement, should, therefore, be rejected. However, the real interest in *Nicolo* was in the question of the legal basis for rejecting M Nicolo's second argument: should it simply be, in conformity with the traditional case law of the Conseil d'Etat, a rejection based on an interpretation of the electoral statute, simpliciter and without even considering the compatibility of that statute with the Treaty of Rome or should the Conseil d'Etat break new ground by holding that the statute could only have legal effect by virtue of the fact that it did conform with the Treaty of Rome.]

Submissions of the Commissaire du Gouvernement

This raises, once again, before the Conseil d'Etat, the question of the application of Article 55 of the constitution **[C50]**. [It] is well known that the Conseil d'Etat has [held], by a celebrated decision in [*Semoules* **[C51]**] that an administrative court cannot give precedence to treaties over subsequently enacted statutes which are contrary to them and this case law holds good both with regard to Community law and to ordinary international agreements. [The] theoretical basis for those decisions which does not come from any allegation of principle of the hierarchical superiority of treaties over statutes – that comes expressly from Article 55 – must, on the other hand, be traced from your desire to respect the principle according to which the administrative court has no power to control the validity of a statute.

The principal considerations which have led you to adopt this solution, numbering three in all, are all devoted to this fundamental rule. In the first place, it seems to you that to set aside a statute for the reason that it is contrary to an earlier treaty would constitute a violation of the separation of powers. Now this principle [forbidding] courts from suspending the application of a statute has, undoubtedly, a constitutional status of the same level as Article 55. In the second [place,] if it is true that the Constitution of 1958 no longer adheres to the dogma of the unassailable character of statutes, it is only to the Conseil constitutionnel that the constitution confers the power to control, as the case may be, the validity of statutes. [Finally your] role in controlling the administration is made more effective by avoiding all conflict with the legislature. [This] is why you have always until now, without concerning yourselves with the developing case law of other jurisdictions, confirmed your decision of 1968.

Let me first of all indicate, as certain commentators have stated **[C52]**, that the control which the courts could be led to exercise over the conformity of statutes to antecedent treaties does not necessarily mean a control of the constitutionality of statutes, properly so called. Such a proposition is identical to the position of the Conseil constitutionnel [which] has expressly held that 'a statute contrary to a treaty is not, on that ground, contrary to the constitution', before deducing from this that it had no power to examine [the] conformity of statutes to international treaties currently in force. [In] truth, I wish to add further to my basic submission that the majority of learned writers customarily oppose your traditional case law and according to them the court, in giving precedence to a treaty over a statute in order to resolve a legal dispute, is in reality confining itself to choosing the proper norm to apply, without even impliedly criticising the legislative provision which it has discarded.

On the other hand, I believe it possible to hold [that] Article 55 itself necessarily implies an enabling power for judges in effect to control the conformity of statutes to treaties. It is necessary in effect to attribute to the framers of the constitution the intention of instituting an effective method of ensuring the supremacy of treaties and that this was to be implemented by Article 55. Now this article was addressed not to the legislator. [In] truth in the words in which it was enacted, this constitutional provision, which has the sole purpose of defining a hierarchy of legal norms, appears to me to be addressed principally to the judges. The judges regard themselves as thus entrusted with a mission to disregard statutes contrary to treaties, and have at their disposal in order to do this an enabling power granted by the constitution which, although it is only implied, nevertheless appears to be specifically contained in Article 55. I would add that such an interpretation allows for the resolution of all the legal problems which the Conseil d'Etat has encountered up till now. Without a doubt there is control of the conformity of statutes, but this derogation from the constitutional principle of the separation of powers finds its basis in the constitution itself. And this theory of the *loi écran* is not by this reasoning questioned. The enabling power impliedly given to the judges can only be implemented, according to Article 55, within the strict limits laid down by Article 55 and only relates to the control of conformity of statutes to treaties.

On the basis of the above reasoning, I propose that the Conseil d'Etat henceforth gives precedence to treaties over statutes made after the treaty. In doing this you would only be following the same approach already taken by the ordinary courts. [He referred to *Vabre* **[C53]**].

[A] reversal of [*Semoules* **[C51]**] therefore appears to me to be legally possible. And several factors lead me to think that it would be extremely apposite. This opportunity relates, first, to the need to fill the gap between the various jurisdictions in the French legal system. Because of the stand adopted since 1975 by the Conseil constitutionnel, the case law of the Conseil d'Etat in effect leads to a complete absence of any effective sanction against a breach of Article 55. This one knows was precisely the principal reason for which [the Cour de Cassation in *Vabre* **[C53]**] declared the superiority of treaties over statutes. [To] take the other line would lead to giving permission to Parliament easily to put a stop to the effective application of those international legal norms, especially Community norms, which Parliament deemed inopportune and this is not justifiable in the light of Article 55. [Secondly] the legal inconsistencies which result from [*Semoules*] are as important as they are numerous. On the one hand, one can see that the case law would lead to treaties repudiated by subsequent statutes having no force within the French internal legal system while at the same time continuing to bind France on the international legal plane and in international law. [On] the other hand, the [existence of two lines of case law, one by the Conseil d'Etat and one by the Cour de Cassation] leads to absurd practical consequences. And this is not intellectually justified. As [one commentator notes:] 'If one jurisdiction applies private law and one public law, that can be logical; but if one applies the treaty and one applies the statute, there is no logic.' [It] is an indisputable scandal, this time specifically emphasising the European Community dimension, that the ordinary citizens cannot rely before the French administrative judge on a rule which they would be allowed to invoke in the other Member States, for the sole reason that in our country the rule had been abrogated by a statute contrary to it. There is here a difference of treatment which is incompatible with the very principles of Community law. [Thirdly] it is clear [that] the current case law constitutes henceforth a tangible obstacle to the introduction in France of international law, especially Community law. One can never repeat too often the fact that the era of unconditional supremacy of the internal law of a state is over. International legal norms, and especially European Community ones, have gradually conquered our legal world, moreover without hesitating to encroach on the legislative province of Parliament. [Thus] certain entire branches of our law, such as the law of the economy, of employment or the protection of human rights, are today very largely the children of international legislation. The inability to give precedence to a treaty over the statute constitutes a real hindrance to this evolutionary process. France cannot at the same time accept limitations on her sovereignty and maintain the supremacy of her statutes before the courts; there is an illogicality that your decision of 1968 appears to have underestimated. [With] regard to the courts of other Community countries, and let us limit ourselves to the framework of European law, I feel constrained to state that the Conseil d'Etat is the last jurisdiction to disregard Community legal norms which are countermanded by subsequent statutes. [He referred to decisions of the constitutional courts of Germany and Italy.]

The attitude of the Conseil constitutionnel assuredly deserves your attention [because that body], even if it has no power to insist upon it, has suggested very firmly that you reverse your case law. [In 1986 it held:] 'it behoves the various institutions of the state within the framework of their respective jurisdictions to watch over the implementation of international agreements' [and in 1988 the] Conseil constitutionnel clearly expressed its way of thinking in agreeing to control the conformity of a statute with a treaty where it is acting in its capacity as an electoral court and, moreover, with the same terms of reference as the administrative courts when they sit as an electoral court. [You should borrow and learn from the Conseil constitutionnel] and it would not harm your freedom of choice to condemn your traditional approach.

[I] therefore propose that you base your decision on Article 55 of the constitution and to extend its scope to the totality of international agreements. If you follow me, you will henceforth [take] care to state expressly [in your judgment] that the electoral law is compatible with the Treaty of Rome [and] for all these reasons, I submit that the [claim of M Nicolo] be rejected.

The Conseil d'Etat

Whereas, according to the exact words of Article 4 of the [statute] of 7 July 1977 relating to the elections of representatives to the European Assembly 'the territory of the Republic forms a single constituency' for the election of the French representatives to the European Parliament; that by virtue of that statutory provision, combined with [the 1958 Constitution], from which it follows that the overseas departments and territories form an integral part of the French Republic, the said overseas departments and territories are necessarily included in the single constituency within which the election of the representatives to the European Parliament took place;

Whereas, according to the exact words of Article 227-1 of the treaty of 25 March 1957 establishing the European Economic Community: 'This Treaty applies . . . to the French Republic'; that the rules cited above, laid down by the statute of 7 July 1977, are not incompatible with the clear provisions of the above-mentioned Article 227-1 of the Treaty of Rome;

Whereas, it follows from what has been stated above that persons having, by virtue of [the] electoral code, the capacity of elector in the overseas departments and territories also have that capacity for the election of representatives to the European Parliament; that they are also eligible, by virtue of the provisions of [the] electoral code, applied to the elections to the European Parliament by Article 5 of the above-mentioned statute of 7 July 1977; that, consequently, it follows that M Nicolo has not succeeded in maintaining that either the participation of French citizens from the overseas departments and territories in the election of representatives to the European Parliament or the presence of certain of these persons on the lists of candidature had rendered the aforementioned election null and void; that, therefore, the application of M Nicolo must be rejected.

[C60]   Boisdet (Conseil d'Etat, 24 September 1990)

[A statute of 8 August 1962 provided (Article 16) that agricultural marketing committees, established in certain regions, could request the Minister of Agriculture that certain rules, accepted by their members in relation to the organisation and marketing of agricultural products, be made obligatory for the whole of the producers in the region, whether members of the committee or not. The 1962 enabling power was later re-enacted by a statute of 4 July 1980 (Article 7). Purporting to use the enabling power, the Ministers of Finance and Agriculture made two orders, the first (dated 29 March 1978) extending certain rules relating to production, quality, size, weight and presentation of apples, together with rules relating to the imposition of levies, which had been accepted by the relevant committee, to all producers in the region (including non-members) and the second (dated 28 April 1981) extending the operation of the first order for a further period of three years. Boisdet claimed that as he was not a member of the committee he was not bound to pay certain levies imposed on members and non-members alike by the orders and sought aid and comfort from Community law. Regulation 1035/72 laid down a régime for the common organisation of the market in fruit and vegetables. The compatibility of the enabling power and the regulation was considered in Case 218/85 *Association comité économique agricole régional fruits et légumes de Bretagne v A Le Campion* [1986] ECR 3513, 25 November 1986, where the Court of Justice held that the regulation 'leaves Member States no power to extend rules laid down by a producers' organisation to all the producers in a specified region where those rules concern the grading, size, weight and presentation of products or require producers to offer all their products for public sale exclusively at markets approved by the producers' organisation and to make contributions to the operation of the withdrawal scheme established by that organisation'.]

The Conseil d'Etat

Whereas, [Regulation 1035/72 laid] down especially with regard to apples a régime for the common organisation of the market including quality standards and intervention methods; that it follows from the interpretation given in its judgment of 25 November 1986 by the Court of Justice following a request for a preliminary ruling, that if this régime does not forbid associations of producers to impose different schemes on their members, the régime does not give jurisdiction to the authorities of Member States to extend to all producers of a specified region the rules laid down by the committee; that it follows from this that the Ministers of Finance and Agriculture did not have jurisdiction to extend those of the rules laid down by the fruit and vegetable agricultural marketing committee of the [region] which are mentioned in their order of 29 March 1978 [relating] to rules for the production, quality, size, weight and presentation of apples [and] relating to the participation by producers in the financing of the organisation [by means of levies]; that in prolonging for a further period of three years the illegal provisions of [the 1978 order] the Ministers of Finance and Agriculture have acted illegally in making their order of 28 April 1981; that the extension for a further period of three years of the rules mentioned in the order of 29 March 1976 could only have for its legal basis the provisions of Article 7 of [the] statute of 4 July 1980 which has re-enacted the provisions of Article 16 of the statute of 8 August 1962, it follows that in as much as it authorises for certain purposes the extension of the rules laid down by the economic agricultural committees, the statute is incompatible with the provisions then in force of [Regulation 1035/72]; [it] follows [that] M Boisdet has succeeded in maintaining that the order of 28 April 1981 [has no validity].

[C61]   SA Rothmans (Conseil d'Etat, 28 February 1992)

[This continues the saga of the French state tobacco monopoly referred to in *International Sales* **[C56]** but in the post-*Nicolo* context. Rothmans objected to ministerial orders relating to prices of tobacco for 1983, signed by a non-European minded Finance Minister, and brought an action seeking the annulment of a decision of the Finance Minister refusing their request to re-value the sales price of tobacco products. In order to appear to be complying with the judgment of the Court of Justice in Case 90/82 *Commission v French Republic* [1983] ECR 2011, 21 June 1983 and referred to in *International Sales*), the French government issued an administrative measure and, after even more complaints, the Commission initiated yet another Article 169 action for continued infringement of Directive 72/464, Article

5(1), for continued infringement of Article 30 and for the infringement of Article 171 in that the French Republic had failed to transpose into its national law the amendments needed to fulfil the court's earlier decision. The court accepted its Advocate General's submissions that the French government's explanations were 'quite inadequate' and that its position was 'untenable', emphasised that Directive 72/464 imposed on Member States the obligation to comply with the directive as long ago as 1 July 1973, and held that 'by not taking the measures necessary to comply' with the court's earlier decision 'the French Republic has failed to fulfil its obligations under Article 171 of the EEC Treaty' (Case 169/87, [1988] ECR 4093, 13 July 1988).]

The Conseil d'Etat

Whereas [the] Court of Justice of the European Community has held in its decisions relating to a failure to comply with Treaty obligations of 21 June 1983 and 13 July 1988 that the only provisions outside the rule laid down by Article 5(1) of the directive are those of national legislation of a general character, designed to keep prices under control; that the provisions [of] Article 6 of the statute of 24 May 1976, confer on the government a specific power to fix the prices of tobacco imported from other Member States of the European Community, independently of the application of national legislation on the control of price levels; that they thus allow the government to fix the price of imported tobacco in circumstances not laid down in Article 5(1) of [Directive 72/464] and are incompatible with the objectives defined by this directive; that it follows from this that Article 10 of the ministerial decree of 31 December 1976, which was based on Article 6 of the statute of 24 May 1976, is itself deprived of a legal basis, because the legal effect of the statute must be set aside; that it follows from the foregoing that the Minister of the Economy and Finance could not legally, in maintaining the price of manufactured tobacco at a different level from that which had been determined by the plaintiff company, [reject] the requests of Rothmans to increase by 50 centimes the price of imported products or distributed wholesale by them in France from 1 September 1983; that, consequently, the aforesaid minister's decisions must be annulled.

Further reading

Bebr, G, 'Article 177 of the EEC Treaty in the Practice of National Courts' [1977] ICLQ 241.

Collins, L, *European Community Law in the United Kingdom* (4th edn, 1990).

Dashwood, A, and Arnull, A, 'English Courts and Article 177 of the EEC Treaty' (1984) 4 YEL 255.

de Burca, G, 'Giving Effect to Community Directives' (1992) 55 MLR 215.

Gormley, L, 'The Application of Community Law in the United Kingdom, 1976–1985' (1986) 23 CMLR 287.

Gravells, N, 'Effective Protection of Community Rights: Temporary Disapplication of an Act of Parliament' [1991] Public Law 180.

Hartley, T, *The Foundations of European Community Law* (3rd edn, 1994).

Hunnings, N, 'Constitutional Implications of Joining the Common Market' (1968) 6 CMLR 50.

Jacobs, F, 'When to Refer to the European Court' (1974) 90 LQR 486.

Lang, T, 'Community Constitutional Law: Article 5 EEC Treaty' (1990) 27 CMLR 645.

Lasok, K, *The European Court of Justice: Practice and Procedure* (1984).

Pescatore, P, 'The Doctrine of Direct Effect: An Infant Disease in Community Law' (1983) 8 ELR 155.

Pollard, D, 'The Conseil d'Etat is European – Official' (1990) 15 ELR 267.

Pollard, D, and Hughes, D, *Constitutional and Administrative Law* (1990).

Rasmussen, 'The European Court's Acte Clair Strategy in CILFIT' (1984) 9 ELR 242.

Ross, M, 'Beyond Francovich' (1993) 56 MLR 55.

Wade, H, 'Sovereignty and the European Communities' (1972) 88 LQR 1.

Winter, J, 'Direct Applicability and Direct Effect: two Distinct and Different Concepts in Community Law' (1972) 9 CMLR 425.

C Broekmeulen v Huisarts Registratie Commissie 246/80 [1981] ECR 2311.

Commission of the EEC v French Republic 232/78 [1979] ECR 2729.

Commission of the EEC v Government of the Italian Republic 7/61 [1961] ECR 317.

Commission of the EEC v Italian Republic 31/69 [1970] ECR 25.

Commission of the EEC v Italian Republic 8/70 [1970] ECR 961.

Commission of the EEC v Italian Republic 28/81 [1981] ECR 2577.

Commission of the EEC v Kingdom of Denmark 211/81 [1982] ECR 4547.

Commission of the EEC v United Kingdom of Great Britain and Northern Ireland 31, 53/77R [1977] ECR 921.

Da Costa en Shaak NV v Nederlandse Belastingadministratie 28-30/62 [1963] ECR 31.

Hoffman-La Roche v Centrafarm Vertriebsgesellschaft Pharmazeutischer Erzeugnisse mbH 107/76 [1977] ECR 957.

Nordsee Deutsche Hochseefischerei v Reederei Mond 102/81 [1982] ECR 1095.

Chapter Four

The European Citizen

SECTION ONE

WORKERS

Introduction

In the beginning there were the workers. In a European Economic Community designed to integrate the economies of the Member States it was necessary to abolish restrictions on factors of production, one of which was the supply of labour. It was essential that freedom of movement for workers should be secured within the Community by the end of the transitional period at the latest and early secondary legislation was designed to eliminate discrimination based on nationality between workers of the Member States as regards conditions of work and employment (Article 48 [**D1**]), together with the ability to obtain social security for migrant workers and for those workers to take accrued social security benefits with them. Workers were to be permitted to move freely within the territory of Member States for this purpose, to stay in a Member State for the purpose of employment and to remain in the territory of a Member State after having been employed there.

The essence of freedom of movement for workers is that restrictions are abolished for, and rights are granted to, human factors of production who cross Community national borders to work or to seek work in the situations envisaged by Community law, in other words the freedom is for migrant workers. The Treaty provisions do not apply to situations of which every element is confined within a single Member State. The free movement of workers provisions require that there has to be some Community dimension in evidence. If a situation arises where there is no connection with trans-border activity, this part of Community law cannot be invoked (*Saunders* [**D2**], *Moser* [**D3**]). In particular, regulations on social security for migrant workers, which require equality of treatment between migrant workers and nationals, do not authorise nationals to demand equality of treatment with migrant workers (Case C-153/91 *Camille Petit v Office National des Pensions* [1993] 1 CMLR 476. See, further, criminal proceedings against *A Lopez Brea and CH Palacios* [**D37**], relating to establishment).

A 'worker' is interpreted as a Community concept (*Hoekstra* [**D4**]) in keeping with the principles of the supremacy and uniform application of

Community law discussed in Chapter Three. The essential feature of an employment relationship is that for a certain period of time a person performs services for and under the direction of another person in return for which he or she receives remuneration. Problems have arisen with regard to part or short-time employment where a person works fewer hours, and consequently receives less remuneration, than full-time workers and the person has to supplement his or her income in other ways (including national social assistance). The Court of Justice has taken a broad perspective. It has determined that the term 'worker' must not be interpreted restrictively and the rules on freedom of movement for workers cover persons in pursuit of effective and genuine activities (*Levin* **[D5]**, *Kempf* **[D6]**, *Lowrie-Blum* **[D7]**), but to the exclusion of activities on such a small scale as to be regarded as purely marginal and ancillary and to the exclusion of persons 'employed' on a scheme of social rehabilitation (*Bettray* **[D8]**). The duration of the activities pursued by the person concerned is a factor which may be taken into account by the national court when assessing whether they are effective and genuine or whether they are so limited as to be merely marginal and ancillary and, in assessing whether a person is a worker, account should be taken of all the occupational activities which the person concerned has pursued within the host Member State but not the activities which he or she has pursued elsewhere within the Community (Case C-357/89 *Raulin v Netherlands Ministry of Education and Science* [1992] ECR I-1027).

A general scheme for abolishing restrictions on the movement and residence of workers is laid down by Directive 68/360 **[D9]**, which refers to rights to leave one Member State and to enter and reside in another Member State and stipulates the documentary requirements for granting residence permits. Member States may take measures to regulate migrant workers, within the limits laid down by Community law, but these measures and any sanctions imposed for their breach must be proportionate to the gravity of any infringement (*Watson* **[D10]**, *Pieck* **[D11]**). Member States cannot impose obligations additional to those laid down by Community law (*Pieck* **[D11]**) and regulatory measures must not be implemented in a systematic or arbitrary manner (*Commission v Belgium* **[D12]**). Since freedom of movement for workers is to be interpreted broadly, Community nationals are entitled to move to another Member State to look for employment (ie provision is made for 'work seekers') and to reside there for a sufficient time (*Antonissen* **[D13]**).

When a worker has exercised migratory rights and crossed a Community border, free movement for workers entails the abolition of any discrimination within the host Member State which is based on nationality and which relates to employment, remuneration and other conditions of employment. Detailed provisions are laid down by Regulation 1612/68 **[D14]** and this (see Chapter Two, Section Three) is automatically incorporated within the domestic legal systems of each Member State. Regulation 1612/68 provides for non-discrimination with regard to eligibility for employment (Articles 1–6), but make an exception with regard to linguistic capability (*Groener* **[D15]**). The regulation also particularises equality of employment treatment for migrant workers (Articles 7–9) (*Sotgiu* **[D16]**).

Of special importance in the development of workers' rights from employment-related movement rights towards recognition of the migrant worker as a citizen integrated with the citizens of the host Member State has been the emphasis by the Court of Justice on non-discrimination in respect of 'social advantages'. Early on, the court applied this to fare reduction cards for national railways (*Cristini* [D17]) and developed a broadly defined form of words (or formula) (*Even* [D18]) which now encompasses, inter alia, loans related to childbirth (*Reina* [D19]), social welfare benefits (*Castelli* [D20], *Frascogna* [D21]), the ability to use one's own language in legal proceedings (*Mutsch* [D22]), the right, when accorded to nationals of the host Member State, to instal an unmarried partner (*Reed* [D23]) and certain educational grants (*Lair* [D24]). Social advantages are designed for workers themselves and not their descendants who are independent or who are work seekers (*Lebon* [D25]). In Case C-243/91 *Belgian State v Taghavi* 8 July 1992, it was shown that entitlement to a benefit for handicapped persons was reserved to Belgian nationals residing in Belgium. It was a personal right and a person who was not a national of an EEC Member State could not be entitled to the benefit by reason solely of the fact that his or her spouse was a Belgian national. It was held that since the spouse of a Belgian worker who was not him or herself an EEC national could not claim the benefit in question, there was in these circumstances no 'social advantage' for national workers and Article 7(2) was not applicable.

The regulation (Articles 10–12) affords rights to the family of a worker, including his or her spouse (but not an unmarried partner: *Reed* [D23]), even if the spouses are separated (*Diatta* [D26]), and dependent children (*Lebon* [D25]), provided that suitable housing accommodation is available at the time the family instals itself with the worker (*Commission v Germany* [D27]). Family members may obtain employment in the host Member State (*Diatta* [D26]) and enjoy educational opportunities (*Casagrande* [D28]).

Finally, when employment has ended, either by retirement or by certain unfortunate circumstances, the freedom of movement for workers permits, in specified circumstances, a worker to remain in the territory of a Member State after having been employed there. This is governed by Regulation 1251/70 [D29].

MATERIALS

[D1]   EEC Treaty, Article 48

1. Freedom of movement for workers shall be secured within the Community by the end of the transitional period at the latest.

2. Such freedom of movement shall entail the abolition of any discrimination based on nationality between workers of the Member States as regards employment, remuneration and other conditions of work and employment.

3. It shall entail the right, subject to limitations justified on grounds of public policy, public security or public health [see Section Three of this chapter]:

(a)   to accept offers of employment actually made;
(b)   to move freely within the territory of Member States for this purpose;
(c)   to stay in a Member State for the purpose of employment in accordance with the provisions governing the employment of nationals of that state laid down by law, regulation or administrative action;
(d)   to remain in the territory of a Member State after having been employed in that state, subject to conditions which shall be embodied in implementing regulations to be drawn up by the Commission.

4. The provisions of this Article shall not apply to employment in the public service [see Section Three of this chapter].

[D2]   Case 175/78 R v Vera Ann Saunders [1979] ECR 1129

The European Court of Justice (at p 1135)

10. Although the rights conferred upon workers by Article 48 may lead the Member States to amend their legislation, where necessary, even with respect to their own nationals, this provision does not however aim to restrict the power of the Member States to lay down restrictions, within their own territory, on the freedom of movement of all persons subject to their jurisdiction in implementation of domestic criminal law.

11. The provisions of the Treaty on freedom of movement for workers cannot therefore be applied to situations which are wholly internal to a Member State, in other words, where there is no factor connecting them to any of the situations envisaged by Community law.

12. The application by an authority or court of a Member State to a worker who is a national of that same state of measures which deprive or restrict the freedom of movement of that worker within the territory of that state as a penal measure provided for by national law by reason of acts committed within the territory of that state is a wholly domestic situation which falls outside the scope of the rules contained in the Treaty on freedom of movement for workers.

[D3] Case 180/83 Moser v Land Baden-Württemberg [1984] ECR 2539

[Moser, a German national, was refused to be allowed to undertake the post-graduate training necessary to secure entry to the teaching profession. The Land based its refusal on the ground that there was insufficient certainty as regards Moser's loyalty to the German Constitution, as Moser was a member of the German Communist Party and had, for a long time and quite openly, been active in the party's affairs.]

The European Court of Justice (at pp 2547–2548)

14. [It] must be pointed out that, as the court held in [*Saunders* **[D2]**], [Article 48] aims, in implementation of the general principle laid down in Article 7, to abolish in the legislation of the Member States provisions regarding employment, remuneration and other conditions of work and employment by virtue of which a worker who is a national of another Member State is subject to more severe treatment or is placed in an unfavourable situation in law or in fact as compared with the situation of a national in the same circumstances.

15. It follows that the provisions of the Treaty concerning the free movement of workers and particularly Article 48 cannot be applied to situations [where] there is no factor connecting them to any of the situations envisaged by Community law.

16. [The case concerns] a German national who has always lived and maintained his residence in the Federal Republic of Germany and who contests the refusal by the German authorities to allow him access, under the legislation of that state, to a particular kind of vocational training.

17. In order to establish a connection with the Community provisions, Mr Moser claimed in the observations which he submitted to the court that the application to him of the German legislation in question, by making it impossible for him to complete his training as a teacher, entails the result that he is precluded from applying for teaching posts in schools in the other Member States.

18. That argument cannot be upheld. A purely hypothetical prospect of employment in another Member State does not establish a sufficient connection with Community law to justify the application of Article 48 of the Treaty.

19. It follows that there is no factor connecting a personal situation of the kind referred to by the national court with the provisions of Community law on the free movement of workers.

[D4] Case 75/63 Mrs MKH Hoekstra (née Unger) v Bestuur der Bedrijfsvereniging voor Detailhandel en Ambachten [1964] ECR 177

[The national court asked whether the concept of a 'wage-earner or assimilated worker' as used in an early regulation on social security for migrant workers should be defined by the legislation of each Member State or by Community law as having a supranational meaning.]

The European Court of Justice (at pp 184–185)

Articles 48 to 51 of the Treaty, by the very fact of establishing freedom of movement for 'workers', have given Community scope to this term.

If the definition of this term were a matter within the competence of national law, it would therefore be possible for each Member State to modify the meaning of the concept of 'migrant worker' and to eliminate at will the protection afforded by the Treaty to certain categories of person.

Moreover nothing in Articles 48 to 51 of the Treaty leads to the conclusion that these provisions have left the definition of the term 'worker' to national legislation.

On the contrary, the fact that Article 48(2) mentions certain elements of the concept of 'workers', such as employment and remuneration, shows that the Treaty attributes a Community meaning to that concept.

Articles 48 to 51 would therefore be deprived of all effect and the above-mentioned objectives of the Treaty would be frustrated if the meaning of such a term could be unilaterally fixed and modified by national law.

The concept of 'workers' in the said articles does not therefore relate to national law, but to Community law.

The expression 'wage-earner or assimilated worker' used by [the regulation] has a meaning only within the framework and the limits of the concept of 'workers' provided for in the Treaty to the application of which this regulation is limited.

The said expression, which is intended to clarify the concept of 'workers' for the purposes of [the regulation], has therefore, like that concept, a Community meaning.

Even if, for the sake of argument, the expression 'wage-earner or assimilated worker' appeared in the legislation of each of the Member States, it could not possibly have a comparable meaning and rôle, so that it is impossible to establish the meaning by reference to similar expressions which may appear in national legislation.

The concept of 'wage-earner or assimilated worker' has thus a Community meaning, referring to all those who, as such and under whatever description, are covered by the different national systems of social security.

[D5]   Case 53/81 DM Levin v Staatssecretaris van Justitie [1982] ECR 1035

[Mrs Levin, a British national and married to a national of a non-EEC country, applied for a permit to reside in the Netherlands. The permit was refused, on the basis of Netherlands legislation, on the ground, amongst others, that Mrs Levin was not engaged in a gainful occupation in the Netherlands and therefore could not be described as a 'favoured EEC citizen' within the meaning of the Netherlands legislation (below). Mrs Levin applied to the Secretary of State for Justice to have the decision reconsidered. The application was rejected and she appealed to a court (the Raad van State) claiming that she had, in the meantime, commenced activity as an employed person in the Netherlands (as a part-time chambermaid, earning low wages) and that, in any event, she and her husband had property and income more than sufficient to support themselves, even without undertaking the employment. The Raad van State referred three questions for a preliminary ruling:

1. Should the concept of 'favoured EEC citizen', which in the Netherlands legislation is taken to mean a national of a Member State as described in Article 1 of Directive 64/221 **[D42]** and is used in that legislation to determine the category of persons to whom Article [48, Regulation 1612/68 and Directives 64/221 and 68/360] apply, also be taken to mean a national of a Member State who in the territory of another Member State pursues an activity, whether paid or not as an employed person, or provides services to such a limited extent that in so doing he earns income which is less than that which in the last-mentioned Member State is considered as the mimimum necessary to enable him to support himself?

2. In the answer to Question 1, should a distinction be drawn between, on the one hand, persons who apart from or in addition to their income derived from limited employment have other income (for example from property or from the employment of their spouses living with them who are not nationals of a Member State) as a result of which they have sufficient means of support as referred to in Question 1 and, on the other hand, persons who do not have such additional income at their disposal and yet for reasons of their own wish to make do with an income less than what is generally considered to be the minimum required?

3. Assuming that question 1 is answered in the affirmative, can the right of such a worker to free admission into and establishment in the Member State in which he pursues or wishes to pursue an activity or provides or wishes to provide services to a limited extent still be relied upon if it is demonstrated or seems likely that his chief motive for residing in that Member State is for a purpose other than the pursuit of an activity or provision of services to a limited extent?]

The European Court of Justice (at pp 1047–1052)

5. Although these questions, as worded, are concerned not only with freedom of movement for workers but also with freedom of establishment and freedom to provide services, it is apparent from the particulars of the dispute in the main proceedings that the national court really has in mind only the issue of freedom of movement for workers. The answers to be given should therefore be confined to those aspects which have a bearing on that freedom.

First and second questions

6. In its first and second questions, which should be considered together, the national court is essentially asking whether the provisions of Community law relating to freedom of movement for workers also cover a national of a Member State whose activity as an employed person in the territory of another Member State provides him with an income less than the minimum required for subsistence within the meaning of the legislation of the second Member State. In particular the court asks whether those provisions cover such a person where he either supplements his income from his activity as an employed person with other income so as to arrive at that minimum or is content with means of support which fall below it.

. . .

9. Although the rights deriving from the principle of freedom of movement for workers and more particularly the right to enter and stay in the territory of a Member State are thus linked to the status of a worker or of a person pursuing an activity as an employed person or desirous of so doing, the terms 'worker' and 'activity as an employed person' are not expressly defined in any of the provisions on the subject. It is appropriate, therefore, in order to determine their meaning, to have recourse to the generally recognised principles of interpretation, beginning with the ordinary meaning to be attributed to those terms in their context and in the light of the objectives of the Treaty.

10. The Netherlands and Danish governments have maintained that the provisions of Article 48 **[D1]** may only be relied upon by persons who receive a wage at least commensurate with the means of subsistence considered as necessary by the legislation of the Member State in which they work, or who work at least for the number of hours considered as usual in respect of full-time employment in the sector in question. In the absence of any provisions to that effect in Community legislation, it is suggested that it is necessary to have recourse to national criteria for the purpose of defining both the mimimum wage and the minimum number of hours.

11. That argument cannot, however, be accepted. As the court has already stated in [*Hoekstra* **[D4]**] the terms 'worker' and 'activity as an employed person' may not be defined by reference to the national laws of the Member States but have a Community meaning. If that were not the case, the Community rules on freedom of movement for workers would be frustrated, as the meaning of those terms could be fixed and modified unilaterally, without any control by the Community institutions, by national laws which would thus be able to exclude at will certain categories of persons from the benefit of the Treaty.

12. Such would, in particular, be the case if the enjoyment of the rights conferred by the principle of freedom of movement for workers could be made subject to the criterion of what the legislation of the host state declares to be a minimum wage, so that the field of application *rationae personae* of the Community rules on this subject might vary from one Member State to another. The meaning and the scope of the terms 'worker' and 'activity as an employed person' should thus be clarified in the light of the principles of the legal order of the Community.

13. In this respect it must be stressed that these concepts define the field of application of one of the fundamental freedoms guaranteed by the Treaty and, as such, may not be interpreted restrictively.

14. In conformity with this view the recitals in the preamble to [Regulation] 1612/68 **[D14]** contain a general affirmation of the right of all workers in the Member States to pursue the activity of their choice within the Community, irrespective of whether they are permanent, seasonal or frontier workers or workers who pursue their activities for the purpose of providing services. Furthermore, although Article 4 of Directive 68/360 **[D9]** grants the right of residence to workers upon the mere production of the document on the basis of which they entered the territory and of a confirmation of engagement from the employer or a certificate of employment, it does not subject this right to any condition relating to the kind of employment or to the amount of income derived from it.

15. An interpretation which reflects the full scope of these concepts is also in conformity with the objectives of the Treaty which include, according to Articles 2 and 3, the abolition, as between Member States, of obstacles to freedom of movement for persons, with the purpose inter alia of promoting throughout the Community a harmonious development of economic activities and a raising of the standard of living. Since part-time employment, although it may provide an income lower than what is considered to be the minimum required for subsistence, constitutes for a large number of persons an effective means of improving their living conditions, the effectiveness of Community law would be impaired and the achievement of the objectives of the Treaty would be jeopardised if the enjoyment of rights conferred by the principle of freedom of movement for workers were reserved solely to persons engaged in full-time employment and earning, as a result, a wage at least equivalent to the guaranteed minimum wage in the sector under consideration.

16. It follows that the concepts of 'worker' and 'activity as an employed person' must be interpreted as meaning that the rules relating to freedom of movement for workers also concern persons who pursue or wish to pursue an activity as an employed person on a part-time basis only and who, by virtue of that fact, obtains or would obtain only remuneration lower than the minimum guaranteed remuneration in the sector under consideration. In this regard no distinction may be made between those who wish to make do with their income from such an activity and those who supplement that income with other income, whether the latter is derived from property or from the employment of a member of their family who accompanies them.

17. It should however be stated that whilst part-time employment is not excluded from the field of application of the rules on freedom of movement for workers, those rules cover only the pursuit of effective and genuine activities, to the exclusion of activities on such a small scale as to be regarded as purely marginal and ancillary. It follows both from the statement of the principle of freedom of movement for workers and from the place occupied by the rules relating to that principle in the system of the Treaty as a whole that those rules guarantee only the free movement of persons who pursue or are desirous of pursuing an economic activity.

18. The answer to be given to the first and second questions must therefore be that the provisions of Community law relating to freedom of movement for workers also cover a national of a Member State who pursues, within the territory of another Member State, an activity as an employed person which yields an income lower than that which, in the latter state, is considered as the minimum required for subsistence, whether that person supplements the income from his activity as an employed person with other income so as to arrive at that minimum or is satisfied with means of support lower than the said minimum, provided that he pursues an activity as an employed person which is effective and genuine.

Third question

19. The third question essentially seeks to ascertain whether the right to enter and reside in the territory of a Member State may be denied to a worker whose main objectives, pursued by means of his entry and residence, are different from that of the pursuit of an activity as an employed person as defined in the answer to the first and second questions.

20. Under Article 48(3) [the] right to move freely within the territory of the Member States is conferred upon workers for the 'purpose' of accepting offers of employment actually made. By virtue of the same provision workers enjoy the right to stay in one of the Member States 'for the purpose' of employment there. Moreover, it is stated in the preamble to Regulation [1612/68] that freedom of movement for workers entails the right of workers to move freely within the Community 'in order to' pursue activities as employed persons, whilst Article 2 of Directive [68/360] requires the Member States to grant workers the right to leave their territory 'in order to' take up activities as employed persons or to pursue them in the territory of another Member State.

21. However, these formulations merely give expression to the requirement, which is inherent in the very principle of freedom of movement for workers, that the advantages which Community law confers in the name of that freedom may be relied upon only by persons who actually pursue or seriously wish to pursue activities as employed persons. They do not, however, mean that the enjoyment of this freedom may be made to depend upon the aims pursued by a national of a Member State in applying for entry upon and residence in the territory of another Member State, provided that he there pursues or wishes to pursue an activity which meets the criteria specified above, that is to say, an effective and genuine activity as an employed person.

22. Once this condition is satisfied, the motives which may have prompted the worker to seek employment in the Member State concerned are of no account and must not be taken into consideration.

23. The answer to be given to the third question put to the court by the Raad van State must therefore be that the motives which may have prompted a worker of a Member State to seek employment in another Member State are of no account as regards his right to enter and reside in the territory of the latter state provided that he there pursues or wishes to pursue an effective and genuine activity.

[D6]   Case 139/85 Kempf v Staatssecretaris van Justitie [1986] ECR 1741

[Kempf, a German national, worked in the Netherlands as a part-time music teacher, giving 12 lessons a week. He received social assistance out of public funds to supplement his income. He applied for a residence permit but this was refused on the ground, inter alia, that he was not a favoured EEC citizen according to Netherlands law (see *Levin* [D5]) because he had recourse to public funds in the Netherlands and was manifestly unable to meet his needs out of the income from his employment. The Raad van State submitted the following question for a preliminary ruling:

Where a national of a Member State pursues within the territory of another Member State an activity which may in itself be regarded as effective and genuine work within the meaning of the Court's judgment in [*Levin*], does the fact that he claims financial assistance payable out of the public funds of the latter Member State in order to supplement the income he receives from that activity exclude him from the provisions of Community law relating to freedom of movement for workers?]

The European Court of Justice (at pp 1749–1751)

8. It is clear [that] the Raad van State seeks in essence a clarification of the criteria laid down by the court in [*Levin*].

11. As regards, first, the criterion of effective and genuine work as opposed to marginal and ancillary activities not covered by the relevant Community rules, the Netherlands government expressed doubts [as] to whether the work of a teacher who gives 12 lessons a week may be regarded as constituting in itself effective and genuine work within the terms of the judgment in *Levin*.

12. There is, however, no need to consider that question since the Raad van State, in the grounds of the judgment making the reference, expressly found that Mr Kempf's work was not on such a small scale as to be purely a marginal and ancillary activity. According to the division of jurisdiction between national courts and the Court of Justice in connection with references for a preliminary ruling, it is for the national courts to establish and to evaluate the facts of the case. The question submitted for a preliminary ruling must therefore be examined in the light of the assessment made by the Raad van State.

13. The court has consistently held that freedom of movement for workers forms one of the foundations of the Community. The provisions laying down that fundamental freedom and, more particularly, the terms 'worker' and 'activity as an employed person' defining the sphere of application of those freedoms must be given a broad interpretation in that regard, whereas exceptions to and derogations from the principle of freedom of movement for workers must be interpreted strictly.

14. It follows that the rules on this topic must be interpreted as meaning that a person in effective and genuine part-time employment cannot be excluded from their sphere of application merely because the remuneration he derives from it is below the level of the minimum means of subsistence and he seeks to supplement it by other lawful means of subsistence. In that regard it is irrelevant whether those supplementary means of subsistence are derived from property or from the employment of a member of his family, as was the case in *Levin*, or whether, as in this instance, they are obtained from financial assistance drawn from the public funds of the Member State in which he resides, provided that the effective and genuine nature of his work is established.

. . .

16. For those reasons, it must be stated in answer to the question submitted for a preliminary ruling that where a national of a Member State pursues within the territory of another Member State by way of employment activities which may in themselves be regarded as effective and genuine work, the fact that he claims financial assistance payable out of the public funds of the latter Member State in order to supplement the income he receives from those activities does not exclude him from the provisions of Community law relating to freedom of movement for workers.

[D7]   Case 66/85 Deborah Lawrie-Blum v Land Baden-Württemberg [1986] ECR 2121

[The question arose as to whether a trainee teacher was a 'worker'.]

The European Court of Justice (at p 2144)

17. [The concept of 'worker'] must be defined in accordance with objective criteria which distinguish the employment relationship by reference to the rights and duties of the persons concerned. The essential feature of an employment relationship, however, is that for a certain period of time a person performs services for and under the direction of another person in return for which he receives remuneration.

18. In the present case, it is clear that during the entire period of preparatory service the trainee teacher is under the direction and supervision of the school to which he is assigned. It is the school that determines the services to be performed by him and his working hours and it is the school's instructions that he must carry out and its rules that he must observe. During a substantial part of the preparatory service he is required to give lessons to the school's pupils and thus provides a service of some economic value to the school. The amounts which he receives may be regarded as remuneration for the services provided and for the duties involved in completing the period of preparatory service. Consequently, the three criteria for the existence of an employment relationship are fulfilled in this case.

. . .

21. The fact that trainee teachers give lessons for only a few hours a week and are paid remuneration below the starting salary of a qualified teacher does not prevent them from being regarded as workers. In [*Levin* [D5]], the court held that the expressions 'worker' and 'activity as an employed person' must be understood as including persons who, because they are not employed full-time, receive pay lower than that for full-time employment, provided that the activities performed are effective and genuine. The latter requirement is not called into question in this case.

[D8]   Case 344/87 I Bettray v Staatssecretaris van Justitie [1989] ECR 1621

[Bettray, a German national, entered the Netherlands and twice applied for a residence permit there, giving as the reason for his stay 'a period of residence with his fiancée and later marriage' and adding, on the second occasion, 'a stay in a rehabilitation centre for drug addicts'. Both applications were rejected by the Netherlands authorities. Because of his drug addiction, Bettray was employed under the system set up by the Wet Sociale Werkvoorziening (Social Employment Law). This law was intended to provide work for the purpose of maintaining, restoring or improving the capacity for work of persons who, for an indefinite period, were unable, because of circumstances related to their situation, to work under normal conditions. Netherlands local authorities set up, with financial support from the state, undertakings or work associations, the sole purpose of which was to provide the persons involved with an opportunity to engage in paid work under conditions corresponding as far as possible to the legal rules and practices applicable to paid employment under normal conditions, having regard to their physical and mental capacities. Bettray submitted a third application for a residence permit giving as the reason for his stay 'work as an employed person'. The residence permit was refused and Bettray brought an action before the Raad van State, claiming that he was a worker.]

The European Court of Justice (at pp 1644–1646)

9. The question raised by the national court seeks essentially to ascertain whether Article [48(1) **[D1]**] must be interpreted as meaning that a national of a Member State employed in another Member State in the framework of a scheme such as that provided for in the Social Employment Law may be regarded on that ground alone as a worker for the purposes of Community law.

10. The Commission and [Bettray] consider that the reply to the national court's question must be in the affirmative, having regard to the court's case law on the concept of worker, while the Netherlands government argues that having regard to the special characteristics of the scheme set up by the Social Employment Law persons working under that scheme should not be regarded as workers for the purposes of Community law. It points in particular to the *sui generis* nature of the employment relationship under the Social Employment Law, the very low productivity of the persons employed, whose remuneration is financed largely by subsidies from public funds, and the pre-eminently social and non-economic nature of the scheme.

11. [According to the now] established case law the term 'worker' in Article 48 [has] a Community meaning and, inasmuch as it defines the scope of one of the fundamental freedoms of the Community, must be interpreted broadly (see [*Lawrie-Blum* **[D7]**]).

12. According to [*Lawrie-Blum*], that concept must be defined in accordance with objective criteria which distinguish the employment relationship by reference to the rights and duties of the persons concerned, and the essential feature of an employment relationship is that for a certain period of time a person performs services for and under the direction of another person in return for which he receives remuneration.

13. It is clear both from the terms in which the principle of freedom of movement for workers is expressed and the place occupied by the provisions concerning that principle in the structure of the Treaty that those provisions guarantee freedom of movement only for persons pursuing or wishing to pursue an economic activity and that, consequently, they cover only the pursuit of an effective and genuine activity (see [*Levin* **[D5]**]).

14. It appears [that] persons employed under the scheme set up by the Social Employment Law perform services under the direction of another person in return for which they receive remuneration. The essential feature of an employment relationship is therefore present.

15. That conclusion is not altered by the fact that the productivity of persons employed in the scheme is low and that, consequently, their remuneration is largely provided by subsidies from public funds. Neither the level of productivity nor the origin of the funds from which the remuneration is paid can have any consequence in regard to whether or not the person is to be regarded as a worker.

16. Nor can the person cease to be regarded as a worker merely by virtue of the fact that the employment relationship under the Social Employment Law is of a sui generis nature in national law. As the court has

held ([*Sotgiu* **[D16]**]), the nature of the legal relationship between the employee and the employer is of no consequence in regard to the application of Article [48].

17. However, work under the Social Employment Law cannot be regarded as an effective and genuine economic activity if it constitutes merely a means of rehabilitation or reintegration for the persons concerned and the purpose of the paid employment, which is adapted to the physical and mental possibilities of each person, is to enable those persons sooner or later to recover their capacity to take up ordinary employment or to lead as normal as possible a life.

18. It appears [that] the jobs in question are reserved for persons who, by reason of circumstances relating to their situation, are unable to take up employment under normal conditions and that the social employment ends once the local authority is informed by the employment office that the person concerned will be able within a short period to take up employment under normal conditions.

19. It also appears [that] persons employed under the Social Employment Law are not selected on the basis of their capacity to perform a certain activity; on the contrary, it is the activities which are chosen in the light of the capabilities of the persons who are going to perform them in order to maintain, re-establish or develop their capacity for work. Finally, the activities involved are pursued in the framework of undertakings or work associations created solely for that purpose by local authorities.

20. The reply to the national court's question must therefore be that Article 48(1) [is] to be interpreted as meaning that a national of a Member State employed in another Member State under a scheme such as that established under the Social Employment Law, in which the activities carried out are merely a means of rehabilitation or reintegration, cannot on that basis alone be regarded as a worker for the purposes of Community law.

[D9]   Directive 68/360 on the abolition of restrictions on movement and residence within the Community for workers of Member States and their families

[Whereas] measures should be adopted for the abolition of restrictions which still exist concerning movement and residence within the Community.

. . .

Whereas the rules applicable to residence should, as far as possible, bring the position of workers from other Member States and members of their families into line with that of nationals. . .

Article 1

Member States shall, acting as provided in this directive, abolish restrictions on the movement and residence of nationals of the said states and of members of their families to whom [Regulation] 1612/68 **[D14]** applies.

Article 2

1. Member States shall grant the nationals referred to in Article 1 the right to leave their territory in order to take up activities as employed

persons and to pursue such activities in the territory of another Member State. Such right shall be exercised simply on production of a valid identity card or passport. Members of the family shall enjoy the same right as the national on whom they are dependent.

2. Member States shall, acting in accordance with their laws, issue to such nationals, or renew, an identity card or passport, which shall state in particular the holder's nationality.

3. The passport must be valid at least for all Member States and for countries through which the holder must pass when travelling between Member States. Where a passport is the only document on which the holder may lawfully leave the country, its period of validity shall be not less than five years.

4. Member States may not demand from the nationals referred to in Article 1 any exit visa or any equivalent document.

Article 3

1. Member States shall allow the persons referred to in Article 1 to enter their territory simply on production of a valid identity card or passport.

2. No entry visa or equivalent document may be demanded save from members of the family who are not nationals of a Member State. Member States shall accord to such persons every facility for obtaining any necessary visas.

Article 4

1. Member States shall grant the right of residence in their territory to the persons referred to in Article 1 who are able to produce the documents listed in paragraph 3.

2. As proof of the right of residence, a document entitled 'Residence Permit for a National of a Member State of the EEC' shall be issued. This document must include a statement that it has been issued pursuant to [Regulation] 1612/68 and to the measures taken by the Member States for the implementation of the present directive. The text of such a statement is given in the Annex to this directive.

3. For the issue of a Residence Permit for a National of a Member State of the EEC, Member States may require only the production of the following documents:

- by the worker:
  - (a) the document with which he entered their territory;
  - (b) a confirmation of engagement from the employer or a certificate of employment;
- by the members of the worker's family:
  - (c) the document with which they entered the territory;
  - (d) a document issued by the competent authority of the state of origin or the state whence they came, proving their relationship;
  - (e) in the cases referred to in Article 10(1) and (2) of [Regulation] 1612/68, a document issued by the competent authority of the state of origin or the state whence they came, testifying that they are dependent on the worker or that they live under his roof in such country.

4. A member of the family who is not a national of a Member State shall be issued with a residence document which shall have the same validity as that issued to the worker on whom he is dependent.

Article 5

Completion of the formalities for obtaining a residence permit shall not hinder the immediate beginning of employment under a contract concluded by the applicants.

Article 6

1. The residence permit:

(a)   must be valid throughout the territory of the Member State which issued it;

(b)   must be valid for at least five years from the date of issue and be automatically renewable.

2. Breaks in residence not exceeding six consecutive months and absence on military service shall not affect the validity of a residence permit.

3. Where a worker is employed for a period exceeding three months but not exceeding a year in the service of an employer in the host state or in the employ of a person providing services, the host Member State shall issue him a temporary residence permit, the validity of which may be limited to the expected period of the employment.

Subject to the provisions of Article 8(1)(c), a temporary residence permit shall be issued also to a seasonal worker employed for a period of more than three months. The period of employment must be shown in the documents referred to in [Article] 4(3)(b).

Article 7

1. A valid residence permit may not be withdrawn from a worker solely on the grounds that he is no longer in employment, either because he is temporarily incapable of work as a result of illness or accident, or because he is involuntarily unemployed, this being duly confirmed by the competent employment office.

2. When the residence permit is renewed for the first time, the period of residence may be restricted, but not to less than 12 months, where the worker has been involuntarily unemployed in the Member State for more than 12 consecutive months.

Article 8

1. Member States shall, without issuing a residence permit, recognise the right of residence in their territory of:

(a)   a worker pursuing an activity as an employed person, where the activity is not expected to last for more than three months. The document with which the person concerned entered the territory and a statement by the employer on the expected duration of the employment shall be sufficient to cover his [stay];

(b)   a worker who, while having his residence in the territory of a Member State to which he returns as a rule, each day or at least once a week, is employed in the territory of another Member State. The competent authority of the state where he is employed may issue such worker with a special permit valid for five years and automatically renewable;

(c) a seasonal worker who holds a contract of employment stamped by the competent authority of the Member State on whose territory he has come to pursue his activity.

2. In all cases referred to in paragraph 1, the competent authorities of the host Member State may require the worker to report his presence in the territory.

Article 9

1. The residence documents granted to nationals of a Member State of the EEC referred to in this directive shall be issued and renewed free of charge or on payment of an amount not exceeding the dues and taxes charged for the issue of identity cards to nationals.

2. The visa referred to in Article 3(2) and the stamp referred to in Article 8(1)(c) shall be free of charge.

3. Member States shall take the necessary steps to simplify as much as possible the formalities and procedure for obtaining the documents mentioned in paragraph 1.

Article 10

Member States shall not derogate from the provisions of this directive save on grounds of public policy, public security or public health [see Section Three of this chapter].

. . .

ANNEX

Text of the statement referred to in Article 4(2)

This permit is issued pursuant to Regulation (EEC) 1612/68 of the Council of the European Communities of 15 October 1968 and to the measures taken in implementation of the Council Directive of 15 October 1968. In accordance with the provisions of the above-mentioned regulation, the holder of this permit has the right to take up and pursue an activity as an employed person in [a Member State's] territory under the same conditions as [the Member State's national] workers.

[D10] Case 118/75 Lynne Watson and Allessandro Belmann [1976] ECR 1185

[Lynne Watson, a United Kingdom national, was alleged to have failed to report, within three days of her entry into Italy, to the police authorities of the place where she was staying 'in order to notify [her] presence and to make a declaration of residence'. This obligation was imposed by Italian legislation on all foreign nationals, with the exception of certain categories of employed workers from other Member States, and the penalties provided for in the event of a failure to discharge it were a fine or a maximum of three months' detention and, in addition, possible deportation from Italy, entailing a prohibition on re-entry without the permission of the Italian Minister for the Interior. Allessandro Belmann, an Italian national, was charged with having failed to inform the police authorities within 24 hours of the identity of Lynne Watson. This obligation was imposed by Italian legislation on 'any person who provides board and lodging, on whatever basis, to a foreign national [or] for any reason whatever takes such person into his employment'. Failure to discharge this obligation rendered the person concerned liable to a fine or a maximum of six months' detention. By way of defence to the criminal charges, Watson and Belmann claimed that the Italian law was contrary to Articles 7 and 48–66 of the Treaty, on the ground that they constituted discrimination based on nationality and a restriction on freedom of movement for persons within the Community. They also argued that the above Community rules constituted fundamental principles which created individual rights and took precedence over national rules to the contrary. Note how the court uses the principle of proportionality (discussed in Chapter Two, Section Four).]

The European Court of Justice (at pp 1197–1201)

12. [Articles 48, 52 and 59 of the Treaty], which may be construed as prohibiting Member States from setting up restrictions or obstacles to the entry into their territory of nationals of other Member States, have the effect of conferring rights directly on all persons falling within the ambit of the above-mentioned articles, as later given closer articulation by certain provisions adopted by the Council in implementation of the Treaty.

[The Court of Justice referred, inter alia, to Article 1 of Regulation 1612/68 **[D14]** and Article 4 of Directive 68/360 **[D9]**].

16. The provisions of the Treaty and of secondary Community law to which reference has just been made implement a fundamental principle contained in Article 3(c) of the Treaty, which states that, for the purposes set out in Article 2, the activities of the Community shall include the abolition, as between Member States, of obstacles to freedom of movement for persons, services and capital.

These provisions take precedence over any national rule which might conflict with them.

17. By creating the principle of freedom of movement for persons and by conferring on any person falling within its ambit the right of access to the territory of the Member States, for the purposes intended by the Treaty, Community law has not excluded the power of Member States to adopt measures enabling the national authorities to have an exact knowledge of population movements affecting their territory.

18. Under the terms of Article 8(2) of Directive [68/360], the competent authorities in the Member States may require nationals of the other Member States to report their presence to the authorities of the state concerned.

Such an obligation could not in itself be regarded as an infringement of the rules concerning freedom of movement for persons.

However, such an infringement might result from the legal formalities in question if the control procedures to which they refer were such as to restrict the freedom of movement required by the Treaty or to limit the right conferred by the Treaty on nationals of the Member States to enter and reside in the territory of any other Member State for the purposes intended by Community law.

19. In particular as regards the period within which the arrival of foreign nationals must be reported, the provisions of the Treaty are only infringed if the period fixed is unreasonable.

20. Among the penalties attaching to a failure to comply with the prescribed declaration and registration formalities, deportation, in relation to persons protected by Community law, is certainly incompatible with the provisions of the Treaty since, as the court has already confirmed in other cases, such a measure negates the very right conferred and guaranteed by the Treaty.

21. As regards other penalties, such as fines and detention, whilst the national authorities are entitled to impose penalties in respect of a failure to comply with the terms of provisions requiring foreign nationals to notify their presence which are comparable to those attaching to infringements of provisions of equal importance by nationals, they are not justified in imposing a penalty so disproportionate to the gravity of the infringement that it becomes an obstacle to the free movement of persons.

22. In so far as national rules concerning the control of foreign nationals do not involve restrictions on freedom of movement for persons and on the right, conferred by the Treaty on persons protected by Community law, to enter and reside in the territory of the Member States, the application of such legislation, where it is based on objective factors, cannot constitute 'discrimination on grounds of nationality', prohibited under Article 7 of the Treaty.

23. Provisions which require residents of the host state to inform the public authorities of the identity of foreign nationals for whom they provide accommodation, and which are for the most part connected with the internal order of the state, can only be called into question from the point of view of Community law if they place an indirect restriction on freedom of movement for persons.

[D11]   Case 157/79 R v Stanislaus Pieck [1980] ECR 2171

[Criminal proceedings were brought in a magistrates' court against Pieck, a Netherlands national residing in Cardiff, and pursuing an activity as an employed person, who was charged that, being a person who was not 'patrial' (a British national having the right of abode in the United Kingdom) and having only been granted leave to enter the United Kingdom or to remain there for a limited period, knowingly remained beyond the time limited by the leave. The accused held no residence permit. When he last entered the United Kingdom, an endorsement containing the words 'Given leave to enter the United Kingdom for six months' was stamped on his passport.]

The European Court of Justice (at pp 2183–2187)

The first question

3. In its first question the court asks what is the meaning of 'entry visa or equivalent document' in Article 3(2) of Council Directive 68/360 **[D9]**?

4. This court has already stated on several occasions that the right of

nationals of a Member State to enter the territory of another Member State and reside there for the purposes intended by the Treaty is a right conferred directly by the Treaty or, as the case may be, by the provisions adopted for its implementation.

5. The aim of Directive 68/360, as the recitals in the preamble thereto show, is to adopt measures for the abolition of restrictions which still exist concerning movement and residence within the Community, which conform to the rights and privileges accorded to nationals of Member States by [Regulation 1612/68] on freedom of movement for workers within the Community. To this end the directive lays down the conditions on which nationals of Member States may exercise their right to leave their state of origin to take up activities as employed persons in the territory of another Member State and their right to enter the territory of that state and to reside there.

6. [The Court of Justice referred to Article 3(1) and (2) of the directive.]

7. In the course of the procedure before the court the British government maintained that the phrase 'entry visa' means exclusively a documentary clearance issued before the traveller arrives at the frontier in the form of an endorsement on his passport or of a separate document. On the contrary an endorsement stamped on a passport at the time of arrival giving leave to enter the territory may not be regarded as an entry visa or equivalent document.

8. This argument cannot be upheld. For the purpose of applying the directive, the object of which is to abolish restrictions on movement and residence for Community workers within the Community, the time at which clearance to enter the territory of a Member State has been given and indicated on a passport or by another document is immaterial. Furthermore the right of Community workers to enter the territory of a Member State which Community law confers may not be made subject to the issue of a clearance to this effect by the authorities of that Member State.

9. Admittedly the right of entry for the workers in question is not unlimited. Nevertheless the only restriction which Article 48 [lays] down concerning freedom of movement in the territory of Member States is that of limitations justified on grounds of public policy, public security or public health. This restriction must be regarded not as a condition precedent to the acquisition of the right of entry and residence but as providing the possibility, in individual cases where there is sufficient justification, of imposing restrictions on the exercise of a right derived directly from the Treaty. It does not therefore justify administrative measures requiring in a general way formalities at the frontier other than simply the production of a valid identity card or passport.

10. The answer to the first question should therefore be that Article 3(2) of Directive 68/360 prohibiting Member States from demanding an entry visa or equivalent document for Community workers moving within the Community must be interpreted as meaning that the phrase 'entry visa or equivalent document' covers any formality for the purpose of granting leave to enter the territory of a Member State which is coupled with a passport or identity card check at the frontier, whatever may be the place or time at which that leave is granted and in whatever form it may be granted.

The second question

11. In its second question the national court seeks to ascertain whether, upon entry into a Member State by an EEC national, the granting by that

Member State of an initial leave to remain for a period limited to six months is compatible with Articles 7 and 48 of the Treaty and with [Directives 64/221 and 68/360].

12. Article 4 of Directive 68/360 provides that Member States shall grant the right of residence in their territory to the persons referred to in the directive and goes on to say that as 'proof' of this right a special residence permit shall be issued. This provision must be interpreted in the light of the recitals in the preamble to the directive, according to which the rules applicable to residence should, as far as possible, bring the position of workers from other Member States into line with that of nationals.

13. The court has already stated in [Case 8/77 *Sagulo, Brenca and Bakhouche* [1977] ECR 1495] that the issue of a special residence document provided for in Article 4 [has] only a declaratory effect and that, for aliens to whom Article 48 [or] parallel provisions give rights, it cannot be assimilated to a residence permit such as is prescribed for aliens in general, in connection with the issue of which the national authorities have a discretion. The court went on to say that a Member State may not therefore require from a person enjoying the protection of Community law that he should possess a general residence permit instead of the document provided for in Article 4 of Directive 68/360.

14. It follows that the answer to the second question has already been given by the court in the above-mentioned judgment.

The third question

15. The third question asks whether a national of a Member State of the Community who has overstayed the leave granted in the residence permit may be punished in that Member State by measures which include imprisonment and/or a recommendation for deportation.

16. In [*Sagulo* (above)] the court has already decided that the imposition of penalties or other coercive measures is ruled out in so far as a person protected by the provisions of Community law does not comply with national provisions which prescribe for such a person possession of a general residence permit instead of the document provided for in Directive 68/360, since the national authorities should not impose penalties for disregard of a provision which is incompatible with Community law.

17. Having regard however to the circumstances of this case as stated by the national court and in the light of the answer just given to the second question, the third question may also be understood as raising the problem whether the failure on the part of a national of a Member State of the Community, to whom the rules on freedom of movement for workers apply, to obtain the special residence permit prescribed in Article 4 of Directive 68/360 may be punished by measures which include imprisonment or a recommendation for deportation.

18. Among the penalties attaching to a failure to comply with the formalities required as proof of the right of residence of a worker enjoying the protection of Community law, deportation is certainly incompatible with the provisions of the Treaty since, as the court has already confirmed in other cases, such a measure negates the very rights conferred and guaranteed by the Treaty.

19. As regards other penalties such as fines and imprisonment, whilst the national authorities are entitled to impose penalties in respect of failure

to comply with the terms of provisions relating to residence permits which are comparable to those attaching to minor offences by nationals, they are not justified in imposing a penalty so disproportionate to the gravity of the infringement that it becomes an obstacle to the free movement of persons. This would be especially so if that penalty included imprisonment.

20. It follows that the failure on the part of a national of a Member State of the Community, to whom the rules on freedom of movement for workers apply, to obtain the special residence permit prescribed in Article 4 of Directive 68/360 may not be punished by a recommendation for deportation or by measures which go as far as imprisonment.

[D12]   Case 321/87 Commission of the European Communities v Kingdom of Belgium [1989] ECR 997

[According to a Belgian Royal Decree governing aliens' access to, residence and establishment in and expulsion from its territory, 'any alien of more than 15 years of age must at all times carry his residence or establishment permit or any other residence documents and produce the same on request by any agent of the public authorities'. That obligation corresponded to the obligation imposed on Belgian nationals by another Royal Decree on identity cards for Belgians. In both cases, non-compliance constituted an offence punishable by a fine. Upon entry into Belgium, the authorities responsible for frontier controls, on a non-systematic basis and in various circumstances, asked non-Belgian Community nationals, residing in Belgium to produce, in addition to their passport or identity card, their residence or establishment permit. If the person concerned did not produce the latter document, he could continue his journey but might be liable to a fine.]

The European Court of Justice (at pp 1009–1011)

6. The Belgian government contends, for its part, that inspection of residence or establishment permits is not a frontier control but part of a general system of police checks carried out habitually throughout Belgian territory to which all inhabitants are liable, and it may incidentally be carried out at the same time as the frontier control.

[The Court of Justice referred, inter alia, to Directive 68/360, Article 3 **[D9]**.]

9. As the court has already held in [*Pieck* **[D11]**], the term 'entry visa or equivalent requirement' covers any formality for the purpose of granting leave to enter the territory of a Member State which is coupled with a passport or identity card check at the frontier, whatever may be the place or time at which that leave is granted and in whatever form it may be granted.

10. It is apparent from [*Pieck*] that the restriction which the EEC Treaty lays down concerning free movement of persons on grounds of public policy, public security or public health must be regarded not as imposing a condition precedent to the acquisition of the right of entry and residence but as providing the possibility, in individual cases where there is sufficient justification, of imposing restrictions on the exercise of a right derived directly from the Treaty. It does not therefore justify administrative measures

imposing in a general way formalities at the frontier other than the mere production of a valid identity card or passport.

11. Consequently, the only precondition which Member States may impose on the right of entry into their territory for the persons covered by the [directive] is the production of a valid identity card or passport.

12. The controls at issue are not a condition for the exercise of the right of entry into Belgian territory and it is undisputed that Community law does not prevent Belgium from checking, within its territory, compliance with the obligation imposed on persons enjoying a right of residence under Community law to carry their residence or establishment permits at all times, where an identical obligation is imposed upon Belgian nationals as regards their identity card.

13. The Commission disputes the compatibility with Community law of the controls at issue in so far as they are carried out at the time of entry into Belgian territory and are thus added to the requirement of production of a valid identity card or passport.

14. It must be stated in the first place that provided that the controls criticised by the Commission are not a condition of entry into Belgian territory, they are not prohibited by the wording of the provisions of the [directive] relied upon by the Commission.

15. However, the carrying out of such controls upon entry into the territory of a Member State may, depending on the circumstances, constitute a barrier to the free movement of persons within the Community, a fundamental principle of the EEC Treaty to which the [directive is] intended to give full effect. That would be the case in particular if it were found that the controls in question were carried out in a systematic, arbitrary or unnecessarily restrictive manner.

16. It is not disputed in the present case that the controls at issue are carried out sporadically and unsystematically. Moreover, the Commission merely alleged that the controls are in themselves contrary to Community law, without providing further information concerning the circumstances in which they are carried out. Accordingly, the Kingdom of Belgium cannot be held to have failed to fulfil any obligation.

[D13] Case C-292/89 R v Immigration Appeal Tribunal, ex parte Gustaff Desiderius Antonissen [1991] ECR I-745

[Antonissen, a Belgian national, entered the United Kingdom in October 1984. He had not yet found work there when, on 30 March 1987, he was sentenced by the Liverpool Crown Court to two terms of imprisonment for unlawful possession of cocaine and possession of cocaine with intent to supply. On 27 November 1987, the Secretary of State for Home Affairs decided to deport Antonissen from the United Kingdom, basing his decision on the Immigration Act 1971, s 3(5)(b), which authorises the Secretary of State to deport foreign nationals if he considers that it would be 'conducive to the public good'. Antonissen appealed against this decision to the Immigration Appeal Tribunal and then, as his appeal was dismissed, made an application for judicial review to the High Court, which referred to the Court of Justice the following questions:

1. For the purpose of determining whether a national of a Member State is to be treated as a 'worker' within the meaning of Article 48 [when] seeking employment in the territory of another Member State so as to be immune from deportation save in accordance with [Directive 64/221 **[D42]**], may the legislature of the second Member State provide that such a national may be required to leave the territory of that state (subject to appeal) if after six months from admission to that territory he has failed to enter employment?

2. In answering the foregoing question what weight if any is to be attached by a court or tribunal of a Member State to the declaration contained in the minutes of the meeting of the Council when the Council adopted Directive 68/360 **[D9]**?

The European Court of Justice (at pp 776–779)

8. [The] national court essentially seeks to establish whether it is contrary to the provisions of Community law governing the free movement of workers for the legislation of a Member State to provide that a national of another Member State who entered the first state in order to seek employment may be required to leave the territory of that state (subject to appeal) if he has not found employment there after six months.

9. In that connection it has been argued that, according to the strict wording of Article [48], Community nationals are given the right to move freely within the territory of the Member States for the purpose only of accepting offers of employment actually made (Article 48(3)(a) and (b)) whilst the right to stay in the territory of a Member State is stated to be for the purpose of employment (Article 48(3)(c)).

10. Such an interpretation would exclude the right of a national of a Member State to move freely and to stay in the territory of the other Member States in order to seek employment there, and cannot be upheld.

11. Indeed, as the court has consistently held, freedom of movement for workers forms one of the foundations of the Community and, consequently, the provisions laying down that freedom must be given a broad interpretation (see, in particular [*Kempf* **[D6]**]).

12. Moreover, a strict interpretation of Article 48(3) would jeopardise the actual chances that a national of a Member State who is seeking employment will find it in another Member State, and would, as a result, make that provision ineffective.

13. It follows that Article 48(3) must be interpreted as enumerating, in a non-exhaustive way, certain rights benefiting nationals of Member States in the context of the free movement of workers and that that freedom also entails the right for nationals of Member States to move freely within the territory of the other Member States and to stay there for the purposes of seeking employment.

14. Moreover, that interpretation of the Treaty corresponds to that of the Community legislature, as appears from the provisions adopted in order to implement the principle of free movement, in particular Articles 1 and 5 of Regulation [1612/68 **[D14]**], which presuppose that Community nationals are entitled to move in order to look for employment, and hence to stay, in another Member State.

15. It must therefore be ascertained whether the right, under Article 48

and the provisions of Regulation [1612/68], to stay in a Member State for the purposes of seeking employment can be subjected to a temporal limitation.

16. In that regard, it must be pointed out in the first place that the effectiveness of Article 48 is secured in so far as Community legislation or, in its absence, the legislation of a Member State gives persons concerned a reasonable time in which to apprise themselves, in the territory of the Member State concerned, of offers of employment corresponding to their occupational qualifications and to take, where appropriate, the necessary steps in order to be engaged.

17. The national court referred to the declaration recorded in the Council minutes at the time of the adoption of [Regulation 1612/68 and Directive 68/360]. That declaration reads as follows:

Nationals of a Member State as referred to in Article 1 [of the directive] who move to another Member State in order to seek work there shall be allowed a minimum period of three months for the purpose; in the event of their not having found employment by the end of that period, their residence on the territory of this second state may be brought to an end.

However, if the above-mentioned persons should be taken charge of by national assistance (social welfare) in the second state during the aforesaid period they may be invited to leave the territory of this second state.

18. However, such a declaration cannot be used for the purpose of interpreting a provision of secondary legislation where, as in this case, no reference is made to the content of the declaration in the wording of the provision in question. The declaration therefore has no legal significance.

19. For their part, the United Kingdom and the Commission argue that, under Article 69(1) of Council Regulation 1408/71 on the application of social security schemes to employed persons, to self-employed persons and to members of their families moving within the [Community], the Member States may limit to three months the period during which nationals from other Member States may stay in their territory in order to seek employment. According to the provision in question, an unemployed person who has acquired entitlement to benefits in a Member State and goes to another Member State to seek employment there retains entitlement to those benefits for a maximum period of three months.

20. That argument cannot be upheld. As the Advocate General has rightly observed, there is no necessary link between the right to employment benefit in the Member State of origin and the right to stay in the host state.

21. In the absence of a Community provision prescribing the period during which Community nationals seeking employment in a Member State may stay there, a period of six months, such as that laid down in the national legislation at issue in the main proceedings, does not appear in principle to be insufficient to enable the persons concerned to apprise themselves, in the host Member State, of offers of employment corresponding to their occupational qualifications and to take, where appropriate, the necessary steps in order to be engaged and, therefore, does not jeopardise the effectiveness of the principle of free movement. However, if after the expiry of that period the person concerned provides evidence that he is continuing to seek employment and that he has genuine chances of being engaged, he cannot be required to leave the territory of the host Member State.

22. It must therefore be stated in reply to the questions submitted by the national court that it is not contrary to the provisions of Community law governing the free movement of workers for the legislation of a Member State to provide that a national of another Member State who entered the first state in order to seek employment may be required to leave the territory of that state (subject to appeal) if he has not found employment there after six months, unless the person concerned provides evidence that he is continuing to seek employment and that he has genuine chances of being engaged.

[D14]   Regulation 1612/68 on freedom of movement for workers within the Community

Whereas freedom of movement for workers should be secured within the Community by the end of the transitional period at the latest; whereas the attainment of this objective entails the abolition of any discrimination based on nationality between workers of the Member States as regards employment, remuneration and other conditions of work and employment, as well as the right of such workers to move freely within the Community in order to pursue activities as employed persons subject to any limitations justified on grounds of public policy, public security or public health;

. . .

Whereas freedom of movement constitutes a fundamental right of workers and their families; whereas mobility of labour within the Community must be one of the means by which the worker is guaranteed the possibility of improving his living and working conditions and promoting his social advancement, while helping to satisfy the requirements of the economies of the Member States; whereas the right of all workers in the Member States to pursue the activity of their choice within the Community should be affirmed;

Whereas such right must be enjoyed without discrimination by permanent, seasonal and frontier workers and by those who pursue their activities for the purpose of providing services;

Whereas the right of freedom of movement, in order that it may be exercised, by objective standards, in freedom and dignity, requires that equality of treatment shall be ensured in fact and in law in respect of all matters relating to the actual pursuit of activities as employed persons and to eligibility for housing, and also that obstacles to the mobility of workers shall be eliminated, in particular as regards the worker's right to be joined by his family and the conditions for the integration of that family into the host country;

Whereas the principle of non-discrimination between Community workers entails that all nationals of Member States have the same priority as regards employment as is enjoyed by national workers; . . .

PART I – EMPLOYMENT AND WORKERS' FAMILIES

TITLE I – ELIGIBILITY FOR EMPLOYMENT

Article 1

1. Any national of a Member State shall, irrespective of his place of residence, have the right to take up an activity as an employed person, and to pursue such activity, within the territory of another Member State in accordance with the provisions laid down by law, regulation or administrative action governing the employment of nationals of that state.

2. He shall, in particular, have the right to take up available employment in the territory of another Member State with the same priority as nationals of that state.

Article 2

Any national of a Member State and any employer pursuing an activity in the territory of a Member State may exchange their applications for and offers of employment, and may conclude and perform contracts of employment in accordance with the provisions in force laid down by law, regulation or administrative action, without any discrimination resulting therefrom.

Article 3

1. Under this regulation, provisions laid down by law, regulation or administrative action or administrative practices of a Member State shall not apply:

– where they limit application for and offers of employment, or the right of foreign nationals to take up and pursue employment or subject these to conditions not applicable in respect of their own nationals; or
– where, though applicable irrespective of nationality, their exclusive or principal aim or effect is to keep nationals of other Member States away from the employment offered.

This provision shall not apply to conditions relating to linguistic knowledge required by reason of the nature of the post to be filled.

2. There shall be included in particular among the provisions or practices of a Member State referred to in the first subparagraph of paragraph 1 those which:

(a) prescribe a special recruitment procedure for foreign nationals;
(b) limit or restrict the advertising of vacancies in the press or through any other medium or subject it to conditions other than those applicable in respect of employers pursuing their activities in the territory of that Member State;
(c) subject eligibility for employment to conditions of registration with employment offices or impede recruitment of individual workers, where persons who do not reside in the territory of that state are concerned.

Article 4

1. Provisions laid down by law, regulation or administrative action of the Member States which restrict by number or percentage the employment of

foreign nationals in any undertaking, branch of activity or region, or at a national level, shall not apply to nationals of the other Member States.

. . .

Article 5

A national of a Member State who seeks employment in the territory of another Member State shall receive the same assistance there as that afforded by the employment offices in that state to their own nationals seeking employment.

Article 6

1. The engagement and recruitment of a national of one Member State for a post in another Member State shall not depend on medical, vocational or other criteria which are discriminatory on grounds of nationality by comparison with those applied to nationals of the other Member State who wish to pursue the same activity.

2. Nevertheless, a national who holds an offer in his name from an employer in a Member State other than that of which he is a national may have to undergo a vocational test, if the employer expressly requests this when making his offer of employment.

TITLE II – EMPLOYMENT AND EQUALITY OF TREATMENT

Article 7

1. A worker who is a national of a Member State may not, in the territory of another Member State, be treated differently from national workers by reason of his nationality in respect of any conditions of employment and work, in particular as regards remuneration, dismissal and, should he become unemployed, reinstatement or re-employment.

2. He shall enjoy the same social and tax advantages as national workers.

3. He shall also, by virtue of the same right and under the same conditions as national workers, have access to training in vocational schools and retraining centres.

4. Any clause of a collective or individual agreement or of any other collective regulation concerning eligibility for employment, employment, remuneration and other conditions of work or dismissal shall be null and void in so far as it lays down or authorises discriminatory conditions in respect of workers who are nationals of the other Member States.

Article 8 [as amended by Regulation 312/76]

A worker who is a national of a Member State and who is employed in the territory of another Member State shall enjoy equality of treatment as regards membership of trade unions and the exercise of rights attaching thereto, including the right to vote and to be eligible for the administration or management posts of a trade union; he may be excluded from taking part in the management of bodies governed by public law and from holding an office governed by public law. Furthermore, he shall have the right of eligibility for workers' representative bodies in the undertaking. The provisions of this Article shall not affect laws or regulations in certain Member States which grant more extensive rights to workers coming from the other Member States.

Article 9

1. A worker who is a national of a Member State and who is employed in the territory of another Member State shall enjoy all the rights and benefits accorded to national workers in matters of housing, including ownership of the housing he needs.

2. Such worker may, with the same right as nationals, put his name down on the housing lists in the region in which he is employed, where such lists exist; he shall enjoy the resultant benefits and priorities.

If his family has remained in the country whence he came, they shall be considered for this purpose as residing in the said region, where national workers benefit from a similar presumption.

TITLE III – WORKERS' FAMILIES

Article 10

1. The following shall, irrespective of their nationality, have the right to install themselves with a worker who is a national of one Member State and who is employed in the territory of another Member State:

(a) his spouse and their descendants who are under the age of 21 years or are dependants;

(b) dependent relatives in the ascending line of the worker and his spouse.

2. Member States shall facilitate the admission of any member of the family not coming within the provisions of paragraph 1 if dependent on the worker referred to above or living under his roof in the country whence he comes.

3. For the purposes of paragraphs 1 and 2, the worker must have available for his family housing considered as normal for national workers in the region where he is employed; this provision, however, must not give rise to discrimination between national workers and workers from the other Member States.

Article 11

Where a national of a Member State is pursuing an activity as an employed or self-employed person in the territory of another Member State, his spouse and those of the children who are under the age of 21 years or dependent on him shall have the right to take up any activity as an employed person throughout the territory of that same state, even if they are not nationals of any Member State.

Article 12

The children of a national of a Member State who is or has been employed in the territory of another Member State shall be admitted to that state's general educational, apprenticeship and vocational training courses under the same conditions as the nationals of that state, if such children are residing in its territory.

Member States shall encourage all efforts to enable such children to attend these courses under the best possible conditions.

[D15]   Case 379/87 Anita Groener v Minister for Education and the City of Dublin Vocational Education Committee [1989] ECR 3967

[Under the appropriate Irish legislation, the approval of the Minister of Education was required for the numbers, qualifications, remuneration and appointment of all employees of each vocational education committee. Exercising his statutory powers, the minister took two administrative measures. By a memorandum, the minister laid down that the competent committee could not appoint a person to a permanent full-time post in certain areas of teaching, in particular art, unless that person held the Ceard-Testas Gaelige (certificate of proficiency in the Irish language) or had an equivalent qualification recognised by the minister. In that memorandum, the minister also reserved the right to exempt candidates from countries other than Ireland from the obligation to know Irish, provided that there were no other fully qualified candidates for the post. By a circular, the minister laid down that, for posts of Assistant Lecturer and Lecturer, Scale I, preference must be given to suitably qualified candidates holding the Ceard-Testas Gaelige. Appointees not holding that certificate could be required to undergo a special examination in Irish consisting of an oral test. The candidates concerned could not be appointed to a temporary or permanent full-time post until they had passed the examination. The circular confirmed that the provision in the memorandum, under which exemption from the liguistic qualification requirement could be granted in a case where there was no fully qualified candidate, was to continue to apply. Mrs Groener, a Netherlands national, was engaged on a temporary basis as a part-time art teacher in the College of Marketing and Design, Dublin, which was under the authority of the Education Committte. She then applied for a permanent full-time post as lecturer at that college. Since she did not have the Ceard-Testas Gaelige, Mrs Groener asked for an exemption, but that request was refused, on the ground that there were other fully qualified candidates for the post. The minister agreed to her being appointed provided that she first passsed the oral examination. Mrs Groener followed a beginners' course under the auspices of the Gael Linn Institute and took the examination during the last week of that course, but she did not pass. Subsequent steps to secure her engagement as a full-time lecturer under a temporary contract or for her to be granted an exemption from the obligation to prove her knowledge of Irish were unsuccessful. Mrs Groener then institituted proceedings for judicial review against the Minister and the Education Committtee before the High Court, Dublin, maintaining that the conditions laid down by the memorandum and the circular were contrary to Article 48 and to Regulation 1612/68. The High Court referred, inter alia, the following question to the Court of Justice:

> In considering the meaning of the phrase 'the nature of the post to be filled' in Article 3 of Regulation [1612/68], is regard to be had to a policy

of the Irish State that persons holding the post should have a competent knowledge of the Irish language, where such knowledge is not required to discharge the duties attached to the post?

The European Court of Justice (at pp 3991–3994)

12. [The court referred to Article 3(1) of Regulation 1612/68 **[D14]**.]

13. It is apparent [that] the obligation to prove a knowledge of the Irish language imposed by the national provisions in question applies without distinction to Irish and other Community nationals, except as regards the exemptions which may be allowed for nationals of other Member States.

14. [The] question submitted by the national court [is] essentially whether the nature of a permanent full-time post of lecturer in art in public vocational education institutions is such as to justify the requirement of a knowledge of the Irish language.

15. According to the documents before the court, the teaching of art, like that of most other subjects taught in public vocational education schools, is conducted essentially or indeed exclusively in the English language. It follows that, as indicated by the terms of [the] question submitted, knowledge of the Irish language is not required for the performance of the duties which teaching of the kind at issue specifically entails.

16. However, that finding is not in itself sufficient to enable the national court to decide whether the linguistic requirement in question is justified 'by reason of the nature of the post to be filled', within the meaning of [Article 3(1) of Regulation 1612/68].

17. To apprehend the full scope of [the] question, regard must be had to the special linguistic situation in [Ireland]. By virtue of Article 8 of the 'Bunreacht na hEireann' (Irish Constitution):

(1) The Irish language as the national language is the first official language.

(2) The English language is recognised as a second official language.

(3) Provision may, however, be made by law for the exclusive use of either of the said languages for any one or more official purposes, either throughout the State or in any part thereof.

18. As is [apparent] although Irish is not spoken by the whole Irish population, the policy followed by Irish governments for many years has been designed not only to maintain but also to promote the use of Irish as a means of expressing national identity and culture. It is for that reason that Irish courses are compulsory for children receiving primary education and optional for those receiving secondary education. The obligation imposed on lecturers in public vocational education schools to have a certain knowledge of the Irish language is one of the measures adopted by the Irish government in furtherance of that policy.

19. The EEC Treaty does not prohibit the adoption of a policy for the protection and promotion of a language of a Member State which is both the national language and the first official language. However, the implementation of such a policy must not encroach upon a fundamental freedom such as that of the free movement of workers. Therefore, the requirements deriving from measures intended to implement such a policy must not in any circumstances be disproportionate in relation to the aim pursued and the manner in which they are applied must not bring about discrimination against nationals of other Member States.

20. The importance of education for the implementation of such a policy must be recognised. Teachers have an essential role to play, not only through the teaching which they provide but also by their participation in the daily life of the school and the privileged relationship which they have with their pupils. In those circumstances, it is not unreasonable to require them to have some knowledge of the first national language.

21. It follows that the requirement imposed on teachers to have an adequate knowledge of such a language must, provided that the level of knowledge required is not disproportionate in relation to the objective pursued, be regarded as a condition corresponding to the knowledge required by reason of the nature of the post to be filled within the meaning of [Article 3(1) of Regulation 1612/68].

22. It must also be pointed out that where the national provisions provide for the possibility of exemption from that linguistic requirement where no other fully qualified candidate has applied for the post to be filled, Community law requires that power to grant exemptions to be exercised by the minister in a non-discriminatory manner.

23. Moreover, the principle of non-discrimination precludes the imposition of any requirement that the linguistic knowledge in question must have been acquired within the national territory. It also implies that the nationals of other Member States should have an opportunity to retake the oral examination, in the event of their having previously failed it, when they again apply for a post of assistant lecturer or lecturer.

24. Accordingly, the reply to [the] question must be that a permanent full-time post of lecturer in public vocational education institutions is a post of such a nature as to justify the requirement of linguistic knowledge, within the meaning of [Article 3(1) of Regulation 1612/68], provided that the linguistic requirement in question is imposed as part of a policy for the promotion of the national language which is, at the same time, the first official language and provided that that requirement is applied in a proportionate and non-discriminatory manner.

[D16]   Case 152/73 Giovanni Maria Sotgiu v Deutsche Bundespost [1974] ECR 153

[Sotgiu, an Italian national, was employed as a worker by the Deutsche Bundespost (the German Federal Post Office) in Stuttgart, although his family lived in Italy. Part of the collective wages agreement which applied to Post Office workers was that a 'separation allowance' could be paid for workers who lived away from the family home. However, the Ministry of the Interior fixed this allowance at a higher rate for workers employed away from the family home whose home was situated within the territory of the Federal Republic and at a lower rate for such workers whose normal residence was situated abroad. Sotgiu brought an action before the Bundesarbeitsgericht (a labour court) which referred the case to the Court of Justice.]

The European Court of Justice (at pp 163–164)

7. The [question] asks whether Article 7(1) and (4) of Regulation 1612/68 **[D14]** is to be interpreted as meaning that the separation

allowance paid in addition to wages falls within the concept of 'conditions of employment and work'.

This question is raised both in view of the nature of this payment and having regard to the fact that according to the relevant national provisions it is a matter of an optional payment.

8. The aim of Article 7 [is] to ensure equality of treatment of workers who are nationals of Member States with regard to all statutory or contractual provisions determining their position and in particular their financial rights.

The separation allowance, in so far as it constitutes compensation for the inconveniences suffered by a worker who is separated from his home, represents supplementary remuneration and is thus one of the 'conditions of employment and work' within the meaning of the regulation.

In this respect it is of little consequence whether the allowance is paid by reason of a statutory or contractual obligation or merely at the option of the state in its capacity as employer.

As soon as the state avails itself of this option on behalf of its own nationals, it is obliged to extend the advantage to workers who are nationals of other Member States in the same situation.

9. It is therefore appropriate to reply that Article 7(1) and (4) of Regulation 1612/68 is to be interpreted as meaning that a separation allowance, paid in addition to wages, falls within the concept of 'conditions of employment and work' without its being necessary to define whether the payment is made by virtue of an option or of an obligation, either statutory or contractual.

[D17] Case 32/75 Anita Cristini v Société nationale des chemins de fer français [1975] ECR 1085

[A French statute provided that in families with three or more children under the age of 18, the father, the mother and each child should, at the request of the head of the family, receive an identity card entitling them to certain reductions in the fares of the SNCF (the French national railway company). The SNCF refused the request for such a reduction card, submitted by an Italian national, residing in France, whose husband, also of Italian nationality, worked in France where he died as the result of an industrial accident, leaving his widow and four infant children. The refusal of the request, on the ground of the widow's nationality, was based on provisions of the French statute which stated that the reduction card for large families was, in principle, reserved solely for French nationals. The Cour d'Appel, Paris, requested a ruling on whether the reduction card issued by the SNCF for large families constituted, for the workers of the Member States, a 'social advantage' within the meaning of Article 7(2) of Regulation 1612/68 **[D14]**.]

The European Court of Justice (at pp 1094–1095)

10. The [SNCF] has argued that the advantages thus prescribed [in Article 7(2)] are exclusively those attaching to the status of worker since they are connected with the contract of employment itself.

11. Although it is true that certain provisions in this article refer to relationships deriving from the contract of employment, there are others, such

as those concerning reinstatement and re-employment should a worker become unemployed, which have nothing to do with such relationships and even imply the termination of a previous employment.

12. In these circumstances the reference to 'social advantage' in Article 7(2) cannot be interpreted restrictively.

13. It therefore follows that, in view of the equality of treatment which the provision seeks to achieve, the substantive area of application must be delineated so as to include all social and tax advantages, whether or not attached to the contract of employment, such as reductions in fares for large families.

14. It then becomes necessary to examine whether such an advantage must be granted to the widow and children after the death of the migrant worker when the national law provides that, at the request of the head of the family, each member of the family shall be issued with an identity card entitling him or her to the reduction.

15. If the widow and infant children of a national of the Member State in question are entitled to such cards provided that the request had been made by the father before his death, the same must apply where the deceased father was a migrant worker and a national of another Member State.

16. It would be contrary to the purpose and the spirit of the Community rules on freedom of movement for workers to deprive the survivors of such a benefit following the death of the worker whilst granting the same benefit to the survivors of a national.

[The court referred to Regulation 1251/70, Articles 3(1) and 7 **[D29]**.]

19. Accordingly, the answer to the question should be that Article 7(2) of Regulation [1612/68] must be interpreted as meaning that the social advantages referred to by that provision include fares reduction cards issued by a national railway authority to large families and that this applies, even if the said advantage is only sought after the worker's death, to the benefit of his family remaining in the same Member State.

[D18]   Case 207/78 Ministère Public v Gilbert Even [1979] ECR 2019

The European Court of Justice (at p 2034)

22. [The] advantages which [Article 7(2) of Regulation 1612/68] extends to workers who are nationals of other Member States are all those which, whether or not linked to a contract of employment, are generally granted to national workers primarily because of their objective status as workers or by virtue of the mere fact of their residence on the national territory and the extension of which to workers who are nationals of other Member States therefore seems suitable to facilitate their mobility within the Community.

Note.   This passage has been repeated constantly by the Court of Justice and is referred to below as the 'social advantage formula'.

[D19] Case 65/81 Francesco Reina and Letizia Reina v Landeskreditbank Baden-Württemberg [1982] ECR 33

[The Landeskreditbank granted loans related to the birth of a child. The loans system was introduced to stimulate the German birth rate and to reduce the number of abortions. An interest-free childbirth loan could be granted to married couples only where at least one of the spouses was a German national and the family income did not exceed a specified amount. The Reinas were workers, both of Italian nationality, residing in Germany and applied for a loan when Mrs Reina gave birth to twins. The request was refused.]

The European Court of Justice (at pp 43–45)

9. In its [question], the national court asks in substance whether [Regulation 1612/68, Article 7(2), must] be construed as meaning that the concept of 'social advantage' [encompasses] interest-free loans granted on childbirth by a credit institution incorporated under public law, on the basis of guidelines and with financial assistance from the state, to families with a low income and with a view to stimulating the birth rate.

10. The Landeskreditbank contends [that] Article 7(2) may not be applied to the loans in question in view of the absence of any connection between the grant of the loan and the recipient's status as a worker and on the ground that the refusal to grant the loan in no way hinders the mobility of workers within the Community.

[The Court of Justice cited the 'social advantage formula' **[D18]**.]

13. Consequently, childbirth loans such as those referred to by the national court satisfy in principle the criteria enabling them to be classified as social advantages to be granted to workers of all the Member States without any discrimination whatever on grounds of nationality, in particular in view of their aim which is to alleviate, in the case of families with a low income, the financial burden resulting from the birth of a child.

14. The Landeskreditbank disputes that conclusion by maintaining that childbirth loans, such as those at issue, fall outside the scope of the concept of 'social advantage' within the meaning of [Article 7(2)] since they are granted principally for reasons of demographic policy in order to counteract the decline in the birth rate of the German population. It is therefore a measure adopted in the area of political rights, necessarily linked to nationality, and which as a result falls outside the ambit of [the free movement provisions].

15. It should be stated that, since the Community has no powers in the field of demographic policy as such, the Member States are permitted, in principle, to pursue the achievement of the objectives of such a policy, even by means of social measures. This does not mean, however, that the Community exceeds the limits of its jurisdiction solely because the exercise of its jurisdiction affects measures adopted in pursuance of that policy. Accordingly, childbirth loans of that kind may not be considered as falling outside the scope of the rules of Community law relating to the free movement of persons and, more specifically, of [Article 7(2)], solely because they are granted for reasons of demographic policy.

16. The Landeskreditbank contends [that] the loans in question

constitute voluntary benefits within the limits of the budgetary resources allocated for that purpose, with the result that no entitlement to those benefits is created. Similarly, it is proper to take into account the fact that many foreign workers return to their countries of origin before the expiry of the period prescribed for the repayment of the loan, so that the repayment is put in jeopardy.

17. However, it must be observed [that] the concept of 'social advantage' referred to in [Article 7(2)] encompasses not only the benefits accorded by virtue of a right but also those granted on a discretionary basis. In the latter case, the principle of equal treatment requires the benefits to be made available to nationals of other Member States on the same conditions as those which apply to a state's own nationals and on the basis of the same guidelines as those which govern the grant of the loans to the latter.

18. The answer to the [question must] be that [Article 7(2) is] to be interpreted as meaning that the concept of 'social advantage' referred to in that provision encompasses interest-free loans granted on childbirth by a credit institution incorporated under public law, on the basis of guidelines and with financial assistance from the state, to families with a low income with a view to stimulating the birthrate. Such loans must therefore be granted to workers of other Member States on the same conditions as those which apply to national workers.

[D20]   Case 261/83 Carmela Castelli v Office National des Pensions pour Travailleurs Salariés [1984] ECR 3199

[Mrs Castelli, an Italian national, left Italy after the death of her husband to settle with her son in Belgium. She did not work in Belgium. She received a small pension based on insurance contributions paid by her late husband as an employed person in Italy. She asked for a supplementary 'guaranteed income for old people' under Belgian law, but this was refused, inter alia, on the ground that there was no reciprocal agreement between Belgium and Italy permitting this.]

The European Court of Justice (at pp 3213–3214)

9. [The court cited Regulation 1612/68, Article 10 **[D14]**, and referred to Regulation 1251/70 **[D29]**.] It is therefore clear that [Mrs Castelli] comes within the class of beneficiaries of [Regulation 1612/68].

10. It follows from [*Cristini* **[D17]**] that the equality of treatment provided for in [Regulation 1612/68, Article 7] is also intended to prevent discrimination against a worker's dependent relatives in the ascending line, such as [Mrs Castelli].

11. [The court cited the 'social advantage formula' **[D18]**.] The effect of that definition, which has been consistently used by the court, is that the concept of social advantage includes the income guaranteed to old people by the legislation of a Member State.

12. [Article 7(2)] must be interpreted as meaning that the grant of a social advantage, such as the income guaranteed to old people by the legislation of a Member State, to dependent relatives in the ascending line

of a worker cannot be conditional on the existence of a reciprocal agreement between that Member State and the Member State of which such a relative is a national.

[D21]   Case 157/84 Maria Frascogna v Caisse des dépôts et consignations [1985] ECR 1739

[This concerned the entitlement of an Italian national (the widow of an Italian national) to a 'special old-age allowance', under French law. Her application was refused on the ground that she had failed to satisfy a 15-year residence qualification.]

The European Court of Justice (at p 1749)

[The court cited the 'social advantage formula' **[D18]** and referred to *Castelli* **[D20]**.]

22. It must therefore be concluded that the special old-age allowance granted to old persons whose income is insufficient falls within the scope of [Regulation] 1612/68.

23. It follows from the court's previous decisions that the fundamental principle of non-discrimination in the sphere of the free movement of persons, laid down in [Regulation 1612/68, Article 7(2)], prohibits any discrimination against the relatives in the ascending line of a worker from another Member State where those relatives have exercised the right conferred upon them under Article 10 of [Regulation] 1612/68 to instal themselves with the worker.

24. Consequently, a requirement that relatives in the ascending line of workers who are nationals of other Member States must have resided in the territory of a Member State for a specified number of years constitutes discrimination contrary to [Regulation 1612/68, Article 7(2)], if that requirement is not also imposed on relatives in the ascending line of workers who are nationals of that Member State.

[D22]   Case 137/84 Ministère public v Robert Heinrich Maria Mutsch [1985] ECR 2681

The European Court of Justice (at p 2696)

16. The right to use his own language in proceedings before the courts of the Member State in which he resides, under the same conditions as national workers, plays an important rôle in the integration of a migrant worker and his family into the host country, and thus in achieving the objective of free movement for workers.

17. In these circumstances, that right must be held to fall within the meaning of the term 'social advantage' **[D18]**.

[D23]   Case 59/85 State of the Netherlands v Ann Florence Reed [1986] ECR 1283

[Miss Reed, a United Kingdom national, lived with her partner, also a United Kingdom national, and requested a residence permit from the Netherlands authorities. She was neither a worker nor a person seeking work as she had been in the Netherlands for over a year. The question arose as to whether she could be treated as the 'spouse' of her partner. Furthermore, under the Netherlands policy on aliens, an alien who had a stable relationship with a Netherlands national could under certain circumstances be permitted to reside in the Netherlands. In particular, the persons concerned had to live together as one household or have lived together as such before arriving in the Netherlands, be unmarried and possess adequate means of support for the foreign partner plus appropriate accommodation. The Court of Justice took a strict view of the meaning of 'spouse' but held that Article 7(2) of Regulation 1612/68 must be interpreted as meaning that a Member State which permits the unmarried companion of its nationals, who are not themselves nationals of that Member State, to reside in its territory cannot refuse to grant the same advantage to migrant workers who are nationals of other Member States.]

The European Court of Justice (at pp 1300–1303)

[On the meaning of 'spouse']

13. [The court referred to Article 189 **[B19]**.] It follows that an interpretation given by the court to a provision [of Regulation 1612/68] has effects in all of the Member States and that any interpretation of a legal term on the basis of social developments must take into account the situation in the whole Community, not merely in one Member State.

. . .

15. In the absence of any indication of a general social development which would justify a broad construction, and in the absence of any indication to the contrary in the regulation, it must be held that the term 'spouse' in Article 10 of the regulation refers to a marital relationship only.

[On the social advantage]

[The court referred to the social advantage formula **[D18]**, *Cristini* **[D17]** and *Mutsch* **[D22]**.]

28. In the same way it must be recognised that the possibility for a migrant worker of obtaining permission for his unmarried companion to reside with him, where that companion is not a national of the host Member State, can assist his integration in the host state and thus contribute to the achievement of freedom of movement for workers. Consequently, that possibility must also be regarded as falling within the concept of a social advantage for the purposes of [Article 7(2)].

[D24] Case 39/86 Sylvie Lair v Universität Hannover [1988] ECR 3161

[Mrs Lair, a French national, had resided since January 1979 in Germany, where she worked as a bank clerk until June 1981. Between July 1981 and September 1984, she went through alternate periods of unemployment and retraining, interspersed with brief periods of employment, the last of which came to an end in July 1985. Since 1 October 1984, she had been studying Romance and Germanic languages and literature at the University of Hanover and it was not disputed that that course of study led to a professional qualification. Under the German statute on grants for training and further education, assistance for training, including university study, could be awarded not only to German nationals but also to certain categories of foreigners, including those who had resided and been engaged in regular occupational activity in Germany for a total period of five years prior to the commencement of the part of the training course for which assistance was available. There was no equivalent requirement of previous occupational activity where German nationals were concerned. The grant for which Mrs Lair applied was refused by the university on the ground that she did not fulfil the condition for the award of assistance to foreigners, since she had not been engaged in occupational activity in Germany for at least five years. The university considered that only periods during which a foreigner was engaged in occupational activity and in that capacity paid taxes and social security contributions, which funded Germany's social investments such as maintenance and training grants, could be regarded as periods of occupational activity for the purposes of the statute on training grants. The national court referred the following to the Court of Justice:

(1) Does Community law entitle nationals of Member States [who] take up employment in another Member State and there, after giving up their employment, commence a course of higher education leading to a professional qualification [to] claim a training grant on the same basis of aptitude and need as that social advantage is accorded to nationals of the host Member State?]

The European Court of Justice (at pp 3195–3201)

Interpretation of Article 7 of Regulation 1612/68 (first question)

17. The first question, relating to the interpretation of Article 7 of Regulation 1612/68, comprises three distinct branches involving, respectively, the following questions:

Whether maintenance and training grants awarded for university studies leading to a professional qualification constitute a 'social advantage' within the meaning of Article 7(2) of Regulation 1612/68.

Whether a national of another Member State who undertakes university studies in the host state after having [been] engaged in occupational activity in that state is to be regarded as having retained his status as a 'worker' and is entitled in that capacity to the benefit of Article 7(2) of Regulation 1612/68.

Finally, whether a host Member State may make the right to the 'same social advantages' provided for in Article 7(2) of Regulation 1612/68 conditional upon a minimum period of prior occupational activity within its territory.

The concept of social advantage

18. In order to define the concept of social advantage within the meaning of [Article 7(2)], it must first be recalled that the aim of that regulation is to enable the objectives laid down in Articles 48 and 49 of the EEC Treaty in the field of freedom of movement for workers to be achieved. That freedom forms part of the freedom of movement for persons referred to in Article 3(c) of the EEC Treaty and the fundamental freedoms guaranteed by the Treaty.

19. A worker who is a national of a Member State and who has exercised that fundamental freedom is, under [Article 7(2)], to enjoy 'the same social . . . advantages as national workers' in the host Member State.

20. In addition to the specific right mentioned in Article 7(1) of that regulation not to be treated differently from national workers in respect of any conditions of employment and work, in particular as regards reinstatement or re-employment, 'social advantages' include all other advantages by means of which the migrant worker is guaranteed, in the words of the third recital in the preamble to the regulation, the possibility of improving his living and working conditions and promoting his social advancement.

21. [The court cited the 'social advantage formula' **[D18]**.]

22. It follows that a worker who is a national of another Member State and has exercised his right as such to freedom of movement is entitled in the same way as national workers to all the advantages available to such workers for improving their professional qualifications and promoting their social advancement.

23. It must now be considered whether or not a grant such as that at issue in the present case is covered by the concept of social advantage as interpreted above. It should be pointed out that such assistance, awarded for the student's maintenance and training, is particularly appropriate from a worker's point of view for improving his professional qualifications and promoting his social advancement. Moreover, the grant and the repayment of the benefits received are linked in national law to the beneficiary's means and are thus dependent on social criteria.

24. It follows that such a grant constitutes a social advantage within the meaning of [Article 7(2)].

25. It was argued before the court that the application of [Article 7(2)] was precluded by Article 7(3) of the same regulation by virtue of the specific content of the latter, which provides that a worker who is a national of a Member State 'shall also, by virtue of the same right and under the same conditions as national workers, have access to training in vocational schools and retraining centres'.

26. In that regard, it should be noted that in order for an educational institution to be regarded as a vocational school for the purposes of that provision the fact that some vocational training is provided is not sufficient. The concept of a vocational school is a more limited one and refers exclusively to institutions which provide only instruction either alternating with or closely linked to an occupational activity, particularly during apprenticeship. That is not true of universities.

27. However, while it is true that Article 7(3) of the regulation provides for a specific social advantage, that does not mean that a grant awarded for

maintenance and training with a view to the pursuit of studies in an institution which does not fall within the concept of a vocational school under that provision cannot be held to be a social advantage within the meaning of Article 7(2).

28. The answer to the first branch of the first question must therefore be that a grant awarded for maintenance and training with a view to the pursuit of university studies leading to a professional qualification constitutes a social advantage within the meaning of [Article 7(2)].

The concept of worker

29. In this connection, the three Member States which have submitted observations argue that a person loses the status of worker, on which the social advantages depend, when, in the host state, he gives up either his previous occupational activity or, if unemployed, his search for employment in order to pursue full-time studies. The Commission disagrees with that view.

30. It should be noted first of all that neither [Article 7(2)] nor Articles 48 or 49 of the EEC Treaty provides an express answer to the question whether a migrant worker who has interrupted his occupational activity in the host state in order to pursue university studies leading to a professional qualification is to be regarded as having retained his status as a migrant worker for the purposes of Article 7 of the regulation.

31. Although the wording of those provisions does not provide an express answer to that question, there is nevertheless a basis in Community law for the view that the rights guaranteed to migrant workers do not necessarily depend on the actual or continuing existence of an employment relationship.

32. With regard to nationals of another Member State who have not yet taken up employment in the host state, it should first be noted that Article 48(3)(a) and (b) guarantees such persons the right to accept offers of employment actually made and to move freely within the territory of the Member States for that purpose. Those provisions were implemented by Part I, Title I of Regulation 1612/68.

33. Persons who have previously pursued in the host Member State an effective and genuine activity as an employed person as defined by the court (see [*Levin* [D5]] and [*Kempf* [D6]]) but who are no longer employed are nevertheless considered to be workers under certain provisions of Community law.

34. First, under Article 48(3)(d) of the EEC Treaty, persons who remain in the territory of a Member State after having been employed in that state are regarded as workers. Regulation [1251/70 [D29]] which implemented that provision of the Treaty, gives workers whose occupational activity has terminated and their families the right, under certain conditions, to remain permanently in the territory of a Member State. Secondly, [Directive 68/360 [D9]] prohibits Member States in certain circumstances from withdrawing a residence permit from a worker solely on the ground that he is no longer in employment. Thirdly, and lastly, under Article 7(1) of Regulation 1612/68 a migrant worker who has become unemployed may not be treated differently from national workers in the same position as regards reinstatement or re-employment.

35. Furthermore, Article 7(3) of Regulation 1612/68 guarantees migrant workers access, by virtue of the same right and under the same conditions

as national workers, to training in vocational schools and retraining centres. That right to specific training, guaranteed by Community legislation, does not depend on the continued existence of an employment relationship.

36. It is therefore clear that migrant workers are guaranteed certain rights linked to the status of worker even when they are no longer in an employment relationship.

37. In the field of grants for university education, such a link between the status of worker and a grant awarded for maintenance and training with a view to the pursuit of university studies does, however, presuppose some continuity between the previous occupational activity and the course of study; there must be a relationship between the purpose of the studies and the previous occupational activity. Such continuity may not, however, be required where a migrant has involuntarily become unemployed and is obliged by conditions on the job market to undertake occupational retraining in another field of activity.

38. Such a conception of freedom of movement for migrant workers corresponds, moreover, to current developments in careers. Continuous careers are less common than was formerly the case. Occupational activities are therefore occasionally interrupted by periods of training or retraining.

39. The answer to the second part of the first question should therefore be that a national of another Member State who has undertaken university studies in the host state leading to a professional qualification, after having engaged in occupational activity in that state, must be regarded as having retained his status as a worker and is entitled as such to the benefit of [Article 7(2)], provided that there is a link between the previous occupational activity and the studies in question.

The fixing of a minimum period of prior occupational activity as a condition for the granting of the same social advantages

40. In this regard, the three Member States which have submitted observations argue that any Member State is entitled to require that a national of another Member State applying for a maintenance and training grant with a view to the pursuit of university studies must first have engaged in occupational activity for a minimum period within its territory. The Commission disagrees with that point of view.

41. It should be stressed that a student who is a national of another Member State may claim such a grant for university training only in his capacity as a worker within the meaning of Article 48 [and Regulation] 1612/68. The court has held (see [*Hoekstra* **[D4]** and *Levin* **[D5]**]) that the concept of worker has a specific Community meaning and may not be defined on the basis of criteria laid down in national legislation.

42. Member States cannot therefore unilaterally make the grant of the social advantages contemplated in [Article 7(2)] conditional upon the completion of a given period of occupational activity (see [*Frascogna* **[D21]**]).

43. In so far as the arguments submitted by the three Member States in question are motivated by a desire to prevent certain abuses, for example where it may be established on the basis of objective evidence that a worker has entered a Member State for the sole purpose of enjoying, after a very short period of occupational activity, the benefit of the student assistance system in that state, it should be observed that such abuses are not covered by the Community provisions in question.

44. The answer to the third part of the first question must therefore be that the host Member State cannot make the right to the same social advantages provided for in [Article 7(2)] conditional upon a minimum period of prior occupational activity within the territory of that state.

[D25] Case 316/85 Centre public d'aide sociale de Courcelles v Marie-Christine Lebon [1987] ECR 2811

[Mrs Lebon, a French national, lived with her father in Belgium and had, apart from a period of two years when she worked in France, always lived in Belgium. Her father, also a French national, was in receipt of a retirement pension in Belgium. She applied to the Centre public d'aide sociale (a social welfare centre) for the grant of the minimum means of subsistence provided for by Belgian law (called a 'minimex'). There was a dispute as to which social welfare centre should deal with her claim and the adjudicating court referred the following questions for a preliminary ruling:

(1) Where a national of a Member State [has] settled with his family within the territory of another Member State and remains there after having obtained a retirement pension, do his descendants who were living with him retain the right to equality of treatment granted by Regulation 1612/68 when they have reached the age of majority, are no longer dependent upon him and do not have the status of workers?

(2) If so, do such descendants continue to retain that right where they no longer live with the migrant worker and have returned to the Member State of which they are nationals and have lived there independently for a certain period either for more than one year or for more than two years (see Article 5 of Regulation 1251/70 [D29])?

(3) If not, does the status of a 'dependent member of a worker's family' result from a factual situation, to be assessed in each specific case, or from objective circumstances independent of the will of the person concerned which make it necessary for him to have recourse to the support of the worker?

(4) If not, in order that a national of a Member State may rely on his status as a worker in order to enter and establish himself within the territory of another Member State, is it sufficient for him to claim that he wishes or intends to work? Must there be actual evidence of that wish in the form of serious and genuine efforts to find work or must he hold an offer of employment?]

The European Court of Justice (at pp 2836–2839)

First question

11. The equality of treatment enjoyed by workers who are nationals of Member States and are employed within the territory of another Member State in relation to workers who are nationals of that state, as regards the advantages which are granted to the members of a worker's family, contributes to the integration of migrant workers in the working environment of the host country in accordance with the objectives of the free movement of workers.

12. However, the members of a worker's family, within the meaning of Article 10 of Regulation 1612/68 **[D14]**, qualify only indirectly for the equal treatment accorded to the worker himself by Article 7 of Regulation 1612/68. Social benefits such as the income guaranteed to old people by the legislation of a Member State (see [*Castelli* **[D20]**]) or guaranteeing in general terms the minimum means of subsistence operate in favour of members of the worker's family only if such benefits may be regarded as a social advantage, within the meaning of [Regulation 1612/68, Article 7(2)], for the worker himself.

13. It follows that, where a worker who is a national of one Member State was employed within the territory of another Member State and exercised the right to remain there, his descendants who have reached the age of 21 and are no longer dependent on him may not rely on the right to equal treatment guaranteed by Community law in order to claim a social benefit provided for by the legislation of the host Member State and guaranteeing in general terms the minimum means of subsistence. In the circumstances, that benefit does not constitute for the worker a social advantage within the meaning of [Article 7(2)], inasmuch as he is no longer supporting his descendant.

14. The answer to the first question must therefore be that, where a worker who is a national of one Member State was employed within the territory of another Member State and remains there after obtaining a retirement pension, his descendants do not retain the right to equal treatment with regard to a social benefit provided for by the legislation of the host Member State and guaranteeing in general terms the minimum means of subsistence where they have reached the age of 21, are no longer dependent on him and do not have the status of workers.

15. In view of the answer given to the first question, there is no need to answer the second question.

Third question

16. In its third question, the national court seeks essentially to ascertain whether the status of dependent member of a worker's family, to which Article 10 of Regulation 1612/68 refers, results from a factual situation, namely the provision of support by the worker, without there being any need to determine the reasons for recourse to the worker's support.

. . .

20. It must be pointed out, in the first place, that a claim for the grant of the minimex submitted by a member of a migrant worker's family who is dependent on the worker cannot affect the claimant's status as a dependent member of the worker's family. To decide otherwise would amount to accepting that the grant of the minimex could result in the claimant forfeiting the status of dependent member of the family and consequently justify either the withdrawal of the minimex itself or even the loss of the right of residence. Such a solution would in practice preclude a dependent member of a worker's family from claiming the minimex and would, for that reason, undermine the equal treatment accorded to the migrant worker. The status of dependent member of a worker's family should therefore be considered independently of the grant of the minimex.

21. It must be pointed out, secondly, that the status of dependent member of a worker's family does not presuppose the existence of a right to maintenance either. If that were the case, the composition of the family would depend on national legislation, which varies from one state to another, and that would lead to the application of Community law in a manner that is not uniform.

22. Article 10(1) and (2) of Regulation 1612/68 must be interpreted as meaning that the status of dependent member of a worker's family is the result of a factual situation. The person having that status is a member of the family who is supported by the worker and there is no need to determine the reasons for recourse to the worker's support or to raise the question whether the person concerned is able to support himself by taking up paid employment.

23. That interpretation is dictated by the principle according to which the provisions establishing the free movement of workers, which constitutes one of the foundations of the Community, must be construed broadly (see [*Kempf* **[D6]**]). Moreover, it corresponds to the wording of the provision in question, whose German language version (*Unterhalt gewähren*) and Greek language version (*efoson synthreitai*) are particularly clear in that respect.

24. The answer to the third question must therefore be that the status of dependent member of a worker's family [is] the result of a factual situation, namely the provision of support by the worker, without there being any need to determine the reasons for recourse to the worker's support.

Fourth question

25. It is clear from the context that the fourth question seeks, in substance, to ascertain whether equal treatment with regard to social and tax advantages, which is laid down by Article 7(2) of Regulation 1612/68, also applies to persons who move in search of employment.

26. It must be pointed out that the right to equal treatment with regard to social and tax advantages applies only to workers. Those who move in search of employment qualify for equal treatment only as regards access to employment in accordance with Article 48 of the EEC Treaty and Articles 2 and 5 of Regulation 1612/68.

27. The answer to the fourth question must therefore be that the equal treatment with regard to social and tax advantages which is laid down by Article 7(2) of Regulation 1612/68 operates only for the benefit of workers and does not apply to nationals of Member States who move in search of employment.

[D26] Case 267/83 Aissatou Diatta v Land Berlin [1985] ECR 567

[Mrs Diatta, a Senegalese national, married a French national who had lived and worked in West Berlin for several years. They lived together for a year and then separated and lived in separate accommodation. Mrs Diatta intended to divorce her husband as soon as this was legally possible. Mrs Diatta had obtained a temporary residence permit but when this expired her application for an extension was rejected on the ground that she was no longer a member of the family of a national of a Member State and that she no longer lived with her husband. Mrs Diatta argued that Regulation 1612/68, Article 10 **[D14]**, could not be interpreted as requiring a married couple to live together and that it was the status of being married which was important.]

The European Court of Justice (at pp 589–590)

18. In providing that a member of a migrant worker's family has the right to instal himself with the worker, Article 10 [does] not require that the member of the family in question must live permanently with the worker, but, as is clear from Article 10(3), only that the accommodation which the worker has available must be such as may be considered normal for the purpose of accommodating his family. A requirement that the family must live under the same roof permanently cannot be implied.

19. In addition such an interpretation corresponds to the spirit of Article 11 of the regulation, which gives the member of the family the right to take up any activity as an employed person throughout the territory of the Member State concerned, even though that activity is exercised at a place some distance away from the place where the migrant worker resides.

20. It must be added that the marital relationship cannot be regarded as dissolved so long as it has not been terminated by the competent authority. It is not dissolved merely because the spouses live separately, even where they intend to divorce at a later date.

21. As regards Article 11 of [Regulation] 1612/68, it is clear from the terms of that provision that it does not confer on the members of a migrant worker's family an independent right of residence, but solely a right to exercise any activity as employed persons throughout the territory of the state in question. Article 11 cannot therefore constitute the legal basis for a right of residence without reference to the conditions laid down in Article 10.

[D27]   Case 249/86 Commission of the European Communities v Federal Republic of Germany [1989] ECR 1263

[According to the German Law on the residence of EEC nationals, paragraph 7 (referred to below as 'the German law'), 'a residence permit must be granted on demand to members of the family of a person who has such a permit and has housing for himself and the members of his family of a nature considered appropriate according to the criteria applied in that regard in the place of residence'; 'a residence permit granted to members of the family of workers must be extended on demand for a period of at least five years if the conditions for the issue thereof continue to be fulfilled'; and 'the period of validity of a residence permit may subsequently be reduced if the conditions required for its issue are no longer fulfilled'. The Commission received complaints from individuals that the German authorities had refused, in certain cases, to renew residence permits for members of the family of migrant workers and threatened them with administrative measures such as expulsion to their country of origin where the housing occupied by the worker and his family no longer corresponded to the prevailing conditions in the place of residence. The Commission brought an action under Article 169 (see Chapter Three, Section One). The Commission and the Federal Republic of Germany differed as to the interpretation of Article 10(3) of Regulation 1612/68 **[D14]** and as to the scope of derogations from the right of free movement of persons. Note how the Court of Justice refers to general principles of law and the protection of human rights (discussed in Chapter Two, Section Four). This case is also important with regard to the public policy derogation discussed in Section Three of this chapter.]

The European Court of Justice (at pp 1289–1293)

[On Article 10(3)]

6. [Germany] contends first that the purpose of [Article 10(3)] is to regulate the right of residence during the entire period of the stay in the host Member State and that the requirement of appropriate housing applies to the entire stay. It must, consequently, be verified both upon the arrival of each new family member and during the stay in the territory of the host Member State, in particular on each occasion that a residence permit is to be renewed. [The German law] therefore does not infringe Community law.

7. The Commission, on the other hand, claims that [Article 10(3)] relates only to the moment when the members of the migrant worker's family instal themselves with him. The condition concerning housing contained in [Article 10(3)] must therefore be interpreted as meaning that it may be required by the Member States only when the members of the worker's family are first admitted to their territory.

8. It should first of all be pointed out that Regulation [1612/68] defines more precisely the principle of freedom of movement for workers as formulated in Articles 48 and 49 of the EEC Treaty. Consequently, that regulation must be interpreted in the light of those provisions of the [Treaty].

9. Furthermore, as the court held in [*Royer* **[D46]**], the right of nationals of a Member State to enter the territory of another Member State and reside there for the purposes intended by the Treaty – in particular to look for or pursue an occupation or activities as employed or self-employed persons, or to rejoin their spouse or family – is a right conferred directly by the Treaty or, as the case may be, by the provisions adopted for its implementation, and that right is acquired independently of the issue of a residence permit by the competent authority of a Member State.

10. Regulation [1612/68] must also be interpreted in the light of the requirement of respect for family life set out in Article 8 of the Convention for the Protection of Human Rights and Fundamental Freedoms. That requirement is one of the fundamental rights which, according to the court's settled case law, restated in the preamble to the Single European Act **[B41]**, are recognised by Community law.

11. Finally, [Article 10(3)] must be interpreted in the context of the overall structure and purpose of that regulation. It is apparent from the provisions of the regulation, taken as a whole, that in order to facilitate the movement of members of workers' families the Council took into account, first, the importance for the worker, from a human point of view, of having his entire family with him and, secondly, the importance, from all points of view, of the integration of the worker and his family into the host Member State without any difference in treatment in relation to nationals of that state.

12. It follows from the foregoing that Article 10(3) must be interpreted as meaning that the requirement to have available housing considered as normal applies solely as a condition under which each member of the worker's family is permitted to come to live with him and that once the family has been brought together, the position of the migrant worker cannot be different in regard to housing requirements from that of a worker who is a national of the Member State concerned.

13. Consequently, if the housing regarded as normal at the time of the arrival of members of the migrant worker's family no longer fulfils that requirement as a result of a new event, such as the birth or arrival at the age of majority of a child, the measures which may be adopted in regard to members of the worker's family cannot be different from those required in regard to nationals of that Member State and cannot lead to discrimination between those nationals and nationals of other Member States.

14. A different solution would be compatible with the objectives which [Article 10(3)] seeks to achieve only if the migrant worker had obtained suitable housing solely in order to obtain the right to have members of his family living with him and had left that housing once he had obtained such authorisation.

15. The German legislation is therefore incompatible with the obligations arising under Community law in so far as it provides for non-renewal of a residence permit or a reduction *a posteriori* of the period of validity of a residence permit for a member of the family of a migrant worker by virtue of the fact that the family's housing can no longer be regarded as suitable according to the criteria applied in that regard in the place of residence, whereas sanctions of comparable severity are not provided for in regard to German nationals.

[On the public policy derogation]

16. [Germany] contends that the right to free movement must be limited where public security and public policy are threatened. The lack of suitable housing is contrary to public security and public policy, concepts, which, in the view of [Germany], must be determined on the basis of national criteria. [The German law] is not essentially repressive but preventive; it is an indispensable means of inducing workers to comply with the housing requirement. Consequently, that provision is justified under Article 48 of the Treaty.

17. As the court held in [*Bouchereau* **[D47]**], recourse to the concept of public policy presupposes the existence, in addition to the perturbation of the social order which any infringement of the law involves, of a genuine and sufficiently serious threat affecting one of the fundamental interests of society.

18. Furthermore, in regard to Articles 3(1) and (2) of [Directive 64/221 **[D42]**], the court held in [*Bonsignore* **[D44]**] that 'measures adopted on grounds of public policy and for the maintenance of public security against the nationals of Member States of the Community cannot be justified on grounds extraneous to the individual case' or be based 'on reasons of a "general preventive nature" '.

19. The court also held in [*Adoui* **[D48]**] that although Community law does not impose upon the Member States a uniform scale of values as regards the assessment of conduct which may be considered contrary to

public policy, conduct may not be regarded as being of a sufficiently serious nature to justify restrictions on the admission to or residence within the
territory of a Member State of a national of another Member State in a case
where the former Member State does not adopt, with respect to the same
conduct on the part of its own nationals, repressive measures or other genuine and effective measures intended to combat such conduct.
Consequently, that Member States may not, by virtue of the reservation relating to public policy contained in Articles 48 and 56 of the Treaty, expel a
national of another Member State from its territory or refuse him access to
its territory by reason of conduct which, when attributable to the former
state's own nationals, does not give rise to repressive measures or other
genuine and effective measures intended to combat such conduct.

20. Finally, as the court has consistently held, in particular in [*Watson*
[D10]], deportation negates the very right conferred and guaranteed by the
Treaty, and the imposition of such a penalty is not justified if it is so disproportionate to the gravity of the infringement that it becomes an obstacle to
the free movement of persons.

21. [Germany] also claims that the application in practice by the German
authorities of [the German law] does not entail any discrimination against
the families of migrant workers and that no member of a worker's family
has been deported.

22. As the court has consistently held, mere administrative practices
which can be modified as and when the administration pleases cannot be
regarded as constituting proper fulfilment of the obligations contained in the
Treaty.

23. In the light of the foregoing it must be held that by adopting and retaining provisions in its national legisation which make renewal of the
residence permit of members of the family of Community migrant workers
conditional on their living in appropriate housing, not only at the time when
they instal themselves with the migrant worker concerned but for the entire
duration of their residence, [Germany] has failed to fulfil its obligations
under Article 10(3) of Regulation [1612/68].

[D28]   Case 9/74 Donato Casagrande v Landeshauptstadt München [1974] ECR 773

[This concerned the application, by the child of an Italian national, working
in Germany, who was attending secondary school in Munich, for a monthly
educational grant. This was refused on the ground that the relevant
German law only permitted such a grant for German nationals, stateless
persons and aliens granted asylum. The Bayersches Verwaltungsgericht
(Bavarian administrative court) sought a preliminary ruling as to whether
the German law was compatible with Regulation 1612/68, Article 12 **[D14]**.
The court referred to the fifth recital to the regulation, emphasising the word
'integration'.]

The European Court of Justice (at pp 778–779)

7. Such integration presupposes that, in the case of the child of a foreign worker who wishes to have secondary education, this child can take
advantage of benefits provided by the laws of the host country relating to

educational grants, under the same conditions as nationals who are in a similar position.

8. It follows from [Article 12(2)] that the Article is intended to encourage special efforts, to ensure that children may take advantage on an equal footing of the education and training facilities available.

9. It must be concluded that in providing that the children in question shall be admitted to educational courses 'under the same conditions as the nationals' of the host state, Article 12 refers not only to rules relating to admission but also to general measures intended to facilitate educational attendance.

. . .

14. As regards Article [12], although the determination of the conditions referred to there is a matter for the authorities competent under national law, they must however be applied without discrimination between the children of national workers and those of workers who are nationals of another Member State who reside in the territory.

[D29]   Regulation 1251/70 on the right of workers to remain in the territory of a Member State after having been employed in that state

[Whereas] the right of residence acquired by workers in active employment has as a corollary the right, granted by the Treaty to such workers, to remain in the territory of a Member State after having been employed in that state; whereas it is important to lay down the conditions for the exercise of such right;

[Whereas] the right to remain, referred to in Article 48(3)(d) of the Treaty, is interpreted therefore as the right of the worker to maintain his residence in the territory of a Member State when he ceases to be employed there;

Whereas the mobility of labour in the Community requires that workers may be employed successively in several Member States without thereby being placed at a disadvantage;

Whereas it is important, in the first place, to guarantee to the worker residing in the territory of a Member State the right to remain in that territory when he ceases to be employed in that state because he has reached retirement age or by reason of permanent incapacity to work; whereas, however, it is equally important to ensure that right for the worker who, after a period of employment and residence in the territory of a Member State, works as an employed person in the territory of another Member State, while still retaining his residence in the territory of the first state;

Whereas, to determine the conditions under which the right to remain arises, account should be taken of the reasons which have led to the termination of employment in the territory of the Member State concerned and, in particular, of the difference between retirement, the normal and foreseeable end of working life, and incapacity to work which leads to a premature and unforeseeable termination of activity; whereas special conditions must be laid down where termination of activity is the result of an accident at work or occupational disease, or where the worker's spouse is or was a national of the Member State concerned;

Whereas the worker who has reached the end of his working life should have sufficient time in which to decide where he wishes to establish his final residence;

Whereas the exercise by the worker of the right to remain entails that such right shall be extended to members of his family; whereas in the case of the death of the worker during his working life, maintenance of the right of residence of the members of his family must also be recognised and be the subject of special conditions;

Whereas persons to whom the right to remain applies must enjoy equality of treatment with national workers who have ceased their working lives;

. . .

Article 1

The provisions of this regulation shall apply to nationals of a Member State who have worked as employed persons in the territory of another Member State and to members of their families, as defined in Article 10 of [Regulation] 1612/68 **[D14]** on freedom of movement for workers within the Community.

Article 2

1. The following shall have the right to remain permanently in the territory of a Member State:

(a)   a worker who, at the time of termination of his activity, has reached the age laid down by the law of that Member State for entitlement to an old-age pension and who has been employed in that state for at least the last 12 months and has resided there continuously for more than three years;

(b)   a worker who, having resided continuously in the territory of that state for more than two years, ceases to work there as an employed person as a result of permanent incapacity to work. If such incapacity is the result of an accident at work or an occupational disease entitling him to a pension for which an institution of that state is entirely or partially responsible, no condition shall be imposed as to length of residence;

(c)   a worker who, after three years' continuous employment and residence in the territory of that state, works as an employed person in the territory of another Member State, while retaining his residence in the territory of the first state, to which he returns, as a rule, each day or at least once a week.

Periods of employment completed in this way in the territory of the other Member State shall, for the purposes of entitlement to the rights referred to in sub-paragraphs (a) and (b), be considered as having been completed in the territory of the state of residence.

2. The conditions as to length of residence and employment laid down in paragraph 1(a) and the condition as to length of residence laid down in paragraph 1(b) shall not apply if the worker's spouse is a national of the

Member State concerned or has lost the nationality of that state by marriage to that worker.

Article 3

1. The members of a worker's family referred to in Article 1 of this regulation who are residing with him in the territory of a Member State shall be entitled to remain there permanently if the worker has acquired the right to remain in the territory of that state in accordance with Article 2, and to do so even after his death.

2. If, however, the worker dies during his working life and before having acquired the right to remain in the territory of the state concerned, members of his family shall be entitled to remain there permanently on condition that:

– the worker, on the date of his decease, had resided continuously in the territory of that Member State for at least two years; or
– his death resulted from an accident at work or an occupational disease; or
– the surviving spouse is a national of the state of residence or lost the nationality of that state by marriage to that worker.

Article 4

1. Continuity of residence as provided for in Articles 2(1) and 3(2) may be attested by any means of proof in use in the country of residence. It shall not be affected by temporary absences not exceeding a total of three months per year, nor by longer absences due to compliance with the obligations of military service.

2. Periods of involuntary unemployment, duly recorded by the competent employment office, and absences due to illness or accident shall be considered as periods of employment within the meaning of Article 2(1).

Article 5

1. The person entitled to the right to remain shall be allowed to exercise it within two years from the time of becoming entitled to such right pursuant to Article 2(1)(a) and (b) and Article 3. During such period he may leave the territory of the Member State without adversely affecting such right.

2. No formality shall be required on the part of the person concerned in respect of the exercise of the right to remain.

Article 6

1. Persons coming under the provisions of this Regulation shall be entitled to a residence permit which:

(a)   shall be issued and renewed free of charge or on payment of a sum not exceeding the dues and taxes payable by nationals for the issue or renewal [of] identity documents;
(b)   must be valid throughout the territory of the Member State issuing it;
(c)   must be valid for at least five years and be renewable automatically.

2. Periods of non-residence not exceeding six consecutive months shall not affect the validity of the residence permit.

Article 7

The right to equality of treatment, established by [Regulation] 1612/68, shall apply also to persons coming under the provisions of this regulation.

SECTION TWO

ESTABLISHMENT

Introduction

Freedom of establishment (see Articles 52–58 of the EC Treaty **[D30]**) broadly relates to movement by three groups: natural persons who seek to practise occupations for which qualifications are necessary, the self-employed and companies or businesses wishing to operate in another state. The characteristics of these groups mean that special problems may arise with regard to their movement within the Community which are not applicable to workers. For traditional professions such as medicine, law or accountancy there may be differences in the exact qualifications demanded by the governing bodies or regulatory instruments applicable in the various Member States. In other areas, such as estate agency or management consultancy, the difficulty may be that some Member States impose regulatory controls which are wholly absent in others.

Developments in the law relating to establishment closely mirror other patterns in EC law. The direct effect of Article 52 was swiftly confirmed by the Court of Justice in *Reyners* **[D31]**, despite protestations that the only permissible scope for promoting establishment was through Community-level directives channelled through Article 57. This filling of a legislative vacuum can be traced right back to the approach taken in *Van Gend en Loos* towards the justifications for direct effect as a general principle. Later cases have refined the rights of those seeking to exercise their freedom of establishment to the point where a suitable process must be available with which to assess the equivalence of qualifications and to justify any outcome of non-recognition. An important but fairly limited position was taken by the court in *Thieffry* **[D32]**, where the recognition of the foreign diploma that had already taken place by one body in the host state could not then be ignored by the relevant professional organisation. This may be compared with the more extensive protection conferred in *Heylens* **[D33]** and *Vlassopoulou* **[D34]**, where the parties claimed establishment on the footing of their original qualifications. The need for a host authority to justify non-recognition or the imposition of further requirements on the migrant has in turn spawned a development whereby the court has acknowledged the legitimate interest of a state in securing certain safeguards for the exercise of particular activities (*Ramrath* **[D35]**). It will be seen in Chapter Five that this approach is consistent with an already familiar line of trade cases (see, for example, *Cassis de Dijon* **[E21]**).

A further parallel with trade law in particular can be seen from the change in legislative policy with regard to establishment. In its early days the Community sought to achieve the consensus necessary to produce an EC regime to govern a particular profession, such as the requisite qualifications relating to architects or branches of medicine. However, influenced perhaps both by the court's rejection of the need for legislation under Article 57 for the protection of establishment rights (*Thieffry* **[D32]**) and by the developments in trade law (see McGee and Weatherill **[E39]**), the Commission moved away from tailor-made legislation that was specific to particular occupations. Hence the enactment of Directive 89/48 on the mutual recognition of higher education diplomas (see **[D40]**).

Limits nevertheless remain to the claiming of establishment rights. First, it is clear from *Brea* [D37] that Article 52 does not, so far as nationals of that state who have acquired no training or qualifications elsewhere are concerned, deregulate a profession for which a Member State has prescribed a framework of control . The concern of the case law is with the obligation on national authorities to assess and take proper account of foreign qualifications. Adequate machinery must be available for redress against default (*Heylens* [D33] echoed in the later legislation of Directive 89/48 [D40]). Secondly, the court has clearly stated that the position of natural persons is different from that of companies and other artificial persons (*Daily Mail and General Trust plc* [D38] and Directive 73/148 [D36]). Nevertheless, discrimination against companies whose activity falls within the scope of the exercise of establishment will still be prohibited (*Commerzbank AG* [D39]).

Finally, it should not be forgotten that rights of establishment may not always be easily discernible from the provision of services (see 'Free movement of services' [E45]–[E47] below). The former involves a more permanent status in the host state than the latter.

MATERIALS

[D 30]   The right of establishment, EC Treaty provisions

Article 52

Within the framework of the provisions set out below, restrictions on the freedom of establishment of nationals of a Member State in the territory of another Member State shall be abolished by progressive stages in the course of the transitional period. Such progressive abolition shall also apply to restrictions in the setting up of agencies, branches, or subsidiaries by nationals of any Member State established in the territory of any Member State.

Freedom of establishment shall include the right to take up and pursue activities as self-employed persons and to set up and manage undertakings, in particular companies or firms within the meaning of the second paragraph of Article 58, under the conditions laid down for its own nationals by the law of the country where such establishment is effected, subject to the provisions of the Chapter relating to capital.

Article 54

1. Before the end of the first stage, the Council shall . . . draw up a general programme for the abolition of existing restrictions on freedom of establishment within the Community.

. . .

2. In order to implement this general programme or, in the absence of such programme, in order to achieve a stage in attaining freedom of establishment as regards a particular activity, the Council, acting in accordance with the procedure referred to in Article 189b and after consulting the Economic and Social Committee, shall act by means of directives.

3. The Council and the Commission shall carry out the duties devolving upon them under the preceding provisions, in particular:

. . .

(c) by abolishing those administrative procedures and practices, whether resulting from national legislation or from agreements previously concluded between Member States, the maintenance of which would form an obstacle to freedom of establishment;

. . .

(g) by co-ordinating to the necessary extent the safeguards which, for the protection of the interests of members and others, are required by Member States of companies or firms within the meaning of the second paragraph of Article 58 with a view to making such safeguards equivalent throughout the Community;

. . .

Article 55

The provisions of this Chapter shall not apply, so far as any given Member State is concerned, to activities which in that state are connected, even occasionally, with the exercise of official authority.

The Council may, acting by a qualified majority on a proposal from the Commission, rule that the provisions of this Chapter shall not apply to certain activities.

Article 56

1. The provisions of this Chapter and measures taken in pursuance thereof shall not prejudice the applicability of provisions laid down by law, regulation or administrative action providing for special treatment for foreign nationals on grounds of public policy, public security or public health.

. . .

Article 57

1. In order to make it easier for persons to take up and pursue activities as self-employed persons, the Council shall, acting in accordance with the procedure referred to in Article 189b, issue directives for the mutual recognition of diplomas, certificates and other evidence of formal qualifications.

. . .

Article 58

Companies or firms formed in accordance with the law of a Member State and having their registered office, central administration or principal place of business within the Community shall, for the purposes of this Chapter, be treated in the same way as natural persons who are nationals of Member States.

'Companies or firms' means companies or firms constituted under civil or commercial law, including co-operative societies, and other legal persons governed by public or private law, save for those which are non-profit making.

[D31]   Case 2/74 Reyners v Belgium [1974] ECR 631

[See also extract at **[D56]**.]

The European Court of Justice

. . .

26. In laying down that freedom of establishment shall be attained at the end of the transitional period, Article 52 thus imposes an obligation to attain a precise result, the fulfilment of which had to be made easier by, but not made dependent on, the implementation of a programme of progressive measures.

27. The fact that this progression has not been adhered to leaves the obligation itself intact beyond the end of the period provided for its fulfilment.

. . .

30. After the expiry of the transitional period the directives provided for by the Chapter on the right of establishment have become superfluous with regard to implementing the rule on nationality, since this is henceforth sanctioned by the Treaty itself with direct effect.

31. These directives have however not lost all interest since they pre-serve an important scope in the field of measures intended to make easier the effective exercise of the right of freedom of establishment.

32. It is right therefore to reply to the question raised that, since the end of the transitional period, Article 52 of the Treaty is a directly applicable pro-vision despite the absence in a particular sphere, of the directives prescribed by Articles 54(2) and 57(1) of the Treaty . . .

[D32]   Case 71/76 Thieffry v Conseil de L'Ordre des Avocats à la Cour de Paris [1977] ECR 765

The European Court of Justice

2. The case before the Cour d'Appel concerns the admission to the [Paris Bar] of a Belgian advocate, who is the holder of a Belgian diploma of Doctor of Laws which has been recognised by a French university as equivalent to the French licentiate's degree in law, and who subsequently obtained the *Certificat d'Aptitude à la Profession d'Avocat* (qualifying certifi-cate for the profession of advocate), having sat and passed that examination, in accordance with French legislation.

3. The appellant in the main action applied for admission to the Paris Bar, but . . . the [Bar Council] rejected his application on the ground that the person concerned 'offers no French diploma evidencing a licentiate's de-gree or a doctor's degree'.

. . .

5. According to the [Bar Council], although the effect of the Treaty is to abolish any discrimination on grounds of nationality in this field, the equiva-lence of diplomas does not follow automatically from the application of its provisions, since such equivalence can result only from directives concern-ing recognition adopted pursuant to Article 57 of the Treaty, which do not yet exist for the profession of advocate.

6. The person concerned appealed to the Cour d'Appel [which made a reference under Article 177].

. . .

12. [Article 57] is . . . directed towards reconciling freedom of establish-ment with the application of national professional rules justified by the general good, in particular rules relating to organisation, qualifications, pro-fessional ethics, supervision and liability, provided that such application is effected without discrimination.

. . .

17. . . . if the freedom of establishment provided for by Article 52 can be ensured in a Member State either under the provisions of the laws and regulations in force, or by virtue of the practices of the public service or of

professional bodies, a person subject to Community law cannot be denied the practical benefit of that freedom solely by virtue of the fact that, for a particular profession, the directives provided for by Article 57 of the Treaty have not yet been adopted.

18. Since the practical enjoyment of freedom of establishment can thus in certain circumstances depend upon national practice or legislation, it is incumbent upon the competent public authorities – including legally recognised professional bodies – to ensure that such practice or legislation is applied in accordance with the objective defined by the provisions of the Treaty relating to freedom of establishment.

19. In particular, there is an unjustified restriction on that freedom where, in a Member State, admission to a particular profession is refused to a person covered by the Treaty who holds a diploma which has been recognised as an equivalent qualification by the competent authority of the country of establishment and who furthermore has fulfilled the specific conditions regarding professional training in force in that country, solely by reason of the fact that the person concerned does not possess the national diploma corresponding to the diploma which he holds and which has been recognised as an equivalent qualification.

. . .

24. . . . it is for the competent national authorities, taking account of the requirements of Community law . . ., to make such assessments of the facts as will enable them to judge whether a recognition granted by a university authority can, in addition to its academic effect, constitute valid evidence of a professional qualification.

25. The fact that a national legislation provides for recognition of equivalence only for university purposes does not of itself justify the refusal to recognise such equivalence as evidence of a professional qualification . . .

[D33]   Case 222/86 UNECTEF v Heylens [1987] ECR 4097

The European Court of Justice

3. It appears . . . that in order to practise the occupation of football trainer in France a person must be the holder of a French football trainer's diploma or a foreign diploma which has been recognised as equivalent by decision of the competent member of the government after consulting a special committee.

4. The defendant in the main proceedings, Georges Heylens, is a Belgian national and the holder of a Belgian football trainer's diploma and was engaged by the Lille Olympic Sporting Club as trainer of the club's professional football team. An application for recognition of the equivalence of the Belgian diploma was rejected by decision of the competent member of the government, which referred, by way of statement of reasons, to an adverse opinion of the special committee, which itself contained no statement of reasons. Since Mr Heylens continued to practise as a football trainer, the French football trainers' trade union summoned him and the directors of the football club which had engaged him before the Lille criminal court.

5. Since it had doubts about the compatibility of the French legislation with the rules on the free movement of workers, the tribunal de grande

instance de Lille (Eighth Criminal Chamber) suspended the proceedings until the court had delivered a preliminary ruling.

. . .

7. The question put by the national court essentially seeks to establish whether, where in a Member State access to an occupation as an employed person is dependent upon the possession of a national diploma or a foreign diploma recognised as equivalent thereto, the principle of the free movement of workers laid down in Article 48 of the Treaty requires that it must be possible for a decision refusing to recognise the equivalence of a diploma granted to a worker who is a national of another Member State by that Member State to be made the subject of judicial proceedings, and that the decision must state the reasons on which it is based.

8. In order to answer that question it must be borne in mind that Article 48 of the Treaty implements, with regard to workers, a fundamental principle contained in Article 3(c) of the Treaty, which states that, for the purposes set out in Article 2, the activities of the Community are to include the abolition, as between Member States, of obstacles to freedom of movement for persons and services (see . . . Case 118/75 *Watson and Belmann* [1976] ECR 1185 **[D10]**).

9. In application of the general principle set out in Article 7 of the Treaty under which discrimination on grounds of nationality is prohibited, Article 48 aims to eliminate in the legislation of the Member States provisions as regards employment, remuneration and other conditions of work and employment under which a worker who is a national of another Member State is subject to more severe treatment or is placed in an unfavourable situation in law or in fact as compared with the situation of a national in the same circumstances (see . . . Case 175/78 *R v Saunders* [1979] ECR 1129 **[D2]**).

10. In the absence of harmonisation of the conditions of access to a particular occupation, the Member States are entitled to lay down the knowledge and qualifications needed in order to pursue it and to require the production of a diploma certifying that the holder has the relevant knowledge and qualifications.

11. However, as the court held in its judgment . . . in Case 11/77 *Patrick v Ministre des affaires culturelles* [1977] ECR 1199, the lawful requirement, in the various Member States, relating to the possession of diplomas for admission to certain occupations constitutes a restriction on the effective exercise of the freedom of establishment guaranteed by the Treaty the abolition of which is to be made easier by directives for the mutual recognition of diplomas, certificates and other evidence of formal qualifications. As the court also held in that judgment, the fact that such directives have not yet been issued does not entitle a Member State to deny the practical benefit of that freedom to a person subject to Community law when that freedom can be ensured in that Member State, in particular because it is possible under its laws and regulations for equivalent foreign diplomas to be recognised.

12. Since freedom of movement for workers is one of the fundamental objectives of the Treaty, the requirement to secure free movement under existing national laws and regulations stems, as the court held in its judgment . . . in Case 71/76 *Thieffry* [1977] ECR 765, from Article 5 of the Treaty, under which the Member States are bound to take all appropriate measures, whether general or particular, to ensure fulfilment of the obligations arising out of the Treaty and to abstain from any measure which could

jeopardise the attainment of the objectives of the Treaty.

13. Since it has to reconcile the requirement as to the qualifications necessary in order to pursue a particular occupation with the requirements of the free movement of workers, the procedure for the recognition of equivalence must enable the national authorities to assure themselves, on an objective basis, that the foreign diploma certifies that its holder has knowledge and qualifications which are, if not identical, at least equivalent to those certified by the national diploma. That assessment of the equivalence of the foreign diploma must be effected exclusively in the light of the level of knowledge and qualifications which its holder can be assumed to possess in the light of that diploma, having regard to the nature and duration of the studies and practical training which the diploma certifies that he has carried out.

14. Since free access to employment is a fundamental right which the Treaty confers individually on each worker in the Community, the existence of a remedy of a judicial nature against any decision of a national authority refusing the benefit of that right is essential in order to secure for the individual effective protection for his right. As the court held in its judgment . . . in Case 222/84 *Johnston v Chief Constable of the Royal Ulster Constabulary* [1986] ECR 1651 **[C32]**, . . . that requirement reflects a general principle of Community law which underlies the constitutional traditions common to the Member States and has been enshrined in Articles 6 and 13 of the European Convention for the Protection of Human Rights and Fundamental Freedoms.

15. Effective judicial review, which must be able to cover the legality of the reasons for the contested decision, presupposes in general that the court to which the matter is referred may require the competent authority to notify its reasons. But where, as in this case, it is more particularly a question of securing the effective protection of a fundamental right conferred by the Treaty on Community workers, the latter must also be able to defend that right under the best possible conditions and have the possibility of deciding, with a full knowledge of the relevant facts, whether there is any point in their applying to the courts. Consequently, in such circumstances the competent national authority is under a duty to inform them of the reasons on which its refusal is based, either in the decision itself or in a subsequent communication made at their request.

16. In view of their aims those requirements of Community law, that is to say, the existence of a judicial remedy and the duty to state reasons, are however limited only to final decisions refusing to recognise equivalence and do not extend to opinions and other measures occurring in the preparation and investigation stage.

17. Consequently, the answer to the question put by the tribunal de grande instance, Lille, must be that where in a Member State access to an occupation as an employed person is dependent upon the possession of a national diploma or a foreign diploma recognised as equivalent thereto, the principle of the free movement of workers laid down in Article 48 of the Treaty requires that it must be possible for a decision refusing to recognise the equivalence of a diploma granted to a worker who is a national of another Member State by that Member State to be made the subject of judicial proceedings in which its legality under Community law can be reviewed, and for the person concerned to ascertain the reasons for the decision.

[D34]   Case C-340/89 Vlassopoulou [1991] ECR I-2357

The European Court of Justice

15. It must be stated . . . that, even if applied without any discrimination on the basis of nationality, national requirements concerning qualifications may have the effect of hindering nationals of the other Member States in the exercise of their right of establishment guaranteed to them by Article 52 of the EEC Treaty. That could be the case if the national rules in question took no account of the knowledge and qualifications already acquired by the person concerned in another Member State.

16. Consequently, a Member State which receives a request to admit a person to a profession to which access, under national law, depends upon the possession of a diploma or professional qualification must take into consideration the diplomas, certificates and other evidence of qualifications which the person concerned has acquired in order to exercise the same profession in another Member State by making a comparison between the specialised knowledge and abilities certified by those diplomas and the knowledge and qualifications required by the national rules.

17. That examination procedure must enable the authorities of the host Member State to assure themselves, on an objective basis, that the foreign diploma certifies that its holder has knowledge and qualifications which are, if not identical, at least equivalent to those certified by the national diploma. That assessment of the equivalence of the foreign diploma must be carried out exclusively in the light of the level of knowledge and qualifications which its holder can be assumed to possess in the light of that diploma, having regard to the nature and duration of the studies and practical training to which the diploma relates (see . . . Case 222/86 *Heylens* [D33]).

18. In the course of that examination, a Member State may, however, take into consideration objective differences relating to both the legal framework of the profession in question in the Member State of origin and to its field of activity. In the case of the profession of lawyer, a Member State may therefore carry out a comparative examination of diplomas, taking account of the differences identified between the national legal systems concerned.

19. If that comparative examination of diplomas results in the finding that the knowledge and qualifications certified by the foreign diploma correspond to those required by the national provisions, the Member State must recognise that diploma as fulfilling the requirements laid down by its national provisions. If, on the other hand, the comparison reveals that the knowledge and qualifications certified by the foreign diploma and those required by the national provisions correspond only partially, the host Member State is entitled to require the person concerned to show that he has acquired the knowledge and qualifications which are lacking.

20. In this regard, the competent national authorities must assess whether the knowledge acquired in the host Member State, either during a course of study or by way of practical experience, is sufficient in order to prove possession of the knowledge which is lacking.

21. If completion of a period of preparation or training for entry into the profession is required by the rules applying in the host Member State, those national authorities must determine whether professional experience acquired in the Member State of origin or in the host Member State may be regarded as satisfying that requirement in full or in part.

22. Finally, it must be pointed out that the examination made to determine whether the knowledge and qualifications certified by the foreign diploma and those required by the legislation of the host Member State correspond must be carried out by the national authorities in accordance with a procedure which is in conformity with the requirements of Community law concerning the effective protection of the fundamental rights conferred by the Treaty on Community subjects. It follows that any decision taken must be capable of being made the subject of judicial proceedings in which its legality under Community law can be reviewed and that the person concerned must be able to ascertain the reasons for the decision taken in his regard (see . . . *Heylens* **[D33]**).

23. Consequently, the answer to the question submitted by the [national court] must be that Article 52 . . . must be interpreted as requiring the national authorities of a Member State to which an application for admission to the profession of lawyer is made by a Community subject who is already admitted to practise as a lawyer in his country of origin and who practises as a legal adviser in the first-mentioned Member State to examine to what extent the knowledge and qualifications attested by the diploma obtained by the person concerned in his country of origin correspond to those required by the rules of the host state; if those diplomas correspond only partially, the national authorities in question are entitled to require the person concerned to prove that he has acquired the knowledge and qualifications which are lacking.

[D35] Case C-106/91 Ramrath v Ministre de la Justice [1992] 3 CMLR 173

The European Court of Justice

The questions have arisen in the course of proceedings brought by Mr Ramrath against the Luxembourg Minister of Justice ('the Minister'), in the presence of the Institut des Réviseurs d'Entreprises (Institute of Company Auditors). The proceedings concern the withdrawal, ordered by the Minister in 1989, of Mr Ramrath's authorisation as a company auditor.

In Luxembourg the profession of company auditor is organised by the Act of 28 June 1984. Section 3 of the Act provides that:

> The statutory audit of the documents referred to by section 1 can be carried out only by persons authorised by the Minister of Justice.
> (1) In order to obtain authorisation, natural persons must satisfy the following conditions:
>   (a) they must be nationals of a member State of the European Community . . .;
>   (b) they must furnish proof of professional qualification and good repute; . . .
>   (c) they must have a professional establishment in Luxembourg.
> (2) In order to obtain authorisation, legal persons must satisfy the conditions set out in indent (1)(a) and (c) and the following conditions:
>   (a) the natural persons who carry out the statutory audit of the documents referred to by section 1 on behalf of the legal person must satisfy the conditions laid down by indent (1) above and have power to bind the legal person;

. . .

(3)   The Minister of Justice shall withdraw the authorisation of persons who no longer fulfil any one of the conditions set out above.

Pursuant to s 6 of the Act of 28 June 1984:

The profession of company auditor shall be incompatible with any activity likely to affect the professional independence of a member of that profession. He shall not take salaried employment except with a person authorised pursuant to s 3.

At the Community level the authorisation of company auditors is the subject of the Eighth Council Directive 84/253, based on Article 54(3)(g) EEC, on the approval of persons responsible for carrying out statutory audits of accounting documents ('the Eighth Directive').

Article 3 of the directive provides as follows:

The authorities of a member State shall grant approval only to persons of good repute who are not carrying on any activity which is incompatible, under the law of that member State, with the statutory auditing of the documents referred to. . .

Articles 23, 24, 25 and 26 of . . . the Eighth Directive are worded as follows:

Article 23
Member States shall prescribe that persons approved for the statutory auditing of the documents referred to in Article 1(1) shall carry out such audits with professional integrity.

Article 24
Member States shall prescribe that such persons shall not carry out statutory audits which they have required if such persons are not independent in accordance with the law of the Member State which requires the audit.

Article 25
Articles 23 and 24 shall also apply to natural persons who satisfy the conditions imposed in Articles 3 to 19 and carry out the statutory audit of the documents referred to in Article 1(1) on behalf of a firm of auditors.

Article 26
Member States shall ensure that approved persons are liable to appropriate sanctions when they do not carry out audits in accordance with Articles 23, 24 and 25.

On 11 February 1985 the Minister granted Mr Ramrath authorisation to practise the profession of company auditor. At that time he was employed by Société Civile Treuarbeit, which is established in Luxembourg ('Treuarbeit Luxembourg') and which, as a legal person, also had such authorisation for Luxembourg.

In 1988 Mr Ramrath stated that he was then employed by Treuarbeit AG Düsseldorf ('Treuarbeit Düsseldorf') in Germany and that his professional establishment was in that city. While pointing out that he himself and Treuarbeit Düsseldorf were authorised as company auditors by the German authorities, Mr Ramrath added that Treuarbeit Düsseldorf had refrained from exercising any influence over him when Treuarbeit Luxembourg asked him to carry out audits in Luxembourg. Treuarbeit Luxembourg subsequently stated that he was in fact employed by it during the time he worked in Luxembourg.

On 19 May 1989 the Minister withdrew Mr Ramrath's authorisation on the grounds, firstly, that he had implicitly admitted, when stating that his professional address was in Düsseldorf, that he no longer had a professional establishment in Luxembourg within the meaning of s 3(1)(c) of the Act . . . and, secondly, that, being an employee of Treuarbeit Düsseldorf, he no longer fulfilled the condition of professional independence laid down by s 6 of the Act.

In support of his appeal against the Minister's decision, Mr Ramrath contended . . . that he was the victim of discrimination. The Act of 28 June 1984 accepted that the fact that a company auditor was employed by a legal person authorised as such by the Luxembourg authorities was compatible with professional independence, whereas it did not permit an auditor to be employed by a legal person authorised as a company auditor by the authorities of another Member State, even though the law of that state laid down similar requirements of independence vis-à-vis persons engaging in business activity.

By order of 12 March 1991 the Conseil d'Etat stayed judgment [and referred questions under Article 177] . . .

It should be observed at the outset that, at the present stage of the proceedings, the national court has not finally assessed Mr Ramrath's situation by reference to the relevant provisions of Community law. The facts found by the national court and the choice of Community law provisions mentioned by the questions indicate various possibilities in this connection, depending on whether Mr Ramrath is covered by Community law by reason of a profession which he himself practises, or employment which he has himself sought or as an employee of a person covered by Community law by reason of that person's own profession.

Consequently his situation could fall within the chapter of the Treaty concerning workers, particularly Article 48, or the chapters relating to the right of establishment and services, particularly Articles 52, 56 and 59.

It should also be stressed that a comparison of these different provisions shows that they are based on the same principles with regard to persons covered by Community law entering and remaining in the territory of the Member States as with regard to the prohibition of discrimination against them by reason of nationality.

. . .

First question

In essence the national court's first question seeks to ascertain whether the Treaty provisions relating to the right of establishment prevent a Member State from prohibiting a person from establishing himself in its territory and practising as a company auditor there on the ground that he is established and authorised as such in another Member State.

On this point it is the court's settled case law (see Case 107/83 *Klopp* [1984] ECR 2971, Case 143/87 *Stanton* [1988] ECR 3877, Joined Cases 154/87 and 155/87 *Wolf* [1988] ECR 3897) that the right of establishment includes the freedom to set up and maintain, subject to observance of the professional rules of conduct, more than one place of work within the Community.

It follows that the right of establishment prevents a Member State from requiring a person practising a profession to have only one establishment in the Community.

Consequently the reply to the first question should be that the provisions of the Treaty relating to the right of establishment prevent a Member State from prohibiting a person from establishing himself in its territory and practising as a company auditor there on the ground that he is established and authorised as such in another Member State.

Second and third questions

These questions seek in essence to determine whether the provisions of the Treaty relating to the freedom of movement of persons prevent a Member State from imposing conditions on the practice of the profession of company auditor in that state by a person who is already authorised to practise as such in another Member State, the conditions in question relating to a permanent professional infrastructure, actual presence in that state and supervision of compliance with the rules of professional conduct or, if the person in question is an employee, relating to the fact that the main employer must be an authorised company auditor in that state.

It is unnecessary to determine whether an auditor who intends to carry out company audits in another Member State has the status of an employee, self-employed person or supplier of services, this being a matter for the national court to decide if the need arises. All the provisions of the Treaty concerning the freedom of movement of persons must be examined in turn to ascertain whether they preclude conditions such as those laid down by the Act of 28 June 1984.

The principle of the freedom of movement for workers, set out in Article 48 EEC, secures the right of a national of a Member State to enter another Member State and to remain there for the purposes specified by that article. The same principle guarantees the right of any employee to take up temporary employment in another Member State. He cannot be refused such employment on the ground that he is already employed in his state of origin or that the work in the other Member State is part-time.

It should also be observed that the court stated in the above-mentioned cases *Stanton* and *Wolf* . . . that the considerations which are set out above in the framework of the reply to the first question relating to the right of establishment apply equally to a person who is employed in one Member State and wishes in addition to work in another Member State in a self-employed capacity.

Finally it should be noted that the freedom to provide services within the meaning of Article 59 et seq EEC involves the elimination of any discrimination against the provider of services by reason of his nationality or the circumstance that he is established in a Member State other than that where the service must be provided (see Case 279/80 *Webb* [1981] ECR 3305).

It follows from what has been said that Articles 48 and 59 EEC are intended to facilitate the pursuit by Community nationals of occupational activities of all kinds throughout the Community, and preclude national legislation which might place Community nationals at a disadvantage when they wish to extend their activities beyond the territory of a single Member State . . .

However, it should be pointed out that, in view of the particular nature of certain professional or business activities, the imposition of specific requirements arising from application of the rules governing those types of activity should not be regarded as incompatible with the Treaty. Nevertheless, the freedom of movement of persons, as a fundamental principle of the Treaty, can only be limited by measures justified by the general interest and applying to any person or enterprise engaged in such activities in the state in question, in so far as that interest is not already safeguarded by rules to which the Community national is subject in the Member State where he is established (see Case C-180/89 *Commission v Italy* [1991] ECR I-709).

Furthermore, the said requirements must be objectively necessary to ensure compliance with professional rules and to safeguard the interests which constitute the objective thereof.

. . .

It follows that those requirements cannot be regarded as compatible with the provisions concerning the freedom of movement of persons unless it is shown that, in the sphere of the profession or business concerned, there are imperative reasons connected with the general interest which justify restrictions on the freedom of movement, that such interest is not already safeguarded by rules of the state where the Community national is established, and that the same result cannot be attained by rules which are less restrictive.

Accordingly it must be verified that the conditions imposed by the Member State where the statutory audit of the accounting documents is carried out are objectively necessary, being conditions relating to a permanent professional infrastructure, actual presence in that state, compliance with the rules governing the profession of company auditor, or to status as an employee of such an auditor who is authorised by the authorities of that state.

. . .

. . . it should be stressed that the Eighth Directive leaves it to the Member States to assess by reference to national law the repute and independence of company auditors practising in their territory.

It must be accepted that the Member State can carry out this task by requiring compliance with professional rules justified by the general interest, concerning the repute and independence of company auditors and applying to any person practising as a company auditor in that state. In this connection, requirements relating to the existence of an infrastructure there and a certain degree of physical presence of the auditor seem justified to safeguard that interest.

However, such requirements are not objectively necessary where the statutory audit of accounting documents is carried out by a company auditor who, while established and authorised as such in another Member State, is temporarily in the service of a natural or legal person authorised to practise as a company auditor by the authorities of the Member State where the audit is carried out. Under these circumstances, it is in relation to that person that the Member State can satisfy itself that the auditor periodically carrying out audits in its territory complies with the rules.

[D36]   Directive 73/148 on the abolition of restrictions on movement and residence within the Community for nationals of Member States with regard to establishment and the provision of services (OJ 1973 L172/14)

Article 1

1. The Member States shall, acting as provided in this directive, abolish restrictions on the movement and residence of:

(a)   nationals of a Member State who are established or who wish to establish themselves in another Member State in order to pursue activities as self-employed persons, or who wish to provide services in that state;

(b)   nationals of Member States wishing to go to another Member State as recipients of services;

(c)   the spouse and the children under 21 years of age of such nationals, irrespective of their nationality;

(d)   the relatives in the ascending and descending lines of such nationals and of the spouse of such nationals, which relatives are dependent on them, irrespective of their nationality.

2. Member States shall favour the admission of any other member of the family of a national referred to in paragraph 1(a) and (b) or of the spouse of that national, which member is dependent on that national or spouse of that national or who in the country of origin was living under the same roof.

. . .

Article 2

1. Member States shall grant the persons referred to in Article 1 the right to leave their territory. Such right shall be exercised simply on production of a valid identity card or passport. Members of the family shall enjoy the same right as the national on whom they are dependent.

. . .

Article 3

1. Member States shall grant to the persons referred to in Article 1 right to enter their territory merely on production of a valid identity card or passport.

. . .

Article 4

1. Each Member State shall grant the right of permanent residence to nationals of other Member States who establish themselves within its territory in order to pursue activities as self-employed persons, when the restrictions on these activities have been abolished pursuant to the Treaty.

. . .

2. The right of residence for persons providing and receiving services

shall be of equal duration with the period during which the services are provided.

. . .

3. A member of the family who is not a national of a Member State shall be issued with a residence document which shall have the same validity as that issued to that national on whom he is dependent.

[D37] Joined Cases C-330/90 and C-331/90 Ministerio Fiscal v Angel López Brea and Carlos Hidalgo Palacios

The European Court of Justice (Judgment 28 January 1992)

2. These questions were raised in proceedings brought by the Ministerio Fiscal against . . . Spanish nationals residing in Spain, who set up business in Alicante as estate agents without the required professional qualifications and authorisations.

. . .

6. . . . the first question [referred by the Spanish court] must be construed in the sense that the national court is seeking to ascertain whether Community law, and in particular the Treaty rules on freedom of establishment and Directive 67/43, is to be interpreted as precluding national rules which reserve certain activities in the real-estate sector to persons practising as estate agents within a regulated profession.

7. In this connection, the court has consistently held that the Treaty provisions on the freedom of movement for persons cannot be applied to activities which are confined in all respects within a single Member State (see . . . Case C-41/90 *Höfner and Elser v Macrotron* [1991] ECR I-1979).

8. It is clear from the facts set out by the national court in its orders for reference that the main proceedings concern Spanish nationals who are practising as estate agents in Spain and do not claim to have obtained in another Member State the professional qualifications required for carrying out such activities.

9. There is thus no connecting factor between such situations and any of those contemplated by Community law, and accordingly the Treaty rules on freedom of establishment are inapplicable.

10. It is also appropriate to examine the scope of Directive 67/43 in order to ascertain whether it contains provisions on harmonisation which are also applicable to purely internal situations, like those in the main proceedings.

11. Article 1 of Directive 67/43 provides that Member States must abolish, in respect of the natural persons and companies or firms covered by Title I of the General Programmes for the abolition of restrictions on freedom of establishment and freedom to provide services . . . the restrictions referred to in Title III of those General Programmes affecting the right to take up and pursue the activities specified in Articles 2 and 3 of the directive.

12. Article 2(1) of Directive 67/43 states that the provisions of the directive are to apply to activities of self-employed persons in matters

concerning immovable property as referred to in Annex I to the above-mentioned General Programme for the abolition of restrictions on freedom of establishment, and to activities of self-employed persons engaging in 'business services not elsewhere classified' which are referred to in the same Annex.

13. An analysis of the above-mentioned General Programmes for the abolition of restrictions of freedom of establishment and freedom to provide services reveals that the restrictions envisaged by those provisions are essentially measures discriminating, directly or indirectly, between nationals of other Member States and nationals of the host country.

14. This interpretation of Directive 67/43 is also confirmed by the wording of Article 5, paragraph 1 of which requires Member States to abolish restrictions which in particular:

(a)   prevent beneficiaries from establishing themselves or providing services in the host country under the same conditions and with the same rights as nationals of that country;

(b)   exist by reason of administrative practices which result in treatment being applied to beneficiaries that is discriminatory by comparison with that applied to nationals.

15. It should accordingly be held that Directive 67/43 merely requires the abolition of all direct or indirect discrimination based on nationality, but does not aim to harmonise the conditions laid down in national rules regulating the taking up or pursuit of the profession of estate agent.

16. In those circumstances, the reply to be given to the first question, as reformulated, should be that Directive 67/43 does not preclude national rules which reserve certain activities in the real-estate sector to persons practising as estate agents within a regulated profession.

[D38]   Case 81/87 R v HM Treasury and Commissioners of Inland Revenue, ex parte Daily Mail and General Trust plc [1988] ECR 5483

The European Court of Justice

17. In the case of a company, the right of establishment is generally exercised by the setting-up of agencies, branches or subsidiaries, as is expressly provided for in the second sentence of the first paragraph of Article 52. Indeed, that is the form of establishment in which the applicant engaged in this case by opening an investment management office in the Netherlands. A company may also exercise its right of establishment by taking part in the incorporation of a company in another Member State, and in that regard Article 221 of the Treaty ensures that it will receive the same treatment as nationals of that Member State as regards participation in the capital of the new company.

18. The provision of United Kingdom law at issue in the main proceedings imposes no restriction on transactions such as those described above. Nor does it stand in the way of a partial or total transfer of the activities of a company incorporated in the United Kingdom to a company newly incorporated in another Member State, if necessary after winding up and, consequently, the settlement of the tax position of the United Kingdom

company. It requires Treasury consent only where such a company seeks to transfer its central management and control out of the United Kingdom while maintaining its legal personality and its status as a United Kingdom company.

19. In that regard it should be borne in mind that, unlike natural persons, companies are creatures of the law and, in the present state of Community law, creatures of national law. They exist only by virtue of the varying national legislation which determines their incorporation and functioning.

20. As the Commission has emphasised, the legislation of the Member states varies widely in regard to both the factor providing a connection to the national territory required for the incorporation of a company and the question whether a company incorporated under the legislation of a Member State may subsequently modify that connecting factor. Certain states require that not merely the registered office but also the real head office, that is to say the central administration of the company, should be situated on their territory, and the removal of the central administration from that territory thus presupposes the winding up of the company with all the consequences that winding up entails in company law and tax law. The legislation of other Member States permits companies to transfer their central administration to a foreign country but certain of them, such as the United Kingdom, make that right subject to certain restrictions, and the legal consequences of a transfer, particularly in regard to taxation, vary from one Member State to another.

. . .

22. . . . none of the directives on the co-ordination of company law adopted under Article 54(3)(g) **[D30]** . . . deals with the differences at issue here.

23. It must therefore be held that the Treaty regards the differences in national legislation concerning the required connecting factor and the question whether – and if so how – the registered office or real head office of a company incorporated under national law may be transferred from one Member State to another as problems which are not resolved by the rules concerning the right of establishment but must be dealt with by future legislation or conventions.

24. Under those circumstances, Articles 52 and 58 of the Treaty cannot be interpreted as conferring on companies incorporated under the law of a Member State a right to transfer their central management and control and their central administration to another Member State while retaining their status as companies incorporated under the legislation of the first Member State.

. . .

27. In its second question, the national court asks whether the provisions of Council Directive 73/148 **[D36]** . . . on the abolition of restrictions on movement and residence within the Community for nationals of Member States with regard to establishment and the provision of services give a company a right to transfer its central management and control to another Member State.

28. It need merely be pointed out in that regard that the title and provisions of that directive refer solely to the movement and residence of natural persons and that the provisions of the directive cannot, by their nature, be applied by analogy to legal persons.

29. The answer to the second question must therefore be that Directive 73/148, properly construed, confers no right on a company to transfer its central management and control to another Member State.

[D39]   Case C-330/91 R v Inland Revenue Commissioners, ex parte Commerzbank AG

The European Court of Justice (Judgment, 13 July 1993)

12. The file shows that the national court's question is designed to ascertain, first, whether Articles 52 and 58 and Articles 5 and 7 of the Treaty prevent the legislation of a Member State from granting repayment supplement on overpaid tax to companies resident for tax purposes in that state whilst refusing that supplement to companies which are resident for tax purposes in another Member State and, secondly, whether such a rule is still discriminatory where the exemption from tax which gave rise to the refund applies only to companies which are not resident for tax purposes in that Member State.

13. As the Court held in . . . Case C-270/83 *Commission v France* [1986] ECR 273 . . . the freedom of establishment which Article 52 grants to nationals of a Member State, and which entails the right for them to take up and pursue activities as self-employed persons under the conditions laid down for its own nationals by the law of the Member State where such establishment is effected, includes, pursuant to Article 58 of the EEC Treaty, the right of companies or firms formed in accordance with the law of a Member State and having their registered office, central administration or principal place of business within the Community to pursue their activities in the Member State concerned through a branch or agency. With regard to companies, it should be noted in this context that it is their seat in the above-mentioned sense that serves as the connecting factor within the legal system of a particular state, like nationality in the case of natural persons. In the same judgment the court held that acceptance of the proposition that the Member State in which a company seeks to establish itself may freely apply to it different treatment solely by reason of the fact that its seat is situated in another Member State would deprive the provision of all meaning.

14. Moreover, it follows from the court's judgment in Case 152/73 *Sotgiu* [D16] that the rules regarding equality of treatment forbid not only overt discrimination by reason of nationality or, in the case of a company, its seat, but all covert forms of discrimination which, by the application of other criteria of differentiation, lead in fact to the same result.

15. Although it applies independently of a company's seat, the use of the criterion of fiscal residence within national territory for the purpose of granting repayment supplement on overpaid tax is liable to work more particularly to the disadvantage of companies having their seat in other Member States. Indeed, it is most often those companies which are resident for tax purposes outside the territory of the Member State in question.

16. In order to justify the national provision at issue in the main proceedings, the United Kingdom government argues that, far from suffering discrimination under the United Kingdom tax rules, non-resident companies which are in Commerzbank's situation enjoy privileged treatment. They are

exempt from tax normally payable by resident companies. In those circumstances, there is no discrimination with respect to repayment supplement: resident companies and non-resident companies are treated differently because, for the purposes of corporation tax, they are in different situations.

17. That argument cannot be upheld.

18. A national provision such as the one in question entails unequal treatment. Where a non-resident company is deprived of the right to repayment supplement on overpaid tax to which resident companies are always entitled, it is placed at a disadvantage by comparison with the latter.

19. The fact that the exemption from tax which gave rise to the refund was available only to non-resident companies cannot justify a rule of a general nature withholding the benefit. That rule is therefore discriminatory.

20. It follows from those considerations that the reply to be given to the national court is that Articles 52 and 58 of the Treaty prevent the legislation of a Member State from granting repayment supplement on overpaid tax to companies which are resident for tax purposes in that state whilst refusing the supplement to companies which are resident for tax purposes in another Member State. The fact that the latter would not have been exempt from tax if they had been resident in that state is of no relevance in that regard.

21. Since legislation such as that in issue in the main proceedings is contrary to Articles 52 and 58 of the Treaty, it is unnecessary to consider its compatibility with Articles 5 and 7.

[D40] Directive 89/48 on a general system for the recognition of higher education diplomas awarded on completion of professional education and training of at least three years' duration (OJ 1989 L19/16)

The Council of the European Communities, . . .

Whereas the provisions so far adopted by the Council, and pursuant to which Member States recognise mutually and for professional purposes higher education diplomas issued within their territory, concern only a few professions; whereas the level and duration of the education and training governing access to those professions have been regulated in a similar fashion in all the Member States or have been the subject of the minimal harmonisation needed to establish sectoral systems for the mutual recognition of diplomas;

Whereas, in order to provide a rapid response to the expectations of nationals of Community countries who hold higher education diplomas awarded on completion of professional education and training issued in a Member State other than that in which they wish to pursue their profession, another method of recognition of such diplomas should also be put in place such as to enable those concerned to pursue all those professional activities which in a host Member State are dependent on the completion of post-secondary education and training, provided they hold such diploma preparing them for those activities awarded on completion of a course of studies lasting at least three years and issued in another Member State;

Whereas this objective can be achieved by the introduction of a general system for the recognition of higher education diplomas awarded on completion of professional education and training of at least three years' duration;

. . .

Whereas the term 'regulated professional activity' should be defined so as to take account of differing national sociological situations; whereas the term should cover not only professional activities access to which is subject, in a Member State, to the possession of a diploma, but also professional activities, access to which is unrestricted when they are practised under a professional title reserved for the holders of certain qualifications; whereas the professional associations and organisations which confer such titles on their members and are recognised by the public authorities cannot invoke their private status to avoid application of the system provided for by this directive;

Whereas it is also necessary to determine the characteristics of the professional experience or adaptation period which the host Member State may require of the person concerned in addition to the higher education diploma, where the person's qualifications do not correspond to those laid down by national provisions;

Whereas an aptitude test may also be introduced in place of the adaptation period; whereas the effect of both will be to improve the existing situation with regard to the mutual recognition of diplomas between Member States and therefore to facilitate the free movement of persons within the Community; whereas their function is to assess the ability of the migrant, who is a person who has already received his professional training in another Member State, to adapt to this new professional environment; whereas, from the migrant's point of view, an aptitude test will have the advantage of reducing the length of the practice period; whereas, in principle, the choice between the adaptation period and the aptitude test should be made by the migrant; whereas, however, the nature of certain professions is such that Member States must be allowed to prescribe, under certain conditions, either the adaptation period or the test; whereas, in particular, the differences between the legal systems of the Member States, whilst they vary in extent from one Member State to another, warrant special provisions since, as a rule, the education or training attested by the diploma, certificate or other evidence of formal qualifications in a field of law in the Member State of origin does not cover the legal knowledge required in the host Member State with respect to the corresponding legal field;

. . . .

Has adopted this Directive:

Article 1

For the purposes of this directive the following definitions shall apply:

(a) diploma: any diploma, certificate or other evidence of formal qualifications or any set of such diplomas, certificates or other evidence:
 – which has been awarded by a competent authority in a Member State, designated in accordance with its own laws, regulations or administrative provisions;

- which shows that the holder has successfully completed a post-secondary course of at least three years' duration, or of an equivalent duration part-time, at a university or establishment of higher education or another establishment of similar level and, where appropriate, that he has successfully completed the professional training required in addition to the post-secondary course, and
- which shows that the holder has the professional qualifications required for the taking up or pursuit of a regulated profession in that Member State, provided that the education and training attested by the diploma, certificate or other evidence of formal qualifications were received mainly in the Community, or the holder thereof has three years' professional experience certified by the Member State which recognised a third-country diploma, certificate or other evidence of formal qualifications.

The following shall be treated in the same way as a diploma, within the meaning of the first sub-paragraph: any diploma, certificate or other evidence of formal qualifications or any set of such diplomas, certificates or other evidence awarded by a competent authority in a Member State if it is awarded on the successful completion of education and training received in the Community and recognised by a competent authority in that Member State as being of an equivalent level and if it confers the same rights in respect of the taking up and pursuit of a regulated profession in that Member State;

(b) host Member State: any Member State in which a national of a Member State applies to pursue a profession subject to regulation in that Member State, other than the state in which he obtained his diploma or first pursued the profession in question;

(c) a regulated profession: the regulated professional activity or range of activities which constitute this profession in a Member State;

(d) regulated professional activity: a professional activity, in so far as the taking up or pursuit of such activity or one of its modes of pursuit in a Member State is subject, directly or indirectly by virtue of laws, regulations or administrative provisions, to the possession of a diploma. The following in particular shall constitute a mode of pursuit of a regulated professional activity:

- pursuit of an activity under a professional title, in so far as the use of such a title is reserved to the holders of a diploma governed by laws, regulations or administrative provisions,
- pursuit of a professional activity relating to health, in so far as remuneration and/or reimbursement for such an activity is subject by virtue of national social security arrangements to the possession of a diploma.

Where the first sub-paragraph does not apply, a professional activity shall be deemed to be a regulated professional activity if it is pursued by the members of an association or organisation the purpose of which is, in particular, to promote and maintain a high standard in the professional field concerned and which, to achieve that purpose, is recognised in a special form by a Member State and:

- awards a diploma to its members,
- ensures that its members respect the rules of professional conduct which it prescribes, and
- confers on them the right to use a title or designatory letters, or to benefit from a status corresponding to that diploma.

A non-exhaustive list of associations or organisations which, when this directive is adopted, satisfy the conditions of the second sub-paragraph is contained in the Annex [not reproduced here]. Whenever a Member State grants the recognition referred to in the second sub-paragraph to an association or organisation, it shall inform the Commission thereof, which shall publish this information in the Official Journal of the European Communities.

(e)   professional experience: the actual and lawful pursuit of the profession concerned in a Member State;

(f)   adaptation period: the pursuit of a regulated profession in the host Member State under the responsibility of a qualified member of that profession, such period of supervised practice possibly being accompanied by further training. This period of supervised practice shall be the subject of an assessment. The detailed rules governing the adaptation period and its assessment as well as the status of a migrant person under supervision shall be laid down by the competent authority in the host Member States;

(g)   aptitude test: a test limited to the professional knowledge of the applicant, made by the competent authorities of the host Member State with the aim of assessing the ability of the applicant to pursue a regulated profession in that Member State.

In order to permit this test to be carried out, the competent authorities shall draw up a list of subjects which, on the basis of a comparison of the education and training required in the Member State and that received by the applicant, are not covered by the diploma or other evidence of formal qualifications possessed by the applicant.

The aptitude test must take account of the fact that the applicant is a qualified professional in the Member State of origin or the Member State from which he comes. It shall cover subjects to be selected from those on the list, knowledge of which is essential in order to be able to exercise the profession in the host Member State. The test may also include knowledge of the professional rules applicable to the activities in question in the host Member State. The detailed application of the aptitude test shall be determined by the competent authorities of that state with due regard to the rules of Community law.

The status, in the host Member State, of the applicant who wishes to prepare himself for the aptitude test in that state shall be determined by the competent authorities in that state.

Article 2

This directive shall apply to any national of a Member State wishing to pursue a regulated profession in a host Member State in a self-employed capacity or as an employed person.

This directive shall not apply to professions which are the subject of a separate directive establishing arrangements for the mutual recognition of diplomas by Member States.

Article 3

Where, in a host Member State, the taking up or pursuit of a regulated profession is subject to possession of a diploma, the competent authority may not, on the grounds of inadequate qualifications, refuse to authorise a national of a Member State to take up or pursue that profession on the same conditions as apply to its own nationals:

(a)   if the applicant holds the diploma required in another Member State for the taking up or pursuit of the profession in question in its territory, such diploma having been awarded in a Member State; or

(b)   if the applicant has pursued the profession in question full-time for two years during the previous ten years in another Member State which does not regulate that profession, within the meaning of Article 1(c) and the first sub-paragraph of Article 1(d), and possesses evidence of one or more formal qualifications:

    – which have been awarded by a competent authority in a Member State, designated in accordance with the laws, regulations or administrative provisions of such state,

    – which show that the holder has successfully completed a post-secondary course of at least three years' duration, or of an equivalent duration part-time, at a university or establishment of higher education or another establishment of similar level of a Member State and, where appropriate, that he has successfully completed the professional training required in addition to the post-secondary course and

    which have prepared the holder for the pursuit of his profession.

The following shall be treated in the same way as the evidence of formal qualifications referred to in the first sub-paragraph: any formal qualifications or any set of such formal qualifications awarded by a competent authority in a Member State if it is awarded on the successful completion of training received in the Community and is recognised by that Member State as being of an equivalent level, provided that the other Member States and the Commission have been notified of this recognition.

Article 4

1. Notwithstanding Article 3, the host Member State may also require the applicant:

(a)   to provide evidence of professional experience, where the duration of the education and training adduced in support of his application, as laid down in Article 3(a) and (b) is at least one year less than that required in the host Member State. In this event, the period of professional experience required:

    – may not exceed twice the shortfall in duration of education and training where the shortfall relates to post-secondary studies and/or to a period of probationary practice carried out under the control of a supervising professional person and ending with an examination,

    – may not exceed the shortfall where the shortfall relates to professional practice acquired with the assistance of a qualified member of the profession.

    In the case of diplomas within the meaning of the last sub-paragraph of Article 1(a), the duration of education and training recognised as being of an equivalent level shall be determined as for the education and training defined in the first sub-paragraph of Article 1(a).

When applying these provisions, account must be taken of the professional experience referred to in Article 3(b).

At all events, the professional experience required may not exceed four years;

(b)   to complete an adaptation period not exceeding three years or take an aptitude test:

–   where the matters covered by the education and training he has received as laid down in Article 3(a) and (b), differ substantially from those covered by the diploma required in the host Member State, or

–   where, in the case referred to in Article 3(a), the profession regulated in the host Member State comprises one or more regulated professional activities which are not in the profession regulated in the Member State from which the applicant originates or comes and that difference corresponds to specific education and training required in the host Member State and covers matters which differ substantially from those covered by the diploma adduced by the applicant, or

–   where, in the case referred to in Article 3(b), the profession regulated in the host Member State comprises one or more regulated professional activities which are not in the profession pursued by the applicant in the Member State from which he originates or comes, and that difference corresponds to specific education and training required in the host Member State and covers matters which differ substantially from those covered by the evidence of formal qualifications adduced by the applicant. Should the host Member State make use of this possibility, it must give the applicant the right to choose between an adaptation period and an aptitude test. By way of derogation from this principle, for professions whose practice requires precise knowledge of national law and in respect of which the provision of advice and/or assistance concerning national law is an essential and constant aspect of the professional activity, the host Member State may stipulate either an adaptation period or an aptitude test. Where the host Member State intends to introduce derogations for other professions as regards an applicant's right to choose, the procedure laid down in Article 10 shall apply.

2. However, the host Member State may not apply the provisions of paragraph 1(a) and (b) cumulatively.

Article 5

Without prejudice to Articles 3 and 4, a host Member State may allow the applicant, with a view to improving his possibilities of adapting to the professional environment in that state, to undergo there, on the basis of equivalence, that part of his professional education and training represented by professional practice, acquired with the assistance of a qualified member of the profession, which he has not undergone in his Member State of origin or the Member State from which he has come.

Article 6

1. Where the competent authority of a host Member State requires of persons wishing to take up a regulated profession proof that they are of good character or repute or that they have not been declared bankrupt, or suspends or prohibits the pursuit of this profession in the event of serious professional misconduct or a criminal offence, that state shall accept as sufficient evidence, in respect of nationals of Member States wishing to pursue that profession in its territory, the production of documents issued by competent authorities in the Member State of origin or the Member State from which the foreign national comes showing that those requirements are met.

Where the competent authorities of the Member State of origin or of the Member State from which the foreign national comes do not issue the documents referred to in the first sub-paragraph, such documents shall be replaced by a declaration of oath – or, in states where there is no provision for declaration on oath, by a solemn declaration – made by the person concerned before a competent judicial or administrative authority or, where appropriate, a notary or qualified professional body of the Member State of origin or the Member State from which the person comes; such authority or notary shall issue a certificate attesting the authenticity of the declaration on oath or solemn declaration.

2. Where the competent authority of a host Member State requires of nationals of that Member State wishing to take up or pursue a regulated profession a certificate of physical or mental health, that authority shall accept as sufficient evidence in this respect the production of the document required in the Member State of origin or the Member State from which the foreign national comes.

Where the Member State of origin or the Member State from which the foreign national comes does not impose any requirements of this nature on those wishing to take up or pursue the profession in question, the host Member State shall accept from such nationals a certificate issued by a competent authority in that state corresponding to the certificates issued in the host Member State.

3. The competent authorities of host Member States may require that the documents and certificates referred to in paragraphs 1 and 2 are presented no more than three months after their date of issue.

4. Where the competent authority of a host Member State requires nationals of that Member State wishing to take up or pursue a regulated profession to take an oath or make a solemn declaration and where the form of such oath or declaration cannot be used by nationals of other Member States, that authority shall ensure that an appropriate and equivalent form of oath or declaration is offered to the person concerned.

Article 7

1. The competent authorities of host Member States shall recognise the right of nationals of Member States who fulfil the conditions for the taking up and pursuit of a regulated profession in their territory to use the professional title of the host Member State corresponding to that profession.

2. The competent authorities of host Member States shall recognise the right of nationals of Member States who fulfil the conditions for the taking up and pursuit of a regulated profession in their territory to use their lawful

academic title and, where appropriate, the abbreviation thereof deriving from their Member State of origin or the Member State from which they come, in the language of that state. Host Member State may require this title to be followed by the name and location of the establishment or examining board which awarded it.

3. Where a profession is regulated in the host Member State by an association or organisation referred to in Article 1(d), nationals of Member States shall only be entitled to use the professional title or designatory letters conferred by that organisation or association on proof of membership.

Where the association or organisation makes membership subject to certain qualification requirements, it may apply these to nationals of other Member States who are in possession of a diploma within the meaning of Article 1(a) or a formal qualification within the meaning of Article 3(b) only in accordance with this directive, in particular Articles 3 and 4.

Article 8

1. The host Member State shall accept as proof that the conditions laid down in Articles 3 and 4 are satisfied the certificates and documents issued by the competent authorities in the Member States, which the person concerned shall submit in support of his application to pursue the profession concerned.

2. The procedure for examining an application to pursue a regulated profession shall be completed as soon as possible and the outcome communicated in a reasoned decision of the competent authority in the host Member State not later than four months after presentation of all the documents relating to the person concerned. A remedy shall be available against this decision, or the absence thereof, before a court or tribunal in accordance with the provisions of national law.

Article 9

1. Member States shall designate, within the period provided for in Article 12, the competent authorities empowered to receive the applications and take the decision referred to in this Directive.

They shall communicate this information to the other Member States and to the Commission.

2. Each Member State shall designate a person responsible for co-ordinating the activities of the authorities referred to in paragraph 1 and shall inform the other Member States and the Commission to that effect. His role shall be to promote uniform application of this directive to all the professions concerned. A co-ordinating group shall be set up under the aegis of the Commission, composed of the co-ordinators appointed by each Member State or their deputies and chaired by a representative of the Commission.

The task of this group shall be:

– to facilitate the implementation of this directive,
– to collect all useful information for its application in the Member States.

The group may be consulted by the Commission on any changes to the existing system that may be contemplated.

3. Member States shall take measures to provide the necessary information on the recognition of diplomas within the framework of this directive.

They may be assisted in this task by the information centre on the academic recognition of diplomas and periods of study established by the Member States within the framework of the Resolution of the Council and the Ministers of Education meeting within the Council of 9 February 1976 and, where appropriate, the relevant professional associations or organisations. The Commission shall take the necessary initiatives to ensure the development and co-ordination of the communication of the necessary information.

Article 10

1. If, pursuant to the third sentence of the second sub-paragraph of Article 4(1)(b), a Member State proposes not to grant applicants the right to choose between an adaptation period and an aptitude test in respect of a profession within the meaning of this directive, it shall immediately communicate to the Commission the corresponding draft provision. It shall at the same time notify the Commission of the grounds which make the enactment of such a provision necessary.

The Commission shall immediately notify the other Member States of any draft it has received; it may also consult the co-ordinating group referred to in Article 9(2) of the draft.

2. Without prejudice to the possibility for the Commission and the other Member States of making comments on the draft, the Member State may adopt the provision only if the Commission has not taken a decision to the contrary within three months.

3. At the request of a Member State or the Commission, Member States shall communicate to them, without delay, the definitive text of a provision arising from the application of this article.

Article 11

Following the expiry of the period provided for in Article 12, Member States shall communicate to the Commission, every two years, a report on the application of the system introduced.

In addition to general remarks, this report shall contain a statistical summary of the decisions taken and a description of the main problems arising from application of the directive.

Article 12

Member States shall take the measures necessary to comply with this directive within two years of its notification. They shall forthwith inform the Commission thereof.

Member States shall communicate to the Commission the texts of the main provisions of national law which they adopt in the field governed by this directive.

Article 13

Five years at the latest following the date specified in Article 12, the Commission shall report to the European Parliament and the Council on the state of application of the general system for the recognition of higher education diplomas awarded on completion of professional education and training of at least three years' duration.

After conducting all necessary consultations, the Commission shall, on this occasion, present its conclusions as to any changes that need to be made to the system as it stands. At the same time the Commission shall, where appropriate, submit proposals for improvements in the present system in the interest of further facilitating the freedom of movement, right of establishment and freedom to provide services of the persons covered by this directive.

Article 14

The directive is addressed to the Member States.

Question

In what ways, if any, does this directive confer any more protection on those seeking recognition of qualifications than that available under the Court of Justice's jurisprudence as to the interpretation of Article 52 in [D31]–[D34]?

SECTION THREE

DEROGATIONS FROM THE FREE MOVEMENT PRINCIPLE

1   Public policy, public security and public health

Although Community law emphasises a wide free movement principle and both secondary legislation and case law have developed the social dimension attaching to the basic right of free movement, the free movement principle does not completely mirror, within the Community, the rights which may be accorded to citizens by a national state. A national state will be expected to accommodate all its citizens and by international law cannot deny them access to the territory of the state, even if these citizens commit criminal offences, are a financial burden on the state or present some form of health risk. However, within the Community, Member States are not obliged to accept or permit to reside on their territory every Community national and derogations from the free movement principle are permitted on the grounds of public policy, public security and public health **[D41]** (cf the analogous provisions relating to free movement of goods: **[E29]–[E35]**).

Directive 64/221 **[D42]** co-ordinates special measures concerning the movement and residence of foreign nationals which are justified on grounds of public policy, public security or public health, specifically limits the areas of competence of Member States (Articles 2–5), and lays down essential procedural safeguards for persons who may be refused a residence permit or may be expelled (Articles 6–9). These provisions are capable of producing the direct effects discussed in Section Three of Chapter Three (*van Duyn* **[D43]**) and the Court of Justice has emphasised that the conduct which might justify the refusal or expulsion of an individual must be personal to that individual (*van Duyn* **[D43]**, *Bouchereau* **[D47]**), as opposed to measures of a general preventive nature (*Commission v Germany* **[D27]**, *Bonsignore* **[D44]**). The conduct must be of a sufficiently serious nature (*Bouchereau* **[D47]**, *Adoui* **[D48]**) and there must be no discrimination between guest nationals and nationals of the host Member State (*Rutili* **[D45]**).

Derogation provisions are construed strictly (*Rutili* **[D45]**) because the free movement rights are conferred by the Treaty and failure to comply with any necessary immigration formalities is not in itself a threat to public policy or public security (*Royer* **[D46]**).

The principles relating to effective legal protection and procedural safeguards (discussed in Section Three of Chapter Three) are applied to the free movement derogations. The principle of strict interpretation of derogations applies not merely to legislative acts of Member States but also to decisions taken by the authorities (including the courts: *Bouchereau* **[D47]**) against individuals (*Rutili* **[D45]**). In addition, individuals must be allowed to utilise and exhaust the procedural remedies granted by the directive (*Royer* **[D46]**, *Adoui* **[D48]**, *Santillo* **[D49]**, *Dzodzi* **[D50]**).

2   Public service and official authority

The second derogation from the free movement principle is founded on the desire by Member States to restrict access to certain occupations to their own nationals. Consequently, the Treaty creates exceptions with regard to 'the public service' and to 'official authority' [D51].

There is, of course, a danger that an over-reliance on the public service and official authority derogations, especially in times of economic depression, might result in Member States attempting to protect their economies and the jobs of their own nationals and this would severely limit the employment opportunities of nationals of other Member States and jeopardise the embryo concept of the European citizen. The danger is that Member States might impose measures equivalent to (or of equivalent effect to) nationality quotas and, in the same way and for the same purpose that the Court of Justice has taken a strict view of measures having a similar effect to quantitative measures with regard to free movement of goods (see [E11]–[E37]), the public service and official authority derogations have been construed strictly as Community concepts which limit the unilateral application of those derogations by the Member States (*Sotgiu* [D52], *Reyners* [D56], *Allué* [D55]). The Commission has on several occasions brought Article 169 proceedings (discussed in Section One of Chapter Three) wherein the Court of Justice has limited the derogations to situations where there is a special relationship between the specific occupation and the state (*Commission v Belgium* [D53], *Commission v Belgium* [D54], *Commission v Hellenic Republic* [D57]).

MATERIALS

[D41]   The public policy derogation, Treaty provisions

Article 48

3. [Freedom of movement for workers] shall entail the right, subject to limitations justified on grounds of public policy, public security or public health.

. . .

Article 56

1. The provisions of this Chapter [on Establishment] and measures taken in pursuance thereof shall not prejudice the applicability of provisions laid down by law, regulation or administrative action providing for special treatment for foreign nationals on grounds of public policy, public security or public health.

. . .

Article 66

The provisions of [Article 56] shall apply to the matters covered by this Chapter [on Services] [cf **[E45]**].

[D42]   Directive 64/221 on the co-ordination of special measures concerning the movement and residence of foreign nationals which are justified on grounds of public policy, public security or public health

[Whereas] co-ordination of provisions laid down by law, regulation or administrative action which provide for special treatment for foreign nationals on grounds of public policy, public security or public health should in the first place deal with the conditions for entry and residence of nationals of Member States moving within the Community either in order to pursue activities as employed or self-employed persons, or as recipients of services;

Whereas such co-ordination presupposes in particular an approximation of the procedures followed in each Member State when invoking grounds of public policy, public security or public health in matters connected with the movement or residence of foreign nationals;

Whereas, in each Member State, nationals of other Member States should have adequate legal remedies available to them in respect of the decisions of the administration in such matters;

Whereas it would be of little practical use to compile a list of diseases and disabilities which might endanger public health, public policy or public security and it would be difficult to make such a list exhaustive; whereas it is sufficient to classify such diseases and disabilities in groups;

. . .

Article 1

1. The provisions of this directive shall apply to any national of a Member State who resides in or travels to another Member State of the Community, either in order to pursue an activity as an employed or self-employed person, or as a recipient of services.

2. These provisions shall apply also to the spouse and to members of the family who come within the provisions of the regulations and directives adopted in this field in pursuance of the Treaty.

Article 2

1. This directive relates to all measures concerning entry into their territory, issue or renewal of residence permits, or expulsion from their territory, taken by Member States on grounds of public policy, public security or public health.

2. Such grounds shall not be invoked to service economic ends.

Article 3

1. Measures taken on grounds of public policy or of public security shall be based exclusively on the personal conduct of the individual concerned.

2. Previous criminal convictions shall not in themselves constitute grounds for the taking of such measures.

3. Expiry of the identity card or passport used by the person concerned to enter the host country and to obtain a residence permit shall not justify expulsion from the territory.

4. The state which issued the identity card or passport shall allow the holder of such document to re-enter its territory without any formality even if the document is no longer valid or the nationality of the holder is in dispute.

Article 4

1. The only diseases or disabilities justifying refusal of entry into a territory or refual to issue a first residence permit shall be those listed in the Annex to this directive.

2. Diseases or disabilities occurring after a first residence permit has been issued shall not justify refusal to renew the residence permit or expulsion from the territory.

3. Member States shall not introduce new provisions or practices which are more restrictive than those in force at the date of notification of this directive.

Article 5

1. A decision to grant or to refuse a first residence permit shall be taken as soon as possible and in any event not later than six months from the date of application for the permit.

The person concerned shall be allowed to remain temporarily in the territory pending a decision either to grant or to refuse a residence permit.

2. The host country may, in cases where this is considered essential, request the Member State of origin of the applicant, and if need be other Member States, to provide information concerning any previous police

record. Such enquiries shall not be made as a matter of routine. The Member State consulted shall give its reply within two months.

Article 6

The person concerned shall be informed of the grounds of public policy, public security, or public health upon which the decision taken in his case is based, unless this is contrary to the interests of the security of the state involved.

Article 7

The person concerned shall be officially notified of any decision to refuse the issue or renewal of a residence permit or to expel him from the territory. The period allowed for leaving the territory shall be stated in this notification. Save in cases of urgency, this period shall be not less than 15 days if the person concerned has not yet been granted a residence permit and not less than one month in all other cases.

Article 8

The person concerned shall have the same legal remedies in respect of any decision concerning entry, or refusing the issue or renewal of a residence permit, or ordering expulsion from the territory, as are available to nationals of the state concerned in respect of acts of the administration.

Article 9

1. Where there is no right of appeal to a court of law, or where such appeal may be only in respect of the legal validity of the decision, or where the appeal cannot have suspensory effect, a decision refusing renewal of a residence permit or ordering the expulsion of the holder of a residence permit from the territory shall not be taken by the administrative authority, save in cases of urgency, until an opinion has been obtained from a competent authority of the host country before which the person concerned enjoys such rights of defence and of assistance or representation as the domestic law of that country provides for.

This authority shall not be the same as that empowered to take the decision refusing renewal of the residence permit or ordering expulsion.

2. Any decision refusing the issue of a first residence permit or ordering expulsion of the person concerned before the issue of the permit shall, where that person so requests, be referred for consideration to the authority whose prior opinion is required under paragraph 1. The person concerned shall then be entitled to submit his defence in person, except where this would be contrary to the interests of national security.

Article 10

1. Member States shall within six months of notification of this directive put into force the measures necessary to comply with its provisions and shall forthwith inform the Commission thereof.

2. Member States shall ensure that the texts of the main provisions of national law which they adopt in the field governed by this directive are communicated to the Commission.

Annex

A.   *Diseases which might endanger public health*

1. Diseases subject to quarantine listed in International Health Regulation No 2 of the World Health Organisation of 25 May 1951;
2. Tuberculosis of the respiratory system in an active state or showing a tendency to develop;
3. Syphilis;
4. Other infectious diseases or contagious parasitic diseases if they are the subject of provisions for the protection of nationals of the host country.

B.   *Diseases and disabilities which might threaten public policy or public security*

1. Drug addiction;
2. Profound mental disturbance; manifest conditions of psychotic disturbance with agitation, delirium, hallucinations or confusion.

[D43]   Case 41/74 Yvonne van Duyn v Home Office (No 2) [1974] ECR 1337

[The Church of Scientology was considered by the United Kingdom government to be socially harmful. There was no legal power to prohibit the practice of Scientology, the government allowed the Church to function through a college in East Grinstead and did not place restrictions on United Kingdom nationals wishing to become members of, or to take up employment with, the Church. However, with regard to foreign nationals, the government considered that the Church was so objectionable that steps would be taken to curb the Church's activities by refusing work permits for foreign nationals for work at a Scientology establishment. Miss van Duyn, a Dutch national, was offered employment at the East Grinstead college but was refused entry to the United Kingdom on the ground that 'the Secretary of State considers it undesirable to give anyone leave to enter the United Kingdom on the business of or in the employment of' the Church. Miss van Duyn brought an action in the High Court for a declaration that she was entitled to enter and remain in the United Kingdom under Article 48 **[D1]** and that the public policy exceptions contained in Directive 64/221, Article 3 **[D42]** did not apply as the refusal to grant entry was not based exclusively or at all on her personal conduct but on the general policy of refusal stated above. Since it was essential to seek, as a matter of interpretation, whether Miss van Duyn could rely upon these provisions, Pennycuick VC stayed the action and referred three questions for a preliminary ruling.]

The European Court of Justice (at pp 1346–1351)

First question

4. By the first question, the court is asked to say whether Article 48 [is] directly applicable so as to confer on individuals rights enforceable by them in the courts of a Member State.
5. It is provided, in Article 48 (1) and (2), that freedom of movement for

workers shall be secured by the end of the transitional period and that such freedom shall entail 'the abolition of any discrimination based on nationality between workers of Member States as regards employment, remuneration and other conditions of work and employment'.

6. These provisions impose on Member States a precise obligation which does not require the adoption of any further measure on the part either of the Community institutions or of the Member States and which leaves them, in relation to its implementation, no discretionary power.

7. [Article 48(3)], which defines the rights implied by the principle of freedom of movement for workers, subjects them to limitations justified on grounds of public policy, public security or public health. The application of these limitations is, however, subject to judicial control, so that a Member State's right to invoke the limitations does not prevent the provisions of Article 48, which enshrine the principle of freedom of movement for workers, from conferring on individuals rights which are enforceable by them and which the national courts must protect.

8. The reply to the first question must therefore be in the affirmative.

Second question

9. The second question asks the court to say whether [Directive 64/221] is directly applicable so as to confer on individuals rights enforceable by them in the courts of a Member State.

10. [The] only provision of the directive which is relevant is that contained in Article 3(1) which provides that 'measures taken on grounds of public policy or public security shall be based exclusively on the personal conduct of the individual concerned'.

11. The United Kingdom observes that, since Article 189 [distinguishes] between the effects ascribed to regulations, directives and decisions, it must therefore be presumed that the Council, in issuing a directive rather than making a regulation, must have intended that the directive should have an effect other than that of a regulation and accordingly that the former should not be directly applicable.

12. If, however, by virtue of the provisions of Article 189 regulations are directly applicable and, consequently, may by their very nature have direct effects, it does not follow from this that other categories of acts mentioned in that Article can never have similar effects. It would be incompatible with the binding effect attributed to a directive by Article 189 to exclude, in principle, the possibility that the obligation which it imposes may be invoked by those concerned. In particular, where the Community authorities have, by directive, imposed on Member States the obligation to pursue a particular course of conduct, the useful effect of such an act would be weakened if individuals were prevented from relying on it before their national courts and the latter were prevented from taking it into consideration as an element of Community law. Article 177, which empowers national courts to refer to the court questions concerning the validity and interpretation of all acts of the Community institutions, without distinction, implies furthermore that these acts may be invoked by individuals in the national courts. It is necessary to examine, in every case, whether the nature, general scheme and wording of the provision in question are capable of having direct effects on the relations between Member States and individuals.

13. By providing that measures taken on grounds of public policy shall

be based exclusively on the personal conduct of the individual concerned, Article 3(1) of [Directive] 64/221 is intended to limit the discretionary power which national laws [confer] on the authorities responsible for the entry and expulsion of foreign nationals. First, the provision lays down an obligation which is not subject to any exception or condition and which, by its very nature, does not require the intervention of any act on the part either of the institutions of the Community or of Member States. Secondly, because Member States are thereby obliged, in implementing a clause which derogates from one of the fundamental principles of the Treaty in favour of individuals, not to take account of factors extraneous to personal conduct, legal certainty for the persons concerned requires that they should be able to rely on this obligation even though it has been laid down in a legislative act which has no automatic direct effect in its entirety.

14. If the meaning and exact scope of the provision raise questions of interpretation, these questions can be resolved by the courts, taking into account also the procedure under Article 177 of the Treaty.

15. Accordingly, in reply to the second question, Article 3(1) of [Directive 64/221] confers on individuals rights which are enforceable by them in the courts of a Member State and which the national courts must protect.

Third question

16. By the third question the court is asked to rule whether Article 48 [and] Article 3 of Directive No 64/221 must be interpreted as meaning that

a Member State, in the performance of its duty to base a measure taken on grounds of public policy exclusively on the personal conduct of the individual concerned is entitled to take into account as matters of personal conduct:
(a)   the fact that the individual is or has been associated with some body or organisation the activities of which the Member State considers contrary to the public good but which are not unlawful in that State;
(b)   the fact that the individual intends to take employment in the Member State with such a body or organisation it being the case that no restrictions are placed upon nationals of the Member State who wish to take similar employment with such a body or organisation.

17. It is necessary, first, to consider whether association with a body or an organisation can in itself constitute personal conduct within the meaning of Article 3 of Directive 64/221. Although a person's past association cannot in general justify a decision refusing him the right to move freely within the Community, it is nevertheless the case that present association, which reflects participation in the activities of the body or of the organisation as well as identification with its aims and its designs, may be considered a voluntary act of the person concerned and, consequently, as part of his personal conduct within the meaning of [Article 3].

18. The third question further raises the problem of what importance must be attributed to the fact that the activities of the organisation in question, which are considered by the Member State as contrary to the public good are not however prohibited by national law. It should be emphasised that the concept of public policy in the context of the Community and where, in particular, it is used as a justification for derogating from the

fundamental principle of freedom of movement for workers, must be interpreted strictly, so that its scope cannot be determined unilaterally by each Member State without being subject to control by the institutions of the Community. Nevertheless, the particular circumstances justifying recourse to the concept of public policy may vary from one country to another and from one period to another, and it is therefore necessary in this matter to allow the competent national authorities an area of discretion within the limits imposed by the Treaty.

19. It follows from the above that where the competent authorities of a Member State have clearly defined their standpoint as regards the activities of a particular organisation and where, considering it to be socially harmful, they have taken administrative measures to counteract these activities, the Member State cannot be required, before it can rely on the concept of public policy, to make such activities unlawful, if recourse to such a measure is not thought appropriate in the circumstances.

20. The question raises finally the problem of whether a Member State is entitled, on grounds of public policy, to prevent a national of another Member State from taking gainful employment within its territory with a body or organisation, it being the case that no similar restriction is placed upon its own nationals.

21. In this connection, the Treaty, while enshrining the principle of freedom of movement for workers without any discrimination on grounds of nationality, admits, in Article 48(3), limitations justified on grounds of public policy, public security or public health to the rights deriving from this principle. Under the terms of the provision cited above, the right to accept offers of employment actually made, the right to move freely within the territory of Member States for this purpose, and the right to stay in a Member State for the purpose of employment are, among others, all subject to such limitations. Consequently, the effect of such limitations, when they apply, is that leave to enter the territory of a Member State and the right to reside there may be refused to a national of another Member State.

22. Furthermore, it is a principle of international law, which the EEC Treaty cannot be assumed to disregard in the relations between Member States, that a state is precluded from refusing its own nationals the right of entry or residence.

23. It follows that a Member State, for reasons of public policy, can, where it deems necessary, refuse a national of another Member State the benefit of the principle of freedom of movement for workers in a case where such a national proposes to take up a particular offer of employment even though the Member State does not place a similar restriction upon its own nationals.

24. Accordingly, the reply to the third question must be that Article 48 [and] Article 3(1) of Directive No 64/221 are to be interpreted as meaning that a Member State, in imposing restrictions justified on grounds of public policy, is entitled to take into account, as a matter of personal conduct of the individual concerned, the fact that the individual is associated with some body or organisation the activities of which the Member State considers socially harmful but which are not unlawful in that state, despite the fact that no restriction is placed upon nationals of the said Member State who wish to take similar employment with these same bodies or organisations.

520   *The European Citizen*

[D44]   Case 67/74 Carmelo Angelo Bonsignore v Oberstadtdirektor der Stadt Köln [1975] ECR 297

[Bonsignore, an Italian national residing in Germany, was unlawfully in possession of a firearm and accidentally caused the death of his brother by his careless handling of that firearm. He was sentenced to a fine for an offence against the German firearms legislation. He was also found guilty of causing death by negligence but the court imposed no punishment on this count, evidently considering that no purpose would be served by such a punishment, in view of the circumstances, especially the mental suffering caused to Bonsignore as a result of the consequences of his carelessness. Following the convictions, the Ausländerbehörde (the German Aliens Authority) ordered Bonsignore to be deported. Bonsignore appealed to the Verwaltungsgericht, Köln (the local Administrative Court) against the deportation order. The Verwaltungsgericht considered that, because of the particular circumstances of the case, the deportation order could not be justified on grounds of a 'special preventive nature' based either on the facts which had given rise to the criminal conviction or on the present and foreseeable conduct of Bonsignore. The Verwaltungsgericht considered that the only possible justification for the deportation would be the reasons of a 'general preventive nature', which were emphasised by the Ausländerbehörde, and were based on the deterrent effect which the deportation of an alien found in possession of a firearm would have in immigrant circles, having regard to the resurgence of violence in the large urban centres. The Verwaltungsgericht referred to the Court of Justice the following two questions:

1. Is Article 3(1) and 3(2) of Directive No 64/221 **[D42]** to be interpreted as excluding the deportation of a national of a Member State [by] the state authority of another Member State for the purpose of deterring other foreign nationals from committing such criminal offences as those with which the person deported was charged or similar offences or other infringements of public security or public policy, that is, for reasons of a general preventive nature?

2. Does the said provision mean that the deportation of a national of a Member State [is] possible only when there are clear indications that the EEC national, who has been convicted of an offence, will commit further offences or will in some other way disregard public security or public policy of a Member [State], that is, for reasons of a special preventive nature?

The European Court of Justice (at pp 306–307)

5. [Article 3(1) and (2) of Directive 64/221 must] be interpreted in the light of the objectives of the directive which seeks in particular to co-ordinate the measures justified on grounds of public policy and for the maintenance of public security envisaged in Articles 48 and 56 of the Treaty, in order to reconcile the application of these measures with the basic principle of the free movement of persons within the Community and the elimination of all discrimination, in the application of the Treaty, between the nationals of the state in question and those of the other Member States.

6. With this in view, Article 3 of the directive provides that measures adopted on grounds of public policy and for the maintenance of public security against the nationals of Member States of the Community cannot be justified on grounds extraneous to the individual case, as is shown in particular by the requirement set out in [Article 3(1)] that 'only' the 'personal conduct' of those affected by the measures is to be regarded as determinative.

As departures from the rules concerning the free movement of persons constitute exceptions which must be strictly construed, the concept of 'personal conduct' expresses the requirement that a deportation order may only be made for breaches of the peace and public security which might be committed by the individual affected.

7. The reply to the questions referred should therefore be that Article 3(1) and (2) of Directive 64/221 prevents the deportation of a national of a Member State if such deportation is ordered for the purpose of deterring other aliens, that is, if it is based, in the words of the national court, on reasons of a 'general preventive nature'.

[D45]   Case 36/75 Roland Rutili v Minister for the Interior [1975] ECR 1219

[Rutili, an Italian national, was the subject of a decision of the French Minister for the Interior whereby Rutili's residence permit was subject to a prohibition on residence in specified regions of France. The court before which he brought an action to annul the decision limiting the territorial validity of his residence permit submitted two questions to the Court of Justice. Compare this case with *Cohn-Bendit* **[C55]**.]

The European Court of Justice (at pp 1228–1235)

First question

8. The first question asks whether the expression 'subject to limitations justified on grounds of public policy' in Article [48(4) **[D41]** concerns] only the legislative decisions which each Member State has decided to take in order to limit within its territory the freedom of movement and residence for nationals of other Member States or whether it also concerns individual decisions taken in application of such legislative provisions.

. . .

16. The effect of [Article 48, Regulation 1612/68 **[D14]** and Directive 64/221 **[D42]**], without exception, is to impose duties on Member States and it is, accordingly, for the courts to give the rules of Community law which may be pleaded before them precedence over the provisions of national law if legislative measures adopted by a Member State in order to limit within its territory freedom of movement or residence for nationals of other Member States prove to be incompatible with any of those duties.

17. Inasmuch as the object of the provisions of the Treaty and of secondary legislation is to regulate the situation of individuals and to ensure their protection, it is also for the national courts to examine whether individual decisions are compatible with the relevant provisions of Community law.

. . .

20. It is all the more necessary to adopt this view of the matter inasmuch as national legislation concerned with the protection of public policy and security usually reserves to the national authorities discretionary powers which might well escape all judicial review if the courts were unable to extend their consideration to individual decisions taken pursuant to the reservation contained in Article [48(3)].

21. The reply to the question referred to the court must therefore be that the expression 'subject to limitations justified on grounds of public policy' in Article 48 concerns not only the legislative provisions which each Member State has adopted to limit within its territory freedom of movement and residence for nationals of other Member States but concerns also individual decisions taken in application of such legislative provisions.

Second question

22. The second question asks what is the precise meaning to be attributed to the word 'justified' in the phrase 'subject to limitations justified on grounds of public policy' in Article [48(3)].

. . .

26. By virtue of the reservation contained in Article 48(3), Member States continue to be, in principle, free to determine the requirements of public policy in the light of their national needs.

27. Nevertheless, the concept of public policy must, in the Community context and where, in particular, it is used as a justification for derogating from the fundamental principles of equality of treatment and freedom of movement for workers, be interpreted strictly, so that its scope cannot be determined unilaterally by each Member State without being subject to control by the institutions of the Community.

. . .

32. Taken as a whole, [Directive 64/221, Articles 2 and 3, and Regulation 1612/68, Article 8] are a specific manifestation of the more general principle, enshrined in [the European Convention on Human Rights which provides that] no restrictions in the interests of national security or public safety shall be placed on the rights secured by [the Convention] other than such as are necessary for the protection of those interests 'in a democratic society'.

. . .

40. The questions put by the [national court] were raised in connection with a measure prohibiting residence in a limited part of the national territory.

41. [The French government] stated that such measures may be taken in the case of its own nationals either, in the case of certain criminal convictions, as an additional penalty, or following the declaration of a state of emergency.

42. The provisions enabling certain areas of the national territory to be prohibited to foreign nationals are, however, based on legislative instruments specifically concerning them.

. . .

46. Right of entry into the territory of Member States and the right to stay there and to move freely within it is defined in the Treaty by reference to the whole territory of these states and not by reference to its internal subdivisions.

47. The reservation contained in Article 48(3) concerning the protection of public policy has the same scope as the rights the exercise of which may, under that paragraph, be subject to limitations.

48. It follows that prohibitions on residence under the reservation inserted to this effect in Article 48(3) may be imposed only in respect of the whole of the national territory.

49. On the other hand, in the case of partial prohibitions on residence, limited to certain areas of the territory, persons covered by Community law must, under Article 7 of the Treaty and within the field of application of that provision, be treated on a footing of equality with the nationals of the Member State concerned.

50. It follows that a Member State cannot, in the case of a national of another Member State covered by the provisions of the Treaty, impose prohibitions on residence which are territorially limited except in circumstances where such prohibitions may be imposed on its own nationals.

51. The answer to the second question must, therefore, be that an appraisal as to whether measures designed to safeguard public policy are justified must have regard to all rules of Community law the object of which is, on the one hand, to limit the discretionary power of Member States in this respect and, on the other, to ensure that the rights of persons subject thereunder to restrictive measures are protected.

52. These limitations and safeguards arise, in particular, from the duty imposed on Member States to base the measures adopted exclusively on the personal conduct of the individuals concerned, to refrain from adopting any measures in this respect which service ends unrelated to the requirements of public policy or which adversely affect the exercise of trade union rights and, finally, unless this is contrary to the interests of the security of the state involved, immediately to inform any person against whom a restrictive measure has been adopted of the grounds on which the decision taken is based to enable him to make effective use of legal remedies.

53. In particular, measures restricting the right of residence which are limited to part only of the national territory may not be imposed by a Member State on nationals of other Member States who are subject to the provisions of the Treaty except in the cases and circumstances in which such measures may be applied to nationals of the state concerned.

[D46]   Case 48/75 Jean Noël Royer [1976] ECR 497

[Criminal proceedings were brought against Royer, a French national, for illegal entry into and illegal residence in Belgium. In France, Royer had been convicted and sentenced to imprisonment for procuring and had also been prosecuted for various armed robberies without, however, having been convicted of them. Royer's wife, also a French national, ran a café and dance hall in Belgium. Royer had joined her but failed to comply with the administrative formalities of entry on the Belgian population register.

The Belgian authorities ordered him to leave the country and initiated proceedings against him for illegal residence which resulted in conviction by a court. After a brief stay in Germany, Royer returned to Belgium and rejoined his wife, once again failing to comply with the legal formalities for the control of aliens. He was again apprehended by the police and committed to prison but the committal was not confirmed by the judicial authorities. Before his release, however, Royer was served with a ministerial decree of expulsion on the ground that 'Royer's personal conduct shows his presence to be a danger to public policy' and that 'he has not observed the conditions attached to the residence of aliens and he has no permit to establish himself in the Kingdom'. Following this expulsion order, Royer appeared to have left Belgium, but the prosecutions for illegal entry and illegal residence followed their course before a Belgian criminal court.]

The European Court of Justice (at pp 508–517)

The relevant Community provisions

10. At the present stage of the proceedings the national court has not yet finally determined the position of the accused with regard to the provisions of Community law applicable to him.

11. The facts submitted by the national court and the choice of the provisions of Community law of which it seeks interpretation allow of different hypotheses according to whether the accused falls within the provisions of Community law by virtue of an occupation which he carried out himself or by virtue of a post which he had himself found or again as the husband of a person subject to the provisions of Community law because of her occupation so that the accused's position may be regulated by either [the workers' provisions or those of establishment and services].

12. Nevertheless comparison of these different provisions shows that they are based on the same principles both in so far as they concern the entry into and residence in the territory of Member States of persons covered by Community law and the prohibition of all discrimination between them on grounds of nationality.

13. In particular Article 10 of Regulation [1612/68 **[D14]**], Article 1 of Directive [68/360 **[D9]**] and Article 1 of Directive [73/148 **[D36]**] extend in indentical terms the application of Community law relating to entry into and residence in the territory of the Member States to the spouse of any person covered by these provisions.

14. Further, Article 1 of Directive [64/221 **[D42]**] states that the directive shall apply to any national of a Member State who resides in or travels to another Member State of the Community either in order to pursue an activity as an employed or self-employed person, or as a recipient of services, and his or her spouse and members of their family.

15. It is apparent from the foregoing that substantially identical provisions of Community law apply in a case such as the one at issue if there exists either with regard to the party concerned or his spouse a connection with Community law under any of the above-mentioned provisions.

[Source] of rights conferred by the Treaty in respect of entry into and residence in the territory of the Member States

23. [Articles 48, 52 and 59], which may be construed as prohibiting

Member States from setting up restrictions or obstacles to the entry into and residence in their territory of nationals of other Member States, have the effect of conferring rights directly on all persons falling within the ambit of the above-mentioned [articles].

. . .

29. It is therefore evident that the exception concerning the safeguard of public policy, public security and public health contained in Articles 48(3) and 56(1) [must] be regarded not as a condition precedent to the acquisition of the right of entry and residence but as providing the possibility, in individual cases where there is sufficient justification, of imposing restrictions on the exercise of a right derived directly from the Treaty.

. . .

31. [It] follows from the foregoing that the right of nationals of a Member State to enter the territory of another Member State and reside there for the purposes intended by the Treaty – in particular to look for or pursue an occupation or activities as employed or self-employed persons, or to rejoin their spouse or family – is a right conferred directly by the Treaty, or, as the case may be, by the provisions adopted for its implementation.

32. It must therefore be concluded that this right is acquired independently of the issue of a residence permit by the competent authority of a Member State.

33. The grant of this permit is therefore to be regarded not as a measure giving rise to rights but as a measure by a Member State serving to prove the individual position of a national of another Member State with regard to provisions of Community Law.

. . .

38. [The] logical consequence of the foregoing is that the mere failure by a national of a Member State to complete the legal formalities concerning access, movement and residence of aliens does not justify a decision ordering expulsion.

39. Since it is a question of the exercise of a right acquired under the Treaty itself, such conduct cannot be regarded as constituting in itself a breach of public policy or public security.

40. Consequently any decision ordering expulsion made by the authorities of a Member State against a national of another Member State covered by the Treaty would, if it were based solely on that person's failure to comply with the legal formalities concerning the control of aliens or on the lack of a residence permit, be contrary to the provisions of the Treaty.

41. It must nevertheless be stated in this respect that on the one hand the Member States may still expel from their territory a national of another Member State where the requirements of public policy and public security are involved for reasons other than the failure to comply with formalities concerning the control of aliens without prejudice to the limits placed on their discretion by Community law as stated by the court [in *Rutili* **[D45]**].

42. On the other hand Community law does not prevent the Member States from providing, for breaches of national provisions concerning the control of aliens, any appropriate sanctions – other than measures of expulsion from the territory – necessary in order to ensure the efficacy of those provisions.

43. As to the question whether a Member State may take measures for the temporary deprivation of liberty of an alien covered by the terms of the Treaty with a view to expelling him from the territory it must first be stated that no measure of this nature is permissible if a decision ordering expulsion from the territory would be contrary to the Treaty.

44. Moreover the validity of a measure of provisional deprivation of liberty taken in the case of an alien who was unable to prove that he was covered by the Treaty or who could be expelled from the territory for reasons other than failure to comply with the formalities concerning the control of aliens depends on the provisions of national law and the international obligations assumed by the Member States concerned since Community law as such does not yet impose any specific obligations on Member States in this respect.

[The Court of Justice referred to Article 3(1) of Directive 64/221 **[D42]**.]

47. Nevertheless it is evident from the foregoing that the failure to comply with the legal formalities concerning the entry, movement and residence of aliens does not in itself constitute a threat to public policy and public security within the meaning of the Treaty.

48. In itself such conduct cannot therefore give rise to the application of the measures referred to in Article 3 of the above-mentioned directive.

. . .

51. The mere failure by a national of a Member State to comply with the formalities concerning entry, movement and residence of aliens is not of such a nature as to constitute in itself conduct threatening public policy and public security and cannot therefore by itself justify a measure ordering expulsion or temporary imprisonment for that purpose.

[Implementation] of measures of expulsion and legal remedies

52. In substance the [national court] asks whether a decision ordering expulsion or a refusal to issue a residence or establishment permit may, in view of the requirements of Community law, give rise to immediate measures of execution or whether such a decision only takes effect after remedies before the national courts have been exhausted.

[The Court of Justice referred to Articles 8 and 9 of Directive 64/221 **[D42]**.]

55. It is appropriate to state in this respect that all steps must be taken by the Member States to ensure that the safeguard of the right of appeal is in fact available to anyone against whom a restrictive measure of this kind has been adopted.

56. However this guarantee would become illusory if the Member States could, by the immediate execution of a decision ordering expulsion, deprive the person concerned of the opportunity of effectively making use of the remedies which he is guaranteed by Directive 64/221.

57. In the case of the legal remedies referred to in Article 8 of Directive 64/211, the party concerned must at least have the opportunity of lodging an appeal and thus obtaining a stay of execution before the expulsion order is carried out.

58. This conclusion also follows from the link established by the directive between Articles 8 and 9 thereof in view of the fact that the procedure set out in the latter provision is obligatory inter alia where the legal remedies referred to in Article 8 'cannot have suspensory effect'.

59. Under Article 9 the procedure of appeal to a competent authority must precede the decision ordering expulsion in cases of urgency.

60. Consequently where a legal remedy referred to in Article 8 is available the decision ordering expulsion may not be executed before the party concerned is able to avail himself of the remedy.

61. Where no such remedy is available, or where it is available but cannot have suspensory effect, the decision cannot be taken – save in cases of urgency which have been properly justified – until the party concerned has had the opportunity of appealing to the authority designated in Article 9 of Directive 64/221 and until this authority has reached a decision.

62. The question must therefore be answered to the effect that a decision ordering expulsion cannot be executed, save in cases of urgency which have been properly justified, against a person protected by Community law until the party concerned has been able to exhaust the remedies guaranteed by Articles 8 and 9 of Directive 64/221.

[D47] Case 30/77 R v Pierre Bouchereau [1977] ECR 1999

[Bouchereau, a French national employed in the United Kingdom since May 1975, was found guilty in June 1976 of an offence punishable under the Misuse of Drugs Act 1971, namely, unlawful possession of drugs. Some six months earlier, Bouchereau had pleaded guilty to an identical offence before another court and had been conditionally discharged for 12 months. The magistrates' court which convicted Bouchereau was minded to make a recommendation for his deportation to the Secretary of State and referred certain questions to the Court of Justice on the interpretation of Article 3 of Directive 64/221 **[D42]**.]

The European Court of Justice (at pp 2009–2014)

The first question

6. The first question asks 'whether a recommendation for deportation made by a national court of a Member State to the executive authority of that State (such recommendation being persuasive but not binding on the executive authority) constitutes a "measure" within the meaning of Article 3(1) and (2) of [Directive] 64/221'.

7. That question seeks to discover whether a court which, under national legislation, has jurisdiction to recommend to the executive authority the deportation of a national of another Member State, such recommendation not being binding on that authority, must, when it does so, take into account the limitations resulting from the Treaty and from [Directive] 64/221 on the exercise of the powers which, in that area, are reserved to the Member States.

8. According to the observations submitted by the government of the United [Kingdom], the question referred to the court raises two separate problems: whether a judicial decision can constitute a 'measure' for the purposes of the directive and, if the answer is in the affirmative, whether a mere 'recommendation' by a national court can constitute a measure for the purposes of that same directive.

(a)   As regards the first point

9. Article 2 of [Directive] 64/221 states that the directive relates to all 'measures' (dispositions, Vorschriften, provvedimenti, bestemmelser, voorschriften) concerning entry into the territory, issue or renewal of residence permits or expulsion from their territory taken by Member States on grounds of public policy, public security or public health.

10. Under [Article 3(1) and (2)] of that directive, 'measures' (mesures, Maßnahmen, provvedimenti, forholdsregler, maatregelen) taken on grounds of public policy or public security shall be based exclusively on the personal conduct of the individual concerned and previous criminal convictions shall not in themselves constitute grounds for the taking of such measures.

11. Although the government of the United Kingdom declares that it accepts unreservedly that [Article 3(1) and (2)] are directly applicable and confer rights on nationals of Member States to which the national courts must have regard, with the result that it is not open to a court of a Member State to ignore those provisions on any matter coming before the court to which they are relevant, it submits that a judicial decision of a national court cannot constitute a 'measure' within the meaning of [Article 3].

12. On that point the government observes that the fact that the term 'measures' is used in the English text in both Articles 2 and 3 shows that it is intended to have the same meaning in each case and that it emerges from the first recital in the preamble to the directive that when used in Article 2 the expression only refers to provisions laid down by law, regulation or administrative action, to the exclusion of actions of the judiciary.

13. A comparison of the different language versions of the provisions in question shows that with the exception of the Italian text all the other versions use different terms in each of the two articles, with the result that no legal consequences can be based on the terminology used.

14. The different language versions of a Community text must be given a uniform interpretation and hence in the case of divergence between the versions the provision in question must be interpreted by reference to the purpose and general scheme of the rules of which it forms a part.

15. By co-ordinating national rules on the control of aliens, to the extent to which they concern the nationals of other Member States, [Directive] 64/221 seeks to protect such nationals from any exercise of the powers resulting from the exception relating to limitations justified on grounds of public policy, public security or public health, which might go beyond the requirements justifying an exception to the basic principle of free movement of persons.

16. It is essential that at the different stages of the process which may result in the adoption of a decision to make a deportation order that protection may be provided by the courts where they are involved in the adoption of such a decision.

17. It follows that the concept of 'measure' includes the action of a court which is required by the law to recommend in certain cases the deportation of a national of another Member State.

18. When making such a recommendation, therefore, such a court must ensure that the directive is correctly applied and must take account of the limits which it imposes on the action of the authorities in the Member States.

19. That finding is, moreover, in line with the point of view of the

government of the United Kingdom which 'is not suggesting that it would be open to a court of a Member State to ignore the provisions of Article 3(1) and (2) on any matter coming before the court to which the articles are relevant' but on the contrary accepts 'that the provisions of those articles are directly applicable and confer rights on nationals of Member States to which the national courts must have regard'.

(b)   As regards the second point

20. As regards the second aspect of the first question, the government of the United Kingdom submits that a mere recommendation cannot constitute a 'measure' within the meaning of Article 3(1) and (2) of [Directive] 64/221, and that only the subsequent decision of the Secretary of State can amount to such a measure.

21. For the purposes of the directive, a 'measure' is any action which affects the right of persons coming within the field of application of Article 48 to enter and reside freely in the Member States under the same conditions as the nationals of the host state.

22. Within the context of the procedure laid down by [the United Kingdom] Immigration Act 1971, the recommendation referred to in the question raised by the national court constitutes a necessary step in the process of arriving at any decision to make a deportation order and is a necessary prerequisite for such a decision.

23. Moreover, within the context of that procedure, its effect is to make it possible to deprive the person concerned of his liberty and it is, in any event, one factor justifying a subsequent decision by the executive authority to make a deportation order.

24. Such a recommendation therefore affects the right of free movement and constitutes a measure within the meaning of Article [3].

The second question

25. The second question asks 'whether the wording of Article 3(2) of [Directive] 64/221, namely that previous criminal convictions shall not "in themselves" constitute grounds for the taking of measures based on public policy or public security means that previous criminal convictions are solely relevant in so far as they manifest a present or future propensity to act in a manner contrary to public policy or public security; alternatively, the meaning to be attached to the expression "in themselves" in Article 3(2) of Directive No 64/221'.

26. [That] question seeks to discover whether, as [Bouchereau] maintained before the national court, 'previous criminal convictions are solely relevant in so far as they manifest a present or future intention to act in a manner contrary to public policy or public security' or, on the other hand, whether, as Counsel for the prosecution sought to argue, although 'the court cannot make a recommendation for deportation on grounds of public policy based on the fact alone of a previous conviction [it] is entitled to take into account the past conduct of the defendant which resulted in the previous conviction'.

27. The terms of Article [3(2)], which states that 'previous criminal convictions shall not in themselves constitute grounds for the taking of such measures' must be understood as requiring the national authorities to carry out a specific appraisal from the point of view of the interests inherent in protecting the requirements of public policy, which does not necessarily

coincide with the appraisals which formed the basis of the criminal conviction.

28. The existence of a previous criminal conviction can, therefore, only be taken into account in so far as the circumstances which gave rise to that conviction are evidence of personal conduct constituting a present threat to the requirements of public policy.

29. Although, in general, a finding that such a threat exists implies the existence in the individual concerned of a propensity to act in the same way in the future, it is possible that past conduct alone may constitute such a threat to the requirements of public policy.

30. It is for the authorities and, where appropriate, for the national courts, to consider that question in each individual case in the light of the particular legal position of persons subject to Community law and of the fundamental nature of the principle of the free movement of persons.

The third question

31. The third question asks whether the words 'public policy' in Article 48(3) are to be interpreted as including reasons of state even where no breach of the public peace or order is threatened or in a narrower sense in which is incorporated the concept of some threatened breach of the public peace, order or security, or in some other wider sense.

32. Apart from the various questions of terminology, this question seeks to obtain a definition of the interpretation to be given to the concept of 'public policy' referred to in Article 48.

33. In its judgment in [*van Duyn* **[D43]**] the court emphasised that the concept of public policy in the context of the Community and where, in particular, it is used as a justification for derogating from the fundamental principle of freedom of movement for workers, must be interpreted strictly, so that its scope cannot be determined unilaterally by each Member State without being subject to control by the institutions of the Community.

34. Nevertheless, it is stated in [*van Duyn*] that the particular circumstances justifying recourse to the concept of public policy may vary from one country to another and from one period to another and it is therefore necessary in this matter to allow the competent national authorities an area of discretion within the limits imposed by the Treaty and the provisions adopted for its implementation.

35. In so far as it may justify certain restrictions on the free movement of persons subject to Community law, recourse by a national authority to the concept of public policy presupposes, in any event, the existence, in addition to the perturbation of the social order which any infringement of the law involves, of a genuine and sufficiently serious threat to the requirements of public policy affecting one of the fundamental interests of society.

[D48]   Cases 115, 116/81 Rezguia Adoui v Belgian State and City of Liège and Dominique Cornvaille v Belgian State [1982] ECR 1665

[The plaintiffs, of French nationality, were refused residence permits by the Belgian authorities on the ground that their conduct was considered to be contrary to public policy because they were waitresses in a bar which was suspect from the point of view of morals (cf *Henn* **[E29]** and *Conegate* **[E30]**).]

The European Court of Justice (at pp 1707–1709)

[On 'public policy']

7. The reservations contained in Articles 48 and 56 of the EEC Treaty permit Member States to adopt, with respect to the nationals of other Member States and on the grounds specified in those provisions, in particular grounds justified by the requirements of public policy, measures which they cannot apply to their own nationals, inasmuch as they have no authority to expel the latter from the national territory or to deny them access thereto. Although that difference of treatment, which bears upon the nature of the measures available, must therefore be allowed, it must nevertheless be stressed that, in a Member State, the authority empowered to adopt such measures must not base the exercise of its powers on assessments of certain conduct which would have the effect of applying an arbitrary distinction to the detriment of nationals of other Member States.

8. It should be noted in that regard that reliance by a national authority upon the concept of public policy presupposes, as the court held in [*Bouchereau* **[D47]**], the existence of a 'genuine and sufficiently serious threat affecting one of the fundamental interests of society'. Although Community law does not impose upon the Member States a uniform scale of values as regards the assessment of conduct which may be considered as contrary to public policy, it should nevertheless be stated that conduct may not be considered as being of a sufficiently serious nature to justify restrictions on the admission to or residence within the territory of a Member State of a national of another Member State in a case where the former Member State does not adopt with respect to the same conduct on the part of its own nationals repressive measure or other genuine and effective measures intended to combat such conduct.

[On Directive 64/221, Article 6]

13. [It] is clear from the purpose of the directive that the notification of the grounds must be sufficiently detailed and precise to enable the person concerned to defend his interests. As regards the language to be used, it appears [that the plaintiffs] are of French nationality and that the decisions affecting them were drawn up in [French]. It is sufficent in any event if the notification is made in such a way as to enable the person concerned to comprehend the content and effect thereof.

[D49]   R v Secretary of State for Home Affairs, ex parte Santillo

(a)   Case 131/79 R v Secretary of State for Home Affairs, ex parte Santillo [1980] ECR 1585
[The United Kingdom Immigration Act 1971 provided that any person described as a non-patrial was subject in the United Kingdom to controls which included liability to be deported in the following circumstances:

Section 3(5)(a) if, having only a limited leave to enter or remain, he does not observe a condition attached to the leave or remains beyond the time limited by the leave; or
(b) if the Secretary of State deems his deportation to be conducive to the public good; or
(c) if another person to whose family he belongs is or has been ordered to be deported;

Section 3(6) [if] he is convicted of an offence for which he is punishable with imprisonment and on his conviction is recommended for deportation by a [court].

The system of appeals differed according to whether the case fell within s 3(5), where the decision by the Secretary of State to make a deportation order was subject to an appeal to an adjudicator from whose decision there was a further appeal to the Immigration Appeal Tribunal, or s 3(6), where the recommendation for deportation made by a court could be appealed against but no appeal could be brought after the making of a subsequent deportation order and there was no machinery for making representations before the decision to make the order was taken.

In December 1973, Mario Santillo was convicted before the Central Criminal Court of buggery and rape committed on a prostitute and of indecent assault occasioning bodily harm on another prostitute. He was sentenced to a total of eight years' imprisonment for the four offences. When giving judgment the trial judge made a recommendation for deportation under the Immigration Act 1971. The trial judge had adjourned the case for ten days for investigation and had been informed that Santillo's wife and children lived in a council flat and did not want to leave the United Kingdom. The judge, in sentencing Santillo to eight years' imprisonment, stated that the offences were 'callous, cruel and ruthless' and that the medical reports showed that he was not in need of medical or psychiatric treatment. The judge took into account the position of the wife and small daughters but stated that 'my duty requires me to recommend that an order of deportation be made in your case in the interests of the community and the protection of the community'. The Court of Appeal, Criminal Division, refused Santillo leave to appeal against the prison sentence and the recommendation for deportation.

Six months before Santillo's expected release, the Secretary of State had to decide on the question of deportation and he considered the original offences, the fact that the prison parole board had twice refused to recommend Santillo for parole, together with the views of the senior medical officer at the prison to the effect that there was a risk that Santillo might commit similar offences again. The Secretary of State reached the conclusion 'that in all the circumstances there would be an excessive risk to the public' if Santillo were allowed to remain in the United Kingdom and made a deportation order against him to take effect when his prison sentence was completed. Having completed his prison sentence in April 1979, after remission of one-third for good behaviour, Santillo was due to be released but remained in detention under the Immigration Act 1971. In April 1979, Santillo applied to the High Court to set aside the deportation order on the ground that, having been made more than four years after the recommendation for deportation by the Central Criminal Court, it infringed his individual rights for failure to comply with the provisions of Article 9(1) of

Directive 64/221 **[D42]**. The High Court referred the following questions to the Court of Justice for a preliminary ruling:

  1. Whether Article 9(1) of [Directive] 64/221 confers on individuals rights which are enforceable by them in the national courts of a Member State and which the national courts must protect?

  2(a) What is the meaning of the phrase 'an opinion has been obtained from a competent authority of the host country' within Article 9(1) of [Directive] 64/221 (an 'opinion');

  2(b) in particular, can a recommendation for deportation made by a criminal court on passing sentence (a 'recommendation') constitute an 'opinion'?

  3. If the answer to question 2(b) is Yes,

  3(a) must 'a recommendation' be fully reasoned?

  3(b) in what (if any) circumstances does the lapse of time between the making of 'a recommendation' and the taking of the decision ordering the expulsion preclude 'a recommendation' from constituting 'an opinion'?

  3(c) in particular, does the lapse of time involved in serving a sentence of imprisonment have the effect that 'a recommendation' ceases to be 'an opinion'?]

The European Court of Justice (at pp 1598–1602)

  9. It is settled in English law that the legal remedies available against a deportation order relate only to the legal validity of that order. It follows that the deportation order itself may be made only in accordance with the provisions of Article 9 of the directive, which makes express provision for such a case.

. . .

  11. Article 9(1) of the directive is one of a number of provisions designed to ensure that the rights of nationals of a Member State regarding the freedom of movement and residence in the territory of other Member States are observed.

. . .

  12. The provisions of Article 9 are complementary to those of Article 8. Their object is to ensure a minimum procedural safeguard for persons affected by one of the measures referred to in the three cases set out in paragraph (1) of that article. Where the right of appeal relates only to the legal validity of a decision, the purpose of the intervention of the 'competent authority' referred to in Article 9(1) is to enable an exhaustive examination of all the facts and circumstances including the expediency of the proposed measure to be carried out before the decision is finally taken. Furthermore the person concerned must be able to exercise before that authority such rights of defence and of assistance or representation as the domestic law of that country provides for.

  13. These provisions, taken together, are sufficiently well defined and specific to enable them to be relied upon by any person concerned and capable, as such, of being applied by any court. This conclusion justifies a positive reply to the first question submitted by the national court.

  14. The requirement contained in Article 9(1) that any decision ordering expulsion must be preceded by the opinion of a 'competent authority' and

that the person concerned must be able to enjoy such rights of defence and of assistance or representation as the domestic law of that country provides for, can only constitute a real safeguard if all the factors to be taken into consideration by the administration are put before the competent authority, if the opinion of the competent authority is sufficiently proximate in time to the decision ordering expulsion to ensure that there are no new factors to be taken into consideration, and if both the administration and the person concerned are in a position to take cognisance of the reasons which led the 'competent authority' to give its opinion – save where grounds touching the security of the state referred to in Article 6 of the directive make this undesirable.

15. As regards the question what is the significance of the phrase 'opinion . . . obtained from a competent authority of the host country' and whether a recommendation for deportation made by a criminal court at the time of conviction constitutes such an opinion, it should be noted that the directive does not define the expression 'a competent authority'. It refers to an authority which must be independent of the administration, but it gives Member States a margin of discretion in regard to the nature of the authority.

16. It is common ground that the criminal courts in the United Kingdom are independent of the administration, which is responsible for making the deportation order, and that the person concerned enjoys the right to be represented and to exercise his rights of defence before such courts.

17. A recommendation for deportation made by a criminal court at the time of conviction under British legislation may, therefore, constitute an opinion within the meaning of Article 9 of the directive provided that the other conditions of Article 9 are satisfied. As the court has already stressed in [*Bouchereau* **[D47]**], a criminal court must take account in particular of the provisions of Article 3 of the directive inasmuch as the mere existence of criminal convictions may not automatically constitute grounds for deportation measures.

18. As regards the time at which the opinion of the competent authority must be given, it must be observed that a lapse of time amounting to several years between the recommendation for deportation and the decision by the administration is liable to deprive the recommendation of its function as an opinion within the meaning of Article 9. It is indeed essential that the social danger resulting from a foreigner's presence should be assessed at the very time when the decision ordering expulsion is made against him as the factors to be taken into account, particularly those concerning his conduct, are likely to change in the course of time.

19. These considerations lead to a reply in the following terms to the second and third questions submitted by the High Court of Justice:

The directive leaves a margin of discretion to Member States for defining the 'competent authority'. Any public authority independent of the administrative authority called upon to adopt one of the measures referred to by the directive, which is so constituted that the person concerned enjoys the rights of representation and of defence before it, may be considered as such an authority.

A recommendation for deportation made under British legislation by a criminal court at the time of conviction may constitute an opinion under Article 9 of the directive provided that the other conditions of Article 9 are satisfied. The criminal court must take account in particular of the provisions

of Article 3 of the directive inasmuch as the mere existence of criminal convictions may not automatically constitute grounds for deportation measures.

The opinion of the competent authority must be sufficiently proximate in
time to the decision ordering expulsion to ensure that there are no new factors to be taken into consideration, and both the administration and the
person concerned should be in a position to take cognisance of the reasons which led the 'competent authority' to give its opinion – save where
grounds touching the security of the state referred to in Article 6 of the directive make this undesirable.

A lapse of time amounting to several years between the recommendation for deportation and the decision by the administration is liable to
deprive the recommendation of its function as an opinion within the meaning of Article 9. It is indeed essential that the social danger resulting from a
foreigner's presence should be assessed at the very time when the decision ordering expulsion is made against him as the factors to be taken into
account, particularly those concerning his conduct, are likely to change in
the course of time.

(b)   R v Secretary of State for the Home Department, ex parte Santillo
[1981] 2 All ER 897, QBD
[Following the Court of Justice's decision the application for judicial review
was heard by the Divisional Court of the Queen's Bench Division.]

Donaldson LJ (at pp 913–915)

[This] court referred to the Court of Justice of the European Communities
several questions arising in connection with [the application for judicial re-
view]. We now have to reach a decision on the application in the light of the
judgment of that court. [That] guidance is expressed in general terms and it
is our duty to apply it to the facts of this case.

The only opinion from a competent authority which can be relied upon in
this case is the recommendation of the trial judge. That was expressed [a]
little under five years before the decision was taken to make a deportation
order. It was thus stale and liable to have ceased to perform its functions as
an opinion of the competent authority within the meaning of [Article] 9. I
take the word 'liable' from the European Court's answer to question 3(b).
But in fact there is not a scintilla of evidence that the position had in any
way changed or that any of the considerations which caused the trial judge
to make his recommendation had been altered at least in a sense
favourable to the applicant. [Whilst] the Secretary of State could have
sought an updated opinion from some competent authority, on the facts of
this case Community law did not require him to do so because the orginal
recommendation was still effective for the purpose of [Article] 9. And, even
if he had done so, there is not the slightest ground for believing that such
an updated opinion would have differed from that of the trial court.

(c)   R v Secretary of State for the Home Department, ex parte Santillo
[1981] 2 All ER 897, CA
[Santillo appealed to the Court of Appeal.]

Lord Denning MR (at p 919)

[The] opinion of the competent authority (the Central Criminal Court) was
sufficiently proximate in point of time to be a valid opinion, on which the

administrative authority (the Home Secretary) could act, because there were no new factors which were such as to invalidate the opinion. The only new factors were factors which were adverse to Mario Santillo, and these served to reinforce the recommendation for deportation.

Shaw LJ (at p 920)

The heart of the matter so far as the applicant is concerned lies in the proposition that, where a recommendation relates to a person who is sentenced to a long term of imprisonment, his personality and character may have changed in a radical way by the date of his release. His deportation may no longer be necessary for the good health of society and there should accordingly be a further review on or before that date. In such circumstances it would, as I see it, be for the prospective deportee to raise the matter by making representations in that regard when the time for his release approached. If he should do so the Secretary of State would be bound to consider them and to act fairly in making his decision. He may indeed take the initiative and decide that further consideration is appropriate even though no representations in that regard are made to him. The lapse of time, even of a long time, may bring no material change. The telling factors remain as the conviction and the circumstances which gave rise to it. There are ample safeguards in the English system which meet the total requirements of the directive. In my view it is unnecessary to change that system in any respect.

Templeman LJ (at pp 921–923)

[The] Divisional Court was obliged to turn its back on reality and to propound certain questions to the European Court. Immersed in the cloudy generality of its [function], the European Court was also obliged to ignore reality but furnished replies which enable this court now to approach the moment of truth.

. . .

[In] the present case no new factor has been suggested by the applicant. The evidence in this case makes it clear that no new factor has emerged, let alone a new factor which might militate against the making of a deportation order, and it is plain from the uncontradicted and uncontradictable evidence of the senior medical officer of [the] prison that the lapse of time between the deportation recommendation and the deportation order had and could have had no effect whatsoever and did not operate to deprive the deportation recommendation of its force and effect or raise any doubts concerning the continuing validity of the deportation recommendation at the date of the deportation order.

[Appeal dismissed. Leave to appeal to the House of Lords refused. The Appeal Committee of the House of Lords dismissed a petition for leave to appeal.]

[D50] Cases I-297/88, 197/89 Massam Dzodzi v Belgian State [1990] ECR I-3763

[Massam Dzodzi, a Togolese national, entered Belgium and married a Belgian national, Mr Herman. As the spouse of a Belgian national, she then applied to the administrative authorities for permission to remain in Belgium by virtue of a right which she maintained was conferred by Community law. There was no response to her application. The couple then went to Togo and resided there for a few months, but without informing the Belgian authorities. Mr Herman died, shortly after returning to Belgium. Further applications for the issue of a permit for an extended period of residence in Belgium were rejected. Massam Dzodzi was ordered to leave Belgium and she applied to the Tribunal de première instance, Brussels, for interim relief in the form of the suspension of the execution of that decision and an order that Belgium should issue her with a residence permit valid for five years. The Cour d'appel, Brussels, asked two questions on Articles 8 and 9 of Directive 64/221 **[D42]**. It pointed out that in 'Belgium, nationals of the State who are threatened with imminent harm which might be caused to them by an act of the administration whose legality is open to dispute may bring before the President of the Tribunal de première instance proceedings for interim relief in the form of an order requiring the public authority to take measures to preserve their interests that are under threat or to suspend provisionally the effects of the act complained of'. The first question was whether it was permitted, in the light of the requirements laid down by Directive 64/221, to prohibit those to whom the directive applies from having recourse to the procedure for obtaining interim relief. The second question was whether Article 9 must be interpreted as meaning that the persons concerned must be entitled to bring an action which would enable them to apply as a matter of urgency for the intervention of a national court or tribunal, prior to the enforcement of the measure complained of, in order to obtain in good time measures protecting the rights under threat. On the question of interim relief, cf *Factortame* **[C47]**, **[C48]**, **[C49]**.]

The European Court of Justice (at pp 3798–3801)

Article 8 of the directive

58. [Article 8] defines the decisions referred to by the directive as 'acts of the administration' and imposes upon the Member States the obligation to make available to any person affected by such acts the same legal remedies as are available to nationals in respect of acts of the administration. Accordingly, a Member State cannot, without being in breach of the obligation imposed by Article 8, organise, for persons covered by the directive, legal remedies governed by special procedures affording lesser safeguards than those pertaining to remedies available to nationals in respect of acts of the administration (judgment in Case 98/79 *Pecastaing v Belgium* [1980] ECR 691, paragraph 10).

59. It follows that if, in a Member State, the administrative courts are not empowered to grant a stay of execution of an administrative decision or interim protective measures with regard to the execution of such a decision, but such power is vested in the ordinary courts, that state is obliged to permit persons covered by the directive to apply to those courts on the same

terms as nationals. It must nevertheless be emphasised that such rights depend essentially on the organisation of the courts and the division of jurisdiction of judicial bodies in the various Member States, since the only obligation imposed upon the Member States by Article 8 is to grant to persons protected under Community law rights of appeal which are not less favourable than those available to nationals of the state concerned against acts of the administration (judgment in *Pecastaing v Belgium*, cited above, paragraph 11).

60. Accordingly, the reply to be given is that under Article 8 [the] Member States are under a duty to secure for the persons covered by that directive judicial protection which is not less favourable, in particular as regards the authority before which an appeal may be brought and the powers of that authority, than the protection which those states afford their own nationals as regards appeals against acts of the administration.

Article 9 of the directive

61. The question essentially seeks to establish whether, as a result of Article 9 of the directive, the Member States are under a duty to recognise a right on the part of persons covered by the directive to bring an appeal, prior to the execution of a decision refusing a residence permit or ordering expulsion from the territory, before a court empowered, under an urgency procedure, to adopt interim protective measures in connection with rights of residence.

62. The object of [Article 9(1)] is to ensure a minimum procedural safeguard for persons affected by a decision refusing renewal of a residence permit or ordering the expulsion of the holder of a residence permit from the territory. That provision, which applies only where there is no right of appeal to a court of law, or where such appeal may be only in respect of the legal validity of the decision, or where the appeal cannot have suspensory effect, provides for the intervention of a competent authority other than the authority empowered to take the decision. Save in cases of urgency, the administrative authority may not take its decision until an opinion has been obtained from that consultative body. In proceedings before that body the person concerned must enjoy such rights of defence and of assistance or representation as the domestic law of that country provides for.

63. Article 9(2) provides that persons who are the subject of a decision refusing the issue of a first residence permit or ordering their expulsion before any permit is issued may refer the matter to the authority whose opinion is required under Article 9(1). In such a case, the person concerned is then entitled to submit his defence in person, except where this would be contrary to the interests of national security.

64. That authority must deliver an opinion which, as is evident from the objectives of the system provided for by the directive, must be duly notified to the person [concerned].

65. The directive does not specify how the competent authority referred to in Article 9 is appointed. It does not require that authority to be a court or to be composed of members of the judiciary. Nor does it require the members of the competent authority to be appointed for a specific period. The essential requirement is, first, that it should be clearly established that the authority is to perform its duties in absolute independence and is not to be directly or indirectly subject, in the exercise of its duties, to any control by

the authority empowered to take the measures provided for in the [directive] and, secondly, that the authority should follow a procedure enabling the person concerned, on the terms laid down by the directive, to put forward his arguments in defence.

66. Although there is no provision empowering the authority in question to take interim protective decisions in connection with the right of residence, it must none the less be observed that, under Article [9] as interpreted by the court (judgment in *Pecastaing v Belgium*, cited above, paragraph 18), once the matter has been brought before that authority, an expulsion order covered by Article 9 may not be executed, save in cases of urgency, before the opinion of that consultative body has been obtained and notified to the person concerned. It must further be noted that the order may not be enforced in breach of the right of that person to stay in the territory for the time necessary to avail himself of the remedies accorded to him under Article [8] (judgment in *Pecastaing v Belgium*, cited above, paragraph 12).

67. It follows from the whole of the foregoing that Article 9 cannot be construed as requiring the provision, for the benefit of persons covered by the directive, of a judicial appeal of the kind described by the Belgian court.

. . .

69. Accordingly, the reply must be that Article 9 [does] not require the Member States to make available to persons covered by the directive a right of appeal, prior to the execution of a decision refusing a residence permit or ordering expulsion from the territory, to a court empowered, under an urgency procedure, to adopt interim protective measures in connection with rights of residence.

[D51] Public service and official authority, EC Treaty provisions

Article 48

. . .

4. The provisions of this article shall not apply to employment in the public service.

Article 55

The provisions of this Chapter [on Establishment] shall not apply, so far as any given Member State is concerned, to activities which in that state are connected, even occasionally, with the exercise of official authority. . .

Article 66

The provisions of [Article 55] shall apply to the matters covered by this Chapter [on Services (see **[E45]**)].

[D52]   Case 152/73 Giovanni Maria Sotgiu v Deutsche Bundespost [1974] ECR 153

[For the facts, see **[D16]**. This was the first case on the meaning of 'employment in the public service'. The court was faced with an old problem in a new field, namely, the extent to which Member States remain competent, in this case to regulate their public service and to define their administration and their decentralised organisations, where power has devolved upon the Community, in this case to guarantee freedom of movement and equality of treatment for workers. It was argued by Advocate General Mayras that the primacy of Community law and the necessity for a uniform application of that law could not permit each Member State to fashion Community rules to their taste and thereby limit freedom of movement for workers. Just as the term 'worker' must have a Community meaning (*Hoekstra* **[D4]**), 'employment in the public service' must be given an independent definition unaffected by variable national criteria which depend upon the conception which each state has of its structure. Whereas, in most states, the 'public' authorities would include the police, the judiciary, policy-making civil servants, these being different to organisations which employ people, such as industry, commerce and agriculture, the position of workers in nationalised industries came somewhere in between.]

The European Court of Justice (at pp 161–163)

2. The [question] asks whether, having regard to the exception provided for in Article [48(4) **[D51]**], workers employed in the public service of a Member State [by] virtue of a contract of employment under private law, may be excluded from the rule of non-discrimination set out in Article 7(1) and (4) of Regulation [1612/68 **[D14]**].

. . .

4. Taking account of the fundamental nature, in the scheme of the Treaty, of the principles of freedom of movement and equality of treatment of workers within the Community, the exception made by Article 48(4) cannot have a scope going beyond the aim in view of which this derogation was included.

The interests which this derogation allows Member States to protect are satisfied by the opportunity of restricting admission of foreign nationals to certain activities in the public service.

On the other hand this provision cannot justify discriminatory measures with regard to remuneration or other conditions of employment against workers once they have been admitted to the public service.

The very fact that they have been admitted shows indeed that those interests which justify the exceptions to the principle of non-discrimination permitted by Article 48(4) are not at issue.

5. It is necessary to establish further whether the extent of the exception provided for by Article 48(4) can be determined in terms of the designation of the legal relationship between the employee and the employing administration.

In the absence of any distinction in the provision referred to, it is of no interest whether a worker is engaged as a workman, a clerk, or an official or even whether the terms on which he is employed come under public or private law.

These legal designations can be varied at the whim of national legislatures and cannot therefore provide a criterion for interpretation appropriate to the requirements of Community law.

6. The answer to the question put to the court should therefore be that Article 48(4) [is] to be interpreted as meaning that the exception made by this provision concerns only access to posts forming part of the public services and that the nature of the legal relationship between the employee and the employing administration is of no consequence in this respect.

[D53] Case 149/79 Commission of the European Communities v The Kingdom of Belgium [1980] ECR 3881

[The Commission brought Article 169 proceedings against Belgium on the grounds that many posts advertised by the National Railway Company, the National Local Railway Company, the City of Brussels and the Commune of Auderghem were reserved to Belgian nationals. Belgium's defence was based on Article 48(4) **[D51]**. Note how the Court of Justice refers to the principle of proportionality (discussed in Chapter Two, Section Four) and, in a case on free movement of persons, takes an analogous stand to that taken with regard to free movement of goods (see *Cassis de Dijon* **[E21]**)]

The European Court of Justice (at pp 3900–3904)

10. [Article 48(4)] removes from the ambit of Article 48(1) to (3) a series of posts which involve direct or indirect participation in the exercise of powers conferred by public law and duties designed to safeguard the general interests of the state or of other public authorities. Such posts in fact presume on the part of those occupying them the existence of a special relationship of allegiance to the state and reciprocity of rights and duties which form the foundation of the bond of nationality.

11. The scope of the derogation made by Article 48(4) to the principles of freedom of movement and equality of treatment laid down in [Article 48(1)–(3)] should therefore be determined on the basis of the aim pursued by that article. However, determining the sphere of application of Article 48(4) raises special difficulties since in the various Member States authorities acting under powers conferred by public law have assumed responsibilities of an economic and social nature or are involved in activities which are not identifiable with the functions which are typical of the public service yet which by their nature still come under the sphere of application of the Treaty. In these circumstances the effect of extending the exception contained in Article 48(4) to posts which, while coming under the state or other organisations governed by public law, still do not involve any association with tasks belonging to the public service properly so called, would be to remove a considerable number of posts from the ambit of the principles set out in the Treaty and to create inequalities between Member States according to the different ways in which the state and certain sectors of economic life are organised.

12. Consequently it is appropriate to examine whether the posts covered by the [Commission's reasoned] opinion may be associated with the concept of public service within the meaning of Article 48(4), which requires

uniform interpretation and application throughout the Community. It must be acknowledged that the application of the distinguishing criteria indicated above gives rise to problems of appraisal and demarcation in specific cases. It follows from the foregoing that such a classification depends on whether or not the posts in question are typical of the specific activities of the public service in so far as the exercise of powers conferred by public law and responsibility for safeguarding the general interests of the state are vested in it.

13. Where, in the case of posts which, although offered by public authorities, are not within the sphere to which Article 48(4) applies, a worker from another Member State is, like a national worker, required to satisfy all other conditions of recruitment, in particular concerning the competence and vocational training required, the provisions of [Article 48(1)–(3)] and Regulation [1612/68 **[D14]**] do not allow him to be debarred from those posts simply on the grounds of his nationality.

14. In support of the argument put forward by the Belgian government and supported by the interveners to the effect that the exception clause in Article 48(4) of the Treaty has general scope covering all the posts in the administration of a Member State, that government has invoked the special provisions of Article 8 of Regulation 1612/68 by which a worker from another Member State 'may be excluded from taking part in the management of bodies governed by public law and from holding an office governed by public law'.

15. Far from supporting the case of the Belgian government that provision confirms on the contrary the interpretation of Article 48(4) given above. Indeed, as the Belgian government itself admits, Article 8 of Regulation 1612/68 is not intended to debar workers from other Member States from certain posts, but simply permits them to be debarred in some circumstances from certain activities which involve their participation in the exercise of powers conferred by public law, such as – to use the examples given by the Belgian government itself – those involving 'the presence of trade-union representatives on the boards of administration of many bodies governed by public law with powers in the economic sphere'.

16. The Belgian government further mentions that the constitutional laws of certain Member States refer expressly to the problem of employment in the public service, the principle being the exclusion of non-nationals, save for any possible derogations. Such is also, it claims, the effect of Article 6 of the Belgian Constitution by which 'Belgians [only] shall be admitted to civil and military posts save in special cases for which exception may be made'. The Belgian government has itself stated that it does not deny that 'Community rules override national rules' but it believes that the similarity between the constitutional laws of those Member States should be used as an aid to interpretation to cast light on the meaning of Article 48(4) and to reject the interpretation given to that provision by the Commission, which would have the effect of creating conflict with the constitutional provisions referred to.

17. The French government has propounded an argument of similar tenor, drawing attention to the principles applied in French law on the public service, which is founded on a comprehensive idea based on the requirement of French nationality as a condition of entry to any post in the public service appertaining to the state, municipalities or other public establishments, without any possibility of making a distinction on the basis of the

nature and the characteristics of the post in question.

18. It is correct that Article 48(4) is indeed intended to operate, in the scheme of the provisions on freedom of movement for workers, to take account of the existence of provisions of the kind mentioned. But at the same time, as is admitted in the observations of the French government, the demarcation of the concept of 'public service' within the meaning of Article 48(4) cannot be left to the total discretion of the Member States.

19. Irrespective of the fact that the wording of the Belgian Constitution does not rule out the possibility of exceptions being made to the general requirement of the possession of Belgian nationality, it should be recalled, as the court has constantly emphasised in its case law, that recourse to provisions of the domestic legal systems to restrict the scope of the provisions of Community law would have the effect of impairing the unity and efficacy of that law and consequently cannot be accepted. That rule, which is fundamental to the existence of the Community, must also apply in determining the scope and bounds of Article [48(4)]. Whilst it is true that that provision takes account of the legitimate interest which the Member States have in reserving to their own nationals a range of posts connected with the exercise of powers conferred by public law and with the protection of general interests, at the same time it is necessary to ensure that the effectiveness and scope of the provisions of the Treaty on freedom of movement of workers and equality of treatment of nationals of all Member States shall not be restricted by interpretations of the concept of public service which are based on domestic law alone and which would obstruct the application of Community rules.

20. Finally, the Belgian and French governments argue that the exclusion of foreign workers from posts which do not at the outset involve any participation in the exercise of powers conferred by public law becomes necessary, for instance, if recruitment takes place on the basis of service regulations and the holders of the posts are eligible for a career which in the higher grades involves duties and responsibilities involving the exercise of powers conferred by public law. The German and British governments add that such an exclusion is also necessitated by the fact that flexibility in assignment to posts is a characteristic of the public service and the duties and responsibilities of an employee may consequently change, not only on promotion, but also after a transfer within the same branch, or to a different branch at the same level.

21. Those objections do not however take account of the fact that, in referring to posts involving the exercise of powers conferred by public law and the conferment of responsibilities for the safeguarding of the general interests of the state, Article 48(4) allows Member States to reserve to their nationals by appropriate rules entry to posts involving the exercise of such powers and such responsibilities within the same grade, the same branch or the same class.

22. The argument of the German government on that last point, to the effect that any exclusion of nationals of other Member States from promotion or transfer to certain posts in the public service would have the effect of creating discrimination within such service, does not take into consideration the fact that the interpretation which that government puts on Article 48(4), and which has the effect of debarring those nationals from the totality of posts in the public service, involves a restriction on the rights of such nationals which goes further than is necessary to ensure observance of the

objectives of the provision as construed in the light of the foregoing considerations.

23. The court takes the view that, in general, so far as the posts in dispute are concerned, information available in this case, which has been provided by the parties during the written and oral procedures, does not enable a sufficiently accurate appraisal to be made of the actual nature of the duties involved so as to make it possible to identify, in the light of the foregoing considerations, those of the posts which do not come within the concept of public service within the meaning of Article [48(4)].

24. In these circumstances the court does not consider itself to be in a position at this stage to give a decision on the allegation that the Belgian government has failed to fulfil its obligations. Consequently it invites the Commission and the Kingdom of Belgium to re-examine the issue between them in the light of the foregoing considerations and to report to the court, either jointly or separately, within a specified period, either any solution to the dispute which they succeed in reaching together or their respective viewpoints, having regard to the matters of law arising from this judgment. An opportunity will be provided for the interveners to submit their observations to the court on any such report or reports at the appropriate time.

[D54]   Case 149/79 Commission of the European Communities v The Kingdom of Belgium [1982] ECR 1845

[The Commission and Belgium could not agree on a joint report, despite the time limit being extended, and they finally submitted two separate reports, with a list of specified posts, as follows:

(a)   With the Belgian National Railways: Shunters, loaders, drivers, platelayers and signalmen;
(b)   With the National Local Railways: Office cleaners, painters' assistants, assistant furnishers, battery servicers, coil winders, armature servicers, night watchmen, cleaners, canteen staff, workshop hands;
(c)   With the City of Brussels: Joiners, garden hands, hospital nurses, children's nurses, night watchmen, head technical supervisors, principal supervisors, works supervisors, stock controllers, inspectors, architects;
(d)   With the Commune of Auderghem: Architects, children's nurses, creche nurses, garden hands, joiners, electricians, plumbers.

It was, therefore, up to the court to undertake the duty, as guardian of the Treaty in place of the Commission, to settle the dispute by examining whether and to what extent the posts at issue were posts within the ambit of Article 48(4).]

The European Court of Justice (at pp 1851–1852)

7. [Employment] within the meaning of Article 48(4) [must] be connected with the specific activities of the public service in so far as it is entrusted with the exercise of powers conferred by public law and with responsibility for safeguarding the general interests of the state, to which the specific interests of local authorities such as municipalities must be assimilated.

8. The Commission has rightly acknowledged that, regard being had to the duties and responsibilities attached to some of the posts at issue described in the aforesaid reports, they may have characteristics which bring them within the scope of the exception in Article 48(4) [in] the light of the criteria established in [[D53]]. The posts are those described as head technical office supervisor, principal supervisor, works supervisor, stock controller and nightwatchman with the municipality of Brussels and architect with the municipalities of Brussels and Auderghem. These matters may therefore be regarded as being no longer at issue.

9. However, as far as the other posts dealt with in the two reports in question are concerned, it does not appear from the nature of the duties and responsibilities which they involve that they constitute 'employment in the public service'.

[D55] Case 33/88 Pilar Allué and Carmel Mary Coonan v Università degli studi di Venezia [1989] ECR 1591

The European Court of Justice (at pp 1609–1610)

6. [The] national court asks essentially whether employment as a foreign-language assistant at a university must be regarded as employment in the public service, within the meaning of Article [48(4) **[D51]**], to which nationals of other Member States may be refused access.

7. In that regard it must be recalled [that] a teaching post does not involve direct or indirect participation in the exercise of powers conferred by public law and in the discharge of functions whose purpose is to safeguard the general interests of the state or of other public authorities and which therefore require a special relationship of allegiance to the state on the part of persons occupying them and reciprocity of rights and duties which form the foundation of the bond of nationality.

8. Furthermore, the court has consistently held (in particular in its judgment [in] Case 225/85 *Commission v Italy* [1987] ECR 2625) that even if employment in the public service within the meaning of Article 48(4) is involved, that provision cannot justify discriminatory measures with regard to remuneration or other conditions of employment against workers from other Member States once they have been admitted to the public service.

9. The answer to [the] question must therefore be that employment as a foreign-language assistant at a university is not employment in the public service within the meaning of Article 48(4) of the EEC Treaty.

[D56] Case 2/74 Jean Reyners v Belgian State [1974] ECR 631

[Reyners, a Dutch national, was the holder of a legal diploma giving the right to take up the profession of avocat in Belgium but was excluded from that profession by reason of his nationality. The Belgian Conseil d'Etat asked, by way of preliminary ruling, first, whether Article 52 **[D30]** was of direct effect, despite the absence of implementing directives envisaged for implementing a general programme relating to the right of establishment, and, secondly, for a definition of what is meant in Article 55 by 'activities which in the State are connected, even occasionally, with the exercise of official authority'. Note the use by the Court of Justice of Treaty provisions (Articles 52 and 55) to counteract the failure of the Member States to implement the establishment programme. For mutual recognition of qualifications, see Directive 89/48 **[D40]**.]

The European Court of Justice (at pp 651–656)

[On direct effect]

26. In laying down that freedom of establishment shall be attained at the end of the transitional period, Article 52 thus imposes an obligation to attain a precise result, the fulfilment of which had to be made easier by, but not made dependent on, the implementation of a programme of progressive measures.

27. The fact that this progression has not been adhered to leaves the obligation itself intact beyond the end of the period provided for its fulfilment.

28. This interpretation is in accordance with Article 8(7) of the Treaty, according to which the expiry of the transitional period shall constitute the latest date by which all the rules laid down must enter into force and all the measures required for establishing the common market must be implemented.

29. It is not possible to invoke against such an effect the fact that the Council has failed to issue the directives provided for by Articles 54 and 57 or the fact that certain of the directives actually issued have not fully attained the objective of non-discrimination required by Article 52.

30. After the expiry of the transitional period the directives provided for by the Chapter on the right of establishment have become superfluous with regard to implementing the rule on nationality, since this is henceforth sanctioned by the Treaty itself with direct effect.

. . .

32. It is right therefore to reply to the question raised that, since the end of the transitional period, Article 52 of the Treaty is a directly applicable provision despite the absence in a particular sphere of the [directives].

[On 'official authority']

34. More precisely, the question is whether, within a profession such as that of avocat, only those activities inherent in this profession which are connected with the exercise of official authority are excepted from the application of the Chapter on the right of establishment, or whether the whole of this profession is excepted by reason of the fact that it comprises activities connected with the exercise of this authority.

35. The Luxembourg government and the Ordre national des avocats de Belgique consider that the whole profession of avocat is exonerated from the rules in the Treaty on the right of establishment by the fact that it is connected organically with the functioning of the public service of the administration of justice.

36. This situation (it is argued) results both from the legal organisation of the Bar, involving a set of strict conditions for admission and discipline, and

from the functions performed by the avocat in the context of judicial procedure where his participation is largely obligatory.

37. These activities, which make the avocat an indispensable auxiliary of the administration of justice, form a coherent whole, the parts of which cannot be separated.

38. [Reyners] contends that at most only certain activities of the profession of avocat are connected with the exercise of official authority and that they alone therefore come within the exception created by Article 55 to the principle of free establishment.

39. The German, Belgian, British, Irish and Dutch governments, as well as the Commission, regard the exception contained in Article 55 as limited to those activities alone within the various professions concerned which are actually connected with the exercise of official authority, subject to their being separable from the normal practice of the profession.

40. Differences exist, however, between the governments referred to as regards the nature of the activities which are thus excepted from the principle of the freedom of establishment, taking into account the different organisation of the professions corresponding to that of avocat from one Member State to another.

41. The German government in particular considers that by reason of the compulsory connection of the Rechtsanwalt with certain judicial processes, especially as regards criminal or public law, there are such close connections between the profession of Rechtsanwalt and the exercise of judicial authority that large sectors of this profession, at least, should be excepted from freedom of establishment.

42. [The court cited Article 55(1).]

43. Having regard to the fundamental character of freedom of establishment and the rule on equal treatment with nationals in the system of the Treaty, the exceptions allowed by [Article 55(1)] cannot be given a scope which would exceed the objective for which this exemption clause was inserted.

44. [Article 55(1)] must enable Member States to exclude non-nationals from taking up functions involving the exercise of official authority which are connected with one of the activities of self-employed persons provided for in Article 52.

45. This need is fully satisfied when the exclusion of nationals is limited to those activities which, taken on their own, constitute a direct and specific connection with the exercise of official authority.

46. An extension of the exception allowed by Article 55 to a whole profession would be possible only in cases where such activities were linked with that profession in such a way that freedom of establishment would result in imposing on the Member State concerned the obligation to allow the exercise, even occasionally, by non-nationals of functions appertaining to official authority.

47. This extension is on the other hand not possible when, within the framework of an independent profession, the activities connected with the exercise of official authority are separable from the professional activity in question taken as a whole.

48. In the absence of any directive issued under Article 57 for the purpose of harmonising the national provisions relating, in particular, to professions such as that of avocat, the practice of such professions remains governed by the law of the various Member States.

49. The possible application of the restrictions on freedom of establishment provided for by [Article 55(1)] must therefore be considered separately in connection with each Member State having regard to the national provisions applicable to the organisation and the practice of this profession.

50. This consideration must however take into account the Community character of the limits imposed by Article 55 on the exceptions permitted to the principle of freedom of establishment in order to avoid the effectiveness of the Treaty being defeated by unilateral provisions of Member States.

51. Professional activities involving contacts, even regular and organic, with the courts, including even compulsory co-operation in their functioning, do not constitute, as such, connection with the exercise of official authority.

52. The most typical activities of the profession of avocat, in particular, such as consultation and legal assistance and also representation and the defence of parties in court, even when the intervention or assistance of the avocat is compulsory or is a legal monopoly, cannot be considered as connected with the exercise of official authority.

53. The exercise of these activities leaves the discretion of judicial authority and the free exercise of judicial power intact.

54. It is therefore right to reply to the question raised that the exception to freedom of establishment provided for by [Article 55(1)] must be restricted to those of the activities referred to in Article 52 which in themselves involve a direct and specific connection with the exercise of official authority.

55. In any case it is not possible to give this description, in the context of a profession such as that of avocat, to activities such as consultation and legal assistance or the representation and defence of parties in court, even if the performance of these activities is compulsory or there is a legal monopoly in respect of it.

[D57]   Case 147/86 Commission of the European Communities v Hellenic Republic [1988] ECR 1637

[The Commission alleged that under Greek legislation nationals of other Member States were not authorised: (1) to set up 'frontistiria' (organised courses which have as their purpose to supplement and consolidate instruction forming part of the curriculum for primary, secondary or higher education (the latter whether or not preparatory to university entrance)), or to teach foreign languages or music or to provide general training in extra-curricular activities; (2) to set up private vocational training schools, that is to say schools which do not exhibit the characteristics of 'frontistiria' and which provide vocational training; (3) to give private lessons at home. Taking the view that this legislation introduced a system that discriminated against nationals of other Member States on grounds of nationality and was therefore contrary to Articles 52 and 59, the Commission instituted Article 169 proceedings.]

The European Court of Justice (at pp 1654–1655)

6. The Greek government challenges [the Commission's] argument [on] the ground that the principle of freedom of establishment laid down by

Article 52 cannot be applied in this case since, by virtue of [Article 55(1)], that principle does not apply to activities connected, even occasionally, with the exercise of official authority. According to the Greek government, it is for each Member State to define which activities in the state are connected with the exercise of official authority. That is the case as regards teaching activities in Greece, in view of the fact that, under the Greek Constitution, the provision of instruction is a fundamental duty of the state designed to ensure in particular the moral and spiritual education of its citizens and the development of their national consciousness, and that private individuals who carry on such activities do so in their capacity as repositories of official authority.

7. In that regard it must be emphasised that, since it derogates from the fundamental rule of freedom of establishment, Article 55 [must] be interpreted in a manner which limits its scope to what is strictly necessary in order to safeguard the interests which it allows the Member States to protect.

8. It is true that, in the absence of a Community directive designed to harmonise national provisions on the setting-up of teaching establishments, the possible application of restrictions on freedom of establishment provided for by Article 55 must be appraised separately in respect of each Member State. However, that appraisal must take account of the Community character of the limits set by Article 55 to the exceptions which are permitted to the principle of freedom of establishment, in order to prevent the effectiveness of the Treaty in this area from being undermined by unilateral provisions adopted by the Member States.

9. Although it is for each Member State to determine the role of, and the responsibilities attaching to, official authority with regard to instruction, it cannot be accepted that the mere fact that a private individual sets up a school such as a 'frontistirion' or a vocational training school, or gives private lessons at home, is connected with the exercise of official authority within the meaning of Article [55].

10. Those private activities remain subject to supervision by the official authorities which have at their disposal appropriate means for ensuring, in any event, the protection of the interests entrusted to them, without there being any need to restrict freedom of establishment for that purpose.

11. The Greek government's [objection] must therefore be rejected.

SECTION FOUR

SOCIAL POLICY

Introduction

The term 'social policy' is capable of embracing an enormous range of activity which might include, for example, health, education or regional development. There has always been some provision for social policy in the evolving Treaty base to the European Community. Unlike the rules relating to workers and establishment, the social policy framework is not dependent on migration across borders. Ms Defrenne **[C23 and D59]** was thus able simply to invoke EC law **[D58]** in a domestic setting to challenge discrimination based on sex. However, the principal developments in social policy have still been in the employment context, thereby reinforcing the association of the Community with economic priorities. The emphasis of the materials in this section is upon the policy which is or should be pursued, rather than on a detailed rehearsal of the many cases which have, for example, extensively refined the concept of 'pay' for the purposes of Article 119.

Criticism of the interpretation and application of Community law in relation to women's interests has concentrated upon the extent to which the jurisprudence of the European Court of Justice has embraced goals which go beyond narrow views of sex discrimination. Colneric **[D60]** measures the case law against the objectives of removing domination rather than differentiation on grounds of sex, and points to the scope for the court's concept of 'indirect indiscrimination' to be used in this way. This analysis may be compared to the models adopted by McCrudden **[D61]**. Whilst the court has clearly stated that social policy is not confined to economic goals **[D59]**, it is also to some degree circumscribed in its action by the secondary legislation which it has to interpret, as can be seen from its discussion of the protection of women in the context of a ban on nightwork (*Stoeckel* **[D62]**).

As would be expected, the social policy cases are microcosms of wider issues. For example, the sex discrimination cases have played a key part in the development of the characteristics of the legal order established by the court. Just as *Defrenne* and *Marshall (No 1)* gave significant impetus to the jurisprudence on direct effect, so *Marshall (No 2)* **[D63]** provides a very stark example of the Community law principle of effective protection in operation. Coupling effective protection at enforcement level with the widest notions of the discussion of the goals of social policy would bring enormous repercussions.

Secondly, the political sensitivity of the economic impact of what might be canvassed as an advanced social policy has meant that the Court of Justice has been faced with the dilemma of how to secure its view of necessary legal rights without engendering significant and damaging effects in the real world. Both the *Defrenne* and *Barber* judgments contained temporal limits as to their application in order to moderate their economic and political impact (although debate may rage as to which of these concerns was uppermost). At a political level, the negotiation of the Maastricht Treaty led to the 'opting-out' by the United Kingdom from the proposed new social policy arrangements. As a result, a Protocol and Agreement on Social Policy were adopted by the other 11 Member States, the status and operation of which has created considerable doubt and controversy (**[D65]** and **[D67]**).

In trying to concentrate upon the interests of persons rather than workers, social policy has opened up or encountered resistance sufficient to trigger potentially major constitutional problems for the Community. An over-adventurous Court of Justice may meet with a severe rap on the knuckles by politicians, as seems to have been successfully achieved, also by Protocol, in the attempt under Maastricht to limit the impact of the *Barber* judgment **[D64]**. Future interest may concentrate not just on whether the worst-case scenarios envisaged by Barnard **[D65]** and Whiteford **[D67]** materialise, but also on alternative ways forward such as Hepple's arguments for a strengthened European Social Charter **[D66]**.

MATERIALS

[D58]   EC Treaty provisions on social policy

TITLE VIII – SOCIAL POLICY, EDUCATION, VOCATIONAL TRAINING AND YOUTH

CHAPTER 1 – SOCIAL PROVISIONS

Article 117

Member States agree upon the need to promote improved working conditions and an improved standard of living for workers, so as to make possible their harmonisation while the improvement is being maintained.

They believe that such a development will ensue not only from the functioning of the common market, which will favour the harmonisation of social systems, but also from the procedures provided for in this Treaty and from the approximation of provisions laid down by law, regulation or administrative action.

Article 118

Without prejudice to the other provisions of this Treaty and in conformity with its general objectives, the Commission shall have the task of promoting close co-operation between Member States in the social field, particularly in matters relating to:
– employment;
– labour law and working conditions;
– basic and advanced vocational training;
– social security;
– prevention of occupational accidents and diseases;
– occupational hygiene; the right of association, and collective bargaining between employers and workers.

To this end, the Commission shall act in close contact with Member States by making studies, delivering opinions and arranging consultations both on problems arising at national level and on those of concern to international organisations.

Before delivering the opinions provided for in this article, the Commission shall consult the Economic and Social Committee.

Article 118a

1. Member States shall pay particular attention to encouraging improvements, especially in the working environment, as regards the health and safety of workers, and shall set as their objective the harmonisation of conditions in this area, while maintaining the improvements made.

2. In order to help achieve the objective laid down in the first paragraph, the Council, acting in accordance with the procedure referred to in Article 189c and after consulting the Economic and Social Committee, shall adopt, by means of directives, minimum requirements for gradual implementation, having regard to the conditions and technical rules obtaining in each of the Member States.

Such directives shall avoid imposing administrative, financial and legal constraints in a way which would hold back the creation and development of small and medium-sized undertakings.

3. The provisions adopted pursuant to this Article shall not prevent any Member State from maintaining or introducing more stringent measures for the protection of working conditions compatible with this Treaty.

Article 118b

The Commission shall endeavour to develop the dialogue between management and labour at European level which could, if the two sides consider it desirable, lead to relations based on agreement.

Article 119

Each Member State shall during the first stage ensure and subsequently maintain the application of the principle that men and women should receive equal pay for equal work. For the purpose of this Article, 'pay' means the ordinary basic or minimum wage or salary and any other consideration, whether in cash or in kind, which the worker receives, directly or indirectly, in respect of his employment from his employer.

Equal pay without discrimination based on sex means:

(a) that pay for the same work at piece rates shall be calculated on the basis of the same unit of measurement;
(b) that pay for work at time rates shall be the same for the same job.

Note.   See also **[A8]** and **[A9]** for the Maastricht Protocol and Agreement on Social Policy.

[D59]   Case 43/75 Defrenne v Sabena (No 2) [1976] ECR 455

The European Court of Justice

Article 119 pursues a double aim. First, in the light of the different states of the development of social legislation in the various Member States, the aim of Article 119 is to avoid a situation in which undertakings established in states which have actually implemented the principle of equal pay suffer a competitive disadvantage in intra-Community competition as compared with undertakings established in states which have not yet eliminated discrimination against women workers as regards pay.

Secondly, this provision forms part of the social objectives of the Community, which is not merely an economic union, but is at the same time intended, by common action, to ensure social progress and seek the constant improvement of the living and working conditions of their peoples.

[See also **[C23]**.]

[D60]   Ninon Colneric: 'The prohibition on discrimination against women under Community law' (1992) International Journal of Comparative Labour Law and Industrial Relations 191

Applicability of the principle of equal treatment of sexes in Community law

Community law prescribes equal treatment of men and women in the following, partly overlapping fields: pay, access to employment, vocational training and promotion, working conditions, in statutory social security schemes, occupational social security schemes, in establishment, the equipping or expansion of the undertaking, the establishment or amendment of rules governing the independent occupations, and financial facilities for self-employed persons. The European Court of Justice has repeatedly concluded that the principle of equal treatment of sexes is part of the fundamental rights of Community law, the observance of which it has to ensure. [See Case 149/77 *Defrenne (No3)* [1978] ECR 1365.]

. . .

In the field of social security, the principle of equal treatment of men and women was realised gradually. Consequently, the Directive regarding the statutory social security schemes [Directive 79/7 (OJ 1979 L6/24)] contains numerous exceptions. According to Article 3(2) it does not apply to survivors' benefits and (basically) family benefits. Furthermore, Article 7 makes it possible for the Member States to exclude a list of specified topics from the field of application of the directive; ie the determination of the pensionable age for the purpose of granting old age and retirement pension. The establishment of different minimum pensionable ages for men and women in the framework of legal systems of social security, therefore, is not a form of discrimination considered to be prohibited under Community law.

The directive on occupational social security schemes [Directive 86/378 (OJ 1986 L225/40)] is also influenced by the notion of gradual realisation of equal treatment. First, it provides for a very long period for the implementation. The Member States are to ensure that provisions in occupational schemes contrary to the principle of equal treatment are revised by 1 January 1993. According to Article 9 of the directive, however, Member States may postpone compulsory application of the principle of equal treatment with regard to certain topics: ie survivors' pensions may be postponed until a directive requires the principle of equal treatment in statutory social security schemes in that regard. The applicability of the principle of equal treatment with regard to old age pension can, for the determination of the pensionable age, be postponed either until the date on which such equality is achieved in statutory schemes or, at the latest, until such equality is required by a directive.

However, with its recent judgment in the *Barber* case [Case C-262/88 *Barber v Guardian Royal Exchange Assurance* [1990] ECR I-1889], the European Court of Justice has upset the Council of Ministers' apple-cart. In that case, the issue at stake was an occupational pension scheme of an English enterprise, setting a different pensionable age for men and women. Earlier (in May 1986), it had been decided by the court, in the *Bilka* case

[Case 170/84 [1986] ECR 1607], that benefits for occupational pension schemes were to be included within the term 'pay' in Article 119 of the EEC Treaty. The court decided that it is contrary to Article 119 of the Treaty to use different pensionable ages with regard to the determination of benefits, even if this difference is in accordance with the regulations of the national statutory schemes. The dilemma with which the court was faced was that a directive cannot restrict the application of Article 119 of the EEC Treaty, while – by means of the exception allowed under Article 9 of the Equal Treatment Directive – the impression was created that Article 119 would not apply to occupational social security schemes. The court resolved this dilemma by using the same method which it had used in the second *Defrenne* case **[D59]**. It limited the effect in time of its judgment in such a way that, with the exception of already pending actions no claim can be brought for pension benefits from the period before the date on which the judgment was made.

According to a press release from the German Social Democrat Party, the European Ministers of Social Affairs reacted to the *Barber* case by making plans for challenging Article 119 of the EEC Treaty. However, the Federal Chancellery reassured the alarmed Euro MP Ranzio-Plath in a letter dated 4 December 1991 which stated that 'on behalf of the Federal Chancellor I can assure you that there is no intention at all to water down or delete Article 119'. On 7 February 1992, however, it was decided to water down Article 119 of the EEC Treaty in the form of a Protocol, which provides:

> The high Contracting Parties have agreed upon the following provision, which shall be annexed to the Treaty establishing the European Community:
> For the purposes of Article 119 of this Treaty, benefits under occupational social security schemes shall not be considered as remuneration if and in so far as they are attributable to periods of employment prior to 17 May 1990, except in the case of workers or those claiming under them who have before that date initiated legal proceedings or introduced an equivalent claim under the applicable national law.

The European Commission had lodged a proposal for a directive as early as 1987, the purpose of which was to establish complete equal treatment of men and women in statutory and occupational social security schemes. In its Social Action Programme for the implementation of the Community Charter of Fundamental Social Rights of Workers, the Commission points out how important it is that the Council should put this proposal on the agenda again, in order to reach a positive decision.

The three exceptions contained in the directive on the implementation of the principle of equal treatment for men and women as regards access to employment, vocational training and promotion, and working conditions (the so-called Equal Treatment Directive [76/207 (OJ 1976 L39/40)]) are not drafted as transitional law.

According to Article 2(2) of the Equal Treatment Directive, the Member States can exclude from the field of applicability of the directive those occupational activities (and, where appropriate, the training leading thereto) for which the sex of the workers constitutes a determining factor. According to Article 2(3), the directive shall not prejudice provisions concerning the protection of women, particularly as regards pregnancy and maternity. The third exception, in Article 2(4), refers to measures promoting equal opportunity for men and women.

It was known that the interpretation of the first two exceptions would depend upon social views of the relations between men and women. The directive itself institutionalises a dynamic perspective: the Member States are periodically to assess the occupational activities referred to in Article 2(2), in order to decide, in the light of social developments, whether there is justification for maintaining the exclusions concerned . . . In addition, the Member States are obliged to revise provisions where the concern for protection, originally inspired in the principle of equal treatment, is no longer well founded.

. . .

The content of the principle of equal treatment in Community law

The meaning of the principle of equal treatment in Community law is defined in the first articles of the various regulations on equal treatment. Therefore, the notion 'discrimination on grounds of sex' forms a starting point for each regulation. The directives on equal treatment of men and women explicitly prohibit, with the exception of the directive on equal pay, both direct and indirect discrimination on grounds of sex. As an example, one may cite Article 2(1) of the Equal Treatment Directive 76/207:

> For the purpose of the following provisions the principle of equal treatment shall mean that there shall be no discrimination whatsoever on grounds of sex either directly or indirectly by reference in particular to marital or family status.

After some initial hesitation, the European Court of Justice affirmed the prohibition of indirect discrimination in the field of equal pay. The directive on occupational social security schemes is particularly precise. Apart from the general definition, it contains, in Article 6, an additional list of regulations which are considered to be incompatible with the principle of equal treatment. Finally, the principle of equal treatment may not be excluded, either by way of provisions in an individual employment contract or by collective agreement.

The precept of effective means

The directive on the principle of equal pay [Directive 75/117 (OJ 1975 L45/19)] explicitly lays down the obligation of Member States to see to it that effective means are available in order to ensure that this principle is observed (Article 2, second phrase). The European Court of Justice also extended, using the interpretative method of the 'principle of effectiveness' (*effet utile*), the precept of effective means outside the scope of the directive on equal pay. Effective equal opportunities cannot be obtained without an appropriate set of sanctions. If a Member State grants compensation as a means of sanctioning the violation of the prohibition of discrimination it should make sure that this compensation, in order to be effective and to guarantee a sufficient deterrence, is reasonably proportionate to the damage suffered, which, therefore, must exceed a purely symbolic compensation (such as mere reimbursement of the costs of application).

The struggle for effectiveness also explains the European Court of Justice case law with regard to the question whether a person who initiates a discrimination case can invoke either grounds of justification or the absence of liability. The European Court of Justice concluded, in the *Dekker* case [Case C-177/88 [1990] ECR I-3841], on that point:

If it was a condition for the liability of an employer for contravention of the principle of equal treatment that fault had to be shown and that no grounds for justification recognised by the national law exist, the effect of those principles would be considerably weakened.

It came to the conclusion that in the framework of civil liability, any violation of the prohibition on discrimination as such would be sufficient to establish full liability of the discriminator. Finally, the bold decision of the European Court of Justice to declare Article 119 directly applicable for private persons – even though it is, according to its wording, only directed to the Member States – must be seen in this perspective.

. . .

The notion of equal treatment in Community law

So far, it has been tacitly taken for granted that in this field only the prohibition of discrimination against women is in question. The prohibition of discrimination against men, which is also enshrined in Community law, is left out of account. This is due to a certain notion of the sex to be protected, implied in the prohibition of discrimination on grounds of sex in Community law. This gives cause to some fundamental remarks about conceptions of special protection for equality. In what follows, I shall consider the question of how the Community rules on equal treatment are to be placed within this analytical framework.

Particular protection of equality, superseding general equality principles, can be realised in two ways; ie by a prohibition on differentiation, or by a prohibition on domination.

The prohibition of differentiation forbids the differentiation on the basis of a certain characteristic. The difference between human beings, on which this characteristic is based, should be irrelevant in law, as such a difference cannot justify the determination of differing legal consequences. When the characteristic 'race' is at stake, then 'colour blindness' will be regulated as well, so to speak; and when the characteristic 'sex' is considered, so is the blindness to the difference between sexes. With regard to the groups selected by the characteristic the prohibition of differentiation is symmetrical. If differentiation on grounds of sex is prohibited, this prohibition applies because of its distinguishing feature, regardless as to whether a man or woman has been placed at a disadvantage. The prohibition of differentiation is a formal principle in two aspects: in the first place, it is of no importance what the consequences of different treatment may be. However, it only applies when the differentiation is based upon the prohibited distinguishing feature. A prohibition of differentiation cannot be a measure for regulations which are neutral towards the characteristic itself, but in practice turn out to be different for both groups, because of the distinguishing feature. Prohibitions on differentiation lose practical sense, in as far as the differentiation on the basis of forbidden criteria is concerned.

The protection of equality by means of a prohibition to dominate is based on a material perspective as to groups of people. An abstract prohibition on the use of certain distinguishing characteristics is not at issue, but, rather, the protection of groups which are traditionally disadvantaged by unjustified and unfavourable treatment. The prohibition to dominate refers to the consequences of a measure for a specifically protected group. It also includes structural prejudice based upon the prohibited distinguishing feature as a problem of discrimination. If women were fully protected by a prohibition on domination, it would, for example, be forbidden to force them into a traditional role or keep them within such a role. Measures connecting unjustified disadvantages to the fulfilment of the traditional role would also be prohibited. Preferential treatment of the dominated group, with the aim of dismantling the domination, is not contrary to the prohibition on domination.

At this stage, I shall examine three options upon which the concept of the special protection for equality in Community regulations is based. These are:

1   norms and activities which differentiate on the basis of traditional views as to the division between men and women;
2   norms and activities which work out differently for men and women, even though they do not relate to the characteristic of sex; and
3   norms and activities relating to the criterion of sex, intended to create realistic opportunities for women and to escape the traditional division between men and women.

Norms and activities which differentiate on the basis of traditional views on the division between men and women are covered by the prohibition on direct discrimination on the basis of sex. If this prohibition were interpreted strictly as a prohibition to differentiate, it would mean that direct discrimination on grounds of sex means no more or less than connecting the different treatment to the variation of sex. It is not relevant to know whether there are plausible reasons for a different treatment. Exceptions to the prohibition of different treatment are allowed only in so far as the exceptions permit.

Unfortunately, it cannot be concluded that the European Court of Justice has always adhered to this obvious conception. In 1983, in infringement proceedings against the Italian Republic, the court had to deal with a regulation on the basis of which only an adopting mother, and not an adopting father, was entitled to three months' leave after reception of the child into the family. The court did not consider this to be a violation of the Equal Treatment Directive, even though the exceptions in the directive were not relevant to this exception. It took into consideration the proposition that the differentiation was justified because it was based upon the legitimate aim of bringing the circumstances under which the child is, in this difficult period, to be received into the adoptive family into line with the circumstances under which a newly-born child is received into the family. Therefore, the different treatment could not be regarded as a form of discrimination envisaged by the directive, as had been alleged by the Commission [Case 163/82 [1983] ECR 3273].

The term discrimination is used here as a gateway for values, which are obviously rooted in traditional views as to the allocation of roles between men and women. It is materialistic in such a way that it fixes women to the traditional role and, thereby, contributes to the reinforcement of male domination.

In the older case law of the European Court of Justice, the same result was reached by an extensive interpretation of the exceptions. In the 1986 *Johnston* case **[C32]**, the exclusion of women from the armed police force in Northern Ireland was at issue. It was argued by the Chief Constable that if female officers were armed this would increase the risk that they might become targets for assassination; that their weapons would fall into the hands of an attacker; and that it would be regarded by the public as a much greater departure from the ideal of an unarmed police force if women were to carry weapons; as well as that armed women officers would be less effective in certain areas for which women are better suited, in particular, welfare-type work which involves dealing with families and children. The court came to the following conclusion:

Article 2(2) of Directive 76/207 must be interpreted as meaning that in deciding whether, by reason of the context in which the activities of a police officer are carried out, the sex of the officer constitutes a determining factor for that occupational activity, a Member State may take into consideration requirements of public safety in order to restrict general policing duties, in an internal situation characterised by frequent assassinations, to men equipped with fire-arms.

It was positive to see that the court did not take the exception in Article 2(3) into consideration as well. The argument that women were to be protected against becoming targets for assassination was not accepted. It was not apparent that women in Northern Ireland were exposed to risks and dangers in their service with the police other than the risks to which men were exposed in the same service. The concept of protection behind Article 2(3) of the Equal Treatment Directive is not aimed at risks and dangers to which women, in themselves, are not particularly exposed. This judgment – by which the monopoly of men on violence is strengthened – is of particular importance for expectations as to future judgments of the European Court of Justice with regard to the problem of 'Women and military service'.

In the 1984 *Hoffmann* case [1984] ECR 3047, the court gave an extensive interpretation of the exceptions with regard to the protection of women. Under consideration here was whether a Member State which ensures maternity leave after compulsory confinement leave, financed by a sickness fund, is obliged, by virtue of the Equal Treatment Directive, to ensure such leave for men as well. The court denied the existence of such an obligation. It argued that the directive was designed to settle questions dealing with the organisation of the family, or to alter the division of responsibility between parents. The directive recognises the legitimacy of protecting a woman's needs in two ways. In the first place, it concerns the protection of a woman's biological condition during pregnancy and, thereafter, until such time as her physiological and mental functions have returned to normal after childbirth. In the second place, the special relationship between a woman and her child may be protected by preventing the relationship from being disturbed by the multiple burdens which would result from the simultaneous exercise of a profession.

This interpretation is far from convincing. Article 2(3) does not mention the protection of the special relationship between mother and child, but the protection of the woman in particular in case of maternity. It would have been more convincing to interpret this stipulation restrictively, in a way that only regulations which are objectively necessary for the protection of mothers are covered by the exception clause. The protection afforded above this level must be realised without making any distinction on the basis of sex. The complainant in this case justly claimed that maternity leave involved a double discrimination: in the first place, gainfully employed fathers are discriminated against in an improper way compared to gainfully employed mothers; in the second place, such a law impairs the position of women on the labour market, because it makes their employment more disadvantageous in comparison to the employment of men. Parental leave, afforded to both men and women, would relieve this disadvantageous situation, since employers then must be prepared for fathers taking parental leave as well.

The European Commission submitted a proposal for a directive on parental leave in 1983, which was revised in 1984. However, the Council has so far been unable to reach unanimity on this proposal.

The European Court of Justice has interpreted the Equal Treatment Directive in line with the prohibition on differentiation in its judgment of 25 July 1991 concerning the prohibition of nightwork for women **[D62]**. According to this judgment, regulations for the protection of female workers can be guaranteed only if the need to treat men and women unequally is justified. It is not foreseeable that, with the exception of pregnancy and maternity, the dangers incurred by nightwork are generally substantially different from those imposed on men. The danger of attacks can be countered by appropriate measures, without impairing the fundamental principle of equal treatment of men and women. The argument that a prohibition of night work for women is justified, having regard to the heavier burdens of family life imposed upon women, is rejected by the court, thereby referring to the thesis as formulated in the *Hoffmann* case; ie that the directive is not designed to settle questions concerned with the internal organisation of the family, or to alter the division of responsibility between parents. This thesis has, however, in the context of the decision on the prohibition of nightwork, a different function – it serves here to resist a breach of the principle of equal treatment. After the decision that there is no exception to Article 2(3), the court concludes from the term discrimination, without any consideration, that the directive imposes an obligation upon the Member States not to lay down a prohibition on nightwork for women as a legal principle, if no prohibition on nightwork exists for men.

. . .

In the already mentioned *Barber* decision, the precept of equal treatment is also interpreted as a strict prohibition on differentiation. Article 119 of the EEC Treaty prohibits different pay for men and women, regardless of the reason for this different treatment . . . [T]he contrast between the attitude of the European Court of Justice and the German Constitutional Court is revealing. In its judgment on different benefit payments for men and women in statutory pension schemes, the Constitutional Court exercised the role of legislator when it established – motivated by a welfare state preconception – a list of disadvantages which, in its view, are based on biological differences between men and women. Behind them there is no unequal treatment on grounds of sex, but measures that are aimed at compensation of disadvantages suffered. Such an extension of equal treatment is unknown in Community law.

The impression that the European Court has recently considered a prohibition of discrimination as a strict prohibition on differentiation is strengthened by another aspect of the *Barber* decision. There, the court rejected an attempt to remove the obligation (based upon Article 119) of the national courts to evaluate and compare the total complexity of different treatment of male and female employees in individual cases of granted benefits. The principle of equal pay should be guaranteed for each individual element of pay, and not merely after the measurement of the benefits paid to the employees in their totality. The court stresses that, otherwise, judicial control would become problematic and, consequently, the practical applicability of Article 119 of the EEC Treaty reduced. In this way, it takes account of the precedence for the strict sense of the prohibition on differentiation in a dogmatic perspective: the judge controls on the basis of fixed measures – evaluations of values are not demanded – the safeguarding of legal security follows automatically.

By contrast, with regard to the legal effects of its judgments, the court takes an attitude which would be in line with a prohibition on domination. It is not indifferent to the way in which the differentiation on grounds of sex is eliminated, but ensures the restriction of disadvantageous treatment by bringing it into line with higher levels. Thus, in the second *Defrenne* case it decided:

> In particular, since Article 119 appears in the context of the harmonisation of working conditions while the improvement is being maintained, the objection that the terms of this article may be observed in other ways than by raising the lowest salaries may be set aside.

In more recent decisions on discrimination against women in labour law and social security, it holds that,

> women are entitled to have the same rules applied to them as are applied to men who are in the same situation, since, where the directive has not been implemented, those rules remain the only valid point of reference. [See for example, Case 286/85 *McDermott and Cotter v Minister for Social Welfare* [1987] ECR 1453.]

Materialisation is undertaken with the aim of improving the status of disadvantaged groups. Prohibitions on discrimination are powerless with regard to norms and activities which, without referring to the characteristic of sex, have different consequences for men and women. They can only be overcome by a prohibition on domination. The prohibition of indirect discrimination on grounds of sex in Community law is modelled as a prohibition of domination. It protects the traditionally discriminated group of women against disadvantages. Hence, so far as this author is aware, there are no cases in which the prohibition of indirect discrimination in Community law has ever been referred to by the court for the protection of men as a group.

It has been a great merit of Community law that, through the prohibition of indirect discrimination, the structural discrimination of women has caught the attention of lawyers. If it had been limited to the protection against direct discrimination, it would slowly have become a claim for the protection of men. Norms expressly differentiating on grounds of sex have become rare. The remains would have worked to the advantage of women. A prohibition on domination, therefore, cannot but improve the situation of women under the present circumstances. From a prohibition on direct discrimination, considerable impetus towards equality may be expected.

It has not been expressly stipulated in Community law what exactly constitutes indirect discrimination. After its first opinions in the *Jenkins* case

[Case 96/80 *Jenkins v Kingsgate* [1981] ECR 911], the court gave a more extensive view of this question in the *Bilka* case. In both cases, the disadvantageous treatment of part-time workers was at issue. In the *Bilka* judgment, the court developed a 'multi-stage test scheme'. Thus, it should first be examined whether the use of a neutral criterion in fact affects a larger number of women than men. Secondly, it should be examined whether the use of the criterion can be justified. For such justification the Court of Justice sets the following criteria:

1   The measure which treats one sex disadvantageously as compared to the other sex must serve a real objective of the undertaking;
2   It must be capable of achieving the objective;
3   It must be necessary for achieving the objective.

In cases referring to social policy measures, the court referred to social policy objectives of the undertaking, rather than the satisfaction of its needs. In the *Rinner–Kühn* case [Case 171/88 [1989] ECR 2743], for example, it decided that:

> If . . . the Member State is in a position to establish that the means selected correspond to an objective necessary for its social policy and are appropriate and necessary to the attainment of that objective, the mere fact that the legislative provision affects a considerably greater number of female than of male workers cannot be regarded as an infringement of Article 119.

In some cases, the court even decided whether the justifications invoked were sufficient, while, in other cases, this decision was left to the national court. It would promote mutual co-operation with national courts and uniform application of Community law if the European Court could decide to make its opinion clear with regard to the validity of justifications invoked.

Unfortunately, the court has not always stuck to its own criteria by which the justifications are to be judged. For example, it has given its consent to the principle of seniority with regard to granting benefits (which is disadvantageous for women) without applying the strict set of criteria formulated in the *Bilka* case.

In 1988, the Commission submitted a proposal for a Directive [COM (88) 269 final] which contains, apart from a rule on the burden of proof, a definition of indirect discrimination. This stated:

1   For the purposes of the principle of equality referred to in Article 1(2), indirect discrimination exists where an apparently neutral provision, criterion or practice disproportionately disadvantages the members of one sex, by reference in particular to marital or family status, and is not objectively justified by any necessary reason or condition unrelated to the sex of the person concerned.
2   Member States shall ensure that the intentions of the respondent are not taken into account in determining whether the principle of equality has been infringed in any individual case.

This proposal for a directive is still with the Council. With regard to the definition of indirect discrimination, it is not as precise as the standard developed by the European Court of Justice.

The proposals for directives which aim at regulating the most important forms of indirect discrimination (ie the unequal treatment of part-time workers) have so far not been accepted. In accordance with a recommendation of the European Parliament, the Commission had already submitted its first proposal for a directive on part-time work in 1982, which was revised in 1983. Recently, the Commission has been attempting to take advantage of the circumstance that Article 100a of the EEC Treaty makes decisions by qualified majority possible for the realisation of the internal market. On this basis, employment relationships of more than eight hours per week must be covered by statutory social security schemes.

. . .

A broad field in which direct discrimination plays a role is the determination of pay. Community law does not only prescribe equal pay for equal work, but also equal pay for work of equal value. The directive on equal pay therefore stipulates that:

> In particular, where a job classification system is used for determining pay, it must be based on the same criteria for both men and women and so drawn up as to exclude any discrimination on grounds of sex.

In the *Rummler* case [Case 237/85 [1986] ECR 2101], the court decided that a job classification system is 'not discriminatory solely because one of its criteria is based on characteristics more commonly found among men' since, in order to be non-discriminatory, 'it must, however, be so designed that, if the nature of the work under discussion so permits, it includes as "work to which equal value is attributed" work in which other criteria are taken into account for which female employees may show particular aptitude'.

If this judgment were implemented consistently it would result in profound changes in pay systems.

Especially problematic is discrimination against pregnant women. This belongs to those patterns of behaviour from which, without formally referring to the characteristic of sex, different treatment of men and women is the result. Since only women can be affected, the court does not deal with it in relation to the rules on indirect discrimination, but the rules on direct discrimination. As a consequence, the examination of grounds for justification is not carried out. An employer who refuses to employ a woman because of her pregnancy cannot claim that he has only chosen between female candidates. The rule to be blind to differences between sexes in employment procedures implies that the occurrence of pregnancy must be disregarded, regardless of the position of the applicant. Thus, a pregnant woman is to be treated as a male person in the same situation.

For a discriminated woman, the chances of winning an action will depend upon the rules concerning the burden of proof. The case law of the European Court of Justice with regard to this question ensures the prohibition of indirect discrimination by means of a mixed decision on the burden of proof. In cases of indirect discrimination, the employer bears the burden of proof as regards grounds of justification. It may suffice for the employee to produce statistical evidence as to the disproportionately unequal treatment of members of her sex.

The proposal for a directive on the division of the burden of proof, as mentioned above, leans in the same direction. Article 3(1) of the proposal places the burden of proof on the opponent if the complainant submits facts supporting a suspicion of the existence of discrimination. According to

Article 3(2), such a suspicion will emerge if the complainant produces facts, or a constellation of facts, which indicate the existence of indirect or direct discrimination if they are not refuted.

Norms and activities which relate to the criterion of sex and which are intended to give the woman real possibilities to escape the traditional division of roles are to be judged by Article 2(4) of the Equal Treatment Directive, which provides that:

This directive shall be without prejudice to measures to promote equal opportunity for men and women, in particular by removing existing inequalities which affect women's opportunities in the areas referred to in Article 1(1) .

The European Court of Justice has not yet given its opinion with regard to the interpretation of this paragraph. In the light of the system of the directive, this paragraph should be regarded as an exception to the prohibition against individual discrimination, which should improve the collective promotion of chances for the under-represented sex. The provision is not formulated in a symmetrical manner for both sexes. Women are particularly emphasised as a target group. Furthermore, Article 2(4) of the Equal Treatment Directive is in line with Article 4(1) of the United Nations Convention on the Elimination of All Forms of Discrimination against Women, which declares that:

Adoption by State Parties of temporary special measures aimed at accelerating *de facto* equality between men and women shall not be considered discrimination as defined in the present Convention, but shall in no way entail as a consequence the maintenance of unequal or separate standards; these measures shall be discontinued when the objectives of equality of opportunity and treatment have been achieved.

Article 2(4) ot the Equal Treatment Directive opens the possibility of ensuring protection for equality modelled as a protection against domination, exceeding the protection of equality in the form of a prohibition on domination. Measures promoting equal opportunities for men and women are allowed to differentiate on grounds of sex, in so far as they are in accordance with the aim of removing domination of women by men.

The promotion of training for girls in traditionally male professions, or the offer of special courses for women (eg in order to qualify them for managing positions), are compatible with the Equal Treatment Directive. Measures promoting the employment of women in the form of quotas are also covered. The elimination of currently existing inequalities, which affect men less, and which endanger the chances of women, are only named as an example of measures to promote equal opportunity in Article 2(4). The definition of measures to promote equal opportunity is not limited to the protected group itself. A legal obligation to take measures for the promotion of equal opportunity for men and women is not yet enshrined in Community law, which merely includes a non-legally binding Council recommendation to adopt positive measures for the promotion of women [1984 OJ L331/34].

The effect of Article 2(4) of the Equal Treatment Directive does not extend so far as to allow measures which differentiate on the basis of sex in order to promote equal chances. In the area of competition law, it has been recognised by the European Court of Justice in the *Walt Wilhelm* case [Case 14/68 [1969] ECR 1] that national authorities cannot prohibit conduct of trans-national cartels on the basis of national distortion procedures, if such conduct is permitted, under Community law. It would be in line with the *Walt Wilheim* decision to interpret Community law so that measures to promote the equal opportunity of women, permitted under Article 2(4) of the Equal Treatment Directive, cannot be prohibited under national law.

. . .

So far as future perspectives are concerned, it should be noted that the eventual Maastricht Agreement on Social Policy, as signed by all of the Member States of the European Communities except for the United Kingdom, provides for the following complementation to Article 119:

This Article shall not prevent any Member State from maintaining or adopting measures providing for specific advantages in order to make it easier for women to pursue a vocational activity or to prevent or compensate for disadvantages in their professional careers.

The meaning of this paragraph, however, is limited to an exception to the principle of equal pay for men and women for equal work.

. . .

Conclusion

The general outcome from all of this is, at one and the same time, positive and depressing. The legal instruments to combat discrimination against women have been considerably improved by the Commission and the European Court of Justice. Attempts to push ahead with the equal treatment of sexes by way of further Directives have for a long time proved unsuccessful because of the consistent resistance of the Council. However, the Maastricht Agreement on Social Policy stipulates that Directives on equal treatment for men and women should, in future, require qualified voting. This would be an important step towards overcoming the stagnation caused by the principle of unanimity. Furthermore, in the Community Charter on Fundamental Social Rights of Workers, the Member States of the Community (with the exception of the United Kingdom) have declared that:

Equal opportunities for men and women must be developed. . . . Measures should also be developed enabling men and women to reconcile their occupational and family obligations

It is now to be hoped that these words may come true.

[D61]   C McCrudden: 'The effectiveness of European equality law: national mechanisms for enforcing gender equality law in the light of European requirements' (1993) 13 Oxford Journal of Legal Studies 320

4.   The objectives of European equality law

A.   The original objective of Article 119: the prevention of 'social dumping'

Article 119 was introduced into the Treaty of Rome because, without it, some countries with national equal pay laws feared that they would be at a competitive disadvantage to those Member States without such laws. Despite the primarily economic rationale for the equal pay provision in the Treaty, the requirement of non-discrimination on grounds of sex has become part of what might be described as the 'fundamental rights' aspect of the Community, an aspect which has become more prominent due to the activities of both the Community institutions, institutions in the Member States, and concerned individuals. Thus a platform of rights has been created by the Community. However, when one attempts to unpack this 'fundamental rights' justification for European equality law, searching for the deeper aims of the law, there is considerable difficulty. To explain why, it will be useful to sketch out two alternative models of the objectives of anti-discrimination law: the individual justice model and the group justice model.

B.   Individual justice model

The individual justice model is generally consistent with a view that the aim of anti-discrimination law is to secure the reduction of discrimination by eliminating from decisions illegitimate considerations based on gender which have harmful consequences for individuals. Some have argued that a reduction in gender discrimination is necessary because discriminatory actions are said to be unfair to the individual discriminated against, because (for example) that person is being judged on the basis of personal characteristics which are immutable (their gender) and therefore ones over which the person discriminated against has no choice. The individual justice approach concentrates on cleansing the process of decision making, and is not concerned with the result, except as an indicator of a flawed process. It is markedly individualistic in its orientation: concentrating on securing fairness for the individual. It is generally expressed in universal and symmetrical terms: women and men are equally protected. It reflects respect for efficiency, merit and achievement and, given the limited degree of intervention permitted, it preserves and possibly enhances the operation of the market. It is 'manageable' in that its aims can be stated with some degree of certainty, and its application does not depend on extensive factual inquiries and judgments of a social scientific kind.

Despite its obvious attractions, this model has been criticised as limited. It is said to underestimate the deep structure of gender discrimination, which is seen to be as often institutional as individual. The individual justice model, it is said, misconceives the nature of the problem as being one of an individual's intention rather than the effect of institutionalised processes.

The model is said not to take adequately into account the surrounding and reinforcing nature of women's disadvantage, and concentrates only on particular actions in assessing whether there should be legal intervention, ignoring the wider picture.

C.   Group justice model

Out of these criticisms come various alternative approaches. Some have argued for an approach which is concerned with the results of decision making and which seeks to redistribute resources from the group of advantaged men to the group of disadvantaged women. Common to such approaches is a view that the aim of anti-discrimination law should be to fix on the outcomes of the decision-making processes. The basic aim is the improvement of the relative position of women and men, whether to redress past subordination and discrimination, or out of a concern for distributive justice at the present time. These approaches tend to be redistributive and to be concerned with the relative position of groups or classes, rather than individuals. The principle is often expressed in asymmetrical terms as focusing on the betterment of women and is less concerned with symmetrical protection for men.

D.   The alternative models and European equality law

The difficulty with specifying the aims of European equality law is that it would seem most consistent with the evidence to view the legislators as intending to adopt modified versions of both the individual justice *and* the group justice models. The intention to further the individual justice model is reflected in the following attributes of the legislation: the individualistic nature of the requirement that individuals must be provided with an adequate remedy through a judicial process; the concentration on the eradication of discrimination as the prime target of legal enforcement, rather than on the broader aim of achieving equality of opportunity, for example; and the generally symmetrical nature of the protection accorded. The European Court of Justice has adopted the individual justice model as an underlying objective of Article 119 and the directives. Indeed, A G Tesauro has gone so far as to say that the major principle underlying the court's approach is to make individual rights more effective, and to create the circumstances by which the individual is used as the instrument for securing more general social policy goals through litigation. The limitations of this approach may lead to the group justice objective, the more social engineering of the two objectives, being neglected except as an indirect result of the successes of the individual justice approach, unless the group justice objective is enforced in other ways.

However, the individual rights model as adopted in the directives is modified by the adoption of aspects of the group justice model. The intention to further a limited version of the group justice model is reflected in the following attributes of the legislation: the prohibition of indirect discrimination (and its expansive interpretation by the European Court of Justice); the inclusion of the exception relating to maternity in Article 2(3) of the 1976 Directive; the inclusion of exceptions permitting limited positive action in Article 2(4) of the 1976 Directive, which would otherwise have amounted to reverse discrimination; the provisions in the directives requiring Member States to take the necessary measures to ensure that provisions in collective agreements which are contrary to the equality principle be declared null and void or be amended, and in the recent case law of the European Court of Justice dealing with pregnancy in which the concern is with disadvantages to women and no symmetrical comparison was required. In assessing what the objectives of European equality law are, we have therefore a complex picture of mixed intentions. Aspects of both the individual justice and group justice models seem to have been adopted.

Question

How far does McCrudden's distinction between individual and group justice correspond to the interests protectable under Colneric's division **[D60]** between differentiation and domination?

[D62]   Case C-345/89 Alfred Stoeckel [1991] ECR I-4047

[This was a preliminary reference made by a French court on the interpretation of Directive 76/207 on the implementation of the principle of equal treatment for men and women as regards access to employment, vocational training and promotion, and working conditions.]

The European Court of Justice

2. That question was raised in criminal proceedings against Mr Stoeckel, an executive of Suma, who was charged with employing 77 women to work at night on 28 October 1988 contrary to Article L 213-1 of the French [Labour Code].

3. Pursuant to Article 5 of Directive 76/207, application of the principle of equal treatment with regard to working conditions means that men and women are to be offered the same conditions without discrimination on grounds of sex. To that end, the Member States are to take the measures necessary to ensure that any provisions contrary to the principle of equal treatment are to be abolished (paragraph 2(a)) and that any provisions contrary to that principle are to be revised when the concern for protection which originally inspired them is no longer well founded (paragraph 2(c)). However, by virtue of Article 2(3), the directive is to be without prejudice to provisions concerning the protection of women, particularly as regards pregnancy and maternity.

. . .

5. Pursuant to Article L213-1 of the French [Labour Code], women may not be employed for any nightwork, in particular in plants, factories or workshops of any kind whatsoever. However, the same article provides for a number of exceptions, relating for example to management posts or executive technical posts and to situations where, because of particularly serious circumstances, provision must be made for the prohibition of nightwork by women employees working in successive shifts to be suspended when the national interest so requires, under the conditions and in the circumstances envisaged in the [Labour Code].

6. It is apparent from the documents before the court that, as a result of economic difficulties brought about by foreign competition, Suma found it necessary to consider laying off about 200 people at its Obenheim factory.

However, having calculated that the number and the effects of the redundancies could be limited if a continuous shift-work system were adopted, involving nightwork for all the workforce, Suma undertook negotiations with the unions with a view to concluding an agreement between them and the company.

7. In an agreement concluded for that purpose . . ., it was stipulated that recourse to nightwork was an exceptional measure and that Suma would revert to day-work only as soon as the economic constraints had ceased. In view of the fact that the female workers in the company had the necessary skills for the posts that had been retained, the parties, wishing to ensure that women were given the same opportunities as men, agreed to make all posts available to both men and women, subject to approval by a majority vote of the female workers. A majority voted in favour of the shift-work system and it was introduced with effect from 1 October 1988.

. . .

12. As the court stated in its judgment in Case 152/84 *Marshall v Southampton and South West Hampshire Health Authority* [C27], . . . Article 5 of Directive 76/207 does not confer on the Member States the right to limit the application of the principle of equal treatment in its field of operation or subject it to conditions and that provision is sufficiently precise and unconditional to be capable of being relied upon by an individual before a national court in order to avoid the application of any national provision not conforming to Article 5(1), which lays down the principle of equal treatment with regard to working conditions.

13. Moreover, pursuant to Article 2(3), the directive is to be without prejudice to provisions concerning the protection of women, particularly as regards pregnancy and maternity. In its judgment in Case 222/84 *Johnston v Chief Constable of the Royal Ulster Constabulary* [C32] . . ., the court held that it was clear from the express reference to pregnancy and maternity that the directive was intended to protect a woman's biological condition and the special relationship which exists between a woman and her child.

14. The French and Italian governments submit that the prohibition of nightwork by women, which is in any case subject to numerous exceptions, is in conformity with the general aims of protecting female workers and with particular considerations of a social nature relating, for example, to the risks of attack and the heavier domestic workload borne by women.

15. As far as the aims of protecting female workers are concerned, they are valid only if, having regard to the principles mentioned above, there is a justified need for a difference of treatment as between men and women. However, whatever the disadvantages of nightwork may be, it does not seem that, except in the case of pregnancy or maternity, the risks to which women are exposed when working at night are, in general, inherently different from those to which men are exposed.

16. As regards the risks of attack, if it is assumed that they are greater at night than during the day, appropriate measures can be adopted to deal with them without undermining the fundamental principle of equal treatment for men and women.

17. As far as family responsibilities are concerned, the court has already held that the directive is not designed to settle questions concerned with the organisation of the family or to alter the division of responsibility

between parents (see the judgment in Case 184/83 *Hofman* [1984] ECR 3047).

18. Thus, the concern to provide protection, by which the general prohibition of nightwork by women was originally inspired, no longer appears to be well founded and the maintenance of that prohibition, by reason of risks that are not peculiar to women or preoccupations unconnected with the purposes of Directive 76/207, cannot be justified by the provisions of Article 2(3) of the Directive.

. . .

19. As regards the numerous exceptions provided for in the legislation of the Member States which retain a prohibition of nightwork by women, to which the French and Italian governments refer, they cannot adequately uphold the objectives of the directive, since the latter prohibits the laying down of a general principle excluding women from undertaking nightwork, and, moreover, they may be a source of discrimination.

[D63]   Case C-271/91 Marshall v Southampton and South West Hampshire Area Health Authority (No 2) [1993] ECR I-4367

In the light of the Court of Justice's earlier ruling in *Marshall (No 1)* **[C27]**, the English Court of Appeal had remitted her claim against dismissal to the industrial tribunal for consideration of the amount of compensation to be awarded. The latter assessed Miss Marshall's loss at £18,405, including £7,710 by way of interest, and awarded her £19,405, including a sum of £1,000 compensation for injury to feelings. However, at the relevant time there was a ceiling to the amount of compensation payable for unlawful sex discrimination under the Sex Discrimination Act 1975, the limit being £6,250. There was also doubt as to whether an industrial tribunal could award interest on compensation. The case was referred by the House of Lords under Article 177 to ascertain the compatibility of these restrictions with Article 6 of Directive 76/207, which provides:

> Member States shall introduce into their national legal systems such measures as are necessary to enable all persons who consider themselves wronged by failure to apply to them the principle of equal treatment . . . to pursue their claims by judicial process after possible recourse to other competent authorities.

The European Court of Justice (Judgment, 2 August 1993)

19. The purpose of the directive is to put into effect in the Member States the principle of equal treatment for men and women as regards the various aspects of employment, in particular working conditions, including the conditions governing dismissal.

20. To that end, Article 2 establishes the principle of equal treatment and its limits, whilst Article 5(1) defines the scope of that principle with regard specifically to working conditions, including conditions governing dismissal, to the effect that men and women are to be guaranteed the same conditions without discrimination on grounds of sex.

21. As the court held in Case 152/84 *Marshall* . . . since Article 5(1) prohibits generally and unequivocaly all discrimination on grounds of sex, in particular with regard to dismissal, it may be relied upon as against a state authority acting in its capacity as an employer, in order to avoid the application of any national provision which does not conform to that article.

22. Article 6 of the directive puts Member States under a duty to take the necessary measures to enable all persons who consider themselves wronged by discrimination to pursue their claims by judicial process. Such obligation implies that the measures in question should be sufficiently effective to achieve the objective of the directive and should be capable of being effectively relied upon by the persons concerned before national courts.

23. As the court held in . . . Case 14/83 *Von Colson and Kamann v Land Nordrhein-Westfalen* **[C29]** . . . Article 6 does not prescribe a specific measure to be taken in the event of a breach of the prohibition of discrimination, but leaves Member States free to choose between the different solutions suitable for achieving the objective of the directive, depending on the different situations which may arise.

24. However, the objective is to arrive at real equality of opportunity and cannot therefore be attained in the absence of measures appropriate to restore such equality when it has not been observed. As the court stated in . . . *Von Colson* . . . those measures must be such as to guarantee real and effective judicial protection and have a real deterrent effect on the employer.

25. Such requirements necessarily entail that the particular circumstances of each breach of the principle of equal treatment should be taken into account. In the event of discriminatory dismissal contrary to Article 5(1) of the directive, a situation of equality could not be restored without either reinstating the victim of discrimination or, in the alternative, granting financial compensation for the loss and damage sustained.

26. Where financial compensation is the measure adopted in order to achieve the objective indicated above, it must be adequate, in that it must enable the loss and damage actually sustained as a result of the discriminatory dismissal to be made good in full in accordance with the applicable national rules.

The first and second questions

27. In its first question, the House of Lords seeks to establish whether it is contrary to Article 6 of the directive for national provisions to lay down an upper limit on the amount of compensation recoverable by a victim of discrimination.

28. In its second question, the House of Lords asks whether Article 6 requires (a) that the compensation for the damage sustained as a result of the illegal discrimination should be full and (b) that it should include an award of interest on the principal amount from the date of the unlawful discrimination to the date when compensation is paid.

29. The court's interpretation of Article 6 as set out above provides a direct reply to the first part of the second question relating to the level of compensation required by that provision.

30. It also follows from that interpretation that the fixing of an upper limit of the kind at issue in the main proceedings cannot, by definition, constitute proper implementation of Article 6 of the directive, since it limits the amount of compensation a priori to a level which is not necessarily consistent with

the requirement of ensuring real equality of opportunity through adequate reparation for the loss and damage sustained as a result of discriminatory dismissal.

31. With regard to the second part of the second question relating to the award of interest, suffice it to say that full compensation for the loss and damage sustained as a result of discriminatory dismissal cannot leave out of account factors, such as the effluxion of time, which may in fact reduce its value. The award of interest, in accordance with the applicable national rules, must therefore be regarded as an essential component of compensation for the purposes of restoring real equality of treatment.

32. Accordingly, the reply to be given to the first and second questions is that the interpretation of Article 6 of the directive must be that reparation of the loss and damage sustained by a person injured as a result of discriminatory dismissal may not be limited to an upper limit fixed a priori or by excluding an award of interest to compensate for the loss sustained by the recipient of the compensation as a result of the effluxion of time until the capital sum awarded is actually paid.

[D64] Cases C-109/91, C-110/91, C-152/91 and C-200/91 Ten Oever v Stichting Bedrijfspensioenfonds voor het Glazenwassers-en Schoonmaakbedrijf, Moroni v Firma Collo GmbH, Neath v Hugh Steeper Ltd, Coloroll Pension Trustees Ltd v Russell, Mangham and others

Opinion of Advocate General Van Gerven (28 April 1993)

The court's case law on Article 119 of the EEC Treaty and the judgment in Barber

3. As is well known, Article 119 of the Treaty lays down the obligation that the Member States must ensure in principle that men and women receive equal pay for equal work. 'Pay' is defined in the second paragraph of Article 119 as 'the ordinary basic or minimum wage or salary and any other consideration, whether in cash or in kind, which the worker receives, directly or indirectly, in respect of his employment from his employer'. Since its judgment in the first *Defrenne* case the court has developed a broad interpretation of the concept of pay as thus defined: it includes 'any other consideration, whether in cash or in kind, whether immediate or future, provided that the worker receives it, albeit indirectly, in respect of his employment from his employer' [Case 80/70 *Defrenne v Belgium* [1971] ECR 445].

Moreover, in the second *Defrenne* case the court went on to hold that Article 119 'applies directly, and without the need for more detailed implementing measures on the part of the Community or the Member States, to all forms of direct and overt discrimination which may be identified solely with the aid of the criteria of equal work and equal pay referred to by the article in question'. [Quotation from Case 129/79 *Macarthys Ltd v Wendy Smith* [1980] ECR 1275, referring to Case 43/75 *Defrenne (No 2)* [1976] ECR 455.]

As far as the interpretation of 'consideration' in Article 119 is concerned, the court had held in *Defrenne (No 1)* that social security schemes and benefits, in particular old age pensions, although in principle not entirely separate from the concept of pay, did not fall under the concept of consideration. The court came to this decision on the basis of the following characteristics of social security systems: (1) they are directly governed by legislation without any element of agreement within the undertaking or trade concerned and are obligatorily applicable to general categories of workers; and (2) they provide workers with the benefit of a statutory scheme to which workers, employers and in some cases the public authorities contribute financially in a measure determined less by the employment relationship between the employer and the worker than by considerations of social policy, so that the employer's contribution cannot be regarded as a direct or indirect payment to the worker for the purposes of Article 119. However, in its judgment . . . in the *Bilka-Kaufhaus* case [Case 170/84 [1986] ECR 1607], the court, applying those criteria, came to the view that benefits paid under an occupational pension scheme originating in an agreement between the employer and the staff committee and forming an integral part of the contract of employment are to be classified as 'consideration' within the meaning of Article 119.

4. In the *Barber* case [Case C-262/88 *Barber v Guardian Royal Exchange Assurance Group* [1990] ECR I-1889] the court had to consider a 'contracted-out' pension scheme approved under United Kingdom legislation, that is to say an occupational pension scheme established in consultation between the social partners or by unilateral decision of the employer, financed by the employer alone or by employer and employees combined, and which employees may join in partial substitution for their statutory pension. From the principles set out above the court deduced that 'a pension paid under a contracted-out scheme constitutes consideration paid by the employer to the worker in respect of his employment and consequently falls within the scope of Article 119 of the Treaty'.

Asked whether a scheme under which a man made compulsorily redundant was entitled only to a deferred pension at the normal pensionable age whilst a woman in the same circumstances was entitled to a pension which was payable immediately was compatible with Article 119, the court replied in the negative. The reasons given by the court in paragraph 32 of its judgment were that:

> Article 119 prohibits any discrimination with regard to pay as between men and women, whatever the system which gives rise to such inequality. Accordingly, it is contrary to Article 119 to impose an age condition which differs according to sex in respect of pensions paid under a contracted-out scheme, even if the difference between the pensionable age for men and that for women is based on the one provided for by the national statutory scheme.

5. The court was, however, aware of the tremendous financial implications of its judgment. It also considered that, in view of the exceptions to the principle of equal treatment regarding pensionable age provided for in Directives 79/7 and 86/738, the Member States could reasonably have taken the view that Article 119 was not applicable to pensions paid under a contracted-out scheme. For those two reasons the court decided to limit the effect of its judgment in time:

In those circumstances, overriding considerations of legal certainty preclude legal situations which have exhausted all their effects in the past from being called in question where that might upset retroactively the financial balance of many contracted-out pension schemes. It is appropriate, however, to provide for an exception in favour of individuals who have taken action in good time in order to safeguard their rights. Finally, it must be pointed out that no restriction on the effects of the aforesaid interpretation can be permitted as regards the acquisition of entitlement to a pension as from the date of this judgment.

The court therefore held that:

The direct effect of Article 119 of the Treaty may not be relied upon in order to claim entitlement to a pension with effect from a date prior to that of this judgment, except in the case of workers or those claiming under them who have before that date initiated legal proceedings or raised an equivalent claim under the applicable national law.

Upon the phrases 'legal situations which have exhausted all their effects in the past', 'the acquisition of entitlement to a pension as from the date of this judgment' and 'a pension with effect from a date prior to this judgment' the issues arising in the present cases from the limitation in time of the effects of the *Barber* judgment turn.

. . .

The operation in time of the Barber judgment

10. *Possible interpretations* . . . Apparently, there are some four possible interpretations of the limitation which the court sought to place on the operation in time of its judgment in the *Barber* case.

A *first interpretation* would be to apply the principle of equal treatment only to workers who became members of, and began to pay contributions to, an occupational scheme as from 17 May 1990 [the date of the *Barber* judgment]. This view would deprive the *Barber* judgment of almost all retroactive effect. In practical terms, it would mean that the full effect of the judgment would be felt only after a period of about 40 years.

A *second interpretation* is that the principle of equal treatment should only be applied to benefits payable in respect of periods of service after 17 May 1990. Periods of service prior to that date would not be affected by the direct effect of Article 119.

According to a *third interpretation*, the principle of equal treatment must be applied to all pensions which are payable or paid for the first time after 17 May 1990, irrespective of the fact that all or some of the pension accrued during, and on the basis of, periods of service completed or contributions paid prior to that date. In other words, it is not the periods of service (before or after the judgment in *Barber*) which are decisive, but the date on which the pension falls to be paid.

A *fourth interpretation* would be to apply equal treatment to all pension payments made after 17 May 1990, including benefits or pensions which had already fallen due and, here again, as in the previous interpretation, irrespective of the date of the periods of service during which the pension accrued. This interpretation undoubtedly has the most far-reaching effect.

. . .

12. In order to put the issues arising in these cases in their full setting, attention must also be drawn to the 'Protocol concerning Article 119 of the Treaty Establishing the European Community' annexed to the Treaty on European Union, although that Treaty, signed at Maastricht on 7 February 1992, is not yet in force. The Protocol provides:

> For the purposes of Article 119 of this Treaty, benefits under occupational social security schemes shall not be considered as remuneration if and in so far as they are attributable to periods of employment prior to 17 May 1990, except in the case of workers or those claiming under them who have before that date initiated legal proceedings or introduced an equivalent claim under the applicable national law.

The significance of that Protocol for the interpretation to be given to the effect in time of the judgment in *Barber* is a matter to which I shall soon return.

. . .

21. *Proposed interpretation* . . . I choose the second interpretation mentioned in paragraph 10 above.

This interpretation sits most easily with the good faith of employers and of occupational pension schemes since account must indeed be taken of their belief that conditions as to pensionable age varying according to sex were permissible. In *Barber* this was recognised by the court in as many words.

. . .

The fact that the good faith of the parties concerned, in particular of employers and occupational pension funds, is to be taken into account means that, before *Barber*, those parties, in the belief that Article 119 was not applicable, could promise pensions and make payments based on a different pensionable age for men and women. The *financial balance* of the pension schemes concerned could therefore be maintained on that basis before the judgment. Only in respect of periods of service *after Barber* did employers know that in administering occupational pension schemes and calculating the contributions to be made to them account had to be taken of a pensionable age which was the same for men and women. If no account were taken of their good faith and that of pension scheme administrators, this would entail serious financial problems for pension schemes. All these factors argue in favour of not allowing obligations entered into and payments made before the date of the *Barber* judgment to be affected.

. . .

23. The interpretation of the temporal limitation of the effects of the *Barber* judgment which I propose here largely coincides with that adopted in the Protocol on Article 119 annexed to the Treaty on European Union. I would, moreover, point out that if the court should come to a different conclusion, its decision would be entirely superseded as soon as the Treaty on European Union comes into force.

Article 239 of the EEC Treaty will be applicable to the Protocol which is to be annexed to the EEC Treaty: as soon as the Treaty on European Union comes into force, that Protocol will become an integral part of the EEC Treaty. In other words, it will have the same legal force as a provision of the Treaty. I would, however, emphasise that the Protocol is not intended to amend Article 119 nor does it appear to call in question the decisions of the court. Indeed, the fifth indent of Article B of the Treaty on European Union expressly confirms that one of the Union's objectives is 'to maintain in full the *acquis communautaire* and build on it', that is to say the entire body of the existing Community rules as interpreted and applied by the court. Accordingly, I see in the Protocol no more than a *declaratory determination of meaning* adopted in relation to Article 119 and the case law of the court.

Note.   In its judgment of 6 October 1993, dealing only with the *Ten Oever* case, the Court of Justice adopted the Advocate General's view as to the temporal limitations of *Barber*.

[D65]   Catherine Barnard: 'A social policy for Europe: Politicians 1: 0 Lawyers' (1992) 8 International Journal of Comparative Labour Law and Industrial Relations 15

European social policy is currently a hotchpot of declarations and principles, the consequence of political expediency rather than a coherent strategy. The fiasco at the Maastricht summit over the now infamous Social Chapter illustrates the extent to which social policy, certainly so far as Britain is concerned, has become a political football – a rallying point for the Tory faithful which has successfully diverted attention away from the more contentious issue of economic and monetary union and the sovereignty-threatening questions of federalism.

But now the dust has begun to settle, the legality of the political compromises must be considered. Important practical questions must be addressed – what is the status of the Social Chapter and to what extent is Britain bound by it? This article aims to demonstrate that first, Britain's refusal to sign the Chapter does not mean that it is immune from its consequences and, indeed, may be bound in more ways than it suspects; secondly, that a legal challenge to the validity of the British government's stance will unearth a Pandora's box of difficulties; thirdly, that the Chapter is not the hot bed of radicalism that has been portrayed; and, fourthly, that Britain's stance may set a precedent that does long-term damage to the integrity of the European community as a whole. The inevitable conclusion is that the Social Chapter is a political compromise to a political crisis: in the face of such forces, the law is largely impotent.

1.   *European social policy*

In order to consider the impact of the Social Chapter, it is first necessary to examine the existing provisions of the Treaty of Rome relating to social policy.

(a)   *The Treaty of Rome and the Social Charter*

The Treaty of Rome, as amended by the Single European Act, makes fairly extensive specific provision for secondary legislation regarding social policy. Most obviously, Article 118a provides the legal basis for directives concerning the health and safety of workers, and Article 100a(2) provides the legal basis for legislation concerning the rights and interests of employed persons. In addition, Article 119 lays down the principle of equal pay for men and women. More broadly, Article 51 permits the European Community to adopt measures in the field of social security necessary to facilitate the free movement of workers, and Articles 49, 57 and 63 grant the community the power to legislate for free movement of workers, the provision of services and the right of establishment.

Where these legal powers have proved inadequate, Articles 100 (approximation of laws) and 235 (residual legal basis where the Treaty has not provided the necessary powers) – both articles requiring unanimity in Council – have been used as general bases to fill the gap. For example, Directive 75/117 on equal pay was based on Article 100, and Directive 76/207 was based on Article 235.

. . .

The Social Charter, agreed by 11 (not including the United Kingdom) of the 12 Member States during the Strasbourg summit in 1989, was designed to extend the social dimension of the European Community. In fact, this 'solemn declaration of fundamental social rights' has no legal effect: it does not constitute an amendment to the Treaty . . ., nor does it fit the description of one of the forms of secondary legislation recognised by Article 189 EEC. It is, therefore, a purely political proclamation.

The implementation of the principles set out in the Social Charter, and, consequently, the creation of legally enforceable norms, is entirely dependent on the Commission's Action Programme, drawn up to implement them. However, every proposal put forward by the Commission as part of the Action Programme has to follow the conventional course of any piece of secondary legislation: it has to find a legal basis in the Treaty of Rome itself. This means that the United Kingdom is bound by any social legislation resulting from the Action Programme, irrespective of the fact that it has refused to sign the Charter.

The legal basis debate came to the fore during discussions concerning the adoption of the working time directive. The Commission, anxious to secure the enactment of the directive, argued that Article 118a (requiring qualified majority voting in Council) was the appropriate basis, while the British government, far less enthusiastic about the directive, argued that Article 100a(2) (requiring unanimity in Council) was more suitable. Had the directive been approved on the basis of Article 118a, the British government could have sought annulment of the directive in judicial review proceedings using Article 173 EEC.

(b) The Social Chapter

The compromise on the Social Chapter is the next episode in what is becoming a long-running saga. In a last-ditch attempt to forge an agreement on the Political Union Treaty, the Dutch Presidency was forced to remove the Social Chapter from the main body of the Treaty and list it in a protocol with an annexed agreement approved by all of the Member States except Britain. The 11 noted their intention 'to continue along the path laid down in the Social Charter of 1989', and agreed to have recourse to the Community institutions, procedures and mechanisms, adapted as necessary to take into account the British absence, in order to take decisions. The United Kingdom will not take part in the deliberations in Council meetings and acts adopted by the Council. Any financial consequences, other than administrative costs entailed by the institutions, will not apply to the United Kingdom.

The 11 Member States have agreed that the following issues can be decided by qualified majority vote:

- health and safety
- working conditions
- information and consultation of workers
- equality at work between men and women
- integration of persons excluded from the labour market.

Issues for unanimous vote include:

- social security and social protection of workers
- protection of workers where their employment contract is terminated
- representation and collective defence of the interests of workers and employers, including co-determination
- conditions of employment for third-country nationals
- financial contributions for promotion of employment and job creation.

Pay, the right of association, and the right to strike or the right to impose lock-outs, are not covered by these provisions.

So how will this work in practice? It seems most likely that new measures will first be proposed on the strength of existing specific legal bases contained in the Treaty of Rome, in an effort to ensure that Britain is securely bound by any new legislation.

. . .

2.   Is the United Kingdom bound by the provisions of the Social Chapter?

As far as the law is concerned, the answer is a qualified 'No'. However, so far as practicalities are concerned, the answer is a qualified 'Yes'.

(a)   International law

The Social Chapter, as an agreement between 11 out of the 12 Member States, cannot constitute an amendment to the Treaty of Rome in accordance with Article 236. The procedure required . . . has not been satisfied. Consequently, the Social Chapter must constitute an agreement between the 11 Member States which is binding at the level of international law.

. . .

(b)   European Community law

The first question must inevitably be: are the Maastricht Treaties, including the Social Chapter, part of European Community law? Is it possible to have some form of hybrid agreement whereby the 12 agree to the majority of the Treaty but only 11 agree to the remainder? . . . It is therefore important for the European Court to give a ruling, first, on the legality of such a hybrid agreement and, secondly, on the Social Chapter itself.

This begs the next two questions: first, how can the matter be brought before the court, and on what basis can the challenge be made; and, secondly, if the European Court finds that the Maastricht Treaty constitutes a valid amendment to the Treaty of Rome and that it is lawful to have a separate Protocol which is agreed upon by the 11, to what extent is the European Court's decision binding on the United Kingdom?

It seems that objections to the British exclusion from the Social Chapter can be raised on two grounds. First, that it contravenes basic fundamental rights, and, secondly, that it is anti-competitive. These arguments will be developed below. However, it also seems that, whatever procedure is chosen as the appropriate method for challenge, it will be so fraught with difficulty that non-legal solutions may be the only answer.

(i)   Proceedings before the national court and the problem of Article 177 references

The first possibility of challenge would be by virtue of judicial review proceedings in the national court, brought under the Order 53 procedure. If, for example, a foreign trade union was prepared to take up the cudgels, it could seek a declaration from the Divisional Court that the British government's action, in refusing to sign the Social Chapter, was illegal. It could argue that the government has acted unlawfully in setting up barriers to the free movement of persons within the Community, contrary to Articles 3(c) and 48 EEC. The argument would run as follows: the government's refusal to sign the Social Chapter will inevitably act as a potential deterrent to the fundamental principle of free movement, since workers will not be guaranteed the same standards of rights in the United Kingdom as elsewhere in the Community.

Alternatively, a British trade union could seek judicial review proceedings in order to argue that the government's actions are potentially anti-competitive and, therefore, unlawful. One of the reasons which the government gave for refusing to sign the Social Chapter is that the United Kingdom would lose its competitive edge if labour costs were forced to increase. Mr Jacques Delors, the President of the European Commission, recognised this in his angry exclamation after the Maastricht summit that 'Britain will become a paradise for investment'. There is an element of truth in this fear . . . The British government's stance is, however, a classic example of a desire to distort competition within the European Community, contrary to the principles contained in Article 2 (approximation of the economic policies of the Member States), Article 3(f) ('ensuring that competition in the common market is not distorted'), and, most significantly, Article 5 [duty of solidarity] . . . This Article has assumed a new significance in the light of the momentous decisions of *Marleasing* [C31] and *Francovich* [C33]. Whether Article 5 represents a free-standing right, or is dependent on other directly applicable articles for its force, is not entirely clear. *Francovich* does, however, make clear that Article 5 imposes an obligation on a Member State 'to make good the unlawful consequences of a breach of Community law'. In either case, if uncertainty does arise as to interpretation, the Divisional Court would be able to refer the matter to the European Court for assistance, under Article 177 EEC.

However, in both potential applications for judicial review, the various unions may experience difficulty in satisfying the locus standi requirements. Section 31(3) of the Supreme Court Act 1981 requires the applicant to have 'sufficient interest in the matter to which the application relates'.

. . .

The second possibility of challenge would involve an action brought by an individual. The following examples illustrate the point.

It is 1994, the Maastricht agreements and the Social Chapter have come into force and various legislation, including a 'directive' on the consultation of individual workers prior to redundancy, has been based on the Social Chapter protocol. The United Kingdom is apparently not bound by the directive. Fred, an employee in a small company, is made redundant without the necessary consultation required by the 'directive'. He brings an action for unfair dismissal before the industrial tribunal and seeks to rely on the 'directive' to assist his case. His employer maintains that the United Kingdom is not bound by the 'directive'. Fred, in reply, argues that first, national law should be interpreted in the light of Community law and, secondly, that he has been denied equality of treatment on the grounds of his nationality under Article 7 EEC. Once again, the tribunal might be persuaded to make a reference to the European Court for an interpretation of the status of legislation based on the Social Chapter and its implications for the United Kingdom.

. . .

But all of this is mere speculation if the court does not have jurisdiction or declines to give a ruling under Article 177. While the European Court would clearly have jurisdiction to interpret Articles 2, 3, 5, 7 and 48 EEC, it may not have jurisdiction to examine the operation of these articles in the light of the Social Chapter. Article 177 references are only available for the interpretation of 'this Treaty' and 'acts of the institutions of the Community'. If the Social Chapter does not constitute an effective amendment to the Treaty of Rome, then does the Social Chapter, and any legislation emanating from it, become 'acts of the institutions'?

. . .

(c)   Practical implications of the Social Chapter

The Protocol on social policy envisages that the 11 will 'borrow' the machinery and procedures of the institutions. However, while it has been made very clear that any British employment minister would not be welcome at Council meetings discussing Social Chapter issues, the use of the institutional machinery will inevitably mean that British Commission officials will be involved in initiating policy, British MEPs will be involved in Parliamentary debates and a British judge may be involved in adjudicating any questions arising in connection with the Chapter.

In addition, the CBI, as part of UNICE, the European employers' organisation, is likely to be involved in the consultation between management and labour envisaged by Article 3 of the new agreement, as will the TUC and the European TUC. By November [1991], the CBI had already agreed, albeit reluctantly, to support a proposal designed to give the 'social partners' the opportunity to amend Commission directives and then make recommendations on them. The Social Chapter proposals will build on this understanding. Such European co-operation will inevitably have knock-on consequences: a greater involvement by the British trade union movement in negotiations at a European level will raise awareness of the advantages enjoyed by workers on the continent who have benefited from European social legislation. This will inevitably lead to comparisons being drawn between the situation in Europe and that at home, which may have a long-term impact on national collective bargaining.

Furthermore, whatever directives the 11 states decide to enact under the Maastricht protocol, could still have an impact on British companies and employees. Many multinationals operating in different European countries tend to see Europe as one administrative zone. Large companies, such as Unilever, have already indicated that they are likely to ignore the British 'opt-out' altogether, not wishing to differentiate between parts of Europe regarding employment conditions, particularly if the current United Kingdom stance is viewed as resulting from political expediency rathen than conviction. Other personnel managers have suggested that they would probably include the United Kingdom in low-cost protocol measures such as works councils, but try to opt out of the more costly measures. Furthermore, British multinationals with companies elsewhere in the European Community will be obliged to give effect, in the other Member States at least, to any directives enacted under the Social Protocol. As a result, some British employees and British companies will be affected by legislation over which the British government will have no influence. This has prompted some of the larger employers to argue that Britain should have fought for a diluted version of the Social Chapter which could be signed by all 12.

[D66] House of Lords Select Committee on the European Communities, Session 1992-93 3rd Report: Human rights re-examined. Memorandum by Professor Bob Hepple of University College, London

Introduction

1. This memorandum discusses the relevance of the Council of Europe's European Social Charter (the ESC) to the inquiry into Community Accession to the European Convention on Human Rights (the ECHR).

. . .

2. . . . this issue has now assumed some importance because of developments since 1986 . . .:

(1) The third paragraph of the Preamble to the Single European Act 1986 (SEA) expressly refers to the fundamental rights recognised in the ESC as well as those in the ECHR.

(2) Since 1986 the European Court of Justice has, on at least one occasion, used the ESC as a source of general principles of Community law (Case 24/86 *Blaizot v Belgium* [1988] ECR 379, in which Article 10 of the ESC was used to support an interpretation of 'vocational training' as including university education).

(3) The Parliamentary Assembly of the Council of Europe (Resolution 931/1989) has put forward a number of arguments in favour of accession by the Community to the ESC and called on the Community to enter into discussions with the Council of Europe in order for it to adapt its ESC so that the Community could accede to it.

(4) Following the recent ratifications by Belgium . . ., Luxembourg . . .

and Portugal . . ., all Member States of the Community have now accepted the ESC.

(5) The Preamble to the Community Charter of the Fundamental Social Rights of Workers, adopted in December 1989 as a 'solemn declaration' by all the Heads of Government apart from the United Kingdom, recites that it draws inspiration 'from the Conventions of the International Labour Organisation and from the European Social Charter of the Council of Europe'. There is a considerable degree of overlap between the rights guaranteed in the ESC and those set out in the Community Charter (see below).

(6) The Maastricht Treaty of European Union contains an undertaking to 'respect fundamental human rights as guaranteed by the European Convention on Human Rights'. Although the Treaty makes no express reference to the ESC, it includes similar objectives to those of the ESC, for example 'to promote economic and social progress' and the 'strengthening of economic and social cohesion'. Article 2 of the revised Community Treaty contains principles very similar to those in Part I of the ESC, namely 'a high level of employment and of social protection, the raising of the standard and quality of living, and economic and social cohesion and solidarity among Member States'.

(7) The Maastricht Protocol on Social Policy notes that 11 Member States 'wish to continue along the path laid down in the Social Charter of 1989' and authorises them 'to have recourse to the institutions, procedures and mechanisms of the Community for the purposes of taking among themselves and applying as far as they are concerned the necessary decisions'. The Agreement adopted by the 11 extends the principle of qualified majority voting established by the SEA for health and safety matters to new areas of social policy, many of which are to be found in the ESC and the Additional Protocol of 1988.

. . .

3. These developments mean that there is now a real danger of three overlapping supra-national systems of social law emerging in the Community, with much resulting confusion and uncertainty:

(1) Social law based on Title VIII, Chapter 1 (Social Provisions) of the revised Community Treaty, binding on all Member States, and to some extent directly effective in those states.

(2) Social law based on the Maastricht Protocol and Agreement, binding on 11 Member States, and of uncertain effect in those states.

(3) Social law subject to the system of supervision under the ESC, accepted by all Member States of the Community and also Austria, Cyprus, Finland, Iceland, Malta, Norway, Sweden and Turkey. Other recent signatories of the ESC are Liechtenstein, Poland and Hungary.

4. In my view, the developments make it desirable to enlarge the discussion of Community accession to the ECHR to include, as well, the question of accession to the ESC.

. . .

The Convention and the European Social Charter

5. The ESC which was signed in 1961 . . . and came into force in 1965, has been described as 'in a sense, a big footnote' to the Convention. The Preamble affirms that it is the counterpart in the social field to the Convention. The content of the ESC overlaps to a small extent with that of the Convention, notably ESC Article 1(2) and ECHR Article 4(2) (forced or compulsory labour), ESC Article 5 (right to organise) and ECHR Article 11(1) (freedom of association), ESC Article 16 and ECHR Article 8 (right to family life). But even in these areas the ESC goes further than the Convention in recognising social rights, for example the right to organise is complemented by the right to bargain collectively in ESC Article 6, and ESC Article 16 contains wide undertakings, not found in the Convention, to promote the social, legal and economic welfare of the family. Part I of the ESC is a declaration of general principles listing 19 economic and social rights. Part II translates each of these general principles into specific obligations in 19 articles consisting of 72 numbered paragraphs. A ratifying state must accept at least 10 of the 19 articles of 45 of the 72 numbered paragraphs. In practice this selective acceptance does not present a problem so far as the link with Community law is concerned for two reasons: (1) all states must accept Part I and these form part of the 'general principles of law' applied by the European Court of Justice; and (2) Belgium, France, Italy and Spain have accepted all numbered paragraphs, and the Netherlands, Luxembourg and Portugal have also done so with limited reservations; Germany and Greece have each not accepted five paragraphs, Ireland nine, the United Kingdom 12, and Denmark 27. With the exception of Greece's non-acceptance of Articles 5 and 6, the reservations and non-accepted paragraphs are not of much importance in practice. This means that there should not be any major obstacle to Community acceptance of the required minimum number of paragraphs.

6. The ESC contains obligations of an international character, the application of which is submitted solely to the system of supervision provided for . . . Unlike the ECHR there is no provision for individual petition, and the ESC is not within the jurisdiction of the Court of Human Rights or the Commission on Human Rights. Instead there is a system of national reports, once every two years.These reports are examined by the seven-member Committee of Independent Experts (CIE), whose 'Conclusions' are submitted to the Governmental Committee (GC) consisting of national civil servants, and to the Parliamentary Assembly which adopts an opinion based on their reports. The Committee of Ministers must then decide (by a two-thirds majority) whether to make a binding recommendation to the Contracting Party.

. . .

The ESC and the Community Charter

7. The scope of the ESC is far wider than that of the Community Charter. The former applies to 'everyone' in the Contracting States and not only to 'workers of the European Community' (in some contexts such as freedom of movement the latter appears to be further restricted to workers who are nationals of the Member States). Moreover, the ESC applies to 23 Contracting Parties and not only to the 12 Community Member States. In this respect one should note that Resolution 831/1989 of the Parliamentary

Assembly declared that 'it is important to preserve the concept of a European social space covering all the countries of the Council of Europe, including those of the European Community, EFTA, and which may be extended to the countries of Central and Eastern Europe which are likely to accede in increasing numbers to the Council of Europe'.

. . .

8. The content of the ESC is also far wider and more detailed than the Community Charter. Among the ESC subjects not found in the Community Charter are general health protection, some social security rights, the right to social and medical assistance, the right to benefit from social welfare services, the right of the family to social, legal and economic protection, the right of mothers and children to social and economic protection, and the rights of migrant workers who are not Community nationals. On the other hand, it has to be said that several of the ESC's provisions are out of date (eg the right to two weeks' paid holiday in Article 2.3 is much lower than the current minimum in Contracting States) and there are important gaps, the most significant being the right to education and cultural rights generally, the right to protection of the environment, substantive protection against racial discrimination and xenophobia, and certain employment rights such as protection from arbitrary dismissal. However, many of these gaps also exist in the Community Charter. The Additional Protocol to the ESC of 5 May 1988 has updated the ESC in some respects, by adding the right to equal opportunities and equal treatment in matters of employment and occupation without discrimination on the grounds of sex, the right of workers or their representatives to information and consultation, the right to take part in the determination and improvement of working conditions and the working environment, and the right of elderly persons to social protection. In these respects the Additional Protocol provides a broader framework of principle than the Community Charter. (The Additional Protocol was opened for signature on 5 May 1988 but has not yet entered into force. No EC Member State has yet ratified it.) If the Community were to accede to the ESC it would be necessary to negotiate changes in the content of the ESC to update it and make it fully compatible with Community objectives.

8. Unlike the ESC, the Community Charter is not a treaty but simply a 'solemn declaration' to which the United Kingdom is not a party. The obligation of the signatory states to implement the Community Charter, as provided for in Title II thereof, is not subject to a supervisory system analogous to that under the ESC. There is simply a provision for an annual report by the Commission (Articles 29 and 30). At Community level, the Charter is the basis of the 'Action Programme' of 29 November 1989 which contains 47 specific proposals for Community action. Progress on the implementation has been very slow, partly due to United Kingdom opposition and the uncertain legal basis for Community acts to implement some aspects of the Programme. Community accession to the ESC would mean that the Community institutions would be brought under the ESC's supervisory system, and the jurisprudence of the CIE would be an integral part of the body of general principles against which Community acts could be evaluated and judged.

The ESC, the Community Treaty and the new Social Chapter

9. The final puzzle in the new jigsaw of European social law is the relationship of the ESC, the Community Treaty and the Maastricht Protocol and Agreement on Social Policy (the latter sometimes being referred to as the 'new Social Chapter'). One of the objections voiced in the 1980 Report [House of Lords Select Committee on the European Communities, *Human Rights*] against Community accession to the Convention was that the Convention, with its emphasis on classical civil and political rights, is not well-suited to the economic and social objectives of the Community. This objection is far less cogent in the case of the ESC when this is compared with the unamended Title III, Chapter 1, Articles 117–122 (social provisions) of the EC Treaty, and even more so in comparison with the new Social Chapter. The Protocol makes it clear that the Protocol and the new Social Chapter are 'without prejudice to the Chapter of the Treaty establishing the European Community . . . which relates to social policy, and whose provisions constitute an integral part of the *acquis communautaire*'. Article 117 provides for harmonisation and approximation to promote an improvement of working conditions and an improved standard of living. Article 118 requires the Commission to promote co-operation in respect of matters such as employment, labour law and working conditions, vocational training, prevention of accidents and diseases, occupational hygiene and the right of association and collective bargaining. Article 118a allows qualified majority voting for the adoption of directives which encourage improvements 'especially in the working environment, as regards the health and safety of workers'. Article 118b gives the Commission the task of developing the social dialogue between management and labour at European level. Article 119 contains the (directly effective) right to equal remuneration for men and women for the same work (extended by Directive 75/117 to work of equal value). Article 120 requires states to endeavour to maintain the existing equivalence of paid holiday schemes. All of these substantive matters are to be found in a somewhat different form in the ESC and Additional Protocol of 1988.

10. The Maastricht 'Social Chapter' adds a number of objectives to Article 117, including the promotion of employment, proper social protection, dialogue between management and labour, the development of human resources with a view to lasting high employment and 'the combating of exclusion'. The measures to implement these objectives must take account of national practices, 'in particular in the field of contractual relations', and the need to maintain the competitiveness of the Community economy. Article 118(2) of the new Social Chapter will allow qualified majority voting not only in respect of workers' health and safety but also working conditions, information and consultation of workers, equality between men and women with regard to labour market opportunities and treatment at work, and the integration of persons excluded from the labour market. Article 118(3) still requires unanimity in respect to social security and social protection of workers, protection of workers where their employment contract is terminated, representation and collective defence of workers and employers including co-determination, conditions of employment for third country nationals lawfully residing in Community territory, and financial contributions for protection of employment and job creation. The state may entrust management and labour with the implementation of directives on matters under Articles

118(2) and (3), but must take powers so as to guarantee the required result. The provisions of the new Article 118 do not, however, apply to pay, the right of association, the right to strike or the right to impose lock-outs. The new Article 118a extends the social dialogue provisions, which according to Article 118b may now lead to 'contractual relations including agreements' and may be implemented either through procedures in the Member State or, in matters covered by Article 118, on a joint request by a Council decision which may be adopted by a majority except on matters covered by Article 118(3). Article 118c requires the Commission to encourage co-operation and to facilitate co-ordination of action by Member States in the social policy field. Article 119 is retained, but a new Article 119(3) for the first time allows limited positive action for women (compare the Additional Protocol to the ESC, Article 1(4) which allows 'the adoption of specific measures aimed at removing de facto inequalities').

11. It is not possible in the scope of this memorandum to consider the many difficult legal questions to which the Maastricht Protocol on Social Policy gives rise, such as whether the measures agreed by the 11 (in some cases by a majority) will become Community law, whether the Protocol and Agreement offend the Community legal order . . . and when the Commission should act under the Community Treaty and when under the Protocol. Nor is it possible to explore the effect of the principles of 'subsidiarity' and 'necessity' in the new Article 3b of the Community Treaty on the adoption of social measures by the Community. The point here is that the Community is gradually extending its legal competence in the social field, but is doing so in a piecemeal, uncertain and confusing way. Accession to the ESC would, at the very least, be an important symbolic act which would place these developments within a broad framework of principle.

Advantages of accession to the ESC

12. The main advantages may be summarised as follows:
(1) The Community institutions would be subject to the supervisory machinery of the ESC, in particular reports would have to be made by these institutions and would be scrutinised by the independent CIE. Those institutions would be able to draw directly on the jurisprudence of the CIE.
(2) It would be possible, on the basis of (a revised) ESC, to develop a single harmonious code of social policy instead of the current 'three-track' approach.
(3) The European Court of Justice is unlikely to have much opportunity to develop 'general principles' on its own in this field. When the European Court of Justice considers 'fundamental rights', such as freedom of movement, and equal treatment of men and women, it should be able to do so explicitly in the context of the ESC as well as the ECHR. Moreover, the development of the social dialogue under the new Social Chapter, may involve the European Court of Justice in questions not only of freedom of association (ECHR Article 11 and ESC Article 5) but also of the right to bargain collectively (ESC Article 6). It is important that these fundamental rights be interpreted by the European Court of Justice in a way which is consistent not only with the case law of the Strasbourg Court (which

is narrowly confined by the wording of ECHR Article 11) but also the jurisprudence of the CIE (with its wider basis in ESC Articles 5 and 6).

(4) The ESC is attractive to, and provides a basis for social action, within a far wider geographical area than the present Community, in particular in Central and Eastern Europe. It is important for the Community to be seen to be in full support of this wider 'social constitution of Europe'. A separate Community Charter is damaging to European integration because it builds a social wall around the Community (and, since Maastricht, an inner wall of 11 states?).

(5) Accession to the ESC would provide a more solid guarantee of basic social rights than the Community Charter which is simply a 'solemn declaration' with no binding force, and which may be disregarded in practice.

Disadvantages of Accession to the ESC

13. The main disadvantages may be summarised as follows:

(1) Although, on the whole, the ESC is suited to the activities of the Community in the social field, it is in some respects wider in its scope (eg rights of the family, of mothers and children, protection of non-EC migrants, etc).

(2) The ESC will be of no direct benefit to individuals because there is no system of individual petition.

(3) The ESC is outdated in various respects, and a revision of the ESC would be necessary in order to make it more compatible with Community standards. It would take many years to negotiate such changes, and the effort could arguably be more productively directed towards ensuring compliance with the ESC by the national Contracting Parties.

(4) Economic and social rights are controversial (as shown by the disagreements over the new Social Chapter) and the consensus which existed in 1961 when the ESC was signed by the United Kingdom has diminished.

Conclusions

14. There are differing views among the experts as to whether Community accession to the ESC would be a good idea. On balance, the arguments seem to me to favour Community accession to the ESC *whether or not the Community also accedes to the ECHR*. Indeed, it could be argued that it would be *more appropriate* to accede to the ESC than the ECHR, although such an argument may have been pre-empted by Article F of the Treaty of European Union. The content of the ESC is far closer to the Community Treaty, Articles 117–119, the Community Charter and the new Social Chapter, than the content of the ECHR is to the Community Treaty. In any event, the Community would only participate in the ESC in respect of matters within its (expanding) competence. The major institutional objections which apply to accession to the ECHR – such as possible conflicts between the Strasbourg and Luxembourg courts – do not arise. The absence of a right of individual petition makes it easier to accede to the ESC than to the ECHR. There would still be some problems of Community participation in the Council of Europe and its committees, but these could be

resolved as they have been in respect of those Council of Europe conventions in which the Community already participates. There remain the political arguments, but of these the most powerful seems to me to be the need, identified by the Parliamentary Assembly, to preserve the concept of a geographically wider European 'social space' by using a revised ESC as the basis of principle and international obligation for Community social policy.

[D67]   Elaine Whiteford: 'Social Policy after Maastricht' (1993) 18 European Law Review 202

[See **[A8]** and **[A9]** for the text of the Maastricht Protocol and Agreement on Social Policy.]

The legal status of the Agreement

The negotiating history of the Agreement makes it clear that it was intended as the new Social Chapter of the EC Treaty, a plan which was doomed to failure by the obstinacy of the British. When this opposition had clearly become insurmountable, it was decided at the last minute to adopt the solution of a Protocol and Agreement of the 11. This suggests that the intention of the signatories of the Agreement was that the Agreement would result in the adoption of Community law, binding on the 11 only, a conclusion which would seem to be confirmed by the use of the term 'Community' in the Agreement itself. Nevertheless, the Agreement is dependent upon the Protocol to which it forms an Annex, for it is only by virtue of the authorisation contained in the Protocol that the signatories of the Agreement can gain access to the Community institutions, procedures and mechanisms which are necessary for the creation of Community law. It is clear, therefore, that it is the terms of the Protocol which are important for determining the precise status of the Agreement.

The text of the Protocol is, however, ambiguous as to the status to be accorded to the Agreement and its results, providing merely that the 12:

> authorise those 11 Member States to have recourse to the institutions, procedures and mechanisms of the Treaty for the purposes of taking among themselves and applying as far as they are concerned the acts and decisions required for giving effect to the above-mentioned Agreement.

The key expressions for the determination of the status of the Agreement are 'among themselves' and 'applying as far as they are concerned' which can be interpreted as authorising either 'mere' inter-governmental co-operation or Community law binding the 11 only. The fact that the Agreement is part of the EC Treaty and the Maastricht Treaty is of little importance in this regard, since the existing Treaties do contain inter-governmental forms of co-operation beside Community procedures and the Maastricht Treaty introduces new examples in the form of co-operation in home and judicial affairs and the provisions on common foreign and security policy. However, the problem with the Agreement is that the Protocol provides that the operation of the Agreement is to be without prejudice to the *acquis communautaire* with the text of the Agreement echoing this in providing that its implementation is to be based on the *acquis*. The *acquis* contains:

the contents, principles and political objectives of the Treaties . . . the legislation adopted in implementation of the Treaties and the jurisprudence of the court; the declarations and resolutions adopted in the Community framework; the international agreements, and the agreements between Member States connected with the Community's activities . . .

[European Commission report on the criteria and conditions for accession of new members to the Community, Europe Documents No 1790 of 3 July 1992, at p 3]

and thus covers the whole body of Community law, both hard and soft. From this it seems possible to infer that it was not the intention of the signatories of the Protocol and Agreement to introduce any fundamental changes into the Community legal order, and therefore to conclude that the Agreement is to operate within the established boundaries of the *acquis*. Given this intention, by examining the consistency of the Agreement – first as mandating inter-governmental co-operation and secondly as mandating Community law binding the 11 – with the *acquis*, some guidance as to the proper interpretation of the ambiguous terms of the Protocol may be gleaned. This examination will also cast light on the main question being considered in this paper, namely, to what extent do the Maastricht Treaty's social provisions represent a departure from existing Community law.

The Protocol authorises the 11 to use the institutions, procedures and mechanisms of the EC Treaty for the purposes of implementing the Agreement. Provision is made to alter the voting procedures in the Council to take account of the British absence, but otherwise, no alterations are required. Thus, the Protocol seems to envisage that the Parliament, Commission and Court [of Justice] will function as usual as regards the working of the Agreement. In the case of the court in particular, there need not be any change in composition because the judges do not represent any particular legal system, nor is there a requirement that a judge hold the nationality of a Member State. They act in the interests of the observation of the law rather than representing any particular national interest. It is difficult to find any convincing reason to exclude the British judge from consideration of the legislation flowing from the Agreement.

The Protocol as mandating inter-governmental co-operation

If the interpretation apparently favoured by the British government is adopted, namely that the Agreement and its results are inter-governmental in nature, the court will have been granted jurisdiction over an inter-governmental Agreement. In the face of the existence of two sets of social provisions (Articles 117–122 EEC and the Protocol and Agreement), the court will be asked to exercise two separate but related functions. The first will be the interpretation of the provisions of the EC Treaty which bind the 12. The second function will be the interpretation of the inter-governmental Agreement signed by the 11. This is a different function from that normally exercised by the court, and to this extent can be seen as a different court for these purposes. In interpreting the scope of the Agreement, the 'social' court will also indirectly be adjudicating on the scope of the EC Treaty itself, something which the Court of Justice alone is competent authoritatively to do. This exclusive jurisdiction is intended to safeguard the autonomous development of Community law and the court has, in the past, rejected any arrangement which it found to threaten this [see **A56**]. For this reason, if the Agreement is interpreted as resulting in purely inter-governmental obligations for the signatories, the operation of the system as envisaged appears to diverge from the *acquis communautaire* in certain respects . . .

Another . . . question as to the working of the inter-governmental Agreement is the uncertain status which is to be accorded the judgments of the court under the Agreement. The Protocol authorises use of the institutions, procedures and mechanisms of the Treaty but does not make it mandatory. The court is lent to the 11 and it is possible that since the procedures and mechanisms are also lent, the binding force of the court's pronouncements is also included, but this is nowhere expressly stated. Legal certainty requires that 'the application of the law to a specific situation must be predictable' prompting the court to require that its judgments are always binding, and providing support for the assertion that the court's judgments pursuant to the Agreement should also be treated as binding on the signatories. However, the requirements of legal certainty are still not completely satisfied since it remains possible for a United Kingdom judge to refer a question on the scope of the working environment in Article 118a EEC, for example, to the court which then hands down a judgment binding the 12. It is equally possible to envisage a reference on the same legal point but asked in relation to Article 2 of the Agreement by a judge of one of the 11 other Member States. The judgment of the court in this case will not bind the United Kingdom judges. In such a situation, it is clear that national judges could become confused as to the status which is to be accorded to judgments of the court on Community law, thereby jeopardising the uniformity of Community law which is said to be a basic premise for the operation of the Community. It would therefore seem that the operation of the inter-governmental Agreement is not entirely in accordance with a number of principles established in the *acquis*. This apparent conflict raises doubts as to the accuracy of an interpretation of the Protocol as mandating inter-governmental co-operation.

The Protocol as mandating Community law

The arguments outlined above in relation to the operation of the inter-governmental Agreement are also partially applicable to its operation as Community law. If the court hands down a judgment pursuant to the Agreement, the domestic courts of the United Kingdom, and all within British jurisdiction, will not be bound by this. If the non-binding status of judgments on the inter-governmental Agreement as regards the United Kingdom was undesirable because of the threat it would pose to legal certainty, this argument gains even more force when it is placed with the Community legal order itself, since it would then concern Community law as such which was not binding on one Member State.

. . .

The Protocol and the Agreement could be described as creating a de facto two-speed Europe. However, in the academic debate which has raged on the subject of a two-speed Europe, the background has always been that of one uniform legal system. In constructing a framework for the existence of different degrees of integration, the basis for such constructions has been that the policy from which derogation is allowed is a Community policy – that is, that all Member States have accepted the objective in question as a Community objective. The . . . derogation envisaged in the framework for a two-speed Europe can clearly be seen to be temporary.

. . .

When the Agreement on social policy is examined against this background, it can be seen that it fails to satisfy these criteria according to which some derogation from the basic principle of the uniformity of the Community legal system can be countenanced. The objectives laid down in the Agreement are simply not accepted by the United Kingdom government and the derogation from these social provisions is unlimited in time. This suggests that the Protocol and Agreement represent a departure from some of the fundamental principles on which the Community legal order has been constructed, in so far as Community objectives – the improvement of living and working conditions, equal pay for women and men, health and safety, social dialogue at Community level – are to be pursued by other than common action. It would appear therefore that if the Protocol is interpreted as mandating Community law binding on 11 Member States only, this represents a significant departure from traditional Community law procedures.

SECTION FIVE

CITIZENSHIP

Introduction

This chapter is called 'The European Citizen', a title deliberately chosen to illustrate and emphasise the developing and transient nature of the relationship between the European Community and the nationals of the Member States. The people of Europe are now no longer considered simply as a factor of economic production and, as the Community has diversified and expanded its role and activities, Community law has conferred upon these people some of the features of citizenship of a nation state.

Evidence of an ever-wider view of the protectable interests of persons under Community law can be seen from the Court of Justice's approach pre-Maastricht. The cases comprising **[D68]** and **[D69]** might be narrowly construed as concerning the recognisable Treaty categories of recipients of services and vocational training respectively. However, care should be taken to see the tourist and student elements that more properly represent their heart. It was also seen in Chapter One how the notion of a European citizenship has been openly embraced in some quarters, particularly by Advocate General Jacobs in *Konstantinidis* **[A21]**.

But it is in the Maastricht Treaty on European Union that a concept of citizenship of the Union receives formal recognition (see earlier **[A50]**). This can be seen as a consolidation of existing rights under the previous Treaties, together with the particular political and civic rights established by Article 8. Nevertheless, it should be remembered that citizenship is itself a dynamic and complex concept which is subject to varied analyses by sociologists, political scientists and others. The approach taken by Meehan **[D71]** argues that there is a place for a citizenship of a multiple character, which is neither purely national nor cosmopolitan. Vogel's feminist argument **[D72]** may usefully be compared with the materials contained in the earlier section of this chapter on the values and goals underpinning social policy (see especially **[D60]** and **[D61]**). Indeed, there are clearly unanswered questions as to the actual, let alone desirable, content of citizenship rights. The triad of political, economic and social rights is not necessarily uniformly supported in extent by legal recognition or institutional frameworks. Developments in relation to questions of identity and allegiance, also important to the notion of citizenship, may depend on the content and impact of the new competences adopted under Maastricht, such as cultural policy **[D70]**. You should also consider the relationship between the court's use to date of fundamental human rights and the likely content of citizenship rights.

The limits of the express provisions on citizenship under the Maastricht Treaty are examined by Closa **[D73]** and Lodge **[D74]**, although both subscribe to the progressive expansion of the content of citizenship in the post-Maastricht phase of the Community's development. Our own attempts to place the present in the context of the future follow at the end of the chapter.

Before embarking on the materials in this section, it is worth re-reading **[A50]** on the notion of citizenship set out in the new Article 8 of the EC Treaty.

MATERIALS

[D68]   Case 186/87 Cowan v Trésor Public [1989] ECR 195

The European Court of Justice

2. [The] question arose in a dispute between the French Trésor Public (Treasury) and a British citizen, Ian William Cowan, concerning compensation for injury resulting from a violent assault suffered by him at the exit of a metro station during a brief stay in Paris.

3. Since his assailants could not be identified Mr Cowan applied to the Commission d'indemnisation des victimes d'infraction attached to the Tribunal de grande instance, Paris, for compensation under Article 706-3 of the Code de procédure pénale. That provision allows compensation to be obtained from the state inter alia when the victim of an assault which has caused physical injury with consequences of a certain severity is unable to obtain effective and adequate compensation for the harm from any other source.

4. Before the Commission d'indemnisation the Law Officer of the Treasury submitted that Mr Cowan did not satisfy the conditions for obtaining the above-mentioned compensation provided for in Article 706-3 . . . That article provides that only the following persons may receive the compensation in question:

Persons who are of French nationality or foreign nationals who prove:
  (i) that they are nationals of a State which has concluded a reciprocal agreement with France for the application of the said provisions and that they satisfy the conditions laid down in the agreement; or
  (ii) that they are holders of a residence permit.

5. Mr Cowan then relied on the prohibition of discrimination laid down, in particular, in Article 7 of the EEC Treaty. He argued that the conditions set out above were discriminatory and that such conditions prevented tourists from going freely to another Member State to receive services there. The representative of the Treasury and the Ministère public replied that the rules in question treated resident foreigners in the same way as French nationals and that to distinguish their situation from tourists was compatible with Community law, which itself makes periods spent by nationals of one Member State in another Member State subject to different conditions according to the length of the stay.

6. In those circumstances the Commission d'indemnisation [submitted a question to the Court of Justice for a preliminary ruling].

. . .

8. The preliminary question asks in essence whether the prohibition of discrimination laid down in particular in Article 7 of the EEC Treaty precludes a Member State, in respect of persons in a situation covered by Community law, from making the award of state compensation for harm caused in that state to the victim of an assault resulting in physical injury subject to the condition that he hold a residence permit or be a national of a country which has entered into a reciprocal arrangement with that Member State.

9. As a preliminary point it should be recalled that the first paragraph of Article 7 of the Treaty provides that 'within the scope of application of this Treaty, and without prejudice to any special provisions contained therein, any discrimination on grounds of nationality shall be prohibited'. These terms lay down both the content and the scope of the prohibition of discrimination.

The content of the prohibition of discrimination

10. By prohibiting 'any discrimination on grounds of nationality' Article 7 of the Treaty requires that persons in a situation governed by Community law be placed on a completely equal footing with nationals of the Member State. In so far as this principle is applicable it therefore precludes a Member State from making the grant of a right to such a person subject to the condition that he reside on the territory of that state – that condition is not imposed on the state's own nationals.

11. It should also be emphasised that the right to equal treatment is conferred directly by Community law and may not therefore be made subject to the issue of a certificate to that effect by the authorities of the relevant Member State (. . . see . . . Case 157/79 *R v Pieck* [1980] ECR 2171 **[D11]**).

12. Finally, it should be recalled, as the court first stated in its judgment . . . in Case 1/72 *Frilli v Belgium* [1972] ECR 457, that the right to equal treatment laid down in Community law may not be made dependent on the existence of a reciprocal agreement between the relevant Member State and the country of which the person concerned is a national.

13. It follows that in so far as the prohibition of discrimination is applicable it precludes a Member State from making the award of a right to a person in a situation governed by Community law subject to the condition that he hold a residence permit or be a national of a country which has entered into a reciprocal agreement with that Member State.

The scope of the prohibition of discrimination

14. Under Article 7 of the Treaty the prohibition of discrimination applies 'within the scope of application of this Treaty' and 'without prejudice to any special provisions contained therein'. This latter expression refers particularly to other provisions of the Treaty in which the application of the general principle set out in that article is given concrete form in respect of specific situations. Examples of that are the provisions concerning free movement of workers, the right of establishment and the freedom to provide services.

15. On that last point, in its judgment . . . in Joined Cases 286/82 and 26/83 *Luisi and Carbone v Ministero del Tesoro* [1984] ECR 377, the court held that the freedom to provide services includes the freedom for the recipients of services to go to another Member State in order to receive a service there, without being obstructed by restrictions, and that tourists, amongst others, must be regarded as recipients of services.

16. At the hearing the French government submitted that as Community law now stands a recipient of services may not rely on the prohibition of discrimination to the extent that the national law at issue does not create any barrier to freedom of movement. A provision such as that at issue in the main proceedings, it says, imposes no restrictions in that respect. Furthermore, it concerns a right which is a manifestation of the principle of national solidarity. Such a right presupposes a closer bond with the state

than that of a recipient of services, and for that reason it may be restricted to persons who are either nationals or that state or foreign nationals resident on the territory of that state.

17. That reasoning cannot be accepted. When Community law guarantees a natural person the freedom to go to another Member State the protection of that person from harm in the Member State in question, on the same basis as that of nationals and persons residing there, is a corollary of that freedom of movement. It follows that the prohibition of discrimination is applicable to recipients of services within the meaning of the Treaty as regards protection against the risk of assault and the right to obtain financial compensation provided for by national law when that risk materialises. The fact that the compensation at issue is financed by the Public Treasury cannot alter the rules regarding the protection of the rights guaranteed by the Treaty.

18. The French government also submitted that compensation such as that at issue in the main proceedings is not subject to the prohibition of discrimination because it falls within the law of criminal procedure, which is not included within the scope of the Treaty.

19. Although in principle criminal legislation and the rules of criminal procedure, among which the national provision in issue is to be found, are matters for which the Member States are responsible, the court has consistently held (see inter alia . . . Case 203/80 *Casati* [1981] ECR 2595) that Community law sets certain limits to their power. Such legislative provisions may not discriminate against persons to whom Community law gives the right to equal treatment or restrict the fundamental freedoms guaranteed by Community law.

20. In the light of all the foregoing the answer to the question submitted must be that the prohibition of discrimination laid down in particular in Article 7 of the Treaty must be interpreted as meaning that in respect of persons whose freedom to travel to a Member State, in particular as recipients of services, is guaranteed by Community law that state may not make the award of state compensation for harm caused in that state to the victim of an assault resulting in physical injury subject to the condition that he hold a residence permit or be a national of a country which has entered into a reciprocal agreement with that Member State.

[D69] Case 293/83 Gravier v City of Liège [1985] ECR 593

The European Court of Justice

2. The questions [referred by the Belgian court under Article 177] were raised in the course of summary proceedings in which Françoise Gravier, a student at the Académie Royale des Beaux-Arts, Liège, claimed that the City of Liège should be prohibited from requiring her to pay a fee called the 'minerval' (enrolment fee) which students of Belgian nationality are not required to pay. The City of Liège joined as third parties the Belgian State, which issued the circulars requiring that the fee be charged, and the Communauté Française, the regional institution responsible for art education.

. . .

7. . . . . [The plaintiff] argued that she could not be obliged to pay a fee which was not required of Belgian nationals since on the one hand such an obligation constituted discrimination on grounds of nationality prohibited by Article 7 of the Treaty and on the other hand a national of another Member State going to Belgium to study must be free to do so as a person to whom services are provided according to Article 59 of the Treaty.

. . .

15. Such unequal treatment based on nationality must be regarded as discrimination prohibited by Article 7 of the Treaty if it falls within the scope of the Treaty.

. . .

18. . . . In the first place, the questions referred concern neither the organisation of education nor even its financing, but rather the establishment of a financial barrier to access to education for foreign students only. Secondly, they concern a particular type of education, referred to as 'vocational training' in the first question and as 'a course in strip cartoon art' in the second question.

19. The first remark which must be made in that regard is that although educational organisation and policy are not as such included in the spheres which the Treaty has entrusted to the Community institutions, access to and participation in courses of instruction and apprenticeship, in particular vocational training, are not unconnected with Community law.

. . .

23. The common vocational training policy referred to in Article 128 of the Treaty is . . . gradually being established. It constitutes, moreover, an indispensable element of the activities of the Community, whose objectives include inter alia the free movement of persons, the mobility of labour and the improvement of the living standards of workers.

24. Access to vocational training is in particular likely to promote free movement of persons throughout the Community, by enabling them to obtain a qualification in the Member State where they intend to work and by enabling them to complete their training and develop their particular talents in the Member State whose vocational training programmes include the special subject desired.

25. It follows from all the foregoing that the conditions of access to vocational training fall within the scope of the Treaty.

26. The answer to the first question must therefore be that the imposition on students who are nationals of other Member States, of a charge, a registration fee or the so-called 'minerval' as a condition of access to vocational training, where the same fee is not imposed on students who are nationals of the host Member State, constitutes discrimination on grounds of nationality contrary to Article 7 of the Treaty.

27. In its second question the national court wishes to know what criteria must be used in deciding whether courses in strip cartoon art constitute vocational training.

. . .

30. . . . any form of education which prepares for a qualification for a particular profession, trade or employment or which provides the necessary

training and skills for such a profession, trade or employment is vocational training, whatever the age and the level of training of the pupils or students, and even if the training programme includes an element of general education.

Note. A broader reference to education is included in the EC Treaty as amended by the Treaty of Union. Article 3(p) refers to 'education and training of quality' as being an activity of the Community. According to the new Article 126:

1. The Community shall contribute to the development of quality education by encouraging co-operation between Member States and, if necessary, by supporting and supplementing their action, while fully respecting the responsibility of the Member States for the content of teaching and the organisation of education systems and their cultural and linguistic diversity . . .

[D70] Commission of the European Communities: New prospects for Community cultural action ((1992) COM 149 final, 29 April 1992)

Introduction

The cultural challenge

The challenge is two-fold: cultural action should contribute to the flowering of national and regional cultural identities and at the same time reinforce the feeling that, despite their cultural diversity, Europeans share a common cultural heritage and common values.

The frontier-free area must provide a stimulating environment for intellectual life, cultural activities and artistic creativity for the ever-growing numbers of European citizens now demanding greater access to culture. In the face of growing intolerance the aim will also be to help them understand, appreciate and respect other cultures in the same way as their own.

The aims of Community cultural action must consequently be:

- to preserve Europe's past by helping to conserve and increase awareness of our common cultural heritage in all its forms;
- to generate an environment conducive to the development of culture in Europe by taking cultural aspects into account in other policies and programmes and by supporting artistic and literary creation and non-commercial cultural exchanges and networks;
- to help ensure that the influence of European culture is felt throughout the world by encouraging co-operation with non-member countries; as a major partner in an ever-changing international scene, the Community should capitalise more on its cultural relations in its political dialogue with the countries and continents with which it has historical ties with a view to promoting mutual understanding.

. . .

Setting up a new reference framework and a cultural dialogue

1992 is a pivotal year, which must be used to provide the Community with a working framework for common action. By stepping up the dialogue with all those concerned – the professionals and the competent authorities in the Member States – it should subsequently be possible for the Commission to prepare specific target-oriented proposals and programmes, and the related budgetary estimates, on the basis of the options selected.

With such an ambitious goal and such a vast field to cover consensus will be the key to success. Special care must be taken to respect the cultural diversity which constitutes the very essence and wealth of Europe and to highlight its common cultural heritage.

The need for a new reference framework is therefore two-fold: to improve the structuring of cultural action, thereby ensuring a more coherent development; and to replace the previous framework, which covered the period 1987 to 1992 [see COM (87) 603 final, Supplement 4/87 Bulletin EC].

Looking ahead to the new areas of Community competence, the high degree of cultural sensitivity of all the Member States means that concertation at all levels must be encouraged to promote the emergence of consensus. The Commission has already embarked on this route by holding initial consultations on the preparation of this communication with the professionals and the competent authorities in the Member States. This dialogue should be stepped up by closely involving Parliament and the new Committee of the Regions in the process.

Compliance with subsidiarity and improved prioritisation

Only through compliance with the principle of subsidiarity and by improved prioritisation can Community action maximise its impact and be truly significant. Increased selectivity will mean fewer Community measures but greater visibility.

As and when cultural action develops, and in particular whenever specific programme proposals are made, care should be taken to ensure that the principle of subsidiarity is fully respected. This subsidiarity will produce action of Community interest geared primarily to the breaking down of barriers, to transparency and to genuine added value throughout the Community.

To this end the Community will encourage cultural co-operation only when it complements action by the Member States and, if necessary, continue to support their action in the areas listed in the article on culture. In addition, action undertaken by the Community must be regularly assessed in the light of the objectives set by the Council and Parliament.

. . .

The aim of this communication is to prepare the ground for discussions in the Council and Parliament with a view to producing the above reference framework and establishing the necessary priorities.

I.   Contributing to the flowering of culture in the frontier-free area

The economic and political integration which will be the hallmark of tomorrow's Community must be accompanied by a stronger cultural dimension which respects national, regional and local diversity.

Cultural co-operation between Member States must be encouraged; their action must be supported and supplemented; and cultural aspects must be taken into account in all Community policies and programmes.

. . .

B. Taking cultural aspects into account in Community policies and programmes

The development of Community policies and programmes can have a direct or indirect impact on culture.

The point here is that cultural aspects must be taken into account as soon as any new action or policy is devised, subject obviously to Community law.

A growing number of measures with a cultural dimension have already been developed as part of various Community policies and programmes including the free movement of cultural goods and persons, the environment, research, the new technologies, social and regional policies, tourism, training and external relations.

And the Community has already attempted to incorporate the cultural dimension into other policies, including audiovisual policy [(1990) COM 78 final] and VAT [(1988) COM 846 final, (1987) COM 324 final]. On the sensitive issue of the protection of national treasures [(1991) COM 447 final] efforts have been made to take account of the cultural dimension at every stage in the discussions.

Important decisions have also been taken in the audiovisual sector [Council Directive of 3 October 1989 ((1989) COM 552)] and on copyright and neighbouring rights [(1990) COM 584 final]; to protect these rights is to preserve and develop cultural creativity and diversity.

Experience has shown that constructive progress has been made in these areas thanks to the consultation of various professionals and experts in the Member States. The Commission believes that this approach should be consolidated and systematically extended to all Community policies with a cultural component.

The development of exchanges which will follow 1992 enhances the need for this approach. The Maastricht Treaty singles out for special attention 'aid to promote culture and heritage conservation' [Article 92(3)(d)].

The Commission feels it is important:

– to improve the flow of information on measures with a significant impact on culture, notably by means of a stocktaking exercise;
– to develop co-ordination with professionals and national experts through consultations, hearings and ad hoc working parties.

II. Bringing the common cultural heritage to the fore by providing support for specific areas

The role of the Community in contributing to the flowering of our cultures must be subsidiary to that of the Member States. Given the vast area covered by culture careful prioritisation is essential if the dissipation of effort is to be avoided.

Community action must therefore be efficient, coherent and a valuable example and motive force.

Action undertaken hitherto . . ., albeit limited, has already made it possible to produce a basic structure and to develop specific measures with practical impact.

With this in mind the Commission is proposing a horizontal approach based primarily on increasing the involvement of all those active in the field of culture and on constantly taking account of the cultural dimension in Community policies and programmes. Priority will be given to the development of this approach in the areas already approved by the Council: cultural heritage, books and reading, and the audiovisual sector. At the same time the Commission feels that the Community should also gradually be turning its attention to other cultural areas. It has already demonstrated its commitment on many occasions to music and the performing arts – the theatre in particular – and to the visual arts but there has as yet been no common action on this front.

In the Commission's view this should be done through transnational networking and encouraging artistic creation. Both priorities have already been partially incorporated in the Kaleidoscope programme [Kaleidoscope – Community scheme of awards for artistic and cultural events (OJ C205, 6 August 1991)] alongside the support provided for cultural events of a European nature, theatre and music in particular.

The Commission feels that by focusing on economies of scale and the exemplary function of Community action on this front, even with relatively limited financial resources, this could have a significant impact.

The starting point for action in the above three areas was different:

– for the cultural heritage, a pilot scheme to conserve the architectural heritage;
– for books and reading, a general analysis and a pilot project on literary translation;
– for the audiovisual media, a three-fold objective: rules of the game, technology, and promotion of the programmes industry.

A.   Cultural heritage

Visible evidence of Europe's historic and artistic past, our architectural and cultural heritage is of fundamental importance for European culture. It reflects both the different stages in the development of our civilisation and the various expressions of our identity. It is both irreplaceable and vulnerable and must be preserved for future generations, providing as it always has done a constant source of inspiration for contemporary creativity.

Community action must, first, be extended notably to include cultural goods, thereby conferring on the concept of cultural heritage the meaning indicated by the new Article 128 and, secondly, do more to exploit the existing resources and highlight the wealth and diversity of our common heritage.

Quite apart from its intrinsic cultural value this heritage is closely bound up with many aspects of economic and social life and support for it could benefit more from the development of the various Community policies with which it is directly or indirectly linked, such as quality of life and the environment, tourism, research and new technology, training and employment, and so on.

The Commission will consequently be presenting the Council with a paper outlining prospects for protecting and enhancing the cultural heritage; this could be combined with an action programme. In order to focus more attention on the model nature of its operations on the ground and to encourage common approaches such action should be systematically accompanied by the wide-scale dissemination of research findings and methods for the conservation of our cultural heritage.

[D71]   Elizabeth Meehan: Citizenship and the European Community (Sage, 1993)

1.   National or European citizenship?

'There are no such animals as "European citizens". There are only French, German, or Italian citizens.' This was the view of Raymond Aron (1974) when he was asked to consider whether multinational or European citizenship were possible. Seventeen years later Lord Jenkins, despite his own Europeanism, told an audience at the Queen's University of Belfast that he could not foresee the day when citzens of Member States of the European Community (EC) would say in Japan that they were European instead of French, German or Italian – unlike the Texan would say that he or she was American. These views contrast with the territorially more inclusive language of Community institutions which speaks of 'a People's Europe' (note the position of the apostrophe), sometimes of 'industrial citizens' and now 'Citizens of the Union'. The argument of this book is that the language of the European Community is justifiable.

My thesis is not that Aron's concept of national citizenship is being relocated to a new level. It is that a new kind of citizenship is emerging that is neither national nor cosmospolitan but that is multiple in the sense that the identities, rights and obligations, associated by Heater (1990) with citizenship, are expressed through an increasingly complex configuration of common Community institutions, states, national and transnational voluntary associations, regions and alliances of regions. This is not to say that the emergence of a new 'public space' for citizens (Tassin, 1992) is inevitable in a form that is precisely identifiable now. But, if unpredictable, the form will not be accidental. The new order comprises states and peoples which have some common experiences and intellectual traditions and some differences. Sometimes, different national traditions are deliberately welded in new institutions. Sometimes, they seem to appear in their new form by default. Conversely, Community institutions and policies are sometimes the subject of difficult disputes about the proper concepts to use and the proper way to go about things. Then, the outcome will depend upon what concessions may or may not be made when a plurality of different interests confront one another in the common 'public space' that exists because of the creation of the Community. What is certain is that the European Community now provides a framework that coexists with those of its Member States, through which nationals of those Member States can claim certain rights. These are economic and social rights which will be extended in these fields and into the political sphere [under the] Maastricht Treaty . . . The nature of European citizenship may continue to have a national focus, enriched with a European dimension . . .; or, it may become more like, as I believe it is now, citizenship of the Roman Empire in which citizens were able to appeal to more than one set of enforceable standards when claiming their rights.

My belief that something like the neo-imperial model exists now has to depend on the view that social rights, together with civil and political rights, form a triad, which must be regarded as interlocked if we are to be able to speak of the existence of equal citizenship. This is a disputed position . . . the meaning of citizenship is bound to the historical, sociological and cultural contexts which provide the reasons for particular understandings. But, if my understanding is one of various positions that could reasonably be held, it follows that Aron's cannot be the only truth about the European Community. Indeed, both of us are obliged to explore what citizenship has meant to participants in the European Community and how these meanings might affect the outlook of governments and what might be the expectations of those whose lives are regulated by national and common institutions.

. . .

Raymond Aron's case for national citizenship

Aron distinguishes between the rights of man and the rights of the citizen in the 1789 French Declaration on the Rights of Man and in the 1948 United Nations Universal Declaration of Human Rights, which also declares the rights of woman. Though a single belief – in the natural equality of human beings – justifies natural or human rights and citizenship rights, the two sets are not the same. To show this, Aron draws upon the Hegelian distinction, also used in a transformed way by Marx, between burghers and citizens. The first are participants (subjects, for Marx) in the economic life of civil society. Their roles may be associated with natural property rights, as in the 18th century, or with the right to have socio-economic needs met, as in the 20th century. Citizens are recognisable by the status conferred upon them in rules about the administration of justice and political participation. Human or burghers' rights may be recognised or denied, irrespective of political status. Citizenship rights may also be denied but they cannot be guaranteed except in the context of nationality and the state – often a nation-state, sometimes a state of several nations which are culturally distinct but share the same legal nationality. Together, Aron's distinctions inform his separation of regulation by the EC of the lives of its economic participants from the civil and political rights guaranteed by their different (nation-)states.

There are four main elements to Aron's case that European citizenship is logically impossible and politically unlikely. First, as indicated, national and Community authorities provide sets of rights of a different order from one another. Secondly, European citizenship would have to involve a transfer of legal and political powers from the national to the EC level (similar to the transfer of Scottish and English citizenship to a single set of British entitlements). Thirdly, Aron argues that citizens can insist that a nation-state respect their rights because the state can demand that citizens fulfil their duties to defend the state, whereas there is no inter- or multi-national polity which has such authority. Usually, this has meant military service and makes men citizens, while women have been said to have a duty to be mothers, a duty traditionally without corresponding rights. The fourth element in Aron's case is that there was, in 1974, no popular demand for a European federation which would be simultaneously responsible for legal-political rights and economic regulation and which could command duties of citizens. Moreover, there was every sign then, perhaps unlike the 1940s, that national leaders intended the Community to remain a regime in which the burghers or economic subjects co-operated in the absence of a political federation. In so far as people criticised nation-states and the association of citizenship with legal nationality, they did so because of the treatment of nationalities submerged within contemporary boundaries. Aron observed cynicism about the idea that domestic problems could be resolved by regulation at a still more remote level and was sceptical, himself, of views that burghers and economic subjects could be made more equal through changes closer to home – such as workers' control, which is one component of Community aspirations.

Aron's thesis can be criticised for three reasons. First, it is based on only one conception of citizenship, although there are others. Secondly, he links his conception of citizenship to an understanding of international relations that emphasises the significance of states as the determinants of the world order, while others contain elements that are compatible with alternative ideas about citizenship. Thirdly, his evidential judgment about lack of support for the transformation that would be necessary to be able to speak of European citizenship has not stood the test of time – a claim I make despite controversy at the time of writing over the Maastricht Treaty of Union.

Alternative conceptions of citizenship

Though both Aron and Leca (1990) emphasise connections between nationality and citizenship, the link is mainly logical for the former and sociological for the latter. In building the logical case, Aron does what Leca says we must not. That is, though he refers to historical ideas and practice in order to elucidate *a* conception of citizenship, this conception is based on a specific historical experience and, once elucidated, has the status of making others incorrect. A broader sweep is taken by Heater (1990), who provides grounds for being persuaded by van Gunsteren's view (1978) that citizenship is a contestable concept and Leca's that its meanings are socially contextual, both of which mean that different meanings must be explored. Heater reminds us that:

> from very early in its history the term [citizenship] already contained a cluster of meanings related to a defined legal or social status, a means of political identity, a focus of loyalty, a requirement of duties, an expectation of rights and a yardstick of good social behaviour . . . No subsequent discussion of the topic has required any more components nor would have been complete with any fewer.

Moreover:

> the early history of citizenship may also lead us to question the *modern* assumption that the status necessarily adheres to the sovereign nation-state. [It] can be associated with any geographical unit from a small town to the whole globe itself (emphasis added).

The 'cluster of meanings' as to the content of rights and duties, the question of who inside a regime has entitlements and the territorial basis of inclusion have been defined and redefined in five distinct contexts: the Greek city-state, the Roman Republic and Empire, the medieval and Renaissance city, the nation-state (from the late 18th century) and in the long-lived Stoic ideal of the cosmopolis. Where direct engagement in the process of ruling, not merely the 'crude indicator' of suffrage is emphasised,

> the intimacy of the Greek or medieval city seemed seemed essential. If loyalty [is] to a moral code, then the whole of humanity must be embraced. If legal status is the essence, the Romans revealed the flexibility of dual city and imperial citizenship. Only if the nation-state is sovereign, commands the complete loyalty of its inhabitants and is the sole source of rights and duties must citizenship necessarily be exercised in that particular geographical context.

Though the link between citizenship and nationality is strong for strategic . . . and ideological . . . reasons, Heater's account shows that it is neither inevitable nor the defining feature of being a citizen. His discussion of Roman Imperial citizenship, where nationality and legal rights were not coterminous, will recur. For the moment, I concentrate on how his perspective modifies Aron's claims that workers' and welfare rights are not part of citizenship rights.

Heater draws attention to a remarkable continuity in the belief that citizenship includes what Aron counts as human rights – a collective memory which transcends the rise of the nation-state. One example is his discussion of John Stuart Mill's idea that workers' rights could be a substitute in large societies for the direct democracy of the Greek city-state – as a means of fulfilling the human need for participation and of developing civic virtues . . . and not merely for the purposes of pursuing self-interest . . . The move towards common standards of workers' rights in the European Community certainly embodies the idea that individual self-interest lies in avoiding disadvantages arising from migration and that this should be dealt with. But Community language also often refers to the need to construct a common moral order if not, I grant, as an end in itself but as a way of inspiring loyalty to a new and wider regime . . . If belittled by Aron in their *social* promise and defined out of the search for *political* equality, Heater's approach means that we must at least consider the possibility that workers' rights might be part of an emergent notion of European citizenship.

Another area in which a historical approach provides a different way of viewing current European developments stems from ideas about rights to welfare . . . Even if people in the 18th century *did* distinguish, as Aron suggests, between natural rights and citizenship in abstract thought, practical political arrangements linked human circumstances and political status. The ideas that only those who are rational ought to participate in politics and that rationality was demonstrated by the accumulation of property together justified the denial of rights for the poor and women, the latter also being debarred for other reasons . . . In the 20th century it has seemed obvious that there can be a different conclusion. That is, not to exclude, but to provide the deprived with the material basis for rationality and, hence, to enable their political participation (King and Waldron, 1988) – a conclusion that can also be accepted by those whose primary concern is not with entitlements but the maintenance of order.

Modern advocates of social citizenship are shown by Jordan (1989) to be of two types. One sort inherits a version of human nature that radicals see in individualism and capitalism; that is, the individual as private and instrumental, albeit, in the new formulation, with welfare needs. This justification for social rights undermines the 19th century view that meeting need was an obligation of *charity* towards those who, because of economic deprivation, had ceased to be citizens . . . But, though it posits rights instead of charity, it is not a fundamental challenge to individualism because these rights are thought of as enabling people to function effectively as persons or relatively equally in civil society. For the other type of social rights advocate, the concepts of the individual and interests are Aristotelian and/or Idealist; that is . . . individuals are human beings only when they belong to a community and, being essentially political, their humanity is expressed when they take part in constructing and maintaining their community. The good society is not only the same as participatory society but is also a moral order of well-being and conviviality. Private interests (of the self-interested type) and public interests cannot exist distinctly from one another since they converge on the common human need for the good society in all its dimensions. Political rights to discharge public duties entail trying to find a fair distribution of social justice. In the modern version of this approach, social rights are *not* an instrument for the pursuit of personal ends but are both the cause and reflection of a solidaristic moral order – which, unlike its Greek predecessors, claims not to include male property rights over slaves and women.

Though the origins of a nation-state concept of citizenship coincided with a period in which the 'cluster of meanings' emphasised legal and political rights, the creation and development of the EC took place at a time when it was accepted in a substantial body of political theory, by citizens and even by governments . . ., that there was a connection – natural, logical, instrumental or expedient – amongst civil, political and social rights. Community regulation of social security, social assistance and sex equality in income maintenance (from paid work and social security) embodies bits of both the individualistic and collectivist understandings referred to above. On the one hand, its legal rights and 'permissive' measures are designed to reduce national and sex discrimination in the exercise of economic and social opportunities in a transnational order. But, as in the case of workers' rights, traces of the idea of a common moral order can be found in many references to common standards of living, social cohesion and harmonious regional development to facilitate the exercise of economic and social roles in a transnational regime. Even if not self-consciously intended by Member State governments as a step towards a common citizenship, these policies cannot be discounted, in the life of their own that they have acquired, as a dimension of European citizenship.

Nor should it be overlooked that Community instruments confer a legally defined status on citizens as 'Community nationals' or, in the words of the Maastricht Treaty, 'Citizens of the Union'. The consolidation of this process, which is discussed in most of this book, means Community policies *do* contribute to Aron's political transformation as a result of 'spill-overs' from social regulation into the legal and political competences of Member States . . .

However, Aron is, of course, right that the governments of nation-states remain the primary actors and that the Member States of the EC vary in their traditions and practices of nationality and citizenship . . . This is acknowledged in the regulation of a common order through twelve, diverse national orders. But, as Heater's historical account shows, this need not necessarily rule out the possibility of common citizenship rights. While the

Stoic ideal of cosmopolitan citizenship has remained largely, though not entirely, abstract (the Nuremburg trials assumed there were 'higher duties'
than loyalty to temporal authority wrongly exercised), the Romans developed 'a form of citizenship which was both pragmatic and extensible in
application' . . . They extended the status of Roman citizenship to residents
of parts of the Empire taken by conquest. Thus, St Paul, declaring himself a
citizen of Tarsus when arrested in Jerusalem, was able to claim also his
Roman citizenship and to demand a trial under the Roman, not local, system of justice.

This early practice of dual citizenship, continuing intellectual interest in it
and in the Stoic ideal, as well as the modern practice of popular participation in the work of international organisations, inspire Heater to think that
propositions about dual and multinational citizenship are not unrealistic . . .
His final reference is to the European Community. But the Community is
not an expression of Stoic universalism, given its distinction between
Community migrants and those from outside ('third country migrants'). Nor,
obviously, is it an empire; sovereign states voluntarily founded it and agree
to its developments. But, as noted before, there is more than one set of
standards that can be appealed to by claimants of rights. In this neo-imperial regime of rights, as in any other, certain issues need to be addressed
which include: identities, loyalties, obligations and institutional frameworks
for participation and the exercise of rights and duties . . .

References in [D71]

Aron, R, 'Is multinational citizenship possible?' (1974) 41(4) *Social
Research* 638–656.
Heater, D, *Citizenship. The Civic Ideal in World History, Politics and
Education* (London, New York: Longman, 1990).
Jordan, B, *The Common Good. Citizenship, Morality and Self-Interest.*
(Oxford: Basil Blackwell, 1989).
King, D, and Waldron, J, 'Citizenship, social citizenship and the defence of
welfare provision' (1988) 18 *British Journal of Political Science* 415–43.
Leca, J, 'Nationalità e cittadinanza nell'Europa delle immigrazioni', in vari-
ous authors, *Italia, Europa e Nuove Immigrazioni* (Turin: Edizione della
Fondazione Giovanni Agnelli, 1990).
Tassin, E, 'Europe: a political community?' in Chantal Mouffe (ed),
Dimensions of Radical Democracy. Pluralism, Citizenship, Community
(London: Verso, 1992).
van Gunsteren, H, 'Notes on a theory of citizenship', in P Birnbaum, J
Lively and G Parry (eds), *Democracy, Consensus and Social Contract*
(London and Beverly Hills, CA: Sage/ECPR, 1978).

[D72]   Ursula Vogel: 'Is citizenship gender-specific?', in U Vogel and M Moran (eds), The Frontiers of Citizenship (Macmillan, 1991)

Conclusion: At the frontiers of citizenship

Feminist political theories today do not speak with one voice. They bring
different priorities and diverse strategies to the debates on citizenship. But

there is general agreement that the task cannot be to improve upon existing models of citizen participation by simply adding a number of women's issues 'to the agenda'. Any attempt to explore the conditions of women's citizenship must centre on the assumption of their autonomy.

Within this framework of shared assumptions one can sketch out four different approaches: (1) a gender-neutral model aimed at establishing women's and men's common citizenship; (2) a model based upon the assumption of women's particular identity; (3) the projection of the 'woman-friendly state' derived from the unique experiences of the Scandinavian welfare states; (4) a new potential for active citizenship that reflects women's strong presence in the New Social Movements.

It should be noted that these efforts of rethinking citizenship are not undertaken within the narrow confines of a 'woman and . . .' scheme. The issues raised address the generally problematic status of citizenship today. Thus, to challenge the traditional distinctions between public and private, political and non-political spheres as they have affected women will lead us to a question of wider implications – whether the spatial categories in which we tend to convey the meanings of citizenship are still adequate. Similarly, the prerequisites of women's participation refer to the obstruction of citizen equality by the unequal access to the resources of participation – money, knowledge, work-patterns and, most pertinently, time. Finally, women's experimenting with new modes of political involvement outside institutional politics underlines the general sense of uncertainty as to the type of community of which we can be active members and to which we should owe the allegiance of citizens (the nation-state? the local neighbourhood? the European dimension of women's networks?).

1. We can say that the first approach opts for a direct route towards a 'fully human theory' of women's and men's common citizenship from which all traces of ascribed gender roles would have disappeared. This project would engage us from the outset in the task of redefining the enabling conditions of citizen participation so as to include not only institutional politics and the workplace but also family relations in the demand for gender equality. Equal opportunities for citizenship will remain illusory until work inside and for the household, and in particular the task of social reproduction, comes to be shared between its adult members.

. . .

2. Different strategies of feminist theory and practice have developed from the premise of gender particularity. They begin with the rejection of all homogeneous, all-inclusive models of citizenship. The traditional languages of participatory politics are seen as defective precisely because they deal in abstracts, ie they focus on citizens as unsituated individuals rather than on 'embodied, gendered persons'. This critique does not necessarily imply, as is sometimes feared, a return to biological essentialism. Rather, it calls upon feminist theory to develop a new vocabulary capable of expressing the specific ways in which women have, *historically*, perceived and practised citizenship. This approach is based on two assumptions. First, in a society whose institutions have always been divided by gender inequality, we can expect that women's and men's experiences, moral perceptions and modes of knowledge will differ significantly. To the extent that women have been disproportionately involved in the female world of the household,

in the concerns of everyday life and in the activities of nurturing and caring, they have developed 'their own voice'. And that voice manifests itself also in different modes of citizen responsibilities and in different modes of citizen participation. It follows, secondly, that women's experience should not be reconstructed primarily within an 'oppressed-group model', not merely from the position of victims but, positively, from the assumption of valuable perspectives on society and politics.

. . .

3. To observers from outside, the Scandinavian countries offer the enviable example of successful '*state feminism*' (or, more cautiously, models of possible developments towards a 'woman-friendly state'). The most pertinent feature – and the major contrast with the condition of women in other European welfare states – is that here the rights of social citizenship have actually empowered women for political participation. Their more securely-rooted material independence must be understood less as the result of policies especially aimed at women than as a consequence of Social Democracy's systematic and pervasive pursuit of social equality – of membership based upon universal rather than status-linked entitlements. On this basis the relationship between the state and various social groups could develop into forms of partnership. The comprehensive institutionalisation of social care is such an example of the partnership between the state and the family. Moreover, given that women now have a massive presence in the public sector – as clients (recipients of benefits), as consumers of services and, importantly, as employees – the welfare state itself could become the central arena for women's citizenship.

Feminists do, on the other hand, not deny that these favourable circumstances cannot by themselves guarantee women's active citizenship. The fact that women are now less dependent upon individual men might mean little more than that they have become more dependent on the state. State feminism, enacted from above, might become entrenched in a dependency culture in which women are citizens as clients and consumers, but not as actors. Especially if we take into consideration that the high degree of women's political mobilisation at local level has so far not been matched at the elite level, there might then be again (as in Britain and in the United States) two classes of citizens separated by gender – electoral citizens and client citizens. This danger can only be countered by 'feminism from below', by the expansion of citizen competence and citizen participation in all decision-making structures of the welfare state. Politics has not been made redundant by social reform. More important for women than material welfare alone is the expansion of representation rights which can add 'citizen aspects to all our public roles'.

4. While women are still inadequately represented in the dominant institutions of the state they have displayed a strong presence in the various groups that make up the New Social Movements (environment, peace, women's movements, Green parties, etc). Women often hold overlapping memberships in these groups, are active not only at grass-roots level but also in the leadership and have considerable influence in the discussions of programmes and strategies. The New Social Movements in general represent a challenge to 'the boundaries of institutional politics', a response to the marginality of political participation in the post-war consensus on growth, prosperity and security. Both on the practical and theoretical level

they document what one might call the 'rebirth of the citizen'. Theoretical reflection in this environment has focused upon the idea of 'civil society' as an intermediate sphere between the state and private life, a space distinct from institutional politics but filled with issues and activities of collective concern. These movements do not primarily aim at gaining power nor, on the other hand, at merely a politics of symbolic gestures. Both in their internal organisation (informal, discontinuous, context-sensitive) and their public activities they experiment with new modes and meanings of participation. And it is this emphasis, rather than the values of autonomy and self-government themselves, that they have brought to the renewed debates about citizenship.

[D73]   Carlos Closa: 'The concept of citizenship in the Treaty on European Union' (1992) 29 Common Market Law Review 1137

3.1   The discussion of the concept of citizenship during the [Inter-governmental Conference] on political union

In the preliminary stage of the IGC, citizenship was not considered in the scope of reform; indeed, the initial mentions of the concept of citizenship were subsumed in the broader and more vague proposals on democratic legitimacy. Thus, the Belgian memorandum of institutional relaunch, which can be considered as the first informal contribution to the IGC process, did not specifically mention the concept of citizenship, although it referred to the old notion of a 'People's Europe' which was considered to be inextricably linked to basic human rights. Therefore, the Belgian government proposed the inclusion of provisions on human rights in the Treaties, and the accession of the Community to the Strasbourg Convention on Human Rights. Both points were regarded as devices to strengthen the democratic nature of the institutions of the Community. Two other measures proposed were a uniform electoral procedure for European Parliament elections, which would allow all Community citizens to take part wherever they reside within the Community, and an effort to progress in granting voting rights in local elections on the lines of former Commission proposals.

The first reported reference to the concept of citizenship in the framework of the political union discussions was contained in a letter by the Spanish Prime Minister to the President in Office of the Council. In that letter, citizenship was defined as one of the three pillars of European political union, the other two being EMU and a common foreign and security policy. The basic elements in the Spanish view would be the unlimited freedom of movement, establishment and access to employment and the right to vote and stand for election irrespective of their country of residence. Although the idea was backed by the Italian and the Danish delegations, it was regarded as a rather vague notion by some other Member States. Thus, the Belgian representatives argued that citizenship should be seen rather as an objective to be achieved and the UK believed that it was premature to consider citizenship as a constitutive element of political union. In the Spanish view, the creation of a new instance of political power, ie the Union, would require the definition of rights and duties of the affected individuals, as happens in national states.

Eventually, the question of citizenship was incorporated in the prepara-tory work of the COREPER and, finally, the 1990 June Dublin European Council included citizenship in the framework of the 'overall objective of po-litical Union'. The indications provided by the European Council endorsed the development of the concept from the limited form of citizenship already existing within the EC and not created ex novo. The Council was asked to examine 'How will the Union include and extend the notion of Community citizenship carrying with it specific rights (human, political, social, the right of complete free movement and residence, etc) for the citizens of the Member States by virtue of these states belonging to the Union?'

The first systematic contribution to the elaboration of the concept was the *Spanish Memorandum on European Citizenship*. This text dismissed the concept of 'citizen of the Community', as developed around the Rome Treaty, as insufficient because the measures and initiatives taken to de-velop it did not allow the notion of 'privileged foreigners' applied to citizens from other Member States to be overcome. From this limited notion, the Spanish proposal called for a further step which would eliminate the nega-tive effects currently accompanying the condition of foreigner for a citizen of a Member State living in another Member State.

The emphasis that the Spanish text put on the autonomous character of citizenship as one of the bases of the Union was reduced in the other two contributions which mentioned the concept of citizenship before the open-ing of the IGC. The Commission opinion, delivered on 21 October, made clear that the development of the concept of citizenship was central to its objective of strengthening democratic legitimacy, explicitly pointing out that the exclusion of the 'people of Europe' by the neofunctionalist dynamic based on the 1992 programme. In its view, involvement of citizens in Community activities should be at every stage of the definition of policies in fields directly affecting them. The second document was the *Danish Memorandum on the IGC on Political Union*, which proposed the inclusion of some political rights in the section under the heading 'Strengthening the democratic basis for Community co-operation'. The Danish delegation pro-posed the right to vote in local elections to citizens residing in a Member State other than their own and the introduction of an ombudsman system under the aegis of the European Parliament [EP].

Functionally, the conclusions of the Presidency after the December Rome summit, which formed the basis for the mandate to the IGC, estab-lished that citizenship would be considered one of the autonomous elements to create the Union (together with democratic legitimacy, common foreign and security policy, extension and strengthening of Community action, and effectiveness and efficiency of the Union). The conclusions recorded the consensus between Member States on the necessity of ex-amining the concept of European citizenship. The Heads of State and Government proposed the study of a catalogue of rights to be included in the Treaty as elements of citizenship, although they pointed out that the im-plementation of such provisions should give appropriate consideration to particular problems in some Member States in a clear reference to Luxembourg's problems with voting rights in local elections.

The substance of the concept of citizenship was, in the view of the Council, to be built around three groups of rights. The first group were 'civic rights', a euphemistic designation for political rights strictu sensu. The Council listed participation in elections to the European Parliament in the country of residence and possible participation in municipal elections. The second group of rights, social and economic rights, were largely an enlarged version of rights under the EEC treaty; ie freedom of movement and equality of opportunities and treatment for all Community citizens. Thirdly, the Council included the joint protection of Community citizens outside Community borders. The Council opined also that the IGC should consider a mechanism for the defence of citizens' rights regarding Community matters (ombudsman). It is particularly significant that human rights were not regarded in connexion to citizenship, as the Spanish memorandum had argued. In its terms, human rights and basic freedoms are a distinct and independent part of the quality of European citizens and the Conference should examine uniform guarantees for residents of the Community, independent of their nationalities. This vague wording would imply indeed a political will to universalise the guarantee of human rights even to nationals from non-Member States. The two institutional contributions from the Commission and the EP argued the opposite case. The Commission's opinion considered that basic human rights were an essential element, and it therefore proposed a reference to the Strasbourg Convention. Consistently, the Commission contribution entitled Union citizens to invoke the rights guaranteed by the Convention. Although the wording of the article establishes that the Union accepts the Convention, the Commission did not call for accession but refers to the proposal already lodged before the Counoil for the Community (and not the Union) to accede. This opinion was also shared by the EP which in its Resolution on Union citizenship considered that such citizenship must imply the guarantee of basic human and fundamental rights. From the rapporteur's point of view, 'it is inconceivable to base citizenship on anything other than the expansion of fundamental rights and freedoms in addition to their recognition and protection'. In any case, human rights were not regarded during the conference in the dispositions creating the citizenship of the Union. In the Treaty, they appear in the Article F2 of the Common Provisions of the Treaty on Political Union, as the Spanish thesis argued.

In comparison with any of the other major issues discussed during the conference, citizenship was not a very controversial topic. Discussion proceeded on the basis of two documents elaborated in the form of draft articles. Those were a text by the Spanish delegation which developed in ten articles the ideas advanced in the memorandum, and the Contribution of the Commission, which contained 12 articles. Basic agreement was already possible around the first draft text of the Luxembourg Presidency and the final shape of the citizenship of the union was almost entirely established by the final draft of the Presidency in June. The EP, however, criticised the achievements of the conference, whose drafts were considered not to institute a Union citizenship but to list a number of special rights of a partial nature whose exercise was subject to inter-governmental agreement.

3.2 The constitutionalisation of the citizenship of the Union

Previous to the IGC, the concept of citizenship had been built on a body of heterogeneous provisions dispersed throughout the Rome Treaty. The lack of an explicit legal acknowledgement of citizenship allowed this ambit to be kept for the discretion of inter-governmental arrangements. The introduction of the citizenship of the Union has implied the generalisation of the rights of residence and movement, the constitutionalising of the right of petition and the establishment of a clear foundation for regulating voting rights in local and EP elections regardless of residence.

Citizenship of the Union is included in Part Two of the 'Provisions Amending the Treaty establishing the European Economic Community with a view to establishing the European Community' and developed through six articles which contain a definition (Article 8), the catalogue of rights attached to the condition of citizen (Articles 8a to 8d) and a procedure for further development of this Part (Article 8e). Significantly, the Treaty has overcome opinions which argued in favour of including the principles in the Treaty, but leaving the application to be effected through derived law. The linkage between the citizenship of the Union developed through the dispositions of the EC Treaty and the Union itself is created by recognising citizenship as one of the objectives of the Union. This is enshrined by the Common Provisions of the Treaty, as had been anticipated by the final text of the Luxembourg Presidency. In this, the Treaty follows the ideas forwarded by the contribution of the Commission. By including the articles regulating the citizenship of the Union in Title I of Part Two (Foundations of the Union) rather than in the Preamble or in the introductory articles, which set out the objectives of the Union, the Commission's intention was to stress that these were implementing measures and not mere declaratory clauses.

The inclusion of the citizenship of the Union in the provisions on the Community implies that some citizenship rights will be governed mainly by Community law and through the involvement of Community institutions. Furthermore, legislation may be directly applicable and the jurisdiction of the European Court of Justice will cover it. This offers the possibility for any individual to have recourse to national courts to make them prevail. Not surprisingly, opposition to the principle of direct applicability, as it would stem from the Project of Articles, was voiced by Denmark. The British government also objected [to] the possible direct applicability of the right of movement throughout the Community without time limits.

The primacy of Community law in the development of the Union enshrined by the Treaty is made uncertain by two aspects. First, during the conference there was no in-depth discussion on the problems and implications of establishing a Union citizenship which would be affected by Union policies (eg legal or police co-operation), but which could only be protected in the framework and with the means of the EC. Secondly, the provisions regulating citizenship are a blend of two different natures, as the Commission pointed out in its contribution. First, there is a group of articles conferring rights which citizens derive directly from the Treaty (non-discrimination, freedom of movement, granting of union citizenship itself) which only need a judicial guarantee and/or improving existing provisions for their exercise. Not surprisingly, this list coincides with the rights already available under the Rome Treaties. The second group is composed by rights whose effective development will require bringing into effect ad hoc legislation together with the necessary detailed rules and conditions. Voting rights and diplomatic protection are included in this category of rights for which the Treaty has failed to establish a proper Community procedure. They might be implemented through multilateral agreements between Member States rather than through Community legal instruments.

. . .

3.5 Modification of the catalogue of rights

The catalogue of rights enshrined by the Treaty is not intended to be a definitive one; current rights may be strengthened and/or new ones added (Article 8e). The final wording of the Treaty has rejected the restrictive version contained in the first Presidency draft, which empowered the Council to modify the catalogue of rights. Modification meant that the Council could eventually *restrict* the foreseen rights through majority voting. Clearly this restrictive option was not acceptable to most of the parties and, therefore, the Council will only be allowed to act in a positive way: *the Council may adopt provisions to strengthen or add to the rights* laid down in Part Two. In any case, future provisions are not automatically binding, since the Council *shall recommend to the Member States for adoption with their respective constitutional rules*. Therefore, the future development of Union citizenship is left to the discretion of the Member States.

Finally, the Commission has been entrusted with guiding the dynamic evolution of citizenship and its parallel development alongside the Union itself. The Commission would report before 31 December 1993 and every three years thereafter on the implementation of the provisions of Part Two. This Commission report will become a basis for Council decisions acting unanimously on a Commission proposal after consulting the EP.

Therefore, the character of the union citizenship is determined by the progressive acquisition of rights stemming from the dynamic development of the Union. That is, the gradual acquisition by the European citizen of specific rights in the new policy areas transferred to the Union. This evolutive character, which is in itself the most characteristic feature of the citizenship of the Union, was developed by the contributions to the conference as a channel for incorporating controversial socio-economic rights. As it has been recorded above, the Spanish proposal differentiated citizenship from the status civitatis which is linked to the degree of union achieved. Lastly, a 'real Union' would require a European citizenship of great content, that is 'real union' should aim to overcome the inequalities which subsist between Community citizens through the promotion of economic and social cohesion, this being a constant claim of the Spanish government.

The Commission also endorsed this dynamic character (ie citizenship would be progressively developed) in its opinion. Indeed, the Commission included as one element of Union citizenship the establishment of targets for the civic, economic and social rights of the individuals to be properly defined at a later stage. When it presented its contribution to the IGC, the Commission explained that the dynamic character was one of the principles on which Union citizenship was based: it *reflects the aims of the Union, involving as it does an indivisible body of rights and obligations stemming from the gradual and coherent development of the Union's political, economic and social dimension.* The Commission wanted to avoid the concept of citizenship being restricted to economic rights in the framework of the Rome Treaties and, at the same time, it sought to provide the basis for its future updating as the Union developed. Therefore, the provisions proposed laid down objectives for the granting of rights in the future and for defining obligations, specially in the social field, with the possibility of eventually *enlarging* (and only enlarging, not reducing) the catalogue of citizens' rights by a unanimous Council vote on a Commission proposal.

[D74]   Juliet Lodge: 'Towards a political union?', in J Lodge (ed), The European Community and the Challenge of the Future (2nd edn, Pinter, 1993)

A People's Europe

The idea of a People's Europe (as one of the tangible and not merely symbolic advantages of the single-market phase in integration) was not sufficiently publicised or clearly presented to capture the public imagination. The replacement of earlier efforts to promote integration by harmonising regulations and technical norms through the mutual recognition of standards, qualifications and practices and by focusing on a limited number of sectors benefited corporate cross-border networking and the goal of realising the single market. Its ramifications were felt outside the business community and outside the territory of the EC where the Community had begun to consolidate and politicise its international identity. But inside the EC, it was questionable whether people not directly engaged in EC policies and programmes were aware of the EC and its policies, let alone identified themselves in any positive way with the Community. The multitude of EC initiatives and non-structural fund schemes designed to enhance mobility, the use of human resources and to promote mobility certainly took off, but they remained visible to a small minority. Moreover, an instrumental switch in loyalty by the beneficiaries could not be assumed or demonstrated. Few saw themselves as EC citizens. As the EC inched towards realising the goal of an ever-closer union, and as it set out a treaty to establish a European Union, the issues of the appropriateness, proximity, visibility, tangibility, transparency and legitimacy of the EC and its institutions had to be faced. It was no longer enough to claim that the EC rested on the direct legitimacy conferred through Euro-elections on the European Parliament and the indirect legitimacy possessed by the Council. It was argued that popular consent was necessary to underpin the Union.

The Adonnino Committee set up by the Fontainebleau European Council in 1984 outlined measures to promote a sense of identity for people in the EC. These included proposals for rights for citizens, culture, youth exchanges, health and social security, symbols like the flag, anthem, passport, common driving licence, and educational and labour opportunities. In short, the idea was to go beyond symbolism to tangible political and social rights to consolidate the idea of common membership in a common venture. Precise obligations as a counterpart to rights have yet to be specified.

A Union based on an EC in which the Four Freedoms are meaningful inevitably has to be recognised as a political union. The concept of citizenship is essentially political. It goes beyond the earlier idea of full-time workers enjoying labour mobility and entitlements to social security wherever they worked in the EC. It builds on the social policy (including its provisions on sexual equality and promoting opportunities for special groups like the young unemployed, disabled etc), the Social Chapter and the commitment to social and economic cohesion to embrace a concept of shared citizenship and multiple loyalty holding common to federal systems. The Treaty on European Union Article 8 states:

1. Citizenship of the Union is hereby established.

Every person holding the nationality of a Member State shall be a citizen of the Union.

2. Citizens of the Union shall enjoy the rights conferred by this Treaty and shall be subject to the duties imposed thereby.

Subsidiarity is being applied here. It remains the right of states to confer or deny a status which then automatically grants a person EC citizenship. The rights derived from this status are mainly those of labour mobility; the right to move and reside freely within the territory of the Member States; the right to vote in and contest municipal elections (in states in which citizens are resident but of which they are not nationals) and in elections to the European Parliament. Beyond that Union citizens have the right to be protected, when in third states, by the diplomatic or consular authorities of any Member State, on the same conditions as that state's nationals; the right to petition the European Parliament; and the right to apply to the Ombudsman. The rights of minorities are not explicitly recognised, but deliberations on these issues and the associated issues of the status of legal immigrants and genuine political refugees, and the development of immigration policies under the Justice and Home Affairs ['pillar'], mean that even more delicate questions need answering. It is inconceivable that this embryonic conception of Union citizenship will not be progressively expanded during the next two decades.

Postscript

Below you will see a (selective and non-exhaustive) list of ten rights, duties and attributes commonly associated with the concept of nationality or citizenship of a nation state, forming an embryo Citizens' Charter (or a social contract between the individual and the state, based on the rule of law). Since citizenship has traditionally been associated with the gaining of personal and political freedom, the list of rights is longer than the list of duties, and such rights, duties and attributes may already be found (expressly or by necessary implication) in the several constitutions of the Member States of the Community.

Consider, in the light of the foregoing chapter, to what extent (in whole or in part) these rights, duties and attributes (and any others which may come to mind) are mirrored within the European Community (let us call it the state of Euro-Utopia) and are possessed by all citizens of Euro-Utopia. When you have done this, consider further whether certain rights, duties and attributes can only be realised by the full political union (whether unitary or federal) of the individual Member States to form the brave new world of Euro-Utopia.

The list
1. The right to Euro-Utopian nationality (or citizenship), by reason of birth in Euro-Utopia, by reason of Euro-Utopian parentage or by naturalisation in accordance with rules treating all applicants for Euro-Utopian nationality in an equal manner.

2. The right to be granted a Euro-Utopian passport, with the right to leave (and not be refused entry into) Euro-Utopia, and, when in a country other than Euro-Utopia, to be given diplomatic protection by representatives to that country from Euro-Utopia, together with the right, irrespective of status, political affiliation, health or financial situation, to travel and reside in every region of Euro-Utopia.

3. The right, in accordance with principles of a common and universal suffrage and subject only to minimalist restrictions (such as age and mental capacity), to vote (within the appropriate electoral constituency) at all national, regional and local elections in Euro-Utopia, together with the co-relative right to stand as a candidate for any elective office in Euro-Utopia.

4. The right, subject to reasonable conditions as to qualifications, competence and expertise, to be appointed to all categories of judicial office in Euro-Utopia, to all levels of the Euro-Utopian civil service, and to all ranks in the police, security and armed forces of Euro-Utopia.

5. The right to personal and political liberty and to equality of treatment in all aspects of public and private life in accordance with the Euro-Utopian Declaration of Fundamental Rights.

6. The right to be governed in accordance with the rule of law and democratic principles of political accountability, to exercise effective enjoyment of the benefits conferred on citizens by Euro-Utopian law, including effective political and legal remedies against unlawful and unreasonable exercise of governmental power.

7. The right to the health, education and other welfare services provided by Euro-Utopia, including the right to dependence on social security provision when unemployed, disabled or old.

8. The duty of allegiance to Euro-Utopia, including the duty not to demonstrate disloyalty to Euro-Utopia or to act against Euro-Utopia's stated interests (as laid down in the criminal code of Euro-Utopia), coupled with the duty to perform such military or other forms of national service as may be determined in accordance with Euro-Utopia's defence policy and international obligations.

9. The duty of all citizens to contribute, according to their means, to the Euro-Utopian economy by the payment of taxes and other financial charges.

10. The attributes (some might say trappings) which contribute to the Euro-Utopian citizen's sense of belonging to a national society, including a national anthem, flag and honours system, national symbols or famous citizens or the Head of State of Euro-Utopia being represented on coins, banknotes and official documents, national sports teams and Euro-Utopian Olympic representation (and, of course, a Euro-Utopian singer in the Global Song Contest!).

Further reading

Green, N, Hartley, T, and Usher, J, 'The Legal Foundations of the Single European Market' (1991).

Handoll, J, 'Article 48(4) EEC and Non-Nationals; Access to Public Employment' (1988) 13 ELR 223.

Marias, E (ed) *European Citizenship* (EIPA, 1994).

O'Keeffe, D, & Twomey, P, (eds) *Legal Issues of the Maastricht Treaty* (Chancery Law, 1993).

Van Steenbergen, B, (ed) *The Condition of Citizenship* (Sage, 1994).

Wyatt, D, and Dashwood, A, *European Community Law* (3rd edn, 1993).

Commission of the EEC v French Republic 307/84 [1986] ECR 1725.

Commission of the EEC v Italian Republic 225/85 [1987] ECR 2625.

Concetta Sagulo, Gennaro Brenca and Addelmadjid Backhouche v Public Ministry Amtsgericht Reutlingen 8/77 [1977] ECR 1495.

Criminal Proceedings against Messner 265/88 [1989] ECR 4209.

Elestina Esselina Christina Morson and Sewradjie Jhanjan v State of the Netherlands 35, 36/82 [1982] ECR 3723.

Emir Gül v Regierungspräsident Düsseldorf 131/85 [1986] ECR 1573.

Mr & Mrs F v Belgian State 7/75 [1975] ECR 679.

Josette Pecastaing v Belgian State 98/79 [1980] ECR 691.

Kenneth Scrivner and Carol Cole v Centre public d'aide sociale de Chastre 122/84 [1985] ECR 1027.

Office national de l'emploi v Joszef Deak 94/84 [1985] ECR 1873.

Udo Steyman v Staatssecretaris van Justitie 196/87 [1989] ECR 6159.

Vera Hoeckx v Openbarr Centrum voor Maatschappelijk Welzijn, Kalmthout 249/83 [1985] ECR 973.

Württembergische Milchverwertung- Südmilch-AG v Salvatore Ugliola 15/69 [1969] ECR 363.

Chapter Five

The European Trader

The economic evolution of the European Community can be charted from the limited concept of a customs union to the pursuit of the much more ambitious goals of economic and monetary union via the single internal market (see earlier [A1]–[A4] and [A14], together with [E1]).That development has brought with it significant changes in the substantive content of the rights and obligations of participants in the market place, whether as individuals, enterprises or Member States. This chapter explores the extent to which, and methods by which, common levels of protection and enjoyment of economic rights have been established by the European Court of Justice (and of late also the Court of First Instance) by synthesis of the various strands of Community law relating to goods, services and competition.

The EC Treaty framework is not textually consistent as to the degree of entitlement or freedom that was originally envisaged as the platform for the creation of a single market or deeper economic union. This in itself may have shaped the preference seemingly displayed by the Court of Justice for relying on certain provisions rather than others. In particular, the huge concentration upon the application of Article 30 (free movement of goods) [E11]–[E37] has highlighted the fact that it is not only discriminatory rules or behaviour that can be caught by the prohibitions of Community law. The notion of a 'mere' restriction on trade brought about by a state measure is capable, on the *Dassonville* [E12] formula at least, of being outlawed even though it may apparently not distinguish between domestic and imported products. In contrast, other rules, such as Article 95(1) (taxation of products of other Member States) [E4] and Article 37 (adjustment of state monopolies) [E83]–[E84], require a discriminatory element before infringement occurs. Yet a different formulation is to be found in the prohibition against protectionist taxation under Article 95(2) [E4]. An interesting question thus arises as to whether there is a progressive ladder of enjoyment available to Community traders under the market provisions of the Treaty, as interpreted by the Court of Justice, ranging from the right to challenge pecuniary charges attaching only by reason of importation [E2]–[E3], through to protection against the most subtle examples of trade restrictions and state interference.

For some, the Court of Justice's willingness to entertain ambitious propositions as to the scope of a trade restriction has gone too far. However, some attempt should be made to distinguish between the defects of inappropriate tools for achieving justifiable objectives, and claims that the objectives themselves have been overreached. Certainly, the cases reveal that the so-called

Dassonville formula may have outlived its obvious usefulness as a flexible net to cast in the direction of evasive state distortions **[E41]**. The impact of judicial activity itself demands credible reasoning to maintain its legitimacy. Hence, perhaps, the alternative explanations sometimes invoked by the court based on causation, scale or immediacy of effect as ways of demarcating the boundaries of the Article 30 prohibition **[A18]**, **[E18]**, **[E19]**. The division of cases along the somewhat murky lines of their discriminatory or non-discriminatory nature (see the *Irish Souvenirs* case **[E22]**) has produced its own boomerang by creating a self-inflicted problem of classification for the court if that distinction does not fit the conclusion most apt in a particular case for the promotion of the purposes of the Community **[E28]**.

However, overstressing definitional aspects of what is a 'trade restriction' may itself be to miss the essential point. From a purposive angle, the relevant question is whether a particular measure impedes the attainment of the goals of the Community (whether that is the single market following the Single European Act or the economic and monetary convergence of Maastricht). Seen in that light, there is a greater interest in what is necessary to attain those goals, or indeed whether more than one path is acceptable.

One of the signal achievements of the jurisprudence of the Court of Justice is the creation of a set of criteria to underpin and limit acceptable restrictions or distortions in the market. What began as the *Cassis* doctrine **[E21]** (also known as imperative or mandatory requirements or the rule of reason) may have looked like a set of exceptions for Member States to sweeten the pill, in the case of non-discriminatory measures, as the incentive for accepting the court's imposition of the Article 30 prohibition upon actions within this wider category. Subsequent cases have extended the range of particular legitimate interests **[A18]**, **[E23]**–**[E27]**, but with the subtle reasoning that this very legitimacy is predicated upon the compatibility with the Community's goals of those selfsame interests. In other words, the socio-cultural characteristics protectable by laws against trading on Sundays **[A18]** are not the preserve of national competence but simply acceptable within the framework of a single market because their negative effects are not distortive enough or sufficiently objectionable in principle. The application of subsidiarity **[A22]**–**[A29]** is an interesting exercise in this context: should the more recent Article 30 cases be viewed as about the most effective method of attaining the single market or as competence being returned to the Member States? These concerns may explain *Keck* **[E20]**.

At the same time as the Court of Justice has been producing a range of Community-compatible criteria of public interest defensible at national level, it has subjected the utilisation of these criteria in individual cases to an additional hurdle in the form of the proportionality test. This notion, embracing aspects of both necessity and reasonableness, seeks to ensure that departures from Treaty goals are not excessive in scope or scale. The overall impression of the cases may be that the court's real concerns are twofold: is the aim of a particular measure capable of being tolerated in a single market, and could it be achieved in any other, less restrictive, fashion **[E32]**–**[E35]**?

What is particularly striking about the emergence of these concerns is that the court has produced principles which are not confined to the context of goods, or indeed markets. The rule of reason has been overtly recognised in relation to services **[E46]**–**[E47]**. The proportionality principle is well-established as a general principle of Community law, as applicable to acts of

Community institutions as it is to Member States or individuals (see Chapter Two, Section Four). For the purpose of this chapter, however, its application in the field of competition policy and regulation should be appreciated.

Goods and competition are two sides of the same market coin. The freedom of movement across frontiers should bring about the penetration which is then to be enjoyed by fair competition in the open market place. The reference in the Treaty to a system of undistorted competition **[E49]** has been treated as the authorisation for a freedom capable of overriding other considerations such as the organisation of national intellectual property rights. However, the natural economic interdependence of goods and competition has not always received legal embodiment. Indeed, the assimilation of Articles 30 and the competition rules by the court in the *Telecoms Terminal Equipment* case **[E86]** is a comparatively rare overt acknowledgement.

Just as the Article 30 cases reveal a concern with whether a particular measure meets a goal or need compatible with other aspects of Community activity, so developments in the interpretation of Articles 85-86 (restrictive agreements etc between undertakings and abuse of a dominant position) **[E49]** show an increasing concern with the functional approach. Although not the only explanation (increased workload on the Commission and the political desirability of decentralisation being others), the willingness to acknowledge that some agreements or practices might not infringe Article 85(1) at all may reflect a value-judgment by the court as to the compatibility of certain business activities with the Community's overall direction. Thus, selective distribution and franchising agreements may escape prohibition altogether if certain criteria are satisfied **[E54]–[E56]**. Given that Article 85(3) provides a schematic system for exemptions, it may seem odd that these developments in relation to the scope of the prohibition should have occurred. Indeed, the earlier case law may have suggested **[E53]** a stricter demarcation between an expansive prohibition under Article 85(1) and the exemption scrutiny using the specific criteria of Article 85(3). However, seen against the avowed 'effects' basis of EC competition law, it may be wholly consistent with the spirit of the jurisprudence under Article 30 to consider whether some other, higher, goal is served by an agreement than just an examination of its apparent, and often inevitable, restrictive effects.

The construction of a unitary approach at law to market rights has brought with it a resulting hierarchy of obligations. It is now clear that Article 222 **[E83]**, apparently safeguarding the national systems of property ownership from the assault of Community law, is vulnerable to values which the court sees as more important. At one time, especially in the context of intellectual property **[E36]–[E37]**, this was delicately put in terms of a distinction between the existence of rights (which Community law could not challenge) and their exercise (which it could). It is hard to see how this distinction is maintainable any longer in the light of several cases involving state monopolies or entrusted undertakings **[E86]**, **[E88]–[E91]**, as well as some of the intellectual property decisions **[E74]–[E75]**. The upshot is to raise question marks as to the compatibility of any public sector with Community law at all. At the very least, there may be a need to identify a core of legitimate interests which that sector is to pursue before it can be compatible with the needs of a single, open market **[E90]**. This core can be seen as strongly analogous to the 'specific subject matter' test used to assess the compatibility with the Treaty of intellectual property rights **[E36]**.

A further conflict, this time within the court's own priorities, may also be discernible in this same case law, especially in the rapidly expanding litigation under Article 86 and abuse of a dominant position. Whereas at one time an emphasis may have been placed on achieving a fair balance of the interests of abuser and abused **[E72]–[E73]**, the single market programme may have produced greater concentration upon integrationist forces. Thus, for example, the early cases on refusal to supply all had an element of pre-existing relationship between dominant party and alleged victim. The distortion or abrogation of that relationship was the very unfairness that created the abuse. However, more recent decisions, especially those relating to exclusive or special rights or the licensing of intellectual property rights **[E75]–[E76]**, **[E88]–[E90]**, seem to give greater weight to the demands of a market in which access is available to all who wish to play. Indeed, one of the pressing concerns in this area is the extent to which the statement in *Michelin* **[E66]** that dominant parties have special responsibilities may have an even longer hidden agenda than first feared by those who protest the inalienable right of a business to choose with whom it wishes to deal **[E77]**.

One of the most informative benchmarks as to the success or otherwise of the implementation of a single market is the extent to which state interference is subject to the same rules as the private sector **[E84]**, **[E87]**. After lengthy periods dormant, provisions such as Article 90 and 92–94 **[E83]**, governing public undertakings and state aids respectively, now appear to be acquiring real teeth **[E92]–[E93]**, **[E95]**. The court's approach has been typically inventive and expansive in this regard. The somewhat nebulous obligations of Article 90 have been held to be a manifestation of the Article 5 duty of solidarity, already used elsewhere as the *fons et origo* of fundamental developments in Community law, such as *Factortame* **[C47]**, **[C48]**, **[C49]** and *Francovich* **[C33]**, **[E97]**. The state aids rules, often criticised in the past for being conditional upon detection and effective supervision by an embattled Commission, have been slotted into the framework of individual protection evolved by the court. Thus, whilst the assessment of a state aid remains the exclusive concern of the Commission **[E94]**, **[E95]**, a national court may protect an individual against any harmful effects he or she may suffer as a result of wrongful implementation of it **[E96]**.

This clever balancing between the roles of Commission and national court demonstrates some of the arguments about subsidiarity, at least in so far as one view of that concept limits it to ensuring appropriate levels of effectiveness. Thus, at one point the individual can receive financial compensation from a national court or obtain an injunction against non-notified aid being given to a competitor. At another, the Commission is treated as the only informed body to be able to take an effective decision as to the compatibility of a national subsidy with the interests of the Community. These levels of assessment and protection, as claimed by the court itself in *French Salmon* **[E96]**, are qualitatively different. However, there is an inevitable interaction between the two processes which is likely to create tension. If, as may be the case **[E97]**, an individual can claim damages from the state for failing to notify an aid, can this justifiably exist alongside the lawfulness of that aid if it subsequently satisfies a Commission assessment?

As discussed in Chapter One, part of the conceptual difficulty posed by subsidiarity is whether it is a drive for more effective application of agreed laws or whether it is authority for increased decentralisation of competences. Trade law rules provide ample evidence of such tensions already in the pre-Maastricht *acquis communautaire.* Addressing the right balance between Commission and local enforcement has been subject to two different forces. First, the court has used the broad obligations of solidarity under Article 5 as a way of encouraging co-operation between national authorities and the Commission **[E60]–[E61]**. This has led to the setting out of guidance principles in the form of a Co-operation Notice **[E63]**. Secondly, the Commission has successfully defended its view that it is not obliged to pursue all the complaints it receives when adequate redress would be available to an individual through national courts **[E62]**. What might yet prove an acid test for the proponents of competence-centred subsidiarity is the extent to which the meaning of 'affecting inter-state trade' **[E70]**, **[E87]** might be re-evaluated for the purposes of the goods and competition rules. But how this could be compatible with the idea of preservation of the *acquis* is a difficult question.

It should be remembered that the single market is only a staging post towards the next goal in the post-Maastricht phase of Community development. Micro-level protection of individual rights is not necessarily easily compatible with attainment of macro-level economic and political goals. Hitherto, the Court of Justice has almost invariably given priority to the micro-solution, as seen in its creation of direct effect and the duty of national courts to provide effective protection (including the application of Community law remedies). The severance principle adopted towards the division between Article 30 and the non-directly effective Article 92 is a stark illustration of pragmatic, and more short-term, answers **[E43]**. However, maturity in the Community's development may require acknowledgement of limits to that micro approach. Two examples may clarify the point.

First, the Treaty on European Union places a greater emphasis than before upon the goal of economic and social cohesion **[A13]**, ie the levelling up of standards of living between the different geographical parts of the Community. One reaction might be to deploy a policy on state aids that was sensitive to regional disparities. When this argument is reduced to a question of choosing the appropriate legal base for action, the relationship between Articles 30 and 92 may require significant revision **[E44]**.

Secondly, the Community has always been faced with the potential conflict, in the area of trade at least, between promoting strong internal competition and permitting the establishment of Community competitors to take on rivals from the United States, Japan and other parts of the world. This political decision is one which does not sit comfortably in the localised, directly effective environment of Articles 85–86. Even in those situations where it has needed to be addressed, the solutions adopted may perhaps seem short-term rather than principled. Under the Merger Regulation **[E78]**, for example, little has yet been made of the opportunities for developing Community strength or, indeed, an industrial policy embracing criteria other than competition **[E79]–[E82]**. A similar caution can be seen in the court's reluctance to authorise various attempts to endow Community law with extensive extraterritorial jurisdiction **[E58]**.

These considerations raise a familiar legal problem: the extent to which the regulation of trading conditions and structures is the proper province of judicial or, indeed, legislative activity. The tests for an abuse of a dominant position or a restriction on trade are essentially legal, not economic, although recognisable economic arguments may be adduced to justifiy particular conclusions **[E64]**, **[E68]**, **[E71]**. It would be somewhat disingenuous to claim that EC trade law is a genuine 'effects'-oriented system when it relies so heavily on the blueprints of block exemptions to make Article 85 workable. Nor is it always obvious to see the consistency between the apparently strongly consumer-favoured priorities in assessing competition provisions and the effects of a harmonisation programme which some commentators claim has a highly dilutory effect on trading standards or consumer participation [E38]–[E42].

Ultimately, the direction taken in resolving these problems depends upon the justiciability of the goals to be achieved and the initiative taken by the Court of Justice in the litigation that comes before it. The background to the single market demonstrates that legislation responded to the conceptual basis (mutual recognition) adopted by the court [E21], [E39]. The court has also backed crucial stages in legislative development [E84], [E86]. In its creation of the *acquis communautaire*, the court has already distilled a set of Community-compatible criteria with which to evaluate the legitimacy of the purpose and application of rules and behaviour which impinge on the market. These tools, essentially consisting of a judicially-defined core of protectable interests to be applied in accordance with proportionality, may form the basis for the court's future view of the justiciability of claims which will follow any failure to achieve economic and social cohesion or, however distantly, economic and monetary union.

SECTION ONE

CREATION OF THE SINGLE MARKET IN GOODS AND SERVICES

MATERIALS

1 The barriers to opening up markets

[E1] Frank McDonald: 'The Single European Market' in McDonald and Dearden (eds) European Economic Integration (Longman, 1992)

The Cecchini Report

The Cecchini Report established the main barriers which were to be removed by implementing Article 13 of the Single European Act. These barriers were identified by references to those outlined in the 1985 White Paper, 'Completing the Internal Market', and by a series of surveys of businesses in tho EC. The White Paper lists three main types of barriers to be eliminated.

1. Physical barriers – frontier controls, and customs formalities.
2. Technical barriers – restriction on economic activities resulting from national rules and regulations. These include technical specifications which hinder or prevent trade in goods; rules and regulations governing services which hinder non-domestic companies from trading across frontiers; discriminatory public procurement rules which limit tendering for government contracts to domestic companies, and legal obstacles faced by foreign companies seeking to set up subsidiaries in other Member States.
3. Fiscal barriers – the need to adjust VAT and excise duties as goods cross EC frontiers. This is necessary as Member States operate different coverage, and levy different rates of VAT and excise duties.

The Cecchini Report reclassifies these barriers in order to estimate the benefits of removing these NTBs [non tariff barriers]. Hence five main barriers are defined by Cecchini: tariffs, quotas, cost-increasing barriers, market-entry restrictions, and market-distorting activities practised by governments.

Tariffs and quotas have largely been eliminated by the CU [customs union], but some remain, in particular VERs [voluntary export restraints] relating to cars and electronic equipment, and quotas on textiles connected to the Multi Fibre Arrangement. These are national quotas and must be removed or harmonised once frontier controls are eliminated. The bulk of the benefits arise from eliminating the remaining barriers. Cost-increasing barriers include customs formalities like VAT and excise duty assessments, verification of technical regulations and also costs incurred by companies in adhering to different technical regulations. These can include modification to products, changes to packaging etc. Market-entry restrictions include prohibiting or restricting access by foreign companies to the services sector, and rules and regulations which prevent foreign firms from bidding for public procurement contracts. Market-distorting activities arise from state aids such as subsidies, tax concessions, and other financial help given to domestic companies.

. . .

Using this taxonomy of barriers, estimates of the benefits of removing them were made. This was generally done for the EC as a whole, and few attempts were made to estimate the redistribution effects of removing these trade barriers.

. . .

These benefits . . . would . . . increase the GDP of the EC as illustrated in Diagram 1.

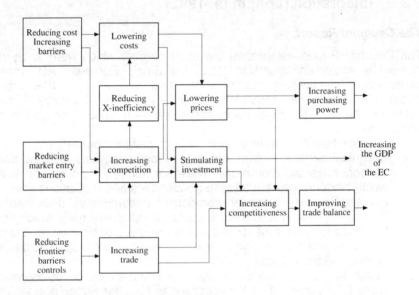

Diagram 1
The bulk of the benefits are seen to derive from the effects of increased competition and lower costs which lead to lower prices, and also stimulate investment. New market opportunities allow for increased economies of scale, and the rationalisation of artificially segmented markets. The increase in competition allows for considerable improvements in the effective use of inputs, and reductions in the anti-competitive practices of companies. This process is further aided by reductions in the costs of business and consumer services made possible by the liberalisation of the service sector. The creation of the Single European Market (SEM) is seen by Cecchini as a programme which boosts the effectiveness of the supply-side of the economy. This improvement in the supply-side leads to an increase in aggregate demand by increasing real purchasing power, increasing investment, and improving the competitiveness of the EC relative to the rest of the world. These changes to the supply-side also lead to improvements in public sector budgetary positions, because of reductions in the costs of public procurement, and the growth of GDP which increases taxation

revenues. This could allow for the consideration of a policy of expansion of the economy led by government expenditure. Such an expansion could help with temporary unemployment problems associated with the recon-struction of the economy, which will be induced by the creation of the SEM. These supply-side changes would improve the productive potential of the economy and should enhance the ability to reach higher levels of non-infla-tionary growth. Such government-led expansion of aggregate demand would need to be co-ordinated to avoid problems of inconsistent growth levels. The Cecchini Report does not have much to say on this issue, but the implication of such a policy is that monetary policies would need to be co-ordinated to prevent the growth of monetary instability. Cecchini esti-mated these accompanying macro-economic policies to have very significant effects on the overall benefits of creating the SEM.

. . .

Criticism of the Cecchini Report

This rather rosy picture has been subjected to a great deal of criticism. This criticism may be classified under three main headings:
1. the assumption that the legislative programme will be completed by 1992;
2. inadequacies in the legislative programme;
3. the view that N I Bs are the main obstacles to free movement.

. . .

In many sectors worries exist over the sufficiency of the mutual recognition approach. This was recently highlighted by the BSE (mad cow disease) scare where mutual recognition of health standards for food was called into question by some EC members. This resulted in the imposition of controls on the import of British beef by some Member States, although this was contrary to EC law on free movement.

Worries also exist over mutual recognition of testing and certification pro-cedures, as there is concern that some Member States may not have adequate facilities and experience to ensure that these procedures are car-ried out with appropriate attention to important details. Similar concerns exist over the regulatory systems of control for financial services. A strong case is being made for expanding the scope of selective harmonisation of essential requirements to ensure that minimum standards apply in these areas. Problems relating to the policing of legislation are also considered to be inadequately dealt with. For example, the legislation to open up public procurement systems is making good progress. However, policing this legislation and investigating breaches of tendering rules is an enormous task, as there exist thousands of government agencies in the EC with the power to issue and process procurement tenders. The record of some EC members in implementing existing Community legislation is not good . . . The extension of Community legislation brought about by the creation of the SEM is likely to intensify conflicts between Member States on these issues.

. . .

The third criticism is more fundamental. It brings into question whether NTBs are a significant barrier in many sectors of the economy. The reaping of benefits from removing NTBs is crucially dependent upon fundamental reconstruction in many industries. This largely depends on achieving economies of scale, and integrating activities by firms to overcome fragmented markets. This implies that many European firms are too small. There is according to Neuburger (*The Economics of 1992*, 1989), no strong evidence to suggest that this is the case. Some industries do seem to be rather small relative to the size of the EC market, thus there are ten manufacturers of electricity-generating equipment in the EC and only two in the USA (Curzon-Price, *1992: Europe's Last Change?* 1988). Many of these industries seem to be heavily involved in the public procurement sector, and the benefits of increased size could be limited to companies with large interests in this area.

. . .

There is also a view (Davis et al, *1992: Myths and Realities*, 1989) that market segmentation is often caused by cultural and regional factors leading to different qualities and specifications being demanded for goods and services. Such differences could mean that homogeneous products could not be effectively marketed on a Pan-European basis. There are also trading barriers such as a lack of detailed marketing and distribution and other sorts of business information, which could restrict the ability of companies to conduct cross-frontier operations. Therefore, simply to remove NTBs does not mean that increased trade and the rationalisation of production processes will necessarily follow. Many of the industries which are most able to operate on a European-wide basis are probably already doing so. In industries such as car production many companies such as Ford, General Motors and Volkswagen are already Pan-European in their operations; this is also true in areas such as food processing, and many types of consumer durables. It is unlikely that these sorts of companies will be able to benefit greatly from increased economies of scale/size as a result of the creation of the SEM. The main benefits for such companies are likely to arise from reductions in costs caused by the emergence of common European standards. The major sector to be affected by the removal of NTBs could well be small to medium-sized companies. The reduction of trading costs which will result from the creation of the SEM could lead to many such companies expanding into cross-frontier trading activities. Many of these companies may also benefit from economies of scale as they expand into such activities. In the service sector there is also evidence that the removal of NTBs will not, at least in the near future, have significant effects upon the bulk of retail financial services (Bank of England, *The Single European Market: Survey of the UK Financial Services Industry*, 1989). This follows from the goodwill and experience which existing national firms possess. In financial services there is also an issue of customer credibility for unknown foreign firms seeking business in other EC countries. Free movement of labour is likely to be hindered by cultural, linguistic, and social security differences (see Turner, *The Living Market*, 1989). Generally, economic factors such as unemployment rates, trade and capital flows, seem to be the main determinants of labour mobility. These factors along with demographic trends and recent events in Eastern Europe are likely to have more influence on labour mobility than the legislation programme to allow for free movement of labour.

. . .

The main effect of the 1992 programme may well turn out to be psychological, that is to turn the attention of producers from the EC, and other developed economies, towards the European market and to encourage them to gather information on the markets of Europe. This effect may also induce a European sense of identity among the citizens of the Member States, and this could have implications for some of the cultural barriers to free movement . . . It is possible that some of the biggest changes from the creation of the SEM could arise from placing companies, institutions and citizens on learning curves.

The Cecchini Report has also been criticised because certain key factors are said to have been omitted. Four main factors may be identified:

1. the effects on Member States;
2. the effects caused by the redistribution of income;
3. the importance of institutional arrangements;
4. the external effects of creating the SEM.

Although the Cecchini Report provided some estimates of the likely changes in prices in the Member States, there has not been much investigation of these issues. It has been argued that lower productivity countries such as the Southern European states, Ireland and the UK could suffer from the creation of the SEM. This would occur as more efficient companies in the rest of the EC displaced domestic companies in these countries.

. . .

The redistribution effects of creating the SEM are also largely ignored by the Cecchini Report. The Report does imply that the reconstruction process will give rise to a temporary increase in unemployment. This follows from the redistribution effects . . . of allowing free movement. However, the temporary nature of this unemployment is disputed by Cutler et al (1989 above) and Grahl and Teague (*1992: The Big Market*, 1990), who lay some stress on the effects that increased competition has on labour. These include not only downward pressure on wages, but also on employment conditions. Hence, the development of 'Social Europe' by imposing high minimum employment standards, is crucial if large sections of labour are not to suffer losses from the creation of the SEM. Free movement of capital may well reinforce these effects because capital movements are deemed to be mainly determined by technological and market operation reasons, rather than by simple rate of return calculations. In this scenario, capital flows tend towards areas with high technology and high productivity. Such movements could add to the downward spiral which the poorer productivity countries would experience from the SEM programme.

. . .

There are theoretical models which suggest that effective markets depend on legal and institutional factors as well as the operation of the price mechanism . . . The importance of information and transaction costs to the working of modern economies is highlighted by Grahl and Teague (1990 above). They maintain that these factors require markets to be backed by a set of institutional and cultural frameworks to correct for the inadequacies of the market, in particular the need for non-market-based contracts and arrangements between economic agents . . . These factors imply that not only the setting-up of institutions' arrangements, but also the growth of common cultural attitudes to the conducting of business activities, are a necessary component in the establishing of an effective SEM.

The neglect of the external effects of creating the SEM is a pronounced feature not only of the Cecchini Report, but also of most of the literature on the SEM . . . Some of the American literature . . . [is] concerned that the growth of regional trading blocs, such as the EC, is harming the growth of free trade in the world as a whole. This results from the trade diversion effects of eliminating trade barriers within a subset of the world, rather than from use of the multilateral methods of the GATT. These harmful effects can also be exacerbated by the adoption of increased protectionist measures by trading blocs against non-bloc countries . . . In the study by Brainard and Perry (*Brookings Papers on Economic Activity, No 2*, 1989), [the] fear is expressed by Dornbusch . . . that the increased pressures of competition induced by the SEM will lead to calls by the lower productivity Member States to increase the levels of external protection to allow them to maintain their threatened industrial structures. These pressures could be increased if the creation of the SEM is accompanied by the imposition of high minimum standards in the social and environmental fields as this would put further competitive pressures on the low productivity Member States. However, Dornbusch also considers that the creation of the SEM will stimulate world trade. This would be caused by the expansionary effect on the GDP of the EC which would follow from the implementation of the SEM, and would lead to an increase in the imports of the EC. It is possible that this expansionary effect could be stronger than the contractionary effect on world trade caused by the trade diversionary effects of the SEM. Given that the first best solution of achieving SEM type trade liberalisation on a global basis is not possible because of very large economic and political problems, the second best SEM programme may not be harmful to world trade providing that an expansion in world trade takes place as a result of this programme.

2   The creation of the customs union

[E2]   Articles 9 and 12 of the EC Treaty

Article 9

The Community shall be based upon a customs union which shall cover all trade in goods and which shall involve the prohibition between Member States of customs duties on imports and exports and of all charges having equivalent effect, and the adoption of a common customs tariff in their relations with third countries.

Article 12

Member States shall refrain from introducing between themselves any new customs duties on imports or exports or any charges having equivalent effect, and from increasing those which they already apply in their trade with each other.

[E3]   Case C-111/89 Netherlands v Bakker Hillegom
[1990] ECR I-1735

The European Court of Justice

9. As the court has held on many occasions, the justification for the prohibition of customs duties and any charges having an equivalent effect lies in the fact that any pecuniary charge, however small, imposed on goods by reason of the fact that they cross a frontier constitutes an obstacle to the movement of goods which is aggravated by the resulting administrative formalities. It follows that any pecuniary charge, whatever its designation and mode of application, which is imposed unilaterally on goods by reason of ' the fact that they cross a frontier and is not a customs duty in the strict sense constitutes a charge having an effect equivalent to a customs duty.

. . .

10. However, the court has held that such a charge escapes that classification if it relates to a general system of internal dues applied systematically and in accordance with the same criteria to domestic products and imported products (. . . Case 132/78 *Denkavit v France* [1979] ECR 1923), if it constitutes payment for a service in fact rendered to the economic operator of a sum in proportion to the service (. . . Case 158/82 *Commission v Denmark* [1983] ECR 3573), or again, subject to certain conditions, if it attaches to inspections carried out to fulfil obligations imposed by Community law (. . . Case 46/76 *Bauhuis v The Netherlands* [1977] ECR 5).

11. It appears from the national court's judgment that the fees in issue in the main proceedings relate to plant health inspections on exportation provided for by an international convention intended to encourage the free importation of plants into the countries of destination by establishing a system of inspections in the exporting state, recognised and organised on a reciprocal basis. In its judgment . . . in Case 89/76 *Commission v The Netherlands* [1977] ECR 1355, the court held that such fees were compatible with the rules of the Treaty 'provided that their amount does not exceed the actual cost of the operations in respect of which they are charged'.

. . .

12. It must be observed that that condition cannot be considered to have been satisfied unless there is a direct link between the amount of the fee and the actual inspection in respect of which the fee is charged. Without such a link, it would be impossible to ensure that the amount of the fee did not exceed the actual cost of the operation in respect of which it was charged.

13. As the Commission rightly submitted, such a link is present when the amount of the fees is calculated on the basis of the duration of the inspection, the number of persons required, the cost of materials, overheads or other similar factors, which does not preclude a fixed-rate assessment of inspection costs, such as, for example, a fixed hourly rate.

14. However, there is no direct link between the actual inspection and the amount of the fee when the calculation of that amount is based on the weight or invoice value of the products exported. Under a system of that

sort, the fees must therefore be regarded as charges having equivalent effect, and incompatible with Articles 12 and 16 of the Treaty.

3   The elimination of discriminatory and protectionist taxation

[E4]   Taxation under Article 95 of the EC Treaty

Article 95

No Member State shall impose, directly or indirectly, on the products of other Member States any internal taxation of any kind in excess of that imposed directly or indirectly on similar domestic products.

Furthermore, no Member State shall impose on the products of other Member States any internal taxation of such a nature as to afford indirect protection to other products.

[E5]   Case 193/85 Co-operativa Co-Frutta Srl v Amministrazione delle Finanze dello Stato [1987] ECR 2085

The European Court of Justice

7. The . . . questions are concerned with the distinction between a charge having an effect equivalent to a customs duty, within the meaning of Articles 9 and 12 . . ., and internal taxation within the meaning of Article 95, and are designed to enable the national court to determine which category the tax on the consumption of bananas falls into.

. . .

8. According to established case law of the court, the prohibition laid down by Articles 9 and 12 . . . in regard to charges having equivalent effect covers any charge exacted at the time of or on account of importation which, being borne specifically by an imported product to the exclusion of the similar domestic product, has the result of altering the cost price of the imported product, thereby producing the same restrictive effect on the free movement of goods as a customs duty.

9. The essential feature of a charge having an effect equivalent to a customs duty which distinguishes it from an internal tax therefore resides in the fact that the former is borne solely by an imported product as such whilst the latter is borne both by imported and domestic products.

10. The court has however recognised that even a charge which is borne by a product imported from another Member State, when there is no identical or similar domestic product, does not constitute a charge having equivalent effect but internal taxation within the meaning of Article 95 of the Treaty if it relates to a general system of internal dues applied systematically to categories of products in accordance with objective criteria irrespective of the origin of the products.

11. Those considerations demonstrate that even if it were necessary in some cases, for the purpose of classifying a charge borne by imported products, to equate extremely low domestic production with its non-existence, that would not mean that the levy in question would necessarily have to be regarded as a charge having an effect equivalent to a customs duty. In particular, that will not be so if the levy is part of a general system of internal dues applying systematically to categories of products according to the criteria indicated above.

12. A tax on consumption of the type at issue in the main proceedings does form part of a general system of internal dues. The 19 taxes on consumption are governed by common tax rules and are charged on categories of products irrespective of their origin in accordance with an objective criterion, namely the fact that the product falls into a certain category of goods. Some of those taxes are charged on products intended for human consumption, including the tax on the consumption of bananas. Whether those goods are produced at home or abroad does not seem to have a bearing on the rate, the basis of assessment or the manner in which the tax is levied. The revenue from those taxes is not earmarked for a specific purpose; it constitutes tax revenue identical to other tax revenue and, like it, helps to finance state expenditure generally in all sectors.

13. Consequently, the tax at issue must be regarded as being an integral part of a general system of internal dues within the meaning of Article 95 of the Treaty and its compatibility with Community law must be assessed on the basis of that article rather than Articles 9 and 12.

[E6] Case 112/84 Humblot v Directeur des services fiscaux [1985] ECR 1367

The European Court of Justice

2. The question was raised in proceedings between Michel Humblot and the [Director General of Revenue] in which Mr Humblot seeks repayment of the special tax imposed on certain vehicles.

3. It appears . . . that there are in France two different types of tax due annually on motor vehicles. First there is a differential tax to which cars rated at 16 CV [. . . horsepower] or less are subject and secondly a special tax on vehicles rated at more than 16 CV. Whereas the amount of differential tax payable increases progressively and uniformly with the power rating for tax purposes, the special tax is levied at a single and considerably higher rate.

4. In 1981 Mr Humblot became the owner of a car rated at 36 CV. Before he could put the vehicle on the road Mr Humblot had to pay the special tax, which, at that time, amounted to FF 5,000. After paying that sum Mr Humblot brought a complaint before the tax administration with a view to obtaining a refund of the difference between that sum and the highest rate of the differential tax (at the time, FF 1,100).

. . .

7. It appears . . . that the essence of the question is whether Article 95 prohibits the charging on cars exceeding a given power rating for tax

purposes of a special fixed tax the amount of which is several times the highest amount of the progressive tax payable on cars of less than the said power rating for tax purposes, where the only cars subject to the special tax are imported, in particular from other Member States.

8. In his observations . . . Mr Humblot points out that the special tax affects imported vehicles only, since no French car is rated for tax purposes at more than 16 CV. Mr Humblot argues that nevertheless vehicles of 16 CV or less and vehicles exceeding 16 CV are completely comparable as regards their performance, price and fuel consumption. As a result, he contends that the French State, by subjecting imported vehicles alone to a special tax much greater in amount than the differential tax, has created discrimination contrary to Article 95 of the Treaty.

9. For its part, the French government contends that the special tax is contrary neither to the first nor to the second paragraph of Article 95. It argues that the special tax is charged solely on luxury vehicles, which are not similar, within the meaning of the first paragraph of Article 95, to cars liable to the differential tax. Moreover, whilst the French government concedes that some vehicles rated at 16 CV or less and others rated at more than 16 CV are in competition and so subject to the second paragraph of Article 95, it maintains that the special tax is not contrary to that provision, since it has not been shown that the tax has the effect of protecting domestic products. It argues that there is no evidence that a consumer who may have been dissuaded from buying a vehicle of more than 16 CV will purchase a car of French manufacture of 16 CV or less.

10. The Commission considers that the special tax is contrary to the first paragraph of Article 95 . . . It argues that all cars, irrespective of their power rating for tax purposes, are similar within the meaning of the case law of the court. That being so, it is no longer possible for a Member State to create discrimination between imported and domestically-produced vehicles. The only exception is where a Member State taxes products differently – even identical products – on the basis of neutral criteria consistent with objectives of economic policy which are compatible with the Treaty, whilst avoiding discrimination between domestic and imported products. The Commission contends, however, that the criterion adopted by France in this instance, namely power rating for tax purposes, is not geared to an economic policy objective, such as heavier taxation of luxury products or vehicles with high fuel consumption. Accordingly, the Commission considers that the special tax, which is almost five times the highest rate of differential tax, affects imported vehicles only and does not pursue an economic policy objective compatible with the Treaty, is contrary to the first paragraph of Article 95 of the Treaty.

11. The United Kingdom government considers that vehicles of more than 16 CV are in a competitive relationship with some cars with a lower power rating for tax purposes, from which it follows that the special tax is contrary to the second paragraph of Article 95 of the Treaty since it diverts consumers from imported cars to French prestige models.

12. It is appropriate in the first place to stress that as Community law stands at present the Member States are at liberty to subject products such as cars to a system of road tax which increases progressively in amount depending on an objective criterion, such as the power rating for tax purposes, which may be determined in various ways.

13. Such a system of domestic taxation is, however, compatible with

Article 95 only in so far as it is free from any discriminatory or protective effect.

14. That is not true of a system like the one at issue in the main proceedings. Under that system there are two distinct taxes . . . Although the system embodies no formal distinction based on the origin of products it manifestly exhibits discriminatory or protective features contrary to Article 95, since the power rating determining liability to the special tax has been fixed at a level such that only imported cars, particularly from other Member States, are subject to the special tax whereas all cars of domestic manufacture are liable to the distinctly more advantageous differential tax.

15. In the absence of considerations relating to the amount of the special tax, consumers seeking comparable cars as regards such matters as size, comfort, actual power, maintenance costs, durability, fuel consumption and price would naturally choose from among cars above and below the critical power rating laid down by French law. However, liability to the special tax entails a much larger increase in taxation than passing from one category of car to another in a system of progressive taxation embodying balanced differentials like the system on which the differential tax is based. The resultant additional taxation is liable to cancel out the advantages which certain cars imported from other Member States might have in consumers' eyes over comparable cars of domestic manufacture, particularly since the special tax continues to be payable for several years. In that respect the special tax reduces the amount of competition to which cars of domestic manufacture are subject and hence is contrary to the principle of neutrality with which domestic taxation must comply.

[E7] Case C-132/88 Commission v Greece [1990] ECR I-1567

[This Article 169 action was brought on the basis of two aspects of the Greek system of taxing private cars: the special consumption tax and the single supplementary special tax. In both cases there were sharp increases in rates above two points of cylinder capacity, namely 1200 cc and 1800 cc. The only cars produced in Greece were of a cylinder capacity of less than 1600 cc.]

The European Court of Justice

16. . . . The Hellenic Republic contended in the course of the written procedure that the differential thresholds adopted for the two taxes in question . . . were objectively justified because they reflected the social circumstances prevailing in Greece and, to some extent, in Europe as a whole: cars of less than 1200 cc are for people with modest incomes; those with a cylinder capacity of between 1201 and 1800 cc are bought by people whose income is in the middle range; and those of above 1800 cc are, above all in Greece, only for people with very substantial incomes.

17. It must be emphasised in this regard that Article 95 of the Treaty does not provide a basis for censuring the excessiveness of the level of taxation which the Member States might adopt for particular products in the light of considerations of social policy.

. . .

18. It must be made clear that a system of taxation cannot be regarded as discriminatory solely because only imported products, in particular those from other Member States, come within the most heavily taxed category (see . . . Case 140/79 *Chemial Farmaceutici SpA v DAF SpA* [1981] ECR 1).

19. In order to determine whether the special consumption tax and the single supplementary special tax have a discriminatory or protective effect, it is necessary to consider whether they are capable of discouraging consumers from purchasing cars of a cylinder capacity in excess of 1800 cc, which are all manufactured abroad, in such a way as to benefit domestically produced cars.

20. If it is assumed that the particular features of the system of taxation at issue actually discourage certain consumers from purchasing cars of a cylinder capacity greater than 1800 cc, those consumers will choose either a model in the range of cars having cylinder capacities between 1600 and 1800 cc or a model in the range of cars having cylinder capacities below 1600 cc. All the models in the first-mentioned range are of foreign manufacture. The second range includes cars of both foreign and Greek manufacture. Consequently, the Commission has not shown how the system of taxation at issue might have the effect of favouring the sale of cars of Greek manufacture.

[E8]   Case 243/84 John Walker & Sons Ltd v Ministeriet for Skatter og Afgifter [1986] ECR 875

[This was a reference under Article 177 concerning the compatibility with Article 95 of a system of differential taxation applied under Danish tax legislation to Scotch whisky and fruit wine of the liqueur type.]

The European Court of Justice

The first paragraph of Article 95

11. In order to determine whether products are similar within the terms of the prohibition laid down in the first paragraph of Article 95 it is necessary to consider . . . whether they have similar characteristics and meet the same needs from the point of view of consumers. The court endorsed a broad interpretation of the concept of similarity in its judgments . . . in Case 168/78 *Commission v France* [1980] ECR 347 and . . . Case 216/81 *Cogis v Amministrazione delle Finanze dello Stato* [1982] ECR 2701 and assessed the similarity of the products not according to whether they were strictly identical, but according to whether their use was similar and comparable. Consequently, in order to determine whether products are similar it is necessary first to consider certain objective characteristics of both categories of beverages, such as their origin, the method of manufacture and their organoleptic properties, in particular taste and alcoholic content, and secondly to consider whether or not both categories of beverages are capable of meeting the same needs from the point of view of consumers.

12. It should be noted that the two categories of beverages exhibit manifestly different characteristics. Fruit wine of the liqueur type is a fruit-based product obtained by natural fermentation, whereas Scotch whisky is a cereal-based product obtained by distillation. The organoleptic properties of

the two products are also different . . ., the fact that the same raw material, for example alcohol, is to be found in the two products is not sufficient reason to apply the prohibition contained in the first paragraph of Article 95. For the products to be regarded as similar that raw material must also be present in more or less equal proportions in both products. In that regard, it must be pointed out that the alcoholic strength of Scotch whisky is 40% by volume, whereas the alcoholic strength of fruit wine of the liqueur type, to which the Danish legislation applies, does not exceed 20% by volume.

13. The contention that Scotch whisky may be consumed in the same way as fruit wine of the liqueur type, as an aperitif diluted with water or with fruit juice, even if it were established, would not be sufficient to render Scotch whisky similar to fruit wine of the liqueur type, whose intrinsic characteristics are fundamentally different.

. . .

The second paragraph of Article 95

14. In its second question the national court seeks to ascertain whether, if they are not similar products, Scotch whisky and fruit wine of the liqueur type are to be regarded as competing products.

. . .

21. It is clear . . . that the product which bears the lightest tax burden is manufactured almost exclusively in Denmark and that whisky, which is exclusively an imported product, is taxed not as such but as an alcoholic beverage included in the tax category of spirits – that is to say beverages with a high alcoholic content – which comprises other products, the vast majority of which are Danish.

22. In order to enable the national court to determine whether, in those circumstances, the differential taxation imposed by the Danish tax system constitutes an infringement of the second paragraph of Article 95, it is necessary to recall that the court has consistently held . . . that Community law at its present stage of development does not restrict the freedom of each Member State to lay down tax arrangements which differentiate between certain products on the basis of objective criteria, such as the nature of the raw materials used or the production processes employed.

. . .

23. Accordingly, without there being any need to ascertain whether there exists a competitive relationship between Scotch whisky and fruit wine of the liqueur type, the answer to the second question must be that at the present stage of its development Community law, and in particular the second paragraph of Article 95 . . ., does not preclude the application of a system of taxation which differentiates between certain beverages on the basis of objective criteria. Such a system does not favour domestic producers if a significant proportion of domestic production of alcoholic beverages falls within each of the relevant tax categories.

[E9] Case 170/78 Commission v United Kingdom [1980] ECR 417

[The Commission brought proceedings under Article 169 for a declaration that, by imposing on still light wine higher excise duty than on beer, the

United Kingdom had failed to fulfil its obligations under the second paragraph of Article 95.]

The European Court of Justice (Judgment No 1)

The interpretation of Article 95

5. The aim of Article 95 as a whole is to eliminate the adverse effects on the free movement of goods and on normal conditions of competition between Member States of the discriminatory or protective application of internal taxation.

. . .

6. In order to determine the existence of a competitive relationship under the second paragraph of Article 95, it is necessary to consider not only the present state of the market but also the possibilities for development within the context of free movement of goods at the Community level and the further potential for the substitution of products for one another which may be revealed by intensification of trade, so as fully to develop the complementary features of the economies of the Member States in accordance with the objectives laid down by Article 2 of the Treaty.

. . .

9. It is true that the first and second paragraphs of Article 95 lay down different conditions as regards the characteristics of the tax practices prohibited by that article. Under the first paragraph . . ., which relates to products which are similar and therefore hypothetically broadly comparable, the prohibition applies where a tax mechanism is of such a nature as to impose higher taxation on imported products than on domestic products. On the other hand, the second paragraph of Article 95, precisely in view of the difficulty of making a sufficiently precise comparison between the products in question, employs a more general criterion, in other words the indirect protection afforded by a domestic tax system.

10. It is however appropriate to emphasise that the above-mentioned provision is linked to the 'nature' of the tax system in question so that it is impossible to require in each case that the protective effect should be shown statistically. It is sufficient for the purposes of the application of the second paragraph of Article 95 for it to be shown that a given tax mechanism is likely, in view of its inherent characteristics, to bring about the protective effect referred to by the Treaty. Without therefore disregarding the importance of the criteria which may be deduced from statistics from which the effects of a given tax system may be measured, it is impossible to require the Commission to supply statistical data on the actual foundation of the protective effect of the tax system complained of.

. . .

The question of competition between wine and beer

12. According to the Commission, there is a competitive relationship between wine and beer; in the case of certain consumers they may therefore actually be substituted for one another and in the case of others they may, at least potentially, be so substituted. The two beverages in fact belong to the same category of alcoholic beverages which are the product of natural

fermentation; both may be used for the same purposes, as thirst-quenching drinks or to accompany meals.

13. The government of the United Kingdom contests this attitude. Without denying the common characteristics of the two beverages, it emphasises that they are both the products of entirely different manufacturing processes. The alcoholic content of wine is three times . . . that of beer . . . The price structure of the two products is entirely different, since wine is appreciably more expensive than beer. As regards consumer habits, the government of the United Kingdom states that in accordance with long-established tradition in the United Kingdom, beer is a popular drink consumed preferably in public houses or in connection with work; domestic consumption and consumption with meals is negligible. In contrast, the consumption of wine is more unusual and special from the point of view of social custom.

14. The court considers that the Commission's argument is well-founded in that it is impossible to deny that to a certain extent the two beverages in question are capable of meeting identical needs, so that it must be acknowledged that there is a certain degree of substitution for one another. For the purpose of measuring the possible degree of substitution, it is impossible to restrict oneself to consumer habits in a Member State or in a given region. In fact, those habits, which are essentially variable in time and space, cannot be considered to be a fixed rule; the tax policy of a Member State must not therefore crystallise given consumer habits so as to consolidate an advantage acquired by national industries concerned to comply with them.

15. At the same time it is however necessary to recognise, together with the government of the United Kingdom, the great differences between wine and beer from the point of view of the manufacturing processes and the natural properties of those beverages. Wine is an agricultural product which is the outcome of intensive farming methods and is closely linked to the properties of the soil and climatic factors; for that reason its characteristics are extremely variable, whereas beer, which is produced from raw materials less susceptible to risks of that nature, is at the same time better suited to methods of industrial manufacture. The difference between the conditions of production leads, in the case of both products, to price structures which are so extremely different that in spite of the competitive relationship between the finished products it seems particularly difficult to make comparisons from the tax point of view.

16. These differences between the two products disclose an aspect of the problem which forms the prerequisite for any legal appraisal and which has not been taken into consideration . . . The Commission did not indicate what it considers to be the appropriate tax ratio between two products which it regards as competing.

. . .

The method of comparison of the two products

17. In its reasoned opinion and when it lodged its application, the Commission emphasised above all the fact that by equal volume wine is subject in the United Kingdom to a tax burden approximately five times that of the burden imposed on beer. Since this criterion for comparison was keenly contested by the government of the United Kingdom because the products involved have a different alcoholic strength, the Commission

put forward other criteria for comparison: first, the alcoholic content by unit of volume which once more shows heavier taxation on wine of the order of 50%; secondly, the relationship between the fiscal element and the price of the goods offered to consumers. The latter method of comparison also shows discrimination against wine. All these criteria of comparison are contested by the government of the United Kingdom which considers that when relying simply upon volume it is necessary to compare the measures in which the two types of beverage are usually offered to consumers, in other words a 'glass of wine' and a 'pint of beer'; in fact, those two typical units of consumption carry a tax burden which is approximately identical.

. . .

19. Of the criteria put forward by the parties, the only factor which may enable an appropriate and somewhat objective comparison to be made consists . . . in the appraisal of the incidence of the tax burden in relation to the alcoholic strength of the beverages in question. By taking into consideration that criterion it may be ascertained that wine is at present subject in the United Kingdom to a tax which is approximately 50% higher than that on beer.

. . .

The question of the protective nature of the tax system in question

21. In this respect, the government of the United Kingdom claims that according to the second paragraph of Article 95 the Commission should have examined the question whether the tax system complained of affords protection to national beer production. Instead of showing this, the Commission has been exclusively concerned to show the disparity between the tax burden imposed on those two products. However, according to the government of the United Kingdom, the tax system complained of did not prevent an increase in imports of wine during the period under consideration and the changes in the rates of duty have had no perceptible repercussions on the consumption figures, so that it is impossible to accept that the system of taxation applied is protective in effect.

. . .

24. The court considers that a comparison of the development of the two tax systems in question shows a protective trend as regards imports of wine in the United Kingdom. However, in view of the uncertainties remaining both as to the characteristics of the competitive relationship between wine and beer and as to the question of the appropriate tax ratio between the two products from the point of view of the whole of the Community, the court considers that it is unable to give a ruling at this stage on the failure to fulfil its obligations under the Treaty for which the United Kingdom is criticised. It therefore requests the Commission and the United Kingdom to resume examination of the question at issue . . . and to report to the court within a prescribed period.

The European Court of Justice (Judgment No 2) [1983] ECR 2265

12. . . . . In view of the substantial differences in the quality and, therefore, in the price of wines, the decisive competitive relationship between

beer, a popular and widely consumed beverage, and wine must be established by reference to those wines which are the most accessible to the public at large, that is to say, generally speaking, the lightest and cheapest varieties. Accordingly, that is the appropriate basis for making fiscal comparisons by reference to the alcoholic strength or to the price of the two beverages in question.

. . .

18. The exchange of views between the parties which followed the [first] judgment . . . showed that, although none of the criteria for comparison applied with a view to determining the tax ratio between the two products in question is capable of yielding reliable results on its own, it is none the less the case that each of the three methods used, that is to say assessment of the tax burden by reference to the volume, the alcoholic strength and the price of the products, can provide significant information for the assessment of the contested tax system.

. . .

26. After considering the information provided by the parties, the court has come to the conclusion that, if a comparison is made on the basis of those wines which are cheaper than the types of wine selected by the United Kingdom and of which several varieties are sold in significant quantities on the United Kingdom market, it becomes apparent that precisely those wines which, in view of their price, are most directly in competition with domestic beer production are subject to a considerably higher tax burden.

27. It is clear, therefore, following the detailed inquiry conducted by the court – whatever criterion for comparison is used, there being no need to express a preference for one or the other – that the United Kingdom's tax system has the effect of subjecting wine imported from other Member States to an additional tax burden so as to afford indirect protection to domestic beer production, inasmuch as beer production constitutes the most relevant reference criterion from the point of view of competition. Since such protection is most marked in the case of the most popular wines, the effect of the United Kingdom tax system is to stamp wine with the hallmarks of a luxury product which, in view of the tax burden which it bears, can scarcely constitute in the eyes of the consumer a genuine alternative to the typical domestically produced beverage.

Questions

1. What had to be done to enable the protective effect to be removed?
2. What would the remedial steps be in the case of similar, as distinct from competing, products?

[E10] Case 356/85 Commission v Belgium ('taxation of wine and beer') [1987] ECR 3299

[This was an action under Article 169 alleging infringement of Article 95 by Belgium in applying a higher rate of VAT to wine of fresh grapes, an imported product, than to beer, a domestic product.]

The European Court of Justice

The protective nature of the tax system

14. In its judgment [in] . . . Case 168/78 *Commission v France* [1980] ECR 347 the court held that whilst the criterion indicated in the first paragraph of Article 95 consists in the comparison of tax burdens whether in terms of the rate, the mode of assessment or other detailed rules for their application, in view of the difficulty of making sufficiently precise comparisons between the products in question the second paragraph of that article is based upon a more general criterion, namely the protective nature of the system of internal taxation.

15. It follows that any assessment of the compatibility of a given tax with the second paragraph of Article 95 must take account of the impact of that tax on the competitive relationship between the products concerned. The essential question is therefore whether or not the tax is of such a kind as to have the effect, on the market in question, of reducing potential consumption of imported products to the advantage of competing domestic products.

16. Consequently, in considering to what extent a protective effect actually exists, the difference between the respective selling prices of beer and wine competing with beer cannot be disregarded. The Belgian government has stated that the price of a litre of beer, including tax, is on average BFR 29.75, whereas the corresponding price of a litre of ordinary wine is around BFR 125, four times the price of beer . . . In the Belgian government's view it follows that even if a single rate were applied to both products, the price difference between the two would continue to be substantial; the reduction in that difference would be so insignificant that it could not influence consumer preference.

. . .

18. . . . it must be concluded that the Commission has not shown that the difference between the respective prices for comparable qualities of beer and wine is so small that the difference of 6% between the VAT rates applied to the two products is capable of influencing consumer behaviour. The Commission has thus not shown that that difference gives rise to any protective effect favouring beer intended for domestic consumption.

19. Nor do the statistics produced by the Commission comparing trends in beer and wine consumption indicate the existence of any protective effect. The Commission stated that beer consumption in Belgium reached a peak in 1973 and has been on the decline since then. By contrast, wine consumption has tripled during the last 20 years; however, from 1980 onwards, the growth in wine consumption slowed down and it levelled off in 1982 and 1983.

20. Whilst those figures show the general trends in the consumption of the products in question, they do not show with any certainty that there is any causal connection between the patterns of consumption described and the introduction in 1977 of a higher rate of VAT for wine . . . Moreover, . . . between 1978 and 1983 the rate of VAT applicable to beer was increased on three occasions without there being in the medium term any restrictive effect on the consumption of beer to the advantage of wine.

21. It follows that the Commission has not established that the tax system in question actually has a protective effect. Accordingly, the application must be dismissed.

4   The free movement of goods

[E11]   Free Movement of Goods, Articles 30-36 of the EC Treaty

Article 30

Quantitative restrictions on imports and all measures having equivalent effect shall, without prejudice to the following provisions, be prohibited between Member States.

Article 34

Quantitative restrictions on exports, and all measures having equivalent effect, shall be prohibited between Member States.

Article 36

The provisions of Articles 30 to 34 shall not preclude prohibitions or restrictions on imports, exports or goods in transit justified on grounds of public morality, public policy or public security; the protection of health and life of humans, animals or plants; the protection of national treasures possessing artistic, historic or archaeological value; or the protection of industrial and commercial property. Such prohibitions or restrictions shall not, however, constitute a means of arbitrary discrimination or a disguised restriction on trade between Member States.

(a)   The notion of a trade restriction

[E12]   Case 8/74 Procureur du Roi v Dassonville [1974] ECR 837

The European Court of Justice

2. By the first question it is asked whether a national provision prohibiting the import of goods bearing a designation of origin where such goods are not accompanied by an official document issued by the government of the exporting country certifying their right to such designation constitutes a measure having an effect equivalent to a quantitative restriction within the meaning of Article 30 of the Treaty.

3. This question was raised within the context of criminal proceedings instituted in Belgium against traders who duly acquired a consignment of Scotch whisky in free circulation in France and imported it into Belgium without being in possession of a certificate of origin from the British customs authorities, thereby infringing Belgian rules.

4. It emerges from the file and from the oral proceedings that a trader, wishing to import into Belgium Scotch whisky which is already in free circulation in France, can obtain such a certificate only with great difficulty, unlike the importer who imports directly from the producer country.

5. All trading rules enacted by Member States which are capable of hindering, directly or indirectly, actually or potentially, intra-Community trade

are to be considered as measures having an effect equivalent to quantitative restrictions.

6. In the absence of a Community system guaranteeing for consumers the authenticity of a producer's designation of origin, if a Member State takes measures to prevent unfair practices in this connexion, it is however subject to the condition that these measures should be reasonable and that the means of proof required should not act as a hindrance to trade between Member States and should, in consequence, be accessible to all Community nationals.

7. Even without having to examine whether or not such measures are covered by Article 36, they must not, in any case, by virtue of the principle expressed in the second sentence of that Article, constitute a means of arbitrary discrimination or a disguised restriction on trade between Member States.

8. That may be the case with formalities, required by a Member State for the purpose of proving the origin of a product, which only direct importers are really in a position to satisfy without facing serious difficulties.

9. Consequently, the requirement by a Member State of a certificate of authenticity which is less easily obtainable by importers of an authentic product which has been put into free circulation in a regular manner in another Member State than by importers of the same product coming directly from the country of origin constitutes a measure having an effect equivalent to a quantitative restriction as prohibited by the Treaty.

[E13]   Case 15/79 P B Groenveld BV v Produktschap voor Vee en Vlees [1979] ECR 3409

[The national law in question prohibited, subject to express exceptions, any manufacturer of sausages from having in stock or processing horsemeat. This measure had been adopted to protect Dutch exports to important markets where there might be objections or prohibitions in relation to horsemeat.]

The European Court of Justice

7. [Article 34] concerns national measures which have as their specific object or effect the restriction of patterns of exports and thereby the establishment of a difference in treatment between the domestic trade of a Member State and its export trade in such a way as to provide a particular advantage for national production or for the domestic market of the state in question at the expense of the production or of the trade of other Member States. This is not so in the case of a prohibition like that in question which is applied objectively to the production of goods of a certain kind without drawing a distinction depending on whether such goods are intended for the national market or for export.

8. The foregoing appreciation is not affected by the circumstance that the regulation in question has as its objective, inter alia, the safeguarding of the reputation of the national production of meat products in certain export markets within the Community and in non-member countries where there are obstacles of a psychological or legislative nature to the consumption of horsemeat when the same prohibition is applied identically to the product in

the domestic market of the state in question. The objective nature of that prohibition is not modified by the fact that the regulation in force in the Netherlands permits the retail sale of horsemeat by butchers. In fact that concession at the level of local trade does not have the effect of bringing about a prohibition at the level of industrial manufacture of the same product regardless of its destination.

9. The reply to the question submitted must therefore be that in the present state of Community law a national measure prohibiting all manufacturers of meat products from having in stock or processing horsemeat is not incompatible with Article 34 of the Treaty if it does not discriminate between products intended for export and those marketed within the Member State in question.

Question

Why should the Court of Justice treat imports and exports differently when considering whether a trade restriction exists? For a possible implied change in attitude see now Case C-47/90 *Établissements Delhaize Frères et Compagnie Le Lion v Promalvin and AGE Bodegas Unidas* (Judgment of 9 June 1992).

[E14]   Case 249/81 EC Commission v Ireland ('buy Irish') [1982] ECR 4005

The European Court of Justice

21. The Irish government maintains that the prohibition against measures having an effect equivalent to quantitative restrictions in Article 30 is concerned only with 'measures', that is to say, binding provisions emanating from a public authority. However, no such provision has been adopted by the Irish government, which has confined itself to giving moral support and financial aid to the activities pursued by the Irish industries.

22. The Irish government goes on to emphasise that the campaign has had no restrictive effect on imports since the proportion of Irish goods to all goods sold on the Irish market fell from 49.2% in 1977 to 43.4% in 1980.

23. The first observation to be made is that the campaign cannot be likened to advertising by private or public undertakings, or by a group of undertakings, to encourage people to buy goods produced by those undertakings. Regardless of the means used to implement it, the campaign is a reflection of the Irish government's considered intention to substitute domestic products for imported products on the Irish market and thereby to check the flow of imports from other Member States.

24. It must be remembered here that a representative of the Irish government stated when the campaign was launched that it was a carefully thought-out set of initiatives constituting an integrated programme for promoting domestic products; that the Irish Goods Council was set up at the initiative of the Irish government a few months later; and that the task of implementing the integrated programme as it was envisaged by the government was entrusted, or left, to that Council.

25. Whilst it may be true that the two elements of the programme which have continued in effect, namely the advertising campaign and the use of

the 'Guaranteed Irish' symbol, have not had any significant success in winning over the Irish market to domestic products, it is not possible to overlook the fact that, regardless of their efficacy, those two activities form part of a government programme which is designed to achieve the substitution of domestic products for imported products and is liable to affect the volume of trade between Member States.

26. The advertising campaign to encourage the sale and purchase of Irish products cannot be divorced from its origin as part of the government programme, or from its connection with the introduction of the 'Guaranteed Irish' symbol and with the organisation of a special system for investigating complaints about products bearing that symbol. The establishment of the system for investigating complaints about Irish products provides adequate confirmation of the degree of organisation surrounding the 'Buy Irish' campaign and of the discriminatory nature of the campaign.

27. In the circumstances the two activities in question amount to the establishment of a national practice, introduced by the Irish government and prosecuted with its assistance, the potential effect of which on imports from other Member States is comparable to that resulting from government measures of a binding nature.

28. Such a practice cannot escape the prohibition laid down by Article 30 of the Treaty solely because it is not based on decisions which are binding upon undertakings. Even measures adopted by the government of a Member State which do not have binding effect may be capable of influencing the conduct of traders and consumers in that state and thus of frustrating the aims of the Community as set out in Article 2 and enlarged upon in Article 3 of the Treaty.

29. That is the case where, as in this instance, such a restrictive practice represents the implementation of a programme defined by the government which affects the national economy as a whole and which is intended to check the flow of trade between Member States by encouraging the purchase of domestic products, by means of an advertising campaign on a national scale and the organisation of special procedures applicable solely to domestic products, and where those activities are attributable as a whole to the government and are pursued in an organised fashion throughout the national territory.

[E15]   Joined Cases 266 and 267/87 R v Royal Pharmaceutical Society of Great Britain, ex parte Association of Pharmaceutical Importers [1989] ECR 1295

The European Court of Justice

13. Before the question whether the measures at issue fall under the prohibition in Article 30 of the Treaty or whether they are justified under Article 36 of the Treaty is considered, the point raised by the national court's third question, which is whether a measure adopted by a professional body such as the Pharmaceutical Society of Great Britain may come within the scope of the said articles, should be resolved.

14. According to the documents before the court, that Society, which was incorporated by Royal Charter in 1843 and whose existence is also recognised in United Kingdom legislation, is the sole professional body for pharmacy. It maintains the register in which all pharmacists must be enrolled in order to carry on their business. As can be seen from the order for reference, it adopts rules of ethics applicable to pharmacists. Finally, United Kingdom legislation has established a disciplinary committee within the Society which may impose disciplinary sanctions on a pharmacist for professional misconduct; those sanctions may even involve his removal from the register. An appeal lies to the High Court from decisions of that committee.

15. It should be stated that measures adopted by a professional body on which national legislation has conferred powers of that nature may, if they are capable of affecting trade between Member States, constitute 'measures' within the meaning of Article 30 of the Treaty.

[E16]   Case 21/84 EC Commission v France ('franking machines') [1985] ECR 1355

The European Court of Justice

1. By an application lodged at the Court Registry on 23 January 1984 the Commission . . . brought an action before the court under Article 169 of the EEC Treaty for a declaration that by refusing, without proper justification, to approve postal franking machines from another Member State [France] has failed to fulfil its obligations under Article 30 of the EEC Treaty.

2. In France, as in the other Member States, the users of the postal service are in general authorised by the post office to use letter-franking machines, which enable them to save time and money. As those machines are used to collect postal charges, their release on to the market is made subject to the grant of approval by the postal authorities in order to prevent their fraudulent use. In France the rules for granting such approval were laid down most recently in Article 2 of the Interministerial Decree of 28 January 1980 on the use of letter-franking machines . . . That provision states that 'every type of franking machine must be approved by the Administration of Posts and Telecommunications following a favourable opinion from the Conseil technique [technical advisory board]'. Before it was amended on 7 March 1984, Article 3 of the decree provided that 'the machines, including the components and spare parts, must be exclusively of French manufacture, subject to any provisions of international agreements which may be applicable'.

3. The action now before the court arises out of a complaint lodged with the Commission by a leading United Kingdom manufacturer whose postal franking machines are approved in a considerable number of countries but which has attempted unsuccessfully, since 1 January 1973, to obtain the approval of the French postal authorities.

. . .

6. At the hearing the Commission stated that, in view of [the March 1984

amendment to include imports from other Member States], the action now concerned only the question of the compatibility with Article 30 of the attitude adopted by the French post office towards the complainant company.

7. In its application the Commission set out the following summary of the steps which the complainant company took, to no avail, between 1973 and 1980:
- delays in replying to letters and abortive contacts;
- correspondence resulting in various requests by the [National Technical Research Centre] for technical modifications to be made to the machines submitted for testing;
- rejection of the application for approval because of 'latent design faults', although the applicant company was in the process of carrying out the modifications to the machines requested by the [Centre];
- rejection of a fresh application . . . on the ground that the French market was already adequately supplied with franking machines;
- [rejection] of a further application, stating that the French government's position had not changed but the application might be reconsidered once electronic equipment had been developed.

. . .

10. . . . Those facts must be assessed in the light of the following principles.

11. The fact that a law or regulation such as that requiring prior approval for the marketing of postal franking machines conforms in formal terms to Article 30 of the EEC Treaty is not sufficient to discharge a Member State of its obligations under that provision. Under the cloak of a general provision permitting the approval of machines imported from other Member States, the administration might very well adopt a systematically unfavourable attitude towards imported machines, either by allowing considerable delay in replying to applications for approval or in carrying out the examination procedure, or by refusing approval on the grounds of various alleged technical faults for which no detailed explanations are given or which prove to be inaccurate.

12. The prohibition on measures having an effect equivalent to quantitative restrictions would lose much of its useful effect if it did not cover protectionist or discriminatory practices of that type.

13. It must however be noted that for an administrative practice to constitute a measure prohibited under Article 30 that practice must show a certain degree of consistency and generality. That generality must be assessed differently according to whether the market concerned is one on which there are numerous traders or whether it is a market, such as that in postal franking machines, on which only a few undertakings are active. In the latter case, a national administration's treatment of a single undertaking may constitute a measure incompatible with Article 30.

14. In the light of those principles it is clear from the facts of the case that the conduct of the French postal administration constitutes an impediment to imports contrary to Article 30 of the EEC Treaty.

[E17]   Case 82/77 Openbaar Ministerie of the Netherlands v Van Tiggele [1978] ECR 25

[This was a reference under Article 177 in the course of criminal proceedings instituted against a licensed victualler who was accused of selling alcoholic beverages at prices below the minimum prices fixed by national law.]

The European Court of Justice

12. For the purposes of [the Article 30] prohibition it is sufficient that the measures in question are likely to hinder, directly or indirectly, actually or potentially, imports between Member States.

13. Whilst national price control rules applicable without distinction to domestic products and imported products cannot in general produce such an effect they may do so in certain specific cases.

14. Thus imports may be impeded in particular when a national authority fixes prices or profit margins at such a level that imported products are placed at a disadvantage in relation to identical domestic products either because they cannot profitably be marketed in the conditions laid down or because the competitive advantage conferred by lower cost prices is cancelled out.

15. These are the considerations in the light of which the question submitted must be settled since the present case concerns a product for which there is no common organisation of the market.

16. First a national provision which prohibits without distinction the retail sale of domestic products and imported products at prices below the purchase price paid by the retailer cannot produce effects detrimental to the marketing of imported products alone and consequently cannot constitute a measure having an effect equivalent to a quantitative restriction on imports.

17. Furthermore the fixing of the minimum profit margin at a specific amount, and not as a percentage of the cost price, applicable without distinction to domestic products and imported products is likewise incapable of producing an adverse effect on imported products which may be cheaper, as in the present case where the amount of the profit margin constitutes a relatively insignificant part of the final retail price.

18. On the other hand this is not so in the case of a minimum price fixed at a specific amount which, although applicable without distinction to domestic products and imported products, is capable of having an adverse effect on the marketing of the latter in so far as it prevents their lower cost price from being reflected in the retail selling price.

19. This is the conclusion which must be drawn even though the competent authority is empowered to grant exemptions from the fixed minimum price and though this power is freely applied to imported products, since the requirement that importers and traders must comply with the administrative formalities inherent in such a system may in itself constitute a measure having an effect equivalent to a quantitative restriction.

Question

How can the national court carry out the task assigned to it here?

[E18]   Case 75/81 Blesgen v Belgium [1982] ECR 1211

[This was a reference under Article 177 in the course of criminal proceedings brought by the Belgian authorities against a restaurateur accused of infringing Belgian rules inasmuch as, being a retailer of drinks for consumption on the premises, he held in stock and sold in his establishment spirits of an alcoholic strength exceeding 22° at a temperature of 15° Centigrade.]

The European Court of Justice

6. In the view of the Belgian government the law in question does not fall under the prohibition of Article 30 of the EEC Treaty because it has no restrictive effect upon intra-Community trade in the absence of any discrimination between imported and domestic products. The objective of the [law in question] is a general one and forms part of the campaign against alcoholism. The Belgian government points out that the ban on keeping and consuming certain spirits in places open to the public is intended to combat alcoholism and its spread and in particular to protect youth against its harmful effects both from a personal and social point of view. It therefore constitutes a legitimate choice of social policy in accordance with the objectives of general interest pursued by the Treaty. The absence of Community rules in the matter justifies national action in so far as it is considered necessary to satisfy imperative requirements which in any event have precedence over the requirements of free movements of goods.

7. Article 30 of the EEC Treaty provides that quantitative restrictions on imports and all measures having equivalent effect shall be prohibited between Member States. It follows that any national measure likely to hinder, directly or indirectly, actually or potentially, intra-Community trade is to be regarded as a measure having an effect equivalent to quantitative restrictions. As the court pointed out in . . . Case 152/78 *Commission v France* [1980] ECR 2299, even though a law on the marketing of products does not directly concern imports, it may, according to the circumstances, affect prospects for importing products from other Member States and thus fall under the prohibition in Article 30 of the Treaty.

8. Moreover according to Article 3 of Commission Directive 70/50 . . . (OJ, English Special Edition 1970 (I) p 17) on the abolition of measures which have an effect equivalent to quantitative restrictions on imports and are not covered by other provisions adopted in pursuance of the EEC Treaty, the prohibition in Article 30 of the Treaty also covers national measures governing the marketing of products even though equally applicable to domestic and imported products, where the restrictive effect of such measures on the free movement of goods exceeds the effects intrinsic to trade rules.

9. That is not however the case with a legislative provision concerning only the sale of strong spirits for consumption on the premises in all places open to the public and not concerning other forms of marketing the same drinks. It is to be observed in addition that the restrictions placed on the sale of the spirits in question make no distinction whatsoever based on their nature or origin. Such a legislative measure has therefore in fact no connection with the importation of the products and for that reason is not of such a nature as to impede trade between Member States.

10. The same considerations also apply to the prohibition of keeping the

drinks in question in premises appurtenant to the establishment open to the public. In so far as that provision is ancillary to the prohibition on consumption on the premises its effect cannot be to restrict the importation of products originating in other Member States.

Question

Could the Court of Justice have reached the same outcome by a different route? Look at **[A18]** and **[E35]**.

[E19] Case C-23/89 Quietlynn and Richards v Southend-on-Sea Borough Council [1990] I-ECR 3059

[On whether national legislation prohibiting the sale of lawful sex articles from unlicensed sex establishments was compatible with Articles 30–36.]

The European Court of Justice

9. First, it must be noted that national legislation prohibiting the sale of sex articles from unlicensed sex establishments applies without distinction to imported and domestic products. It thus does not constitute an absolute prohibition on the sale of the products in question, but merely a rule regarding their distribution, regulating the outlets through which the products may be marketed. In principle, therefore, the marketing of products imported from other Member States is not rendered any more difficult than that of domestic products.

10. It must be pointed out that in similar cases concerning rules governing the marketing of certain products the court has held Article 30 of the Treaty not to be applicable. In its judgment in Case 155/80 *Oebel* [1981] ECR 1993, the court held that national rules governing working hours in bakeries and the hours of delivery and sale of bakers' wares were compatible with Article 30 of the Treaty since trade within the Community remained possible at all times. Likewise, in its judgment in Case 75/81 *Blesgen v Belgium* **[E18]**, the court considered that a legislative provision that concerned only the sale of strong spirits for consumption on the premises in all places open to the public and did not concern other forms of marketing the same drinks had in fact no connection with the importation of the products and for that reason was not of such a nature as to impede trade between Member States.

11. It must also be pointed out that the provisions prohibiting the sale of sex articles from unlicensed sex establishments have in fact no connection with intra-Community trade, since the products covered by the Act may be marketed through licensed sex establishments and other channels, that is to say through shops in which sex articles account for only an insignificant proportion of sales and which are therefore not required to be licensed, or by mail order. Moreover, those provisions are not intended to regulate trade in goods within the Community and they are therefore not of such a nature as to impede trade between Member States.

[E20]   Joined Cases C-267 and C-268/91 Keck and Mithouard (Judgment, 24 November 1993)

[Reference under Article 177 arising from prosecutions under French laws prohibiting reselling products in an unaltered state at prices lower than their actual purchase price ('resale at a loss').]

The European Court of Justice

. . .

11. By virtue of Article 30, quantitative restrictions on imports and all measures having equivalent effect are prohibited between Member States. The court has consistently held that any measure which is capable of directly or indirectly, actually or potentially, hindering intra-Community trade constitutes a measure having equivalent effect to a quantitative restriction.

12. It is not the purpose of national legislation imposing a general prohibition on resale at a loss to regulate trade in goods between Member States.

13. Such legislation may, admittedly, restrict the volume of sales, and hence the volume of sales of products from other Member States, in so far as it deprives traders of a method of sales promotion. But the question remains whether such a possibility is sufficient to characterise the legislation in question as a measure having equivalent effect to a quantitative restriction on imports.

14. In view of the increasing tendency of traders to invoke Article 30 of the Treaty as a means of challenging any rules whose effect is to limit their commercial freedom even where such rules are not aimed at products from other Member States, the court considers it necessary to re-examine and clarify its case law on this matter.

15. In *Cassis de Dijon* **[E21]** it was held that, in the absence of harmonisation of legislation, measures of equivalent effect prohibited by Article 30 include obstacles to the free movement of goods where they are the consequence of applying rules that lay down requirements to be met by such goods (such as requirements as to designation, form, size, weight, composition, presentation, labelling, packaging) to goods from other Member States where they are lawfully manufactured and marketed, even if those rules apply without distinction to all products unless their application can be justified by a public interest objective taking precedence over the free movement of goods.

16. However, contrary to what has previously been decided, the application to products from other Member States of national provisions restricting or prohibiting certain selling arrangements is not such as to hinder directly or indirectly, actually or potentially, trade between Member States within the meaning of the *Dassonville* judgment **[E12]**, provided that those provisions apply to all affected traders operating within the national territory and provided that they affect in the same manner, in law and in fact, the marketing of domestic products and of those from other Member States.

17. . . . Such rules therefore fall outside the scope of Article 30 of the Treaty.

Question

How does this judgment affect **[A18]**, **[E12]** and **[E21]**? Can indistinctly applicable measures contravene Article 30 any more?

(b) The mandatory requirements and the notion of Community-compatible interests

[E21]   Case 120/78 Rewe-Zentral AG v Bundesmonopolverwaltung für Branntwein ('Cassis de Dijon') [1979] ECR 649

[This was a reference under Article 177 concerning the compatibility with Community law of a provision of the German rules relating to the marketing of alcoholic beverages fixing a minimum alcoholic strength for various categories of alcoholic products.]

The European Court of Justice

2. It appears . . . that the plaintiff in the main action intends to import a consignment of 'Cassis de Dijon' originating in France for the purpose of marketing it in . . . Germany.

. . .

3. . . . [The German] provisions lay down that the marketing of fruit liqueurs, such as 'Cassis de Dijon', is conditional upon a minimum alcohol content of 25%, whereas the alcohol content of the product in question, which is freely marketed as such in France, is between 15 and 20%.

4. The plaintiff takes the view that the fixing by the German rules of a minimum alcohol content leads to the result that well-known spirits products from other Member States of the Community cannot be sold in . . . Germany and that the said provision therefore constitutes a restriction on the free movement of goods between Member States which exceeds the bounds of the trade rules reserved to the latter.

In its view it is a measure having an effect equivalent to a quantitative restriction on imports contrary to Article 30 of the EEC Treaty.

Since, furthermore, it is a measure adopted within the context of the management of the spirits monopoly, the plaintiff considers that there is also an infringement of Article 37, according to which the Member States shall progressively adjust any State monopolies of a commercial character so as to ensure that when the transitional period has ended no discrimination regarding the conditions under which goods are procured or marketed exists between nationals of Member States.

. . .

7. It should be noted in this connexion that Article 37 relates specifically to state monopolies of a commercial character.

That provision is therefore irrelevant with regard to national provisions which do not concern the exercise by a public monopoly of its specific function – namely, its exclusive right – but apply in a general manner to the production and marketing of alcoholic beverages, whether or not the latter are covered by the monopoly in question.

That being the case, the effect on intra-Community trade of the measure referred to by the national court must be examined solely in relation to the requirements under Article 30.

. . .

8. In the absence of common rules relating to the production and marketing of alcohol . . . it is for the Member States to regulate all matters relating to the production and marketing of alcohol and alcoholic beverages on their own territory.

Obstacles to movement within the Community resulting from disparities between the national laws relating to the marketing of the products in question must be accepted in so far as those provisions may be recognised as being necessary in order to satisfy mandatory requirements relating in particular to the effectiveness of fiscal supervision, the protection of public health, the fairness of commercial transactions and the defence of the consumer.

9. [The German government] put forward various arguments which, in its view, justify the application of provisions relating to the minimum alcohol content of alcoholic beverages, adducing considerations relating on the one hand to the protection of public health and on the other to the protection of the consumer against unfair commercial practices.

10. As regards the protection of public health the German government states that the purpose of the fixing of minimum alcohol contents by national legislation is to avoid the proliferation of alcoholic beverages on the national market, in particular alcoholic beverages with a low alcohol content, since, in its view, such products may more easily induce a tolerance towards alcohol than more highly alcoholic beverages.

11. Such considerations are not decisive since the consumer can obtain on the market an extremely wide range of weakly or moderately alcoholic products and furthermore a large proportion of alcoholic beverages with a high alcohol content freely sold on the German market is generally consumed in a diluted form.

12. The German government also claims that the fixing of a lower limit for the alcohol content of certain liqueurs is designed to protect the consumer against unfair practices on the part of producers and distributors of alcoholic beverages.

This argument is based on the consideration that the lowering of the alcohol content secures a competitive advantage in relation to beverages with a higher alcohol content, since alcohol constitutes by far the most expensive constituent of beverages by reason of the high rate of tax to which it is subject.

Furthermore, according to the German government, to allow alcoholic products into free circulation wherever, as regards their alcohol content, they comply with the rules laid down in the country of production would have the effect of imposing as a common standard within the Community the lowest alcohol content permitted in any of the Member States, and even of rendering any requirements in this field inoperative since a lower limit of this nature is foreign to the rules of several Member States.

13. As the Commission rightly observed, the fixing of limits in relation to the alcohol content of beverages may lead to the standardisation of products placed on the market and of their designations, in the interests of a greater transparency of commercial transactions and offers for sale to the public.

However, this line of argument cannot be taken so far as to regard the mandatory fixing of minimum alcohol contents as being an essential guarantee of the fairness of commercial transactions, since it is a simple matter to ensure that suitable information is conveyed to the purchaser by requiring the display of an indication of origin and of the alcohol content on the packaging of products.

14. It is clear from the foregoing that the requirements relating to the minimum alcohol content of alcoholic beverages do not serve a purpose

which is in the general interest and such as to take precedence over the requirements of the free movement of goods, which constitutes one of the fundamental rules of the Community.

In practice, the principal effect of requirements of this nature is to promote alcoholic beverages having a high alcohol content by excluding from the national market products of other Member States which do not answer that description.

It therefore appears that the unilateral requirement imposed by the rules of a Member State of a minimum alcohol content for the purposes of the sale of alcoholic beverages constitutes an obstacle to trade which is incompatible with the provisions of Article 30 of the Treaty.

There is therefore no valid reason why, provided that they have been lawfully produced and marketed in one of the Member States, alcoholic beverages should not be introduced into any other Member State; the sale of such products may not be subject to a legal prohibition on the marketing of beverages with an alcohol content lower than the limit set by the national rules.

[E22] Case 113/80 EC Commission v Ireland ('Irish souvenirs') [1981] ECR 1625

The European Court of Justice

2. According to the explanatory notes thereto, Statutory Instrument No 306 (hereinafter referred to as 'the Sale Order') prohibits the sale or exposure for sale of imported articles of jewellery depicting motifs or possessing characteristics which suggest that they are souvenirs of Ireland, for example an Irish character, event or scene, wolfhound, round tower, shamrock etc and Statutory Instrument No 307 (hereinafter referred to as 'the Importation Order') prohibits the importation of such articles unless, in either case, they bear an indication of their country of origin or the word 'foreign'.

3. The articles concerned are listed in a schedule to each order. However, in order to come within the scope of the orders the article must be made of precious metal or rolled precious metal or of base metal, including polished or plated articles suitable for setting.

. . .

5. The Irish government does not dispute the restrictive effects of these orders on the free movement of goods. However, it contends that the disputed measures are justified in the interests of consumer protection and of fairness in commercial transactions between producers. In this regard, it relies upon Article 36 of the Treaty which provides that Articles 30 to 34 shall not preclude prohibitions or restrictions on imports justified on grounds of public policy or the protection of industrial and commercial property.

6. The defendant is, however, mistaken in placing reliance on Article 36 of the Treaty as the legal basis for its contention.

7. In fact, since the court stated in its judgment . . . in Case 46/76 *Bauhuis* [1977] ECR 5 that Article 36 of the Treaty 'constitutes a derogation from the basic rule that all obstacles to the free movement of goods

between Member States shall be eliminated and must be interpreted strictly', the exceptions listed therein cannot be extended to cases other than those specifically laid down.

8. In view of the fact that neither the protection of consumers nor the fairness of commercial transactions is included amongst the exceptions set out in Article 36, those grounds cannot be relied upon as such in connection with that Article.

9. However, since the Irish government describes its recourse to these concepts as 'the central issue in the case', it is necessary to study this argument in connection with Article 30 and to consider whether it is possible, in reliance on those concepts, to say that the Irish orders are not measures having an effect equivalent to quantitative restrictions on imports within the meaning of that article, bearing in mind that, according to the established case law of the court, such measures include 'all trading rules enacted by Member States which are capable of hindering, directly or indirectly, actually or potentially, intra-Community trade' [*Dassonville* **[E12]**].

10. In this respect, the court has repeatedly affirmed . . . that 'in the absence of common rules relating to the production and marketing of the product in question, it is for Member States to regulate all matters relating to the production, distribution and consumption on their own territory subject, however, to the condition that those rules do not present an obstacle . . . to intra-Community trade' and that 'it is only where national rules, which apply without discrimination to both domestic and imported products, may be justified as being necessary in order to satisfy imperative requirements relating in particular to . . . the fairness of commercial transactions and the defence of the consumer that they may constitute an exception to the requirements arising under Article 30'.

11. The orders concerned in the present case are not measures which are applicable to domestic products and to imported products without distinction but rather a set of rules which apply only to imported products and are therefore discriminatory in nature, with the result that the measures in issue are not covered by the decisions cited above which relate exclusively to provisions that regulate in a uniform manner the marketing of domestic and imported products.

12. The Irish government recognises that the contested measures apply solely to imported articles and render their importation and sale more difficult than the sale of domestic products. However, it maintains that this difference in the treatment awarded to home-produced articles and to imported articles does not constitute discrimination on the ground that the articles referred to in the contested orders consist mainly of souvenirs; the appeal of such articles lies essentially in the fact of their being manufactured in the place where they are purchased and they bear in themselves an implied indication of their Irish origin, with the result that the purchaser would be misled if the souvenir bought in Ireland was manufactured elsewhere. Consequently, the requirement that all imported 'souvenirs' covered by the two orders must bear an indication of origin is justified and in no way constitutes discrimination because the articles concerned are different on account of the differences between their essential characteristics.

13. The Commission rejects this reasoning . . . [I]t submits that it is unnecessary for a purchaser to know whether or not a product is of a particular origin, unless such origin implies a certain quality, basic materials or process of manufacture or a particular place in the folklore or tradition of

the region in question; since none of the articles referred to in the orders displays these features, the measures in question cannot be justified and are therefore 'overtly discriminatory'.

14. It is therefore necessary to consider whether the contested measures are indeed discriminatory or whether they constitute discrimination in appearance only.

15. The souvenirs referred to in the Sale Order and in the Importation Order are generally articles of ornamentation of little commercial value representing or incorporating a motif or emblem which is reminiscent of an Irish place, object, character or historical event or suggestive of an Irish symbol and their value stems from the fact that the purchaser, more often than not a tourist, buys them on the spot. The essential characteristic of the souvenirs in question is that they constitute a pictorial reminder of the place visited, which does not by itself mean that a souvenir, as defined in the orders, must necessarily be manufactured in the country of origin.

16. Furthermore, leaving aside the point argued by the Commission – with regard to the articles covered by the contested orders – that it would not be enough to require a statement of origin to be affixed to domestic products also, it is important to note that the interests of consumers and fair trading would be adequately safeguarded if it were left to domestic manufacturers to take appropriate steps such as affixing, if they so wished, their mark of origin to their own products or packaging.

17. Thus by granting souvenirs imported from other Member States access to the domestic market solely on condition that they bear a statement of origin, whilst no such statement is required in the case of domestic products, the provisions contained in the Sale Order and the Importation Order indisputably constitute a discriminatory measure.

Question

Why should the Court of Justice be so insistent upon distinguishing the so-called imperative requirements from Article 36 derogations?

[E23] Case 286/81 Oosthoek's Uitgeversmaatschappij BV [1982] ECR 4575

The European Court of Justice

7. In its question, the national court seeks in substance to ascertain whether Articles 30 and 34 of the EEC Treaty preclude the application by a Member State to products from, or intended for, another Member State of national legislation which prohibits the offering of giving, for sales promotion purposes, of free gifts in the form of books to purchasers of an encyclopaedia and requires, for the application of an exception to that prohibition, the existence of a relationship between the consumption or use of the free gift and the product sold.

8. In their observations, the Netherlands, German and Danish governments express the view, in limine, that national legislation such as that at issue has no particular impact on intra-Community trade and does not fall within the scope of Articles 30 and 34 of the EEC Treaty.

9. In that regard, it must be stated that the application of the Netherlands legislation to the sale in the Netherlands of encyclopaedias produced in that country is in no way linked to the importation or exportation of goods and does not therefore fall within the scope of Articles 30 and 34 of the EEC Treaty. However, the sale in the Netherlands of encyclopaedias produced in Belgium and the sale in other Member States of encyclopaedias produced in the Netherlands are transactions forming part of intra-Community trade. In the view of the question raised by the national court, it is therefore necessary to determine whether provisions of the type contained in the Netherlands legislation are compatible with both Article 30 and Article 34 of the EEC Treaty.

10. Oosthoek maintains that the Netherlands legislation obliges it to adopt different sales promotion schemes in the various Member States which constitute a single market, involves it in additional costs and further difficulties and thus hinders the importation and exportation of the encyclopaedias in question. The requirement of related consumption or use is not justified by the need either to protect consumers or to safeguard competition.

11. The Commission considers that although the possibility that such a measure may indirectly hinder the importation of encyclopaedias cannot be ruled out, it is not contrary to Article 30 since it applies to all products without distinction and is justified by the objectives of consumer protection and organisation of the economy.

12. In order to answer the question raised by the national court, it is necessary to consider the question relating to exportation separately from that relating to importation.

13. As regards exportation, Article 34 is concerned with national measures the aim or effect of which is specifically to restrict the flow of exports and thus establish a difference in treatment between the domestic trade of a Member State and its export trade, in such a way as to confer a particular advantage on domestic production or on the domestic market of the state in question. That is evidently not the position in the case of legislation such as that at issue as regards the sale in other Member States of the Community of encyclopaedias produced in the Netherlands. That legislation merely imposes certain restrictions on marketing conditions within the Netherlands without affecting the sale of goods intended for exportation.

14. As regards the restrictions on imports referred to in Article 30 . . . it must be remembered that the court has repeatedly held . . . that in the absence of common rules relating to marketing, obstacles to movement within the Community resulting from disparities between national rules must be accepted in so far as those rules, being applicable to domestic products and imported products without distinction, are justifiable as being necessary in order to satisfy mandatory requirements relating, inter alia, to consumer protection and fair trading.

15. Legislation which restricts or prohibits certain forms of advertising and certain means of sale promotion may, although it does not directly affect imports, be such as to restrict their volume because it affects marketing opportunities for the imported products. The possibility cannot be ruled out that to compel a producer either to adopt advertising or sales promotion schemes which differ from one Member State to another or to discontinue a scheme which he considers to be particularly effective may constitute an obstacle to imports even if the legislation in question applies to domestic

products and imported products without distinction.

16. It is therefore necessary to consider whether a prohibition of a free gift scheme, such as that contained in the Netherlands legislation, may be justified by requirements relating to consumer protection and fair trading.

17. In that regard, it is clear from the evidence before the court that the [Netherlands law] pursues a twofold objective which is, in the first place, to prevent the disruption of normal competition by undertakings which offer products as free gifts or at very low prices with a view to promoting the sale of their own range of goods and, secondly, to protect consumers by the attainment of greater market transparency.

18. It is undeniable that the offering of free gifts as a means of sales promotion may mislead consumers as to the real prices of certain products and distort the conditions on which genuine competition is based. Legislation which restricts or even prohibits such commercial practices for that reason is therefore capable of contributing to consumer protection and fair trading.

19. The question raised by the national court with regard to legislation of that kind concerns, in particular, the criterion of related consumption or use the purpose of which, in the present case, is to define the scope of one of the exceptions relaxing the rule which in principle prohibits the offering of free gifts.

20. Even though no such criterion has been incorporated in the laws of other Member States, and in particular that of Belgium, it does not appear to be unrelated to the above-mentioned objectives of the Netherlands legislation or, in particular, to the desire to achieve market transparency to the extent considered necessary for the protection of consumers and to ensure fair trading. Accordingly, the incorporation of such a criterion in national legislation in order to define the scope of an exception to a rule which prohibits the offering of free gifts does not exceed what is necessary for the attainment of the objectives in question.

[E24] Joined Cases 60 and 61/84 Cinéthèque and others v Fédération Nationale des Cinémas Français [1985] ECR 2605

[Under French law, cinematographic work being shown in cinemas could not be exploited through video until the expiry of one year from the date of the cinema performance certificate. In proceedings brought for breach of this rule, producers of video-cassettes claimed that the French provisions contravened Community law relating to the free movement of goods and services.]

Opinion of Advocate General Slynn

It seems to me in summary that a measure is in breach of Article 30 (a) if it forbids imports or restricts imports quantitatively; (b) if it discriminates against imports by eg imposing more stringent standards on importers than on domestic producers so that in practice importation may be made more difficult and thereby imports may be restricted; (c) if, although not directed to importation as such but covering both national goods and imports, it requires a producer or distributor to take steps additional to those which he would normally and lawfully take in the marketing of his goods, which thereby render importation more difficult, so that imports may be restricted and national producers be given protection in practice. The last category (c) will not be in breach of Article 30 if it can be shown that the measure is justified by mandatory requirements of the kind contemplated in Cassis de Dijon.

On the other hand, in an area in which there are no common Community standards or rules, where a national measure is not specifically directed at imports, does not discriminate against imports, does not make it any more difficult for an importer to sell his products than it is for a domestic producer, and gives no protection to domestic producers, then in my view, prima facie, the measure does not fall within Article 30 even if it does in fact lead to a restriction or reduction of imports.

The European Court of Justice

8. It is necessary to consider first whether the Treaty provisions relating to the free movement of services, especially Article 59, are relevant in assessing the compatibility of such national legislation with Community law.

9. Cinematographic works belong to the class of artistic works which may be transmitted to the public either directly by showing the film on television or in cinemas, or indirectly by means of recordings such as video-cassettes. In the latter case the transmission to the public merges with the putting of the works on the market.

10. The provision of French law which gave rise to the main proceedings in the two cases prohibits the 'exploitation' of cinematographic works in the form of recordings, in particular in the form of video-cassettes. The question may therefore be asked whether that prohibition, whilst not applying to the mere grant of a licence which is not immediately followed by the production of the video-cassettes in question, nevertheless extends to an instruction to produce them. In that respect it must be emphasised that it is not possible to regard the process of production of video-cassettes as the provision of 'services' within the meaning of the Treaty since the services of a manufacturer of such products result directly in the manufacture of a material object which is, moreover, the subject of classification in the Common Customs Tariff . . . According to Article 60 of the Treaty services are only to be considered as such if they are provided for remuneration 'in so far as they are not governed by provisions relating to freedom of movement for goods'.

11. It follows from the foregoing considerations that the questions raised by the Tribunal de grande instance fall to be considered solely with regard to Articles 30 to 36 of the Treaty.

. . .

15. . . . [The] defendant in the main proceedings contends that the legislation in question applies to imported and national products alike, that it was adopted in the absence of Community legislation in a field falling within the exclusive competence of the Member States and that it was justified by the mandatory requirements of the general interest. What was at issue was the protection of the cinema as a means of cultural expression, which protection was necessary in view of the rapid development of other modes of film distribution.

16. The French government . . . observes that the legislation in question forms part of a body of rules intended to establish a chronological order between different methods of exploiting a cinematographic work in order to ensure priority for exploitation in cinemas. Exploitation through television was already regulated in France . . . and the aim of Article 89 of Law 82-652 was to apply the same system to exploitation by video, but subject to a shorter interval. Such an arrangement was necessary in order to ensure the continued creation of cinematographic works since their exploitation in cinemas produces the bulk of their revenue (80%) and income from other forms of exploitation is very small. Cinema showings were essential for the film industry to remain profitable, and thus for the continued production of films.

. . .

18. The Commission states that the national legislation in question, by prohibiting the marketing of video-cassettes of cinematographic works shown in cinemas, undeniably has the effect of hindering imports of video-recordings lawfully produced and marketed in another Member State and in free circulation there . . . The Commission maintains, however, that cultural aims may justify certain restrictions on the free movement of goods provided that those restrictions apply to national and imported products without distinction, that they are appropriate to the cultural aim which is being pursued and that they constitute the means of achieving them which affects intra-Community trade the least.

. . .

20. It must be stated . . . that, in the light of [information produced by the Commission at the court's request], the national legislation at issue in the main proceedings of these cases forms part of a body of provisions applied in the majority of Member States, whether in the form of contractual, administrative or legislative provisions and of variable scope, but the purpose of which, in all cases, is to delay the distribution of films by means of video-cassettes during the first months following their release in the cinema in order to protect their exploitation in the cinema, which protection is considered necessary in the interests of the profitability of cinematographic production, as against exploitation through video-cassettes. It must also be observed that, in principle, the Treaty leaves it to the Member States to determine the need for such a system, the form of such a system and any temporal restrictions which ought to be laid down.

21. In that connection it must be observed that such a system, if it applies without distinction to both video-cassettes manufactured in the national territory and to imported video-cassettes, does not have the purpose of regulating trade patterns; its effect is not to favour national production as against the production of other Member States, but to encourage cinematographic production as such.

22. Nevertheless, the application of such a system may create barriers to intra-Community trade in video-cassettes because of the disparities between the system operated in the different Member States and between the conditions for the release of cinematographic works in the cinemas of those states. In those circumstances a prohibition of exploitation laid down by such a system is not compatible with the principle of the free movement of goods provided for in the Treaty unless any obstacle to intra-Community

trade thereby created does not exceed that which is necessary in order to ensure the attainment of the objective in view and unless that objective is justified with regard to Community law.

23. It must be conceded that a national system which, in order to encourage the creation of cinematographic works irrespective of their origin, gives priority, for a limited initial period, to the distribution of such works through the cinema, is so justified.

. . .

25. The plaintiffs and the interveners in the main action also raised the question whether Article 89 of the French law on audio-visual communication was in breach of the principle of freedom of expression recognised by Article 10 of the European Convention for the Protection of Human Rights and Fundamental Freedoms and was therefore incompatible with Community law.

26. Although it is true that it is the duty of this court to ensure observance of fundamental rights in the field of Community law, it has no power to examine the compatibility with the European Convention of national legislation which concerns, as in this case, an area which falls within the jurisdiction of the national legislator.

Questions

Compare **[A18]**. In the latter, did the Court of Justice treat the Sunday trading legislation as justified by imperative requirements, or beyond the scope of Article 30 for other reasons? Does proportionality govern whether justifications are established, or the existence of a restriction in the first place?

[E25]   Case C-362/88 GB-INNO-BM v Confédération du Commerce Luxembourgeoise [1990] ECR I-667

The European Court of Justice

2. The question was raised in proceedings between [CCL], a non-profit-making association which claims to represent the interests of Luxembourg traders, and GB-INNO-BM, which operates supermarkets in Belgian territory, inter alia in Arlon, near the Belgian–Luxembourg border. The Belgian company had distributed advertising leaflets on Luxembourg territory as well as on Belgian territory and CCL applied to the Luxembourg courts for an injunction against the company to stop the distribution of those advertising leaflets. CCL claimed that the advertising contained in the leaflets was contrary to the Grand-Ducal Regulation of 23 December 1974 on unfair competition . . ., according to which sales offers involving a temporary price reduction may not state the duration of the offer or refer to previous prices.

3. The presiding judge of the Tribunal d'arrondissement (District Court), Luxembourg, competent for commercial matters, granted the injunction, taking the view that the distribution of the leaflets in question constituted a sales offer prohibited by the Grand-Ducal Regulation of 1974 and an unfair practice prohibited by the same regulation. The Cour d'appel upheld the

injunction, whereupon GB-INNO-BM appealed to the Cour de cassation. It argued that the advertising contained in the leaflets complied with the Belgian provisions on unfair competition and that it would thus be contrary to Article 30 of the EEC Treaty to apply to it the prohibitions laid down in the Luxembourg legislation.

[The Cour de Cassation stayed proceedings and made a reference under Article 177.]

. . .

7. . . . The court has already held, in its judgment . . . in Case 286/81 *Oosthoek's Uitgeversmaatschappij* **[E23]**, that legislation which restricts or prohibits certain forms of advertising and certain means of sales promotion may, although it does not directly affect trade, be such as to restrict the volume of trade because it affects marketing opportunities.

8. Free movement of goods concerns not only traders but also individuals. It requires, particularly in frontier areas, that consumers resident in one Member State may travel freely to the territory of another Member State to shop under the same conditions as the local population. That freedom for consumers is compromised if they are deprived of access to advertising available in the country where purchases are made. Consequently a prohibition against distributing such advertising must be examined in the light of Articles 30, 31 and 36 of the Treaty.

9. It is therefore clear that the question referred to the court for a preliminary ruling concerns the compatibility with Article 30 of the Treaty of an obstacle to the free movement of goods resulting from disparities between the applicable national legislation. It is apparent from the documents before the court that the advertising of sales offers involving a price reduction and stating the duration of the offer and the prices previously charged is prohibited by the Luxembourg legislation but permitted by the provisions in force in Belgium.

10. The court has consistently held that in the absence of common rules relating to marketing, obstacles to the free movement of goods within the Community resulting from disparities between national laws must be accepted in so far as such rules, applicable to domestic and imported products without distinction, may be justified as being necessary in order to satisfy mandatory requirements relating inter alia to consumer protection or the fairness of commercial transactions.

. . .

11. According to CCL and the Luxembourg government, the two prohibitions in question – against stating the duration of a special offer and against specifying the previous price – are justified on the grounds of consumer protection. The purpose of the prohibition concerning the duration of the special offer is to avoid the risk of confusion between special sales and half-yearly clearance sales the timing and duration of which is restricted under Luxembourg legislation. The prohibition against allowing the previous price to appear in the offer is justified, they say, by the fact that the consumer is not normally in a position to check that a previous reference price is genuine. In addition, the marking of a previous price might exert excessive psychological pressure on the consumer. In substance the German government shares that point of view.

12. That view is contested by GB-INNO-BM and the Commission, who

point out that any normally aware consumer knows that price sales take place only twice a year. As regards comparison of prices, the Commission has submitted an overview of the relevant legislation in various Member States and concludes that, with the exception of the Luxembourg and German provisions, they all allow both prices to be indicated if the reference price is genuine.

13. The question thus arises whether national legislation which prevents the consumer from having access to certain information may be justified in the interest of consumer protection.

14. It should be observed first of all that Community policy on the subject establishes a close link between protecting the consumer and providing the consumer with information. Thus the 'preliminary programme' adopted by the Council in 1975 (OJ 1975 C92/1) provides for the implementation of a 'consumer protection and information policy'. By a Resolution of 19 May 1981 (OJ 1981 C133/1), the Council approved a 'second programme of the European Economic Community for a consumer protection and information policy' the objectives of which were confirmed by the Council Resolution of 23 June 1986 concerning the future orientation of the policy of the Community for the protection and promotion of consumer interests (OJ 1986 C167/1).

15. The existence of a link between protection and information for consumers is explained in the introduction to the second programme. There it is stressed that measures taken or scheduled in accordance with the preliminary programme contribute towards improving the consumer's situation by protecting his health, his safety and his economic interest, by providing him with appropriate information and education, and by giving him a voice in decisions which involve him. It is stated that often those same measures have also resulted in harmonising the rules of competition by which manufacturers and retailers must abide.

16. The introduction goes on to specify that the purpose of the second programme is to continue and intensify the measures in this field and to help establish conditions for improved consultation between consumers on the one hand and manufacturers and retailers on the other. To that end the programme sets out five basic rights to be enjoyed by the consumer, amongst which appears the right to information and education. One of the measures proposed in the programme is the improvement of consumer education and information . . . The part of the programme which lays down the principles which must govern the protection of the economic interests of consumers includes passages which aim to ensure the accuracy of information provided to the consumer, but without refusing him access to certain information. Thus, according to one of the principles . . ., no form of advertising should mislead the buyer; an advertiser must be able to 'justify, by appropriate means, the validity of any claims he makes'.

17. As the court has held, a prohibition against importing certain products into a Member State is contrary to Article 30 where the aim of such a prohibition may be attained by appropriate labelling of the products concerned which would provide the consumer with the information he needs and enable him to make his choice in full knowledge of the facts (judgments . . . in Case 193/80 *Commission v Italy* [1981] ECR 3019, and . . . in Case 178/84 *Commission v Germany* **[E32]**).

18. It follows from the foregoing that under Community law concerning consumer protection the provision of information to the consumer is

considered one of the principal requirements. Thus Article 30 cannot be interpreted as meaning that national legislation which denies the consumer access to certain kinds of information may be justified by mandatory requirements concerning consumer protection.

19. In consequence, obstacles to intra-Community trade resulting from national rules of the type at issue in the main proceedings may not be justified by reasons relating to consumer protection. They thus fall under the prohibition laid down in Article 30 of the Treaty. The exceptions to the application of that provision contained in Article 36 are not applicable; indeed, no reliance was placed on them during the proceedings before the court.

Question

If consumers must be allowed to travel to the goods of their choice and have the information to do so, why did the Court of Justice not apply the same reasoning to abortion information in *Grogan* **[A19]**?

[E26] Case 302/86 Commission v Denmark ('drinks containers') [1988] ECR 4607

[Action was brought under Article 169 by the Commission for a declaration that by introducing and applying a system under which all containers for beer and soft drinks had to be returnable, Denmark was in breach of Article 30.]

The European Court of Justice

2. The main feature of the system which the Commission challenges as incompatible with Community law is that manufacturers must market beer and soft drinks only in re-usable containers. The containers must be approved by the National Agency for the Protection of the Environment, which may refuse approval of new kinds of container, especially if it considers that a container is not technically suitable for a system for returning containers or that the return system envisaged does not ensure that a sufficient proportion of containers are actually re-used or if a container of equal capacity, which is both available and suitable for the same use, has already been approved.

3. Order 95 of 16 March 1984 amended the aforementioned rules in such a way that, provided that a deposit-and-return system is established, non-approved containers, except for any form of metal container, may be used for quantities not exceeding 3,000 hectolitres a year per producer and for drinks which are sold by foreign producers in order to test the market.

. . .

7. In the present case the Danish government contends that the mandatory collection system for containers of beer and soft drinks applied in Denmark is justified by a mandatory requirement related to the protection of the environment.

8. The court has already held in its judgment . . . in Case 240/83 *Procureur de la République v Association de défense des brûleurs d'huiles usagées* [1985] ECR 531 that the protection of the environment is 'one of

the Community's essential objectives', which may as such justify certain limitations of the principle of the free movement of goods. That view is moreover confirmed by the Single European Act.

9. In view of the foregoing, it must therefore be stated that the protection of the environment is a mandatory requirement which may limit the application of Article 30 of the Treaty.

10. The Commission submits that the Danish rules are contrary to the principle of proportionality in so far as the aim of the protection of the environment may be achieved by means less restrictive of intra-Community trade.

. . .

12. It is therefore necessary to examine whether all the restrictions which the contested rules impose on the free movement of goods are necessary to achieve the objectives pursued by those rules.

13. First of all, as regards the obligation to establish a deposit-and-return system for empty containers, it must be observed that this requirement is an indispensable element of a system intended to ensure the re-use of containers and therefore appears necessary to achieve the aims pursued by the contested rules. That being so, the restrictions which it imposes on the free movement of goods cannot be regarded as disproportionate.

14. Next, it is necessary to consider the requirement that producers and importers must use only containers approved by the National Agency for the Protection of the Environment.

. . .

19. The provision in Order 95 restricting the quantity of beer and soft drinks which may be marketed by a producer in non-approved containers to 3,000 hectolitres a year is challenged by the Commission on the ground that it is unnecessary to achieve the objectives pursued by the system.

20. It is undoubtedly true that the existing system for returning approved containers ensures a maximum rate of re-use and therefore a very considerable degree of protection of the environment since empty containers can be returned to any retailer of beverages. Non-approved containers, on the other hand, can be returned only to the retailer who sold the beverages, since it is impossible to set up such a comprehensive system for those containers as well.

21. Nevertheless, the system for returning non-approved containers is capable of protecting the environment and, as far as imports are concerned, affects only limited quantities of beverages compared with the quantity of beverages consumed in Denmark owing to the restrictive effect which the requirement that containers should be returnable has on imports. In those circumstances, a restriction of the quantity of products which may be marketed by importers is disproportionate to the objective pursued.

22. It must therefore be held that by restricting, by Order 95 . . . the quantity of beer and soft drinks which may be marketed by a single producer in non-approved containers to 3,000 hectolitres a year, the Kingdom of Denmark has failed, as regards imports of those products from other Member States, to fulfil its obligations under Article 30 of the EEC Treaty.

[E27] Case C-239/90 SCP Boscher, Studer et Fromentin v SA British Motors Wright and others [1991] ECR I-2023

The European Court of Justice

2. The questions were raised in proceedings between SCP Boscher, Studer et Fromentin, a firm of auctioneers (*commissaires-priseurs*) operating in Paris, and SA British Motors Wright, which sell luxury second-hand cars, concerning the prohibition of an auction sale.

3. Pursuant to Article 1(1) of the French Law of 25 June 1841 on public auction sales, sale by public auction may not be used as a habitual means of carrying on business. Article 1(3) provides that the voluntary retail sale by that means of any second-hand goods or articles whatever belonging to or held by a trader who has not been registered for at least two years in the Registre de Commerce (Trade Register) and the Role des Patentes (Business Tax Roll) within the jurisdiction of the Tribunal de grande instance (Regional Court) in which the sale is to take place is also prohibited.

4. SCP Boscher, Studer et Fromentin was instructed by the German company Nado ('Nado'), whose registered office is in Hamburg, to sell by public auction on 6 November 1988 a number of second-hand vehicles some of which, according to the findings of the court before which an application for interim relief was initially brought, were collectors' items and some were high-priced vehicles of recent manufacture and low mileage. SA British Motors Wright and three other companies made an application to the Tribunal de grande instance (Regional Court), Paris, for an interim order prohibiting the sale pursuant to Article 1 of the Law of 25 June 1841. On the basis of that provision, on 4 November 1988 the court ordered the auctioneers not to proceed with the sale until it was proved that the owner or person in possession of the vehicles was entered in the trade register or the business tax roll pursuant to Article 1 of the Law of 25 June 1841.

[The Cour de Cassation, faced with appeals by Boscher, Studer et Fromentin from a judgment of the Cour d'Appel, referred several questions under Article 177.]

The first question (freedom to provide services)

7. The national court's first question seeks to determine whether or not legislation of a Member State which lays down the conditions governing the sale by a trader established in another Member State of goods belonging to him falls within the scope of Article 59 of the Treaty.

8. Such legislation, which concerns the conditions laid down for the marketing of goods traded between Member States, is subject to the provisions of the Treaty concerning the free movement of goods.

9. Pursuant to Article 60 of the Treaty, services provided for remuneration are considered to be 'services' within the meaning of the Treaty, in so far as they are not governed by the provisions relating inter alia to the free movement of goods.

10. Accordingly, it must be stated in reply to the first question that legislation of a Member State laying down the conditions governing the sale by

a trader established in another Member State of goods belonging to him does not fall within the scope of Article 59 of the Treaty.

. . .

The third and fourth questions (free movement of goods)

12. These questions seek to determine whether or not national legislation which makes the sale by public auction of second-hand goods from another Member State conditional upon the prior entry of the undertaking which owns the goods offered for sale in the trade register at the place of sale is compatible with Articles 30 and 36 of the Treaty.

13. According to the principle laid down in the judgment in Case 8/74 *Dassonville* **[E12]**, the prohibition of measures having an effect equivalent to quantitative restrictions laid down in Article 30 of the Treaty applies to all trading rules that are capable of hindering intra-Community trade directly or indirectly, actually or potentially.

14. The court has consistently held (judgments in Case 286/81 *Oosthoek* **[E23]** and Case C-362/88 *GB-INNO* **[E25]**) that the possibility cannot be ruled out that to compel a producer either to adopt advertising or sales promotion schemes which differ from one Member State to another or to discontinue a scheme which he considers to be particularly effective may constitute an obstacle to imports even if the legislation in question applies to domestic products and imported products without distinction. In its judgment in Case 382/87 *Buet* [1989] ECR 1235, the court stated that that finding applies, a fortiori, when the rules in question deprive the trader concerned of the possibility of using not a means of advertising but a method of marketing.

15. Moreover, the court has held that legislation which causes undertakings established in another Member State to incur the additional expenditure involved in complying with the obligation to have a representative in the importing Member State must be regarded as a measure having an effect equivalent to a quantitative restriction (judgments in Case 155/82 *Commission v Belgium* [1983] ECR 531 and Case 247/81 *Commission v Germany* [1984] ECR 1111).

16. National legislation that imposes on a seller the requirement of prior entry in the trade register at the place where the auction sale takes place is liable to impede the free movement of goods, since its effect is to require the owner of the goods either to use the services of a trader operating at the place of the sale or to refrain from selling goods by public auction.

17. Since the rules at issue apply without distinction to the sale of domestic and imported products, it is necessary to determine whether they may be justified by imperative requirements relating to the protection of consumers.

18. It has been contended that the requirement of prior entry of the seller in the trade register at the place of sale is necessary since otherwise the system of public auctions might not provide adequate safeguards for the consumer as to the origin and condition of an article which he purchases without the benefit of any period of reflexion.

19. As the court has made clear on several occasions, rules intended to satisfy a mandatory requirement must be proportionate to the goals pursued, and if a Member State has at its disposal less restrictive means of attaining the same goals it is under an obligation to use them.

20. The system of public auctions, as described in the documents before the court, usually involves buyers who are specially informed; furthermore, there are sufficient safeguards for the consumer. In any event, it is possible to impose conditions which are capable of protecting consumers and have a less restrictive effect on the free movement of goods than the requirement of prior entry of the owner of the goods offered for sale in the trade register at the place of sale.

21. It follows that legislation of the kind referred to by the national court cannot be justified by mandatory requirements relating to the protection of consumers and, consequently, that it is incompatible with Article 30 of the Treaty.

22. Nor can such legislation be justified on grounds of public policy under Article 36 of the Treaty.

23. The goal purportedly pursued, namely prevention of the sale of stolen cars, may be attained by appropriate control measures, such as checking of the chassis number.

24. It must therefore be stated in reply to the questions submitted by the national court that national legislation which makes the sale by public auction of second-hand goods from another Member State conditional upon the prior entry of the undertaking which owns the goods offered for sale in the trade register at the place of the sale is incompatible with Articles 30 and 36 of the Treaty.

[E28] Case C-2/90 Re Imports of Waste: EC Commission v Belgium [1993] 1 CMLR 365

First Opinion of Advocate General Jacobs

In these proceedings the Commission seeks a declaration that, by prohibiting the storage, tipping or dumping in Wallonia of waste from other Member States or from Belgian regions other than Wallonia, Belgium has failed to fulfil its obligations under:

1. Council Directive 75/442 on waste.
2. Council Directive 84/631 on the supervision and control within the European Community of the transfrontier shipment of hazardous waste.
3. Articles 30 and 36 EEC.

. . .

In my view, breach of Directive 75/442 has not been established. It is true that the objective of the directive, as its first recital indicates, is not only the protection of health and the environment, but also the prevention of disparities in national laws which may create unequal conditions of competition and affect the operation of the Common Market: it can thus be said to take as its point of departure the free movement of goods. However, beyond that the directive merely establishes a general framework of rules for the supervision of waste disposal operations: it contains no substantive provision which is specifically concerned with inter-state trade in waste products or which expressly or by necessary implication excludes the type of measure adopted by the Walloon Regional Executive.

The position is different as regards Directive 84/631. That directive also, as the fourth recital indicates, seeks to ensure that differences between the provisions on disposal of hazardous waste do not distort conditions of competition and thus directly affect the functioning of the common market. But, in contrast to Directive 75/442 Directive 84/631 is also specifically concerned with the transfrontier movement of dangerous waste, setting up a detailed, uniform system of supervision and control, including in particular the obligatory prior authorised disposal or regenerating undertaking in another Member State.

Once it is accepted that all waste is covered by the Treaty provisions on free movement of goods, then it is in my view plain that a measure which, by prohibiting the storage, tipping and dumping of waste, has the effect of restricting imports of waste from other Member States, must be viewed as a measure of equivalent effect. In that regard, it is irrelevant that the ban also extends to waste from other Belgian regions. The fact that a measure restricting intra-Community trade also restricts trade as between the regions of the Member State concerned cannot have the effect of removing the measure from the scope of Article 30. Moreover, . . . exceptions to the ban are possible by virtue of agreements made with the other Belgian regions, a possibility which does not exist in respect of imports from other Member States. In any event, as the Commission points out in answer to a written question from the court, the ban on imports from other Belgian regions is capable of reinforcing the ban on imports from other Member States, in that it will prevent the treatment of waste from other Member States in the Flanders or Brussels regions, followed by final disposal in Wallonia.

It is in my view also irrelevant that by virtue of s 2 of the decree derogations may be granted to the prohibition on the influx of waste from other countries. According to well-established case law, the mere requirement that importers and traders must comply with certain administrative formalities may itself constitute a measure having an effect equivalent to a quantitative restriction: see, for example, Case 82/77 *Van Tiggele* **[E17]**.

. . .

The question then arises whether reliance on Article 36 is possible. Directive 75/442, which contains only a general framework for the supervision of waste disposal, does not in my view displace Article 36. However, I consider that Directive 84/631 does exclude reliance on Article 36, at any rate as regards the categories of *dangerous* waste covered by that directive. As already stated, Directive 84/631 establishes a detailed, uniform system for the supervision and control of the transfrontier shipment of dangerous waste. As the court has indicated, where in application of Article 100 EEC, Community directives provide for the harmonisation of measures necessary to ensure the protection of animal and human health and establish Community procedures to check that they are observed, recourse to Article 36 is no longer justified and the appropriate checks must be carried out and the measures of protection adopted within the framework outlined by the harmonising directive: see Case 5/77 *Tedeschi* [1977] ECR 1555 and Case 148/78 *Ratti* [1979] ECR 1629 **[C26]**.

In my view it is not in any event open to Belgium to rely on Article 36 in order to restrict imports of non-dangerous waste. According to well-established case law, Article 36 must be interpreted restrictively . . . and I therefore do not think it possible to adopt a wide interpretation of the 'human health' exception so as to permit restrictions on substances which do not threaten health or life but at the most 'the quality of life'. Nor is it possible to rely on the 'mandatory requirements' exceptions to Article 30, which include the protection of the environment: see Case 302/86 *Commission v Denmark* **[E26]**. Those exceptions can be invoked only for measures which are not discriminatory. But the measure in question, which favours waste produced in one region or a Member State, is plainly not indistinctly applicable to domestic and imported products.

The result is that Belgium might in principle rely on Article 36 only in relation to the categories of dangerous waste excluded from the scope of Directive 84/631, such as the radioactive waste excluded by Article 3 of Directive 78/319, or the chlorinated and organic solvents excluded by Article 2(1)(a) of Directive 84/631. Without it being necessary to consider the possible justification for restrictions on the imports of such products into Wallonia, it is sufficient to say that a global, a priori ban on imports of waste from other Member States is clearly neither necessary nor proportionate to avert any danger to public health which might be posed by those products.

Second Opinion of Advocate General Jacobs

Oral argument was presented at a hearing on 27 November 1990, and I delivered my opinion on 10 January 1991. However, by an order dated 2 May 1991 made pursuant to Article 61 of the Rules of Procedure, the court reopened the oral procedure in order to give the parties, the other Member States and the other institutions an opportunity to express their view on the following question: Is the movement of unusable and non-recyclable waste which is devoid of commercial value covered by the Treaty provisions concerning the free movement of goods, or are the commercial transactions relating to the disposal, tipping or destruction of such waste covered by the Treaty provisions concerning the free movement of services?

Waste and the free movement of goods

. . . The Treaty provisions concerning the free movement of goods are the cornerstone of the Community. According to Article 9 EEC, the Community 'shall be based upon a customs union which shall cover all trade in goods . . .'. The Treaty does not, however, contain any definition of the term 'goods' (unlike, for instance, the ECSC Treaty, which contains a definition of the terms 'coal' and 'steel'). This lack of a definition is perhaps already an indication that the term is to be given a wide meaning. In contrast, the term 'services' does receive at least a partial definition in Article 60 EEC, which provides that:

> Services shall be considered to be 'services' within the meaning of this Treaty where they are normally provided for remuneration, in so far as they are not governed by the provisions relating to freedom of movement for goods, capital and persons.

As Article 60 makes clear, the concept of services covers a residual category of transactions not covered by the free movement of goods, capital or persons: see . . . *Cinéthèque* **[E24]**. The residual character of the services provisions of the Treaty have recently been demonstrated by Case C-239/90 *Boscher, Studer et Fromentin v British Motors Wright* **[E27]**.

There, a national provision which restricted the sale of goods by public auction, by imposing a local registration requirement on the owners of the goods, was held to be incompatible with Article 30 EEC. Article 59 did not apply, even though the restriction was also no doubt a barrier to the provision of services by the auctioneers to clients established in another Member State.

Thus, the provisions of the Treaty concerning the free movement of goods can apply, whether or not the transactions in question also provide the occasion for the provision of services. Even if it is accepted that the waste disposal contractor provides a 'service', within the meaning of the Treaty, to the producer of the waste, that would not be enough in itself to bring the transaction within the services provisions of the Treaty. Indeed, the latter provisions will only apply if the transaction in question is not covered by those concerning the free movement of goods. That is not to say that there are no circumstances in which a transaction involving both the movement of goods and the provision of services can properly be regarded as falling under Article 59; an example might be where goods are temporarily moved to another Member State for the purposes of restoration or repair. In such cases the movement of the goods is only an incidental feature of the transaction in question. However where, as in the present case, the whole point of the transaction is permanently to remove the object from one Member State to another in order that it can be stored, tipped or destroyed, the movement of goods cannot be regarded as merely incidental to the provision of services, even if the operations of storage, tipping or destruction are regarded as 'services' within the meaning of the Treaty.

. . .

The next question . . . is whether there is any feature of the transactions concerned – namely, those involving the transportation across national frontiers of non-recyclable waste for the purpose of storage, tipping or disposal – which removes them from the ambit of Articles 30 to 36 EEC.

It should first be observed that objects can benefit from the Treaty provisions concerning the free movement of goods, whether or not they are being transported across national frontiers for the purposes of sale or resale. The principle of the free movement of goods is not limited to those goods which are intended to be traded in the Member State of importation; the principle extends, for instance, to the importation of goods by a private individual for the purposes of personal consumption: see Case 215/87 *Schumacher v Hauptzollamt Frankfurt am Main-Ost* [1989] ECR 617 and Case C-362/88 *GB-INNO-BM v Confédération du Commerce Luxembourgeois* **[E25]**.

. . .

It seems to me, moreover, that it would be wrong in principle to confine the free movement of goods to the movement of objects having a positive value. An object with a negative value, just as much as one with a positive value, is something to which property rights and obligations can attach. Among such rights and obligations must be numbered those relating to the safe disposal of the object. Under national law, the owner of an object will typically enjoy, not only the right to its lawful use, but also the right to decide, again within the limits of the law, upon the proper method of its disposal. It does not seem to me that any useful distinction can be drawn, for the present purposes, between the right to dispose of an object by consumption and the right to do so by storage, tipping or dumping. To an ecologist, for instance, the latter right may be more significant than the former. It follows, in my view, that the free movement of goods includes the freedom to move articles across a national frontier in order to dispose of them more cheaply or more safely in another Member State, just as much as it includes the freedom to move personal possessions across a national frontier for the purpose of private consumption, as in Case 215/87 *Schumacher*, cited above. Thus, the free movement of goods applies not only to goods intended for further trading, but also those destined for consumption, storage or disposal.

. . .

In my opinion, therefore, 'goods' for the purposes of the Treaty must be taken to include any movable physical object to which property rights or obligations attach (and which can therefore be valued in monetary terms, whether positive or negative). If the exercise of such rights, or the fulfilment of such obligations, involves the selection of a method of disposal, and if the method selected entails the movement of the object between Member States, national provisions restricting such movement fall to be examined under Articles 30 to 36 EEC.

For all the above reasons, I reach the conclusion that the term 'goods' for the purposes of the Treaty covers non-recyclable and unusable waste, and that restrictions on the movement of such waste between Member States are covered by the Treaty provisions concerning the free movement of goods, rather than those concerning the free movement of services. Thus, notwithstanding that the national legislation at issue in these proceedings applies exclusively to waste which cannot be, or is not in fact, re-used or recycled, I remain of the opinion that such legislation infringes Article 30 EEC.

At the hearing, there was some discussion of what measures a Member State might be permitted to take in order to safeguard particular regions or localities from an unwanted influx of non-recyclable waste. It is clear that such measures would have to be capable of justification, in accordance with well-established principles, either under Article 36 or under one or other of the mandatory requirements recognised by Community law, among which is included environmental protection . . . If justification is sought in terms of a mandatory requirement not mentioned in Article 36 itself, the measures in question must be indistinctly applicable to domestic and imported waste. Even if the transactions were to be classified as the provision of services, the justification for any restriction would in my opinion fall to be examined in accordance with similar principles. Thus, Article 56, which applies to services by virtue of Article 66, provides an exception to the free movement of services on grounds of public health; and in the case of indistinctly applicable measures, restrictions on services can be justified as measures taken in accordance with imperative requirements pertaining to the general interest: Case C-288/89 *Stichting Collectieve Antennevoorziening Gouda* [E47].

Applying those principles, it seems to me that at least some restrictions on the transfer of waste could be justified on environmental grounds. Since environmental protection is a mandatory requirement not mentioned in Article 36, any such measure would, however, have to be indistinctly applicable to domestic and foreign waste. As I suggested in my previous opinion, that condition may not be satisfied by a measure which simply restricts the use of the waste disposal facilities of a particular region or locality to waste produced in that locality or region. A provision of that type clearly favours domestically produced waste, especially where, as is the case with the decrees of the Walloon Regional Executive, exceptions may be made in the case of waste coming from other regions of the same Member State. Hence, in the circumstances of the present case, the measures in issue cannot be justified on grounds of environmental protection. In contrast, a provision applying throughout a region of a Member State, requiring waste to be disposed of within its locality of generation, might be said to be indistinctly applicable. Such a provision would prevent the exportation of locally produced waste to another locality or another Member State in exactly the same way that it prevented the disposal of waste coming from another state or locality. Such a measure might moreover be justified in terms of the need to reduce the amount of waste in transit and to limit the areas used for waste disposal. Whether or not the measure was in fact proportionate to those objectives could of course only be decided in the light of all the relevant circumstances.

The European Court of Justice

[The Court of Justice held there to be no breach of Directive 75/442 but an infringement of Directive 84/631, for the reasons given by the Advocate General.]

22. It remains to examine the Belgian measures in question, in so far as they relate to waste which is outside the ambit of Directive 84/631, in the light of Articles 30 and 36 EEC.

23. It is common ground that waste which can be recycled and re-used, after processing if necessary, has an intrinsic commercial value and therefore amounts to goods for the purpose of applying the Treaty, and that such waste is therefore within the ambit of Article 30 et seq.

24. The question whether waste which is non-recyclable and cannot be re-used is also covered by Article 30 et seq was argued before the court.

25. On this point the Belgian government contended that such waste cannot be considered as goods within the meaning of Article 30 et seq EEC because it has no intrinsic commercial value and could not therefore be sold. The Belgian government adds that the operations for disposing of such waste are covered by the provisions of the Treaty relating to the freedom to supply services.

26. In reply to these arguments it is sufficient to point out that objects which are transported over a frontier in order to give rise to commercial transactions are subject to Article 30, irrespective of the nature of those transactions.

27. Secondly, it should be observed that the distinction between recyclable and non-recyclable waste raises a serious difficulty of practical application with regard to frontier controls, as was explained to the court. Such a distinction is based on uncertain factors which may change in the course of time, depending on technical progress. Moreover, whether any

particular waste is recyclable or not also depends on the cost of recycling and therefore the profitability of the proposed further use, so that a decision in this connexion is necessarily subjective and depends on variable factors.

28. Therefore it must be concluded that waste, whether recyclable or not, should be regarded as a product the movement of which must not in principle, pursuant to Article 30 EEC, be impeded.

29. The defendant state contends that the obstacles to the movement of waste are justified on the grounds, first, that the contested provisions conform to mandatory requirements relating to the protection of the environment and the safeguarding of human health, which overrides the objective of the free movement of goods and, secondly, that those provisions are an exceptional, temporary measure to safeguard Wallonia from an influx of waste from neighbouring countries.

30. So far as the environment is concerned, it should be observed that waste has a special characteristic. The accumulation of waste, even before it becomes a health hazard, constitutes a threat to the environment because of the limited capacity of each region or locality for receiving it.

31. In the present case the Belgian government contended, and the Commission accepted, that an abnormal, massive influx of waste had taken place from other regions for the purpose of dumping in Wallonia, thus constituting a genuine threat to the environment in view of the region's limited capacity.

32. It follows that the argument that the contested measures are justified by mandatory requirements relating to the protection of the environment must be regarded as well founded.

33. However, the Commission contends that these mandatory requirements cannot be invoked in the present case because the measures in question discriminate against waste from other Member States which is no more harmful than the waste produced in Wallonia.

34. It is true that the mandatory requirements are to be taken into account only with regard to measures which apply to national and imported products without distinction: see Case C-1/90 *Aragónesa de Publicidad* **[E35]**. However, in order to determine whether the obstacle in question is discriminatory, the particular type of waste must be taken into account. The principle that environmental damage should as a priority be rectified at source – a principle laid down by Article 130r(2) EEC for action by the Community relating to the environment – means that it is for each region, commune or other local entity to take appropriate measures to receive, process and dispose of its own waste. Consequently waste should be disposed of as close as possible to the place where it is produced in order to keep the transport of waste to the minimum practicable.

35. Furthermore this principle accords with the principles of self-sufficiency and proximity set out in the Basle Convention of 22 March 1989 on the control of transborder movements of hazardous waste and the disposal thereof, to which the Community is a party.

36. It follows that, having regard to the differences between waste produced in one place and that in another and its connection with the place where it is produced, the contested measures cannot be considered to be discriminatory.

37. Therefore it must be concluded that the application should be dismissed in so far as it relates to waste which is not covered by Directive 84/631.

Questions

1. Do you agree that this measure was not discriminatory, in the sense that the Court of Justice had used the term in previous cases?

2. Why is the 'particular type of waste' relevant to the reasoning here? Was the particular type of souvenir relevant to the court in **[E22]**?

(c)   The derogations of Article 36

(I)   PUBLIC MORALITY

[E29]   Case 34/79 R v Henn and Darby [1979] ECR 3795

[The defendants had been charged with the offence of having been 'knowingly concerned in the fraudulent evasion of the prohibition of the importation of indecent or obscene articles'. The House of Lords referred certain questions under Article 177, including the meaning of the 'public morality' ground contained in Article 36. The defendants in the main proceedings claimed that divergences within the laws applied in this area within the constituent parts of the United Kingdom meant that no consistent policy existed which could be relied upon with regard to indecent and obscene articles (see, further, **[C40]**).]

The European Court of Justice

15. Under the terms of Article 36 of the Treaty the provisions relating to the free movement of goods within the Community are not to preclude prohibitions on imports which are justified inter alia 'on grounds of public morality'. In principle, it is for each Member State to determine in accordance with its own scale of values and in the form selected by it the requirements of public morality in its territory. In any event, it cannot be disputed that the statutory provisions applied by the United Kingdom in regard to the importation of articles having an indecent or obscene character come within the powers reserved to the Member States by the first sentence of Article 36.

16. Each Member State is entitled to impose prohibitions on imports justified on grounds of public morality for the whole of its territory, as defined in Article 227 of the Treaty, whatever the structure of its constitution may be and however the powers of legislating in regard to the subject in question may be distributed. The fact that certain differences exist between the laws enforced in the different constituent parts of a Member State does not thereby prevent that state from applying a unitary concept in regard to prohibitions on imports imposed, on grounds of public morality, on trade with other Member States.

17. The answer . . . must therefore be that the first sentence of Article 36 upon its true construction means that a Member State may, in principle, lawfully impose prohibitions on the importation from any other Member State of articles which are of an indecent or obscene character as understood by its domestic laws and that such prohibitions may lawfully be applied to the whole of its territory even if, in regard to the field in question, variations exist between the laws in force in the different constituent parts of the Member State concerned.

. . .

19. In [its other questions] the House of Lords takes account of the appellants' submissions based upon certain differences between, on the one hand, the prohibition on importing the goods in question, which is absolute, and, on the other, the laws in force in the various constituent parts of the United Kingdom, which appear to be less strict in the sense that the mere possession of obscene articles for non-commercial purposes does not constitute a criminal offence anywhere in the United Kingdom and that, even if it is generally forbidden, trade in such articles is subject to certain exceptions, notably those in favour of articles having scientific, literary, artistic or educational interest. Having regard to those differences the question has been raised whether the prohibition on imports might not come within the second sentence of Article 36.

20. According to the second sentence of Article 36 the restrictions on imports referred to in the first sentence may not 'constitute a means of arbitrary discrimination or a disguised restriction on trade between Member States'.

21. In order to answer the questions which have been referred to the court it is appropriate to have regard to the function of this provision, which is designed to prevent restrictions on trade based on the grounds mentioned in the first sentence of Article 36 from being diverted from their proper purpose and used in such a way as either to create discrimination in respect of goods originating in other Member States or indirectly to protect certain national products. That is not the purport of a prohibition, such as that in force in the United Kingdom, on the importation of articles which are of an indecent or obscene character. Whatever may be the differences between the laws on this subject in force in the different constituent parts of the United Kingdom, and notwithstanding the fact that they contain certain exceptions of limited scope, these laws, taken as a whole, have as their purpose the prohibition, or at least, the restraining, of the manufacture and marketing of publications or articles of an indecent or obscene character. In these circumstances it is permissible to conclude, on a comprehensive view, that there is no lawful trade in such goods in the United Kingdom. A prohibition on imports which may in certain respects be more strict than some of the laws applied within the United Kingdom cannot therefore be regarded as amounting to a measure designed to give indirect protection to some national product or aimed at creating arbitrary discrimination between goods of this type depending on whether they are produced within the national territory or another Member State.

22. The answer to the . . . question must therefore be that if a prohibition on the importation of goods is justifiable on grounds of public morality and if it is imposed with that purpose the enforcement of that prohibition cannot, in the absence within the Member State concerned of a lawful trade in the same goods, constitute a means of arbitrary discrimination or a disguised restriction on trade contrary to Article 36.

[E30]   Case 121/85 Conegate Ltd v HM Customs and Excise [1986] ECR 1007

[Conegate had sought to import a number of articles described as 'window display models' but which the customs authorities discovered to be inflatable rubber dolls and other items of a sexual nature. The goods were ordered to be forfeited under national provisions governing indecent and obscene articles. Conegate contended that forfeiture constituted an infringement of Article 30 which could not be justified under the public morality grounds of Article 36. The Queen's Bench Division referred questions under Article 177 which sought to clarify the 'lawful trade' element in the preliminary ruling already given by the Court of Justice in *R v Henn and Darby* **[E29]**.]

The European Court of Justice

15. . . . although Community law leaves the Member States free to make their own assessments of the indecent or obscene character of certain articles, it must be pointed out that the fact that goods cause offence cannot be regarded as sufficiently serious to justify restrictions on the free movement of goods where the Member State concerned does not adopt, with respect to the same goods manufactured or marketed within its territory, penal measures or other serious and effective measures intended to prevent the distribution of such goods in its territory.

16. It follows that a Member State may not rely on grounds of public morality in order to prohibit the importation of goods from other Member States when its legislation contains no prohibition on the manufacture or marketing of the same goods on its territory.

17. It is not for the court, within the framework of the powers conferred upon it by Article 177 of the EEC Treaty, to consider whether, and to what extent, the United Kingdom legislation contains such a prohibition. However, the question whether or not such a prohibition exists in a state comprised of different constituent parts which have their own internal legislation, can be resolved only by taking into consideration all the relevant legislation. Although it is not necessary, for the purposes of the application of the above-mentioned rule, that the manufacture and marketing of the products whose importation has been prohibited should be prohibited in the territory of all the constituent parts, it must at least be possible to conclude from the applicable rules, taken as a whole, that their purpose is, in substance, to prohibit the manufacture and marketing of those products.

18. In this instance, . . . the High Court took care to define the substance of the national legislation the compatibility of which with Community law is a question which it proposes to determine. Thus it refers to rules in the importing Member State under which the goods in question may be manufactured freely and marketed subject only to certain restrictions, which it sets out explicitly, namely an absolute prohibition on the transmission of such goods by post, a restriction on their public display and, in certain areas of the Member State concerned, a system of licensing of premises for the sale of those goods to customers aged 18 years and over. Such restrictions cannot however be regarded as equivalent in substance to a prohibition on manufacture and marketing.

Question

In what way, if at all, is this a more difficult test for the Member State to satisfy than **[E29]**? Note the comparison with the test used in connection with workers in the *Adoui and Cornuaille* case **[D48]**.

(II)   PUBLIC POLICY AND PUBLIC SECURITY

[E31]   Case 231/83 Cullet v Centre Leclerc, Toulouse [1985] ECR 305

[The case arose from an action by the plaintiffs which sought to prevent the two Centres Leclerc from selling fuels at below the minimum prices fixed by French law. The French government claimed that the price controls were justified by Article 36.]

Opinion of Advocate General Verloren van Themaat

In order to justify the rules at issue, the French government has . . . put forward the following grounds in particular: (1) the attempt to limit the use of petroleum products; (2) the desire to guarantee the availability of distribution points throughout the entire French territory; (3) the protection of public policy and public security. My opinion on those grounds can be relatively brief. The first two grounds are clearly of an economic nature; it is quite impossible, moreover, to classify them under any of the grounds set out in Article 36. For those two reasons alone, they must be rejected on the basis of the established case law of the court on Article 36. In that connexion I refer inter alia to the judgment of the court in Case 95/81 *Commission v Italy* ([1982] ECR 2187). The reference to public policy and public security is elucidated solely by reference to the social unrest, and even blockades and violence, to which the price war unleashed by the Centre Leclerc has given rise. However, there is no support in the judgments of the court for such a wide interpretation of the concept of public policy. In that connection the Commission refers especially to the court's judgment in Case 7/78 *R v Thompson and others* ([1978] ECR 2247 . . .). However, I would add that the acceptance of civil disturbances as justification for encroachments upon the free movement of goods would, as is apparent from experiences of the last year (and before, during the Franco-Italian 'wine war') have unacceptably drastic consequences. If road-blocks and other effective weapons of interest groups which feel threatened by the importation and sale at competitive prices of certain cheap products or services, or by immigrant workers or foreign businesses, were accepted as justification, the existence of the four fundamental freedoms of the Treaty could no longer be relied upon. Private interest groups would then, in the place of the Treaty and Community (and, within the limits laid down in the Treaty, national) institutions, determine the scope of those freedoms. In such cases, the concept of public policy requires, rather, effective action on the part of the authorities to deal with such disturbances. Somewhat superfluously, the Commission further points out that even if one of those grounds were accepted as justification in principle, the second sentence of Article 36 would prevent their ultimate acceptance. In fact it also follows from its analysis, which I accept, of the de facto effects of the French rules in question that they constitute a disguised protection of French refineries and thus a disguised restriction on trade between Member States.

For the sake of completeness, however, I wish in conclusion to devote some attention to the judgment of the court . . . in Case 72/83 *Campus Oil* . . . [1984] ECR 2727. . . It will be remembered that the court decided in that case that a Member State which is totally or almost totally dependent on imports for its supplies of petroleum products 'may rely on grounds of public security within the meaning of Article 36 . . . for the purpose of requiring importers to cover a certain proportion of their needs by purchases from a refinery situated in its territory at prices fixed by the competent minister on the basis of the costs incurred in the operation of that refinery, if the production of the refinery cannot be freely disposed of at competitive prices on the market concerned'. However, the court then added that 'the quantities of petroleum products covered by such a system must not exceed the minimum supply requirement without which the public security of the State concerned would be affected or the level of production necessary to keep the refinery's production capacity available in the event of a crisis and to enable it to continue to refine at all times the crude oil for the supply of which the State has entered into long-term contracts'.

I do not need to consider here the significance of that judgment in relation to the interpretation of Article 36 as a whole. In any case, I think certain crucial differences of fact militate against applying that judgment by analogy in the present case. First, in periods in which there is a shortage of oil supplies a country such as France can, as a result of its geographical location, make use of the emergency arrangements for mutual assistance adopted within the Community and at international level more easily than a Member State such as Ireland, which is surrounded by sea. Secondly, it is apparent from the statistical data . . . that the proportion of the French needs which is supplied by the French refineries is approximately double the share of the domestic market guaranteed to the Irish refineries as a result of the Irish rules which were at issue. Thirdly, it is apparent from . . . the judgment in *Campus Oil* that reliance upon public security can be justified only in so far as the production capacity in question is necessary for the proper functioning of Irish public institutions and essential public services and even the survival of its inhabitants. In addition to public utilities and a limited number of genuine public services, this will also include hospitals. On the other hand, it is clear from the facts . . . that the French government is motivated by the need to guarantee an optimal geographical spread of supplies of purely individual needs. From . . . *Campus Oil* it is apparent that such interests are regarded as purely economic and cannot justify reliance upon Article 36. . .

The European Court of Justice

30. In order to justify the rules at issue in the main proceedings, the French government has also relied on the imperative requirements of the protection of the interests of consumers. In its opinion, destructive competition over the price of fuel could lead to the disappearance of a large number of service-stations and therefore to an inadequate supply network throughout the national territory.

31. On that point it should be noted that national rules compelling retailers to observe fixed retail selling prices, which make it more difficult to distribute imported products on the market, can be justified only on the grounds set out in Article 36.

. . .

32. As regards the application of Article 36 the French government referred to the threat to public order and security represented by the violent

reactions which would have to be anticipated on the part of retailers affected by unrestricted competition.

33. In that regard, it is sufficient to state that the French government has not shown that it would be unable, using the means at its disposal, to deal with the consequences which an amendment of the rules in question in accordance with the principles set out above would have upon public order and security.

Question

Why does the Court of Justice not adopt a principled approach to the problem here?

(III)   PUBLIC HEALTH

[E32]   Case 178/84 Commission v Germany ('beer purity') [1987] ECR 1227

[The Commission brought proceedings under Article 169 against Germany on the basis of two national rules concerning beer purity. First, a prohibition against marketing under the designation 'bier' any beers manufactured in other Member States which did not comply with the contents specified in Article 10 of the German Biersteuergesetz. Secondly, there was an absolute ban on the marketing of beers containing additives.]

The European Court of Justice

29. It is not contested that the application of Article 10 . . . to beers from other Member States in whose manufacture raw materials other than malted barley have been lawfully used, in particular rice and maize, is liable to constitute an obstacle to their importation into . . . Germany.

30. Accordingly, it must be established whether the application of that provision may be justified by imperative requirements relating to consumer protection.

31. The German government's argument that Article 10 . . . is essential in order to protect German consumers because, in their minds, the designation 'Bier' is inseparably linked to the beverage manufactured solely from the ingredients laid down in Article 9 . . . must be rejected.

32. First, consumers' conceptions which vary from one Member State to the other are also likely to evolve in the course of time within a Member State. The establishment of the common market is, it should be added, one of the factors that may play a major contributory role in that development. Whereas rules protecting consumers against misleading practices enable such a development to be taken into account, legislation of the kind contained in Article 10 . . . prevents it from taking place. As the court has already held in another context (. . . Case 170/78 *Commission v United Kingdom* **[E9]**), the legislation of a Member State must not 'crystallise given consumer habits so as to consolidate an advantage acquired by national industries concerned to comply with them'.

. . .

35. It is admittedly legitimate to seek to enable consumers who attribute specific qualities to beers manufactured from particular raw materials to

make their choice in the light of that consideration. However, as the court has already emphasised (. . . Case 193/80 *Commission v Italy* [1981] ECR 3019), that possibility may be ensured by means which do not prevent the importation of products which have been lawfully manufactured and marketed in other Member States and, in particular, 'by the compulsory affixing of suitable labels given the nature of the product sold'. By indicating the raw materials utilised in the manufacture of beer 'such a course would enable the consumer to make his choice in full knowledge of the facts and would guarantee transparency in trading and in offers to the public'. It must be added that such a system of mandatory consumer information must not entail negative assessments for beers not complying with the requirements of Article 9.

. . .

36. Contrary to the German government's view, such a system of consumer information may operate perfectly well even in the case of a product which, like beer, is not necessarily supplied to consumers in bottles or in cans capable of bearing the appropriate details. That is borne out, once again, by the German legislation itself. [National law] . . . provides for a system of consumer information in respect of certain beers, even where those beers are sold on draught, when the requisite information must appear on the casks or the beer taps.

37. It follows . . . that by applying the rules on designation in Article 10 of the Biersteuergesetz to beers imported from other Member States which were manufactured and marketed lawfully in those states . . . Germany has failed to fulfil its obligations under Article 30 of the EEC Treaty.

The absolute ban on the marketing of beers containing additives

43. . . . the application to imported products of prohibitions on marketing products containing additives which are authorised in the Member State of production but prohibited in the Member State of importation is permissible only in so far as it complies with the requirements of Article 36 of the Treaty as it has been interpreted by the court.

44. It must be borne in mind . . . that in its judgments in the *Sandoz*, *Motte* and *Muller* cases [Case174/82 [1983] ECR 2445, Case 247/84 [1985] ECR 3887 and Case 304/84 [1986] ECR 1511 respectively], . . . the court inferred from the principle of proportionality underlying the last sentence of Article 36 of the Treaty that prohibitions on the marketing of products containing additives authorised in the Member State of production but prohibited in the Member State of importation must be restricted to what is actually necessary to secure the protection of public health. The court also concluded that the use of a specific additive which is authorised in another Member State must be authorised in the case of a product imported from that Member State where, in view, on the one hand, of the findings of international scientific research, and in particular of the work of the Community's Scientific Committee for Food, the Codex Alimentarius Committee of the Food and Agriculture Organisation of the United Nations (FAO) and the World Health Organisation, and, on the other hand, of the eating habits prevailing in the importing Member State, the additive in question does not present a risk to public health and meets a real need, especially a technical one.

45. Secondly, it should be remembered that, as the court held in . . . the

Muller case, . . . by virtue of the principle of proportionality, traders must also be able to apply, under a procedure which is easily accessible to them and can be concluded within a reasonable time, for the use of specific additives to be authorised by a measure of general application.

46. It should be pointed out that it must be open to traders to challenge before the courts an unjustified failure to grant authorisation. Without prejudice to the right of the competent national authorities of the importing Member State to ask traders to produce the information in their possession which may be useful for the purpose of assessing the facts, it is for those authorities to demonstrate . . . that the prohibition is justified on grounds relating to the protection of the health of its population.

47. It must be observed that the German rules on additives applicable to beer result in the exclusion of all the additives authorised in the other Member States and not the exclusion of just some of them for which there is concrete justification by reason of the risks which they involve in view of the eating habits of the German population; moreover those rules do not lay down any procedure whereby traders can obtain authorisation for the use of a specific additive in the manufacture of beer by means of a measure of general application.

48. As regards more specifically the harmfulness of additives, the German government, citing experts' reports, has referred to the risks inherent in the ingestion of additives in general. It maintains that it is important, for reasons of general preventive health protection, to minimise the quantity of additives ingested, and that it is particularly advisable to prohibit altogether their use in the manufacture of beer, a foodstuff consumed in considerable quantities by the German population.

49. However, it appears from the tables of additives authorised for use in the various foodstuffs submitted by the German government itself that some of the additives authorised in other Member States for use in the manufacture of beer are also authorised under the German rules, in particular the Regulation on Additives, for use in the manufacture of all, or virtually all, beverages. Mere reference to the potential risks of the ingestion of additives in general and to the fact that beer is a foodstuff consumed in large quantities does not suffice to justify the imposition of stricter rules in the case of beer.

. . .

53. Consequently, in so far as the German rules on additives in beer entail a general ban on additives, their application to beers imported from other Member States is contrary to the requirements of Community law as laid down in the case law of the court, since that prohibition is contrary to the principle of proportionality and is therefore not covered by the exception provided for in Article 36 of the EEC Treaty.

[E33]   Case C-42/90 Bellon [1990] ECR I-4863

The European Court of Justice

2. . . . Mr Bellon had imported and offered for sale in France light-pastry products from Italy, which were manufactured in that country under the name 'panettone' and contained sorbic acid, a preservative permitted under Italian law.

3. It appears from the case file that the relevant French legislation . . . prohibits the addition to foodstuffs of any substance for which express prior authorisation has not been granted by joint ministerial order. A circular . . . regulates the form of applications for authorisation which must establish, inter alia, both the usefulness of the substance for users and consumers and its harmlessness when used under normal conditions.

4. The Tribunal de grande instance, Marseille, before which [criminal proceedings were] brought, decided to stay proceedings until the Court of Justice had given a preliminary ruling on the following question:

> Is it lawful under Community law to refuse entry into France to a food-stuff lawfully produced and marketed by a Member State on the ground that it contains sorbic acid, a preservative which is permitted under Directive 64/54 [as amended], but which, under French law, may be used only in a limited number of stipulated foodstuffs, although no overriding reason is given?

. . .

7. The national court's question must . . . be understood as seeking to determine whether Articles 30 and 36 of the EEC Treaty are to be interpreted as precluding a Member State from prohibiting, pursuant to national legislation proscribing fraud and falsification in the sale of foodstuffs, the marketing in its territory of a product lawfully manufactured in another Member State, containing sorbic acid, a preservative the use of which is permitted by Directive 64/54.

8. It must be observed first of all that under Article 1 of Directive 64/54 . . . Member States may not authorise the use, for the protection of food-stuffs against deterioration caused by micro-organisms, of any preservatives other than those listed in the annex to the directive, which include sorbic acid.

9. According to its preamble, the directive is merely the first stage in the approximation of national laws in that field. At this stage, therefore, Member States are not obliged to authorise the use of all the substances listed in the annex to the directive. However, their freedom to determine their own rules concerning the addition of preservatives to foodstuffs may be exercised only subject to the twofold condition that no preservative not listed in the annex to the directive may be authorised for use and that the use of a preservative which is listed there may not be totally prohibited except, in the case of foodstuffs produced and consumed within their own territory, in special cases where the use of such a preservative does not meet any technological need (see the judgments in Case 88/79 *Ministère Public v Grunert* [1980] ECR 1827 and in Case 108/80 *Ministère Public v Kugelmann* [1981] ECR 433).

10. Since the products concerned in the main proceedings are products imported from another Member State where they are lawfully produced and marketed, the application of national rules of the kind in issue in the main proceedings must be regarded as hindering intra-Community trade and thereby constituting in principle a measure having an effect equivalent to a quantitative restriction within the meaning of Article 30 of the EEC Treaty. However, since there has been partial harmonisation within the Community in the area concerned, it must be examined whether such a measure may be justified on the ground of the protection of human health, as provided for in Article 36 of the Treaty.

11. It must be borne in mind that, as the court has consistently held (see, inter alia, the judgment in Case 174/82 *Sandoz BV* [1983] ECR 2445), in so far as there are uncertainties in the present state of scientific research, it is for the Member States, in the absence of harmonisation, to decide what degree of protection of the health and life of humans they intend to assure, having regard, however, for the requirements of the free movement of goods within the Community.

12. It is also clear from the court's case law (especially the judgments in *Sandoz*, cited above, in Case 247/84 *Motte* [1985] ECR 3887, in Case 304/84 *Ministère public v Muller* [1986] ECR 1511 and in Case 178/84 *Commission v Germany* **[E32]**) that in those circumstances Community law does not preclude the adoption by the Member States of legislation whereby the use of additives is subjected to prior authorisation granted by a measure of general application for specific additives, in respect of all products, for certain products only or for certain uses. Such legislation meets a genuine need of health policy, namely that of restricting the uncontrolled consumption of food additives.

13. However, the application to imported products of prohibitions on marketing products containing additives which are authorised in the Member State of production but prohibited in the Member State of importation is permissible only in so far as it complies with the requirements of Article 36 of the Treaty as it has been interpreted by the court.

14. It must be borne in mind that in its judgments [cited above] . . . the court inferred from the principle of proportionality underlying the last sentence of Article 36 of the Treaty that prohibitions on the marketing of products containing additives authorised in the Member State of production but prohibited in the Member State of importation must be restricted to what is actually necessary to secure the protection of public health. The court also concluded that the use of a specific additive which is authorised in another Member State must be authorised in the case of a product imported from that Member State where, in view, on the one hand, of the findings of international scientific research, and in particular of the work of the Community's Scientific Committee for Food, the Codex Alimentarius Committee of the Food and Agriculture Organisation of the United Nations (FAO) and the World Health Organisation, and, on the other hand, of the eating habits prevailing in the importing Member State, the additive in question does not present a risk to public health and meets a real need, especially a technological one.

15. Secondly, it should be remembered that, as the court held in its judgments in [*Ministère public v Muller* and . . . *Commission v Germany*], cited above, by virtue of the principle of proportionality, traders must also be able to apply, under a procedure which is easily accessible to them and can be concluded within a reasonable time, for the use of specific additives to be authorised by a measure of general application.

16. It should be pointed out that it must be open to traders to challenge before the courts an unjustified failure to grant authorisation. Without prejudice to the right of the competent national authorities of the importing Member State to ask traders to produce the information in their possession which may be useful for the purpose of assessing the facts, it is for those authorities to demonstrate . . . that the prohibition is justified on grounds relating to the protection of the health of its population.

Question

Do you agree with the conclusions of the Court of Justice in **[E32]** and **[E33]** as to the best-equipped party to assume responsibility for the assessment of risk? Should these arguments apply to the assessment of security or morality issues? The next extract also shows the court refusing to decide on a matter of scientific doubt.

[E34]   Joined Cases 266 and 267/87 R v Royal Pharmaceutical Society of Great Britain, ex parte Association of Pharmaceutical Importers [1989] ECR 1295

[See also the other extract from this case **[E15]**.]

The European Court of Justice

The first two questions

18. . . . it is common ground between the parties to the main proceedings that the 50 or so products imported in parallel, which have brand names different from those of the equivalent products previously authorised in the United Kingdom, were marketed in that Member State in significant quantities for several years but their importation practically ceased during . . . 1986, which is the time when the Pharmaceutical Society of Great Britain published its statement drawing attention to the ethical rule prohibiting pharmacists from substituting another product for a specifically named product even if the other product has identical therapeutic effect and confirming that that rule applied to imported products as well as to domestic products.

19. In those circumstances, and although the existence of a causal link is a matter of dispute between the parties, the court cannot exclude the possibility that, in the particular circumstances of the case, the said rule is capable of hindering intra-Community trade. For that reason, and without there being any need to decide whether a rule prohibiting a pharmacist from substituting another product with the same therapeutic effect for the medicinal product prescribed by the doctor treating the patient generally constitutes a measure having equivalent effect within the meaning of Article 30 of the Treaty, it is necessary to consider whether such a rule may be justified under Article 36.

. . .

20. In that regard, it should be noted that among the grounds of public interest set out in Article 36, only the protection of health could be relevant. A rule prohibiting a trader from substituting, even with the consumer's consent, another product for the brand ordered would go beyond what could be necessary for the protection of industrial and commercial property.

. . .

21. On the other hand, the rules concerning the relationship between doctors and pharmacists and in particular those rules relating to the

attending doctor's freedom to prescribe any product he chooses and to any possibility which the pharmacist may have to dispense a medicinal product other than that prescribed in the prescription are part of the national public health system. As long as those matters have not been regulated by Community legislation, it is for the Member States, within the limits laid down in Article 36, to decide on the degree to which they wish to protect human health and life and how that degree of protection is to be achieved.

22. There is no evidence in this case to justify a conclusion by the court that a rule prohibiting pharmacists from substituting another medicinal product for one designated by name in the prescription, even if the other product has the same therapeutic effect, goes beyond what is necessary to achieve the objective in view, which is to leave the entire responsibility for the treatment of the patient in the hands of the doctor treating him. In particular, the court finds itself unable to discount the reasons, based on psychosomatic phenomena, for which, according to the observations submitted by the Pharmaceutical Society of Great Britain and by the governments of several Member States, a specific proprietary medicinal product might be prescribed rather than a generic product or any other proprietary medicinal product having the same therapeutic effect.

23. Furthermore, the arguments put forward by the Association of Pharmaceutical Importers do not disclose any evidence that the application of such a general rule to products imported from other Member States, in which they may be marketed lawfully, constitutes a means of arbitrary discrimination or a disguised restriction on trade between Member States within the meaning of the last sentence of Article 36.

[E35] Joined Cases C-1/90 and C-176/90 Aragonesa de Publicidad Exterior SA and Publivía SAE v Departamento de Sanidad y Seguridad Social de la Generalitat de Cataluña [1991] ECR I-4151

[Fines had been imposed on the appellants in the main proceedings for infringing a Law enacted by the Parliament of the Autonomous Community of Catalonia on the prohibition of the advertising of beverages having an alcoholic strength of more than 23° in the media, on streets and highways (except to indicate centres of production and sale) and in cinemas and on public transport.]

The European Court of Justice (Judgment, 25 July 1991)

8. It should first be pointed out that Article 30 of the Treaty may apply to measures adopted by all the authorities of the Member States, be they the central authorities, the authorities of a federal state, or other territorial authorities.

. . .

10. As the court held, inter alia, in its judgment in Case C-362/88 *GB-INNO-BM v Confédération du Commerce Luxembourgoise* [1990] ECR I-667 **[E25]**, . . . legislation which restricts or prohibits certain forms of advertising and certain means of sales promotion may, although it does not

directly affect trade, be such as to restrict the volume of trade because it affects marketing opportunities.

11. Accordingly, national legislation such as that at issue in the main proceedings, which prohibits the advertising in certain places of beverages having an alcoholic strength of more than 23° may constitute a hindrance to imports from other Member States and, therefore, must in principle be regarded as a measure having equivalent effect within the meaning of Article 30.

12. However, in its observations to the court, the Commission argues that such legislation, which applies without distinction to domestic and imported products, must be upheld by reference to Article 30 alone without its being necessary to have recourse, as the national court does, to Article 36, because that legislation is justified by an imperative requirement, namely the protection of public health.

13. That form of reasoning cannot be accepted. The protection of public health is expressly mentioned amongst the grounds of public interest which are set out in Article 36 and enable a restriction on imports to escape the prohibition laid down in Article 30. In those circumstances, since Article 36 also applies where the contested measure restricts only imports, whereas according to the court's case law the question of imperative requirement for the purposes of the interpretation of Article 30 cannot arise unless the measure in question applies without distinction to both national and imported products, it is not necessary to consider whether the protection of public health might also be in the nature of an imperative requirement for the purposes of the application of Article 30.

14. In those circumstances it is first of all necessary to ascertain whether the legislation at issue is of such a nature as to protect public health and, secondly, is proportionate to the objective to be attained.

15. On the first point it is sufficient to observe, as the court pointed out in its judgment in Case 152/78 *Commission v France* [1980] ECR 2299, paragraph 17, that advertising acts as an encouragement to consumption and the existence of rules restricting the advertising of alcoholic beverages in order to combat alcoholism reflects public health concerns.

16. On the second point it must be stated that in the present state of Community law, in which there are no common or harmonised rules governing in a general manner the advertising of alcoholic beverages, it is for the Member States to decide on the degree of protection which they wish to afford to public health and on the way in which that protection is to be achieved. They may do so, however, only within the limits set by the Treaty and must, in particular, comply with the principle of proportionality.

17. A national measure such as that at issue restricts freedom of trade only to a limited extent since it concerns only beverages having an alcoholic strength of more than 23°. In principle, the latter criterion does not appear to be manifestly unreasonable as part of a campaign against alcoholism.

18. On the other hand, the measure at issue does not prohibit all advertising of such beverages but merely prohibits it in specified places, some of which, such as public highways and cinemas, are particularly frequented by motorists and young persons, two categories of the population in regard to which the campaign against alcoholism is of quite special importance. It thus cannot in any event be criticised for being disproportionate to its stated objective.

19. Secondly, in order to benefit from the derogation provided for in Article 36, a national provision must not constitute a means of arbitrary

discrimination or a disguised restriction on trade between Member States, to use the precise terms of the second sentence of that article.

20. As the court held in Case 34/79 *R v Henn and Darby* **[E29]** . . . the function of the second sentence of Article 36 is to prevent restrictions on trade based on the grounds mentioned in the first sentence from being diverted from their proper purpose and used in such a way as to create discrimination in respect of goods originating in other Member States or indirectly to protect certain national products.

21. In that connection, Aragónesa de Publicidad Exterior and Publivía argue that, in assessing the discriminatory and protective nature of the measure, it is necessary to take more into account than the fact that the Catalan law makes no formal distinction between the domestic or foreign origin of the beverages in question. It should be borne in mind that that law applies only within the territorial jurisdiction of the parliament of Catalonia.

22. According to the applicants in the main proceedings, what should be compared, therefore, is not the situation of imported products with that of products from Spain as a whole but the situation of imported products with that of Catalan products. Since the majority of Catalan-produced alcoholic beverages have an alcohol content of less than 23°, the measure at issue should be regarded as discriminatory and protective in nature, inasmuch as it seeks to discourage the consumption of beverages with a high alcohol content and thus places at a disadvantage beverages originating outside Catalonia, and inasmuch, on the other hand, as it does not restrict the advertising of beverages with a lower alcohol content, thus protecting locally-produced beverages.

23. Those arguments cannot be upheld.

24. It is true that, when a national measure has limited territorial scope because it applies only to a part of the national territory, it cannot escape being characterised as discriminatory or protective for the purposes of the rules on the free movement of goods on the ground that it affects both the sale of products from other parts of the national territory and the sale of products imported from other Member States. For such a measure to be characterised as discriminatory or protective, it is not necessary for it to have the effect of favouring national products as a whole or of placing only imported products at a disadvantage and not national products.

25. However, national legislation such as that in question . . . does not constitute arbitrary discrimination or a disguised restriction on intra-Community trade. On the one hand, it is clear from the documents before the court that such legislation does not distinguish between products according to their origin. The restrictions which it imposes do not apply to beverages having an alcoholic strength of less than 23° and therefore do not restrict imports of such beverages from other Member States. In regard to beverages having an alcoholic strength of more than 23°, those restrictions affect both products, in not inconsiderable quantities, originating in the part of the national territory to which they apply and products imported from other Member States. On the other hand, the fact that that part of the national territory produces more beverages having an alcoholic strength of less than 23° than beverages with a higher alcoholic content is not in itself sufficient to cause such legislation to be regarded as liable to give rise to arbitrary discrimination or a disguised restriction on intra-Community trade.

26. Accordingly, the reply to be given to the questions submitted . . . should be that Articles 30 and 36 of the EEC Treaty, viewed together, do

not preclude legislation such as the law at issue in the main proceedings which, in part of the territory of a Member State, prohibits the advertising of beverages having an alcoholic strength of more than 23°, in the media, on streets and highways (with the exception of signs indicating centres of production and of sale) in cinemas and on public transport, where that legislation, even if it constitutes a measure having equivalent effect within the meaning of Article 30 of the EEC Treaty, can be justified under Article 36 of that Treaty on grounds of the protection of public health, and where, in view of its characteristics and the circumstances set out in the documents before the court, it does not appear to be a means, even an indirect means, of protecting certain local products.

Note.   Compare this approach with that taken in **[E18]**.

Questions

   1. Why does it matter whether the Court of Justice thinks a measure is justified by Article 36 or that it is not caught by the prohibition of Article 30 in the first place?
   2. Are there any implications in the discussion of public health for the relationship between the imperative requirements and Article 36 generally?

(IV)   THE PROTECTION OF INDUSTRIAL AND COMMERCIAL PROPERTY

[The phrase relates to intellectual property: patents, trade marks, copyright, design rights etc.]

[E36]   Case 15/74 Centrafarm BV v Sterling Drug Inc [1974] ECR 1147

The European Court of Justice

   2. In the . . . reference the [Dutch Supreme Court] set out as follows the elements of fact and of national law in issue in relation to the questions referred:

   – a patentee holds parallel patents in several of the states belonging to the EEC,
   – the products protected by those patents are lawfully marketed in one or more of those Member States by undertakings to which the patentee has granted licences to manufacture and/or sell,
   – those products are subsequently exported by third parties and are marketed and further dealt in in one of those other Member States,
   – the patent legislation in the last-mentioned state gives the patentee the right to take legal action to prevent products thus protected by patents from being there marketed by others, even where these products were previously lawfully marketed in another country by the patentee or by the patentee's licence.

. . .

   7. . . . it is clear from [Article 36], in particular its second sentence, as well as from the context, that whilst the Treaty does not affect the existence

of rights recognised by the legislation of a Member State in matters of industrial and commercial property, yet the exercise of these rights may nevertheless, depending on the circumstances, be affected by the prohibitions in the Treaty.

8. Inasmuch as it provides an exception to one of the fundamental principles of the Common Market, Article 36 in fact only admits of derogations from the free movement of goods where such derogations are justified for the purpose of safeguarding rights which constitute the specific subject matter of this property.

9. In relation to patents, the specific subject matter of the industrial property is the guarantee that the patentee, to reward the creative effort of the inventor, has the exclusive right to use an invention with a view to manufacturing industrial products and putting them into circulation for the first time, either directly or by the grant of licences to third parties, as well as the right to oppose infringements.

10. An obstacle to the free movement of goods may arise out of the existence, within a national legislation concerning industrial and commercial property, of provisions laying down that a patentee's right is not exhausted when the product protected by the patent is marketed in another Member State, with the result that the patentee can prevent importation of the product into his own Member State when it has been marketed in another Member State.

11. Whereas an obstacle to the free movement of goods of this kind may be justified on the ground of protection of industrial property where such protection is invoked against a product coming from a Member State where it is not patentable and has been manufactured by third parties without the consent of the patentee and in cases where there exist patents, the original proprietors of which are legally and economically independent, a derogation from the principle of free movement of goods is not, however, justified where the product has been put on to the market in a legal manner, by the patentee himself or with his consent, in the Member State from which it has been imported, in particular in the case of a proprietor of parallel patents.

12. In fact, if a patentee could prevent the import of protected products marketed by him or with his consent in another Member State, he would be able to partition off national markets and thereby restrict trade between Member States, in a situation where no such restriction was necessary to guarantee the essence of the exclusive rights flowing from the parallel patents.

. . .

15. The question referred should therefore be answered to the effect that the exercise, by a patentee, of the right which he enjoys under the legislation of a Member State to prohibit the sale, in that state, of a product protected by the patent which has been marketed in another Member State by the patentee or with his consent is incompatible with the rules of the EEC Treaty concerning the free movement of goods within the Common Market.

[E37]   Case 58/80 Dansk Supermarked A/S v A/S Imerco [1981] ECR 181

The European Court of Justice

2. The file shows that A/S Imerco, the respondent in the main action, a group of Danish hardware merchants commissioned in the United Kingdom on the occasion of the 50th anniversary of its foundation in 1978 a china service decorated with pictures of Danish royal castles and bearing on the reverse side the words 'Imerco Fiftieth Anniversary'. The sale of that service was reserved exclusively to hardware merchants who were members of Imerco. It was agreed between Imerco and the British manufacturer that the substandard pieces which, owing to the quality standards applied, amounted to approximately 20% of the production, might be marketed by the manufacturer in the United Kingdom but might not in any circumstances be exported to Denmark or to other Scandinavian countries.

3. Dansk Supermarked A/S, the appellant in the main action, the proprietor of several supermarkets, was able to obtain through dealers a number of services marketed in the United Kingdom and offered them for sale in Denmark at prices appreciably lower than those of the services sold by Imerco's members. The file does not establish whether the services in question were sold as substandard in the United Kingdom; in any case the customers of Dansk Supermarked do not appear to have been notified of that fact.

. . .

9. [The question referred by the Danish court] must be understood as asking whether goods which have been lawfully marketed in one Member State with the consent of the undertaking which is entitled to sell them may be prohibited, under an agreement concluded between that undertaking and the manufacturer, from being marketed in another Member State either on the basis of national provisions on the protection of copyright or trade marks or under legislation on marketing.

The legislation on the protection of copyright and trade marks

11. In this matter it is sufficient to refer to the settled case law of the court as it has been set out in particular in the judgment of [Case 119/75 *Terrapin (Overseas) Ltd* [1976] ECR 1039]. It may be recalled that the effect of the provisions of the Treaty on the free movement of goods and in particular of Article [30], is to prohibit between Member States quantitative restrictions on imports and all measures having equivalent effect. However, according to Article 36 that provision does not preclude prohibitions or restrictions on imports justified on grounds of the protection of industrial and commercial property. Nevertheless it is clear from that article, in particular the second sentence, as well as from the context, that whilst the Treaty does not affect the existence of rights recognised by the legislation of a Member State in matters of industrial and commercial property, yet the exercise of those rights may none the less, depending on the circumstances, be restricted by the prohibitions of the Treaty. Inasmuch as it provides an exception to one of the fundamental principles of the common market, Article 36 in fact admits exceptions to the free movement of goods only to

the extent to which such exceptions are justified for the purpose of safeguarding rights which constitute the specific subject-matter of that property. The exclusive right guaranteed by the legislation on industrial and commercial property is exhausted when a product has been lawfully distributed on the market in another Member State by the actual proprietor of the right or with his consent.

. . .

The application of the rules on marketing

13. The Danish Law of 14 June 1974 upon which Imerco relies, requires undertakings in their dealings to comply with the requirements of approved marketing usage. It authorises the competent courts to issue injunctions prohibiting all acts in breach of the provisions of the law and prescribes penalties for breach of such injunctions. As the Danish government has explained, that Law is comparable in certain respects to the legislation in force in other Member States against unfair competition, but it has in addition other objectives in that sphere, in particular the protection of consumers.

. . .

15. In order to reply to [the] question it must first of all be remarked that Community law does not in principle have the effect of preventing the application in a Member State to goods imported from other Member States of the provisions on marketing in force in the state of importation. It follows that the marketing of imported goods may be prohibited if the conditions on which they are sold constitutes an infringement of the marketing usages considered proper and fair in the Member State of importation.

16. It must nevertheless be emphasised, as the Court of Justice has stressed in another context in its judgment [in Case 22/71 *Béguelin* [1971] ECR 949], that the actual fact of the importation of goods which have been lawfully marketed in another Member State cannot be considered as an improper or unfair act since that description may be attached only to offer or exposure for sale on the basis of circumstances distinct from the importation itself.

17. It must furthermore be remarked that it is impossible in any circumstances for agreements between individuals to derogate from the mandatory provisions of the Treaty on the free movement of goods. It follows that an agreement involving a prohibition on the importation into a Member State of goods lawfully marketed in another Member State may not be relied upon or taken into consideration in order to classify the marketing of such goods as an improper or unfair commercial practice.

Notes.

1. The Court of Justice extracts a 'core' of protectable interests to solve the problem of how to balance free movement against exclusive rights. Consider how this approach is mirrored elsewhere in the court's reasoning, eg **[A18]**, **[E56]**, **[E86]** and **[E90]**.

2. The purported distinction between existence and exercise is not watertight. See, for example, G Friden (1989) 26 Common Market Law Review 193.

5 Operating a single market

(a)   The harmonisation process

[E38]   Article 100a

[The first three paragraphs of this provision are set out at **[A33]**; see also **[A30]**—**[A32]** and **[A34]**.]

4. If, after the adoption of a harmonisation measure by the Council acting by a qualified majority, a Member State deems it necessary to apply national provisions on grounds of major needs referred to in Article 36, or relating to protection of the environment or the working environment, it shall notify the Commission of these provisions.

The Commission shall confirm the provisions involved after having verified that they are not a means of arbitrary discrimination or a disguised restriction on trade between Member States.

By way of derogation from the procedure laid down in Articles 169 and 170, the Commission or any Member State may bring the matter directly before the Court of Justice if it considers that another Member State is making improper use of the powers provided for in this Article.

5. The harmonisation measures referred to above shall, in appropriate cases, include a safeguard clause authorising the Member States to take, for one or more of the non-economic reasons referred to in Article 36, provisional measures subject to a Community control procedure.

[E39]   A McGee and S Weatherill: 'The evolution of the single market – harmonisation or liberalisation' (1990) 53 Modern Law Review 578

Introduction

The evolution of the single market is both a legal process and a political process. The concept of a single market requires the elimination of all barriers to inter-state trade and all national prohibitions on establishment and the ultimate harmonisation of laws and regulations throughout the Community. The political reality is that vested interests, both of national governments and of trade and professional organisations, seek to delay the creation of this kind of single market. In these circumstances the choice facing the Community may be seen as being that between delaying the single market process until these obstacles can be overcome or reaching a pragmatic compromise by allowing the retention, at least temporarily, of some of the existing barriers. If it is accepted that some barriers can be retained, the next problem is to identify which these are. Some barriers must be seen as entirely incompatible with the single market, whilst others may be regarded as tolerable . . . An important theme . . . is the relative effectiveness of different interest groups in securing the recognition of particular trade barriers as legitimate and in obtaining for themselves the power to determine the content of those barriers. This point is related to the crucial distinction between changes which are intended to make it easier to conduct business on a Community-wide basis (referred to here as 'facilitative legislation'), and changes which are designed to regulate business activity, usually in the interests of protecting groups such as consumers and employees (referred to here as 'protective legislation') . . .

Lawful barriers

It is necessary to begin by establishing that it is in fact possible to have lawful trade barriers once the single market comes into existence. Certainly there may not be any barrier which breaches the Treaty of Rome. This rule is absolute and not subject to modification by the agreement of national governments. Any breach of this rule is actionable before the Court of Justice at the instance of the European Commission or before national courts, since the majority of the relevant provisions are directly effective. However, . . . not all trade barriers are prohibited by the Treaty. Harmonisation legislation may be introduced to replace divergent national rules which act as trade barriers with a single Community rule. However, harmonisation need not mean uniformity, nor the elimination of all trade barriers, since the application of a common Community principle may differ from one state to another. In addition, derogation or opting-out by Member States may be permitted, either by virtue of the legal base of the measure or within the measure itself. Accepting that this is so, it remains to establish a procedure for deciding which barriers are to be retained and to determine the substantive content of those barriers. It has been customary, in dealing with trade barriers, to identify three classes of barrier, namely the physical (ie customs barriers at frontiers), the fiscal (ie those arising from differences in taxation systems) and the technical (ie those caused by disparities in national legislation governing production and marketing). A fourth category may be identified, consisting of the more general problem of barriers created by the existence of differing legal systems within the Member States (for example, problems resulting from divergences in company law between Member States). This is in itself a valid classification of barriers, but the evolution of the single market . . . requires an alternative classification based on the approach which the Community has taken to particular barriers. There are essentially three ways in which the Community may treat a barrier which is lawful under the Treaty:

1. It may pass legislation which covers the entire field in question, albeit in a very general way. This approach is referred to here as 'Exhaustive regulation' because it involves Community rule-making which excludes Member States' competence to regulate the area. A good example of this is provided by product safety.
2. It may pass legislation which deals with some issues in the area under consideration, but leaves others to the national law. This approach is referred to here as 'Partial regulation'. Two good examples of this are provided by the Product Liability Directive [Directive 85/374] and the regulation creating the European Economic Interest Grouping [Regulation 2137/85]. It is expected that the scheme for the European Company Statute will follow the same pattern.
3. It may not act at all; there are numerous possible reasons for this. One is simple lack of resources, since there is much to be done in the pursuit of the single market, and some matters inevitably have higher

priority than others. Another possibility is political difficulty in reaching an agreed position. This may in turn take either of two forms. There may be agreement that regulation is required, but no consensus about the form of regulation, or there may be disagreement as to whether any form of regulation is called for. Finally, there may have been a conscious choice to leave the particular area unregulated at Community level. Such failure to act, for whatever reason, is referred to here as 'No regulation'.

Clearly, any of these three approaches may have been adopted in respect of any of the four classes of barrier previously identified, and this classification should therefore be regarded as cutting across the traditional one. It concentrates on responding to problems rather than on defining them. It remains to examine these three approaches in more detail.

Exhaustive regulation

Exhaustive regulation refers to the replacement of divergent national systems by a Community rule, where that Community rule becomes the sole regulation governing the area. No assumption is made here about the content of the Community regime, which may be rigorous or liberal; it may even prohibit regulation throughout the Community. The essential point is the exclusion of Member States' competence in the area.

As a result of a comprehensive reassessment of its regulatory policy, the Community has since 1985 followed the 'New Approach' to technical harmonisation. Old-style harmonisation which, put crudely, tried to create uniform, mandatory rules for the Community stands discredited. It produced 'Europroducts', which alienated the consumer. It stifled national tradition and discouraged innovation by producers. It demanded arduous negotiation to produce even minor legislation. The 'New Approach' shifts the focus to a concept of 'mutual recognition'. A product lawfully manufactured in one Member State should be taken in principle to be of sufficient quality to be sold throughout the Community. Harmonisation will be limited to aspects of health and safety, where a Community notion of 'essential safety requirements' will be set out in the harmonisation measure (usually a directive). These essential requirements indicate the performance standard which must be attained by a product in order to secure the right of free movement throughout the Community and they will be given shape by a supporting body of standards. There is to be no harmonisation for harmonisation's sake. To borrow the words of Lord Cockfield, 'gone are the days when it could be said that "if it moves, harmonise it" '. In a sense, this constitutes deregulation in that the mandatory content of Community rule is vastly reduced. A uniform Community standard is established, but its precise content is left inexplicit. The Community regulation is exhaustive in that the Member State is deprived of the ability to establish rules at variance with the Community régime, but this does not imply that a single inflexible rule is set in stone for the whole Community.

Consumer protection supplies useful examples. Lawful trade barriers within the Community are caused by the divergent regimes in different states relating to toy safety. Consequently, a Community harmonisation measure, the Toy Safety Directive [Directive 88/378: **[B22]–[B28]**], was passed in 1988 and this came into force in the UK on 1 January 1990 by virtue of the implementing Toy (Safety) Regulations. The directive follows the New Approach. It does not tell toy manufacturers how to make their toys. What is demanded of a toy, to entitle it to free movement in the Community, is that it shall satisfy the 'essential safety requirements'. These are broadly phrased performance levels relating to protection from health hazards and including reference to matters such as the flammability and toxicity of the toy. There are two methods of meeting the 'essential safety requirements'. First a toy can be made in accordance with CEN [the European standards-making body; the acronym is French] standards which are drawn up by experts in the field and which in effect represent a crystallised version of the essential safety requirements. For the United Kingdom, these CEN standards are adopted as British Standards. But, alternatively, the manufacturer can seek approval for a toy which does not conform to the CEN standards but which none the less is claimed to meet the overall performance level of the essential safety requirements. The manufacturer can choose. He or she can either comply with the CEN standard or else select an alternative though equally safe design. Flexibility is the virtue of the New Approach. The legislator is not laying down strict rules, merely overall performance goals. Standards drawn up by experts at CEN amplify the goals, but even then innovation remains possible in the context of the alternative approval procedure. Because harmonisation is limited to the safety aspects of the toy, national diversity is successfully preserved in the framework of a Community measure

. . .

The object of the New Approach, apart from the obvious practical point that it saves the Commission time and money, is to reconcile the diversity of cultural and commercial tradition in the Community with the need for a common Community approach in the pursuit of free trade and economic integration. To focus more precisely on the particularly difficult area of consumer protection, it aims to accommodate the different levels of consumer protection among the Member States within the internal market framework. Thus, the approach possesses both facilitative and protective elements.

The New Approach is an exercise in deregulation at two levels. First, it involves the creation of a single Community rule to replace several national rules. The range of diverse national legislation which tends to partition the market is thereby reduced. Secondly, although the purpose of the rule, safety, remains applicable equally throughout the Community, the rule itself is couched in sufficiently broad terms to permit a choice of methods selected according to national and local taste. In this second sense, the policy of deregulation connects with a policy of privatisation. The standards-making process, which is vital in giving shape to the broadly-phrased legal rule, is delegated to private parties with expertise in the field acting within the CEN framework.

In this context, the link between deregulation and privatisation needs careful consideration. It has been said that 'the New Approach is based on the principle that the Government should only regulate that which falls under its responsibility. The private sector must handle other matters itself.' However, such an analysis requires support from a definition of the ambit of governmental responsibility. It should be realised that broad issues of democratic accountability are raised by the present Community 'philosophy of clearer separation of responsibilities towards the public authority and the private sector'.

In addressing such issues relating to responsibility and accountability, one must ask whether the new system of deregulation and privatisation takes account of the interest of all affected parties. It is submitted that there are structural reasons why the New Approach might serve the European consumer ill. The difficulty lies in the privatisation of the standards-making process which supports the New Approach. For financial reasons it is likely that business will capture the standardisation process within CEN. Consumer organisations lack resources to participate fully in CEN committee work; in any event, consumer representation is ill-organised and haphazard in several Member States. Enforcement authorities should have an input, but in the United Kingdom the parlous state of local authority funding makes this a vain hope. If standards-making becomes the province of business alone, the balance between consumer protection and free trade will be distorted, prejudicing overall public confidence in the Community. It may be that states with traditionally high standards of consumer protection will find that standards which are set by CEN will fall below their expectations. Yet the New Approach Directive, as an exercise in exhaustive regulation, will mean that they will be obliged to accept on to their market goods conforming to those standards.

. . .

Partial regulation

. . . It might at first be thought that partial regulation would commonly be encountered in connection with directives, since these are binding only as to the end to be achieved, whilst leaving the method of achieving that end to the national authority. In fact, the concept of partial regulation does not extend to the situation where all Member States are required to achieve the same result (that is what is meant in the present context by 'Exhaustive regulation') so that directives generally are not intended to achieve partial regulation. Partial regulation refers to the scope of a measure, not to its form, so that partial regulation may be achieved either by regulation or by directive.

The reason why the Directive on Product Liability is an example of partial regulation is that it contains a provision allowing Member States to choose whether or not to include in their legislation the 'development risks defence' ie the defence that the defect contained in the product was one which could not have been discovered having regard to the state of scientific and technical knowledge at the time when the product was supplied. The United Kingdom has adopted this defence [Consumer Protection Act 1987, s 4(1)(e)], as have about half the other Member States. The inevitable consequence of this is that the laws on product liability differ between different Member States, so that in this respect at least there is not a genuine single market, nor is there now any prospect that a genuine single market will be achieved. In political terms the explanation for this untidy state of affairs is to be found in the view of a number of Member States, including the United Kingdom, that the very strict form of liability originally proposed by the Commission was unacceptable because it would unduly hinder business innovation. The fundamental question to be asked is, how significant are such breaches of the single market principle? The answer must depend upon the nature and effect of the individual breach. It is instructive to consider the possible effects of the derogation contained in the Product

Liability Directive. At present there are two systems of product liability operating within the Community. Each state's rules apply to products supplied within that state; in so far as the availability of the development risks defence makes any difference to the attitudes of manufacturers and suppliers, it may be supposed that they will be more ready to supply goods within those states which allow the development risks defence than in those which do not. In the short term this is likely to distort the pattern of trade within and between Member States, though the extent of this distortion is very difficult to estimate in advance and doubtless varies according to product category. A more interesting question is what is likely to happen in the longer term. One of the major arguments in favour of refraining from exhaustive regulation has been that the market place should be left to decide which system is best. Applying this theory, the expected result is that over a period of years it will eventually become apparent either that consumers are prepared to accept the existence of the defence in order to secure products more readily and at a cheaper price, or that manufacturers are prepared to accept the absence of the defence in order to overcome consumer resistance to buying. Gradually, the laws of the various Member States will be amended so that all reflect whichever solution is found by the market to be preferable.

A number of obvious difficulties with this theory of market response may be raised. In the first place it may be doubted whether any element of consumer reaction will ever be capable of being directly attributed to the presence or absence of the defence, not least since relatively few consumers will even be aware of the legal position. Secondly, even if consumers are aware of the legal position, it is not clear that they can really change their behaviour in response to it, since choosing not to buy particular goods may not be a realistic option when there is no available substitute which is supplied under a different legal régime. Third, even where consumer reaction exists and is measurable, it should not necessarily be assumed that the result will be the same in all Member States, so that in theory the disparities could remain, with some states belatedly adopting the defence and others belatedly abandoning it. Fourth, it is in any event unrealistic to suppose that a matter of this kind is likely to attract the level of political interest necessary to produce rapid legal change, so that even well-documented deficiencies in the existing law are likely to remain uncorrected for some considerable time.

A number of conclusions may be drawn from these observations. The first is that decisions made now about the choice between partial and exhaustive regulation are likely to remain effective for some considerable time to come. The second is that the choice is closely bound up with pressure from interest groups and with the perceptions of the government of the day in each individual Member State. Finally, it may be noted that an initial choice for partial regulation may well be susceptible of later conversion into exhaustive regulation, either by the operation of market forces or by a change at Community level, whereas it seems unlikely that an initial choice for exhaustive regulation will ever be followed by a reversion to partial regulation.

. . .

No regulation

There are of course many areas which have not yet been regulated at all at Community level. Indeed, virtually the whole of private law falls into this category. However, the example which will be considered here is tax law. Differences in tax laws between different Member States may operate as a barrier to the operation of a free market since these differences are likely to distort the choice of where to establish a business, and, possibly, the choice of where to seek more business (assuming that receipts are likely to be taxed, at least initially, in the state where they arise). In connection with indirect taxation, the fact that the basic system of value added tax is itself a Community concept has assisted in making some limited progress. By contrast, direct taxation provides an example of an area where there is as yet no regulation. Direct taxes generally pre-date the formation of the Community and there are differences between Member States in underlying concepts as well as in tax rates. It is much more difficult to pursue the objective of harmonisation when not comparing like with like. The Treaty of Rome appears to recognise this: Article 99 calls for the harmonisation of indirect taxes, whereas Article 100 speaks of the approximation of direct taxes. It is unclear whether the two concepts are in practice different. So far very little progress has been made in the direction of harmonisation/approximation. This is partly explained by the requirement of unanimous consent for proposals in this area [this applies even after the introduction of the Single European Act: Article 100a(2)], and the existence of this requirement recognises the extreme political sensitivity of measures related to taxation. This is one area where governments are very concerned to protect their own interest, as distinct from the interest of any group within their own societies. The power to raise revenue (and implicitly the power to determine rates of taxation) are fundamental attributes of sovereignty, and it is not surprising that progress in this area is so difficult to achieve. The foregoing appears to suggest that tax law is one area where it will be necessary to allow the retention of some form of trade barrier beyond the end of 1992, for there is surely no prospect that the objectives of Articles 99 and 100 can be fully achieved within that time. It is noticeable that a disproportionate number of the sectors which have proved most resistant to the introduction of harmonised Community rules are those traditionally supervised or influenced by the state, such as energy, communication and transport.

Choice of legal base: the court's role reasserted

The choice between the different forms of Community response, examined above, might be thought to be fundamentally an economic and/or political decision. A general touchstone is found in the Delors Report's principle of subsidiarity, which holds that the Community should only assume competence in areas where Community authority is more efficient than national regulation. However, the fact of heterogeneity within the Community has been regularly referred to in the course of this article and there is every likelihood that on many matters no agreement will be reached, either because of a different interpretation of the economic evidence or a different ideological perception, or a combination of both. In these circumstances, the nature of the Community's response will depend to a significant extent on the view taken by the Court of Justice of the correct Treaty legal base for the adoption of the legislation.

Assume that a lawful trade barrier exists as a result of divergence in Member States' legislation. The matter may concern employment protection rights, environmental protection legislation, civil law liability systems or road safety laws. Varied though such matters are, all may to some degree distort trade patterns in the Community, because business is subject to different costs according to the legislation of the state in which it happens to be operating.

. . .

The court's task, though important, is unenviable. It is obliged to determine the purpose of a Community act in order to select the appropriate Treaty base. Yet few Community acts have a single purpose. The problem is well illustrated by the present debate about the nature of Community Social Policy. The Community has always possessed a Social Policy, the most familiar feature of which is Article 119 EEC, dealing with sex discrimination. Such policies are in one sense aspects of Community protective regulation, but they also bear directly on the completion of the common market. Differences in national social policies in any field may distort the competitive structure of the market and therefore action at Community level to harmonise such regulation may be seen as a means of facilitating the free movement of persons. However, disputes about the nature and purpose of such legislation are a feature of recent Community activity and in this context the draft Social Charter proved particularly controversial.

. . .

It is . . . difficult to believe that the court, when . . . legislation is challenged before it on the ground that the incorrect legal base has been chosen, is able to find the 'right' answer. Indeed, the court itself has been moved to comment on the lack of coherence between the different rules under the different Treaty provisions [Case 242/87 *Commission v Council* **[B58]**]. However, a decision which may be difficult, if not logically impossible to make, will have fundamentally important constitutional consequences. Accordingly, the court has in this respect a central role in shaping the nature of the Community response.

Conclusion

. . . it is important to ask the fundamental question, what sort of single market is being created here? The answer seems to be that it is a market in which business flourishes, relatively free from protective regulation, but the legitimate interests of other social groups are at risk of being ignored. This is a conclusion which may please the United Kingdom government, but which may be of rather more concern to the governments of other Member States. It must be accepted that those who find themselves in the minority in any discussion of Community policy are likely to seek a means of preserving their own freedom of action . . . In some cases the preservation of national legislative competence may be justifiable; if one Member State has its own system of protective legislation, which is more generous to those protected than the scheme proposed by the Community, then there is every reason why that scheme should be retained, even though this preserves national divergences. A principle such as this is doubly necessary at a time when business interests are having some success in blocking protective legislation at Community level. In the absence of Community protection the maintenance of protection at national level must be respected. Integration is not a goal in itself.

At present a number of disturbing aspects of the evolution of the single market may be identified. These include the insistence by individual Member States on partial regulation which permits their protective standards to fall short of those of the Community as a whole (as in the case of product liability), the adoption of exhaustive regulation which subordinates the objective of protection to the workings of the free market (as in the case of the Merger Regulation **[E78]**) [and] the introduction of standards-setting machinery which is likely to be dominated by business interests (as in the case of the New Approach to technical harmonisation) . . . Such developments emerge from an emphasis on facilitative legislation to the detriment of protective legislation. This emphasis can only be seen as inadequate to satisfy all interest groups in the Community.

It is to be hoped that the coming decade will see a greater willingness on the part of Member States to accept the legitimacy of the call for protective legislation within the Single Market and a greater determination on the part of the Commission to press for such legislation. Nevertheless it is apparent that the commercial interests have secured a considerable head start, and the fierce opposition offered even to the non-binding Social Charter demonstrates a determination not to surrender this perceived advantage. It will take a long time to redress the balance effectively.

[E40]   Case C-11/92 R v Secretary of State for Health, ex parte Gallaher Ltd and others (Judgment, 22 June 1993)

[The English High Court made a reference under Article 177 on the interpretation of certain provisions of Council Directive 89/622 on the approximation of the laws, regulations and administrative provisions of the Member States concerning the labelling of tobacco products (OJ 1989 L359/1). In particular, the applicants in the main proceedings, various cigarette companies, claimed that they were entitled to market cigarette packets in the United Kingdom, other than those imported from another Member State, which complied with the directive but did not meet the stricter standards imposed by domestic legislation as regards the space to be given to health warnings on the packets.]

Report for the hearing

4. The Commission first of all points out that the harmonisation of laws provided for under the Treaty can be of three main types:
   (1) *total*: the national rules are replaced by a uniform set of standards from which Member States cannot derogate in any circumstances other than those provided for by Community law;
   (2) *optional*: Member States are prevented from using their national standards as barriers to the free circulation of goods but remain free to maintain lower standards for the sale of goods on their own territory, adoption of the harmonisation standards in each Member State being at the option of the Member States;
   (3) *minimal*: Member States may introduce or maintain stricter standards which may be applied to imported goods on a non-discriminatory basis, whereby the harmonisation establishes a

baseline for the laying down of national standards. The compatibility of minimal harmonisation with the Treaty can be ensured by using a differentiated approach: the free movement of goods can be guaranteed on the basis of the minimum standard laid down, leaving Member States free only to apply a stricter standard in situations which do not impinge on the free movement of goods.

According to the Commission, Article 100a of the EEC Treaty permits the approximation of national laws carried out pursuant to that article to be a total harmonisation (Council Directive 89/458 . . . amending with regard to European emission standards for cars below 1.4 litres Directive 70/220 . . . OJ 1989 L226/1 . . .), an optional harmonisation (Council Directive 88/436 . . . amending Directive 70/220 . . . OJ 1988 L214/1) or a minimal harmonisation (Council Directive 90/314 . . . on package travel, package holidays and package tours, OJ 1990 L158/59 . . .). It is therefore for the Community legislature to decide if the achievement of the internal market requires the imposition of total harmonisation or if, taking into account the nature of the goods in question and the principle of subsidiarity, it suffices to lay down a minimal harmonisation.

The Commission goes on to point out that the Treaty confers no special competence on the Community in the area of public health generally and that the directive [in question] constitutes the first Community legislation on the subject of health warnings on cigarette packets. In ensuring the free movement of goods, the Commission would not wish to undermine Member States' efforts in this area of public health. To this end, it may take as a base for its proposal a high level of protection (Article 100a(3)) and keep medical developments under review (eighth recital in the preamble to the directive) or ensure that the directive leaves Member States free to develop their own policies in this area where this is consistent with the principle of the free movement of goods.

The Commission notes in this regard that Member States have an unconditional right (subject to the rules of the Treaty) to introduce more stringent measures under Article 118a(3). The fact that Article 100a contains no unconditional safeguard of this kind does not mean that the possibility of Member States taking such measures is excluded in an Article 100a directive, as is demonstrated by, inter alia, Council Directive 80/117 . . . on the protection of workers from the risks related to exposure to chemical, physical and biological agents at work (OJ 1980 L327/8), which is based on Article 100.

Similarly, in the area of control of the free movement of firearms, Council Directive 91/477 . . . on the control of the acquisition and possession of weapons (OJ 1991 L256/51), which was adopted pursuant to Article 100a, lays down certain minimum standards to be applied by Member States in issuing firearm permits in their territory (Article 5) but also confers on Member States the right to adopt more stringent provisions (Articles 3 and 12(2)). It is thus an area in which the Community legislature took the view that it was not opportune totally to harmonise national rules in an effort to accommodate both the interests of free movement and public safety.

With regard to the directive in question, the Commission takes the view that Article 8(1) thereof serves to render the minimal nature of the directive compatible with the objective of the free movement of goods by requiring each Member State to permit the sale of cigarettes imported from another Member State whose laws are in conformity with those minimal rules.

. . .

The Commission also takes the view that the approach of differentiated minimal harmonisation followed by the directive meets the same concerns as motivated the adoption of Article 100a(4) of the EEC Treaty, whilst being less restrictive of the free movement of goods. In the Commission's view, where the Commission is legislating for the first time in an area relating to one of the 'major needs' referred to in Article 100a(4), the possibility of Member States wishing to invoke Article 100a(4) in the event of a total harmonisation should be deflected by recourse to the differentiated approach to minimal harmonisation if the Community legislature considers it opportune in order to avoid the creation of the obstacles to the free movement of goods which would result from the use of Article 100a(4).

The European Court of Justice (Judgment, 22 June 1993)

3. The directive provides that certain indications and warnings must appear on cigarette packets. Article 3(3), for example, provides that the indications of tar and nicotine yields must be printed on the side of cigarette packets, in the official language or languages of the country of final marketing, in clearly legible print on a contrasting background so that at least 4% of the corresponding surface is covered.

4. Article 4(1) requires all unit packets of tobacco products to carry, on the most visible surface, the general warning 'Tobacco seriously damages health'. With regard to cigarette packets, Article 4(2) requires the other large surface of the packet to carry specific warnings to be selected from those contained in the list drawn up by each Member State exclusively on the basis of the warnings listed in the annex to the directive. Article 4(4) provides that the warnings on cigarette packets provided for in Article 4(1) and (2) must cover at least 4% of each large surface of the unit packet, excluding the indication of the authority that is their author.

. . .

5. Regulation 5(2)(d) of the United Kingdom regulations provides that in the case of cigarette packets the general warning and the specific warning must cover at least 6% of the surfaces on which they are printed. Regulation 6(3)(b) of the United Kingdom regulations provides that the statement of tar and nicotine yields on cigarette packets must also cover an area amounting to at least 6% of the side of the packet.

6. Regulations 8(c) and (d) of the United Kingdom regulations provide that a person who imports cigarettes of any brand from another Member State with a view to marketing them in the United Kingdom is to be regarded as complying with the requirements of the United Kingdom regulations if the packets in question carry warnings in English which comply with the requirements of that other Member State imposed pursuant to the directive.

. . .

10. It should be borne in mind that the directive, which was adopted pursuant to Article 100a of the EEC Treaty, is designed to eliminate barriers to trade which might arise as a result of differences in national provisions on the labelling of tobacco products and thereby impede the establishment and operation of the internal market. With that end in view, the directive contains common rules concerning the health warnings to appear on the

unit packet of tobacco products and the indications of the tar and nicotine yields to appear on cigarette packets.

11. These common rules are not always identical in nature.

12. Some of them give Member States no discretion to impose requirements stricter than those provided for in the directive, or even to impose more detailed or at any rate different requirements, with regard to the labelling of tobacco products.

13. According to Article 8(1) of the directive, Member States may not, for reasons of labelling, prohibit or restrict the sale of products which comply with the directive. Under Article 8(2), Member States still have the right to lay down, so far as compatible with the Treaty, requirements concerning the import, sale and consumption of tobacco products which they deem necessary in order to protect public health, but only in so far as such requirements do not imply any changes to labelling as laid down in the directive.

14. Other provisions of the directive allow the Member States a degree of discretion to adapt the labelling of tobacco products to the requirements of public health protection. One such provision is Article 4(2), which allows the Member States to select the specific warnings which must appear on cigarette packets by choosing them from those listed in the annex to the directive. Another is Article 4(3), which allows Member States to stipulate that the general warning 'Tobacco seriously damages health', as well as the specific warnings, must be combined with the indication of the authority that is their author.

15. The existence of provisions containing minimum requirements is accounted for by the Resolution of the Council and of the representatives of the governments of the Member States, meeting within the Council, of 7 July 1986 on a programme of action of the European Communities against cancer (OJ 1986 C184/19), to which the fifth recital in the preamble to the directive refers. Under that programme, the measures to be adopted by the Community with a view to limiting and reducing the consumption of tobacco were to be based on the practical experience gained in the various Member States and were to contribute to increasing the effectiveness of national programmes and actions.

16. Member States which have made use of the powers conferred by the provisions containing minimum requirements cannot, according to Article 8 of the directive, prohibit or restrict the sale within their territory of products imported from other Member States which comply with the directive.

17. In order to reply to the question referred by the national court, it is therefore necessary to determine whether Articles 3(3) and 4(4) of the directive still allow the Member States a degree of latitude to require, with regard to domestic production, that the indications and warnings in question cover in each case more than 4% of the relevant surface area.

18. The applicants in the main proceedings consider that the rules in the directive requiring the indications and warnings to cover at least 4% of the relevant surface area must be incorporated as such by the Member States into their national law because the provisions in question confer on them no discretion. They argue that it is for manufacturers of tobacco products to decide whether the indications and warnings should cover a larger surface area. First of all, the applicants submit that this interpretation is confirmed by the court's case law relating to certain directives on labelling, according

to which the common rules laid down by those directives must be interpreted as excluding any additional or different national requirement, in the absence of provisions to the contrary. With particular regard to Council Directive 73/173 . . . on the approximation of Member States' laws, regulations and administrative provisions relating to the classification, packaging and labelling of dangerous preparations (solvents) (OJ 1973 L189/7), the applicants in the main proceedings argue that, nothwithstanding Article 6(1) of that directive, which provides that 'each symbol must cover at least one tenth of the surface area of the label', the court made it clear that the labelling rules laid down in that directive applied uniformly in the same fashion to both domestic goods and imported goods (judgment in Case 148/78 *Pubblico Ministero v Ratti* [1979] ECR 1629). They go on to argue that any different interpretation would result in the imposition on national products of stricter conditions than those imposed as regards the marketing of products imported from other Member States, which would lead to discrimination and would be likely to jeopardise the free movement of tobacco products and affect conditions of competition.

19. Those arguments cannot be accepted.

20. Articles 3(3) and 4(4) of the directive contain provisions directed to the Member States, to whom the directive is addressed, and not to the manufacturers of tobacco products, who have no interest in using a greater surface area for the indications and warnings in question. The expression 'at least' contained in both articles must be interpreted as meaning that, if they consider it necessary, Member States are at liberty to decide that the indications and warnings are to cover a greater surface area in view of the level of public awareness of the health risks associated with tobacco consumption.

21. The case law on labelling cited by the applicants in the main proceedings concerns directives whose scope differs from that of Directive 89/622. So far as the decision in *Ratti* is concerned, the court there ruled not on the interpretation of Article 6(1) of Directive 73/173, which also contains the expression 'at least', but on other provisions of that directive and on the nature of its provisions in general.

22. Admittedly, as the applicants in the main proceedings have pointed out, this interpretation of the provisions may imply less favourable treatment for national products in comparison with imported products and leaves in existence some inequalities in conditions of competition. However, those consequences are attributable to the degree of harmonisation sought by the provisions in question, which lay down minimum requirements.

23. The answer to the question referred by the national court must therefore be that Articles 3(3) and 4(4) of Council Directive 89/622 are to be interpreted as allowing the Member States to require, so far as domestic production is concerned, that the indications concerning tar and nicotine yields provided for in Article 3 of that directive and the general and specific warnings provided for in Article 4 of the directive be printed on cigarette packets so as to cover at least 6% of each of the relevant surface areas.

(b) Market integration and subsidiarity

[E41] D Chalmers: 'Free movement of goods within the European Community: an unhealthy addiction to Scotch whisky?' (1993) 42 International and Comparative Law Quarterly 269

C. The evolution of the regulatory line of reasoning

. . .

1. The development of an incipient doctrine of subsidiarity in the case law on Article 30

In *Cinéthèque* [E24] there were already indications of a sensitivity on the part of the court towards recognition of regional autonomy within the common market. Having acknowledged that the French régime was restrictive of free movement of goods the court stated: 'It must be conceded that a national system which, in order to encourage the creation of cinematographic works irrespective of their origin, gives priority for a limited period, to the distribution of such works through the cinema is so justified.'

The court does not ascertain whether the measure is the least restrictive of trade necessary to protect French cinema; rather, it considers that the *institution* of giving priority to certain works through the cinema is justified under Community law. Unlike the 'mandatory requirements' doctrine in *Cassis de Dijon* [E21], the court did not consider that the aims of the Treaty required that such a measure be harmonised. If this is correct, the judgment provides implicit recognition by the court that certain measures taken by Member States which indirectly restrict trade may still be compatible with the common market.

This reasoning was more clearly articulated in *Torfaen*. The court considered there that the arrangement of working hours in accordance with 'national or regional socio-cultural characteristics' was, in the present state of Community law, a matter for Member States. Sunday trading legislation, despite being restrictive of free movement of goods, would therefore breach Article 30 only if it exceeded the effects intrinsic to rules of that kind. It is questionable, therefore, whether the evolution of a common market ever requires this matter to be regulated at a Community level. Regional diversity in this area being held to be compatible with the Treaty, it can equally well be regulated at either a national or local level.

It is still unclear whether the court now recognises a general ground of justification which allows national provisions to reflect political or economic choices in keeping with national or regional socio-cultural characteristics. This matter has been considered by Advocate General Van Gerven in both *SPUC v Grogan* [A19] and *Stoke-on-Trent City Council v B & Q plc* [A18]. He considered that Member States could use such a justification only if they could either link the measure in question to a 'mandatory requirement' that already existed in the case law or could establish a close connection between it and the grounds provided in Article 36 of the EEC Treaty.

The author questions the wisdom of such an approach. The ground in Article 36 which is most likely to be invoked is that of public policy. According to *Bouchereau* [D47] a Member State may take measures on grounds of public policy, however, only if there is a genuine and serious threat to a fundamental interest of its society. According to Van Gerven's reasoning, a Member State would thus only be free to regulate matters that were considered to be fundamental social interests. This concept is not only extremely restrictive but also very vague. The content will fluctuate from one Member State to another, resulting in a lack of unity in the case law. For the court to suggest that certain national choices are legitimate, whereas others are not, is not only likely to lead to arbitrary distinctions but is almost certainly inconsistent with the notion of judicial restraint that is the rationale behind this case law in the first place.

In parallel areas of Community law, when faced with the difficult task of determining which measures are a reflection of legitimate political or economic choices taken by Member States, the court has consequently resorted to leaving the category very open. In *Koestler* the court considered that a German refusal to recognise certain speculative transactions as legally enforceable was compatible with Article 59 of the EEC Treaty on the grounds that it was non-discriminatory and was based on reasons founded on the '*social order*' – namely that Germany did not consider that wagers should be contractually binding. Similarly, in *Bond van Adverteerders* the court considered that Dutch restrictions on television subtitling were compatible with Article 59, despite the fact that the Dutch government could have achieved its aims in less restrictive manner, on the grounds that every Member State had the power to regulate television advertising on its territory on grounds of *public interest*.

It is tempting to speculate that Advocate General Van Gerven might not have wanted to create a general justification that allows national rules to reflect political or economic choices in keeping with national or regional socio-cultural characteristics for fear of creating a situation where a Member State will always raise this defence to excuse any restrictions on free movement of goods. This fear could be met if certain restrictions were held to be per se illegal, subject to Article 36 of the EEC Treaty and the *Cassis de Dijon* 'mandatory requirements' jurisprudence, and thus be unable to benefit from this ground on the basis that they were incompatible with a fully developed common market. Measures that would fall under this proviso would be those that either discriminated against imports or put a condition precedent on access to the national market. If this were so, in the light of the above difficulties, it is suggested that it might be better to leave the category of national or regional socio-cultural characteristics undefined. The court should consider all areas of regulation that do not place a condition precedent on entry to the national market as being capable of being regulated at the national level, unless the measure either discriminates, de jure or de facto, against imports or excessively restricts trade.

2.   Reconciling regionalism and the needs of a common market: the need for a new proportionality test

The type of measure considered in *Cinéthèque* or the Sunday shopping cases, as they can be permanently regulated at a national level, is not being examined against some external value or interest but in the light of the institution it creates. If that institution is found to be justified under Community law, the question of whether the measure taken was the least restrictive necessary to create that institution is an empty one. As Mattera pointed out, in relation to the *Torfaen* judgment, in such circumstances proportionality does not act to circumscribe an exception to Article 30, as in the *Cassis de Dijon* case law but, rather, delimits Article 30 itself. The justification for such restrictions is therefore markedly different from those restrictions the court has traditionally considered as justified to satisfy some 'mandatory requirement' such as consumer or environmental protection whose justification stems from their protection of certain fundamental values pending action at a Community level.

Their differing rationales indicate consequently that they should be evaluated differently, and that the mode of application of the proportionality principle, the primary means of assessing such measures, should vary respectively. This matter was touched upon in the opinion of Advocate General Van Gerven in *Stoke-on-Trent*:

> *First* of all, it must be determined whether a national measure in question is *objectively necessary* in order to further the attainment of the objective pursued by it. That means that the measure must be *relevant* (effective), that is to say of such a nature as to afford effective protection of the public interest involved, and must be essential in order to attain the objective, which implies that the competent legislator does not have an equally effective alternative available to it which would have a *less restrictive* effect on the free movement of goods. Secondly, even if the national measure is effective and essential with regard to the objective pursued, it must be determined whether the restriction caused thereby to intra-Community trade is *in relation*, that is to say *proportionate* to that objective. It may be seen from the foregoing that the proportionality test in the broad understanding of the term essentially contains both a dual necessity criterion (relevance and indispensability of the measure) and a proportionality criterion in the strict sense.

The Advocate General had previously indicated in *SPUC v Grogan* what he understood by proportionality in the strict sense: 'Such proportionality may arise, for instance where the rule gives rise to serious screening off of the market. See in this connection my Opinions in *Torfaen* . . . and in *Conforama*.'

It is suggested that this latter application of the principle will rarely be relevant in the case of national measures which are taken in pursuit of a traditional 'mandatory requirement' under the *Cassis de Dijon* case law. In that instance and in the case of measures taken under Article 36 of the EEC Treaty it has been generally held by the court, either expressly or implicitly, that the level of protection that should be offered is a matter of discretion for the Member State, subject to the proviso that the protection offered be effective. The Member State is, however, required to take the measure the least restrictive of trade to achieve that level of protection. It would thus appear that if a Member State requires a high level of protection in an area, pending harmonisation of the matter, the measure will be legal if, despite its having highly restrictive effects, it is the least restrictive measure available. Only in the *Danish Bottles* judgment **[E26]** did the court depart from this and say that a measure was still illegal, despite fulfilling these requirements, as it was excessively restrictive of trade. This judgment has rightly been criticised as engaging in an arbitrary balancing exercise between the principles of free movement of goods and environmental protection which served to weaken environmental protection in the

Community. It was thus unsurprising that in *Commission v Belgium* **[E28]** when the court was faced with a Belgian ban on the import of non-recyclable waste, it reverted to its former approach. Having found that the measure was the least restrictive necessary to fulfil a 'mandatory requirement' recognised by Community law, namely environmental protection, the court did not go on to consider whether it was still excessively restrictive of trade but held it to be compatible with Article 30.

The position is different with regard to measures which are found to be restrictive of trade but a justifiable expression of regional autonomy. These measures are synonymous with the aims they pursue. It is consequently circular to ask whether they are a necessary means of achieving these aims or whether they do this through the least restrictive means possible. The Sunday trading legislation jurisprudence provides a good example of this. The objective justified under Community law, which, according to the court, Sunday trading legislation pursues, is the arrangement of working hours in accordance with national or regional socio-cultural characteristics. Sunday trading legislation reflects and shapes these national socio-cultural characteristics, however. It is consequently unsurprising that the court has never considered whether it is the least restrictive means of achieving these aims; rather, stating that the rules must not exceed the effects intrinsic to rules of that kind.

In such instances the second branch of the proportionality principle is more relevant. The measure, being prima facie permissible, will be held to contravene Article 30 only if it is unduly restrictive. Thus in *Stoke-on-Trent* the court stated that in order to ascertain whether national Sunday trading legislation was compatible with the Treaty, the court had to weigh the interest in the national measure against the principle of free movement of goods and verify whether its restrictive effects were direct, indirect or purely speculative and whether its effects did not impede the marketing of imported products more than the marketing of national products. Such criteria are quantitative. Being of a quantitative nature, moreover, they will necessitate the use of economic criteria, for example increases in cost, restrictions on outlets of supply and curtailment of demand. Where the threshold should be is clearly a matter of judgment. A parallel can be drawn from the application of the de minimis rule in EC competition law. Commission Notice of 3 September 1986 on Minor Agreements states that where the products subject to the anti-competitive practice represent less than 5 per cent of the total affected market and the aggregate turnover of the undertakings does not exceed ECU 200m, the measure will not be caught by EC competition law. Where it is forecast that imports of a good will be restricted by less than 5 per cent as a result of a particular measure, current practice suggests, therefore, that such a measure should be held to be legal.

A heavy demand will also be imposed upon national courts. If there is to be consistency in application and such a matter is not to be a source of constant reference from national courts to the European Court, it is important that the latter issues clear guidelines on when a measure is excessively restrictive. It was consequently regrettable that in its case law on Sunday trading the court has not been able to articulate these guidelines in a more detailed manner. The vagueness of the criteria which were finally spelled out in *Stoke-on-Trent* as to when a measure is excessively restrictive will in all likelihood be only a source for further litigation.

[E42] N Reich: 'Competition between legal orders: a new paradigm of EC law?' (1992) 29 Common Market Law Review 861

1. Introduction

The competition rules have a prominent place in EC law, but, in addition to that, their underlying principles may also present a new paradigm for understanding the evolution of Community law in creating the internal market, and for adapting to the challenge of implementing new policies, such as environmental and consumer protection. Competition between legal orders, instead of centralised regulation – this seemed to be the 'new approach' of the EC harmonisation process as initiated by the White Paper of the Commission on completing the internal market [(1985) COM 310 final]. Its underlying principle of 'home country control', combined with a per se access of products or services conforming to the standards of the country of origin to the entire internal market, implicitly recognises competition between legal orders as a substitute for harmonisation.

. . .

6. Interbrand competition: subsidiarity and minimum protection

6.1 Subsidiarity and public choice

Subsidiarity has been debated as a new political principle within the EC to allow for a redistribution of powers between the ever-growing competence of the Community, the loss of jurisdiction by Member States, and the non-recognition of regional entities or states as political actors within the EC. It starts from the principle that 'things should not be done at Community level unless they cannot be done at national level'.

We do not want to enter into the entire debate about subsidiarity, but prefer to discuss very tentatively some [of] its legal implications. Our paradigm of competition between legal orders might be helpful for conceptually clarifying some of the issues involved, provided we keep in mind that competition here will be increased between Community and Member State (eventually regional) law. We will call this 'interbrand competition'. The concept suggests that more choice should be left to local actors on how they regulate certain areas of social policy which, as M Porter has said, should not be subject to competitive advantage. On the other hand, we take Kitch's public choice theory seriously, [attacking integration theory and putting trust in competing, decentralised jurisdictions to provide adequate regulatory patterns] because a centralised regulation of certain areas of social policy, with which we are specifically concerned here, eg environmental, consumer and workplace protection, is hardly a realistic option for the EC given its character as 'market without government'. Community law based on the principle of subsidiarity encourages decentralised measures which, of necessity, will be divergent and therefore allow competing choices; this should, however, not endanger integration. As a legal consequence of this withdrawal of authority, the Community will usually enact only minimum provisions which allow a competition for 'better rules'. The principles of precedence and direct effect, an important *acquis communautaire* recently reiterated by the court in its opinion on the draft European

Economic Area agreement **[A56]**, will be applied more flexibly to allow for more choice between legal orders and to experiment among different solutions in order to attain social objectives which are only indirectly caught by the EEC Treaty. However, subsidiarity may lead to 'distortions of competition' and therefore needs careful monitoring by the European Court as 'umpire'.

. . .

A good example is presented by the extensive debate on a general Community directive on product safety. It tries to implement consumers' (and workers') right to safety and is therefore centred on a delimitation of jurisdictions between the Community and Member States. The proposal of 1990, now adopted as Directive 92/59 of 29 June 1992, on general product safety [1992] OJ L228/24, codifies the principle of subsidiarity as the ruling one, by allowing a Community action in case of a dangerous product presenting a 'serious and immediate risk' only if one Member State has acted already and if a measure on a Community level is indispensable. The Community should therefore not interfere with responsibilities of Member States which they take for the safety and health of their citizens stemming from hazardous products. Weatherill therefore insists on 'developing Community consumer policy from below' [(1991) JCP 171]. The Community will act only if the territorial limits of state jurisdiction require concertation. The pre-emptive scope of Community action is again limited and does not set aside Member State action, especially if based on criminal law or on consumer critique.

6.2   A new reading of Article 100a(4)

As far as the establishment of the internal market is concerned, the Single Act seemed keen to give exclusive jurisdiction to the Community and thereby exclude competition between legal orders as an element of disintegration. But it did not do so without exceptions, the best known being Article 100a(4), the so-called opt-out provision. Can one interpret this clause as an implicit recognition of the principle of minimum protection, and hence as a recognition of a (limited) 'interbrand competition of legal orders' within the framework of Community law? Or is it to be regarded as an exception to the principle of total harmonisation left to the exclusive jurisdiction of the Community, which must therefore be construed narrowly?

. . .

Commission officials have . . . attempted to limit [Article 100a(4)'s] scope of application by restrictive interpretation, eg by insisting that Member States may not introduce *new* protective measures once the Community has acted. On the other hand, many authors pointed out that the principle of *best possible protection* was enshrined in Article 100a(4). In such a reading, the *practical* differences between the minimum protection clause in Article 130t, 118a(3) on the one hand, and the opt-out clause of Article 100a(4) on the other become blurred and should not be overemphasised, even if they exist in theory.

We will not try to give a definite answer to this controversy. Its practical importance – except for the different form of participation of the Parliament in Community law making – has been rather limited. Pipkorn mentions that, till the end of 1990, no Member State had used the opt-out proviso of paragraph (4) of Article 100a to safeguard the 'application' of its standards. The danger of opting-out was overcome by the Community in the drafting and negotiation stage of directives. Directives on product standards, which usually involve important workplace, consumer and environmental safety issues, are accompanied by safeguard clauses and procedures which allowing for 'provisional measures' under Article 100a(5) are thereby leading to a healthy 'competition of legal orders' and administrative practices, monitored by the Commission and finally the court.

As a consequence of this reading of the relationship betwen paras (4) and (5) of Article 100a we suggest that, even where the Community enjoys its most intense form of jurisdiction, namely to complete the internal market, there remains room for choices between different legal orders. The Community is responsible for the functioning of the internal market and therefore will have exclusive and not only subsidiary jurisdiction here. Member States on the other hand are still primarily responsible for the social welfare of their people, which is recognised by Community law either by allowing for a safeguard or – as a more radical step – for an opting-out procedure. This 'flexibility' doctrine under Article 100a implies the recognition that Member States have to take Community interests into account when they want to go their own ways in using the safeguard clauses, respectively paragraph 4, of Article 100a. They are bound by Article 5, and in doing so they must be regarded as acting as 'trustees of the common interest' . . . The real difference between Article 130t, 118a on the one hand and Article 100a(4) and (5) on the other can be found in the intensity of monitoring by the Commission, which is more stringent where the internal market is concerned.

6.3 The Maastricht Treaty on Political Union and its recognition of the principle of subsidiarity

It is interesting to see that, the more the Community occupies fields which were traditionally those left to the Member States, the more the principles of subsidiarity and minimum protection find recognition, thereby allowing increased competition of legal orders within the EC. The extension of Community jurisdiction is paralleled by an extension of competition of legal orders!

The best example for this seemingly contradictory trend is to be found in the Maastricht Treaty on European Union . . . It will expressly recognise the principle of subsidiarity. The latter will become an overall rule of Community policy in areas where it has no exclusive competence, per Article 3b. This continues a rule already laid down with relation to environmental policy, per Article 130r(4), and is the basis of new policies like consumer protection, per Article 129a(3), public health, Article 129(1), or industrial policy, Article 130(2). However, there is as yet no express mechanism of judicial control of subsidiarity as proposed by some authors. On the other hand, if the Community has acted under the new provisions and if Member States take action themselves under the minimum protection clause, the court may look at whether the requirements for Community action have been fulfilled. It is however unlikely, as experiences with other federal jurisdictions demonstrate, that such a legal control will be very effective.

It is also not clear how subsidiarity can be invoked if the Community takes measures under its exclusive competence to complete the internal market, per Article 100a, which is expressly mentioned in Article 129a(1)(a) on consumer policy **[A6]**. Community measures protecting the economic interests of consumers had till now been enacted first under Article 100 or, since 1987, Article 100a, based upon a broad reading of Community jurisdiction to establish the common market or to complete the internal market. Will the Community take these measures now as 'specific actions' under Article 129a(1)(b) which would always imply the adoption of a minimum protection standard? On the other hand, the harmonisation measures taken by the Community in the past, eg to protect the economic interests of consumers, have usually been minimum directives; this will not change after ratification of the Maastricht Treaty.

The underlying principle of this discussion seems to imply an inherent logic of Community law. The more competences the Community is acquiring, the less exclusive will be its jurisdiction, and the more 'interbrand' competition between legal orders will take place. So the public choice theory of Kitch might find a prominent place in Community law-making. On the other hand, an unfettered competition between legal orders may lead to distortions of competition and would thereby allow for unjustified competitive advantages, which is not to be welcomed . . . In our opinion, the basic objective of Community law today is exactly to develop rules which allow a delimitation between workable and distorted competition. Efficiency does not come from competition alone, but only by applying conflict rules 'ensuring that competition in the common market is not distorted', per Article 3(f) EEC . . . The free movement and competition rules of Community law are, as the court has said in its opinion on the draft EEA Treaty, not an end in themselves but a means to accomplish the overall objectives of Articles 2, 8a and 102a of the EEC Treaty.

Note.   Article 102a of the EEC Treaty refers to co-operation between Member States to ensure the convergence of economic and monetary policies. This is replaced by a new provision in the EC Treaty: see **[A14]**.

(c)   Market integration and cohesion

[E43]   Case C-21/88 Du Pont de Nemours Italiana SpA v Unità sanitaria locale No 2 di Carrara [1990] ECR I-889

The European Court of Justice

7. In its first question, the national court seeks to ascertain whether national rules reserving to undertakings established in certain regions of the national territory a proportion of public supply contracts are contrary to Article 30, which prohibits quantitative restrictions on imports and all measures having equivalent effect.

. . .

9. It must be pointed out . . . that according to the first recital in the preamble to Council Directive 77/62 of 21 December 1976 co-ordinating procedures for the award of public supply contracts [OJ 1977 L13/1], which was in force at the material time, 'restrictions on the free movement of

goods in respect of public supplies are prohibited by the terms of Articles 30 et seq of the Treaty'.

10. Accordingly, it is necessary to determine the effect which a preferential system of the kind at issue in this case is likely to have on the free movement of goods.

11. It must be pointed out in that regard that such a system, which favours goods processed in a particular region of a Member State, prevents the authorities and public bodies concerned from procuring some of the supplies they need from undertakings situated in other Member States. Accordingly, it must be held that products originating in other Member States suffer discrimination in comparison with products manufactured in the Member State in question, with the result that the normal course of intra-Community trade is hindered.

12. That conclusion is not affected by the fact that the restrictive effects of a preferential system of the kind at issue are borne in the same measure both by products manufactured by undertakings from the Member State in question which are not situated in the region covered by the preferential system and by products manufactured by undertakings established in other Member States.

13. It must be emphasised in the first place that, although not all the products of the Member State in question benefit by comparison with products from abroad, the fact remains that all the products benefiting by the preferential system are domestic products; secondly, the fact that the restrictive effect exercised by a state measure on imports does not benefit all domestic products but only some cannot exempt the measure in question from the prohibition set out in Article 30.

14. Furthermore, it must be observed that, on account of its discriminatory character, a system such as the one at issue cannot be justified in the light of the imperative requirements recognised by the court in its case law; such requirements may be taken into consideration only in relation to measures which are applicable to domestic products and to imported products without distinction (. . . Case 113/80 *Commission v Ireland* **[E22]**).

15. It must be added that neither does such a system fall within the scope of the exceptions exhaustively listed in Article 36 of the Treaty.

. . .

19. In its second question, the national court seeks to establish whether in the event that the rules in question might be regarded as aid within the meaning of Article 92 that might exempt them from the prohibition set out in Article 30.

20. In that regard, it is sufficient to recall that, as the court has consistently held (see, in particular, the judgment of 5 June 1986 in Case 103/84 *Commission v Italy* [1986] ECR 1759), Article 92 may in no case be used to frustrate the rules of the Treaty on the free movement of goods. It is clear from the relevant case law that those rules and the Treaty provisions relating to state aid have a common purpose, namely to ensure the free movement of goods between Member States under normal conditions of competition. As the court made clear in the judgment cited above, the fact that a national measure might be regarded as an aid within the meaning of Article 92 is therefore not a sufficient reason to exempt it from the prohibition contained in Article 30.

Questions

1. In the light of other cases on the meaning of 'restrictions' for the purpose of Article 30, do you agree that this was a discriminatory rule?

2. Why should the Court of Justice wish to give the application of Article 30 priority over the use of Article 92, the latter provision (it might be said) being specifically designed to monitor at Community level the particular benefits and disadvantages of schemes such as the one involved here?

[E44]   José Maria Fernández Martin and Oliver Stehmann: 'Product market integration versus regional cohesion in the Community' (1991) 16 European Law Review 216

The conflict between Articles 92 et seq with Article 30: a critical view

. . . we believe that the court's approach is . . . unsatisfactory in so far as it is excessively formalistic, confuses the scope and functions of different EEC Treaty provisions and thereby disregards economic reality. First of all, one of the grounds on which the Court of Justice justifies its position is that both sets of rules have a common objective, that is, to ensure the free movement of goods under normal conditions of competition. Although this is true, it is only partially so. One should not ignore that there is a second objective underlying Articles 92(3) and 93, namely, to grant the Commission the possibility to declare compatible with the EEC Treaty those aids which are intended to close the economic, social and regional gaps existing inside the Community. Therefore, the fact that some competition-distorting state aids may be permitted to operate proves that certain exceptions to the free movement of goods and to the free competition principles are to be admitted. This affirmation flows directly from Article 92(3)(a) which states that aids may be exempted from the general incompatibility principle laid down in Article 92(1), inter alia, those aids intended 'to promote the economic development of areas where the standard of living is abnormally low or where there is serious underemployment' in order to reduce 'the differences existing between the various regions and the backwardness of the less favoured regions'. Thus, state aids within the meaning of Article 92(3) have as a second but no less important function to act as incentive measures to close regional and economic gaps, that is, an economic cohesion function.

Secondly, the relation of both sets of rules maintained in this judgment may have certain undesirable consequences. Whereas this position might be justifiable on the basis of the *nemo auditur* principle in those cases in which no prior notification has taken place, applying Article 30 as interpreted in *Dassonville* [E12] without engaging in a deeper economic (or other) analysis risks obliterating Articles 92 and 93. After the *Dassonville* definition, almost anything would come under the 'imperium' of Article 30. State aids, by nature, always have a negative effect on inter-state trade when they strengthen national industry or regions. By artificially improving the competitiveness of national firms, competitive advantages of foreign firms are reduced or eliminated. Therefore, the imports that would have taken place are partly or entirely foreclosed. It is difficult to imagine any state aid that does not have any restrictive effect on trade. If one follows strictly the court's reasoning of giving priority to the application of Article 30, which is moreover not subject to a de minimis rule, Articles 92 and 93 would lose much of their sense.

Thirdly, from a procedural point of view the court's reasoning may also bring difficulties. Article 30 is directly applicable while Articles 92 and 93 are not so. Therefore, national courts are entitled to apply the former article as regards measures fulfilling the requirements of a measure equivalent to a quantitative restriction in the sense of the *Dassonville* case law. Following the court's *iter logicus*, when national courts detect restrictive effects on trade in a contested aid scheme – which is quite likely – in the sense of the *Dassonville* case law, they should give application to Article 30 and as a consequence declare void the contested measure. If the aid scheme has been notified to the Commission pursuant to Article 93, the latter could be faced with a national judicial decision which may not be in line with its own evaluation, which poses obvious problems as far as legal certainty is concerned. In other words, where is now the line dividing national courts and Community institutions competences as regards those cases where a pretended state aid is challenged as contrary to Article 30? These problems would not be resolved until the Court of Justice pronounced itself on the specific case, declaring the measure either as a state aid or a measure equivalent to a quantitative restriction, or established unequivocal guide lines for national judges to be followed. Moreover, the Commission's wide discretion, recognised in Article 93 and sanctioned by the court to accept aids as compatible with the common market, would remain impaired since it appears that no state aids with restrictive effects on trade in the sense of the *Dassonville* case law may be admitted. This can not certainly be the intention of the court, and further clarification in next cases is required.

From an economic point of view the court's position leads to favouring rapid market integration – represented by the free movement of goods provisions – to the detriment of regional cohesion – represented by the state aids provisions. In the context of the '1992' internal market this attitude is worrying. The transition from national economies to an European one should be achieved smoothly so as to avoid the increase of regional economic divergences. The speed with which trade barriers are dismantled in the Community increases sharply the need for quick measures to balance adverse effects on disfavoured regions. This pressure is especially borne by national governments as final responsible political actors before their own citizens. The whole picture is aggravated by the fact that measures undertaken at European level to balance these effects are far from sufficient. The Community's subsidiary role for regional policy has not been adapted to the new situation. Thus, with respect to the specific issue of public procurement, the Commission itself has recognised that the total opening of public markets to European competition will bring a need for transitional restructuring measures in the short run. It has therefore proposed some policies in order to facilitate this restructuring. These policies are however still far from being implemented. Thereby in the short run pressure on Member States is increased to alleviate unilaterally, the effects of increasing regional divergence. As a result, transitional corrective measures become mainly the responsibility of Member States.

These measures, which are objectively necessary, should be carefully evaluated in the light of Articles 92 and 93. It does not seem reasonable to pursue radical positions as regards state aids when no substitute mechanism has been developed at Community level. The founders of the Community provided for different legal means, amongst which were state aids provisions, to ensure that market integration was accompanied by an harmonious development within the Community. Therefore legal formalism should not neglect these considerations, and the court should be at least asked to reason its decisions in a more detailed manner, weighing the political and economic consequences of such a policy. This formalistic application of Article 30 may therefore generate at a political level, a sharp reaction of Member States.

6   Free movement of services

[E45]   Articles 59, 60 and 56 of the EC Treaty

Article 59

Within the framework of the provisions set out below, restrictions on freedom to provide services within the Community shall be progressively abolished . . . in respect of nationals of Member States who are established in a state of the Community other than that of the person for whom the services are intended.

The Council may, acting by a qualified majority on a proposal from the Commission, extend the provisions of this Chapter to nationals of a third country who provide services and who are established within the Community.

Article 60

Services shall be considered to be 'services' within the meaning of this Treaty where they are normally provided for remuneration, in so far as they are not governed by the provisions relating to freedom of movement for goods, capital and persons.

'Services' shall in particular include:

(a)   activities of an industrial character;
(b)   activities of a commercial character;
(c)   activities of craftsmen;
(d)   activities of the professions.

Without prejudice to the provisions of the Chapter relating to the right of establishment, the person providing a service may, in order to do so, temporarily pursue his activity in the state where the service is provided, under the same conditions as are imposed by that state on its own nationals.

Article 56 (applicable also to services by virtue of Article 66)

1. The provisions of this Chapter and measures taken in pursuance thereof shall not prejudice the applicability of provisions laid down by law, regulation or administrative action providing for special treatment for foreign nationals on grounds of public policy, public security or public health.

Note.   See also the comments made as to the residual nature of the services provisions made in extracts **[E27]** and **[E28]**.

[E46] Case C-198/89 Commission v Greece ('tourist guides') [1991] ECR I-727

The European Court of Justice

1. . . . [T]he Commission brought an application under Article 169 of the EEC Treaty for a declaration that by making the provision of services by tourist guides accompanying groups of tourists from another Member State subject to possession of a licence which requires specific training evidenced by a diploma where those services consist in guiding tourists in places other than museums or historical monuments which may be visited only with a specialised professional guide, the Hellenic Republic has failed to fulfil its obligations under Article 59 of the Treaty.

2. . . . Under [the provisions in issue], tourist guides are persons who accompany foreign or national tourists or visitors to the country, guide them and show them local points of interest, historic or ancient monuments, works of art of each period, and explain their significance, their purpose and their history, and give general information on classical and present-day Greece.

. . .

5. As a preliminary matter it should be pointed out that the activities of a tourist guide from a Member State other than Greece who accompanies tourists on an organised tour from that other Member State to Greece may be subject to two distinct sets of legal rules. A tour company established in another Member State may itself employ guides. In that case it is the tour company that provides the service to tourists through its own guides. A tour company may also engage self-employed tourist guides established in that other Member State. In that case, the service is provided by the guide to the tour company.

6. The two cases described above thus relate to the provision of services by the tour company to tourists and by the self-employed tourist guide to the tour company respectively. Such services, which are of limited duration and are not governed by the provisions on the free movement of goods, capitals and persons, constitute activities carried on for remuneration within the meaning of Article 60 of the EEC Treaty.

7. It must be determined whether such activities fall within the scope of Article 59 of the Treaty.

8. In that connection the Greek government argued that Article 59 of the Treaty applies only where a person providing services and their recipients are established in different Member States.

9. Although Article 59 of the Treaty expressly contemplates only the situation of a person providing services who is established in a Member State other than that in which the recipient of the service is established, the purpose of that Article is nevertheless to abolish restrictions on the freedom to provide services by persons who are not established in the state in which the service is to be provided (see judgment in Case 76/81 *Transporoute v Minister of Public Works* [1982] ECR 417 . . .). It is only when all the relevant elements of the activity in question are confined within a single Member State that the provisions of the Treaty on freedom to provide services cannot apply (judgment in Case 52/79 *Procureur du Roi v Debauve* [1980] ECR 833 . . .).

10. Consequently, the provisions of Article 59 must apply in all cases where a person providing services offers those services in a Member State other than that in which he is established, wherever the recipients of those services may be established.

11. Since the present case and the two situations described in paragraph 5 of this judgment concern the provision of services in a Member State other than that in which the person providing them is established, Article 59 of the Treaty must apply.

. . .

15. It is therefore necessary to examine whether, in the absence of any Community harmonisation, the application of the Greek legislation in question to tourist guides accompanying a group of tourists from another Member State is compatible with Articles 59 and 60.

. . .

16. It should further be pointed out that Articles 59 and 60 of the Treaty require not only the abolition of any discrimination against a person providing services on account of his nationality but also the abolition of any restriction on the freedom to provide services imposed on the ground that the person providing a service is established in a Member State other than the one in which the service is provided. In particular, the Member State cannot make the performance of the services in its territory subject to observance of all the conditions required for establishment; were it to do so the provisions securing freedom to provide services would be deprived of all practical effect.

17. The requirement imposed by the above-mentioned provisions of Greek legislation amounts to such a restriction. By making the provision of services by tourist guides accompanying a group of tourists from another Member State subject to possession of a specific qualification, that legislation prevents both tour companies from providing that service with their own staff and self-employed tourist guides from offering their services to those companies for organised tours. It also prevents tourists from taking part in such organised tours from availing themselves at will of the services in question.

18. However, in view of the specific requirements in relation to certain services, the fact that a Member State makes the provision thereof subject to conditions as to the qualifications of the person providing them, pursuant to rules governing such activities within its jurisdiction, cannot be considered incompatible with Articles 59 and 60 of the Treaty. Nevertheless, as one of the fundamental principles of the Treaty the freedom to provide services may be restricted only by rules which are justified in the general interest and are applied to all persons and undertakings operating in the territory of the state where the service is provided, in so far as that interest is not safeguarded by the rules to which the provider of such a service is subject in the Member State where he is established. In addition, such requirements must be objectively justified by the need to ensure that professional rules of conduct are complied with and that the interests which such rules are designed to safeguard are protected (see inter alia . . . Case 205/84 *Commission v Germany* [1986] ECR 3755 . . .).

19. Accordingly, those requirements can be regarded as compatible with Articles 59 and 60 of the Treaty only if it is established that with regard to

the activity in question there are overriding reasons relating to the public interest which justify restrictions on the freedom to provide services, that the public interest is not already protected by the rules of the state of establishment and that the same result cannot be obtained by less restrictive rules.

20. The Greek government contends that the legislation in question is justified by the general interest in proper appreciation of the artistic and archaeological heritage of the country and in consumer protection. In that connection, it stresses the fundamental difference between the written and oral transmission of information on that heritage. In its view, the Greek authorities regulate the quality of printed material circulating within the country and take care that material disseminated outside Greece presents in a correct manner the country's artistic and cultural heritage. Control of information communicated orally by a tourist guide to a specific group of tourists would on the other hand be more difficult. The Greek government considers that the legislation in issue is all the more justified since in some Member States the occupation of tourist guide may be carried on without any occupational qualification.

21. The general interest in the proper appreciation of the artistic and archaeological heritage of a country and in consumer protection can constitute an overriding reason justifying a restriction on the freedom to provide services. However, the requirement in question contained in the Greek legislation goes beyond what is necessary to ensure the safeguarding of that interest inasmuch as it makes the activities of a tourist guide accompanying groups of tourists from another Member State subject to possession of a licence.

22. The service of accompanying tourists is performed under quite specific conditions. The independent or employed tourist guide travels with the tourists and accompanies them in a closed group; in that group they move temporarily from the Member State of establishment to the Member State to be visited.

23. In those circumstances a licence requirement imposed by the Member State of destination has the effect of reducing the number of tourist guides qualified to accompany tourists in a closed group, which may lead a tour operator to have recourse instead to local guides employed or established in the Member State in which the service is to be performed. However, that consequence may have the drawback that tourists who are the recipients of the services in question do not have a guide who is familiar with their language, their interests and their specific expectations.

24. Moreover, the profitable operation of such group tours depends on the commercial reputation of the operator, who faces competitive pressure from other tour companies; the need to maintain that reputation and the competitive pressure themselves compel companies to be selective in employing tourist guides and exercise some control over the quality of their services. Depending on the specific expectations of the groups of tourists in question, that factor is likely to contribute to the proper appreciation of the artistic and archaeological heritage and the protection of consumers, in the case of conducted tours of places other than museums or historical monuments which may be visited only with a professional guide.

25. It follows that in view of the scale of the restrictions it imposes, the legislation in issue is disproportionate in relation to the objective pursued, namely to ensure the proper appreciation of places and things of historical interest, the widest possible dissemination of knowledge and the artistic

and cultural heritage of the Member State in which the tour is conducted, and the protection of consumers.

26. The Greek government further submits that it is impossible to reconcile the Commission's point of view as expressed in its application with the action taken by it at the same time with a view to the adoption of the proposal for a directive on a second general system for the recognition of professional education and training (1989 OJ C263/1), which complements Council Directive 89/48 . . . on a general system for the recognition of higher education diplomas awarded on completion of professional education and training of at least three years' duration (OJ 1989 L19/16).

27. It is true that in the case of occupations in respect of which the Community has laid down no minimum level of necessary qualifications, that proposal for a directive allows Member States themselves to determine that minimum level.

28. Nevertheless, it should be recalled that provisions of secondary legislation can only concern national measures which are compatible with the requirements of Article 59 of the Treaty, as defined in the case law of the court.

29. It must consequently be held that by making the provision of services by tourist guides travelling with a group of tourists from another Member State, where those services consist in guiding such tourists in places other than museums and historical monuments which may be visited only with a specialised professional guide, subject to possession of a licence which requires specific training evidenced by a diploma, the Hellenic Republic has failed to fulfil its obligations under Article 59 of the Treaty.

[E47]   Case C-288/89, Stichting Collectieve Antennevoorziening Gouda and others v Commissariaat voor de Media [1991] ECR I-4007

The European Court of Justice

1. By decision of 30 August 1989, which was received at the court on 19 September 1989, the Administrative Appeal Section of the Raad van State (State Council), the Netherlands, referred to the court for a preliminary ruling three questions on the interpretation of the provisions of the EEC Treaty concerning the freedom to provide services, in order to assess the compatibility with Community law of national legislation laying down conditions for the transmission by cable of radio and television programmes broadcast from other Member States which contain advertising specifically intended for the Dutch public.

2. Those questions were raised in proceedings between ten operators of cable networks and the Commissariaat voor de Media, the institution responsible for supervising the operation of cable networks, regarding conditions imposed by the Dutch law of 21 April 1987 governing the supply of radio and television programmes, radio and television licence fees and press subsidies *(Staatsblad* No 249 of 4 June 1987, hereinafter referred to as 'the Mediawet') on the transmission of advertising contained in radio or television programmes broadcast from abroad. The cable network

operators consider that these conditions are contrary to Article 59 et seq of the EEC Treaty.

3. The conditions in question are contained in Article 66 of the Mediawet, which provides as follows:

(I) The operator of a cable network may:
(a) transmit programmes which are broadcast by a foreign broadcasting body by means of a broadcasting transmitter and which may, most of the time, be received directly in the area served by the cable network by means of a normal individual aerial with a reasonable standard of quality;
(b) transmit programmes other than those mentioned in (a) which are broadcast by a foreign broadcasting body or a group of such bodies as broadcasting programmes, in accordance with the legislation in force in the broadcasting country. If such programmes contain advertisements, they may be transmitted solely provided that the advertisements are produced by a separate legal person, that they are clearly identifiable as such and clearly separated from other parts and are not broadcast on Sundays, that the duration of such advertisements does not exceed 5% of the total air time utilised, that the broadcasting body fulfils the conditions laid down in Article 55(1) and that the entire revenue is used for the production of programmes. Nevertheless, if those conditions are not fulfilled, such a programme may also be transmitted provided that the advertisements contained therein are not specifically intended for the Dutch public;

. . .

(2) For the purposes of the application of paragraph I(b), advertisements shall, in any event, be deemed to be intended specifically for the Dutch public if they are broadcast during or immediately after a portion of a programme or a coherent group of programmes containing Dutch sub-titles or a portion of a programme in Dutch.

(3) Our Minister may grant an exemption from the prohibition contained in paragraph I(b) in respect of programmes broadcast in Belgium intended for the Dutch-speaking public in that country.

4. Article 55(1) of the Mediawet provides that in principle 'bodies which have obtained air time may not be used to enable a third party to make a profit . . .'.

5. By decision of 6 January 1988 a fine was imposed by the Commissariaat voor de Media on each of the ten cable network operators on the ground they had transmitted programmes broadcast by foreign broadcasting bodies containing advertising entirely or partly in Dutch which did not fulfil the conditions laid down in Article 66(1)(b), set out above.

6. The cable network operators appealed against that decision to the Administrative Appeal Section of the Raad van State on the ground that Article 66(1)(b) of the Mediawet was contrary to Articles 56 and 59 of the EEC Treaty.

7. The Raad van State then decided that it was necessary to refer to the court for a preliminary ruling three questions on the interpretation of Article 59 et seq of the Treaty.

The field of application of Article 59 of the Treaty

9. By those questions the national court seeks to establish whether conditions such as those imposed by the Mediawet on the transmission by operators of cable networks of radio or television programmes broadcast from the territory of other Member States are covered by Article 59 of the Treaty and, if so, whether they may be justified.

10. In this respect, the court has consistently held (see, most recently, the judgments in Case C-154/89 *Commission v France* [1991] ECR I-659, paragraph 12, Case C-180/89 *Commission v Italy* [1991] ECR I-709, paragraph 15, and Case C-198/89 *Commission v Greece* **[E46]**, paragraph 16) that Article 59 of the Treaty entails, in the first place, the abolition of any discrimination against a person providing services on account of his nationality or the fact that he is established in a Member State other than the one in which the service is provided.

11. As the court held in its judgment in Case 352/85 *Bond van Adverteerders* [1988] ECR 2085, at paragraphs 32 and 33, national rules which are not applicable to services without discrimination as regards their origin are compatible with Community law only if they can be brought within the scope of an express exemption, such as that contained in Article 56 of the Treaty. It also appears from that judgment (paragraph 34) that economic aims cannot constitute grounds of public policy within the meaning of Article 56 of the Treaty.

12. In the absence of harmonisation of the rules applicable to services, or even of a system of equivalence, restrictions on the freedom guaranteed by the Treaty in this field may arise in the second place as a result of the application of national rules which affect any person established in the national territory to persons providing services established in the territory of another Member State who already have to satisfy the requirements of that state's legislation.

13. As the court has consistently held (see, most recently, the judgments in *Commission v France,* cited above, paragraph 15; *Commission v Italy,* cited above, paragraph 18; and *Commission v Greece,* cited above, paragraph 18), such restrictions come within the scope of Article 59 if the application of the national legislation to foreign persons providing services is not justified by overriding reasons relating to the public interest or if the requirements embodied in that legislation are already satisfied by the rules imposed on those persons in the Member State in which they are established.

14. In this respect, the overriding reasons relating to the public interest which the court has already recognised include professional rules intended to protect recipients of the service (Joined Cases 110/78 and 111/78 *Van Wesemael* [1979] ECR 35, paragraph 28); protection of intellectual property (Case 62/79 *Coditel* [1980] ECR 881); the protection of workers (Case 279/80 *Webb* [1981] ECR 3305, paragraph 19; Joined Cases 62/81 and 63/81 *Seco v EVI* [1982] ECR 223, paragraph 14; Case C-113/89 *Rush Portuguesa* [1990] ECR I-1417, paragraph 18); consumer protection (Case 220/83 *Commission v France* [1986] ECR 3663, paragraph 20; Case 252/83 *Commission v Denmark* [1986] ECR 3713, paragraph 20; Case 205/84 *Commission v Germany* [1986] ECR 3755, paragraph 30; Case 206/84 *Commission v Ireland* [1986] ECR 3817, paragraph 20; *Commission v Italy* cited above, paragraph 20; and *Commission v Greece,*

cited above, paragraph 21), the conservation of the national historic and artistic heritage *(Commission v Italy,* cited above, paragraph 20); turning to account the archaeological, historical and artistic heritage of a country and the widest possible dissemination of knowledge of the artistic and cultural heritage of a country *(Commission v France,* cited above, paragraph 17, and *Commission v Greece,* cited above, paragraph 21).

15. Lastly, as the court has consistently held, the application of national provisions to providers of services established in other Member States must be such as to guarantee the achievement of the intended aim and must not go beyond that which is necessary in order to achieve that objective. In other words, it must not be possible to obtain the same result by less restrictive rules (see, most recently, Case C-154/89 *Commission v France,* . . . Case C-180/89 *Commission v Italy,* . . . Case C-198/89 *Commission v Greece,* [all] cited above . . .).

16. It is in the light of those principles that it should be examined whether a provision such as Article 66(1)(b) of the Mediawet, which, according to the national court, is not discriminatory, contains restrictions on freedom to provide services and, if so, whether those restrictions may be justified.

The existence of restrictions on the freedom to provide services

17. It must be noted at the outset that conditions such as those imposed by the second sentence of Article 66(1)(b) of the Mediawet contain a twofold restriction on freedom to provide services. First, they prevent operators of cable networks established in a Member State from transmitting radio or television programmes supplied by broadcasters established in other Member States which do not satisfy those conditions. Secondly, they restrict the opportunities afforded to those broadcasting bodies to include in their programmes for the benefit in particular of advertisers established in the state in which the programmes are received advertising intended specifically for the public in that state.

18. Accordingly, the reply to be given to the national court's first question should be that conditions such as those set out in the second sentence of Article 66(1)(b) of the Mediawet constitute restrictions on the freedom to provide services covered by Article 59 of the Treaty.

The possibility of justifying those restrictions

19. As the Commission rightly pointed out, those conditions fall into two different categories. First, there are those relating to the structure of the broadcasters: they must entrust advertising to a legal person independent of the suppliers of programmes; they must use all their advertising revenue for the production of programmes; and they may not permit third parties to make a profit. Secondly, there are conditions relating to the advertisements themselves: they must be clearly recognisable as such and separated from the other parts of the programme; they may not exceed 5% of air time; and they must not be broadcast on Sundays.

20. In order to answer the national court's second and third questions, which essentially seek to establish whether such restrictions may be justified, those conditions should be examined separately.

A . The conditions relating to the structure of broadcasting bodies established in other Member States

21. As regards the conditions relating to the structure of broadcasting bodies established in other Member States, the Netherlands government explains that these are identical to the conditions which Dutch broadcasting bodies must fulfil. Thus, the requirement that the advertisements must be produced by a legal person separate from the producers of the programmes corresponds to the prohibition imposed by the Mediawet on national bodies' broadcasting commercial advertising, as this is reserved to the Stichting Etherreclame (television advertising foundation) (hereinafter referred to as 'the STER'). The obligation imposed on broadcasting bodies in other Member States not to permit a third party to make a profit is intended to guarantee the non-commercial nature of broadcasting, which the Mediawet seeks to maintain for national broadcasting bodies. Lastly, the purpose of the requirement relating to the assignment of advertising revenue, namely that it must be reserved for the production of programmes, is to provide broadcasting bodies in other Member States with funds at least equivalent to those obtaining under the national system, where most of the STER's advertising revenue covers radio and television operating costs.

22. The Netherlands government maintains that those restrictions are justified by imperatives relating to the cultural policy which it has implemented in the audiovisual sector. It explains that the aim of this policy is to safeguard the freedom of expression of the various — in particular social, cultural, religious and philosophical — components of the Netherlands in order that that freedom may be capable of being exercised in the press, on the radio or on television. It says that that objective may be jeopardised by the excessive influence of advertisers over the content of programmes.

23. A cultural policy understood in that sense may indeed constitute an overriding requirement relating to the general interest which justifies a restriction on the freedom to provide services. The maintenance of the pluralism which that Dutch policy seeks to safeguard is connected with freedom of expression, as protected by Article 10 of the European Convention on Human Rights and Fundamental Freedoms, which is one of the fundamental rights guaranteed by the Community legal order (Case 4/73 *Nold v Commission* [1974] ECR 491, paragraph 13 **[B44]**).

24. However, it should be observed that there is no necessary connection between such a cultural policy and the conditions relating to the structure of foreign broadcasting bodies. In order to ensure pluralism in the audiovisual sector it is not indispensable for the national legislation to require broadcasting bodies established in other Member States to align themselves on the Dutch model should they intend to broadcast programmes containing advertisements intended for the Dutch public. In order to secure the pluralism which it wishes to maintain the Netherlands government may very well confine itself to formulating the statutes of its own bodies in an appropriate manner.

25. Conditions affecting the structure of foreign broadcasting bodies cannot therefore be regarded as being objectively necessary in order to safeguard the general interest in maintaining a national radio and television system which secures pluralism.

B. The conditions relating to advertising

26. Contrary to the view advanced by the Commission, the Netherlands government maintains that neither the prohibition on the broadcasting of advertisements on certain days, the limitation of their duration or the obligation to identify them as such and to separate them from other parts of programmes is discriminatory. The services provided by the STER are subject to the same restrictions. In this connection, the Netherlands government referred to Article 39 of the Mediawet. It appears from that provision that the Commissariaat voor de Media allocates to the STER air time available on the national network, which must be allocated in such a manner that the programmes of the national broadcasting bodies are not interrupted. Moreover, under the same provision, no air time is to be allocated on Sundays.

27. In this respect, it must be observed in the first place that restrictions on the broadcasting of advertisements, such as a prohibition on advertising particular products or on certain days, a limitation of the duration or frequency of advertisements or restrictions designed to enable listeners or viewers not to confuse advertising with other parts of the programme, may be justified by overriding reasons relating to the general interest. Such restrictions may be imposed in order to protect consumers against excessive advertising or, as an objective of cultural policy, in order to maintain a certain level of programme quality.

28. Next, it should be observed that the restrictions in question relate solely to the market in advertising intended specifically for the Dutch public. That market was also the only market covered by the prohibition on advertising contained in the Kabelregeling which gave rise to the questions which were referred to the court for a preliminary ruling in the *Bond van Adverteerders* case (cited above). Even if the advertising relates to products which may be consumed in the Netherlands, the restrictions apply only if the advertisements accompany programmes in Dutch or subtitled in Dutch. Moreover, the restrictions may be lifted with regard to programmes in Dutch broadcast in Belgium and intended for the Belgian Dutch-speaking public.

29. Unlike the Kabelregeling, the provisions of the Mediawet at issue in this case no longer reserve to the STER all the revenue from advertising intended specifically for the Dutch public. However, by laying down rules on the broadcasting of such advertisements they restrict the competition to which the STER may be exposed in that market from foreign broadcasting bodies. Accordingly the result is that they protect the revenue of the STER — albeit to a lesser degree than the Kabelregeling — and therefore pursue the same objective as the previous legislation. As the court held in the *Bond van Adverteerders* case (cited above), at paragraph 34, that objective cannot justify restrictions on the freedom to provide services.

30. Accordingly, the reply to be given to the national court's second and third questions should be that restrictions of the kind at issue are not justified by overriding requirements relating to the general interest.

Notes

1. Technological advance has meant that the provision of services need no longer entail physical crossing of borders by provider or recipient, a fact which the Court of Justice has had to recognise, especially in the field of broadcasting.

2. Although taking longer to develop, the services case law has yielded a notion of public interest which seems to correspond to the various *Cassis* heads applied to goods. See also Article 90(2) **[E83]** for another possible source for building a unitary notion of the 'Community interest'.

SECTION TWO

COMPETITION POLICY

MATERIALS

1 Directions

[E48] EC Commission: XXIInd Report on Competition Policy ((1993) COM 162 final, 5 May 1993)

Introduction

Alongside the establishment of a common market, competition policy is one of the two great strategies by which the Treaty of Rome sets out to achieve the Community's fundamental objectives: the promotion of harmonious and balanced economic development throughout the Community, an improved standard of living, and closer relations between the Member States. Competition policy cannot therefore be pursued in isolation, as an end in itself, without reference to the legal, economic, political and social context.

Rapid changes in that context call for rigorous consistency and steadfastness in applying the competition rules, combined with greater flexibility in adapting to the new situation and staying in tune with the objectives which the Community has set itself for economic and social cohesion, industrial competitiveness, research and technological development, and the environment.

In addition to the completion of the internal market, the progress being made in technology, and the globalisation of markets, there are two new factors which competition policy must take into account:
 – the slowdown in economic growth, with its social consequences, and
 – the application of the principle of subsidiarity.
These developments are combining to create an environment in which competition between firms is fiercer than ever, while the tendency to adopt a defensive and protectionist posture has never been so strong. At the same time the Maastricht debate shows that the greatest possible clarity is needed in the Commission's efforts to ensure that competition is not distorted.

. . .

The policy priorities detailed in previous reports remain unchanged; in particular, competition policy seeks to contribute to the achievement of a genuinely frontier-free area, and to economic and social cohesion, by throwing open markets which might otherwise be protected by exclusive rights, restrictive practices, the abuse of dominant positions, or state aid.

. . .

The main challenges facing competition policy are without any doubt the introduction of competition into regulated sectors and the monitoring of state aid. State monopolies and exclusive rights have to be seen in their new context, which is the single market: change and competition are vital if the four fundamental freedoms are to be given practical effect, and the benefits of the single market are to materialise. This is particularly so as technological progress and the demands of users are removing the rationale of some monopolies, for example in telecommunications. But there has to be a proper balance between this drive for economic efficiency and the need to take account of the social dimension and to maintain a universal service, or in the case of sectors such as gas and electricity to maintain security of supply as well.

There is just as delicate a balance to be observed in the field of state aid, particularly at a time when the economic going is difficult and strong pressure is being brought to bear on the public authorities by firms which face more intense competition and a slowdown in demand. The Commission looks at cases from a Community rather than a national angle, and seeks to distinguish aid whose harmful effect on competition is offset by its contribution to economic growth, to structural adjustment and to economic and social cohesion from aid which impedes development towards more efficient structures and serves merely to export problems to other Member States.

The globalisation of markets and the knock-on effects of certain anti-competitive behaviour outside the Community mean that policy must broaden to take account of the international dimension. The scope of Community law is confined to conduct or measures implemented inside the Community. But some practices outside the Community may affect the Community market; and Community firms may have to contend with anti-competitive practices on non-Community markets. The main competition policy response to this situation is to seek to encourage the application of similar policies by the Community's main trading partners, by means of bilateral agreements or through multilateral negotiation. Unlike protectionism, a broadening of competition policy of this kind is ultimately in the interests both of the Community and of its partners.

The transparency and subsidiarity debates have also highlighted the need for wider familiarity with the objectives of the rules and mechanisms of competition policy as a factor in industrial competitiveness. The policy cannot be effective if its objectives are not embraced by the business community. The Commission accordingly pressed ahead with its policy of transparency; it approved a considerable number of regulations and codes and published various explanatory booklets.

. . .

A successful competition policy depends very much on proper application of the principle of subsidiarity, with matters being handled at the level at which they can be dealt with most effectively. The Commission is firmly in favour of a decentralised application of competition law, which would allow the appropriate authorities in the Member States to deal with cases, whose implications are essentially domestic, leaving the Commission free to concentrate its resources on the cases which it alone is capable of resolving. The process should be facilitated by the notice which the Commission approved this year on co-operation between national courts and the Commission in applying Articles 85 and 86 of the EEC Treaty **[E63]**. The measures taken to improve transparency should help to ensure the wide awareness which decentralisation will require.

[E49]   The EC Treaty framework

Article 3(f) (renumbered by the Treaty of Union as Article 3(g))

For the purposes of Article 2 **[A1]**, the activities of the Community shall include . . . the institution of a system ensuring that competiton in the common market is not distorted.

Article 85 (restrictive agreements, decisions and concerted practices between undertakings)

1. The following shall be prohibited as incompatible with the common market: all agreements between undertakings, decisions by associations of undertakings and concerted practices which may affect trade between Member States and which have as their object or effect the prevention restriction or distortion of competition within the common market, and in particular those which:

(a)   directly or indirectly fix purchase or selling prices or any other trading conditions;
(b)   limit or control production, markets, technical development, or investment;
(c)   share markets or sources of supply;
(d)   apply dissimilar conditions to equivalent transactions with other trading parties, thereby placing them at a competitive disadvantage;
(e)   make the conclusion of contracts subject to acceptance by the other parties of supplementary obligations which, by their nature or according to commercial usage, have no connection with the subject of such contracts.

2. Any agreements or decisions prohibited pursuant to this Article shall be automatically void.

3. The provisions of paragraph 1 may, however, be declared inapplicable in the case of:

– any agreement or category of agreements between undertakings;
– any decision or category of decisions by associations of undertakings;
– any concerted practice or category of concerted practices;

which contributes to improving the production or distribution of goods or to promoting technical or economic progress, while allowing consumers a fair share of the resulting benefit, and which does not:

(a)   impose on the undertakings concerned restrictions which are not indispensable to the attainment of these objectives;
(b)   afford such undertakings the possibility of eliminating competition in respect of a substantial part of the products in question.

Article 86 (abuse of a dominant position)

Any abuse by one or more undertakings of a dominant position within the common market or in a substantial part of it shall be prohibited as incompatible with the common market in so far as it may affect trade between Member States. Such abuse may, in particular, consist in:

(a)   directly or indirectly imposing unfair purchase or selling prices or unfair trading conditions;

(b)   limiting production, markets or technical development to the prejudice of consumers;

(c)   applying dissimilar conditions to equivalent transactions with other trading parties, thereby placing them at a competitive disadvantage;

(d)   making the conclusion of contracts subject to acceptance by the other parties of supplementary obligations which, by their nature or according to commercial usage, have no connection with the subject of such contracts.

[See also the measures aimed at state intervention **[E83]**.]

2   Analysing objectionable collusion under Article 85

[E50]   Cases C-89/85 and others Re Wood Pulp [1993] 4 CMLR 407

Opinion of Advocate General Darmon

A.   The concept of concerted practices

166. In prohibiting concerted practices, Article 85(1) EEC did not define that concept. The court has had the matter raised before it on numerous occasions and has therefore been able to provide guidance of some value in a number of noted cases. However, I cannot dissemble the fact that there is still, in my view, some uncertainty regarding the definition of concerted practices. Quite clearly, it is necessary to proceed with caution in order to avoid general forms of words which are too constricting in areas in which the law is faced with changing and complex economic realities. Courts must not engage in academic theorising. However, one is not succumbing to the temptation to theorise if one seeks to clarify certain concepts where the requirements of legal certainty are at stake. Traders must have a clear frame of reference to ascertain which practices are prohibited by competition law rules. Besides, who would deny that the effectiveness of the law depends on its precision? Let us therefore now attempt to identify the elements which make up the concept of concerted practices.

167. One point may already be considered established: a concerted practice is to be distinguished from a formal agreement between undertakings. In *Dyestuffs*, the court made it clear that:

[although] Article 85 draws a distinction between the concept of 'concerted practices' and that of 'agreements between undertakings' . . . the object is to bring within the prohibition of that Article a form of co-ordination between undertakings which, without having reached the stage where an agreement properly so-called has been concluded . . . substitutes practical co-operation between them for the risks of competition.

A concerted practice 'by its very nature, then, does not have all the elements of' an agreement and therefore constitutes a legal category *sui generis*, independent of the latter.

. . .

168. Far more delicate is the question which then arises: what is the substance of the concertation required between undertakings? In *Suiker Unie,* the court stated that

the criteria of *co-ordination and co-operation* . . ., which *in no way require the working out of an actual plan,* must be understood in the light of the concept inherent in the provisions of the Treaty relating to competition that each economic operator must determine *independently* the policy which he intends to adopt on the Common Market.

The court added that:

this requirement of independence . . . however strictly preclude[s] *any direct or indirect contact* between . . . [competitors], the object or effect whereof is either to influence the conduct on the market of an actual or potential competitor or to disclose to such a competitor the course of conduct which they themselves have decided to adopt or contemplate adopting on the market.

169. Those indicators are very broad in scope. They cover every form and method of contact between undertakings. From that point of view, the court has quite rightly drawn the conclusions from the *informality* that is implicit in the very concept of a concerted practice. Similarly, the court has considered that contacts for the joint *determination* and *fixing* of future conduct are unnecessary, once again in accordance with the specific nature of that concept in relation to that of an agreement. However, certain commentators have taken the view that the court has widened the concept of concerted practices by including unilateral action by undertakings not capable of constituting concertation which presupposes joint discussions or the exchange of views.

170. I doubt whether it is possible to restrict to those two specific situations the instances of prohibited concertation. The *form* of the contacts between undertakings matters little. On the other hand, it is clear to me that *by definition* concertation requires *reciprocation* of communications between competitors. Article 85(1) cannot apply to unilateral action by undertakings. But that is what would happen if the requirement of reciprocal communications, by whatever means, was not laid down. In its aforesaid case law the court does not seem to me to have laid sufficient emphasis on that requirement. There are, however, some indications in more recent judgments that seem to postulate some reciprocity.

171. Thus, in *Züchner,* the court stated that a national court:

must consider whether between the banks conducting themselves in like manner there are contacts or, at least, exchanges of information.

Clearly, such reciprocity of communication between competitors is something that must be defined in each individual case. At this stage, therefore, it is apparent that concertation presupposes reciprocal communications between undertakings, whatever the form. That being so, what must their purpose be?

172. As I have said, it is not necessary that by means of such communications competitors jointly determine their future conduct. It is apparent from some of the court's decisions that it is necessary, though sufficient, that by virtue of their communications the competitors have removed the uncertainty as to their future market conduct. Thus, in *Dyestuffs,* the court stated that:

it is contrary to the rules on competition contained in the Treaty for a producer to co-operate with his competitors, in any way whatsoever, in order to determine a co-ordinated course of action relating to a price increase and to ensure its success by *prior elimination of all uncertainty* as to each other's conduct regarding the essential elements of that action, such as the amount, subject matter, date and place of the increases.

In *Züchner*, the court referred to an identical requirement in connexion with the exchange of information on:

the rate of the charges actually imposed for comparable transfers *which have been carried out or are planned for the future.*

173. In other words, concertation must *at the very least* give the participants an *assurance* as to the conduct to be expected of their competitors; each of them can foresee the future actions of the others.

174. It follows from those observations that the concept of concerted practices refers to reciprocal communications between competitors with the aim of giving each other assurances as to their conduct on the market. As one writer has pointed out [Joliet [1974] CDE 251], the definition proposed by the Commission in the *Dyestuffs* case synthesises those elements perfectly:

it is enough that they (the competitors) *let each other* know beforehand what attitude they intended to adopt, so that each of them could regulate his conduct, *safe in the knowledge* that his competitors would act in a similar fashion.

175. It is further necessary that the competitors' knowledge of each other's conduct stem from communications between them, and not simply from monitoring the market.

176. In its case law, the court has been at pains to point out that:

every producer is free to change his prices, *taking into account in so doing the present or foreseeable conduct of his competitors.*

It has also stated that

this requirement of independence does not deprive traders of the right to adapt themselves intelligently to the existing or anticipated conduct of their competitors.

The court therefore recognises that each undertaking is entitled to align itself independently on the conduct of its competitors, if knowledge of such conduct is obtained solely by monitoring the market.

177. That is a vital factor having regard to the principles of economic theory. Parallel conduct is not necessarily the result of prior concertation. It can be explained, or even dictated, by the very structure of certain markets. As a summary outline, let me refer to the two examples most frequently mentioned in that regard. The first situation involves a concentrated oligopoly, in which undertakings are interdependent: each undertaking must take account in its decisions of the conduct of its rivals. Alignment on each other's conduct constitutes a rational response, independently of any concertation. 'Price leadership' constitutes the second situation: undertakings align themselves on a 'price leader' on account of the latter's power on the market. Mention may also be made of spontaneous alignment on a price leader which acts as a barometer, with its decisions reflecting

changes in market conditions for reasons linked, for instance, to its previous knowledge of that market.

178. In view of the findings made in the contested decision, two further sets of remarks are called for.

179. In the first place, the question may arise whether in itself monitoring the conduct of competitors falls in any event outside the scope of the rules of competition. What is the position where the decisions of each undertaking operating on the market immediately or very rapidly come to the knowledge of its competitors? In the 1970s the United States anti-trust authorities instituted proceedings against conduct known as 'price signalling' with a view to prohibiting in certain cases indirect 'discussions' in public between competitors or even public price announcements.

180. In my view, the greatest caution must be exercised in calling in question the practices known as 'price signalling'. To begin with, challenging public price announcements even when made in advance seems to me to call for very serious reservations. It must be borne in mind that such announcements do meet quite legitimate and normal business requirements. Who would deny, in particular, that purchasers may in some cases need to know prices some time in advance so as to be able to determine their own costs and their own prices in order to notify those prices to their own customers? In a market economy, information which a producer communicates to his customers, whether actual or potential, is of fundamental importance.

. . .

181. That, in my view, is the basic consideration which must be borne in mind in connection with 'price signalling'. However, it would be irrational to deny as a matter of principle that concertation between competitors may take the form of exchanges of information which, whilst being public, are none the less reciprocal and are such as to remove any uncertainty regarding the conduct of rival undertakings. From that point of view, the difficulty clearly lies in eliciting the criteria for demarcating 'permissible' public price announcements from a public exchange of information which is open to criticism. In that regard, reference has been made to 'complex, unusual and artificial' [Kestenbaum, (1980) 91 Anti-trust Law Journal 914] practices which, lacking any commercial justification, in fact establish a public dialogue between undertakings by giving mutual assurances as regards each other's conduct.

182. If it were possible to identify the reciprocal nature of the communications in question, I would see no reason not to treat them as an element of concertation just because it is exchanged publicly, when the same exchanges recorded in the minutes drawn up at the end of a meeting held behind closed doors would constitute a breach of the competition rules. Let me emphasise, however, that a situation of that kind is not connected in any way with 'mere' price announcements which are, in principle, unilateral acts on the market and cannot therefore by themselves constitute a concerted practice.

183. It remains to be determined, and this is my second point, what is the scope of a finding of identical conduct on the market, that is to say parallel conduct, in relation to the concept of concerted practices.

184. In other words, is similar conduct by undertakings included in an 'objective' element within the concept of concerted practices? Some of my predecessors have answered that question in the affirmative [see Advocate

General Mayras in the *Dyestuffs* case]. However, the view has also been taken that it is wrong to include parallel conduct within the actual concept of concerted practices. It is in the field of evidence that parallelism of conduct should be situated: it may point to the existence of concertation if it cannot be explained other than by concertation.

185. The first view may be supported by reference to the actual wording of the Treaty: does the use of the term 'practice' not seem to refer to actual conduct on the market? However, attention must be drawn to the scheme of Article 85(1) which prohibits not only concerted practices having the effect of restricting competition but also those whose *object* is to achieve that result. If parallel conduct is included within the concept of concerted practices as an 'objective criterion', how can the prohibition in Article 85(1) not extend to types of concertation which, albeit not implemented, nevertheless pursued a restrictive object? Accordingly, to take the view that de facto identical conduct forms part of the concept of concerted practices would lead to a particularly restrictive conception of the Treaty, which is contrary to the scheme of Article 85(1).

186. The major obstacle here was clearly identified by Advocate General Mayras when he pointed out that:

> There can be no doubt that it would seem curious for a concerted practice which has not had any material effect on the competitive situation, despite the intention of the participants and because of the circumstances beyond their control, to escape the application of Article 85.

Yet that is the conclusion which follows from the inclusion within the concept of concerted practices of de facto common conduct which was the view held by my predecessor. In order to overcome the resultant obstacle, he suggested that:

> in such a case merely to attempt or to initiate execution would be enough to justify the application of Article 85(1).

Hence the need to have recourse to categories of criminal law, which are alien to the concepts of Community competition law, reveals in my view the impasse resulting from the inclusion of an 'objective criterion' derived from the parallelism of undertakings' conduct in the definition of a concerted practice.

187. No doubt the ambiguity of the term 'practice' lies at the root of this discussion. I believe, however, that, in the light of the scheme of Article 85 the scope of the concept of concerted practices is quite clear: a concerted practice does not refer to identical conduct by undertakings. In fact, within that concept, in my view, the Treaty distinguishes between and contrasts de facto concertation or concertation in practice, on the one hand, and formal concertation resulting from an agreement, on the other. Ultimately, the Treaty precludes co-operation amongst traders in whatever form:

> Article 85 does not rule out uniformity of conduct but only certain ways by which it is achieved [Wathelet [1975] 4 RTDE 663].

188. I therefore share the view that 'mere concomitant conduct does not constitute a concerted practice but may at best point, on the basis of further evidence, to the existence of an agreement between the parties concerned' [Bortolotti, *Pratiques concertées et notion d'ententes dans le traité CEE*, Droit et Affaires CEE, 1970, No 176, Doc No 17, p 1].

189. No doubt, certain forms of words used by the court in its case law might lead to the assumption that the court regards parallel conduct as constituting in itself an objective criterion for establishing a concerted practice.

190. In *Dyestuffs*, however, the court seemed to consider, at least as regards only the principles which it laid down, that it was in connection with evidence that the scope of parallel conduct had to be assessed, stating that although such conduct:

> may not be itself be identified with a concerted practice, it may however amount to strong evidence of such a practice if it leads to conditions of competition which do not correspond to the normal conditions of the market, having regard to the nature of the products, the size and number of the undertakings, and the volume of the said market.

191. In any event, it must be emphasised that parallel conduct does not in itself constitute proof of a concerted practice. From parallel conduct it is possible to deduce evidence of concertation where it cannot have arisen as a result of individual and rational decisions taken by the undertakings concerned having regard to the characteristics of the market in question.

192. Those principles, it may be worth noting, are ultimately no different from the solutions which seem to emerge from the development of United States case law.

. . .

194. . . . So far as concerns Article 85 EEC, parallel conduct cannot be equated with a concerted practice . . . On the other hand, however, such conduct may serve as evidence of concertation.

195. In that regard, since recourse to indirect forms of evidence is involved, caution must be exercised in establishing the existence of a concerted practice. According to the court's case law, the evidence must be 'sufficiently precise and coherent . . . to justify the view that the parallel behaviour . . . was the result of concerted action'. [Joined Cases 29-30/83 *CRAM v Commission* [1984] ECR 1679]. In other words, it is necessary to establish a degree of certainty that goes beyond any reasonable doubt. In accordance with the principles governing the burden of proof, it is for the Commission to demonstrate that: the burden of proof cannot be shifted simply by a finding of parallel conduct. Unless the court can be satisfied by a set of presumptions having a solid basis, concertation is not established. In any event, if there is a plausible explanation for the conduct found to exist which is consistent with an independent choice by the undertakings concerned, concertation remains unproven.

196. That is the principle which can be elicited from the court's judgment in *CRAM*. The Commission had established the existence of a concerted practice by those two undertakings which had interrupted in quick succession their deliveries to a single producer who had re-exported the products concerned to the German market, contrary to the terms of the contracts of sale concluded with the suppliers concerned. CRAM and Rheinzink explained the reasons which allegedly prompted each of them individually to interrupt its deliveries and the court held that:

> it is sufficient for the applicants to prove circumstances which cast the facts established by the Commission in a different light and which thus allow another explanation of the facts to be substituted for the one adopted by the contested decision.

197. Of course, the existence of direct evidence of concertation may be conclusive by itself and, in circumstances in which it is sufficient, it may even render devoid of purpose recourse to indicia drawn from parallel conduct. In this case, however, the Commission treats the analysis based on parallel prices as primary evidence, since the documents referred to in the decision play a secondary role, merely providing, as the defendant puts it, 'independent support'.

The European Court of Justice

59. According to the Commission's first hypothesis, it is the system of quarterly price announcements in itself which constitutes the infringement of Article 85 EEC.

60. First, the Commission considers that that system was deliberately introduced by the pulp producers in order to enable them to ascertain the prices that would be charged by their competitors in the following quarters. The disclosure of prices to third parties, especially to the press and agents working for several producers, well before their application at the beginning of a new quarter, gave the other producers sufficient time to announce their own, corresponding, new prices before that quarter and to apply them from the commencement of that quarter.

61. Secondly, the Commission considers that the implementation of that mechanism had the effect of making the market artificially transparent by enabling producers to obtain a rapid and accurate picture of the prices quoted by their competitors.

. . .

64. In this case, the communications arise from the price announcements made to users. They constitute in themselves market behaviour which does not lessen each undertaking's uncertainty as to the future attitude of its competitors. At the time when each undertaking engages in such behaviour, it cannot be sure of the future conduct of the others.

65. Accordingly, the system of quarterly price announcements on the pulp market is not to be regarded as constituting in itself an infringement of Article 85(1).

66. In the second hypothesis, the Commission considers that the system of price announcements constitutes evidence of concertation at an earlier stage.

. . .

70. Since the Commission has no documents which directly establish the existence of concertation between the producers concerned, it is necessary to ascertain whether the system of quarterly price announcements, the simultaneity or near-simultaneity of the price announcements and the parallelism of price announcements as found during the period from 1975 to 1981 constitute a firm, precise and consistent body of evidence of prior concertation.

. . .

126. Following [an experts' report requested by the court], it must be stated that, in this case, concertation is not the only plausible explanation for the parallel conduct. To begin with, the system of price announcements

may be regarded as constituting a rational response to the fact that the pulp market constituted a long-term market and to the need felt by both buyers and sellers to limit commercial risks. Further, the similarity in the dates of price announcements may be regarded as a direct result of the high degree of market transparency, which does not have to be described as artificial. Finally, the parallelism of prices and the price trends may be satisfactorily explained by the oligopolistic tendencies of the market and by the specific circumstances prevailing in certain periods. Accordingly, the parallel conduct established by the Commission does not constitute evidence of concertation.

127. In the absence of a firm, precise and consistent body of evidence, it must be held that concertation regarding announced prices has not been established by the Commission.

[E51]   T-7/89 Re the Polypropylene Cartel: Hercules Chemicals NV SA v Commission [1992] 4 CMLR 84

Court of First Instance

Arguments of the parties

[246] The applicant claims that it did not participate in any agreement or in any concerted practice and seeks to demonstrate that the factors constituting both the agreement and the concerted practice are absent in its case.

[247] First, it claims that it did not participate in any agreement. In its view, in order for a party to incur obligations under an agreement, it must have the intention to be bound, it must have expressed consent to be bound, it must be competent to do so and, finally, there must have been a meeting of minds.

[248] Secondly, it contends that it did not engage in concerted practices either. Although employees of the company did have contact with competitors, those contacts did not have the object or effect of influencing the conduct on the market of a competitor or of disclosing Hercules' course of conduct. Hercules' conduct did not meet the criteria defining a concerted practice, namely a 'practice', co-ordination and co-operation: *Suiker Unie* [Cases 40/73 etc [1975] ECR 1663], parallelism of behaviour not being capable by itself of constituting a concerted practice: Case 48/69 *ICI v Commission* [1972] ECR 619.

[249] Finally, the applicant takes the view that, in order for the terms 'co-operation' and 'co-ordination' to have any meaning, they must imply a measure of mutual expectation of performance, even if such expectations fall short of an 'agreement' . . . In the present case, the evidence makes clear that the other producers neither had any such expectation nor reasonably could have formed any such expectation, in view of the conduct of Hercules' employee at the meetings and Hercules' conduct in the market place. Likewise, the behaviour of other producers in the market place gave no expectation that the targets set during the discussions would actually be observed. This phenomenon, which Mr B was able to observe, served to deprive him of any expectation that other producers would co-ordinate their behaviour with his.

[250] The Commission refers to what it stated previously about the participation of the applicant's employee in the meetings. However, as regards Hercules' participation in a concerted practice, it also states that as long as the evidence shows that Hercules participated in meetings and had other contacts during which prices and quotas were discussed, thereby signifying its interest in, and support of, such discussions, it is not open to it to seek to escape its responsibility, even by asserting that it never, or rarely, gave a certain type of information to the other producers, or that it never sought in express terms to persuade its competitors to act in any particular way in the market place.

[251] In the Commission's view, there is a concerted practice as soon as there is concerted action having as its purpose the restriction of the autonomy of the undertakings in relation to one another, even if no actual conduct has been found on the market. In its view, the argument revolves around the meaning of the word 'practice'. It opposes the argument advanced by the applicant that the word has the narrow meaning of 'conduct on the market'. In its view, the word can cover the mere act of participating in contacts, provided that they have as their purpose the restriction of the undertakings' autonomy.

[252] The Commission goes on to argue that if the two requirements – concerted action and conduct on the market – were required for the existence of the concerted practice, as the applicant maintains, a whole gamut of practices having as their purpose, but not necessarily as their effect, the distortion of competition on the common market would not be caught by Article 85. Part of the purpose of Article 85 would thus be thwarted. Furthermore, that view of the applicant is not in accordance with the case law of the Court of Justice concerning the concept of concerted practice . . . If that case law mentions each time practices on the market, they are not mentioned as an element constituting the infringement, as the applicant maintains, but as a factual element from which the concerted action may be deduced. According to that case law, no actual conduct on the market is required. All that is required is contact between economic operators, characteristic of their abandonment of their necessary autonomy.

[253] In the Commission's view, it is not therefore necessary, in order for there to be an infringement of Article 85, for the undertakings to have put into practice that which they have discussed together. The offence under Article 85(1) exists in full once the intention to substitute co-operation, without there necessarily being, after the event, conduct on the market which may be found.

Assessment by the court

[254] The Commission characterised each factual element found against the applicant as either an agreement or a concerted practice for the purposes of Article 85(1). In fact, it is apparent from [paragraphs of] the Decision, when read together, that the Commission characterised each of those different elements primarily as an 'agreement'.

[255] It is likewise apparent . . . that the Commission in the alternative characterised the elements of the infringement as 'concerted practices' where either those elements did not enable the conclusion to be drawn that the parties had reached agreement in advance on a common plan defining their action on the market but had adopted or adhered to collusive devices

which facilitated the co-ordination of their commercial behaviour, or they did not, owing to the complexity of the cartel, make it possible to establish that some producers had expressed their definite asssent to a particular course of action agreed by the others though they had indicated their general support for the scheme in question and conducted themselves accordingly. Thus, the Decision concludes that in certain respects the continuing co-operation and collusion of the producers in the implementation of an overall agreement may display the characteristics of a concerted practice.

[256] Since it is clear from the case law of the Court of Justice that in order for there to be an agreement within the meaning of Article 85(1) it is sufficient if the undertakings in question have expressed their joint intention to conduct themselves on the market in a specific way: see Case 41/69 *ACF Chemiefarma NV v Commission* [1970] ECR 661, and . . . Cases 209-215 and 218/78 *Heintz van Landewyck v Commission* [1980] ECR 3125 this court holds that the Commission was entitled to treat the common intentions existing between the applicant and other polypropylene producers, which the Commission has proved to the requisite legal standard and which related to target prices for the period from July to December 1989 and sale volume targets for the years 1979 and 1980, as agreements within the meaning of Article 85(1).

[257] Furthermore, having established to the requisite legal standard that the effects of the price initiatives continued to last until November 1983, the Commission was fully entitled to take the view that the infringement continued until at least November 1983. It is indeed clear from the case law of the Court of Justice that Article 85 is also applicable to agreements which are no longer in force but which continue to produce their effects after they have formally ceased to be in force (Case 243/83 *Binon & Cie SA v Agence et Messagerie de la Presse SA* [1985] ECR 2015).

[258] For a definition of the concept of concerted practice, reference must be made to the case law of the Court of Justice, which shows that the criteria of co-ordination and co-operation previously laid down by the court must be understood in the light of the concept inherent in the competition provisions of the EEC Treaty according to which each economic operator must determine independently the policy which he intends to adopt on the Common Market. Although this requirement of independence does not deprive economic operators of the right to adapt themselves intelligently to the existing and anticipated conduct of their competitors, it does however strictly preclude any direct or indirect contact between such operators, the object or effect whereof is either to influence the conduct on the market of an actual or potential competitor or to disclose to such a competitor the course of conduct which they themselves have decided to adopt or contemplate adopting on the market: *Suiker Unie*.

. . .

[259] In the present case, the applicant participated in meetings having as their purpose the fixing of price and sale volume targets during which information was exchanged between competitors about the prices they wished to see charged on the market, about the prices they intended to charge, about their profitability thresholds, about the sale volume restrictions they judged to be necessary, about their sales figures or about the identity of their customers. Through its participation in those meetings, it took part, together with its competitors, in concerted action the purpose of

which was to influence their conduct on the market and to disclose to each other the course of conduct which each of the producers itself contemplated adopting on the market.

[260] Thus, not only did the applicant pursue the aim of eliminating in advance uncertainty about the future conduct of its competitors but also, in determining the policy which it intended to follow on the market, it could not fail to take account, directly or indirectly, of the information obtained during the course of those meetings. Similarly, in determining the policy which they intended to follow, its competitors were bound to take into account, directly or indirectly, the information disclosed to them by the applicant about the course of conduct which the applicant itself had decided upon or which it contemplated adopting on the market.

[261] The Commission was accordingly justified, in the alternative, having regard to their purpose, in categorising the regular meetings of polypropylene producers in which the applicant participated between the beginning of 1979 and August 1983 and its participation in fixing sale volume targets for the years 1979 to 1982 as concerted practices within the meaning of Article 85(1).

. . .

Consequently, the applicant's ground of challenge must be dismissed.

[E52]   Jan Peeters: 'The rule of reason revisited: prohibition on restraints of competition in the Sherman Act and the EEC Treaty' (1989) American Journal of Comparative Law 521

It is generally recognised that some restraints of competition can be useful and therefore should be encouraged. This policy decision will be based on the goals of the competition policy. Fikentscher distinguished in this regard between:

(a)   *wirtschaftspolitische* (economic policy) rule of reason: the restraint of trade is upheld for economic reasons;

(b)   *rechtspolitische* (legal policy): the restraint of trade is upheld on legal grounds, such as unfair competition laws, ancillary restraints considerations and opportunistic grounds (so-called de minimis concept: the minor importance of the restraint does not justify the expenditure of legal efforts to analyse it);

(c)   *sozialpolitische* (socio-political) rule of reason: the restraint is upheld by taking into account such factors as the protection of small businesses, consumers, and other societal interests;

(d)   *allgemeinpolitische* (political) rule of reason: the restraint of trade will be upheld on purely political grounds.

These last two types of policy rules of reason clearly indicate that the goals of competition policy can be very broad . . . Dissipation of market power, protection of small enterprises, the entrepreneurial freedom of retailers and other non-economic goals can give a special character to a system of competition law. One can argue whether a competition policy should ever further such goals. The problem of the weight to be given to these different goals is further aggravated by the different economic models that underlie the *economic policy rule of reason*: certain of the socio-political goals might be indirectly taken into account within this type of rule of reason analysis, depending on the economic model adhered to.

Such rule of reason analysis is furthermore based upon the premise that restraints of trade are objectionable and should therefore be prohibited. It imposes on competitors the task of arguing the reasonableness of the restraint in view of the policy goals administered. In order to maintain the workability of the administration of the competition policy, however, it might sometimes be useful to develop modes of analysis for certain types of agreements that are generally considered objectionable but are difficult to deal with individually under the policy rule of reason. Such types of agreements will therefore be approached as per se illegal, without a need to address their unreasonableness at a policy level. Such per se rules of illegality tend to lead, however, to inconsistencies within the legal system: rather than concentrating on the main issue, whether the restraint of trade has some beneficial effects and should therefore be upheld, the debate will focus on whether a restraint comes within the category of restraints that are per se illegal or not.

The history of the development of the rule of reason as applied to s 1 of the Sherman Act and to the relationship between Article 85(1) and 85(3) of the EEC Treaty can be analysed and compared against this background. Under both legal systems, the legislative provisions are phrased as a general prohibition on restraints of competition. The American courts, entrusted with the administration of the system, have decided to narrow this general prohibition by reading a rule of reason into it. In Europe, on the other hand, the prohibition principle as laid down in Article 85(1) was completed with Article 85(3), which provides for the possibility of an explicit exemption. Exclusive jurisdiction to administer this exemption was given to the European Commission (subject to review by the European Court of Justice), whereas national courts were concurrently granted jurisdiction to administer the general prohibition as laid down in Article 85(1). Could a policy rule of reason nevertheless be read into Article 85(1) itself?

[E53] Joined Cases 56 and 58/64 Consten and Grundig v Commission [1966] ECR 299

The European Court of Justice

The complaints concerning the criterion of restriction on competition

The applicants and the German government maintain that since the Commission restricted its examination solely to Grundig products the decision was based upon a false concept of competition and of the rules on prohibition contained in Article 85(1), since this concept applied particularly to competition between similar products of different makes; the Commission, before declaring Article 85(1) to be applicable, should, by basing itself upon the 'rule of reason', have considered the economic effects of the disputed contra[c]t upon competition between the different makes. There is a presumption that vertical sole distributorship agreements are not harmful to competition and in the present case there is nothing to invalidate that presumption. On the contrary, the contract in question has increased the competition between similar products of different makes.

The principle of freedom of competition concerns the various stages and manifestations of competition. Although competition between producers is generally more noticeable than that between distributors of products of the same make, it does not thereby follow that an agreement tending to restrict the latter kind of competition should escape the prohibition of Article 85(1) merely because it might increase the former.

Besides, for the purpose of applying Article 85(1), there is no need to take account of the concrete effects of an agreement once it appears that it has as its object the prevention, restriction or distortion of competition.

Therefore the absence in the contested decision of any analysis of the effects of the agreement on competition between similar products of different makes does not, of itself, constitute a defect in the decision.

It thus remains to consider whether the contested decision was right in founding the prohibition of the disputed agreement under Article 85(1) on the restriction on competition created by the agreement in the sphere of the distribution of Grundig products alone. The infringement which was found to exist by the contested decision results from the absolute territorial protection created [by] the said contract in favour of Consten on the basis of French law. The applicants thus wished to eliminate any possibility of competition at the wholesale level in Grundig products in the territory specified in the contract essentially by two methods.

First, Grundig undertook not to deliver even indirectly to third parties products intended for the area covered by the contract. The restrictive nature of that undertaking is obvious if it is considered in the light of the prohibition on exporting which was imposed not only on Consten but also on all the other sole concessionaires of Grundig, as well as the German wholesalers. Secondly, the registration in France by Consten of the GINT trade mark, which Grundig affixes to all its products, is intended to increase the protection inherent in the disputed agreement, against the risk of parallel imports into France of Grundig products, by adding the protection deriving from the law on industrial property rights. Thus no third party could import Grundig products from other Member States of the Community for resale in France without running serious risks.

The defendant properly took into account the whole distribution system thus set up by Grundig. In order to arrive at a true representation of the contractual position the contract must be placed in the economic and legal context in the light of which it was concluded by the parties. Such a procedure is not to be regarded as an unwarrantable interference in legal transactions or circumstances which were not the subject of the proceedings before the Commission.

The situation as ascertained above results in the isolation of the French market and makes it possible to charge for the products in question prices which are sheltered from all effective competition. In addition, the more producers succeed in their efforts to render their own makes of product individually distinct in the eyes of the consumer, the more the effectiveness of competition between producers tends to diminish. Because of the considerable impact of distribution costs on the aggregate cost price, it seems important that competition between dealers should also be stimulated. The efforts of the dealer are stimulated by competition between distributors of products of the same make. Since the agreement thus aims at isolating the

French market for Grundig products and maintaining artificially, for products of a very well-known brand, separate national markets within the Community, it is therefore such as to distort competition in the Common Market.

It was therefore proper for the contested decision to hold that the agreement constitutes an infringement of Article 85(1). No further considerations, whether of economic data (price differences between France and Germany, representative character of the type of appliance considered, level of overheads borne by Consten) or of the corrections of the criteria upon which the Commission relied in its comparisons between the situations of the French and German markets, and no possible favourable effects of the agreement in other respects, can in any way lead, in the face of the above-mentioned restrictions, to a different solution under Article 85(1).

[E54]   Case 26/76 Metro v Commission [1977] ECR 1875

The European Court of Justice

20. The requirement contained in Articles 3 and 85 of the EEC Treaty that competition shall not be distorted implies the existence on the market of workable competition, that is to say the degree of competition necessary to ensure the observance of the basic requirements and the attainment of the objectives of the Treaty, in particular the creation of a single market achieving conditions similar to those of a domestic market.

In accordance with this requirement the nature and intensiveness of competition may vary to an extent dictated by the products or services in question and the economic structure of the relevant market sectors.

In the sector covering the production of high-quality and technically advanced consumer durables, where a relatively small number of large- and medium-scale producers offer a varied range of items which, or so consumers may consider, are readily interchangeable, the structure of the market does not preclude the existence of a variety of channels of distribution adapted to the peculiar characteristics of the various producers and to the requirements of the various categories of consumers.

On this view the Commission was justified in recognising that selective distribution systems constituted, together with others, an aspect of competition which accords with Article 85(1), provided that resellers are chosen on the basis of objective criteria of a qualitative nature relating to the technical qualifications of the reseller and his staff and the suitability of his trading premises and that such conditions are laid down uniformly for all potential resellers and are not applied in a discriminatory fashion.

21. It is true that in such systems of distribution price competition is not generally emphasised either as an exclusive or indeed as a principal factor.

This is particularly so when, as in the present case, access to the distribution network is subject to conditions exceeding the requirements of an appropriate distribution of the products.

However, although price competition is so important that it can never be eliminated, it does not constitute the only effective form of competition or that to which absolute priority must in all circumstances be accorded.

The powers conferred upon the Commission under Article 85(3) show that the requirements for the maintenance of workable competition may be reconciled with the safeguarding of objectives of a different nature and that to this end certain restrictions on competition are permissible, provided that they are essential to the attainment of those objectives and that they do not result in the elimination of competition for a substantial part of the Common Market.

For specialist wholesalers and retailers the desire to maintain a certain price level, which corresponds to the desire to preserve, in the interests of consumers, the possibility of the continued existence of this channel of distribution in conjunction with new methods of distribution based on a different type of competition policy, forms one of the objectives which may be pursued without necessarily falling under the prohibition contained in Article 85(1), and, if it does fall thereunder, either wholly or in part, coming within the framework of Article 85(3).

This argument is strengthened if, in addition, such conditions promote improved competition inasmuch as it relates to factors other than prices.

22. Although the figures submitted by both sides concerning the existence of price competition amongst SABA distributors ultimately indicate that the price structure is somewhat rigid, they do not, especially in view of the existence at the same time of competition between products of the same brand (intra-brand competition) and the existence of effective competition between different brands, permit the conclusion that competition has been restricted or eliminated on the market in electronic equipment for leisure purposes.

Nevertheless, the Commission must ensure that this structural rigidity is not reinforced, as might happen if there were an increase in the number of selective distribution networks for marketing the same product.

[E55]   Case 75/84 Metro v Commission (no 2) [1986] ECR 3021

The European Court of Justice

40. It must be borne in mind that, although the court has held in previous decisions that 'simple' selective distribution systems are capable of constituting an aspect of competition compatible with Article 85(1) of the Treaty, there may nevertheless be a restriction or elimination of competition where the existence of a certain number of such systems does not leave any room for other forms of distribution based on a different type of competition policy or results in a rigidity in price structure which is not counterbalanced by other aspects of competition between products of the same brand and by the existence of effective competition between different brands.

41. Consequently, the existence of a large number of selective distribution systems for a particular product does not in itself permit the conclusion that competition is restricted or distorted. Nor is the existence of such systems decisive as regards the granting or refusal of an exemption under Article 85(3), since the only factor to be taken into consideration in that regard is the effect which such systems actually have on the competitive situation.

. . .

42. It follows that an increase in the number of 'simple' selective distribution systems after an exemption has been granted must be taken into consideration, when an application for renewal of that exemption is being considered, only in the special situation in which the relevant market was already so rigid and structured that the element of competition inherent in 'simple' systems is not sufficient to maintain workable competition. Metro has not been able to show that a special situation of that kind exists in the present case.

[E56]   Case 161/84 Pronuptia [1986] ECR 374

The European Court of Justice

13. It should be pointed out first of all that franchise agreements, the legality of which has not previously been put in issue before the court, are very diverse in nature. It appears from what was said in argument before the court that a distinction must be drawn between different varieties of franchise agreements. In particular, it is necessary to distinguish between (1) service franchises, under which the franchisee offers a service under the business name or symbol and sometimes the trademark of the franchisor, in accordance with the franchisor's instructions, (2) production franchises, under which the franchisee manufactures products according to the instructions of the franchisor and sells them under the franchisor's trademark, and (3) distribution franchises, under which the franchisee simply sells certain products in a shop which bears the franchisor's business name or symbol. In this judgment the court is concerned only with this third type of contract, to which the questions asked by the national court expressly refer.

14. The compatibility of franchise agreements for the distribution of goods with Article 85(1) cannot be assessed in abstracto but depends on the provisions contained in such agreements.

. . .

15. In a system of distribution franchises of [the kind in question] an undertaking which has established itself as a distributor on a given market and thus developed certain business methods grants independent traders, for a fee, the right to establish themselves in other markets using its business name and the business methods which have made it successful. Rather than a method of distribution, it is a way for an undertaking to derive financial benefit from its expertise without investing its own capital. Moreover, the system gives traders who do not have the necessary experience access to methods which they could not have learned without considerable effort and allows them to benefit from the reputation of the franchisor's business name. Franchise agreements for the distribution of goods differ in that regard from dealerships or contracts which incorporate approved retailers into a selective distribution system, which do not involve the use of a single business name, the application of uniform business methods or the payment of royalties in return for the benefits granted. Such a system, which allows the franchisor to profit from his success, does not in itself interfere with competition. In order for the system to work two conditions must be met.

16. First, the franchisor must be able to communicate his know-how to the franchisees and provide them with the necessary assistance in order to enable them to apply his methods, without running the risk that that know-how and assistance might benefit competitors, even indirectly. It follows that provisions which are essential in order to avoid that risk do not constitute restrictions on competition for the purposes of Article 85(1). That is also true of a clause prohibiting the franchisee, during the period of validity of the contract and for a reasonable period after its expiry, from opening a shop of the same or a similar nature in an area where he may compete with a member of the network. The same may be said of the franchisee's obligation not to transfer his shop to another party without the prior approval of the franchisor; that provision is intended to prevent competitors from indirectly benefiting from the know-how and assistance provided.

17. Secondly, the franchisor must be able to take the measures necessary for maintaining the identity and reputation of the network bearing his business name or symbol. It follows that provisions which establish the means of control necessary for that purpose do not constitute restrictions on competition for the purposes of Article 85(1).

18. The same is true of the franchisee's obligation to apply the business methods developed by the franchisor and to use the know-how provided.

19. That is also the case with regard to the franchisee's obligation to sell the goods covered by the contract only in premises laid out and decorated according to the franchisor's instructions, which is intended to ensure uniform presentation in conformity with certain requirements. The same requirements apply to the location of the shop, the choice of which is also likely to affect the network's reputation. It is thus understandable that the franchisee cannot transfer his shop to another location without the franchisor's approval.

20. The prohibition of the assignment by the franchisee of his rights and obligations under the contract without the franchisor's approval protects the latter's right freely to choose the franchisees, on whose business qualifications the establishment and maintenance of the network's reputation depend.

21. By means of the control exerted by the franchisor on the selection of goods offered by the franchisee, the public is able to obtain goods of the same quality from each franchisee. It may in certain cases – for instance, the distribution of fashion articles – be impractical to lay down objective quality specifications. Because of the large number of franchisees it may also be too expensive to ensure that such specifications are observed. In such circumstances a provision requiring the franchisee to sell only products supplied by the franchisor or by suppliers selected by him may be considered necessary for the protection of the network's reputation. Such a provision may not however have the effect of preventing the franchisee from obtaining those products from other franchisees.

22. Finally, since advertising helps to define the image of the network's name or symbol in the eyes of the public, a provision requiring the franchisee to obtain the franchisor's approval for all advertising is also essential for the maintenance of the network's identity, so long as that provision concerns only the nature of the advertising.

23. It must be emphasised on the other hand that, far from being necessary for the protection of the know-how provided or the maintenance of the network's identity and reputation, certain provisions restrict competition

between the members of the network. That is true of provisions which share markets between the franchisor and franchisees or between franchisees or prevent franchisees from engaging in price competition with each other.

24. In that regard, the attention of the national court should be drawn to the provision which obliges the franchisee to sell goods covered by the contract only in the premises specified therein. That provision prohibits the franchisee from opening a second shop. Its real effect becomes clear if it is examined in conjunction with the franchisor's undertaking to ensure that the franchisee has the exclusive use of his business name or symbol in a given territory. In order to comply with that undertaking the franchisor must not only refrain from establishing himself within that territory but also require other franchisees to give an undertaking not to open a second shop outside their own territory. A combination of provisions of that kind results in a sharing of markets between the franchisor and the franchisees or between franchisees and thus restricts competition within the network. As is clear from the judgment [in] . . . *Consten and Grundig v Commission* **[E53]**, a restriction of that kind constitutes a limitation of competition for the purposes of Article 85(1) if it concerns a business name or symbol which is already well known. It is of course possible that a prospective franchisee would not take the risk of becoming part of the chain, investing his own money, paying a relatively high entry fee and undertaking to pay a substantial annual royalty, unless he could hope, thanks to a degree of protection against competition on the part of the franchisor and other franchisees, that his business would be profitable. That consideration, however, is relevant only to an examination of the agreement in the light of the conditions laid down in Article 85(3).

25. Although provisions which impair the franchisee's freedom to determine his own prices are restrictive of competition, that is not the case where the franchisor simply provides franchisees with price guidelines, so long as there is no concerted practice between the franchisor and the franchisees or between the franchisees themselves for the actual application of such prices. It is for the national court to determine whether that is indeed the case.

26. Finally, it must be added that franchise agreements for the distribution of goods which contain provisions sharing markets between the franchisor and the franchisees or between the franchisees themselves are in any event liable to affect trade between Member States, even if they are entered into by undertakings established in the same Member State, in so far as they prevent franchisees from establishing themselves in another Member State.

[E57] Joined Cases 25 and 26/84 Ford v Commission [1985] ECR 2725

The European Court of Justice

44. There remains to be considered the last submission which is based on alleged inadequacies in the reasoning of the decision. The applicants claim that the Commission has not indicated how the circular . . . could have aggravated the restrictive effects of the main dealer agreement. Even

if the Commission was justified in regarding the withdrawal of deliveries of right-hand-drive cars on the German market as the diminution of an advantage flowing from the agreement, it ought in any event to have considered the extent to which the loss of that advantage made it impossible to grant an exemption under Article 85(3) in respect of that agreement.

45. The Commission admits that it regarded the availability of right-hand-drive cars on the German market as one of the advantages of the agreement. It maintains that the decision at issue shows however that Ford AG's behaviour led not only to the loss of that advantage but also to a significant reduction in the other advantages likely to flow from the agreement . . . The balance between advantages and disadvantages was significantly affected by the fact that Ford AG prevented parallel imports from being carried out and such conduct constitutes a decisive reason for not granting an exemption in respect of the agreement under Article 85(3).

46. With regard to that argument, it should be noted that, as the Commission rightly contends, the Commission is not obliged to carry out a detailed examination of all the advantages and disadvantages likely to flow from a selective distribution system when it has good reason to believe that a manufacturer has used such a system to prevent parallel imports and thus artificially to partition the common market. Moreover, the contested decision does consider what advantages and disadvantages may flow from the main dealer agreement.

[E58]   Joined Cases 89, 104, 114, 116, 117 and 125-129/85 Åhlström Osakeyhtiö and others v EC Commission (Wood Pulp) [1988] ECR 5193

Opinion of Advocate General Darmon

IV . Suggested jurisdictional criteria

47. The difficulties encountered in this area illustrate clearly that territoriality, as a connecting factor, does not make it possible to resolve all the problems connected with the scale and nature of contemporary international trade. According to Professor Mann, an inflexible territoriality principle is no longer suited to the modern world. The same view is taken by Professor Prosper Weil in the following passage:

The picture before us is that of an international society made up of adjacent cells, separated by frontiers; the concept of territory, which lies at the very heart of the concept of territoriality, illustrates that division between separate entities by physical and geographical boundaries. But it is clear . . . that frontiers are not only barriers but also crossing points and economic life makes light of such barriers.

48. This assessment has led different writers to devise different criteria for the extraterritorial application of laws. Sir Robert Jennings, for example, considers that under international law a state is entitled to exercise international jurisdiction where its legitimate interests are concerned but that it may not abuse that right. There is abuse where the exercise of extraterritorial jurisdiction constitutes interference with the exercise of the local

territorial jurisdiction. According to Professor Mann, the real problem is that of identifying what he calls the 'legally relevant facts' and the state whose connection with those facts is of such a kind as to render the assertion of jurisdiction fair and reasonable. Advocating that jurisdiction should be based on 'closeness of connection', Professor Mann considers 'that a State has (legislative) jurisdiction, if its contact with a given set of facts is so close, so substantial, so direct, so weighty, that legislation in respect of them is in harmony with international law and its various aspects (including the practice of States, the principles of non-interference and reciprocity and the demands of inter-dependence)'.

Professor Mann points out at the same time that a mere political, economic, commercial or social interest does not constitute a close connection. In the case, more particularly, of the law of competition, he considers that the effect, whether intended, foreseeable or, a fortiori, unanticipated, cannot establish a connection of that kind.

49. Other writers suggest that the jurisdiction of the state in which 'the primary effect' of the act is felt should be recognised. In order to determine whether the effect is primary or secondary, it is necessary to take a twofold factor into consideration: is the effect produced within the state concerned more direct and more substantial than the effect produced in other states? It is suggested that that approach permits jurisdiction to be exercised only by states having a legitimate interest therein. Finally, it is generally acknowledged that international law does not preclude concurrent jurisdiction. I would point out, however, that, according to some writers, the development of customary international law leads to the emergence of certain specific limitations on the extraterritorial exercise of a state's jurisdiction. Thus, international law would prohibit the extraterritorial application of domestic law where it might give rise to conflicting obligations or provoke conflicts of jurisdiction.

50. In my view, those various concerns are, for the most part, taken into account by the adoption of the criterion of qualified effect. That criterion, which does not conflict with any prohibitive rule of international law, has gained wide acceptance in the practice of states. Moreover, it is, on objective grounds, particularly appropriate in view of the specific nature of competition law, as a law designed to regulate market conditions and safeguard *ordre public* in the economic context. It is on the basis of those considerations and of the criteria of international law that it is necessary to define the characteristics of an effect whose location justifies the assertion of prescriptive jurisdiction over undertakings established outside the Community.

51. According to some writers, such effects should correspond to those which are covered where the interference with competition is the result of conduct within the territory of the state which claims jurisdiction. However, . . . it is unclear whether the concept of effect provided for in Article 85 . . . in order to establish the *existence* of an infringement of the competition rules is identical to that required by Community law, and accepted by international law, in order to *determine whether there is jurisdiction* over undertakings established outside the Community.

52. According to the substantive provisions of Community law, the restriction of competition must be 'perceptible' or 'appreciable'. The adverse effects on competition may be either direct or indirect and objectively or reasonably foreseeable. Those are the characteristics of the effect

envisaged as a constituent element of interference with freedom of competition within the Community.

53. In my view, not all of those characteristics have to be adopted if the effect is taken as the criterion of extraterritorial jurisdiction. The most important reservation in that regard concerns indirect effect. I would remind the court that Mr Advocate General Mayras suggested . . . in the *Dyestuffs* cases [1972] ECR 665, the adoption of the criterion of the direct and immediate, reasonably foreseeable and substantial effect. I agree with that solution and, for the reasons which he sets forth, I would adopt his analysis which is as follows:

> Surely the Commission would be disarmed if, faced with a concerted practice, the initiative for which was taken and the responsibility for which was assumed exclusively by undertakings outside the common market, it was deprived of the power to take any decision against them? This would also mean giving up a way of defending the common market and one necessary for bringing about the major objectives of the European Economic Community.

. . .

57. . . . there is no rule of international law which is capable of being relied upon against the criterion of the direct, substantial and foreseeable effect. Nor does the concept of international comity, in view of its uncertain scope, militate against that criterion either.

58. In the absence of any such prohibitive rule and in the light of widespread state practice, I would therefore propose that in view of its appropriateness to the field of competition, it be adopted as a criterion for the jurisdiction of the Community.

. . .

V.   The position of KEA

60. KEA is an association of United States undertakings which – the Commission essentially alleges – made recommendations on prices which were followed by its members and contributed to the transparency of the market, thereby favouring concertation with other producers unconnected with the association. In general terms, KEA is said to have constituted the framework for concertation between the producers concerned.

61. If it is satisfied, the criterion which I suggest the court should adopt is such as to justify, in principle, the assertion of jurisdiction by the Community even though KEA does not have any branches, subsidiaries or agencies in the Community, that is to say it lacks the type of territorial connection which, according to the United Kingdom, constitutes the sole basis for the exercise of jurisdiction by the Community.

62. Nor does the nature of the activities carried on by KEA, which has not itself traded in the Community, constitute in my view an obstacle to the applicability of Community law. The fact that an association of undertakings does not engage, as such, in economic activities does not preclude the application of the competition rules to it.

The European Court of Justice

Incorrect assessment of the territorial scope of Article 85 of the Treaty and incompatibility of the decision with public international law. . .

(a)   The individual undertakings

12. It should be noted that the main sources of supply of wood pulp are outside the Community, in Canada, the United States, Sweden and Finland and that the market therefore has global dimensions. Where wood pulp producers established in those countries sell directly to purchasers established in the Community and engage in price competition in order to win orders from those customers, that constitutes competition within the common market.

13. It follows that where those producers concert on the prices to be charged to their customers in the Community and put that concertation into effect by selling at prices which are actually co-ordinated, they are taking part in concertation which has the object and effect of restricting competition within the common market within the meaning of Article 85 of the Treaty.

14. Accordingly, it must be concluded that by applying the competition rules in the Treaty in the circumstances of this case to undertakings whose registered offices are situated outside the Community, the Commission has not made an incorrect assessment of the territorial scope of Article 85.

15. The applicants have submitted that the decision is incompatible with public international law on the grounds that the application of the competition rules in this case was founded exclusively on the economic repercussions within the common market of conduct restricting competition which was adopted outside the Community.

16. It should be observed that an infringement of Article 85, such as the conclusion of an agreement which has had the effect of restricting competition within the common market, consists of conduct made up of two elements, the formation of the agreement, decision or concerted practice and the implementation thereof. If the applicability of prohibitions laid down under competition law were made to depend on the place where the agreement, decision or concerted practice was formed, the result would obviously be to give undertakings an easy means of evading those prohibitions. The decisive factor is therefore the place where it is implemented.

17. The producers in this case implemented their pricing agreement within the common market. It is immaterial in that respect whether or not they had recourse to subsidiaries, agents, sub-agents, or branches within the Community in order to make their contacts with purchasers within the Community.

18. Accordingly the Community's jurisdiction to apply its competition rules to such conduct is covered by the territoriality principle as universally recognised in public international law.

. . .

(b)   KEA

24. According to its articles of association, KEA is a non-profit-making association whose purpose is the promotion of the commercial interests of its members in the exportation of their products and it serves primarily as a clearing-house for its members for information regarding their export markets. KEA does not itself engage in manufacture, selling or distribution.

25. It should further be pointed out that within KEA a number of groups have been formed, including the Pulp Group, to cover the different sectors of the pulp and paper industry. Under Article 1 of the bye-laws of KEA, undertakings may only join KEA by becoming a member of one of those

groups. Article 2 of the bye-laws provides that the groups enjoy full independence in the management of their affairs.

26. It should lastly be noted that according to a policy statement adopted by the Pulp Group . . ., the members of the group may conclude price agreements at meetings which they hold from time to time provided that each member is informed in advance that prices will be discussed and that the meeting is quorate. The unanimous agreement of the members present is also binding on members who are absent when the decision is adopted.

27. It is apparent from the foregoing that KEA's price recommendations cannot be distinguished from the pricing agreements concluded by undertakings which are members of the Pulp Group and that KEA has not played a separate role in the implementation of those agreements.

28. In those circumstances the decision should be declared void in so far as it concerns KEA.

Question

What, if anything, is the difference between the 'effects' test proposed by the Advocate General and the 'implementation' notion employed by the Court of Justice?

3   Application of competition policy

[E59]   Regulation 17/62, First Regulation implementing Articles 85 and 86 of the EEC Treaty

The Council of the European Economic Community,
Having regard to the Treaty establishing the European Economic Community, and in particular Article 87 thereof;
Having regard to the proposal from the Commission;
Having regard to the Opinion of the Economic and Social Committee;
Having regard to the Opinion of the European Parliament;

Whereas, in order to establish a system ensuring that competition shall not be distorted in the common market, it is necessary to provide for balanced application of Articles 85 and 86 in a uniform manner in the Member States;

Whereas in establishing the rules for applying Article 85(3) account must be taken of the need to ensure effective supervision and to simplify administration to the greatest possible extent;

Whereas it is accordingly necessary to make it obligatory, as a general principle, for undertakings which seek application of Article 85(3) to notify to the Commission their agreements, decisions and concerted practices;

Whereas, on the one hand, such agreements, decisions and concerted practices are probably very numerous and cannot therefore all be examined at the same time and, on the other hand, some of them have special features which may make them less prejudicial to the development of the common market;

Whereas there is consequently a need to make more flexible arrangements for the time being in respect of certain categories of agreement, decision and concerted practice without prejudging their validity under Article 85;

Whereas it may be in the interest of undertakings to know whether any agreements, decisions or practices to which they are party, or propose to become party, may lead to action on the part of the Commission pursuant to Article 85(1) or Article 86;

Whereas, in order to secure uniform application of Articles 85 and 86 in the common market, rules must be made under which the Commission, acting in close and constant liaison with the competent authorities of the Member States, may take the requisite measures for applying those Articles;

Whereas for this purpose the Commission must have the co-operation of the competent authorities of the Member States and be empowered, throughout the common market, to require such information to be supplied and to undertake such investigations as are necessary to bring to light any agreement, decision or concerted practice prohibited by Article 85(1) or any abuse of a dominant position prohibited by Article 86;

Whereas, in order to carry out its duty of ensuring that the provisions of the Treaty are applied, the Commission must be empowered to address to undertakings or associations of undertakings recommendations and decisions for the purpose of bringing to an end infringements of Articles 85 and 86;

Whereas compliance with Articles 85 and 86 and the fulfilment of obligations imposed on undertakings and associations of undertakings under this regulation must be enforceable by means of fines and periodic penalty payments;

Whereas undertakings concerned must be accorded the right to be heard by the Commission, third parties whose interests may be affected by a decision must be given the opportunity of submitting their comments beforehand, and it must be ensured that wide publicity is given to decisions taken;

Whereas all decisions taken by the Commission under this regulation are subject to review by the Court of Justice under the conditions specified in the Treaty; whereas it is moreover desirable to confer upon the Court of Justice, pursuant to Article 172, unlimited jurisdiction in respect of decisions under which the Commission imposes fines or periodic penalty payments;

Whereas this regulation may enter into force without prejudice to any other provisions that may hereafter be adopted pursuant to Article 87;
Has adopted this regulation:

Article I Basic provision

Without prejudice to Articles 6, 7 and 23 of this regulation, agreements, decisions and concerted practices of the kind described in Article 85(1) of the Treaty and the abuse of a dominant position in the market, within the meaning of Article 86 of the Treaty, shall be prohibited, no prior decision to that effect being required.

Article 2 Negative clearance

Upon application by the undertakings or associations of undertakings concerned, the Commission may certify that, on the basis of the facts in its possession, there are no grounds under Article 85(1) or Article 86 of the Treaty for action on its part in respect of an agreement, decision or practice.

Article 3   Termination of infringements

1. Where the Commission, upon application or upon its own initiative, finds that there is infringement of Article 85 or Article 86 of the Treaty, it may by decision require the undertakings or associations of undertakings concerned to bring such infringement to an end.

2. Those entitled to make application are:

(a)   Member States;
(b)   natural or legal persons who claim a legitimate interest.

3. Without prejudice to the other provisions of this regulation, the Commission may, before taking a decision under paragraph 1, address to the undertakings or associations of undertakings concerned recommendations for termination of the infringement.

Article 4   Notification of new agreements, decisions and practices

1. Agreements, decisions and concerted practices of the kind described in Article 85(1) of the Treaty which come into existence after the entry into force of this regulation and in respect of which the parties seek application of Article 85(3) must be notified to the Commission. Until they have been notified, no decision in application of Article 85(3) may be taken.

. . .

Article 8   Duration and revocation of decisions under Article 85(3)

1. A decision in application of Article 85(3) of the Treaty shall be issued for a specified period and conditions and obligations may be attached thereto.

2. A decision may on application be renewed if the requirements of Article 85(3) of the Treaty continue to be satisfied.

3. The Commission may revoke or amend its decision or prohibit specified acts by the parties:

(a)   where there has been a change in any of the facts which were basic to the making of the decision;
(b)   where the parties commit a breach of any obligation attached to the decision;
(c)   where the decision is based on incorrect information or was induced by deceit;
(d)   where the parties abuse the exemption from the provisions of Article 85(1) of the Treaty granted to them by the decision.

In cases to which sub-paragraphs (b), (c) or (d) apply, the decision may be revoked with retroactive effect.

Article 9   Powers

1. Subject to review of its decision by the Court of Justice, the Commission shall have sole power to declare Article 85(1) inapplicable pursuant to Article 85(3) of the Treaty.

2. The Commission shall have power to apply Article 85(1) and Article 86 of the Treaty; this power may be exercised notwithstanding that the time

limits specified in Article 5(1) and in Article 7(2) relating to notification have not expired.

3. As long as the Commission has not initiated any procedure under Articles 2, 3 or 6, the authorities of the Member States shall remain competent to apply Article 85(1) and Article 86 in accordance with Article 88 of the Treaty; they shall remain competent in this respect notwithstanding that the time limits specified in Article 5(1) and in Article 7(2) relating to notification have not expired.

. . .

Article 11   Request for information

1. In carrying out the duties assigned to it by Article 89 and by provisions adopted under Article 87 of the Treaty, the Commission may obtain all necessary information from the governments and competent authorities of the Member States and from undertakings and associations of undertakings.

2. When sending a request for information to an undertaking or association of undertakings, the Commission shall at the same time forward a copy of the request to the competent authority of the Member State in whose territory the seat of the undertaking or association of undertakings is situated.

3. In its request the Commission shall state the legal basis and the purpose of the request and also the penalties provided for in Article 15(1)(b) for supplying incorrect information.

4. The owners of the undertakings or their representatives and, in the case of legal persons, companies or firms, or of associations having no legal personality, the persons authorised to represent them by law or by their constitution shall supply the information requested.

5. Where an undertaking or association of undertakings does not supply the information requested within the time limit fixed by the Commission, or supplies incomplete information, the Commission shall by decision require the information to be supplied. The decision shall specify what information is required, fix an appropriate time limit within which it is to be supplied and indicate the penalties provided for in Article 15(1)(b) and Article 16(1)(c) and the right to have the decision reviewed by the Court of Justice.

6. The Commission shall at the same time forward a copy of its decision to the competent authority of the Member State in whose territory the seat of the undertaking or association of undertakings is situated.

. . .

Article 13   Investigations by the authorities of the Member States

1. At the request of the Commission, the competent authorities of the Member States shall undertake the investigations which the Commission considers to be necessary under Article 14(1), or which it has ordered by decision pursuant to Article 14(3). The officials of the competent authorities of the Member States responsible for conducting these investigations shall exercise their powers upon production of an authorisation in writing issued by the competent authority of the Member State in whose territory the investigation is to be made. Such authorisation shall specify the subject matter and purpose of the investigation.

2. If so requested by the Commission or by the competent authority of the Member State in whose territory the investigation is to be made, the officials of the Commission may assist the officials of such authorities in carrying out their duties.

Article 14   Investigating powers of the Commission

1. In carrying out the duties assigned to it by Article 89 and by provisions adopted under Article 87 of the Treaty, the Commission may undertake all necessary investigations into undertakings and associations of undertakings. To this end the officials authorised by the Commission are empowered:

(a)   to examine the books and other business records;
(b)   to take copies of or extracts from the books and business records;
(c)   to ask for oral explanations on the spot;
(d)   to enter any premises, land and means of transport of undertakings.

2. The officials of the Commission authorised for the purpose of these investigations shall exercise their powers upon production of an authorisation in writing specifying the subject matter and purpose of the investigation and the penalties provided for in Article 15(1)(c) in cases where production of the required books or other business records is incomplete. In good time before the investigation, the Commission shall inform the competent authority of the Member State in whose territory the same is to be made of the investigation and of the identity of the authorised officials.

3. Undertakings and associations of undertakings shall submit to investigations ordered by decision of the Commission. The decision shall specify the subject matter and purpose of the investigation, appoint the date on which it is to begin and indicate the penalties provided for in Article 15(1)(c) and Article 16(1)(d) and the right to have the decision reviewed by the Court of Justice.

4. The Commission shall take decisions referred to in paragraph 3 after consultation with the competent authority of the Member State in whose territory the investigation is to be made.

5. Officials of the competent authority of the Member State in whose territory the investigation is to be made may, at the request of such authority or of the Commission, assist the officials of the Commission in carrying out their duties.

6. Where an undertaking opposes an investigation ordered pursuant to this Article, the Member State concerned shall afford the necessary assistance to the officials authorised by the Commission to enable them to make their investigation. Member States shall, after consultation with the Commission, take the necessary measures to this end before 1 October 1962.

Article 15   Fines

1. The Commission may by decision impose on undertakings or associations of undertakings fines of from 100 to 5,000 units of account where, intentionally or negligently:

(a)   they supply incorrect or misleading information in an application pursuant to Article 2 or in a notification pursuant to Articles 4 or 5; or
(b)   they supply incorrect information in response to a request made pursuant to Article 11(3) or (5) or to Article 12, or do not supply information within the time limit fixed by a decision taken under Article 11(5); or
(c)   they produce the required books or other business records in incomplete form during investigations under Articles 13 or 14, or refuse to

submit to an investigation ordered by decision issued in implementation of Article 14(3).

2. The Commission may by decision impose on undertakings or associations of undertakings fines from 1,000 to 1,000,000 units of account, or a sum in excess thereof but not exceeding 10% of the turnover in the preceding business year of each of the undertakings participating in the infringement where, either intentionally or negligently:

(a) they infringe Article 85(1) or Article 86 of the Treaty; or
(b) they commit a breach of any obligation imposed pursuant to Article 8(1).

In fixing the amount of the fine, regard shall be had both to the gravity and to the duration of the infringement.

3. Article 10(3) to (6) shall apply.

4. Decisions taken pursuant to paragraphs 1 and 2 shall not be of a criminal law nature.

5. The fines provided for in paragraph 2(a) shall not be imposed in respect of acts taking place:

(a) after notification to the Commission and before its decision in application of Article 85(3) of the Treaty, provided they fall within the limits of the activity described in the notification;
(b) before notification and in the course of agreements, decisions or concerted practices in existence at the date of entry into force of this regulation, provided that notification was effected within the time limits specified in Article 5(1) and Article 7(2).

6. Paragraph 5 shall not have effect where the Commission has informed the undertakings concerned that after preliminary examination it is of opinion that Article 85(1) of the Treaty applies and that application of Article 85(3) is not justified.

. . .

Article 17   Review by the Court of Justice

The Court of Justice shall have unlimited jurisdiction within the meaning of Article 172 of the Treaty to review decisions whereby the Commission has fixed a fine or periodic penalty payment; it may cancel, reduce or increase the fine or periodic penalty payment imposed.

. . .

Article 19   Hearing of the parties and of third persons

1. Before taking decisions as provided for in Articles 2, 3, 6, 7, 8, 15 and 16, the Commission shall give the undertakings or associations of undertaking concerned the opportunity of being heard on the matters to which the Commission has taken objection.

2. If the Commission or the competent authorities of the Member States consider it necessary, they may also hear other natural or legal persons. Applications to be heard on the part of such persons shall, where they show a sufficient interest, be granted.

3. Where the Commission intends to give negative clearance pursuant to Article 2 or take a decision in application of Article 85(3) of the Treaty, it

shall publish a summary of the relevant application or notification and invite all interested third parties to submit their observations within a time limit which it shall fix being not less than one month. Publication shall have regard to the legitimate interest of undertakings in the protection of their business secrets.

Article 20   Professional secrecy

1. Information acquired as a result of the application of Articles 11, 12, 13 and 14 shall be used only for the purpose of the relevant request or investigation.

2. Without prejudice to the provisions of Articles 19 and 21, the Commission and the competent authorities of the Member States, their officials and other servants shall not disclose information acquired by them as a result of the application of this regulation and of the kind covered by the obligation of professional secrecy.

3. The provisions of paragraphs 1 and 2 shall not prevent publication of general information or surveys which do not contain information relating to particular undertakings or associations of undertakings.

Article 21   Publication of decisions

1. The Commission shall publish the decisions which it takes pursuant to Articles 2, 3, 6, 7 and 8.

2. The publication shall state the names of the parties and the main content of the decision; it shall have regard to the legitimate interest of undertakings in the protection of their business secrets.

[E60]   Case C-2/88 Imm JJ Zwartveld and others [1990] ECR I-3365

The European Court of Justice

16. In its judgment in Case 294/83 *Les Verts v European Parliament* [1986] ECR 1357 **[B49]**, the court established the principle that the European Economic Community is a Community based on the rule of law, inasmuch as neither its Member States nor its institutions can avoid a review of whether the measures adopted by them are in conformity with the basic constitutional charter, the Treaty (paragraph 23). The EEC Treaty established the Court of Justice as the judicial body responsible for ensuring that both the Member States and the Community institutions comply with the law.

17. In that community subject to the rule of law, relations between the Member States and the Community institutions are governed, according to Article 5 of the EEC Treaty, by a principle of sincere co-operation. That principle not only requires the Member States to take all the measures necessary to guarantee the application and effectiveness of Community law, if necessary by instituting criminal proceedings (see the judgment in Case 68/88 *Commission v Greece* [1989] ECR 2965, at p 2984, paragraph 23) but also imposes on Member States and the Community institutions mutual duties of sincere co-operation (see the judgment in Case 230/81 *Luxembourg v European Parliament* [1983] ECR 255, paragraph 37).

18. This duty of sincere co-operation imposed on Community institutions is of particular importance vis-à-vis the judicial authorities of the Member States, who are responsible for ensuring that Community law is applied and respected in the national legal system.

. . .

22. In this case, the request has been made by a national court which is hearing proceedings on the infringement of Community rules, and it seeks the production of information concerning the existence of the facts constituting those infringements. It is incumbent upon every Community institution to give its active assistance to such national legal proceedings, by producing documents to the national court and authorising its officials to give evidence in the national proceedings; that applies particularly to the Commission, to which Article 155 of the Treaty entrusts the task of ensuring that the provisions of the Treaty and the measures taken by the institutions pursuant thereto are applied.

. . .

25. Under those circumstances, the Commission must produce to the Rechter-commissaris the documents which it has requested, unless it presents to the court imperative reasons relating to the need to avoid any interference with the functioning and independence of the Communities justifying its refusal to do so.

[E61] Case C-234/89 Delimitis v Henninger Bräu AG [1991] ECR I-935

The European Court of Justice

The compatibility of beer supply agreements with Article 85(1) of the Treaty

10. Under the terms of beer supply agreements, the supplier generally affords the reseller certain economic and financial benefits, such as the grant of loans on favourable terms, the letting of premises for the operation of a public house and the provision of technical installations, furniture and other equipment necessary for its operation. In consideration for those benefits, the reseller normally undertakes, for a predetermined period, to obtain supplies of the products covered by the contract only from the supplier. That exclusive purchasing obligation is generally backed by a prohibition on selling competing products in the public house let by the supplier.

11. Such contracts entail for the supplier the advantage of guaranteed outlets, since, as a result of his exclusive purchasing obligation and the prohibition on competition, the reseller concentrates his sales efforts on the distribution of the contract goods. The supply agreements, moreover, lead to co-operation with the reseller, allowing the supplier to plan his sales over the duration of the agreement and to organise production and distribution effectively.

12. Beer supply agreements also have advantages for the reseller, inasmuch as they enable him to gain access under favourable conditions and with the guarantee of supplies to the beer distribution market. The reseller's and supplier's shared interest in promoting sales of the contract

goods likewise secures for the reseller the benefit of the supplier's assistance in guaranteeing product quality and customer service.

13. Even if such agreements do not have the object of restricting competition within the meaning of Article 85(1), it is nevertheless necessary to ascertain whether they have the effect of preventing, restricting or distorting competition.

14. In its judgment in Case 23/67 *Brasserie de Haecht v Wilkin* [1967] ECR 407, the court held that the effects of such an agreement had to be assessed in the context in which they occur and where they might combine with others to have a cumulative effect on competition. It also follows from that judgment that the cumulative effect of several similar agreements constitutes one factor amongst others in ascertaining whether, by way of a possible alteration of competition, trade between Member States is capable of being affected.

15. Consequently, in the present case it is necessary to analyse the effects of a beer supply agreement, taken together with other contracts of the same type, on the opportunities of national competitors or those from other Member States, to gain access to the market for beer consumption or to increase their market share and, accordingly, the effects on the range of products offered to consumers.

16. In making that analysis, the relevant market must first be determined. The relevant market is primarily defined on the basis of the nature of the economic activity in question, in this case the sale of beer. Beer is sold through both retail channels and premises for the sale and consumption of drinks. From the consumer's point of view, the latter sector, comprising in particular public houses and restaurants, may be distinguished from the retail sector on the grounds that the sale of beer in public houses does not solely consist of the purchase of a product but is also linked with the provision of services, and that beer consumption in public houses is not essentially dependent on economic considerations. The specific nature of the public house trade is borne out by the fact that the breweries organise specific distribution systems for this sector which require special installations, and that the prices charged in that sector are generally higher than retail prices.

17. It follows that in the present case the reference market is that for the distribution of beer in premises for the sale and consumption of drinks. That finding is not affected by the fact that there is a certain overlap between the two distribution networks, namely inasmuch as retail sales allow new competitors to make their brands known and to use their reputation in order to gain access to the market constituted by premises for the sale and consumption of drinks.

18. Secondly, the relevant market is delimited from a geographical point of view. It should be noted that most beer supply agreements are still entered into at a national level. It follows that, in applying the Community competition rules, account is to be taken of the national market for beer distribution in premises for the sale and consumption of drinks.

. . .

24. If . . . such examination reveals that it is difficult to gain access to the relevant market, it is necessary to assess the extent to which the agreements entered into by the brewery in question contribute to the cumulative effect produced in that respect by the totality of the similar contracts found

on that market. Under the Community rules on competition, responsibility for such an effect of closing off the market must be attributed to the breweries which make an appreciable contribution thereto. Beer supply agreements entered into by breweries whose contribution to the cumulative effect is insignificant do not therefore fall under the prohibition under Article 85(1).

25. In order to assess the extent of the contribution of the beer supply agreements entered into by a brewery to the cumulative sealing-off effect mentioned above, the market position of the contracting parties must be taken into consideration. That position is not determined solely by the market share held by the brewery and any group to which it may belong, but also by the number of outlets tied to it or to its group, in relation to the total number of premises for the sale and consumption of drinks found in the relevant market.

26. The contribution of the individual contracts entered into by a brewery to the sealing-off of that market also depends on their duration. If the duration is manifestly excessive in relation to the average duration of beer supply agreements generally entered into on the relevant market, the individual contract falls under the prohibition under Article 85(1). A brewery with a relatively small market share which ties its sales outlets for many years may make as significant a contribution to a sealing-off of the market as a brewery in a relatively strong market position which regularly releases sales outlets at shorter intervals.

. . .

The jurisdiction of the national court to apply Article 85 to an agreement not enjoying the protection of an exemption regulation

. . .

44. . . . it should be stressed, first of all, that the Commission is responsible for the implementation and orientation of Community competition policy. It is for the Commission to adopt, subject to review by the Court of First Instance and the Court of Justice, individual decisions in accordance with the procedural rules in force and to adopt exemption regulations. The performance of that task necessarily entails complex economic assessments, in particular in order to assess whether an agreement falls under Article 85(3). Pursuant to Article 9(1) of [Regulation 17/62: **[E59]**] . . . the Commission has exclusive competence to adopt decisions in implementation of Article 85(3).

45. On the other hand, the Commission does not have exclusive competence to apply Articles 85(1) and 86. It shares that competence with the national courts. As the court stated in its judgment in Case 127/73 *BRT v SADAM* [1974] ECR 51, Articles 85(1) and 86 produce direct effect in relations between individuals and create rights directly in respect of the individuals concerned which the national courts must safeguard.

46. The same is true of the provisions of the exemption regulation (judgment in Case 63/75 *Fonderies Roubaix* [1976] ECR 111). The direct applicability of those provisions may not, however, lead the national courts to modify the scope of the exemption regulations by extending their scope of application to agreements not covered by them. Any such extension, whatever its scope, would affect the manner in which the Commission exercises its legislative competence.

47. It now falls to examine the consequences of that division of competence as regards the specific application of the Community competition
rules by national courts. Account should here be taken of the risk of
national courts taking decisions which conflict with those taken or envisaged by the Commission in the implementation of Articles 85(1) and 86,
and also of Article 85(3). Such conflicting decisions would be contrary to
the general principle of legal certainty and must, therefore, be avoided
when national courts give decisions on agreements or practices which may
subsequently be the subject of a decision by the Commission.

48. As the court has consistently held, national courts may not, where
the Commission has given no decision under Regulation 17, declare automatically void under Article 85(2) agreements which were in existence prior
to 13 March 1962, when that regulation came into force, and have been
duly notified (judgment in Case 48/72 *Brasserie de Haecht v Wilkin* [1973]
ECR 77; and judgment in Case 59/77 *De Bloos v Bouyer* [1977] ECR
2359). Those agreements in fact enjoy provisional validity until the
Commission has given a decision (judgment in Case 99/79 *Lancôme v
Etos* [1980] ECR 2511).

49. The contract at issue in the main proceedings was entered into on
14 May 1985 and there is nothing in the file to indicate that that contract
represents an exact reproduction of a standard contract concluded before
13 March 1962 and duly notified . . . The contract would not therefore appear to enjoy provisional validity. Nevertheless, in order to reconcile the
need to avoid conflicting decisions with the national court's duty to rule on
the claims of a party to the proceedings that the agreement is automatically
void, the national court may have regard to the following considerations in
applying Article 85.

50. If the conditions for the application of Article 85(1) are clearly not
satisfied and there is, consequently, scarcely any risk of the Commission
taking a different decision, the national court may continue the proceedings
and rule on the agreement in issue. It may do the same if the agreement's
incompatibility with Article 85(1) is beyond doubt and, regard being had to
the exemption regulations and the Commission's previous decisions, the
agreement may on no account be the subject of an exemption decision
under Article 85(3).

51. In that connection it should be borne in mind that such a decision
may only be taken in respect of an agreement which has been notified or is
exempt from having to be notified. Under Article 4(2) of Regulation 17, an
agreement is exempt from the notification obligation when only undertakings from a single Member State are parties to it and it does not relate to
imports or exports between Member States. A beer supply agreement may
satisfy those conditions, even if it forms an integral part of a series of similar contracts.

. . .

52. If the national court finds that the contract in issue satisfies those
formal requirements and if it considers in the light of the Commission's
rules and decision-making practices, that that agreement may be the subject of an exemption decision, the national court may decide to stay the
proceedings or to adopt interim measures pursuant to its national rules of
procedure. A stay of proceedings or the adoption of interim measures

should also be envisaged where there is a risk of conflicting decisions in the context of the application of Articles 85(1) and 86.

53. It should be noted in this context that it is always open to a national court, within the limits of the applicable national procedural rules and subject to Article 214 of the Treaty, to seek information from the Commission on the state of any procedure which the Commission may have set in motion as to the likelihood of its giving an official ruling on the agreement in issue pursuant to Regulation 17. Under the same conditions, the national court may contact the Commission where the concrete application of Article 85(1) or of Article 86 raises particular difficulties, in order to obtain the economic and legal information which that institution is bound by a duty of sincere co-operation with the judicial authorities of the Member State, who are responsible for ensuring that Community law is applied and respected in the national legal system (Order . . . in Case C-2/88 *Zwartveld* **[E60]**).

54. Finally, the national court may, in any event, stay the proceedings and make a reference to the court for a preliminary ruling under Article 177 of the Treaty.

[E62] Case T-24/90 Automec Srl v Commission [1992] 5 CMLR 431

The Court of First Instance

(a) First ground: contravention of Article 155 EEC, Article 3 of Regulation 17 and Article 6 of Regulation 99/63; second ground: statement of reasons of contested decision

. . .

Assessment by the court

[71] The court considers that the question raised by this submission seeks in effect to ascertain the Commission's obligations when it receives an application pursuant to Article 3 of Regulation 17 from a natural or legal person.

[72] It should be observed that Regulations 17 and 99 have conferred procedural rights upon persons submitting an application to the Commission, such as the right to be informed of the reasons why the Commission proposes to reject their complaint and the right to submit observations in this connection. Thus the Community legislature has imposed certain specific obligations upon the Commission. However, neither Regulation 17 nor Regulation 99 contain express provisions as to the action to be taken concerning the substance of a complaint and as to the Commission's obligations, if any, to carry out investigations.

[73] To ascertain the Commission's obligations in this context it should be observed . . . that the Commission is responsible for implementing and guiding Community competition policy: see Case C-234/89 *Delimitis* **[E61]**. Accordingly, Article 89(1) EEC has given the Commission the task of ensuring the application of the principles laid down by Articles 85 and 86, and measures adopted on the basis of Article 87 have conferred wide powers upon it.

[74] The extent of the Commission's obligations in the field of competition law must be examined in the light of Article 89(1) EEC which, in this area, is the specific manifestation of the general task of supervision entrusted to the Commission by Article 155. However, as the Court of Justice observed in relation to Article 169 EEC: Case 247/87 *Star Fruit v Commission* [1989] ECR 291, this task does not entail an obligation for the Commission to commence proceedings seeking to establish the existence of infringements of Community law.

[75] On this point the court observes that it is clear from the case law of the Court of Justice (Case 125/78 *GEMA* [1979] ECR 3173) that the rights conferred upon complainants by Regulations 17 and 99/63 do not include a right to obtain a decision, within the meaning of Article 189 EEC, as to the existence or otherwise of the alleged infringement. It follows that the Commission cannot be required to give a ruling in that connection unless the subject matter of the complaint is within its exclusive remit, such as the withdrawal of an exemption granted pursuant to Article 85(3) EEC.

[76] As the Commission has no obligation to rule on the existence or otherwise of an infringement it cannot be compelled to conduct an investigation, because this could have no purpose other than to seek evidence of the existence or otherwise of an infringement the existence of which it is not required to establish. On this point it should be noted that, unlike the provision contained in Article 89(1), sentence 2, in relation to applications by Member States, Regulations 17 and 99/63 do not expressly oblige the Commission to investigate the complaints referred to it.

[77] In this connection it should be observed that, for an institution performing a public service task, the power to take all the organisational measures necessary for the fulfilment of that task, including settling priorities in the framework laid down by law, where those priorities have not been settled by the legislature, is an inherent part of the work of administration. This must apply particularly where an authority has been given a supervisory and regulatory function as general and extensive as that assigned to the Commission in the field of competition. Therefore the fact that the Commission allocates different degrees of priority to the matters referred to it in the field of competition is compatible with its obligations under Community law.

. . .

[79] However, although the Commission cannot be compelled to conduct an investigation, the procedural safeguards provided for by Article 3 of Regulation 17 and Article 6 of Regulation 99/63 oblige it nevertheless to examine carefully the factual and legal aspects of which it is notified by the complainant in order to decide whether they indicate behaviour likely to distort competition in the Common Market and affect trade between the Member States.

. . .

[80] Where, as in the present case, the Commission has decided to close the file relating to the complaint without conducting an investigation, the review to be made by the court of the legality of that decision seeks to ascertain whether the contested decision is based on materially wrong facts, is flawed by a mistake in law or a manifest error of assessment or by a misuse of powers.

[81] It is for the court to verify, in the light of these principles, first,

whether the Commission has carried out the examination of the complaint which it is required to do by evaluating with all the requisite care the factual and legal aspects adduced by the applicant in his complaint and, secondly, whether the Commission has given proper reasons for closing the file on the complaint on the basis of its power 'to accord different degrees of priority to pursuing the matters referred to it' on the one hand, and on the basis of the Community interest in the matter as a criterion of priority on the other.

[82] In this connection the court finds, first, that the Commission carried out a careful examination of the complaint, in the course of which it not only took account of the factual and legal aspects adduced in the complaint itself, but also conducted an exchange of views and information with the applicant and its lawyers. The Commission rejected the complaint only after noting the further details supplied by the applicant in this way and the observations submitted in reply to the letter sent pursuant to Article 6 of Regulation 99/63. Therefore, having regard to the factual and legal aspects contained in the complaint, the Commission carried out an appropriate examination thereof and it cannot be charged with a want of diligence.

[83] Secondly, concerning the reasons for the contested decision to close the file, the court points out in the first place that the Commission is entitled to accord different degrees of priority to examining the complaints it receives.

[84] The second point to be considered is whether it is legitimate, as the Commission contends, to refer to the Community interest of a matter as a criterion of priority.

[85] In this connection it should be observed that, unlike the civil courts, whose task is to safeguard the subjective rights of private persons in their mutual relations, an administrative authority must act in the public interest. Consequently it is legitimate for the Commission to refer to the Community interest in order to determine the degree of priority to be accorded to the different matters before it. This does not mean removing the Commission's acts from judicial review: as Article 190 EEC requires the reasons on which decisions are based to be stated, the Commission cannot merely refer to the Community interest in isolation. It must set out the legal and factual considerations which lead it to conclude that there is not a sufficient Community interest which would justify the adoption of measures of investigation. Thus by reviewing the legality of those reasons the court can review the Commission's acts.

[86] To assess the Community interest in pursuing the examination of a matter, the Commission must take account of the circumstances of the particular case, particularly the legal and factual aspects set out in the complaint referred to it. It is for the Commission in particular to weigh up the importance of the alleged infringement for the functioning of the Common Market, the probability of being able to establish the existence of the infringement and the extent of the investigation measures necessary in order to fulfil successfully its task of securing compliance with Articles 85 and 86.

[87] In this context the question for the court is whether the Commission was right, in this particular case, to conclude that there was not a sufficient Community interest in pursuing the examination of the matter on the ground that the applicant, who had already referred to the Italian courts the dispute concerning the termination of the distribution agreement, could also submit to those courts the question of whether BMW Italia's distribution

system was compatible with Article 85(1) EEC.

[88] On this point it should be observed that, in doing so, the Commission did not confine itself to stating that as a general rule it ought not to proceed with a matter solely on the ground that the national court had jurisdiction to deal with it. The fact is that associated disputes between Automec and BMW Italia concerning the latter's distribution system had already been referred to the national courts and the applicant did not deny that the Italian courts had already taken cognisance of the contractual relationship between BMW Italia and its distributors. Under the particular circumstances of the case, reasons pertaining to saving unnecessary proceedings and the proper administration of justice militate in favour of examination of the matter by the court already dealing with associated questions.

[89] However, to assess the legality of the contested decision to close the file, the Court must determine whether, in referring the complainant enterprise to the national court, the Commission misconstrued the extent of the protection which the national court can provide to safeguard the rights derived by the applicant from Article 85(1) EEC.

[90] In this connection it should be observed that Articles 85(1) and 86 take direct effect in relations between individuals and create rights for individuals which the national courts must safeguard (see Case 127/73 *BRT* [1974] ECR 51). The power to apply those provisions is vested simultaneously in the Commission and the national courts (see Case C-234/89 *Delimitis*, cited above). Such power is however characterised by the obligation of loyal co-operation between the Commission and the national courts arising from Article 5 EEC (see . . . *Delimitis* . . .).

[91] Therefore the court must consider whether the Commission could rely upon such co-operation to ensure an assessment of the question whether BMW Italia's distribution system is compatible with Article 85(1).

[92] To this end, the Italian court is in a position to determine, first, whether the system entails restrictions of competition within the meaning of Article 85(1). In the event of doubt, it can seek a preliminary ruling from the Court of Justice. If it finds that there is a restriction of competition contrary to Article 85(1), it must next consider whether the system has the benefit of a group exemption under Regulation 123/85. This question is also within its jurisdiction (see *Delimitis* . . .). If there is any doubt as to the validity or interpretation of the regulation, the court may also make a reference to the Court of Justice pursuant to Article 177 EEC. In each of these situations the national court is able to give a ruling on the conformity of the distribution system with Article 85(1).

[93] Although the national court does not have power to order an end to any infringement it finds and to impose fines on the enterprises responsible, as the Commission can, it is nevertheless for the national court to apply Article 85(2) in relations between individuals. By making express provision for this civil sanction, the Treaty postulates that national law gives the court power to preserve the rights of enterprises which are victims of anti-competitive practices.

[94] In the present case the applicant has produced nothing to indicate that Italian law provides no legal remedy which would enable the Italian court to safeguard its rights in a satisfactory manner.

[95] It should be added that the existence in the present case of an exemption regulation, assuming that it applies, was a factor which could

legitimately be taken into account by the Commission to assess the Community public interest in carrying out an investigation into such a distribution system. As the Commission rightly points out, the main aim of a group exemption regulation is to limit the individual notification and examination of distribution agreements used in the sector concerned. The existence of such a regulation also facilitates the application of competition by the national court.

[96] Consequently, in referring the applicant to the national court, the Commission has not misconstrued the extent of the protection which the latter can give to the rights which the applicant derives from Article 85(1) and (2).

[97] It follows from what has been said that the court's examination of the contested decision reveals no mistake in law or in fact and no manifest error in assessment. It follows that the objection based on the contravention of Community law, particularly Article 155 EEC, Article 3 of Regulation 17 and Article 6 of Regulation 99/63 is unfounded.

[98] Furthermore, it follows necessarily from the foregoing that the reasons stated for the contested decision are sufficient because the applicant has been able to assert his rights before this court and the court has been able to carry out its review of legality.

[E63]   Commission Notice on co-operation between national courts and the Commission in applying Articles 85 and 86 of the EEC Treaty (OJ 1993 C39/6)

II. Powers

4. The Commission is the administrative authority responsible for the implementation and for the thrust of competition policy in the Community and for this purpose has to act in the public interest. National courts, on the other hand, have the task of safeguarding the subjective rights of private individuals in their relations with one another.

5. In performing these different tasks, national courts and the Commission possess concurrent powers for the application of Article 85(1) and Article 86 of the Treaty. In the case of the Commission, the power is conferred by Article 89 and by the provisions adopted pursuant to Article 87. In the case of the national courts, the power derives from the direct effect of the relevant Community rules.

. . .

6. In this way, national courts are able to ensure, at the request of the litigants or on their own initiative, that the competition rules will be respected for the benefit of private individuals. In addition, Article 85(2) enables them to determine, in accordance with the national procedural law applicable, the civil law effects of the prohibition set out in Article 85.

7. However, the Commission, pursuant to Article 9 of Regulation 17 **[E59]**, has sole power to exempt certain types of agreements, decisions and concerted practices from this prohibition. The Commission may exercise this power in two ways. It may take a decision exempting a specific

agreement in an individual case. It may also adopt regulations granting block exemptions for certain categories of agreements, decisions or concerted practices, where it is authorised to do so by the Council, in accordance with Article 87.

8. Although national courts are not competent to apply Article 85(3), they may nevertheless apply the decisions and regulations adopted by the Commission pursuant to that provision. The court has on several occasions confirmed that the provisions of a regulation are directly applicable. The Commission considers that the same is true for the substantive provisions of an individual exemption decision.

. . .

III.   The exercise of powers by the Commission

13. . . . The administrative resources at the Commission's disposal to perform its task are necessarily limited and cannot be used to deal with all the cases brought to its attention. The Commission is therefore obliged, in general, to take all organisational measures necessary for the performance of its task and, in particular, to establish priorities.

14. The Commission intends, in implementing its decision-making powers, to concentrate on notifications, complaints and own-initiative proceedings having particular political, economic or legal significance for the Community. Where these features are absent in a particular case, notifications will normally be dealt with by means of a comfort letter and complaints should, as a rule, be handled by national courts or authorities.

15. The Commission considers that there is not normally a sufficient Community interest in examining a case when the plaintiff is able to secure adequate protection of his rights before the national courts. In these circumstances the complaint will normally be filed.

16. In this respect the Commission would like to make it clear that the application of Community competition law by the national courts has considerable advantages for individuals and companies:
- the Commission cannot award compensation for loss suffered as a result of an infringement of Article 85 or Article 86. Such claims may be brought only before the national courts. Companies are more likely to avoid infringements of the Community competition rules if they risk having to pay damages or interest in such an event,
- national courts can usually adopt interim measures and order the ending of infringements more quickly than the Commission is able to do,
- before national courts, it is possible to combine a claim under Community law with a claim under national law. This is not possible in a procedure before the Commission,
- in some Member States, the courts have the power to award legal costs to the successful applicant. This is never possible in the administrative procedure before the Commission.

IV.   Application of Articles 85 and 86 by national courts

. . .

1.   Application of Articles 85(1) and (2) and Article 86

20. The first question which national courts have to answer is whether the agreement, decision or concerted practice at issue infringes the

prohibitions laid down in Article 85(1) or Article 86. Before answering this question, national courts should ascertain whether the agreement, decision or concerted practice has already been the subject of a decision, opinion or other official statement issued by an administrative authority and in particular by the Commission. Such statements provide national courts with significant information for reaching a judgment, even if they are not formally bound by them. It should be noted in this respect that not all procedures before the Commission lead to an official decision, but that cases can also be closed by comfort letters. Whilst it is true that the Court of Justice has ruled that this type of letter does not bind national courts, it has nevertheless stated that the opinion expressed by the Commission constitutes a factor which the national courts may take into account in examining whether the agreements or conduct in question are in accordance with the provisions of Article 85.

21. If the Commission has not ruled on the same agreement, decision or concerted practice, the national courts can always be guided, in interpreting the Community law in question, by the case law of the Court of Justice and the existing decisions of the Commission.

. . .

22. On these bases, national courts should generally be able to decide whether the conduct at issue is compatible with Article 85(1) and Article 86. Nevertheless, if the Commission has initiated a procedure in a case relating to the same conduct, they may, if they consider it necessary for reasons of legal certainty, stay the proceedings while awaiting the outcome of the Commission's action. A stay of proceedings may also be envisaged where national courts wish to seek the Commission's views in accordance with the arrangements referred to in this Notice. Finally, where national courts have persistent doubts on questions of compatibility, they may stay proceedings in order to bring the matter before the Court of Justice, in accordance with Article 177 of the Treaty.

23. However, where national courts decide to give judgment and find that the conditions for applying Article 85(1) or Article 86 are not met, they should pursue their proceedings on the basis of such a finding, even if the agreement, decision or concerted practice at issue has been notified to the Commission. Where the assessment of the facts shows that the conditions for applying the said Articles are met, national courts must rule that the conduct at issue infringes Community competition law and take the appropriate measures, including those relating to the consequences that attach to infringement of a statutory prohibition under the civil law applicable.

2. *Application of Article 85(3)*

24. If the national court concludes that an agreement, decision or concerted practice is prohibited by Article 85(1), it must check whether it is or will be the subject of an exemption by the Commission under Article 85(3). Here several questions may arise.

25. (a) The national court is required to respect the exemption decisions taken by the Commission. Consequently, it must treat the agreement, decision or concerted practice at issue as compatible with Community law and fully recognise its civil law effects. In this respect mention should be made of comfort letters in

which the Commission states that the conditions for applying Article 85(3) have been met. The Commission considers that national courts may take account of these letters as factual elements.

26. (b) Agreements, decisions and concerted practices which fall within the scope of application of a block exemption regulation are automatically exempted from the prohibition laid down in Article 85(1) without the need for a Commission decision or comfort letter.

27. (c) Agreements, decisions and concerted practices which are not covered by a block exemption regulation and which have not been the subject of an individual exemption decision or a comfort letter must, in the Commission's view, be examined in the following manner.

28. The national court must first examine whether the procedural conditions necessary for securing exemption are fulfilled, notably whether the agreement, decision or concerted practice has been duly notified in accordance with Article 4(1) of Regulation 17. Where no such notification has been made, and subject to Article 4(2) of Regulation 17, exemption under Article 85(3) is ruled out, so that the national court may decide, pursuant to Article 85(2), that the agreement, decision or concerted practice is void.

29. Where the agreement, decision or concerted practice has been duly notified to the Commission, the national court will assess the likelihood of an exemption being granted in the case in question in the light of the relevant criteria developed by the case law of the Court of Justice and the Court of First Instance and by previous regulations and decisions of the Commission.

30. Where the national court has in this way ascertained that the agreement, decision or concerted practice at issue cannot be the subject of an individual exemption, it will take the measures necessary to comply with the requirements of Article 85(1) and (2). On the other hand, if it takes the view that individual exemption is possible, the national court should suspend the proceedings while awaiting the Commission's decision. If the national court does suspend the proceedings, it nevertheless remains free, according to the rules of the applicable national law, to adopt any interim measures it deems necessary.

. . .

32. The Commission realises that the principles set out above for the application of Articles 85 and 86 by national courts are complex and sometimes insufficient to enable those courts to perform their judicial function properly. This is particularly so where the practical application of Article 85(1) and Article 86 gives rise to legal or economic difficulties, where the Commission has initiated a procedure in the same case or where the agreement, decision or concerted practice concerned may become the subject of an individual exemption within the meaning of Article 85(3). National courts may bring such cases before the Court of Justice for a preliminary ruling, in accordance with Article 177. They may also avail themselves of the Commission's assistance according to the procedures set out below.

V. *Co-operation between national courts and the Commission*

33. Article 5 of the EEC Treaty establishes the principle of constant and sincere co-operation between the Community and the Member States with a view to attaining the objectives of the Treaty, including implementation of Article 3(f) [now 3(g)], which refers to the establishment of a system ensuring that competition in the common market is not distorted. This principle involves obligations and duties of mutual assistance, both for the Member States and for the Community institutions. The court has thus ruled that, under Article 5 of the EEC Treaty, the Commission has a duty of sincere co-operation vis-à-vis judicial authorities of the Member States, who are responsible for ensuring that Community law is applied and respected in the national legal system.

34. The Commission considers that such co-operation is essential in order to guarantee the strict, effective and consistent application of Community competition law. In addition, more effective participation by the national courts in the day-to-day application of competition law gives the Commission more time to perform its administrative task, namely to steer competition policy in the Community.

35. In the light of these considerations, the Commission intends to work towards closer co-operation with national courts in the following manner.

36. The Commission conducts its policy so as to give the parties concerned useful pointers to the application of competition rules. To this end, it will continue its policy in relation to block exemption regulations and general notices. These general texts, the case law of the Court of Justice and the Court of First Instance, the decisions previously taken by the Commission and the annual reports on competition policy, are all elements of secondary legislation or explanations which may assist national courts in examining individual cases.

37. If these general pointers are insufficient, national courts may, within the limits of their national procedural law, ask the Commission and in particular its Directorate General for Competition for the following information.

First, they may ask for information of a procedural nature to enable them to discover whether a certain case is pending before the Commission, whether a case has been the subject of a notification, whether the Commission has officially initiated a procedure or whether it has already taken a position through an official decision or through a comfort letter sent by its services. If necessary, national courts may also ask the Commission to give an opinion as to how much time is likely to be required for granting or refusing individual exemption for notified agreements or practices, so as to be able to determine the conditions for any decision to suspend proceedings or whether interim measures need to be adopted. The Commission, for its part, will endeavour to give priority to cases which are the subject of national proceedings suspended in this way, in particular when the outcome of a civil dispute depends on them.

38. Next, national courts may consult the Commission on points of law. Where the application of Article 85(1) and Article 86 causes them particular difficulties, national courts may consult the Commission on its customary practice in relation to the Community law at issue. As far as Articles 85 and 86 are concerned, these difficulties relate in particular to the conditions for applying these articles as regards the effect on trade between Member States and as regards the extent to which the restriction on competition resulting from the practices specified in these provisions is appreciable. In its

replies, the Commission does not consider the merits of the case. In addition, where they have doubts as to whether a contested agreement, decision or concerted practice is eligible for an individual exemption, they may ask the Commission to provide them with an interim opinion. If the Commission says that the case in question is unlikely to qualify for an exemption, national courts will be able to waive a stay of proceedings and rule on the validity of the agreement, decision or concerted practice.

39. The answers given by the Commission are not binding on the courts which have requested them. In its replies the Commission makes it clear that its view is not definitive and that the right for the national court to refer to the Court of Justice, pursuant to Article 177, is not affected. Nevertheless, the Commission considers that it gives them useful guidance for resolving disputes.

40. Lastly, national courts can obtain information from the Commission regarding factual data: statistics, market studies and economic analyses. The Commission will endeavour to communicate these data, within the limits laid down in the following paragraph, or will indicate the source from which they can be obtained.

41. It is in the interests of the proper administration of justice that the Commission should answer requests for legal and factual information in the shortest possible time. Nevertheless, the Commission cannot accede to such requests unless several conditions are met. First, the requisite data must actually be at its disposal. Secondly, the Commission may communicate this data only in so far as permitted by the general principle of sound administrative practice.

42. For example, Article 214 of the Treaty, as spelt out in Article 20 of Regulation 17 for the purposes of the competition rules, requires the Commission not to disclose information of a confidential nature. In addition, the duty of sincere co-operation deriving from Article 5 is one applying to the relationship between national courts and the Commission and cannot concern the position of the parties to the dispute pending before those courts. As amicus curiae, the Commission is obliged to respect legal neutrality and objectivity. Consequently, it will not accede to requests for information unless they come from a national court, either directly, or indirectly through parties which have been ordered by the court concerned to provide certain information. In the latter case, the Commission will ensure that its answer reaches all the parties to the proceedings.

43. Over and above such exchange of information, required in specific cases, the Commission is anxious to develop as far as possible a more general information policy. To this end, the Commission intends to publish an explanatory booklet regarding the application of the competition rules at national level.

. . .

46. This Notice is issued for guidance and does not in any way restrict the rights conferred on individuals or companies by Community law.

47. This Notice is without prejudice to any interpretation of the Community competition rules which may be given by the Court of Justice of the European Communities.

48. A summary of the answers given by the Commission pursuant to this Notice will be published annually in the Competition Report.

Question

How far does this document amount to the application of subsidiarity to competition policy?

4   Abuse of a dominant position

Article 86 is set out in **[E49]**.

(a)   The relationship between Articles 85 and 86

[E64]   Case 6/72 Europemballage Corpn and Continental Can Co Inc v Commission [1973] ECR 215

The European Court of Justice

24. . . . . if Article 3(f) [now 3(g)] provides for the institution of a system ensuring that competition in the Common Market is not distorted, then it requires a fortiori that competition must not be eliminated. This requirement is so essential that without it numerous provisions of the Treaty would be pointless. Moreover, it corresponds to the precept of Article 2 of the Treaty according to which one of the tasks of the Community is 'to promote throughout the Community a harmonious development of economic activities'. Thus the restraints on competition which the Treaty allows under certain conditions because of the need to harmonise the various objectives of the Treaty, are limited by the requirements of Articles 2 and 3. Going beyond this limit involves the risk that the weakening of competition would conflict with the aims of the Common Market.

25. With a view to safeguarding the principles and attaining the objectives set out in Articles 2 and 3 of the Treaty, Articles 85 to 90 have laid down general rules applicable to undertakings. Article 85 concerns agreements between undertakings, decisions of associations of undertakings and concerted practices, while Article 86 concerns unilateral activity of one or more undertakings. Articles 85 and 86 seek to achieve the same aim on different levels, viz the maintenance of effective competition within the Common Market. The restraint of competition which is prohibited if it is the result of behaviour falling under Article 85, cannot become permissible by the fact that such behaviour succeeds under the influence of a dominant undertaking and results in the merger of the undertakings concerned. In the absence of explicit provisions one cannot assume that the Treaty, which prohibits in Article 85 certain decisions of ordinary associations of undertakings restricting competition without eliminating it, permits in Article 86 that undertakings, after merging into an organic unity, should reach such a dominant position that any serious chance of competition is practically rendered impossible. Such a diverse legal treatment would make a breach in the entire competition law which could jeopardise the proper functioning of the Common Market. If, in order to avoid the prohibitions in Article 85, it sufficed to establish such close connections between the undertakings that they escaped the prohibition of Article 85 without coming within the scope of that of Article 86, then, in contradiction to the basic principles of the Common Market, the partitioning of a substantial part of this market would

be allowed. The endeavour of the authors of the Treaty to maintain in the market real or potential competition even in cases in which restraints on competition are permitted, was explicitly laid down in Article 85(3)(b) of the Treaty. Article 86 does not contain the same explicit provisions, but this can be explained by the fact that the system fixed there for dominant positions, unlike Article 85(3), does not recognise any exemption from the prohibition. With such a system the obligation to observe the basic objectives of the Treaty, in particular that of Article 3(f), results from the obligatory force of these objectives. In any case Articles 85 and 86 cannot be interpreted in such a way that they contradict each other, because they serve to achieve the same aim.

[E65]   Case 66/86 Ahmed Saeed Flugreisen v Zentrale zur Bekämpfung unlauteren Wettbewerbs [1989] ECR 803

[The Court of Justice was asked to deliver a preliminary ruling on the compatibility with the Treaty of certain practices in connection with the fixing of tariffs applicable to scheduled passenger flights.]

The European Court of Justice

5. It should be pointed out that when the written procedure in this case was still in progress the court delivered its judgment in Joined Cases 209 to 213/84 *Ministère Public v Asjes and others* [1986] ECR 1425 in which it held that in the absence of rules on the application of Article 85 . . . to air transport, to be adopted by the Council pursuant to Article 87, agreements between undertakings and decisions by associations of undertakings could be prohibited under Article 85(1) and automatically void under Article 85(2) only in so far as they had been held by the authorities of the Member States, pursuant to Article 88, to fall under Article 85(1) and not to qualify for exemption under Article 85(3) or in so far as the Commission had recorded an infringement pursuant to Article 89(2). It follows that in the absence of implementing rules relating to air transport the transitional provisions set out in Articles 88 and 89 have continued to be applicable.

6. After an initial hearing in this case, the Council adopted . . . a series of measures concerning in particular the application of the rules on competition to undertakings in the air transport sector.

. . .

7. On the basis of those rules adopted by the Council, the Commission adopted . . . regulations on the application of Article 85(3) of the Treaty to certain categories of agreements between undertakings, decisions of associations of undertakings and concerted practices.

. . .

32. . . . The sole justification for the continued application of the transitional rules set out in Articles 88 and 89 is that the agreements, decisions and concerted practices covered by Article 85(1) may qualify for exemption under Article 85(3) and that it is through the decisions taken by the

institutions which have been given jurisdiction, under the implementing rules adopted pursuant to Article 87, to grant or refuse such exemption that competition policy develops. In contrast, no exemption may be granted, in any manner whatsoever, in respect of an abuse of a dominant position; such abuse is simply prohibited by the Treaty and it is for the competent national authorities or the Commission, as the case may be, to act on that prohibition within the limits of their powers.

33. It must therefore be concluded that the prohibition laid down in Article 86 of the Treaty is fully applicable to the whole of the air transport sector.

[E66] Case T-51/89 Tetra Pak Rausing SA v Commission [1990] ECR II - 309

The Court of First Instance

15. The applicant maintains that the Commission cannot apply Article 86 to behaviour exempt under Article 85(3) because Articles 85 and 86 both pursue the same objective.

. . .

16. In support of that argument, the applicant claims that the finding against it in the decision relates essentially to the exclusivity granted by the licensing agreement. The applicant goes on to argue that the Commission based the application of Article 86 on a distinction, for which there is no justification in competition law, between an exclusive licence enjoying block exemption on the one hand and, on the other, acquisition of the exclusivity afforded by the licence through takeover of a competing company (in this case Liquipak), such acquisition having been held in the decision to constitute infringement of Article 86. Both, according to the applicant, have the same restrictive effects on competition.

17. The applicant further argued . . . that since, on this view, Article 86 cannot be applied to an agreement enjoying exemption under Article 85(3), the fact that an undertaking in a dominant position becomes party to an agreement enjoying such exemption cannot constitute an abuse within the meaning of Article 86 unless a supplementary element, extrinsic to the agreement and attributable to the undertaking, is present.

. . .

18. The applicant points out that the inapplicability of Article 86 to an exempt agreement does not jeopardise achievement of the objectives of Article 86 since it is always within the discretion of the Commission to withdraw the exemption.

. . .

20. In reply . . ., the Commission points out that in the judgment in [Case 66/86 *Ahmed Saeed* [E65]] the Court of Justice expressly stated that no exemption may be granted in respect of an abuse of a dominant position . . . It concludes that the applicant's argument [in paragraph 18 above] cannot be accepted since that would be tantamount to recognising the existence of exemption for abuse of a dominant position, withdrawal of exemption being effective only *ex nunc*.

21. This court notes at the outset that the problem of reconciling application of Article 86 with enjoyment of block exemption, which is the crux of the present case and arises because of the need for logical coherence in the implementation of Articles 85 and 86, has not yet been expressly determined by the Community Court. However, it must be borne in mind that the relationship between Articles 85 and 86 has, to an extent, been clarified by the Court of Justice, in that the court has expressly said that the applicability to an agreement of Article 85 does not preclude application of Article 86. The court held that in such a case the Commission may apply either of the two provisions to the act in question: 'the fact that agreements . . . might fall within Article 85 and in particular within paragraph 3 thereof does not preclude the application of Article 86 . . . so that in such cases the Commission is entitled, taking into account the nature of the reciprocal undertakings entered into and the competitive position of the various contracting parties on the market or markets on which they operate, to proceed on the basis of Article 85 or Article 86' (Case 85/76 *Hoffman-la-Roche* . . .). The Court of Justice confirmed that position in *Ahmed Saeed* where it said that, in certain circumstances, 'the possibility that Articles 85 and 86 may both be applicable cannot be ruled out' . . . But the problem raised in *Ahmed Saeed* . . . was the question of principle as to whether implementation of an agreement capable of falling under Article 85(1) can also constitute abuse of a dominant position. The relationship between exemption under Article 85(3) and the applicability of Article 86 was not at issue.

. . .

23. Turning to the specific nature of the conduct whose compatibility with Article 86 is considered in the decision, this court holds that the mere fact that an undertaking in a dominant position acquires an exclusive licence does not per se constitute abuse within the meaning of Article 86. For the purpose of applying Article 86, the circumstances surrounding the acquisition, and in particular its effects on the structure of competition in the relevant market, must be taken into account . . . The decisive factor in the finding that acquisition of the exclusive licence constituted an abuse . . . lay quite specifically in the applicant's position in the relevant market and in particular . . . in the fact that at the material time the right to use the process protected by the BTG licence was alone capable of giving an undertaking the means of competing effectively with the applicant in the field of the aseptic packaging of milk. The takeover of Liquipak was no more than the means – to which the Commission has attached no particular significance in applying Article 86 – by which the applicant acquired the exclusivity of the BTG licence, the effect of which was to deprive other undertakings of the means of competing with the applicant.

. . .

25. In these circumstances, this court holds that in the scheme for the protection of competition envisaged by the Treaty the grant of exemption, whether individual or block exemption, under Article 85(3) cannot be such as to render inapplicable the prohibition set out in Article 86. This principle follows both from the wording of Article 85(3) which permits derogation, through a declaration of inapplicability, only from the prohibition of agreements, decisions and concerted practices set out in Article 85(1), and also from the general scheme of Articles 85 and 86 which . . . are independent

and complementary provisions designed, in general, to regulate distinct situations by different rules . . . If the Commission were required in every case to take a decision withdrawing exemption before applying Article 86, this would be tantamount, in view of the non-retroactive nature of the withdrawal of exemption, to accepting that an exemption under Article 85(3) operates in reality as a concurrent exemption from the prohibition of abuse of a dominant position . . . Moreover, in view of the principles governing the hierarchical relationship of legal rules, grant of exemption under secondary legislation could not, in the absence of any enabling provision in the Treaty, derogate from a provision of the Treaty, in this case Article 86.

26. Having established that, in principle, the grant of exemption cannot preclude application of Article 86, the question remains whether, in practice, findings made with a view to the grant of exemption under Article 85(3) preclude application of Article 86.

. . .

28. The way in which the question of exemption arises may in practice be different depending on whether an individual or block exemption is involved. The grant of individual exemption presupposes that the Commission has found that the agreement in question complies with the conditions set out in Article 85(3). So, where an individual exemption decision has been taken, characteristics of the agreement which would also be relevant in applying Article 86 may be taken to have been established. Consequently, in applying Article 86, the Commission must take account, unless the factual and legal circumstances have altered, of the earlier findings made when exemption was granted under Article 85(3).

29. Now it is true that regulations granting block exemption, like individual exemption decisions, apply only to agreements which, in principle, satisfy the conditions set out in Article 85(3). But unlike individual exemptions, block exemptions are, by definition, not dependent on a case by case examination to establish that the conditions laid down in the Treaty are in fact satisfied. In order to qualify for a block exemption, an agreement has only to satisfy the criteria laid down in the relevant block exemption regulation. The agreement itself is not subject to any positive assessment with regard to the conditions set out in Article 85(3). So a block exemption cannot, generally speaking, be construed as having effects similar to negative clearance in relation to Article 86. The result is that, where agreements to which undertakings in a dominant position are parties fall within the scope of a block exemption regulation (that is, where the regulation is unlimited in scope), the effects of block exemption on the applicability of Article 86 must be assessed solely in the context of the scheme of Article 86.

(b) Determination of the market

[E67] Case 27/76 United Brands v Commission [1978] ECR 207

The European Court of Justice

The relevant market

10. In order to determine whether UBC has a dominant position on the banana market it is necessary to define this market both from the

standpoint of the product and from the geographic point of view.

11. The opportunities for competition under Article 86 of the Treaty must be considered having regard to the particular features of the product in question and with reference to a clearly defined geographic area in which it is marketed and where the conditions of competition are sufficiently homogeneous for the effect of the economic power of the undertaking concerned to be able to be evaluated.

The product market

12. As far as the product market is concerned it is first of all necessary to ascertain whether, as the applicant maintains, bananas are an integral part of the fresh fruit market, because they are reasonably interchangeable by consumers with other kinds of fresh fruit such as apples, oranges, grapes, peaches, strawberries, etc or whether the relevant market consists solely of the banana market which includes both branded bananas and unlabelled bananas and is a market sufficiently homogeneous and distinct from the market of other fresh fruit.

13. The applicant submits in support of its argument that bananas compete with other fresh fruit in the same shops, on the same shelves, at prices which can be compared, satisfying the same needs: consumption as a dessert or between meals.

. . .

19. The Commission maintains that there is a demand for bananas which is distinct from the demand for other fresh fruit, especially as the banana is a very important part of the diet of certain sections of the community.

21. The Commission draws the conclusion from the studies quoted by the applicant that the influence of the prices and availabilities of other types of fruit on the prices and availabilities of bananas on the relevant market is very ineffective and that these effects are too brief and too spasmodic for such other fruit to be regarded as forming part of the same market as bananas or as a substitute therefor.

22. For the banana to be regarded as forming a market which is sufficiently differentiated from other fruit markets it must be possible for it to be singled out by such special features distinguishing it from other fruits that it is only to a limited extent interchangeable with them and is only exposed to their competition in a way that is hardly perceptible.

23. The ripening of bananas takes place the whole year round without any season having to be taken into account.

24. Throughout the year production exceeds demand and can satisfy it at any time.

25. Owing to this particular feature the banana is a privileged fruit and its production and marketing can be adapted to the seasonal fluctuations of other fresh fruit which are known and can be computed.

26. There is no unavoidable seasonal substitution since the consumer can obtain this fruit all the year round.

27. Since the banana is a fruit which is always available in sufficient quantities the question whether it can be replaced by other fruits must be determined over the whole of the year for the purpose of determining the degree of competition between it and other fresh fruit.

28. The studies of the banana market on the court's file show that on the

latter market there is no significant long-term cross-elasticity any more than
. . . there is any seasonal substitutability in general between the banana
and all the seasonal fruits, as this only exists between the banana and two
fruits (peaches and table grapes) in one of the countries (West Germany)
of the relevant geographic market.

29. As far as concerns the two fruits available throughout the year (oranges and apples) the first are not interchangeable and in the case of the
second there is only a relative degree of substitutability.

30. This small degree of substitutability is accounted for by the specific
features of the banana and all the factors which influence consumer choice.

31. The banana has certain characteristics, appearance, taste, softness,
seedlessness, easy handling, a constant level of production which enable it
to satisfy the constant needs of an important section of the population consisting of the very young, the old and the sick.

32. As far as prices are concerned two FAO studies show that the banana is only affected by the prices – falling prices – of other fruits (and only
of peaches and table grapes) during the summer months and mainly in July
and then by an amount not exceeding 20%.

33. Although it cannot be denied that during these months and some
weeks at the end of the year this product is exposed to competition from
other fruits, the flexible way in which the volume of imports and their marketing on the relevant geographic market is adjusted means that the conditions
of competition are extremely limited and that its price adapts without any
serious difficulties to this situation where supplies of fruit are plentiful.

34. It follows from all these considerations that a very large number of
consumers having a constant need for bananas are not noticeably or even
appreciably enticed away from the consumption of this product by the arrival of other fresh fruit on the market and that even the seasonal peak
periods only affect it for a limited period of time and to a very limited extent
from the point of view of substitutability.

35. Consequently the banana market is a market which is sufficiently
distinct from the other fresh fruit markets.

(c)   The notion of dominance

[E68]   Case 322/81 Michelin v Commission [1983] ECR 3461

The European Court of Justice

30. . . . Article 86 prohibits . . . any abuse of economic strength enjoyed
by an undertaking which enables it to hinder the maintenance of effective
competition on the relevant market by allowing it to behave to an appreciable extent independently of its competitors and customers and ultimately of
consumers.

31. The various criteria and evidence relied upon by the parties regarding the existence of a dominant position must be examined in that light.
They concern first Michelin's share of the relevant product market and secondly the other factors which must be taken into consideration in the
assessment of Michelin's position in relation to its competitors, customers
and consumers.

[The Court of Justice upheld the Commission's view that the relevant market was in new replacement tyres for heavy vehicles in the Netherlands and continued:]

55. . . . it should be observed that in order to assess the relative economic strength of Michelin and its competitors on the Netherlands market the advantages which those undertakings may derive from belonging to groups of undertakings operating throughout Europe or even the world must be taken into consideration. Amongst those advantages, the lead which the Michelin group has over its competitors in the matters of investment and research and the special extent of its range of products, to which the Commission referred in its decision, have not been denied. In fact in the case of certain types of tyre the Michelin group is the only supplier on the market to offer them in its range.

56. That situation ensures that on the Netherlands market a large number of users of heavy-vehicle tyres have a strong preference for Michelin tyres. As the purchase of tyres represents a considerable investment for a transport undertaking and since much time is required in order to ascertain in practice the cost-effectiveness of a type or brand of tyre, Michelin therefore enjoys a position which renders it largely immune to competition. As a result, a dealer established in the Netherlands normally cannot afford not to sell Michelin tyres.

57. It is not possible to uphold the objections made against those arguments by Michelin, supported on this point by the French government, that Michelin is thus penalised for the quality of its products and services. A finding that an undertaking has a dominant position is not in itself a recrimination but simply means that, irrespective of the reasons for which it has such a dominant position, the undertaking concerned has a special responsibility not to allow its conduct to impair genuine undistorted competition in the common market.

58. Due weight must also be attached to the importance of Michelin's network of commercial representatives, which gives it direct access to tyre users at all times. Michelin has not disputed the fact that in absolute terms its network is considerably larger than those of its competitors or challenged the description, in the decision at issue, of the services performed by its network whose efficiency and quality of service are unquestioned. The direct access to users and the standard of service which the network can give them enables Michelin to maintain and strengthen its position on the market and to protect itself more effectively against competition.

59. As regards the additional criteria and evidence to which Michelin refers in order to disprove the existence of a dominant position, it must be observed that temporary unprofitability or even losses are not inconsistent with the existence of a dominant position. By the same token, the fact that the prices charged by Michelin do not constitute an abuse and are not even particularly high does not justify the conclusion that a dominant position does not exist. Finally, neither the size, financial strength and degree of diversification of Michelin's competitors at the world level nor the counterpoise arising from the fact that buyers of heavy-vehicle tyres are experienced trade users are such as to deprive Michelin of its privileged position on the Netherlands market.

60. It must therefore be concluded that the other criteria and evidence relevant in this case in determining whether a dominant position exists confirm that Michelin has such a position.

Note. This case imposes a duty on dominant firms: is this fair or appropriate if the firm cannot discern, or makes an erroneous assessment, whether it is dominant on the Court of Justice's criteria?

[E69] Cases T-68/89 and T–77-78/89 Re Italian Flat Glass [1992] 5 CMLR 302

The Court of First Instance

Application of Article 86 EEC

Arguments of the parties

[341] According to the United Kingdom, the Commission was not entitled to find an infringement of Article 86 by considering that SIV, FP and VP held a collective dominant position on the Italian market for flat glass and by finding an abuse of that collective dominant position. Consequently, Article 2 of the decision should be annulled in so far as it finds an infringement of Article 86.

. . .

[342] In the opinion of the United Kingdom, it is only in very special circumstances that two or more undertakings may jointly hold a dominant position within the meaning of Article 86, namely, when the undertakings concerned fall to be treated as a single economic unit in which the individual undertakings do not enjoy a genuine autonomy in determining their conduct on the market and are not to be treated as economically independent of one another.

. . .

[343] The United Kingdom points out that, according to the case law of the Court of Justice, Article 85 does not apply to an agreement between a parent and its subsidiary which, although having separate legal personality, enjoys no economic independence: Cases 22/71 *Béguelin* [1971] ECR 949, Case 15/74 *Centrafarm* [1974] ECR 1147, Case 170/83 *Hydrotherm* [1984] ECR 2999 and Case 30/87 *Bodson* **[E87]**. When undertakings form part of one and the same economic unit, their conduct must be considered under Article 86 . . . The court considers that that view is supported by Case 66/86 *Ahmed Saeed* **[E65]**.

[344] According to the United Kingdom, the only matters relied on by the Commission to show that the three undertakings form a 'single entity' are the very same matters as the Commission relies on as constituting infringements of Article 85. The Commission has not demonstrated either the existence of institutional links between the undertakings analogous to those that exist between parent and subsidiary nor the loss of their individual autonomy nor the absence of competition among them.

. . .

[346] The applicants express their agreement with the arguments put forward by the United Kingdom.

. . .

[350] The Commission, for its part, refers to [its] decision with regard to the circumstances in which the concept of collective dominant position may be applied to independent undertakings. It in no way intended to apply the concept . . . to the undertakings in question solely on the ground that they form part of a tight oligopoly controlling more than 80 per cent of the Italian market in flat glass. It applied the concept of collective dominant position to the undertakings in question because, not only did they hold collectively a very large share of the market, they presented themselves on the market as a single entity and not as individuals. That emerges not from the structure of the oligopoly but from the agreements and concerted practices which led the three producers to create structural links amongst themselves, such as, in particular, the systematic exchanges of products. The Commission defends itself for having adopted the position that Article 86 may be applied to undertakings in an oligopolistic position regardless of whether or not there are agreements or concerted practices among them.

[351] The Commission adds that, even if there were certain differences in behaviour, such as in the case of VP which especially favoured processing wholesalers, those differences did not prevent the producers from observing one and the same global market strategy: they, in fact, conducted themselves as undertakings belonging to a single group.

. . .

Assessment by the court

[357] The court notes that the very words of Article 86(1) provide that 'one or more undertakings' may abuse a dominant position. It has consistently been held . . . that the concept of agreement or concerted practice between undertakings does not cover agreements or concerted practices among undertakings belonging to the same group if the undertakings form an economic unit . . . It follows that when Article 85 refers to agreements or concerted practices between 'undertakings' it is referring to relations between two or more economic entities which are capable of competing with one another.

[358] The court considers that there is no legal or economic reason to suppose that the term 'undertaking' in Article 86 has a different meaning from the one given to it in the context of Article 85. There is nothing, in principle, to prevent two or more independent economic entities from being, on a specific market, united by such economic links that, by virtue of that fact, together they hold a dominant position vis-à-vis the other operators on the same market. This could be the case, for example, where two or more independent undertakings jointly have, through agreements or licences, a technological lead affording them the power to behave to an appreciable extent independently of their competitors, their customers and ultimately of their consumers.

. . .

[359] The court finds support for that interpretation in the wording of Article 8 of Council Regulation 4056/86 laying down detailed rules for the application of Articles 85 and 86 EEC to maritime transport. Article 8(2) provides that the conduct of a liner conference benefiting from an exemption from a prohibition laid down by Article 85(1) may have effects which are incompatible with Article 86. A request by a conference to be exempted from

the prohibition laid down by Article 85(1) necessarily presupposes an agreement between two or more independent economic undertakings.

[360] However, it should be pointed out that for the purposes of establishing an infringement of Article 86, it is not sufficient, as the Commission's agent claimed at the hearing, to 'recycle' the facts constituting an infringement of Article 85, deducing from them the finding that the parties to an agreement or to an unlawful practice jointly hold a substantial share of the market, that by virtue of that fact alone they hold a collective dominant position, and that their unlawful behaviour constitutes an abuse of that collective dominant position. Amongst other considerations, a finding of a dominant position, which is in any case not in itself a matter of reproach, presupposes that the market in question has been defined . . . The court must therefore examine, first, the analysis of the market made in the decision and, secondly, the circumstances relied on in support of the finding of a collective dominant position.

. . .

[366] . . . even supposing that the circumstances of the present case lend themselves to application of the concept of 'collective dominant position' (in the sense of a position of dominance held by a number of independent undertakings), the Commission has not adduced the necessary proof. The Commission has not even attempted to gather the information necessary to weigh up the economic power of the three producers against that of Fiat, which could cancel each other out.

. . .

[368] It follows that Article 2 of the decision must be annulled.

Question

Is this conclusive acceptance of the application of Article 86 to collective dominance?

[E70]   Case 22/78 Hugin v Commission [1979] ECR 1869

The European Court of Justice

3. As regards the question whether Hugin occupies a dominant position on the market the Commission takes the view that the facts of the case have shown that while Hugin has only a relatively small share of the cash register market – which is very competitive – it has a monopoly in spare parts for machines made by it and that consequently it occupies a dominant position for the maintenance and repair of Hugin cash registers in relation to independent companies which need a supply of Hugin spare parts. As regards the reconditioning of used machines and the renting out of such machines the Commission also takes the view that Hugin occupies a dominant position as regards cash registers of its own manufacture, since undertakings engaged in such activities depend on supplies of Hugin spare parts.

4. Hugin contests the validity of the Commission's findings . . . In its principal argument it states that the supply of spare parts and of

maintenance services is certainly not a separate market but is an essential parameter of competition in the market for cash registers as a whole. It states that on that market after-sales service and the quality of repair and maintenance services, including the supply of spare parts, constitute such a significant factor that Hugin runs those services at a loss.

5. To resolve the dispute it is necessary, first, to determine the relevant market. In this respect account must be taken of the fact that the conduct alleged against Hugin consists in the refusal to supply spare parts to Liptons and, generally, to any independent undertaking outside its distribution network. The question is, therefore, whether the supply of spare parts constitutes a specific market or whether it forms part of a wider market. To answer that question it is necessary to determine the category of clients who require such parts.

6. In this respect it is established, on the one hand, that cash registers are of such a technical nature that the user cannot fit the spare parts into the machine but requires the services of a specialised technician and, on the other, that the value of the spare parts is of little significance in relation to the cost of maintenance and repairs. That being the case, users of cash registers do not operate on the market as purchasers of spare parts, however they have their machines maintained and repaired. Whether they avail themselves of Hugin's after-sales service or whether they rely on independent undertakings engaged in maintenance and repair work, their spare part requirements are not manifested directly and independently on the market. While there certainly exists amongst users a market for maintenance and repairs which is distinct from the market in new cash registers, it is essentially a market for the provision of services and not for the sale of a product such as spare parts, the refusal to supply which forms the subject matter of the Commission's decision.

7. On the other hand, there exists a separate market for Hugin spare parts at another level, namely that of independent undertakings which specialise in the maintenance and repair of cash registers, in the reconditioning of used machines and in the sale of used machines and the renting out of machines. The role of those undertakings on the market is that of businesses which require spare parts for their various activities. They need such parts in order to provide services for cash register users in the form of maintenance and repairs and for the reconditioning of used machines intended for resale or renting out. Finally, they require spare parts for the maintenance and repair of new or used machines belonging to them which are rented out to their clients. It is, moreover, established that there is a specific demand for Hugin spare parts, since those parts are not interchangeable with spare parts for cash registers of other makes.

8. Consequently the market thus constituted by Hugin spare parts required by independent undertakings must be regarded as the relevant market for the purposes of the application of Article 86 of the facts of the case. It is in fact the market on which the alleged abuse was committed.

. . .

The effects on trade between the Member States

. . .

17. The interpretation and application of the condition relating to effects on trade between Member States contained in Articles 85 and 86 of the

Treaty must be based on the purpose of that condition which is to define, in the context of the law governing competition, the boundary between the areas respectively covered by Community law and the law of the Member States. Thus Community law covers any agreement or any practice which is capable of constituting a threat to freedom of trade between Member States in a manner which might harm the attainment of the objectives of a single market between the Member States, in particular by partitioning the national markets or by affecting the structure of competition within the common market. On the other hand conduct the effects of which are confined to the territory of a single Member State is governed by the national legal order.

18. For the purpose of applying these criteria to the facts in this case it is necessary to examine separately the effects on Liptons' commercial activities, on the one hand, and on trade in spare parts in general, on the other.

19. It is established that the centre of Liptons' activities is the London region and that, in any event, its commercial activities have never extended beyond the United Kingdom. As regards the future, there is no indication that Liptons envisages extending its activities beyond those geographical limits. That limitation is explained, moreover, by the particular nature of the activities in question. The maintenance, repair and renting out of cash registers and the sale of used machines cannot constitute profitable operations beyond a certain area around the commercial base of an undertaking. This characteristic is reflected in the structure of the undertakings concerned. It appears from the file that in the United Kingdom there exist large numbers of small, local undertakings which specialise in the provision of the services in question. There are grounds for believing that the commercial structure of this trade is the same in the other Member States in which Hugin also applies its policy of not supplying spare parts outside its own distribution network.

20. The conclusion to be drawn from these considerations is therefore that trade between Member States is not affected by the obstacles which Hugin's conduct places in the way of the activities of independent undertakings which specialise in the provision of maintenance services.

21. As regards the distribution of Hugin spare parts as a distinct commercial activity it is established that Liptons has tried in vain to obtain such parts from Hugin distributors in certain other Member States. Moreover, Hugin does not deny that its policy of not supplying spare parts outside its own network, whilst it does not involve a prohibition on exports, necessarily implies that the refusal to supply independent undertakings applies whatever the geographical location of the undertaking.

22. The question is therefore, whether it may be assumed that trade between Member States in Hugin spare parts would exist if the market conditions were entirely free and not subject to restrictive practices such as those applied by Hugin in this instance.

23. It should be recalled in this respect that the value of the spare parts is in itself relatively insignificant. Accordingly they are not such as to constitute a commodity of commercial interest in trade between Member States, quite apart from the fact that an independent undertaking would derive no economic advantage from buying them from a Hugin subsidiary in another Member State rather than from the parent company. Indeed, it has not been alleged that Hugin applies differentiated prices on the various local markets. It is logical to suppose that an independent undertaking which could not obtain a spare part from the Hugin subsidiary established in its

country would turn to the parent company, that is to say, in this instance, to a supplier based in a non-member country, rather than to a subsidiary in another Member State. If the latter course were followed it would constitute an exception rather than a normal commercial transaction.

24. In the present case Liptons turned to Hugin subsidiaries and distributors in certain other Member States precisely because Hugin's restrictive policy prevented it from satisfying its spare parts requirements through normal commercial channels. Its attempts to obtain spare parts in the other Member States can therefore not be regarded as an indication of the existence, whether actual or potential, of a normal pattern of trade between the Member States in spare parts. In other words, if Liptons had been able to obtain spare parts from a Hugin subsidiary in another Member State it would have been because Hugin was willing to sell those parts outside its own distribution network. In such a case, however, it would be customary for Liptons to apply to the Hugin subsidiary in its own country rather than to a subsidiary in another Member State.

25. In those circumstances Hugin's conduct cannot be regarded as having the effect of diverting the movement of goods from its normal channels, taking account of the economic and technical factors peculiar to the sector in question.

26. It must therefore be concluded that Hugin's conduct is not capable of affecting trade between Member States. Consequently, the Commission's decision does not satisfy all the conditions laid down by Article 86 of the Treaty. It must therefore be annulled.

Note.   Given that the 'affecting inter-state trade' element represents the division between Community and national competence for both Articles 85 and 86, the arguments of the Court of Justice in this case may seem surprising. Should competence be determined by effects above a de minimis level?

(d)   The concept of abuse

[E71]   Case C-62/86 AKZO Chemie BV v EC Commission [1991] ECR I-3359

The European Court of Justice

35. In the decision it is primarily the organic peroxides market (including the benzoyl peroxide used in the plastics industry) that is held to be the relevant market, because that was the market from which AKZO sought in the long term to exclude ECS. Alternatively, according to the decision, the abuse took place in the flour additives market (including the benzoyl peroxide used in the milling sector) in the United Kingdom and Ireland.

36. It must be determined, first, whether the Commission was right to define the relevant market as the organic peroxides market.

37. AKZO disputes this definition in view of the subject matter of the decision, which relates solely to its allegedly unlawful behaviour in the flour additives sector. It points out in this respect that in the judgment in Joined Cases 6 and 7/73 *Commercial Solvents v Commission* [E72] . . ., the court held that the market in which the effects of the abuse appear is 'irrelevant as regards the determination of the relevant market to be considered for the purpose of a finding that a dominant position exists'.

38. That argument must be examined in the light of the particular circumstances of this case.

39. In that respect it must first be observed that benzoyl peroxide, one of the main organic peroxides, used in the manufacture of plastics, is also one of the main additives for flour because of its use as a bleaching agent for flour in the United Kingdom and Ireland.

40. Secondly, it should be pointed out that before 1979 ECS operated solely in the flour additives sector. It was only in the course of that year that it decided to extend its activities to the plastics sector. Consequently, when the dispute arose, ECS had only an extremely small market share in that sector.

41. Moreover, it is not disputed that the plastics sector was more important to AKZO than the flour additives sector, since it had a much higher turnover in that sector.

42. AKZO therefore applied price reductions in a sector (that of flour additives) which was vital to ECS but only of limited importance to itself.

43. Furthermore, AKZO was able to set off any losses that it incurred in the flour additives sector against profits from its activity in the plastics sector, a possibility not available to ECS.

44. Finally, . . . AKZO did not adopt its behaviour in order to strengthen its position in the flour additives sector, but to preserve its position in the plastics sector by preventing ECS from extending its activities to that sector.

45. The Commission was in those circumstances justified in regarding the organic peroxides market as the relevant market, even though the abusive behaviour alleged was intended to damage ECS's main business activity in a different market.

. . .

51. In its judgment in Case 31/80 *L'Oréal v De Nieuwe AMCK* [1980] ECR 3775 the court held that when considering the possibly dominant position of an undertaking within a particular market, 'the possibilities of competition must be judged in the context of the market comprising the totality of the products which, with respect to their characteristics, are particularly suitable for satisfying constant needs and are only to a limited extent interchangeable with other products'.

52. It should be observed that organic peroxides may, indeed, be individualised with regard to their formula, their concentration or their presentation in order to meet the particular requirements of customers. Nevertheless, 90% of their use is in various operations in the plastics industry and they are therefore suitable for satisfying constant needs, in the sense expressed in the judgment cited above. Moreover, they are not exposed to competition from other products, such as sulphur-based compounds used in the limited field of vulcanisation of synthetic rubber, since the latter products cannot replace them completely as they do not have all the technical properties required.

53. Finally, it may be seen from AKZO's internal documents . . . that AKZO itself regarded organic peroxides as a single market, since it calculates its market share in relation to those products as a totality.

. . .

The dominant position

. . .

60. With regard to market shares the court has held that very large shares are in themselves, and save in exceptional circumstances, evidence of the existence of a dominant position (. . . Case 85/76 *Hoffman-la-Roche v Commission* [1979] ECR 461 . . .). That is the situation where there is a market share of 50% such as that found to exist in this case.

61. Moreover, the Commission rightly pointed out that other factors confirmed AKZO's predominance in the market. In addition to the fact that AKZO regards itself as the world leader in the peroxides market, it should be observed that, as AKZO itself admits, it has the most highly developed marketing organisation, both commercially and technically, and wider knowledge than that of their competitors with regard to safety and toxicology.

. . .

The existence of an abuse of a dominant position

. . .

63. According to the contested decision AKZO had abusively exploited its dominant position by endeavouring to eliminate ECS from the organic peroxides market mainly by massive and prolonged price-cutting in the flour additives sector.

64. According to the Commission, Article 86 does not make costs the decisive criterion for determining whether price reductions by a dominant undertaking are abusive. Such a criterion does not take any account of the general objectives of the EEC competition rules as defined in Article 3(f) of the Treaty and in particular the need to prevent the impairment of an effective structure of competition in the common market. A mechanical criterion would not give adequate weight to the strategic aspect of price-cutting behaviour. There can be an anti-competitive object in price-cutting whether or not the aggressor sets its prices above or below its own costs, whatever the manner in which those costs are understood.

65. A detailed analysis of the costs of the dominant undertaking might, however, according to the Commission, be of considerable importance in establishing the reasonableness or otherwise of its pricing conduct. The exclusionary consequences of a price-cutting campaign by a dominant producer might be so self-evident that no evidence of intention to eliminate a competitor is necessary. On the other hand, where the low pricing could be susceptible of several explanations, evidence of an intention to eliminate a competitor or restrict competition might also be required to prove an infringement.

66. AKZO disputes the relevance of the criterion of lawfulness adopted by the Commission, which it regards as nebulous or at least inapplicable. It maintains that the Commission should have adopted an objective criterion based on its costs.

67. In that respect, it states that the question of the lawfulness of a particular level of prices cannot be separated from the specific market situation in which the prices were fixed. There is no abuse if the dominant undertaking endeavours to obtain an optimum selling-price and a positive coverage margin. A price is optimum if the undertaking may reasonably expect that

the offer of another price or the absence of a price would produce a less favourable operating profit in the short term. Furthermore, a coverage margin is positive if the value of the order exceeds the sum of the variable costs.

68. According to AKZO, a criterion based on an endeavour to obtain an optimal price in the short term cannot be rejected on the grounds that it would jeopardise the viability of the undertaking in the long term. It is only after a certain time that the undertaking in question could take measures to eliminate the losses or withdraw from a loss-making branch of business. In the meantime the undertaking would have to accept 'optimum orders' in order to reduce its deficit and to ensure continuity of operation.

69. It should be observed that, as the court held in its judgment in Case 85/76 *Hoffman-la-Roche* . . . the concept of abuse is an objective concept relating to the behaviour of an undertaking in a dominant position which is such as to influence the structure of a market where, as a result of the very presence of the undertaking in question, the degree of competition is weakened and through recourse to methods which, different from those which condition normal competition in products or services on the basis of the transactions of commercial operators, has the effect of hindering the maintenance of the degree of competition still existing in the market or the growth of that competition.

70. It follows that Article 86 prohibits a dominant undertaking from eliminating a competitor and thereby strengthening its position by using methods other than those which come within the scope of competition on the basis of quality. From that point of view, however, not all competition by means of price can be regarded as legitimate.

71. Prices below average variable costs (that is to say, those which vary depending on the quantities produced) by means of which a dominant undertaking seeks to eliminate a competitor must be regarded as abusive. A dominant undertaking has no interest in applying such prices except that of eliminating competitors so as to enable it subsequently to raise its prices by taking advantage of its monopolistic position, since each sale generates a loss, namely the total amount of the fixed costs (that is to say, those which remain constant regardless of the quantities produced) and, at least, part of the variable costs relating to the unit produced.

72. Moreover, prices below average total costs, that is to say, fixed costs plus variable costs, but above average variable costs, must be regarded as abusive if they are determined as part of a plan for eliminating a competitor. Such prices can drive from the market undertakings which are perhaps as efficient as the dominant undertaking but which, because of their smaller financial resources, are incapable of withstanding the competition waged against them.

73. These are the criteria that must be applied to the situation in the present case.

[E72]   Joined Cases 6 and 7/73 Commercial Solvents v Commission [1974] ECR 223

Opinion of Advocate General Warner

My Lords, I have no doubt that, if an undertaking has a dominant position in the market for a raw material, that undertaking abuses that position if, without reasonable justification, it refuses to supply a particular user of the raw material. It may, I think, be different if, the raw material being itself a manufactured product that exists only thanks to the efforts in research and development of the dominant undertaking, that undertaking decides to sell it to no-one, but to maximise its profits by itself supplying all the demand for the end product.

The European Court of Justice

25. However, an undertaking being in a dominant position as regards the production of raw material and therefore able to control the supply to manufacturers of derivatives, cannot, just because it decides to start manufacturing these derivatives (in competition with its former customers) act in such a way as to eliminate their competition which in the case in question, would amount to eliminating one of the principal manufacturers of ethambutol in the Common Market. Since such conduct is contrary to the objectives expressed in Article 3(f) of the Treaty and set out in greater detail in Articles 85 and 86, it follows that an undertaking which has a dominant position in the market in raw materials and which, with the object of reserving such raw material for manufacturing its own derivatives, refuses to supply a customer, which is itself a manufacturer of these derivatives, and therefore risks eliminating all competition on the part of this customer, is abusing its dominant position within the meaning of Article 86.

[E73]   Case 77/77 BP v Commission [1978] ECR 1513

Opinion of Advocate General Warner

The origin of this action lies in the oil 'crisis' that occurred in 1973–74 as a result of the decision of certain major oil-producing countries . . . sharply to increase their prices for crude oil and, at the same time, to reduce their production. For some importing countries, whose attitude was considered to have been inimical to the Arab cause in the Yom Kippur war, the resultant scarcity of oil was rendered particularly acute by an embargo on shipments to them imposed by Arab governments. The countries that were subject to that embargo included the Netherlands.

The action is brought under Article 173 of the EEC Treaty by three Dutch companies, which are . . . wholly-owned subsidiaries of BP, to challenge a decision of the Commission . . ., whereby the Commission declared that their conduct, during the period November 1973 to March 1974, in reducing deliveries of motor spirit to a particular customer to a greater degree than to other customers, constituted an abuse of a dominant position.

. . .

That customer is . . . ABG.

. . .

The history of the commercial relationship between ABG and BP is important.

Up to 1968 BP supplied ABG on the basis of contracts under which prices, quantities and other terms were agreed annually. Thereafter supplies were governed by contracts of indefinite duration, which were subject to six months' notice of cancellation by either side. On 21 November 1972 BP gave ABG notice terminating the current contract as from the end of May 1973. It appears that it did so because of action taken by the governments of countries where its oilfields were situate which reduced the reliability of its supplies of crude oil.

. . .

At the end of October 1973 the crisis arose . . . In the allocation of the available supplies as between national markets, the oil companies appear to have applied, or at all events BP applied, what it called the principle of 'equal misery'.

Within the Dutch market BP divided its customers into three categories:
(1)   those to whom it was bound by contract,
(2)   non-contractual but regular customers, and
(3)   customers towards whom it felt it had no particular responsibility.

. . .

Among the third category BP placed those who had been only casual customers in the past and also ABG.

. . .

The real question here is, in my view, whether the Commission is right in thinking that Article 86 is, on its correct interpretation, applicable to a situation in which, owing to an emergency causing a temporary scarcity of supplies of a particular commodity, the customers or the 'normal' customers of each supplier may become dependent on him.

I do not think so.

. . .

In a temporary emergency of the kind here in question, . . . a trader cannot distribute his scarce supplies regardless of the attitude of his customers. He must have it in mind that, once the emergency is over, they will have memories of the way in which they were treated by him during the period of scarcity. Contractual customers will expect the favourable treatment to which their contracts entitle them, both as a matter of law and as a matter of commercial honour . . . Non-contractual but regular customers will expect the loyalty shown by them in normal competitive times to be repaid by loyalty to them on the part of their supplier in the period of scarcity. A supplier can disregard those considerations only at the peril of losing customers to his competitors after the emergency is over. So I do not think that he is, during the emergency, in a dominant position in the sense in which that expression is used in Article 86.

Secondly, if Article 86 is to be held applicable to a supplier in such an emergency, there must be found in the terms of that Article some rule, either express or implicit, that suppliers are required to observe in such a situation. I cannot discern any such rule . . . We are here concerned not with the terms on which a trader supplies different customers, but with his selection of customers to supply and his decision as to the quantity to be supplied to each. Denial of supplies may of course constitute an abuse of a dominant position, as in . . . *Commercial Solvents* **[E72]**. . .

In my opinion it was legitimate for BP, in all the circumstances, to take the view it did. That being so, if it did have a dominant position, it cannot be held to have abused that position.

The European Court of Justice

14. . . . Article 103 of the Treaty . . . lays down that 'Member States shall regard their conjunctural policies as a matter of common concern', whilst providing the Community with the opportunity to meet conjunctural difficulties by appropriate measures subject to the observance of Community objectives.

. . .

15. . . . the absence of appropriate rules, based in particular on Article 103 . . ., which would make it possible to adopt suitable conjunctural measures, whilst revealing a neglect of the principle of Community solidarity which is one of the foundations of the Community, and a failure to act which is all the more serious since Article 103(4) provides in terms that 'the procedures provided for in this article shall also apply if any difficulty should arise in the supply of certain products', still cannot release the Commission from its duty to ensure in all circumstances, both in normal and special market conditions, when the competitive position of traders is particularly threatened, that the prohibition in Article 86 of the Treaty is scrupulously observed.

. . .

19. The contested decision accuses BP of having abused its dominant position on the market in question by reducing its supplies to ABG substantially and proportionately to a much greater extent than in relation to all its other customers and of having been unable to provide any objective reasons for its behaviour.

20. It thus accuses the company of having imposed on ABG an obvious, immediate and substantial competitive disadvantage and states that this behaviour might have jeopardised ABG's continued existence.

21. Whilst admitting that undertakings holding a dominant position may take into consideration certain peculiarities and differences in the situation of their customers the decision states that, to avoid abusing a dominant position within the meaning of Article 86 of the Treaty an undertaking in such a position must distribute 'fairly' the quantities available amongst all its customers.

. . .

29 . . . at the time of the crisis and even from November 1972, ABG's position in relation to BP was no longer, as regards the supply of motor spirit, that of a contractual customer but that of an occasional customer.

30. The principle laid down by the contested decision that reductions in supplies ought to have been carried out on the basis of a reference period fixed in the year before the crisis, although it may be explicable in cases in which a continued supply relationship has been maintained, during that period, between seller and purchaser, cannot be applied when the supplier ceased during the course of that same period to carry on such relations with its customer, regard being had in particular to the fact that the plans of any undertaking are normally based on reasonable forecasts.

. . .

32. . . . since ABG's position had been, for several months before the crisis occurred, that of an occasional customer, BP cannot be accused of

having applied to it during the crisis less favourable treatment than that which it reserved for its traditional customers.

33. Having regard to the general shortage of petroleum products during the period under review and the difficult position in which the whole of the Netherlands market was placed, the application to ABG by BP of a rate of reduction identical or very close to that applied to its traditional customers would have resulted in a considerable diminution of the deliveries which those customers expected.

34. A duty on the part of the supplier to apply a similar rate of reduction in deliveries to all its customers in a period of shortage without having regard to obligations contracted towards its traditional customers could only flow from measures adopted within the framework of the Treaty, in particular Article 103, or, in default of that, by the national authorities.

. . .

43. Hence, in view of these circumstances, it does not appear that BP in this case abused a dominant position in relation to ABG within the meaning of Article 86 of the Treaty.

[E74]   Case 238/87 Volvo v Veng [1988] ECR 6211

The European Court of Justice

7. It must first be observed, as the court held in its judgment . . . in Case 144/81 *Keurkoop v Nancy Kean Gifts* [1982] ECR 2853 with respect to the protection of designs and models, that, as Community law stands at present and in the absence of Community standardisation or harmonisation of laws, the determination of the conditions and procedures under which protection of designs and models is granted is a matter for national rules. It is thus for the national legislature to determine which products are to benefit from protection, even where they form part of a unit which is already protected as such.

8. It must also be emphasised that the right of the proprietor of a protected design to prevent third parties from manufacturing and selling or importing, without its consent, products incorporating the design constitutes the very subject matter of his exclusive right. It follows that an obligation imposed upon the proprietor of a protected design to grant to third parties, even in return for a reasonable royalty, a licence for the supply of products incorporating the design would lead to the proprietor thereof being deprived of the substance of his exclusive right, and that a refusal to grant such a licence cannot in itself constitute an abuse of a dominant position.

9. It must however be noted that the exercise of an exclusive right by the proprietor of a registered design in respect of car body panels may be prohibited by Article 86 if it involves, on the part of the undertaking holding a dominant position, certain abusive conduct such as the arbitrary refusal to supply spare parts to independent repairers, the fixing of prices for spare parts at an unfair level or a decision no longer to produce spare parts for a particular model even though many cars of that model are still in circulation, provided that such conduct is liable to affect trade between Member States.

[E75]   Case T-76/89 Independent Television Publications Ltd v Commission [1991] 4 CMLR 745

The Court of First Instance

Facts and procedure

[1]. . . . ITP sought the annulment of the Commission Decision of 21 October 1988 (hereinafter referred to as 'the decision') in which the Commission found that ITP's policies and practices, at the material time, in relation to the publication of its weekly listings for television and radio programmes which may be received in Ireland and Northern Ireland constituted infringements of Article 86 of the Treaty in so far as they prevented the publication and sale of comprehensive weekly television guides in Ireland and Northern Ireland. This action is linked with the concurrent actions for the annulment of that decision brought by the two other organisations to which it was addressed, namely *Radio Telefis Eirann ('RTE')* (Case T-69/89) and the *British Broadcasting Corporation and BBC Enterprises Ltd ('the BBC')* (Case T-70/89).

. . .

[2]. . . . Each of those organisations published a specialised television guide containing only its own programmes and, under the United Kingdom Copyright Act 1956 and the Irish Copyright Act 1963, claimed copyright in its weekly programme listings, preventing their reproduction by third parties.

Those listings indicate programme content and specify the broadcasting channel, together with the date, time and title of each programme. They go through a series of drafts, which become increasingly detailed and precise at each stage, until a weekly schedule is finalised approximately two weeks before transmission. At that stage, as the decision states, the programme schedules become a marketable product.

. . .

[7] The publisher Magill TV Guide Ltd (hereinafter referred to as 'Magill'), a company governed by Irish law, . . . was established in order to publish in Ireland and Northern Ireland a weekly magazine containing information on the television programmes available to television viewers in that area, the *Magill TV Guide* . . . After the publication on 28 May 1986 of an issue . . . containing all the weekly listings for all the television channels available in Ireland – including ITV and Channel 4 – an Irish court, in response to an application from BBC, RTE and ITP, issued an interim injunction restraining Magill from publishing weekly listings for those organisations' programmes.

. . .

[8] Previously, on 4 April 1986, with a view to the publication of complete weekly listings, Magill had lodged a complaint with the Commission under Article 3 of Regulation 17 [E59], seeking a finding that the ITP, BBC and RTE were abusing their dominant position by refusing to grant licences for the publication of their respective weekly listings . . . On 21 December 1988 [the Commission] adopted the decision with which the present action is concerned.

[9] In the decision, the relevant products are defined as follows for the three organisations concerned: they are the advance weekly listings of ITP, the BBC and RTE, and also the television guides in which those listings are published. In the Commission's definition, a programme listing is 'a list of programmes to be broadcast by or on behalf of a broadcasting organisation within a given period of time, the list including the following information: the title of each programme to be broadcast, the channel, the date and time of transmission'.

The Commission finds that because of the factual monopoly enjoyed by the broadcasting organisations over their respective weekly listings, third parties interested in publishing a weekly television guide are 'in a position of economic dependence which is characteristic of the existence of a dominant position'. Furthermore, the Commission adds, that monopoly is strengthened into a legal monopoly in so far as those organisations claim copyright protection for their respective listings. In those circumstances, the Commission observes, 'no competition from third parties is permitted to exist on [the relevant] markets'. From that it infers that 'ITP, BBC and RTE each hold a dominant position within the meaning of Article 86'.

[10] To establish the existence of an abuse, the decision relies more particularly on Article 86(2)(b) of the Treaty, pursuant to which an abuse is committed if an undertaking holding a dominant position limits production or markets to the prejudice of consumers. The Commission considers in particular that 'substantial potential demand . . . for comprehensive TV guides' exists on the market. It finds that, by using its dominant position 'to prevent the introduction on to the market of a new product, that is, a comprehensive weekly TV guide', the applicant is abusing that dominant position. It adds that a further element of the abuse is that, by virtue of the offending policy regarding information on its programmes, the applicant retains for itself the derivative market for weekly guides for those programmes.

The Commission therefore rejects the argument that the conduct to which it objects is justified by copyright protection and states that in the present case ITP, the BBC and RTE 'use copyright as an instrument of the abuse, in a manner which falls outside the scope of the specific subject-matter of that intellectual property right'.

. . .

Legal assessment

[46]. . . . the court, in its review of the merits of the plea based on a breach of Article 86 and an inadequate statement of reasons, must examine three points. First of all, the definition of the relevant product market must be considered; then, secondly, the applicant's position on that market must be determined. As a third stage, the court must decide whether or not the conduct at issue constitutes an abuse.

The definition of the relevant products

. . .

[48] In fact, the markets for weekly listings and for the television magazines in which they are published constitute submarkets within the market for television programme information in general. They offer a product – information on weekly programmes – for which there is a specific demand,

both from third parties wishing to publish and market comprehensive television guides and from television viewers. The former are unable to publish such guides unless they have at their disposal all the weekly programme listings for the channels which can be received within the relevant geographical market. As regards the latter, it must be observed that, as the Commission rightly established in its decision, the programme information available on the market at the time of the adoption of the decision, namely the complete lists of programmes for a 24-hour period – and for a 48-hour period at weekends and before public holidays – published in certain daily and Sunday newspapers, and the television sections of certain magazines covering in addition 'highlights' of the week's programmes, are only to a limited extent substitutable for advance information to viewers on all the week's programmes. Only weekly television guides containing comprehensive listings for the week ahead enable users to decide in advance which programmes they wish to follow and arrange any leisure activities for the week accordingly.

That limited substitutability of weekly programme information is evidenced in particular by the success enjoyed, at the material time, by the specialised television magazines which were all that was available on the market in weekly guides in the United Kingdom and Ireland and, in the rest of the Community, by the comprehensive television guides available on the market in the other Member States. That clearly demonstrates the existence of a potential specific, constant and regular demand on the part of viewers, in this case in Ireland and Northern Ireland, for television magazines containing comprehensive television programme listings for the week ahead, irrespective of any other sources of programme information available on the market.

The existence of a dominant position

[49]. . . . the court notes that ITP enjoyed, as a consequence of its copyrights in ITV and Channel 4 listings, . . . the exclusive right to reproduce and market those listings. It was thus able, at the material time, to secure a monopoly over the publication of its weekly listings in the TV Times, a magazine specialising in the programmes of ITV and Channel 4. Consequently, the applicant clearly held at that time a dominant position both on the market represented by its weekly listings and on the market for the magazines in which they were published in Ireland and Northern Ireland. Third parties such as Magill . . . were in a situation of economic dependence on the applicant, which was thus in a position to hinder the emergence of any effective competition on the market for information on its weekly programmes.

The existence of an abuse

. . .

[51] In the absence of harmonisation of national rules or Community standardisation, the determination of the conditions and procedures under which copyright is protected is a matter for national rules. That division of powers with regard to intellectual property rights was explicitly endorsed by the Court of Justice in Case 144/81 (*Keurkoop v Nancy Kean Gifts* [1982] ECR 2853) and confirmed, in particular, in Case 53/87 (*CICRA v Renault*

[1988] ECR 6039) and Case 238/87 (*Volvo v Veng* **[E74]**).

[52] The relationship between national intellectual property rights and the general rules of Community law is governed expressly by Article 36 of the Treaty, which provides for the possibility of derogating from the rules relating to the free movement of goods on grounds of the protection of industrial or commercial property. However, that derogation is explicitly made subject to certain reservations.The protection of intellectual property rights conferred by national law is recognised, in Community law, only subject to the conditions set out in the second sentence of Article 36 **[E11]** . . . Article 36 thus emphasises that the reconciliation between the requirements of the free movement of goods and the respect to which intellectual property rights are entitled must be achieved in such a way as to protect the legitimate exercise of such rights, which alone is justified within the meaning of that article, and to preclude any improper exercise thereof likely to create artificial partitions within the market or pervert the rules governing competition within the Community. The exercise of intellectual property rights conferred by national legislation must consequently be restricted as far as is necessary for that reconciliation.

[53] Within the system of the Treaty, Article 36 must be interpreted 'in the light of the Community's objectives and activities as defined by Articles 2 and 3 of the EEC Treaty', as the Court of Justice held in Case 270/80 [*Polydor v Harlequin* [1982] ECR 329]. That assessment must take into account, in particular, the requirements arising out of the establishment of a system of free competition within the Community, referred to in Article 3(f) [now 3(g)], which take the form, inter alia, of the prohibitions laid down in Article 85 and 86 of the Treaty.

[54] Under Article 36, as it has been interpreted by the Court of Justice in the light of the objectives pursued by Articles 85 and 86 and the provisions governing the free movement of goods or services, only those restrictions on freedom of competition, free movement of goods or freedom to provide services which are inherent in the protection of the actual substance of the intellectual property right are permitted in Community law. In Case 78/70 *Deutsche Grammophon* [1971] ECR 487 . . ., which concerned a right similar to copyright, the Court of Justice held: 'Although it permits prohibitions or restrictions on the free movement of products, which are justified for the purpose of protecting industrial and commercial property, Article 36 only admits derogations from that freedom to the extent to which they are justified for the purpose of safeguarding rights which constitute the specific subject matter of such property'.

[55] It is common ground that in principle the protection of the specific subject matter of copyright entitles the copyright-holder to reserve the exclusive right to reproduce the protected work. The Court of Justice expressly recognised that in Case 158/86 *Warner Bros Inc v Christiansen* [1988] ECR 2605 . . ., in which it held that '[t]he two essential rights of the author, namely the exclusive right of performance and the exclusive right of reproduction, are not called in question by the rules of the Treaty'.

[56] However, while it is plain that the exercise of the exclusive right to reproduce a protected work is not in itself an abuse, that does not apply when, in the light of the details of each individual case, it is apparent that that right is exercised in such ways and circumstances as in fact to pursue an aim manifestly contrary to the objectives of Article 86. In that event, the copyright is no longer exercised in a manner which corresponds to its

essential function, within the meaning of Article 36 of the Treaty, which is to protect the moral rights in the work and ensure a reward for the creative effort, while respecting the aims of, in particular, Article 86. In that case, the primacy of Community law, particularly as regards principles as fundamental as those of the free movement of goods and freedom of competition, prevails over any use of a rule of national intellectual property law in a manner contrary to those principles.

[57] That analysis is borne out by the case law of the Court of Justice which in . . . *Volvo v Veng* and *CICRA v Renault* . . . held that the exercise of an exclusive right which, in principle, corresponds to the substance of the relevant intellectual property right may nevertheless be prohibited by Article 86 if it involves, on the part of the undertaking holding a dominant position, certain abusive conduct.

. . .

[59]. . . . it must also be stressed that . . . the applicant's refusal to authorise third parties to publish its weekly programme listings may be distinguished from the refusal of Volvo and Renault . . . in the above-mentioned judgments . . . to grant third parties licences to manufacture and market spare parts. In the present case, the aim and effect of the applicant's exclusive reproduction of its programme listings was to exclude any potential competition from the derivative market represented by information on the weekly programmes broadcast on ITV and Channel 4, in order to maintain the monopoly enjoyed, through the publication of the TV Times, by the applicant on that market. For the point of view of outside undertakings interested in publishing a television magazine, the applicant's refusal to authorise, on request and on a non-discriminatory basis, any third party to publish its programme listings is therefore comparable, as the Commission rightly stresses, to an arbitrary refusal by a car manufacturer to supply spare parts – produced in the course of his main activity of car making – to an independent repairer carrying on his business on the derivative market of automobile maintenance and repair. Moreover, the applicant's conduct stifled the emergence on the market of a certain type of product, namely general television magazines. Consequently, in so far as it was in particular characterised, in that regard, by a failure to take consumer needs into consideration, that conduct also presented a certain similarity to a decision by a car manufacturer – envisaged as a hypothesis by the Court of Justice in the above-mentioned judgments – no longer to produce spare parts for certain models even though there was still a market demand for such parts. It is thus clear from that comparison that the applicant's conduct is not related, according to the criteria established in the case law to which the parties refer, to the actual substance of its copyright.

[60] In the light of the foregoing considerations, the court finds that, although the programme listings were at the material time protected by copyright as laid down by national law, which still determines the rules governing that protection, the conduct at issue could not qualify for such protection within the framework of the necessary reconciliation between intellectual property rights and the fundamental principles of the Treaty concerning the free movement of goods and freedom of competition. The aim of that conduct was clearly incompatible with the objectives of Article 86.

[E76] Decision of the EC Commission 92/213 British Midland Airways Ltd v Aer Lingus plc (OJ 1992 L96/34)

I. Facts

B. The refusal to interline

3. Interlining is hailed as one of IATA's major achievements. It essentially consists of an agreement (Multilateral Interline Traffic Agreement – MITA . . .), pursuant to which airlines are authorised to sell each other's services. As a result a single ticket can be issued which comprises segments to be performed by different airlines. Applicable tariffs and conditions are those of the party over whose route the passenger is to be carried. The airline which issues the ticket collects the price for all segments from the passenger. The issuing airline then pays the fare due to the carrying airline (less a 9% interline service charge . . .) through the IATA clearing house.

In order to become a party to the MITA an interested airline (which must not necessarily be an IATA member) makes an application to IATA which is circulated to all participating airlines. Traditionally agreement or 'concurrence' to an application is hardly ever refused, the exception being where currency convertibility or the financial stability of the applicant are not assured. In the latter case airlines may conclude specific agreements, providing eg for unilateral interlining (ie that the applicant accepts the flag carriers' authority to issue tickets on its behalf but not vice versa).

The interlining system benefits from the participation of the vast majority of the world's airlines, accounting for approximately 95% of all scheduled traffic.

4. In addition airlines accept to change tickets at passengers' request. This technically relates to 'voluntary changes' rather than 'interlining' . . . but normally operates in conjunction with interlining.

. . .

5. The main advantages of the multilateral interline and voluntary change system (jointly referred to hereafter, for the purpose of this decision, as 'interline system') are that passengers can buy a single ticket providing for transportation by different carriers (eg leaving on the issuing airline and returning on another airline serving the same route, or leaving on the issuing airline and continuing to destinations not served by that airline), and that passengers can easily change the reservations, routings or airlines mentioned on the ticket.

. . .

7. Since 1964, Aer Lingus [the national airline of Ireland] concurred with British Midland's participation in the MITA.

After having been awarded the right to operate a London (Heathrow)–Dublin service, British Midland announced on 22 February 1989 its intention to commence services on that route from 28 April 1989. On 7 April 1989 Aer Lingus gave notice that it terminated its concurrence with British Midland's participation in MITA, effective 7 May. Furthermore Aer Lingus did not accept interchangeability of its and British Midland's tickets on the London (Heathrow)–Dublin route. British Midland was able to interline with British Airways until the latter's withdrawal from the route at the end of March 1991.

Aer Lingus did not cancel its interline agreement with the other airline operating on the route, British Airways.

In statements to the press issued at that time, Aer Lingus declared:

> We have established ourselves as the dominant carrier on the routes between the two capitals, and intend to remain so . . . . British Midland does not have the resources to offer a similar frequency of service, so they want us to provide product for them via an interline agreement (*Airline World*, 24 April 1989).

. . .

II. Legal assessment

A. Article 86

(a) Dominance

20. The very high share of the relevant market [60–75%] enjoyed by Aer Lingus, and the presence of barriers to entry on the route concerned are indicative of dominance. Furthermore Aer Lingus is the national Irish airline and would be the preferred choice of most passengers on the route, who are Irish nationals. Aer Lingus has the most extensive network out of Ireland and accounts for a very large share of air transport out of the country. This position gives it commercial power in the local market which smaller, foreign-based airlines do not possess.

21. The mere fact that Aer Lingus was able to disregard the complaints of travel agents and business travellers suffering from the refusal to interline suggests that Aer Lingus enjoys considerable freedom of action.

. . .

22. Even though British Midland has been able to obtain a significant market share in the years following entry on the route, its presence does not negate the evidence of dominance by Aer Lingus.

Aer Lingus maintained and even increased the absolute number of passengers carried on the route. Its share of passengers carried and of sales relative to that of other airlines on the route decreased following British Midland's entry, but only by a fairly small margin and recovered again after British Airways' exit. British Midland's success appears to be due to a large extent to its ability to benefit from the significant growth of the number of passengers on the route between 1989 and 1990 by providing extra capacity at a time when there was demand for it.

23. All of this indicates that Aer Lingus has an appreciable freedom of action. While Aer Lingus has been exposed to a certain amount of competition, it has been able to contain that competition successfully at relatively low cost to itself.

(b) Abuse

24. Abusive conduct is defined as 'practices which are likely to affect the structure of a market where, as a result of the presence of the undertaking in question, competition has already been weakened and which, through recourse to methods differing from those governing normal competition in goods or services based on traders' performance, have the effect of

hindering the maintenance or development of the level of competition existing on the market' (judgment of the Court . . . in Case 85/76
Hoffman-la-Roche v Commission [1979] ECR 541).

25. Refusing to interline is not normal competition on the merits.
Interlining has for many years been accepted as industry practice, with
widely acknowledged benefits for both airlines and passengers. A refusal to
interline . . . is a highly unusual step and has up to now not been seen by
the European airline industry as a normal competitive strategy. Aer Lingus
itself has maintained interline agreements with the other airlines competing
with it on London–Dublin services, British Airways and Dan Air.

Aer Lingus has argued that, whereas interlining in most circumstances is
beneficial to all participating airlines, it would suffer from interlining with
British Midland by losing several points of market share to the new entrant.
Even if this could be demonstrated, the argument that interlining would
result in a loss of revenue would not in itself make the refusal legitimate.
Aer Lingus has not argued that interlining with British Midland would have a
significant effect on its own costs, whereas there is evidence that a refusal
to interline would impose a significant handicap on British Midland.

26. Both a refusal to grant new interline facilities and the withdrawal of existing interline facilities may, depending on the circumstances, hinder the
maintenance or development of competition. Whether a duty to interline
arises depends on the effects on competition of the refusal to interline; it
would exist in particular when the refusal or withdrawal of interline facilities by
a dominant airline is objectively likely to have a significant impact on the other
airline's ability to start a new service or sustain an existing service on account
of its effects on the other airline's costs and revenue in respect of the service
in question, and when the dominant airline cannot give any objective commercial reason for its refusal (such as concerns about creditworthiness) other
than its wish to avoid helping this particular competitor. It is unlikely that there
is such justification when the dominant airline singles out an airline with which
it previously interlined, after that airline starts competing on an important
route, but continues to interline with other competitors.

. . .

29. It is true that Aer Lingus' strategy in the event has not resulted in
British Midland's departure from the route, and that British Midland has succeeded in building up a reasonable schedule and in obtaining a significant
market share. It is also true that the refusal to interline does not entirely
preclude British Midland from attracting business travellers . . . However, if
Aer Lingus had continued to accept interlining, British Midland would have
incurred lower costs, it would have earned higher revenues, its services
would have been more attractive to its passengers and it would have been
a stronger and more successful competitor than it now is.

[The decision of the Commission imposed fines on Aer Lingus for the
breach of Article 86.]

Question

In the light of extracts **[E72]–[E76]**, does a duty not to abuse dominance include a duty to grant access to the market place to actual or potential
competitors? Read also **[E88]**, and consider the arguments in **[E77]** below.

[E77]   R Subiotto: 'The right to deal with whom one pleases under EEC competition law: a small contribution to a necessary debate' [1992] 6 European Competition Law Review 234

Note.   This article was written before the Court of Justice heard the appeals in the TV listings cases.

The duty to share and intellectual property rights

The benefits to society of technical and creative innovation are undeniable. Innovation is unlikely to occur unless the innovator can be assured of some recompense. The best incentive for technical and creative innovation is considered to be the provision to the innovator of exclusive rights over his new technological process, product, creation or design for a limited duration. This duration reflects the compromise struck by the state between the need to encourage innovation and the 'evil' of granting a monopoly to an undertaking. Thus:

- A patent rewards the creative effort of the owner of, for example, a patented process by granting him the exclusive right for a limited duration to use the patented process to manufacture products and sell them for the first time (that is, he will be able to control the first sale but not subsequent sales of the same product). As a consequence of his exclusive right, he will be able to prevent its use by third parties.
- Copyright rewards the creative effort of the author of the copyrighted product by granting him the exclusive right for a limited duration to manufacture and sell the product for the first time as well as granting him exclusive rights over the performance of the copyrighted product. As a consequence of his exclusive rights, the copyright holder will be able to prevent the reproduction and unauthorised performance of the work by third parties.
- A design right rewards the creative effort of the proprietor of the protected design by granting him the exclusive right for a limited duration to manufacture and sell for the first time products incorporating the design. As a consequence of his exclusive rights, a proprietor of the protected design will be able to prevent its use by third parties.
- A trade mark rewards the manufacturer that consistently produces high-quality goods by granting him the exclusive right to use the trade mark for the first marketing of the marked product. As a consequence of his exclusive right, the owner of a trade mark will be able to prevent its use by third parties that wish to take advantage of its status and reputation.

Therefore, since the intellectual property laws are concerned with the creation and commercial exploitation of a statutory grant of monopoly power and competition law is concerned with proscribing various kinds of monopoly power, reconciling the interrelationship between the two requires caution.

By contrast, the pronouncements of the Commission and the Court of First Instance in *Magill* **[E75]** seem not to reflect this caution. They suggest that a holder of an intellectual property right which is in a monopoly position might, depending on the circumstances, be forced to share it with third parties in order to enable them to create a new product for which there is substantial potential consumer demand, even though the new product might compete with the intellectual property owner's existing product. This, despite the fact that legislation has granted the holder of the intellectual property right an exclusivity over its use, and that it has already operated a compromise between the grant of that exclusivity and the public interest by providing the right in most cases only for a limited duration.

. . .

The obligation to deal with others under US anti-trust law

. . . Unqualified upholding of *Magill* by the court would represent an extension of the existing case law and may well confirm Article 86 as a sufficient legal basis to impose on dominant undertakings a general obligation to help competitors, in particular by sharing their assets with or providing services to new customers. Dominant undertakings that refused to assist could then be accused of using their dominance in a manner which was 'manifestly contrary' to the objective of Article 86. But at what price to the achievement of the objectives of the EEC Treaty set forth in Article 2?

. . .

Reference is often made in the United States to the 'essential facilities' doctrine. In a judgment of 29 October 1991, the US Court of Appeals, Ninth Circuit, indicated that '[S]tated most generally, the essential facilities doctrine imposes liability when one firm, which controls an essential facility, denies a second firm reasonable access to a product or service that the second firm must obtain in order to compete with the first.' [*Alaska Airlines v United Airlines* (948 F 2d 536 (9th Cir. 1991)].

Professor Phillip Areeda calls it the so-called 'essential facilities' doctrine:

> 'so-called' because most Supreme Court cases invoked in support do not speak of it and can be explained without reference to it. Indeed the cases support the doctrine only by implication and in highly qualified ways. You will not find any case that provides a consistent rationale for the doctrine or that explores the social costs and benefits or the administrative costs of requiring the creator of an asset to share it with a rival. [(1990) 58 Anti-trust Law Journal 841.]

. . .

The cases usually cited in the United States in connection with the so-called 'essential facilities' doctrine were based either on circumstances similar to those in *Commercial Solvents* **[E72]** or involved 'natural monopolies' operating within specific regulatory frameworks.

In the light of the absence of clear principles underpinning the so-called 'essential facilities' doctrine, Professor Areeda sets forth the following propositions as best responding to the policy objectives of competition law, namely optimum allocative and productive efficiency:
- There is no general duty to share. Compulsory access, if it exists at all, should be very exceptional.
- A company's facility is 'essential' only when it is both:
   (i) critical to the plaintiff's competitive vitality; and
   (ii) the plaintiff is essential for competition in the market place.
   'Critical to the plaintiff's competitive vitality' means that the plaintiff

cannot compete effectively without it and that duplication or practical alternatives are not available.
- No-one should be forced to deal unless doing so is likely substantially to improve competition in the market place by reducing price or by increasing output. Such an improvement would be unlikely, in particular, when it would chill desirable activity. This is, of course, a very important point in the case of intellectual property rights.
- Even when all these conditions are satisfied, denial of access is never per se unlawful; legitimate business purpose may justify not sharing a facility with third parties.
- The monopolist's intention is irrelevant because every firm that denies its facilities to rivals does so to limit competition with itself and increase its profits.

The principles, although not entirely followed, appear to have had some influence on recent judgments in the United States. For example, in *City of Anaheim v Southern California* (955 F2d 1373), it was held that an electricity network operator had not violated s 2 of the Sherman Act – the equivalent of Article 86 – and could not therefore be required to permit access to the network by the third party claimants because it had legitimate business reasons to refuse access. It was using all the available capacity in order to carry cheap power to be sold to all its customers, including the third party claimants. The network operator could not transmit all of the power it wanted if a portion of its capacity rights were being used by the third party claimants at the same time. To allow access by the third party claimants would have allowed them to benefit at the expense of the network operator's other customers.

5   Merger control

Prior to the so-called Merger Regulation **[E78]**, the Commission had used the limited tools of Articles 85 and 86 to exert some Community law regulation over merger activity. But neither provision was especially suitable. Article 86 only covered acquisitions which strengthened existing dominance and would not involve any advance notification of a merger. The elements of Article 85 need not always be easy to establish in all concentrations, and the framework of notification and exemption might not give adequate supervision.

The Merger Regulation, enacted after protracted negotiation, purportedly represents a 'one-stop shopping' system for merger control. The extracts **[E78]–[E82]** give a flavour of the controversies relating to the purpose of merger control in the Community, the relationship of the substantive tests with those of Article 86 and the extent to which merger control constitutes subsidiarity in practice.

[E78]   Council Regulation 4064/89 on the control of concentrations between undertakings (amended version OJ 1990 L257/14)

The Council of the European Communities,
Having regard to the Treaty establishing the European Economic Community, and in particular Articles 87 and 235 thereof,
Having regard to the proposal from the Commission,
Having regard to the opinion of the European Parliament,
Having regard to the opinion of the Economic and Social Committee,

(1) Whereas, for the achievement of the aims of the Treaty establishing the European Economic Community, Article 3(f) [now 3(g)] gives the Community the objective of instituting 'a system ensuring that competition in the common market is not distorted';

(2) Whereas this system is essential for the achievement of the internal market by 1992 and its further development;

(3) Whereas the dismantling of internal frontiers is resulting and will continue to result in major corporate reorganisations in the Community, particularly in the form of concentrations;

(4) Whereas such a development must be welcomed as being in line with the requirements of dynamic competition and capable of increasing the competitiveness of European industry, improving the conditions of growth and raising the standard of living in the Community;

(5) Whereas, however, it must be ensured that the process of reorganisation does not result in lasting damage to competition; whereas Community law must therefore include provisions governing those concentrations which may significantly impede effective competition in the common market or in a substantial part of it;

(6) Whereas Articles 85 and 86, while applicable, according to the case law of the Court of Justice, to certain concentrations, are not, however, sufficient to control all operations which may prove to be incompatible with the system of undistorted competition envisaged in the Treaty;

(7) Whereas a new legal instrument should therefore be created in the form of a regulation to permit effective control of all concentrations from the point of view of their effect on the structure of competition in the Community and to be the only instrument applicable to such concentrations;

(8) Whereas this regulation should therefore be based not only on Article 87 but, principally, on Article 235 of the Treaty, under which the Community may give itself the additional powers of action necessary for the attainment of its objectives,

. . .

(9) Whereas the provisions to be adopted in this regulation should apply to significant structural changes the impact of which on the market goes beyond the national borders of any one Member State;

(10) Whereas the scope of application of this regulation should therefore be defined according to the geographical area of activity of the undertakings

concerned and be limited by quantitative thresholds in order to cover those concentrations which have a Community dimension; whereas, at the end of an initial phase of the application of this regulation, these thresholds should be reviewed in the light of the experience gained;

(11) Whereas a concentration with a Community dimension exists where the combined aggregate turnover of the undertakings concerned exceeds given levels worldwide and within the Community and where at least two of the undertakings concerned have their sole or main fields of activities in different Member States or where, although the undertakings in question act mainly in one and the same Member State, at least one of them has substantial operations in at least one other Member State; whereas that is also the case where the concentrations are effected by undertakings which do not have their principal fields of activities in the Community but which have substantial operations there;

(12) Whereas the arrangements to be introduced for the control of concentrations should, without prejudice to Article 90(2) of the Treaty, respect the principle of non-discrimination between the public and the private sectors; whereas, in the public sector, calculation of the turnover of an undertaking concerned in a concentration needs, therefore, to take account of undertakings making up an economic unit with an independent power of decision, irrespective of the way in which their capital is held or of the rules of administrative supervision applicable to them;

(13) Whereas it is necessary to establish whether concentrations with a Community dimension are compatible or not with the common market from the point of view of the need to maintain and develop effective competition in the common market; whereas, in so doing, the Commission must place its appraisal within the general framework of the achievement of the fundamental objectives referred to in Article 2 of the Treaty, including that of strengthening the Community's economic and social cohesion, referred to in Article 130a;

(14) Whereas this regulation should establish the principle that a concentration with a Community dimension which creates or strengthens a position as a result of which effective competition in the common market or in a substantial part of it is significantly impeded is to be declared incompatible with the common market;

(15) Whereas concentrations which, by reason of the limited market share of the undertakings concerned, are not liable to impede effective competition may be presumed to be compatible with the common market; whereas, without prejudice to Articles 85 and 86 of the Treaty, an indication to this effect exists, in particular, where the market share of the undertakings concerned does not exceed 25% either in the common market or in a substantial part of it;

(16) Whereas the Commission should have the task of taking all the decisions necessary to establish whether or not concentrations with a Community dimension are compatible with the common market, as well as decisions designed to restore effective competition;

. . .

(23) Whereas it is appropriate to define the concept of concentration in

such a manner as to cover only operations bringing about a lasting change in the structure of the undertakings concerned; whereas it is therefore necessary to exclude from the scope of this regulation those operations which have as their object or effect the co-ordination of the competitive behaviour of undertakings which remain independent, since such operations fall to be examined under the appropriate provisions of the regulations implementing Articles 85 and 86 of the Treaty; whereas it is appropriate to make this distinction specifically in the case of the creation of joint ventures;

. . .

(26) Whereas the Commission should be given exclusive competence to apply this regulation, subject to review by the Court of Justice;

(27) Whereas the Member States may not apply their national legislation on competition to concentrations with a Community dimension, unless this regulation makes provision therefor; whereas the relevant powers of national authorities should be limited to cases where, failing intervention by the Commission, effective competition is likely to be significantly impeded within the territory of a Member State and where the competition interests of that Member State cannot be sufficiently protected otherwise by this regulation; whereas the Member States concerned must act promptly in such cases; whereas this regulation cannot, because of the diversity of national law, fix a single deadline for the adoption of remedies;

(28) Whereas, furthermore, the exclusive application of this regulation to concentrations with a Community dimension is without prejudice to Article 223 of the Treaty, and does not prevent the Member States from taking appropriate measures to protect legitimate interests other than those pursued by this regulation, provided that such measures are compatible with the general principles and other provisions of Community law;

(29) Whereas concentrations not covered by this regulation come, in principle, within the jurisdiction of the Member States; whereas, however, the Commission should have the power to act, at the request of the Member State concerned, in cases where effective competition could be significantly impeded within that Member State's territory;

. . .

HAS ADOPTED THIS REGULATION:

Article 1 Scope

1. Without prejudice to Article 22 this regulation shall apply to all concentrations with a Community dimension as defined in paragraph 2.

2. For the purposes of this regulation, a concentration has a Community dimension where:

(a) the combined aggregate worldwide turnover of all the undertakings concerned is more than ECU 5,000m; and

(b) the aggregate Community-wide turnover of each of at least two of the undertakings concerned is more than ECU 250m, unless each of the undertakings concerned achieves more than two-thirds of its aggregate Community-wide turnover within one and the same Member State.

3. The thresholds laid down in paragraph 2 will be reviewed before the end of the fourth year following that of the adoption of this regulation by the Council acting by a qualified majority on a proposal from the Commission.

Article 2   Appraisal of concentrations

1. Concentrations within the scope of this regulation shall be appraised in accordance with the following provisions with a view to establishing whether or not they are compatible with the common market.

In making this appraisal, the Commission shall take into account:

(a)   the need to maintain and develop effective competition within the common market in view of, among other things, the structure of all the markets concerned and the actual or potential competition from undertakings located either within or outwith the Community;

(b)   the market position of the undertakings concerned and their economic and financial power, the alternatives available to suppliers and users, their access to supplies or markets, any legal or other barriers to entry, supply and demand trends for the relevant goods and services, the interests of the intermediate and ultimate consumers, and the development of technical and economic progress provided that it is to consumers' advantage and does not form an obstacle to competition.

2. A concentration which does not create or strengthen a dominant position as a result of which effective competition would be significantly impeded in the common market or in a substantial part of it shall be declared compatible with the common market.

3. A concentration which creates or strengthens a dominant position as a result of which effective competition would be significantly impeded in the common market or in a substantial part of it shall be declared incompatible with the common market.

Article 3   Definition of concentration

1. A concentration shall be deemed to arise where:

(a)   two or more previously independent undertakings merge, or
(b)   − one or more persons already controlling at least one undertaking, or
    − one or more undertakings

acquire, whether by purchase of securities or assets, by contract or by any other means, direct or indirect control of the whole or parts of one or more other undertakings.

2. An operation, including the creation of a joint venture, which has as its object or effect the co-ordination of the competitive behaviour of undertakings which remain independent shall not constitute a concentration within the meaning of paragraph 1(b).

The creation of a joint venture performing on a lasting basis all the functions of an autonomous economic entity, which does not give rise to co-ordination of the competitive behaviour of the parties amongst themselves or between them and the joint venture, shall constitute a concentration within the meaning of paragraph 1(b).

3. For the purposes of this regulation, control shall be constituted by rights, contracts or any other means which, either separately or in

combination and having regard to the considerations of fact or law involved, confer the possibility of exercising decisive influence on an undertaking, in particular by:

(a) ownership or the right to use all or part of the assets of an undertaking;
(b) rights or contracts which confer decisive influence on the composition, voting or decisions of the organs of an undertaking.

   4. Control is acquired by persons or undertakings which:

(a) are holders of the rights or entitled to rights under the contracts concerned; or
(b) while not being holders of such rights or entitled to rights under such contracts, have the power to exercise the rights deriving therefrom.

. . .

Article 4   Prior notification of concentrations

   1. Concentrations with a Community dimension defined in this regulation shall be notified to the Commission not more than one week after the conclusion of the agreement, or the announcement of the public bid, or the acquisition of a controlling interest. That week shall begin when the first of those events occurs.
   2. A concentration which consists of a merger within the meaning of Article 3(1)(a) or in the acquisition of joint control within the meaning of Article 3(1)(b) shall be notified jointly by the parties to the merger or by those acquiring joint control as the case may be. In all other cases, the notification shall be effected by the person or undertaking acquiring control of the whole or parts of one or more undertakings.

[Article 5, relating to calculation of turnover, is omitted.]

Article 6   Examination of the notification and initiation of proceedings

   1. The Commission shall examine the notification as soon as it is received.

(a) Where it concludes that the concentration notified does not fall within the scope of this regulation, it shall record that finding by means of a decision.
(b) Where it finds that the concentration notified, although falling within the scope of this regulation, does not raise serious doubts as to its compatibility with the common market, it shall decide not to oppose it and shall declare that it is compatible with the common market.
(c) If, on the other hand, it finds that the concentration notified falls within the scope of this regulation and raises serious doubts as to its compatibility with the common market, it shall decide to initiate proceedings.

   2. The Commission shall notify its decision to the undertakings concerned and the competent authorities of the Member States without delay.

. . .

Article 8   Powers of decision of the Commission

1. Without prejudice to Article 9, all proceedings initiated pursuant to Article 6(1)(c) shall be closed by means of a decision as provided for in paragraphs 2 to 5.

2. Where the Commission finds that, following modification by the undertakings concerned if necessary, a notified concentration fulfils the criterion laid down in Article 2(2), it shall issue a decision declaring the concentration compatible with the common market.

It may attach to its decision conditions and obligations intended to ensure that the undertakings concerned comply with the commitments they have entered into vis-à-vis the Commission with a view to modifying the original concentration plan. The decision declaring the concentration compatible shall also cover restrictions directly related and necessary to the implementation of the concentration.

3. Where the Commission finds that a concentration fulfils the criterion laid down in Article 2(3), it shall issue a decision declaring that the concentration is incompatible with the common market.

4. Where a concentration has already been implemented, the Commission may, in a decision pursuant to paragraph 3 or by separate decision, require the undertakings or assets brought together to be separated or the cessation of joint control or any other action that may be appropriate in order to restore conditions of effective competition.

. . .

Article 9   Referral to the competent authorities of the Member States

1. The Commission may, by means of a decision notified without delay to the undertakings concerned and the competent authorities of the other Member States, refer a notified concentration to the competent authorities of the Member State concerned in the following circumstances.

2. Within three weeks of the date of receipt of the copy of the notification a Member State may inform the Commission, which shall inform the undertakings concerned, that a concentration threatens to create or to strengthen a dominant position as a result of which effective competition would be significantly impeded on a market, within that Member State, which presents all the characteristics of a distinct market, be it a substantial part of the common market or not.

3. If the Commission considers that, having regard to the market for the products or services in question and the geographical reference market within the meaning of paragraph 7, there is such a distinct market and that such a threat exists, either:

(a) it shall itself deal with the case in order to maintain or restore effective competition on the market concerned; or

(b) it shall refer the case to the competent authorities of the Member State concerned with a view to the application of that state's national competition law.

If, however, the Commission considers that such a distinct market or threat does not exist it shall adopt a decision to that effect which it shall address to the Member State concerned.

. . .

7. The geographical reference market shall consist of the area in which the undertakings concerned are involved in the supply and demand of products or services, in which the conditions of competition are sufficiently homogeneous and which can be distinguished from neighbouring areas because, in particular, conditions of competition are appreciably different in those areas. This assessment should take account in particular of the nature and characteristics of the products or services concerned, of the existence of entry barriers or of consumer preferences, of appreciable differences of the undertakings' market shares between the area concerned and neighbouring areas or of substantial price differences.

8. In applying the provisions of this article, the Member State concerned may take only the measures strictly necessary to safeguard or restore effective competition on the market concerned.

9. In accordance with the relevant provisions of the Treaty, any Member State may appeal to the Court of Justice, and in particular request the application of Article 186, for the purpose of applying its national competition law.

10. This article will be reviewed before the end of the fourth year following that of the adoption of this regulation.

. . .

Article 19   Liaison with the authorities of the Member States

1. The Commission shall transmit to the competent authorities of the Member States copies of notifications within three working days and, as soon as possible, copies of the most important documents lodged with or issued by the Commission pursuant to this regulation.

. . .

3. An Advisory Committee on concentrations shall be consulted before any decision is taken pursuant to Article 8(2) to (5), 14 [fines] or 15 [periodic penalty payments], or any provisions are adopted pursuant to Article 23.

4. The Advisory Committee shall consist of representatives of the authorities of the Member States. Each Member State shall appoint one or two representatives; if unable to attend, they may be replaced by other representatives. At least one of the representatives of a Member State shall be competent in matters of restrictive practices and dominant positions.

. . .

6. The Advisory Committee shall deliver an opinion on the Commission's draft decision, if necessary by taking a vote. The Advisory Committee may deliver an opinion even if some members are absent and unrepresented. The opinion shall be delivered in writing and appended to the draft decision. The Commission shall take the utmost account of the opinion delivered by the Committee. It shall inform the Committee of the manner in which its opinion has been taken into account.

7. The Advisory Committee may recommend publication of the opinion. The Commission may carry out such publication. The decision to publish shall take due account of the legitimate interest of undertakings in the protection of their business secrets and of the interest of the undertakings concerned in such publications taking place.

Article 20   Publication of decisions

1. The Commission shall publish the decisions which it takes pursuant to Article 8(2) to (5) in the Official Journal of the European Communities.

2. The publication shall state the names of the parties and the main content of the decision; it shall have regard to the legitimate interest of undertakings in the protection of their business secrets.

Article 21   Jurisdiction

1. Subject to review by the Court of Justice, the Commission shall have sole jurisdiction to take the decisions provided for in this regulation.

2. No Member State shall apply its national legislation on competition to any consideration that has a Community dimension.

The first sub-paragraph shall be without prejudice to any Member State's power to carry out any inquiries necessary for the application of Article 9(2) or after referral, pursuant to Article 9(3), first sub-paragraph, indent (b), or (5), to take the measures strictly necessary for the application of Article 9(8).

3. Notwithstanding paragraphs 1 and 2, Member States may take appropriate measures to protect legitimate interests other than those taken into consideration by this regulation and compatible with the general principles and other provisions of Community law.

Public security, plurality of the media and prudential rules shall be regarded as legitimate interests within the meaning of the first sub-paragraph.

Any other public interest must be communicated to the Commission by the Member State concerned and shall be recognised by the Commission after an assessment of its compatibility with the general principles and other provisions of Community law before the measures referred to above may be taken. The Commission shall inform the Member State concerned of its decision within one month of that communication.

Article 22   Application of the Regulation

1. This regulation alone shall apply to concentrations as defined in Article 3.

2. Regulations 17, 1017/68, 4056/86 and 3975/87 shall not apply to concentrations as defined in Article 3.

3. If the Commission finds, at the request of a Member State, that a concentration as defined in Article 3 that has no Community dimension within the meaning of Article 1 creates or strengthens a dominant position as a result of which effective competition would be significantly impeded within the territory of the Member State concerned it may, in so far as the concentration affects trade between Member States, adopt the decisions provided for in Article 8(2), second sub-paragraph, (3) and (4).

. . .

5. Pursuant to paragraph 3 the Commission shall take only the measures strictly necessary to maintain or restore effective competition within the territory of the Member State at the request of which it intervenes.

. . .

Article 23   Implementing provisions

The Commission shall have the power to adopt implementing provisions concerning the form, content and other details of notifications pursuant to Article 4, time limits pursuant to Article 10 and hearings pursuant to Article 18.

. . .

Article 25   Entry into force

1. This regulation shall enter into force on 21 September 1990.

. . .

This regulation shall be binding in its entirety and directly applicable in all Member States.

[E79]   Sir Leon Brittan, 'The law and policy of merger control in the EEC' (1990) 15 European Law Review 351

. . . Let there be no doubt: the fundamental analysis to bo oarricd out [under the Merger Regulation] by the Commission is whether the merger impedes competition. A dominant position analysis, along the lines of that carried out under Article 86, will be necessary in all cases to see whether the merged company has a sufficient degree of market power to stand in the way of competition by acting without the restraints which competition imposes in normal circumstances on its relations with suppliers, customers or competitors. In other words, as is always the case in competition policy, our concern will be whether the merged company could raise prices, discriminate unfairly or restrict output with impunity or in a way which would not be possible in normal competitive conditions. The various factors listed in Article 2 of the regulation provide assistance to the Commission in making that analysis. Allow me to focus on three or four of the most controversial issues.

Market definition is always crucial in competition cases . . . Indeed, market power makes no sense whatsoever as a concept unless a market is first defined, both in product or service terms and in geographical terms. Geography here is not political, it is economic. For some products or services, there is a Community market; for others there are still markets covering one or more Member States. There are even world markets for some products or services and in such cases we would take account of the competition brought to the Community by companies situated outside it. But our only concern is for competition *within* the Community and I reject the argument that a competitive world market may justify a dominant position in the Community. Companies will be competitive abroad only if they are used to competing at home. There can be no trade-off between competition in the Community and competitiveness elsewhere. This would be economic nonsense and bad law. Fortunately, the regulation follows, as it must, the EEC Treaty in providing for a system of undistorted competition in the Common Market and I shall resist any attempt to distort competition by distorting the regulation's meaning.

Another issue which seems to have caused concern is the inclusion of the words borrowed from Article 85(3) EEC – 'technical and economic progress' – in the substantive criteria of the Merger Regulation. It has even been suggested that this opens the back door to industrial policy. This is no more true of the Merger Regulation than it ever has been of Article 85(3). The notion of technical and economic progress must be seen in the context of the competition policy thrust of the regulation and in conjunction with the specific reference to the consumer interest and the requirement that no obstacle be placed in the way of competition which accompany the notion in the text . . . The technical and economic progress which a merger may bring about will certainly form part of the Commission's analysis of the reasons for a merger. However, this does not mean that such progress is a legitimate defence for a merger which creates a dominant position.

. . .

Some of the difficulties in understanding these problems of market definition and technical and economic progress seem to arise from a misapprehension of the nature of competitive policy analysis. We are not taking a snapshot of a market situation at a particular time. We are looking at the dynamic development of a market and considering the short, medium and long-term impact of a given merger. In a time frame in which foreseeable market developments are taken into account, it is perfectly proper to consider wider market issues and the merger's contribution to technical and economic progress. It is in this context too that the reference in a recital to the Community's goal of social and economic cohesion must be understood. Of course, we all seek to encourage economic development in the poorer areas of the Community. Indeed, we believe that competition policy has an important role to play in bringing cohesion about. It would be retrograde and patronising to want to shelter the Community's poorer regions from competition at a time when all over Europe, within and outside the Community's frontiers, people are crying out for the efficiencies and choice which only a market economy can bring alongside democratic political structures. Competition will lead to cohesion and the dynamics of the Community's integration process require that merger policy be part of that general movement. Once again, this means that there is no cohesion defence to dominant positions. But it does mean that market integration as part of the cohesion process is a factor of which account is properly taken in analysing a given merger case.

Finally, on the substantive criteria in the regulation, the question is bound to be asked whether it is sufficient to know what Article 86 means to understand the dominant position test or whether the qualification 'as a result of which effective competition would be significantly impeded' gives rise to a new test altogether. In my view, we are at the beginning of a new legal development and the Council did not wish to create a pure dominant position test. A dominant position as such is not prohibited. One may ask whether a dominant position without the effect of impeding competition is at all conceivable. I think that in most cases it is not. However, the dynamic factor of time is again important here. A short-lived market share of some size in a market with no or low barriers to entry is not really a threat to competition at all. The European Court has traditionally defined dominance in Article 86 cases in terms of independence or the ability to act with scant regard to competitive pressures. This is not quite the same as impeding competition and I expect a new line of case law to develop.

[E80] EC Commission: XXIInd Report on Competition Policy ((1993) COM 162 final, 5 May 1993)

Merger control

7. Merger control occupies a central place in Community competition policy; it aims to reconcile two imperatives. First, the mergers envisaged by industry will generally help to adapt industrial structures to the single market so that the market can in fact generate the desired efficiency gains. The notifications which firms submit have to be dealt with efficiently and rapidly in order to avoid the harm which would be caused by a prolonged period of uncertainty. It is fair to say that that objective has been achieved, since at the first stage of inquiry the Commission is settling a large number of cases which raise no serious doubts from a competition point of view. Another fundamental consideration here is the principle of the 'one-stop shop', which means that a merger is considered once, at Community level, and that firms do not find themselves having to approach a number of different authorities.

8. Secondly it is likewise vital that mergers should not be allowed to establish dominant positions in the Community, with the holders of such positions no longer exposed to sufficient competitive pressure. They would not then need to pass on to consumers the benefit of the increased efficiency secured through the merger; instead they could exploit consumers' new dependence on them. In such cases the Commission must be able to take the measures necessary to maintain a competitive market structure in the Community, which is the only way of ensuring that the beneficial effects of the single market materialise in practice.

9. This was the second full year of Community merger control, and for the most part the Commission continued with the policy followed in 1991. In the great majority of cases a decision not to oppose the merger was taken at the first stage in the procedure. It did not happen, as it had the previous year, that the original plans could not be adjusted satisfactorily and a decision to prohibit the merger had to be taken. There were in fact more cases in which the plans notified were amended . . . in order to allow a favourable decision to be taken. This is a welcome development from the point of view both of the Commission and of business, since it produces a result which is at the same time in the interests of competition and acceptable to the firms involved. The conditions which the Commission imposed consisted mainly of obligations either to sell off part of the new group which the merger would create or to withdraw from particular markets where the new group would enjoy a dominant position. The Commission's objective was always to maintain a competitive structure on the relevant markets by preventing the establishment of a dominant position. This made it necessary to ensure a proper market access for existing or potential competitors.

10. There were several cases which presented novel aspects of some importance in the development of Commission merger control policy. The *Mannesmann/Hoesch* case is of special interest: the Commission there allowed the establishment of an enterprise holding a very significant share of a national market, because it was clear that the position would be only a temporary one given that Community directives liberalising the market were to enter into force very rapidly. The case provides an example of the need to take a dynamic view of markets; analysis may reveal that a market which

at present is still a national one is likely to become a Community market in the near future. This approach allows account to be taken of the probable developments which firms themselves seek to anticipate, and of those developments' probable impact on the firms.

11. The Commission considerably clarified the scope of its merger control powers in its decision in the *Nestlé/Perrier* case **[E81]**, where it stated the principle that the purpose of the regulation, which was to maintain competitive structures, required that the Commission be able to prevent the creation or strengthening not just of a dominant position held by a single firm but also of a dominant position held jointly by a number of firms. Thus the Commission has power to prevent restrictions of competition resulting from the creation or strengthening of a duopoly or oligopoly.

[E81]   Commission Decision of 22 July 1992 relating to a proceeding under Council Regulation 4064/89 (Case No IV/M 190 – Nestlé/Perrier)

[Nestlé notified a public bid by which it intended to acquire control over Perrier, amounting to a concentration within the meaning of the Merger Regulation. The proposed concentration affected primarily the business of bottling water originating from a natural spring or source ('source water'). Source waters can be labelled 'mineral waters' provided that they fulfil certain legal requirements as to content and quality. Other source waters can be marketed as 'spring waters'. Nestlé's activities in France were concentrated upon the still mineral water part of the market, whilst Perrier operated in both still and sparkling mineral waters. Both companies exported from their sources in France. The third major supplier on the French source water market was BSN. Part of the notified proposals included an agreement whereby Nestlé would sell the Volvic source brand of Perrier to BSN in the event of Nestlé acquiring control of Perrier.]

The European Commission

H.   Impact on the maintenance or development of effective competition

(a)   In the case of implementation of the sale of Volvic to BSN: duopolistic dominance

108. Given the high market shares and capacities of Nestlé and BSN after the merger and sale of Volvic to BSN, the insufficient competitive counterweight from local mineral and spring waters, the increased dependency of retailers and wholesalers on the portfolio of brands of Nestlé and BSN, the absence of effective price-constraining potential competition from newcomers and the other characteristics outlined hereafter, the Commission must conclude that the proposed merger between Nestlé and Perrier would create a duopolistic dominant position which would significantly impede effective competition on the French bottled water market. This market constitutes a substantial part of the common market.

109. Nestlé, supported by BSN, has submitted that Article 2(3) of the Merger Regulation does not apply to oligopolistic dominance and, if it did, that the Commission has not proved the absence of significant competition

between the established national suppliers and the absence of actual or potential competition from outside the oligopoly.

(i) Application of Article 2(3) of the Merger Regulation to oligopolies

110. Article 2(3) of the Merger Regulation stipulates: A concentration which creates or strengthens a dominant position as a result of which effective competition would be significantly impeded in the common market or in a substantial part of it shall be declared incompatible with the common market.

The question is whether this provision covers only a market situation where effective competition is significantly impeded by one firm which alone has the power to behave independently of its competitors, customers and consumers, or whether this provision also covers market situations where effective competition is significantly impeded by more than one firm which together have the power to behave to an appreciable extent independently of the remaining competitors, of customers and ultimately of consumers.

111. Nestlé has not denied the fact that from an economic point of view, both single firm dominance and oligopolistic dominance can significantly impede effective competition under certain market structure conditions.

. . .

112. The Commission considers that the distinction between single firm dominance and oligopolistic dominance cannot be decisive for the application or non-application of the Merger Regulation because both situations may significantly impede effective competition under certain market structure conditions. This is in particular the case if there is already before the merger weakened competition between the oligopolists which is likely to be further weakened by a significant increase in concentration and if there is no sufficient price-constraining competition from actual or potential competition from outside the oligopoly.

113. Article 3(f) [now 3(g)] provides for the institution of a system ensuring that competition in the common market is not distorted. One of the principal goals of the Treaty is thus the maintenance of effective competition. The restriction of effective competition which is prohibited if it is the result of a dominant position held by one firm cannot become permissible if it is the result of more than one firm. If, for instance, as a result of a merger, two or three undertakings acquire market power and are likely to apply excessive prices this would constitute an exercise of a collective market power which the Merger Regulation is intended to prevent by the maintenance of a competitive market structure. The dominant position is only the means by which effective competition can be impeded. Whether this impediment occurs through single firm power or collective power cannot be decisive for the application or non-application of Article 2(3) of the Merger Regulation.

114. In the absence of explicit exclusion of oligopolistic dominance by Article 2(3) it cannot be assumed that the legislator intended to permit the impediment of effective competition by two or more undertakings holding the power to behave together to an appreciable extent independently on the market. This would create a loophole in the fundamental Treaty objective of maintaining effective competition at all times in order not to jeopardise the proper functioning of the common market. If, in order to

avoid the application of the Merger Regulation, it sufficed to divide the dominant power between for instance two companies in order to escape the prohibition of Article 2(3), then, in contradiction to the basic principles of the common market, effective competition could be significantly impeded. In such a hypothesis the objective of Article 3(f) of the EEC Treaty could be overturned.

115. Seen in the light of these legal and economic considerations, Article 2(3) must be interpreted as covering both single firm and oligopolistic dominance. It is also significant to note that all other major anti-trust systems with a merger control system apply or can apply their rules to both single firm and oligopolistic dominance, eg the American system, the French law (Article 38 of the Law of 1 December 1986); German law (22 GWB) and UK law (Fair Trading Act, s 6(2)). In most of these systems, it is an established practice to control mergers raising a problem of oligopolistic dominance. It cannot be the case that following the adoption of the Merger Regulation mergers which previously were subject to such control would now be subject only to single firm dominance control. The Merger Regulation would not only have transferred the national merger control powers to the Community but those Member States which had a system with oligopolistic dominance control would at the same time have abandoned such control altogether without any substitute for it at Community level. In the absence of any express provision to that effect, such a cession of control cannot be assumed.

116. The argument of BSN that the Commission would be violating the principle of legal certainty because this case would be the first case to apply the oligopolistic dominance concept cannot be accepted. As explained above, the correct interpretation of the Merger Regulation leads to the conclusion that Article 2(3) has always covered dominance which significantly impedes effective competition independently of whether such a situation is the result of one or more than one firm. Furthermore, if the argument of BSN was right, it would mean that the Commission could never develop any of its administrative case law. Although BSN's argument could under other circumstances have some relevance in particular where a posteriori control takes place and involves interference in acquired rights, the merger control system is an a priori control system which by definition does not allow the implementation of mergers without prior authorisation by the Commission.

(ii)   Creation of a duopolistic dominant position

117. Although Nestlé has stated that the Commission has not proved absence of significant competition between the suppliers, it has not brought forward any arguments to rebut the indicators mentioned by the Commission . . . to the effect that, even before the merger, price competition between these suppliers was greatly weakened, in particular the high degree of price parallelism over a long period of time, the very high production cost-price margin, and the large gap between ex-works prices of national mineral waters and local spring waters.

118. The Commission has not asserted that there existed an oligopolistic dominance between Nestlé, Perrier and BSN even before the merger. The facts and market structures show, however, that the French bottled water market is already a highly concentrated market where price competition is considerably weakened. The maintenance or development of

whatever competition there remains on that market therefore requires particular protection. Any structural operation restricting even more the scope for competition in such a situation has to be judged severely. The combination of the market structure arising from the merger and of certain additional factors (see recitals 119 to 120) lead to the conclusion that the proposed merger would have the effect of creating a duopolistic dominant position allowing Nestlé and BSN to jointly maximise profits by avoiding competition among themselves and acting to a large extent independently of their customers and competitors.

119. After the merger, the degree of concentration would be extremely high with Nestlé and BSN holding over 82% of the total French water market by value and 75% by volume (nearly 95% of all still mineral waters). There would only be two national still and sparkling mineral water suppliers on the French market. Both suppliers would operate in the most profitable segment of bottled water and have a strong interest and incentive to jointly defend their position.

After the merger, there would be no competitor in the Community approaching the size, the range of well-known brands and the geographic spread of either Nestlé or BSN.

. . .

120. The reduction from three to two suppliers (duopoly) is not a mere cosmetic change in the market structure. The concentration would lead to the elimination of a major operator who has the biggest capacity reserves and sales volumes in the market. Perrier sources and brands would be divided between the two remaining suppliers. In addition, the reduction from three to only two national suppliers would make anti-competitive parallel behaviour leading to collective abuses much easier.

121. The mineral water suppliers in France have developed instruments of transparency facilitating a tacit co-ordination of pricing policies.

Retail prices of bottled water are transparent. The packaging and product size of the main products are the same in this market. Retail prices can easily be checked, and statistics are regularly supplied by different organisations.

. . .

122. Companies have developed instruments allowing control and monitoring of each other's behaviour.

Homogeneity and transparency of tariffs allow the mutual monitoring of pricing policies of competitors. In addition, Perrier, BSN and [another] have implemented a mechanism of regular exchange of information on quantities sold each month, broken down by major brands.

. . .

It also needs to be remembered that these suppliers carry out the bulk of their sales with the same customers.

123. The two players remaining in the market are similar in size and nature.

After the merger, there would remain two national suppliers on the market which would have similar capacities and similar market shares (symmetric duopoly).

. . .

Given this equally important stake in the market and their high sales volumes, any aggressive competitive action by one would have a direct and significant impact on the activity of the other supplier and most certainly provoke strong reactions with the result that such actions could considerably harm both suppliers in their profitability without improving their sales volumes. Their reciprocal dependency thus creates a strong common interest and incentive to maximise profits by engaging in anti-competitive parallel behaviour. This situation of common interests is further reinforced by the fact that Nestlé and BSN are similar in size and nature, are both active in the wider food industry and already co-operate in some sectors of that industry.

124. Demand is relatively price-inelastic; prices might be increased without fear of offsetting losses in volume.

Because of the motivation of consumers to buy and consume mineral water on a daily basis, there are no real substitutes for mineral water. The overall image of branded water and brand loyalty accentuate the price-inelasticity of demand.

. . .

125. Costs are similar. No company seems to enjoy a significant cost advantage.

. . .

126. Technology is mature. R & D play no major role.

. . .

127. The notified operation in itself weakens the likelihood of the development of competition among Nestlé and BSN.

Nestlé and BSN have together reacted strongly to the attempt by an external actor (Ifint) to acquire Perrier. Since BSN and Vittel have smaller spare capacities than Perrier, Perrier under ownership of a third party coming from outside the water market could have constituted an element of uncertainty and disruption in the market. The joint reaction of Nestlé and BSN to Ifint's bid can be viewed in this sense as a joint entry deterrence action.

. . .

(iii)　Conclusion

131. It must be concluded from all the above that the market structure resulting from the merger between Nestlé and Perrier (followed by a sale of the Volvic source to BSN) would create a duopolistic dominant position on the French bottled water market which would significantly impede effective competition and would be very likely to cause a considerable harm to consumers.

. . .

(b)　Without the sale of Volvic to BSN: single firm dominance

132. If the Volvic agreement was not implemented, the proposed merger . . . would create a dominant position for the new entity by affording it the power to behave alone to an appreciable extent independently of its competitors, its customers and ultimately its consumers.

VI.   COMMITMENTS PROPOSED BY NESTLÉ

136. Nestlé has offered to modify the original concentration plan as notified by entering into the following commitments:

. . .

In order to meet the requirements of the Commission to facilitate the entry of a viable competitor with adequate resources in the bottled water market or the increase in the capacity of an existing competitor so that in either case such competitor could effectively compete on the French bottled water market with Nestlé and BSN, Nestlé has undertaken that it will make available for sale both brand names and sufficient capacity of water for bottling to such competitor as will permit that competitor to have not less than 3,000m litres of water capacity per annum.

. . .

Nestlé agrees to hold separate from its own operations all assets and interests acquired from Perrier, until it has completed the sale of all bottled water operations described above to a single entity which is approved by the Commission. The buyer must be an entity that has no structural, financial or personal relationships with Nestlé, Perrier or BSN or any of the parent entities, or any of the subsidiaries of, or any officers, directors, employees, or agents of Nestle, Perrier or BSN, which relationships are of such a nature that it would be unlikely that the buyer would compete effectively with Nestlé and BSN.

. . .

Nestle acknowledges that the approval of the purchaser by the Commission is of the essence for the acceptance of its undertaking by the Commission. The establishment of an effective competitor vis-à-vis Nestlé and BSN depends on the strength of the purchaser to develop the sources and brands which will be sold to it. The purchaser must in particular have:
  − sufficient financial resources to develop a nation-wide distribution organisation and to adequately promote the acquired brands; and
  − sufficient expertise in the field of branded beverage or food products.
These are the two main criteria. The Commission will withhold approval only if it can show that the proposed purchaser will not be a credible competitor or is unlikely to compete effectively with Nestlé and BSN, despite meeting these two criteria.

. . .

Nestlé is enjoined and restrained from re-acquiring, directly or indirectly, any of the sources or brands which it divests pursuant to this undertaking, for a period of ten years from the date of this decision, without the prior written approval of the Commission. In this context, the Commission will take into consideration any changes in the market structure of the French bottled water market.

. . .

137. . . . Therefore, subject to the fulfilment of the conditions and obligations set out in Nestlé's commitment, the Commission has concluded that the sale of a capacity of 3,000m litres and of the agreed portfolio of brands

to a strong buyer acceptable to the Commission would be sufficient to create a viable competitor able effectively to compete with Nestlé and BSN and thus to prevent the collective dominant position which would otherwise be created by the proposed concentration and the subsequent sale of Volvic to BSN.

. . .

138. If the sale of the assets to be divested has not taken place by the end of the time period set out in Nestlé's commitment, or if any of the other obligations accepted by Nestlé are breached, then the Commission reserves the right . . . to revoke its decision to accept the modifications proposed here and to require that Nestlé divest all assets and interests in Perrier and thereby that Nestlé and Perrier be fully separated in order to restore conditions of effective competition.

Note.   This decision is subject to an appeal to the Court of First Instance.

[E82]   Aidan Robertson: 'Competition policy or industrial policy?' In Competition, Issue 5, 25 May 1993 (Sweet & Maxwell Ltd)

The appointment of Karel Van Miert as EC Competition Commissioner in place of Sir Leon Brittan has led to much speculation about the future content of EC competition policy. Though there is unlikely to be drastic change, it is possible to detect some signs of a move away from a policy based on the primacy of competition, towards a wider assessment of the requirements of European industrial policy.

The 1980s may be seen in retrospect as forming the high water mark of competition policy as such. Sir Leon Brittan's appointment to the European Commission led to an infusion of Thatcherite dogma to a body previously more associated with a French-style *dirigiste* approach to European industry. In particular, Sir Leon proved more willing than his predecessors to adopt competition as the primary means of moving towards the goal of the internal market. For the first time, significant steps were taken at the European level to begin the dismantling of state monopolies and to opening up previously protected national markets to competition from both elsewhere in the EC and internationally. This process is thus far most advanced in the telecommunications field, though the first steps have also been initiated in gas and electricity.

However, the Commission as a body was never united behind what was seen by some, notably Martin Bangemann (until this year the Industry and Internal Market Commissioner), as a doctrinaire adherence to competition as a policy goal in itself. This openly manifested itself in the Commission's narrow decision in October 1991 to prohibit the *Aerospatiale/Alenia* joint venture's takeover of De Havilland, a substantial minority considering that the merger would have created a strong EC force in world aircraft manufacture, the value of which would have outweighed any detriment to competition. Subsequent merger decisions, particularly *Nestlé/Perrier* in July 1992 **[E81]** and *ICI/Du Pont* in September 1992, have demonstrated a willingness to accept concentrations of market power which would have been unlikely to have passed scrutiny by the United Kingdom's Monopolies and Mergers Commission (MMC). The suspicion is growing that competition as a policy end is being subordinated to other considerations, particularly of promoting strong European businesses.

This suspicion seems to be confirmed by a couple of recent decisions in December 1992, the first by the President of the Court of First Instance in *Nestlé/Perrier* and the second, ironically, by Sir Leon Brittan in *Ford/Volkswagen.*

The *Nestlé/Perrier* case arose out of the Commission's approval of Nestlé's takeover of the Perrier bottled water business, subject to undertakings to divest four brands to a third party in order to create a third force on what would otherwise have been a duopolistic French mineral water market. The Perrier workforce sought to challenge the decision on the basis that both the merger and the divestiture would lead to redundancies, thus requiring the President of the Court of First Instance to order immediate interim measures halting the merger. This argument was rejected on the merits, but in doing so the President . . . made some interesting comments on the policy considerations to be taken into account by the Commission in assessing mergers. While accepting that competition considerations had been predominant, the President stressed that the Commission must place its appraisal within the general framework of the Treaty of Rome's fundamental objectives, which include strengthening economic and social cohesion, and noted that the Commission had accepted this was correct. The question then arises as to how economic and social cohesion is to be attained: through a rigid application of a competition policy, or by allowing other considerations to be balanced against competition?

The Commission's decision eight days later to approve a *Ford/Volkswagen* joint venture indicates that the latter approach may be the one currently finding favour and, what is more intriguing, that this represents a policy shift that was under way before Mr Van Miert's arrival. The *Ford/VW* joint venture was set up to build a new model of 'Multi Purpose Vehicle', more popularly known as a people carrier, the market leader in the EC being the Renault Espace. In granting an exemption to this joint venture under Article 85(3), the Commission noted that a factor that had been taken into account was that the vehicle would be built in Portugal, creating 5,000 jobs directly and another 10,000 indirectly, together with other associated investment and development, thus leading to the reduction of regional disparities, one of the basic aims of the Treaty. Renault is seeking to challenge this exemption before the Court of First Instance, arguing, not unreasonably, that both Ford and Volkswagen had the necessary resources to set up plant to manufacture the MPV independently of each other, and, perhaps less reasonably, that the Commission is effectively granting *Ford/VW* a future dominant position (Renault currently has a 55% market share, Ford and VW less than 1%).

While one must wait about two years to learn the ultimate outcome of both sets of proceeding, they provide an indication that arguing wider industrial and social issues before the Commission is a far from futile exercise. The Commission appears to be more receptive than ever to these sorts of arguments. Nor is one restricted to factors appearing on the face of their decisions. It seems certain that the Commission in *Ford/VW*, for example, must have taken into account the end of Japanese voluntary export restraints in the year 2000 and the need then for European motor industry to be in a position to compete. One might reconcile this with competition policy by saying that the Commission is taking a long-run view of future potential world competition; a more realistic view would be to acknowledge that the Commission is beginning to take industrial policy more overtly into its deliberations when exercising its competition policy powers.

Note.   The President of the Court of First Instance, on a further application arising from the *Nestlé/Perrier* case, later suspended the sale of one of the brands and sources acquired by Nestlé.

6   State intervention in the market and competition

[E83]   EC Treaty provisions on state intervention

Article 222

This Treaty shall in no way prejudice the rules in Member States governing the system of property ownership.

Article 37

1. Member States shall progressively adjust any state monopolies of a commercial character so as to ensure that when the transitional period has ended no discrimination regarding the conditions under which goods are procured and marketed exists between nationals of Member States.

The provisions of this Article shall apply to any body through which a Member State, in law or in fact, either directly or indirectly supervises, determines or appreciably influences imports or exports between Member States. These provisions shall likewise apply to monopolies delegated by the state to others.

. . .

Article 90

1. In the case of public undertakings and undertakings to which Member States grant special or exclusive rights, Member States shall neither enact nor maintain in force any measure contrary to the rules contained in this Treaty, in particular to those rules provided for in Article 7 and Articles 85 to 94.

2. Undertakings entrusted with the operation of services of general economic interest or having the character of a revenue-producing monopoly shall be subject to the rules contained in this Treaty, in particular to the rules on competition, in so far as the application of such rules does not obstruct the performance, in law or in fact, of the particular tasks assigned to them. The development of trade must not be affected to such an extent as would be contrary to the interests of the Community.

3. The Commission shall ensure the application of the provisions of this article and shall, where necessary, address appropriate directives or decisions to Member States.

Article 92

1. Save as otherwise provided in this Treaty, any aid granted by a Member State or through state resources in any form whatsoever which distorts or threatens to distort competition by favouring certain undertakings or the production of certain goods shall, in so far as it affects trade between Member States, be incompatible with the common market.

2. The following shall be compatible with the common market:

(a) aid having a social character, granted to individual consumers, provided that such aid is granted without discrimination related to the origin of the products concerned;
(b) aid to make good the damage caused by natural disasters or other exceptional occurrences;
(c) aid granted to the economy of certain areas of the Federal Republic of Germany affected by the division of Germany, in so far as such aid is required in order to compensate for the economic disadvantages caused by that division.

3. The following may be considered to be compatible with the common market:

(a) aid to promote the economic development of areas where the standard of living is abnormally low or where there is serious underemployment;
(b) aid to promote the execution of an important project of common European interest or to remedy a serious disturbance in the economy of a Member State;
(c) aid to facilitate the development of certain economic activities or of certain economic areas, where such aid does not adversely affect trading conditions to an extent contrary to the common interest . . .
(d) aid to promote culture and heritage conservation where such aid does not affect trading conditions and competition in the Community to an extent that is contrary to the common interest;
(e) such other categories of aid as may be specified by decision of the Council acting by a qualified majority on a proposal from the Commission.

Article 93

1. The Commission shall, in co-operation with Member States, keep under constant review all systems of aid existing in those states. It shall propose to the latter any appropriate measures required by the progressive development or by the functioning of the common market.

2. If, after having given notice to the parties concerned to submit their comments, the Commission finds that aid granted by a state or through state resources is not compatible with the common market having regard to Article 92, or that such aid is being misused, it shall decide that the state concerned shall abolish or alter such aid within a period of time to be determined by the Commission.

If the state concerned does not comply with this decision within the prescribed time, the Commission or any other interested state may, in derogation from the provisions of Articles 169 and 170, refer the matter to the Court of Justice direct.

On application by a Member State, the Council may, acting unanimously, decide that aid which that state is granting or intends to grant shall be considered to be compatible with the common market, in derogation from the provisions of Article 92 or from the regulations provided for in Article 94, if such a decision is justified by exceptional circumstances. If, as regards the aid in question, the Commission has already initiated the procedure provided for in the first sub-paragraph of this paragraph, the fact that the state concerned has made its application to the Council shall have the effect of suspending that procedure until the Council has made its attitude known.

If, however, the Council has not made its attitude known within three months of the said application being made, the Commission shall give its decision on the case.

3. The Commission shall be informed, in sufficient time to enable it to submit its comments, of any plans to grant or alter aid. If it considers that any such plan is not compatible with the common market having regard to Article 92, it shall without delay initiate the procedure provided for in paragraph 2. The Member State concerned shall not put its proposed measures into effect until this procedure has resulted in a final decision.

Article 94

The Council, acting by a qualified majority on a proposal from the Commission, and after consulting the European Parliament, may make any appropriate regulations for the application of Articles 92 and 93 and may in particular determine the conditions under which Article 93(3) shall apply and the categories of aid exempted from this procedure.

[E84]   Joined Cases 188-190/80 France, Italy and United Kingdom v Commission [1982] ECR 2545

[These were actions brought by three Member States for a declaration that Commission Directive 80/723 on the transparency of financial relations between Member States and public undertakings was void.]

The European Court of Justice

2. The directive, which was adopted on the basis of Article 90(3) of the Treaty, requires the Member States to keep available for five years information concerning public funds made available by public authorities to public undertakings and also concerning the use to which those funds are actually put by those undertakings. It is clear from the preamble to the directive that its essential objective is to promote the effective application to public undertakings of the provisions contained in Articles 92 and 93 of the Treaty concerning state aids. Moreover, the preamble emphasises the principle of equal treatment of public and private undertakings as well as the need for transparency of financial relations between the former and the Member States because of the complexity of those relations.

. . .

First submission (Commission's lack of competence)

. . .

8. . . . the three applicant governments claim that the rules contained in the contested directive could have been adopted by the Council [under Article 94].

. . .

11. . . . in order to assess the argument relating to Article 94, it is necessary to compare the provisions of that article with those of Article 90 in the light of the objectives and purposes of the two articles.

12. In that regard, it should be noted that the two provisions have different objectives. Article 94 is one of a set of provisions which regulate the sphere of aids granted by states, regardless of the form and recipients of such aids. On the other hand, Article 90 concerns only undertakings for whose actions states must take special responsibility by reason of the influence which they may exert over such actions. It emphasises that such undertakings are subject to all the rules laid down in the Treaty, subject to the provisions contained in paragraph 2; it requires the Member States to respect those rules in their relations with those undertakings and in that regard imposes on the Commission a duty of surveillance which may, where necessary, be performed by the adoption of directives and decisions addressed to Member States.

. . .

14. In comparison with the Council's power under Article 94, that which is conferred upon the Commission under Article 90(3) thus operates in a specific field of application and under conditions defined by reference to the particular objective of that article. It follows that the Commission's power to issue the contested directive depends on the needs inherent in its duty of surveillance provided for in Article 90 and that the possibility that rules might be laid down by the Council, by virtue of its general power under Article 94, containing provisions impinging upon the specific sphere of aids granted to public undertakings does not preclude the exercise of that power by the Commission.

15. It follows from all those considerations that the first submission relied upon by the applicant governments must be rejected.

Second submission (absence of necessity)

. . .

18. In view of the diverse forms of public undertakings in the various Member States and the ramifications of their activities, it is inevitable that their financial relations with public authorities should themselves be very diverse, often complex and therefore difficult to supervise, even with the assistance of the sources of published information to which the applicant governments have referred. In those circumstances there is an undeniable need for the Commission to seek additional information on those relations by establishing common criteria for all the Member States and for all the undertakings in question. So far as the precise determination of those criteria is concerned, the applicant governments have not established that the Commission has exceeded the limits of the discretion conferred upon it by Article 90(3).

. . .

Third submission (discrimination against public undertakings as compared with private undertakings)

20. The French and Italian governments claim that it is clear both from Article 222 and from Article 90 that public and private undertakings must be treated equally. The effect of the directive is to place the former in a less favourable position than the latter, especially in so far as it imposes on public undertakings special obligations, in particular in relation to accounts, which are not required of private undertakings.

21. In that regard, it should be borne in mind that the principle of equality, to which the governments refer in connection with the relationship between public and private undertakings in general, presupposes that the two are in comparable situations. Within the limits laid down by the applicable legislation, private undertakings determine their industrial and commercial strategy by taking into account in particular requirements of profitability. Decisions of public undertakings, on the other hand, may be affected by factors of a different kind within the framework of the pursuit of objectives of public interest by public authorities which may exercise an influence over those decisions. The economic and financial consequences of the impact of such factors lead to the establishment between those undertakings and public authorities of financial relations of a special kind which differ from those existing between public authorities and private undertakings. As the directive concerns precisely those special financial relations, the submission relating to discrimination cannot be accepted.

Fourth submission (infringement of Articles 90, 92 and 93 inasmuch as the directive defines the concepts of public undertakings and state aid)

. . .

23. Those criticisms are not justified. In relation to the definition contained in Article 3 of the financial relations which are subject to the rules contained in the directive, it is sufficient to state that that is not an attempt by the Commission to define the concept of aid which appears in Articles 92 and 93 of the Treaty, but only a statement of the financial transactions of which the Commission considers that it must be informed in order to check whether a Member State has granted aids to the undertakings in question, without complying with its obligation to notify the Commission under Article 93(3).

. . .

24. In relation to the provisions of Article 2, which defines the concept of public undertaking 'for the purpose of this directive', it should be emphasised that the object of those provisions is not to define that concept as it appears in Article 90 of the Treaty, but to establish the necessary criteria to delimit the group of undertakings whose financial relations with the public authorities are to be subject to the duty laid down by the directive to supply information. In order to assess that delimitation, which is moreover indispensable in order to make known to the Member States the extent of their obligations under the directive, it is therefore necessary to compare the criteria laid down with the considerations on which the duty of surveillance imposed on the Commission by Article 90 is based.

25. According to Article 2 of the directive, the expression 'public undertakings' means any undertaking over which the public authorities may

exercise directly or indirectly a dominant influence. According to the second paragraph, such influence is to be presumed when the public authorities directly or indirectly hold the major part of the undertakings's subscribed capital, control the majority of the votes, or can appoint more than half of the members of its administrative, managerial or supervisory body.

26. As the court has already stated, the reason for the inclusion in the Treaty of the provisions of Article 90 is precisely the influence which the public authorities are able to exert over the commercial decisions of public undertakings. That influence may be exerted on the basis of financial participation or of rules governing the management of the undertaking. By choosing the same criteria to determine the financial relations on which it must be able to obtain information in order to perform its duty of surveillance under Article 90(3), the Commission has remained within the limits of the discretion conferred upon it by that provision.

27. It follows that the fourth submission must also be rejected [as were the remaining submissions].

[E85]   Case 59/75 Pubblico Ministero v Manghera [1976] ECR 91

Tho European Court of Justice

2. The national court is concerned with the application of the Italian criminal law to facts described as constituting an infringement of the legal provisions granting an exclusive right of import to the state monopoly in manufactured tobacco.

. . .

5. Without requiring the abolition of the said monopolies, [Article 37] prescribes in mandatory terms that they must be adjusted in such a way as to ensure that . . . discrimination shall cease to exist.

. . .

12. The exclusive right to import manufactured products of the monopoly in question . . . constitutes, in respect of Community exporters, discrimination prohibited by Article 37(1).

[E86]   Case C-202/88 France v Commission ('telecommunications terminal equipment') [1991] ECR I-1223

The European Court of Justice

1. [France] brought an action before the court under the first paragraph of Article 173 of the EEC Treaty for the annulment of Articles 2, 6, 7 and, in so far as necessary, Article 9 of Commission Directive 88/301 of 16 May 1988 on competition in the markets in telecommunications terminal equipment (OJ 1988 L131, p 73).

2. Directive 88/301 was adopted on the basis of Article 90(3) of the Treaty. According to Article 2 of that directive, Member States which have

granted special or exclusive rights to undertakings for the importation, marketing, connection, bringing into service of telecommunications terminal equipment and/or maintenance of such equipment are to ensure that those rights are withdrawn and are to inform the Commission of the measures taken or draft legislation introduced to that end.

. . .

4. According to Article 6 of the directive, Member States are to ensure that, from 1 July 1989, responsibility for drawing up specifications, monitoring their application and granting type approval is entrusted to a body independent of public or private undertakings offering goods and/or services in the telecommunications sector.

5. Article 7 requires Member States to take the necessary steps to make it possible for customers to terminate, with maximum notice of one year, leasing or maintenance contracts relating to terminal equipment which at the time of when the contracts were concluded were subject to exclusive or special rights granted to certain undertakings.

6. Finally, according to Article 9, Member States are to provide the Commission at the end of each year with a report allowing it to monitor compliance with the provisions of Articles 2, 3, 4, 6 and 7.

. . .

8. The French government relies on four pleas in law, alleging misuse of procedure, lack of powers of the Commission, breach of the principle of proportionality and infringement of essential procedural requirements. As part of its plea in law alleging lack of powers, the French government also claims that the Commission has misapplied the rules of the Treaty. Since that allegation in fact constitutes a separate plea, it will be considered on its own.

Legal background to the dispute

9. The pleas in law and arguments put forward in this case relate essentially to the interpretation of Article 90 of the Treaty. According to paragraph (3) of that article, on the basis of which the contested regulation was adopted, 'the Commission shall ensure the application of the provisions of this article and shall, where necessary, address appropriate directives or decisions to Member States'.

10. In the case of public undertakings and undertakings to which Member States grant special or exclusive rights, Article 90(1) prohibits the Member States generally from enacting or maintaining in force any measure contrary to the rules contained in the Treaty, in particular to those rules provided for in Article 7 and Articles 85 to 94.

11. Article 90(2) provides that undertakings entrusted with the operation of services of general economic interest are to be subject to those rules, in particular to the rules on competition, in so far as the application of such rules does not obstruct the performance, in law or in fact, of the particular tasks assigned to them, on condition, however, that the development of trade is not affected to such an extent as would be contrary to the interests of the Community.

12. In allowing derogations to be made from the general rules of the Treaty on certain conditions, that provision seeks to reconcile the Member

States' interest in using certain undertakings, in particular in the public sector, as an instrument of economic or fiscal policy with the Community's interest in ensuring compliance with the rules on competition and the preservation of the unity of the Common Market.

13. In paragraph 11 of the preamble to the contested directive, the Commission states that the conditions for applying the exception in Article 90(2) of the Treaty are not fulfilled. Neither the French government nor the interveners have challenged that. It follows that this dispute falls within the scope of paragraphs (l) and (3) of Article 90 of the Treaty.

14. Inasmuch as it makes it possible for the Commission to adopt directives, Article 90(3) of the Treaty empowers it to lay down general rules specifying the obligations arising from the Treaty which are binding on the Member States as regards the undertakings referred to in Article 90(1) and (2).

15. Accordingly, the parties' pleas in law and arguments must be considered in the light of the question whether in this case the Commission has remained within the bounds of the legislative power thus conferred upon it by the Treaty.

Misuse of procedure

16. In its first plea in law the French government claims that the Commission adopted the contested directive pursuant to Article 90(3) of the Treaty instead of initiating the procedure provided for in Article 169. In its view, Article 90(3) is intended to enable the Commission to inform the Member States, in cases where it is unclear how compliance with the Treaty is to be achieved, of the means which must be used in order to ensure such compliance. In contrast, recourse must be made to Article 169 where it is clear that a measure is wholly contrary to the Treaty and must be brought to an end forthwith.

17. It must be held in that regard that Article 90(3) of the Treaty empowers the Commission to specify in general terms the obligations arising under Article 90(1) by adopting directives. The Commission exercises that power where, without taking into consideration the particular situation existing in the various Member States, it defines in concrete terms the obligations imposed on them under the Treaty. In view of its very nature, such a power cannot be used to make a finding that a Member State has failed to fulfil a particular obligation under the Treaty.

18. However, it appears from the content of the directive at issue in this case that the Commission merely determined in general terms obligations which are binding on the Member States under the Treaty. The directive therefore cannot be interpreted as making specific findings that particular Member States failed to fulfil their obligations under the Treaty, with the result that the plea in law relied upon by the French government must be rejected as unfounded.

Competence of the Commission

19. In its second plea in law the French government, supported by the interveners, argues that by adopting a directive providing simply for the withdrawal of special and exclusive rights for the importation, marketing, connection, bringing into service and/or maintenance of telecommunications terminal equipment, the Commission exceeded the supervisory

powers conferred upon it by Article 90(3) of the Treaty. In the French government's view, that provision presupposes the existence of special and exclusive rights. Accordingly, to take the view that the maintenance of those rights constitutes in itself a measure within the meaning of Article 90 disregards the scope of that article.

20. The Belgian and French governments further consider that a policy on the restructuring of the telecommunications sector, as envisaged by the directive, fell within the sole competence of the Council, acting under Article l00a. The Belgian and Italian governments maintain in addition that the directive is contrary to Article 87 of the Treaty inasmuch as only the Council is empowered to lay down rules for the application of Articles 85 and 86 of the Treaty in specific sectors.

21. As far as the first argument is concerned, it must be held in the first place that the supervisory power conferred on the Commission includes the possibility of specifying, pursuant to Article 90(3), obligations arising under the Treaty. The extent of that power therefore depends on the scope of the rules with which compliance is to be ensured.

22. Next, it should be noted that even though that article presupposes the existence of undertakings which have certain special or exclusive rights, it does not follow that all the special or exclusive rights are necessarily compatible with the Treaty. That depends on different rules, to which Article 90(1) refers.

23. As regards the allegation that the Commission has encroached on the powers conferred on the Council by Articles 87 and 100a of the Treaty, those provisions have to be compared with Article 90, taking into account their respective subject matter and purpose.

24. Article l00a is concerned with the adoption of measures for the approximation of the provisions laid down by law, regulation or administrative action in Member States which have as their object the establishment and functioning of the internal market. Article 87 is concerned with the adoption of any appropriate regulations or directives to give effect to the principles set out in Articles 85 and 86, that is to say the competition rules applicable to all undertakings. As for Article 90, it is concerned with measures adopted by the Member States in relation to undertakings with which they have specific links referred to in the provisions of that article. It is only with regard to such measures that Article 90 imposes on the Commission a duty of supervision which may, where necessary, be exercised through the adoption of directives and decisions addressed to the Member States.

25. It must therefore be held that the subject matter of the power conferred on the Commission by Article 90(3) is different from, and more specific than, that of the powers conferred on the Council by either Article l00a or Article 87.

26. It should also be noted that, as the court held in Joined Cases 188 to 190/80 (*France, Italy and United Kingdom v Commission* **[E84]**, at paragraph 14), the possibility that rules containing provisions which impinge upon the specific sphere of Article 90 might be laid down by the Council by virtue of its general power under other articles of the Treaty does not preclude the exercise of the power which Article 90 confers on the Commission.

27. The plea in law alleging lack of powers on the part of the Commission must therefore be rejected.

. . .

Application of the rules of the Treaty

29. The French government and the interveners allege that Articles 2, 6, 7 and 9 of the directive are unlawful, on the ground that those provisions are wrongly based on an infringement by the Member States of Articles 30, 37, 59 and 86 of the Treaty.

30. On the basis of the observations set out above, that complaint must be construed as being directed against the misapplication by the Commission of the aforesaid provisions of the Treaty. Articles 2, 6, 7 and 9 of Directive 88/301 must therefore be considered in the light of the grounds on which they are based.

Legality of Article 2 of Directive 88/301 (withdrawal of special and exclusive rights)

31. Article 2 of the contested directive requires Member States which have granted undertakings special or exclusive rights regarding the importation, marketing, connection, bringing into service of telecommunications terminal equipment and/or maintenance of such equipment to withdraw those rights and to inform the Commission of the measures taken or draft legislation introduced to that end.

32. It follows that the directive is concerned with exclusive rights, on the one hand, and special rights, on the other. It is appropriate to follow that classification in considering this complaint.

33. With regard to exclusive importation and marketing rights, it should be borne in mind that, as the court has consistently held (see, in particular, the judgment in Case 8/74 *Procureur du Roi v Dassonville* **[E12]**, at paragraph 5), the prohibition of measures having an effect equivalent to quantitative restrictions laid down in Article 30 of the Treaty applies to all trading rules enacted by Member States which are capable of hindering, directly or indirectly, actually or potentially, intra-Community trade.

34. In that regard it should be noted first that the existence of exclusive importing and marketing rights deprives traders of the opportunity of having their products purchased by consumers.

35. It should be pointed out, secondly, that the terminals sector is characterised by the diversity and technical nature of the products concerned and by the ensuing constraints. In those circumstances there is no certainty that the holder of the monopoly can offer the entire range of models available on the market, inform customers about the state and operation of all the terminals and guarantee their quality.

36. Accordingly, exclusive importation and marketing rights in the telecommunications terminal sector are capable of restricting intra-Community trade.

37. With regard to the question whether such rights can be justified, it should be noted that in Article 3 of the contested directive the Commission specified the extent and the limits of the withdrawal of special and exclusive rights so as to take into account certain requirements such as those listed in Article 2(17) of Council Directive 86/361, namely user safety, safety of employees of public telecommunications network operators, protection of public telecommunications networks from harm and interworking of terminal equipment in justified cases.

38. For its part, the French government has not challenged Article 3 of the contested directive, nor has it argued that there are other essential requirements which the Commission should have complied with.

39. In those circumstances, the Commission was right to consider exclusive importation and marketing rights in the telecommunications terminal sector incompatible with Article 30 of the Treaty.

40. So far as concerns exclusive rights regarding the connection, bringing into service and maintenance of telecommunications terminal equipment, paragraph 6 of the preamble to the directive states that:

> . . . The retention of exclusive rights in this field would be tantamount to retention of exclusive marketing rights . . . .

41. In that regard it should be borne in mind, in the first place, that, as the court has consistently held, Articles 2 and 3 of the Treaty set out to establish a market characterised by the free movement of goods where the terms of competition are not distorted (see, in particular, the judgment in Case 229/83 *Leclerc v Au Blé Vert* [1985] ECR 1, at paragraph 9). Article 30 et seq must therefore be interpreted in the light of that principle, which means that the competition aspect of Article 3(f) [now 3(g)] of the Treaty has to be taken into account.

42. Next, it should be noted that in a market which exhibits the characteristics described above (see paragraph 35), there is no certainty that a holder of exclusive rights regarding the connection, bringing into service and maintenance of terminal equipment can guarantee the reliability of those services for every type of terminal available on the market and thereby enable them all to be used, nor that he will have any incentive to do so. Accordingly, when the exclusive marketing right has been withdrawn, an economic agent must himself be able to connect, bring into service and maintain equipment in order to be able to carry on his marketing activity in conditions of competition which are not distorted.

43. Accordingly, the Commission rightly regarded exclusive rights regarding the connection, bringing into service and maintenance of telecommunications terminal equipment as incompatible with Article 30.

44. It follows from the foregoing that the Commission was justified in requiring the withdrawal of exclusive rights regarding the importation, marketing, connection, bringing into service of telecommunications terminal equipment and/or maintenance of such equipment.

45. As far as special rights are concerned, it should be noted that neither the provisions of the directive nor the preamble thereto specify the type of rights which are actually involved and in what respect the existence of such rights is contrary to the various provisions of the Treaty.

46. It follows that the Commission has failed to justify the obligation to withdraw special rights regarding the importation, marketing, connection, bringing into service and/or maintenance of telecommunications terminal equipment.

47. Accordingly, Article 2 must be declared void in so far as it concerns the withdrawal of those rights.

. . .

55. In [regard to Article 7 of the Directive], it should be noted that Article 90 of the Treaty confers powers on the Commission only in relation to state measures (see paragraph 24) and that anti-competitive conduct engaged in by undertakings on their own initiative can be called in question only by individual decisions adopted under Articles 85 and 86 of the Treaty.

56. It does not appear either from the provisions of the directive or from

the preamble thereto that the holders of special or exclusive rights were compelled or encouraged by state regulations to conclude long-term contracts.

57. Article 90 cannot therefore be regarded as an appropriate basis for dealing with the obstacles to competition which are purportedly created by the long-term contracts referred to in the directive. It follows that Article 7 must be declared void.

[E87]   Case 30/87 Bodson v Pompes funèbres des régions libérées [1988] ECR 2479

The European Court of Justice

1. . . . the French Cour de Cassation (Court of Cassation) referred to the Court of Justice for a preliminary ruling under Article 177 of the EEC Treaty a number of questions on the interpretation of Articles 37, 85, 86 and 90 of the EEC Treaty, in order to assess the compatibility with those provisions of national rules on exclusive concessions of communal monopolies for certain funeral services.

2. Those questions arose in a dispute between . . . PFRL . . ., a subsidiary of Pompes funèbres générales, which has since 1972 been given an exclusive concession by the town of Charleville-Mézières to provide the 'external services' for funerals, on the one hand, and Mrs Corinne Bodson, who had engaged in certain activities forming part of the 'external services' for funerals within the territory of that commune, on the other.

3. A French Law of 1904 . . . entrusted the 'external services' for funerals to the communes. Those services cover exclusively the carriage of the body after it has been placed in the coffin, the provision of hearses, coffins and external hangings of the house of the deceased, conveyances for mourners, the equipment and staff needed for burial and exhumation and cremation. In particular, the 'external services' do not include either the 'internal services', which relate to the religious services, or the 'non-regulated services' which cover non-essential funeral services such as the supply of flowers and marblework.

4. It is apparent from the documents before the court that 5,000 French communes, out of a total of some 36,000, with 25 million inhabitants, approximately 45% of the population of France, have granted to a private undertaking a concession to provide the 'external services'. Pompes funèbres générales and its subsidiaries hold the concession in 2,800 communes. They carry out a large proportion of burials in France.

. . .

5. Mrs Bodson operates an undertaking business under a franchise from Mr Michel Leclerc, who has set up a network of such firms in France which provide their services at prices substantially lower than those normally charged in that sector, in particular by Pompes funèbres générales and its subsidiaries. When Mrs Bodson organised funerals within the territory of the town of Charleville-Mézières, the holder of the exclusive concession instituted proceedings for an injunction against her.

[The Court of Justice recited the questions referred by the national court and then continued:]

9. The first question relates to the interpretation of the Treaty in the context of state monopolies, whilst the other three questions, which should be considered together, are concerned with the interpretation of the competition rules applicable to undertakings.

10. With regard to the interpretation of Article 37 of the EEC Treaty, it must be borne in mind that, as the court has consistently held . . ., it follows both from the place occupied by Article 37 in the chapter of the EEC Treaty on the elimination of quantitative restrictions and from the wording used in that provision that it refers to trade in goods and cannot relate to a monopoly over the provision of services. However, the possibility cannot be ruled out that a monopoly over the provision of services may have an indirect influence on trade in goods between Member States, in particular where the monopoly over the provision of services established by an undertaking or by a group of undertakings leads to discrimination against imported goods as opposed to products of domestic origin.

. . .

13. . . . Article 37 applies in particular to situations in which the national authorities are in a position to supervise, determine or even appreciably influence trade between Member States through a body established for that purpose or a monopoly delegated to others. That provision therefore covers a situation in which the monopoly in question is operated by an undertaking or group of undertakings, or by the territorial units of a state such as communes.

14. However, the situation described by the national court is not covered by either of those alternatives. The national rules entrust the provision of the 'external services' for funerals to the communes, which are at liberty to grant private undertakings the concession to provide the service, to leave it entirely unregulated or to operate it themselves. The fact that the holders of concessions in a number of communes covering a large part of the national territory belong to a single group of undertakings and can thus influence patterns of trade is the result of the conduct of the undertakings in question and not of the national or municipal authorities.

15. It is apparent from those considerations that the situation envisaged by the national court must be dealt with in the light of the Treaty provisions applicable to undertakings, and in particular Articles 85, 86 and 90, rather than in the light of the rules relating to state monopolies in Article 37.

16. It must be pointed out, in the first place, that the aim of Article 90 is to specify in particular the conditions for the application of the competition rules laid down by Articles 85 and 86 to public undertakings, to undertakings granted special or exclusive rights by the Member States and to undertakings entrusted with the operation of services in the general economic interest. Accordingly, it is necessary to start by examining the problems relating to the applicability of Articles 85 and 86.

17. With regard to Article 85, the national court asks . . . whether that provision is applicable to contracts for concessions concluded in the field of funeral services between certain undertakings or a group of undertakings and communes.

18. As the Commission has rightly pointed out, Article 85 of the Treaty applies, according to its actual wording, to agreements 'between undertakings'. It does not apply to contracts for concessions concluded between communes acting in their capacity as public authorities and undertakings entrusted with the operation of a public service.

19. With regard to the applicability of Article 85 to relations between holders of concessions belonging to the same group of undertakings, it must be borne in mind that . . . that provision is not concerned with agreements or concerted practices between undertakings belonging to the same concern and having the status of parent company and subsidiary, if the undertakings form an economic unit within which the subsidiary has no real freedom to determine its course of action on the market, and if the agreements or practices are concerned merely with the internal allocation of tasks as between the undertakings.

. . .

22. Article 86 prohibits abusive practices resulting from the exploitation by one or more undertakings of a dominant position within the common market or in a substantial part of it. However, that prohibition applies only in so far as those practices may affect trade between Member States.

23. According to the French government, the latter condition is not fulfilled in a case such as this. The Commission shares that view, pointing out that it had received complaints concerning the prices charged by concession holders belonging to the Pompes funèbres générales group and that, after considering those complaints, it came to the conclusion that the activities of the group could have only an imperceptible influence on transactions with other Member States. In that regard, the Commission took the view that the monopoly in the 'external services' for funerals does not involve the supply of any goods other than coffins and that a monopoly exists in only some 14% of communes in France, the Pompes funèbres générales group holding the concession in only two-thirds of those communes. However, the Commission points out that the same group also provides funeral services in other Member States, in particular the Netherlands, where it handles 14% of all burials, and in the United Kingdom and . . . Germany.

24. In that regard, it must be borne in mind that, in order to determine whether trade between Member States is capable of being affected by an abuse of a dominant position, within the meaning of Article 86, account must be taken of the consequences for the effective competitive structure in the common market. In the case of services, those consequences may, in particular, . . . consist in the activities of an undertaking or group of undertakings being conducted in such a way that their effect is to partition the common market and thereby to restrict the freedom to provide services which constitutes one of the objectives of the Treaty.

. . .

26. The second condition laid down by Article 86 is that an undertaking must have a dominant position within the common market or in a substantial part of it. A dominant position of that kind is characterised . . . by a position of economic strength enjoyed by an undertaking which enables it to hinder the maintenance of effective competition on the market by allowing it to behave to an appreciable extent independently of its competitors and its customers. It also follows from the case law of the court that the application of Article 86 is not precluded by the fact that the absence or restriction of competition is facilitated by laws or regulations.

27. In order to examine whether a dominant position of that kind exists in a case such as this, it is appropriate to determine the economic strength of the group of undertakings holding concessions on the relevant market,

that is to say the market in funerals. As the concept of a dominant position relates to a factual situation, it is also necessary to take into consideration the position of the group of undertakings in question in the communes in which it does not hold the exclusive concession, in addition to the services provided and the goods supplied by the group apart from the 'external services', such as, for instance, the supply of flowers or marblework forming part of the 'non-regulated service'.

28. According to the information in the documents before the court, the group of undertakings of which Pompes funèbres générales is the parent company holds the exclusive concession in less than 10% of communes in France. However, the population of those communes accounts for more than one-third of the total population of France. It is the size of the population, rather than the number of communes covered by the exclusive concessions granted to the group in question, which determines the number of burials and which must therefore be taken into consideration in order to ascertain whether a dominant position exists.

29. While the existence of such a dominant position is a question of factual assessment for the national court, it is appropriate for it to base its appraisal on the following criteria:

  − the size of the market share held by the group which is shielded from any competition at all as a result of the exclusive concession;
  − the influence of that monopolistic situation on the position of the group with regard to supplies of goods and services not covered by the exclusive concession;
  − the position of the group in communes which have not granted a concession to an undertaking for the 'external services' for funerals and the market share held by the group in other Member States;
  − the financial resources of the group as apparent, for instance, from the fact that the group belongs to a powerful conglomerate of undertakings or groups of undertakings.

30. The third condition laid down by Article 86 is the abuse of a dominant position . . . In this case, the complaints addressed to the Commission were concerned . . . with the imposition of unfair prices by the concession holders. In these proceedings, Mrs Bodson contended that Pompes funèbres générales and its subsidiaries charge excessive prices.

31. The French government and PFRL have denied that the prices charged by the subsidiaries of Pompes funèbres générales are unfair. The documents before the court do not contain any information enabling that problem to be resolved. Since over 30,000 communes in France have not granted to an undertaking the concession to provide 'external services' for funerals, but have left that service unregulated or operate it themselves, it must be possible to make a comparison between the prices charged by the group of undertakings which hold concessions and prices charged elsewhere. Such a comparison could provide a basis for assessing whether or not the prices charged by the concession holders are fair.

. . .

33. In so far as the communes imposed a given level of prices on the concession holders, in the sense that they refrained from granting concessions for the 'external services' to undertakings if the latter did not agree to charge particularly high prices, the communes are covered by the situation referred to in Article 90(1) of the Treaty. That provision governs the

obligations of the Member States – which includes, in this context, the public authorities at the regional, provincial or communal level – towards undertakings 'to which [they] grant special or exclusive rights'. That situation covers precisely the grant of an exclusive concession for the 'external services' for funerals.

34. It follows from that finding that public authorities may not, in circumstances such as those of this case, either enact or maintain in force any 'measure' contrary to the rules of the Treaty, in particular the rules laid down by Articles 85 and 86. They may not therefore assist undertakings holding concessions to charge unfair prices by imposing such prices as a condition for concluding a contract for a concession.

[E88]   Case C-41/90 Höfner & Elser v Macrotron GmbH [1993] 4 CMLR 306

[Employment in Germany was governed by the Arbeitsförderungsgesetz (AFG). This statute entrusted the attainment of its general aims to the Bundesanstalt, whose activity principally consisted of bringing prospective employees into contact with employers and administering unemployment benefits. Notwithstanding the Bundesanstalt's exclusive right to undertake employment procurement, various executive recruitment consultants had sprung up, including Hofner and Elser. Although these activities were tolerated by the Bundesanstalt, acts constituting infringements of the statutory prohibition contained in the AFG were void under German law. The dispute in the main proceedings arose when Macrotron did not appoint a candidate found for it under contract by Höfner and Elser and refused to pay the latter's fees. Höfner and Elser then sued for payment, only to meet the argument that the contract was void under national law. The national court referred questions under Article 177 in relation to discrimination, establishment, and Articles 86 and 90 of the EEC Treaty.]

The European Court of Justice

21. It must be observed, in the context of competition law, first that the concept of an undertaking encompasses every entity engaged in an economic activity, regardless of the legal status of the entity and the way in which it is financed and, secondly, that employment procurement is an economic activity.

22. The fact that employment procurement activities are normally entrusted to public agencies cannot affect the economic nature of such activities. Employment procurement has not always been, and is not necessarily, carried out by public entities. That finding applies in particular to executive recruitment.

23. It follows that an entity such as a public employment agency engaged in the business of employment procurement may be classified as an undertaking for the purpose of applying the Community competition rules.

24. It must be pointed out that a public employment agency which is entrusted, under the legislation of a Member State, with the operation of services of general economic interest, such as those envisaged in . . . the AFG, remains subject to the competition rules pursuant to Article 90(2) EEC unless and to the extent to which it is shown that their application is

incompatible with the discharge of its duties: see Case 155/73 *Sacchi* [1974] ECR 409.

25. As regards the manner in which a public employment agency enjoying an exclusive right of employment procurement conducts itself in relation to executive recruitment undertaken by private recruitment consultancy companies, it must be stated that the application of Article 86 EEC cannot obstruct the performance of the particular task assigned to that agency in so far as the latter is manifestly not in a position to satisfy demand in that area of the market and in fact allows its exclusive rights to be encroached on by those companies.

26. Whilst it is true that Article 86 concerns undertakings and may be applied within the limits laid down by Article 90(2) to public undertakings or undertakings vested with exclusive rights or specific rights, the fact nevertheless remains that the Treaty requires the Member States not to take or maintain in force measures which could destroy the effectiveness of that provision: see Case 13/77 *INNO* [1977] ECR 2115. Article 90(1) in fact provides that the Member States are not to enact or maintain in force, in the case of public undertakings and the undertakings to which they grant special or exclusive rights, any measure contrary to the rules contained in the Treaty, in particular those provided for in Articles 85 to 94.

27. Consequently, any measure adopted by a Member State which maintains in force a statutory provision that creates a situation in which a public employment agency cannot avoid infringing Article 86 is incompatible with the rules of the Treaty.

28. It must be remembered, first, that an undertaking vested with a statutory monopoly may be regarded as occupying a dominant position within the meaning of Article 86 EEC: see Case 311/84 *CBEM* [1985] ECR 3261 and that the territory of a Member State, to which that monopoly extends, may constitute a substantial part of the Common Market: Case 322/81 *Michelin* **[E66]**.

29. Secondly, the simple fact of creating a dominant position of that kind by granting an exclusive right within the meaning of Article 90(1) is not as such incompatible with Article 86 EEC . . . A Member State is in breach of the prohibition contained in those two provisions only if the undertaking in question, merely by exercising the exclusive right granted to it, cannot avoid abusing its dominant position.

30. Pursuant to Article 86(b), such an abuse may in particular consist in limiting the provision of a service, to the prejudice of those seeking to avail themselves of it.

31. A Member State creates a situation in which the provision of a service is limited when the undertaking to which it grants an exclusive right extending to executive recruitment activities is manifestly not in a position to satisfy the demand prevailing on the market for activities of that kind and when the effective pursuit of such activities by private companies is rendered impossible by the maintenance in force of a statutory provision under which such activities are prohibited and non-observance of that prohibition renders the contracts concerned void.

32. It must be observed, thirdly, that the responsibility imposed on a Member State by virtue of Articles 86 and 90(1) EEC is engaged only if the abusive conduct on the part of the agency is liable to affect trade between Member States. That does not mean that the abusive conduct in question must actually have affected such trade. It is sufficient to establish

that that conduct is capable of having such an effect: see Case 322/81 *Michelin*.

33. A potential effect of that kind on trade between Member States arises in particular where executive recruitment by private companies may extend to the nationals or to the territory of other Member States.

[E89]   Case C-260/89 ERT v Dimotiki [1991] ECR I-2925

The European Court of Justice

10. In Case C-155/73 *Sacchi* [1974] ECR 409 . . . the court held that nothing in the Treaty prevents Member States, for considerations of a non-economic nature relating to the public interest, from removing radio and television broadcasts from the field of competition by conferring on one or more establishments an exclusive right to carry them out.

11. Nevertheless, it follows from Article 90(1) and (2) of the Treaty that the manner in which the monopoly is organised or exercised may infringe the rules of the Treaty, in particular those relating to the free movement of goods, the freedom to provide services and the rules on competition.

. . .

Free movement of goods

15. . . . the grant to a single undertaking of exclusive rights in relation to television broadcasting and the grant for that purpose of an exclusive right to import, hire or distribute material and products necessary for that broadcasting does not as such constitute a measure having an effect equivalent to a quantitative restriction within the meaning of Article 30.

. . .

16. It would be different if the grant of those rights resulted, directly or indirectly, in discrimination between domestic products and imported products to the detriment of the latter. It is for the national court, which alone has jurisdiction to determine the facts, to consider whether that is so in the present case.

. . .

Freedom to provide services

. . .

20. . . . although the existence of a monopoly in the provision of services is not as such incompatible with Community law, the possibility cannot be excluded that the monopoly may be organised in such a way as to infringe the rules relating to the freedom to provide services. Such a case arises, in particular, where the monopoly leads to discrimination between national television broadcasts and those originating in other Member States, to the detriment of the latter.

. . .

22. As the Commission has observed, the concentration of the monopolies to broadcast and retransmit in the hands of a single undertaking gives that undertaking the possibility both to broadcast its own programmes and

to restrict the retransmissions of programmes from other Member States. That possibility, in the absence of any guarantee concerning the retransmission of programmes from other Member States, may lead the undertaking to favour its own programmes to the detriment of foreign programmes. Under such a system equality of opportunity as between broadcasts of its own programmes and the retransmission of programmes from other Member States is therefore liable to be seriously compromised.

23. The question whether the aggregation of the exclusive right to broadcast and the right to retransmit actually leads to discrimination to the detriment of programmes from other Member States is a matter of fact which only the national court has jurisdiction to determine.

24. It should next be pointed out that the rules relating to the freedom to provide services preclude national rules which have such discriminatory effects unless those rules fall within the derogating provisions contained in Article 56 of the Treaty to which Article 66 refers. It follows from Article 56, which must be interpreted strictly, that discriminatory rules may be justified on grounds of public policy, public security or public health.

25. It is apparent from the observations submitted to the court that the sole objective of the rules in question was to avoid disturbances due to the restricted number of channels available. Such an objective cannot however constitute justification for those rules for the purposes of Article 56 of the Treaty, where the undertaking in question uses only a limited number of the available channels.

. . .

The rules on competition

27. As a preliminary point, it should be observed that Article 3(f) [now 3(g)] of the Treaty states only one objective for the Community which is given specific expression in several provisions of the Treaty relating to the rules on competition, including in particular Articles 85, 86 and 90.

28. The independent conduct of an undertaking must be considered with regard to the provisions of the Treaty applicable to undertakings, such as, in particular, Articles 85, 86 and 90(2).

. . .

31. . . . it should be borne in mind that an undertaking which has a statutory monopoly may be regarded as having a dominant position within the meaning of Article 86 of the Treaty (see . . . Case C-311/84 *CBEM v CLT and IBP* [1985] ECR 3261 . . .) and that the territory of a Member State over which the monopoly extends may constitute a substantial part of the common market (see . . . Case C-322/81 *Michelin v Commission* [1983] ECR 3461 **[E66]**. . .).

32. Although Article 86 . . . does not prohibit monopolies as such, it nevertheless prohibits their abuse. For that purpose Article 86 lists a number of abusive practices by way of example.

33. In that regard it should be observed that, according to Article 90(2) of the Treaty, undertakings entrusted with the operation of services of general economic interest are subject to the rules on competition so long as it is not shown that the application of those rules is incompatible with the performance of their particular task.

. . .

34. Accordingly it is for the national court to determine whether the practices of such an undertaking are compatible with Article 86 and to verify whether those practices, if they are contrary to that provision, may be justified by the needs of the particular task with which the undertaking may have been entrusted.

35. As regards state measures, and more specifically the grant of exclusive rights, it should be pointed out that while Articles 85 and 86 are directed exclusively to undertakings, the Treaty none the less requires the Member States not to adopt or maintain in force any measure which could deprive those provisions of their effectiveness.

. . .

37. In that respect it should be observed that Article 90(1) of the Treaty prohibits the granting of an exclusive right to retransmit television broadcasts to an undertaking which has an exclusive right to transmit broadcasts, where those rights are liable to create a situation in which that undertaking is led to infringe Article 86 of the Treaty by virtue of a discriminatory broadcasting policy which favours its own programmes.

38. The reply to the national court must therefore be that Article 90(1) of the Treaty prohibits the granting of an exclusive right to transmit and an exclusive right to retransmit television broadcasts to a single undertaking, where those rights are liable to create a situation in which that undertaking is led to infringe Article 86 by virtue of a discriminatory broadcasting policy which favours its own programmes, unless the application of Article 86 obstructs the performance of the particular tasks entrusted to it.

. . .

Article 10 of the European Convention on Human Rights

41. With regard to Article 10 of the European Convention on Human Rights . . ., it must first be pointed out that, as the court has consistently held, fundamental rights form an integral part of the general principles of law, the observance of which it ensures. For that purpose the court draws inspiration from the constitutional traditions common to the Member States and from the guidelines supplied by international treaties for the protection of human rights on which the Member States have collaborated or of which they are signatories (see, in particular, the judgment in Case C-4/73 *Nold v Commission* [1974] ECR 491 **[B44]** . . .). The European Convention on Human Rights has special significance in that respect (see in particular Case C-222/84 *Johnston v Chief Constable of the Royal Ulster Constabulary* [1986] ECR 1651 **[C32]** . . .). It follows that, as the court held in . . . Case C-5/88 *Wachauf v Germany* [1989] ECR 2609 . . ., the Community cannot accept measures which are incompatible with the observance of the human rights thus recognised and guaranteed.

42. As the court has held (see . . . *Cinéthèque* **[E24]** . . . and the judgment in Case C-12/86 *Demirel v Stadt Schwäbisch Gmünd* [1987] ECR 3719 . . .), it has no power to examine the compatibility with the European Convention on Human Rights of national rules which do not fall within the scope of Community law. On the other hand, where such rules do fall within the scope of Community law, and reference is made to the court for a preliminary ruling, it must provide all the criteria of interpretation needed by the national court to determine whether those rules are compatible with the fundamental rights

the observance of which the court ensures and which derive in particular from the European Convention on Human Rights.

43. In particular, where a Member State relies on the combined provisions of Articles 56 and 66 in order to justify rules which are likely to obstruct the exercise of the freedom to provide services, such justification, provided for by Community law, must be interpreted in the light of the general principles of law and in particular of fundamental rights. Thus the national rules in question can fall under the exceptions provided for by the combined provisions of Articles 56 and 66 only if they are compatible with the fundamental rights the observance of which is ensured by the court.

44. It follows that in such a case it is for the national court, and if necessary, the Court of Justice to appraise the application of those provisions having regard to all the rules of Community law, including freedom of expression, as embodied in Article 10 of the European Convention on Human Rights, as a general principle of law the observance of which is ensured by the court.

[E90]   Case C-320/91 Corbeau ((1993) Times, 21 July)

The European Court of Justice

The national court sought, in substance, to establish whether Article 90 of the Treaty was to be interpreted as preventing the legislation of a Member State, which granted a body such as the *Régie des postes*, the exclusive right to collect, transport and distribute mail from prohibiting, subject to criminal penalties, a trader established in that Member State from offering certain specific services on that market.

A body such as the *Régie des postes* was to be regarded as an undertaking to which a Member State had granted special or exclusive rights within the meaning of Article 90(1) of the EEC Treaty.

That . . . provision was to be read in combination with paragraph 2 of the same Article which provided that undertakings entrusted with the services of general economic interest were to be subject to the rules on competition, in so far as the application of such rules did not obstruct the performance, in law or in fact, of the particular tasks assigned to them.

That last provision thereby enabled Member States to grant undertakings, which they entrusted with the operation of services of general economic interest, exclusive rights which might prevent the application of the rules on competition contained in the Treaty, to the extent to which restrictions on competition, or even an exclusion of any competition by other traders, was necessary in order to ensure the performance of the specific task which was conferred on the undertakings which held those exclusive rights.

With regard to the services in question in the main proceedings, it could not be denied that the *Régie des postes* was responsible for a service of general economic interest consisting in the obligation to ensure the collection, transport and distribution of mail, for all users, throughout the territory of the Member State concerned, at uniform tariffs and under similar conditions relating to quality, without regard to specific situations or to the level of profitability of each individual transaction.

Consequently, it was necessary to examine to what extent a restriction on competition, or even the exclusion of all competition by other traders, was necessary to enable the holder of the exclusive right to carry out its task of general interest, and in particular to benefit from economically acceptable conditions.

For the purposes of that examination, it was necessary to start from the premise that the obligation on the undertaking responsible for that task to provide its services under economically balanced conditions presupposed the possibility of a set-off between profitable activities and less profitable activities and therefore justified a limitation of competition from individual undertakings in economically profitable areas.

To authorise individual undertakings to compete with the holder of exclusive rights in sectors which they might choose which were covered by those rights would enable competitors to concentrate on profitable activities and to offer lower prices for them than those applied by the holders of exclusive rights, given that, by contrast with the latter, they were not economically obliged to carry out a set-off between losses arising in non-profitable sectors and profits arising in the more profitable areas.

The exclusion of competition could not, however, be justified where certain specific services were concerned which were dissociable from the service of general economic interest, which satisfied specific needs of traders and which required certain additional services which the traditional postal service did not offer, such as collection from the sender, greater speed or reliability of distribution or the possibility of changing the destination of an item while in transit, and to the extent to which those services, by their nature and the conditions under which they were offered, such as the geographical area in which they were provided, did not call in question the economic equilibrium of the service of general economic interest which was provided by the holder of the exclusive right.

. . .

It was for the referring court to examine whether the services at issue in the case before it fell within those criteria.

Question

The headline of this law report in *The Times* reads: 'Postal service monopoly cannot be justified'; is this true, and does the same claim apply to public ownership as a whole?

[E91] C-D Ehlermann: 'Managing monopolies: the role of the state in controlling market dominance in the European Community' [1993] 2 European Competition Law Review 61

. . . Are there limits for the definition of the scope of exclusive rights granted by Member States? And what are these limits?

In addition to Article 90(1), the Treaty contains only one other provision dealing expressly with exclusive rights, that is Article 37. Article 37 requires the progressive adjustment of state monopolies of a commercial character so as to ensure that exclusive rights to import and export goods are eliminated.

Until the end of the 1980s specialists in Community law interpreted Articles 37 and 90(1) as meaning that only monopolies over the importation and exportation of goods caught by Article 37 are prohibited. By contrast, exclusive rights not caught by Article 37 are authorised; Article 90(1) presupposes their existence. Of course, the *exercise* of an exclusive right is governed by the Treaty's provisions on the abuse of dominant positions. But this control of the *exercise* of an exclusive right does not involve any control of the statutory limits of its scope, that is the structure of that right. The national legislator is free to create such a right and to define its limits.

These views have been overtaken by events in the form of two developments. The *first* of these developments rests on Article 90(1) in combination with Article 86. If the extension of an exclusive right to include an ancillary activity constitutes an abuse on the part of the enterprise enjoying that right, why should the extension, without any objective justification, of the exclusive right itself by the Member State not constitute an abuse prohibited by Article 90(1)? The Commission has applied this simple reasoning for the first time in its 1988 and 1990 directives on liberalisation of the markets in telecommunications terminal equipment and in certain telecommunications services. The Court of Justice has endorsed it fully in its judgment concerning the Belgian RTT. In addition, an exclusive right cannot be structured in such a way that it leads inevitably to abuses prohibited by Article 86. This is the line of reasoning followed by the Court of Justice in its judgment in the German federal employment office **[E88]** and in the Greek radio and television case **[E89]**. The scope of exclusive rights is therefore clearly limited by the combination of Articles 90(1) and 86.

The *second* development which has led to a reappraisal of traditional thinking on the compatibility of exclusive rights – not caught by Article 37 – with the Treaty stems from the interpretation of the fundamental freedoms, or more precisely the free movement of goods and freedom to provide services. Here also, two trends are apparent in the case law of the Court of Justice.

First, the scope of the prohibition laid down in Article 37 is becoming broader as far as the free movement of goods is concerned. The prohibition on import and export monopolies is ultimately nothing more than a specific instance of the fundamental prohibition of unjustified obstacles to intra-Community trade in goods. Any exclusive right, any channelling of trade in goods, must be justified by 'imperative reasons'. If the exclusive right is justified by an 'imperative reason', which must by definition be non-economic, it may be maintained in force. Otherwise it is incompatible with the Treaty and must be abolished. This is the line which the court took, most spectacularly, in its recent judgment on the 1988 Commission directive prohibiting exclusive rights in relation to telecommunications terminal equipment **[E86]**.

Secondly, at the Commission's prompting, the court has gradually aligned the principle of freedom to provide services more closely on that of the free movement of goods. Recent judgments seem to indicate that exclusive rights which constitute obstacles to freedom to provide services except where they are justified – as in the case of goods – by imperative reasons. It is necessary henceforth to justify the extent – and even the very existence – of exclusive rights to provide services in the telecommunications and postal sectors, and in that of energy (in so far as services, and not goods, are involved) on public-interest grounds of a non-economic nature.

That leaves the third fundamental freedom, that of establishment. Until now, the great majority of legal practitioners have considered that this freedom does not affect the exclusive rights in relation to production which exist, notably, in the energy field. Thus, according to this view, production monopolies are alone in not having to be justified by 'imperative reasons'.

There are a host of reasons which militate in favour of a horizontal approach to exclusive rights as far as the four fundamental freedoms are concerned. Therefore, production monopolies must also be justified by 'imperative reasons' if they are to be deemed compatible with the Treaty.

The principle of undistorted competition and the fundamental freedoms therefore go hand in hand and lead together to the same conclusion: exclusive rights created by the Member States may be maintained in force if and to the extent that they are justified on public-interest grounds. Such grounds include the need to provide and exploit a universal network or a universal service to the general public under reasonable, fair and non-discriminatory conditions in the fields of voice telephony, electricity, gas and postal services. On the other hand, exclusive rights must be reduced or abolished altogether if and to the extent that such public-interest grounds are lacking or no longer exist owing, for example, to technological developments.

The underlying economic reasons for the review of exclusive rights

It is not for ideological reasons that exclusive rights granted yesterday are called into question today and restricted or abolished tomorrow. This process is due to changes in objective circumstances. The three following seem to be the most important.

The internal market project necessarily involves a detailed discussion of state monopolies which partition national markets in goods and services. In a genuine internal market, such monopolistic situations can be tolerated only if they are indispensable both from the point of view of the Member States and from that of the Community.

The second factor is technological development. This development is most apparent in the field of telecommunications, as these are helping, more than any other branch of technology, to transform business, our habits and our way of thinking. The new technologies are gradually breaking down the natural monopolies which underlie most of the exclusive rights granted by states. Witness the public monopolies of radio and television. These monopolies used to be necessary owing to the shortage of frequencies. Technological breakthroughs, notably cable and satellite, have profoundly modified the situation by removing the technical justification for the monopolies, thereby opening the door to other operators and to competition.

The third reason why exclusive rights are being called into question is the enormous need for funds which characterises the sectors concerned. This need cannot be satisfied by the state in its capacity as owner of public enterprises owing to the pressure on public finances, the high level of existing taxation and international competition, which encourages governments to reduce taxes rather than increase them. Hence the need to resort to private capital and to operate on the financial markets with the same flexibility and the same attractiveness as private enterprises. This helps to explain at least in part the general move towards privatisation that is taking place even in Western Europe.

[E92]   Case C-142/87 Belgium v Commission (Re Tubemeuse) [1990] ECR I-959

The European Court of Justice

25. It should be pointed out that, according to settled case law, investment by the public authorities in the capital of undertakings, in whatever form, may constitute state aid where the conditions set out in Article 92 are fulfilled (see the judgments . . . in Case 323/82 *Intermills* [1984] ECR 3809 and . . . Cases 296/82 and 318/82 *Netherlands and Leeuwarder Papierwarenfabriek v Commission* [1985] ECR 809).

. . .

29. . . . there is nothing which suggests any error in the Commission's statement that Tubemeuse's prospects of profitability were not such as to induce private investors operating under normal market economy conditions to enter into the financial transactions in question, that it was unlikely that Tubemeuse could have obtained the amounts essential for its survival on the capital markets and that, for that reason, the Belgian government's support for Tubemeuse constituted state aid.

. . .

54. With regard to the application of Article 92(3)(c), the Commission states in the contested decision that the measures taken by the Belgian State in favour of Tubemeuse could not be said to be conducive to the economic development of the region concerned because Tubemeuse was not in a position to ensure its own viability.

55. The Belgian government claims that the social and economic situation has changed since the Commission carried out the above-mentioned analysis and that the aid in question ought to have been considered to come within the exceptions provided for in Article 92(3)(a) and (c) inasmuch as it was intended to promote the economic development of the Liège area which has been severely hit recently by factory closures and job losses.

56. The applicant's arguments cannot be accepted. In that regard to Article 92(3), the Commission has a wide discretion the exercise of which implies economic and social assessments which must be carried out in a Community context.

57. Having regard to the Commission's powers in this matter, the Belgian government's submission, in which it confines itself to making a general criticism of the assessments on which the measure is based, without adducing any evidence capable of casting doubt upon them, must be rejected.

The submission that it was impossible to implement the contested decision immediately

58. Belgium claims that it was impossible to implement the Commission's decision immediately, in so far as it ordered the recovery of the contested aid. Recovery of aid granted contrary to the Treaty may be effected only in accordance with the relevant rules of national law. In this case, the composition proceedings to which Tubemeuse was subject prevented any claim by

the Belgian State. The undertaking's assets have been assigned to its creditors and the state no longer has any power to order the recovery of the aid in question.

59. Belgium adds that, like a judgment of the court, the Commission's decision cannot create any privilege in its favour which would permit it to derogate, to the disadvantage of Tubemeuse's creditors, from the rules applicable to such cases. In the context of the composition procedure, the Belgian State can only declare its debt as an unsecured creditor of the undertaking. In so far as the contested decision orders the immediate recovery of the aid, it thus infringes the general principles common to the Member States in regard to company law and the law of insolvency.

60. It should be noted that the Belgian government's argument is based on the premiss that the contested decision orders the recovery of the aid in question on a privileged basis. However, the contested decision confines itself to ordering recovery of the aid, without prescribing the way in which that is to be done.

61. In principle the recovery of aid unlawfully paid must take place in accordance with the relevant procedural provisions of national law, subject however to the proviso that those provisions are to be applied in such a way that the recovery required by Community law is not rendered practically impossible (see the judgment . . . in Case 94/87 *Commission v Germany* [1989] ECR 175).

62. Moreover, that is the reason why the Commission stated at the hearing that the Belgian government had fulfilled its obligations under the contested measure in regard to the recovery of the aid since, after the dismissal of its application for interim measures . . ., the Belgian government sought to have its debt registered as one of Tubemeuse's unsecured liabilities and lodged an appeal against the judgment rejecting that application.

63. It should be added that any procedural or other difficulties in regard to the implementation of the contested measure cannot have any influence on the lawfulness of the measure.

64. Consequently, the submission must be rejected.

65. Belgium also claims that the obligation to recover the aid laid down in the contested decision is disproportionate to the objectives laid down in Articles 92 and 93, inasmuch as the declaration of the debt by the Belgian State in the composition procedure would cause serious damage to other creditors.

66. It should be pointed out in that regard that it follows from the court's previous decisions (see, for example, the judgment . . . in Case 310/85 *Deufil v Commission* [1987] ECR 901) that recovery of unlawful aid is the logical consequence of the finding that it is unlawful. Consequently, the recovery of state aid unlawfully granted for the purpose of re-establishing the previously existing situation cannot in principle be regarded as disproportionate to the objectives of the Treaty in regard to state aids.

67. That submission must therefore be rejected.

[E93]   Commission Communication to Member States on the application of Articles 92 and 93 of the EEC Treaty and Article 5 of Commission Directive 80/723 to public undertakings in the manufacturing sector (OJ 1991 C273/2)

V.   Practicality of the market economy investor principle

27.   The practical experience gained by the Commission from the application of state aid rules to public enterprises and the general support among the Community institutions for the basic themes of the market economy investor principle confirm the Commission's view that it is as such an appropriate yardstick to determine whether or not aid exists. However, it is noted that the majority of cases to which the mechanism has been applied have been of a particular nature and the wider application of the mechanism may appear to cause certain difficulties. Some further explanations are therefore warranted. In addition, the fear has been expressed that the application of the market economy investor principle could lead to the Commission's judgment replacing the investor and his appreciation of investment projects. In the first place this criticism can be refuted by the fact that this principle has already shown itself to be both an appropriate and practical yardstick for determining which public funds constitute aid in numerous individual cases. Secondly it is not the aim of the Commission in the future, just as it has not been in the past, to replace the investor's judgment. Any request for extra finance naturally calls for public undertakings and public authorities, just as it does for private undertakings and private providers of finance, to analyse the risk and the likely outcome of the project. In turn, the Commission realises that this analysis of risk requires public undertakings, like private undertakings, to exercise entrepreneurial skills, which by the very nature of the problem implies a wide margin of judgment on the part of the investor. Within that wide margin the exercise of judgment by the investor cannot be regarded as involving state aid. It is in evaluation of the justification for the provision of funds that the Member State has to decide if a notification is necessary in conformity with its obligation under Article 93(3).

. . .

28.   There is no question of the Commission using benefit of hindsight to state that the provision of public funds constituted state aid on the sole basis that the out-turn rate of return was not adequate. Only projects where the Commission considers that there were no objective or bona fide grounds to reasonably expect an adequate rate of return in a comparable private undertaking at the moment the investment/financing decision is made can be treated as state aid. It is only in such cases that funds are being provided more cheaply than would be available to a private undertaking, ie a subsidy is involved. It is obvious that, because of the inherent risks involved in any investment, not all projects will be successful and certain investments may produce a sub-normal rate of return or even be a complete failure. This is also the case for private investors . . . Moreover such an approach makes no discrimination between projects which have short or long-term pay back periods, as long as the risks are adequately and

objectively assessed and discounted at the time the decision to invest is made, in the way that a private investor would.

. . .

VI. Compatibility of aid

32. Each Member State is free to choose the size and nature of its public sector and to vary it over time. The Commission recognises that when the state decides to exercise its right to public ownership, commercial objectives are not always the essential motivation. Public enterprises are sometimes expected to fulfil non-commercial functions alongside or in addition to their basic commercial activities. For example, in some Member States public companies may be used as a locomotive for the economy, as part of efforts to counter recession, to restructure troubled industries or to act as catalysts for regional development. Public companies may be expected to locate in less developed regions where costs are higher or to maintain employment at levels beyond purely commercial levels. The Treaty enables the Commission to take account of such considerations where they are justified in the Community interest. In addition the provision of some services may entail a public service element, which may even be enforced by political or legal constraints. These non-commercial objectives/functions (ie social goods) have a cost which ultimately has to be financed by the state (ie taxpayers) either in the form of new finance (eg capital injections) or a reduced rate of return on capital invested. This aiding of the provision of public services can in certain circumstances distort competition. Unless one of the derogations of the Treaty is applicable, public undertakings are not exempted from the rules of competition by the imposition of these non-commercial objectives.

[E94]   Case C-301/87 France v Commission (Boussac) [1990] ECR I-307

The European Court of Justice

2. It is apparent from the document before the court that the French authorities granted financial contributions between June 1982 and August 1984 to a French producer of textiles, clothing and paper products, Compagnie Boussac Saint Frères (hereinafter referred to as 'CBSF'). That financial assistance took the form of capital investment which was approved by the Institut de développement industriel (hereinafter referred to as 'IDI') and then transferred to the Société de participation et de restructuration industrielle (hereinafter referred to as 'Sopari'), which itself provided CBSF with new capital, loans at reduced rates of interest and reductions in social security charges made under the aid scheme for the textile and clothing industry.

. . .

8. The submissions made by the French government in support of its application are based on infringement of the procedural rules under Article 93 of the Treaty, on the insufficient reasoning on which the contested decision is based, the incorrect application of Article 92 of the Treaty and breach of the general principle of proportionality.

A.   The effects of the failure to notify

9. It is necessary, as a preliminary point, to consider a problem raised by the Commission. It takes the view that, since the court has already recognised the direct effect of the final sentence of Article 93(3) of the Treaty, a clear, binding provision involving public policy, failure to comply with that provision is in itself sufficient to render that aid unlawful. Such illegality, it contends, makes it unnecessary to examine the matter in detail and entitles the Commission to order recovery of the aid. For that reason, the Commission believes that the court should refuse to entertain the objections raised by the French government against that part of the contested decision in which the Commission concludes that the aid in question is incompatible with Article 92 of the Treaty.

10. The French government contends that a possible failure to comply with the procedural rules in Article 93(3) of the Treaty cannot by itself render the financial assistance illegal and justify recovery of the aid. The Commission ought, in any case, to have carried out a detailed examination of the disputed contributions.

11. It must be observed that each of these two arguments is liable to give rise to major practical difficulties. On the one hand, the argument put forward by the Commission implies that aid which is compatible with the common market may be declared unlawful because of procedural irregularities. On the other hand, it is not possible to accept the French government's argument to the effect that the Commission, when faced with aid which has been granted or altered by a Member State in breach of the procedure laid down in Article 93(3) of the Treaty, has only the same rights and obligations as those which it has in the case of aid duly notified at the planning stage. Such an interpretation would in effect encourage the Member State concerned not to comply with Article 93(3) and would deprive that paragraph of its effectiveness.

12. In the light of those arguments, it is necessary to examine the problem by analysing the powers and responsibilities which the Commission and the Member States have in cases where aid has been granted or altered.

13. In the first place, it should be noted that Articles 92, 93 and 94, which form part of Section 3 of the Treaty entitled 'Aids granted by States', lay down procedures which imply that the Commission is in a position to determine, on the basis of the material at its disposal, whether the disputed financial assistance constitutes aid within the meaning of those articles.

14. Secondly, it should be noted that the Council has not as yet adopted any recommendation under Article 94 of the Treaty for the application of Articles 92 and 93 thereof.

15. Furthermore, it is necessary to bear in mind the established case law of the court. In its judgment . . . in Case 78/76 *Steinike und Weinlig v Germany* [1977] ECR 595, the court held that the prohibition contained in Article 92(1) of the Treaty is neither absolute nor unconditional, since paragraph (3) in particular of that article confers on the Commission a wide discretion to admit aid by way of derogation from the general prohibition in Article 92(1). The assessment in such cases of whether a state aid is or is not compatible with the common market raises problems which presuppose the examination and appraisal of economic facts and conditions which may be both complex and liable to change rapidly.

16. That was the reason for which the Treaty provided in Article 93 for a special procedure under which the Commission would monitor aid schemes and keep them under constant review. With regard to new aid which Member States might be intending to grant, a preliminary procedure was established; if this procedure was not followed, the aid could not be regarded as having been properly granted. By providing under Article 93 for the Commission to monitor and keep under constant review all aid schemes, the Treaty intended that any finding that aid might be incompatible with the common market should, subject to review by the court, be the outcome of an appropriate procedure for the implementation of which the Commission was responsible.

17. The court has also held (see . . . Joined Cases 91/83 and 127/83 *Heineken Brouwerijen BV v Inspecteurs der Vennootschapsbelasting, Amsterdam and Utrecht* [1984] ECR 3435) that the purpose of the first sentence of Article 93(3) of the Treaty is to provide the Commission with the opportunity to review, in sufficient time and in the general interest of the Communities, any plan to grant or alter aid. The final sentence of Article 93(3) of the Treaty constitutes the means of safeguarding the machinery for review laid down by that article, which, in turn, is essential for ensuring the proper functioning of the common market. The prohibition laid down in that article on putting any proposed measures into effect is designed to ensure that a system of aid cannot become operational before the Commission has had a reasonable period in which to study the proposed measures in detail and, if necessary, to initiate the procedure provided for in Article 93(2).

18. In order for it to be effective, the system analysed above presupposes that measures may be taken to counteract any infringement of the rules laid down in Article 93(3) of the Treaty and that such measures may, with a view to protecting the legitimate interests of the Member States, form the subject of an action. With regard to this system, there can be no dispute as to the need to introduce conservatory measures in cases where the effect of practices engaged in by certain Member States with regard to aid is to render nugatory the system established by Articles 92 and 93 of the Treaty.

19. Once it has established that aid has been granted or altered without notification, the Commission therefore has the power, after giving the Member State in question an opportunity to submit its comments on the matter, to issue an interim decision requiring it to suspend immediately the payment of such aid pending the outcome of the examination of the aid and to provide the Commission, within such period as it may specify, with all such documentation, information and data as are necessary in order that it may examine the compatibility of the aid with the common market.

20. The Commission has the same power in cases where it has been notified of aid but the Member State in question, instead of awaiting the outcome of the procedure provided for under Article 93(2) and (3) of the Treaty, has instead proceeded to put the aid into effect, contrary to the prohibition contained in Article 93(3).

21. Where a Member State has complied in full with the Commission's order, the Commission is obliged to examine the compatibility of the aid with the common market, in accordance with the procedure laid down in Article 93(2) and (3) of the Treaty.

22. If the Member State, notwithstanding the Commission's order, fails to provide the information requested, the Commission is empowered to

terminate the procedure and make its decision, on the basis of the information available to it, on the question whether or not the aid is compatible with the common market. If appropriate, such a decision may call for the recovery of the amount of aid which has already been paid.

23. It has to be recognised that if the Member State fails to suspend payment of the aid, the Commission is entitled, while carrying out the examination on the substance of the matter, to bring the matter directly before the court by applying for a declaration that such payment amounts to an infringement of the Treaty. Such a referral is justified in respect of urgency because there has been a decision embodying an order, taken after the Member State in question has been given all opportunity to submit its comments and thus at the conclusion of a preliminary procedure in which it has been enabled to put its case, as in the case of the means of redress provided under the second sub-paragraph of Article 93(2) of the Treaty. This means of redress is in fact no more than a variant of the action for a declaration of failure to fulfil Treaty obligations, specifically adapted to the special problems which state aid poses for competition within the common market.

24. With regard to the present case, it is not disputed that the Commission did examine whether or not the aid was compatible with the common market, even though it did so as a matter of secondary importance. That examination is therefore capable of forming the subject of the present proceedings.

B.   *Infringement of the procedural rules*

25. In this submission, the French government contends first of all that the Commission infringed the general principle of legal certainty through its failure to act within a reasonable period, bearing in mind the detailed information which the French authorities provided to the Commission in good time. It also believes that its right to a fair hearing was infringed in the present case because the Commission failed to inform it of the observations of interested third parties received pursuant to Article 93(2) of the Treaty.

26. With regard to the first complaint, it should be noted that, according to the documents before the court, the French authorities started to provide the information, which the Commission had requested on numerous occasions, after most of the aid in question had already been paid out. It is therefore not in dispute that the Commission was not informed in sufficient time, within the meaning of Article 93(3) of the Treaty, to enable it to submit its comments on the proposed aid for CBSF. Moreover, the information which the French government provided to the Commission in March 1984 was far from complete. Thus, it was not until 23 August 1984 that it confirmed, though without providing full particulars, the holding of IDI, and then Sopari, in the capital of CBSF.

27. In the light of those circumstances, it was thus reasonable for the Commission to allow itself three months from 23 August 1984 in which to consider the matter and to carry out investigations before issuing the formal notice on 3 December 1984. Furthermore, it should be noted that part of the information sent to the Commission was on several occasions corrected and supplemented by the French government. It was not until the letters of 27 March and 21 May 1987 that the French government supplied the Commission with the necessary particulars and sent to it the definitive information on the basis of which the Commission was able to adopt the decision of 15 July 1987.

28. While it is true to say that fairly long periods elapsed between, in the first place, the initial letter of 22 March 1984 from the French government and the formal notice of 3 December 1984 and, secondly, between that formal notice and the decision of 15 July 1987, it was not until 21 May 1987 that the Commission was in possession of all the facts and material necessary for it to examine the compatibility of the aid with the common market. Given those circumstances, it must be held that the Commission's conduct did not infringe the general principle of legal certainty.

29. With regard to the second complaint, based on infringement of the right to be heard, it should be stressed that the court has consistently held (see the judgments . . . in Cases 234/84 and 40/85 *Belgium v Commission* [1986] ECR 2263 and 2321, and . . . in Case 259/85 *France v Commission* [1987] ECR 4393) that observance of the right to be heard is, in all proceedings initiated against a person which are liable to culminate in a measure adversely affecting that person, a fundamental principle of Community law which must be guaranteed even in the absence of any rules governing the procedure in question.

30. The court recognised in those judgments that this principle requires the Member State in question to be placed in a position in which it may effectively make known its views on the observations submitted by interested third parties under Article 93(2) of the Treaty and on which the Commission proposes to base its decision. The court held that in so far as the Member State had not been afforded the opportunity to comment on such observations, the Commission could not incorporate them in its decision against that state.

31. However, in order for such an infringement of the right to be heard to result in annulment, it is necessary to establish that, had it not been for such an irregularity, the outcome of the procedure might have been different. In that regard, it should be noted that the observations in question, which were lodged with the court at its request, do not contain any information in addition to that which the Commission already possessed and of which the French government was aware. Under those circumstances, the fact that the French government did not have an opportunity to comment on those observations was not likely to influence the outcome of the administrative procedure. This complaint must therefore also be rejected.

C.   The statement of the reasons on which the decision is based

32. The French government claims that the statement of the reasons on which the contested decision is based is inadequate inasmuch as it contains no assessment of the real effect of the aid already granted on competition and on trade between Member States, and inasmuch as it appears to be contradictory in view of the closure of production sites. The French government also criticises the reasoning of the decision by claiming that it is based on an incorrect assessment of the market share held by CBSF and of the patterns of trade between the Member States. The latter complaint also relates, in substance, to the question whether the financial contributions were compatible with the common market and will for that reason be considered together with the submission based on infringement of Article 92.

33. The first complaint must be rejected. If the Commission were required in its decision to demonstrate the real effect of aid which had already

been granted, that would ultimately favour those Member States which grant aid in breach of the duty to notify laid down in Article 93(3) of the Treaty, to the detriment of those which do notify aid at the planning stage. It was therefore not necessary that the reasoning on which the contested decision was based should contain an up-to-date assessment of the effect of aid granted without being notified at the planning stage.

. . .

[The second complaint was also rejected.]

. . .

D.   The application of Article 92 of the Treaty

37. The French government takes the view, primarily, that the financial contributions do not constitute aid, that they do not affect trade between Member States and that they neither distort nor threaten to distort competition by favouring certain undertakings. In the alternative, the French government claims that the aid is compatible with the common market on the basis of Article 92(3)(a) and (c) of the Treaty and that it is consistent with the various guidelines and notices drawn up by the Commission in 1971, 1977 and 1984.

38. In support of its main contention, the French government first points out that the capital contributions, loans at reduced rates of interest and reductions in social security charges which are here at issue do not constitute aid because they were granted to CBSF under conditions of a market economy and were made in conjunction with private investment. The French authorities thus decided to grant financial assistance in association with private investors on the basis of a market analysis and an evaluation of the undertaking which permitted the conclusion that it could, subject to restructuring, become profitable within a reasonable period of time. Such restructuring consisted, in particular, in the elimination of overcapacity, a reduction in manpower, the conversion of non-profitable or excessively vulnerable activities into profitable ones, rationalisation of production and improved productivity.

39. For the purpose of deciding whether such measures constitute state aid, it is appropriate to apply the criterion, suggested by the Commission in its decision and in any case not disputed by the French government, which is based on the opportunities open to the undertaking of acquiring the amounts in question on the capital market.

40. In the present case, it is apparent from the documents before the court that, in the first place, the financial situation of the company in 1981 was such that it did not give cause to believe that investments would reach an acceptable level of profitability within a reasonable period, and, secondly, that CBSF would not, in view of its inadequate margin of self-financing, have been in a position to acquire the necessary funds on the capital market. It should also be noted that the first private investments, which in any case were much lower than the contributions of public funds, were only made after the latter had been allocated. The capital contributions which Sopari granted to CBSF following the transfer of IDI therefore do constitute state aid within the meaning of Article 92(1) of the Treaty.

41. The same is true of the loans at reduced rates of interest and the reduction in social security charges, because they also enabled CBSF to

avoid having to bear costs which would normally have had to be met out of the undertaking's own financial resources, and thereby prevented market forces from having their normal effect.

42. The French government also claims that the financial assistance does not affect trade patterns and neither distorted nor threatened to distort competition between Member States. Thus, the market share held by CBSF is less than 0.5% of the European textile market, which represents approximately ECU 115,000m, and CBSF'S exports, rather than increasing, fell between 1982 and 1986 by 33%. The figures given by the Commission relate to sectors of CBSF'S activity which did not receive public aid and also fail to take account of the short-term increase in activity within the linen sector during 1983 and 1984.

43. It should be noted that the contested decision contains an analysis of all these factors. The statement of the reasons on which the decision is based includes an examination of the textile and clothing market in France. After finding that the French industry in those sectors accounts for approximately 20% of value added in the common market and plays a very active role in intra-Community trade, since approximately 40% of its total production is exported to other Member States, the decision points out that CBSF is the third largest producer in France of textiles and clothing and that this sector accounts for 56% of its total turnover, which in 1986 came to FF 4,700m. According to that decision, CBSF is the fifth-largest producer in the Community and participates in intra Community trade by exporting 16% of its textile production to other Member States and a further 9% elsewhere. The Commission also states in its decision that the period which must be examined in order to determine whether the financial assistance is compatible with the common market is that during which the aid was granted. During that period, which ran from July 1982 to the end of 1984, textile exports to other Member States increased by 32% and more than half of CBSF's turnover was achieved in the textiles and clothing sector.

44. The Commission also notes, among the reasons for its decision, that the pecuniary assistance intended to restore CBSF's financial position reduced the costs which it would normally have incurred to an extent which placed it at an advantage over its competitors, who must be regarded as having been affected thereby. As it reduced the price which CBSF would normally have had to pay for its rationalisation and modernisation, the aid at issue did affect trade between Member States and distorted or threatened to distort competition.

45. It should be pointed out that the considerations set out by the Commission, taken as a whole, can support the conclusion which it reached as regards the illegality of the aid. Consequently, the complaints based on the nature of the aid and its incompatibility with the common market, together with those directed against the reasons on which the decision is based, must be rejected.

46. The French government requests the court, in the alternative, to consider whether the aid may be compatible with the common market under Article 92(3) of the Treaty. It contends that the recovery of CBSF is beyond dispute and that the aid facilitated the development and reconversion of its industrial activities within the meaning of Article 92(3)(c) of the Treaty.

47. It goes on to maintain that the aid to CBSF was granted in areas affected by serious underemployment in comparison with the Community average, within the meaning of Article 92(3)(a) of the Treaty.

. . .

49. The arguments put forward by the applicant cannot be accepted. It should be borne in mind that the Commission enjoys a wide discretion under Article 92(3) of the Treaty and that the exercise of that discretion involves assessments of an economic and social nature which must be made within a Community context.

50. In that context, the Commission was entitled, without exceeding the limits of its discretionary power, to form the view that the aid granted to CBSF could not come within the exemption provided for in Article 92(3)(c) of the Treaty in favour of aid designed to facilitate the development of certain economic activities or of certain economic areas, where such aid did not adversely affect trading conditions to an extent contrary to the common interest. The aid lowered CBSF's costs and thereby reduced the competitiveness of other manufacturers within the Community, at the risk of forcing them to withdraw from the market even though they had hitherto been able to continue their activities by virtue of restructuring and improvements in productivity and quality, financed by their own resources.

51. With regard to the argument based on the application of Article 92(3)(a) of the Treaty, it should be borne in mind that the Commission is obliged to take account of the economic situation in the areas concerned as compared with that in the Community as a whole. It is clear from the statistics provided by the Commission and the intervener, which were not disputed by the French government, that the areas containing the production sites of CBSF to which aid was granted were not areas where the standard of living was abnormally low or where there was serious underemployment.

. . .

58. It follows that the submission based on the application of Article 92 of the Treaty must be rejected.

E.   The submission based on infringement of the general principle of proportionality

59. In the view of the French government, the contested decision infringes the general principle of proportionality, in the first place, because it fails to take account either of the restructuring costs incurred by CBSF or of the fact that CBSF, had it not been for its recovery, would have been put into liquidation, with serious consequences for both creditors and the community as a whole, and, secondly, because the recovery of aid which is sought is disproportionate to the adverse effects on competition.

60. That submission must be rejected. As the Commission has made clear in its decision, the aid granted cannot be regarded as having resulted in a proper restructuring of CBSF. The undertaking limited itself to a modernisation of its production plants, without making any fundamental alterations, by replacing machinery which had become totally obsolete and by adapting production techniques and procedures to the technological developments which had taken place many years previously throughout the rest of the Community textile industry. In the light of the information in the decision relating to reductions in manpower and capacity, the Commission was entitled to form the view that the aid did not represent investment for restructuring and to disregard in its decision the costs of the alleged restructuring.

61. As the Commission has pointed out in its decision, out of 27 production sites and 4,730 persons transferred to independent companies, 13 sites, representing a work-force of 3,153 or 66.66% of the total number of jobs transferred, were closed down and textile production there was permanently discontinued. The Commission considered the aid paid to facilitate those 13 transfers as money lost. In seeking recovery, therefore, of only 33% of total aid paid, the Commission did comply with the principle of proportionality.

62. This last submission must therefore also be rejected.

As none of the submissions made by the French government has been upheld, the application must be dismissed in its entirety.

[E95]   Case C-292/90 British Aerospace plc and Rover Group Holdings plc v Commission [1992] 1 CMLR 853

The European Court of Justice

1. [British Aerospace and Rover] brought an action under Article 173(2) EEC for the partial annulment of a Commission Decision of 17 July 1990 OJ 1991 C21/2, in so far as it requires the United Kingdom to recover £44.4m of alleged state aid.

2. In the preamble to the contested decision the Commission refers to a previous decision, Decision 89/58/EEC of 13 July 1988 OJ 1989 L25/92, concerning aid provided by the United Kingdom government to the Rover Group, an undertaking producing motor vehicles. By that decision the Commission authorised aid consisting of a capital contribution intended to absorb certain debts of the Rover Group in connection with its acquisition by British Aerospace. The aid was authorised on inter alia the following conditions:

- that the United Kingdom government would not alter the proposed terms of sale and in particular those specifying that the acquisition price paid by British Aerospace would be £150m and that British Aerospace would bear all future restructuring costs;
- that the United Kingdom government would refrain from granting any further aid to Rover in the form of capital contributions or any other form of discretionary aid except for limited regional aid.

3. Following the publication in November 1989 of a report and secret memorandum by the Comptroller and Auditor General of the United Kingdom National Audit Office, the Commission discovered that the United Kingdom government had granted British Aerospace a number of financial concessions which were not covered by Decision 89/58.

4. The Commission took the view that the additional concessions constituted aid for the purposes of Article 92(1) EEC and that they were incompatible with the Common Market since they had been granted in breach of Article 1 of Decision 89/58. The Commission therefore adopted the contested measure in which it decided:

- that the additional £44.4m aid granted in the context of the sale of [Rover] to [British Aerospace] constitutes illegal aid which was paid in breach of Decision 89/58 EEC and that [the United Kingdom authorities] are required to recover it from the beneficiaries (ie the £9.5m payment to cover the purchase cost of minority shares and the £33.4m benefit to [British Aerospace] which resulted from the deferment of the payment of the sales price) and £1.5m from [Rover] (which it obtained to cover external advice costs linked to the sale).

. . .

6. The applicants plead a breach of Articles 92 and 93 EEC, the existence of an error in the calculation of the amount to be recovered, failure to respect the principle of proportionality and failure to provide an adequate statement of reasons.

7. The applicants contend first that, if the Commission considered that the concessions granted to British Aerospace and to Rover constituted state aid incompatible with the Common Market, it should have instituted the procedure laid down in Article 93(2) EEC and thereby given the parties concerned the opportunity to submit their comments. The Commission cannot, in the applicants' view, deny that the contested decision is independent of Decision 89/58 EEC, inasmuch as it characterises the concessions as state aid, finds them incompatible with the Common Market, quantifies them and orders their recovery.

8. The Commission replies that the contested decision is not independent of Decision 89/58 EEC, which laid down a series of conditions for the approval of the aid which had been notified at that time by the United Kingdom and was directly enforceable.

9. In considering the merits of this plea it is necessary to bear in mind the system established by Article 93(2) EEC and the powers conferred upon the Commission by that provision.

10. The first sub-paragraph of Article 93(2) makes the Commission responsible for implementing, subject to review by the court, a special procedure involving the constant review and monitoring of aid which Member States intend to introduce: see Case C-301/87 *France v Commission* **[E94]**. Any finding that aid is incompatible with the Common Market may be made only on completion of that procedure, during which the Commission is required inter alia to give notice to the parties concerned to submit their comments.

11. If a state does not comply with a Commission decision finding proposed aid to be incompatible with the Common Market or does not observe the conditions on which the Commission approved the aid, the Commission is entitled, under the second sub-paragraph of Article 93(2), to refer the matter directly to the Court of Justice by way of derogation from the provisions of Articles 169 and 170 EEC.

12. It follows from the foregoing that, if the Commission considered that the United Kingdom had not complied with certain conditions laid down by Decision 89/58EEC, it should have instituted proceedings against the United Kingdom directly before the court by virtue of the second sub-paragraph of Article 93(2).

13. If the Commission considered that the United Kingdom had paid new aid which had not been examined under the procedure leading to the adoption of Decision 89/58 EEC, it was obliged to institute the special procedure provided for by the first sub-paragraph of Article 93(2) and to give notice to the parties concerned to submit their comments.

14. It is true that in its judgment in Case C-261/89 *Italy v Commission* [1991] ECR I-4437 the court held that, where in such circumstances the

Commission examines the compatibility of state aid with the Common Market, it must take account of all relevant matters, including in appropriate cases the circumstances already considered in any previous decision and any obligations which that previous decision may have imposed on the Member State. However, such an examination must be made in accordance with the procedures laid down by the Treaty.

15. Consequently, without there being any need to consider the other pleas, the Commission Decision of 17 July 1990 must be annulled in so far as it requires the United Kingdom to recover £44.4m of alleged state aid.

Note. The Commission subsequently reopened proceedings to have the 'sweeteners' treated as an aid. In a negotiated outcome, interest was agreed to be payable on the repayment, down to the date of settlement.

[E96] Case C-354/90 Fédération Nationale du Commerce Extérieur des Produits Alimentaires and others v France

The European Court of Justice (Judgment, 21 November 1991 – unofficial translation, as published in the Weekly Proceedings of the Court of Justice and Court of First Instance, No 20/91)

As far as the national courts were concerned, the court stated that proceedings could be brought before them requiring them to interpret and apply the concept of aid, referred to in Article 92, with a view to determining whether a state measure introduced without observance of the prior review procedure under Article 93(3) should be subject thereto.

The court stated that the validity of acts involving the implementation of aid measures was affected by disregard by the national authorities of the last sentence of Article 93(3) of the Treaty. The national court has to ensure that individuals were in a position to enforce rights of action in respect of any such disregard, from which all the proper consequences would follow, in accordance with their national law, both regarding the validity of acts involving the implementation of aid measures and the recovery of financial support granted in breach of that provision or of any provisional measures.

The court stated that the central executive role reserved to the Commission by Articles 92 and 93 of the Treaty concerning identification of any incompatibility of an aid with the common market was fundamentally different from the role of the national courts regarding protection of the rights attaching to individuals by virtue of the direct effect of the prohibition laid down in the last sentence of Article 93(3) of the Treaty. Whilst the Commission was required to examine the compatibility of the planned aid with the common market, even in cases where the Member State infringed the prohibition of implementing aid measures, national courts, for their part, merely safeguarded, pending a final decision by the Commission, the rights of individuals against any disregard by the state authorities of the prohibition laid down in the last sentence of Article 93(3) of the Treaty. Where those courts delivered a decision in that regard, they did not therefore adjudicate on the compatibility of aid measures with the common market since that final assessment was the exclusive responsibility of the Commission, subject to review by the Court of Justice.

The court stated that the Commission's final decision did not have the effect of regularising, ex post facto, implementing measures that were invalid in that they were adopted in breach of the prohibition laid down in that article, otherwise the direct effect of the last sentence of Article 93(3) of the Treaty would be undermined and the interests of individuals, which, as stated above, the national courts are responsible for safeguarding, would be encroached upon. Any other interpretation would encourage non-observance by the Member State concerned of the last sentence of Article 93(3) and would deprive it of useful effect.

Note. Judgment here was given two days after the ruling in *Francovich* **[C33]**. If a non-notified aid is implemented, what are the rights of a disadvantaged competitor against the Member State? Is this case a *lex specialis* in relation to state aids, or part of a general right conferred by *Francovich*? Does it matter?

[E97] Malcolm Ross: 'Beyond Francovich' (1993) 56 Modern Law Review 55

C. *Express obligations lacking direct effect*

. . . For the purposes of the discussion that follows, it is assumed that the three conditions attached in the *Francovich* judgment **[C33]** would apply whatever the source or guise of the instrument of Community law. This seems a reasonable assumption to make on the footing that each of the three stated criteria is geared to tying the action to individual interests and the particular loss suffered by the litigant. There appears no attempt in *Francovich* to circumscribe the liability of states other than by these criteria. Thus, if the measure or principle of Community law can be seen as for individuals' interests, can be described as such in the relevant source or instrument, and if a sufficient causal link is established between the state's default and the plaintiff's loss, then an arguable claim arises for damages.

The search for Community law rules satisfying these criteria is likely to prove controversial. Three obligations on Member States are considered below. The first, concerning Article 90(1) EEC, is included because it represents a specific obligation upon Member States which has hitherto not been seen as giving rise to direct effect on its own. It has been interpreted by the court as a specific embodiment of Article 5 EEC, thereby offering opportunities for developing the application of *Francovich* to the latter. The second illustration, concerning the scope for *Francovich* actions in the context of state aids, presents the dilemma as to whether such claims are *sui generis,* parasitic or secondary in nature according to whether adequate individual protection already exists within the scheme of supervision as previously interpreted by the court. The final, and most controversial, scenario asks whether the logical development of *Francovich is* to hold that the duty of solidarity owed under Article 5 EEC itself creates directly effective rights for individuals.

Article 90(1) EEC

This provision requires that in the case of public undertakings and undertakings to which Member States grant special or exclusive rights, Member

States shall neither enact nor maintain in force any measure contrary to the rules contained in the Treaty, in particular those relating to discrimination on grounds of nationality and to competition policy. Conventional wisdom on Article 90(1) has distinguished the act of a Member State in permitting (or even requiring) a public or entrusted undertaking to break Treaty competition rules from the behaviour of the undertakings themselves. So, to take a recent example, it would be an abuse of a dominant position under Article 86 for a concessionaire granted a monopoly over particular services by regional authorities to charge customers excessive prices. If this price were laid down in the contract constituting the concession, it would seem that the state would, separately and additionally, directly infringe Article 90(1). The 'victim' would, without consideration of *Francovich,* have a directly enforceable right against the abuser in a national court, for which that court would have to find an effective remedy.

Equally, the Commission would be able to take action against the Member State (assuming for the moment that an organ 'of the state' can be identified as having brought about the abusive behaviour by the undertaking) for breach of Article 90(1), but there is no unequivocal support in the case law for allowing the 'victim' to sue the state.

However, the advent of *Francovich* appears to simplify matters considerably here. Given that the express function of Article 90(1), both in terms of the provision and in the court's case law, is to ensure that the state both itself abides by the rules of the Treaty and ensures that certain types of privileged or state-influenced undertakings do likewise, it appears that the requisite level of individual interest is established. The only reason for abstaining in the past from endowing the provision with direct effect has been the difficulty of severing it from the other parts of the Treaty (which might or might not be directly effective) which it seeks to underpin. This is not an obstacle to the *Francovich* route to remedy, since it is the very failure to provide that guarantee which constitutes the material content of the default giving rise to damages. Moreover, part of the essential contribution of the *Francovich* principle is that it does not have to be linked to provisions that are themselves directly effective.

The next question is whether failure to ensure that others comply with their Treaty obligations is sufficient causal nexus to justify compensation for the plaintiff's loss. Here, too, the potential difficulties to an action do not appear insuperable. At first sight it might be thought that the failure is qualitatively different from that involved, for example, in not transposing (accurately or at all) a directive into national legislation. In the latter case, there is a direct obligation by virtue of Article 189 upon the Member State to carry out such implementation. But, in the same way, the duty to monitor is expressly provided for in Article 90(1).

An instructive example can be seen in the *Macrotron* case **[E88]**. A German statute had reserved the task of professional job placements to a particular organisation, although in practice this monopoly was not observed. One of the businesses breaching this code de facto then sued a client for fees, having fulfilled its part of the contract. The client, however, responded that the arrangement was void under national law because it infringed the statutory monopoly. In reply, the plaintiff claimed that the existence of the monopoly itself was incompatible with the EEC Treaty. Whilst not accepting this view in its most extreme form, the court was willing to hold that there could be an abuse of a dominant position where exclusive rights were not satisfying the demands of the market place.

Translating this into the terms of *Francovich,* could it be said that the granting of exclusivity which proves ineffective or inefficient would make the state liable in damages to the players who were prevented by the existence of the statutory monopoly from entering the game? The basis of the argument would be that the state had infringed its obligations under Article 90(1). Since the effect of that default was to prevent individuals from participating in the market place, the rule could be considered to be designed for individual benefit. There might be some issue as to causation, to the extent that there would need to be some criteria for determining when and how market failure is to be deemed to occur. However, the fact that the court seems to have countenanced this as a workable test under Article 86 may indicate that it does not see the difficulty as insuperable.

However, developing the scenario in *Macrotron* in the way suggested brings another complication. Is the effect of using *Francovich* to translate the liability of the grantee of exclusive rights as an abuser under Article 86 into the liability of the state under Article 90(1) for allowing it to happen, or is the plaintiff now free to choose either (or even both) routes for redress? At first sight, there seems no reason why the plaintiff cannot have two independent claims. Article 86 is directly effective, so it would run counter to the court's notion of the fundamental nature of this doctrine to subject it to any general rules about dual recovery. Moreover, the court has already made it clear that Article 90 may be infringed by a Member State in addition to any breach by an undertaking of the competition rules of the Treaty, thereby implying that the actions involved are distinct.

However, there are objections to this highly plaintiff-oriented solution. First, there may be moral or policy difficulties in accepting that there should be double recovery in damages for what is in effect the same loss (the inability to enter the market place because the privileged undertaking is permitted or required by the state to prevent it). Secondly, but with the effect of removing the dual element to liability, it may be argued that Article 86 should not be applicable to circumstances where the undertaking is not engaged in a voluntary act. Thus, only the claim for damages against the Member State would be available, if it can be said that the undertaking's exclusion of the plaintiff is the result of a monopoly or privilege conferred by the state. The difficulty with this approach, although carrying with it the benefit of clarification, would be that it requires the court to address the question of intention in the context of liabilities under the competition rules.

A third consideration, also affecting whether the plaintiff would be left with only one potential defendant, is whether all the criteria of *Francovich* are satisfied if dual recovery is permitted. In particular, if the plaintiff can recover against the undertaking through Article 86 and damages are consequently given by the national court as the appropriate remedy to constitute effective enjoyment, is there any loss left that can be said to have been caused by the state? This argument, of course, would also work in reverse if the plaintiff chose to sue the state first before attempting to take the undertaking to court. Even if this view of causation is to be adopted, there would seem little point in preventing the plaintiff from having the choice as to which party to claim against. Financial considerations would dictate a fairly obvious outcome!

State aids

Turning to the rules on state aids, the situation at present governing individual protection is as follows. Member States must notify new aids to the Commission for approval against specific criteria for assessing whether the proposed aid is compatible with the common market. Only after this assessment has been carried out can the aid properly be put into operation. It is clear that the obligation to notify is capable of giving rise to individual rights. Thus, a competitor disadvantaged by the failure to notify an aid could seek effective redress in its national court (leaving aside for the moment what form that might take). On the other hand, it emerges from the decision in *Boussac* **[E94]** that an aid is not rendered incompatible with the Treaty and unlawful merely because of its non-notification. The Commission is thus unable to proceed directly to a claim to have the aid repaid.

In recent decisions, the court has stated that the position of individuals must nevertheless still be protected in order to avoid the supervisory system being rendered nugatory. It appears to have invited national courts to declare prematurely implemented aids as unlawful, whilst preventing the Commission from being able to follow the same path. One avenue for reconciling this apparently conflicting approach is to use the *Francovich* action to compensate individuals whilst maintaining the stance that review of the compatibility of aids with the common market can only be undertaken at Community level by the Commission.

In this role, the *Francovich* action provides a distinct and independent form of protection for individuals. It does not undermine the non-directly effective nature of the rules on state aids, which specifically contain a discretionary element for the supervisory agency in order to monitor the various forms of support in an appropriate and co-ordinated fashion. Moreover, it clarifies the uncertainty previously associated with the notion that non-notification was directly effective but lacking a defined remedy. Certainly, English courts have had to consider whether a bare declaration might be the limit of protection against non-notification, given that the Commission might subsequently declare the aid perfectly lawful once the proper process of notification and evaluation has taken place.

Adopting this analysis reinforces the view that the liability established by *Francovich* arises from the need to provide effective protection for individuals against state default affecting their interests, and does not attempt to encroach upon the methods of assessing state aids in the context of Community-wide competition policy. If this is indeed the function of the new development, its possible extension to a wider range of state obligations under Community law must be considered. Is there any reason why *Francovich* should be confined to areas where states are under specific obligations, such as Articles 90(1) and 92, or are given powers by instruments such as the Merger Regulation? This question invites discussion of whether individuals have a right to have Member States comply with their duties under the Treaties and general principles of law, in particular the obligations contained in Article 5 EEC.

Article 5 EEC and the duty of solidarity

Is the far-reaching implication of *Francovich* that Article 5 can now give rise to directly effective rights for individuals? Such a view has not hitherto prevailed, although the provision has become the *fons et origo* of several key extensions of court jurisprudence. There is, of course, direct reference to Article 5 in the *Francovich* judgment, although put in terms that justification for the action can be found in the cornerstone principle of solidarity, rather than that the principle of damages flows directly from it. Framing the judgment expressly in terms of the direct effect of Article 5 would have been too adventurous a claim to be met with anything other than resistance from the Member States.

However, on closer scrutiny it may be argued that the effective application of the *Francovich* action achieves similar results. It is true that there are limiting criteria, but it has already been seen that these are not elaborate obstacles to lawyers trained in Euro-interpretation and creative claims. The startling result that could follow is that the obligations arising from Article 5 would allow for actions that do not have any specific base elsewhere in the Treaty. Unlike the previous illustrations relating to the specific obligations contained in Articles 90(1) and 92–94, a dynamic approach to Article 5 allows any failure by a Member State to make at least the starting gate of litigation. Of course, it must then be evaluated against the three *Francovich* criteria. It remains to be seen whether the court's future jurisprudence will elaborate upon these tests to allay conservative fears of an avalanche of open-ended and unjustified actions.

To identify the potential type of Article 5 claim, it is important to remember the fundamental, cohesive character of the provision as it has already been interpreted. The duty of solidarity, whilst express, is not specific. Its flexibility has allowed the creation of the very notion of effective protection, so unequivocally articulated previously in *Factortame* **[C48]**. Hence the suggestion put forward earlier in this paper that the failure of national courts to come up with adequate and sufficient remedies under national law for the protection of Community law rights would itself give rise to a claim under *Francovich*.

This approach raises a serious question as to the function of the limiting criteria adopted within the *Francovich* formula. It might be suggested that the requirement that individuals are affected and intended to be protected is only a particular expression of a fundamentality element as to the interests which can give rise to damages against the Member State. This approach would help clarify the ambiguous reference by the court in *Francovich* to the significance of the nature of the breach when determining the conditions for state liability. It is suggested that it is the breach of a fundamental Community obligation which should be decisive, not the gravity of infringement. Moreover, the court has on many occasions defended the initiation and expansion of the doctrine of direct effect as a necessary but natural response to the central position to be attached to individuals within most spheres of application of the Treaty. Article 5 may be seen as the archetypal expression of and vehicle for protection of the most important constitutional values. Therefore, the argument might run, it is for the entrenchment and emphasis of the fundamentality of certain rights that the presence of a *Francovich* action is most suited. Conversely, this same argument can be made to limit *Francovich* if it proves necessary to assuage fears that all defaults would render the Member State liable in damages. Only those breaches or lapses which are incompatible with fundamental rights could qualify as sufficiently important to be construed as affecting individuals.

Seen in these terms, an obvious candidate for *Francovich* protection is infringement by a Member State of human rights recognised as embodied within Community law. There could hardly be any argument against the 'individuality' of such claims; that is the very purpose of the protection demanded by codes of human rights. The adoption of *Francovich* remedies in this area would underline the importance to be attached to observance of these perceived cornerstones of individual entitlement. However, such a stance would require a shift in the court's apparent priorities in the use of human rights as part of the general principles of Community law. Instead of concentrating upon their 'offensive' capacity to make inroads into areas hitherto reserved for national competence, the court would be in a position to consider the intrinsic protection afforded by human rights.

In essence, therefore, *Francovich* potentially creates two types of state liability. The first, and most easily identified, relates to breaches of express and specific duties contained in the Treaty and secondary legislation. These would be actionable according to the conditions laid down in *Francovich* without any additional requirements to be satisfied. The second type of liability concerns more nebulous claims, such as breach of an obligation created by general principles recognised by the court to be generated by Article 5. Such actions would demand the additional requirement of fundamentality to render them specific enough. In other words, the capacity for a breach of Article 5 to trigger an action for damages by an individual would work in a similar fashion to the current operation of Article 90, that is, as a reference provision which depends for its availability to individuals upon the nature of the rule or principle which it seeks to underscore.

Question

Would *Francovich* be of any assistance to an individual seeking to enjoy any benefits from social and economic cohesion **[A13]** or any of the other goals of the post-Maastricht European Community?

Further reading

Barents, R, 'The internal market unlimited: some observations on the legal basis of Community legislation' (1993) 30 CMLRev 85.

Bright, C, 'Article 90, economic policy and the duties of Member States' (1993) 6 ECLR 263.

Downes, T, & MacDougall, D, 'Significantly impeding effective competition: substantive appraisal under the Merger Regulation' (1994) 19 ELRev 286.

Hancher, L, 'State aids and judicial control in the European Community' (1994) 2 ECLR 134.

Maduro, M, '*Keck:* The end? The beginning of the end? Or just the end of the beginning?' (1994) 3 Irish Journal of European Law 30.

Reich, N, 'The "November Revolution" of the European Court of Justice: *Keck, Meng* and *Audi* revisited' (1994) 31 CMLRev 459.

Van Gerven, G, and Navarro Varana, E, 'The *Wood Pulp* case and the future of concerted practices' (1994) 31 CMRLRev 575.

Whish, R, 'The enforcement of EC competition law in the domestic courts of Member States' (1994) 2 ECLR 60.

Wils, W, 'The search for the rule in Article 30 EC: much ado about nothing?' (1993) 18 ELRev 475.

Winter, J, 'Supervision of state aid: Article 93 in the Court of Justice' (1993) 30 CMLRev 311.

Index